UNDERSTANDING ABNORMAL CHILD PSYCHOLOGY

THE WILEY BICENTENNIAL—KNOWLEDGE FOR GENERATIONS

$\mathcal{E}$ach generation has its unique needs and aspirations. When Charles Wiley first opened his small printing shop in lower Manhattan in 1807, it was a generation of boundless potential searching for an identity. And we were there, helping to define a new American literary tradition. Over half a century later, in the midst of the Second Industrial Revolution, it was a generation focused on building the future. Once again, we were there, supplying the critical scientific, technical, and engineering knowledge that helped frame the world. Throughout the 20th Century, and into the new millennium, nations began to reach out beyond their own borders and a new international community was born. Wiley was there, expanding its operations around the world to enable a global exchange of ideas, opinions, and know-how.

For 200 years, Wiley has been an integral part of each generation's journey, enabling the flow of information and understanding necessary to meet their needs and fulfill their aspirations. Today, bold new technologies are changing the way we live and learn. Wiley will be there, providing you the must-have knowledge you need to imagine new worlds, new possibilities, and new opportunities.

Generations come and go, but you can always count on Wiley to provide you the knowledge you need, when and where you need it!

WILLIAM J. PESCE
PRESIDENT AND CHIEF EXECUTIVE OFFICER

PETER BOOTH WILEY
CHAIRMAN OF THE BOARD

UNDERSTANDING ABNORMAL CHILD PSYCHOLOGY

Second Edition

VICKY PHARES, PH.D.
University of South Florida

BICENTENNIAL
1807
WILEY
2007
BICENTENNIAL

JOHN WILEY & SONS, INC.

Vice President & Publisher	Jay O'Callaghan
Executive Editor	Christopher T. Johnson
Assistant Editor	Maureen Clendenny
Editorial Assistant	Eileen McKeever
Marketing Manager	Emily Streutker
Senior Production Editor	Sandra Dumas
Creative Director	Harry Nolan
Senior Designer	Kevin Murphy
Photo Department Manager	Hilary Newman
Senior Photo Editor	Jennifer MacMillan
Media Editor	Lynn Pearlman
Production Management Services	Pine Tree Composition
Cover Photo	Patrisha Thomson/Stone/Getty/Images
Bicentennial Logo Design	Richard J. Pacifico

This book was set in 10/12 Times Ten by Laserwords Private Limited, Chennai, India and printed and bound by R.R. Donnelley/Willard. The cover was printed by Phoenix Color Corporation.

The book is printed on acid-free paper. ∞

To order books or for customer service please, call 1-800-CALL WILEY (225-5945).

Library of Congress Cataloging-in-Publication Data:

Phares, Vicky.
  Understanding abnormal child psychology / Vicky Phares.—2nd ed.
    p. ; cm.
  Includes bibliographical references and index.
  ISBN 978-0-471-72411-7 (alk. paper)
 1. Child psychopathology. 2. Adolescent psychopathology. I. Title.
  [DNLM: 1. Psychopathology. 2. Adolescent Psychology. 3. Adolescent. 4.
Child Psychology. 5. Child. WS 350 P536u 2008]
  RJ499.P46 2008
  618.92′89—dc22

                            2007006917

Printed in the United States of America

10 9 8 7 6 5 4 3 2 1

To Nikki and Kelly—
For showing me the perfect outcome of childhood
And to Carson—
For showing me the perfect beginning (and middle)

CONTENTS

PREFACE

Wow, has a lot changed since the first edition of this book. The fields of developmental psychopathology and clinical child psychology are moving at a rapid pace to help understand why children develop problems and how to help children and families with effective therapies. In this second edition, a wealth of new research is reviewed and a number of features have been added to make the book more student friendly.

Whereas the first edition of the book had 17 chapters, this second edition only has 15 chapters to more easily fit into a semester. (Did I hear a cheer from you students?) The chapter on ethics was deleted, but a lot of that information was infused into other relevant chapters (e.g., ethical research is discussed in the context of research methodology, ethical treatment is discussed in the context of effective therapies). The chapters on assessment and therapy have been combined into one comprehensive chapter that shows the continuity of assessing problems and then treating them.

Additional emphasis has been placed on developmental disabilities and mental retardation. This material is now covered in the chapter with learning disorders. Additional information has been highlighted in a number of areas, including the new Individuals with Disabilities Education Act (IDEA), childhood obesity, binge eating disorder, new nationwide outcome studies for the treatment of attention-deficit/hyperactivity disorder (ADHD) and depression, multicultural issues, young children and feeding disorders, and the parent–child relationship. Current controversies and issues that have received a great deal of media attention are also included, such as the use of antidepressant medication with youth and the controversies associated with the diagnosis of ADHD and bipolar disorder.

A new feature to the book is called "You Decide," where students are provided with research data on a "hot topic" regarding children, and they are invited to make up their minds on the topic. This feature is meant to help students remain engaged in critical thinking and for them to remain engaged in the material that is relevant to the well-being of children these days.

With all these changes, note that the emphasis and the perspective of the second edition remain the same as in the first edition. In *Understanding Abnormal Child Psychology*, students will learn about both normative and abnormal development throughout children's lives. If you already love children, this book should provide you with a glimpse into what makes them "tick" and how their behavior can give us a clue as to their individual functioning. After reading this book, you may grow to love children even more. If you are not that fond of children at this point, my hope is that this book will help you learn to appreciate them for who they are. Instead of groaning the next time you hear a child screaming in the video store, you might learn to pay attention to what happens when the child screams and how the parents or caretakers handle the child's request (e.g., Does the 8-year-old get to rent the violent and sexually explicit movie that he or she wants, or does the parent set limits and give the child more appropriate choices?). Although no book can make everyone love children, I am hopeful that this book will give everyone a greater appreciation. Consistent with the first edition, you will notice that certain themes run throughout this book.

Developmental psychopathology. The first concept that you will learn about in chapter 1 is developmental psychopathology. I will not spoil the surprise and define the concept for you here, but suffice it to say that this book is not just about listing disorders that children and adolescents experience. Rather, this book will help you see that children's and adolescents' behaviors are on a continuum (from very adaptive to very maladaptive), with only the very severe ends of the spectrum being conceptualized as disorders. A cornerstone in the philosophy of this book is the importance of knowing the range of normal behavior before trying to identify and treat abnormal behavior. One way of understanding children's and adolescents' behavior that helps take the focus away from labeling children with a specific disorder is to understand that many factors relate to the development of troubled behavior in children. Specifically, factors (such as physical abuse, sexual abuse, interparental conflict, poverty) that put children at greater risk for problems and factors (such as secure attachment to a stable primary caretaker, family strength and support, and role models outside the family) that protect children from the development of problems will be discussed in individual chapters as well as throughout the discussion of specific disorders. After reading this book, you should feel comfortable with knowing about specific disorders of childhood as well as knowing about the factors that are related consistently to the development and prevention of these problems.

Strengths and healthy outcomes. Inherent in the developmental psychopathology perspective is a focus on strengths and adaptive functioning in children's and adolescents' behavior, rather than solely focusing on children's deficits and problems. With this in mind, problematic behavior will be discussed with an eye toward how the behavior might have served an adaptive function at some time. In addition, because focusing on a child's strengths is a cornerstone of working to decrease problematic behavior through therapy, strengths and healthy outcomes will be discussed in relation to effective therapies that help children and families. Prevention of emotional/behavioral problems is also a goal in creating psychologically healthy children. For this reason, preventive efforts will be highlighted throughout the book.

Making abnormal child psychology come to life. You can read all of the research that you want, but until you meet a child with problems or at least read a story about a child with problems, you might not be able to understand the magnitude of these problems. For this reason, case studies and stories about children, adolescents, and families will be presented throughout the book to make the scholarly literature more real. In addition, readings and films will be suggested at the end of each chapter if you want more firsthand accounts of abnormal child psychology. Reading an in-depth memoir by someone who was touched by abnormal child psychology is a wonderful way to gain a better understanding of the personal side of these issues. Finally, you will be given the opportunity to become involved with child and adolescent cases actively by creating treatment plans, considering therapeutic options, imagining progress in therapy, and learning how to document treatment effectiveness. To understand abnormal child psychology, you need to know both the professional research literature and the personal side of abnormal child psychology. Hopefully, this book will provide a good balance between the professional side of the field and the personal side of the experience.

Diversity, inclusion, and understanding. A critique of early work in psychology and education was the focus on middle- and upper-class, Caucasian boys and men. The scholarly field has changed greatly since those early days, with greater awareness of the differences and commonalities across diverse groups. Throughout this book, special attention will be given to issues of race/ethnicity, gender, family constellation, religious orientation, primary language, socioeconomic status, and physical differences. In addition, there are highlighted sections that help you to see the commonalities and differences of abnormal child behavior within a cross-cultural and international context.

Fathers as well as mothers. Nearly every book I have seen on abnormal child psychology, abnormal psychology, developmental psychology, and even introductory psychology has all but ignored the father–child relationship as it relates to children's well-being and men's well-being. Although this book continues to explore the knowledge base regarding mothers and their children, fathers and their children will also be emphasized. In addition to this focus on fathers, other primary figures within families (i.e., siblings, stepparents, caretaking grandparents, foster parents) will be discussed in relation to abnormal child psychology as well as healthy outcomes of children.

Abnormal child psychology in everyday life. When you hear the screaming infant on the airplane or see the child throwing a tantrum in the cookie aisle of the grocery store, you know that child behavior is everywhere. Even if you do not have children in your life right now, you are bound to run into them somewhere during your life. From "SpongeBob SquarePants" to the latest installment of "Harry Potter," popular culture is filled with examples of child behavior (or childlike behavior). This book will illustrate how understanding abnormal child behavior can help you understand events that are specific to your life, as well as specific to the local, national, and international communities. When you read the newspaper and see stories of child abuse or of children and teenagers hurting themselves and others, you probably wonder why such horrific things happen. This book will try to help you understand events that occur in your everyday life and in everyday society. Although I cannot promise an answer to "why" such troubling events occur, this book will attempt to explain the factors that are related to disturbing events that affect children and adolescents in society today.

Settings that relate to abnormal child psychology. Not only is child behavior everywhere you look in your life and in popular culture, but it is also evident in a number of settings where you might want to work eventually (e.g., schools, medical hospitals, mental health facilities, day-care facilities). This book will cover abnormal child psychology within the fields of psychology, education, social work, and psychiatry. Given that children are influenced by so many environments, and in turn have an influence on so many environments, this book will provide a full overview of the many areas in which abnormal child psychology is evident. For example, children and adolescents spend a great deal of their time in school. Not only are schools a setting for education, but they are also a setting for socialization, for developing friendships, and for modeling others' behavior (both good and bad). Thus, the school environment will be mentioned throughout this book to understand one of the locations where children might develop maladaptive behavior and one of the locations where children might be treated for abnormal behavior.

How to make a difference. One chapter that is relatively unique to this book is a chapter on how to help children and families who experience problems. In many universities, students might find it hard to access information about career paths that are open to them. The last chapter of this book focuses on the many ways that nonprofessionals and professionals can make a difference in children's lives. Whether you plan a career in the helping field or not, this chapter should illustrate the diverse ways in which children and families can be helped.

As you may have gathered from this overview, this book is intended as a textbook that will be used in departments of psychology, education, counseling, and social work. The book is intended for advanced undergraduate students (i.e., juniors and seniors), as well as beginning graduate students who are just starting to learn about abnormal child behavior.

I am hopeful that both the scholarly and personal side of abnormal child psychology will intrigue you throughout this book. As for myself, I have been intrigued with children for as long as I can remember. In fact, I first began volunteering at an inpatient mental health facility when I was in high school. Throughout my undergraduate and graduate training, I remained intrigued with children and adolescents in all of their complexities. As a professor, director of clinical training, and licensed psychologist, I remain intrigued with what we can learn from youth and what we can teach them in return. I hope that you enjoy this sometimes painful, sometimes uplifting adventure to understand abnormal child psychology.

ACKNOWLEDGMENTS

I began the acknowledgments section of my dissertation by stating that I would keep it short and sweet (kind of like some children I know). I'll try to follow the same sentiments here.

To begin with, the editorial staff at John Wiley and Sons, Inc., have been instrumental in getting this book published. The reviewers for the first edition (Catherine L. Bagwell, University of Richmond; Myra Beth Bundy, Eastern Kentucky University; Mari L. Clements, Pennsylvania State University; David Crystal, Georgetown University; Deidre Beebe Fitzgerald, Eastern Connecticut State University; Laura Freberg, California Polytechnic State University; Gerald P. Koocher, Harvard Medical School; Kristin Lindahl, University of Miami; C. H. Madsen, Jr., Florida State University; Erin McClure, Emory University; Jill Norvilitis, Buffalo State College; Nina Parker-Cohen, University of Utah; and Charles Schaefer, Fairleigh Dickinson University) and the second edition (Jill M. Norvilitis, Buffalo State College; Jon B. Ellis, East Tennessee State University; Penny A. Leisring, Quinnipiac University; Michael C. Wolff, Penn State University; and Martin D. Murphy, University of Akron) have been exceedingly helpful.

There are too many people to thank in my own professional realm, but suffice it to say that I've learned from some of the best. My graduate students have also taught me a lot, especially about having fun and getting work done (usually in that order). There are also too many people to thank in the personal realm, where there too I've learned from some of the best. I continue to appreciate my friends from graduate school and from my academic jobs who have allowed a seamless integration of work and fun. My nonwork friends have taught me about life beyond working.

There are also too many people in my family to thank, but here again, they are the best. On both sides of the aisle, the Phares/Brandt families and the Owen families, have made me appreciate family ties more each day.

Of special note are the people who tolerated my work on both the first and second edition of this textbook. My thanks go to Chuck, Nikki, Jimmy, Kelly, Anita, and Carson for their support. Most of you made it into a picture or two so I hope that it was worth it.

CONCEPTUALIZATIONS OF NORMALITY AND ABNORMALITY IN CHILDREN AND ADOLESCENTS

CHAPTER SUMMARY

When they said "sit down," I stood up. Ooh . . . growin' up.

—Bruce Springsteen, "Growin' Up" (1973)

NORMALITY AND ABNORMALITY IN CHILDREN AND ADOLESCENTS

Let's put your life on fast-forward for a moment. Imagine that you are a well-established clinical psychologist working in a community mental health center. You get a call from a father who is extremely upset about his daughter's behavior. The father states that his daughter recently began seeing things that no one else can see, and she talks to the visions that she sees. In addition, the daughter seems to think that she has special powers, such as the ability to read her puppy's mind. The father goes further to state that he's very worried about her behavior, and he thinks she needs therapy or medication to help her with these behaviors.

Once you have listened to this father's concerns, what is the first question that you would ask him? Before reading further, you may want to take a minute to jot down the questions that you think are necessary to help this father.

Lots of questions might come to mind. Has the daughter had any recent traumas in her life, such as parental divorce, death of a loved one, or some type of abuse? Is there a history of schizophrenia or other psychotic disorders in the family? What type of attention does the girl receive from her parents and teachers, both when she is not seeing things and when she reports that she sees things? What type of friends does she have, if any? Are any relevant religious beliefs held by the family that include seeing visions? What

Developmental psychopathology is concerned with children from diverse ages and backgrounds.

type of television shows and movies has the girl been allowed to watch? A few business-minded students might even want to ask first about whether or not the family has insurance that covers assessment and therapy services.

Although all these questions are good ones, and you probably thought of other good questions yourself, the one question that is screaming out to be asked is: How old is the girl? Read the first paragraph again with a $2\frac{1}{2}$-year-old in mind and then read it again with a 17-year-old in mind. Obviously, those behaviors deserve a lot more concern if the daughter is a teenager rather than a toddler. In fact, many of the behaviors are considered very developmentally appropriate for a young child (e.g., having imaginary playmates, feeling special powers). In contrast, these same behaviors in an adolescent might be related to very serious problems, such as schizophrenia or use of hallucinogenic substances. The main point is that we need to know a child's age and developmental level to understand her or his behavior. The same behavior may be developmentally appropriate in a certain age group but very inappropriate and maladaptive in other age groups. Although some behaviors are never considered part of normal development (e.g., suicidal behaviors), many behaviors can be considered normal at one age and troubling at another age.

This is where I get to say: Welcome to the study of developmental psychopathology. The term **developmental psychopathology** is the combination of two important areas of study: developmental, which relates to the course and causes of changes over a person's life span, and psychopathology, which involves the patterns of behaviors, cognitions, and emotions that are abnormal, maladaptive, disruptive, or distressing to either the person or others around the person. Thus, developmental psychopathology is a developmental approach to the study of psychopathology "to help us understand troublesome behavior in light of the developmental tasks and processes that characterize human growth" (Achenbach, 1982, p. 9). Developmental psychopathology takes into consideration maturational and developmental processes when conceptualizing abnormal behavior (Kuperminc & Brookmeyer, 2006; Luthar, 2003). In other words, we need to know what is normal for girls and boys in that age range before we can define what is abnormal. This concept applies to people of all ages, but it is especially relevant for children and adolescents. Think of the changes and growth that occur in the first 12 months of life and then consider the changes that the average person goes through from the age of 22 to the age of 23. To be sure, many 22-year-olds grow and change a lot in those 12 months. On average, however, the amount of developmental changes and challenges in the younger years are more immense than the changes at any other time of life. Thus, professionals tend to focus on developmental processes much more during infancy, childhood, and adolescence than in adulthood.

Also central to the study of developmental psychopathology is the understanding of risk and protective factors. **Risk factors** are characteristics, events, or processes that put the individual at risk for the development of psychological problems. Thus, risk factors increase the likelihood that a problem may occur in the future. Risk factors can be centered in the individual (e.g., difficult child temperament), in the family (e.g., parental psychopathology, interparental conflict, large number of siblings), or in the school and community (e.g., over-crowded schools, poverty, violence; Masten & Powell, 2003; Werner & Smith, 2001). The study of risk factors leads naturally to the question of protective factors. **Protective factors** are characteristics, events, or processes that seem to protect an individual from the development of psychological problems, even when faced with adverse circumstances (Luthar, Cicchetti, & Becker, 2000; Masten et al., 2004). Thus, protective factors serve to decrease the likelihood that a problem will occur in the future. Like risk factors, protective factors can be centered in the individual (e.g., at least average intelligence, good coping skills), in the family (e.g., warm and supportive parents, stable role models), or in the school and community (e.g., competent and caring teachers,

Case Study: The Case of Al—The Boy with the Unique Behaviors

Al was the first-born child of parents who would remain married throughout his childhood. In general, Al was well behaved, but there were a number of odd behaviors that were noted during his early years. For example, when Al was a little over 2 years old, his maternal grandmother referred to him as "dear" and "good" but also mentioned that he had "droll ideas," which were apparently communicated in a nonverbal fashion. Al's parents consulted a doctor because Al was still not talking by the age of three. At the age of four or five, Al's father gave him a magnetic compass to play with while Al was ill in bed. Al became obsessed with the compass and discussed it as though it had changed his life. There were other similar obsessions later in his childhood. For example, at the age of 12, Al became obsessed with a book on Euclidean geometry and referred to it as "the holy geometry booklet." Al had a number of other peculiar behaviors. He was a loner and did not play games with other children. Instead, he would spend hour upon hour building houses of cards that sometimes reached fourteen stories high. In older childhood, Al admitted that he had the "peculiarity" of repeating his own words softly. In addition, he often refused to eat certain foods, such as pork.

Al's schooling also showed signs of trouble. Although he did quite well in school, he seemed to hate school (especially the rote instruction). Al acknowledged that he had a poor memory for words and that he had trouble concentrating on subjects that did not interest him. One teacher pointedly told him, "You will never amount to anything." In 7th grade, this teacher asked Al to transfer to another school because of his attitude toward school and the teachers. By the age of 15, Al's family moved to another country, but left him behind to complete his schooling. He was so miserable and lonely that he dropped out of school and left to join his family. He did not enroll in school when he moved to be with his family.

Given what you know about this case and the ages at which the behaviors occurred, what types of diagnoses might come to mind? You might want to pursue an assessment of one of the pervasive developmental disorders, given the difficulty in social connections, the delayed speech, and the perseveration (i.e., repeated focus) on specific objects and activities. This perseveration on specific objects and activities, along with the obsessive nature of Al's interests, also might lead you to assess for obsessive-compulsive disorder. You might also want to consider a learning disorder, given the difficulty with certain subjects in school and Al's failure to remain in school during his adolescence.

Although all these behaviors might be indicators of a clinical disorder, you might be interested to know that "Al" (better known as Albert Einstein) went on to change the world with the theory of relativity and other advances in physics and the sciences. If you reread those symptoms and behaviors with the knowledge that they were exhibited by someone who was obviously brilliant and a revolutionary thinker, it might allow you to gain an appreciation that unusual behavior in children is not necessarily a bad thing. Albert Einstein's fascination with a compass and with building houses of cards were probably reflective of a very active and intelligent mind. His refusal to eat pork as a child was related to his strong beliefs in the Jewish faith. His difficulty in school was probably related to his intrinsic interest in certain subjects, which is sometimes difficult for school personnel to handle.

Overall, this case should highlight the importance of not pathologizing unusual behaviors in children. Throughout this book, you will read about cases of children with unusual and unique behaviors. You will learn the diagnostic criteria for clinical disorders, and you will learn about the treatment methods used to decrease or even eliminate these unusual behaviors. But keep in mind that sometimes unique and unusual behaviors are signs of creativity or even brilliance and, thus, should not always be viewed as problematic. One of the challenges for any professional working with children is trying to determine which unique behaviors are harmful and which are reflective of the strong diversity that exists in human beings. Hopefully, this book will help you grapple with this issue, which is partially an empirical question and partly a philosophical question.

Ironically, an article published in *Biography* speculated that a number of well-known, successful professionals, such as Einstein, the comedian Andy Kaufman, and artist Andy Warhol, could have met criteria for Asperger's disorder if it had existed while they were alive (Attwood, 2003). This disorder will be discussed in more detail in the chapter on pervasive developmental disorders, but suffice it to say that Einstein's accomplishments are impressive regardless of, or perhaps partly due to, the uniqueness of his behaviors.

Source: Hoffman (1972).

stable role model outside the family, involvement in prosocial organizations; Masten & Powell, 2003; Werner & Smith, 2001). There is also recent interest in exploring biological contributors to children's well-being (Curtis & Cicchetti, 2003). Overall, the concepts of risk and protective factors are central to understanding psychopathology from a developmental perspective. These concepts will be addressed in separate chapters as well as being addressed throughout each chapter individually.

One other concept that is central to developmental psychopathology is the continuity/discontinuity continuum. Specifically, developmental psychopathologists are interested in how behavior stays the same (i.e., continuity) or changes (i.e., discontinuity) over time. It is important to note that the same behaviors may have very different meaning at various ages (Caspi & Moffitt, 1995; Cicchetti, Rogosch, & Toth, 1997; Maughan & Rutter, 1998). For example, a toddler's crying may mean something very different than a teenager's crying. Conversely, different behaviors may have the same essential meaning at various points in time. For example, social isolation might be shown by a 6-year-old who sits alone in the corner of the playground and by a 17-year-old who drives around aimlessly alone. Overall, researchers interested in developmental psychopathology examine changes and similarities in behavior over the life span.

The field of developmental psychopathology is relatively new. Approximately 50 years ago, theorists such as Piaget, Vygotsky, and Werner used developmental theories to define and assess intellectual and emotional disabilities in children (Hodapp, 1997). In the 1960s, Zigler applied developmental theories to the understanding of intellectual limitations (Hodapp, 1997; Hodapp & Zigler, 1995; Zigler & Phillips, 1961). In 1974, Dr. Tom Achenbach's first edition of *Developmental Psychopathology* was published. He began the book by noting, "This is a book about a field that hardly exists yet" (Achenbach, 1974). Since that time, there has been a wealth of information on developmental psychopathology. Notably, a professional journal entitled *Development and Psychopathology* was first published in 1989, with Dr. Dante Cicchetti as the first editor. These facts are not meant to suggest, however, that children's abnormal behavior was only investigated from a developmental perspective beginning in 1974. Although the history of understanding children's behavior lags behind the study of abnormal behavior in adults, there is a long history of trying to understand children's and adolescents' abnormal behavior.

One of the most obvious facts about grown-ups, to a child, is that they have forgotten what it is like to be a child.

—Randall Jarrell

HISTORY OF UNDERSTANDING ABNORMAL CHILD BEHAVIOR

Unfortunately, the history of dealing with troubled children is riddled with painful and sometimes abhorrent treatment of these children. The majority of this history has been documented in Western cultures (Reagan, 2000). Troubled children were dealt with in ways that were influenced by the **Zeitgeist** (the spirit or outlook that was characteristic of a period of time) in dealing with children in general. In ancient Greece, boys and girls with either mental or physical disabilities were often scorned in public or abandoned by their family (Donohue, Hersen, & Ammerman, 2000). Some children were even put to death, in a practice known as **infanticide,** which was the intentional murder of an infant or child. These practices were also thought to have occurred in ancient Rome, during the Roman empire (Donohue et al., 2000).

During the Middle Ages (500–1300), children were often neglected and treated as laborers and slaves, regardless of whether they were well functioning or not (Donohue et al., 2000). Severe beatings of children were not uncommon, and child mortality rates were high. Mental differences and "insanity" in children and adults were thought to be due to the work of the devil and other evil spirits (Achenbach, 1982). These beliefs were largely espoused by the Catholic Church and by Calvin and Luther (Donohue et al., 2000). In order to rid disturbed children of these evil spirits, children were often imprisoned, publicly humiliated, and rejected, and some were tortured or burned at the stake. Although there is some evidence of more humane and compassionate treatment of these troubled children (Neugebauer, 1979), there is overwhelming evidence that disturbed children suffered greatly during this time in history.

The belief in demonic possession continued into the Renaissance period (1300–1600). Punishment for what we now consider to be psychological symptoms was routine for children in both wealthy and poor families (Donohue et al., 2000). Over the course of the Renaissance period, infanticide was eventually stopped, and troubled children were often put in orphanages rather than being put to death. Unfortunately, mortality rates in European orphanages were high, and most abandoned

Case Study: The Case of Mary Ellen — The Tragic Case That Started a Movement

"My mother and father are both dead. I don't know how old I am. I have no recollection of a time when I did not live with the Connollys. I call Mrs. Connolly mamma ... I have had no shoes or stockings on this Winter. I have never been allowed to go out of the room where the Connollys were, except in the night time, and then only in the yard ... My bed at night has been only a piece of carpet stretched on the floor underneath a window, and I sleep in my little under-garments, with a quilt over me. I am never allowed to play with any children, or to have any company whatever. Mamma (Mrs. Connolly) has been in the habit of whipping and beating me almost every day. She used to whip me with a twisted whip—a raw-hide. The whip always left a black and blue mark on my body. I have now the black and blue marks on my head which were made by mamma and also a cut on the left side of my forehead which was made by a pair of scissors. She struck me with the scissors and cut me. I have no recollection of ever having been kissed by any one ... Whenever mamma went out I was locked up in the bedroom. I do not know for what I was whipped—mamma never said anything to me when she whipped me. I do not want to go back to live with mamma, because she beats me so ..." (*New York Times,* April 10, 1874).

This heart-wrenching account was given by Mary Ellen in a statement to the court that was investigating this case of abuse. Ironically, there were only statutes at the time for the prevention of cruelty to animals, but not to humans. This case served as a catalyst to begin the New York Society for the Prevention of Cruelty to Children. In reading the account of how Mary Ellen was identified, it is obvious that many of the neighbors knew about the abuse but did nothing to report it. Many people still felt that parents' treatment of children was a family matter and not an issue in which neighbors should get involved. Unfortunately, it was not until 100 years later that abuse was legally mandated to be reported by teachers, psychologists, physicians, and other professionals.

---

children in orphanages did not survive into adolescence (Rie, 1971).

The same harsh circumstances also existed for children in Colonial America in the 1600s (Donohue et al., 2000). Children were often thought of as cheap labor, and they were treated in an abusive manner, regardless of their level of mental health. In fact, the Stubborn Child Law of 1654 allowed parents in Colonial America to put "stubborn" children to death if the children were not following orders and were not compliant with adults. Children in Europe and Colonial America, and especially children in wealthy families, began to receive better treatment toward the end of the 1600s (Rie, 1971).

From the late 1600s and into the 1700s, there was a growing focus on humane treatment of troubled children in both Colonial America and Europe (Rie, 1971). Mental health problems were now thought to be an organic disease, so there was a focus on treatment rather than punishment. There was also an increased interest in the study of children. Benjamin Rush (1745–1813), who was the first psychiatrist in the United States, began to study mental problems in children around this time.

In the late 1700s and early 1800s, a well-publicized case caught the attention of many individuals who were interested in the psychological and intellectual functioning of children. A young boy, who was later named Victor but who was most commonly known as the Wild Boy of Aveyron, was found in a forest near Aveyron, France, in 1798. Victor had apparently grown up in the forest without any caretaking by humans. He could not speak other than limited guttural sounds, and he did not behave in a civilized manner. Jean Itard had been successful in training deaf children with a technique known as sensory-motor instruction, and he tried to train this "wild" boy with the same techniques (Achenbach, 1982). Although Itard had some success with training Victor, he eventually concluded that Victor was retarded and would not develop adequate behavior. This case was an early example of relatively humane treatment, rather than punishment, of a troubled child.

In the mid-1800s, a former schoolteacher, Dorthea Dix (1802–1887), observed that many troubled children in the United States were put in cages and in cellars with deplorable living conditions. She advocated for more humane treatment of troubled children, and she was instrumental in helping to develop federal funding for treatment centers that would help children with problems. Based on her tireless efforts to advocate for the rights of children, 30 new mental hospitals were developed that offered humane and moral treatment of troubled children (Achenbach, 1982).

In 1874, the American Society for the Prevention of Cruelty to Animals brought attention to a case of child abuse, with the suggestion that human children should have the same rights and protections as animals (see The Case of Mary Ellen). In the late 1800s, the National Society for the Prevention of Cruelty to Children was founded to try to prevent child abuse. With all these movements toward more humane treatment of children, there were still limits to the humane treatment of children. For example, the mental health hospitals that Dorthea Dix helped to develop often became overcrowded and underfunded. Thus, the humane treatment that was provided initially was not always continued (Donohue et al., 2000).

During the late 1800s, there continued to be an interest in studying children to understand the factors that might lead to the development of problems. In fact, the field of psychology was in the process of being founded. In 1879, Wilhelm Wundt (1832–1920) founded the scientific field of psychology in Leipzig, Germany. There was also attention to children's functioning specifically. Toward the end of the 1800s, G. Stanley Hall (1844–1924), who founded the first journal of psychology in the United States (in 1887) and who was the first president of the American Psychological Association (in 1892), began to study children's development systematically (Achenbach, 1982). In what was referred to as a "baby biography," Hall sent out questionnaires to parents, teachers, mental health professionals, and children themselves to document normative developmental changes in children and adolescents. In 1904, he published a two-volume book that summarized these data and helped identify adolescence as a distinctly different period of development than earlier childhood.

At the same time that there was a focus on studying children, there was also an attempt to categorize disturbing behavior in adults as well as in children. In 1883, Emil Kraepelin (1856–1926), who was a psychiatrist in Germany, published his first edition of a taxonomy of mental disorders. Kraepelin focused on adult disorders, with an assumption that mental disorders were evidence of brain pathology. Kraepelin's series of books set the stage for the development of taxonomies of childhood disorders. By the end of the 1800s, there had been some attempts to codify abnormal behavior in children. There was a great deal of attention to the classification of different levels of mental retardation in children, but there were also efforts to define and categorize problems in children such as hyperactivity, psychoses, aggression, and "masturbatory insanity" (Rie, 1971).

With regard to the treatment of children with problems, there was increased attention in the late 1800s and early 1900s to helping children without hospitalizing them. In 1896, Lightner Witmer (1867–1956) founded the first psychological clinic in the world. Notably, the clinic served as a child guidance clinic, where the first client was a boy who showed both learning and behavior problems. As a professor of psychology at the University of Pennsylvania, Witmer coined the term "clinical psychology" with the idea that psychological knowledge and therapeutic skills would lead to improved lives for both children and adults (Trull, 2005). Witmer's clinic focused on addressing observable behavior in children, and the emphasis was clearly on rehabilitation rather than punishment of emotional, behavioral, learning, and intellectual problems in children.

Continuing with this modality of humane treatment and with a goal toward helping children, William Healy (a psychiatrist) and Grace Fernald (a psychologist) established the Juvenile Psychopathic Institute in Chicago in 1909 to help delinquent children. This clinic was used as a model for the development of many other child guidance clinics (Rie, 1971). In 1917, William Healy and his wife Augusta Bronner (a psychologist) founded the Judge Baker Guidance Center in Boston to help troubled children. In the early 1920s, psychiatrists began working in the school system, with the idea that they could help prevent problems in children related to learning difficulties (Rie, 1971). Also in the early 1920s, the National Committee on Mental Hygiene and the Commonwealth Fund began programs to establish additional child guidance clinics (Rie, 1971). There were 200 child guidance clinics in the United States by 1932 (Donohue et al., 2000).

The focus on children's mental health in the United States decreased due to World War II (Trull, 2005). Before WWII, there tended to be a focus on helping children, sometimes to the detriment of helping adults. Given the heavy mental health needs of veterans returning from World War II, the fields of psychology and psychiatry turned to helping adults, often to the detriment of programs that helped children (Trull, 2005). This focus on adults, to the exclusion of children and adolescents, was reflected in the early categorizations of mental disorders.

Not until we have fallen do we know how to rearrange our burden.

—Proverb of Africa

MORE RECENT DIAGNOSTIC CLASSIFICATION SYSTEMS

In 1952, the American Psychiatric Association published the first edition of the *Diagnostic and Statistical Manual of Mental Disorders,* known as the *DSM-I.* As will be seen later, the *DSM* series has been and continues to be very influential in the categorization of children's, adolescents', and adults' mental disorders. Overall, disorders were referred to as "reactions of the psychobiologic unit" (Achenbach, 1982). As can be inferred from this term, disorders were considered to be evident when an individual had difficulty adjusting to some type of life situation, both from a physical perspective and from a mental perspective. In some respects, the *DSM* system is counter to developmental psychopathology because it categorizes behavior into diagnoses rather than exploring behavior on a continuum. As will be discussed later in this chapter and throughout the book, behavior exists on a continuum and can be understood more thoroughly from a dimensional perspective. The *DSM* system is not consistent with a dimensional perspective.

With regard to the history of the *DSM* system, *DSM-I* paid only limited attention to children and adolescents. Possibly because of the continued focus on adults to the exclusion of children, very few disorders were specified for children and adolescents. This pattern also could have been due to the fact that children were conceptualized as miniature adults at that time (Achenbach, 1982), which is known as **adultomorphism.** Because children were thought to fall into the categories that were developed for adults, there was no need to create specific diagnoses for children.

The few disorders that were identified for children and adolescents were somewhat vague and diffuse (Donohue et al., 2000). Although children and adolescents could also be diagnosed with disorders listed for adults when appropriate, the majority of children and adolescents either received a diagnosis of adjustment reaction or they received no diagnosis (Achenbach, 1982).

Although the first *DSM* was relatively well received within the United States, the World Health Organization published an international diagnostic system in 1965, which included both medical disorders and mental disorders by the time of the sixth edition. Known as the *International Classification of Diseases (ICD),* the tenth edition of this system is used currently (World Health Organization, 1992). The *ICD-10* is especially helpful for allowing comparable diagnostic processes in cross-cultural and international research.

In 1968, the American Psychiatric Association published the second edition of the *DSM.* Known as *DSM-II,* this revision was more inclusive of disorders related specifically to childhood and adolescence (e.g., hyperkinetic reaction, overanxious reaction, runaway reaction, adjustment reactions, learning disturbances). Like

DSM-I, there were few operational definitions for any of these disorders, so the process of diagnosis remained subjective. *DSM-II* has also been criticized for having a psychodynamic theoretical orientation in the conceptualization of mental disorders. Although there were additional diagnoses relevant to children and adolescents, the majority of youth continued to be diagnosed with adjustment reaction (Achenbach, 1982).

Due to some of these limitations in *DSM-II,* the third revision of the DSM was published by the American Psychiatric Association in 1980. *DSM-III* proved to be a great departure, and most would say improvement, compared to *DSM-II. DSM-III* provided operational definitions that were observable and behavioral in nature. Thus, the diagnostic categories were thought to be well defined and well articulated in an objective manner. *DSM-III* was also considered to be **atheoretical** (i.e., without any theoretical orientation). Although some might argue that a psychodynamic orientation was replaced by a behavioral orientation, the behavioral descriptions in *DSM-III* were intended to make the diagnostic criteria more objective but not to imply the etiology or causation of disorders. A strength of *DSM-III* was the addition of decision trees to aid with **differential diagnosis** (the attempt to distinguish one disorder from another in an individual client). Clinicians must perform differential diagnosis when there are symptoms that are common across two or more disorders, or when there is not a clear-cut diagnosis.

In addition to these improvements, *DSM-III* also introduced a method of **multiaxial evaluation,** which means that individuals were rated on multiple axes or dimensions of functioning. The rationale behind multiaxial evaluation is that there is more to an individual than his or her clinical problems. Thus, individuals were not only diagnosed on their clinical problem, but also on long-standing problems, physical functioning, life stressors, and global functioning.

DSM-III also proved to be a major improvement in the categorization of disorders experienced by children and adolescents. There were nine major categories of disorders related to infants, children, and adolescents. There was also a section for other conditions that were not considered mental disorders but that were the focus of attention or treatment (known as **V-Codes**). In addition to the disorders listed in the section, "Disorders usually first evident in infancy, childhood, or adolescence," children and adolescents could still be diagnosed with a number of other disorders, such as major depression, alcohol abuse, and adjustment disorder, that were listed in other sections of *DSM-III*.

Overall, *DSM-III* was comparable to the diagnostic system that is in current use. The thoroughness of the diagnostic system helped to allow an explosion of research into child and adolescent disorders.

Partially in reaction to a large part of this research, *DSM-III-Revised* (known as *DSM-III-R*) was published in 1987. Like *DSM-III*, *DSM-III-R* continued to add more specific diagnoses related to child and adolescent disorders. There were 11 major categories of disorders specific to infancy, childhood, and adolescence, and a number of other diagnoses could be used for individuals of any age.

Further research and refining of the diagnostic system led to the publication of *DSM-IV* in 1994. In 2000, the American Psychiatric Association published *DSM-IV-TR* (Text Revision), with revisions in the written information but no revisions in the majority of diagnostic categories (American Psychiatric Association, 2000). Given that *DSM-IV* is the current diagnostic system used in the United States as well as in many other countries, a thorough description of *DSM-IV* is warranted. As can be seen in Table 1.1, there are 10 major categories of disorders that fall into the section entitled "Disorders usually first diagnosed in infancy, childhood, and adolescence." Within these categories, there are a total of 38 specific disorders (not including disorders listed as "Not Otherwise Specified"). In addition, there are over 200 other disorders that can be diagnosed for children and adolescents as well as for adults, approximately 150 of which are mentioned in Table 1.1. Specifics of many disorders will be covered in later chapters, but the overview of these diagnoses in Table 1.1 shows that a range of disorders is covered by *DSM-IV*. Interested students should consider reading *DSM-IV Training Guide for Diagnosis of Childhood Disorders* (Rapoport & Ismond, 1996), which provides a clear and comprehensive overview of the diagnostic process with children and adolescents.

DSM-IV continues *DSM-III*'s use of a multiaxial evaluation system to help professionals diagnose and understand children and adolescents (American Psychiatric Association, 2000). Each axis includes information about different domains in a child's or adolescent's life to help clinicians plan and evaluate appropriate treatments for the client. The five axes are listed in Table 1.2. The inclusion of all five axes is meant to allow a broad view of the child's or adolescent's overall functioning, rather than simply focusing on the presenting clinical symptoms (American Psychiatric Association, 2000). Given that all five axes are important to understand, each axis will be described separately.

TABLE 1.1   Clinical Disorders in *DSM-IV* That Can Be Diagnosed in Children and Adolescents*

Disorders Usually First Diagnosed in Infancy, Childhood, or Adolescence:

Mental Retardation (Coded on Axis II)
  5 levels of diagnoses (based on functioning)
Learning Disorders
  Reading Disorder
  Mathematics Disorder
  Disorder of Written Expression
Motor Skills Disorder
  Developmental Coordination Disorder
Communication Disorders
  Expressive Language Disorder
  Mixed Receptive-Expressive Language Disorder
  Phonological Disorder
  Stuttering
Pervasive Developmental Disorders
  Autistic Disorder
  Rett's Disorder
  Childhood Disintegrative Disorder
  Asperger's Disorder
Attention-Deficit and Disruptive Behavior Disorders
  Attention-Deficit/Hyperactivity Disorder (3 types)
  Conduct Disorder (2 types)
  Oppositional Defiant Disorder
Feeding and Eating Disorders of Infancy or Early Childhood
  Pica
  Rumination Disorder
  Feeding Disorder of Infancy or Early Childhood
Tic Disorders
  Tourette's Disorder
  Chronic Motor or Vocal Tic Disorder
  Transient Tic Disorder (2 types)
Elimination Disorders
  Encopresis
  Enuresis (3 types)
Other Disorders of Infancy, Childhood, or Adolescence
  Separation Anxiety Disorder
  Selective Mutism
  Reactive Attachment Disorder of Infancy or Early Childhood (2 types)
  Stereotypic Movement Disorder

Other Clinical Disorders That Can Be Diagnosed in Childhood or Adolescence:

Substance-Related Disorders
  Alcohol Use Disorders (2 types)
  Alcohol-Induced Disorders (12 types)
  Specific Substance-Related Disorders (97 types)
Schizophrenia and Other Psychotic Disorders
  Schizophrenia (5 types)
  Schizophreniform Disorder
  Schizoaffective Disorder
Mood Disorders
  Major Depressive Disorder (2 types)
  Dysthymic Disorder (2 types)
  Bipolar I Disorder

TABLE 1.1 *(continued)*

Bipolar II Disorder
Cyclothymic Disorder
Anxiety Disorders
  Panic Disorder (3 types)
  Specific Phobia
  Social Phobia
  Obsessive-Compulsive Disorder
  Posttraumatic Stress Disorder
  Acute Stress Disorder
  Generalized Anxiety Disorder
Somatoform Disorders
  Somatization Disorder (2 types)
  Conversion Disorder
  Pain Disorder (2 types)
  Hypochondriasis
  Body Dysmorphic Disorder
Eating Disorders
  Anorexia Nervosa
  Bulimia Nervosa
Impulse-Control Disorders Not Elsewhere Classified
  Intermittent Explosive Disorder
  Kleptomania
  Pyromania
  Pathological Gambling
  Trichotillomania
Adjustment Disorders (6 types)

* Unless otherwise noted, all disorders are coded on Axis I. This list is not exhaustive. There are other categories of disorders (such as Delirium, Amnestic, and Other Cognitive Disorders, Factitious Disorders, Dissociative Disorders, Sexual and Gender Identity Disorders, Sleep Disorders, and Personality Disorders) that can be diagnosed in children and adolescents, but are quite rare in youngsters. Also note that diagnoses referred to as "Not Otherwise Specified" (or NOS for short) are not listed in this table.

Source: American Psychiatric Association (2000).

Reprinted with permission from the *Diagnostic and Statistical Manual of Mental Disorders, Fourth Edition, Text Revision.* Copyright 2000 American Psychiatric Association.

TABLE 1.2 **Multiaxial Evaluation in *DSM-IV***

Axis I:	Clinical Disorders
	Other Conditions That May Be a Focus of Clinical Attention
Axis II:	Personality Disorders
	Mental Retardation
Axis III:	General Medical Conditions
Axis IV:	Psychosocial and Environmental Problems
Axis V:	Global Assessment of Functioning

Source: American Psychiatric Association (2000).

Reprinted with permission from the *Diagnostic and Statistical Manual of Mental Disorders, Fourth Edition, Text Revision.* Copyright 2000 American Psychiatric Association.

In some respects, Axis I contains what most people think about when they think about a clinical diagnosis.

A child's or adolescent's primary clinical disorder or mental disorder is listed on Axis I along with any other conditions that may be a focus of clinical attention. Based on the definition in *DSM-IV*, a **mental disorder** "is conceptualized as a clinically significant behavioral or psychological syndrome or pattern that occurs in an individual and that is associated with present distress (e.g., a painful symptom) or disability (i.e., impairment in one or more important areas of functioning) or with a significantly increased risk of suffering death, pain, disability, or an important loss of freedom" (American Psychiatric Association, 2000, p. xxxi). Inherent in this definition is that

- The behavior is beyond what is expected for the individual of that age, gender, culture, and background.

- The behavior is either distressing or is related to impairments in daily life.

- The behavior can put the individual at risk for further harm or distress.

The terms *clinical disorder* and *mental disorder* are used interchangeably in *DSM-IV*. In either case, these problems are noted on Axis I.

If a child or adolescent meets criteria for more than one clinical disorder, multiple disorders can be listed on Axis I. If a client does not meet criteria for any clinical disorder or V-Code, a clinician would note that there was no diagnosis or condition on Axis I. All the clinical disorders and other conditions listed in Table 1.1 would be noted on Axis I, except Mental Retardation and Personality Disorders (which are listed on Axis II). Table 1.3 lists other conditions that may be a focus of clinical attention (i.e., V-Codes). The inclusion of V-Codes is a laudable effort to acknowledge subthreshold diagnoses. V-Codes, however, remain a controversy in both child and adult diagnoses.

V-Codes can be listed on Axis I (or on Axis II in the case of Borderline Intellectual Functioning) with or without other disorders. Unfortunately, very little research has been completed on the V-Codes. For those who wish to help children access mental health services, it is also unfortunate to note that most insurance companies and other third-party payers (such as health maintenance organizations and preferred provider organizations) do not cover mental health services for V-Codes (Patterson & Lusterman, 1996). One possibility is that these "conditions" may not be perceived as serious as clinical disorders. In fact V-Codes and other relationship problems have often been considered "second-class" diagnoses in the diagnostic system

TABLE 1.3 Selected Other Conditions That May Be a Focus of Clinical Attention (V-Codes)

Relational Problems
  Relational Problem Related to a Mental Disorder or
    General Medical Condition
  Parent–Child Relations Problem
  Partner Relational Problem
  Sibling Relational Problem
Problems Related to Abuse or Neglect
  Physical Abuse of Child
  Sexual Abuse of Child
  Neglect of Child
Additional Conditions That May Be a Focus of Clinical
    Attention
  Noncompliance with Treatment
  Malingering
  Child or Adolescent Antisocial Behavior
  Borderline Intellectual Functioning (Coded on Axis II)
  Bereavement
  Academic Problem
  Identity Problem
  Religious or Spiritual Problem
  Acculturation Problem
  Phase of Life Problem

Source for V-Codes: American Psychiatric Association (2000).

Reprinted with permission from the *Diagnostic and Statistical Manual of Mental Disorders, Fourth Edition, Text Revision.* Copyright 2000 American Psychiatric Association.

(Borduin, Schaeffer, & Heiblum, 1999). Another possibility for the lack of insurance coverage for V-Codes is that they are not considered to be illnesses like clinical disorders and physical illnesses (Simola, Parker, & Froese, 1999). Ironically, when children and adolescents diagnosed with V-Codes were studied, they were found to have clinically significant problems that lead to impairment (Simola et al., 1999). Thus, a number of writers have argued that V-Codes should be covered by insurance companies (Patterson & Lusterman, 1996; Simola et al., 1999). V-Codes are considered to be less stigmatizing for children and are also thought by many therapists to be more reflective of children's and adolescents' problems than specific diagnoses of the individual youngster. Relationship difficulties that are exemplified through V-Codes are often at the heart of children's and adolescents' problematic behavior (Doucette, 2002) Even in the *DSM-IV Training Guide for Diagnosis of Childhood Disorders,* it is noted that V-Codes are especially useful when the real focus of the problem is the parent or family, rather than the child him- or herself (Rapoport & Ismond, 1996). Thus, it appears that V-Codes are worthy of additional research to explore whether or not they capture children's and adolescents' experience of problems in a meaningful way and to try

to establish whether or not these categorizations should be given the same coverage that other clinical disorders receive.

In order to provide individual attention to mental retardation and personality disorders, Axis II was developed (American Psychiatric Association, 2000). For children and adolescents, the majority of Axis II diagnoses are related to mental retardation rather than personality disorders (American Psychiatric Association, 2000). Although most of the long-standing personality disorders can be diagnosed in childhood and adolescence, these disorders tend to be diagnosed more consistently in adults when compared to youngsters. There is some interest in diagnosing personality disorders in children and adolescents, but there is also resistance to diagnosing personality disorders in youth, given that the disorders are considered to be long standing and maladaptive for long-term functioning (Johnson et al., 2005). Because personality disorders in children and adolescents are rare compared with other disorders, they will not be addressed in any depth in this book.

Axis III allows the clinician to note any general medical conditions that are relevant for the child or adolescent. Specifically, any medical conditions that might be relevant to the understanding or treatment of the child's or adolescent's clinical disorders should be listed on Axis III. Diseases of the nervous system (such as Tay-Sachs disease), diseases of the respiratory system (such as cystic fibrosis), neoplasms (such as leukemia), endocrine diseases (such as childhood diabetes), nutritional diseases (such as obesity), and hematological diseases (such as sickle-cell anemia) are among the different types of medical conditions that would be listed for children and adolescents. The inclusion of Axis III is meant to highlight the need for a thorough evaluation of the client and to facilitate communication among professionals working with the client (American Psychiatric Association, 2000).

Attention is given to psychosocial and environmental problems by listing them on Axis IV. These problems are relevant to the diagnosis, treatment, and prognosis of clinical disorders in children and adolescents. Psychosocial and environmental problems include, but are not limited to:

- Problems with the primary support group (such as parental overprotection, inadequate discipline, and disruption of family by separation, divorce or estrangement, sexual abuse, and physical abuse)

- Problems related to the social environment (such as difficulty with acculturation, death or loss of a significant friend, and inadequate social support system)

- Educational problems (such as discord with classmates or teachers, inadequate school environment, and academic problems)

- Occupational problems (such as stressful work schedule and discord with boss or coworkers)

- Housing problems (such as homelessness, inadequate housing, and living in an unsafe neighborhood)

- Economic problems (such as living in extreme poverty)

- Problems with access to health-care services (such as inadequate health-care services)

- Problems related to interaction with the legal system/ crime (such as being arrested or incarcerated and being the victim of a crime)

- Other psychosocial and environmental problems (such as exposure to war and discord with non-family caregivers, such as a counselor or social worker)

As can be surmised from this list, a great deal of psychosocial and environmental problems can be noted on Axis IV. The inclusion of Axis IV was meant to encourage clinicians to consider the relevant contexts in which clients' clinical disorders develop and are maintained.

The final axis, Axis V, lists the clinician's global assessment of functioning (known as a GAF score). Specifically, the clinician rates the client on a scale of 1 to 100 (with higher numbers reflecting better functioning). This rating system can be used for adults as well as for youth. Clinicians consider information on the child's or adolescent's psychological, social, and academic functioning to determine the GAF score. Most often, clinicians rate the child's or adolescent's current GAF, but sometimes clinicians rate an intake and discharge GAF (i.e., to note how children or adolescents were functioning when they were first brought to the mental health facility and then to note how they were functioning when they were discharged or to note children's and adolescents' highest functioning within the past year. Scores can be any number between 1

Case Study: The Case of Eric—An Example of Multiaxial Evaluation using *DSM-IV*

Eric is 9 years old and lives with his two brothers, his mother, and his father. For the past 3 months, he has been afraid of attending the 3-hour religious classes at his church after school. He had been performing quite well in these classes, but said that he was afraid of failing the classes. His progress in regular school classes had begun to deteriorate, partially due to the fact that he missed a lot of school and had trouble concentrating when he was at school. In addition to having trouble sleeping, he also had many somatic complaints, such as headaches and stomachaches. He often felt sad and did not seem to enjoy activities that used to be enjoyable. Eric often cried for what seemed to be no apparent reason. Eric had always been shy, but he did have some friends with whom he would occasionally spend the night.

Eric's parents had been married for over 20 years, but they often fought with each other and had many marital problems. Eric and his brothers were often the topic of their parents' arguments. In addition, Eric's mother had received treatment for Major Depressive Disorder on three separate occasions.

When interviewed, Eric reported that he was distressed about causing his parents to worry about him. He quickly began to sob and stated that he felt awful nearly all of the time. He acknowledged that he and his family would be better off if he were dead, but he did not seem to have a specific plan to attempt suicide.

Diagnosis

Axis I:	Major Depressive Disorder, Single Episode
Axis II:	No Diagnosis
Axis III:	None
Axis IV:	Problems with primary support group
	Parent–child problems
	Psychiatric disorder in mother
	Family discord
Axis V:	GAF = 70 (Current)
	GAF = 85 (Highest level in the past year)

Eric met criteria for Major Depressive Disorder, which is coded as a clinical disorder on Axis I. Although he reported symptoms of anxiety, these symptoms were not enough to warrant diagnosis of an anxiety disorder. There was no evidence of a personality disorder or mental retardation, so no diagnosis was warranted on Axis II. The somatic complaints were thought to be due to his depression and symptoms of anxiety, rather than an actual physical problem. If he had experienced a physical problem, it would have been coded on Axis III. Axis IV was used to note that Eric had experienced many psychosocial and environmental problems. Axis V was used to note Eric's Global Assessment of Functioning, both currently and within the past year.

Source: Rapoport & Ismond (1996).

and 100, and although there is more detail provided in the *DSM-IV*, the highlights of the GAF are presented following (American Psychiatric Press, 2000).

- **1–10:** Persistent danger of severely hurting self or others or persistent inability to maintain minimal personal hygiene
- **11–20:** Some danger of hurting self or others
- **21–30:** Inability to function in almost all areas
- **31–40:** Major impairment in several areas, such as work or school
- **41–50:** Serious symptoms (e.g., suicidal ideation, severe obsessional rituals)
- **51–60:** Moderate symptoms (e.g., occasional panic attacks)
- **61–70:** Some mild symptoms (e.g., depressed mood)
- **71–80:** If symptoms are present, they are transient
- **81–90:** Absent or minimal symptoms
- **91–100:** Superior functioning in a wide range of activities. No symptoms.

RELIABILITY AND VALIDITY OF DIAGNOSTIC CATEGORIES

Now that you understand the current *DSM-IV* system, you might be wondering about the reliability and validity of this system. **Reliability** refers to the consistency of the diagnostic system, such that the same diagnosis would be reached across time and across clinicians. **Validity** refers to the degree to which the diagnostic system is accurate for diagnoses as they actually exist. Together, reliability and validity can be combined to refer to the **psychometric properties** of a diagnostic system. It is interesting to note that psychometric properties were not included in the *DSM-IV* itself. Four years after the publication of *DSM-IV*, the fourth volume of the *DSM-IV Sourcebook* was published with reliability and validity data on some, but not all, of the disorders of childhood and adolescence (American Psychiatric Association, 1998).

As you might imagine, it is difficult to establish meaningful ways to measure reliability and validity for a diagnostic system. One way of exploring the reliability of a diagnostic system is to study **test-retest reliability** (i.e., when a clinician conducts diagnostic interviews at two points in time, usually one or two weeks apart). In general, the test-retest reliabilities for disorders in childhood and adolescence are not as strong as for disorders in adulthood (American Psychiatric Association, 1998). For

example, disorders such as attention-deficit/hyperactivity disorder, oppositional defiant disorder, and conduct disorder all have test-retest reliabilities that are considered to be in the fair range (.51 to .64 for kappas; American Psychiatric Association, 1998), but not in the strong or excellent range.

Another way of exploring reliability is to assess the correspondence between two clinicians' ratings, which is known as **inter-rater reliability.** In studies of childhood disorders with experienced clinicians, clinician-to-clinician agreement was stronger for some disorders, such as autism (with a kappa of .85), than for other disorders, such as oppositional defiant disorder (with a kappa of .55; American Psychiatric Association, 1998). Note that the **kappa statistic** for inter-rater reliability is the percentage of agreement between two raters, while controlling for chance agreement. Overall, inter-rater reliability and other types of reliability tend to be stronger for disorders that are more objective and observable than other disorders. For example, the average correspondence between parents' and adolescents' reports of adolescents' psychopathology was .30. This average, however, hides a wide range of correspondence for different disorders. Parent–adolescent correspondence was stronger for observable disorders, such as conduct disorder (.79) and anorexia nervosa (.75) than for other less observable disorders, such as major depressive disorder (.31) and alcohol abuse (.19; Cantwell, Lewinsohn, Rohde, & Seeley, 1997). When all eating disorders were considered, including anorexia nervosa (a highly observable disorder) and bulimia nervosa (a somewhat less observable disorder), the average kappa was .64 (Nicholls, Chater, & Lask, 2000). Overall, reliabilities of disorders in childhood and adolescence have lagged behind reliabilities of disorders in adulthood. Validity has also been a challenge to establish, though there are indications that certain more observable disorders (such as autism and anorexia nervosa) have shown evidence of strong validity (American Psychiatric Association, 1998).

Education, in short, cannot be better described than by calling it the organization of acquired habits of conduct and tendencies to behavior.

—William James

CHILDREN IN THE SCHOOL SYSTEM

Because children are in school for so much of their time, schools have become a central setting for diagnosing and treating mental health problems (House, Elliott, & Witt, 2002). A number of laws have been established to ensure that children receive appropriate services in school systems nationwide.

- **Public Law 94–142: Education for All Handicapped Children Act:** This national law, which was established in 1975, has a number of crucial components. To begin with, all special-needs children should be provided with free, appropriate public education. Special-needs children must be evaluated in a nondiscriminatory manner, which means that they should be assessed in their native language with tests that have been validated appropriately for that specific purpose. Each child should have an Individualized Education Program (IEP), which should include documentation of the child's current level of functioning, yearly goals, short-term objectives, and evaluation procedures to verify accomplishment of the short

The school environment can be an important part of children's lives.

term goals. Although an example of an IEP would be too lengthy for this textbook, note that IEPs can focus on children's academic, emotional/behavioral, and adaptive needs. All children should be educated and treated in the least-restrictive environment that is possible and appropriate (e.g., a mainstreamed classroom with special pullout services is considered less restrictive than a special education classroom, which is in turn considered less restrictive than a residential setting). Finally, the law established the legal right for parents to be informed about decisions regarding their children and to encourage parental participation in the educational and therapeutic process for their children.

- **Public Law 99–457: Education of the Handicapped Act Amendments of 1986:** This law was used to amend PL 94–142 to include children from birth to 3 years old (see also Box 1.1). The focus of this law was to mandate the availability of free, appropriate assessment and intervention services for infants and toddlers. In addition, it clarified the fact that PL 94–142 funds were to be used to establish diagnostic and treatment services for children aged 3 to 5.

- **Public Law 101–476: Education of the Handicapped Act Amendments of 1990:** This act served to change the name of the law to Individuals with Disabilities Education Act (IDEA). Any references to "handicaps" in PL 94–142 and its subsequent revisions were changed to "disabilities." More conscientious terminology was also established, such as stating "infants and toddlers with disabilities" rather than "handicapped infants and toddlers." The IDEA was established to serve individuals from birth to the age of 21. Note that there is now a proposed set of changes in the IDEA, which should be finalized by 2006 (Wright & Wright, 2005).

- **Public Law 101–336: Americans with Disabilities Act (ADA):** In 1990, the ADA served as civil rights legislation for all individuals with any type of disability (including certain clinical disorders). The law established the need to maintain accessibility to education and other publicly funded activities. The ADA is a far-reaching law, covering everything from the physical accessibility of a building (by use of wheelchair ramps) to allowing special provisions for taking tests when a student has a documented learning disorder. The ADA served as sweeping legislation to protect the rights of the disabled from infancy into elderly adulthood.

BOX *1.1*

DIAGNOSTIC CLASSIFICATION OF MENTAL HEALTH AND DEVELOPMENTAL DISORDERS OF INFANCY AND EARLY CHILDHOOD

Many people do not realize that even infants and toddlers can experience mental health problems. Although *DSM-IV* lists some disorders relevant to infants and toddlers, the *Diagnostic Classification of Mental Health and Developmental Disorders of Infancy and Early Childhood: Revised Edition* (DC: 0-3R; Zero to Three/National Center for Clinical Infant Programs, 2005) is meant to classify a breadth of disorders and problems that occur in the first three years of life. As can be seen following, both primary disorders (within the youngster) and relationship disorders (between the youngster and the caretaker) can be classified.

Primary Diagnosis:

Posttraumatic Stress Disorder
Deprivation/Maltreatment Disorder
Prolonged Bereavement/Grief Reaction
Anxiety Disorders of Infancy and Early Childhood

Separation Anxiety Disorder
Specific Phobia
Social Anxiety Disorder (Social Phobia)
Generalized Anxiety Disorder
Anxiety Disorder Not Otherwise Specified (NOS)

Depression of Infancy and Early Childhood

Major Depression
Depressive Disorder Not Otherwise Specified (NOS)

Mixed Disorder of Emotional Expressiveness
Adjustment Disorder
Regulation Disorders of Sensory Processing

Hypersensitive
Fearful/Cautious
Negative/Defiant
Hyposensitive/Underresponsive
Sensory Stimulation-Seeking/Impulsive

Sleep Behavior Disorder

Sleep-Onset Disorder
Night-Waking Disorder

Feeding Behavior Disorder

Feeding Disorder of State Regulation
Feeding Disorder of Caregiver–Infant Reciprocity

Infantile Anorexia
Sensory Food Aversions
Feeding Disorder Associated with Concurrent Medical Condition
Feeding Disorder Associated with Insults to the Gastrointestinal Tract

Disorders of Relating and Communicating
Multisystem Developmental Disorder
Other Disorders

Relationship Disorder Classification:

Overinvolved
Underinvolved
Anxious/Tense
Angry/Hostile
Verbally Abusive
Physically Abusive
Sexually Abusive

Like *DSM-IV*, *Diagnostic Classification: 0-3R* uses a multiaxial evaluation system. Also like *DSM-IV*, there are five axes on which to code infants' and toddlers' functioning:

Axis I:	Primary Classification
Axis II:	Relationship Disorder Classification
Axis III:	Medical and Developmental Disorders and Conditions
Axis IV:	Psychosocial Stressors
Axis V:	Emotional and Social Functioning

Compared with more well-established diagnostic systems like *DSM-IV*, this system is in its infancy (no pun intended). Further research is needed to establish the reliability and validity of the diagnostic system, but this system provided a good start to classifying problems in infants, toddlers, and their primary caretakers. Students interested in mental health issues of infancy and toddlerhood should also consider reading *Handbook of Infant Mental Health* (2nd ed.) (Zeanah, 2005), which is a compendium of research on mental health issues in infants and their caretakers.

Case Study: The Case of Carl—The Boy with Problems in School

On the suggestion of a school psychologist, 7-year-old Carl was given a full battery of assessment measures to find out why he might be struggling in school. Although Carl's parents did not report any problems at home, Carl's teachers reported that he had difficulty with his schoolwork, that he did not pay attention to them, that he seemed immature, and that he had poor coordination.

Upon examination, Carl seemed like a sweet, friendly, and cooperative child. His speech was clear, but it was not as developed as would be expected for a child of his age. He was found to meet criteria for an Expressive Language Disorder (coded on Axis I). A full evaluation of his learning abilities showed that there was a possibility of a Reading Disorder, so the diagnosis was noted as Reading Disorder/Provisional (coded on Axis I). Finally, there was also some evidence that Carl had heightened problems with attention, so a provisional diagnosis of Attention-Deficit/Hyperactivity Disorder, Predominantly Inattentive Type was made (coded on Axis I). Note that the provisional diagnoses are meant to highlight the need to monitor Carl in these areas and to reevaluate for these problems at a later date. It was thought that the Expressive Language Disorder, which falls into the category of Communication Disorders, played the central role in Carl's difficulties.

Source: Rapoport & Ismond (1996).

Overall, these public laws have had a drastic effect on the educational and therapeutic services provided to special-needs children in the school system (Rathvon, Witt, & Elliott, 2004). For children who do not meet criteria for services under the IDEA, they can still access help through Section 504 of the Rehabilitation Act of 1973, which mandates that accommodations and modifications be provided to children identified by professionals outside the school system (such as physicians or private psychologists; Witt, Elliott, Daly, Gresham, & Kramer, 1998).

The IDEA requires that assessment and classification be performed by a multidisciplinary team, which includes at least one professional (such as a special education teacher) who has expertise in the area of the suspected disability. Decisions regarding placement of the child must be made by professionals who know the child, who know the placement options, and who can understand and interpret the assessment results (Wright & Wright, 2005). Classification in educational settings is most often consistent with the IDEA, but school psychologists and other professionals within the school system can refer to the *DSM-IV* criteria for help in understanding diagnoses of clinical disorders in children (Wright & Wright, 2005).

In addition to the identification and remediation of learning and emotional/behavioral disorders that disrupt the educational experience, there are a number of other factors related to children's functioning that are salient in the school environment. Issues such as problem solving, achievement-related beliefs, social competence, and self-efficacy are all important in the school setting (Rathvon et al., 2004). In addition, language, communication, and adaptive functioning are all crucial components to children's success in the school setting (Rathvon et al., 2004). As can be seen in Box 1.2, schools have also been a useful site for programs that are meant to help prevent the development of problems in children.

All kids need is a little help, a little hope, and somebody who believes in them.

—Earvin "Magic" Johnson

DISORDERS IN THE FUTURE OF *DSM*

In an effort to help encourage research on possible new diagnoses, an Appendix in *DSM-IV* describes disorders that are being considered for inclusion of *DSM-V.* Although none of the disorders are specific to children or adolescents, two disorders will be highlighted to show some possible diagnoses of the future. If included in *DSM-V,* these disorders could be used for children and adolescents as well as adults.

- Mixed anxiety-depressive disorder, which is reflective of symptoms of both anxiety and depression that are not severe enough to warrant a diagnosis of major depressive disorder or an anxiety disorder

- Factitious disorder by proxy, which is when a parent or other caretaker intentionally inflects harm or psychological symptoms on a child (or pretends that such harm or psychological symptoms exist in the child) so that the parent or caretaker can receive the social and emotional benefits of the child's illness (e.g., others will give them attention and

BOX 1.2

PREVENTION AND THE SCHOOLS: TWO SCHOOL-BASED PREVENTION PROGRAMS THAT WORK

The prevention of mental health problems, and concomitant promotion of competence in children, is a central theme in developmental psychopathology. There has been increasing interest in evidence-based prevention programs that are shown to work well (Weisz, Sandler, Durlak, & Anton, 2005). A great deal of prevention programs have been instituted in the school system. Because children can be accessed relatively easily in the school system, many preventionists have focused on reaching children and adolescents within the school system to prevent problems from occurring in the future. The following examples highlight two excellent prevention programs that have been instituted in schools nationwide to help prevent children from experiencing distress and psychological problems.

- **Primary Mental Health Project (PMHP):** Developed by Dr. Emory Cowen and his colleagues, the PMHP has been in existence for over 45 years and is now located in several thousand schools nationally and internationally. The PMHP is considered a selective prevention program, which means that the program identifies children "at risk" for the development of problems before any difficulties develop. Although the project began with a focus on preventing school failure, it soon began to focus on other characteristics related to school functioning, such as problem solving, social competence, and personal empowerment. Children who are identified as at risk for school failure are given extra help and guidance by a volunteer in the program. Often, these volunteers serve as mentors and role models for children. The PMHP has been extraordinarily successful in preventing school failure and also in preventing the development of emotional/behavioral problems (Cowen, Work, & Wyman, 1997; Johnson, Pedro-Carroll, & Demanchick, 2005).

- **The Improving Social Awareness–Social Problem Solving (ISA-SPS) Project:** The ISA-SPS Project has been in existence for over 25 years (Bruene-Butler, Hampson, Elias, Clabby, & Schuyler, 1997). The program is aimed at helping children transition from elementary school to middle school without developing emotional/behavioral problems. The main focus of the program centers around teaching children social problem-solving skills. This program is considered a universal prevention program because it allows all children, not just those at risk, to be exposed to the prevention program. Through classes conducted at school, children are taught eight steps that encompass social decision making and problem solving:

1. "Look for signs of different feelings.
2. Tell yourself what the problem is.
3. Decide on your goal.
4. Stop and think of as many solutions to the problem as you can.
5. For each solution, think of all the things that might happen next.
6. Choose your best solution.
7. Plan it and make a final check.
8. Try it and rethink it." (Bruene-Butler et al., 1997, p. 249)

These steps are consistent with a number of other cognitive–behavioral programs designed to help children learn impulse control and social skills. In the ISA-SPS Project, children not only learn these strategies, but they are offered many opportunities to role-play their new skills and to try out their newly acquired solutions to social problem solving. The program has been successful at teaching children new skills and in decreasing the social and emotionally difficulties that often accompany transition from elementary school to middle school. The program now is instituted in a number of schools, from elementary through high schools (Sukhodolsky, Golub, Stone, & Orban, 2005).

---

sympathy). This problem has often been referred to as Munchausen by proxy.

It is unclear whether these disorders will be listed in the upcoming edition of *DSM-V*. These examples illustrate the attempt to develop more specific diagnoses that might help classify abnormal behavior across the life span. In addition, the task force for *DSM-V* plans to pay more attention to dimensional conceptualizations of psychopathology (Hankin, Fraley, Lahey, & Waldman, 2005; Widiger & Clark, 2000). There has also been some discussion of including clients and parents of clients in the revision process for *DSM-V* (Sadler, 2004). According to the American Psychiatric Publishing, Inc., which publishes the *DSM* for the American Psychiatric Association, *DSM-V* is scheduled to be published in 2011 (Kupfer, First, & Regier, 2002).

ADVANTAGES AND DISADVANTAGES OF *DSM-IV*

With any system of classification like *DSM-IV,* there are bound to be strengths and weaknesses. The strengths of DSM-IV are many. Probably the most salient strength of the *DSM* system is the wide acceptance and use of the system. It has been estimated that over 500,000 mental health professionals in the United States utilize *DSM-IV* in their work (Nathan, 1997). Thus, when a client is diagnosed in California, the client would have probably received the same diagnosis if she or he had lived in New York. Similarly, researchers from across the nation can use the same terminology to compare and contrast their research samples. Having such a widely followed system also allows for professionals from many different disciplines and many different countries to share a common diagnostic language. Thus, even though the *DSM* system was developed by psychiatrists, many different types of mental health professionals utilize *DSM-IV* currently, including school psychologists, social workers, clinical psychologists, counselors, and psychiatrists. This commonality reaches to many other countries as well, so that cross-cultural research can use the same diagnostic system (e.g., Muris, Schmidt, Engelbrecht, & Perold, 2002; Yang, Wang, Qian, Biederman, & Faraone, 2004).

In keeping with the benefit of a common diagnostic language, another advantage of *DSM-IV* is that many insurance companies have adopted its use to establish coverage for certain clinical disorders. Although not all insurance companies cover treatment of mental health problems, *DSM-IV* is often the diagnostic system that is used when services for mental health are covered.

As mentioned previously, *DSM-IV* represents an improvement on earlier versions, with the inclusion of multiaxial evaluation, adequate conceptualizations of psychosocial and environmental problems, greater attention to some disorders of childhood and adolescence, an attempt to be atheoretical, and increased attention to details in diagnostic criteria (American Psychiatric Association, 2000; Gruenberg & Goldstein, 2003). In addition, the *DSM-IV* classification system is thought to be as good or better than the previous versions regarding reliability and validity, even though there are limited psychometric data published at this time (Helzer & Hudziak, 2002). Overall, *DSM-IV* has been helpful in allowing researchers and clinicians to have a common language with which to discuss clients.

The limitations of the *DSM-IV* system are reflected in the terminology related to diagnosis itself. Achenbach (1998) distinguished between diagnosis for solely classification purposes in contrast to diagnostic formulations, which explore the nature, etiology, and conclusions about a particular problem. Unfortunately, *DSM-IV* is usually used solely for classification. Children and adolescents are classified into diagnostic categories, and little attention is given to what led to the problems or what would help alleviate the problems. Diagnostic formulations, on the other hand, would not only evaluate the appropriateness of an actual diagnosis, but would also consider the child's functioning in other areas (such as developmental history, genetic predisposition, physical functioning, educational functioning, cognitions, family issues, social network, strengths, and interests). Although the *DSM-IV* system does not prevent more thorough diagnostic formulations from occurring, it may inadvertently allow clinicians to think that the evaluation process is concluded when a diagnosis is reached.

Another significant criticism of *DSM-IV* and *ICD-10* is that they both are formulated within the medical model. The **medical model** occurs when the medical system is applied to mental health issues. The medical model is evident when behaviors are referred to as symptoms, when mental health problems are referred to as diseases or disorders, and when the individual's problem is located within the individual her or himself, rather than in the context or environment (Trull, 2005). The medical model has been criticized for a number of reasons, including encouraging biological rather than social, psychological, familial, or environmental views of mental health problems, focusing attention on deficits rather than strengths of individuals, and conceptualizing clients as passive in the therapeutic process (Korchin, 1976). In fact, even the terminology that clinicians use is sometimes reflective of the medical model. In many settings, individuals receiving services are referred to as patients, rather than clients or consumers. The terms *clients* and *consumers* imply a much more active role on the part of the individual and should convey the message that professionals are not the only ones who have expertise in healthy functioning (Trull, 2005). The medical model can be contrasted to the new paradigm of disability, which focuses on strengths rather than deficits, promotion of health and resilience rather than risk for problems, and focuses on the social, political, economic, and legal influences on functioning rather than difficulties internal to the individual (Olkin & Pledger, 2003).

The bulk of limitations of *DSM-IV* listed so far are related to the diagnostic system in general. There are, however, specific limitations to *DSM-IV* when considering the diagnostic classification of children and adolescents, rather than adults. First of all, the reliability of diagnoses of children and adolescents lags far behind the reliability of diagnoses of adults (American Psychiatric Association, 1998). Because the process of diagnosing children and adolescents is newer to the field than diagnosing adults, it may be that the process of diagnosing children and adolescents will eventually "catch up" with the process of diagnosing adults. It could also be that the current diagnoses just do not capture the actual behaviors of children and adolescents in a meaningful and distinct manner. In light of the fact that so many disorders can be diagnosed in the same child or adolescent, some researchers have raised the question as to the utility of the diagnostic system altogether (Caplan, 1995; Caplan & Cosgrove, 2004; Kutchins & Kirk, 1997).

The poor reliability of diagnoses in childhood and adolescents may merely be a reflection of the complexity of youth. Even in very reliable assessment systems,

different informants, such as mothers, fathers, and teachers, often have very different perspectives on children's behavior (DeLosReyes & Kazdin, 2004; Youngstrom, Findling, & Calabrese, 2003). Thus, the difficulty with reliable diagnoses may be related to the complexity of children's behavior and the possibility of children behaving differently in different environments.

A related issue is the lack of developmental sensitivity and specificity in the diagnostic criteria for child and adolescent disorders. As illustrated at the beginning of the chapter, age and developmental level are extremely important factors to consider when evaluating children's and adolescents' behavior. Although there is a specific section on disorders first evident in infancy, childhood, and adolescents in *DSM-IV*, the diagnostic criteria throughout the entire system lack developmental sensitivity (Doucette, 2002). Clinicians are left to use their own judgement about what is expected for a child of that particular age, developmental level, gender, racial or ethnic background, and culture. Most of the diagnostic criteria for childhood disorders do continue to note the importance of diagnosing only behavior that is maladaptive and inconsistent with developmental level, but clinicians are left to make this judgement themselves rather than relying on empirically validated assessment measures.

Finally, but probably most importantly, a diagnostic system such as *DSM-IV* allows children and adolescents

---

YOU DECIDE: IS THE DSM-IV GOOD FOR CHILDREN AND ADOLESCENTS?

Throughout the book, controversial topics will be presented with both ends of the spectrum provided. Data will be provided so that you can consider where you stand on the issue. To begin with, we will ask: Is the *DSM-IV* good for children and adolescents?

Yes

- The *DSM-IV* has been revised with the most up-to-date clinical evidence regarding mental disorders (First & Pincus, 2002), and dimensional characterizations of mental disorders can be encompassed in *DSM-IV* because considerations of subthreshold mental disorders (i.e., problems that do not meet criteria for a diagnosis) are allowed (Pincus, McQueen, & Elinson, 2003).

- Given the current health-care system, the majority of children and adolescents would not be eligible for mental health services without a formal psychiatric diagnosis (Patterson & Lusterman, 1996).

No

- Labeling children leads to negative interpretations of their behavior and allows individuals to ignore the strengths within children (Fewster, 2002). Further, the *DSM-IV* and other systems of psychiatric diagnosis are inherently biased, especially against females and racial/ethnic minorities (Poland & Caplan, 2004).

- Difficulties in the child's environment and family, such as poverty, abuse, and poor parenting, are at the heart of children's difficulties, so assigning a diagnosis that implies that the problem is within the child is incorrect and potentially damaging (Hines, Heinlen, Enochs, Etzbach, & Etzbach, 2005).

So, is the *DSM-IV* good for children and adolescents? You decide.

to be labeled for behavior that may or may not be an important part of their character. **Labeling** occurs when information about a child's diagnostic classification is communicated in a negative manner that leads to stigma for the child (Penn et al., 2005; Sternberg & Grigorenko, 2000; Stolzer, 2005). There is concern that labeling and diagnoses might lead to **self-fulfilling prophecies,** in which children and adolescents act in a manner that confirms the diagnosis simply because they know about the diagnosis (Hobbs, 1975). For example, if a boy is diagnosed with attention-deficit/hyperactivity disorder—combined type, he may inadvertently act even more overactive, impulsive, and inattentive than he did before the diagnosis simply because he has been told of the diagnosis. Sometimes parents and professionals unwittingly reinforce self-fulfilling prophecies by acting as though the diagnosis is a central characteristic of that child. For example, if teachers lower their expectations of children who are identified with a problem, then the children may not be motivated to achieve their full potential in school (Cullinan, 2007).

For this, and many other reasons, many mental health professionals have advocated for more careful usage of terminology related to diagnoses (Hupp & Adams, 2004). Think about the different implications in the following two sentences: She's an autistic child versus she's a child with autism. The first sentence might lead you to think that there is nothing else important to know about this child other than her autism. The second sentence will hopeful convey that, although the child has been diagnosed with autism, there are many other important characteristics to know about her. Although labeling can occur no matter what terminology is used, these issues of language were even noted in *DSM-IV* (American Psychiatric Association, 2000) to encourage professionals to be conscientious when discussing their clients. Overall, there has been mixed support of the usefulness of the *DSM* system with children, as is evident from the "You Decide" section.

Youth is the turning point of life, the most sensitive and volatile period, the state that registers most vividly the impressions and experience of life.

—Richard Wright

DIFFERENCES BETWEEN CATEGORICAL AND DIMENSIONAL UNDERSTANDING OF BEHAVIOR

To counteract many of the limitations in the diagnostic process, and especially to address the somewhat subjective process of decision making that led to the inclusion or exclusion of diagnoses into diagnostic systems such as *DSM-IV* or *ICD-10,* a number of researchers and clinicians have opted for a more empirically based (i.e., research based) understanding of children's and adolescents' emotional/behavioral problems. To understand these contrasting approaches, we need to step back and think about the essence of the diagnostic process in its current form. Both *DSM-IV* and *ICD-10* represent a **categorical approach** to the description of children's mental health problems. As the name implies, a categorical approach attempts to categorize mental health problems into distinct diagnoses. The categorical approach is based on the idea that children either meet criteria for a specific disorder or they do not. This conceptualization allows a clinician to make a dichotomous decision (i.e., yes the child meets criteria or no the child does not meet criteria for that disorder).

Categorical approaches are thought to be most appropriate when there is great homogeneity within each category (i.e., a lot of similarity among children diagnosed with the same disorder), when there are clear boundaries and differences between categories (i.e., the disorders do not overlap in descriptions), and when categories are mutually exclusive (i.e., if you meet criteria for one disorder then you can not meet criteria for another disorder, American Psychiatric Association, 2000). Although some of these assumptions are accurate for certain disorders in the *DSM-IV* diagnostic system, many professionals have expressed hesitation about a categorical system of classifying mental health problems (e.g., Achenbach, 1982; Clark, Watson, & Reynolds, 1995). Many professionals think that the categorical approach is inappropriate for understanding child psychopathology and limits research advances regarding child psychopathology (Sonuga-Barke, 1998). There are empirical data to question the use of dichotomous categories for some childhood problems, such as depression (Hankin, Fraley, et al., 2005). For these reasons, many professionals have tried to identify appropriate alternatives to the categorical approach of diagnostic classification.

The **dimensional approach** is an alternative way of conceptualizing children's mental health problems. As the name implies, this approach focuses on different dimensions or different levels of a child's behavior. Rather than determine whether or not a child meets criteria for a particular disorder, a clinician using the dimensional system would look at the varying levels of different behaviors that a child exhibits. The range of behaviors would be evaluated on a continuum, without an artificial limit that puts the child

Case Study: The Case of Julie—An Example of the Dimensional Conceptualization of Behavior

By the age of 14, Julie was arrested for shoplifting a sweater from a local clothing store. Although this was her first arrest, Julie had experienced a troubled childhood. Her biological parents had a conflicted and violent marriage that ended when Julie was 5. From the age of 5 to 10, Julie was transferred back and forth from her mother's and father's homes and was often left unsupervised in both homes. Her parents both experienced alcohol and drug abuse problems. In addition, her mother was diagnosed with bipolar disorder (often known as manic-depression). When Julie was 10 years old, the state protective agency intervened and took Julie away from her parents due to her mother's neglect and her father's and mother's boyfriend's physical abuse. Eventually, parental rights were terminated.

Julie was placed in a foster home, with a couple who eventually adopted her. She initially appeared sad, sullen, moody, and irritable. In addition, she had few friends. Her adoptive parents tried to talk with her and attempted to provide her a stable, nurturing environment. By the age of 13, Julie appeared to be happier and more outgoing. Her adoptive parents became concerned, however, when Julie began associating with "troublemakers" in the community and staying out past her curfew. Julie became more involved in illicit activities with her friends and also became involved in sexual activities with three different boys.

The profile shown below illustrates Julie's adoptive parents' reports of her behavior at the age of 10 and at the age of 14 (after the arrest for shoplifting). Higher scores represent more problems. Scores above the highest dotted line are considered to be in the clinical range. At the age of 10, Julie's greatest problems, according to her parents, were related to being withdrawn, having social problems, and having attention problems. At the age of 14, Julie's most salient problem was in the area of delinquency, with some continuing problems in being withdrawn.

After the arrest, Julie received counseling services and was encouraged to become involved in prosocial activities at school, such as band, drama, and after-school clubs. She also volunteered in a hospital to honor the community service hours that were required after her shoplifting arrest. By the age of 15, there were dramatic reductions in Julie's delinquent behavior, and she appeared to be happy and well adjusted. She continued in counseling to deal with her feelings of anger and abandonment from her biological parents.

This case illustrates a way of conceptualizing a child's behavior from a dimensional, rather than categorical, framework. The assessment showed higher and lower levels of problems, without categorizing Julie's behavior into a specific diagnostic category.

Source: Achenbach & McConaughy (1997).

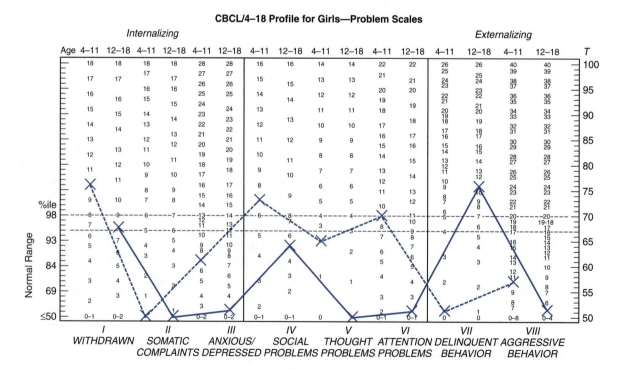

Hand-Scored CBCL Problem Profiles for Julie at Age 14 (Solid Line) and Age 10 (Broken Line).

into a diagnostic category or keeps the child from meeting a diagnosis. Dimensional conceptualizations are advantageous because they reduce large numbers of diagnoses into smaller numbers of dimensions of behaviors and because they highlight the level of severity for remediation and treatment of behaviors that are considered problematic (Clark et al., 1995). In addition, behavior exists on a continuum (i.e., different individuals show varying levels of behaviors) rather than in distinct units (i.e., it is unlikely that certain individuals show lots of a particular behavior, whereas other individuals show almost none of that particular behavior), so the dimensional approach is consistent with behavior as it actually exists (Clark et al., 1995). In a comprehensive review of mental health by the then-surgeon general, psychological problems were noted to be on a continuum (Satcher, 2000, 2001).

Dimensional approaches to children's and adolescents' emotional/behavioral problems are consistent with **empirically based taxonomies.** Given that the term *empirical* means research, an empirically based taxonomy is a system in which "assessment of behavioral and emotional functioning is viewed as a measurement process that identifies quantitative gradations in the target phenomena" (Achenbach & McConaughy, 1997, p. 3). In other words, empirically based taxonomies rely on actual data to understand and interpret children's and adolescents' behavior (Achenbach, 2002). Most other diagnostic systems (such as the *DSM* system and the *ICD* system) use data as only one part of the process to inform committees and professionals who establish the diagnostic criteria.

In contrast, an empirically based taxonomy originates from research data and is modified solely on research data, Achenbach and McConaughy (1997, 2003) developed an empirically based taxonomy guided by the following principles:

- Collect information in a standardized manner from a large, representative sample of youth by asking different informants (such as parents, teachers, and children themselves) about the competencies and problems of the youth.

- Analyze the assessment data through empirical and quantitative methods to explore connections and associations among the behaviors reported for the children and adolescents.

- After associations are identified among children's and adolescents' problem behaviors, syndromes are identified to show higher order groupings of the behavior problems.

- Scales (such as anxious/depressed or aggressive) are developed based on the behavioral items. To score individual youngsters on these scales, normative data are utilized so that an individual child's behavior can be compared with what would be expected from children of that age range and gender.

- An individual child or adolescent can be assessed with the same standard instruments that were used in the original development of the empirically based taxonomy.

Because dimensional systems tend to be conceptualized within empirically based taxonomies, dimensional systems also tend to be oriented toward empirical data. One of the primary reasons a dimensional approach is advantageous over a diagnostic system such as *DSM-IV* is that it is based on research data that are reflective of children's and adolescents' behavior.

Note that, although there is a history of polarizing the categorical and dimensional approaches, there has been some attention to the mutual strengths of both approaches. Both the categorical and dimensional approaches have strengths that are necessary for thorough evaluations of children and adolescents (Jensen & Watanabe, 1999). In a study that compared a categorical evaluation process with a dimensional evaluation process, children who showed problems through one approach but not the other were still thought to have problems that were in need of attention (Jensen & Watanabe, 1999). In other words, children who met diagnostic criteria but did not score high on a dimensional evaluation and, conversely, children who did not meet diagnostic criteria but did score high on a dimensional evaluation were still likely to need help regardless of what pattern they showed. Thus, both categorical and dimensional approaches were necessary for understanding children's and adolescents' emotional/behavioral problems (Jensen & Watanabe, 1999). Both systems could be used in a complimentary rather than adversarial manner to understand children's and adolescents' functioning in a comprehensive manner (Beauchaine, 2003; Youngstrom, Findling, & Calabrese, 2003). Some recent empirically based dimensional scales also provide information on how each child's scores correspond to *DSM* criteria (Achenbach, Dumenci, & Rescorla, 2003; Achenbach & Rescorla, 2001), and there are suggestions that using both a categorical and dimensional analysis of children's behavior is superior to using only one or the other (Ferdinand et al., 2004).

Regardless of whether you use a categorical or dimensional approach to understand children's and adolescents' functioning, it is crucial to remember that

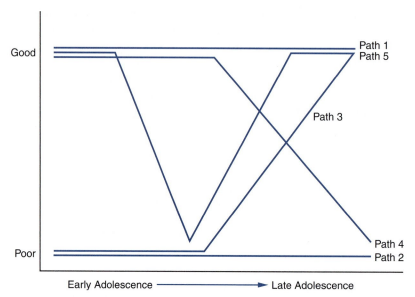

FIGURE 1.1 There are multiple pathways of development throughout childhood and adolescence

Path 1: Stable adaptation (few problems, good self-worth, low risk exposure)

Path 2: Stable maladaptation (chronic adversities, little parental protection)

Path 3: Reversal of maladaptation (important life change creates new opportunity, such as transfer to new school with caring teachers and a prosocial peer group)

Path 4: Decline of adaptation (environmental or biological shifts bring adversity, such as parental divorce that contributes to problems)

Path 5: Temporal maladaptation (can reflect transient experimental risk taking, such as use of illegal drugs).

Source: Compas, Hinden, & Gerhardt (1995). With permission, from the *Annual Review of Psychology,* Volume 46, (c) 1995 by Annual Reviews www.AnnualReviews.org.

behavior can change over time. If a child shows elevated levels of a problem at a particular point in time, it does not necessarily mean that she or he will always show high levels of that problem. As can be seen in Figure 1.1, even in adolescence, there are many possible pathways of developmental adaptation.

PREVALENCE OF CHILDREN'S AND ADOLESCENTS' PROBLEM BEHAVIOR

After understanding the different conceptualizations of children's and adolescents' emotional/behavioral problems, the next logical issue is the extent to which youth experience these problems. The term **epidemiology** refers to the study of the prevalence, incidence, and distribution of mental disorders or emotional/behavioral

problems within a particular population. **Prevalence** refers to the total number of cases (e.g., number of youth with a clinical disorder, or number of youth who score in the clinical range on a particular measure) at a particular point in time. **Incidence,** on the other hand, refers to the number of new cases in a given period of time (such as how many youth developed a particular problem within the past year). Prevalence rates are usually cited when describing the commonality or rarity of specific clinical disorders (e.g., this disorder is more common than that disorder). Incidence rates are usually discussed when looking at changes over time in rates of clinical disorders (e.g., Has there been an increase in children experiencing a particular clinical disorder over the past ten years?). The study of epidemiology can help inform clinical practice (Walker-Barnes, 2003), public policy (Mason, 2003), and prevention programs (Yale, Scott, Gross, & Gonzalez, 2003). The epidemiology of different disorders and emotional/behavioral problems will be discussed in each chapter separately, but a few comments on overall prevalence rates are in order to put abnormal child behavior in context.

EPIDEMIOLOGICAL RATES BASED ON THE CATEGORICAL APPROACH

Although there have been a number of epidemiological studies over the years, the largest and most comprehensive epidemiological study of children and adolescents in the United States has been the Methods for the Epidemiology of Child and Adolescent Mental Disorders (MECA) Study (Goodman et al., 1998). Funded by the National Institute of Mental Health (NIMH), the MECA study was completed by over 30 psychologists, psychiatrists, public health researchers, and other professionals (as well as their research staffs). The MECA study was meant to parallel the National Institute of Mental Health Epidemiologic Catchment Area (ECA) study of clinical disorders in adults (Robins & Regier, 1991). Based on the ECA study, it was estimated that 29.5% of adults experienced a clinical disorder at some point in the past year.

Data from the MECA study continue to be published, and there are a number of interesting and enlightening papers published from this important study (Goodman et al., 1998; Goodman, Schwab-Stone, Lahey, Shaffer, & Jensen, 2000; Gordon et al., 2003; Kandel et al., 1999; King et al., 2001; Lahey et al., 1996; Lahey et al., 2000; Leaf et al., 1996; Shaffer et al., 1996). The sample was comprised of nearly 1,300 children and adolescents (aged 9–17) and their parents, who were recruited from four primary sites in the United States: Connecticut, Georgia, New York, and San Juan, Puerto Rico. Parents and youth were interviewed with the Diagnostic Interview Schedule for Children (DISC; Shaffer et al., 1996), which is a structured interview that can be completed by parents and youth separately. In the sample, there were approximately equal numbers of boys and girls (53% and 47%, respectively). There was an attempt to recruit youth and their parents from ethnically diverse and socioeconomically diverse areas, however, the final distribution of race/ethnicity in the MECA study showed an overrepresentation of Hispanic/Latino/Latina participants and a slight underrepresentation of African-American participants (Lahey et al., 1996). The median family income was somewhat higher than what would be expected from families in those target areas. Overall, the sample in the MECA study was somewhat more representative than previous epidemiological studies, but the sample was still not truly representative of children and adolescents in the United States.

Given this caveat, it is still worthwhile to explore the information that was gained from the MECA study. Overall, when parents were interviewed, 19.2% of children and adolescents met criteria for a clinical disorder and showed the level of impairment that was necessary for being diagnosed with that disorder (Shaffer et al., 1996). When children and adolescents were interviewed, the prevalence rate was shown to be 19.6%. When parents and youth were combined, a total of 32.8% of the sample met criteria for a clinical disorder (Shaffer et al., 1996). In a refined analysis of these data, it appeared that only 6.6% of children and adolescents met criteria for a diagnosis (with impairment) when both the youth and the parent reported the same types of problems (Leaf et al., 1996). Thus, when trying to summarize the prevalence data from the MECA study, the answer depends on who you ask. This issue is relevant in any type of research with children and adolescents, so it is not unique to the MECA study.

Given the range of prevalence rates from 6.6% to 32.8%, it should be noted that the most consistent reports of prevalence rates of child and adolescent disorders usually fall between 14% and 20% (Brandenburg, Friedman, & Silver, 1990; Costello, Mustillo, Erkanli, Keller, & Anglold, 2003). It is also important to consider lifetime prevalence rates, which explore whether or not the child has ever experienced a psychiatric disorder in his or her lifetime. Estimates in the United States and New Zealand are comparable for lifetime prevalence rates at 39.0% and 38.3%, respectively (Jaffee, Harrington, Cohen, & Moffitt, 2005). Overall, these prevalence data suggest that a significant number of children and adolescents experience some type of psychopathology at some point during their childhood. Table 1.4 shows the prevalence rates that were listed in *DSM-IV* for specific disorders. Note that prevalence rates are significantly higher for children living in families who receive public assistance, with some researchers suggesting that nearly half (47.9%) of children in the welfare system experienced elevated problems in mental health (Burns et al., 2004). Other studies of children in foster care suggest that 37% met criteria for a disorder within the past year (McMillen et al., 2005).

Epidemiological rates vary by country. In a study of adolescent self-reports across seven countries, Verhulst

TABLE 1.4 Prevalence Estimates of Selected Clinical Disorders in Children and Adolescents

Clinical Disorder	Estimated Prevalence*
Mental retardation	1%
Learning disorders	2%–10%
Autistic disorder	< 1%
Attention-deficit/hyperactivity disorder (in school-age children)	3%–7%
Conduct disorder	1%–10%
Oppositional defiant disorder	2%–16%
Separation anxiety disorder	4%

*Note that prevalence rates vary according to a number of factors, including the methodology, the sample characteristics, and the assessment measures. These prevalence rates are the estimates presented in *DSM-IV* for children and adolescents (American Psychiatric Association, 2000). Prevalence rates for children and adolescents were not listed in *DSM-IV* for a number of disorders (such as major depressive disorder and a number of the anxiety disorders). Epidemiological information will be discussed at greater length in each chapter.

Source: American Psychiatric Association (2000).

and colleagues (2003) found that adolescents from China and Jamaica reported the highest levels of psychopathology, whereas adolescents from Israel and Turkey reported the lowest levels. Adolescents' self-reported psychopathology in the United States, Australia, and the Netherlands fell between these other four countries. Another review explored prevalence rates of childhood psychopathology in a number of different countries and found rates of psychopathology of 12.4% in France, 17.6% in New Zealand, 25.4% in Ireland, and 26.0% in the Netherlands (Bird, 1996). Prevalence rates of childhood disorders were found to range from 10% to 18% in Germany (Barkmann & Schulte-Markwort, 2005) and were found to be 15% in Bangladesh (Mullick & Goodman, 2005). It is important, however, not to diagnose children in one culture with the definitions of psychopathology from another culture (Alarcon et al., 2002; Kress, Eriksen, Rayle, & Ford, 2005; Lopez & Guarnaccia, 2000).

As you might expect, the rates of different disorders vary according to a number of factors such as gender and age. Epidemiological data on specific disorders will be presented in each chapter separately, but some patterns of prevalence rates might be helpful to keep in mind when considering psychopathology in childhood. Girls, and especially adolescent girls, tend to experience major depressive disorder, some types of anxiety disorders, eating disorders, and adjustment disorders to a greater extent than do adolescent boys

(American Psychiatric Association, 2000; Crick & Zahn-Waxler, 2003). Before adolescence, boys show higher rates of oppositional defiant disorder than do girls. Both before and during adolescence, boys show higher rates of other disruptive disorders (such as attention-deficit/hyperactivity disorder and conduct disorder) than do girls (American Psychiatric Association, 2000; Crick & Zahn-Waxler, 2003; McCabe et al., 2004). As you might already have noticed, girls show higher rates of problems that are not disruptive in nature, and boys show higher rates of problems that are disruptive in nature. These patterns of gender differences have been found internationally (Verhulst et al., 2003). Specific patterns of gender differences will be explored for individual disorders in later chapters, but suffice it to say that there is a wide range of explanations for these gender differences including, biological, genetic, socialization, and cognitive differences (Winstead & Sanchez, 2005).

Each chapter will also address patterns of the co-occurrence of disorders within children and adolescents of both genders. **Comorbidity** is the term used to describe the co-occurrence of two or more diagnosed disorders in one individual. Within the study of child and adolescent psychopathology, comorbidity is the rule rather than the exception (Doss & Weisz, 2006; Jensen, 2003). There are high rates of comorbidity between attention-deficit/hyperactivity disorder and conduct disorder, major depressive disorder and anxiety disorders, major depressive disorder and conduct disorder, major depression and bulimia, and major depression and substance use disorders (Joiner & Lonigan, 2000; Lilienfeld, 2003; Stice, Burton, & Shaw, 2004; Swendsen & Merikangas, 2000). In addition, high rates of comorbidity are evident between learning disorders and other psychological disorders (Willcutt & Pennington, 2000). These high rates of comorbidity have been interpreted in a number of different ways, from establishing the fact that distressed children are often distressed in many different ways, to suggesting that the categorical approach is inadequate due to the overlap between categories that were meant to be separate and distinct. Specifically, high rates of comorbidity call into question a categorical system such as *DSM-IV* (Jensen, 2003; Meehl, 2001; Waldman & Lilienfeld, 2001). Comorbidity rates have, however, been used to support genetic influences for multiple disorders (Simonoff, 2000). The issue of comorbidity is relevant to the understanding of psychopathology from a dimensional perspective, given that the dimensional perspective by definition allows children and adolescents to show lower and higher levels of problems in different areas of functioning.

EPIDEMIOLOGICAL RATES BASED ON THE DIMENSIONAL APPROACH

Dr. Tom Achenbach and colleagues (Achenbach, Howell, McConaughy, & Stanger, 1995a, 1995b, 1995c; Achenbach, Howell, Quay, & Conners, 1991; Achenbach & Rescorla, 2001) have conducted some of the most well-designed and comprehensive studies to explore children's and adolescents' functioning from a dimensional approach. Using measures such as the Child Behavior Checklist (CBCL; Achenbach & Rescorla, 2001), which is completed by parents, Achenbach and his colleagues have conducted large-scale national and international investigations into the occurrence of children's and adolescents' emotional/behavioral problems.

To understand children's and adolescents' functioning from a dimensional perspective, it is important to understand the distinction between internalizing and externalizing emotional/behavioral problems. **Internalizing problems** are feelings or behaviors that are over-controlled and primarily experienced internally by the child (such as anxiety, depression, and withdrawal). **Externalizing problems** are behaviors that are under-controlled and primarily experienced externally to the child (such as breaking rules and aggression). These two broad dimensions of children's and adolescents' emotional/behavioral functioning have been well established within the United States (Achenbach & Rescorla, 2001), as well as many other countries (Heubeck, 2000).

Based on a study of over 3,200 parents' reports of matched clinical and nonclinical children, a number of items showed clear distinctions between youth who were receiving mental health services and those who were not. As can be seen in Table 1.5, behaviors ranging from inattention to sadness were helpful in distinguishing troubled children from well-functioning children. As will be discussed in the assessment chapter, the use of a measure like the CBCL allows children's and adolescents' behavior to be compared with a normative sample and to be evaluated on a continuum. Although there are clinical cutoffs to help in the identification of troubled children and adolescents, this type of dimensional system allows children's and adolescents' behavior to be considered on a continuum rather than in a dichotomous or categorical fashion. It is interesting to note that the referral status of children (i.e., whether or not they were referred for therapy) was the most salient characteristic that showed differences between the items. Differences between boys and girls were very limited, as were differences between younger and older

TABLE 1.5   Gender, Age, and Race: Items on the Child Behavior Checklist That Showed More Than 20% Difference in the Variance between Children in Different Groups

Referred for Treatment vs. Not Referred	
Can't concentrate, can't pay attention for long	**Gender** (None)
Cruelty, bullying, or meanness to others	
Disobedient at home	**Age**
Disobedient at school	(None)
Doesn't get along with other kids	
Breaks rules at home, school, or elsewhere	**Race/Ethnicity**
Impulsive or acts without thinking	(None)
Lying or cheating	
Poor schoolwork	**Socioeconomic Status**
Sudden changes in mood or feelings	(None)
Temper or hot temper	
Unhappy, sad, or depressed	
Total problems	

Note: When items were compared for boys and girls, no item showed a difference of more than 20% of the variance, and in fact, no item showed more than 6% of the variance on the Child Behavior Checklist. When younger children were compared with adolescents, no items showed a difference of greater than 20% and no item showed more than 10% variance. When items were compared for race/ethnicity and socioeconomic status, very few differences emerged (Achenbach & Rescorla, 2001).

TABLE 1.6   Broadband and Narrowband Emotional/Behavioral Problem Factors from the Child Behavior Checklist, Youth Self-Report, and Teacher's Report Form

Internalizing Problems		Externalizing Problems
Anxious/ depressed	Social problems	Rule-breaking behavior
Withdrawn/ depressed	Thought problems	Aggressive behavior
Somatic complaints	Attention problems	

Note: In addition to these emotional/behavioral problem factors, there is also a measure of competence on each of these measures (Achenbach & Rescorla, 2001).

children, youth from different racial and ethnic groups, and youth from higher versus lower socioeconomic brackets (Achenbach & Rescorla, 2001).

Table 1.6 presents the broadband and narrowband factors that have been established through empirically based assessments in national surveys of 6- to 18-year-olds. In a 3 year follow-up study, there were strong correlations from adolescence to adulthood for most of these types of syndromes (Achenbach, Howell, McConaughy, & Stanger, 1995a, 1995b, 1995c).

The exploration of children's and adolescents' emotional/behavioral functioning from a dimensional perspective has allowed an in-depth look at national changes over time. In an article entitled, "Are American Children's Problems Still Getting Worse? A 23-Year Comparison," Achenbach, Dumenci, and Rescorla (2003) compared parents' reports of children's behavior in 1976, 1989, and 1999. Although there had been increases in children's emotional/behavioral problems between 1976 and 1989, there was a significant decrease in children's emotional/behavioral problems from 1989 to 1999. The rates of emotional/behavioral problems in 1999, however, were still higher than those reported in 1976. Overall, this study showed the importance of tracking children's functioning from a dimensional perspective.

HOW CHILDREN'S ENVIRONMENTS INFLUENCE THEIR BEHAVIOR

Within the study of developmental psychopathology, there has been increasing interest in understanding the social context in which children's problematic behaviors occur (Ford, Goodman, & Meltzer, 2004; Gordon et al., 2003; Reijneveld, Brugman, Verhulst, & Verloove-Vanhorick, 2005). Researchers recently began exploring children's and adolescents' behavior within a specific context to identify person by environment interactions. In an intensive observational study of troubled children's social interactions at a therapeutic summer camp, researchers found that children high in internalizing problems tended to withdraw in aversive situations with peers and adults, children with high externalizing problems tended to show higher rates of aggression toward peers but not adults, and children high in both internalizing and externalizing problems tended to show both withdrawal and aggression in reaction to their peers talking and showed surprisingly little withdrawal when they were teased or threatened by their peers (Wright, Zakriski, & Drinkwater, 1999). This research highlights the reciprocal nature of children's behavior, and it allows an important investigation into the interactions between children and their environment (Keiley, Bates, Dodge, & Pettit, 2000; Wright & Zakriski, 2001). Box 1.3 discusses a cross-cultural study that also relates to environmental context.

A crucial aspect of children's and adolescents' environment is their **socioeconomic status (SES)**, which

Poverty strikes children from all walks of life, but is much more prevalent in ethnic minority communities.

refers to a combination of factors, including the family's income, the parents' educational level, and the parents' occupational level (Luthar, 1999). SES and race/ethnicity are highly related within the United States. A total of 29.2% of children under 18 live in families characterized by low income (where the family income is below 200% of the federal poverty threshold; Urban Institute, 2004). This figure varies according to race/ethnicity, where:

- 21.4% of Caucasian American youth live in poverty.
- 44.4% of African-American youth live in poverty.

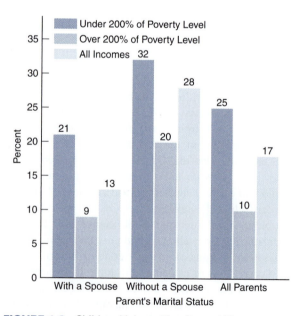

FIGURE 1.2 Children Living with a Parent Whose Symptoms Suggested Poor Mental Health, by Family Income and Parent's Marital Status, 1997.

BOX *1.3*

CROSS-CULTURAL ISSUES: HOW DO PARENTS FROM DIFFERENT NATIONS FEEL ABOUT THEIR CHILDREN'S BEHAVIOR?

In an extraordinary series of investigations, Dr. John Weisz and his colleagues have investigated the similarities and differences between the behaviors of children in the United States and children in Thailand (Weisz, Suwanlert, Chaiyasit, Weiss, Achenbach, & Trevatham, 1988; Weisz & Weiss, 1991; Weisz, Weiss, Suwanlert, & Chaiyasit, 2003; Reviewed in Weisz, McCarty, Eastman, Chaiyasit, & Suwanlert, 1997). One of the interesting findings to emerge from this project was the way in which parents perceive their children's behavior. Overall, parents from both countries felt that externalizing behaviors were more worrisome, more serious, and less likely to improve than internalizing problems. As can be seen below, there were also interesting differences between parents in both countries. Specifically, parents in the United States rated children's behavior problems as more worrisome, more serious, less likely to improve, and more unusual than parents in Thailand. These findings were parallel to the findings from teachers in the United States and in Thailand. Overall, this research highlights the fact that there are both similarities and differences between parents and teachers in different nations and in different cultures. These similarities and differences are important to explore to gain a more complete understanding of children's and adolescents' problems and competencies.

Source: Weisz, Suwanlert, Chaiyasit, Weiss, Walter, & Anderson (1988).

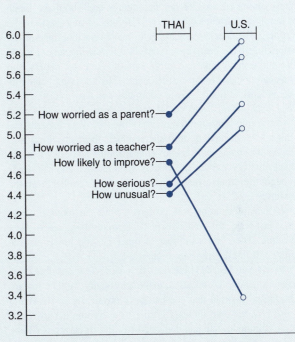

Parents' Perceptions of Child Behavior in Thailand and the United States.

- 54.5% of Hispanic/Latino/Latina youth live in poverty.

Throughout the remaining chapters, whenever differences related to race and ethnicity are discussed, it will be important to keep in mind the confounding factor of family socioeconomic status. For example, rates of many types of psychopathology are higher in children from lower SES families (Gordon et al., 2003; Reijneveld et al., 2005). It appears, however, that the effects of poverty are even more severe for the mental health of African-American children than children of other races and ethnicities (Luthar, 1999). In addition, the connection between children's mental health problems and lower SES may be mediated by harsh, inconsistent parenting and more severe stressors in the children's lives (McLoyd, 1998). As can be seen in Figure 1.2, children in the most severe poverty groups

who live with a singe parent are exposed to more parental psychological symptoms than children in other groups (Urban Institute, 1999a). Thus, the issues of socioeconomic status, racial/ethnic identity, and mental health are very complex.

Nothing that grieves us can be called little: by the eternal laws of proportion a child's loss of a doll and a king's loss of a crown are events of the same size.

—Mark Twain

DIFFERENT PERSPECTIVES ON PROBLEMS

Any discussion of children's and adolescents' emotional/behavioral functioning is not complete without

Case Study: Is it Obsessive Compulsive Disorder or a Troubled Family (or Both)?

Peta is an 8-year-old girl who meets diagnostic criteria for obsessive compulsive disorder (OCD). Peta worries extensively about the loss of her belongings and about the death of family and friends close to her. Before leaving home in the morning, she checks the garbage to make sure that none of her belongings have been thrown out. Before leaving school in the afternoon, she checks and verifies that her pencils, papers, and books are located in the correct places. Her checking behaviors take at least an hour a day to complete, and they interfere with Peta's schoolwork and social relationships. Peta has shown this checking behavior for over six months. Peta experiences a high level of anxiety until she conducts these checking rituals. Although she gains some relief from the anxiety when she checks her belongings, the anxiety soon returns, and she needs to begin the rituals over again to get temporary relief from the anxiety.

If this information was presented with the focus on Peta (as it just was), the diagnosis of OCD would be given without question. There are a number of other factors, however, that might call the diagnosis into question.

Peta's parents, David and Liza, have had an unstable marriage in which David used to be physically violent toward Liza. Liza reported that she had been physically and sexually abused by her own father. In order to overcome her own difficult childhood, she has dedicated her life to caring for Peta, and she has become extremely involved in every aspect of

Peta's life. David, however, makes all the decisions for the family and is overtly disrespectful to Liza and her feelings. David thinks that Peta's problems are due to Liza's lack of discipline. Liza worries that Peta's problems are due to the history of schizophrenia, depression, alcohol abuse, and OCD in David's family. There have also been a number of significant losses in Peta's young life, including the death of her grandfather, with whom she was close, the severe illness of a favorite teacher, and the loss of three cats in car accidents. Peta's grandmother apparently teases her that someone else in the family will die soon.

Overall, there are a number of factors that could be related to the development and maintenance of Peta's OCD behavior. She may have a genetic predisposition to psychopathology given the family history of psychopathology. There are a number of risk factors, such as spousal abuse, teasing, loss, and parental instability that could relate to her behavior. A family therapist would argue that the essence of Peta's problems are rooted in the dysfunction within the family and within the parents, rather than in Peta herself. This case should highlight the complex and multifaceted factors that can relate to children's and families' problems. When learning about each disorder in this book, it is essential that the family context and social context be taken into consideration in addition to understanding the individual's symptoms of psychopathology.

Source: Schwartz (1992).

considering the issue of who is distressed by the behavior. In a classic study, children receiving mental health services were compared with children not receiving mental services (Shepherd, Oppenheim, & Mitchell, 1971). The children were comparable on the severity of behavior problems, but the study sought to identify the factor that distinguished who had been referred for services and who had not been referred. As it turned out, mothers' perceptions of the severity of the problem, along with maternal competence, family dysfunction, and maternal depression were the primary factors that distinguished between the two groups. This study suggests that the definition of problem behavior can be related to more than just the actual behavior.

Not surprisingly, youth, parents, and teachers feel differently about which behaviors are bothersome. In a school-based sample of young adolescents, adolescents thought that their parents would be much more distressed about adolescents' externalizing prob-

lems than internalizing problems (Phares & Compas, 1990). Conversely, adolescents reported greater distress over their own internalizing problems than their externalizing emotional/behavioral problems. In a special education clinical sample of adolescents with elevated emotional/behavioral problems, both parents and teachers reported more distress over externalizing behavior problems than did adolescents (Phares & Danforth, 1994). Parents reported greater distress than either teachers or adolescents about adolescents' internalizing problems. These studies suggest that a part of the evaluation process should include information about how different individuals feel about the child's or adolescent's behavior. Because children and adolescents rarely refer themselves for therapy, it is likely that most clinicians will hear more from parents who are distressed by their children's behavior, regardless of how the children and adolescents feel about the behavior themselves.

If you really want to hear about it, the first thing you'll probably want to know is where I was born, and what my lousy childhood was like, and how my parents were occupied and all before they had me, and all that David Copperfield kind of crap, but I don't feel like going into it.
—J.D. Salinger

TROUBLED FAMILIES RATHER THAN TROUBLED CHILDREN

There is some evidence that exploring family issues can be as useful if not more useful than exploring issues related to the individual child. In the 1950s and 1960s, when *DSM-I* was still being used, a number of researchers and therapists were trying to identify issues within the family that might be related to children's maladaptive behavior (Bateson, Jackson, Haley, & Weakland, 1956; Laing & Esterson, 1965). Emotional and behavioral problems were thought to be due to problems in the family's structure, rather than in the child her or himself (Minuchin, Montalvo, Guerney, Rosman, & Schumer, 1967). In fact, family theorists argue that children's problems are primarily a reflection of actual problems that exist in the family (Cox & Paley, 2003; Kaslow, 2001; McGoldrick, Giordano, & Garcia-Preto, 2005; Reder, McClure, & Jolley, 2000). Given the empirical evidence for the connections between troubled families and troubled children, there has been recent interest in integrating family systems work into the study of developmental psychopathology (Campbell & Davies, 2002; Davies & Cicchetti, 2004; Serbin & Karp, 2003).

Often the family environment can be harmful to children.

Characteristics in families of troubled youth include

- Parental psychopathology
- Verbal and physical fighting between parents
- Dysfunctional family structure
- Troubled expression of emotions within the family

These issues (reviewed in Kaslow, 2001) will be discussed in greater detail in the chapter on theories and mechanisms, as well as throughout the book. As can be seen in the case study of Peta, cases that appear to be related to troubled behavior in the child can actually be due to troubled behavior patterns within the family.

SUMMARY AND KEY CONCEPTS

Normality and Abnormality in Children and Adolescents. A central theme in this book, and in **developmental psychopathology** in general, is that you need to know what is normal before you can determine what is abnormal. Also central to the understanding of developmental psychopathology are the concepts of **risk factors** and **protective factors,** which can put the child at increased risk or decreased risk for the development of problems, respectively.

How Abnormal Child Behavior Was Understood in the Past. There is a long and troubled history of the treatment of children with psychological problems, which was often influenced by the **Zeitgeist** of the time. From public scorn, to **infanticide,** to abandoning troubled children in orphanages, the history of the treatment of troubled children has been less than humane at times.

More Recent Diagnostic Classification Systems. The primary classification system in the United States is the *Diagnostic and Statistical Manual of Mental Disorders* (the fourth edition, text revision, is in use currently). Nationally and internationally, the *International Classification of Diseases (ICD-10)* is also used frequently. Early versions of the DSM system were biased by the belief that children were just miniature adults (a concept known as **adultomorphism**). More recently, there has been an attempt to be cognizant of the developmental processes that might influence disorders of childhood and adolescence. *DSM-IV* is intended to be **atheoretical,** and it allows the use of **differential diagnosis** to distinguish between two or more disorders in a child or adolescent. A strength of *DSM-IV* is that it allows the clinician to complete a **multiaxial evaluation,** which includes an evaluation of a possible **mental**

disorder (or other conditions that are the focus of attention or treatment, known as **V-Codes),** personality disorder, mental retardation, general medical condition, psychosocial and environmental problem, and global functioning.

Reliability and Validity of Diagnostic Categories. Reliability (such as **test-retest reliability, inter-rater reliability,** and use of the **kappa statistic**) and **validity** refer to the **psychometric properties** of a diagnostic system.

Children in the School System. Increasingly, professionals in the school system have had to deal with troubled children. Federal guidelines (such as PL 94–142, PL 99–457, PL 101–476, and PL 101–336) have protected the rights of special-needs children in the school system as well as in other settings.

Disorders in the Future of *DSM*. Research that will help inform the next revision of the *DSM* system is being conducted continuously. Disorders such as mixed anxiety-depressive disorder and factitious disorder by proxy are all under consideration for inclusion in *DSM-V.*

Advantages and Disadvantages of *DSM-IV*. There are a great many strengths to the *DSM* system. The overarching strength of *DSM-IV* is the wide acceptance and use of the diagnostic language. The weaknesses of *DSM-IV* include the use of the **medical model,** the possible harm of **labeling** children's and adolescents' divergent behaviors, and the possibilities of children developing **self-fulfilling prophecies** due to receiving a diagnosis.

Differences between Categorical and Dimensional Understandings of Behavior. *DSM-IV* is based on a **categorical** approach to classification of children's and adolescents' emotional/behavioral problems, in which behavior is classified into distinct diagnoses. In contrast, the **dimensional** approach views behavior in a continuous manner, where children and adolescents can show higher levels of some problems and lower levels of other problems, and the problems are not classified into a distinct category. Dimensional approaches are largely influenced by **empirically based taxonomies,** which are conceptualizations of behavior based on research data.

Prevalence of Children's and Adolescents' Problem Behavior. The study of **epidemiology** includes the investigation of **prevalence rates** and **incidence rates.** Rates vary somewhat depending on whether you are exploring epidemiology from a categorical or dimensional approach.

Epidemiological Rates Based on the Categorical Approach. The largest and most comprehensive study of epidemiology to date is the Methods for the Epidemiology of Child and Adolescent Mental Disorders (MECA) Study. In many studies of epidemiology, high rates of **comorbidity** are found.

Epidemiological Rates Based on the Dimensional Approach. In the investigation of children's and adolescents' emotional/behavioral problems from a dimensional approach, it is crucial to understand that youngsters' problems fall into two primary areas, **internalizing problems** and **externalizing problems.**

How Children's Environments Influence Their Behavior. Another central theme in understanding children's behavior from a developmental psychopathology perspective is to understand the influence of environment and context. Individual characteristics, such as gender, age, race/ethnicity, and **socioeconomic status** are all crucial in understanding children's and adolescents' functioning.

Different Perspectives on Problems. Even with all the sophisticated classification systems and dimensional conceptualizations of children's and adolescents' behavior, it is still important to reflect on different perspectives about children's and adolescents' behavior. It is imperative to determine the different perspectives of various individuals involved in the child's life.

Troubled Families Rather Than Troubled Children. In many cases, the child's problems are merely a reflection of a troubled family system. Factors such as parental psychopathology, interparental conflict and violence, dysfunctional family structure, and troubled expression of emotions within families are related to emotional/behavioral problems in children and adolescents.

KEY TERMS

developmental psychopathology	differential diagnosis	psychometric properties	categorical approach	internalizing problems
risk factors	multiaxial evaluation	test-retest reliability	dimensional approach	externalizing problems
protective factors	V-Codes	inter-rater reliability	empirically based taxonomies	socioeconomic status
Zeitgeist	mental disorder	kappa statistic	epidemiology	
infanticide	reliability	medical model	prevalence rates	
adultomorphism	validity	labeling	incidence rates	
atheoretical		self-fulfilling prophecies	comorbidity	

SUGGESTED READINGS

Kozol, Jonathan. *Ordinary Resurrections: Children in the Years of Hope*. New York: Perennial, 2000. This book describes the lives of a number of children who are being raised in abject poverty in the South Bronx. Neighborhood environment as well as family, peers, and the educational system are discussed in terms of risk factors as well as protective factors.

Lauck, Jennifer. *Blackbird: A Childhood Lost and Found*. New York: Pocket Books, 2000. This powerful memoir describes the sad story of a happy child who loses her mother and father within a short period of time, which results in being raised by an uncaring stepmother and then being shipped off to be raised by a stranger. This book includes consideration of all aspects of behavior, including what is "normal" in abnormal circumstances and how to try to retain some sense of self when no one else supports your own self-identity.

SUGGESTED VIEWINGS

Sisterhood of the Traveling Pants. (2005). In this great coming-of-age film, lifelong girlfriends deal with a whole host of problems that could relate to their functioning, including parental bereavement, sexuality, pediatric issues, body image, and peer networks.

Born into Brothels. (2004). This documentary shows the heart wrenching and yet resilient lives of children whose mothers are prostitutes in Calcutta's impoverished red-light district.

CHAPTER 2

THEORIES OF NORMALITY AND ABNORMALITY IN CHILDREN AND ADOLESCENTS

CHAPTER SUMMARY

THE IMPORTANCE OF THEORY

PSYCHODYNAMIC THEORY

GENETIC AND BIOLOGICAL THEORIES OF DEVELOPMENTAL PSYCHOPATHOLOGY

BEHAVIORAL GENETICS

BEHAVIORAL THEORIES AND DEVELOPMENTAL PSYCHOPATHOLOGY

COGNITIVE–BEHAVIORAL THEORIES AND DEVELOPMENTAL PSYCHOPATHOLOGY

THEORIES OF FAMILY FUNCTIONING AND ABNORMAL BEHAVIOR IN CHILDREN AND ADOLESCENTS

THE INFLUENCE OF SOCIAL CONTEXT ON THE DEVELOPMENT AND MAINTENANCE OF PROBLEM BEHAVIOR

THE OVERARCHING THEORY OF DEVELOPMENTAL PSYCHOPATHOLOGY

SUMMARY AND KEY CONCEPTS

KEY TERMS

SUGGESTED READINGS

SUGGESTED VIEWINGS

In violence, we forget who we are.

—Mary McCarthy

On September 11, 2001, the world watched in horror as four commercial airplanes were hijacked and used as human missiles to attack two of the World Trade Center buildings in New York and the Pentagon building in Washington, D.C. It is estimated that close to 3,000 people lost their lives in the September 11th attacks. Victims represented over 80 countries. It is estimated that over 3,000 infants, children, and adolescents lost at least one parent in these attacks, many losing the only parent they have ever known. For example, 14-year-old, Amy Vazquez, who is already a mother herself, lost her own mother (and her baby's grandmother) in the September 11th attack (Jones, 2001).

Two months later (in an incident that was apparently unrelated to September 11th), five Palestinian boys, aged 7 to 14, were playing peacefully in a refugee camp when a bomb exploded. The bomb killed them instantly. The boys were part of the same extended family (Associated Press, 2001).

In March of 2005 in Red Lake, Minnesota, 16-year-old Jeff Weise killed his grandfather and his grandfather's girlfriend and then proceeded to school on his sovereign Indian reservation, where he killed two school employees and four students before shooting and killing himself. By the end of the day, a total of 10 people were dead (including Weise), and 7 were seriously injured. This school shooting was the deadliest in the United States since the shooting rampage at Columbine High School (Connolly, 2005).

A month later on a Sunday afternoon, 7-year-old Nikeemah Hubanks was playing outside her home in Milwaukee, Wisconsin, where she was shot in the head by what was apparently a stray bullet from some type of drug-related altercation. Nikeemah had already survived severe burns that were due to a house fire when she was 2 months old. She had already narrowly escaped a bullet that was inadvertently fired into her bedroom while she was sleeping the previous year. Nikeemah loved to dance and sing, and she loved to play with dolls. Her favorite color was purple. Nikeemah was described as a "real

Thousands of children were affected by the attacks on the twin towers of the World Trade Center.

sweet child" who was "soft hearted and full of life." She died that Monday morning (Kane, 2005).

After experiencing the horror and sadness related to tragedies like the ones just described, most people have only one question. Why? The nation and the world asked this question after the massacre on September 11, 2001, and after the massacre in Red Lake. A much smaller group of family and friends asked this question after the five Palestinian boys were killed by the bomb and after little Nikeemah Hubanks was shot in the head. The essential question of "why" relates directly to the theories of abnormal or deviant behavior.

Do not confuse the issue, however, between violence and emotional/behavioral difficulties in children and adolescents. Only a small percentage of children and adolescents with psychological problems show the type of violent behavior that results in another person's death (Rappaport & Thomas, 2004; Wiener, 1999). Similarly, only a small percentage of adults with psychological disorders show extremely violent behavior (Wiener,

1999). Conversely, violent behavior is expressed by a great number of adults without any diagnosable clinical disorder (Wiener, 1999). Many people come to the erroneous conclusion that mental problems and violence are connected because of the way they process the information that is available to them. Most often, after a tragedy that receives media attention, there is an investigation into whether or not the person had a history of psychological problems. If psychological problems were apparent, then those problems are highlighted. If psychological problems were not evident, then something else is highlighted—but the fact that no psychological problems were evident is often not even mentioned. In addition, the vast majority of nonviolent children, adolescents, and adults who experience psychological problems remain unnoticed. Given the confidential nature of assessment and treatment of psychological problems, clinicians (or reporters, for that matter) cannot highlight all the accomplishments of people who have experienced psychological problems. Thus, many people are left with only hearing about horrific occurrences and not everyday, quiet and productive lives. Box 2.1 presents information regarding gun violence and the well-being of our nation's children.

Considering the importance of understanding why abnormal behavior occurs, this chapter covers the primary theories that relate to the development of problems in children and adolescents. Note, however, that no one theory predominates the field, and no one theory has been developed that explains all types of child and adolescent psychopathology. For that reason, theories related to specific disorders will be covered separately for those disorders. This chapter is meant to give you a brief overview of the overarching theories of the development of psychopathology.

THE IMPORTANCE OF THEORY

A **theory** is a systematic set of statements designed to help analyze, explain, predict, and even suggest ways of controlling certain phenomena of interest. In the study of childhood disorders, the phenomena of interest are the different types of disorders. Even the most basic theory should serve a number of purposes, including to

- Understand the phenomena of interest

- Predict future associations in relation to the phenomena of interest

- Organize and interpret the research data that are collected in relation to the phenomena of interest

BOX *2.1*

PREVENTION AND CULTURE

"A moral outrage: One American child or teen killed by gunfire nearly every 3 hours" was the headline of a recent press release from the Children's Defense Fund (2005c). Eight children and adolescents are killed by firearms every day, and that is just in the United States. Approximately 40 additional children and adolescents are injured by firearms each day. In children and adolescents aged 10 to 19, firearms are the second leading cause of death. These figures reach every race and ethnicity. For example, Caucasian Americans were killed in 61% of the firearm deaths between 1979 and 2001. Homicide is the leading cause of death among African-American males between the ages of 14 and 24 years old. In 2004, more children and adolescents died from gun-related deaths than from pneumonia, influenza, and cancer combined (Children's Defense Fund, 2005c).

There is a prevalent myth that gun homicides are committed by strangers to the victim. Contrary to this myth, the majority of gun homicides are committed by family members, neighbors, or acquaintances (Children's Defense Fund, 1999). Children are much more likely to be killed by an adult than by another juvenile. Children are more likely to be killed in their own home or in the home of a friend than in school or in a public setting. A total of 35% of homes in the United States with children younger than 18 have at least one firearm, and a survey of those homes suggests that 43% of the homes have at least one firearm that is not locked and is not kept away from the children (Duke, Resnick, & Borowsky, 2005). Interestingly, in states that have enacted laws that make adults responsible for guns that are left accessible to children, there has been an average of 23% fewer accidental shooting deaths of children under the age of 15 (Children's Defense Fund, 1999).

Marian Wright Edelman, the president of the Children's Defense Fund, said Escalating violence against and by our children and youths is no coincidence. What we're witnessing is the cumulative, convergent, and heightened manifestation of a range of serious and too-long neglected problems. Factors such as poverty, economic inequality, racial intolerance, drug and alcohol abuse, domestic violence, violence in popular culture, births to unmarried mothers, and divorce all have contributed to the disintegration of the family, community, and spiritual values. If you add to these crises easy access to deadlier firearms, lonely and neglected children and youths left to fend for themselves by absentee parents of all races and income groups, gangs of inner-city and suburban young people relegated to the margins of American life without education, jobs, or hope, and political leadership that pays more attention to foreign than domestic enemies, and to the rich than to the poor, then you can understand the social and spiritual disintegration of American society that confronts us today. (CDF Reports, 1999)

After discussing the need for better education, support for families, and stricter control of access to guns, Edelman goes on to encourage each person to make a difference. "It takes just one person to change a child's life. Those of us who care about children and the future of our country need to keep on working until we change the odds for all American children by making the violence of guns, poverty, preventable disease, and family neglect un-American" (CDF Reports, 1999).

- Generate future research into the phenomena of interest

In order to evaluate the quality of a theory, there are a number of important characteristics to consider. The characteristics of a good theory include the ability to

- Account for the majority of the existing research information and data related to the phenomena of interest
- Give a relevant explanation that shows logical reasons for believing that the phenomena of interest would exist under the specified conditions

- Show testability and the ability to be tested, in order to make sure that the theory could be refuted if it were not accurate
- Predict new and novel events, in order to ensure that new relevant phenomena could be included in the theory
- Provide parsimony, with the most direct and simple explanation possible (and the fewest assumptions and deductions) for the phenomena of interest
- Provide logical consistency, where the theory does not contradict itself and where the theory shows internal consistency (summarized in Bordens & Abbott, 2003)

Theories are crucial for helping to guide and evaluate research on developmental psychopathology (Rapport, 2001). Without theories, research data would be left up to the subjective interpretations of the researchers and the consumers of the research. In a sense, theories are meant to keep researchers honest so that they will evaluate their findings in light of the other research done on that topic.

As Dr. Tom Achenbach (1982) pointed out, "There is not now (and probably never will be) a *single* developmental theory of *all* psychopathology. Instead, the role of a developmental approach is to help us understand troublesome behavior in light of the developmental tasks, sequences, and processes that characterize human growth" (p. 1). Because of the wide range of children's problem behaviors (e.g., anxiety, abuse, distress, hyperactivity) and the wide range of domains in children's lives that require explanation (e.g., familial, educational, psychosocial, cognitive), it is likely that a matching number of theories will be required to explain the many types of developmental psychopathology (Rapport, 2001). In addition, there is a need to remain somewhat flexible with developmental theories of psychopathology, given that the best explanation of a particular disorder may be an integration of different facets from individual theories. It is possible that "minitheories" will be needed for different components of each separate psychopathology (Kazdin, 1989).

Note that the theories presented here are meant to explain the **etiology** of developmental psychopathology. Etiology refers to the "cause" of emotional/behavioral problems. The reason that the term "cause" is rarely used in professional writing about developmental psychopathology is that the research methods necessary to argue causation are often unethical. As you will see in the chapter on research methods, to argue causality, the researcher must conduct a study with an experimental design where participants are assigned randomly to two or more groups. If differences are found between the two groups after researchers manipulate the groups, then researchers can say that their manipulation caused the change in behavior. Without random assignment, then another third factor could have influenced the results.

If we wanted to argue that physical abuse causes emotional/behavioral difficulties, we would have to recruit healthy children into the study, assign them to either be abused by their parents or to not be abused by their parents, and then measure their emotional/behavioral difficulties at the end of the study. This study would be unethical for obvious reasons and is ridiculous to even contemplate. Given these constraints, researchers are left with having to rely on studies that show connections between physical abuse and emotional/behavioral difficulties as they occur naturally (Jaffee, Caspi, Moffitt, & Taylor, 2004). These studies can only refer to the relations between physical abuse and emotional/behavioral difficulties in children, but cannot be used to argue that the abuse caused the children's emotional/behavioral difficulties. It could be that these connections are related to another factor, such as overall family distress, or dysfunctional parenting, or genetic loading that put the parent at risk for being abusive and put the child at risk for the development of emotional/behavioral problems.

This point is crucial when reading about theories. Although theories attempt to explore the etiology of psychopathology within children and adolescents, most research studies that test theories can only do so through correlational methods that prevent assumptions of causation. With this point in mind, the following etiological theories of developmental psychopathology will be explored: psychodynamic, biological and genetic, behavioral genetics, behavioral, cognitive–behavioral, family systems, social context and peer relationships, and developmental psychopathology. Throughout many of these theories, there is an issue of the importance of fathers in the lives of children, as can be seen in the "You Decide" section.

PSYCHODYNAMIC THEORY

Psychodynamic theory was developed originally by Sigmund Freud (1894). Although the theory has influenced the field of developmental psychopathology from a historical perspective, psychodynamic theory has not been maintained as an active nor effective theory in understanding the development of psychopathology in children and adolescents.

Freud proposed that children advanced through a series of psychosexual stages. If a child were to become stuck or fixated at one of these stages, then certain psychological problems were likely to develop. The following are the psychosexual stages and proposed problems that developed if a child was fixated at that stage:

- The **oral stage** is thought to be a time when infants focus on the world and get pleasure from food and objects through their mouth. Fixation at this stage was thought to lead to orally fixated problems, such as overeating, smoking, alcoholism, childlike dependence, or severe sarcasm.

YOU DECIDE: SHOULD FATHERS BE ENCOURAGED OR EVEN MANDATED TO REMAIN INVOLVED IN THEIR CHILDREN'S LIVES?

Yes

- Responsible fathering is essential for the development of psychologically healthy children, especially boys (Doherty, Kouneski, & Erickson, 1998).
- Children and adolescents who are raised without a father are more likely to show emotional/behavioral problems, to have poor academic progress, and to be involved in criminal activity than children and adolescents raised by both their mother and their father (Popenoe, 2004).

No

- Although well-functioning fathers can enhance children's functioning, the focus on encouraging or mandating father involvement regardless of the father's functioning is potentially harmful to children. For example, children who had a lot of contact with fathers who had high levels of antisocial problems were worse off in terms of emotional/behavioral adjustment than children who had little or no contact with their troubled fathers (Jaffee, Moffitt, Caspi, & Taylor, 2003).
- If paternal involvement enhances interparental conflict, domestic violence, or physical abuse of children, then children are worse off psychologically than if the father was absent from their lives (Cummings, Goeke-Morey, & Raymond, 2004; Flouri, 2005).

So, should fathers be encouraged or even mandated to remain involved in their children's lives? You decide.

- The **anal stage** was characterized by the pleasure that develops from the anal region. Fixation at the anal stage was thought to be symbolic of withholding feces (such as being stingy, obsessive–compulsive, or too neat) or of expelling feces (such as being impulsive or explosive).
- The **phallic stage** was characterized by children experiencing pleasure with their genitals. Fixation at the phallic stage could result in long-standing problems in stable, romantic relationships in adulthood or in difficulties with authority figures.
- The **latency period** was characterized by the lack of attention to sexual pleasures or other sexual matters. Freud did not expand greatly on this stage, nor did he discuss in detail the problems that would occur from becoming fixated at the latency period.
- The **genital stage** was again characterized by a focus on the genitals as related to pleasurable activities. Given that this stage was thought to be the healthy outcome of development, fixation at this stage was not considered problematic.

Overall, Freud's psychodynamic theory and resultant psychodynamic therapies helped the field from a historical perspective. In addition, Freud's focus on childhood in relation to adult development was helpful in focusing attention on the importance of a healthy childhood.

More recent psychodynamic theorists have focused on **object relations,** which is a theory that highlights the importance of the infant's relationship with the parent or caregiver (Goodman, 2002). Object relations theorists, such as Margaret Mahler (1968) and Melanie Klein (1957), argued that individuals' perceptions of themselves and of the world are formulated from their first relationship with their primary caregiver. If this relationship was healthy (i.e., the primary caregiver was stable, nurturing, accepting of the infant, and encouraging of the infant's and child's growing independence), then the infant would grow into a psychologically healthy individual. If this relationship were troubled (i.e., the primary caregiver was inconsistent, too demanding, or not involved enough), then the infant would grow into an individual with troubled emotions and behaviors. Overall, the object relations segment of the psychodynamic theory is followed somewhat currently, but not to the same extent as other theories related to the development of psychopathology in children and adolescents. As seen in Box 2.2, both psychodynamic theory and object relations, as well as many other theories, have tended to blame mothers for their children's emotional/behavioral problems while ignoring the father's role in family functioning.

Attachment theory is related to the theory of object relations, but attachments between the infant and primary caregiver are of central focus. The original theory of attachment was developed by such theorists as Bowlby (1969) and Ainsworth (Ainsworth, Blehar, Waters, & Wall, 1978). The basic premise was that infants are attached to their primary caretaker(s) in a manner that affects children's emotional well-being

BOX 2.2

PARENTAL GENDER: BLAMING MOTHERS AND IGNORING FATHERS

Inherent in a number of theories of developmental psychopathology is the idea that mothers are either directly or indirectly to blame for their children's troubled behavior (summarized in Phares, 1999). In the late 1940s, the term schizophrenogenic mother was used to describe a mother who "caused" schizophrenia in her child (Fromm-Reichmann, 1948). This type of mother was thought to be intermittently overly involved and distant from her child. Another term, refrigerator mother, was also popular in the 1940s to describe a mother who "caused" autism in her child by being aloof and cold to the child (Kanner, 1943). Although these ideas have been shown to be completely inaccurate, remnants of blaming mothers and ignoring fathers remain in clinical research and clinical work even today.

In clinical research, mothers are studied to a much greater extent than fathers (Phares, Fields, Kamboukos, & Lopez, 2005). In a review of research published in well-respected empirical journals, 45% of clinical child research included mothers only, 25% included mothers and fathers and analyzed them separately, 28% included "parents" without specifying whether they were mothers or fathers, and just 2% of the articles included fathers only (Phares, Fields et al., 2005). These findings are similar for research in children's health-related issues and in pediatric research (Phares, Lopez, Fields, Kamboukos, & Duhig, 2005). Similarly in dissertation research, 59% of the studies included mothers only, 30% included both parents, and 11% included fathers only (Silverstein & Phares, 1996). Interestingly, male researchers were more likely to include fathers in their research than were female researchers. No other characteristics (such as type of doctoral degree, gender of advisor, or area of research) were related to the likelihood of including fathers in dissertation research (Silverstein & Phares, 1996).

Therapists also ignore fathers and inadvertently blame mothers in clinical practice. A number of therapists even neglect to invite fathers into therapy sessions that are meant to help deal with the child's emotional/behavioral problems (Phares, Fields, & Binitie, 2006). Unfortunately, mothers and fathers have also taken on some of these beliefs about mothers' responsibility for children's emotional/behavioral problems. Two studies that investigated parents' perceptions of blame for their children's emotional/behavioral problems found that mothers blamed themselves for their children's problems, and fathers blamed mothers for their children's emotional/behavioral problems (Penfold, 1985; Watson, 1986).

Overall, there has been a long history of blaming mothers and ignoring fathers for children's and adolescents' emotional/behavioral difficulties. It is rarely advantageous to place blame, so many professionals have moved toward trying to understand the systems in which children's problems have developed (e.g., the family system, the school system, the community). In addition, many problems in childhood cannot be "blamed" on any one factor. As can be seen in the multitude of theories related to the development of psychopathology in children and adolescents, it is rare that only one factor can be identified as the sole etiology of any type of psychopathology. As a result, it is important not to blame mothers (or fathers) and to look for ways in which children can be helped, rather than looking for something or someone to blame.

---

throughout their lives. Based on this early work as well as more recent research, there are four types of infant–caretaker attachment. **Secure attachment** is shown when the infant uses the parent as a base from which to explore a new environment. After being separated from the parent, a securely attached infant will welcome the parent's return with happiness and joy. Parents with securely attached infants are usually stable, sensitive to the infant's needs, and responsive (Cassidy & Shaver, 1999; Dozier, Manni, & Lindhiem, 2005). **Anxious insecure attachment** is actually split into three primary types: avoidant (where the infant ignores or avoids the parent after a separation), ambivalent (where the infant shows distress when the parent leaves, but shows anger or rejection when the parent returns), and disorganized (where the infant shows an inconsistent pattern of attachment, sometimes reaching out for the parent without looking at the parent and sometimes rejecting the parent on return altogether).

The attachment relationship is thought to serve as a template for relationships in later childhood and adulthood (Waters, Hamilton, & Weinfield, 2000). Intervening factors, however, such as parental divorce, loss of a parent, parental or child illness, and parental psychopathology, can change the course of attachment (Hamilton, 2000; Waters, Merrick, Treboux, Crowell, & Albersheim, 2000). Aside from these intervening factors,

Infants can show equally strong attachment to their father as well as their mother.

attachment during infancy is related to later outcomes. For example, anxious insecure attachment styles are associated with the development of psychopathology (Davila, Ramsay, Stroud, & Steinberg, 2005). Insecure attachment puts children at risk for further complications throughout their lives (Solomon & George, 1999). Disordered attachment has been linked to conduct disorder, hyperactivity, and physical abuse (Davila et al., 2005). In addition, parental psychopathology is linked to the type of attachments parents have with their infants (Davila et al., 2005). Preventive interventions that have focused on increasing parental sensitivity to enhance parent–child attachment have been found to be effective (Bakermans-Kranenburg, van IJzendoorn, & Juffer, 2003). Overall, attachment theory has been helpful in exploring the early parent–child relationship in relation to later functioning in the child and adolescent. Note, however, that secure attachment is defined differently in various cultures, so cultural sensitivity is necessary when conducting research on attachment (Rothbaum, Weisz, Pott, Miyake, & Morelli, 2000). In general, there are parenting behaviors that are associated with well-functioning children and a strong parent–child attachment in many cultures (see Box 2.3).

If you know his father and grandfather, don't worry about his son.

—Proverb of Africa

GENETIC AND BIOLOGICAL THEORIES OF DEVELOPMENTAL PSYCHOPATHOLOGY

Specific genetic and biological theories will be addressed more completely for each disorder. For now, the general principles utilized in research on genetic and biological theories will be considered.

The rationale behind most genetic theories is that genes inherited from biological parents play a central role in the development of emotional/behavioral problems in children and adolescents (Dick & Todd, 2006; Farmer, 2004; Hudziak, 2002). **Genotype** refers to a child's genetic makeup that is inherited from his or her parents. **Phenotype** refers to observable characteristics in the child that are created from the interaction of heredity and environment. The newer concept of **endophenotype** refers to the interaction between genotype and phenotype, which reflects the interactions between nature and nurture (Gottesman & Gould, 2003). **Heritability,** which is the proportion of variation from genetic influences, is calculated by dividing the variance due to genotype by the variance due to phenotype. Thus, heritability estimates are usually given in the form of a proportion that ranges from 0 (no genetic influence) to 1.0 (perfect genetic correspondence). Of course, most psychological and behavioral characteristics are somewhere between 0 and 1 rather than at either extreme.

One of the primary methods used to investigate genetic contribution to the development of psychopathology is to study **monozygotic (MZ) twins** (known as

TEN BASIC PRINCIPLES OF GOOD PARENTING

As a leading researcher in parenting and child development, Dr. Laurence Steinberg has informed generations of clinicians and researchers about the well-being of children and families. He has now synthesized that wealth of knowledge into a book for the popular press called *The 10 Basic Principles of Good Parenting* (Steinberg, 2004).

Regardless of whether the etiologies of problem behavior are from characteristics related to biological, genetic, behavioral genetic, cognitive–behavioral, family, social, or other factors, parents can help their children grow and flourish by following these suggestions, which are supported by decades of research. According to Dr. Steinberg (2004), "the ten basic principles of good parenting (are)

- What you do matters
- You cannot be too loving
- Be involved in your child's life
- Adapt your parenting to fit your child
- Establish rules and set limits
- Help foster your child's independence
- Be consistent
- Avoid harsh discipline
- Explain your rules and decisions
- Treat your child with respect" (Steinberg, 2004, p. ix)

---

identical twins) and **dizygotic (DZ) twins** (known as fraternal twins) who were raised either in the same or different environments. Monozygotic twins develop from the same fertilized egg, so they have the same genotype (i.e., the same genetic material). Dizygotic twins have an average of 50 percent of shared genetic material. Every human, twin or not, has a different phenotype, given that one's phenotype is a combination of both genes and the environment. Thus, studying twins reared together and apart can help clarify the genetic contributions and the environmental contributions to the development of psychopathology in children and adolescents. In essence, the correspondence rates between identical twins are compared with the correspondence rates between fraternal twins, nontwin siblings, biological parents, adoptive parents, and other relatives.

One of the basic formulas to determine an estimate of heritability of a particular characteristic in research with twins is as follows:

Difference between DZ twins' scores	=	Genetic + Environmental Effects
− Difference between MZ twins' scores	=	Environmental Effects
	=	Genetic Effects

The idea is that DZ twins differ in both genetic and environmental effects, whereas MZ twins differ only in environmental effects (Lemery & Doelger, 2005). Thus, the differences between the sets of DZ twins and MZ twins helps identify the genetic contributions to that characteristic or disorder. There are caveats to this

research design, however, given that MZ twins appear to spend more time together, to engage in similar activities, and to be treated by others in similar ways, which makes their environmental experience more similar than the experience of DZ twins or nontwin siblings (Lombroso, Pauls, & Leckman, 1994; State, Lombroso, Pauls, & Leckman, 2000).

With **adoption studies,** this method is studied further by comparing both DZ and MZ twins who are raised apart and those who are raised together. Environmental effects can be controlled somewhat with this method, assuming that twins raised in different households would not necessarily share any common environmental effects. Note, however, that a complicating factor in adoption studies is that children who are adopted tend to be overrepresented in outpatient mental health centers when compared to their nonadopted peers (Miller, Fan, Christensen, Grotevant, & van Dulmen, 2000; Miller, Fan, Grotevant, Christensen, Coyl, & van Dulmen, 2000).

Based on twin studies, certain disorders (such as schizophrenia and bipolar disorder) have been found to be highly genetically loaded, and many temperamental and personality characteristics (such as anger proneness, positive emotionality, emotional regulation) have been found to be highly genetically related (Bouchard, 2004; State et al., 2000). In adoption studies of many personality and behavioral characteristics (e.g., adjustment scores, extroversion, neuroticism, aggression, behavioral inhibition), MZ twins reared apart continue to show higher correspondence than DZ twins reared together (Bouchard, 2004; State et al., 2000).

A number of studies suggest genetic loading for a variety of disorders in childhood and adolescence. The following specific findings highlight the diversity of studies that support genetic influences in developmental psychopathology.

- Some studies suggest that genetic contributions to certain disorders are very high (80% in schizophrenia, 50 to 60% in alcohol abuse; Bouchard, 2004).

- Attention-deficit/hyperactivity disorder is highly influenced by genetic factors, even in adolescence (Larsson, Larsson, & Lichtenstein, 2004).

- Child physical abuse puts children at risk for the development of conduct disorder, especially those children who are already at genetic risk for conduct disorder (Jaffee et al., 2005).

- Anxiety disorders and fears may be more heavily genetically loaded for girls than for boys (Lichtenstein & Annas, 2000).

- Rates of comorbidity suggest some genetic loading (Dick, Viken, Kaprio, Pulkkinen, & Rose, 2005; Simonoff, 2000).

- There may even be genetic influences in the level of socioeconomic status that is attained (Lichtenstein & Pedersen, 1997).

- Children's adjustment to parental divorce is influenced by genetics to some extent (O'Connor, Caspi, DeFries, & Plomin, 2000).

Overall, these studies suggest a high amount of heritability in some characteristics but limited amounts of heritability in other characteristics. Note that genetics research has not been without controversy. In many content areas, and especially in the study of ethnic/racial differences, the interpretation of data from genetic studies has been under intense scrutiny (Anderson & Nickerson, 2005; Smedley & Smedley, 2005). In addition, parents seem to be overly convinced of genetic influences on their children's challenging behavior largely because professionals have emphasized genetic factors (Rosemond, 2005).

The other influence that is often linked with genetic contributions in the development of psychopathology relates to biological contributions to the development of disorders (Pihl & Nantel-Vivier, 2005; Skuse, 2000). The study of biological influences includes, but is not limited to, the study of the connection between psychological and behavioral processes in relation to

- Physiological mechanisms
- Brain structure and functioning
- Central nervous system functioning
- Neuroendocrinology (including hormones and the immune system)
- Neuropharmacological mechanisms
- Maturational rates (especially, the onset of puberty)

Biological factors can be present due to genetic loadings or they can be due to other factors, such as exposure to contaminants while the fetus is still in utero (Newland & Rasmussen, 2003). It is rare to find a clinical disorder that is solely considered to be due to biological influences. For example, although there have been extensive studies that utilize neuroimaging (such as magnetic resonance imaging) on children with developmental disorders such as autism, reading disorders, and attention-deficit/hyperactivity disorder, none of these disorders have been linked to clear-cut discrete focal lesions or other structural differences in the brain (Filipek, 1999). There are, however, a number of biological factors that have been linked to different facets of clinical disorders. For example, impaired attention is thought to be due to biological factors in relation to the development of schizophrenia (Pantelis et al., 2004; Sporn et al., 2005) and in relation to attention-deficit/hyperactivity disorder (Fischer, Barkley, Smallish, & Fletcher, 2005; Nigg, Blaskey, Stawicki, & Sachek, 2004). In addition, the differential gender rates of depression before and after puberty have been linked to biological factors to some extent (Emslie, Weinberg, Kennard, & Kowatch, 1994). Also note that there is some evidence of biological influences related to evolution in some disorders, such as dyslexia (i.e., reading disorders), autism, and attention-deficit/hyperactivity disorder (Barkley, 2004; Siegert & Ward, 2002).

There have been exciting advances in the biological investigation of behavior and abnormal behavior with a relatively new cell known as a "mirror neuron." Mirror neurons are cells in the brain that activate similarly when the individual is performing a task or when the individual is watching someone else perform the task (Winerman, 2005). These cells were first discovered in macaque monkeys, where it was observed that the same cells would fire when either the monkey was picking up a cup or when the monkey observed someone else picking up a cup (Winerman, 2005). Additional research into these cells may provide further clues into human behavior. Researchers are particularly interested in mirror neurons

Case Study: D.S., a Child with Down Syndrome

One example of a problem that develops from chromosomal abnormalities is Down syndrome, which is caused by an extra chromosome. Specifically, children born with a trio rather than a pair of chromosome 21 will be born with Down syndrome. Intellectual functioning of individuals with Down syndrome usually ranges between 40 and 50 (based on IQs where 100 is "average"), although functioning can be much higher or much lower in these individuals. As will be seen in a later chapter, mental retardation is diagnosed when the IQ is below 70 and when there are deficits in adaptive functioning, all of which are present before the age of 18. Physical appearance is also quite distinctive in children with Down syndrome, with these children showing thick facial features, thick folds in the eyelids, a tongue that protrudes slightly, and a noticeable large crease in the palms of the hands. Quite often, unrelated children with Down syndrome look more like each other than they look like their own family members.

"D.S." is a 15-year-old boy who displays all the physical and intellectual signs of Down syndrome. His IQ was 45. Since the time he was 8, D.S. attended "special schools" and lived away from home. Each time his parents would visit, he would beg to be taken home. "Mommy, take me home" was D.S.'s most common response when he saw his mother on visiting days. Racked with guilt, his mother would take him home

about once a year with the idea of raising D.S. at home. Soon thereafter, however, D.S. would become unmanageable, and his mother would have to admit him into yet another "special school."

D.S.'s parents divorced when he was 11 years old, and his father moved to another state. D.S. does not have any brothers or sisters.

By the age of 15, D.S.'s mother had again tried to take care of him at home. After approximately 6 months, D.S.'s mother took him to an emergency room and pleaded, "You've got to admit him; I just can't take it anymore." Over the past 6 months, D.S. had shown more and more behavioral problems. He was a large boy, at about 5'9" and weighing almost 200 pounds. Lately, he began to lose his temper quite often, and he had angry outbursts and tantrums that his mother could not control. On more than one occasion, D.S. hit his mother when she tried to stop him from acting out. For example, D.S. recently was banging a broom on the apartment floor and when his mother tried to stop him, he hit her on the shoulders and arms. D.S.'s mother felt that she had no other alternative than to place him in a special setting again.

Source: Spitzer, Gibbon, Skodol, Williams, & First (1994).

---

for the investigation of empathy, or rather lack of empathy, in children with autism (Dingfelder, 2005).

Parents are like shuttles on a loom. They join the threads of the past with threads of the future and leave their own bright patterns as they go.

—Fred Rogers (Mr. Rogers)

BEHAVIORAL GENETICS

Closely linked to the study of genetics is the study of behavioral genetics. Although many researchers use the terms *genetics* and *behavioral genetics* synonymously (Lenzenweger & Haugaard, 1996), these sections have been separated to highlight the distinct contributions of the study of behavioral genetics. The study of **behavioral genetics** focuses on the connections between inherited genetic influences and environmental influences in relation to the development of psychopathology. Thus, behavioral genetics is the study of the interaction of genetics and the environment (Moffitt, Caspi, & Rutter, 2006). Currently, it is rare to find any researchers

who argue solely for the role of genetic factors or solely for the role of environmental factors in the development of psychopathology (Maccoby, 2000). Given the wealth of knowledge about both genetic and environmental factors, it is more common for researchers to try to understand the different contributions of both genetic heritability (i.e., nature) and the environment (i.e., nurture). Rather than asking if a certain disorder is related to nature or nurture, the more logical question is to ask "To what extent are given behaviors due to variations in genetic endowment, variations within the environment, or the interaction between these two factors?" (Mash & Dozois, 2003, p. 52).

Behavioral geneticists have made exciting contributions to the understanding of environmental influences. Not only do researchers in behavioral genetics explore genetic influences, but they also explore environmental influences in a number of ways. Specifically, researchers acknowledge that children raised in the same environment do not always experience the same environment (Feinberg & Hetherington, 2000; Feinberg, Neiderhiser, Simmens, Reiss, & Hetherington, 2000; Richmond

& Stocker, 2003). Think about your brothers or sisters, if you have them. Chances are that, although there were similarities in the family environment in which you all grew up, there were also differences in your family environments. For example, maybe you were the oldest child and your parents were more strict with you than they were with your younger siblings. Or maybe your sibling was born at a time when your parents were particularly distressed with each other, but you were born at a time when your parents were getting along well. These examples highlight the different family environments that siblings can experience. The term **shared environment** refers to the common experiences in siblings' environments, such as living in the same house, living in the same neighborhood, and having the same family traditions. The term **nonshared environment** refers to the unique aspects of the family that each sibling experiences differently than the others, such as being a favored child by one or both parents or having higher or lower amounts of attention and financial resources at a particular developmental point.

In a book entitled *Why Are Siblings So Different?*, Judy Dunn and Robert Plomin (1990) summarized a number of interesting findings from the behavioral genetics research literature. For example, although the development of schizophrenia is thought to be due largely to genetic factors, there is more to it than that. Based on twin and adoption studies, the percent of variance that accounts for the development of schizophrenia is 45% nonshared environment, 40% genetic, 5% shared environment, and 10% unknown (or measurement error). This distribution is presented graphically in the pie chart in Figure 2.1. Thus, even a disorder that is thought to be highly genetically related is also highly environmentally related in terms of the nonshared environment.

More recently, a number of disorders have been studied within a behavioral genetic theoretical framework, including oppositional defiant disorder (Hudziak, Derks, Althoff, Copeland, & Boomsma, 2005), antisocial behavior (Moffitt, 2005; Taylor, Loney, Bobadilla, Iacono, & McGue, 2003), conduct problems (Gelhorn et al., 2005; Jaffee et al., 2005), attention-deficit/hyperactivity disorder (Larsson et al., 2004), substance use (Hopfer, Crowley, & Hewitt, 2003), depression (Rice, Harold, & Thapar, 2002), and anxiety disorders (Lichtenstein & Annas, 2000). Overall, there is evidence of combined influences between genetics, shared environment, and nonshared environment in the development of psychopathology. Patterns of comorbidity have even been explored and were found to have both genetic and environmental effects (Dick et al., 2005). Note, however, that behavioral genetics research has been criticized for focusing too much on the genetics side of the equation and not enough on the environmental (and especially, parenting) side of the equation (Collins, Maccoby, Steinberg, Hetherington, & Bornstein, 2000; Maccoby, 2000). When parenting and genetics are explored together, both are important in the development of psychopathology (Reiss, 2005). The work in behavioral genetics has led many researchers to consider a biopsychosocial conceptualization of development that focuses on the integration of biological, psychological, and social factors in development (Pennington, 2002).

The thing that impresses me most about America is the way parents obey their children.
—King Edward VIII (Duke of Windsor)

FIGURE 2.1 The Different Sources of Variance that Account for the Development of Schizophrenia.

Source: Dunn & Plomin (1990).

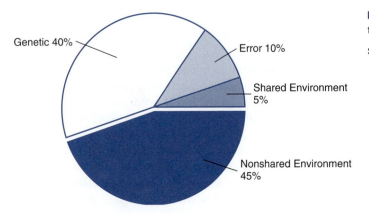

BEHAVIORAL THEORIES AND DEVELOPMENTAL PSYCHOPATHOLOGY

Behavioral theories of developmental psychopathology began primarily with John B. Watson's (1913) suggestion that most human behavior was governed by the consequences that followed the behavior. Thus, behavioral tendencies were learned and not inherited. In addition, Watson highlighted the importance of exploring observable behaviors rather than internal, subjective processes. With regard to the development of psychopathology, Watson demonstrated that a child (known as "Little Albert") could be conditioned to fear a previously neutral stimulus (a fluffy white rat) by pairing it with an aversive experience (a loud bang). Over time, the child not only showed a fear response to white rats, but also to rabbits, and even to a Santa Claus beard (Watson & Rayner, 1920). This work led to the idea that most if not all psychopathologies were the result of behavioral conditioning.

Since that time, there has been growing awareness that some disorders are more linked to behavioral contingencies than others. Phobias (King, Muris, & Ollendick, 2004), enuresis (Houts, 2003), and certain oppositional and antisocial problems in children (Snyder, Reid, & Patterson, 2003) continue to be linked strongly to behavioral contingencies. Imagine the following scenario in your local grocery store:

- James, a cute 4-year-old, and his father are in the cookie aisle.

- James says, "I want lots of chocolate Koala Yummie Bears".

- James's father says, "No, we already have fruit for dessert at home".

- James grabs a package of Koala Yummie Bears and replies loudly, "I want Yummie Bears!"

- James's father again firmly says, "No, you cannot get the Yummie Bears," as he returns the cookies to the shelf.

- James grabs for the Yummie Bears and also knocks down a number of other cookies from the shelf and yells, "Give me my Yummie Bears!"

- James's father says loudly, "James put those Yummie Bears back."

- James then starts stomping on the cookies on the floor and begins yelling, "Yummie Bears! Yummie Bears! Yummie Bears!"

- Exasperated, James's father says, "Okay, you can have your Koala Yummie Bears" as he quickly tries to put the other smashed cookies back on the shelves while averting the stares of the on-looking shoppers.

James's father has inadvertently rewarded James's bad behavior (yelling and throwing a tantrum) by giving him what he wanted in the form of a tangible reinforcement (delicious chocolate-filled Koala Yummie Bears). Based on behavioral principles, this scenario would create a greater likelihood for James's bad behavior to occur in the future. A number of oppositional and defiant behaviors are inadvertently created in children by adults who do not realize what they are doing (Snyder et al., 2003). As we will see in the chapter on therapies and interventions, many behavioral therapies are effective for disorders that seem to be linked to behavioral contingencies.

COGNITIVE–BEHAVIORAL THEORIES AND DEVELOPMENTAL PSYCHOPATHOLOGY

Although many disorders have been linked to behavioral contingencies, many other disorders have been linked to the combination of behavioral and cognitive processes. The idea behind cognitive–behavioral theories is that observable behavior can be influenced by mental processes. Thus, how an individual acts and feels may be related to how the individual thinks about the situation. Much of the work on cognitive–behavioral theories started with Dr. Aaron Beck's (1976) development of the cognitive theory of depression in adults. Dr. Beck argued that clients often have distorted cognitions (i.e., thoughts) about themselves, the world, and the future. The more the client focuses on these negative thoughts, the more depressed they will become. A number of researchers have found these same patterns in children, especially as related to informational processing and cognitive bias (Bijttebier, Vasey, & Braet, 2003; Dalgleish et al., 2003). Cognitive–behavioral theorists have added a behavioral component to these cognitive theories, with regard to conceptualizing depression as well as many other disorders (Dodge, 2003; Hammen & Rudolph, 2003; Mather & Cartwright-Hatton, 2004). Not only might a depressed child experience distorted cognitions and an attributional style that is likely to exacerbate the depression, but he or she might also have discontinued previously enjoyable activities, which increases feelings of depression (Hammen & Rudolph, 2003). Imagine the following scenario.

Case Study: Regina, Who Has the "Terrible Twos" as a 6-Year Old

Regina was 6 years old when her parents brought her to a psychology clinic for help. Her parents reported that she was "ruining their marriage" due to her outbursts and poor behavioral control. Both parents were personally dedicated to Regina, but they both appeared to be overwhelmed by her behavior. Her father thought that her mother "spoiled" Regina and that she did not provide consistent discipline. Her mother reported that she tried to do her best with Regina.

Regina had always been considered a difficult child. Her parents seemed to think that she had never outgrown the "terrible twos." Her mother and father reported that she was extremely difficult and demanding. Regina often ruined family activities due to her misbehavior. In addition, when Regina's friends were playing with her at home, she would often throw a tantrum and the children would be sent home. Her teachers often had her play by herself at school, because she seemed to annoy the other students. Both at home and at school, Regina

would often throw things or slap people when she did not get her way. She was often given what she wanted after her outbursts.

During the first interview at the clinic, Regina seemed to enjoy the individual attention of the clinician, but she showed herself to be very demanding. In addition, she refused to help clean up the toys after the session was over and she demanded that she be allowed to take a number of toys home with her even though she was told that she could not take the toys home.

From a behavioral perspective, Regina had inadvertently been rewarded for these problematic behaviors. It could have been that the parents gave in to her demands when she was younger and then felt trapped to continue giving in to her demands when she was older. Behavioral parent training (Barkley, 1997b) would probably be the most beneficial treatment to alleviate Regina's acting-out behaviors.

Source: Rapoport & Ismond (1996).

- Rosa, a beautiful and intelligent 14-year-old girl, is already somewhat sad because her parents have not been getting along very well lately.

- At school, a boy she likes does not say "hello" to her in the hallway, even though she smiled at him.

- Rosa automatically thinks that the boy does not like her, and she further reasons that she is not worthy of being liked (given that she thinks she is dumb, unattractive, and chubby).

- A few minutes later, a group of her friends invite her to the mall after school to go watch a movie.

- Even though she used to enjoy hanging out with her friends, she declines their offer because she does not feel like she will be good company for them.

- Instead, Rosa stays alone in her room after school and thinks about how she'll never have a boyfriend and wonders if she'll have any friends when she gets older.

This scenario illustrates a number of salient components of cognitive–behavioral theories, especially related to the development and maintenance of depression. Rosa shows negative **automatic thoughts,** which are immediate, unquestioned thoughts that individuals experience when faced with a new or recurrent situation or event. In this situation, Rosa immediately thought that the boy did not like her because he did not say "hello." Although that explanation could have been accurate, it could have

also been that the boy did not see her or that the boy likes her but is too shy to speak with her. As will be discussed in the chapter on therapies and interventions, a therapist would try to help Rosa develop other plausible alternative thoughts that might counteract her negative automatic thoughts.

Rosa also showed **cognitive distortions,** which are thoughts that are distorted or changed from reality. Given that Rosa is considered to be bright and attractive, Rosa's thoughts that she is dumb, unattractive, and chubby are probably distortions of reality. In addition, given that she has friends who invited her to the mall, she probably has little reason to be concerned about not having friends in the future. These cognitive distortions appear to help develop and maintain depressive symptomatology (Moran, Bifulco, Ball, & Campbell, 2001). Finally, the behavioral part of cognitive–behavioral theory was evidenced by Rosa's decision not to go to the mall with her friends. Although Rosa used to enjoy going to the mall, she declined the offer, which limits the possibility of her experiencing pleasant events (Hollon & Beck, 1994). When children withdraw from activities that used to be pleasurable, they limit their opportunity to experience joy and happiness. In cognitive–behavioral therapy, the therapist would not only work on helping Rosa to change her cognitions, but would also help her to increase her opportunities for pleasurable experiences (Rohde, Lewinsohn, Clarke, Hops, & Seeley, 2005). Note that cognitive–behavioral therapies have

BOX *2.4*

TROUBLED CHILDREN IN THE SCHOOL SETTING

Increasingly, teachers and other school professionals are being called on to identify and treat troubled children. In the case of childhood depression, Kevin Stark (1990) gives the following examples in a book that focuses on school-based cognitive–behavioral interventions for childhood depression:

- An English teacher becomes concerned about a student whose journal entries focus solely on death and self-hatred.
- A beautiful sixth-grade girl, who is active in volleyball, cheerleading, and academic excellence, reports to everyone who will listen that she is fat, ugly, stupid, and not worthy of friends.
- A fourth-grade boy is taken to the nurse's office because he falls asleep in class, complains of headaches, and looks tired constantly.
- The grades of a fifth-grade girl drop suddenly, and she is known to alienate herself from peers and to run away from home occasionally.

- Cody is a third-grader who hides under his desk frequently and cries.
- An art teacher becomes alarmed when a student draws a picture of himself on top of a tall building, while he looks closely at the sidewalk far below him.

Although teachers often deal with attention-deficit/hyperactivity disorder and learning disorders, they are exposed to every type of psychopathology that is imaginable in children and adolescents (as well as in parents). Based on a cognitive–behavioral framework, many children and adolescents can be helped in the school setting via group therapies that focus on their thoughts, feelings, and actions. Although these techniques are usually conducted by school psychologists, teachers are a crucial piece of the puzzle because they are often the ones to notice troubled children before anyone else notices. Many school psychologists have tried to help train teachers to identify children and adolescents at risk for the development of psychopathology (Stark, 1990).

also been applied to emotional/behavioral problems that are evident in the classroom (Boxer & Butkus, 2005; Ehntholt, Smith, & Yule, 2005). (Box 2.4 discusses the school setting in particular.) Because of the limited cognitive development in young children, however, cognitive–behavioral theories have not been used extensively with very young children (Stark, Sander, Yancy, Bronik, & Hoke, 2000).

Sticks in a bundle are unbreakable.

—Proverb of Africa

THEORIES OF FAMILY FUNCTIONING AND ABNORMAL BEHAVIOR IN CHILDREN AND ADOLESCENTS

The cognitive–behavioral description in the previous section on Rosa's experience focused almost solely on Rosa (i.e., her cognitions, her interpretation of events, the behavior in which she engaged). You might have wondered about the issue that was making her sad, namely that her parents were not getting along very well. From a family theory perspective, Rosa is the **identified problem (or identified patient)** who is

showing problems that are reflective of troubles within the family system (Cox & Paley, 2003). Most family theorists argue that the majority of problems shown in children and adolescents are due to problems within the family structure and that the child or adolescent is expressing problems (usually unintentionally) so that the family can get the help it needs. Note that the concept of "family" is defined broadly by most family theorists to include a diversity of family constellations, such as families in which the parents are divorced or were never married, single-parent families, stepfamilies, families where the children are being raised by a grandparent or other relative, or families headed by lesbian couples or gay male couples (L'Abate, 1998).

Family theories have existed in the mainstream of psychology and education for over 40 years (Kaslow, 2001; McGoldrick et al., 2005; Wamboldt & Wamboldt, 2000). Although there are a number of different theories of family functioning (e.g., Ackerman, 1958; Bateson et al., 1956; Bowen, 1978; Haley, 1976; Minuchin, 1974; Satir, 1983; Selvini-Palazzoli, Boscolo, Cecchin, & Prata, 1978), certain central themes apply to nearly all family theories of the development of psychopathology.

- Children's problems are a reflection of problems within the family or within the parents' relationship.

Families can provide both strengths and weaknesses in children's development.

- Families have a tendency to want to maintain **homeostasis** (i.e., to stay the same), even when distressing patterns have emerged.

- Structures within the family (e.g., children having more power and control than parents) or alliances within the family (e.g., the son and the noncustodial father are allied against the caretaking mother and the daughter) are often disrupted in troubled families.

- Communication styles are often disrupted in families with problems, such as sharing too much or not enough information with each other or expressing too many or too few emotions when communicating with each other.

- Issues related to personal distance and closeness are often problematic in troubled families, with families who show too much closeness being referred to as **enmeshed** and families who show too much distance being referred to as **disengaged** (summarized and discussed in Cox & Paley, 2003; Kaslow, 2001).

Cultural and ethnic/racial differences and similarities in families are also of central importance (Hall & Barongan, 2002; McGoldrick et al., 2005; Rothbaum, Morelli, Pott, & Liu-Constant, 2000). This point is relevant both within and outside the United States (Rey et al., 2000). Historically, a "healthy" family system was based on the model of a middle-class, Caucasian family of Western European descent, with the idea that a fair amount of emotional distance was appropriate (McGoldrick et al., 2005). Many families from other cultural backgrounds were labeled as enmeshed and

troubled when compared with this biased ideal. More recently, many researchers and writers have highlighted the importance of understanding and respecting the cultural and ethnic/racial heritage of families (Hall & Barongan, 2002; McGoldrick et al., 2005). With this concept in mind, many family therapists now try to understand the family system as well as the cultural and contextual system from which the family developed (see Box 2.5).

Without human companions, paradise itself would be an undesirable place.
—Proverb of Africa

THE INFLUENCE OF SOCIAL CONTEXT ON THE DEVELOPMENT AND MAINTENANCE OF PROBLEM BEHAVIOR

Another system that is crucial to understand when considering the development of psychopathology is the social context of behavior, including the peer network. Overall, there are a number of important aspects to consider in understanding the social context of the development of psychopathology.

- Contexts are multidimensional and nested within each other (e.g., the school system is nested within the community, the family system is nested within both the larger community and a subset of communities, such as the neighborhood or religious community).

BOX 2.5

ETHNICITY, FAMILIES, AND CULTURE

In order to think more personally about ethnicity, culture, and families, you might want to consider answering some of the following questions for yourself:

- How would you describe yourself ethnically?
- Who in your family experience most influenced your sense of ethnic identity?
- Which ethnic group, other than your own, do you think you understand the best?
- Which general characteristics of your ethnic group do you like the most and which do you like the least?
- How do you think that your own family would react if they had to attend family therapy?

These are questions that are often used to train family therapists in ethnic and cultural sensitivity and awareness. One of the issues in working with families is to balance respect for their ethnic and cultural background with their clinical issues about which they are seeking help. For some families, their difficulties may be very tied to their ethnic and cultural identity. For other families, their difficulties may have little to do with their ethnic and cultural identity. Family therapists must try to assess the family's perceptions of the connection between their ethnic identity and their presenting problem.

It is also important for family therapists to acknowledge that the style of therapy may need to differ for families. The perceived usefulness of therapy and talking itself may differ between families from various ethnic and cultural backgrounds. Some of the issues that family therapists need to consider, include some of the general differences that follow.

- Families with a strong Irish heritage may use words and talking as a way of buffering their experience, either to cover up their painful experiences or to embellish their experiences.
- Within families of Italian descent, words are often used for dramatic purposes and to share emotional experiences with each other.
- In the Chinese culture, food is often used as a way of communicating in lieu of words. The dominant idea in America of "laying your cards on the table" is often not accepted.
- Within the Jewish culture, words are often used to articulate, understand, analyze, and acknowledge one's experience.
- Within the Anglo culture, words are often used to achieve particular goals, but not to share any high degree of emotions.
- Within the Sioux Indian culture, the way in which family members talk is often prescribed by the roles in which they find themselves. For example, a woman may never utter a word to her father-in-law, and yet may feel great closeness with him.

Although there are differences for individuals in each ethnic and cultural group, some of these generalities may help therapists to think about a way of approaching families in therapy.

Source: McGoldrick et al. (2005).

- Contexts become more broad, more differentiated, and more specific and have greater depth as children grow older.
- Contexts and children are determined mutually, with a reciprocal nature of influences.
- The meaning of a context to a child influences the effects of the context on the child, which is ultimately based on the ability of the context to provide for the child's fundamental needs.
- When assessing the social contexts that are relevant to the child, it is important to acknowledge specific questions or outcomes that are of interest regarding the child (e.g., assessing parents', peers', and community members' attitudes about substance use would be appropriate in relation to an adolescent who was

abusing marijuana; Boyce et al., 1998; Steinberg & Avenevoli, 2000).

Dr. Urie Bronfenbrenner (1979) provided a necessarily complex diagram of the various contexts in which children and adolescents exist, which are considered part of the Ecological Systems Theory. A multitude of settings and systems must be considered when trying to understand the etiology of the development of psychopathology in children and adolescents. The **macrosystem,** which is most distant from the child, contains the beliefs and values of the cultures. These values might be related to violence and war, the acceptance or nonacceptance of maltreatment of others, and values of family and community functioning. The **exosystem,** which is a bit closer to the child, includes a number of social structures such as the family, the neighborhood, socioeconomic status, support systems, and other aspects of the community in which the child and family live. The **mesosystem** relates to the interconnections between the various community systems, such as peer groups, schools, and religious organizations. The **microsystem** is even closer to the child, with a focus on the immediate environment in which the child lives, including the immediate family, the school, and any work setting. Finally, the **ontogenic development** of the child, which has been added since Dr. Bronfenbrenner's original model, is considered to be the internal state that relates to the child's development and adaptation, such as biological factors, affect regulation, and intellectual level (Cicchetti et al., 1997). This comprehensive conceptualization of ecological factors is good to keep in mind when considering individual facets of children's and adolescents' development.

Social contexts are multidimensional and become more intense and more meaningful as children age (Boyce et al., 1998). With regard to the peer network, peers and friends are usually linked to children through the school system and through children's extracurricular activities (e.g., sports activities, religious organizations, and employment opportunities in older children and adolescents). Peers within the school setting are thought to exert a great deal of influence on children's development of academic-related beliefs, prosocial behaviors, popularity, and the development of emotional/behavioral problems (Cillessen & Rose, 2005; Hintze & Shapiro, 1999). Peers can be so influential that programs have been developed where well-functioning children help other children who are troubled or otherwise in need of assistance (Foot, Morgan, & Shute, 1990). Interestingly, peer relationships appear to be influenced by whether children have same-sexed or opposite-sexed siblings (Updegraff, McHale, & Crouter, 2000). In fact, similar to the research on peer networks, there is growing evidence of the influence of siblings on children's development (Brody, 2004).

There is growing interest in the peer network related to the socialization of children. As can be seen in Box 2.6, there is national interest in the importance of peers. Although the national debate has become extremist at times (e.g., suggesting that parents have no influence and that peers are the only ones who influence children; Harris, 1995), it is important to acknowledge the extensiveness of peers' influences on the development of psychopathology. As early as first grade, bullying and reactive aggression are associated with high peer status (i.e., popularity) in African-American boys from lower- and lower-middle-income families (Coie, Dodge, Terry, & Wright, 1991). Choosing aggressive children as friends is associated with higher rates of externalizing problems and with the development of depressive symptoms in early adolescence (Mrug, Hoza, & Bukowski, 2004). In later years, both antisocial and prosocial behaviors are associated with high peer status, depending on the peer group (Cillessen & Rose, 2005; Luthar, 1999). Peer deviance appears to be related to the development of substance use in young adolescents, perhaps due to

BOX *2.6*

CONTEXT AND CHILDREN'S FRIENDSHIPS

"Do parents have any important long-term effects on the development of their child's personality?" In answer to this provocative question, the even more provocative answer is "no," according to Judith Rich Harris (1995). According to Harris, the group socialization theory of development argues that children are most influenced by their peer group and by their friends. "Children learn how to behave outside the home by becoming members of, and identifying with, a social group" (p. 482). Although these conclusions contradict years of research, Harris and her ideas have received a great deal of attention. Harris's first major article on this issue was published in *Psychological Review* (Harris, 1995), which is a highly respected journal published by the American Psychological Association. Harris (1998a) went on to publish a book on the topic, *The Nurture Assumption:*

Why Children Turn Out the Way They Do. Since then a number of publications, including *The New Yorker* have covered this issue (Gladwell, 1998), and a debate has ensued in the professional literature (Collins et al., 2000; Eisenberg, Spinrad, & Cumberland, 1998; Gifford-Smith, Dodge, Dishion, & McCord, 2005; Harris, 1998b). The work by Harris has raised interesting questions about how much peer influences have been integrated into the professional literature. Although it is unlikely that any extremist, unidimensional view would be supported by the data (e.g., only peers can influence children or only parents can influence children), interesting issues have been raised to explore the many ways children and adolescents are influenced (Masten, 2005).

shared environmental factors (Walden, McGue, Iacono, Burt, & Elkins, 2004). Peer victimization (e.g., being teased, bullied, picked on) is associated with depression, social maladjustment, and psychological maladjustment (Hawker & Boulton, 2000; Keltner, Capps, Kring, Young, & Heerey, 2001).

There is a great deal of research interest in the differential influence of peers versus parents. Overall, a number of studies suggest that parental influence far outweighs peer influence (e.g., Gerrard, Gibbons, Zhao, Russell, & Reis-Bergan, 1999). In a study of inner-city Latino/Hispanic adolescents, deviant peer modeling was associated with use of tobacco, alcohol, and marijuana, as well as gang involvement (Frauenglass, Routh, Pantin, & Mason, 1997). Family support, however, seemed to decrease the impact of deviant peers. Thus, adolescents with higher social support from their parents tended to be less influenced by their peers, especially regarding use of tobacco and marijuana (Frauenglass et al., 1997). In a cross-cultural study of African-American and Caucasian-American adolescents from the United States and Chinese adolescents from Beijing, China, there was a great deal of consistency found across cultural and ethnic groups (Pilgrim, Luo, Urberg, & Fang, 1999). Specifically, adolescents who had parents with an authoritative parenting style (i.e., parents who set age-appropriate, firm control and limits in addition to showing high levels of warmth toward the adolescents) and adolescents who showed low sensation-seeking behavior reported lower rates of illicit substance use. The substance use of a close friend also had some influence on adolescents' substance use, but this finding was true only for the Caucasian-American and Chinese adolescents (Pilgrim et al., 1999).

There is also compelling evidence that adolescents do not just find themselves in a deviant peer group, but rather that it is more of an intentional process (Gerrard et al., 1999). In a process known as **niche-picking,** children and adolescents are thought to choose their peer group and friends based on their own level of deviant behavior (Maughan & Rutter, 1998). Parents' monitoring of their adolescents' behavior and of their friendship networks is related to the types of peers with which adolescents get involved. In a 2-year longitudinal study of adolescents' problem behavior (i.e., antisocial behavior, high-risk sexual behavior, academic failure, and substance use), high rates of family conflict, low levels of parent–child involvement, poor parental monitoring, and association with deviant peers were all associated with adolescents' problem behavior (Ary, Duncan, Duncan, & Hops, 1999). The

pattern appeared to be directional, with high family conflict being linked to low parent–child involvement, which then was linked to poor parental monitoring and association with deviant peers one year later. Parental monitoring (e.g., parents who know the whereabouts of their adolescent most of the time, parents who make it a point to know their adolescent's friends, parents who provide age-appropriate control and guidance over their adolescent's activities) is associated strongly with better behavioral outcomes in adolescents (Ary et al., 1999). Overall, it seems pointless to argue that parents have no influence on their children, just as it seems pointless to argue that peers have no influence on children. There are complex associations in the links between parents, peers, and the behavior of children and adolescents.

The peer network is just one example of a social context. Another salient social context has to do with the cultural context of behavior. Increasing attention has been given to the cultural context of behavior, both in the development of prosocial behaviors and in the development of psychopathology (Hall & Barongan, 2002; Kazarian & Evans, 1998). Culture not only refers to the country in which the child lives, but also the child's and family's ethnic/racial background, religious affiliation, social network, community, and neighborhood (Hall & Barongan, 2002; Luthar, 1999). For example, violence levels in neighborhoods were found to be more predictive of violence in inner-city girls than did the timing of puberty (Obeidallah, Brennan, Brooks-Gunn, & Earls, 2004).

The predominant culture can be conveyed in a number of ways, from print media (e.g., newspapers, magazines, and books) to computer games to the Internet to television and movies. Within the area of eating disorders and body image disturbance, for example, a number of studies have pointed to the unrealistic and unhealthy portrayal of female bodies (i.e., bodies that are significantly underweight) within the media (Birkeland Thompson, Herbozo, et al., 2005). The print media has been examined in the context of body image and the development of eating disorders. Unrealistic images of the thin ideal in girls and women are even prevalent in media geared toward young children. This pattern appears to be more prevalent in children's videos rather than children's books (Herbozo, Tantleff-Dunn, Gokee-Larose, & Thompson, 2004). Higher rates of viewing magazines are associated with more body image disturbance in adolescent and college-age girls and women (Turner, Hamilton, Jacobs, Angood, & Dwyer, 1997). This relationship appears to be stronger for Caucasian-American females than for African-American females, given that Caucasian-American girls appear to have more body image concerns than African-American girls (Lawrence & Thelen, 1995). Overall, the relationship between media images of thin girls and women are associated with body image problems. These issues have been explored within the framework of a feminist critique of the media's role in body image problems and the development of eating disorders (Gilbert, Keery, & Thompson, 2005).

Another factor that is thought to transmit the predominant culture is television and the media. There have been thousands of studies of the influence of violence in the media (Anderson et al., 2003; Bushman & Anderson, 2001; Peterson & Newman, 2000; Villani, 2001). That children and adolescents (as well as adults) are exposed to excessive amounts of violence on television should not be news to you. By the time they graduate from elementary school, the average child will have viewed at least 100,000 acts of violence and more

than 8,000 murders on television (Donnerstein, Slaby, & Eron, 1994; Huston et al., 1992; Kunkel et al., 1996; reviewed in Anderson et al., 2003). Many music videos, such as shown on MTV, are known to be both violent and sexually explicit in relation to violence (Peterson & Newman, 2000; Villani, 2001). In the United States, cartoons average 20 acts of violence per hour, and prime-time programs average 5 acts of violence per hour (Radecki, 1990). Box 2.7 focuses on violence in computer and video games.

Overall, there are links between viewing violence and behaving aggressively (Anderson et al., 2003; Bushman & Anderson, 2001; Peterson & Newman, 2000; Van Evra, 1998; Villani, 2001). Although this research finding might lead you to assume that violence in the media "causes" aggression in children, the issue is not that simple. There are factors related to both the depiction of violence and the individuals viewing the

---

BOX 2.7

COMPUTER GAMES, VIDEO GAMES, AND VIOLENCE

Boy (9 years old): When I've finished playing on my own, I sometimes turn it on to two players and then just leave the other player there so I can just kick and punch them.

Researcher: What's the point if there's no one playing with you who can move the other joystick?

Boy: Well, I like to be able to work out the death moves—I can do torso removal and it rips the other body in half. (He laughs loudly). (Sanger, Wilson, Davies, & Whitakker, 1997, p. 1: Reprinted with permission: Taylor and Francis, *Young children, videos, and computer games*).

Computer games and video games are an integral part of many children's lives these days. What concerns many people is the violence and sexism in many video games. In a survey of the most popular video games, nearly 80% of the games showed high levels of aggression and violence (Dietz, 1998). Although over half of the games (59%) did not include any female characters, those that did include female characters tended to show the females as sex objects.

A number of professionals argue that children's use of video games should be monitored by parents and teachers. It appears, however, that this monitoring is the exception rather than the rule. In a study of children's use of computer games and video games at home and at school, parents and teachers often did not monitor children's use of video games and computer games closely (Sanger et al., 1997). A comprehensive review of research on this topic suggested that exposure to violent video games increased children's aggressiveness (Anderson et al., 2003). This conclusion was based on well-controlled studies, where children were randomly assigned to either play a violent or a nonviolent video game. The results suggest that exposure to violent video games is detrimental to the well-being of children and those around them.

In particular, certain vulnerable or impressionable children are put at greater risk for behaving aggressively when exposed to massive amounts of violent video games (Sanger et al., 1997). It is unlikely, however, that playing a violent video game would make an otherwise well-functioning, nonviolent child express extreme violence him- or herself (Sanger et al., 1997). The research findings do suggest, however, that children behave and think more violently after playing violent video games in comparison to playing nonviolent video games (Anderson et al., 2003). Overall, this is a complicated issue. Solutions to this problem must be similarly complex and thorough.

media violence that are related to the potential impact of the violence.

With regard to media violence, certain types of violence are more heavily associated with higher rates of aggression and aggressive fantasies in children. Depictions of violence and aggression on television and in the media are more harmful when

- There is a lack of punishment, or when there is some type of reward for the violence that is depicted.

- The violence is depicted in a realistic and graphic manner.

- The violence is presented in a way that implies it is justified.

- The viewer's perspective is seen through the perpetrator's viewpoint and identification with the perpetrator is encouraged.

- Sexually explicit violence is related more strongly to attitudes that are conducive to sexual assault. (Anderson et al., 2003; Swan, Meskill, & DeMaio, 1998; Van Evra, 1998).

There are also characteristics of the child or adolescent that are related to the impact of viewing violence. Greater exposure to violent television and media in children and adolescents is associated with

- Children, such as those with oppositional defiant disorder or conduct disorder, who already have tendencies toward aggression

- Less parental monitoring, which is associated with more emotional/behavioral problems in children and adolescents and is associated with greater exposure to peers with maladjusted behavior

- Conflict and aggression within the child's or adolescent's family situation (Anderson et al., 2003; Swan et al., 1998; Van Evra, 1998)

Overall, there is no easy answer to the connection between viewing violent material and perpetrating violence or aggression. Although violence in the media is associated with higher levels of aggression with some impressionable and vulnerable children, not every child is affected adversely by violence in the media (Villani, 2001). Obviously, the media is not the only exposure to violence and aggression that children and adolescents experience. Conversely, the majority of children and adolescents who watch television and movies never show any overt violent behavior. Given the complexity of this issue, it is important to keep in mind all the personal, familial, social, and cultural factors that are associated with problematic behavior in youth.

Violence on television and in video games can be associated with aggression in children.

Note also that television programs have been used to present prevention programs with good results (Sanders, Montgomery, & Brechman-Toussaint, 2000).

It is better to support schools than jails.

—Mark Twain

THE OVERARCHING THEORY OF DEVELOPMENTAL PSYCHOPATHOLOGY

The theory of developmental psychopathology attempts to integrate divergent theories (Achenbach, 1982; Cicchetti & Walker, 2003; Hankin & Abela, 2005; Luthar, Burack, Cicchetti, & Weisz, 1997; Mash & Dozois, 2003). For example, the impact of neurobiological and physiological factors, behavioral and emotional factors, family and genetic factors, and sociocultural factors within both the school and the community are all part of what is explored within developmental psychopathology (Campbell & Davies, 2002; Cicchetti & Walker, 2003). Even differential maturational processes in puberty are associated with different outcomes in childhood (Ellis, 2004). These multiple influences in the development of psychopathology are intertwined and influenced by the context (Cicchetti & Toth, 1997; Lerner, Walsh, & Howard, 1998; Wills & Cleary, 2000). One of the major theorists and writers on developmental psychopathology, Dante Cicchetti (1990), noted that "Developmental psychopathology ... should bridge fields of study, span the life cycle, and aid in the discovery of important new truths about the processes underlying adaptation and maladaptation, as well as the best means of preventing or ameliorating psychopathology" (p. 20). With this perspective in mind, a number of central questions should be explored in studies of the theory of developmental psychopathology.

- Which pathways will lead to similar outcomes?
- What are the variations in outcome associated with a given pathway?
- What factors determine the choice of a given pathway?
- What factors determine whether a child continues on the path initially chosen or is deflected off that path?
- When do pathways become fixed, in the sense that deviation from the existing path becomes significantly less likely? (Sroufe, 1989, 1997).

A central component to developmental psychopathology is understanding **developmental trajectories** (i.e., how behavior changes over time). For example, increasing numbers of studies are looking at changes across the life span, including from infancy to young adulthood (Arnett, 2000). Inherent in the exploration of developmental trajectories are the concepts of **multifinality** and **equifinality.** Multifinality suggests that one particular experience may lead to a number of different outcomes in various children (Cicchetti et al., 1997). For example, having a depressed parent is associated with a variety of outcomes in children such as depression, withdrawal, aggression, and oppositional behavior (Goodman & Gotlib, 2002a, 2002b; Kane & Garber, 2004). Equifinality, on the other hand, suggests that a particular outcome can have many different sources (Cicchetti et al., 1997). For example, oppositional behavior in children may be due to genetic predisposition, poor disciplinary practices, or a poor fit between child temperament and family environment (Frick, 1998b). Overall, developmental psychopathology researchers are focused on trying to understand variabilities in functioning over the life span.

A primary goal of developmental psychopathology is to understand the normative developmental process in order to understand the development of emotional/behavioral problems (Achenbach, 1982; Cicchetti & Walker, 2003; Costello & Angold, 1996). Another central goal is to explore continuities and discontinuities in development (i.e., to explore which behaviors stay the same over time and which behaviors change over time; Rutter, 1996). As can be seen in Table 2.1, there are many examples of normal developmental tasks that must be mastered throughout infancy, childhood, and adolescence.

TABLE 2.1 Examples of Developmental Tasks

Age Period	Task
Infancy to preschool	Attachment to caregiver(s)
	Language
	Differentiation of self from environment
	Self-control and compliance
Middle childhood	School adjustment (attendance, appropriate conduct)
	Academic achievement (e.g., learning to read, do arithmetic)
	Getting along with peers (acceptance, making friends)
	Rule-governed conduct (following rules of society for moral behavior and prosocial conduct)
Adolescence	Successful transition to secondary schooling
	Academic achievement (learning skills needed for higher education or work)
	Involvement in extracurricular activities (e.g., athletics, clubs)
	Forming close friendships within and across gender
	Forming a cohesive sense of self-identity

Source: Masten & Coatsworth (1998).

Although these tasks are not necessarily completed in one specific sequence for all children, it appears that the majority of infants, children, and adolescents master these tasks at some time during childhood (Masten & Coatsworth, 1998). In addition to exploring normative developmental tasks, it is also important to consider the development of problems at different ages. Consistent with the exploration of problems from a developmental level, the types of problems that are investigated by developmental psychopathologists include

- Difficult temperament in infants
- Troubled attachment patterns between infants and caretakers
- Defiance or overly independent strivings in toddlers and preschoolers
- Aggressive behavior
- Social withdrawal
- School problems
- Peer problems (Campbell, 1998; Frick, 2004)

Developmental psychopathology also focuses on **resilience,** which refers to children who overcome adverse environments to achieve healthy developmental

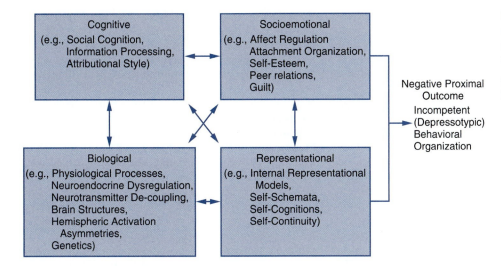

FIGURE 2.2 Emerging competence as the organization of biological and behavioral systems.

Source: Cicchetti & Toth (1995).

outcomes (Fraser, 2004; Goldstein & Brooks, 2005; Luthar, 2003; Luthar, Cicchetti, & Becker, 2000; Masten & Coatsworth, 1998). Resilient children show a number of advantageous characteristics at the level of the individual, the family, and the extrafamilial context. On the individual level, resilient children show good intellectual functioning, self-confidence, faith, and a disposition that is easygoing, sociable, and appealing (Luthar, 2003; Masten & Coatsworth, 1998; Werner & Smith, 2001). On the level of the family, resilient children tend to have at least one close and stable relationship with a caring parental figure, have connections with an extended family network, and have parents who show an authoritative parenting style in which they show high levels of warmth and structure along with providing high expectations of success (Luthar, 2003; Masten & Coatsworth, 1998; Werner & Smith, 2001). At the larger level of the extrafamilial context, resilient children have strong bonds to prosocial adults outside the family (e.g., a caring teacher, a stable coach), show connections with prosocial organizations, and attend effective schools (Luthar, 2003; Werner & Smith, 2001; Wright & Masten, 2005). Note that all these levels of influence are reciprocal and can influence each other individually and collectively. For example, in a long-term longitudinal study of African-American children raised by a single mother, Kim and Brody (2005) found that strong parenting practices were associated with later decreases in problem behaviors, but this process was mediated by the children's self-control. Overall, a central theme in the theory of developmental psychopathology deals with how children in adverse environments are able to avoid developing psychological problems. In addition, there is a strong focus on the malleability of children's behavior, given that a child who is diagnosed with a clinical disorder can still develop into a well-functioning child (Sroufe, 1997).

Figure 2.2 provides an example of a model of the development of psychopathology (in this case, depression). This model shows the complexity of the many variables that are associated with adverse outcomes.

SUMMARY AND KEY CONCEPTS

The Importance of Theory. Nearly all well-respected research into the development of psychopathology is based on a **theory,** which is a systematic set of statements designed to help analyze, explain, predict, and even suggest ways of controlling certain phenomena of interest. The theories discussed in this chapter focus on **etiology** primarily, which is the exploration of what leads to or "causes" the development of a particular type of psychopathology.

Psychodynamic Theory. Based on Freud's work, psychodynamic theory suggests that children and adolescents usually go through five psychosexual stages, the **oral stage,** the **anal stage,** the **phallic stage,** the **latency period,** and the **genital stage.** A more recent psychodynamic theory is referred to as **object relations.** In addition, **attachment theory,** which presupposes the importance of the parent–infant pattern of attachment, focuses on early childhood in relation to later development. Attachment styles fall into two primary categories, **secure attachment** and **anxious insecure attachment,** which are further broken down into avoidant, ambivalent, and disorganized.

Genetic and Biological Theories of Developmental Psychopathology. Most genetic theories focus on the characteristics that are inherited from one's parents. **Genotype** refers to a child's inherited characteristics, **phenotype** refers to a child's observable characteristics, **endophenotype** refers to the interaction between genotype and phenotype, and **heritability** is a term used to refer to the proportion of genetic influence regarding a particular characteristic. In order to assess the genetic versus environmental influences of different characteristics, **monozygotic (MZ) twins** and **dizygotic (DZ) twins** are often studied in what are known as **adoption studies.**

Behavioral Genetics. The study of **behavioral genetics** focuses on the combined influences of genetic and environmental factors in the development of psychopathology. In addition to the focus on inherited genetic factors, environment is explored at two levels: **shared environment** and **nonshared environment.**

Behavioral Theories and Developmental Psychopathology. Behavioral theories argue that observable behaviors are the most important aspect of a child's or adolescent's functioning (although there is some acknowledgment of the importance of cognitions). Behavioral disorders are thought to be developed due to the antecedents and consequences related to the behavior.

Cognitive–Behavioral Theories and Developmental Psychopathology. Closely linked to behavioral theories, cognitive–behavioral theories add a child's or adolescent's cognitions to the understanding of the development of psychopathology. Not only can clinical disorders develop in the context of adverse behavioral conditions, but also adverse cognitions (such as **automatic thoughts** and **cognitive distortions**) can also be linked to the development of certain types of psychopathology.

Theories of Family Functioning and Abnormal Behavior in Children and Adolescents. Within family theories, a main hypothesis is that the problem rarely resides in the child or adolescent him- or herself. Rather, the child is referred to as the **identified problem** (or **identified patient**) who is expressing the problems that are actually present in the family system.

Quite often when families seek help for their child's behavior, they unknowingly might try to maintain **homeostasis** so that nothing in the family changes. Problems within the family are often thought to be related to troubled structures within the family, disrupted communication styles, and difficulty with personal closeness and distance (too much closeness is referred to as **enmeshed,** and too much distance being referred to as **disengaged**).

The Influence of Social Context in the Development and Maintenance of Problem Behavior. Children are embedded within a number of contexts, including peer networks, the school system, religious affiliations, the neighborhood, the community, and the culture as a whole. Based on Urie Bronfenbrenner's conceptualizations of the ecology of childhood, children are nested within all the following contexts: the **macrosystem** (which is represented by the beliefs and values of the child's culture), the **exosystem** (which is represented by the social structures closer to the child, such as the family, the neighborhood, socioeconomic status, support systems, and other aspects of the community), the **mesosystem** (which is represented by the interconnections between many different social systems, such as peer groups, schools, and religious organizations), the **microsystem** (which is reflective of the child's immediate environment including the family, the school, and any work setting), and the **ontogenic development** (which is the internal state of the child). A process known as **niche-picking** suggests that children and adolescents may actually choose their own peer groups that are consistent with their own level of deviant behavior.

The Overarching Theory of Developmental Psychopathology. The study of developmental psychopathology has focused extensively on **developmental trajectories, multifinality, equifinality,** and **resilience.** Developmental trajectories, multifinality, and equifinality are all related to the ways in which children's behavior changes over time. Resilient children develop into well-functioning and exceptional young people in the face of often terrible adverse circumstances. Overall, the theory of developmental psychopathology tries to bridge the gaps between many other theories and tries to help identify the most crucial aspects of the individual or the environment that can help children achieve healthy outcomes.

KEY TERMS

theory	secure attachment	dizygotic (DZ)	identified patient	ontogenic
etiology	anxious insecure	adoption studies	homeostasis	development
oral stage	attachment	behavioral genetics	enmeshed	niche-picking
anal stage	genotype	shared environment	disengaged	developmental
phallic stage	phenotype	nonshared	macrosystem	trajectories
latency period	heritability	environment	exosystem	multifinality
genital stage	endophenotype	automatic thoughts	mesosystem	equifinality
object relations	monozygotic (MZ)	cognitive distortions	microsystem	resilience
attachment theory	twins	identified problem		

SUGGESTED READINGS

Colapinto, John. *As Nature Made Him: The Boy Who Was Raised as a Girl*. New York: Perinnial, 2001. This piece of investigative reporting highlights some egregious unethical behaviors and how some professionals often "cover up" for each others' mistakes. In this case, the "mistake" was to ruin an infant's penis during circumcision and the subsequent decision to raise the boy as a girl without informing him of these difficult circumstances.

Green, Jess. *The Velveteen Father: An Unexpected Journey to Parenthood*. New York: Ballantine Books, 1999. Given the focus on adoption studies as well as the issues around including fathers in research related to the etiology of psychopathology, this book highlights the story of a gay man who adopts two children. Funny and poignant, this memoir highlights that good parenting is good parenting, no matter who provides it.

SUGGESTED VIEWINGS

Mysterious Skin. (2005). A variety of issues are dealt with in this powerful film that explores sexual abuse, sexual orientation, family disengagement, and how children make sense out of the world. This is not a film for the faint of heart.

House of Sand and Fog. (2003). This film speaks to the events that shape our lives and focuses on family, culture, and dealing with financial difficulties.

CHAPTER 3

RESEARCH METHODS IN THE STUDY OF DEVELOPMENTAL PSYCHOPATHOLOGY

CHAPTER SUMMARY

Facts are stubborn things; and whatever may be our wishes, our inclinations, or the dictates of our passions, they cannot alter the state of facts and evidence.

—John Adams

How do you know what you know? That is, how do you know that what you believe to be true is really true? From an existential standpoint, you might just say that you know what you know because of what you've experienced. Or, possibly, you just have a gut feeling about certain topics. From a more objective standpoint, one way of finding out accurate information is to conduct research. Consider the types of headlines that you might read in your local newspaper:

- Children from Single-Parent Homes More Likely to Be Arrested
- Music by Mozart Makes Children Smarter
- Mothers' Love Is Crucial to Child Development

These statements should only be made if there were empirical research studies to back up the findings. Note that each of these statements is biased in one way or another given that research findings were reported incorrectly. Not only should experimental research be conducted before making these types of statements, but also a specific type of experimental research design should be used before making these statements. Results from research must also be conveyed in a fair and objective manner.

This issue is important in any topic area, but it is especially important in the area of developmental psychopathology. What we think we know about children and their problems should be verified and clarified in rigorous research studies. Before acting on clinical "hunches" or techniques that seem to make sense, it is imperative that these issues be examined within research studies. An illustration can be used to make this point.

In 1990, a technique for communicating with autistic children called **facilitated communication (FC)** was popularized in the United States (Biklen, 1990; Biklen, Morton, Saha, & Duncan, 1991). Facilitated communication is a technique in which a facilitator holds a letter board, keyboard, or a typing machine for the autistic individual, and often holds their hand, while the autistic individual types out their thoughts and feelings. The idea behind facilitated communication was that autistic children had the cognitive capacities to communicate, but their disorder hampered their ability to communicate. With this difficulty in mind, facilitated communication was meant to "unlock" their thoughts and feelings in a way that looked to be promising and powerful. Children who were thought to be autistic and mentally retarded were now doing algebra and writing poetry. The words that came from autistic children, who were previously thought to be developmentally delayed and incapable of sophisticated thoughts, were amazing.

- "Autism held me hostage for seventeen years but not any more because now I can talk."
- "I cry a lot about my disability . . . it makes me feel bad when I can't do my work by myself."

The testimonials from teachers and parents were amazing.

- "I thought it was wonderful. At last we were going to help these people communicate."
- "We find that once we open this world for the kids, they are social now, they are appropriate, they do have language, they do understand." (Source for quotes: Frontline documentary, 1993).

Thousands of facilitators were trained to use FC throughout the United States and other countries. Thousands, if not millions, of dollars were spent on buying facilitating machines and on training facilitators and hiring them in special education schools. And why not? Look at those testimonials. The people closest to these children knew that FC was a technique that worked. If you had been in one of those classrooms and seen FC in action, you probably would have been a believer. Why would anyone question the power of this exciting new technique?

Well, as it turns out, FC had not been tested in a rigorous manner to establish that it really worked. Again, with so much evidence and belief that it worked, why would anyone feel the need to study the technique? After FC was used to charge a number of parents and caretakers with sexual abuse, many professionals and families themselves started wondering about who was actually typing those facilitated communications (e.g., Hudson, Melita, & Arnold, 1993). For this reason, a number of empirical studies were instituted that tested the process of FC to ensure that it really was the autistic individual, and not the facilitator, who was authoring the words on the facilitation board.

To test out the facilitated communication technique through an empirically rigorous method, a series of **double blind** studies were developed. Double blind studies allowed the facilitator and the autistic individual

to see the same stimulus in some examples and see a different stimulus in other examples. Thus, each participant was unaware (formerly known as blind) to what the other participant was seeing. The facilitator was placed next to the autistic child and they both looked at pictures at the end of a long table. There was a partition between the facilitator and the autistic child, so that the participants could not see what their partner was seeing. Sometimes the facilitator and the autistic child would be shown the same stimulus. Sometimes they were shown different stimuli. The test of facilitated communication came when they were shown different stimuli. If the child were shown a picture of a cat and the facilitator was shown a picture of a shoe—what would be typed? If FC worked, then the word *cat* should be typed, because that is what the child saw and typed. If the word *shoe* were typed, then the facilitator might actually be authoring the words that were supposed to be the child's words.

Study after study showed that it was really the facilitator who was authoring the words (Moore, Donovan, Hudson, & Dykstra, 1993; Myles & Simpson, 1994). For example, when an autistic child was shown a picture of a key and the facilitator was shown a picture of a dog, the word *dog* was typed. When the child was shown a picture of a box and the facilitator was shown a picture of an apple, the word *apple* was typed. Many studies found comparable results (Prior & Cummins, 1992). Even in the best of circumstances, when the facilitators were highly trained and working with the most capable children who were autistic, the results still suggested that the words were the facilitator's and not the child's.

These findings are not meant to suggest that most facilitators were typing the words consciously. The overwhelming majority of facilitators were concerned individuals who thought that they were unlocking the inner thoughts of children who had been shut out from the world previously. Unfortunately, these beliefs were so unquestioned that even thoughtful, caring individuals were swept up in the hype. Even more unfortunate is that the autistic children were not being helped by this technique, and some may have been harmed by the ramifications of this technique (e.g., bogus reports of sexual abuse that tore up otherwise stable family environments).

In most cases, as more information about the bogus nature of FC was established, FC was dropped as quickly as it was adopted. Although there are still some true believers in FC (Biklen & Cardinal, 1997), academicians and educators have dismissed FC as a useless technique.

The FC debacle illustrates the extraordinary need for empirical research. Even when you "know" something to be true because you have seen it with your own eyes (just like all of those facilitators), you should question whether or not the knowledge has also been established through empirical research. The following description of research methodologies is meant to make you a better consumer of research and also to highlight ways that you can become involved in research. The research process is an exciting and powerful enterprise that can help more children and families than can be helped by any individual therapy session.

If you are interested in a Ph.D. in clinical child psychology, school psychology, education, or a related field, it makes sense for you to get some experience as a research assistant in order to be competitive for those doctoral programs. In addition, serving as a research assistant will help you learn whether or not research is part of what you want to do and might help you to make decisions about what type of graduate program to pursue. I only got involved in research as an undergraduate because I knew I needed the experience to be a competitive applicant to doctoral programs. Until then, I had only heard about research that seemed uninteresting. When I joined a research project that explored mother-child interactions with hyperactive children, I found that research was not just a means to get into graduate school, but it was fascinating and fulfilling. Hopefully, you will find that the research process is yet another way to help children and families. It can be viewed as a puzzle, where the researcher tries to understand why certain behaviors occur in different situations. The research process can be extraordinarily exciting, so here are the basics to get you started.

RESEARCH METHODOLOGIES THAT ARE UTILIZED IN THE STUDY OF DEVELOPMENTAL PSYCHOPATHOLOGY

Research methods used to study developmental psychopathology are comparable to research methods in other areas of inquiry (Drotar, 2000; Roberts & Ilardi, 2005). Thus, if you are familiar with research methodology in any area, the research methodologies used to study developmental psychopathology should sound familiar. There are, of course, specific issues within developmental psychopathology that are not addressed in other areas of research. Issues related to developmental changes, risk factors, and protective factors permeate the study of developmental psychopathology and are often ignored in other fields of study. Thus, although the methodology is comparable to other areas, the focus and application of research methodology is often unique to the study of developmental psychopathology. In addition to the current discussion of these topics, interested readers are referred to *Handbook of Research in Pediatric and Clinical Child Psychology* (Drotar, 2000), *Handbook of Research Methods in Clinical Psychology* (Roberts & Ilardi, 2005), and *Sourcebook of Family Theory and Research* (Bengtson, Acock, Allen, Dilworth-Anderson, & Klein, 2005), all of which are excellent books that should help with the practical issues of conducting research.

As with so many other aspects of research methodology, there is no single research design that is superior above all other designs (Holmbeck, Friedman, Abad, & Jandasek, 2006; Proctor & Capaldi, 2001). The choice of a research design depends on the goals of the study and depends largely on the research questions and hypotheses that are to be tested. A well-designed study might use multiple methods of data collection (e.g., interviews, questionnaires, and direct observation) and might use different facets of many research designs (e.g., within an experimental design, there might also be a component of questionnaires that represent the survey method). Although research studies are often specific in the research questions and hypotheses, greater breadth of methodology usually adds strength to the research findings (Gliner, Morgan, & Harmon, 2000; Morgan, Gliner, & Harmon, 2000).

Experimental Designs

As exemplified in Box 3.1, experimental designs are the cornerstone of the scientific study of psychology. The basic premise of the **experimental design** is that the researcher recruits participants into the study, conducts **random assignment** in which participants are put randomly into one of two or more groups, administers an **independent variable** that is the experimental manipulation provided by the researcher (often a type of treatment intervention or different situation that the child or family has to deal with), and then measures the **dependent variable** in order to see the impact of the independent variable. An example from work on the prevention of psychopathology is highlighted by a study conducted in Minneapolis. Dr. Lauren Braswell and her colleagues (Braswell et al., 1997) identified children at risk for the development of disruptive disorders, randomly assigned children to either receive a

BOX *3.1*

A CLASSIC STUDY OF AGGRESSION IN CHILDHOOD

A study of aggression in childhood conducted by Dr. Albert Bandura, Dr. Dorothea Ross, and Dr. Sheila Ross (1961) was highlighted in a book entitled *Twenty Studies That Revolutionized Child Psychology* (Dixon, 2003) and also in a book called *Forty Studies that Changed Psychology* (Hock, 2004). Dr. Bandura and his colleagues wanted to understand why some children showed aggression and others did not. They proposed to explore the social learning theory of the development of aggression.

The research was conducted at the Stanford University Nursery School, with 36 boys and 36 girls, who ranged in age from 3 to 5 years old. The study utilized an experimental design, whereby children were randomly assigned to one of three conditions: the control group (which was not exposed to any model), the nonaggressive model group (which was exposed to a model who did not show aggression), and the aggressive model group (which was exposed to a model who showed aggression). Half of the participants in each group were boys and half were girls. For children in the modeling groups, half were exposed to a model of the same sex and half viewed a model of the other sex. Thus, there were a total of eight experimental groups and one control group. At the beginning of the study, children in different groups did not differ on levels of aggression.

Children in the control group were left in a playroom for 10 minutes without any other adult present. The playroom was the same for all the children. It contained two different tables, one with craft activities and stickers, and the other with a tinker toy set, and a mallet. This second table was near an inflated Bobo doll that was approximately 5 feet tall. Children in the nonaggressive model group were left in the playroom for 10 minutes with an adult who was playing with tinker toys. Children in the aggressive model group were left in the playroom with the model who played with tinker toys for 1 minute and then interacted aggressively with the Bobo doll for the remaining 9 minutes. The aggressive interactions included punching the Bobo doll, hitting it with the mallet, throwing it in the air, while making statements such as "Sock him in the nose...," "Hit him down...," and "Pow..." These aggressive interactions were standardized so that all children in the aggressive model group witnessed the same amount and the same type of aggression.

After this 10-minute session, all children were taken individually to another room by the experimenter (not the model) and were allowed to begin playing with a number of attractive toys (such as fire engines and doll sets). Each child was soon told that those toys were reserved for other children, so they were escorted to yet another room. This intervention was meant to be a somewhat frustrating situation for the children to allow aggression to be expressed later.

This final room was filled with lots of toys that were both aggressive and nonaggressive in nature. Toys such as mallets, dart guns, a tether ball with a face painted on it, a Bobo doll, tea sets, balls, dolls, cars, trucks, plastic farm animals, crayons, and paper were all presented to the child for his or her enjoyment. The experimenter then left the child alone in the room, and the child was observed through one-way mirrors. Trained observers recorded children's aggressive behavior for 20 minutes.

Results of the study showed that children exposed to the aggressive model showed significantly more aggression during the 20-minute period. Boys showed 38.2 episodes of physical aggression on average, and girls showed 12.7 episodes of physical aggression on average. With regard to verbal aggression, boys showed an average of 17.0 verbal acts of aggression, and girls showed an average of 15.7 verbal acts of aggression. Boys and girls in the control group and in the nonaggressive model group showed virtually no evidence of physical or verbal aggression.

This study was used as compelling evidence that children observe and imitate adult models, even when they themselves are not rewarded for their behavior. This study has been replicated and refined extensively (Dixon, 2003; Hock, 2004). Overall, the conclusions still hold up today as one way of understanding children's and adolescents' tendencies to become aggressive merely by observing aggression in others around them.

multicomponent competence enhancement intervention (MCEI) or information/attention (control group), and measured the outcome of psychological functioning 2 years later. In this example, the preventive intervention (MCEI versus control group) is the independent variable and the outcome (psychological functioning) is the dependent variable. This study found that children in both the intervention group (MCEI) and the control group showed increases in adaptive skills, increases in problem-solving skills, decreases in school problems, and decreases in internalizing symptoms after 2 years. This study highlights the importance of a control group, given that the positive changes were not specific to the intervention (Braswell et al., 1997).

The strength of the experimental design is that researchers can argue **causality** regarding the impact of the independent variable on the dependent variable. That is, the researcher can claim legitimately that the manipulation of the independent variable "caused" the changes that were found in the dependent variable. This point is crucial in understanding research results. Because most other research designs do not allow researchers to claim causality, use of the experimental design provides researchers with unique confidence in their conclusions.

You may be wondering why every researcher does not use the experimental design. Given the strength of the design and the conclusions that can be drawn, why would a researcher use any other design? As you might have already guessed, a huge number of topics cannot be addressed with the experimental design. Imagine that you wanted to assess the real impact of child psychological abuse. In order to argue causality with an experimental design, you would need to recruit young, nonabused children into your study and then randomly assign them to either an abused group (where their parents are required to psychologically abuse them) or to a nonabused group (where their parents are encouraged not to psychologically abuse them). Obviously, this type of research is unthinkable. Thus, the experimental design does not work for many topics within the purview of developmental psychopathology. Sometimes a prospective longitudinal design can help researchers to argue causality (e.g., following children from infancy and then measuring the functioning later in childhood

of those children who were or were not abused). In its truest form, however, the experimental design is the best design to enable conclusions related to causality.

Luckily, a number of clinical child issues have been explored through the experimental design and through laboratory-based procedures, including anxiety (Vasey & Lonigan, 2000), depression (Garber & Kaminski, 2000), conduct problems (Frick & Loney, 2000), and attention-deficit/hyperactivity disorder (Rapport, Chung, Shore, Denney, & Isaacs, 2000).

A torn jacket is soon mended, but hard words bruise the heart of a child.

—Henry Wadsworth Longfellow

Quasi-Experimental Designs

For researchers who want to explore group differences where random assignment is impossible or unethical, the **quasi-experimental design** provides a useful option (Morgan et al., 2000). The quasi-experimental design allows researchers to compare groups that already exist. The primary differences between the experimental method and the quasi-experimental method are the lack of random assignment and the lack of manipulation of the independent variable in the quasi-experimental method. Although the quasi-experimental method can help researchers infer the causal differences between groups, true conclusions of causality can only be obtained with the experimental design.

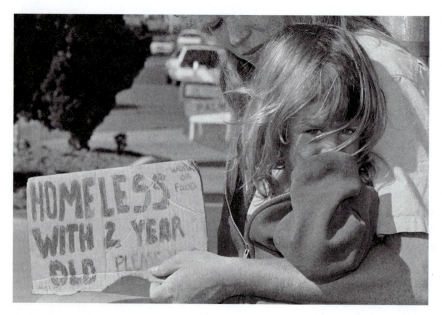

Quasi-experimental research designs have been used to study the functioning of children who are homeless.

When researchers find differences between two already existing groups through the quasi-experimental method, why not claim causality based on the characteristic that differs between the two groups? The main issue is that there may be factors other than the independent variable that allow the two groups to differ. Imagine conducting a study of the health and responsiveness of neonates born to smoking mothers and fathers versus nonsmoking mothers and fathers. The researcher could recruit smoking and nonsmoking couples who were expecting a baby and then measure the baby's health and responsiveness at birth. When differences were found and babies of nonsmoking parents were found to be healthier and more responsive at birth, the researchers still could not claim that smoking was the sole cause of the differences between the infants. Given what we already know about the negative ramifications of smoking during pregnancy, it could be that parents who continue to smoke during pregnancy may also have other characteristics that would make them different from parents who do not smoke during pregnancy. It could be that nonsmoking parents also eat more healthy meals, do not ingest liquor, and exercise appropriately during pregnancy. Thus, when differences were found in the health and responsiveness of the neonates,

it could be due to the smoking but it also could have been due to other health-related behaviors of the parents (or some combination of these factors). Even with a quasi-experimental research design, researchers must be cautious about interpreting results from a causative perspective because the results may be due to other factors that were not controlled in the study (Morgan et al., 2000). Box 3.2 provides another example of a quasi experimental design.

Correlational Designs

In contrast to the experimental and quasi-experimental designs, **correlational designs** can be conducted for almost any topic. The term *correlational design* is actually used to represent a combination of many different types of research that all are correlational in nature. In correlational designs, researchers do not manipulate any variables and cannot argue causality. The **survey method** is common within the field of developmental psychopathology. As the name implies, the survey method utilizes surveys and questionnaires to assess variables that are later analyzed to explore connections between those variables. This type of research can include questionnaire reports from children,

---

BOX *3.2*

A CASE EXAMPLE OF A QUASI-EXPERIMENTAL DESIGN

A number of researchers have explored the psychological ramifications to homelessness. Obviously, this type of research could not be conducted with an experimental design where children and their families would be assigned randomly to either be homeless or to have a home. For this reason, the main research design in this type of research is the quasi-experimental design where known groups of children (in this case, homeless and those who are not homeless) can be compared. The design does not allow formal conclusions of causality, but it does allow a detailed exploration of the differences between children and adolescents who either do or do not have a place to live.

One study explored homeless adolescents (McCaskill, Toro, & Wolfe, 1998). The researchers identified homeless adolescents and compared their functioning with matched adolescents who were housed. Many of the homeless adolescents were recruited from runaway shelters and through advocates for the homeless in an urban community. Housed adolescents were recruited from the neighborhoods in which the homeless adolescents used to reside.

Differences between the two groups emerged for some variables but not for all the variables in the study. Homeless adolescents showed higher rates of disruptive behavior, more alcohol abuse, alcohol dependence, and greater overall emotional/behavioral problems than housed adolescents. There were no significant differences between the groups for rates of drug abuse or depression.

This study highlights the type of important questions that can be addressed with the quasi-experimental design. Although causality might be inferred from the study (e.g., homelessness leads to greater disruptive problems, alcohol problems, and overall emotional/behavioral problems), it could be that another factor was responsible for these findings. For example, it could be that adolescents with higher rates of disruptive behavior and alcohol problems are more likely to run away from home or to be kicked out of their home than adolescents without those problems. For this reason, the quasi-experimental design can only point researchers in a direction that is likely to explain the group differences, but cannot provide causative conclusions with assurance.

parents, teachers, guidance counselors, clinicians, and physicians. Overall, the survey method is a very versatile method through which to collect data.

Case Studies and Single-Subject Designs

Both **case studies** and **single-subject designs** (also known as within-subject designs) allow thorough investigation of one child or a small number of children (Gliner et al., 2000). Case studies tend to be used at the very beginning of a research venture, when almost nothing is known about a particular constellation of behaviors, or in cases of very rare disorders (Linscheid, 2000). Examples of topics investigated with case studies include selective mutism, where a child talks in some situations but does not talk in other situations such as school (Segal, 2003), and autoerotic suicide, where adolescents try to intensive their masturbatory orgasm by limiting blood flow to the brain through some type of constricting rope around their neck and inadvertently end up killing themselves (Sheehan & Garfinkel, 1988). These behaviors are not frequent enough for large-scale survey studies to be conducted, so researchers must piece together a lot of information about the rare cases that come to the attention of clinicians and researchers. Case studies offer a wealth of information about rare or little understood phenomena, but they can be misleading if the individual children or adolescents are not representative of others who experience those phenomena.

The single-subject design is well grounded in the behavioral tradition and is often referred to as a within-subject design. Most often the single-subject design is used to assess changes in behavior related to a behavioral intervention. These types of studies are often done in special education classrooms and in institutionalized settings for children and adolescents. More recently, psychologists have used single-subject designs to assess the effectiveness of therapy in order to be accountable to managed care companies that are paying some portion of the psychologists' fees (Morgan & Morgan, 2001).

One example of the single-subject design is the **A-B-A-B design,** which is also known as the **reversal design.** As illustrated in Figure 3.1 for a child who receives parental attention for appropriate peer interactions, the A-B-A-B design usually allows for baseline data to be collected in the first phase, then a treatment or intervention is administered in the next phase, then the intervention is withdrawn in the third phase, then the intervention is reinstated in the fourth phase. If the intervention works, the desired behavior should be evident in the second and fourth phases (the two "B" phases) but should be less evident in the first and third phases (the two "A" phases). This type of single-subject design is usually used with behaviors that can be modified through situational or environmental changes (e.g., attention, rewards, ignoring maladaptive behavior, etc.). The limitation to this design is that changes in behavior may be due to a factor other than the intervention that had not been controlled. For this reason, researchers who use single-subject designs must control the contingencies related to the behavior of interest carefully (Gliner et al., 2000).

High-Risk Designs

A number of studies within developmental psychopathology utilize a **high-risk design** in which children in a

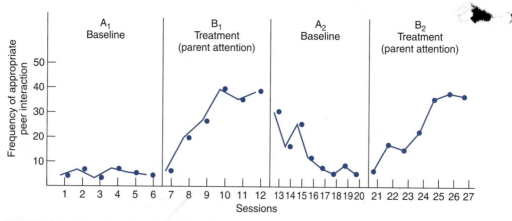

FIGURE 3.1 Example of an A-B-A-B Design.

Source: Clifford J. Drew, Michael L. Hardman, & Ann Weaver Hart, *Designing and Conducting Research* (2nd ed.), 1 Copyright © 1996 by Allyn & Bacon. Reprinted by permission.

disadvantaged situation are studied and compared with children who are not exposed to that disadvantaged situation. Children at high risk for the development of psychopathology include children living in poverty and in the lower socioeconomic status group (Leventhal & Brooks-Gunn, 2004; Luthar, 1999; McLoyd, 1998; Ungar, 2004; Wadsworth, Raviv, Compas, & Connor-Smith, 2005), children from families with high levels of discord or where separation and divorce have occurred (Hetherington, Bridges, & Insabella, 1998), children who have a parent with some type of psychopathology (Connell & Goodman, 2002; Kane & Garber, 2004), and children who have experienced some type of maltreatment (Dixon, Browne, & Hamilton-Giachritsis, 2005). There are also studies that use a high-risk design to explore children who are exposed to a number of risk factors, which is referred to as cumulative risk (Appleyard, Egeland, van Dulmen, & Sroufe, 2005). Most of this research has the ultimate goal of reducing the risk of problems in children (Appleyard et al., 2005; Cicchetti & Rogosch, 1999a).

Behavioral Genetics Designs

As mentioned in the chapter on theories, a great deal of effort has been put into trying to disentangle genetic and environmental factors that might be related to the development of psychopathology. Researchers have used behavioral genetics designs to explore the etiology of a number of childhood problems including conduct problems (Gelhorn et al., 2005; Jaffee et al., 2005), attention-deficit/hyperactivity disorder (Larsson et al., 2004), and

substance use (Hopfer, Crowley, & Hewitt, 2003). Even the exploration of neighborhood derivation (Caspi, Taylor, Moffitt, & Plomin, 2000) and parental divorce (O'Connor, Caspi, DeFries, & Plomin, 2000) have been explored within a behavioral genetics research design.

Behavioral genetics studies typically use either a twin design (where monozygotic and dizygotic twins are compared on a series of characteristics) or an adoption design (where twins or siblings are adopted and raised in different households). Both types of studies can assess the differential contribution of genetic, nonshared environmental, and shared environmental characteristics that are associated with the development of psychopathology in children and adolescents (Cicchetti & Rogosch, 1999a; Deater-Deckard, 2000; Ehringer, Rhee, Young, Corley, & Hewitt, 2006). Although social and biological approaches to understanding behavior have often been investigated separately, behavioral genetics research and other techniques within social neuroscience can lead to a more comprehensive understanding of the development of behavior (Cacioppo, Berntson, Sheridan, & McClintock, 2000; Moffitt, Caspi, & Rutter, 2005).

TIME FRAME OF THE RESEARCH STUDY

There are a number of different time lines during which research can be conducted. There is no one correct way to conduct research from the standpoint of time involvement. Rather, each strategy has strengths and

Studies on twins can help behavioral geneticists clarify the different influences of nature and nurture.

weaknesses that must be considered when choosing a research strategy.

Reason has no age.

—Proverb of Africa

Cross-Sectional Research

Cross-sectional research involves gathering data at one point in time of a child's or adolescent's life (Cicchetti & Rogosch, 1999a). The majority of research is conducted in a cross-sectional manner, largely because it is cheaper and easier to complete than the other methods of data collection. For example, imagine that we wanted to explore the relationship between depressive symptoms and hyperactivity. We could recruit a group of 10-year-olds, some of whom have problems with depression, some of whom have problems with hyperactivity, and some of whom have no known emotional/behavioral problems, and then assess their symptoms of depression and hyperactivity. We would just assess their current symptoms, and we would not re-assess their symptoms at any other point in time.

The cross-sectional research design provides a wealth of information about children at a particular time in their lives, but it is limited by the inability to look at changes over time. This limitation is especially problematic in the area of developmental psychopathology, where a great deal of emphasis is placed on the stability and changes in children's emotional/behavioral functioning over time. For those researchers who can afford it (both in terms of time and money), a stronger research design would involve the prospective longitudinal approach.

Life would be infinitely happier if we could only be born at the age of eighty and gradually approach eighteen.

—Mark Twain

Prospective Longitudinal Research

In contrast to the cross-sectional approach, the **prospective longitudinal research** design allows researchers to follow groups of children and adolescents over time. Often the time frame is somewhat brief (e.g., 6 months), but sometimes prospective longitudinal research projects range from 14 (Hofstra, VanderEnde, & Verhulst, 2000) to over 25 or 30 years (Bell & Bell, 2005; Block & Block, 2006; Werner & Smith, 2001). The advantage of prospective longitudinal research is that researchers can capture the developmental changes that are inevitable

in children and adolescents. The drawback of prospective longitudinal research is that the fact of being in the study might actually alter the behavior that is exhibited by the child or family (a process known as reactivity). Thus, even long-term prospective longitudinal research has limitations. A series of prospective longitudinal studies have been conducted by Caspi and his colleagues who have explored long-term associations between toddlers' temperament and young adults' psychopathology (Caspi, 2000), children's low self-esteem and later development of aggression (Donnellan, Trzesniewski, Robins, Moffitt, & Caspi, 2005), young adolescents' conduct problems and young adults' mental health difficulties (Arseneault, Moffitt, Caspi, Taylor, & Silva, 2000), and adolescents' school attendance and criminal behavior in adulthood (Henry, Caspi, Moffitt, Harrington, & Silva, 1999). Overall, this type of research is time consuming and expensive, but is very helpful in identifying the life-courses of problems found in early childhood. See Box 3.3 for an example of prospective longitudinal research and Box 3.4 for an example of a prospective longitudinal film series.

Accelerated Longitudinal Research

Accelerated longitudinal research is also known as cohort-sequential or cross-sequential research. This design allows researchers to follow groups of children over time, with some attention to overlap in their ages at the start of the study (Cicchetti & Rogosch, 1999a). For example, rather than trying to conduct a 5-year prospective longitudinal research study with 5-year-old children, researchers might begin with a group of 5-year-olds, 6-year-olds, 7-year-olds, 8-year-olds, and 9-year-olds and then follow them for one year. In this manner, information can be gained about the developmental changes that occur between the ages of 5 and 10, but the researchers have only spent 1 year rather than 5 years to conduct the study. The accelerated longitudinal research design combines the strengths of both the cross-sectional and prospective longitudinal research designs.

Overall, there is no single time frame that is ideal for conducting research on developmental psychopathology. In order to remain true to the developmental aspects of developmental psychopathology, it makes sense to follow children, adolescents, and families over time. It is also useful, however, to get a thorough understanding of functioning at one point in time, especially at the beginning of a research endeavor.

BOX *3.3*

A CASE EXAMPLE OF THE PROSPECTIVE LONGITUDINAL DESIGN

An excellent example of a long-term, prospective longitudinal design was conducted in New Zealand. Over 1,200 infants born in 1977 have been followed for over 25 years (Fergusson, Horwood, & Ridder, 2005). The results of the investigation of peer relationships and later psychosocial functioning are highlighted to show the advantages of prospective longitudinal designs (Woodward & Fergusson, 1999).

Peer relationship problems that were reported by teachers when the children were 9 years old were related to externalizing behavior problems (such as criminal involvement and substance abuse) when the children were 18 years old. Other characteristics were assessed when the participants were 25 years old (Fergusson et al., 2005).

Early peer relationship problems were not related to later problems with anxiety disorders or depression. You might be inclined to think that early peer relationships caused the later externalizing problems, but the analyses of these data suggest otherwise. Further investigation showed that the externalizing behavior problems at the age of 18 seemed to be most related to conduct problems in early childhood and poor parent–child relationships in early childhood. Thus, the functioning of children at the age of 18 seemed to be closely related to the functioning of the children at the age of 9 (Woodward & Fergusson, 1999). This series of studies has also been informative on a number of other issues. For example, Fergusson and colleagues (2005) found that conduct problems in children aged 7 to 9 years old were related to criminal behavior, substance dependence, poor mental health, and troubled sexual relationships at the age of 25. In addition, the experiences of child physical abuse and child sexual abuse were associated with the development of panic disorder in young adulthood, but early exposure to parental violence such as spousal abuse was not associated with the development of panic disorder in young adulthood (Goodwin, Fergusson, & Horwood, 2005).

This type of prospective longitudinal design allows the exploration of a wealth of causative and associative relationships between variables. Although this type of research is difficult to conduct, it is well worth the effort given the comprehensiveness of the findings.

Science is built up with facts, as a house is with stones. But a collection of facts is no more a science than a heap of stones is a house.

—Jules Henri Poincare

How are research ideas identified and how are samples chosen?

A good father is a little bit of a mother.

—Lee Salk

THE ACTUAL PROCESS OF RESEARCH

Most professional researchers develop a line of research from which they create a number of different, but related research projects. **Programmatic research,** during which researchers set out to build on their own previous research, is most commonly done by professors and researchers who develop an expertise in a particular area. Most often, this research is driven by a theoretical framework that researchers are investigating (Peterson & Tremblay, 1999). The boxes throughout this chapter highlight programmatic research that has been conducted all over the world (see, for example, Box 3.5). Once a researcher identifies an area of investigation, it is often relatively easy to identify the next study (and sometimes to identify the next 20 studies!). But what about the researcher who is just beginning the empirical process?

Choosing a Research Topic and Identifying Hypotheses

By the time graduate students begin the research process formally, they probably have already had at least some experience with research. Most often, especially in doctoral graduate programs, students choose a graduate program and a mentor that are consistent with their research interests. Sometimes research interests develop from a personal interest in a particular topic (e.g., Uncle Fred devastated his family with his alcoholism, so the student becomes interested in the family ramifications of alcoholism). Research interests can also develop from the sheer fascination with a research topic (e.g., autism is such a perplexing disorder, so the student wants to be part of identifying the etiologies of autism). Sometimes students become interested with the research topic that their undergraduate or graduate mentor is studying, so

BOX *3.4*

A PROSPECTIVE LONGITUDINAL FILM SERIES

In 1964, filmmaker Michael Apted selected 14 children in England to film for a documentary that was part of the "World in Action" series. Children were selected from a diverse array of backgrounds, and some of the earliest interviews had to do with the effects of growing up in privilege or in poverty. The first film was titled "7-up" because the children were 7 years old. Since that time, the filmmakers have interviewed the same individuals every 7 years. Based on the ages of the participants, the resulting films are entitled, "14-up," "21-up," "28-up," "35-up," "42-up" and "49-up." The premise of the film started with the following idea—"Give me the child until he [she] is seven and I will give you the man [woman]."

In the documentary when the participants were 42 years old (Apted, 1999), the interviewer asked the participants to reflect on how their participation in the series has impacted their lives. Although being followed by an international audience from childhood to adulthood is different than participating in prospective longitudinal research privately, the participants' answers give us a glimpse of what participants in research may experience when they are followed over time. Here are some of the responses:

- "It's funny because before the film starts, you think—what on earth have I done in the last seven years? What can I talk about that I've done?"
- "If you came and asked me if you could do this to my children, I certainly wouldn't be enthusiastic. I think it's something that I wouldn't want to wish on someone particularly."

- "I don't think I'd ever have kept a record of my life in the way that we have with this program. So yes, I mean, I enjoy doing it."
- "There's a lot of baggage that gets stirred up every seven years for me that I find quite . . . hard to deal with. And I can put it away for the seven years and then it comes around again and the whole lot comes tumbling out again and I have to deal with it all over again."
- "It has to be said that I bitterly regret that the headmaster of the school where I was when I was seven pushed me forward for this series because every seven years a little pill of poison is injected."
- "There's a certain amount of excitement."
- "It hasn't sort of changed my choices in life. I haven't thought—well I have to be doing this by then or how will this seem to others. . . . It's just a periodic little intrusion."

These reflections show the ambivalence that may be evident in participants from prospective longitudinal research. In addition, these comments suggest that the fact of participating in a project over time may alter the participants' actual developmental trajectory. These films are worth a look for anyone interested in developmental psychopathology as well as normative developmental processes. In addition, Apted's film work has been discussed in relation to how documentaries can inform psychologists and other mental health workers (Apted & Robinson, 2003).

---

they continue on in that research area with their own unique addition to the empirical process.

One of the most common problems that students face in identifying a research topic is their desire to address a research question that is too large. I have heard undergraduate honors students identify research topics like, "I want to find out which therapy is most effective" or "I want to show what causes attention-deficit/hyperactivity disorder." Although these are extraordinarily important research questions, even researchers with millions of dollars of grant money and unlimited time to conduct the research continue to struggle with answering these research questions. It is important for researchers to choose a topic that is feasible within their constraints of time, money, and expertise. No single study can answer these overarching issues. Individual studies can, however, be pieced

together to make more comprehensive statements about a particular area.

Once a feasible topic has been identified, students or professional researchers conduct a literature review to find out what else is known about that topic. Sometimes, the very study that the researcher would like to conduct has already been completed numerous times. Other times, the literature review reveals that similar studies have been conducted, but the exact study of interest has not yet been completed. Overall, researchers need to build their own new research on work that has been completed previously. Different sampling issues, measurement issues, and design issues can be highlighted when reviewing the research literature. Through the literature review, researchers develop their own hypotheses about what they expect to find in their study. It is much better to conduct research that is

The father–child relationship can have both positive and negative ramifications, just like the mother–child relationship.

BOX 3.5

A CASE EXAMPLE OF THE RESEARCH ODYSSEY

In a book entitled, *The Developmental Psychologists: Research Adventures Across the Life Span* (Merrens & Brannigan, 1996), 18 developmental psychologists explain why they investigate their chosen topics and how their research programs have changed over the years. Dr. Ross Parke (1996) provides an interesting explanation of how he came to study fathers. He became intrigued with the father–infant relationship for a number of reasons, including the theoretical importance of the topic, the social and scientific relevance of the topic, and the dearth of

knowledge in this area. When Dr. Parke began much of his classic work in the late 1960s and early 1970s, nearly all the research completed with infants and their parents focused on the mother–infant relationship. He chose to look at the father–infant relationship in addition to the mother–infant relationship. This line of research proved to be very important and productive. Dr. Parke has continued this line of inquiry for over 35 years, and continues to investigate the father–child relationship with regard to play, emotions, and social development (Parke, 2004).

---

driven by hypotheses than to "go fishing" for results. Once the literature has been reviewed thoroughly and the specific study has been identified and the hypotheses have been formulated, it is time to identify the sample of participants who will be part of the study.

Choosing a Sample

In an article that was entitled, "Most of the Subjects Were White and Middle Class," Dr. Sandra Graham (1992) reviewed the distressing pattern that empirical research is based largely on samples of middle-class, Caucasian-American individuals. Although she was discussing research in general, this pattern holds true in research on developmental psychopathology and families (Coley, 2001). Although samples of ethnic

minorities are sometimes more difficult to recruit than nonminorities (Costigan & Cox, 2001), it is imperative that research samples provide a representative (and therefore, generalizable) sample of participants. The issues of representativeness include, but are not limited to, age and developmental level, gender, race and ethnicity, socioeconomic status, cultural diversity (including religion, native language, and acculturation), geographical region (e.g., rural, urban, suburban), and family constellation. A number of researchers have discussed the importance of inclusion of representative samples (e.g., Hall & Maramba, 2001; McLoyd, 1998; Sue, Kurasaki, & Srinivasan, 1999). Notably, a special issue of *Journal of Family Psychology* is dedicated to the issue of cultural variation in families (Parke, 2000). Interested readers should also consider finding

THE FAR SIDE®   BY GARY LARSON

The Far Side® by Gary Larson © 1982 FarWorks, Inc. All Rights Reserved. The Far Side® and the Larson® signature are registered trademarks of FarWorks, Inc. Used with permission.

Late at night, and without permission, Reuben would often enter the nursery and conduct experiments in static electricity.

a copy of *Studying Minority Adolescents: Conceptual, Methodological, and Theoretical Issues* (McLoyd & Steinberg, 1998) and *Multicultural Psychology* (Hall & Barongan, 2002), which both provide comprehensive reviews of research findings of diverse groups of youth and families.

In addition to these issues, it is also important for the researcher to consider which individuals of a family or school system will be invited to participate in the research. Historically, mothers have been overrepresented in clinical child research and fathers have been ignored (Phares, 1992). More recently, there has been attention to the need to include fathers in research related to developmental psychopathology and pediatric psychology, but the majority of studies continue to include mothers and not fathers (Phares, Lopez, Fields, Kamboukos, & Duhig, 2005). Fathers are a bit more difficult to recruit into family-based research than are mothers (Costigan & Cox, 2001), but their presence in studies of developmental psychopathology is important and is worth the extra effort by researchers.

The school system is also a place where careful considerations about sampling must be made (Phillips, 1999). Depending on the research question, researchers may only be interested in children involved in regular education classrooms, or they may be interested in special education programs.

There is no one "right" way to identify a sample of children and adolescents for research on the development of psychopathology, but there are some guiding rules to follow.

- Make sure to consult previous research before identifying a research sample. It may be that the research question has already been answered with a particular population, but has not been addressed with another population.

- Try to recruit a diverse sample.

- When a diverse sample cannot be gathered, explain why a diverse sample was not recruited and highlight the homogeneity of the sample as a possible limitation of the results.

- Do not generalize the data beyond the characteristics of the sample that was collected (e.g., if only boys were studied, then do not try to suggest the research results also apply to girls).

Overall, these guiding rules should increase representative and generalizable samples of children and adolescents in studies of developmental psychopathology (Hall & Barongan, 2002; McLoyd & Steinberg, 1998). No single study can address all of the issues within a research topic, so it is also important to acknowledge that other researchers can address the issues that your study was not able to address (Drotar, 2000). Box 3.6 describes a study that involved a difficult sample to investigate.

Choosing Psychometrically Sound Measures

Empirically based assessments and questionnaires (Achenbach, 2002) are discussed in more detail in the chapter on assessment. For the purposes of understanding the research process, it is important to consider what type of measurements will be used in the research study. Measures with strong psychometric properties (i.e., reliability and validity) are imperative to trust the data that are collected. In addition, a number of methods of measurement can be considered, including direct observation, interviews, questionnaires, educational measures, family measures, neuropsychological measures, physiological assessments, and medical/health measures. Regardless of which methodology is chosen,

BOX 3.6

A CASE EXAMPLE OF A DIFFICULT SAMPLE TO STUDY

A difficult topic to study is the death of a parent. Not only is this issue potentially painful for the children and guardians who might be recruited into the study, but it is difficult to identify enough children in this group to allow an adequate sample. For example, a researcher could not just go to a public school and expect to recruit enough children who had lost their parents to death.

One group of researchers dealt with this topic by recruiting children from a variety of sources (Thompson et al., 1998). The researchers were able to recruit 80 children and adolescents who had experienced parental death within the last 4 to 24 months. Youth were identified through medical records at an inner-city hospital that serves primarily low-income and ethnic minority individuals and families, records from a victim and witness assistance program, referrals from a local hospice (which cares for individuals who are close to death), obituaries, an HIV clinic, and the medical examiner's office. Nonbereaved children and adolescents were recruited from a general medical clinic, a hospital newsletter, and through referrals from bereaved children and adolescents. The researchers recruited the control group of nonbereaved youth so that they were comparable to the bereaved group on their demographic characteristics, such as socioeconomic status, race/ethnicity, gender, and percent receiving federal financial assistance.

Youngsters and their parent or guardian completed measures of emotional/behavioral functioning for the child. When children's and adolescents' reports were compared, there were no significant differences between the bereaved and nonbereaved groups. When parents' and guardians' reports were compared, children and adolescents in the bereaved group showed significantly more internalizing and externalizing problems than children and adolescents in the nonbereaved group. Interestingly, this finding was only significant for Caucasian-American children and adolescents. Thus, when parents and guardians reported on children and adolescents from ethnic minority groups, the bereaved and nonbereaved children and adolescents did not differ between groups.

This study shows the complexity of research findings and the difficulty of interpreting results in group comparisons. It could be that youth do not experience significant emotional/behavioral problems after the death of a parent (as would be suggested by the youngsters' self-reports). It could also be that some children (notably Caucasian-American children according to this study) do experience difficulties that are noticeable to their surviving parent or guardian. More research is needed on this difficult and potentially painful topic in order to understand the factors that lead to adaptive versus maladaptive outcomes after the loss of a parent due to death.

---

it is important to use well-established measures that have been shown to be reliable and valid. It is also helpful to use multiple methods of measurement, such as interviews and direct observation. By not relying on only one method of measurement (e.g., self-reports), researchers can be more confident with their findings.

I pass with relief from the tossing sea of Cause and Theory to the firm ground of Result and Fact.
—Sir Winston Spencer Churchill

Collecting Data

Once the measures and sample have been identified, the data collection process can begin. In most cases, parental consent and child assent are required. These issues are discussed later in this chapter regarding the ethics of conducting research with children and families. After consent and assent have been established, researchers and their assistants collect data. Sometimes the data

collection process is relatively easy (e.g., hand out questionnaires to a group of well-behaved 10-year-olds in the school cafeteria). Sometimes the data collection process is quite arduous (e.g., doing home visits and interviews with troubled families who have chaotic schedules and who are often not available for the interviews when the research assistants show up at the family's place of residence). Depending on the time frame of the research, the data collection process can take years (e.g., in prospective studies where children are followed from birth to 7 years old).

Every experienced researcher has lots of horror stories, as well as lots of poignant anecdotes, about the data collection process. My own favorite horror story is from the beginning stages of data collection for my dissertation. It had taken about 6 weeks to get permission to collect data in a particular school district. The week that I was finally allowed to begin recruiting adolescents for the study was the week that the teachers chose to go on strike. Luckily for everyone concerned (especially the teachers!), the strike was resolved quickly, and I was allowed to get into the school about a month after the strike was resolved (and after the school system and classrooms had gotten back to normal).

One of my favorite positive anecdotes is from a recent family who came to the university for a research project that involved interviews and behavioral observation. The behavior observation required that the mother and the father talk with the adolescent separately for 5 minutes each while being videotaped. The videotapes were later transcribed and coded to explore parent–adolescent interactions. Both parents had a particularly difficult time finding 5 minutes worth of conversation to have with their adolescent. They reported to me later that the behavioral observation had been a wake-up call for them. They felt that they had an open and honest relationship with their adolescent, but when they found that it was a struggle to have a sustained conversation for 5 minutes, they realized that they wanted to spend more "quality" time with their adolescent (rather than always running from one activity to another). Overall, the data collection can be as fascinating as the actual data that are collected. It is a wise researcher who stays closely involved with the process of data collection so that she or he can learn from the research participants.

Data Analyses

Once the data are collected, they must be entered into a computer and analyzed. There are a wide variety of data analyses that can be conducted, including

- Frequencies, means, and standard deviations, which are used as descriptive statistics to describe the characteristics of the sample
- T-tests, analyses of variance (ANOVAs), and multivariate analyses of variance (MANOVAs), which are used to look at either group differences or differences between variables
- Correlations and regressions, which are used to look at the correspondence between variables and to assess how the variables are related to one another
- Path analyses and structural equation modeling (SEM), which are used to explore the connections between variables and can be used to look at the directionality of the relationships between the variables

There are a number of more sophisticated data analyses available, but this list includes the main analyses that are used in research on the development of

psychopathology. Note that it is standard to use a **p-value** (probability value) of $p < .05$ in most research on developmental psychopathology. Although researchers can make arguments about using a stronger or a more lenient p-value, the standard is usually to use $p < .05$ unless otherwise noted. This standard means that as researchers, we acknowledge that there may be significant findings by chance in 5 out of 100 analyses. If researchers wish to have more trust in their results, they might use a p-value of $p < .01$ or $p < .001$, both of which would allow more assurance of few chance findings.

Even when a result is statistically significant, not that it is still incumbent on the research to address whether or not the result is clinically significant and clinically meaningful (Beutler & Moleiro, 2001; Jensen, 2001; Kazdin, 2001). Sometimes results can be statistically significant, but the actual differences between groups, for example, are so small that they are clinically meaningless. Thus, clinical researchers are encouraged to remain cognizant of both statistical significance and clinical significance.

Writing Up, Presenting, and Publishing the Results

Once the data have been analyzed, it is time to write up the results. Specific writing tips can be found in the fifth edition of *The Publication Manual of the American Psychological Association* (2001). Most often, researchers try to present their research findings at a professional conference while they are trying to get their research findings published. There is usually a quicker turnaround time for decisions from professional conferences, and it is legitimate to first present research data at a conference and then publish the data in a journal. It is not, however, appropriate to publish data and then present it at a conference. Professional conferences are meant for the presentation of cutting-edge research, so presenting data that have already been published would defeat that purpose.

A number of conferences and journals are appropriate for research on developmental psychopathology. In addition to the following lists, interested students can look at the reference section to get a sense of other outlets for research on developmental psychopathology. The following organizations usually have conferences on a yearly or biyearly basis and empirical research on developmental psychopathology is often presented at these conferences:

- *American Psychological Association* (APA), which is the largest professional organization of psychologists in the world (Division 15 on educational psychology, Division 16 on school psychology, Division 37 on child, youth, and family services, Division 43 on family psychology, Division 53 on clinical child psychology, and Division 54 on pediatric psychology are especially likely to present research related to developmental psychopathology)

- *American Psychological Society* (APS), which is smaller than APA and more focused on research

- *Society for Research on Child Development* (SRCD), which focuses on developmental psychology, but has many presentations on developmental psychopathology

- *International Society for Research on Child and Adolescent Psychopathology* (ISRCAP), which is a small but distinguished group of researchers who focus on the development of psychopathology

- *National Association of School Psychologists* (NASP), the largest organization of school psychologists in the United States

- *American Association for Marital and Family Therapy* (AAMFT), which focuses on the treatment of marital and family problems

There are also a number of groups that specialize in certain disorders (e.g., alcohol and substance abuse, anxiety disorders) that are possible outlets for research on developmental psychopathology. In addition, each region and state within the United States has separate conferences for that geographical area (e.g., the Western Psychological Association, the Florida Psychological Association). There is no shortage of conferences where research on developmental psychopathology can be presented. If you cannot identify an appropriate outlet for your research, your research mentor or other colleagues may be able to help you identify appropriate outlets. Even if you are not a researcher yet, you may want to attend one or more of these conferences to get a glimpse of the research and scholarly process at academic conferences. I attended my first national APA conference when I was between my sophomore and junior years of undergraduate work. It was fascinating and overwhelming all at the same time—and it was definitely something that I would recommend to interested students.

When considering publishing research results, there are a number of viable venues for research in developmental psychopathology. Some of the primary journals include

- *Journal of Consulting and Clinical Psychology*
- *Journal of Abnormal Psychology*
- *Journal of Family Psychology*
- *Child Development*
- *Developmental Psychology*
- *Journal of Clinical Child and Adolescent Psychology*
- *Journal of Abnormal Child Psychology*
- *Development and Psychopathology*
- *Journal of the American Academy of Child and Adolescent Psychiatry*
- *Journal of Child Psychology and Psychiatry*
- *American Journal of Community Psychology*
- *Journal of School Psychology*
- *Journal of Educational Psychology*

In addition to these journals, interested researchers are also encouraged to find a copy of *Journals in Psychology (5th edition),* which is published by the American Psychological Association (1997b). There are a number of specialty journals in which articles on developmental psychopathology might be published (e.g., *Journal of Affective Disorders, International Journal of Eating Disorders, Cultural Diversity and Ethnic Minority Psychology*). Many journals now also have Web sites, so information on topic coverage, acceptance rates, and length of time for an editorial decision can be shared. The publication process can be arduous, often with the manuscript having many rejections and revisions before finding a place for publication. But the publication process is a crucial link in helping disseminate research findings. When meaningful results are found, it is incumbent on the researcher to try to share those results with the scholarly public through presentations and publications.

The scientist values research by the size of its contribution to that huge, logically articulated structure of ideas which is already, though not yet half built, the most glorious accomplishment of [human]kind.

—Sir Peter Brian Medawar

Continuing the Research Process

Once a study is completed, many researchers are left with even more questions than before the study began. For this reason, the results of one study usually lead nicely into the hypotheses of another study. When good programmatic research is conducted, researchers can use previous research results to formulate the

BOX 3.7

A CASE EXAMPLE OF RESEARCH IN THE COMMUNITY

In order to understand the connections between witnessing violence and experiencing antisocial behavior, one research group explored adolescents who were at risk for the development of antisocial behavior (Miller, Wasserman, Neugebauer, Gorman-Smith, & Kamboukos, 1999). Boys between the ages of 6 and 10 who lived in an urban setting and who had at least one sibling with a juvenile court conviction were recruited into the study. Slightly more than half of the participants were African American and slightly less than half of the participants were Hispanic/Latino. The boys were interviewed at two points in time, which were separated by 15 months.

Results of the study showed that boys' exposure to violence in the community was related to the later development of antisocial behavior (e.g., delinquency, fighting). This

relation, however, was moderated by the family environment. For boys with low levels of parent–child conflict, the witnessing of violence was a significant predictor of increased antisocial behavior over 1 year later. For boys who experienced high levels of parent–child conflict, the additional witnessing of violence in the community did not predict any greater antisocial behavior a year later. Thus, it appeared that either high parent–child conflict or high exposure to community violence were associated with greater levels of antisocial behavior in the future.

This study combined the prospective longitudinal design with the high-risk design. This type of comprehensive and thoughtful research needs to be conducted to establish the many factors that lead to the development of psychopathology in children.

---

questions for research in the future. It is an exciting process that can lead to better ways of understanding and helping children, adolescents, their families, their schools, and their communities (Lerner, Fisher, & Weinberg, 2000). Box 3.7 presents an example of research in the community.

CHOOSING APPROPRIATE SAMPLES OF PARTICIPANTS

The issue of representativeness of samples has already been mentioned, but the topic warrants additional attention. For researchers to conduct research that can be generalized to the larger population of children, they must include representative samples of children and adolescents. This representativeness should include considerations of age/developmental level, gender, race/ethnicity, socioeconomic status, geographic region (such as urban, rural, suburban), cultural diversity (including religion, native language, and acculturation), family constellation, and clinical versus nonclinical status.

Throughout the history of psychological and educational research, there are egregious examples of biased samples that were used to generalize to the broader population. In her book entitled, *In a Different Voice,* Dr. Carol Gilligan (1993) described the early research on moral development that was conducted with only boys and men and then was applied to girls and women. Once research on moral development was conducted with girls and women, it became clear that males and females differ

in the process of moral development. Brown and Gilligan (1998) have gone on to highlight the differences and similarities between girls and boys in their development. As you can see in the "You Decide" section, there are still pros and cons to exploring gender differences.

In his book entitled, *Even the Rat was White,* Dr. Robert Guthrie (2003) illustrated a number of studies that were conducted with Caucasian Americans, the results of which were then applied to individuals of all races and ethnicities often to their detriment. These examples illustrate the importance of trying to identify representative samples of children and adolescents for all research topics. If researchers are not able to recruit a representative sample, then they must be extremely careful to only apply the results to that specific type of sample. Thus, if research is conducted with impoverished children from a rural community, the results should not be applied to impoverished children from the inner city. Similarly, if the process of developing a learning disorder is studied with a sample of children whose native language is English, then the results should not be applied to children who have learned English as their second (or third) language.

Another important consideration in the recruitment of participants is the adequate description of those participants. In a review of published clinical child research, Dr. Joyce Lum and I found that 36.7% of the studies did not include information about socioeconomic status or the racial and ethnic distribution of their sample. A total of 80.4% of the studies did not include any information about parental marital status or family constellation (Phares & Lum, 1996). Given that research results should not be generalized beyond the characteristics of the sample, it is imperative that research samples be described adequately. This study highlighted that many researchers did not describe their samples adequately.

LOCATIONS OF RESEARCH ON DEVELOPMENTAL PSYCHOPATHOLOGY

To some extent, research on developmental psychopathology can be completed whereever children and adolescents are found. A number of research sites are highlighted, but research can be conducted in almost any setting.

School-Based Research

Because children and adolescents spend so much of their week in school, it is not surprising to find that much of the research on developmental psychopathology is conducted within the school setting (Drotar, Timmons-Mitchell et al., 2000). Researchers can choose to conduct research within regular education classrooms to access a broad range of children (most of whom would be expected to fall into the nonclinical range), or they can choose from a number of specialized programs within public schools (such as classrooms for children who are severely emotionally disturbed, children with severe intellectual limitations, and children who have both physical and intellectual limitations).

Researchers of developmental psychopathology try to include representative samples of children in their studies.

Obviously, school-related issues (such as learning disorders, behavioral disorders, peer interaction, issues related to intellectual functioning, and teacher–child interactions) can be studied within the school setting. Many other areas of research have also been conducted within the school setting (e.g., children's emotional/behavioral functioning, eating disorders and body image problems within children and adolescents, gender differences, children's perceptions of family functioning, children's understanding of health issues). Often, researchers introduce the topic of study to children in the classroom and then pull children out of the classroom for the brief period of data collection once the child has received permission to participate in the study. Researchers are often asked to convey their overall results to school officials and teachers to show the value of the research and to educate school personnel about the research process. Overall, the school system is a wonderful place to collect data about children and adolescents. Especially in schools with a diverse student population, researchers have a chance of recruiting representative samples that can be generalized to other children and adolescents in that type of school setting. Box 3.8 presents an example of research in the schools.

Hospital-Based and Clinic-Based Research

Researchers often conduct studies of health and illness issues in medical hospitals (Drotar, Timmons-Mitchell et al., 2000). For example, studies of children's emotional/behavioral functioning regarding their sickle cell anemia (Chen, Cole, & Kato, 2004), cancer (Patenaude & Kupst, 2005), or cystic fibrosis (Chapman & Bilton, 2004) have been conducted in hospital settings and outpatient medical settings. Similarly, sometimes children are recruited into studies based on their parent's medical illness, such as cancer (Faulkner & Davey, 2002) or AIDS (Rotheram-Borus, 2005). The hospital emergency room is a site for research on adolescent suicide, given that the emergency room is often the first contact that adolescents have with mental health professionals (Gothelf et al., 1998). In addition, a great wealth of research on developmental psychopathology has been conducted in inpatient psychiatric settings where children and adolescents are being treated for severe psychopathologies (e.g., Joiner, 1999).

Clinic-based research most often involves children and adolescents who are being seen by a therapist on an outpatient basis. These studies often explore specific types of psychopathology (Southam-Gerow, Weisz, &

BOX 3.8

A CASE EXAMPLE OF RESEARCH IN THE SCHOOLS

One research program in the schools attempted to decrease the stressors associated with the transition from elementary school to middle school (Elias & Clabby, 1989, 1991; Sukhodolsky et al., 2005). The Improving Social Awareness-Social Problem Solving (ISA-SPS) program focused on two central themes during this difficult transitional time: Initial transition difficulties (such as getting used to new routines and having to change classes for each subject) and longitudinal problems (such as peer pressure and acculturation into the social system of the new school). In addition to these central themes, the researchers identified more than 20 specific stressors, such as not remembering the combination to your locker and getting lost in the new school. The preventive intervention included three primary components:

• Development of self-control skills, group participation skills, and social awareness

• Development of social decision making skills and problem-solving skills

• Promoting skill acquisition and application in the school and home environment

Evaluations of this preventive intervention have shown that, when compared with children who did not receive the preventive intervention, children who participated in the program showed better adjustment and fewer conflicts with peers and authorities (Elias & Clabby, 1989, 1991; Sukhodolsky et al., 2005). These studies illustrate the excellent research that can be conducted within the school setting, with the support of teachers and school administrators. In programs such as the ISA-SPS, teachers are often taught strategies for helping their students with psychosocial difficulties, so teachers often receive a direct benefit from these programs in addition to the benefits to their students.

Kendall, 2003), but they can also deal with other topics such as parent–child interactions (McCarty, Lau, Valeri, & Weisz, 2004), parental beliefs about the etiology of children's emotional/behavioral problems (Yeh, Hough, McCabe, Lau, & Garland, 2004), and treatment outcome research (Roberts, Vernberg, & Jackson, 2000; Weisz, Doss, & Hawley, 2005). Because the census of inpatient hospitals has been decreasing over the years (due to deinstitutionalization and limits in funding; Scholle & Kelleher, 1998), research in clinics and in the community has increased while research with inpatient populations has declined (Rappaport & Seidman, 2000).

Community-Based Research

Research can be conducted within the community setting as well. Often, community-based research deals with issues relevant to the community (such as violence, overcrowding, racism) and can be used to inform social policy (Lerner et al., 2000; McCall & Groark, 2000). As highlighted in Box 3.2, studies have explored the similarities and differences of homeless children and children who have homes (Masten, Miliotis, Graham-Bermann, Ramirez, & Neemann, 1993; McCaskill et al., 1998). Interestingly, these studies have found conflicting evidence with some studies showing greater psychopathology in homeless adolescents (McCaskill et al., 1998) and other studies finding no differences between

homeless children and those with homes (Masten et al., 1993). Much of the work on risk and protective factors (such as the Kauai studies; Werner, 1995; Werner & Smith, 2001) has been conducted within the community in which children and families live.

Laboratory-Based Research

When researchers want more of a structured setting in the data collection process, they may choose to do laboratory-based research. Imagine the difference between trying to interview a single mother in her home as opposed to in the laboratory. In the home, the phone might be ringing, the baby might be crying, the television might be blaring, and the information from the interview might be compromised by all of these distractions. Imagine, instead, interviewing a single mother in a laboratory setting, where the researchers have provided free child care during the interview, where the room is quiet and comfortable, and where the mother can focus her attention on the questions at hand. There are clear advantages to laboratory-based research, but there are also some limitations on generalizability given that the setting is probably foreign to the research participants. Especially when conducting behavioral observations in the laboratory, researchers must be aware that research participants might be acting quite differently in the laboratory than they would in

YOU DECIDE: SHOULD THE STUDY OF GENDER DIFFERENCES BE A FOCUS OF RESEARCH IN DEVELOPMENTAL PSYCHOPATHOLOGY?

Yes

- Gender differences are found consistently in prevalence rates for certain disorders (such as girls showing higher rates of depression after puberty, boys showing higher rates of oppositional defiant disorder before puberty, boys showing higher rates of conduct disorder throughout childhood, and boys showing higher rates of ADHD), so they should be continued to be studied (Costello et al., 2003).

- Boys are more likely than girls to be referred for mental health services, so the gender differences in symptoms and referral processes should be studied (Gardner, Pajer, Kelleher, Scholle, & Wasserman, 2002).

No

- Although there are some gender differences found in some studies, boys and girls are more similar than different (Hyde, 2005). The primary gender differences that is found consistently is that boys and men show more aggression, especially physical aggression, in contrast to girls and women, respectively (Hyde, 2005). Thus, although the differences are important, there are far more similarities than there are differences.

- Often when gender differences are found in clinical populations of children, these differences may have more to do with who gets referred for treatment rather than an actual gender difference in the symptomatology. For example, in clinical samples of children with ADHD children, girls are found to have less comorbid disorders and to show fewer learning disorders. In nonclinical samples, however, these differences are not found and boys and girls are quite comparable in the expression of ADHD symptomatology (Biederman et al., 2005). Thus, the differences appear to be more due to the referral process rather than gender differences symptom expression in boys and girls.

So, should the study of gender differences be a focus of research in developmental psychopathology?

their own home. Thus, there are both strengths and weaknesses to conducting research within a laboratory setting.

I've never seen a computer.

—Rosa, 8 years old, Mexico

Research Sites in the Future

Although all these sites are expected to remain viable data collection sites in the future, one methodology is looming large now and in the foreseeable future. A number of studies (especially in the adult research literature) have used the Internet as a way of recruiting participants into studies and as a mechanism for collecting data (Murray & Fisher, 2002; Ritterband, Cox, et al., 2003; Ritterband, Gander-Frederick, et al., 2003). Participants might be contacted by e-mail or they might find a research Web site through advertisements and announcements. Participants can then complete questionnaires or interviews through the Web. Although this methodology has not been well established in the area of developmental psychopathology, it is worth considering that the Internet may be a site for future data collection. As with any site of data collection, the representativeness of the sample must be considered.

With Internet data collection, researchers would only be accessing individuals who have access to a computer and who are comfortable with Internet technology. As the Web becomes more a part of our culture, it is possible that a great deal of research will be conducted over the Internet. Recent data suggest that participants on Web-based surveys are representative of the general community and that the results are comparable with what would have been collected with more traditional paper-and-pencil methods (Ferrando & Lorenzo-Seva, 2005; Gosling, Vazire, Srivastava, & John, 2004).

Overall, there is no single site of research that is better than another (Armstrong & Drotar, 2000; Drotar, Timmons-Mitchell et al., 2000). The research site, just like the participant population, depends on the research questions and the goals of the research. As with selecting representative samples, researchers must take care to select research sites that do not inadvertently bias their sample (e.g., collecting data at a public school would probably yield a more diverse sample than collecting data at an expensive private school). Like most decisions that researchers make, choosing an appropriate research site means that researchers must be aware of the strengths and weaknesses of all possible research sites.

QUANTITATIVE RESEARCH AND QUALITATIVE RESEARCH

Up to this point in the chapter, the majority of research has been **quantitative research.** Quantitative research uses the empirical process to collect data, analyze data, and draw conclusions based on objective and numerical data. Data are quantified into numbers and patterns that allow interpretation (e.g., Deater-Deckard, 2000). In contrast, **qualitative research** is less empirically driven and focuses more on the experience of the participants (Auerbach & Silverstein, 2003). Qualitative research is often conducted through interviews and diaries of research participants. Patterns in the information are ascertained from reviewing the information rather than trying to quantify the information. Both types of research are meaningful in the area of developmental psychopathology.

The bulk of research on developmental psychopathology has been quantitative in nature (Drotar, 2000). There are instances, however, when qualitative research can be helpful. For example, qualitative research can be enlightening at the beginning of a research venture to identify the important and salient issues in need of investigation. Qualitative research can also be helpful in understanding the experience of research participants and in getting a deeper look at the information collected through quantitative research. Thus, both quantitative and qualitative research can be helpful in the process to understand the development, prevention, and treatment of psychopathology in children and adolescents.

AREAS IN NEED OF FURTHER STUDY IN DEVELOPMENTAL PSYCHOPATHOLOGY

Throughout this book, areas in need of further research will be mentioned and highlighted. Compared with other areas within psychology and education, developmental psychopathology is still a relatively young field. For this reason, there are still wide areas of interest that have not received sufficient attention. For example, research is needed on the differences and similarities between the dimensional and categorical conceptualizations of children's and adolescents' functioning (Pincus et al., 2003). More research is needed with sophisticated imaging techniques, such as function MRIs, so that brain functioning can be explored in relation to behavioral functioning (Hendren, DeBacker, & Pandina, 2000). A greater degree of sophisticated research on the

connections between genes and behavior is needed, especially with a focus on resilience (Curtis & Cicchetti, 2003) and gene–environment interactions (Moffitt et al., 2005). More work is needed to explore the impact of managed care companies and the accessibility and quality of therapeutic services that are available to children and families (Morgan & Morgan, 2001).

Research is needed to understand children and adolescents in multiple contexts, such as their family, their school, and their community. More attention is needed to the bidirectionality of parent–child interactions and teacher–child interactions to understand fully the interactions between children and the adults in their lives. Although most developmental psychopathologists are sensitive to diversity issues in their research, there is still a great need to explore underrepresented populations of children, such as children from ethnic minority backgrounds, children from other countries, and children from unique family constellations (e.g., children raised by their grandmother or children born into families headed by lesbians or gay men).

Although no single study can address all of these issues, more cultural diversity in individual samples will lead to more research within developmental psychopathology that is consistent with the lives and experiences of children and adolescents. Findings from these representative samples can then be used to try to help improve the lives of children and adolescents (Lerner et al., 2000; McCall & Groark, 2000).

ETHICS OF CONDUCTING RESEARCH

Now that the research process has been explained, it is worthwhile to reflect on how to conduct ethical research. There are specific ethical guidelines for conducting research with children and adolescents. A few of those ethical standards are presented in Table 3.1, including, gaining institutional approval (Ethical Standard 8.01), obtaining informed consent for research participation (Ethical Standard 8.02), offering inducements to research participants (Ethical Standard 8.06), providing participants with information about the study after it is completed (Ethical Standard 8.08), reporting research findings (Ethical Standard 8.10), and taking credit for publications (Ethical Standard 8.12). All of these ethical standards are relevant to research with children as well as adults (Fisher, 2004). These ethical standards are consistent with the ethical standards followed within other disciplines, such as school psychology (Flanagan,

TABLE 3-1 **Selected Ethical Principles of Psychologists and Code of Conduct Related to Research**

The American Psychological Association (APA) delineates ethical and professional principles for psychologists (American Psychological Association, 2002). Below are a few selected ethical principles related to the research process.

GENERAL PRINCIPLES
Principle A: Beneficence and Nonmaleficence
Principle B: Fidelity and Responsibility
Principle C: Integrity
Principle D: Justice
Principle E: Respect for People's Rights and Eignity

8. RESEARCH AND PUBLICATION

8.01 *Institutional Approval:* When institutional approval is required, psychologists provide accurate information about their research proposals and obtain approval prior to conducting the research. They conduct the research in accordance with the approved research protocol.

8.02 *Informed Consent to Research:* (a) When obtaining informed consent..., psychologists inform participants about (1) the purpose of the research, expected duration, and procedures; (2) their right to decline to participate and to withdraw from the research once participation has begun; (3) the foreseeable consequences of declining or withdrawing; (4) reasonably foreseeable factors that may be expected to influence their willingness to participate such as potential risks, discomfort, or adverse effects; (5) any prospective research benefits; (6) limits of confidentiality; (7) incentives for participation; and (8) whom to contact for questions about the research and research participants' rights....

8.06 *Offering Inducements for Research Participation:* (a) Psychologists make reasonable efforts to avoid offering excessive or inappropriate financial or other inducements for research participation when such inducements are likely to coerce participation....

8.08 *Debriefing:* (a) Psychologists provide a prompt opportunity for participants to obtain appropriate information about the nature, results, and conclusions of the research, and they take reasonable steps to correct any misconceptions that participants may have of which the psychologists are aware.... (c) When psychologists become aware that research procedures have harmed a participant, they take reasonable steps to minimize the harm.

8.10 *Reporting Research Results:* (a) Psychologists do not fabricate data.... (b) If psychologists discover significant errors in their published data, they take reasonable steps to correct such errors in a correction, retraction, erratum, or other appropriate publication means.

8.12 *Publication Credit:* (a) Psychologists take responsibility and credit, including authorship credit, only for work they have actually performed or to which they have substantially contributed.... (b) Principal authorship and other publication credits accurately reflect the relative scientific or professional contributions of the individuals involved, regardless of their relative status.... (c) Except under exceptional circumstances, a student is listed as principal author on any multiple-authored article that is substantially based on the student's doctoral dissertation....

Source: American Psychological Association (2002).

Miller, & Jacob, 2005) and for specific research populations, such as ethnic minority children and their families (Fisher et al., 2002).

The essence of these guidelines suggests that research must be conducted with competence and in an objective manner that is consistent with scientific practice in that area. It is incumbent on researchers to be knowledgeable in their area of research in order to know the current standard practices within that research area (Bersoff, 2003). Any research with children and adolescents must be approved by the **Institutional Review Board** that monitors the researchers' work. Usually this type of board exists at the college or university in which the researcher works, but many schools and mental health facilities also have their own review board for any research that is requested at that facility. In these cases, researchers must acquire permission from all relevant review boards before beginning the research process. For many professors of psychology, education, social work, and psychiatry, this policy means that they have to gain approval from the scientific review committee in their department, from the research review board at the site where they wish to collect data (e.g., the school or mental health facility), and from the university's Institutional Review Board (Bersoff, 2003). Although these multiple levels of review sometimes slow down the research process, they have been established to protect the rights of research participants and to ensure that the research has scientific merit.

Like in therapy, informed consent and assent must be obtained from parents and children, respectively, who are involved in research. Parents must provide their written informed consent before researchers can ever contact individual children for data collection. Depending on the age of the children, informed assent from the children is usually warranted for participation in research. Obviously, different research projects will have to follow different procedures depending on the child's age and level of functioning. No one in their right mind would suggest that infants should provide written informed assent to participate in research. Likewise, if children or adolescents are severely cognitively or psychiatrically impaired (such as due to developmental disabilities or psychosis), it may not be appropriate to request their informed assent for participation in research. Children, adolescents, and individuals who are involved in clinical services are considered to be an "at-risk" group when it comes to research involvement.

For this reason, professionals on Institutional Review Boards are especially careful about reviewing research with these individuals. Care must be taken to ensure that these "at-risk" groups are protected from coercion to participate in research and from inappropriate research that is not in their best interest. A number of researchers have raised concerns about children's ability to assent to research, and they have suggested that clinical child researchers investigate children's understanding of the research process (Fogas, Oesterheld, & Shader, 2001).

There are some rare instances when informed consent and informed assent are not required, such as when behavioral observations are conducted in a naturalistic setting and the identities of the children and parents are never known. For the overwhelming majority of studies in developmental psychopathology, however, strong adherence to the informed consent and informed assent process is required.

Participation in research should be educational to some degree (Bersoff, 2003). Most often, children and families are provided with a summary of the research findings after the study is completed. This summary

Case Study: An Overzealous Researcher

Dr. S worked with disadvantaged youngsters in an elementary school setting. These youngsters had low self-esteem and Dr. S wanted to try to help them improve their self-esteem. The youngsters lived in severe poverty. They tended to be teased and taunted by their classmates and their academic work was difficult because of generations of educational disadvantages. Dr. S decided that she would conduct a study in which she taught the children the correct answers to an intelligence test (the Wechsler Intelligence Scale for Children; WISC), and then test the children's intelligence with the WISC. She reasoned that the children's IQs would show improvements and these improvements would help the children feel better about themselves. Dr. S received written permission from parents for the children's participation in this study. Dr. S conducted the study (i.e., she trained 25 students on the answers to the WISC, then tested them with the WISC and found that their IQ scores had been raised). When a colleague in the school system learned of this research, the colleague reported Dr. S to the ethics committee given that Dr. S had violated an ethical standard that states the professionals must maintain the security of standardized tests.

Dr. S informed the ethics committee that her goals in the study were laudable. She felt that it was necessary to improve the self-esteem of these children if they were going to have a chance at success in school and in larger society. Dr. S also

stated that there were other intelligence tests, so these children could be tested with alternative tests if needed.

The ethics board reprimanded Dr. S on a number of ethical violations. First, she did not receive approval from the school or from any institutional review board to conduct this study. If she had requested this approval, it is likely that her colleagues would have prevented the research from occurring in the first place. Second, Dr. S destroyed the possibility of using the WISC with these children if they required standardized testing in the future. Although there are other standardized intelligence tests, the ethics board reasoned that the WISC was the primary intelligence test used at this school and with this population. In addition, the ethics board noted that there was no empirical basis for attempting to raise self-esteem by falsely inflating IQ scores. They reasoned that this tactic could have done more harm than good.

This case illustrates the need for well-formulated and well-reviewed research protocols. Review by an institutional review board is meant to ensure that researchers' ideas are consistent with standard research practices and that participants will not be harmed by their involvement in research. In addition, the detrimental effects of breaking test security were highlighted in this case.

Source: American Psychological Association (1987).

should be provided in language that is understandable to the children, adolescents, and parents who participated in the research. Sometimes researchers also share their overall findings with teachers or professionals in mental health facilities in which the research was conducted. The idea is that researchers should not just take information from the research participants and the research site, but rather, they should give something back to these individuals and these sites. In this way, researchers cannot only help add to the scholarly literature, but they can also use the research findings to better the lives (or at least add education to the lives) of the participants in the research.

Regarding confidentiality, suffice it to say that confidentiality is protected within research in a similar manner to the way that it is protected within assessment and therapy services. Limits to confidentiality in research are comparable to those in assessment and therapy. Research can also be conducted in an anonymous fashion, so that participants' identities are never linked to any identifying information. Both confidential and anonymous research are allowed with children. In either case, parents and children must be informed as to which type of research is being conducted.

A cornerstone of the ethical guidelines from the American Psychological Association (American Psychological Association, 2002) is that research participants must be treated with dignity and respect. There are too many horror stories of unethical research in the past. Currently, there is an attempt to maintain the highest ethical standards when it comes to research with children and adolescents. One of the subtle changes to encourage respect for individuals involved in research is the use of the term "participants" rather than "subjects." The term *subjects* implies a passive role, in which someone (i.e., the researcher) is doing something to the passive individual (i.e., the subject). The term *participants,* on the other hand, implies a more active role, in which the individual is a member of a team trying to answer interesting research questions. Although the terminology differences are subtle, this change is part of the attempt to be more conscientious about the rights and dignity of individuals involved in research. There is currently a strong spirit of maintaining the dignity of research participants. Although there are still sometimes examples of unethical research that are brought to light, the overwhelming majority of researchers in the field of developmental psychopathology are highly ethical scholars who are greatly concerned about the welfare of children, adolescents, and their families. Box 3.9 highlights an

---

BOX *3.9*

ETHICS IN INTERPRETING DATA—IS CHILD SEXUAL ABUSE OKAY?

Although not discussed at length in this chapter, part of the ethical code also suggests that researchers must be careful with how they interpret and present their research findings. A controversial example of this issue occurred in an unlikely source. In 1998, a premiere journal within the field of psychology, *Psychological Bulletin,* published a review article entitled "A Meta-Analytic Examination of Assumed Properties of Child Sexual Abuse Using College Samples" (Rind, Tromovitch, & Bauserman, 1998). The researchers summarized studies of college students who had experienced sexual abuse during childhood. They concluded that "Self-reported reactions to and effects from child sexual abuse indicated that negative effects were neither pervasive nor typically intense..." (p. 22). In plain English, it appeared that the authors were stating that there were few, if any, problems associated with child sexual abuse.

This article led to a firestorm of controversy. A number of pedophile Web sites used the article as evidence that sex with children was not harmful, Dr. Laura (the radio talk show host) announced her dismay at the article and at the American Psychological Association for publishing the article, and the U.S. Congress even got into the act by condemning the idea that sex with "willing" children was acceptable (Ondersma et al., 2001). The American Psychological Association defended the research as well as academic freedom, but also provided significant space in *Psychological Bulletin* for published commentaries that disputed the conclusions in the original article (e.g., Dallam et al., 2001; Ondersma et al., 2001).

From an ethical standpoint, research findings should be presented in a careful and accurate manner to prevent misinterpretation or inflammatory responses by others. From a research standpoint, the title of one of the commentaries can best sum up the issue: "Sex with children is abuse" (Ondersma et al., 2001). There are myriad well-designed longitudinal studies that have shown that early childhood sexual abuse is associated with later psychological problems (Goodwin et al., 2005). So, overall, the conclusion in the controversial article that sex with children is not harmful was inaccurate.

example of questionable interpretation and presentation of research results.

Overall, guidelines for ethical research are consistent with guidelines for ethical clinical practice. The basic premises of ethical research are, first to be respectful of research participants and clients and to do no harm to research participants and clients (Bersoff, 2003). Although ethical behavior cannot be monitored every second of professionals' lives, the majority of researchers and clinicians working with children and adolescents exhibit extraordinarily ethical behavior in which the best interests of children and adolescents are held as a top priority. Interested readers are encouraged to review these fascinating books on ethical and legal issues, entitled *Decoding the Ethics Code: A Practical Guide for Psychologists* (Fisher, 2003) and *Ethics and Research with Children: A Case-Based Approach* (Kodish, 2005).

SUMMARY AND KEY CONCEPTS

The research process is an integral part of understanding the development of psychopathology. One example that illustrates the need for empirical research is **facilitated communication,** which after empirical study, was found to be bogus. The **double blind** technique was used to study facilitated communication, in which the facilitator and the autistic individual were presented with different stimulus material.

Research Methodologies that are Utilized in the Study of Developmental Psychopathology. A number of research methodologies are utilized to study the development of psychopathology. In an **experimental design,** the researcher recruits participants into the study, conducts **random assignment** to put the participants in one of two groups, administers an **independent variable** which is the experimenter's manipulation, and then measures the **dependent variable** which is thought to be influenced by the independent variable. The experimental design allows for researchers to argue **causality,** which means that they can argue that the independent variable caused the changes that were seen in the dependent variable.

Another common design in the study of developmental psychopathology is the **quasi-experimental design,** which allows for known groups to be tested. The premise behind the **correlational design** is to explore how different variables covary together. Often, correlational designs are conducted through the **survey method,** which allows researchers to administer questionnaires to large numbers of participants and then the researcher assesses how the variables on the measures correlate with each other.

Case studies can be used to investigate thoroughly one or a few individuals who show a rare type of behavior. **Single-subject designs** (also known as within subject designs) are often used with one participant or a small group of participants in order to assess their change in behavior after a behavioral intervention. A common single-subject design is the **A-B-A-B design** (also known as the **reversal design**).

Another research design within developmental psychopathology is the **high-risk design.** In the high-risk design, children who are thought to be at high risk for the development of psychopathology are studied to assess risk and protective factors that are related to the eventual development of psychopathology. The behavioral genetics design allows the development of psychopathology to be explored through twin studies and through adoption studies.

Time Frame of the Research Study. There are a number of ways to conceptualize research when the time frame of the research is taken into account. **Cross-sectional research** is conducted when data are collected at one point in time. **Prospective longitudinal research** is conducted when children are followed over a period of time and data are collected at two or more points in time. **Accelerated longitudinal research** combines cross-sectional and prospective longitudinal research by collecting data from different groups of children at one point in time and then following all of those children over a period of time.

The Actual Process of Research. The majority of researchers conduct **programmatic research,** which means that they have a research program that attempts to answer related research questions (e.g., the study of child abuse could be studied in a variety of different ways by the same research group).

Choosing Appropriate Samples of Participants. It is imperative that researchers attempt to recruit representative samples of participants that can be generalized to the broader population. Researchers must be cognizant of issues related to age/developmental level, gender, race/ethnicity, socioeconomic status, geographic region, cultural diversity, family constellation, and clinical versus nonclinical status of the participants.

Locations of Research on Developmental Psychopathology. There are a number of common sites of research on developmental psychopathology, including schools, hospitals, clinics, communities, and laboratories.

Quantitative Research and Qualitative Research. **Quantitative research** utilizes the empirical process in order to address issues within developmental psychopathology. The majority of studies described in this chapter and in this textbook are quantitative in nature. **Qualitative research** utilizes a less numeric approach to understanding developmental psychopathology.

Areas in Need of Further Study in Developmental Psychopathology. A great deal of areas are in need of further research in the study of developmental psychopathology.

Topics such as dimensional versus categorical approaches to understanding developmental psychopathology and the study of bidirectional influences between children and their parents and teachers are just a couple of the topics that could use more exploration within research on developmental psychopathology.

Ethics of Conducting Research. Ethical principles within research are very similar to ethical principles within other domains of professional work with children, adolescents, and families. Before conducting any study, researchers must first have their studies reviewed by an **Institutional Review Board** to verify that it is ethical and meaningful research.

KEY TERMS

facilitated communication	dependent variable	single-subject designs	prospective longitudinal research	programmatic research
double blind	causality	A-B-A-B design	accelerated longitudinal research	*p*-value
experimental design	quasi-experimental design	reversal design		quantitative research
random assignment	correlational design	high-risk design		qualitative research
independent variable	survey method	cross-sectional research		Institutional Review Board
	case studies			

SUGGESTED READINGS

Angelou, Maya. *The Collected Autobiographies of Maya Angelou*. New York: Random House, 2004. This book represents six autobiographies that illustrate the struggles and triumphs of artist, writer, poet, political activist, and filmmaker, Maya Angelou. Similar to prospective research that observes an individual from childhood to adulthood, this collection of autobiographies is a stellar way to understand a complicated and triumphant life.

Pelzer, Dave. *The Privilege of Youth: A Teenager's Story of Longing for Acceptance and Friendship*. New York: Penguin, 2004. This book is the fourth in a series that describes the author's horrific childhood experiences of abuse and poverty and then goes on to highlight how children can overcome these circumstances. The earlier books in the series are *A Child Called It* (Pelzer, 1995), *The Lost Boy: A Foster Child's Search for the Love of a Family* (Pelzer, 1997), and *Man Named Dave: A Story of Triumph and Forgiveness* (Pelzer, 1999). Taken together, these books read like a longitudinal case study.

SUGGESTED VIEWINGS

49-Up. (2005). Based on a series of documentaries that began in 1964, 14 children from all walks of life in England were filmed when they were 7 years old, and then again every 7 years thereafter. This film uses clips from each of the previous documentaries and is an incredible example of doing longitudinal research with a camera and a microphone.

The Pacifier. (2005). This lighthearted look at parenting illustrates the strengths and weaknesses of different parenting styles (especially authoritarian), which have been researched extensively within developmental psychopathology.

CHAPTER 4

ASSESSMENT AND THERAPEUTIC INTERVENTIONS WITH CHILDREN, ADOLESCENTS, AND FAMILIES

CHAPTER SUMMARY

ASSESSMENTS

MULTIAXIAL ASSESSMENT OF CHILDREN AND ADOLESCENTS

INTERVIEWS WITH CHILDREN AND THEIR PARENTS

BEHAVIORAL ASSESSMENT

CHECKLISTS AND RATING SCALES

PERSONALITY ASSESSMENT

FAMILY ASSESSMENT

ASSESSING INTELLECTUAL FUNCTIONING AND ACADEMIC ACHIEVEMENT

EDUCATIONAL ASSESSMENT

NEUROPSYCHOLOGICAL ASSESSMENT

THERAPEUTIC INTERVENTIONS

SETTINGS WHERE INTERVENTIONS ARE CONDUCTED

PSYCHODYNAMIC THERAPIES

BEHAVIORAL THERAPIES

COGNITIVE–BEHAVIORAL THERAPIES

FAMILY SYSTEMS THERAPIES

PSYCHOPHARMACOLOGICAL INTERVENTIONS

EFFECTIVENESS OF THERAPEUTIC INTERVENTIONS

PREVENTION PROGRAMS THAT WORK

PROFESSIONAL ETHICS IN ASSESSMENT AND INTERVENTIONS

SUMMARY AND KEY CONCEPTS

KEY TERMS

SUGGESTED READINGS

SUGGESTED VIEWINGS

Measurement began our might.

—W. B. Yeats

ASSESSMENTS

When there are concerns about a child's functioning, there are two primary ways of dealing with the child—assessment and therapeutic interventions. In the best of circumstances, assessments and interventions are intertwined and are planned thoughtfully by the professionals involved. Assessment will be described first, and then therapeutic interventions will be reviewed. There is a great deal of focus currently on evidence-based assessments (Achenbach, 2005; Kazdin, 2005a, 2005b; Mash & Hunsley, 2005). Throughout the chapter,

the focus will be on evidence-based practices, which have empirical data to support the assessment or therapeutic techniques.

Assessment of emotional/behavioral problems involves testing and evaluation to ascertain the child's or adolescent's level of functioning and the level of problems. As you may recall from the first chapter, the most important characteristic to know about children or adolescents is their age. But once you know their age, how can you tell if children's or adolescents' behaviors are within the normal range of behavior? This type of question can be answered with the use of developmentally appropriate assessment techniques (Achenbach & McConaughy, 2003; Geisinger, 2000). In fact, the assessment process has many purposes (Schroeder & Gordon, 2002), including to

- Determine the level of problematic emotions and behaviors (e.g., How high or low are the levels of problems in the child or adolescent?)

- Determine the range of problematic emotions and behaviors (e.g., How many different types of problems are being experienced by the child or adolescent?)

- Help to identify the appropriate diagnosis for a child or adolescent, if any

- Identify strengths and competencies of a child or adolescent

- Evaluate the effectiveness of treatment by assessing behaviors before, during, and after treatment

- Determine the etiological factors that might be affecting the child's or adolescent's problems

- Identify children at risk for developing problems in the future

Figure 4.1 shows a flowchart of effective assessment that leads to effective intervention. Even before children are referred for assessments, parents and teachers can intervene to prevent the need for a formal assessment. When assessments occur, they should take into account the ecology or environmental aspects of the child's functioning and the legal and ethical guidelines for assessment, such as the Individuals with Disabilities Education Improvement Act of 2004 (IDEA04), which will be discussed in more depth in the chapter on learning disorders (Wright & Wright, 2005). In addition, assessment measures should have strong psychometric properties (e.g., reliability and validity) and should provide recommendations that are focused and relevant to clinical practice (Johnston & Murray, 2003; Skinner, Freeland, & Shapiro, 2003).

Overall, assessment techniques are almost always utilized when working therapeutically with children and adolescents. Assessments can also calm the fears of worried parents. Imagine the following scenario. A worried mother calls a mental health clinic for an evaluation and treatment of her 11-year-old daughter. She states that her daughter only has three good friends and that, although her daughter talks with the friends on the phone and sees her friends on weekends, she is worried that her daughter is socially isolated and socially anxious. The mother recalls having lots more friends during childhood and she is worried that her daughter is missing out on social opportunities. The mother and daughter come to the clinic for an evaluation, and the results all point to a happy and healthy preadolescent. In addition, the clinician evaluates

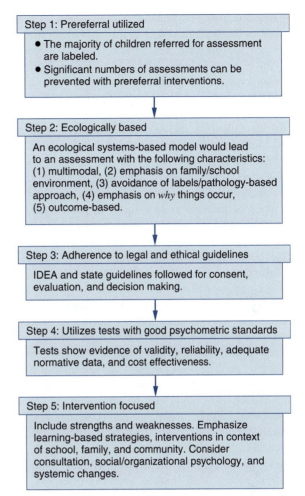

FIGURE 4.1 A model for effective assessment.

Source: Prevatt (1999b).

the mother's functioning, and she is found to be a competent and appropriately concerned mother. Rather than progressing with unneeded treatment, the clinician can allay the mother's fears and suggest ways for the mother to be reassured of her daughter's status as a well-functioning child. Given that the daughter is happy with her friendships and her social support network, no intervention is necessary for the daughter. This example illustrates that assessments do not necessarily end in the identification of problems in children and adolescents.

Assessors must choose between depth versus breadth in assessing the functioning of children and adolescents. That is, if a child is referred for problems of hyperactivity, should the clinician only assess the hyperactivity in depth or should the clinician assess a broader range of emotional/behavioral problems in addition to hyperactivity? Although there is no right or wrong answer to this question, many clinicians choose to assess for depth as well as for breadth. There are a number of specific measures for different emotional/behavioral problems and there are a number of broad-based measures of emotional/behavioral problems. Both of these types of measures can be used in comprehensive assessments of children and adolescents.

In the following sections, you will read about the many different types of assessment measures that are available to assess children's and adolescents' emotional/behavioral functioning. The most comprehensive and conclusive assessment would include many different types of assessment techniques (a process known as **multimethod assessment**) and would include many different types of individuals to report on the child's or adolescent's behavior (a strategy known as **multiple informants**). Thus, a multimethod assessment might start with an interview of the child and the parent, then the completion of behavior checklists from the child, parent, and teacher, then include academic achievement testing and intellectual testing, and then involve behavioral observation of the child in multiple settings. Depending on the age of the child and the referral problem, additional measures for personality functioning and family functioning might also be completed. As for the inclusion of multiple informants, that process most often includes the child, the parent or parents, and the teacher or teachers. Although the use of multiple informants depends on the age of the child and the referral problem, children, parents, and teachers are most often the best informants on children's behavior. Because one informant often has knowledge about the child that other informants do not know (Meyer et al., 2001), the use of multiple informants is an integral part of comprehensive assessments of children and adolescents. Multimethod assessments are also thought to be the "gold standard" for identifying strengths and weaknesses in children and adolescents (DeLosReyes & Kazdin, 2004; Kagan, Snidman, McManis, Woodward, & Hardway, 2002).

The average child is an almost non-existent myth. To be normal one must be peculiar in some way or another.
—Heywood C. Broun

MULTIAXIAL ASSESSMENT OF CHILDREN AND ADOLESCENTS

In the first chapter, you learned that *DSM-IV* uses a multiaxial evaluation system for rating children and adolescents on multiple axes of functioning (Gruenberg &

Goldstein, 2003). Note that the term *multiaxial* means simply that there are different axes or dimensions to consider. Within the realm of assessment of children and adolescents, the term *multiaxial assessment* is used commonly. **Multiaxial assessment** requires that different aspects of children be assessed with different informants (Achenbach & McConaughy, 1997). Although the term *informant* is used to refer to a "snitch" on television shows about police officers, in multiaxial assessment, the term *informant* is used to refer to individuals who can inform the clinician about the child's functioning. As can be seen in Table 4.1, multiaxial assessment includes reports by parents (Axis I), teachers (Axis II), and children (Axis V), in addition to evaluation of cognitive functioning (Axis III), physical functioning (Axis IV), and behavioral, self-concept, and personality functioning (Axis V). Specific measures in Table 4.1 are described later in this chapter.

The point of this multiaxial assessment system is to gain a comprehensive and thorough understanding of the child's or adolescent's functioning, regardless of the specific referral question. Obviously, different referral questions will lead to somewhat different assessment protocols. But with the use of the multiaxial assessment system, the clinician can provide a comprehensive assessment of the child or adolescent. In order to conduct multiaxial assessments, clinicians must know many different assessment techniques and modalities, including interviews, behavioral assessment, behavior checklists and rating scales, personality measures, family methodology, intellectual and achievement testing, educational assessment, and neuropsychological assessment.

No one is without knowledge except him (or her) who asks no questions.
—Proverb of Africa

INTERVIEWS WITH CHILDREN AND THEIR PARENTS

Clinicians usually first conduct an interview to determine whether or not a child or family has a problem. Usually, the interview process begins at the point of the **intake phone call,** which is when the clinician first talks with a family member about the problems the child and family are experiencing. The main goal of any interview (whether it is in the intake phone call or at the time of the first appointment) is to gather information about the child and the family.

TABLE 4.1   Multiaxial Assessment Procedures

Age Range	Axis I Parent Reports	Axis II Teacher Reports	Axis III Cognitive Assessment	Axis IV Physical Assessment	Axis V Direct Assessment of Child
2 to 5	CBCL/2–3 CBCL/4–18 Developmental history Parent interview Vineland Social Maturity Scale (Sparrow et al., 1984)	TCRF/2–5 Preschool record Teacher interview	Ability tests, e.g., McCarthy (1972) Perceptual-motor tests Language tests	Height, weight Medical exam Neurological exam	Observation during testing and play interview
6 to 11	CBCL/4–18 Developmental history Parent interview	TRF School records Teacher interview	Ability tests, e.g., Kaufman & Kaufman (1983) Achievement tests Perceptual-motor tests Language tests	Height, weight Medical exam Neurological exam	SCICA DOF
12 to 18	CBCL/4–18 Developmental history Parent interview	TRF School records Teacher interview	Ability tests, e.g., WAIS-R; WISC-III (Wechsler, 1981, 1991) Achievement tests	Height, weight Medical exam Neurological exam	SCICA DOF YSR Self-concept measures Personality tests

Note: CBCL = Child Behavior Checklist, TCRF = Teacher/Caregiver Report Form, TRF = Teacher's Report Form, WAIS-R = Wechsler Adult Intelligence Scale-Revised, WISC-III = Wechsler Intelligence Scale for Children-Third Edition, SCICA = Semistructured Clinical Interview for Children and Adolescents, DOF = Direct Observation Form, YSR = Youth Self-Report.

Source: (Achenbach & McConaughy (1997).

When clinicians interview children, they must be cognizant of the child's developmental level. Specifically, clinicians may need to ask questions that are more concrete and objective with younger children in comparison to older children and adolescents (McConaughy, 2005).

Interviews can be broken down into three categories: unstructured interviews, semistructured interviews, and structured interviews.

Unstructured Interviews

Unstructured interviews consist of interviews that do not follow a specific, rigid format. That does not mean, however, that clinicians ask questions in a random order. With unstructured interviews, clinicians usually follow their own format for collecting information. If an important topic arises, however, they can deviate from their regular format and pursue questioning related to that new topic. Table 4.2 provides an overview of the types of information that might be collected in an unstructured interview.

Even when clinicians plan to use a structured interview, they usually begin the very first session with an unstructured interview. Both parents and children can be involved in unstructured interviews, but often different information is gathered when children and parents are

interviewed together versus separately (McConaughy, 2000). At the outset of an unstructured interview, clinicians need to build **rapport** with the child and the parents. Rapport refers to the feelings of trust and openness that a client develops toward a therapist. Imagine the different types of information that clinicians would receive if they did or did not have rapport with a client. Think about a surly 15-year-old boy who was brought in by his parents against his will. Without rapport, the clinician might get "yes" and "no" answers from the teen, if he or she is lucky. With rapport, the teen may feel more comfortable disclosing his concerns and fears on the problems that he is experiencing. He might say that all the problems are his parents' or teachers' fault, but at least he would be expressing his own feelings rather than refusing to share any information. Rapport can be developed by clinicians who are caring, warm, attentive, and empathic (Sattler, 1998). Special consideration should be taken in conducting interviews when sexual abuse, physical abuse, or child neglect are suspected. Table 4.3 provides a list of suggestions when interviewing a child for suspected abuse, and Box 4.1 shows an example of this type of interview. These suggests are crucial in cases of suspected abuse, but the suggestions are also relevant to any type of interviewing with children and adolescents.

Michael: A Case Example of Multiaxial Assessment

When Michael was 2 years old, his parents divorced, and he was raised by his mother with his five older brothers and sisters. As he grew up in this impoverished household, Michael fantasized increasingly about violence, aggression, and being a martial arts expert. Although he was Caucasian, Michael was convinced that his father and grandfather were ninja warriors. He spent countless hours watching violent television shows and playing with guns, knives, and other weapons. By the age of 9, Michael attacked his mother with a kitchen knife. After the police and a social worker intervened, Michael was taken to a residential treatment facility, where professionals could monitor his behavior more closely. Michael was in the residential treatment facility for 3 years, where he received behavior management programs, individual therapy, medication, and special education services. At the age of 12, there had been significant improvements, so Michael was moved to

a therapeutic foster home that was more comparable to a family environment. Although Michael continued to see his mother and siblings once a month, she still had difficulty dealing with his behavior, so Michael remained in structured therapeutic living facilities rather than going back to live with his family. Michael's mother agreed with this living arrangement.

Following are some of the results from Child Behavior Checklists that were completed when Michael was 9 and again when he was 12. Although there were obviously improvements in Michael's behavior, he continued to experience social problems and elevated aggression at the age of 12, according to his foster parent. These profiles illustrate how empirically validated assessment tools, such as the Child Behavior Checklist (CBCL), can be used to compare different informants' perspectives on children's behavior and how they can be used to show change over time in children's behavior.

CBCL problem profiles for Michael scored at age 9 by his mother (solid line) and child care worker (dotted line) and at age 12 by his foster parent (broken line).

Source: Achenbach & McConaughy (1997).

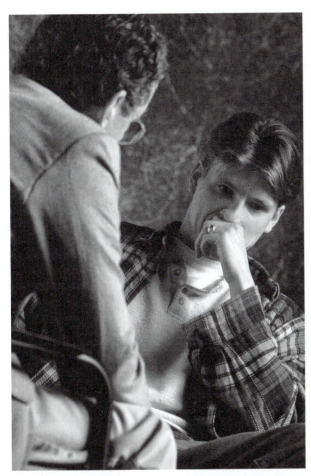

Interviews are almost always the first step in a thorough assessment.

Overall, unstructured interviews are usually used as a foundation on which the rest of the assessment process will be built. Strengths of unstructured interviews are the ability to establish rapport, the wealth of information that is usually generated, and the flexibility of the interviews. There are drawbacks, however, to unstructured interviews. Multiple clinicians may get varied information from the same clients because they chose to follow up on different issues with the clients. For this reason, reliability of unstructured interviews has been questioned repeatedly (Welsh & Bierman, 2003). In order to try to develop more reliable interview techniques, semistructured and structured interviews have been developed.

Semistructured Interviews

Semistructured interviews are more structured than unstructured interviews. Semistructured interviews suggest a specific format that the clinician follows, but allows the clinician some flexibility to follow up on important topics. For example, the Semistructured Clinical Interview for Children and Adolescents (SCICA; McConaughy & Achenbach, 2001) is a comprehensive interview that allows the clinician to follow a set format but also allows the clinician to follow up on relevant questions and themes. As can be seen in Table 4.4, the SCICA covers a broad range of topics and concerns. Based on the interview, the clinician completes a standardized observation form about the child's behavior and a standardized questionnaire about the child's self-reported concerns during the interview. These forms are then analyzed, and standardized scores are calculated from the normative database on these measures. Overall, the SCICA represents an empirically based interview system that still allows clinicians flexibility in the interview process (McConaughy, 2005).

Structured Interviews

In contrast to unstructured and semistructured interviews, **structured interviews** do not allow deviation from the original format. Structured interviews are most often used to determine a diagnosis, so specific questions must be asked in a specific order. Although clinicians have the option to return to important topics after the formal structured interview is completed, the format of the structured interview should be followed closely to retain the psychometric properties of the interview. Examples of structured diagnostic interviews include the Diagnostic Interview for Children and Adolescents–Revised (DICA–R; Reich, 2000), the Child Adolescent Schedule (CAS; Hodges, 1997), the Schedule for Affective Disorders and Schizophrenia for School-Age Children (known as the Kiddie-SADS; Ambrosini, 2000), the Interview Schedule for Children (Sherrill & Kovacs, 2000), and the Diagnostic Interview Schedule for Children–IV (DISC; Shaffer, Fisher, Lucas, Dulcan, & Schwab-Stone, 2000). There are also a number of structured interviews that assess one particular problem in depth, such as the Anxiety Disorders Interview Schedule for *DSM-IV* (ADIS; Albano & Silverman, 1996; Silverman & Albano, 1996). Because the DISC is the most widely used structured diagnostic interview, example questions are provided in Table 4.5 on page 90.

The DISC is highly structured, with little to no room for variations in questions. Because of this rigorous structure, the DISC can be given by trained individuals with a bachelor's degree who do not have formal graduate training. Note that there is a child-report

TABLE 4.2 Information That Can Be Collected in an Unstructured or Semistructured Interview

Information from Both Parents and Children/Adolescents

History of current difficulties (e.g., onset of difficulties, precipitating factors, consequences to the difficulties, how do the child and parents feel about the problems)

Child's educational history (e.g., grades and academic performance, favorite and least favorite subjects, favorite and least favorite teachers)

Home environment (e.g., family activities, family rituals and beliefs, strengths and difficulties within the home)

Expectations for child (e.g., how do parents and child feel about the likelihood of improvement for the child, what do parents and child expect from therapy)

Child's strengths, competencies, and accomplishments (e.g., what are the child and parents most proud of in the child, in which domains does the child excel)

Information from Parents (Usually without Child Present)

Details of pregnancy and birth (e.g., smoking or substance use during pregnancy, delivery complications at birth)

Child's developmental history (e.g., age of sitting, standing, walking, talking, development of self-help skills, and personal–social relationships)

Child's medical history (e.g., dates and types of injuries, major illnesses, hospitalizations)

Family characteristics and family history (e.g., parents' marital status, family constellation, siblings' and parents' mental health history)

Child's interpersonal skills (e.g., child's ability to form friendships, child's social activities, child's relationships with children and adults)

Information from Children/Adolescents (Usually without Parents Present)

Child's or adolescent's occupational history, if any (e.g., jobs held, job training, career aspirations)

Child's or adolescent's friendships (e.g., how many friends, what age and gender, activities that are done with friends)

Child's or adolescent's sexual involvements, if any (e.g., romantic and sexual relationships with others of the same or opposite sex, current involvements and past involvements)

Child's or adolescent's involvement with illicit substances (e.g., drug use, drinking alcohol, smoking cigarettes)

Source: Sattler (1998).

TABLE 4.3 Suggestions for Interviewing Children Who Are Suspected of Being Abused

The interviewer should not:

- Ask leading questions
- Provide answers for the child
- Add to the child's sense of guilt
- Make the child discuss topics with which he or she is extremely uncomfortable
- Allow the child to be interviewed by a "team" of professionals
- Be critical of the way in which the child expresses her or himself
- Make the child think that the interviewer is shocked or disgusted by the events that the child reports

The interviewer should:

- Develop the child's trust through legitimate means
- Be supportive and warm with the child and make sure that the child does not feel that the abuse was her or his fault
- Interview the child in a private setting that feels comfortable to the child
- Sit near the child, without a desk or table in between
- Be as honest as possible about future actions and litigation, without frightening the child or making promises that cannot be kept
- Clarify any misunderstandings with the child (e.g., the meanings of words that the child uses, fears that the child expresses about getting in trouble)

Readers interested in further suggestions for interviewing children who are suspected of being abused are referred to *Recognizing Child Abuse* (Besharov, 1998).

BOX *4.1*

UNSTRUCTURED INTERVIEW WITH A CHILD WHO WAS SEXUALLY ABUSED

The interviewer has provided the 6-year-old child with a number of anatomically correct dolls (i.e., dolls with genitalia that are proportioned appropriately for the size of the doll's body). In this interview, the interviewer is trying not to use leading questions and is also trying not to identify body parts for the child. Rather, an attempt is made to allow the child to use her own language to explain the abuse.

The child chooses the adult male doll and the child female doll and positions the adult male doll on top of the child doll.

Interviewer:	What is happening?
Child:	They are sleeping?
Interviewer:	Is anything else happening?
Child:	He is humping her.
Interviewer:	It is hard for me to see this. Can you show me what humping means?

Child uses the dolls to demonstrate and says, "This thing goes in that thing."

Interviewer:	It looks like you are putting the man's thing in the girl's thing. Is that correct?
Child:	Yes.
Interviewer:	Remind me what you call these parts. A man's thing is …
Child:	Penis.
Interviewer:	Okay, and a girl's thing is …?
Child:	Private.
Interviewer:	Okay, so the man's penis went in the girl's private?
Child:	Yes.
Interviewer:	How do you know this happened?
Child:	Because that is what he did to me.
Interviewer:	The man's penis went into your private?
Child:	Yes.
Interviewer:	How do you know his penis went into your private?
Child:	I could feel it and it hurt!
Interviewer:	Who was the man?
Child:	My dad.

Source: Morgan (1995).

and a parent-report version of the DISC. The primary purpose of the DISC is to establish present and lifetime diagnoses in the child or adolescent. It is appropriate for children aged 6 to 18. Based on extensive psychometric studies, the DISC appears to be very reliable (Shaffer et al., 2000), although there are issues related to the ordering of questions that need to be resolved (Jensen, Watanabe, & Richters, 1999). In addition, there is not a perfect connection between diagnoses based on the DISC interview and clinicians' diagnostic decisions (Jewell, Handwerk, Almquist, & Lucas, 2004). Thus, further work is needed to validate the DISC.

Overall, there are no right or wrong answers when choosing between unstructured, semistructured, and structured interviews. What a clinician gains from a structured interview (e.g., reliable information, clinical diagnoses) is tempered by what is often missed in a structured interview, but what can be gathered in an unstructured or semistructured interview (e.g., breadth of information, well-established rapport, strengths and weaknesses of the child in a number of domains). Thus, the choice between interview formats depends largely on the goals of the assessment and the specific referral

question. As with most other types of assessment, clinical skill and knowledge are used to determine the best and most comprehensive assessment techniques that are appropriate for that particular child or adolescent.

BEHAVIORAL ASSESSMENT

There are three primary types of behavioral assessment: behavioral observation, functional assessment, and self-monitoring. These techniques can be used in nearly any setting (e.g., the clinician's office, the child's home, an inpatient unit where the child is hospitalized) but the most common setting to conduct behavioral assessments is in the school setting (Breen & Fiedler, 2003; Chandler & Dahlquist, 2005).

Behavioral Observation

Behavioral observation consists of the clinician's observing the child at school, at home, in a research laboratory, or in the clinician's office. Having just read about unstructured and structured interviews, you will probably not be surprised to learn that there are

TABLE 4.4 Topics and Sample Questions from the Semistructured Clinical Interview for Children and Adolescents (SCICA) Aged 6 to 18

Topic/Domain	Sample Questions
Activities	What do you like to do in your spare time, like when you're not in school? What is your favorite TV show?
School	What do you like best in school? If you could change something about school, what would it be?
Job (ages 12–18)	Do you have a job? How do you feel about your job/boss?
Friends	How many friends do you have? Tell me about someone you like. Tell me about someone you don't like.
Family Relations	Who are the people in your family? How do your parents get along?
Fantasies	If you had 3 wishes, what would you wish? What would you like to be when you're older?
Self-Perception, Feelings	What makes you happy? What makes you sad? What do you worry about?
Somatic Complaints/Alcohol and Drugs/Trouble with the Law (ages 12–18)	Have you had headaches? Have you drunk beer, wine, or liquor? Have you used tobacco? Have you been in trouble with the police or law?

Source: McConaughy & Achenbach (2001).

TABLE 4.5 Sample Questions from the Diagnostic Interview Schedule for Children (DISC)

Attention-Deficit/Hyperactivity Disorder (AD/HD Module)

Children and adolescents are asked to think about the past 12 months and they are asked to answer these questions in a yes/no format. If a child answers "yes" to one of these questions, then follow-up questions are completed to obtain more details and also to ascertain whether the symptoms have been present for at least 4 weeks. There is also a parent interview with parallel questions.

In the last year, have you often made a lot of mistakes because it's hard for you to do things carefully?

In the last year, did you often have trouble keeping your mind on what you were doing for more than a short time?

In the last year, did you often not listen when people were speaking to you?

In the last year, have you often left your seat when you weren't supposed to?

In the last year, were you often "on the go" or did you move around as if you were "driven by a motor"?

Source: Shaffer et al. (2000). Reprinted with permission.

also unstructured and structured behavioral observation techniques. Nearly any clinician who meets with a child will observe the child's behavior. With the permission of the parents and teacher, clinicians can also visit the school to observe the child in the school setting (Skinner, Rhymer, & McDaniel, 2002). Often, clinicians observe the child's behavior in relation to the **antecedents** (what occurs before the behavior) and **consequences** (what occurs after the behavior). Imagine that a child has been referred for disruptive behavior in the classroom. When observing the child in the classroom, the clinician notices that the child receives no attention (good or bad) when she is staring quietly into space while sitting at her desk. As soon as she starts throwing her pencils around, she receives a great deal of attention (negative attention from the teacher in the form of a reprimand and positive attention from the other children in the form of laughter). These observations might lead the clinician

to hypothesize that the disruptive behavior was at least partially reinforced by the consequences to the behavior.

Although unstructured behavioral observations can collect a wealth of information, they can also be biased by the clinician's own way of viewing the situation. For this reason, structured behavioral observation systems have been developed. One example is the Direct Observation Form (DOF; Achenbach, 1991a). Not only is the child observed in a standardized manner, but also another child of the same age and gender is observed as a comparison child. The DOF allows clinicians to report on a series of behaviors that may have gone unnoticed without the prompt of the DOF stimulus material. Overall, the DOF has strong psychometric properties, and it provides a strong addition to the available tools for observation of children's and adolescents' behaviors. Overall, a great advantage of behavioral observation is the observation of the child's environment rather

Observations of children in their natural environments, such as school, can help clinicians understand a great deal about children's behavior.

	M	T	W	T	F	M	T	W	T	F
Total number assigned										
Total completed										
Percentage completed										

FIGURE 4.2 Example of a self-monitoring worksheet.

Source: Kratochwill et al. (1999).

than just hearing secondhand reports from parents and children (Winsor, 2003). These benefits of behavioral observation are also present in functional assessment.

Functional Assessment

Functional assessment consists of the evaluation of actual behaviors and the child's ability to perform those behaviors. Imagine that you were asked to work with a 7-year-old boy who reportedly had poor social skills. In addition to getting information from the boy's parents, teachers, and day-care workers, you might also want to observe the child interacting with others. Functional assessment allows you to observe the child while he exhibits the behaviors of interest. Not only would functional assessment help you determine whether or not there was a problem, but you would also be able to identify what specific behavioral strengths and weaknesses the boy exhibited (Steege & Watson, 2003). In observing the boy, for example, you might find that he stands far too close when speaking with other children and that he tries to continue conversations even after the other child is ready to leave. With this information, the functional assessment would identify specific target behaviors for treatment. Treatment effectiveness could then be assessed more accurately through functional outcome measures, which would evaluate the changes in the specific target behaviors (Chandler & Dahlquist, 2005).

Self-Monitoring

Self-monitoring is an assessment technique that allows the child to keep track of a specific behavior by recording the occurrence of the behavior (Kratochwill, Sheridan, Carlson, & Lasecki, 1999). For example, imagine a 10-year-old girl who reportedly has a learning disorder. Before going through formal testing, the school psychologist asks the girl to self-monitor her completion of homework assignments. As can be seen in Figure 4.2, the girl is given a grid that lists each day of the week, and she is asked to keep track of her homework completions. The school psychologist would use this information to begin to understand why the girl might be having difficulties in school. If, for example, she never does her homework, then an intervention could be developed to address that problem. If, on the other hand, the girl was completing her assignments but still not doing well on tests at school, then more formal testing for a learning disorder might be appropriate.

Interestingly, all these behavioral assessment techniques have potential problems. The primary concern is related to **reactivity,** which occurs if children behave differently solely because they are being observed (Kratochwill et al., 1999). It is not unusual for a child to try to act more appropriate (or sometimes less appropriate) when being observed. For this reason, clinicians often try to observe behavior in an unobtrusive manner (e.g., before they have met the child so the child does not know their identity) or try to observe behavior for a long enough period of time that reactivity decreases. Overall, behavioral assessment techniques provide a wealth of information about the child in different environments.

Silence is also speech.

—Proverb of Africa

CHECKLISTS AND RATING SCALES

One of the least expensive and most commonly used assessment techniques with children and adolescents is the use of checklists and rating scales. Checklists

Case Study: "B" The Boy Who Set Fires

For the first three years of B's life, he had a relatively stable home life with his mother, father, and four siblings. His parents separated when B was 3 years old, and he had a series of chaotic and unstable caretaking situations after that point. B's mother had psychiatric problems, and she made two suicide attempts during B's childhood, one of which led to hospitalization. By the age of 8, B's mother asked that B and one brother be put up for adoption. For the next two years, B bounced from one foster home to another. He was often kicked out of foster homes for lying, stealing, and acting defiant. He had fewer and fewer contacts with his mother and did not appear to have any close bonds with adults or children in his life. By the age of 10, B's mother's parental rights were terminated formally.

In one of the foster care placements, B had an argument with his roommate. After being reprimanded for something that he did not think was his fault, B set fire to some papers that were in his roommate's dresser. Shortly thereafter, he was placed in a psychiatric hospital for ten months because he set another fire. During this hospitalization, a thorough psychiatric evaluation was completed. The clinician concluded that B was "a depressed and angry boy who idealized a relationship between himself and his mother and father. He could not admit that his mother was rejecting him and appeared to have displaced this anger through fire setting and violent episodes" (Kolko & Ammerman, 1988; p. 247).

B made modest improvements with individual therapy, and he was discharged to a foster home. After 4 months in this foster home, B was found spreading kerosene around the neighbor's house. He was placed in a temporary emergency shelter where he tried to ignite a deodorant can to be used as a torch. At this point, he was $13\frac{1}{2}$ years old, and he was admitted to yet another psychiatric hospital, where a thorough psychological evaluation was completed. Results from this evaluation showed B to be a sad and angry boy who set fires when he reached a peak of sadness and anger.

Based on the results of this assessment, a comprehensive cognitive–behavioral treatment was completed. B was taught better impulse control techniques, and his feelings of sadness and anger were dealt with directly. B was successful in this treatment, and he was eventually discharged to a long-term residential treatment facility for emotionally disturbed children. A follow-up assessment was conducted after 6 months, and B maintained many of his therapeutic gains. Although he was still somewhat defiant and oppositional, B had not set any fires even after a particularly troubling visit with his biological mother. This case illustrates how assessments can be used to formulate treatment plans, to evaluate the effectiveness of treatment, and to verify the stability of treatment gains in a follow-up evaluation.

Source: Kolko & Ammerman (1988).

and rating scales are usually easy to administer, and they provide a wealth of information about children's functioning without being time consuming. Most of the measures discussed in this section take between 5 and 15 minutes to complete. Checklists and rating scales can be broken down into roughly two categories: broad measures and specific measures. Broad measures cover a variety of emotional/behavioral problems, whereas specific measures focus on one or two specific areas of concern. Both types of measures can be used in a comprehensive assessment. For example, if a 14-year-old girl were referred for depression, the clinician would certainly want to administer a specific measure that assessed depression and suicide, but the clinician might also want to administer a broad measure that would assess other possible problems such as anxiety, attentional problems, and somatic complaints. By using both broad and specific measures, the clinician can assess the referral problem in depth while also screening for other problems that were not mentioned in the intake phone call. Broad measures are described here, and

specific measures are discussed in the relevant chapters (e.g., the Children's Depression Inventory is discussed in the chapter on depression).

Broad Measures

Two well-known systems of broad-based measures will be highlighted. Both systems provide checklists to be completed by youth, parents, and teachers. Both systems assess competencies as well as emotional/behavioral problems in children. Both systems are empirically based and well established in the research literature. Finally, both systems have furthered our understanding of children's and adolescents' emotional/behavioral functioning immeasurably.

The most widely used and well established broad-based measure of children's emotional/behavioral functioning was developed originally by Dr. Tom Achenbach and Dr. Craig Edelbrock (1983). Since that time, the system was revised and renormed by Dr. Tom Achenbach and his research group in 1991 (Achenbach, 1991a, 1991b, 1991c, 1992) and revised and renormed again by

Dr. Tom Achenbach and Dr. Leslie Rescorla (Achenbach & Rescorla, 2000, 2001). The assessment system is now referred to as the Achenbach System of Empirically Based Assessment (ASEBA). For school-aged children, the Child Behavior Checklist (CBCL/6–18) is the parent report version within this system, the Teacher's Report Form (TRF) is geared toward teachers' perceptions, and the Youth Self-Report (YSR) is meant to be completed by older children and adolescents (Achenbach & Rescorla, 2001). Parents and teachers can complete the measures for children aged 6 to 18, and children aged 11 to 18 can complete the YSR. There are also parent-report measures (CBCL/1½–5) and caretaker/daycare worker measures (C-TRF) for children between the ages of 1½ and 5 who have not yet begun formal schooling (Achenbach & Rescorla, 2000). Interestingly, this system has also been expanded into young adulthood, with a measure known as the Young Adult Self-Report (YASR) that can be completed by young adults aged 18 to 30 and a measure known as the Young Adult Behavior Checklist (YABC) that can be completed by parents of young adults aged 18 to 30 (Achenbach, 1997). There has been a recent extension of these forms into adulthood (Achenbach & Rescorla, 2003) and older adulthood (Achenbach, Newhouse, & Rescorla, 2004). Although all these measures are dimensional in nature, they can be used to help inform the clinician about the appropriateness of *DSM* diagnoses (Achenbach & Dumenci, 2001; Achenbach & Rescorla, 2001; Krol, De Bruyn, Coolen, & van Aarle, 2006).

The three primary measures (CBCL, TRF, YSR) have been studied extensively and are well normed. Thousands of parents, teachers, and nonclinical as well as clinical youth were involved in the original development and revisions of these measures, so the measures have been extremely well validated. These measures all have excellent reliability as well. Table 4.6 provides sample items from the narrow-band scales. Note that the wordings of the items differ somewhat depending on whether the measure is to be filled out by a parent (CBCL), a teacher (TRF), or an adolescent (YSR). Note that these measures also yield T-scores related to the child's competence in a number of domains. Overall, the CBCL, TRF, and YSR provide a wealth of valid information that can be used to help children in innumerable ways. Because the norms on measures are updated frequently, interested students may want to check the Web site (www.ASEBA.org) for the latest information.

Another strong system of assessment for children is known as the Behavior Assessment System for Children (BASC; Reynolds & Kamphaus, 2005). The BASC system utilizes multiple informants (children, parents, and teachers), and the self-reports can be completed by children as young as 8 years old. There is a structured developmental history that can be used with parents, and a direct observational system (the Systematic Observation System) can be used (Reynolds & Kamphaus, 2005). The BASC system is comparable to the system developed by Achenbach given that the measures are broad based and given that they assess children in multiple contexts. In addition, both emotional/behavioral problems as well as competencies are assessed.

Overall, both the BASC system and the ASEBA system involving the CBCL, TRF, and YSR are well established and well validated in the research literature (Achenbach & McConaughy, 2003; Thorpe, Kamphaus,

TABLE 4.6   Sample Items From the CBCL, TRF, and YSR

Internalizing		Externalizing
Anxious/Depressed	Social Problems	Rule-Breaking Behavior
Cries a lot	Too dependent	Lies and cheats
Fears doing bad things	Doesn't get along with others	Steals
Worries	Gets teased	Swears
Withdrawn/Depressed	Thought Problems	Aggressive Behavior
Refuses to talk	Hears things	Argues a lot
Secretive	Repeats certain acts	Gets in fights
Withdrawn	Sees things	Teases a lot
Somatic Complaints	Attention Problems	
Feels dizzy	Can't concentrate	
Headaches	Daydreams	
Nausea	Poor schoolwork	

Source: Achenbach & Rescorla (2001).

& Reynolds, 2003). Both styles of assessment allow a dimensional approach to understanding children's and adolescents' behavior given that scores are based on a continuum rather than dichotomous categorizations. In a comprehensive assessment of a child or adolescent, it behooves the clinician to use one of these systems to assess broadly for problems and competencies in the child or adolescent and then also to consider using more specific measures of functioning related to the referral problem (e.g., administering the Children's Depression Inventory to assess the child's depression). Overall, clinicians must seek appropriate measures that show strong psychometric properties. Box 4.2 further discusses how children feel about their behavior and Box 4.3 discusses the issue of different perspectives on children's and adolescents' behaviors. Note that ratings on behavior checklists can be influenced by parental symptoms (Chi & Hinshaw, 2002) and by teachers' preconceived notions about appropriate behavior for children of different races and ethnicities (Chang & Sue, 2003), so clinicians should take appropriate caution when interpreting data from assessments.

Measures of Competence and Adaptive Functioning

Competence, self-esteem, and adaptive functioning are all important features to assess in children, even if they are being referred for problem behavior. Although parents and teachers (and often children) tend to focus on the problems that the child is experiencing, it is important for the clinician to assess the strengths and competencies that the child exhibits. Some of the most widely used measures of competence were developed by Dr. Susan Harter and her colleagues. Different developmentally appropriate forms of the Self-Perception Profile have been developed for preschool children, elementary-aged children, adolescents, college students, and adults (Harter, 1985; 1988). The rationale behind the Harter measures is that perceived competence is domain specific. That is, rather than asking children how they feel about themselves overall, it is more accurate to ask how children feel about themselves in different topic areas (such as the social, scholastic, athletic, physical appearance, behavioral conduct, job, and dating domains). In addition to these domains, both children and adolescents are asked for their overall sense of global self-worth, which is comparable to overall ratings of self-esteem.

In order to assess adaptive functioning, the Vineland Adaptive Behavior Scales-II (Sparrow, Cicchetti, & Balla, 2005) are used. Primarily used in assessments for developmental disabilities, the Vineland-II assesses such characteristics as daily living skills, communication, socialization, motor skills, and maladaptive behavior.

BOX 4.2

SUBJECTIVE DISTRESS

Imagine that you are referred a 12-year-old girl who continues to get in trouble at school for talking too much and for being a "class clown." When you meet with the girl and her single father, the girl seems to be unfazed by her "problems," whereas her father is expressing that he is at his "wit's end." The father explains that the girl has been suspended from school multiple times for her antics at school, which necessitates that he take a day off of work and receive no pay for those missed days. After talking with the father, and later talking with the teachers, it is clear that the adults in this girl's life want her behavior changed. It is also clear that the girl does not believe she has a problem. She later confides in you that she likes the attention that children in school give her when she goofs off in class, and she also likes her days of suspension because it is the only time that she can spend with her father.

In formal assessments, usually children and adolescents are asked to report on the occurrence of their behavior, but they are often not asked how they feel about their behavior. There are a number of studies that show interesting patterns when you ask adolescents and parents how they feel about the adolescents' behavior (Duhig & Phares, 2003; Phares & Compas, 1990; Phares & Danforth, 1994). For example, mothers, fathers, and teachers are more distressed by adolescents' externalizing behaviors in contrast to internalizing behaviors (Phares & Danforth, 1994; Duhig & Phares, 2003), whereas adolescents are more distressed about their internalizing problems than their externalizing problems (Phares & Compas, 1990).

Overall, these studies suggest that adolescents, parents, and teachers should not only be asked about the frequency of behaviors, but should also be asked about their feelings about the behaviors. It may be that other forces are at work to reward the behaviors (such as attention from peers, parents, or teachers). These rewards for problematic behaviors are important for clinicians to know about before trying to change the behaviors.

THE FAMILY CIRCUS BY BIL KEANE

BILLY'S FIRST DAY OF SCHOOL

NO, DADDY! NO! NO! I DON'T WANNA GO! NO!

Here's What REALLY Happened! by Billy

"Bye, Daddy!"

The Vineland is most often administered to the parent, caretaker, or teacher and can be used for individuals from infancy through adulthood. The Scales of Independent Behavior–Revised (SIB–R; Bruinink, Woodcock, Weatherman, & Hill, 1996) battery can also be used to assess adaptive functioning and independence in a number of settings, including home, school, work, and the community. These measures are most often used with clients who might have a developmental disability, with the intention of giving specific recommendations to increase the client's independence and development of age-appropriate adaptive skills (Burns, 2003).

PERSONALITY ASSESSMENT

All the previously discussed measures are based on observable behavior in one way or another. Interviews, behavioral assessments, and checklists all rely on either reports of behavior or actual observation of behavior. In contrast, personality assessments often try to look beyond the behavior to find a deeper meaning to the child's or adolescent's functioning. Personality assessments fall into roughly two categories: personality inventories and projective measures. There is less empirical support for children's personality inventories and projectives measures, so these sections will only provide a brief overview of these assessment measures.

Personality Inventories

Personality inventories are paper-and-pencil measures that usually ask about the child's functioning without asking about specific behaviors. For example, the answers on a personality inventory would be compared with the profiles of known reference groups (such as children who are depressed or children who are out of touch with reality) so that the child's or adolescent's profile could be compared with the profiles of those reference groups. Often the items on the measures do not seem to have anything to do with the child's behavior, but there is an inference between the profile of answers and the inferred behavior of the child. This inference is one of the biggest points that separates behavioral measures from personality measures.

Two primary personality inventories are used with children and adolescents: the Personality Inventory for Children–2 (PIC–2; Lachar & Gruber, 2001), which is completed by parents about their children, and the Minnesota Multiphasic Personality Inventory–Adolescent version (MMPI–A; Archer, 2005), which is a self-report measure for adolescents that is an offshoot of the well-known MMPI-2 that was developed for adults (Butcher, Dahlstrom, Graham, Tellegen, & Kaemmer, 1989).

Although there is a wealth of data on the use of personality inventories in adults, there are relatively few studies that use personality inventories with children and adolescents. The majority of research into child and adolescent functioning has relied on more behaviorally based measures, partly because these measures have been validated more extensively than personality measures with children.

Projective Measures

The rationale behind **projective measures** is that an ambiguous stimulus is presented to children and adolescents, and they project their innermost thoughts and concerns onto that ambiguous stimulus (Weiner &

BOX *4.3*

WHO IS RIGHT?

When divergent information is gathered from different informants, who is right? This is actually a trick question because the answer is that everyone is right. There is no "gold standard" of a child's or adolescent's behavior, so multiple informants offer different perspectives on the child's behavior (Achenbach, McConaughy, & Howell, 1987). A classic meta-analysis of different informants (Achenbach et al., 1987) showed that informants in similar roles (e.g., parent with parent, teacher with teacher) tend to see the child's behavior in the most comparable manner (with correlations that average .60). Adults in different roles (e.g., parent with teacher) tend to have ratings that correspond to a significant, but small amount (with correlations that average .28). Children and the adults in their lives (such as parent with child, teacher with child) tend to correspond to a significant, but small degree (with correlations that average .22). Correlations tend to be higher for all informant pairs when externalizing (as opposed to internalizing) problems are rated and when children (as opposed to adolescents) are rated. These findings have been replicated

in a number of other studies (Cai, Kaiser, & Hancock, 2004; DeLosReyes & Kazdin, 2004, 2005) and are somewhat comparable to what is found with adults (Achenbach, Krukowski, Dumenci, & Ivanova, 2005). With children and adolescents, discrepancies between mothers and fathers are related to parental psychological symptoms (Treutler & Epkins, 2003). Disagreements between parents and children are also related to the salience of the behaviors for the parents versus the children (Karver, 2006). Interestingly, the greater the discrepancy between parents' and adolescents' reports, the greater the likelihood of adverse outcomes in later adolescence and young adulthood (Ferdinand, van der Ende, & Verhulst, 2004).

Thus, clinicians are often left with the daunting task of trying to make sense of divergent information. It behooves a clinician to consider all the informants' perspectives on children's and adolescents' behavior. Rather than searching for the "right" information, it is worthwhile to consider the different perspectives from all informants to gain a better understanding of children's and adolescents' functioning.

Kuehnle, 1998). The most widely used projective measures with children and adolescents are the Rorschach (1942) inkblot test; the Children's Apperception Test (CAT; Bellak, 1993), where children write stories about ambiguous pictures; the Draw-A-Person (DAP; Zalsman et al., 2000), where the child draws a picture of a person that is thought to reflect the child's perceptions of him/herself; the House-Tree-Person (HTP; Buck, 1985), which allows the child to draw a house (thought to represent home life and family relationships), a tree (thought to reflect the child's personal feelings about her- or himself), and a person (thought to reflect the child's self-perceptions about their future); and the sentence completion task (Rotter, Lah, & Rafferty, 1992), where children are asked to complete sentence stems such as "I wish..." or "My father..." or "I am afraid of..." Critics of projective techniques worry that there is too much inference beyond the information that is provided by the child or adolescent (Garb, Wood, Lilienfeld, & Nezworski, 2002; Hunsley & Bailey, 1999; Hunsley, Lee, & Wood, 2003). In addition, the psychometric properties of the Rorschach have been called into question, especially when used with children (Hunsley & Bailey, 2001; Wood, Nezworski, Lilienfeld, & Garb, 2003).

Figure 4.3 shows the DAP of a 5-year-old boy whose parents are divorced. The disconnections between the

FIGURE 4.3   A 5-year-old boy's Draw-A-Person.

Source: Di Leo (1973).

Case Study: Alan: A Case Study of Maternal Psychological Problems and Neglect

Alan was first referred to a treatment center for maltreated children and their families when he was 5 years old. His mother, Mary, has had a long history of psychiatric difficulties and has been diagnosed with schizophrenic disorder. Alan's father abandoned his mother one week prior to Alan's birth. Although Mary thought about giving Alan up for adoption, she opted to keep him since she had always wanted a baby. Alan was hospitalized repeatedly for illnesses when he was an infant and toddler.

Mary acknowledged that she had difficulty keeping a job and maintaining her public assistance payments. She often worked part-time cleaning houses and doing laundry, but she reported that these tasks were difficult to manage in her own home. Mary reported that the refrigerator in their apartment was broken frequently, so she kept perishable food on the windowsill.

Mary said that Alan was accident prone at home and that he never followed her directions. Alan would often leave the house at night and run around the neighborhood unattended. By the age of 5, the school counselor noticed that Alan would steal from other children, would eat out of the garbage, would show up for school dirty and unkempt, would rarely complete his homework, and would often be late or absent from school. When asked about eating out of the garbage, Alan reported that "I'm hungry and there isn't enough food at home." The school counselor made the referral to the treatment center.

In order to begin treatment, the clinicians first completed assessments on Alan and his mother. Alan had average intelligence, appropriate academic achievement, and elevated emotional/behavioral problems. He was diagnosed with attention-deficit/hyperactivity disorder, pica (eating nonfood substances), and oppositional defiant disorder. After her own evaluation, Mary was diagnosed with schizophrenic disorder. She reported that she heard voices when no one was around and that she often felt that strangers did not like her and that they talked about her behind her back.

The clinicians began treatment to help Alan in individual sessions and to help Mary with parenting skills. After a year, treatment was terminated because Mary failed to bring Alan in for his therapy appointments, and she often did not show up for her own parenting therapy sessions. After another year, Mary and Alan rejoined the program. At this time, Alan was found to have deteriorated significantly. His IQ was now in the low average range, his academic achievement scores were delayed, his adaptive skills were found to be in the low average range, and he showed elevated levels of impulsivity, anxiety, instability, and confusion.

As Alan approached adolescence, Mary became less and less able to deal with his behavior, and she had difficulty maintaining any therapeutic contacts for herself or for Alan. Alan would often run away from home and would rarely show up for school. For these reasons, Alan was placed in a therapeutic residential center, where he was given a stable, structured, and nurturing environment that provided appropriate adult role models. Although the original goal was to help Mary provide this type of environment for Alan, it did not appear that she was capable of doing so. Thus, a long-term out-of-home placement was deemed necessary.

Source: Green (1991).

---

head, body, and arms in the drawing are interpreted to reflect feelings of insecurity (Di Leo, 1973). Unfortunately, the psychometric properties of DAP techniques have not been well established. DAP techniques, also known as Human Figure Drawings, can be used as another form of open-ended interviewing in cases of alleged sexual abuse, and this technique seems promising (Aldridge et al., 2004).

FAMILY ASSESSMENT

Nearly all the previously discussed measures have focused on children's and adolescents' functioning. In a comprehensive assessment, it is imperative to assess the family's functioning to ascertain whether or not the family is contributing to the child's or adolescent's problems. As mentioned in the chapter on theories,

family theorists believe that many problems in children and adolescents are merely symbolic of larger problems within the family system. An assessment of the family should be included even if the clinician does not consider her- or himself to be a family clinician (Rey et al., 2000). A wealth of research suggests family factors can create or at least exacerbate problems in children and adolescents. Thus, it is crucial to assess family functioning whenever children or adolescents are experiencing problems.

Note that clinicians must be flexible in their definitions of "family." Sometimes children and adolescents have no genetic connection and even no legal connection to those individuals who are raising them and who they consider family. It is important for clinicians to use the child's terminology rather than imposing traditional family terminology onto the child. For example, if a child has been raised since birth by an ex-girlfriend of his deceased father and if the child refers to the woman as "Ann," then the clinician should use Ann's name rather than referring to her as "mother." Similarly, if a child refers to her stepfather as "Dad" because he's the only father she has ever known, then it is important for the clinician to honor that terminology and not to impose the term *stepfather* onto the child. In my own clinical and supervision work, I have seen amazing definitions of families that children have accommodated into their lives. Similarly, work in other countries has shown the importance of culturally sensitive assessment of families (Rey et al., 2000). Like any other topic, it is important for clinicians not to impose their value system onto the family but rather to try to understand the relationships and values within the family who is seeking help.

One of the first things that many clinicians use to understand a family during an assessment is a family **genogram** (McGoldrick, Gerson, & Shellenberger, 1999). As can be seen in Figure 4.4, a family genogram provides a schematic representation of the family structure. Once the major family members have been identified for the current and recent past generations, the clinician can interview the family about any specific patterns of behavior. For example, if a clinician was working with a 15-year-old adolescent girl who was abusing alcohol, the clinician might want to look at the family genogram with an eye toward who else in the family had abused alcohol or other substances. Genograms are usually completed by the clinician while asking the parents and children their recollections. The genogram can be a graphic way of illustrating multigenerational problems that children and adolescents might be experiencing.

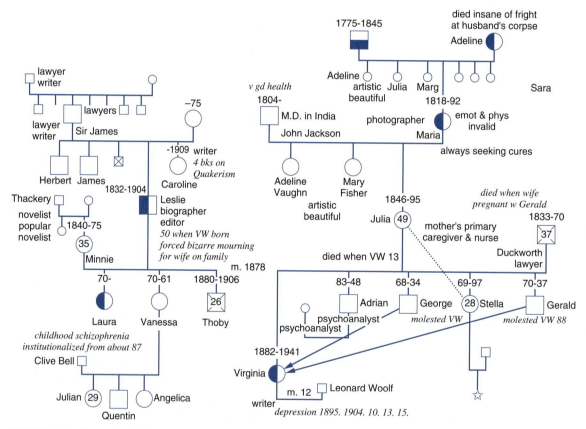

FIGURE 4.4 Example of a family genogram for Virginia Woolf, the novelist.

Note: Circles represent females, squares represent males. A circle and square who are connected by a line were married (with date of marriage marked by m), lines coming down from them are their offspring. Dates above circles and squares are the birth and death dates of that person. Highlighted characteristics, such as lawyer, writer, were chosen to show patterns of creativity within this family system.

Source: McGoldrick, Gerson, & Shellenberger (1999).

Two of the most widely used measures of family functioning are the Family Environment Scale (FES; Moos & Moos, 1994) and the Family Adaptability and Cohesion Scale (FACES; Olson, 2000). Both of these paper-and-pencil measures can be completed by children as well as parents, and both can be used to compare different responses within the family. The FES measures a wide variety of aspects of the family, including expressiveness, conflict, independence, intellectual–cultural orientation, active–recreational orientation, organization, and control (Moos & Moos, 1994). The FACES yields two factors: cohesion and adaptability. Both of these measures have been well validated, and both show strong psychometric properties.

The Kinetic Family Drawing (KFD; Burns, 1982) can be considered a projective technique, but because it focuses on family functioning, it is also considered a measure of family assessment. Children and adolescents are asked to draw a picture of their family doing something. After the picture is drawn, the child is asked to explain what is happening in the picture and what will happen in the characters' future. The picture is then interpreted for issues that are relevant to the child and the family. For example, if a child "forgets" to draw one parent, it may be that the parent is absent a lot from the child's life or that the child feels abandoned emotionally by the parent. Like many projective techniques, there are almost no norms or well-established scoring systems for the KFD technique (Carlson, 2003). Some clinicians use the KFD as another way of interviewing children about their families. With this measure serving as an impetus for an interview, the technique can be useful as long as the clinician's interpretations are consistent with other, more objective information.

Figure 4.5 shows a KFD drawn by an 8-year-old girl, whose father is severely depressed and whose mother is emotionally unavailable (Burns & Kaufman, 1972). The fact that the father is in bed and the mother is working on a church project without interacting with the children might suggest that the girl sees her parents as distant. The fact that the 5-year-old brother and the cat are all the same size as the 8-year-old girl might suggest that she feels inconsequential to her parents and that she also feels connected to her brother and the cat (Burns & Kaufman, 1972).

Another way of assessing functioning within the family is to assess parental functioning within the family. For example, the Parenting Scale can assess strengths and weaknesses within mothers' and fathers' parenting techniques, which provides a measure of parental competence (Arnold, O'Leary, Wolff, & Acker, 1993). Parenting efficacy and control can also be assessed through standardized measures (Lovejoy, Verda, & Hays, 1997). Parent–child relationships can be assessed through the social relations model of family assessment (Cook & Kenny, 2004). Even the potential for abusing one's children can be estimated with a scale known as the Child Abuse Potential Inventory, although this

FIGURE 4.5 Kinetic family drawing by an 8-year-old girl.

Source: Burns & Kaufman (1972).

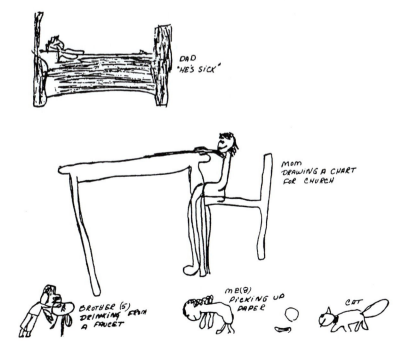

measure sometimes identifies parents incorrectly of having the potential to abuse their children (Ammerman & Patz, 1996; Milner, 1986, 1994). These assessment techniques offer new ways to assess and consider parental functioning within the context of the family. They also offer another way of looking at the context of the child's problems rather than just assessing the child's problems directly.

The test of a first-rate intelligence is the ability to hold two opposed ideas in the mind at the same time, and still retain the ability to function.

—F. Scott Fitzgerald

ASSESSING INTELLECTUAL FUNCTIONING AND ACADEMIC ACHIEVEMENT

Intellectual functioning and academic functioning are important to assess for a number of different referral problems. If a child is thought to be developmentally delayed, then they are often given an intelligence test. A common referral problem that leads to the assessment of intelligence and academic functioning is when a child or adolescent is having problems in school. In these cases, teachers often suggest to parents that they have their child assessed for a learning disorder. In cases where a child is having attentional problems, it also makes sense to have the child's intelligence and cognitive functioning tested.

A number of standardized measures of intelligence and developmental abilities can be used with youngsters. Beginning in infancy, the Bayley Scales of Infant and Toddler Development-III (Bayley, 2005) can be used to assess developmental abilities of infants and toddlers. In most cases, intelligence testing or the assessment of developmental abilities in infants and toddlers is completed only when there are concerns about limited intellectual abilities. In addition, intelligence tests in infancy and early childhood do not provide strong predictions for intellectual functioning in later childhood, adolescence, or adulthood (Rock & Stenner, 2005; Tasbihsazan, Nettelbeck, & Kirby, 2003). For this reason, intellectual testing in infancy is only completed in rare cases.

Beginning in preschool and following into adulthood, a number of tests can be given to assess intelligence. A series of tests originally developed by Dr. David Wechsler can be used from preschool to adulthood. The Wechsler Primary and Preschool Intelligence Scale–III

(WPPSI–III; Wechsler, 2002), the Wechsler Intelligence Scale for Children–Fourth Edition (WISC–IV; Wechsler, 2003), and the Wechsler Adult Intelligence Scale–Third Edition (WAIS–III; Psychological Corporation, 1997) can be used to assess intellectual functioning throughout the life span. The Stanford-Binet Intelligence Scale: Fifth Edition (SB5; Roid, 2003 can be used from 2 years old to adulthood. A number of other intelligence tests can be used with children (reviewed in Reynolds & Kamphaus, 2003), but the WISC–IV will be highlighted because of its widespread use in the United States as well as internationally.

The WISC–IV is used with children aged 6 to 16 years, 11 months and can take between 2 and 3 hours to complete. The test is given in a one-on-one situation with a highly trained examiner, who knows both how to administer the measure and who is fully trained on the psychometric theory behind test development. As can be seen in Table 4.7, the WISC–IV is broken down into subscales that reflect a variety of skills. Each child receives an overall Full Scale Intelligence Quotient (FSIQ), as well as index scores on Verbal Comprehension, Perceptual Reasoning, Working Memory, and Processing Speed. Note that these scores are all established with a mean of 100 and a standard deviation of 15. Thus, only 2% of the population is expected to score above 130 (which is 2 standard deviations above the mean), and only 2% of the population is expected to score below 70 (which is 2 standard deviations below the mean).

Overall, the WISC–IV is well standardized and has been very well validated. The psychometric properties on the measure are excellent, and the utility of the WISC–IV has been well established (Wechsler, 2003). Some of the limitations of the WISC–IV, like most other standardized intelligence measures, include concerns about heavy cultural loadings and school-based qualities of many of the subtests, which inadvertently seems to penalize bilingual, minority, and learning-disordered children (Burns, & O'Leary 2004; Harris & Lilorente, 2005), and the focus on speed of responses (which seems to penalize more methodical, hesitant, careful children, as well as behaviorally disordered children; Calhoun & Mayes, 2005). These criticisms are important to keep in mind, especially when assessing a child who might not be able to perform at her or his maximum capacity because of the test itself.

Some of these same criticisms have been mentioned in relation to the most widely used measure of academic achievement, the Woodcock-Johnson Psycho-Educational Battery–Third Edition (WJ–III; Woodcock,

TABLE 4.7 Subtests on the Wechsler Intelligence Scale for Children–IV (WISC–IV)

Verbal Comprehension	Perceptual Reasoning	Working Memory	Processing Speed
Similarities	Block design	Digit span	Coding
Vocabulary	Picture concepts	Letter-number sequencing	Symbol search
Comprehension	Matrix reasoning	Arithmetic	Cancellation
Information	Picture completion		
Word reasoning			

Source: Wechsler (2003). Wechsler Intelligence Scale for Children: Fourth Edition. Copyright 2003 by The Psychological Corporation Assessment Company. Reproduced by permission. All rights reserved. "Wechsler Intelligence Scale for Children" and "WISC" are trademarks of The Psychological Corporation, a Harcourt Assessment Company, registered in the United States of America and/or other jurisdictions.

McGrew, & Mather, 2000). The WJ–III assesses children's and adolescents' acquired knowledge within the school setting. Different ages are assessed on different subscales, but the broadband factors at all ages include Broad Reading, Broad Mathematics, and Written Expression. The WJ–III can be used in conjunction with an intelligence test to ascertain whether or not the child or adolescent exhibits a learning disorder. In addition, children and adolescents who are struggling in their academic work can be assessed to identify areas of strength and weakness regarding their academic achievement.

It is noble to teach oneself, but still nobler to teach others—and less trouble.

—Mark Twain

EDUCATIONAL ASSESSMENT

Nearly all the assessment techniques discussed so far can be completed within the school system. Most of these assessment techniques are only appropriate for school psychologists and clinical psychologists to complete, given the training that is involved in conducting an assessment in a competent and ethical manner. There are schoolwide testing programs in which teachers participate (such as group achievement testing and scholastic testing), and these tests can be helpful in adding information to the assessment of an individual child or adolescent. Individual testing, however, is most often completed by a school psychologist who can spend time with the child and her or his family.

It is important for professionals within the school system to follow their own state's admission, retention, and dismissal (ARD) procedures for students who might be placed in special education (Stetson, 1992). In most states, there is a five-step process for children to receive special services within the school system:

- Level I: Screening and initial identification
- Level II: Diagnosis to establish eligibility
- Level III: Placement and individualized treatment plan development
- Level IV: Instructional planning
- Level V: Evaluation

It is important to know the options for remediation that are available within the child's school system. As can be seen in Table 4.8, a host of programs offer special education services for children in need. Note that school systems also offer special services and special full-time classrooms for children who are emotionally disturbed, physically disabled, and multiply handicapped (Stetson, 1992).

School psychologists, working in conjunction with teachers, have access to a wealth of information about a child's functioning. They are in an enviable position of not only assessing children and adolescents, but also making recommendations that can be instituted in the school setting. Interestingly, evaluations from school psychologists and private clinical psychologists often look very similar. Often comparable measures are used, similar informants are asked to participate, and similar conclusions are drawn (Kamphaus, Petoskey, & Rowe, 2000).

Nearly all the measures mentioned in this chapter can be used within the school system, and many rely on information from teachers and other school personnel (e.g., observations, functional assessments, behavior rating scales). There is, however, a great deal of overlap between assessments done within the school system and those completed in a community or private setting (Kamphaus et al., 2000; Shapiro & Kratochwill, 2002). In some ways, this commonality works to the benefit of children, given that most professional settings have comparable standards for assessments. Those who are interested in more information about assessment

TABLE 4.8 Special Classes Available in Most School Districts and Criteria for Placement

Type of Class	IQ Criterion	Achievement Criterion	Cognitive Learning Deficiencies
Reading and Title I	70 and above	Functioning 2 years or more below grade level	No requirement
Pull-out resource	70 and above	Achievement is more than 1 standard deviation below potential as measured on standardized tests	No requirement
Full-time learning disabled	70 and above	Achievement is more than 1 standard deviation below potential as measured on standardized tests	Deficiency in one or more areas
Educable mentally retarded	50–70	No requirement	No requirement
Trainable mentally retarded	Below 50	No requirement	No requirement
Academically talented	130 and above	Typically 2 years or more above present grade level	No requirement

Source: Stetson (1992).

procedures within the school setting are encouraged to read *Conducting School-Based Assessments of Child and Adolescent Behavior* (Shapiro & Kratochwill, 2002).

NEUROPSYCHOLOGICAL ASSESSMENT

Neuropsychological assessment has become a specialization within the field of clinical psychology (Riccio & Wolfe, 2003). The field of neuropsychology developed largely to investigate the connections between the brain and behavior (Baron, 2004). Neuropsychological assessment is used to help identify ways in which cognitive or emotional functioning influences intellectual or academic functioning in a particular individual. Neuropsychological assessment can pinpoint functional problems that might be missed by other more broad measures of assessment (D'Amato, Reynolds, & Fletcher-Janzen, 2005). Neuropsychological assessment has been used a great deal when there are concerns about the ramifications of a traumatic brain injury or other medically based illnesses, but it has also been used when children show the possibility of such problems as learning disorders, autism, attention-deficit/hyperactivity disorder, conduct disorder, depression, and anxiety disorders (Riccio & Wolfe, 2003). There is an increasing need for neuropsychological assessments within the field of special education (D'Amato et al., 2005). Common neuropsychological assessment techniques for children include the Halstead-Reitan Neuropsychological Test Batteries for Children, the Nebraska Neuropsychological Children's Battery, and the Wide Range Assessment of Memory and Learning (described by Miller, Bigler, & Adams, 2003; Riccio & Wolfe, 2003). In addition to

using a standardized intellectual test, a thorough neuropsychological evaluation might include assessment of the following areas (Baron, 2004; D'Amato, Rothlisberg, & Rhodes, 1997):

- Perceptual/sensory
- Motor functions
- Verbal functions
- Nonverbal functions
- Attention/learning/processing
- Communication/language skills
- Academic achievement
- Personality/behavior
- Educational/classroom environment

In addition to the many areas that are usually assessed in neuropsychological assessments, more complex and comprehensive assessments might also include neuroimaging with magnetic resonance imaging (MRI) or computerized tomography (CT; Eliez & Reiss, 2000; Johnson, Halit, Grice, & Karmiloff-Smith, 2002). In a review of 10 years of neuroimaging studies, the authors concluded that neuroimaging "holds great promise" for the assessment of psychological disorders (Hendren, DeBacker, & Pandina, 2000). Results from neuroimaging studies, however, suggest that it is not yet specific enough to serve as a primary diagnostic instrument. In addition, neuroimaging is quite expensive and cannot be performed during every neuropsychological assessment. It can, however, provide another avenue of understanding—the brain-related mechanisms—that might be influencing a child's behavior or academic functioning—both through adaptive and maladaptive processes (Johnson et al., 2002).

TABLE 4.9   Examples and Overview of Each Type of Assessment Technique

Type of Assessment	Examples
Interviews	Unstructured
	Semistructured (e.g., SCICA)
	Structured (e.g., DISC)
Behavioral assessment	Behavioral observation
	Functional assessment
	Self-monitoring
Checklists	Broad measures (e.g., CBCL, BASC)
	Adaptive (e.g., Harter)
Personality assessment	Personality inventories (e.g., MMPI-2, PIC)
	Projective measures (e.g., Rorschach, CAT)
Family assessment	Genograms, measures (e.g., FACES, FES)
Intellectual and achievement assessment	WISC-IV, WJ-III
Educational assessment	Screening, diagnosis, placement, instructional planning, and evaluation
Neuropsychological assessment	Halstead-Reitan Neuropsychological Test Batteries
	Nebraska Neuropsychological Children's Battery

Overall, there are a number of well-established and promising assessment techniques to help determine the functioning of children, adolescents, and the family. An overview is provided in Table 4.9. Note also that there is a clear connection between assessments and therapeutic interventions. Assessment can be used to determine the type of problem (if any) that requires therapeutic interventions and then can also be used to assess progress in treatment as well as the maintenance of treatment gains over time.

Identify the problem bring it out
don't kick or punch or even shout
attack the problem and not the fear
listen with your open mind and ear
cause you are you and I am me
but we are us and us are we
Focus on the problem don't leave it behind
treat others with respect and feeling kind
take responsibility for your action
and you'll get a feeling of satisfaction
cause you are you and I am me
but we are us and us are we
　　　　　—Shamar, aged 10 and homeless (Children's Defense
　　　　　　　　　　　　　Fund—Minnesota, 1990; p. 2)

THERAPEUTIC INTERVENTIONS

Like assessment, therapy with children and adolescents is often limited by the reluctance of youth to seek out these services themselves. Parents and school professionals are the most common conduit for children to receive therapy services (Poduska, 2000). It is almost

unheard of to have a child (especially a young child) mention that they want help for a specific behavioral problem (Logan & King, 2001; Srebnik, Cauce, & Baydar, 1996). Some clinicians have an entire lifetime of work with children and families without ever receiving a call from a child or adolescent who wants help. Even when children are brought to therapy by their parents, they often do not understand why their parents have sought services. For example, in one study of children referred for therapy, 63% of the parent–child pairs failed to agree on the specific problems that were in need of treatment (Yeh & Weisz, 2001). Even when problems were grouped into general categories, almost 34% of the parent–child pairs still did not overlap in their identification of behaviors in need of treatment (Yeh & Weisz, 2001). When agreements between children, parents, and therapists are compared, the same pattern appears. A total of 76.8% of child–parent therapist triads did not agree on a single specific target problem at the beginning of the child's therapy (Hawley & Weisz, 2003). When broad categories of behavior were considered, 44.4% of the dyads still did not agree on the target of treatment. Thus, therapy with children, adolescents, and families poses interesting challenges that are often not faced by clinicians working with individual adults in therapy.

In addition to helping future child clinicians understand these issues, another big challenge in teaching undergraduate students and graduate students about therapeutic interventions is the need to use empirical research to identify effective therapies for emotional/behavioral problems. Too often, students find a therapeutic modality that they like or one that fits their personality style, and then they seek training in that modality. Unfortunately, this process can mean that many relatively ineffective therapies are conducted that provide only limited benefits for children and families. Like so many other aspects of psychology, we cannot rely on a "one therapy fits all" approach to helping children. It is imperative that therapeutic interventions be subjected to rigorous empirical testing to verify their effectiveness for specific problems. Increasingly, insurance companies and health maintenance organizations will only cover therapies that have been documented as effective (Compas & Gotlib, 2002; Reed, Levant, Stout, Murphy, & Phelps, 2001). Even with this documentation, however, the large majority of health maintenance organizations and insurance companies within the United States do not cover mental health services for children or adults (Kiesler, 2000).

Outside developed nations, it is important to acknowledge that therapeutic services for children in developing countries are limited at best (Rahman, Mubbashar, Harrington, & Gater, 2000). Although significant advances have been made with helping children in Western cultures, effective intervention and prevention programs are often not available in many developing countries (Rahman et al., 2000).

A number of therapy-oriented books and special issues of journals organize their discussion around treatment of specific types of developmental psychopathology (e.g., Kazdin & Weisz, 2003; Kendall, 2006; Rapport, 2001), whereas other books organize their discussion around specific types of treatment (e.g., Hibbs & Jensen, 1996; LeCroy, 1994; Ollendick, 1998). Although both of these organizational styles have their merits, the latter organizational style is used in this chapter. In order for students to understand the differences and similarities between therapeutic modalities, each type of therapeutic modality is discussed separately. This chapter, therefore, reviews a number of different settings for therapy and a number of different therapeutic modalities, including psychodynamic, behavioral, cognitive–behavioral, and family systems therapies, as well as psychopharmacological interventions (i.e., medications). After discussing these differing modalities, studies of the effectiveness of these therapies will be discussed. Given the importance of preventing problems rather than waiting for them to occur, the chapter ends with a section on prevention programs that work. It is important to know that computers (e.g., software on DVDs) and the Internet (e.g., online services and Web sites) are being targeted for many behavioral health-care interventions with adults

as well as with children (Naglieri et al., 2004; Ritterband, Cox, et al., 2003; Ritterband, Gonder-Frederick, et al., 2003; Spence, Holmes, March, & Lipp, 2006).

SETTINGS WHERE INTERVENTIONS ARE CONDUCTED

Throughout the case studies presented in this book, a number of locations and settings of therapy and other interventions will be highlighted. For the most severe examples of developmental psychopathology, **inpatient settings** can provide intensive treatment around the clock in a safe environment for the child (e.g., Green et al., 2001). Children receiving services in an inpatient setting are usually unable to be stabilized in any other less-restrictive environment, and many are a danger to themselves or others. Although longer stays (sometimes extending into months or years) used to be commonplace in inpatient settings, shorter stays are more common these days (Pottick, Barber, Hansell, & Coyne, 2001; Pottick, McAlpine, & Andelman, 2000). **Treatment plans** that identify problematic behaviors, long-term goals, short-term goals, and specific interventions are often used in inpatient settings to coordinate treatment among these diverse groups of professionals.

Children who require longer term, intensive treatment can be placed in a **residential treatment facility.** Residential treatment facilities are usually located away from a hospital setting and are often housed in a less-populated area of a city (e.g., in the rural outskirts of a city or in a suburb). Residential treatment facilities tend to work with children for long periods of time (sometimes years), during which children cannot function in a less-restrictive environment and cannot live at home. Residential treatment facilities provide a structured, therapeutic environment and also attend to children's academic and educational needs (e.g., Lyons, Uziel-Miller, Reyes, & Sokol, 2000).

Residential treatment facilities usually house relatively large numbers of children, whereas **group homes** and **therapeutic foster care homes** tend to provide comparable services to smaller numbers of children in a homelike environment. Both group homes and therapeutic foster care homes are often run by a small number of staff (sometimes just two adults), who try to run the homes in a comfortable but structured manner (Chamberlain & Smith, 2005). The biggest difference between group homes and therapeutic foster care homes is that children in the foster care system have either temporarily or permanently been separated from their biological parents through the child protective process. In an interesting study that investigated the impact of family reunification of children in therapeutic foster care, children who were reunified with their biological parent or parents were shown to experience an increase in adverse life events, which was correlated with an increase in emotional/behavioral problems (Lau, Litrownik, Newton, & Landsverk, 2003). In addition, children received fewer mental health services after reunifying with their biological family. Overall, the relation between child functioning and family reunification is complex. In addition, as with so many treatment options for children, the quality of group homes and therapeutic foster care homes varies greatly, from therapeutic to harmful. State agencies monitor and license both types of homes, but there is still a great need for improvement in many of these homes.

For children who are discharged from an inpatient setting or a residential treatment facility, but who are still in need of intensive services, **day hospitals** (also known as day treatment) can be utilized. A day hospital, or day program, can be used for children who are able to live at home with their own family, but who require relatively structured and therapeutic activities during the day. Most often, day hospital programs are used to transition children from an inpatient setting to an outpatient setting (e.g., Milin, Coupland, Walker, & Fisher-Bloom, 2000). One study found that children in day hospitals and those receiving treatment on an inpatient unit showed the highest levels of psychological impairment when compared with children receiving services in an outpatient setting (McDermott, McKelvey, Roberts, & Davies, 2002).

One of the most common sites of therapeutic intervention is the **outpatient setting.** When children live with their own family, but need some type of therapeutic intervention, they can obtain services at an outpatient setting. Examples of outpatient settings include community mental health centers, private practice or independent practice offices, and child guidance centers. Children, adolescents, and families can receive therapy or counseling from psychologists, psychiatrists, counselors, or social workers in an outpatient setting. Note that effective treatment can be provided in the public health care system (Xue, Hodges, & Wotring, 2004), but children who remain in the home rather than receiving out-of-home care were less likely to receive therapeutic services (Leslie et al., 2005). As noted in Box 4.4, children appear to be referred for services differentially,

BOX 4.4

WHO RECEIVES SERVICES?

A number of children, adolescents, and families need help for psychological problems but never receive any professional help. One study suggested that at least 17% of children and adolescents who experienced severe psychopathology never received any professional interventions for their problems (Flisher, Kramer, Grosser, et al., 1997). Many researchers have compared characteristics of children and adolescents who receive services with those youngsters who do not receive services (Flisher, Kramer, Grosser, et al., 1997; Goodman et al., 1997; Howard & Hodes, 2000; Leslie et al., 2003). In a national study of nearly 1,300 children and adolescents (Goodman et al., 1997), the researchers found that children who received services:

- Experienced higher levels of psychopathology
- Showed lower levels of competence
- Were more likely to have more than one disorder (i.e., showed comorbid disorders)
- Were more likely to be Caucasian (non-Hispanic/Latino/Latina) Americans
- Were less likely to be prepubertal girls

- Tended to have parents who were more educated, more dissatisfied with their family functioning, less involved in monitoring their children's behavior, and more likely to have received mental health treatment themselves

These findings suggest that more work is needed to reach out to children and adolescents who require services. The fact that children who received services were more disturbed and had more comorbid disorders does suggest that some of the neediest children are receiving services. Other factors (such as race/ethnicity and parental factors), however, suggest that there may be biases in the referral systems for children or conversely may suggest that mental health professionals need to make themselves more available to those who have not typically accessed their services (Goodman et al., 1997). Similar to this study, another study of psychotropic medication use showed that African-American and Latino/Latina children were less likely to be prescribed medication for emotional/behavioral problems than were Caucasian children (Leslie et al., 2003). Thus, there appear to be disparities between racial/ethnic groups in the ways that mental health services are rendered.

depending on their emotional/behavioral problems, gender, race/ethnicity, and parental characteristics.

Increasing numbers of children are also receiving mental health services in the school system. These **school-based mental health services** are often funded through public monies that have been set aside for the mental health needs of children. Both assessments and therapeutic interventions can be conducted in the school setting (Breen & Fiedler, 2003; Millman, Schaefer, & Cohen, 2004; Rathvon, 1999; Shapiro et al., 2002). School psychologists, clinical psychologists, social workers, and other mental health professionals all conduct therapy and counseling for students who need help for emotional/behavioral difficulties. The advantage of school-based mental health services is that the services can be administered without relying on the parent (e.g., for transportation) and can be available to many children in need of services (Weist, Evans, & Lever, 2003). One study of clinically referred children found that parents were more likely to follow through on recommendations regarding school-based interventions in comparison to recommendations regarding professional clinic-based interventions (MacNaughton & Rodrigue, 2001). A disadvantage of school-based mental health services is that, too often, treatment only focuses on the child rather than other factors such as the family or environment (Logan & King, 2001).

An increasing number of public mental health dollars are being targeted for school-based mental health services with the goal of reaching as many troubled children as possible (Martin, 2005). A number of evidence-based interventions have been shown to be effective in the school setting (Vernberg, Jacobs, Nyre, Puddy, & Roberts, 2004; Weiss, Harris, Catron, & Han, 2003; Wilson, Lipsey, & Derzon, 2003). In addition, many prevention programs are housed within the school setting in order to prevent problems from occurring in children and adolescents (August, Egan, Realmuto, & Hektner, 2003; Christenson & Thurlow, 2004; Farrell, Meyer, Kung, & Sullivan, 2001; Greenberg et al., 2003; Weissberg, 2000).

There is no one setting that appears more advantageous than any other (Bickman et al., 1995; Bickman, Lambert, Andrade, & Penaloza, 2000). All these settings have been found to be potentially therapeutic for children and adolescents (Kutash & Rivera, 1996). Throughout all these settings, a diverse array of therapeutic interventions can be conducted. Although the settings differ significantly, it is possible for similar types of therapies to be conducted in varying settings. Therapeutic interventions range from psychodynamic, behavioral,

"You always get to be the therapist! I never get to be the therapist!"

cognitive–behavioral, family systems, and psychopharmacological interventions.

Fortunately [psycho]analysis is not the only way to resolve inner conflicts. Life itself still remains a very effective therapist.

—Karen Horney

PSYCHODYNAMIC THERAPIES

Although psychodynamic therapies are relevant from a historical perspective, they have received very little empirical support for their effectiveness (Roberts, Vernberg, & Jackson, 2000; Russ, 1998; Target & Fonagy, 1998; Weiss, Catron, & Harris, 2000). There is some indication that more well-designed studies may uncover effective therapeutic processes via psychodynamic theories for internalizing disorders (Muratori, Picchi, Bruni, Patarnello, & Romagnoli, 2003). Because there is not a large of body of empirical evidence to support the use of psychodynamic therapies, they are not discussed at length in this book. Long-term psychoanalysis, which provided the foundation of many psychodynamic therapies that were developed initially by Sigmund Freud, tends not to be used with children and adolescents (Target & Fonagy, 1998). Many play therapies are based on the same principles (e.g., working through transference onto the therapist, dealing with unconscious conflicts and

Although play therapy has not received a great deal of empirical support, therapists can use empirically supported treatments within the context of the playroom setting.

motivations) and are used more frequently with children and young adolescents (Reddy, Files-Hall, & Schaefer, 2005; Roberts et al., 2000).

Play therapy is a type of therapy in which the child is exposed to many toys, dolls, and activities in which to engage while the therapist observes and interacts with the child. The primary rationale behind play therapy is that the modality of "playing" allows children to act out their psychological issues through play and allows them to speak more freely about their concerns with the therapist (Reddy et al., 2005).

Although play therapy per se has not received a great deal of empirical support (Roberts et al., 2000), it is possible for play to be incorporated into other more effective modalities. For example, behavioral therapies, cognitive behavioral therapies, and even family therapies can integrate play into sessions that continue to focus

on behavior change (Knell, 1998). One meta-analysis showed that play therapy was most effective when parents were involved and when there were at least 30 to 35 sessions (LeBlanc & Ritchie, 1999). These findings were supported by another comprehensive meta-analysis (Bratton, Ray, Rhine, & Jones, 2005). In addition, child therapy appears to be most effective when parents have a strong connection with the therapist (Nevas & Farber, 2001). Overall, however, psychodynamic therapies with children have not been shown to be effective by any rigorous or well-controlled study, and thus are not a good choice for trying to help children (Roberts et al., 2000). Across many different therapeutic orientations, children and adolescents need to feel comfortable talking about their sexual orientation if they wish (see Box 4.5).

BEHAVIORAL THERAPIES

Behavioral therapies can be broken down into two broad categories: child-oriented interventions and parent-oriented interventions. In general, most behavioral therapies rely on behavioral principles that have been well established.

Child-Oriented Interventions

The purest form of behavioral therapy with individual children is known as **applied behavior analysis** (see www.abainternational.org for the Web site of the Association for Behavior Analysis). Applied behavior analysis usually uses functional assessment to identify the problematic behaviors and then relies primarily on operant conditioning principles to change the problematic behaviors (Chandler & Dahlquist, 2005; Lutzker & Whitaker, 2005; Wolery, Barton, & Hine, 2005). There is a great deal of focus on the antecedents (i.e., what comes before) and the consequences (i.e., what comes after) observable behavior. Table 4.10 provides a list of definitions of concepts that are used extensively in applied behavior analysis and in more complex behavioral therapies.

In addition to these basic behavioral techniques, other more complex behavioral techniques have been used in behavior therapy. **Token economies** (known by many parents as "star charts") are usually used to increase adaptive behaviors. Children are given a small list of behaviors that are to be accomplished each day (e.g., make your bed, set the table for dinner, and brush your teeth at night). For each behavior they accomplish, they receive a token (e.g., a poker chip) or a "star" or other visual indication is written next to the behavior for that

BOX 4.5

HELPING CHILDREN AND ADOLESCENTS WITH THEIR SEXUAL ORIENTATION

Although there is no single therapy designed to help children and adolescents who are struggling with their sexual orientation, a number of issues need to be addressed with these children and adolescents (Division 44, 2000; Savin-Williams & Diamond, 1999). Homosexuality used to be considered a psychiatric disorder in and of itself (American Psychiatric Association, 1968), but it has not been a disorder for over 30 years. In fact, most professionals now believe that homosexuality is a natural part of human diversity.

Little is known about children and adolescents who are dealing with their sexual orientation, but there is a growing empirical literature to help guide work with these youngsters. Children and adolescents who must deal with their sexual orientation, or who have clearly identified themselves as homosexual, have different difficulties in adjustments than youngsters who are not dealing with these issues (Lock & Steiner, 1999). For example, gay male and lesbian youth are more at risk for verbal and physical abuse, both at home and at school, which is associated with greater risk for psychological difficulties (Savin-Williams, 1994). Compared with their heterosexual siblings, lesbian, gay, and bisexual youth reported significantly more childhood psychological and physical abuse by parents and more childhood sexual abuse (Balsam, Rothblum, & Beauchaine, 2005). In a comprehensive review of research, Meyer (2003) found that prevalence rates for nearly all mental disorders were higher in gay, lesbian, and bisexual populations, but these higher rates were thought to be associated with minority stress (e.g., stigma, prejudice, and discrimination).

Not all outcomes are negative, however, for gay children and adolescents. For example, when youth come out to their parents, they are more likely to confide in their mother than their father, and they are likely to receive either supportive or slightly negative reactions (Savin-Williams & Ream, 2003a). Parent–youth relationships tended to remain the same after disclosure or were reported to be better by the adolescents (Savin-Williams & Ream, 2003a). Many gay, lesbian, and bisexual youth have happy, fulfilled lives and do not show heightened risk for mental disorders (Savin-Williams, 2001a, 2001b, 2005). One of the lead researchers in this area, Dr. Ritch Savin-Williams, is quoted in *Time Magazine* as saying that the studies he has done of hundreds of gay, lesbian, and bisexual youth suggest that they "are more diverse than they are similar and more resilient than suicidal. . . . They're adapting quite well, thank you" (Cloud, 2005, p.48).

When gay, lesbian, and bisexual children and adolescents are struggling psychologically, they often seek therapy to deal with issues of:

- Feelings of differentness
- Disclosure to others of their feelings of differentness
- Whether or not to "come out" to different individuals (including parents, friends, and teachers)
- Social and cultural ramifications of being different
- Finding supportive and trusted allies (including parents, friends, and teachers)

These and other issues may be central themes in dealing with youngsters who are dealing with their sexual orientation. Conversely, it is possible to work with a gay male, lesbian, or bisexual youth who has concerns that are irrelevant to their sexual orientation (Savin-Williams & Diamond, 1999). Thus, it is important for therapists to be prepared to deal with issues of sexual orientation with children and adolescents, but not to focus solely on a youngster's sexual orientation. Interested readers are referred to the "Guidelines for Psychotherapy with Lesbian, Gay, and Bisexual Clients," which has a section on working with lesbian, gay, and bisexual youth (Division 44, 2000) or to a book in the popular press called *The New Gay Teenager* (Savin-Williams, 2005).

---

day. Children can then "cash in" these tokens or stars after a predetermined period of time (e.g., 10 tokens equals getting one extra book read at bedtime). Token economies work best if they are simple enough for the child to understand, if the rewards and consequences to behaviors are clear and followed consistently, and if the rewards are truly desirable to the child.

Overall, behavioral therapies and applied behavior analysis are very effective for a number of behavioral problems in children and adolescents (Houts, 2003; Lovaas & Smith, 2003; Lutzker & Whitaker, 2005). One of the clear advantages to behavioral therapies and applied behavior analysis is the ease with which these techniques can be used in the school setting as well as in the home setting (Chandler & Dahlquist, 2005).

Always obey your parents, when they are present.

—Mark Twain

TABLE 4.10 Definitions of Basic Behavioral Concepts

Techniques Used to Strengthen or Increase Adaptive Behaviors

- **Reinforcement:** By definition, reinforcement occurs when a behavior is strengthened or increased after administration of the reinforcer. Most often, the term *positive reinforcement* is used to signify the application of a pleasant reward (such as a smile, pat on the back, token, or food item). Behaviors must already be in the child's repertoire before they can be reinforced.

- **Prompting:** If the desired behavior does not yet exist, prompting can be used to teach the new behavior. Prompting can be in the form of physical prompts (e.g., a parent guides a child's hand with a spoon full of food to the child's mouth), verbal prompts (e.g., a teacher tells a child with a reading problem to sound the word out first before attempting the word), or visual prompts (e.g., a picture of the dog's food dish is put on the refrigerator to remind the child to feed the dog).

- **Shaping:** Reinforcement of successive approximations to the final desired behavior.

- **Chaining:** For complex behaviors, each step in the behavior is taught and then linked to the next step of the behavior (e.g., a child learning to tie her shoes is first taught to pull the laces tight, then to make a loop out of one of the laces, etc.).

- **Modeling:** Desirable behaviors are demonstrated for the child (either by the therapist, by another child, or via videotape) to teach the child the desired behavior.

Techniques Used to Weaken or Decrease Maladaptive Behaviors

- **Differential reinforcement of incompatible, alternative, or other behavior:** Behaviors that are contrary to the maladaptive behavior are reinforced to decrease the maladaptive behavior (e.g., to decrease out-of-seat behavior, a teacher might verbally reward a boy any time he is working on his academic activities at his desk).

- **Extinction:** The eventual disappearance of a problematic behavior because of the withdrawal of rewards that were maintaining the behavior.

- **Time-Out:** In its truest form, time-out is used to remove the child from any reinforcers that are maintaining the maladaptive behavior (e.g., if the child is getting attention for throwing a tantrum, which inadvertently increases the likelihood of tantrums, then time-out would be used to ignore the child's tantrum and to remove the child from any reinforcers for the tantrum).

- **Punishment:** Two methods of punishment are common—the removal of a positive reinforcer (which is also known as response cost; e.g., losing dessert if children do not eat their vegetables) and the administration of an aversive stimulus (e.g., spanking or yelling at a child after a maladaptive behavior).

Source: Hudson (1998).

Parent-Oriented Interventions

Many of the behavioral techniques that were just discussed have been integrated into what is known as **behavioral parent training** (Barkley, 1997b; McMahon & Forehand, 2003). Behavioral parent training is used primarily for children aged 2 to 11, and the treatment is actually administered to the parents. This treatment is most effective with oppositional, aggressive, and antisocial behavior in children (Kazdin, 2005b). In addition to the work with younger children, behavioral parent training programs have also been developed for parents of adolescents (Barkley, Edwards, & Robin, 1999). Behavioral parent training is often administered in a limited number of sessions (e.g., 10 sessions) with parents, and these therapy sessions focus on the following concepts (Barkley, 1997b; Barkley et al., 1999; Webster-Stratton & Hooven, 1998):

- Paying attention to and rewarding good behavior (sometimes parents who think that their children never show good behavior are instructed to "catch their child being good")

- Ignoring bad behavior (if feasible and if it does not endanger the child or another person)

- Allow natural consequences to occur when possible and feasible (e.g., playing roughly with the cat may lead to a natural consequence of getting scratched, which may decrease the likelihood of the child playing roughly with the cat in the future)

- Model appropriate behavior (e.g., if parents want their children to stop yelling all the time, they should examine their own way of communicating to make sure that they are not inadvertently modeling maladaptive behavior)

- Provide consistent and known consequences to behavior (with the idea that consistency includes different situations, by different parents and caretakers, at different times of the day, and no matter what "different" mood the parent is experiencing at the time)

Token economies, such as star charts, are often effective in helping children increase adaptive behaviors.

- Anticipate problem behavior and plan for how it will be handled (e.g., if parents take children grocery shopping and the children always run wild through the aisles, make contingencies for this behavior that are known to the children before they enter the store)
- Follow through on consequences that are established and do not make idle threats that cannot be completed (e.g., "If you don't buckle your seat belt right now, I will never drive you anywhere again.")
- Limited use of punishments (if any)

Behavioral parent training is extraordinarily effective in reducing externalizing behaviors in children, with especially good results for children diagnosed with oppositional defiant disorder (Gross et al., 2003; Sanders, Markie-Dadds, Tully, & Bor, 2000; Webster-Stratton & Hooven, 1998) and AD/HD (Barkley, 1997b, 2006). Better therapeutic outcomes are shown when parents have a good therapeutic alliance with the therapist (Kazdin & Whitley, 2006b). These interventions have been found to be effective with many family constellations, including single and divorcing mothers (Martinez & Forgatch, 2001) and mothers in a battered women's shelter (Jouriles et al., 2001).

A related treatment is known as Parent-Child Interaction Therapy (PCIT), which focuses on the attachment between parent and child and helps parents to develop parenting skills that are healthy and that can be worked into the family routine (Brinkmeyer & Eyberg, 2003).

PCIT has been found to be effective in reducing oppositional behavior in preschoolers (Nixon, Sweeney, Erickson, & Touyz, 2004) and in reducing reports of physical abuse by parents involved in therapy (Chaffin et al., 2004). Long-term gains from PCIT are evident 6 years after treatment (Hood & Eyberg, 2003) and appear to be strengthened by including both fathers and mothers in treatment (Bagner & Eyberg, 2003).

Note also that across many therapeutic interventions, a strong therapeutic alliance (i.e., a supportive connection between therapists and clients) is related to treatment gains. In particular, a strong parent–therapist alliance is related to fewer cancellations, fewer no-shows, and more frequent family participation in child therapy sessions (Hawley & Weisz, 2005). Based on specific studies (Hawley & Weisz, 2005; McLeod & Weisz, 2005) as well as comprehensive meta-analytic studies (Shirk & Karver, 2003) and reviews (Shirk & Karver, 2006), child–therapist alliance is related to improvements in children's and adolescents' emotional/behavioral functioning.

COGNITIVE–BEHAVIORAL THERAPIES

Cognitive–behavioral therapies are comparable to behavioral therapies given the emphasis on behavior change. The difference between these two types of therapy is that cognitive–behavioral therapy focuses on both cognitions and behaviors. The cognitive–behavioral approach pre-supposes that cognitions (i.e., private thoughts experienced by the client) can influence behavior and learning such that behavioral change can occur predominantly through altered cognitions, and that children's and adolescents' behavior and cognitions are "reciprocally determined" such that they are related, and when one is changed the other is likely to change (Finch, Nelson, & Moss, 1993).

Given the focus on both cognitions and behaviors, it makes sense that many of the specific intervention strategies focus on both cognitions and behaviors. There are a diverse array of strategies that are used within cognitive–behavioral therapies (Hart & Morgan, 1993), including

- Cognitive modeling (clients are taught to change their cognitions by observing a model who is verbalizing appropriate cognitions and thought processes)
- Self-instruction (clients are trained to alter self-statements before and after a difficult situation by using contingent consequences or modeling)
- Cognitive restructuring (clients are taught to replace irrational beliefs and faulty thought patterns with adaptive cognitions through logical analyses of the irrational beliefs and thoughts)
- Cognitive problem solving (clients are taught to deal with stressors by preparing for these stressors and by using such techniques as self-instruction, self-monitoring, and cognitive rehearsal)

As can be seen in Figure 4.6, most cognitive–behavioral therapies focus on a number of points of intervention, including the stimulus (e.g., what precedes the cognition or behavior), the organism's internal reaction (e.g., the cognition), the response (e.g., the behavior), and the consequence (e.g., what happens after the behavior; Elliott, Busse, & Shapiro, 1999). This **Stimulus-Organism-Response-Consequence (S-O-R-C) model** highlights a number of places for possible intervention.

Cognitive–behavioral therapies have been used for a wide variety of emotional/behavioral problems, including depression (Curry & Reinecke, 2003; Rohde, Lewinsohn, Clarke, Hops, & Seeley, 2005), anxiety (Compton et al., 2004; Kendall et al., 2005; Velting, Setzer, & Albano, 2004), obsessive–compulsive disorder (March, Franklin, Foa, 2005), impulsivity and hyperactivity (Anastopoulos, Barkley, & Sheldon, 1996; Kendall & Braswell, 1993), aggression (Finch, Nelson, & Moss, 1993; Webster-Stratton, 1993), body image and eating disorders (Bowers, Evans, LeGrange, & Andersen,

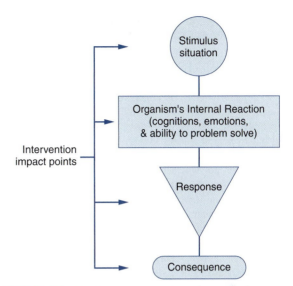

FIGURE 4.6 The Stimulus-Organism-Response-Consequence (S-O-R-C) model of behavior with intervention impact points.

Source: Elliott et al. (1999).

2003), low self-esteem (Shirk, Burwell, & Harter, 2003), and limited social skills (LeCroy, 1994). In general, cognitive–behavioral therapies are quite effective in treating children's and adolescents' emotional/behavioral problems (Schroeder & Gordon, 2002). Characteristics that improve the possibility of effective cognitive–behavioral therapy include a focus on generalizing the newly acquired skills to multiple situations (e.g., trying to generalize the skills to both the home and school environments), integrating naturally occurring reinforcers into the treatment, and finding ways to provide maintenance of the newly acquired skills (Kendall et al., 1998). A number of cognitive–behavioral therapies also include parents in the treatment so that parents become another agent of change (Barmish & Kendall, 2005). Cognitive–behavioral techniques can also be used with individual child clients or in a group therapy setting with a number of children addressing similar clinical problems (Evans & Sullivan, 1993). Overall, cognitive–behavioral therapies are very promising for the treatment of a wide array of children's and adolescents' emotional/behavioral problems.

Parentage is a very important profession, but no test of fitness for it is ever imposed in the interest of the children.
—George Bernard Shaw

Case Study: Cognitive–Behavioral Treatment of Impulsivity

Adam is an 11-year-old boy who was diagnosed with AD/HD. Although he was receiving medication to control his behavior, he remained relatively impulsive. In school, he blurted out answers and interrupted others. The impulsivity was especially noticeable in social situations, during which Adam would push other children and try to grab the ball from others during team sports. Partly because of these behaviors, Adam had no friends nor was he sought out as a playmate by any of his classmates. In order to address these problems with impulsivity, Adam was referred to a psychologist for a cognitive–behavioral treatment known as self-instructional training (Kendall & Braswell, 1993).

The treatment began by teaching Adam five self-instructions to be used when facing a difficult or unique situation. The self-instructional statements are as follows (with the concept that they represent noted in parentheses):

- "Let's see, what am I supposed to do?" (Problem Definition)
- "I have to look at all the possibilities." (Problem Approach)
- "I better concentrate and focus in, and think only of what I'm doing right now." (Focusing of Attention)
- "I think it's this one . . ." (Choosing an Answer)

- Either: "Hey, not bad. I really did a good job" (Self-Reinforcement) or "Oh, I made a mistake. Next time I'll try to go slower and concentrate more and maybe I'll get the right answer." (Coping Statement)

These five "steps" were first said out loud by Adam and then eventually were faded into thoughts that Adam would review in future circumstances. After Adam learned these steps, he practiced and rehearsed them with the therapist. The therapist also modeled self-control in role-play situations in the therapy sessions (e.g., the therapist would play a young child, then be exposed to a stressor such as another child stealing the basketball, then would talk through the steps and make choices accordingly while Adam was watching). This treatment also included behavioral contingencies (both self-reward for a job well done and social rewards from the therapist).

After 20 sessions of treatment, Adam showed significant decreases in his impulsivity and showed greater engagement in friendship networks. By the end of treatment, he was being invited to sleep over at a friend's house, was asked by his classmates to join them on a bicycle trip, and showed significant improvement in his schoolwork.

Source: Kendall & Braswell (1993).

Family therapists see the problem as residing in the family system—not just in the child.

FAMILY SYSTEMS THERAPIES

Family systems therapies are based on family systems theories that suggest children's emotional/behavioral problems are only a reflection of problems within the family system (Kaslow, 2001; Nichols & Schwartz, 2004). The term **identified problem** (or identified

patient) is often used to signify the child whose problem was the impetus for treatment. Most family therapists will only work with children when their family is also willing to be involved in therapy. Some effective family therapies focus on the family management skills of the parents (such as supervising their children's or adolescents' activities, providing appropriate discipline, and creating opportunities for positive parent-youngster activities), in addition to overall family functioning (Eddy & Chamberlain, 2000). Other effective family therapies focus on developing a healthy attachment between the parent and adolescent (Diamond, Reis, Diamond, Siqueland, & Isaacs, 2002). As can be seen in Box 4.6, involving both parents in family therapy can be a challenge.

Overall, family therapy is effective with treatment of children's emotional/behavioral problems (Diamond & Josephson, 2005). Multisystemic treatment, which focuses on helping empower parents to alter their adolescents' antisocial behaviors, has been found to be very effective in working with antisocial adolescents (Curtis, Ronan, & Borduin, 2004). In addition, success has been found when children's emotional/behavioral problems are related to or are exacerbated by difficulties within

BOX *4.6*

ARE FATHERS INCLUDED IN THERAPY FOR CHILD AND ADOLESCENT PROBLEMS?

Like research on family issues, therapy for children's emotional/behavioral problems has a long history of blaming mothers and ignoring fathers (Phares, 1999). One survey of clinicians found that fathers were only included in 30% of therapy sessions, whereas mothers were included in 59% of the sessions (Duhig, Phares, & Birkeland, 2002). This pattern was true for dual-parent families and families headed by single mothers. The remainder of the sessions involved only the individual child. Other studies have found that clinicians are more likely to include fathers in therapy sessions if they are male, hold more egalitarian beliefs, are newer on the job, have more academic work in family

therapy, are employed by an agency that supported parental involvement in treatment, and when they are able to offer flexible scheduling for appointments, including evening and weekend appointments (reviewed in Phares, Fields, & Binitie, 2006). Thus, is appears that sometimes personal characteristics of clinicians have more to do with who is included in therapy than the needs of the family.

Overall, there is a need for therapists to at least consider including fathers in therapy for children's emotional/behavioral difficulties. We must remain vigilant about considering the fathers' role in both the development and treatment of psychopathology in children and adolescents.

---

the family (such as interparental conflict). As is obvious from the connections between interparental conflict and children's emotional/behavioral problems, family therapy or couples therapy that decreases interparental conflict is likely to reduce children's emotional/behavioral problems (Garber, 2004; Gurman, 2001). Family therapy has also been found to ameliorate problems related to child custody disputes (Lebow, 2003).

Most family therapists agree about the importance of acknowledging families' cultural orientation, including issues regarding ethnicity, race, religion, country of origin, level of acculturation, and preferred mode of communication (Hall & Barongan, 2002; McGoldrick, Giordano, & Garcia-Preto, 2005). Across all therapies, including family therapy, Sue (2003) argues that cultural competence and an understanding of similarities and

differences across cultures need to be a focus of effective treatment. Efforts have been made, for example, to establish effective treatments for African-American families (Boyd-Franklin, 2003) and to provide culturally sensitive interventions in the school setting (Frisby & Reynolds, 2005). Note that there are other considerations while conducting culturally informed interventions. As an example, Table 4.11 highlights information about traditional Korean values and mainstream American values that would be important to know when working with a Korean American who had difficulty integrating these two cultures. Cultural issues have been highlighted for family therapists in the United States (Kaslow, 2001), as well as for family therapists in a diverse array of countries, including Israel (Halpern, 2001), the Virgin Islands (Dudley-Grant, 2001), and Japan (Kameguchi

TABLE 4.11   Korean versus American Values

Korean Traditional Values	American Mainstream Values
Family Values	
Family-centered	Individual-oriented
Interdependency	Autonomy and independence
Vertical, authoritarian structure	Horizontal, democratic structure
Life Philosophy	
Collectivism	Individualism
Sense of stoicism and fatalism	Sense of optimism and opportunism
Reciprocity and obligation	Avoidance of obligation
Communication Style	
Subtle, nonverbal, body language	Emphasis on verbal language
Control of feelings	Free expression of feelings
Little eye-to-eye contact	Eye contact important

Source: Adapted from Kim, Kim, & Rue (1997).

& Murphy-Shigematsu, 2001). In general, good family therapy with ethnically diverse clients looks very similar to good family therapy with clients from the same cultural background as the therapist (Paniagua, 1998). It is imperative, however, that family therapists, as well as all other therapists, be alert to issues of culture that may impact on the therapeutic process (Hall & Barongan, 2002; McGoldrick et al., 2005; Paniagua, 1998).

> As our children grow, so must we grow to meet their changing emotional, intellectual, and designer-footwear needs.
>
> —Dave Barry

PSYCHOPHARMACOLOGICAL INTERVENTIONS

In addition to the many psychotherapies and behavioral therapies that are available for children, adolescents, and their families, there are also a number of **psychopharmacological interventions** (i.e., medications) that can help alleviate problematic symptoms of developmental psychopathology. Although only physicians (such as psychiatrists or developmental pediatricians) can prescribe medications, it is incumbent on child therapists and researchers to be informed about medications for children's emotional/behavioral problems (Brown, Carpenter, & Simerly, 2005; DuPaul, McGoey, & Mautone, 2003; Khusman, 2001). Note, however, that the information presented here should not be used as medical advice. If you or someone you care about has questions about medications, please consult a physician directly.

During psychological assessments, it is not uncommon for the assessor to recommend some type of therapy in addition to a medical evaluation for the appropriateness of medication. Many of the most common medications used to treat children's emotional/behavioral problems are listed in Table 4.12.

The medications that are noted as clinically validated in double-blind studies have been tested when the physician, parents, and child or adolescent do not know whether the pill has active medication in it or if it is a placebo. This type of investigation is considered the gold standard in testing pharmaceutical interventions because children or parents may sometimes report improvements just due to the administration of a pill (Phelps, Brown, & Power, 2002). The use of placebos allows a comparison between the child's behavior on active medication with the child's behavior on placebo. Thus, when medications are found to be effective after

double-blind studies, physicians can assume that the behavioral improvements are due to the medication rather than just the expectations of improvements that could have been shown with a placebo.

As with any type of intervention, there are pros and cons to taking medications for children's and adolescents' emotional/behavioral problems. The advantages of medication center around the effectiveness rates and ease of administration (as opposed to more involved psychosocial therapies). It is estimated that over 6% of children and adolescents in the United States are receiving some type of psychiatric medication (DeAngelis, 2004). As the names imply, **antidepressants** are usually used to treat depression, **anxiolytics** (i.e., antianxiety medications) are used to treat symptoms of anxiety; **antipsychotic medications** are used to treat hallucinations, delusions, and other symptoms of schizophrenia; and **stimulants** are used to overactivity and inattention. Of those classes of medications, antipsychotic medications and psychostimulant medications have received the strongest empirical support for use with children and adolescents experiencing schizophrenia and AD/HD, respectively (McClellan & Werry, 2003; Patel et al., 2005; Root & Resnick, 2003; Richmond & Rosen, 2005). Although antipsychotic medications are effective at treating symptoms of schizophrenia, there are a number of potentially severe side effects (such as **tardive dyskinesia,** which is a permanent condition where the child makes repetitive stereotypical movements such as facial grimaces). Thus, antipsychotic medication should only be used in the most severe cases of schizophrenia and should be monitored closely (Patel et al., 2005).

With regard to stimulants, there is a great deal of evidence that stimulants (prescribed primarily for AD/HD) are effective in enhancing children's and adolescents' concentration, attention, and behavioral control (Root & Resnick, 2003). There is mixed evidence, however, regarding whether stimulants can decrease the aggressive behavior that is often associated with AD/HD (Root & Resnick, 2003). Stimulants do not appear to help academic functioning significantly (Root & Resnick, 2003). As effective as stimulants appear to be, there is evidence that approximately 80% of children with AD/HD show improved functioning while taking a psychostimulant, whereas 20% show either no improvement or show decreased levels of functioning (Rowland et al., 2002; Wilens et al., 2002). Of all of these medications, stimulants continue to receive the most rigorous and careful empirical investigation. Ironically, there is concern that stimulants should not be used with adults given that there are few studies to

Case Study: Family Therapy for Michael's Aggression

Brian (aged 8), Michael (aged 9), and Robert (aged 10) all lived with their mother (Jane Smith) and stepfather (Jeff Smith). Mr. Smith used to abuse Mrs. Smith physically, and both parents have a history of spanking the boys severely as a method of punishment. Michael was the identified problem (IP) in that he often showed aggression, impulsivity, and explosiveness when he was told what to do by his parents. Michael's problems emerged at around the same time Mr. Smith joined the family. Michael's behavioral outbursts became so severe that he was admitted to a psychiatric hospital three times in the preceding two years. During each hospitalization, he showed significant improvement in the hospital and then deteriorated rapidly when placed back in the family home.

The therapists hypothesized that Michael's aggression served a function in the family so that Mr. Smith would not abuse Mrs. Smith (e.g., Mr. and Mrs. Smith allied against Michael and hit him for his transgressions, which may have alleviated Mr. Smith's desire to hit Mrs. Smith). As part of therapeutic process, the therapists tried to help the children gain a "voice" in this family and tried to reunify the parents so that the children were not between them. In addition, the parents were referred to couples therapy so that the history of domestic violence could be dealt with separately from the children. Family therapy was continued to ensure that the children were disengaged from their parents' troubled relationship.

Source: Kemenoff, Jachimczyk, & Fussner (1998, pp. 119–120).

---

assess their effectiveness with adults (Consumer Reports Best Buy Drugs, 2005).

There are a number of potential drawbacks to the use of medication for treating emotional/behavioral problems in children and adolescents. The most salient drawback is the possibility of side effects from the medications. All the medications listed in Table 4.12 have the possibility of side effects, which range from mild irritants to serious and life-threatening problems. Table 4.13 lists the medications that are considered so dangerous with children and adolescents that they should either not be prescribed at all or should only be used as a medication of last resort (Phelps et al., 2002). Ironically, some of these medications have been validated through double-blind clinical trials for certain disorders. For example, Clomipramine (Anafranil) and Imipramine (Tofranil), both of which are tricyclic medications, have been found to be effective in double-blind studies with children and adolescents. Specifically, Clomiprimine (Anafranil) has been found to be effective in the treatment of obsessive–compulsive disorder and depression, whereas Imipramine (Tofranil) has been found to be effective in treating enuresis (Phelps et al., 2002). Similarly, Clozapine (Clozaril) has been found to be effective through double-blind trials in the treatment of drug-resistant schizophrenia, and nortriptylin (Aventyl, Pamelor) has been shown to be effective in the treatment of ADHD). These medications, however, have serious enough side effects that the health risks may be too large compared to the benefits of behavioral improvements. Other medications, such as Fenfluramine (Pondimin, Ponderex), which were used to treat the symptoms of autism, have been removed from the market because of the serious, irreversible, and potentially fatal side effects.

Given all the potential side effects for the medications listed in Tables 4.12 and 4.13, physicians and parents must weigh the benefits of the medication against the potential side effects of the medication (Richmond & Rosen, 2005). Notably, some medications are used that have not even been tested with children and adolescents or that have been tested but are found to be ineffective. For example, Amitriptyline (Elavil, Etrafon, Limbitrol, Triavil) appears to be effective and safe in the treatment of depression in adults, but is not effective or safe for children (Phelps et al., 2002). Child psychiatrists and pediatricians can consult a number of resources to choose the most effective and safe treatment for children. For example, there are treatment guidelines and consensus statements for a number of childhood disorders, including ADHD (American Academy of Pediatrics, 2001; National Institutes of Health, 2000), depression (Treatment for Adolescents With Depression Study Team, 2004), bipolar disorder (Kowatch et al., 2005), OCD (The Pediatric OCD Treatment Study Team, 2004), and substance abuse (American Academy of Child and Adolescent Psychiatry, 2005), that provide decision trees and conclusions on the most effective and safest course of treatment. Overall, physicians and parents must monitor children's behavior closely to identify any adverse effects from medications as soon as those effects appear. It should go without saying that physicians prescribing the medications should be consulted before making any changes in medications or before terminating the use of medication.

TABLE 4.12 Common Medications Used to Treat Children's and Adolescents' Emotional/Behavioral Problems

Class of Drug	Generic Name/Trade Name	Indications	Possible Side Effects
ANTIDEPRESSANTS			
Selective Serotonin	Fluoxetine/Prozac	Depression*, OCD*, ADHD*	Restlessness, insomnia, etc.
Reuptake Inhibitors (SSRI)	Sertraline/Zoloft	Depression, OCD*	Nausea, diarrhea, etc.
Atypical Antidepressant	Bupropion/Wellbutrin	ADHD*	Insomnia, dizziness, etc.
Antimanics	Lithium Carbonate/Eskalith, Lithane		
	Lithane	Bipolar*	Diarrhea, nausea, drowsiness
ANXIOLYTICS (ANTIANXIETY)			
Benzo-diazepines	Clonazepam/Klonopin	Separation anxiety* Generalized Anxiety Disorder* Panic attacks*	Drowsiness, dizziness
Others	Buspirone/BuSpar	Anxiety	Dizziness, drowsiness
ANTIPSYCHOTICS			
Phenothiazines	Thioridazine/Mellaril	Autistic Disorder*, PDD*, Schizophrenia*	Sedation, dry mouth, etc
Others	Haloperidol/Haldol	Psychotic Disorder* Developmental Disorders*	Tardive diskinesia, etc
STIMULANTS			
	Dextro-amphetamine/Dexedrine	ADHD*	Insomnia, dizziness, etc.
	Methylphenidate/Ritalin	ADHD*	Appetite suppressant, etc.
	Amphetamine & d-ampheamine compound/Adderall	ADHD*	Insomnia, dizziness, etc.

*Medication is clinically validated in double-blind studies for use with children and adolescents for that specific disorder.

Source: Adapted from Brown, Carpenter, & Simerly, 2005; DuPaul, McGoey, & Mautone (2003), and Phelps, Brown, & Power (2002).

There appear to be growing concerns about a number of psychopharmalogical interventions. In particular, there has been a great deal of concern recently over the use of antidepressants, given the greater potential for suicide in children and adolescents who are taking antidepressants (Consumer Reports, 2004). In fact, on October 15, 2004, the U.S. Food and Drug Administration (FDA) issued a "black box" warning (which is their strongest safety alert) due to the connections between the use of antidepressant medications and suicide in children and adolescents (Richmond & Rosen, 2005; see www.fda.gov/bbs/topics/news/2004/NEW01124). Specifically, a study in England found that between 2% and 3% of children and adolescents who were prescribed an antidepressant showed suicidal tendencies (Jick, Kaye, & Jick, 2004). The risk for suicide was particularly acute within the first 9 days of children and adolescents taking the antidepressant medication.

Upon further federal investigations in both the United States and in England, it became clear that Glaxo-SmithKline, the maker of Paxil, had data in 2003 to suggest that 3.4% of children aged 7 to 18 who received Paxil were at increased risk for suicide compared with 1.2% of the youth given placebo (Consumer Reports,

2004). Specifically, Glaxo-SmithKline had tested Paxil in three different studies and found adverse effects in all the studies. In addition, two of the three studies showed no therapeutic improvements to depression in children compared with placebo. Only the study that showed Paxil to be effective was published, and the increases in suicidal behavior and thoughts were referred to suicidal ideation as "emotional lability" (Consumer Reports, 2004). Because of these concerns about antidepressants, especially those known as Selective Serotonis Reuptake Inhibitors (SSRIs), a "black box" warning was mandated on 34 antidepressant medication, which means that the following warning had to be made to all customers:

Suicidality in Children and Adolescents: Antidepressants increase the risk of suicidal thinking and behavior (suicidality) in children and adolescents with major depressive disorder (MDD) and other psychiatric disorders. Anyone considering the use of [Drug Name] or any other antidepressant in a child or adolescent must balance this risk with the clinical need. Patients who are started on therapy should be observed closely for clinical worsening, suicidality, or unusual changes in behavior....

—(www.fda.gov/cder/drug/antidepressants/SSRIlabelChange)

TABLE 4.13   Medications That Should Only Be Administered to Children and Adolescents with Extreme Caution

Generic Name/Trade Name	Possible Side Effects	Previously Used For
Amitriptyline/Elavil, Etrafon, Limbitrol, Triavil	Cardiac difficulties	Depression
Clomipramine/Anafranil	Seizure, drowsiness, dizziness, tremors, headaches, dry mouth, fatigue	Depression, OCD
Clozapine/Clozaril	Potentially fatal drop in bone marrow and white blood cell counts, seizures	Schizophrenia
Desipramine/Norpramin	Cardiac complications leading to death	Anxiety disorders Depression, ADHD
Imipramine/Tofranil	Cardiac complications leading to death	Anxiety disorders Depression, ADHD
Nortriptyline/Aventyl, Pamelor	Cardiac complications, low blood pressure, drowsiness, insomnia, blurred vision	ADHD
Paroxetine/Paxil	Drowsiness, vomiting, etc.	Depression, OCD
Pemoline/Cylert	Liver failure, appetite reduction, insomnia, tics, headaches	ADHD

Source: Adapted from Brown et al. (2005), Phelps et al. (2002), and Richmond & Rosen (2005).

Given all these concerns about pharmacological interventions for children and adolescents as well as adults, the American Psychological Association has convened a task force to investigate the pros and cons of using psychotropic medication with children and adolescents (DeAngelis, 2004). In addition, books such as *Let Them Eat Prozac: The Unhealthy Relationship Between the Pharmaceutical Industry and Depression* (Healy, 2004) have been written for lay audiences to consider the issues related to the use of medications. Overall, the side effects of medications, especially in relation to children's and adolescents' self-harm, are under strong scrutiny currently (Fortune & Hawton, 2005).

A somewhat less salient, but equally important, drawback to the use of medication is the message that the medication sends to children about their problems (Hobbs, 1975; Johnston & Leung, 2001; Rappaport & Chubinsky, 2000). If children are told to take a pill to control their behavior, they may end up feeling that they have no control over their behavior themselves. An interesting study was conducted to assess children's and parents' attributions of children's behavior in relation to different types of treatment (Brown, Carpenter, & Simerly, 2005). All the children in the study received cognitive therapy to deal with externalizing problems, most of which were consistent with a diagnosis of AD/HD. In addition to the cognitive therapy that focused on self-control, children were assigned randomly to either receive no medication, active medication (Methylphenidate/Ritalin), or a placebo pill that contained no active medication. Parents and children

were later asked to report their attributions of children's abilities to control their behavior and to solve problems.

As can be seen in Figure 4.7, both parents and children tended to attribute successful behavioral control and problem solving to the child when the child was not receiving any type of pill (whether Ritalin or a placebo). Parents and children attributed success to medication when children were taking a pill, and especially when children were taking a placebo. This study suggests that the act of taking a pill (whether it is an actual medication or a placebo) can change the way in which parents and children feel about children's abilities to solve problems and control their own behavior (Borden & Brown, 1989). These external attributions for success (e.g., thinking that the medication helped the child and not giving the child credit for behavioral change) may inadvertently work against children gaining control over their behavior. It may be especially troublesome when children are removed from medication because children and parents may expect children's behavior to deteriorate without psychopharmacological interventions.

When children and adolescents are prescribed medications, there is also a strong message that the problem is within the individual (Hobbs, 1975). Unfortunately, a rush to medicate children might circumvent the possibility of identifying problems that could more effectively be treated (such as interparental conflict, ongoing abuse, learning difficulties). A thorough and thoughtful assessment of children and adolescents with emotional/behavioral problems should consider factors outside the child that may be at the root of the child's

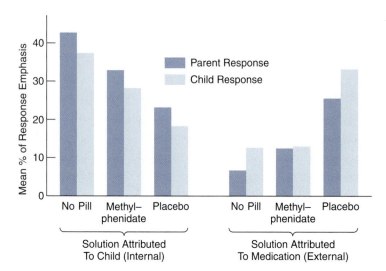

FIGURE 4.7 Similarity of parent and child attributions for the solution of child's presenting problems.

Source: Borden & Brown (1989).

behavior or that may be exacerbating the child's behavior. If medication is administered without exploring these other factors, then it is unlikely that the child's behavior will be improved in the long run (Hobbs, 1975). In addition, medications do not teach the child appropriate behaviors, they can only suppress the maladaptive behaviors.

Overall, medications are useful, especially for problems of AD/HD and schizophrenia in childhood and adolescence. Some medications, however, have potentially serious side effects. Given the potential serious adverse effects of medications, the use of medications must be considered thoughtfully and thoroughly by parents and physicians alike. In addition, medications can be used in conjunction with therapy so that behavioral changes can be instituted that will remain even after the child is removed from the active medication.

I am growing stronger and more serene each day with my therapy and my twelve-step support groups. I do believe I am "over the hill" and am on the downside of all of this. I know that I will carry scars for life, but I am growing in confidence that healing is possible.
—Karen Seal, survivor of incest (Rhodes & Rhodes, 1996; p. 341)

EFFECTIVENESS OF THERAPEUTIC INTERVENTIONS

In national surveys, the large majority of clients report that therapy helped them (Consumer Reports, 1995, 2004). So, why would any further study be required? Although this type of study was important from a consumer standpoint, it tells us little about the

effectiveness of different types of therapies. In addition, it does not provide a rigorous test of the effectiveness of therapy. It may be that any type of intervention (from therapy to reading a self-help book to playing with a puppy) could be rated as helpful, therefore, these results tell us little about the actual effectiveness of professional therapy.

The primary way in which therapies are studied is through **outcome studies.** In an outcome study, the effects of one therapy are compared with some type of control group. In order to maintain experimental control, clients with comparable psychological problems are assigned randomly to either a group who receives the therapy of interest or some type of control group. There are many types of control groups (Kendall, Flannery-Schroeder, & Ford, 1999), including

- No-treatment control groups, in which clients receive no intervention of any kind but are assessed at the same periods of time as clients in the active therapy group
- Wait-list control groups, in which clients receive no intervention at the beginning of the study, but then receive the active treatment at the completion of the study (usually 10 to 16 weeks later)
- Attention-placebo/nonspecific control groups, in which clients receive attention or some other type of contact from the therapist, but do not receive the active treatment
- Standard treatment/routine care control, in which clients receive the regular treatment or services that would have been provided even if they had not been in the study

The importance of including a control group in an outcome study is to verify that improvements in clients' behavior are actually due to the target therapy rather than merely the passage of time (as would be assessed in the no-treatment and wait-list control groups) or attention from a therapist (as would occur in attention-placebo/nonspecific control groups). The strength of including a standard treatment/routine care control group is to compare the effectiveness of the new therapy with the effectiveness of the therapy that is already established.

Although outcome studies are the first step to exploring the effectiveness of a therapy, there is growing concern that therapy conducted within an outcome study is not comparable to therapy that is conducted in the community at large (Henggeler & Randall, 2000; Weisz, Doss, & Hawley, in press). For example, most therapy outcome studies clarify specific techniques that will be used, and many follow a manual that delineates the specific treatment techniques that will be used in the study. In the real world away from the research lab, however, clinicians are often not as structured in their delivery of therapeutic services or do not adhere closely to the therapy manual (Huey, Henggeler, Brondino, & Pickrel, 2000; Scaturo, 2001). One important aspect of conducting therapy outcome studies is to find ways to translate the findings into the larger practicing community of therapists (Henggeler & Randall, 2000). The most effective techniques in the world will not help any children if the techniques are not being utilized in the community (Weisz, Doss, & Hawley, 2005).

Any one outcome study can inform us about a specific treatment with a specific sample of children, adolescents, or families. A more comprehensive way to investigate the effectiveness of therapy is to conduct a **meta-analysis,** which allows the statistical combination of a number of outcome studies to gain an overall understanding of the effectiveness of that type of therapy.

Note that meta-analyses provide the combined results of outcome studies that explored similar types of treatments (e.g., cognitive–behavioral therapy) for similar types of problems (e.g., social phobia). Although meta-analyses provide a powerful tool in establishing the effectiveness of different therapies, they can be misleading if the authors are not careful in explaining the limitations of their meta-analytic reviews. For example, meta-analyses that utilize single-subject designs (where a treatment is administered to only one or two clients) would not have the same statistical power as meta-analyses that utilize studies with larger sample sizes.

In addition, if researchers only select published studies for their meta-analysis, they may inadvertently be stacking the deck toward finding differences between the target therapy and the control groups. Known as the **file-drawer problem,** this issue is of concern because studies that find differences (e.g., between a new treatment and a control group or between a new treatment and an established treatment) are somewhat more likely to be published than studies that do not find these differences (Durlak, 1999). Given this potential bias, many researchers who conduct meta-analyses try to include studies from both published and unpublished sources, such as journals and *Dissertation Abstracts,* respectively (Durlak, 1999). Notably, when dissertation outcome studies were analyzed, smaller effect sizes were found, which suggests that previous meta-analyses may have overestimated the effects of psychotherapy with children and adolescents (McLeod & Weisz, 2004).

One of the first large-scale meta-analyses conducted for child and adolescent therapy was published in 1985 (Casey & Berman, 1985). The researchers found that the mean effect size for all therapies was .71, which means that the average child who received therapy was better off than 76% of the children who did not receive therapy (based on a conversion of the effect size to percentages). Overall, the researchers found that most therapies (other than psychodynamic therapy) were more effective than no treatment. A comparable follow-up meta-analysis found that behavioral therapies were somewhat more effective than nonbehavioral therapies, and that therapies were more effective for children as compared with adolescents (Weisz, Weiss, Alicke, & Klotz, 1987).

Since the time of these meta-analyses, a number of other meta-analyses and other reviews have been completed for treatment of children's and adolescents' emotional/behavioral problems (Baer & Nietzel, 1991; Weisz, Doss, & Hawley, 2005; Weisz, Sandler, Durlak, & Anton, 2005; Weisz & Weiss, 1993; Weisz, Weiss, Han, Granger, & Morton, 1995). Results suggest that children who receive treatment are better off emotionally and behaviorally than 76% to 79% of children who do not receive treatment (reviewed by Kazdin, 1996).

In an effort to synthesize outcome studies and meta-analyses, there has been a recent emphasis on identifying **empirically supported treatments** (Kazdin & Weisz, 1998). A federal task force was developed to help define and identify effective treatments that were supported by empirical research (Chambless et al., 1998; Task Force on Promotion and Dissemination of Psychological Procedures, 1995). Two acceptable categories of empirically supported treatments (EST's) were identified:

- *Well-established treatments,* which are required to have at least two high-quality between-group studies that show the treatment is either better than another therapy or a placebo, or that the treatment is as effective as a well-established treatment that is already in use. The treatments must have been instituted through the use of a structured manual, and the significant results must have been found by at least two different research groups. Sample characteristics must have been identified clearly.

- *Probably efficacious treatments,* which are required to have at least one or two high-quality between-groups studies that show the treatment is better than another therapy or a placebo. The study or studies are allowed to have been conducted by the same research group. Again, the treatment should have been administered with a structured manual, and sample characteristics must have been identified clearly.

Throughout the textbook, specific effective treatments (both well established and probably efficacious) will be identified for each disorder or problem. Rather than stating each of those findings here, suffice it to say that there are a number of effective treatments for a variety of different problems in childhood and adolescence. The overwhelming majority of well-established treatments and probably efficacious treatments can be conceptualized as cognitive–behavioral, behavioral, or cognitive in nature (Weisz & Hawley, 1998). The specific treatments that are most clearly well established within the area of childhood and adolescence are behavior modification for enuresis (not maintaining control of urinary functioning), behavioral parent training programs for children with oppositional problems, and cognitive–behavioral therapy for adolescents with bulimia (Chambless et al., 1998). Unfortunately, many practitioners in the community do not necessarily utilize these empirically supported treatments (Schmidt & Taylor, 2002).

Note, however, that much more work is needed to establish whether empirically supported treatments are effective for different groups of children, such as ethnic minority children or impoverished children (Hall & Barongan, 2002; Sue & Zane, 2006). As noted in the "You Decide" section, there are ongoing debates as to whether evidence-based therapy is effective for children and families from diverse backgrounds. In fact, there is evidence that effective therapies are even more effective for youth who are not disadvantaged in contrast to disadvantaged youth (Ceci & Papierno,

2005). One parent training study found that single-parent, immigrant families were less likely to participate in treatment, whereas poverty, family disturbance, and parental depressive symptoms were not related to treatment involvement (Cunningham et al., 2000). In a study of outpatient treatment for adolescents in Finland, however, low parental socioeconomic status was the most meaningful predictor of early dropout from therapy (Pelkonen, Marttunen, Laippala, & Loennqvist, 2000). In addition to exploring individual and family characteristics that are related to treatment effectiveness, it is also important to identify which treatment factors are associated with better versus worse outcome with specific treatment programs (Southam-Gerow, Kendall, & Weersing, 2001).

Currently, the term **evidence-based treatment** (Kazdin & Weisz, 2003) seems to be replacing empirically supported treatment (partly to get away from the restrictive criteria of Chambless & Hollon, 1998). In fact, the American Psychological Association established another task force, which focused on evidence-based practice (APA Presidential Task Force on Evidence-Based Practice, 2006; DeAngelis, 2005). Either sets of terminology are meant to convey treatments that have empirical data to show their effectiveness. Although the search for evidence-based treatments has been criticized for ignoring therapeutic factors and for not using representative samples (e.g., Westen, 2006; Westen, Novotny, & Thompson-Brenner, 2004, 2005), the overwhelming evidence in the field appears to support the search for evidence-based treatments (Crits-Christoph, Wilson, & Hollon, 2005; Weisz, Weersing, & Henggeler, 2005).

The area of attention-deficit/hyperactivity disorder (ADHD) provides a model that illustrates how treatment outcome research can be done. In a nationwide, multisite assessment of treatment effectiveness, the Multisite Treatment Study of ADHD (MTA) evaluated different modalities of treatment of ADHD in various settings (Arnold et al., 2004; Hoza, Mrug, Hinshaw, et al., 2005; Jensen et al., 2005; Owens et al., 2003). In addition to evaluating behavioral treatments, effectiveness of medications were also evaluated. The results of the MTA will be discussed in more depth in Chapter 9. Overall, the MTA study provides a model for how effective outcome studies can be developed. Although there are promising findings for the treatment of developmental psychopathology (including ADHD), there are also promising findings for the prevention of developmental psychopathology before it ever occurs.

YOU DECIDE: ARE EVIDENCE BASED TREATMENTS RESPONSIVE TO THE NEEDS OF DIVERSE CLIENT POPULATIONS?

<u>Yes</u>

- On average, child clients who receive evidence-based treatments are far better off than children who do not receive treatment, and that is true for children from all walks of life (Weisz, Sandler, Durlak, & Anton, 2005).
- Different evidence-based treatments can be tailored for different communities, such as the brief strategic family therapy model that has been shown to be very effective with Hispanic/Latino/Latina youth and their families (Robbins et al., 2003).

<u>No</u>

- Therapy for adults as well as children has ignored the needs of impoverished clients, and it is not responsive to

their needs (Smith, 2005). One review found that only 6% of studies that explored empirically supported treatments dealt with culture in any manner (Clay, Mordhorst, & Lehn, 2002).

- A number of dimensions of diversity have been ignored in clinical treatment outcome studies, including race/ethnicity (Sue & Zane, 2006), gender (Levant & Silverstein, 2006), sexual orientation (Brown, 2006), and physical disabilities (Olkin & Taliaferro, 2006). Without research into the effectiveness of these therapies with different populations, it is unknown whether they work with diverse populations.

So, are evidence based treatments responsive to the needs of diverse client populations? You decide.

PREVENTION PROGRAMS THAT WORK

Throughout this book, effective prevention programs will be highlighted. Prevention programs often try to enhance protective factors in the lives of children, for example, by working to improve parent–child attachment (Bakermans-Kranenburg, van Ijzendoom, & Juffer, 2003), by creating more supportive teacher–student relationships that can decrease the likelihood of childhood aggression (Hughes, Cavell, & Jackson, 1999), by teaching parents positive parenting skills through a television series (Sanders, Montgomery, & Brechman-Toussaint, 2000), by educating parents about childhood anxiety (Rapee, Kennedy, Ingram, Edwards, & Sweeney, 2005), by teaching adolescents and their parents cognitive and interpersonal skills to prevent adolescent depression (Shochet et al., 2001), or by providing extensive services to impoverished families and communities (Brotman et al., 2003; Knitzer, 2000). Preventive efforts can be located in many settings, including preschools and schools (August et al., 2003; Christenson & Thurlow, 2004; Farrell et al., 2001; Noam & Hermann, 2002; Webster-Stratton, Reid, & Hammond, 2001), the child welfare system (Zeanah et al., 2001), hospitals (Ialongo, Kellam, & Poduska, 2000), and the community (Dawson-McClure, Sandler, Wolchik, & Millsap, 2004; Tolan, Gorman-Smith, & Henry, 2004).

Throughout the history of prevention work, different definitions have sometimes been used to convey the same concepts. For example, for many years the

terms *primary prevention, secondary prevention,* and *tertiary prevention* were used. These terms were used to reflect services provided to the entire community, to children at-risk, and to clients who had completed therapy, respectively (reviewed in Evans & Seligman, 2005). More recently, there has been a move to change these conceptualizations based on the Institute of Medicine (1994) definitions. The main categorizations of prevention programs are as follows:

- Universal mental health prevention
- Selective mental health prevention
- Indicated prevention interventions

Universal mental health prevention is similar to primary prevention in that the prevention efforts are targeted to the entire population. Everyone in the community has an opportunity to be exposed to the prevention efforts, such as a citywide advertising campaign to prevent child abuse or a schoolwide campaign to promote self-esteem (Doll, Zucker, & Brehm, 2004; Felner et al., 2000). The goals of universal mental health programs are to reduce the occurrence of new disorders from developing.

Selective mental health prevention programs are similar to secondary prevention programs in that they focus on certain individuals or groups of people who have experiences that put them at risk for developing emotional/behavioral problems. For example, we know that children of parents who abuse substances are at an increased risk for the development of psychopathology, so a selective mental health prevention program might target those children from a prevention program (Evans & Seligman, 2005).

Indicated prevention interventions, formerly known as tertiary prevention programs, target individuals who are already experiencing emotional/behavioral problems and attempt to prevent additional problems from occurring (Knitzer, 2000).

In order to compare and contrast these different levels of prevention, an example that compares across the same topic is in order. One important concern for children, adolescents, and adults is the prevention of violent behavior. Effective programs for the prevention of violent behavior in children have been targeted at many different levels (Group for the Advancement of Psychiatry, Committee on Preventive Psychiatry, 1999):

• Universal mental health prevention—gun control

• Selective mental health prevention—gun-free zones around schools in violent areas

• Indicated prevention interventions—gun confiscation and conflict resolution training for violent youth

Prevention programs have been targeted at all these levels for many different emotional/behavioral problems in children and adolescents (Weissberg, Kumpfer, & Seligman, 2003; Weisz, Sandler, Durlak, & Anton, 2005), for preventing eating disorders (Stice & Shaw, 2004), for preventing depression (Horowitz & Garber, 2006; Possel, Horn, Groen, & Hautzinger, 2004), for preventing sexual victimization (Davis & Gidycz, 2000), and for preventing violent tendencies, such as sexual coercion (Pacifici, Stoolmiller, & Nelson, 2001) and gun violence (Mulvey & Cauffman, 2001).

In keeping with the focus on developmental processes, it is important to acknowledge that different prevention programs should be targeted at varying age groups. For example, prenatal services and well-baby health services should be geared to pregnant women and infants up to the age of 2, programs that decrease the upheaval at school would be appropriate for elementary school students as they transition to middle school, educational and vocational programs could help young adults who have not yet found their niche, and health and social-service efforts might be most appropriate for elderly individuals (Felner et al., 2000). Prevention programs run the gamut from widely administered programs that are not effective (e.g., DARE, which attempts to prevent substance abuse but is not effective) to highly effective prevention programs such as Life Skills Training, which decreases substance abuse by teaching social skills and personal problem-solving skills (Botvin & Griffin, 2004; Dusenbury, Brannigan, Hansen, Walsh, & Falco, 2005; West & O'Neal, 2004).

Figure 4.8 shows a model of child abuse prevention strategies, where a number of characteristics can be targeted for preventive efforts (including increasing parents' social support, educating parents on child development; Culbertson & Schellenbach, 1992). This type of comprehensive model is usually needed to impact on complex problems like child abuse.

In general, effective prevention programs are thought to be more cost efficient (i.e., it takes fewer dollars to prevent problems than to deal with long-term treatment of problems that develop) and are designed to prevent continued suffering by children and their families

FIGURE 4.8 A model of child abuse prevention.

Source: Culbertson & Schellenbach (1992).

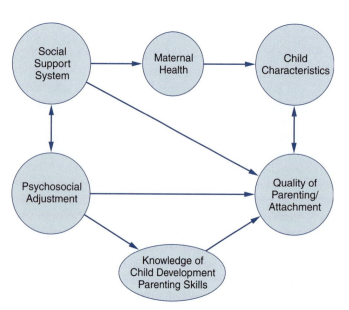

(Albee, 1982; Knitzer, 2000; Weisz, Sandler, Durlak, & Anton, 2005). In addition to the programs that are highlighted in the textbook, there are huge numbers of prevention programs that are effective throughout the world. These programs show a wide range of modalities and focus on the prevention of a great many problems. The following is a brief list of the types of successful prevention programs that are being instituted around the world:

- Preventing emotional/behavioral problems in children of parents with psychopathology in the Netherlands (Verburg, Janssen, Rikken, Hoefnagels, & van Willenswaard, 1992)

- Preventing physical illness and mental health problems through social action in Ghana (Sefa-Dedeh, 1992)

- Preventing emotional/behavioral problems through a public health strategy in Canada (Waddell, McEwan, Shepherd, Offord, & Hua, 2005)

- Preventing disruptive behavior through a television series on families in Australia (Sanders, Montgomery, & Brechman-Toussaint, 2000)

- Prevention of violence through school prevention programs in the United States (Farrell, Meyer, & White, 2001)

- Prevention of mental health problems and intellectual delays through integrated child care services in India (Sonty, 1992)

- Preventing childhood sexual abuse in China by providing preventive strategies and education to parents of young children (Chen & Chen, 2005)

- Prevention of child abuse through fostering parental competence in Poland (Sek, Bleja, & Sommerfeld, 1992)

- Prevention of HIV/AIDS in Africa, Asia, and Latin America through education and health promotion (Kelly et al., 2006)

Overall, prevention is an integral part of helping children. What better humanistic goal than to prevent problems from occurring rather than waiting to treat them after they occur? Given the often devastating consequences of developmental psychopathology for children, families, and society, continued support for prevention programs and public policy changes that help children are warranted (Kamon, Tolan, & Gorman-Smith, 2006; Knitzer, 2000; Ripple & Zigler, 2003; Rotheram-Borus & Duan, 2003).

Leave a good name behind in case you return.

—Proverb of Africa

PROFESSIONAL ETHICS IN ASSESSMENT AND INTERVENTIONS

Professional ethical standards are necessary while conducting effective assessments, treatments, and preventive services. Although different professional organizations have their own ethical and professional guidelines, the majority of professions within the field of mental health and education provide similar guidelines for professionals (Fisher, Hatashita-Wong, & Greene, 1999). For example, school psychologists and clinical psychologists follow strikingly similar ethical codes of conduct and legal statutes (Flanagan, Miller, & Jacob, 2005; Reschly & Bersoff, 1999). As can be seen in Table 4.14, the American Psychological Association (APA) provides a comprehensive set of ethical and professional principles for psychologists and other mental health professionals (American Psychological Association, 2002). The full listings of the ethical principles are too lengthy to reproduce for the purposes of this textbook, but the major ethical principles that relate to mental health professionals working with children are discussed. Readers interested in seeing the full description of psychologists' ethical principles code of conduct should refer to the full text, which is presented in the *American Psychologist* (American Psychological Association, 2002) and which can also be accessed online (www.apa.org/ethics). Issues related to the ethics of competence, multiple relationships, informed consent, and confidentiality will be discussed briefly so that students can understand the range of ethical guidelines for psychologists.

Morals are an acquirement—like music, like a foreign language, like piety, poker, paralysis—no man [or woman] is born with them.

—Mark Twain.

Competence

As noted in Table 4.14, there is an ethical standard (Ethical Standard 2.01) related to **competence,** which mandates that professionals only get involved in professional activities in which they have competence. These activities include, but are not limited to, conducting therapy, conducting assessments, implementation of prevention programs, teaching, and conducting research

TABLE 4.14 Selected Ethical Principles of Psychologists and Code of Conduct Related to Assessment and Therapeutic Interventions

The American Psychological Association (APA) delineates ethical and professional principles for psychologists (American Psychological Association, 2002). Following are a few selected ethical principles related to assessment and therapy.

2. COMPETENCE

2.01 *Boundaries of Competence:* (a) Psychologists provide services, teach, and conduct research with populations and in areas only within the boundaries of their competence, based on their education, training, supervised experience, consultation, study, or professional experience.

3. HUMAN RELATIONS

3.05 *Multiple Relationships:* (a) A multiple relationship occurs when a psychologist is in a professional role with a person and (1) at the same time is in another role with a person, [or] (2) at the same time is in a relationship with a person closely associated with or related to the person with whom the psychologist has the professional relationship.... A psychologist refrains from entering into a multiple relationship if the multiple relationship could reasonably be expected to impair the psychologist's objectivity, competence, or effectiveness in performing his or her functions as a psychologist, or otherwise risks exploitation or harm to the person with whom the professional relationship exists.

3.10 *Informed Consent:* (a) When psychologist conduct research or provide assessment, therapy, counseling, or consulting services in person or via electronic transmission or other forms of communication, they obtain the informed consent of the individual or individuals using language that is reasonably understandable to that person or persons except when conducting such activities without consent is mandated by law or governmental regulation...

4. PRIVACY AND CONFIDENTIALITY

4.01 *Maintaining Confidentiality:* Psychologists have a primary obligation and take reasonable precautions to protect confidential information obtained through or stored in any medium...

Note that state psychology licensing boards sometimes have more strict rules than the American Psychological Association. In those cases, the stricter of the two rules must be followed to ensure compliance with all relevant legislation and ethical codes.

Source: American Psychological Association (2002).

(Snow, Grady, & Goyette-Ewing, 2000). Note that the competence must have been obtained through either formal education, formal training, organized supervised experience, or other appropriate professional experiences (Yanagida, 1998). Thus, psychologists cannot deem themselves competent in an area without some documentation of formalized professional training.

The issue of competence has important ramifications for working with children, adolescents, and families. Professionals who have only been trained in working with adults would need to receive additional training before establishing competence in working with children, adolescents, and families. As discussed throughout this book, working with children is very different than working with adults. Although certain skills (e.g., good listening skills, strong interviewing skills, good therapeutic skills, knowledge of the empirical process) are required with both adults and children, the way in which services are delivered can be very different when working with children versus adults. In addition, a number of issues are relevant in working with children that usually are not as relevant in working with adults, such as dealing effectively with parents, coordinating services with the school, dealing with confidentiality issues when the

parents are the legal holders of confidentiality yet the child is the individual client. These issues often result in decisions related to ethics (Mannheim et al., 2002), so it is imperative that professionals working with children, adolescents, and families receive specialized training and that they remain competent in the provision of these services. Competence in working with clients from diverse backgrounds is also important, as noted in Box 4.7.

Character counts for a great deal more than either intellect or body in winning success in life.

—Theodore Roosevelt

Multiple Relationships

As noted in Table 4.14, Ethical Standard 3.05 states that psychologists must refrain from becoming involved in **multiple relationships** with their clients, research participants, and students. Formerly known as dual relationships, multiple relationships exist when psychologists have more than one role in relation to individuals with whom they work professionally (Yanagida, 1998). For example, a multiple relationship would exist if a psychologist were providing therapy to one of his or her

BOX *4.7*

ETHICS AND COMPETENCE RELATED TO GENDER, RACE/ETHNICITY, AND CULTURE

Within the assessment and therapeutic process, issues often arise that relate to gender, race/ethnicity, and culture. Although these issues are not always present, ethical clinicians must be aware of the potential for these issues at all times. Recommendations for ethical behavior in regard to gender, race/ethnicity, and culture include

- Clinicians should recognize that gender, race/ethnicity, and culture are fundamental issues in all relationships. They should be able to understand clients' individual differences within this broader context.
- In the same way that mental health professionals should refrain from providing services when they are psychologically impaired, they should also refrain from providing services when their personal beliefs (e.g., sexism, racism, homophobia) prevent them from providing services in an objective and productive manner.
- Clinicians must remain abreast of the latest empirical and theoretical information regarding gender, race/ethnicity, and culture. If they are not able to

maintain continued competence in these areas, they should refer clients to other practitioners who have shown competence in these areas.
- Not only should these issues be addressed when clinicians are working with clients, but issues of gender, race/ethnicity, and culture must also be addressed when clinicians provide supervision, conduct research, and teach in a scholarly setting.

Overall, good ethical practice in the areas of gender, race/ethnicity, and culture are consistent with good ethical practice in all areas of concern. The same can be said for the issue of sexual orientation (Crawford, McLeod, Zamboni, & Jordan, 1999; Division 44, 2000). Clinicians must remain vigilant about maintaining competence and proficiency in all areas within their practice and their research.

Sources: American Psychological Association (2003a); Fisher et al., 2002; Hall & Barongan (2002); Hampton & Gottlieb (1997).

---

students. The psychologist would be in the role of a therapist and also in the role of an instructor, which would be considered multiple relationships. The reason that multiple relationships are forbidden is that the dual roles may create a conflict of interest. To stay with the example of a psychologist who is both a therapist and an instructor with the same client/student, imagine that one of the primary themes in therapy is the client's concern about academic excellence. As a therapist, the psychologist could explore the meaning and importance of academic progress and empathically help the client come to terms with his or her academic difficulties. As an instructor, however, the psychologist would need to maintain objective grading criteria and academic rigor, which might mean that he or she would fail the student in that class. Imagine the impact on the therapeutic alliance when the warm, caring therapist has to fail the client for inadequate academic functioning. Imagine the strain in the therapy session after grades are posted. This example illustrates the potential problems with multiple relationships and why they should be avoided at all costs.

Good name and honor are worth more than all the gold and jewels ever mined.
— Harry S Truman

Informed Consent

As discussed in Ethical Standard Table 4.14, **informed consent** is the process through which clients are told about therapy or assessment services that will take place (i.e., they are informed of these services in language that they understand) and through which they willingly agree to these services (i.e., they give their uncoerced consent to take part in these services). **Informed assent** is the term used to discuss the same process with child or adolescent clients. Formally, only competent adults over the age of 18 can give their legal informed consent to therapy or assessment services. Thus, parents need to provide informed consent for their child's therapy or assessment services (Pryzwansky & Wendt, 1999). It is beneficial, however, to involve child and adolescent clients in this process. Children and adolescents can provide their informed assent to services after their parents or legal guardians have provided their informed consent for services.

As part of the informed consent/assent process, it is important for therapists to inform clients about the therapy or assessment services that will take place, the fees associated with the services, the possibility of other more effective services that could be provided elsewhere, the approximate length of time in which

Case Study: A Young Adolescent Who Wanted Help

Jackie is a 13-year-old boy who walked into a community mental health center and asked to speak to someone. He met with Dr. G and proceeded to tell him of the many difficulties and troubles in his life. He also reported to Dr. G that his parents severely abused him. He asked Dr. G not to talk with anyone about these issues, "especially my folks." Dr. G then informed Jackie that he could not provide therapy to anyone under the age of 18 without parental consent and went further to tell Jackie that he was mandated to report the physical abuse. Jackie felt betrayed by Dr. G.

There are two issues that arise in this case study. Dr. G should have mentioned the issue of only being able to provide treatment to someone under the age of 18 with parental consent

immediately upon meeting Jackie. This policy is not consistent across states, and some states allow a limited number of therapy sessions without parental consent if the therapist deems that parental consent would hamper the therapeutic process initially. The issue of limits to confidentiality should also have been discussed with Jackie before he began self-disclosing to Dr. G. Not only did Jackie feel betrayed by Dr. G, but he may have developed a mistrust for other mental health professionals that would prevent him from seeking help in the future. This case illustrates the importance of covering these ground rules at the outset of therapy rather than waiting until a sensitive issue arises.

Source: Koocher & Keith-Spiegel (1998).

---

to expect the services to be completed, and the reasonable estimate of the outcome of the services (e.g., a formal assessment report might be the logical culmination of assessment services, whereas a decrease in emotional/behavioral problems might be a logical and reasonable goal of therapeutic services; Koocher & Keith-Spiegel, 1998).

Whenever children and families are involved in assessments or therapy, it is incumbent on the clinician to clarify who is considered the client and what relationship the clinician will have with each client. As can be seen in Figure 4.9, family relationships, especially within reconstituted stepfamilies, can get very complex and can provide a challenge for clinicians trying to clarify their roles with different family members.

Always do right. This will gratify some people, and astonish the rest.

—Mark Twain

Confidentiality

As noted in Ethical Standard 4.01 in Table 4.14, clinicians and therapists must maintain the confidentiality rights of their clients. **Confidentiality** means that identifying information about clients, personal clinical material about clients, and even the fact that a client is a client should be protected to the legal extent of the law. This type of information is considered private and under the purview of only the therapist and the client. Unless clinicians have the written permission of their clients (or the parents of clients in the case of children), they cannot

disclose any information regarding the therapy or assessment services to anyone other than the client. Clinicians must also clarify the parameters of confidentiality at the outset of services. For example, many clinicians working with older children and adolescents want to be able to talk with the child alone without having to disclose all the information to the parents. If the child felt that everything he or she said would be immediately reported to the parent, then he or she would probably not disclose very much meaningful information to the clinician. For that reason, clinicians often establish these guidelines at the outset of therapy and tell parents that what the child reports to the clinician is confidential unless the child is in significant danger of harming him or herself or if abuse has been reported. If the parents disagree with the ground rules, then they can seek services with someone else.

The ultimate measure of a man [or woman] is not where he [or she] stands in moments of comfort and convenience, but where he [or she] stands at times of challenge and controversy.

—Dr. Martin Luther King

Given the sacred nature of confidentiality, it is important to realize that there are limits to confidentiality that must be discussed with clients at the outset of therapy or assessment services. These limits to confidentiality are usually established by state law. Most states do not allow the following topics to be kept confidential:

- Imminent suicide for clients of any age
- Imminent homicide for clients of any age

Therapists must obtain informed consent from parents and informed assent from children before working with them.

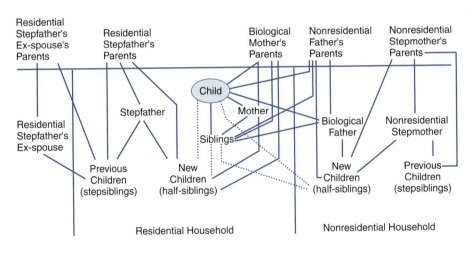

FIGURE 4.9 Potential complexity in stepfamilies. Solid lines represent biological relationships; dashed lines indicated sibling relationships less than full biological relatives.

Source: Anderson & Greene (1999). Wendy K. Silverman & Thomas H. Ollendick, *Developmental issues in the clinical treatment of children*, Copyright © 1999 by Allyn & Bacon. Reprinted by permission.

- Physical abuse of children under the age of 18
- Sexual abuse of children under the age of 18 (or sometimes a younger age, such as under the age of 16, in some states)
- Psychological or emotional abuse of children under the age of 18
- Neglect of children under the age of 18
- Abuse of an elderly or incapacitated adult

These limits to confidentiality are based on the idea that clinicians are in a unique position to prevent harm from coming to children and adolescents. The rationale for these limits to confidentiality is to prevent suicide, homicide, and abuse from occurring or from continuing in the lives of children and adolescents (Pryzwansky & Wendt, 1999). Confidentiality is one of the most basic and fundamental ethical guidelines that clinicians need to follow, but following the limits to confidentiality is equally important to protect clients.

Honesty: the best of all the lost arts.

—Mark Twain

Case Study: Parents of an Adolescent Who Feel Betrayed

Donna is a sexually active 15-year-old who feels alienated from her parents. She has been in therapy with Dr. C, during which time she acknowledged that she contracted genital herpes. At some point, Donna's parents discovered that she had genital herpes, and when they challenged her on her sexual activity, she retorted that they were not as "understanding as Dr. C." Donna's parents were furious with Dr. C for knowing that Donna had been sexually active but not informing them. They felt that Dr. C's knowledge of Donna's sexual activity had implicitly condoned the sexual activity. Donna's parents demanded a meeting with Dr. C and threatened to terminate Donna's treatment if this meeting were not held quickly. They also threatened to file an ethics complaint against Dr. C.

The primary issue that arises in this case is that the rules of confidentiality were not established at the beginning of therapy. Dr. C should have met with the parents and Donna in the first session and described the ground rules of confidentiality within the therapy sessions. When working with adolescents, these ground rules are often made explicit regarding sexual activity and use of illegal substances. If the parents were unwilling to abide by Dr. C's practice of keeping all but life-threatening information confidential between herself and Donna, then Donna's parents could have sought therapy services elsewhere. Most parents agree to this arrangement because they know that their adolescent might only disclose information to a trusted therapist. If these parents had agreed to this type of arrangement at the outset of therapy, they probably would not have been upset by Dr. C's knowledge of Donna's sexual activity and genital herpes. The parents may have still felt jealous or envious of Donna's trust and respect for the therapist, and they would undoubtably have felt distress over Donna's sexual activity and sexually transmitted disease, but at least they would not have felt betrayed by Dr. C.

Source: Koocher & Keith-Spiegel (1998).

SUMMARY AND KEY CONCEPTS

Assessment is the process of testing and evaluating children and adolescents to ascertain their functioning. **Multimethod assessment** includes many methods of assessment (such as interviews, checklists, behavioral observation, and standardized intellectual testing). The use of **multiple informants** is a strategy that includes many different informants on the child's behavior (such as the parents, teachers, and the child him- or herself).

Multiaxial Assessment of Children and Adolescents. **Multiaxial assessment** consists of the evaluation of children and adolescents from multiple perspectives on six axes: parent reports, teacher reports, cognitive functioning, physical assessment, and direct assessment.

Interviews with Children and Their Parents. Most often, the clinical process begins with an *intake phone call,* in which the parents describe the problems their child or their family is experiencing. **Unstructured interviews** are the most common and allow clinicians to ask questions that seem relevant to the referral problem in whatever order they deem appropriate. **Rapport,** which is at the foundation of the therapeutic relationship, is one of the first goals of an unstructured interview. **Semistructured interviews** are more structured than unstructured interviews, in that clinicians are provided with a suggested template for an interview format that they can follow or that they can deviate from as they see fit. **Structured interviews** are usually used for diagnostic purposes, and the interviews must be followed in a very specific sequence with little to no deviation from the format.

Behavioral Assessment. There are three primary types of behavioral assessment, all of which can be done in conjunction with other assessment techniques. **Behavioral observation** is completed when the clinician or other professional observes the child's behavior. A common pattern that is observed by the clinician is to look at the **antecedents** (what comes before the behavior) and the **consequences** (what occurs after the behavior). **Functional assessment** occurs when the child is observed actually conducting the behaviors of interest (such as assessing social skills while the child is actually interacting with other children). **Self-monitoring** allows the child to keep track of his or her own behavior that is in need of changing. There is some concern about **reactivity** in all these behavioral assessment techniques.

Checklists and Rating Scales. The most common broad-based measures of children's behavior are the Achenbach system (comprised of the CBCL, TRF, YSR, and other associated measures) and the BASC system (comprised of parent, teacher, and child/adolescent reports). In addition to these broad-based measures, there are also a number of measures of adaptive functioning.

Personality Assessment. Personality inventories (such as the MMPI–2 and PIC) are paper-and-pencil measures that are used to assess the underlying constructs of personality functioning. **Projective measures** (such as the Rorschach inkblot test, CAT, drawings, and sentence completion tasks) are meant to provide children with an ambiguous stimulus onto which they can project their innermost thoughts, feelings, and concerns.

Family Assessment. **Genograms** are used as a schematic representation of the family constellation and the constellation of previous generations. Paper-and-pencil measures and Kinetic Family Drawings can also be used to assess the family environment and other aspects of family functioning.

Assessing Intellectual Functioning and Academic Achievement. A wide range of standardized measures assess intellectual functioning and academic achievement. These measures are all administered individually to the child, and the child's results are compared with the normative data on the measures to provide standardized scores.

Educational Assessment. Clinical psychologists and school psychologists conduct surprisingly similar assessments for children and adolescents.

Neuropsychological Assessment. Neuropsychological assessment is a specialization within clinical psychology that allows more specific assessments of children's and adolescents' brain-related limitations that influence behavior.

Settings Where Interventions are Conducted. Therapy can be conducted in a number of different settings, most of which institute a **treatment plan** that identifies problem behaviors, long-term goals, short-term goals, and specific interventions that will be administered to help the child. The range of settings varies from inpatient settings (which are usually in a hospital setting and require that children stay in the facility 24 hours a day), **residential treatment facilities** (where children reside for a greater length of time and which are usually away from a hospital setting), **group homes** and **therapeutic foster care homes** (which usually serve fewer children than in residential treatment facilities), **day hospitals** (which allow children to receive services during the day but live at home with their family), **outpatient settings** (which allow children to visit with a therapist on usually a weekly basis in the therapist's office), and **school-based mental health services** (which allow children to receive mental health services at school).

Psychodynamic Therapies. Although traditional psychodynamic therapy is rarely conducted with children or adolescents, **play therapy** is an offshoot of psychodynamic therapy that is still used with children.

Behavioral Therapies. The most traditional form of behavioral therapy is called **applied behavior analysis,** which applies behavioral principles to children's emotional/behavioral problems. Many basic behavioral concepts are used in applied behavior analysis and behavior therapy, including, **reinforcement** (applying a pleasant reward to increase behavior), **prompting** (applying a prompt to help teach a new behavior), **shaping** (reinforcing successive approximations toward the final desired behavior), **chaining** (teaching and rewarding each link in a behavioral chain), **modeling** (showing children the desirable behavior through a live model or through a videotaped model), **differential reinforcement of incompatible, alternative, or other behavior** (reinforcing behaviors that are incompatible with the target maladaptive behavior), **extinction** (gradual disappearance of a behavior due

to the withdrawal of reinforcers that were maintaining the behavior), **time-out** (removal of reinforcers that were maintaining the behavior), and **punishment** (applying an aversive stimulus or withdrawing a pleasant stimulus to decrease the problematic behavior). More complex behavioral therapies are also used extensively with children and adolescents, such as **token economies** (giving a token or other symbol for adaptive behaviors and then allowing children to "cash in" their tokens for a desired object or activity). **Behavioral parent training,** as well as parent–child interaction therapy are the primary therapies that can be conducted with parents from a behavioral perspective.

Cognitive-Behavioral Therapies. Cognitive–behavioral therapies combine principles from behavioral therapies with principles from cognitive therapies. Therapists work with children and adolescents to alter maladaptive cognitions, enhance coping and problem-solving skills, eliminate maladaptive behavior, and enhance adaptive behavior.

Family Systems Therapies. Based on family systems theories, family systems therapies conceptualize children's and adolescents' emotional/behavioral problems as being reflective of a problem within the family system. The child who is experiencing the emotional/behavioral problem is referred to as the **identified problem** (or identified patient). Family therapy is effective, especially when evidence-based techniques are used.

Psychopharmacological Interventions. A number of different **psychopharmacological interventions** (i.e., medications) can be prescribed by a physician to treat children's emotional/behavioral problems, including **antidepressants** (to treat depression), **anxiolytics** (to treat anxiety problems), **antipsychotic medications** (to treat schizophrenia or other psychotic disorders), and **stimulants** (to treat AD/HD). Care must be taken (by both physicians and parents) to monitor any adverse side effects (such as **tardive dyskinesia,** which is a permanent neuromuscular disorder that can develop after using antipsychotic medication).

Effectiveness of Therapeutic Interventions. The primary way that therapeutic effectiveness is studied is through **outcome studies** (where clients are assigned randomly to either a treatment group or a control group). In order to summarize the results of outcome studies statistically, a **meta-analysis** can be completed that combines the results of many outcome studies and evaluates the overall effectiveness of the therapies that are of interest. Note that a potential problem with meta-analyses is that many studies are not published when they do not find differences between treatments (a problem that is known as the **file-drawer problem**). Recently, there has been a focus on **empirically supported treatments** and **evidence-based treatments** that are evaluated for the rigor and strength of research findings.

Prevention Programs That Work. In addition to the therapeutic interventions that are effective in helping children and adolescents with their emotional/behavioral problems, there are also a great deal of prevention programs that have been instituted to prevent emotional/behavioral problems for occurring in the first place. Prevention programs can target entire communities (**universal mental health programs**), at-risk children (**selective mental health prevention programs**), and children who have already experienced problems (**tertiary prevention programs**).

Professional Ethics in Assessment and Interventions. Mental health professionals must show **competence** in their work with children and families. Mental health professionals must guard against **multiple relationships,** which means that they should guard against having different roles with their clients. Before the therapy or assessment process begins, parents of child clients must provide their written **informed** consent, and child clients must provide their **informed assent** to take part in the services. In both cases, parents and children should be informed about what to expect from the professional services and should agree to these services of their own free will. **Confidentiality** is one of the most strictly held principles within the mental health field. Clinicians should assure clients that the information that is shared with the clinician will not be disclosed to anyone other than the client. Limits to confidentiality include suicidality, homicidality, child physical abuse, child sexual abuse, child psychological abuse, child neglect, or abuse of an incapacitated or elderly adult.

KEY TERMS

assessment	functional	school-based mental	token economies	file-drawer problem
multimethod	assessment	health services	behavioral parent	empirically
assessment	self-monitoring	play therapy	training	supported
multiple informants	reactivity	applied behavior	Stimulus-Organism-	treatments
multiaxial	projective measures	analysis	Response-	evidence-based
assessment	genograms	reinforcement	Consequences	treatments
intake phone call	neuropsychological	prompting	(S-O-R-C) model	universal mental
unstructured	assessment in	shaping	identified problem	health prevention
interviews	patient settings	chaining	psychopharmacological	selective mental
rapport	treatment plan	modeling	interventions	health prevention
semistructured	residential treatment	differential	antidepressants	indicated prevention
interviews	facilities	reinforcement of	anxiolytics	interventions
structured	group homes	incompatible,	antipsychotic	competence
interviews	therapeutic foster	alternative, or	medications	multiple
behavioral	care homes	other behavior	stimulants	relationships
observation	day hospitals	extinction	tardive dyskinesia	informed consent
antecedents	outpatient settings	time-out	outcome studies	informed assent
consequences		punishment	meta-analysis	confidentiality

SUGGESTED READINGS

Gordon, Emily Fox. *Mockingbird Years: A Life In and Out of Therapy*. New York: Basic Books, 2000. With five different therapists before she turned 17 years old and a suicide attempt by the age of 18, it is not surprising to find that the author ended up needing inpatient services. This powerful memoir tells the story of therapy that works.

Hayden, Torey. *Twilight Children*. New York: William Morrow, 2005. Consistent with her other books from when she was a special education teacher, the author now describes her work as an educational psychologist. This book tells the story of two children and one adult, all of whom are quite disturbed and who are provided therapy services by the author.

SUGGESTED VIEWINGS

Girl, Interrupted. (1999). Based on an eloquent autobiography of the same name, this film illustrates the inpatient treatment of Susanna Kaysen (1993) for depression, suicidal wishes, and problems with adjustment. Both the film and the book also explore the issue of who is "crazy."

Capturing the Friedmans. (2003). In this powerful documentary, a family is investigated for alleged sexual abuse both inside and outside the family. Family dynamics are captured throughout the process, and the disintegration of the family is documented through the allegations, legal proceedings, and the ultimate attempt at a resolution of these issues.

CHAPTER 5

RISK FACTORS AND ISSUES OF PREVENTION

CHAPTER SUMMARY

TEMPERAMENT AND ATTACHMENT

GENETIC PREDISPOSITION

PARENTAL PSYCHOPATHOLOGY

PARENTAL LOSS DUE TO DEATH

INTERPARENTAL CONFLICT

CHILD PHYSICAL ABUSE

CHILD SEXUAL ABUSE

CHILD PSYCHOLOGICAL MALTREATMENT

FAMILY DYSFUNCTION

INADEQUATE EDUCATIONAL RESOURCES

POVERTY AND LOW SOCIOECONOMIC STATUS

VIOLENCE WITHIN THE COMMUNITY

SUMMARY AND KEY CONCEPTS

KEY TERMS

SUGGESTED READINGS

SUGGESTED VIEWINGS

We are always too busy for our children; we never give them the time or interest they deserve. We lavish gifts upon them; but the most precious gift—our personal association, which means so much to them—we give grudgingly.

—Mark Twain

As mentioned in the first chapter, **risk factors** are characteristics, events, or processes that put the individual at risk for the development of psychological problems. The presence of a risk factor in children's or adolescents' lives puts them at risk for the development of emotional/behavioral problems and other adverse outcomes (Wright & Masten, 2005). Risk factors can be conceptualized as broadly falling into three different categories (Werner & Smith, 2001):

- Individual characteristics of the infant, child, or adolescent (e.g., troubled attachment to the caregiver, difficult temperament)

- Characteristics within the family (e.g., parental psychopathology, interparental conflict, child abuse, family environment)

- Characteristics of the school or community (e.g., overcrowded schools, poverty, violence within the community)

This chapter covers these and many other factors that put youngsters at risk for the development of emotional/ behavioral problems and the development of psychopathology. Note that each chapter on individual types of psychopathology will also address the risk factors that are specific to the development of that clinical disorder. Within this chapter, risk factors that are associated with the development of different types of difficulties are addressed. First, individual characteristics are covered, including attachment and temperament. Then, characteristics within the family are covered, including parental psychopathology, parental death, interparental conflict, child abuse and maltreatment, and family dysfunction. Finally, characteristics within the school and the community are covered, including inadequate educational opportunities, poverty, and violence within the community. Although these topics are separated for ease of discussion, note that many children experience multiple risk factors. For example, in a large community-based study, children were found to have a range of experiences, including low risk (23%), universal high risk with multiple risk factors (7%), family conflict (11%), substance abuse within the family (22%), separated or divorced parents (24%), and parental psychiatric disorders (13%; Menard, Bandeen-Roche, & Chilcoat, 2004).

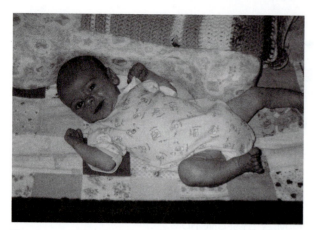

Temperament is evident in infants at the time of birth, and infants can be categorized as easy babies (like the one in this picture), slow-to-warm-up babies, and difficult babies.

The first cry of a newborn baby in Chicago or Zamoango, in Amsterdam or Rangoon, has the same pitch and key, each saying "I am! I have come through! I belong!"

—Carl Sandburg

TEMPERAMENT AND ATTACHMENT

Both temperament and attachment are studied primarily in the beginning years of life. **Temperament** reflects the infant's personal and individual style in relation to the frequency of expression of needs and emotions (Calkins & Degnan, 2006). Temperament is thought to be present at birth and is assumed to be due largely to genetic and constitutional factors with only some influence from environmental factors. There are three primary types of temperament shown in infants:

- Easy babies tend to be relatively predictable in their sleeping and eating habits, seldom cause a fuss, and react to new or novel situations with pleasure and cheer.

- Slow-to-warm-up babies encounter new situations with wariness and trepidation, but they eventually come around to enjoy the new situation.

- Difficult babies do not show regular patterns of eating or sleeping and tend to be irritable the majority of the time (Thomas & Chess, 1977).

The overwhelming majority of babies are easy babies. In general, temperament in infancy is consistent with temperament in later toddlerhood, childhood, and adolescence (Thomas & Chess, 1977).

The difficult temperamental style is considered to be a risk factor for the development of psychopathology in later years. For example, infants who showed a difficult and highly reactive temperamental style as infants were more likely to show problematic levels of anxiety when they were 7 years old (Kagan, Snidman, Zentner, & Peterson, 1999). Difficult temperament during infancy was associated with internalizing problems in young adolescents (Oldehinkel, Hartman, DeWinter, Veenstra, & Ormel, 2004). Similarly, difficult temperament in infancy and toddlerhood has also been associated with the development of externalizing problems such as aggression in adolescents (Mesman & Koot, 2000; Rettew, Copeland, Stanger, & Hudziak, 2004). Although temperament is thought to be somewhat innate, the match between infant temperament and caretaker tolerance for the infant's behavior may relate to the child's adaptational outcome (Campbell, 1998). Rather than remaining focused on temperament in infancy, recent work has also focused on temperamental characteristics in children and adolescents. For example, difficult temperament in children and adolescents, as reflected by negative emotionality, is associated with increased depressive symptoms (Compas, Connor-Smith, & Jaser, 2004). Difficult temperament in childhood and adolescence has also been associated with increased risk for ADHD (Nigg, Goldsmith, & Sachek, 2004), conduct problems (Frick & Morris, 2004), and substance abuse (Wills & Dishion, 2004).

The other primary risk factor within the individual is attachment. As noted in the chapter on theories, **attachment** is the relationship that develops between the infant and the caregiver over the first year of life. Most often, this relationship is a deep, enduring, and affectionate bond between the infant and caretaker (usually a parent). There are four primary types of attachment:

- Secure attachment, in which infants show a desire to be with their parent, use their parent as a secure base from which to explore unfamiliar settings, and show joy when reunited with their parent after a separation

- Avoidant anxious insecure attachment, in which infants ignore or avoid their parent when reunited after a separation

- Ambivalent anxious insecure attachment, in which infants protest when their parent leaves the room but then appear to be angry and rejecting when the parent returns to them after a brief separation

- Disorganized anxious insecure attachment, in which infants provide mixed signals such as crying when being returned to their parent or reaching out for their parent while looking away (Karen, 1994)

The majority of infants show secure attachment with their primary caretaker (Cassidy & Mohr, 2001; Karen, 1994). Attachment style is seen as a risk factor when the infant shows any of the anxious insecure attachment styles (avoidant, ambivalent, or disorganized). Children who showed insecure attachment in infancy showed greater problems with compliance in school, more peer isolation, more emotional/behavioral problems, greater rates of depression, and greater rates of conduct problems in childhood and adolescence (Keller, Spieker, & Gilchrist, 2005; Sund & Wichstrom, 2002). Note that anxious insecure attachment is not itself a type of psychopathology nor does it appear to lead directly to one type of psychopathology. Rather, it appears that anxious insecure attachment leads to additional problems that are linked to the development of psychopathology (Sroufe, Carlson, Levy, & Egeland, 1999). In Box 5.1, a prevention program is described to help parents connect with their infants to prevent abuse and other problems.

It is important to note that attachment can be considered a reciprocal process between infants and caretakers, rather than an individual characteristic of the infant. There is evidence that the parent's or caretaker's behavior with the infant can influence attachment style significantly. Parents and caretakers who tend to be abrupt, angry, and intolerant of their infant are likely to have an infant with some type of anxious insecure attachment (Campbell, 1998). Given that these parental behaviors would most likely continue through the infant's childhood and adolescence, it may be that these parental behaviors serve as a risk factor either separate from or in addition to the attachment style in infancy.

GENETIC PREDISPOSITION

As discussed in the chapter on theories, a number of emotional/behavioral problems are associated with a genetic predisposition toward the problem (Rutter, Silberg, O'Connor, & Simonoff, 1999a, 1999b). Many problems have been associated with a genetic risk toward the emotional/behavioral problem, including depression, anxiety, conduct problems, attention problems, hyperactivity, substance abuse problems, pervasive developmental problems, schizophrenia, learning problems, and intellectual deficits (Bouchard, 2004; State et al., 2000). Surprisingly, even poor achievement and social maladjustment after parental divorce are linked to genetic risk

factors (O'Connor, Caspi, DeFries, & Plomin, 2000). Parental psychopathology is the genetic risk factor that has received the most empirical attention.

> *If there is anything that we wish to change in the child, we should first examine it and see whether it is not something that could better be changed in ourselves.*
>
> —Carl Gustav Jung

PARENTAL PSYCHOPATHOLOGY

Researchers have explored the risk factor of parental psychopathology extensively. As mentioned in the chapter on research methods, the primary research design to study parental psychopathology is called the high-risk design, which presupposes that offspring are at high risk for the development of psychopathology when their parent experiences psychopathology. Beginning with research in the 1950s on parents diagnosed with schizophrenia (Cornblatt, Dworkin, Wolf, & Erlenmeyer-Kimling, 1996), a great number of researchers have explored the ramifications of having a parent with a clinical disorder. In the early days of this research, parents diagnosed with depression were used as a control group to be compared with parents diagnosed with schizophrenia. Ironically, researchers found that the offspring of parents with schizophrenia and the offspring of parents with depression were at increased risk for the development of emotional/behavioral problems (Cornblatt et al., 1996). Thus, control groups were later defined as offspring of parents without any type of psychopathology. Since those early studies, nearly every clinical disorder has been explored within the context of parental psychopathology. Unfortunately, the majority of research has explored psychopathology in mothers and has all but ignored psychopathology in fathers (Phares et al., 2005).

Most research on maternal psychopathology has shown that offspring are at increased risk for the development of psychopathology. Clinical disorders in mothers ranging from depression (Frye & Garber, 2005; Goodman, 2003; McCarty, McMahon, Conduct Problems Prevention Research Group, 2003), anxiety disorders (Mojtabai, 2005; Turner, Beidel, & Roberson-Nay, 2005), substance abuse (Ohannessian et al., 2004), and schizophrenia (Erlenmeyer-Kimling et al., 2005) all put children at risk for the development of psychopathology. Similarly, research on paternal psychopathology has found that children and adolescents are at risk for

BOX 5.1

HELPING PARENTS CONNECT WITH THEIR INFANTS

Many young, impoverished parents, especially teenage mothers, have difficulty with the demands of an infant in addition to other life stressors. Many times, these difficulties lead to the infant being at risk for physical abuse, emotional/behavioral problems, and limited academic and intellectual functioning later in childhood. Some of these problems may be due to the lack of adequate information for the young parents and may be due to the limited attachment that is formed between an infant and a parent under severe stress (Olds, 1997).

The Prenatal/Early Infancy Program is one prevention program that was designed to prevent some of these difficulties (Olds, 1988, 1997). This program targeted parents who were less than 19 years old and who had low socioeconomic status. Although you might think that this type of program would target only teenage mothers, over 40% of the participants in this program were married, and a number of other participants were living with the baby's father. The program recruited parents before the infant was born so that adequate prenatal care could be encouraged and so that a bond could be developed between the parents and the support staff from the research team. A primary component of this program was that support staff would make home visits, so that the parents might be more willing and able to receive the services. The program consisted of a number of different components, including

- Prenatal education (which included helping expectant mothers with healthy food intake and exercise, helping eliminate drugs, alcohol, and cigarettes from expectant parents, teaching parents to identify possible signs of pregnancy complications, educating parents on labor and delivery issues, preparing parents for the demands of early care of their newborn, helping parents learn about appropriate health-care options available to them and the newborn, and helping parents with job training or educational pursuits as needed)
- Infancy education (which included teaching parents about infants' temperaments, helping parents identify ways in which to promote socioemotional and cognitive

development in their infants, helping to promote the physical development of the infant)
- Informal support (which included helping parents identify appropriate family members and friends who could help with the process of becoming new parents, having the support staff serve as a support system for the new parents)
- Connecting to formal services (which included informing parents about the different public resources that were available to them, such as legal aid, child care, and medical and dental services)

These support services were provided from before birth to the time that the child was 2 years of age. For the first 6 weeks of the child's life, the support staff visited the parents on a weekly basis. From the time that the infant was 6 weeks old to 4 months old, the support staff visited the parents every 2 weeks, then every 3 weeks from the ages of 4 to 14 months, every month from the ages of 14 to 20 months, and finally every 6 weeks from the ages of 20 to 24 months.

Positive effects of the program were evidenced at many stages of infants' and children's lives. Babies were less likely to be born prematurely and were less likely to be born at a low birth weight than infants whose parents had not received the program. These changes may have been due to the reduction in smoking, drinking alcohol, and drug use among parents in the program. Infant–parent attachment was significantly stronger and more adaptive than in nonprogram infant–parent dyads. This secure attachment appeared to be connected to a host of other strengths within these families. Notably, there was a 75% reduction of documented cases of child physical abuse at follow-up when compared with children whose parents had not received the program. Overall, this intensive prevention program showed that intervening with young parents can prevent a host of problems that are associated with later development of emotional/behavioral problems in children.

Source: Olds (1997).

psychopathology. Clinical disorders in fathers, including depression (Kane & Garber, 2004), alcohol abuse (Ohannessian et al., 2004; Nigg et al., 2004), and schizophrenia (Erlenmeyer-Kimling et al., 2005), all put children and adolescents at risk for the development of psychopathology (reviewed in Connell & Goodman, 2002). Overall, maternal or paternal psychopathology appears to put children and adolescents at risk for

psychopathology (Rohde, Lewinsohn, Klein, & Seeley, 2005), with a greater connection between maternal psychopathology and internalizing problems in children and no differences between maternal or paternal psychopathology in relation to elevated rates of externalizing problems in children (Connell & Goodman, 2002). Note also that for both mothers and fathers, children who have a parent who is comorbid with at least two disorders show the highest levels of maladjustment themselves (Ohannessian et al., 2004).

Adding to the complexity of this research area is the tendency for individuals to pair up with other individuals with comparable levels of mental health functioning. The term **assortative mating** is used to describe the tendency that clinically disturbed individuals tend to become involved with and have children with other individuals who are clinically disturbed (Foley et al., 2001; Luo & Klohnen, 2005). Given this pattern, it is possible that children may be exposed to two parents with clinical disorders. There is also a greater likelihood for parents who experience psychopathology to show higher rates of interparental conflict, higher rates of separation, and a greater likelihood of divorce (if they were married), so children are often exposed to parental psychopathology in addition to interparental conflict and parental separation (Merikangas et al., 1988). Thus, the study of children at high risk for the development of psychopathology due to parental psychopathology is quite complex.

A central question in the research on parental psychopathology relates to whether the increased risk is based on a genetic predisposition toward the same type of psychopathology as the parent experiences or whether the disturbed parenting influences the functioning of the child. As discussed in the chapter on etiological theories of disorders, it is not clear what percentage of the variance is accounted for by genetic predisposition and what percentage is accounted for by characteristics within the family and environment. For example, parental psychopathology is associated with low levels of positive emotionality (Durbin, Klein, Hayden, Buckley, & Moerk, 2005), low levels of emotional availability (Lum & Phares, 2005), and lax discipline (Leung & Slep, 2006), all of which are associated with emotional/behavioral problems in youth.

Relatedly, few disorders are linked directly from parent to child. For example, studies that show children of depressed mothers and depressed fathers are at increased risk for the development of psychopathology do not show that there is a direct link between parental

---

Case Study: Louie, Son of an Alcoholic Father

Comedian Louie Anderson (1991) wrote a funny and heart-wrenching book called *Dear Dad: Letters from an Adult Child*. The book is a compilation of letters that Louie wrote to his deceased father, who had experienced severe problems with alcohol abuse during Louie's childhood. The letters illustrate the devastation of parental alcohol abuse. Not only was Louie's father often absent (both physically and emotionally) due to the alcohol abuse, but he was often verbally abusive. In Louie's own words (from letters to his father):

"Secretly, I always wished someone would deck you, just once, but the one time I saw you splayed out frightened me in a way your abuse never did. It was a weekend afternoon and you and I were the only ones home. I was watching TV and heard a horrible crash. You were drunk and had fallen down the basement stairs. You were lying there, unconscious. I raced downstairs and tried to get you up. But I couldn't. So I put a pillow under your head and sat there until Mom got home.
"Why is Dad like this?" I asked Mom.
"He's drunk," she said matter-of-factly.
"Why?"
"He's been drinking."
"But why?"

"But why, Dad? I'd still really like to know the answer. It's something I think about when I'm sitting on my balcony on a clear night, gazing at the view of the city." (p. 45)

(When his father wanted to take him into a bar) "Ah, come on," you urged. "It's only for a minute."
"But, Dad. . .?" I whined
"You fucking baby, come on."
"What choice did I have? What twelve-year-old boy wants to be called a fucking baby by his father?" (At the end of this drinking episode, the father piled Louie and his brother into the car and drove while he was intoxicated enough to fall asleep at a stop sign.) (p. 72)

(When describing a shelter for abused, neglected, and runaway children where he worked the night shift, Louie describes his realization about himself in relation to his father) "In the sad eyes and weary, bruised faces of the children I was assigned to watch over, I found an aching emptiness that was similar to what I felt in my own heart. I understood their silence, their refusal to cry, and when they did cry or wake from bad dreams, I could honestly tell them, 'I understand.' " (p. 131)

Source: Anderson (1991).

depression and children's depression. One comprehensive review suggested that parental depression without concomitant interparental conflict was related to internalizing problems in children, such as depression or anxiety, but that parental depression in combination with interparental conflict was associated with externalizing problems in children, such as oppositional defiant disorder and conduct disorder (Downey & Coyne, 1990). This type of review suggests that few disorders are linked directly from parent to child. Rather, there are a complex set of characteristics that relate to the genetic and environmental factors that put children and adolescents at risk for the development of psychopathology when their parent or parents experience psychopathology.

PARENTAL LOSS DUE TO DEATH

As with so many other issues within developmental psychopathology, there are no easy answers to understanding the impact of parental death on children and adolescents. Approximately 3.4% of children and adolescents in the United States have lost one or both parents to death (Wolchik, Tein, Sandler, & Ayers, 2006). Two thirds of the parental loss has been the loss of a father. A number of studies have shown that children and adolescents who have lost a parent to death tend to show grief reactions and often show heightened levels of emotional/behavioral problems long after the death (reviewed by Dowdney, 2000). Approximately one out of five bereaved children develop a diagnosable mental disorder (Dowdney, 2000). Thus, increases in problems after parental death are not always found (Kwok et al., 2005). The risk for problems appears to be influenced by a number of different factors. Specifically, children who lose a parent to death are more likely to develop emotional/behavioral problems if (Dowdney, 2000; Kwok et al., 2005):

Case Study: The Parker Family, A Case of Interparental Conflict and Parental Problems

Alex is 16 years old, and he has been suspended from school for 8 days for fighting at school. He has a twin brother, Andrew, and the boys live with their mother, Leslie, and their father, Jerry. Leslie is a full-time homemaker, and Jerry is a salesperson for retirement plans. The oldest daughter, Barbara, is 20 and lives with her boyfriend in another city. The family sought family therapy due to Alex's suspension and due to other acting-out problems with Andrew. Alex had thrown a knife at Andrew previously, but the family did not seek help after that incident.

Although the presenting problems focused on the boys' behavior, the family therapist who worked with this family soon identified a number of other problems within the family system. Rather than just focusing on the presenting problem, the therapist asked questions about who runs the family (i.e., control), who gets upset the most (i.e., affective involvement), and how the parents get along (i.e., interparental conflict). It soon became evident that there were a host of other problems within the family, and the therapist hypothesized that the boys' acting-out behavior was serving as a shield for the parents' marital difficulties. Some of the parents' problems included:

- The mother felt abandoned by her husband, given that he worked 14-hour days and was not involved in family matters except when she forced his involvement.

- The mother and father argued a lot about how to handle the boys' behavior, about their lack of closeness to each other, and about their different interests (he liked to watch television and she liked to shop).

- The father had experienced a drinking problem for 25 years, but when he finally gave up alcohol 3 years previously, the mother did not even seem to notice. The mother and father argued a great deal when the father was abusing alcohol. After he quit, they had nothing to talk about, so they became even more distant. When the boys' acting-out behavior began (shortly after their father stopped drinking), the parents found something else about which to argue. The therapist hypothesized that arguing was the only way that the parents could communicate with each other, and it was the only closeness that they could feel from each other, even if the closeness was negative.

- The father was currently trying to lose weight, but the mother belittled his success. She felt that no good changes would come from improvements within the family.

After approximately 12 sessions (the majority of which involved only the parents and not the children), the family therapist was able to work with the parents to find more productive ways to communicate and to find ways to become close again without arguing. This case illustrates the connection between interparental conflict and children's acting-out behavior. In addition, this case highlights the need to look beyond children's acting-out behavior for other problems within the family system.

Source: Prevatt (1999a).

- There are multiple deaths at one time (e.g., both parents or a parent and a sibling)
- The parental death was sudden
- The parent's death was due to suicide or homicide
- The child who loses a parent had psychological difficulties even before the parent died
- The child had a conflicted relationship with the deceased parent
- The surviving parent or caretakers are significantly distressed and have limited abilities to deal with the child's needs
- There is an unstable home environment after the parent's death

Overall, parental death appears to be a risk factor for the development of emotional/behavioral problems, but not for all children. Children who have time to deal with the death (both in preparation and in response to the death), children who were well adjusted before losing their parent, those who had a good relationship with the parent prior to the parent's death, and children who have a stable and nurturing family environment after the loss of their parent appear to show no greater risk

for the development of emotional/behavioral problems or psychopathology after the parent's death (Lin, Sandler, Ayers, Wolchik, & Luecken, 2004). These patterns of findings appear to be regardless of the age of the child when they lost their parent to death and whether they lose their mother or their father (Cerel, Fristad, Verducci, Weller, & Weller, 2006).

I remember them arguing a lot. All the time. I mean, I never saw them express any emotional tenderness toward each other.
—Michelle, 14-year-old (Royko, 1999, p. 17).

INTERPARENTAL CONFLICT

One of the most consistent findings in the study of developmental psychopathology is the adverse effects of interparental conflict on child and adolescent functioning (Cummings, Goeke-Morey, & Papp 2004; Grych & Fincham, 2001. These findings are consistent internationally (Liu et al., 2000). Whether or not parents are still together, when parents argue, and especially when parents put their children in the middle of their arguments, children suffer. Interestingly, children and

---

BOX *5.2*

CHILDREN OF DIVORCE TELL IT LIKE IT IS

The arguments were hard to listen to in the evening time or morning time. In the daytime they were just skirmishes, nighttime they were full-blown wars. Yell, yell, yell, yell, yell. About bills, financial disagreements, taxes, all that lovely stuff.
—Arnie, 13 years old (p. 14)

I hated being in the middle. They still say things to me now, seven years after the divorce, about the other parent, and they expect me to laugh at a bad joke about them or to say something bad about them or to agree with something bad that's said about them. That's just a horrible thing to make somebody do, because they both know that I still care a lot about both of them . . .
—Nicole, 19 years old (p. 49)

When your mother and father split up, I don't care what age you are, if you love them at all, it hurts. It hurts bad.
—Leroy, 15 years old (p. 29)

My friend's parents are getting a divorce. I told him, "It won't be fun. You won't like it. But after a while you'll get used to it."
—Ted, 12 years old (p. 189)

When I was little, I thought the divorce was my fault, but it's sort of out of my mind. I don't remember. It's probably just the guilt of it.
—Tom, 12 years old (p. 48)

If I had three wishes, I'd ask for a thousand more wishes. Then I'd make every single wish be that my mom and dad would get back together and stay together forever—plus one wish for my dog, that he didn't die.
—Serena, 11 years old (p. 201)

My parents get along a lot better now than before Dad moved out and they got divorced. He'll come over for dinner and stuff.
—Al, 16 years old (p. 40)

Source: Royko (1999).

adolescents appear to function better in a non-conflicted, divorced family than in a conflicted intact family (Hetherington & Stanley-Hagan, 1999; Kelly, 2000). If, however, the conflict continues both before and after a divorce, then children in divorced homes tend to fare worse than those in intact families (Amato, 2001; Pruett, Williams, Insabella, & Little, 2003). See Box 5.2 to hear the direct experiences of children of divorce.

The issue of interparental conflict (and other psychosocial factors) is integral to the understanding of the connections between family constellation and child functioning. Early research suggested that children from divorced families were more maladjusted and remained more maladjusted than children in two-parent homes (reviewed by Hetherington et al., 1998). More recently, however, there is overwhelming evidence that family constellation is not the most crucial variable in children's functioning (Kelly, 2000). There are often greater numbers of problems found in children in single-parent families and in stepfamilies, but when factors such as interparental conflict, family adversity, and poor socioeconomic status

are considered, the meaningfulness of family constellation disappears (Clarke-Stewart, Vandell, McCartney, Owen, & Booth, 2000; Nicholson, Fergusson, & Horwood, 1999). Thus, when exploring functioning, children's exposure to interparental conflict is more important than whether they live with one or two parents. See Box 5.3 for an exploration of conflict in a laboratory setting.

BOX 5.3

WHY IS THE RESEARCH ASSISTANT YELLING AT DADDY?

Given that children cannot be randomly assigned to experience interparental conflict or not, how can researchers argue that interparental conflict "causes" emotional/behavioral problems in children? With some creative research designs, these issues have been addressed through experimental research methods.

Dr. E. Mark Cummings has headed one research team that explores children's exposure to conflict and anger with an experimental design. Dr. Cummings and his colleagues (reviewed in Cummings & Davies, 1994) have run studies that expose children to background anger to observe how children handle background anger. A typical design is to bring a child into the research room and have them take part in games or activities. After the researcher leaves the room, two people (sometimes the researcher and a stranger, sometimes the researcher and the child's parent, sometimes the child's parent and a stranger) get into a heated argument in the hallway. Sometimes the argument occurs in the room with the child. In other conditions, the two people engage in loud, but congenial conversations (to serve as a control group condition). Children are observed to see how they react to this background anger. Overall, children tend to become quite distressed and agitated when exposed to background anger. In many instances, children (especially

boys) show signs of aggressiveness after exposure to background anger.

This research design allows a closer look at children's reactions to anger and conflict without exposing children to excessive amounts of interparental conflict in the home. With this research design, the investigators have also found that some type of reconciliation or rapprochement observed by the child will help negate the effects of background anger. For example, if the research assistant who yelled at the parent later apologizes and explains that they are under stress, children's functioning tends to return to what it was before the angry interchange. Children and parents in these studies are debriefed about their participation, and there have been no negative long-term effects from these studies.

More recent studies from this research group include collecting diary records of children's reactions to interparental conflict in addition to collecting this type of observational data. Based on mothers', fathers', and children's diary records, children's level of aggression increased when they witnessed or heard their parents arguing (Cummings et al., 2004).

Source: Cummings & Davies (1994) and Cummings et al. (2004).

Case Study: Devastated Darryl

In order to gain more "hands on" experience with developmental psychopathology, you are going to be presented with a case and then you will be asked to formulate a treatment plan. In doing so, you will be challenged to apply your learning in an active manner. This process is similar to what practicing clinicians must take part in when ever they begin seeing a new client.

Once you have developed your own ideas, you will be presented with suggestions from The Adolescent Psychotherapy Treatment Planner *(Jongsma, Peterson, & McInnis, 2000a), which is reprinted from a series called* Practice Planners™ *that provides specific help to practicing clinicians. This case is meant to help you apply and integrate your learning. Hopefully, this exercise will also illustrate some of the actual techniques that are used by practicing clinicians.*

Darryl is a 13-year-old African-American boy whose parents divorced more than 2 years ago. He is currently at risk for being held back in school (due to failure to complete assignments and poor performance on tests). Darryl has missed quite a few days of school in the past year because of illnesses that do not appear to have any medical reason (e.g., stomachaches and headaches). Darryl is intermittently withdrawn and belligerent with his mother. He appears sad quite often, but then appears quite angry at other times. Darryl has gotten into fights with neighborhood teenagers on two occasions recently. Darryl's mother is concerned that he has begun drinking alcohol, though Darryl denies having done so.

Before the divorce, Darryl had a close relationship with both his father and his mother. Although his parents argued a lot before the divorce, Darryl was able to talk with both parents frequently and he seemed to enjoy family dinners together in particular, Darryl and his father used to go running together and they both enjoyed watching professional basketball together. Immediately after Darryl's parents separated, his father withdrew from the family and spent less and less time with Darryl and his twin sister. Darryl has not had any contact with his father in the past year. He wonders if he caused his parents' divorce, since he was beginning to spend more time with his friends right before his parents separated.

Darryl, his mother, and his twin sister took part in the initial interview. Although his father was contacted and invited to be part of the treatment, he declined. During the interview, Darryl appeared sad and upset, especially when talking about his father. He did, however, brighten up when talking about his maternal grandfather, with whom he has a good relationship. Darryl reported that he had some good friends, but that he had begun "hanging out" with other teenagers who tended to get in trouble. Darryl developed good rapport with you, but appeared to want to seem older than his age. For example, when speaking of the possibility of girlfriends, he used phrases that might be spoken by a 17-year-old boy rather than a 13-year-old boy.

Darryl's medical history and developmental milestones were all within the normal range. He and his father had been in a car accident when he was a toddler, but he did not receive any injuries (largely due to the high-quality car seat that his father had purchased).

Treatment Plan

Based on what you have learned from this textbook so far, try to write a treatment plan that would address Darryl and his family's concerns. Make sure to include behavioral definitions, long-term goals, short-term objectives, and therapeutic interventions. After you have written out your treatment plan, turn to the next section to review what is suggested in *The Adolescent Psychotherapy Treatment Planner* (Jongsma et al., 2000a).

Behavioral Definitions

1. _____
2. _____
3. _____
4. _____
5. _____
6. _____
7. _____
8. _____
9. _____
10. _____

Long-Term Goals

1. _____
2. _____
3. _____
4. _____
5. _____
6. _____
7. _____
8. _____
9. _____
10. _____

Short-Term Objectives	*Therapeutic Interventions*
1. _____	1. _____
2. _____	2. _____
3. _____	3. _____
4. _____	4. _____
5. _____	5. _____
6. _____	6. _____
7. _____	7. _____
8. _____	8. _____
9. _____	9. _____
10. _____	10. _____

From *The Child Psychotherapy Treatment Planner*—Jongsma Peterson, and McInnis (2000a)

(continued)

Case Study: Devastated Darryl (*continued*)

DIVORCE REACTION

BEHAVIORAL DEFINITIONS

1. Infrequent contact or loss of contact with a parental figure due to separation or divorce.
2. Loss of contact with a positive support network due to a geographic move.
3. Feelings of guilt accompanied by the unreasonable belief of having behaved in some manner to cause his/her parent's divorce and/or failed to prevent the divorce from occurring.
4. Strong feelings of grief and sadness combined with feelings of low self-worth, lack of confidence, social withdrawal, and loss of interest in activities that normally bring pleasure.
5. Intense emotional outbursts (e.g., crying, yelling, swearing) and sudden shifts in mood due to significant change in the family system.
6. Marked increase in frequency and severity of acting-out, oppositional, and aggressive behaviors since the onset of the parents' marital problems, separation, or divorce.
7. Significant decline in school performance and lack of interest or motivation in school-related activities.
8. Excessive use of alcohol and drugs as a maladaptive coping mechanism to ward off painful emotions surrounding separation or divorce.
9. Pattern of engaging in sexually promiscuous or seductive behaviors to compensate for the loss of security or support within the family system.
10. Pseudomaturity as manifested by denying or suppressing painful emotions about divorce and often assuming parental roles or responsibilities.
11. Numerous psychosomatic complaints in response to anticipated separations, stress, or frustration.

LONG-TERM GOALS

1. Accept the parents' separation or divorce with consequent understanding and control of feelings and behavior.
2. Establish and/or maintain secure, trusting relationships with the parents.
3. Create a strong, supportive social network outside of the immediate family to offset the loss of affection, approval, or support from within the family.
4. Eliminate feelings of guilt and statements that reflect self-blame for the parents' divorce.
5. Elevate and stabilize mood.
6. Refrain from using drugs or alochol and develop healthy coping mechanisms to effectively deal with changes in the family system.
7. Cease maladaptive pattern of engaging in sexually promiscuous or seductive behaviors to meet needs for affection, affiliation, and acceptance.

8. Parents establish and maintain a consistent, yet flexible, visitation arrangement that meets the client's emotional needs.
9. Parents establish and maintain appropriate parent–child boundaries in discipline and assignment of responsibilities.
10. Parents consistently demonstrate mutual respect for one another, especially in front of the children.

SHORT-TERM OBJECTIVES

1. Identify and express feelings related to the parents' separation or divorce.
2. Tell the story of the parents' separation or divorce.
3. Describe how the parents' separation or divorce has impacted personal and family life.
4. Express thoughts and feelings within the family system regarding parental separation or divorce.
5. Parents demonstrate understanding and empathy for how the divorce has impacted the client's life.
6. Recognize and affirm self as not being responsible for the parents' separation or divorce.
7. Parents verbalize an acceptance of responsibility for the dissolution of the marriage.
8. Recognize and verbally acknowledge that the parents will not be reuniting in the future and that he/she cannot bring the parents back together.
9. Identify positive and negative aspects of the parents' separation or divorce.
10. Identify and verbalize unmet needs to the parents.
11. Reduce the frequency and severity of angry, depressed, and anxious moods.
12. Decrease the frequency and intensity of emotional outbursts that occur in response to changes in the family or around periods of transfer from one parent's home to another.
13. Express feelings of anger about the parents' separation or divorce through controlled, respectful verbalizations and healthy physical outlets.
14. Reduce the frequency and severity of acting-out, oppositional, and aggressive behaviors.
15. Parents establish appropriate boundaries and follow through with consequences for acting-out, oppositional, or aggressive behaviors.
16. Parents verbally recognize how their guilt and failure to follow through with limits contributes to client's acting-out or aggressive behaviors.
17. Complete school and homework assignments on a regular basis.
18. Decrease the frequency of somatic complaints.
19. Parents assign an appropriate amount of household responsibilities or tasks to the client and siblings.

(*continued*)

20. Noncustodial parent verbally recognizes his/her pattern of overindulgence and begins to set limits on money and/or time spent in leisure or recreational activities.

21. Noncustodial parent begins to assign household responsibilities and/or require the client to complete homework during visits.

22. Reduce the frequency of immature and irresponsible behaviors.

23. Parents cease making unnecessary, hostile, or overly critical remarks about the other parent in the presence of the children.

24. Parents recognize and agree to cease the pattern of soliciting information about and/or sending messages to the other parent through the children.

25. The disengaged or uninvolved parent follows through with recommendations to spend greater quality time with the client.

THERAPEUTIC INTERVENTIONS

1. Actively build the level of trust with the client in individual sessions through consistent eye contact, active listening, unconditional positive regard, and warm acceptance to improve his/her ability to identify and express feelings connected to the parents' separation or divorce.

2. Explore, encourage, and support the client in verbally expressing and clarifying his/her feelings associated with the separation or divorce.

3. Develop a timeline where the client records significant developments that have positively or negatively impacted his/her personal and family life, both before and after the divorce. Allow the client to verbalize his/her feelings about the divorce and subsequent changes in the family system.

4. Use the empty chair technique to help the client express mixed emotions he/she feels toward both parents about the separation or divorce.

5. Ask the client to keep a journal where he/she explores experiences or situations that evoke strong emotions pertaining to the divorce. Share the journal in therapy sessions.

6. Assist the client in developing a list of questions about the parents' divorce, then finding possible answers for his/her questions.

7. Hold family therapy sessions to allow the client and siblings to express feelings about the separation or divorce in the presence of the parents.

8. Encourage the parents to provide opportunities at home (e.g., family meetings) to allow the client and siblings to express their feelings about the separation or divorce and subsequent changes in the family system.

9. Explore the factors contributing to the client's feelings guilt and self-blame about the parents' separation or divorce.

10. Assist the client in realizing that his/her negative behaviors did not cause the parents' divorce to occur and that he/she does not have the power or control to bring the parents back together.

11. Conduct a family therapy session where the parents affirm that the client and siblings are not responsible for the separation or divorce.

12. Challenge and confront statements by the parents that place blame or responsibility for the separation or divorce on the client or siblings.

13. Assign the client the homework of listing both positive and negative aspects of the parents' divorce. Process the information in the following session and allow the client to express different emotions.

14. Empower the client by reinforcing his/her ability to cope with the divorce and make healthy adjustments.

15. Provide support for the client in session to allow for expression of sad, depressed, or anxious feelings.

16. Direct the parents to spend 10 to 15 minutes of one-on-one time with the client and siblings on a regular or basis.

17. Assist the client in identifying activities (e.g., making popcorn and watching movies, playing a board game) help the client make the transition from one parent's home another without exhibiting excessive emotional distress fighting, or arguing.

18. Assist the client in making a connection between underlying painful emotions about the divorce and angry outbursts or aggressive behaviors.

19. Identify appropriate and inappropriate ways to express anger about the parents' separation or divorce or changes in the family.

Interparental conflict has been linked to a number of problems in children and adolescents, including externalizing problems, internalizing problems, social problems, interpersonal problems, and dating violence (Kelly, 2000; Kinsfogel & Grych, 2004; Lee, Beauregard, & Bax, 2005; O'Leary & Vidair, 2005). There is more evidence that interparental conflict puts children at risk for externalizing problems than for internalizing problems (Cummings et al., 2004; Kelly, 2000). Although some studies find age differences and gender differences in the impact of interparental conflict, most researchers find that interparental conflict impacts negatively on children of all ages and of both genders (Hetherington & Stanley-Hagan, 1999; Schulz, Waldinger, Hauser, & Allen, 2005).

YOU DECIDE: SHOULD PARENTS STAY MARRIED FOR THE SAKE OF THE CHILDREN?

<u>Yes</u>

• Children are better off living with married parents than they are living in single-parent households, especially from the standpoint of having access to better economic resources (Horn, 2006).

• Children whose parents divorce are at greater risk for many maladaptive outcomes, including behavioral difficulties, academic delays, and troubled romantic relationships when they grow up (Zinsmeister, 2006).

<u>No</u>

• If there are high degrees of interparental conflict that can be reduced through separation or divorce, then it is

better for parents to divorce so that the children are not exposed to the harmful effects of interparental conflict (Cummings, Goeke-Morey, & Raymond, 2004).

• If parents stay married and are so unhappy that they become depressed or begin abusing substances (which can happen when individuals are unhappy in their relationship), then the children will be at an increased risk for emotional/behavioral problems due to the parents' psychopathology (Connell & Goodman, 2002).

So, should parents stay married for the sake of the children? You decide.

One of the most damaging types of interparental conflict appears to be **triangulation,** when the child is put in the middle of the parents' arguments (Margolin, Gordis, & John, 2001). In addition, conflict that remains unresolved or that is resolved away from the child appears to be quite detrimental to children and adolescents (Cummings et al., 2004). Parents can help their children deal with conflict by allowing children to understand how the conflict was resolved (e.g., that the parents compromised on their disagreement or that they discussed the issue and then reached a mutually satisfying conclusion). Obviously, not all conflict is meant to be discussed in front of children, but it is important to model good conflict-resolution skills for children so that they understand how to deal with their own anger and conflict in other situations (Cummings et al., 2004).

Note that a number of programs have been developed to help prevent the difficulties that are associated with interparental conflict (e.g., Tein, Sandler, MacKinnon, & Wolchik, 2004). In addition, preventive mediation rather than litigation during divorce and child custody resolution appears to be associated with decreased interparental conflict and better outcome for children 12 years after parental divorce (Emery, Laumann-Billings, Waldron, Sbarra, & Dillon, 2001). These prevention programs appear to be promising for lowering this risk of children's maladjustment due to interparental conflict and divorce. As noted in the "You Decide" section, there continue to be ongoing debates about the importance of marriage for the well-being of children.

When children are abused physically, the wounds can be both physical and psychological.

My mother was with violent men. A series of them. Some of my earliest memories are of my father beating his mule and the mule running away one day. I think there was something in me that thought, he's going to get mad enough, he's going to do the same thing to me. So when he was whipping me with his razor strap, I must have been absolutely terrified.

—David Ray (Rhodes & Rhodes, 1996; p. 66)

CHILD PHYSICAL ABUSE

Physical abuse occurs when aversive or inappropriate control strategies are used with children, including beatings and consistent inappropriate use of physically coercive responses. Parents often do not consider their severe methods of corporal punishment and physical aggression toward their children as abusive, even though

Case Study: Joe and Erin, Physically Abused Children

Erin is 10 years old and her brother, Joe, is 12 years old. They attend the same school and were well-behaved children. Erin was a bit on the quiet side, and Joe was actively involved in many activities. Both children showed up to school with bruises and scratches on a regular basis, but the teachers assumed that they were just active children who received injuries in the course of their activities. Erin and Joe's parents were actively involved in the school and seemed to be conscientious and concerned parents.

Concern was raised when Erin showed up at school with a black eye. She told one of her friends that her father had hit her. When questioned by the teacher, Erin said that she had been hit by a baseball thrown by her brother. During the interview, the therapist noted that Erin had a number of burn marks that appeared to be cigarette burns. When asked about the marks, Erin stated that they were mosquito bites. When Joe was questioned about Erin's black eye, he reported that she had run into the bedroom door by accident. Neither child reported any difficulties with their parents. Given the conflicting stories, the seriousness of the burns, and the multitude of bruises, the child protective services removed the children from the home. Shortly thereafter, the children were allowed to return to the home if the father moved out. The children also began intensive therapy to deal with the abuse.

Over the course of therapy, the children finally admitted that they had received a great deal of "punishment" from their father. He would scold them if they did not have dinner ready when he got home, and he would yell at them when they did not finish their homework. More recently, he spanked them for what he perceived were their misbehaviors. Eventually, his anger became more extreme, and he hit Joe and threw Erin against a wall. One day when Erin had not finished her math homework, her father administered a cigarette burn for each math problem that was left unfinished. The black eye that was noticed by the teachers occurred after Erin had dropped something in the kitchen and her father hit her in the eye with his fist.

The children never wanted to report their father's behavior because they did not want to get him in trouble. They both felt that they deserved the "punishment" to some extent because they misbehaved.

When the parents were interviewed by the same therapist, the father finally admitted to the mother that the abuse allegations were true. The mother was shocked and upset. She had assumed that the allegations were false and that there had been a terrible misunderstanding. The father broke down and cried that he did not want to lose his family, but that he had been stressed about financial issues and he took his stress out on the children. For approximately 1 month, the mother stated that she would divorce the father because of the abuse. She felt immense anger toward him, and she felt a great deal of guilt for leaving her children with their father in the afternoons and evenings due to her work schedule. Both parents began attending group therapy, which included other abusive parents and their nonabusing partners. The father began making strides in his anger control and in attempting to communicate his concerns appropriately. The mother decided to work on saving the marriage and to work toward allowing her husband back in the home with the children.

The children continued to work with the therapist on issues of betrayal and anger management. Joe had become more and more angry at his father, and he began fighting at school. Over the course of therapy, the children seemed ready to be reunited with their father, and the father had made significant improvements in group therapy. The family was reunited, and family therapy sessions were continued for 6 months. Rules were established about how to punish the children's behavior appropriately and how to reward them for good behavior. One year after the case was closed, the child protective services agency did a follow-up to verify that the physical abuse had not reappeared. Both children were well adjusted, and neither reported any abusive incidents. The mother had gone back to college to work on a teaching certificate, and the father had received a promotion in the bank in which he worked.

Source: Morgan (1999).

---

their behavior would be considered physically abusive by professionals and by state law (Chang, Schwartz, Dodge, & McBride-Chang, 2003; Mahoney, Donnelly, Lewis, & Maynard, 2000; Wolfe, Rawana, & Chiodo, 2006). In many states, the indicator of physical abuse is when a mark is left on the child (e.g., from being hit by a hand or belt or by being burned intentionally). Comparable concerns are evident in many other countries, such as India (Hunter, Jain, Sadowski,

& Sanhueza, 2000), China (Chang et al., 2003), and countries within Eastern Europe (Sicher et al., 2000). It is estimated that between 5% and 26% of children and adolescents in the United States and similar countries are victims of physical abuse each year (Children's Defense Fund, 2005b; Cicchetti, 2004; Emery & Laumann-Billings, 1998). This estimate represents a wide range due to the difficulty in identifying child abuse, the secretive nature of this problem, and the difficulty in proving allegations of child abuse. In a study of community mental health clinics in Los Angeles, a total of 46.9% of children referred for mental health services were identified as having a history of maltreatment (Lau & Weisz, 2003). Not all children who are identified as having been abused are given follow-up services after the child protective services investigation. It is estimated that nearly 6 out of 10 (57.1%) of the cases of confirmed abuse did not receive any follow-up services such as medical treatment, psychological treatment, or parenting classes for the abusive parent (Children's Defense Fund, 2005b).

Although both boys and girls are equally at risk for physical abuse, it appears that age and gender interact when epidemiological patterns are considered. Boys under the age of 12 and girls over the age of 12 are the children at highest risk for physical abuse (Azar, Ferraro, & Breton, 1998), with both boys and girls under the age of 3 being at the highest risk for physical maltreatment (Cicchetti, 2004). Children who are exposed to spousal abuse (most often, children whose father physically abuses their mother) are significantly more likely to be physically abused than children who are not exposed to spousal abuse (McGuigan, Vuchinich, & Pratt, 2000). Children with physical and intellectual disabilities are even more likely to be physically abused than nondisabled children (Westcott & Jones, 1999). Children in poorer communities are more at risk for child physical abuse, but this connection appears to be more true for Caucasian-American families than for African-American families (Korbin, Coulton, Chard, Platt-Houston, & Su, 1998). Regardless of the specific number of children who are abused each year, the numbers are staggering.

In general, physical abuse of children and adolescents is associated with childhood depression, conduct disorder, oppositional defiant disorder, agoraphobia, overanxious disorder, generalized anxiety disorder, poor social competence, and global impairment (Cicchetti, 2004; Shonk & Cicchetti, 2001). Physical abuse is also associated with bullying, victimization, and rejection by peers (Bolger & Patterson, 2001; Shields & Cicchetti, 2001). Approximately one quarter to one half or more of children who experience physical abuse go on to experience posttraumatic stress disorder (PTSD; reviewed in Emery & Laumann-Billings, 1998). Physical abuse that is more severe and more long lasting puts children at even greater risk for PTSD (Emery & Laumann-Billings, 1998). Within a treatment setting, children with a history of maltreatment showed greater likelihood than children

without a history of maltreatment to show elevated externalizing problems, to leave treatment prematurely and without therapist approval, and to have elevated externalizing behaviors 2 years after treatment (Lau & Weisz, 2003). Even harsh physical punishment, which may not meet the definition of child physical abuse, is associated with greater emotional/behavioral problems in children (Lynch et al., 2006).

Child physical abuse is thought to put children at much greater risk for a whole host of emotional/behavioral problems. The effects of child physical abuse can often be long lasting and can sometimes continue into adolescence and adulthood if the problems are not dealt with in childhood (Bryant-Davis, 2005). For example, maltreated children were more likely than children without a history of maltreatment to perpetrate dating violence in adolescence or to be the recipient of dating violence (Ehrensaft et al., 2003; Kwong, Bartholomew, Henderson, & Trinke, 2003; Wolfe, Wekerle, Scott, Straatman, & Grasley, 2004). Physically abused children are at greater risk to physically abuse their own children (Dixon, Browne, & Hamilton-Giachritsis, 2005). Adolescent mothers who were abused as children were more likely to have difficulty with their own infant, but having a supportive caretaker and a supportive romantic relationship during the pregnancy appeared to decrease the likelihood of difficulty with the infant (Milan, Lewis, Ethier, Kershaw, & Ickovics, 2004). As can be seen in Table 5.1, a host of difficulties are associated with abusive parents and their abused children.

There are noticeable connections between physical abuse and brain development in children. Specifically, brain development is hampered in physically abused children even when there are not direct head injuries (Cicchetti, 2004; Glaser, 2000). New technology, such as the use of magnetic resonance imaging (MRI) has helped to identify physical abuse in children when the abuse might have gone undetected previously (Chabrol, Decarie, & Fortin, 1999). In addition to these potential changes in brain functioning, there is also evidence that maltreated children process information differently than others. Specifically, Price and Glad (2003) found that when compared to nonmaltreated children, maltreated children were more likely to interpret ambiguous or neutral events with hostile attributions toward their parents, an unfamiliar teacher, an unfamiliar peer, and their best friend. Thus, physical abuse can be associated with brain changes as well as cognitive processing changes.

TABLE 5.1   Parent Problem Areas and Child Problems Areas Related to Abuse.

	Parent problem area	Child problem area
Infancy and toddlerhood	Insensitive and noncontingent responsiveness Poor ability to tolerate stresses such as prolonged crying, sleep problems, and feeding difficulties Failures to engage in behaviors that foster language, social, and emotional development Lack of attention to safety issues and health needs/knowledge deficit Expectancies that infants and toddlers are able to perspective take, are capable of intentional provoking behavior, and can provide the parent comfort Deficits in skills to comfort/soothe child, utilize distraction, redirection, and environmental management as a means to reduce aversive child behavior and mange child behavior	Attachment problems Health-related difficulties, such as under-nourishment, low birth weight, prematurity, and physical trauma (e.g., shaken baby syndrome) Lags in toilet training, motor skills, speech, and language development, and socialization Anxiety In appropriate sexual behavior Nightmares
Early and middle childhood	Inconsistent and Indiscriminant use of discipline Overuse of physical strategies to manage behavior Lack of use of optimal socialization strategies (such as explanantion) General lack of Interaction A negative bias in overlabeling child behavior as evidence of misbehavior (even developmentally appropriate behavior) Poor ability to deal with stress of self-regulation problems in children (e.g., non-compliance) Unrealistic expectations of children's perspective-taking abilities, self-regulation skills, ability to place parental needs ahead of their own, to engage in self-care, and other house-hold duties	High levels of noncompliance Developmental and academic problems Social cognitive difficulties (e.g., expression and recognition of affect; perspective-taking; empathy, social problem-solving) Heightened aggression Poor social skills Conduct problems; firesetting Social withdrawal Cognitive delays such as greater distractibility Inconsistent school attendance Fatigue Low self-esteem Difficulty trusting others Trauma/stress-related symptoms (regressed behavior) Poor conflict resolution skills
Adolescence	Failure to use age-appropriate child management strategies Excessive attempts to control Decreased ability to tolerate teenagers' moves toward autonomy Poor ability to deal with emerging sexuality Unrealistic expectations of taking on adult responsibilities	Overrepresented among runaways, delinquents, and truants Poor academic performance Poor stress/anger management skills Social skill and peer Interaction problems Conduct problems Depression, suicidal, or self-injurious behavior

Source: Azar et al. (1998).

Frequently, children are exposed to physical abuse in the context of other risk factors, which makes them even more vulnerable to the development of problems. For example, children who were physically abused and who also had a parent diagnosed with schizophrenia were even more likely to show heightened levels of aggression and delinquency than those children exposed to either physical abuse or a schizophrenic parent alone (Walker, Downey, & Bergman, 1989). Children who were physically abused and who were exposed to violence within the community were more at risk for the development of emotional/behavioral problems (Lynch & Cicchetti, 1998).

In a study with direct ramifications for prevention of child physical abuse, physically abusive fathers were found to have lower rates of emotional support when compared with their nonabusing peers (Coohey, 2000). Specifically, abusive fathers were disengaged from their social network and their kin. It may be that friends, in-laws, and other kin discourage fathers' abusive behavior toward children (Coohey, 2000). These findings might help design prevention programs that would engage fathers in healthy social networks. Although there are more treatment programs for the effects of physical abuse than there are prevention programs, some outstanding prevention programs have been implemented both within the United States (Cicchetti, Toth, & Rogosch, 2000; Fisher, Gunnar, Chamberlain, & Reid, 2000) and in other countries (Sicher et al., 2000).

Overall, physical abuse often leads to devastating consequences for children and adolescents. Even sadder is the fact that many children who are physically abused are also at risk for sexual abuse.

CHILD SEXUAL ABUSE

Child sexual abuse has many different and complex definitions, but the majority of definitions focus on the sexual exploitation of children due to the inequality of power between the perpetrator and the child (Haugaard, 2000). Sexual abuse can range from anal, oral, genital, or breast contact and can also include exposing children to sexual behaviors or sexual materials that are age-inappropriate for the child. Although official estimates of the prevalence of childhood sexual abuse average around 3.2% for girls and 0.6% for boys, retrospective studies of adolescents who report sexual abuse during childhood suggest that between 12% and 35% of girls and 4% and 9% of boys have been sexually abused (Putnam, 2003). These figures are considered underestimates, given the hesitation that many children and adolescents would have about reporting such abuse. Even so, these figures show that girls are at significantly greater risk for sexual abuse than are boys. In infancy, the ratio between girls and boys is 2:1, in school-aged children the ratio is 3:1, and in adolescence, the ratio of girls to boys is approximately 6:1 (Wekerle & Wolfe, 1996). Children who live with a mother who was physically abused are 12 to 14 times more likely to be sexually abused than children whose mother was not physically abused (Emery & Laumann-Billings, 1998). Girls who live with a stepfather (or other unrelated male) and who live with their substance-abusing mother with a history of sexual abuse are at particularly great risk for being abused sexually (McCloskey & Bailey, 2000). Children with physical or cognitive disabilities are also at greater risk for sexual abuse, and the majority appear to be acquainted with the perpetrator (Keating, 1998). In a study of three generations of African-American families (child, mother, and grandmother), children were more at risk for sexual abuse when their mother was troubled as an adult, when the mother and grandmother had a negative relationship, and when the mother had received inconsistent parenting as a child (Leifer, Kilbane, Jacobsen, & Grossman, 2004). Child sexual abuse appears to occur in all socioeconomic classes and racial/ethnic groups to an equal degree (Putnam, 2003). Comparable rates of childhood sexual abuse have been found in other industrialized countries (Putnam, 2003).

Like child physical abuse, child sexual abuse tends to have devastating consequences for survivors of the abuse. The apparent consequences of childhood sexual abuse, however, vary according to a number of personal, familial, and abuse-related factors (Saywitz, Mannarino, Berliner, & Cohen, 2000). Factors that are relatively well established in showing even greater risk for psychological maladjustment after the sexual abuse include (Noll, Trickett, & Putnam, 2003; Putnam, 2003):

- When the abuse is perpetrated by a father or father figure
- Greater degree of sexual contact, including intercourse
- Greater periods of time over which sexual abuse is perpetrated
- Use of coercion and physical force and threats to perpetrate the sexual abuse
- Lack of support, disbelief, and victim-blaming when the child reports the abuse

The effects of child sexual abuse are variable, with some children never showing any adverse effects and

Case Study: Martha, Sexual Abuse Survivor

At the age of 16, Martha was experiencing severe abdominal pain and pain in her genital area. In addition, she experienced severe anxiety. After a thorough medical evaluation that resulted in no known cause for the pain, Martha was referred to a psychiatric clinic to determine if the pain was related to any emotional distress. Martha had a sister who was 1 year younger and a brother who was 2 years older.

Martha and her mother readily admitted that Martha had been sexually abused by her father from the age of 10 until she was 13 years old. At that time, the father left the house because he did not want to be "bothered" by the family any longer. When the sexual abuse first began, Martha reported it to her mother, who felt helpless to change her husband's behavior and who did not see that there was anything all that harmful about the sexual involvement. Although Martha begged her mother to stop her father from sexually abusing her and her sister, the mother made no attempts to stop the sexual abuse. After he moved out the house, Martha did not have any significant contact with her father, so she did not appear to be in danger of continued sexual abuse. The father was alcoholic and was arrested a number of times

for drunk and disorderly conduct after he moved out of the house.

Although Martha did not show any overt emotional/behavioral troubles in school, she was failing all her classes by the age of 16 and had never been a stellar student. She had a great many friends, but sometimes got into trouble with her friends (e.g., once the police were called when Martha and her sister were having a party when their mother was at work). Martha reported that she began smoking at the age of 14 to settle "her nerves," but she denied any use of alcohol or drugs. The pelvic and abdominal pain became very intense for Martha periodically, but the symptoms would disappear when she became involved in activities or when she got a phone call from a friend.

After a psychological evaluation, Martha was referred for therapy due to her unresolved issues related to the sexual abuse and due to her severe anger at her father. Although both Martha and her mother appeared receptive to Martha's therapy, they never made an appointment for therapy or any other intervention.

Source: Leon (1990).

---

the majority of children showing moderate to extreme negative sequelae after the sexual abuse. Children who have poor coping strategies in relation to the sexual abuse (such as becoming self-destructive or becoming avoidant) are more likely to experience long-term maladjustment into adulthood than are children who show adaptive coping techniques (Merrill, Thomsen, Sinclair, Gold, & Milner, 2001). One retrospective study of childhood sexual abuse suggested that history of sexual abuse was more predictive of suicidality in adults than was current diagnosis of depression (Read, Agar, Barker-Collo, Davies, & Moskowitz, 2001). Even when controlling for other risk factors, women who were sexually abused as children have a 2 to 4 times greater likelihood of attempting suicide than nonabused women, and men have a 4 to 11 times greater risk for suicide attempts than do men who do not have a history of sexual abuse (Molnar, Berkman, & Buka, 2001). There is relatively clear evidence that women who report a history of sexual abuse are more likely than nonabused women to experience more relationship problems and more sexual difficulties (Noll et al., 2003; Rumstein-McKean & Hunsley, 2001; Testa, VanZile-Tamsen, & Livingston, 2006).

There are a number of ways of conceptualizing the negative impact of childhood sexual abuse. The

traumagenic dynamics model highlights four primary factors that relate to adverse outcomes in children after sexual abuse:

- Exposure to age-inappropriate sexual behaviors and traumatic sexualization
- Feelings of powerlessness related to the child's inability to prevent the abuse
- Other individuals stigmatizing the child or otherwise conveying negative feelings about the child because of the sexual abuse
- Feelings of betrayal when a trusted individual breaks that trust by perpetrating abuse or feelings of betrayal at the lack of being protected from the sexual abuse (Finkelhor, 1988)

Another more recent integrative model is shown in Figure 5.1, which shows a number of complex factors that lead to the possibility of psychological symptoms related to child sexual abuse. As can be seen in this **transactional model,** there are bidirectional influences between abuse stress (such as the actual abuse and the response to disclosure of abuse), coping strategies (how the child tries to cope with the sexual abuse), cognitive appraisals (how the child thinks about the sexual abuse), and psychological symptoms. In addition, support resources (such as family

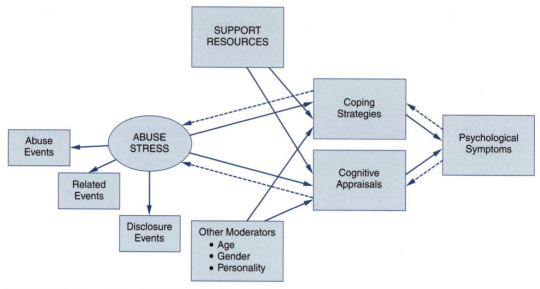

FIGURE 5.1   Transactional Model of Child Sexual Abuse.

Source: Spaccarelli (1994).

or individual supports for the child) and other moderating factors (such as age, gender, and personality variables) can influence both children's coping strategies and cognitive appraisals (Spaccarelli, 1994). This model shows the complexity that is evident when trying to determine the impact of childhood sexual abuse.

Overall, childhood sexual abuse has been linked to PTSD, anxiety, depression, sexual difficulties or sexual acting out, teenage pregnancy, substance abuse, and externalizing problems (Bailey & McCloskey, 2005; Rumstein-McKean & Hunsley, 2001). The link between sexual abuse and later sexual activity is mediated by coping strategies, whereby girls who use avoidant coping strategies are likely to have fewer sexual partners as young adults whereas girls who use self-destructive coping strategies are likely to have more sexual partners as young adults (Merrill, Guimond, Thomsen, & Milner, 2003).

For the majority of children and their loved ones, childhood sexual abuse is a devastating stressor with which to deal. Effective treatments have been developed for posttraumatic symptoms related to childhood sexual abuse (King et al., 2000; Putnam, 2003). Given the often significant adverse effects of childhood abuse and maltreatment, a number of prevention programs have also been developed to prevent the occurrence of abuse and maltreatment in childhood (see Boxes 5.1 and 5.4).

The wound caused by words is worse than the wound of bodies.

—Proverb of Africa

CHILD PSYCHOLOGICAL MALTREATMENT

Psychological or emotional maltreatment of children has received less attention in the research literature than either physical abuse or sexual abuse in childhood. Largely due to the difficulty of defining psychological maltreatment and the difficulty of identifying psychologically maltreated children, this topic has remained unexplored until relatively recently. Psychological abuse can be defined as a pattern of acts or verbalizations that damage the child psychologically with regard to cognitive, affective, behavioral, or physical functioning of the child. Examples of psychological abuse include (Brassard, Germain, & Hart, 1987; Hamarman, Pope, & Czaja, 2002:

- Rejection—When children are actively rejected or made scapegoats in the family and when children are given constant negative evaluations about themselves

- Terrorizing—When children are threatened, inordinately teased, or (depending on age) are intentionally terrified by adults around them

- Isolating—When children are kept from socializing with others, including being locked in a closet or locked in the basement for long periods of time

BOX *5.4*

SCHOOL-BASED PREVENTION OF CHILD SEXUAL ABUSE

Given the devastation of child sexual abuse, there have been efforts across the nation to institute programs to prevent the occurrence of sexual abuse. Many of these programs have been based in preschools and in elementary schools. These programs tend to focus on informing children about "good" touch and "bad" touch, empowering children to say "no" to taking part in activities that make them uncomfortable, and encouraging them to tell a trusted adult about any attempted or actual abuse. These types of programs have been successful with regard to information retention (e.g., giving children an informational test before and after the training, which shows that they learned something during the training; Davis & Gidycz, 2000; Finkelhor, Asdigian, & Dziuba-Leatherman, 1995; Kolko, 1988; Liang, Bogat, & McGrath, 1993). Longer-term programs that utilize behavioral skills training are the most effective (Davis & Gidycz, 2000). In addition, these programs usually train teachers to notice the possible signs of child sexual abuse and inform teachers about how to report occurrences of child sexual abuse (Liang et al., 1993).

These programs, however, are not without their drawbacks. Following are a few of the concerns about the nationwide focus on teaching children how to protect themselves, while little is done to prevent adults from actually abusing children (Conte, Wolf, & Smith, 1989; Melton, 1992; Pelcovitz, Adler, Kaplan, Packman, & Krieger, 1992; Renk, Liljequist, Steinberg, Bosco, & Phares, 2002; Trudell & Whatley, 1988):

- Putting the onus on children, rather than adults, to stop sexual abuse is inappropriate and may send the message that children can just say "no" to sexual abuse and make it stop.
- Even if a child does say "no" or in some other way is able to prevent his or her own sexual abuse, surveys of sexual offenders suggest that the offender would just find another target for the abuse.

- These prevention programs tend to focus on non–family members as abusers, and few programs focus on the fact that the majority of harm (both physical abuse and sexual abuse) comes from within the family or from trusted friends of the family.

Other preventionists have suggested that, in addition to these school-based programs, more attention should be paid to actually preventing sexual offenders from wanting to offend. Many suggestions have been proposed, including early sex education, to promote responsible sexuality that does not include power and domination as in the case of sexual abuse and sexual assault (Renk et al., 2002; Williams, 1983) and disentangling the connections at the societal level (as evidenced in the media as well as in homes across the nation) between sex and power (Tutty, 1991). Interestingly, fathers who are more involved in their child's life during infancy are much less likely to sexually abuse their child, so there has been a call to encourage responsible and involved fathering that could prevent the occurrence of sexual abuse within the family (Parker & Parker, 1986). In addition to these prevention strategies, there has also been increased focus on keeping sexual offenders and sexual predators away from children by either mandating further treatment or by reporting the offenders' whereabouts to the neighborhood and to the community (Myers, 1996).

Overall, the prevention of child sexual abuse is extraordinarily complex. There are no easy answers, yet it appears that multifaceted approaches that include many different levels of prevention (e.g., school-based programs with children, working with teachers to identify signs of sexual abuse, helping parents to understand how to recognize signs of abuse, responsible sexuality training at many grade levels, media messages about the inappropriateness of controlling a child through sexual domination) are most appropriate.

- Degrading—When children are called names and belittled constantly, even when they have accomplished something worthwhile
- Missocializing—When children are encouraged to break the law, such as stealing for their parents, or when children are encouraged to engage in age-inappropriate behaviors such as drinking, smoking, using drugs, or having sex

Although some of these comments or behaviors may be evidenced by even the most competent parents, psychological abuse is identified when there is a consistent pattern of these types of comments and behaviors. As with other types of abuse, psychological maltreatment is associated with a range of problems in children, including internalizing problems, externalizing problems, and low self-esteem (Azar et al., 1998).

Case Study: The D'Niale Family, Psychological and Emotional Abuse

The D'Niale family consists of a mother, father, 2-year-old boy (Sonny Jr.), 5-year-old boy (Joey), and 8-year-old girl (Francine). The two older children are Mrs. D'Niale's children from previous relationships. The family was known to child protective service agents because of multiple generations of abuse and neglect. The family is Caucasian, and they live in poverty.

At the time of the evaluation, Mrs. D'Niale showed signs of severe depression and has also shown inadequate parenting skills. Mr. D'Niale experienced alcohol dependency and often had alcohol-related seizures and periods of violence related to the alcohol dependency. One example of a violent episode was when he ran out of beer, he pushed the refrigerator off the fourth floor balcony. Luckily, no one was underneath the refrigerator when it hit the ground four stories below. Mr. D'Niale recently was arrested for breaking and entering and was awaiting sentencing. Both parents reported a great deal of interparental conflict. All three children show emotional/behavioral problems. The 2-year-old, Sonny Jr., is very aggressive with everyone, including his siblings and parents. The 5-year-old, Joey (who was physically abused as a child and who had witnessed his mother being beaten and raped when he was younger), was very quiet and withdrawn. The 8-year-old, Francine (who had been neglected for long periods of time when she was an infant and who had been physically abused by her mother), showed signs of conduct disorder. Francine had already been taken away from Mrs. D'Niale's custody and was living with her grandmother.

During the evaluation (where Mr. D'Niale was noticeably absent), Mrs. D'Niale showed clear signs of psychological abuse toward her children. She constantly belittled her children and called them names. She referred to Joey as a sissy, a baby, and as stupid. She referred to Sonny Jr. (who had a soiled diaper for the entire 4 hour interview) as "stinker" and "my little shit." Mrs. D'Niale also used terrorizing with her children in an attempt to control them. For example, when Sonny Jr. dropped a glass of milk, Mrs. D'Niale replied, "Clean that up or I'll break your fingers." She also threatened to put Joey in a garbage can, to burn the children with her lit cigarette, and to break their bones. She reported that she forbids the children from playing with neighborhood children, and she often refuses to let the children attend school.

Overall, this case illustrates clear psychological abuse in addition to patterns of physical abuse, neglect, and parental psychopathology. The children were referred for therapy to deal with the effects of the abuse, and the parents were offered numerous services to deal with their issues. Unfortunately, these types of complicated cases (especially when there are multiple generations of dysfunction) are difficult to treat without immense and multifaceted intervention services (including individual therapy, family therapy, parent training, educational support, social service help with employment and financial issues, and possible medical interventions when needed).

Source: Brassard, Hart, & Hardy (1991).

Psychological maltreatment is difficult to identify, given the hidden nature of the trauma and the sometimes ambiguous definitions (Hamarman & Bernet, 2000). Clinicians, teachers, and other caring adults can be on the alert for psychological abuse by listening to how parents talk to their children and by noticing when children make particularly self-disparaging comments about themselves that might represent what they have heard from their parents (Azar et al., 1998).

Although not formally considered a type of psychological maltreatment, it is important to note that racism is associated with increased emotional/behavioral problems in African-American adolescent boys (Nyborg & Curry, 2003). Specifically, when adolescents perceived greater levels of verbal and institutional racism, they reported higher levels of externalizing problems, internalizing problems, and hopelessness and lower levels of self-concept. Thus, psychological maltreatment within the family and within the larger community (as reflected through racism) should be explored more extensively,

given the connection with children's and adolescents' well-being.

FAMILY DYSFUNCTION

In addition to parental functioning and abuse within the family, a number of other family factors can put children and adolescents at risk for the development of psychopathology. Factors within the family that have been associated with the development of emotional/behavioral problems include high rates of hostility and competitiveness (McHale & Rasmussen, 1998), family-related and parent-related stress (Grant et al., 2003; Rudolph & Hammen, 1999), maladaptive family environment (Ford, Goodman, & Meltzer, 2004; Jacobson & Rowe, 1999), low family cohesion (Cuffe, McKeown, Addy, & Garrison, 2005), parental negative affect and negative control (Deater-Deckard, Fulker, & Plomin, 1999), parental criticism (McCarty, Lau, Valeri, & Weisz, 2004), negative expressed emotion (Wamboldt & Wamboldt, 2000), uninvolved parenting (Simons et al., 2002), maladaptive parenting style (Hoge, Andrews, & Leschied, 1996), parental emotional unavailability (Lum & Phares, 2005), and sibling deviance (Stormshak, Comeau, & Shepard, 2004). One study found that older adolescents reported higher rates of mental health problems when they reported retrospectively that their mother was less affectionate than their father (Jorm, Dear, Rodgers, & Christensen, 2003). Many of these risk factors have been identified in other countries, including Nigeria (Omigbodun, 2004). Obviously, in most countries, many family factors are associated with the development of emotional/behavioral problems in children and adolescents. Sometimes these factors are related to risk factors that have already been discussed (e.g., depressed parents may show more hostility toward their children than nondepressed parents). Thus, children are often exposed to multiple risk factors within the family environment.

I used to like school a lot. Now since they got divorced, it's just okay. Really, I don't like anything that much anymore.
—Dexter, 13 years old (Royko, 1999 p. 197).

INADEQUATE EDUCATIONAL RESOURCES

Turning away from family-related risk factors, it is also important to acknowledge the risk factors related to the educational system and the larger community. There are a number of risk factors in the school system, including difficult transitions from elementary to middle school (Holmbeck & Shapera, 1999), lack of school connectedness (Jacobson & Rowe, 1999), and less than optimal school settings (Luthar, 1999).

In general, higher numbers of school transitions that children have to experience are associated with increased risk for emotional/behavioral problems (Richman, Bowen, & Woolley, 2004). The transition between elementary school and middle school seems to be particularly difficult for a great many adolescents, partly due to the many changes that this transition brings (e.g., having one teacher in elementary school and having upward of six teachers in middle school). Higher educational levels tend to be associated with more complex school environments and more complex social systems, so adolescents must deal with a great deal of changes as they move from elementary school to middle school to high school (Holmbeck & Shapera, 1999). Box 5.5 describes

a prevention program that is targeted at making school transitions easier for children and adolescents.

A lack of school connectedness (i.e., when children feel than their teachers care about them, that the school is fair in its policies, that the school is a safe environment, and that they belong at the school) is associated with greater emotional/behavioral problems (Jacobson & Rowe, 1999). The direction of this association is not clear, given that more distressed children could perceive less school connectedness because of possible cognitive distortions related to their level of distress. Regardless of the direction of this association, it appears that children who feel less connected with their school and who feel marginalized within the school system are at greater risk for emotional/behavioral problems (Jacobson & Rowe, 1999).

School environments vary from dismal to optimal. Schools that provide a less than optimal environment for students are associated with a host of risk factors for children's emotional/behavioral problems. For example, greater class size is associated with poorer academic achievement and decreased functioning (Mather & Ofiesh, 2005). Poorer schools tend to be overcrowded, tend to have a poorer teacher–student ratio, tend to have fewer resources for basic educational opportunities as well as enrichment opportunities, and often have teachers and administrators with lower expectations of academic success for their students (Elias, Parker, & Rosenblatt, 2005). All these factors are linked to poorer academic achievement and greater rates of emotional/behavioral problems in children and adolescents (Luthar, 1999). It appears that children and adolescents who are exposed to poorer educational environments are often also those children who are exposed to poverty, low socioeconomic status, and violence within their communities.

Poverty is the worst form of violence.

—Mahatma Gandhi

POVERTY AND LOW SOCIOECONOMIC STATUS

In general, low socioeconomic status and poverty have been linked to greater rates of emotional/behavioral problems in children and adolescents (Evans, 2004; Samaan, 2000; Wadsworth & Achenbach, 2006; Wadsworth & Compas, 2002). Although children who grow up in affluent suburban neighborhoods are not immune from maladaptive outcomes (Luthar & Latendresse,

BOX 5.5

HELPING CHILDREN WITH SCHOOL TRANSITIONS

Because of the problems that often occur when children transition into middle school or high school, a number of prevention programs have been instituted to see if the structure of the school can help children negotiate these transitions more successfully. One such program is called the School Transitional Environment Program (STEP; Felner et al., 2001; Felner, Ginter, & Primavera, 2002). This program has been applied to children who were not only at risk because of their school transition status, but who were also at risk because they were impoverished and of minority ethnic status, they received little support from their families or community, and they were entering puberty.

The STEP program trained teachers and administrators to help children with this transition. In addition, changes in the school environment were made to help children with the transition. Some of these changes included

- Reorganizing the social system so that children had at least four classes with the same group of classmates
- Assigning students to a homeroom, which became a solid base from which students could learn about the rest of the school and where the students could be monitored and helped by the homeroom teacher
- Helping teachers develop teamwork mentalities to help students and to help each other with the emotional and academic support that was needed

Overall, the STEP program was very effective. Children who were involved in the STEP program showed lower absentee rates, were less likely to drop out of school, and had better academic achievement than children who were not exposed to the STEP program.

Note that the STEP program was administered to children in selected schools based on the overall risk factors for most children. This type of prevention program is called selective prevention, because it is targeting a group of children who are at risk for developing problems. Universal prevention programs would target general populations of children whether or not they are risk for the development of problems and indicated prevention programs would select only those children who have already evidenced problems. Prevention programs were discussed in the chapter on therapeutic and preventive interventions. Overall, the STEP program is a nice example of a selective prevention program that can be administered to children to help prevent problems that typically occur due to transition into middle school.

Source: Felner et al. (2001); Felner et al. (2002).

2005b), living in abject poverty appears to put youth at increased risk for a whole host of problems. As can be seen in Figure 5.2, younger children and adolescents at the most severe levels of poverty have higher rates of emotional/behavioral problems than other youth (Urban Institute, 1999b).

Poverty, however, is not a distinct factor as much as it is a constellation of factors that co-occur when there is little money or resources within the family. See Box 5.6 to get a glimpse of the characteristics of children in poverty in the United States currently. Children in poverty are exposed to significantly more risk factors than children who do not live in poverty (Evans, 2004). Teenage mothers are more likely to live within poverty and to raise their children in poverty (Children's Defense Fund, 2005d). Households headed by single parents, most often single mothers, are overrepresented in low socioeconomic neighborhoods (Bradley & Corwyn, 2002). Homelessness (Buckner, Bassuk, Weinreb, & Brooks, 1999; Embry, Vander Stoep, Evens, Ryan,

& Pollock, 2000), housing instability (Adam, 2004), and family instability (Milan, Pinderhughes, & the Conduct Problems Prevention Research Group, 2006) are also associated with living in poverty. Children and adolescents living in poverty are exposed to more chaos than their nonpoor counterparts, as evidenced by less stable and structured households, more housing disruptions, and poorer physical environment of the dwelling (Evans, Gonnella, Marcynyszyn, Gentile, & Salpekar, 2005). Impoverished children living in homes characterized by chaos were also likely to be exposed to poor parental discipline (Dumas et al., 2005). Children in impoverished neighborhoods can be surrounded by social networks of other troubled youth (Leventhal & Brooks-Gunn, 2003). Children from ethnic and racial minority groups are overrepresented in impoverished neighborhoods (Brady & Matthews, 2002). In a litany of the harsh realities of poverty, Evans (2004) noted that when compared to their economically advantaged peers, poor children

Case Study: Oswald, a Boy from a Disadvantaged Environment

Oswald is an 11-year-old, African-American boy living in public housing with his 36-year-old mother and his seven siblings. One other brother died in an accident 2 years ago. Oswald's father was also killed in this accident. Before this accident, there had been five boys and four girls. Oswald was the fourth oldest child. The family has been receiving public assistance in the form of Aid to Families with Dependent Children (AFDC) for over 5 years. The family lived in an apartment that had a total of four rooms (including the living room and kitchen), so the siblings often got in each others' way and would fight to maintain some space for themselves. There were no quiet places to read or do homework in the house.

Oswald's mother, Mrs. Williams, wanted to have Oswald's intelligence tested. Oswald had been in a special education class for children with borderline or retarded intellectual functioning. In addition, Oswald had been showing aggression, which was usually unprovoked, both at school and at home.

Oswald was born prematurely, and he suffered from a number of medical problems when he was a baby. His developmental milestones (such as crawling, walking, and talking) tended to come a bit later than would be expected. When Oswald first began school, he was referred for intelligence testing because of "partial lack of communication and reading impairment." At that time, his intellectual functioning fell into the mildly retarded range (IQ below 70 with limited adaptive abilities). In second grade, Oswald tested in the IQ range of borderline intellectual functioning (IQ between 70 and 80). Oswald had always been in special education classes at school.

The family had experienced many traumas, many of which were related to limited financial resources. Mr. Williams had been marginally employed, but when he died, the family became even more destitute. In addition, the family and Mrs. Williams were devastated by the loss of Mr. Williams and one of the boys. Mrs. Williams reported that Mr. Williams had always been the disciplinarian and he had always made sure to know the children's whereabouts. Mrs. Williams tried to carry on these behaviors after Mr. Williams' death, but she found it difficult to do so. She was especially concerned about the safety of her children, given the dangerous and often violent neighborhood in which they lived. She rarely left the house and rarely let the children leave the house for anything other than school due to her fear of the harm that might come to them. When she did leave the house, Mrs. Williams would phone the children every 15 minutes to make sure that they were alright.

Because of the difficulties with her children, Mrs. Williams started treatment to help with parenting issues and to help make decisions about Oswald's educational future. Oswald also saw a male social worker for counseling in order to work on his anger management and aggression issues. With therapy, Mrs. Williams learned how to set appropriate limits on her children's behavior. She was also encouraged to find enjoyable activities for herself. She became more involved in the church, began dating a man in the same housing project, and began working at a part-time job as a cleaning woman to help with the financial strain on the household. Mrs. Williams reported that she felt very relaxed when she was at work, because she felt that she was helping her children without having to worry about them constantly.

Oswald developed a very therapeutic bond with his social worker, but his behavior became progressively worse. He was suspended a number of times from school. The social worker and teacher worked out a token economy, through which Oswald could earn tokens for good behavior at school, and his mother could reward him at home (e.g., with extra attention or by letting him stay in a room by himself for a certain amount of time without interruption from his brothers and sisters). The token economy appeared to be working well. Unfortunately, Mrs. Williams and Oswald stopped coming to therapy and did not respond to the therapists' repeated invitations to continue their work together.

Source: Leon (1990).

---

are exposed to more family turmoil, violence, separation from their families, instability, and chaotic households. Poor children experience less social support, and their parents are less responsive and more authoritarian,. Low-income children are read to relatively infrequently, watch more TV, and have less access to books and computers. Low-income parents are less involved in their children's school activities. The air and water poor children consume are more polluted. Their homes are more crowded, noisier, and of lower quality. Low-income neighborhoods are more dangerous, offer poorer municipal services, and suffer greater physical deterioration. Predominantly low-income schools and day care are inferior. (p. 77)

As mentioned in the first chapter, the rates of children living in poverty in the United States and other countries are staggering. Approximately 29.2% of all children under the age of 18 in the United States live in families that are characterized by low income (Urban Institute, 2004). This percentage varies widely, depending on the child's ethnic and racial background, with 21.4% of Caucasian-American children, 44.4% of African-American children, and 54.5% of Hispanic/Latino/Latina

BOX 5.6

WHO ARE POOR CHILDREN IN THE UNITED STATES?

- They live with at least one employed parent (e.g., 70% live in families where a family member is employed, and 31.4% live with a full-time, year-round worker).

- They are of every race (e.g., 4.2 million of poor children are White, 3.9 million are Black, and 4.1 million are Hispanic/Latina/Latino).

- They experience serious deprivations throughout the year (e.g., 55% experience serious deprivations such as lack of food, no utilities, substandard housing)

- The majority of poor children do not live in inner-city, urban areas but rather in rural and suburban areas.

- There are an average of 2.2 children in poor families.

There are over 13 million children in the United States currently being raised in poverty, 5.6 million of which are considered to be living in extreme poverty. The poverty line for a three-person family was set at less than $15,219 per year in 2004. Extreme poverty is defined as a three-person family living on less than $7,610 per year.

Source: Children's Defense Fund (2005d).

Poverty is associated with emotional/behavioral problems in children.

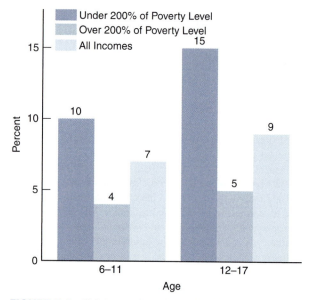

FIGURE 5.2 Children with high levels of behavioral and emotional problems, by age and family income, 1997.

Source: Urban Institute (1999b).

children living in poverty (Urban Institute, 2004). Although many people think of inner-city children when they think of poverty, note that poverty exists in many different types of communities, including rural communities (Murry & Brody, 1999).

Rates of childhood psychopathology are higher in impoverished communities than in communities with adequate resources, even after controlling genetic predispositions (Caspi, Taylor, Moffitt, & Plomin, 2000). Figure 5.3 shows the possible effects of neighborhoods and the community across the life span (Caspi & Moffitt, 1995). The effects of poverty, however, appear to impact African-American children to an even larger degree

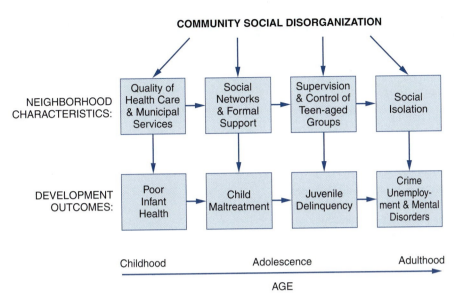

COMMUNITY SOCIAL DISORGANIZATION

NEIGHBORHOOD CHARACTERISTICS:

Quality of Health Care & Municipal Services → Social Networks & Formal Support → Supervision & Control of Teen-aged Groups → Social Isolation

DEVELOPMENT OUTCOMES:

Poor Infant Health → Child Maltreatment → Juvenile Delinquency → Crime Unemployment & Mental Disorders

Childhood   Adolescence   Adulthood

AGE

FIGURE 5.3 Community effects on the developing person across the life span.

Source: Caspi & Moffitt (1995).

than children from other ethnic and racial backgrounds (Luthar, 1999). In addition, children living in poverty who are also exposed to harsh or inconsistent parenting and severe stressors are even more likely to develop emotional/behavioral problems than are children living in poverty who are not exposed to those factors (Brody et al., 2001; Evans, 2004; McLoyd, 1998). Interestingly, harsh parenting such as high rates of parental criticism were associated with poor outcomes in children regardless of their impoverished or affluent living situation (Luthar & Latendresse, 2005a). Low amounts of parental monitoring (e.g., parents who do not keep track of where their children spend their time and who do not set limits on their children's activities) were also associated with greater externalizing problems in a group of children from impoverished and unsafe neighborhoods (Pettit, Bates, Dodge, & Meece, 1999) as well as in a group of children from middle-class neighborhoods (Waizenhofer, Buchanan, & Jackson-Newsom, 2004). Homelessness was related to internalizing problems but not externalizing problems when other factors of poverty were controlled (Buckner et al., 1999). Family instability, which was defined as the number of times families moved or changed settings, was directly related to increased emotional/behavioral problems in children as young as 7 years old (Ackerman et al., 1999). Experiences of racism and criminal victimization were related to the development of depressive symptoms in a sample of impoverished youth (Simons et al., 2002).

Overall, low socioeconomic status and poverty are associated with increased risk for the development of emotional/behavioral problems in children and adolescents. Low socioeconomic status is also associated with physical health, which can influence psychological well-being (Chen, 2004). As with so many other risk factors, the risk factor of low socioeconomic status is compounded by other factors, such as neighborhood safety, single-parent homes, stressors within the family, family instability, and lack of resources (Evans, 2004). Violence within the community also appears to be confounded with living in impoverished neighborhoods. Box 5.7 gives a sense of a day in the life of America's children.

Injustice anywhere is a threat to justice everywhere.
—Dr. Martin Luther King

VIOLENCE WITHIN THE COMMUNITY

Sadly, children living in poverty often witness violence or are the victims of violence themselves. In a national survey of children and adolescents from all SES brackets, nearly one third had witnessed violence or been exposed to indirect victimization, such as household theft or having someone close to them harmed (Finkelhor, Ormrod, Turner, & Hamby, 2005). Overall, 13.0% had witnessed an assault with a weapon, 21.4% had witnessed an assault without a weapon, 0.3% witnessed a murder, 4.7% witnessed a shooting or bombing, and 9.2% had their home burglarized (Finkelhor et al., 2005).

The rates of exposure to violence are even more disturbing in impoverished areas. In a survey of first- and

BOX 5.7

THE STATE OF AMERICA'S CHILDREN

In the United States, here is what a day in the life of a child
looks like:

Every 9 seconds	a student in high school drops out of school
Every 20 seconds	a child or teenager under the age of 18 is arrested
Every 36 seconds	a baby is born into poverty
Every 1 minute	a baby is born to a mother who is a teenager
Every 2 minutes	a baby is born with low birth weight
Every 4 minutes	a child is arrested on drug abuse charges
Every 19 minutes	a baby dies before turning 1 year old
Every 3 hours	a child or teenager is killed by a gun
Every 5 hours	a child or teenager commits suicide
Every 6 hours	a child is killed by abuse or neglect

Source: Children's Defense Fund (2005d).

second-grade students living in the inner city of Washington, D.C., 90% of the children reported having witnessed at least one arrest, and over one third reported that they have seen a dead body in the community (Richters & Martinez, 1993). In Miami, 87% of innercity adolescents reported having witnessed a beating or mugging, 38% reported that they were the victim of a beating or mugging, and nearly 42% reported that they had witnessed a murder (Berman, Kurtines, Silverman, & Serafini, 1996). Over 85% of impoverished children in foster care had witnessed an act of violence within their lives, and the large majority had witnessed violence with the 6 months proceeding the study (Stein et al., 2001). Witnessing or being the victim of violence is unfortunately not a rare event for children and adolescents living in poverty.

Witnessing violence in the community has been associated with a wide range of emotional/behavioral problems. Toddlers and young children tend to show greater sleep disturbance, irritability, poor concentration, depression, and anxiety after being exposed to violence in the community (Finkelhor et al., 2005). Older children and adolescents also show higher rates of depression, aggression, and PTSD when exposed to violence (Henrich, Schwab-Stone, Fanti, Jones, & Ruchkin, 2004; Margolin & Gordis, 2004). When African-American young adolescents spent more time in risky contexts in the face of violence versus protective contexts, they were more likely to show higher rates of delinquent behavior (Richards et al., 2004). It appears that children's reactions to witnessing violence in the community

may be related to how their family deals with the violence. For example, young children showed increased emotional/behavioral problems in relation to community violence when their mothers also showed high levels of distress (Linares et al., 2001). African-American girls who were exposed to neighborhood violence and who were exposed to high levels of interparental conflict were at greater risk than girls whose parents showed low levels of conflict (Forehand & Jones, 2003). It appears that violence in the community limits or erodes social support in children, thereby putting them at greater risk for dysfunction (Margolin & Gordis, 2004).

Violence is not only present in inner-city communities. Violence, such as physical fighting, is evident to some degree in most schools and in most communities. Exposure to excessive amounts of physical fighting can put children at risk for the development of both internalizing and externalizing problems (Fitzpatrick, 1997).

Violence within the family can also be devastating. Child physical abuse has already been covered, but there is also concern about children who witness physical violence between their parents or other caretakers. Exposure to family violence (also known as domestic violence) is associated with increased emotional/behavioral problems, decreased self-esteem, and posttraumatic stress disorder (Grych, Jouriles, Swank, McDonald, & Norwood, 2000; Levendosky, Huth-Bocks, Semel, & Shapiro, 2002). It also appears that exposure to domestic violence in the context of hostile-withdrawn coparenting is associated with an even higher level of emotional/behavioral problems than when parenting is more adaptive (Katz & Low, 2004). Exposure to domestic violence is associated with lower IQ, whereby higher levels of exposure are associated with lower levels of IQ (Koenen, Moffitt, Caspi, Taylor, & Purcell, 2003). Specifically, even when controlling for genetic factors, children exposed to domestic violence were tested to have an average of 8 IQ points less than children who were not exposed to domestic violence (Koenen et al., 2003). In a comprehensive meta-analysis, it was found that children who were exposed to domestic violence were at greater risk for emotional/behavioral problems (Kitzmann, Gaylord, Holt, & Kenny, 2003). Notably, children who witnessed domestic violence had approximately the same level of maladaptive outcomes as children who were physically abused themselves and children who both witnessed domestic violence and were physically abused themselves (Kitzmann et al., 2003).

Exposure to domestic violence is also associated with a greater risk for being physical abused (McGuigan et al., 2000). Children who witness violence within the family are at four times greater the risk for psychopathology than children from nonviolent homes (Cummings, Davies, & Campbell, 2000). There are indications, however, that the ramifications of witnessing domestic violence depend somewhat on how the child interprets the events. In a study of siblings who resided in the same house, siblings showed higher rates of disturbance in relation to the domestic violence if they felt that they were at fault for the domestic violence or if they felt personally threatened by the violence (Skopp, McDonald, Manke, & Jouriles, 2005). Thus, even exposure to the same levels of domestic violence can influence children differently, depending on how they interpret the events.

Beyond the family and the community, children are often exposed to horrendous examples of violence that are experienced in times of war. In one study of Palestinian children who experienced war trauma, an overwhelming number developed PTSD after their exposure to war (Thabet & Vostanis, 1999). The cumulative effects of witnessing greater numbers of war-related traumas were associated with greater numbers of PTSD symptoms.

Overall, the effects of children witnessing violence can be intense and long-standing. These effects, however, are mediated by a number of other factors such as the amount of exposure, how the adults in the child's life handle the exposure to violence, and the amount of other risk factors that the child is exposed to in addition to the violence (Luthar, 1999). Preventive efforts have focused on decreasing access to firearms and increasing conflict resolution skills in youth and their families (Duke, Resnick, & Borowsky, 2005; Group for the Advancement of Psychiatry, Committee on Preventive Psychiatry, 1999).

SUMMARY AND KEY CONCEPTS

Risk factors. are characteristics, events, or processes that put a child or adolescent at risk for the development of psychological difficulties.

Temperament and Attachment. Temperament is the infant's personal and individual style regarding the frequency of expression of needs and emotions. Infants differ at birth in their temperamental style. **Attachment** is the relationship that develops between infants and their caretakers (usually their parents), which is usually characterized by a deep, enduring, and affectionate bond between the infant and the caretaker.

Genetic Predisposition. Most emotional/behavioral problems have been linked, to some extent, to genetic risk factors.

Parental Psychopathology. Nearly every type of parental psychopathology, in both mothers and fathers, has been linked to an increased likelihood of emotional/behavioral problems in children and adolescents. The effects of parental psychopathology are exacerbated when both parents show psychopathology, which is not uncommon given the process of **assortative mating** (when someone with a clinical disorder has children with someone else with a clinical disorder).

Parental Loss Due to Death. Although losing a parent to death is devastating for most children and adolescents, the loss of parent is associated with even greater risk for emotional/behavioral problems when certain characteristics are present (e.g., multiple loses at the same time, sudden parental death).

Interparental Conflict. The connections between interparental conflict (i.e., fighting and arguing between parents) and child maladjustment are among the most consistent findings in the study of developmental psychopathology. Interparental conflict is associated with greater risk for emotional/behavioral problems, whether or not the parents are living together. One of the most devastating types of interparental conflict is **triangulation,** when parents put the child in the middle of their arguments.

Child Physical Abuse. Not surprisingly, child physical abuse is associated with greater risk for the development of emotional/behavioral problems in childhood and adolescence. Often, child physical abuse is evident in the context of other risk factors (e.g., insecure attachment, parental psychopathology, interparental conflict).

Child Sexual Abuse. Like physical abuse, child sexual abuse is associated with a great number of emotional/behavioral problems for children and adolescents. The effects of child sexual abuse are especially devastating when certain factors are present (e.g., the perpetrator is a father or father figure, when the abuse has occurred over a long period of time).

Child Psychological Maltreatment. Psychological maltreatment of children has not been studied as much as child physical abuse or child sexual abuse; however, it appears to be an important risk factor to consider in the lives of children.

Family Dysfunction. Many types of other family dysfunctions have been linked to increased risk for emotional/behavioral problems, including hostility and competitiveness, stress, maladaptive family environments, troubled family systems, negative parental affect, and maladaptive parenting styles.

Inadequate Educational Resources. The school environment can have an impact on children's emotional well-being as well as their academic and intellectual functioning. Problems can arise when there are difficult transitions (e.g., from elementary school to middle school), when there is a lack of school connectedness, and when there are less than optimal school conditions (e.g., overcrowding, limited educational resources).

Poverty and Low Socioeconomic Status. Nearly one out of four children (22%) in the United States lives at or below the poverty line. Poverty and low socioeconomic status have been associated with greater emotional/behavioral problems in children and adolescents.

Violence Within the Community. A surprisingly high number of children and adolescents have been the victims of or have observed violence in their communities. Children who witness violence within their own family (e.g., spousal abuse), show four times more psychopathology than children from nonviolent families.

KEY TERMS

risk factors	attachment	traumagenic	transactional model
temperament	assortative mating	dynamics model	triangulation

SUGGESTED READINGS

Tucker, Neely. *Love in the Driest Season: A Family Memoir*. New York: Three Rivers Press, 2004. Without being adopted and cared for by the author and his wife, baby Chipo would surely have died like so many other infant orphans in Zimbabwe. This compelling memoir tells the story of saving Chipo and trying to save others in her same circumstances.

Lawrence, Barbara Kent. *Bitter Ice: A Memoir of Love, Food, and Obsession*. New York: William Morrow and Company, 1999. In this eloquent memoir, the author describes the devastation on her marriage and on her children's lives due to her husband's struggle with anorexia nervosa and OCD-like tendencies. These behaviors serve as a dramatic risk factor for the children, but the author tries to set up the family situation in such a way that the children are protected from their father's peculiar activities.

SUGGESTED VIEWINGS

The Woodsman. (2004). This somber and serious film shows the life of a pedophile who is released from prison after 12 years in confinement. With sexual abuse as a major risk factor to consider in developmental psychopathology, this films shows the complicated life of a pedophile who struggles with finding an appropriate sexual connection with another adult.

Little Miss Sunshine. (2006). In this quirky film, risk factors such as family dysfunction, death of a family member, interparental conflict, and parental job insecurity are highlighted as the family travels cross-country to attend a beauty pageant.

CHAPTER 6

PROTECTIVE FACTORS AND ISSUES OF PREVENTION

CHAPTER SUMMARY

My kids are resilient because they see the same quality in their parents.

—(p. 227; Cohen, 2004) regarding how his children have coped with his loss of sight, his recurrent battles with cancer, and his multiple sclerosis

Over the past two and a half decades, there has been increasing interest within the field of psychology to explore the positive side of human beings. Often known as positive psychology, this emphasis has led to a better understanding of happiness and subjective well-being (Diener, Oishi, & Lucas, 2003), optimism (Reivich, Gillham, Chaplin, & Seligman, 2005), and the ordinary strengths within human development (Wright & Masten, 2005).

Consistent with these explorations of positive aspects of human behavior, many developmental psychopathologists have been interested in identifying positive factors in children's lives that seem to protect them from adverse circumstances. **Protective factors** are those characteristics within the individual child, the family, or the community that serve to decrease the likelihood of a child developing psychopathology in the face of adversity. Although many characteristics serve as healthy factors in children's lives, these characteristics are referred to as protective factors only when they are associated with children overcoming otherwise adverse circumstances and risk factors (such as poverty, abuse, interparental conflict). Thus, it is not just the absence of risk factors that is important to understand but rather the presence of protective factors when children are at high risk for developing problems. Research studies on protective factors tend to be sensitive to cultural and ethnic issues, but there is still a need for more attention to cultural diversity within the context of research on protective factors (Arrington & Wilson, 2000). Risk factors were covered in the previous chapter, and the current chapter focuses on protective factors and assets.

A primary research strategy in the study of protective factors has been to examine **resilience** within children (Peters, McMahon, & Leadbeater, 2004; Luthar, 2003; Wright & Masten, 2005 for excellent reviews). Resilience is the process by which children overcome adverse circumstances and develop into healthy and competent young adults. More specifically, resilience is "a pattern of positive adaptation in the context of past or present adversity" (Wright & Masten, 2005, p. 18). There were many pioneering efforts into the study of resilience in the 1960s and 1970s (Anthony, 1974; Garmezy, 1974; Rutter, 1979; Werner & Smith, 1982; reviewed in Werner, 2005). These studies laid the groundwork for understanding the strengths within children and their environments that protect children from adverse situations. Most often, researchers collect data from a large group of children who are at risk for developing adverse outcomes due to individual or environmental circumstances. When these children are followed over time, some of them will in fact develop adverse outcomes (such as psychopathology or criminal behavior), but some of them will develop into well-functioning and psychologically healthy adolescents and young adults. Investigation of these resilient children helps to identify the characteristics within the children or

Many aspects of families can serve as protective factors, such as close stable relationships with well-functioning parents and siblings.

within their environment that protect them from the initial adverse circumstances. Box 6.1 highlights the work of Dr. Emmy Werner, whose research has been groundbreaking in the study of resilient children.

The study of resilient children over the past 25 years has led to some promising findings about what factors serve to protect children from adverse environments. As can be seen in Table 6.1, four primary groupings of variables serve as protective factors: characteristics within the child, within the family, within the community, and within the culture or society (Wright & Masten, 2005).

All these factors are important in the development of resilient children, and all of them will be touched on to some extent in this chapter. Note that one limitation in this research knowledge, as is true with so much of what we know about the development and prevention of psychopathology, is that the majority of what we know comes from correlational and longitudinal studies.

Given that research in this area cannot be completed with an experimental design (e.g., randomly assign some children to an adverse environment without the presence of any protective factors and assign other children to an adverse environment with the presence of protective factors), the causal links in this area of research are still somewhat tenuous. Luckily, relatively consistent results have been found and replicated with children from different ethnic groups within the United States, such as African Americans and Asian Americans, as well as within different countries worldwide (Fergusson & Horwood, 2003; Werner, 2005; Werner & Smith, 2001; Wright & Masten, 2005). Even with this solid research base, however, findings should be interpreted cautiously until more research with an experimental design or quasi-experimental design can be completed.

CHARACTERISTICS WITHIN THE CHILD

Adaptable Temperament

As mentioned in the chapter on risk factors, temperament reflects an infant's individual style in relation to the frequency of expression of needs and emotions. An easy temperament in infancy is associated with later resilience in children and adolescents. For example, easy and adaptable temperamental styles were associated with lower risk for internalizing and externalizing problems in young adolescents (Oldehinkel, Hartman, DeWinter, Veenstra, & Ormel, 2004). Similarly, adaptive temperament was associated with lowered risk for ADHD and disruptive behavior disorders in children and adolescents (Rettew, Copeland, Stanger, & Hudziak, 2004). Thus, adaptive temperament appears to serve as a protective factor for children and adolescents exposed to adverse environments.

Good Cognitive Abilities

Good cognitive abilities, as reflected in adequate intelligence, have been identified consistently as a protective factor from adverse environments (Anthony & Cohler, 1987; Masten & Coatsworth, 1998; Werner & Smith, 2001). Note, however, that these findings are not as simple as just finding that better intelligence is related to better outcome. Rather, it appears that at least average intellectual functioning is associated with other characteristics that are related to healthy outcomes. For example, higher verbal abilities (one component of intellectual functioning) in children of depressed mothers

DR. EMMY WERNER'S PIONEERING WORK ON THE ISLAND OF KAUAI

One of the classic series of studies of protective factors and resilience in children was conducted by Dr. Emmy Werner and her colleagues on the island of Kauai (Werner, 1995; Werner & Smith, 1982, 1992, 2001). The research team included pediatricians, psychologists, public health workers, and social workers. Werner and her colleagues collected information on nearly 700 children who were born in 1955 on the Hawaiian island of Kauai. The majority of children born onto the island remain on the island during their entire life, so the island provides an ideal opportunity for longitudinal research that follows children throughout their lives.

Data were collected on these children prenatally and at the ages of 1, 2, 10, 18, 32, and in their early 40s (with continued follow-up interviews planned for the future). Approximately 30% of the children were considered to be at high risk for development of psychological problems due to prenatal stress, perinatal stress, chronic poverty in childhood, chronic interparental conflict, parental divorce, or parental psychopathology during early childhood. Two thirds of the children with four or more risk factors early in life ended up developing serious emotional/behavioral problems or learning problems by the age of 10 or developed mental health problems, criminal problems, or pregnancy by the age of 18. One third of the children with four or more risk factors developed into well-functioning, psychologically healthy adolescents and young adults. The key to identifying protective factors was to investigate the characteristics of the children who were at risk initially, but then who ended up leading healthy and productive lives in later adolescence and early adulthood.

Over the course of their investigation, Werner and her colleagues (summarized in Werner & Smith, 2001) identified a number of factors within the individual, family, and community that served as protective factors for these resilient children. During infancy and early childhood, resilient children were more likely to be described as active,

cuddly, good-natured, affectionate, and "easy to deal with" when compared with children who did not show resilience. During middle childhood and adolescence, resilient children showed good communication skills, good problem-solving skills, interests in special hobbies or activities, internal locus of control and self-efficacy, positive self-concept, and adequate (though not necessarily gifted) intellectual functioning. Protective factors within the family centered around having at least one competent and emotionally stable person with whom the child could bond (such as a competent grandparent if the parents were unable to provide this type of support). Interestingly, resilient children often sought out these competent role models and in turn, became role models and caretakers for younger siblings or others who were in need of help. Protective factors within the community focused on the availability of competent role models outside the family (such as a teacher, coach, religious leader, or competent friend). There were also notable protective factors within the community that helped high-risk, troubled adolescents and young adults to rebound from their troubled lives. In particular, adult education programs, religious activities, marriage to a competent partner, affiliation with a supportive friend, and voluntary military service were noted to help some troubled older adolescents and young adults to become more competent than their background would have suggested.

Overall, the work by Werner and colleagues has been crucial in the understanding of risk and protective factors within children and adolescents. This unique sample, and the continued efforts to follow these grown children and their offspring, has provided a wealth of information about the lives of children and families. Interested students are encouraged to read, *Journeys from Childhood to Midlife: Risk, Resilience, and Recovery* (Werner & Smith, 2001). In addition, Werner (2005) provided an overview of other large-scale, longitudinal studies that have shaped the study of resilience.

were associated with decreased risk for depressive symptoms in the children (Malcarne, Hamilton, Ingram, & Taylor, 2000). In addition, children with at least average intelligence who are raised in adverse environments may have a better chance of doing well in school and in seeking out teachers to help them with their work (Masten & Coatsworth, 1998). Academic achievement can help the child stay more invested in school, rather than disengaging from school and other

prosocial activities. Adequate intellectual functioning is also associated with better information-processing skills, which may in turn help the child to negotiate peer relationships and academic involvements. More intelligent children may be more creative and effective in solving problems, so they may negotiate difficulties in a more effective manner than children with lower intelligence (Werner & Smith, 2001). Higher intelligence was found to be a particularly important protective factor

TABLE 6-1 Examples of Assets and Protective Factors

Source	Characteristic
Child	Social and adaptable temperament in infancy
	Good cognitive abilities and problem-solving skills
	Effective emotional and behavioral regulation strategies
	Positive view of self (self-confidence, high self-esteem, self-efficacy)
	Positive outlook on life (hopefulness)
	Faith and a sense of meaning in life
	Characteristics valued by society and self (talents, sense of humor, attractiveness to others)
Family	Stable and supportive home environment
	Low level of parental discord
	Close relationship to responsive caregiver
	Authoritative parenting style (high on warmth, structure/monitoring, and expectations)
	Positive sibling relationships
	Supportive connections with extended family members
	Faith and religious affiliations
	Parents involved in child's education
	Parents have individual qualities listed above as protective for child
	Socioeconomic advantages
	Postsecondary education of parent
Community	Connections to caring adult mentors and prosocial peers
	High neighborhood quality
	Safe neighborhood
	Low level of community violence
	Affordable housing
	Access to recreational centers
	Clean air and water
	Effective schools
	Well-trained and well-compensated teachers
	After-school programs
	School recreation resources (sports, music, art)
	Employment opportunities for parents and teens
	Good public health care
	Access to emergency services (police, fire, medical)
Cultural or Societal	Value and resources directed at education
	Protective child policies (child labor, child health, and welfare)
	Prevention of and protection from oppression or political violence
	Low acceptance of physical violence

Source: Wright & Masten, 2005.

against the development of antisocial behavior during adolescence (Masten et al., 1999).

Overall, average intelligence has been identified as a protective factor in nearly every study that has investigated the connection between intellectual functioning and healthy outcomes (Masten et al., 1999). Although the mechanisms are not completely clear, it appears that higher intelligence is associated with myriad skills that are predictive of competent outcomes. In fact, some researchers have argued that intellectual functioning, along with parenting quality, are the two most crucial protective factors in the prevention of

psychopathology and other adverse outcomes (Masten et al., 1999).

Parents learn a lot from their children about coping with life.

—Muriel Spark

Effective Emotional and Behavioral Regulation Strategies

There are a number of ways in which children gain control over their emotions (i.e., self-regulate), which allows them to self-soothe and deal with difficult situations. Self-regulation has been associated with

Case Study: A Neurosurgeon Who Grew Up in the Inner City

Dr. Ben Carson gained international attention for coordinating a team of surgeons who were able to separate conjoined twins (also known as Siamese twins) who were joined at the back of the head. The parents of these 7-month-old infants had all but given up hope for being able to have both twins survive such a surgery. Most of the physicians they contacted either would not do the surgery or would do the surgery with the plan of only saving one twin. Dr. Carson planned the complex and dangerous surgery for 5 months with a surgical team of over 70 professionals. The surgery took over 22 hours. Both twins survived and are functioning well.

Given this extraordinary story, it is even more extraordinary to learn that Dr. Carson grew up in a single-parent home in the inner city of Detroit with few prospects for success. As an African American, he experienced a great deal of racism and prejudice when he attended a school in which Caucasian-American children were the clear majority. His mother, who had a third-grade education, had insisted that he be bussed to this school so that he could get an adequate education. His mother also insisted that he study hard, follow her rules (such as only watching three television shows a week and reading

two entire books per week), and be respectful to his elders. In addition to the academic tenacity that Dr. Carson developed as a young child, he also exhibited great intellect even at a very young age. His mother reported that he had always been very bright, but she needed to help him "apply" himself to his academic studies. Obviously, this strategy paid off not only for Dr. Carson, but also for the thousands of children he has helped with his neurosurgical skills.

Not only did Dr. Carson have to overcome obstacles early in his life, but in 2002 he was informed that he had an aggressive form of prostate cancer. Dr. Carson underwent surgery and is now cancer free (Chappell, 2003). As a result of this near-fatal diagnosis, Dr. Carson has tried to find ways to reduce stress in his life and to spend more quality time with his family. The story of Dr. Carson illustrates a number of protective factors, including intelligence, a stable and determined parent, strong beliefs that he would persevere, and good coping mechanisms. For information on the Carson Scholars Fund, which is a nonprofit organization that helps impoverished youth excel in school, see www.carsonscholars.org.

Source: Carson & Murphey (1990) and Chappell (2003).

---

better outcomes in children raised in poverty (Buckner, Mezzacappa, & Beardslee, 2003). Good inhibitory control was associated with decreased use of alcohol in adolescent boys (Pardini, Lochman, & Wells, 2004). In the presence of parental hostility, adolescents who showed better emotional regulation were more likely to have positive outcomes than adolescents who showed less ability to control their emotions (Schulz, Waldinger, Hauser, & Allen, 2005). These patterns are also evident in psychophysiological measures (such as heart rate and timing of breathing), which highlights the connections between biological and emotional functioning (El-Sheikh & Whitson, 2006).

A related construct to self-regulation is coping. Coping style has been identified as an individually based characteristic that can serve to protect children from adverse circumstances (Compas, Connor-Smith, Saltzman, Thomsen, & Wadsworth, 2001; Wadsworth & Compas, 2002). In particular, children show resilience when they are able to appraise a potentially stressful situation in a manner that helps their ability to cope with the situation (Werner & Smith, 2001; Wyman, Sandler, Wolchik, & Nelson, 2000). Children with good problem-solving coping skills tend to be more resilient than children without those skills (Dumont & Provost,

1999). In a study of children exposed to high levels of marital conflict, girls who showed higher levels of active coping and support coping were more likely to show lower depressive symptoms and higher self-esteem (Nicolotti, El-Sheikh, & Whitson, 2003). In a study of urban children, resilient children showed significantly better problem-solving coping skills than did children who were stress-affected (Cowen et al., 1997). Children who seek the help of others when faced with a challenge that exceeds their ability to cope also show better resilience to adverse environments (Dumont & Provost, 1999). Children who can call on stable adults or peers to help them cope with difficult situations show higher rates of competence and lower rates of emotional/behavioral problems (Werner & Smith, 2001). In addition, coping style has been linked to intellectual functioning and problem-solving skills, so coping style can serve as a protective factor directly and can also serve to enhance other protective factors (Masten et al., 1999).

Positive View of Self (Self-Confidence, High Self-Esteem, Self-Efficacy)

Children and adolescents with a positive view of themselves tend to show resilience in the face of

Case Study: A Family Coping with Incest

Amy's maternal grandfather, Melvin, had been sexually abusing her for over 10 years. At the age of 14, she reported the abuse to her mother (Belle), but her mother did not believe her. At the age of 15, Amy reported the abuse to a teacher who reported it to child protective authorities. Although her mother still did not believe her, Amy's mother finally accepted the allegations when Amy's two younger siblings reported that they had also been sexually abused by their grandfather. The child protective agency mandated that the grandfather have no more contact with the children and that Belle take Amy to therapy.

Amy's mother and father have been divorced for many years, and Belle just recently remarried and is expecting a baby within the month. Conflict often arises in the family, in which Amy's mother and stepfather blame Amy for doing something wrong. Frequently, the mother and stepfather are on one side of an argument and Amy and her siblings are on the other side of the argument. Given the family distress, Amy expressed interest in going to live with her biological father. Although Amy's father has told Amy that she can live with him, he informed the child protective agency that Amy cannot live with him.

The following verbatim transcript is from a family therapy session with Amy and her mother, Belle. This portion of the session occurred after Amy asked to speak with her mother about something that made her sad.

Belle: [sitting down] OK.
Amy: [speaks in a high, childlike voice and shrinks back a bit] OK, what?
Belle: You want to speak to me.
Amy: [still in a childlike voice] Yeah, I do.
Belle: [crosses arms and looks guarded] About?
Amy: About our relationship.
Belle: Yeah?
Amy: It's not going too well.
Belle: [tensely] Well, it's not worse than it has been. It's gonna take some time, Amy.
Amy: [voice gets small] I know, Mom, but I don't feel like I'm getting any support from you.
Belle: Like how?
Amy: Just, [pause] you weren't here for [pause] the hearing.
Belle: [slightly interrupting in a sharp voice] I know that and we discussed that, and it was agreed by you that it was okay. Neither of us had any clue what that hearing really was about. [pauses as she continues to look at Amy, whose head is down as if being punished] We discussed that at length before we ever

left. [pause] Isn't that right? And what did you say?
Amy: I don't remember.
Belle: Tsk.
Amy: I don't.
Belle: You said that it was perfectly all right for H and T [a couple from church] to . . .
Amy: I know, but that's . . .
Belle: [starts to finish her sentence but stops]
Amy: . . . because you all planned to go on vacation.
Belle: [sharply] Amy, we were perfectly willing to stay if we needed to.
Amy: But y'all needed to get away.
Belle: Well, that's true too. [pause] But we still discussed it with you, and you said, "no," that it was fine for them to take you. [long pause]
Amy: Just—[pause] I feel neglected by you.
Belle: How?
Amy: [voice gets smaller and words become hard to understand, mumbles] You don't show you love me.
Belle: [sounds impatient] Like how am I supposed to?
Amy: [shoulders hunched, head down, starts to cry] When I do good in school, you don't tell me I do a good job.
Belle: [slightly raises voice] Amy that is not true.
Amy: Yes, it is.
Belle: It is not.
Amy: When I come home and tell you I have 95s [pause] on papers, I don't hear "Good job."
Belle: That is not true. I have commented on every single good paper that you have brought. [Amy shakes her head no and looks at Belle.]

This case illustrates a number of adverse circumstances that Amy has endured (sexual abuse, and lack of support from her mother, stepfather, and father). Some of the protective factors that had strengthened Amy's ability to deal with these difficulties included a supportive teacher, and good coping skills (e.g., she did not blame herself for the sexual abuse, she sought out a supportive teacher frequently). The therapist worked on ways that Belle could reconnect with Amy and tried to help Belle become more supportive of Amy. Mother and daughter began having "girl times" together, many of which were initiated by Belle. Amy's difficult behavior decreased, and both mother and daughter reported greater closeness and harmony within the family.

Source: Lawrence (1999, pp. 176–177).

difficult circumstances. In normative community samples, self-esteem changes developmentally over time. For example, self-esteem is relatively high in childhood, tends to decrease in adolescence (especially for girls), and then tends to rise throughout later adolescence and through adulthood (Robins & Trzesniewski, 2005). There is a sharp decline in self-esteem in older adults, especially after the age of 70. Throughout the life span, there tends to be rank-order stability, which means that individuals with high self-esteem at one point are likely to be on the high end of the continuum (even if the level has decreased from previous rates) at other points in time (Robins & Trzesniewski, 2005). Overall, high self-esteem serves to buffer individuals from adverse circumstances.

In addition to self-confidence and high self-esteem (Brendgen, Vitaro, Turgeon, Poulin, & Wanner, 2004; Niiya, Crocker, & Bartmess, 2004) being linked to resilience, self-efficacy has been shown to be a consistent predictor of resilience. **Self-efficacy** is a term used to describe a cognitive structure in which children have come to expect success and who believe that they can perform successfully in any new challenging situation (Bandura, 1986). In general, self-efficacy is associated with healthy outcomes in children as well as adults (Bandura, 1986). It appears that individuals who have high self-efficacy will try harder and remain more engaged in challenging tasks and, therefore, will succeed in those tasks more often than individuals with low self-efficacy (Bandura, 1986). More recently, self-efficacy has also been associated with pleasure-in-mastery, which occurs when children and adolescents enjoy activities that challenge them to excel (Masten et al., 1999).

Higher rates of self-efficacy have been identified as serving a protective function in children from adverse circumstances (Wright & Masten, 2005; Werner & Smith, 2001). Children with higher rates of self-efficacy stay engaged in tasks longer and succeed at tasks to a greater degree than children with lower rates of self-efficacy (Masten et al., 1999). Given that children from adverse environments often encounter more challenges than children from stable environments, higher rates of self-efficacy appear to help at-risk children in a number of venues, including the home, school, and community. Remember that self-efficacy is a cognitive process, rather than the actual process of succeeding. The idea behind the importance of self-efficacy as a protective factor is that at-risk children with high self-efficacy will persevere even in challenging situations because they believe that they can succeed in these situations. Children with lower levels of self-efficacy

may give up more quickly on a task and will then be less able to succeed in that task. Overall, self-efficacy has been identified consistently as a protective factor that is associated with resilience in children from adverse circumstances (Masten & Coatsworth, 1998).

Other Protective Characteristics within the Child

Other protective factors that have been identified within children are having a positive outlook on life, such as showing hopefulness even in difficult situations, having faith and a sense of meaning in life, and possessing characteristics that are valued by society and by the child him or herself, such as having talents, having a sense of humor, or being attractive to others.

Much of the recent research on hopefulness has focused on optimism and has focused on the prevention of depression in at-risk children (Reivich, Gillham, Chaplin, & Seligman, 2005). Given that a central component of depression is a cognitive triad in which children or adolescents feel hopelessness in themselves, the world, and the future (Greening, Stoppelbein, Dhossche, & Martin, 2005), it is logical that the work on hopefulness would focus on depression. There are promising results in programs that teach hopefulness to children to prevent maladaptive functioning (Reivich et al., 2005). Thus, having a positive outlook on life and showing hopefulness appear to serve as protective factors in the face of adverse circumstances.

In addition to having a positive outlook on life, involvement in religious and spiritual activities appears to serve as a protective factor for children at risk for the development of emotional/behavioral problems (Mahoney, Pargament, Tarakeshwar, & Swank, 2001; McMahon, Singh, Garner, & Benhorin, 2004). Spirituality, regardless of attendance at a place of worship, has also been found to serve in a protective role among children and adolescents at risk for the development of emotional/behavioral problems (Haight, 1998) and substance abuse (Miller, Davies, & Greenwald, 2000). In a sample of older adolescents, religious faith was associated with optimism and better coping skills (Plante, Yancey, Sherman, & Guertin, 2000). Spirituality was identified as an effective coping mechanism in African-American children who were exposed to violence (Bryant-Davis, 2005). Overall, some type of faith or commonly held belief system that is shared either within or outside of the family serves a protective function for at-risk children and adolescents (Masten & Coatsworth, 1998).

The final protective characteristics identified within the child are when the child possesses characteristics that are valued by society and by the child her- or himself. Examples of these types of characteristics include having talents, a sense of humor, and being attractive to others. For example, having a sense of humor was associated with positive long-term outcomes in African-American children who were exposed to violence (Bryant-Davis, 2005).

Overall, all these characteristics within the individual child or adolescent have been shown to serve a protective function in youth who are exposed to adverse circumstances. Interestingly, many of these individual characteristics also make it more likely that the child will engage in activities with others in their family and their community that are also associated with resilience.

Once you bring life into the world, you must protect it. We must protect it by changing the world.

—Elie Wiesel.

CHARACTERISTICS WITHIN THE FAMILY

A number of factors within the family serve as protective factors, including having a stable and supportive home environment, being in a family who has a faith or a

Having a positive relationship with a well-functioning sibling can serve as a protective factor.

religious affiliation, having parents who are involved in children's education, having stable parents, living with socioeconomic advantages, and having parents with at least postsecondary education.

Stable and Supportive Home Environment

A number of aspects are related to having a stable and supportive home environment, including having parents with low levels of discord, having a close relationship to a responsive caregiver, having parents with an authoritative parenting style, having positive relationships with competent siblings, and having supportive connections with extended family members such as grandparents and other relatives. Even the stability of residential living situations, such as remaining in the same community and living in the same dwelling for a long period of time, is associated with resilience in children (Adam, 2004).

To begin with, children and adolescents who are raised by parents who show low levels of parental disorder tend to show resilience in the face of adverse circumstances. This pattern is true whether or not the parents live together (Davies, Cummings, & Winter, 2004).

A close and stable relationship with at least one parent or caretaker has consistently been shown to protect children from adverse circumstances (Brody et al., 2006; Wright & Masten, 2005). For brevity, the term *parent* will be used to signify any adult caretaker who has primary responsibility for the child's well-being. Note that there are few differences in the impact of caring and stable parenting, regardless of whether the parenting is coming from a biological mother, biological father, stepmother, stepfather, grandparent, aunt, uncle, older sibling, or nonrelative (Black, Dubowitz, & Starr, 1999). The important thing to consider in children's well-being is the type of parenting they receive, not from whom they receive the parenting. In some ways, parents are considered to be the most important agents of socialization in a child's life, so competent and caring parenting is a salient protective factor for children born to adverse circumstances (Kim & Brody, 2005).

The protective nature of caring and consistent parenting begins in infancy, where secure attachment serves as a protective factor for infants who have been exposed to trauma or other adverse circumstances (Sroufe, Carlson, Levy, & Egeland, 1999). Similarly, secure attachment was associated with decreased conduct problems in preschoolers who were born to adolescent mothers (Keller, Spieker, & Gilchrist, 2005). Secure attachment was also associated with decreased risk for depressive

Case Study: A Mother's Love

In an extraordinary book that documents the lives of homeless families, Jonathon Kozol (1988) illustrates the devastation of poverty on children and families. There are also illustrations of resilience in the face of horrific living circumstances. One notable family is Rachel and her four children (who are aged 11 months to 12 years old). They live in public housing in the northeast, where there is often little heat during the winter and the living conditions are often deplorable. Rachel noted that she had to sign a statement when she moved into the one-room space that she would not cook anything in her room. She noted that this rule necessitates that children live on inadequate nutrition (such as bologna sandwiches), when she can afford the food.

Even in the face of these horrible life circumstances, Rachel has managed to remain a stable and caring influence in her children's lives. She spends time with them and helps the older children with their homework. She reads the Bible to her children and speaks to them of the day when they will have a better life. Away from her children, she acknowledges that she is scared and that she does not sleep at night so that she can watch over her children and prevent any harm from coming to them. With her children, however, she presents a confident and stable will that keeps the children from worrying when or if they will have a next meal. Rachel has tried her best to allow her children to remain "innocent" and to protect them from the harsh realities of living in extreme poverty.

Source: Kozol (1988).

---

symptoms in young adolescents (Sund & Wichstrom, 2002). Secure attachment is usually associated with parents who provide nurturing and warm interactions with the infant in a stable and consistent manner. These parenting characteristics also serve as protective factors later in the child's life.

As early as 3 years old, an African-American child living in urban poverty showed better cognitive and language competence and fewer behavioral problems when their father was nurturant and satisfied with his parenting role (Black et al., 1999). Similarly, paternal involvement was associated with adaptive outcomes in infants exposed to maternal depression (Mezulis, Hyde, & Clark, 2004). In kindergarten, parents' positive affect and support were associated with children's social competence (Isley, O'Neil, Clatfelter, & Parke, 1999) in an ethnically diverse sample. At-risk children aged 7 to 9 years old who lived in urban poverty showed better overall functioning when they received competent parenting from a caregiver with stable psychosocial resources (Wyman et al., 1999). Within the African-American community, parents who held Africentric values (especially related to collective work and personal responsibility) had children who were less likely to become involved in illicit drug use (Belgrave, Townsend, Cherry, & Cunningham, 1997). Parental involvement, especially as demonstrated through family mealtime, is associated with a host of positive outcomes for children, even in children living in abject poverty (Luthar & Latendresse, 2005b; Schwarzchild, 2000). A strong parent–child relationship was associated with better mental health outcomes for children who had survived cancer (Orbuch, Parry, Chesler, Fritz, & Repetto, 2005).

During adolescence, parental support, stress-buffering interactions, and parental competence were associated with less risk for internalizing and externalizing problems and substance use, including tobacco, alcohol, and marijuana (Brody et al., 2006; Forman & Davies, 2003). Parental and family support have even decreased the influence of deviant peers and decreased the likelihood of Latino/Latina adolescents' substance use (Frauenglass, Routh, Pantin, & Mason, 1997) and have protected African-American adolescents from the adverse effects of violence in the community (Richards et al., 2004).

Parental monitoring of young adolescents' behavior (e.g., knowing the whereabouts of their children, keeping track of adolescents' activities and friends) was associated with more secure attachment and better adolescent outcomes (Kerns, Aspelmeier, Gentzler, & Grabill, 2001). Parental monitoring was also associated with better outcomes for poor, inner-city children exposed to violence (Buckner et al., 2003; Ceballo, Ramirez, Hearn, & Maltese, 2003). Parental monitoring was also associated with lowered risk for adolescent deviance (Waizenhofer et al., 2004). Positive parental behavior and family functioning was associated with better academic functioning and better adjustment in adolescents (Gorman-Smith, Tolan, Henry, & Florsheim, 2000; Voydanoff & Donnelly, 1999). Similarly, urban adolescents living in poverty with parents who provided support and protection from daily hassles had lower rates of depression and antisocial behavior (Seidman et al., 1999). African-American children and adolescents who received high levels of parental warmth tended to show greater emotional/behavioral adjustment (Brennan, LeBrocque, & Hammen, 2003; McCabe, Clark, & Barnett, 1999). Both

BOX 6.2

OUT OF THE MOUTHS OF BABES

A fascinating book, entitled *What Preteens Want Their Parents to Know,* was written by Ryan Holladay and Friends (1994) when Ryan was just 12 years old. The book provides a collection of suggestions from young adolescents to their parents. Although some of the suggestions are specific to parents, many of the suggestions could be useful to teachers, coaches, grandparents, and others who care about young adolescents. Many of these suggestions focus on the positive side of the adolescent–parent relationship, which is consistent with how parents (and others) can help develop a strong and stable relationship with adolescents. Here are their suggestions:

- Listening is one of the best ways to show me you love me (p. 27).
- Have at least one meal as a family each day (p. 60).
- Your praise means more to me than anyone else's (p. 71).
- Teach me right and wrong (p. 94).
- Look at family photo albums with me and tell me about the relatives (p. 137).

African-American and Mexican-American adolescents flourished in families with at least one competent parent (Gorman-Smith et al., 2000). Within Asian-American and Latin-American adolescents in the United States, stronger feelings of family obligations and family connection with their parents were associated with better family relationships, stronger peer relationships, and higher motivations to succeed in school (Fuligni, Tseng, & Lam, 1999). Parental expectations and positive family attention served as protective factors against suicide in a sample of Native American adolescents (Dexheimer Pharris, Resnick, & Blum, 1997). In a sample from Columbia, South America, family support served a protective role after adolescents witnessed violence against a family member (Kliewer, Murrelle, Mejia, Torres, & Angold, 2001). Interestingly, these protective factors are consistent with what adolescents sometimes want from their families (see Box 6.2).

Overall, there is clear support for the protective nature of stable and nurturing caretaking. In fact, there is evidence that parenting resources play a larger protective role than many other protective factors (Masten et al., 1999). Protective factors within the family have been used as a mechanism to help families in therapy (Rutter, 1999) and to serve as the focus of prevention programs (Patterson, DeGarmo, & Forgatch, 2004).

Research findings about protective factors within the family are consistent with the studies on parenting styles that have identified the **authoritative parenting style** as a protective factor. Authoritative parenting is characterized by warmth, age-appropriate structure, and high expectations (Baumrind, 1971). Other parenting styles, which include permissive parents (who do not set any limits or provide any structure for their children's behavior) and authoritarian parents (who provide strict limits and structure to their children, while providing little warmth) are associated with adverse outcomes, such as being withdrawn and unhappy (Baumrind, 1971). Authoritative parenting, on the other hand, is associated with children who are friendly, independent, cooperative, socially responsible, and academically advanced (Baumrind, 1971; Steinberg, Lamborn, Darling, Mounts, & Dornbusch, 1994). Note that authoritative parenting is associated with positive outcomes even in children of separated and divorced parents (Hetherington & Clingempeel, 1992; Hetherington & Stanley-Hagan, 1999). In families of children who have lost one parent to death, authoritative parenting in the remaining parent was associated with better mental health outcomes for children (Kwok et al., 2005; Lin, Sandler, Ayers, Wolchik, & Luecken, 2004). Authoritative parenting has been identified as a protective factor in children from diverse racial and ethnic backgrounds (Varela et al., 2004).

One specific aspect of supportive and authoritative parenting seems to be the use of scaffolding. **Scaffolding** occurs when parents provide structure and support for the child's next level of development (Vygotsky, 1978). One of the most salient examples of scaffolding is when parents take their not-yet-crawling infant and help to shape the infant's legs and arms into the crawling position. The infant may be able to crawl a step or two with this help, and then may eventually learn how to move his or her own legs and arms in the necessary position for crawling. Scaffolding is helpful primarily when the child is at the cusp of making new advancements. Although the example of scaffolding when an infant is learning to crawl is an objective example, scaffolding can occur at any developmental stage. The essence of scaffolding is that parents provide support and structure for the child to move to a more advanced level in their functioning, which might be in an academic, social, moral, or physical domain. Scaffolding is one of the many mechanisms that helps supportive and nurturing parents enhance their children's functioning and protects their children from adverse circumstances (Masten & Coatsworth, 1998).

Consistent with other aspects of a stable family environment, children who have positive sibling relationships appear to be protected from adverse circumstances. For example, a close relationship with a competent and well-functioning sibling is associated with decreased risk for substance abuse in adolescents (Stormshak, Comeau, & Shepard, 2004).

In addition to the protective function of sibling relationships, there is also overwhelming evidence of the protective nature of a child's connections to extended supportive family networks (Wright & Masten, 2005). Figure 6.1 shows a family drawing of a girl who has a large and close extended family (Di Leo, 1973). Studies on extended supportive family networks tend to show findings that are similar to the parenting literature. Specifically, relatives and others in the family system who treat children with support and nurturance serve as protection against otherwise adverse circumstances (Wright & Masten, 2005). Support and warmth from kin (i.e., relatives and other family members) have been associated with a host of positive outcomes, such as decreased acting out, shyness, and anxious behavior, even in the face of great stressors in adolescents' lives (McCabe et al., 1999). As can be seen in Box 6.3, grandparents can often play a particularly important role in their grandchildren's lives.

Faith and Religious Affiliations

Family attendance at a place of worship has been associated with decreased risk for substance abuse in both African-American and Caucasian-American adolescents (Albrecht, Amey, & Miller, 1996) and with decreased risk for suicide in Inuit youth (Kirmayer, Boothroyd, & Hodgins, 1998). Parents' spirituality is associated with more positive parenting, which is in turn associated with better child outcomes (Mahoney et al., 2001). In a sample of children of adolescent mothers, higher levels of mothers' religiosity was associated with adaptive outcomes in offspring over a 10-year period (Carothers, Borkowski, Lefever, & Whitman, 2005). Involvement in spiritual activities appears to expose children and parents to social support and a larger community of role models (Carothers et al., 2005; Samaan, 2000), thus faith and religious involvement appears to serve as a protective factor both within the family and as related to the larger community.

Other Protective Characteristics within the Family

There are a number of other protective characteristics within the family, including having parents who are involved in the child's education, having parents who show strong parenting characteristics, living with socioeconomic advantages, and having a parent who has completed at least postsecondary education. For example, parents who are involved in their children's schools appear to help their children gain academic success (Hill & Taylor, 2004). Competent parents appear to advocate well for their children in the school setting as well as in other settings (Hill & Taylor, 2004). In addition, socioeconomic advantages are associated with a number of protective factors, such as adequate housing, stability in the family environment, and economic resources to enhance familial and educational activities (Evans, 2004). Finally, a minimum of postsecondary education of parents appears to serve as a protective factor, partly because it allows parents to have higher expectations of their children's achievements and to help them navigate difficult educational and social dilemmas (Hill & Taylor, 2004).

Overall, many factors within the family are associated with the development of resilient children who have

FIGURE 6.1 Drawn by a Nine-Year-Old Girl from Puerto Rico Who Was Asked to Draw a Picture of Her Family.

Source: Di Leo (1973).

BOX *6.3*

THE IMPORTANCE OF GRANDPARENTS AND THEIR WISDOM

Nobody can do for little children what grandparents do. Grandparents sort of sprinkle stardust over the lives of little children

—Alex Haley

Whether they are full-time caretakers of their grandchildren or occasional visitors with their grandchildren, grandparents can serve an extraordinarily important role in children's lives. A good grandparent–grandchild relationship has been shown to be a protective factor with at-risk children (Grizenko & Pawliuk, 1994) and with adolescent mothers (Black & Nitz, 1996). The protective function of grandparents is often due to grandparents' focus on the positive aspects of their grandchildren and their ability to serve as competent role models (Werner, 1995; Werner & Smith, 2001). In addition, grandparents help children learn about themselves within a much larger context, that of an extended family and of generations of family members, in order for children to feel part of something larger than themselves (Black & Nitz, 1996). Grandparents can serve important roles for their grandchildren, whether or not the grandchildren are at risk for the development of problems.

The novelist Alice Hoffman (1996) wrote an amusing and poignant recollection of advice from her grandmother, Lillie Lulkin, including,

- When crossing the street, never trust the judgment of drivers. They may not stop for you.
- Anything served in a fancy restaurant can be equaled in your own kitchen. As a matter of fact, everything can be made out of potatoes—bread, soup, pancakes, cake.
- Between men and women, love is not only blind, but stupid.
- Don't kid yourself—nothing lasts forever.
- Sleep is overrated. Who needs it?
- Don't think that good deeds go unforgotten.
- Bathing on a cold day is worse for your health than a little dirt will ever be.
- Being old is not what you think it is. You feel the same. You are the same. The woman beside you is the girl she once was. Remember that. Remember me.

Grandparents and other stable elders can serve an important protective role in children's lives.

faced severe adversity. Sometimes children are put at risk due to factors within the family (e.g., parental psychopathology, interparental conflict, severe poverty, abuse), and there are no available supports within the family to help protect them from this adversity. It is heartening to learn that protective factors can exist outside of the family as well as inside the family.

*I wish I could help people
cuz they need help right now
cuz other people need
to help other people
so they can get more stuff*

*They need a lot of stuff
so they can
eat every day*

> —Dorothy, 11 years old and homeless (Children's Defense Fund—Minnesota, 1990, p. 34).

CHARACTERISTICS WITHIN THE COMMUNITY

In addition to the protective factors within the family, there are a number of protective factors outside the family in the community.

Connections to Caring Adult Mentors and Prosocial Peers.

Even a child from an adverse home environment can be helped significantly by a stable and caring role model

BOX 6.4

MENTORS FROM ALL WALKS OF LIFE

In her eloquent memoir, *Lanterns: A Memoir of Mentors,* Dr. Marian Wright Edelman (1999) describes the many different mentors that she has had in her life. Born into a large, impoverished African-American family living in the segregated south, Edelman went on to become a civil rights attorney and the president of the Children's Defense Fund. She attributes much of her professional and personal success to a number of mentors throughout her life including,

- Her parents
- Community elders
- Religious leaders

- Teachers
- Professors
- Dr. Martin Luther King and other civil rights leaders

While reflecting on her life, Edelman also noted how historical figures (such as Harriet Tubman and Sojourner Truth) can serve as role models and mentors to children who learn about them in school and through reading. As someone who has experienced many cycles of life, Edelman also highlights how children can serve as mentors and role models for adults in a way that will empower both the children and the adults.

or mentor outside the family (Masten & Coatsworth, 1998). Often these role models are teachers, coaches, or friends, but they can also come from other domains such as religious leaders, neighbors, scout troop leaders, and parents of a friend. See Box 6.4 for a description of role models in the life of Dr. Marion Wright Edelman, the president of the Children's Defense Fund.

Many adults can look back on their childhood and recall a teacher who took special interest in their well-being. When children do not have many other appropriate role models within their lives, teachers can serve a very important purpose in the child's growth and development. In fact, many preventionists argue that teachers are among the most appropriate individuals to serve in a protective role with children, given that children spend so much time in the school setting (Consortium on the School-based Promotion

of Social Competence, 1994). Teachers who provide clear expectations of children's educational and personal success can help children develop greater self-efficacy so that children try harder to achieve their goals (Hawkins, 1997). A positive student–teacher relationship decreased the likelihood of aggression, especially in students with unsupportive parents (Hughes, Cavell, & Jackson, 1999). Teachers can also serve to empower children to enhance an appropriate sense of control over their own lives and to encourage children's personal responsibility for their own actions (Meyers, 1989). Overall, teachers can serve as important individuals in children's lives. Not only can they serve as role models and mentors, but they can also show care and consideration to children who might not otherwise experience that type of respect.

Like teachers, coaches can serve an important role for children who are involved in sports activities. Whether it is a volunteer coach from the local recreation center or a professionally trained coach in a competitive high school sport, coaches' behaviors can have an astounding impact on their players' feelings and well-being. Researchers have conducted some fascinating studies on the impact of coaches on youngsters (reviewed in Smith & Smoll, 1997). As you might imagine, coaches who are supportive in their interactions with their child and adolescent players tend to have players who are happier with their performances and who feel better about their athletic abilities (Smith & Smoll, 1997). The best outcomes for child and adolescent athletes are associated with coaches who:

- Show a high degree of positive reinforcement for both desired performance and for effort

- Deal with player mistakes by providing encouragement and technical instruction
- De-emphasize the importance of winning and emphasize the importance of enjoying the game and improving one's own performance

This research also noted that negative, punitive, and hostile actions from coaches can have devastating effects on child and adolescent athletes. Negativity from coaches was associated with lower self-esteem and poorer attitudes in children (Smith & Smoll, 1997). Interestingly, children with high self-esteem before beginning the sport tended to fare better in the context of low supportiveness from the coach. As can be seen in Figure 6.2, child and adolescent athletes evaluated their coaches more positively if the coach was supportive or if the child had adequate self-esteem, even when the coach was not supportive.

Overall, coaches, teachers, and other adults in children's lives can serve to enhance the resilience of children. Friends of children can also serve a protective function. Although sometimes involvement with friends who have deviant behavior can lead to more problematic behavior in children (Frauenglass et al., 1997), having competent and caring friends can serve as a protective factor against adverse environments (Werner, 1995; Werner & Smith, 2001). Notably, there is evidence that

children and adolescents are quite active in their choice of friends (Brook, Whiteman, Brook, & Gordon, 1982). So rather than worrying that children or adolescents will be swayed by the "wrong" group of friends, it appears that troubled children and adolescents seek out other troubled youngsters with which to become friends (Brook et al., 1982).

Based on an extensive meta-analysis, researchers found that children's friendships served to promote social and emotional growth, especially with strong and close friendships (Newcomb & Bagwell, 1995). Childhood friendships also serve as a protective factor against peer victimization in schools, such as being teased or being picked on (Hodges, Boivin, Vitaro, & Bukowski, 1999). Specifically, children with at least one close friend were less likely to be victimized by others, and when they were victimized, they showed less emotional/behavioral problems as a result of the victimization than those children who did not have a close friend (Hodges et al., 1999). Children can also serve as peer-tutors and mentors within the school system (Foot, Morgan, & Shute, 1990). This type of peer-tutoring appears to help both the giver and the recipient of the tutoring, with higher self-esteem, better academic functioning, and better social skills shown by both groups of children (Foot et al., 1990). Thus, children's friendships can serve a strong protective role for children who are at risk for the development of emotional/behavioral problems.

Overall, a variety of individuals outside the family can serve in a protective function to help increase the resilience of children against adverse environments. As will be discussed in chapter 15, one of the best ways to help children as a nonprofessional is to become a mentor or role model for an at-risk child. Many programs, such as Big Brothers/Big Sisters and the Boys and Girls Clubs, serve an integral role in helping find competent mentors for children who might not otherwise have these positive influences in their lives.

High Neighborhood Quality

A number of characteristics that reflect high neighborhood quality are considered protective factors for children in adverse circumstances. For example, growing up in a safe neighborhood, with low levels of violence, affordable housing, access to recreational centers, clean air and water, and effective schools are associated with resilience in children exposed to adverse circumstances (Evans, 2004). These neighborhood contexts appear to protect children from adverse outcomes due to institutional resources (e.g., the quality of the actual resources),

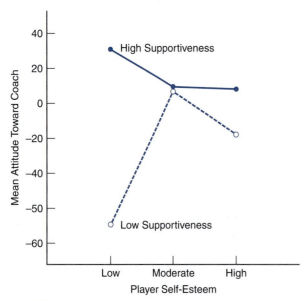

FIGURE 6.2 Mean evaluations of coaches by young athletes as a function of athletes' self-esteem and supportiveness of the coach.

Source: Smith & Smoll (1997).

Case Study: A Competent Friend Serving as a Role Model

Eva is a sophomore in high school in an impoverished, urban area. She was born in Trinidad, then came to the United States to live with her aunt and uncle. She recently moved in with her mother, who came to the United States from Trinidad a few years ago. In addition to living in impoverished circumstances, Eva has a very conflicted relationship with her mother and a somewhat conflicted relationship with her father. Eva had experienced great difficulties in school, but recently her school performance and self-esteem have improved. When an interviewer asked her if there was anyone in her life that she looked up to, she replied:

That I look up to? Yeah, my best friend, Tamara. I've always looked up to her and then, there's like I'm

interested in poetry. I write a lot of poetry. And I like a lot of black poets, like Langston Hughes. Like in my freshman year, I used to be like an average student—a 'C' student. And then I felt good about myself. I don't know, I think I got it from my friend Tamara. She encouraged me. And like this year I'm doing real good. And getting honors and stuff. I don't know, I think it was really her . . . [Tamara] would always compete with me like, you know, "Oh, I bet you can't do it." It wasn't in the negative stuff. Like she used to be like, "I bet you can't get the honor roll before I do." (p. 238).

Source: Way (1998).

---

relationships and ties (the family and friendship networks that are established in these neighborhoods), and norms and collective efficacy through which the community has a shared vision of improving itself and its citizens (Leventhal & Brooks-Gunn, 2003).

Effective Schools.

Similar to the connection with a teacher, children's connections to their schools are also associated with resilient outcomes. Specifically, children and adolescents who feel a sense of community at their school and who feel a sense of identification with their school show better emotional/behavioral and academic outcomes (McMahon et al., 2004; Richman, Bowen, & Woolley, 2004; Shochet, Dadds, Ham, & Montague, 2006). Strong connections with a teacher or other school personnel can enhance this type of school identification in children and adolescents. Competent, well-trained, and well-compensated teachers are also associated with serving in a protective role in the lives of children in adverse circumstances (Wright & Masten, 2005). In addition, after-school programs and school recreational resources are associated with resilient children (Hirsch, 2005). Examples of these characteristics include sports, music, and art programs.

As mentioned in the section on supportive and stable coaches, sports activities can help protect children from the harsh ramifications of an otherwise adverse environment. Not only can sports activities expose children and adolescents to appropriate role models

Involvement in sports activities can serve as a protective factor and can be an important part of living a physically healthy lifestyle.

YOU DECIDE: IS DAY CARE BAD FOR CHILDREN?

Yes

- Day care is associated with increased aggression and defiance (Belsky, 2002).
- Children show troubled attachment to their parents when they were put in day care from very early on in life (Belsky, 2001, 2005).

No

- High-quality day care is associated with increased social competence. In some ways, the question is a moot point because most parents (especially single mothers) have to work outside the home to provide for the family. Over 90% of young children spend some type of regular care away from their parents, so the question should be how to fund quality care rather than asking whether or not it is bad (NICHD Early Child Care Research Network, 2001).

- Children whose parents are lacking in competent parenting skills actually do better in the long run compared with children who are raised solely by parents who are lacking in competent parenting skills. In general, parental factors were more predictive of children's functioning than anything about the child care setting (NICHD Early Child Care Research Network, 2001; Parks, 2006).

So, is day care bad for children? You decide.

---

in coaches and trainers, but involvement in sports can also help children obtain a healthy and active lifestyle (Bar-Or, 1996). Sports activities are helpful for children experiencing cancer (Elkin, Tye, Hudson, & Crom, 1998) as well as many other childhood difficulties such as diabetes, low self-esteem, and poor academic performance (Bar-Or, 1996). The protective nature of activities depends on the type of sports and athletic activities in which children and adolescents are involved. Team sports (also known as refereed sports) such as basketball and soccer seem to serve more of a protective function than individual sports (also known as judged sports) such as gymnastics and competitive dance (Zucker, Womble, Williamson, & Perrin, 1999). Specifically, judged sports such as gymnastics were associated with greater emotional/behavioral problems like eating disorders and body image problems than were refereed sports such as basketball (Zucker et al., 1999). Involvement in team sports was also found to be predictive of lower risk for smoking in adolescents (Rodriguez & Audrain-McGovern, 2004). Overall, the protective nature of sports or athletic involvement depends on the type of involvement and on the role models and mentors available in that activity.

Involvement in extracurricular activities also serves a protective function in children's lives. Note that high-quality after-school programs and day-care facilities often provide these types of enhanced activities, as discussed in the "You Decide" section. Children's involvement in after-school clubs and other enrichment activities predicted better academic achievement in elementary school students (Kurtz-Costes, Meece, & Floryan, 1999). Structured extracurricular activities also predicted emotional adjustment over 2 years later in elementary school students (Posner & Vandell, 1999). Unstructured activities, such as watching television and hanging out, were found to predict maladjustment in children (Posner & Vandell, 1999). Overall, structured extracurricular activities such as after-school clubs, library activities, and crafts activities were associated with resilience in children and adolescents.

Involvement in the arts is also associated with enhanced emotional/behavioral functioning in children and adolescents. Although research on the specific of type of involvement in the arts (e.g., the visual arts versus the musical arts) is limited, artistic and creative activities serve a protective function for at-risk children (Werner & Smith, 2001; Wright & Masten, 2005). The use of popular music such as rap music in prevention programs is associated with decreased risk for transmission of HIV in African-American adolescents (Stephens, Braithwaite, & Taylor, 1998). Artistic involvement is associated with increased self-esteem and decreased rates of substance abuse and is used in prevention programs within low-income, urban families (Emshoff, Avery, Raduka, & Anderson, 1996). Overall, some type of involvement in artistic and creative activities is associated with decreased risk for emotional/behavioral problems. It may be that, like other protective factors, involvement in the arts can help expose at-risk children and adolescents to other opportunities and lifestyles in addition to helping children and adolescents develop feelings of competence and pride in their own skills.

Involvement in volunteer activities and other prosocial activities has not received a great deal of empirical

BOX 6.5

PREVENTION WORKS

The Houston Parent–Child Development Center (Johnson, 1988; Johnson & Blumenthal, 2004) is one of many prevention programs that attempts to enhance the amount of protective factors in children's lives to prevent the development of emotional/behavioral problems. This program was targeted at young Mexican-American families who lived in an impoverished community. Families were invited into the program when their infant was 1 year old, and the program followed these infants for 2 years. Home visits were conducted and enrichment day-care facilities were offered for those interested in such services. Services were provided in both English and in Spanish, depending on the family's choice of language. Among the strategies that were implemented to try to prevent emotional/behavioral problems were

- Parent education to increase parental warmth, support, and structure

- Enhanced enriching activities for the infants and toddlers to increase motor, intellectual, and social-emotional development
- Staff members who helped parents increase their social support network and their involvement with other supportive individuals
- Medical care and education about how to access additional medical resources for the family
- Financial resources and education about how to deal with financial stressors that might arise in the family

At the end of the project, as well as at follow-up after 5 and 8 years, children who received the prevention program showed higher intellectual functioning, better academic performance, and lower emotional/behavior problems than children who did not receive the prevention program. This program illustrates that knowledge about protective factors can be applied to prevention programs to enhance protective factors for at-risk children.

---

attention, but it appears that children's and adolescents' involvement in volunteer activities can serve as a protective factor in at-risk children (McMahon et al., 2004; Werner & Smith, 2001). Interestingly, there has been a wealth of research on elderly individuals' involvement in volunteer activities. In elderly populations, volunteerism has been associated with better physical health, better mental health, and longer life span (Oman, Thoresen, & McMahon, 1999). Volunteerism was an even stronger protective factor than social support or involvement in religious organizations (Oman et al., 1999). Although this research was conducted with an elderly population (aged 55 to 85), these findings have relevance for children's and adolescents' involvement in volunteer activities. Volunteerism can help an individual feel pride in helping others, can expose the individual to other appropriate role models and mentors, and can create feelings of personal competence and personal accomplishment in the individual (Oman et al., 1999). These factors appear to be just as relevant for children and adolescents as they are for older adults.

Although the focus has been on resilience against the development of emotional/behavioral problems, most of these protective factors also serve to decrease the likelihood of other adverse outcomes such as poor physical health (Jessor, Turbin, & Costa, 1998) and poor academic performance (McDonald & Sayger, 1998).

These protective factors are associated with resilience in children and adolescents from a diverse array of ethnic and racial backgrounds, including African American and Caucasian American (Jessor et al., 1998), Latino/Latina Americans (Alva, 1995), Pacific Islanders (Werner & Smith, 2001), Native Americans (McCubbin, Thompson, Thompson, & Fromer, 1998), Asian Americans (Fuligni et al., 1999), and children and adolescents from across the globe (Albee, Bond, & Monsey, 1992; Fuligni, 1998). As can be seen in Box 6.5, knowledge about protective factors can be synthesized into preventive programs that increase the protective characteristics in a child's environment in order to decrease the likelihood of emotional/behavioral problems.

Other Protective Factors within the Community

A number of other factors within the community serve a protective function within children and adolescents from adverse backgrounds, including employment opportunities for parents and teens, good public health care, and access to emergency services, such as police, fire, and medical services. These factors all serve to provide the basic necessities of living (e.g., employment opportunities through which to support the family) and of staying safe and healthy (e.g., having good health care and

Case Study: Beating the Odds

The Children's Defense Fund has a private, nonprofit scholarship fund called "Beat the Odds." Children who are economically deprived but who show academic excellence and commitment to education are honored by this program. Here are two of the many stories of children who grew up and beat the odds:

Shekhinah Jay, New York, New York: After both parents passed away from AIDS during Shekhinah's preteen years, she moved in with her grandmother. "Because of [my grandmother]," she writes, "I was able to use all the grief that I built up to produce potential." She persevered and stayed focused on her studies and is now a junior at Cornell University. Currently, she is on the dean's list and majoring in industrial and labor relations. She participates in the Big Brother/Big Sister Program, the NAACP, and the Minority Industrial and Labor Relations Student Organization. Additionally, she runs an Afrocentric Saturday School for minority children in the Cornell community. . . . Her goal is to attend law school and then run a community center in

her home neighborhood of South Jamaica, Queens, New York. For Shekhinah, "The Beating the Odds scholarship is a constant reminder to me that I am special and I can make it if I put my all into it."

Marino Angulo, Los Angeles, California: Marino's family emigrated from Mexico when he was 6 years old. His mother was imprisoned for drug possession, and his alcoholic father was unemployed. Marino and his sister raised the other eight children. To help make money for his family, Marino sold fruit, did odd jobs, and cleaned at a gas station. While doing all this, he was able to maintain his superior academic standing and participate in varsity athletics. Marino attended Whittier College and then returned to pursue a master's degree in education. Since 1997, he has been teaching social studies and coaching basketball and baseball. He is married to a first-grade teacher, Sandra, and they have two children.

Source: Children's Defense Fund (2005a).

---

access to emergency services; Wright & Masten, 2005). Although these characteristics are ideals for all communities, many are not able to provide these resources for citizens (Evans, 2004).

CHARACTERISTICS WITHIN THE CULTURE OR SOCIETY

Although there is less research on these issues, a growing body of data suggest protective factors within the culture or society. Specifically, protective characteristics within the culture or society for children include being surrounded by a community that values education, living in a culture that has protective child policies (e.g., child labor, health, and welfare laws), having a system in place where there is prevention and protection from oppression or political violence, and living in a culture or society where there is low acceptance of physical violence. Individuals can often advocate for these types of changes through political action and support of

politicians who would support this type of agenda (Kaufmann & Lay, 2004). In general, community-level, cultural, and societal changes can reach many more children and adolescents than services geared at individuals, families, or even schools (Perkins, Crim, Silberman, & Brown, 2004). Thus, intervening at the larger level should provide better outcomes for less investment of resources.

Overall, studies of protective factors, resilience, and prevention programs are well established in the research literature. The study of resilience is considered so important that the American Psychological Association developed a resilience initiative to address national tragedies such as terrorism attacks, the Iraq war, and natural disasters (Newman, 2005). In addition, adopting a focus on resilience in therapeutic interventions has been identified as a way to enhancing well-being in children and adolescents (Alvord & Grados, 2005). A number of recent books (Fraser, 2004; Goldstein & Brooks, 2005; Luthar, 2003) are available with comprehensive updates for interested students.

SUMMARY AND KEY CONCEPTS

Protective factors are characteristics in children's lives that are associated with competent outcomes even in adverse circumstances. Children from adverse environments who overcome these obstacles due to protective factors in their lives are thought to show **resilience** against these adverse circumstances.

Characteristics within the Child.   A number of characteristics that are thought to be located within the child have been shown to be protective factors, such as adaptable temperament, good cognitive abilities, effective emotional and behavioral regulation strategies, and having a positive view of oneself. In particular, **self-efficacy,** which is a well-established protective factor, is shown when children expect success and when they believe that they can perform successfully in any new or challenging situation.

Characteristics within the Family.   Having a stable and supportive home environment is associated with resilience in children. **Parental monitoring,** where parents attend to their children's activities and provide age-appropriate limits for their children, is a well-established protective factor within the family. Relatedly, parents with an **authoritative parenting style,** which is characterized by warmth, age-appropriate structure, and high expectations, tend to have children who show resilience even in the face of adverse circumstances. **Scaffolding** (providing support and structure for the child's next level of development) is one of the many appropriate behaviors that these parents tend to show. In addition to the stable and supportive environment, children who are exposed to a faith framework or who are involved with religious affiliations are more likely to overcome adverse circumstances.

Characteristics within the Community.   A number of protective factors have been identified in the community, including connections to caring adult mentors and prosocial peers, living in a high-quality neighborhood where there is a sense of community, and attending an effective school. Of particular note is that teachers, coaches, and competent friends have been shown to serve in protective functions for at-risk children. Involvement in sports and other athletic activities, after-school clubs, creative and artistic endeavors, and volunteer activities can help to increase resilience in children and adolescents.

Characteristics within the Culture or Society.   A number of cultural and societal characteristics have been established as serving a protective role with children, including living in a society that values and provides adequate resources for education, having a system through which protective child policies are enforced (such as protections regarding child labor, child health, and welfare), living in a society where children are protected from oppression or political violence, and living in a culture where there is a low acceptance of physical violence. All these factors have been found to reduce the risk of adverse outcomes when children are exposed to less-than-optimal circumstances.

KEY TERMS

protective factors	self-efficacy	authoritative	scaffolding
resilience	parental monitoring	parenting style	

SUGGESTED READINGS

Obama, Barack. *Dreams from My Father*. New York: Three Rivers Press, 2004. With a Caucasian-American mother and a black African father who is almost nonexistent in his life, this memoir explains how the author overcame his difficulties with the strength of his family and went on to become a powerful and well-respected politician and social advocate.

Fleming, Keith. *The Boy with the Thorn in His Side: A Memoir*. New York: Perennial, 2000. By the age of 16, the author was hospitalized in a psychiatric facility because he was defiant and depressed. With the help of his uncle, novelist Edmund White (2000), the author is able to get back on track.

SUGGESTED VIEWINGS

Hotel Rwanda. (2005). While hundreds of thousands of individuals were being massacred in Rwanda and the surrounding areas, the protagonist in this film serves as a protective factor by shielding his family and others from these atrocities. Based on a true story.

The Pursuit of Happyness. (2006). Based on the real life story of Chris Gardener, this powerful film shows the difficulties and strengths of a father who becomes homeless with a young son and then is able to succeed in the financial world through perseverance and determination.

MOOD DISORDERS, DEPRESSIVE SYNDROMES, AND DEPRESSIVE MOODS

CHAPTER SUMMARY

> *Night*
> *to sit under a tree*
> *by the light of the moon*
> *listening to the sounds of the night*
> *thinking about the good and bad things that happened in your life*
> *and while you are thinking you think about your favorite but saddest song and cry in a sad way.*
> —Billy, aged 10, and homeless (Children's Defense Fund—Minnesota, 1990, p. 22)

Nearly everyone has felt sad or depressed at some point in their lives. In some ways, depression does not need to be defined because it is so well known to most individuals. There are, however, many misconceptions about depression in infancy, childhood, and adolescence.

From the 1930s to the 1960s, the predominant belief among psychoanalytic theorists was that children could not be depressed (Bemporad, 1994). Serious clinical depression was only thought possible when an individual had a fully developed superego, so children were thought to be immune from depression. Only when an adolescent or young adult developed and internalized a superego could they be at risk for the development of a depressive disorder (Bemporad, 1994). Ironically, some psychodynamic theorists and attachment theorists were identifying depression in infants at approximately the same time that others were questioning the existence of depression in anyone without a fully developed superego.

ANACLITIC DEPRESSION AND FAILURE TO THRIVE IN INFANCY

In the mid-1940s, the term **anaclitic depression** was used to refer to infants who had lost their primary caregiver (or whose primary caregiver was physically or emotionally abusive or distant from the infant). These infants showed signs of whining, withdrawal, weight loss, impaired social interactions, immobile facial expressions, and slowed or stunted growth (Spitz, 1946). Somewhat later, Bowlby (1973) was interested in infants who were institutionalized and who received little or no individual care and attention. These infants would often show **failure to thrive,** which is a condition where infants show apathy, slow motor development, no interest in their surroundings, and sometimes, no interest in food or liquids (Achenbach, 1982). The concepts of anaclitic depression and failure to thrive were related to each other and represent early understandings of depression in infants. Although articles and books still include the concept of anaclitic depression (Blatt, 2004; Luyten, Blatt, & Corveleyn, 2005), there is little empirical evidence to support the concept.

More recently, the *Diagnostic Classification: 0–3R* system conceptualized depression in infants and toddlers with two primary diagnoses (Zero to Three/National Center for Clinical Infant Programs, 2005). **Prolonged bereavement/grief reaction** occurs when an infant loses a primary caretaker and shows signs of crying, withdrawal, disrupted eating and sleeping, regression to previous earlier functioning, detachment, and extreme sensitivity. **Depression of infancy and early childhood** is diagnosed when an infant or toddler shows at least 2 weeks of depressed or irritable mood, decreased interest in activities that were enjoyable previously, decreased capacity to protest, excessive whining, possibilities of disturbances in sleeping and eating, and limited social interactions. These problems are often associated with disrupted attachment patterns for infants, although other etiologies have been found that are comparable to depression in older children (Schwartz, Gladstone, & Kaslow, 1998; Zero to Three/National Center for Clinical Infant Programs, 2005).

Happiness is an imaginary condition, formerly often attributed by the living to the dead, now usually attributed by adults to children and by children to adults.

—Thomas Szasz

MASKED DEPRESSION

Referring back to historical conceptualizations of depression in childhood and adolescence, another popular conceptualization in the late 1960s and early 1970s was masked depression (Cytryn & McKnew, 1972; Glaser, 1968). **Masked depression** was a term used when children showed aggressive, hyperactive, or other acting-out behaviors "to ward off the unbearable feelings of despair" (Cytryn & McKnew, 1979, p. 327). The idea was that children were really depressed, but their observable behavior showed more externalizing types of problems. Given the highly inferential nature of this term, and the lack of established validity, the concept of masked depression has been dropped from more recent conceptualizations of depression in childhood and adolescence (Schroeder & Gordon, 2002). Note, however, that high rates of comorbidity between depression and some externalizing disorders do exist. As will be noted in the section on comorbidity, the coexistence of depression and an externalizing disorder is very different than the idea that the externalizing disorder is "masking" or hiding the true depression. We will now turn to the current conceptualizations of depression in childhood and adolescence.

MAJOR DEPRESSIVE DISORDER

As can be seen in Table 7.1, **major depressive disorder** is defined clearly in the *Diagnostic and*

Children who experience depression are often isolated from their peers.

Case Study: Jacob, the Withdrawn Boy

Jacob Samuels was 7-years-old when his second-grade teacher first became concerned about him. For the first 2 months of school, Jacob just sat at his desk. He did not stand for the pledge of allegiance, he did not go to the chalkboard when asked, and he did not walk around the room when allowed. He followed the other children to and from the cafeteria, but he usually sat by himself, and he rarely ate anything for lunch.

The teacher set up a meeting with Jacob's parents, but they did not show up for the meeting. The teacher then referred Jacob to the school psychologist, who again set up a meeting with Mr. and Mrs. Samuels. The parents did not show up for that meeting, but they did finally attend a meeting that was scheduled personally by the principal. Jacob's father worked for a plumbing company, and Jacob's mother was a full-time homemaker. Mr. and Mrs. Samuels reported that Jacob was not a discipline problem, and they were surprised that the school officials were concerned about him. They acknowledged that he did not have any friends, but stated that he preferred playing with his younger sister and brother.

When interviewed later by the school psychologist, Jacob sat passively in the office and did not make eye contact with the psychologist. Jacob reported that he had a lot of chores, such as making his bed each morning, changing his sheets once a week, taking out the garbage each night, and taking care of the dog. He stated that sometimes he wished he was the youngest in the family so he would not have so many chores. Jacob also reported that he used to love reading, but that lately he did not enjoy it so he quit reading except for homework. He also reported that he often could not fall asleep, given his "bad" thoughts. With much probing, the psychologist was able to find out that Jacob sometimes thought about pushing his younger brother off the swing and fantasized about not doing his chores.

He cried when he acknowledged that his mother loved him very much, but he thought she was too bossy, and he complained that she would not leave him alone to relax and read.

The school psychologist had Jacob complete a Children's Depression Inventory. Jacob scored in the moderately depressed category, with high scores on eating problems, social isolation, feeling sad, sleeping problems, and loss of pleasure in everyday activities.

After diagnosing Jacob with major depressive disorder, the school psychologist developed a treatment plan for Jacob that included cognitive–behavioral therapy with Jacob and family sessions with Jacob's parents. Jacob responded well to the sessions, and his parents' sessions revealed a number of issues that were troubling to the parents. Mrs. Jacobs, for example, felt trapped by her responsibilities as a homemaker, and she often felt overwhelmed with life. She had wanted to attend college, but Mr. Jacobs had not been supportive. Through the parents' therapy sessions, Mr. and Mrs. Jacobs developed a plan for Mrs. Jacobs to begin taking classes at the local community college, and the children's grandmother could care for the children while their mother was at school. Mr. Jacobs began to encourage his wife in her educational pursuits. After 3 months of treatment, both Jacob and his parents were much happier and well functioning.

Two years later, the therapist checked up on Jacob and his family. In the time since therapy, Jacob had not had any recurrence of depression, and his parents were functioning very well. Mrs. Jacobs had continued to attend classes at the local college, and she had decided to become a nurse.

Source: Morgan (1999).

Statistical Manual of Mental Disorders, Fourth Edition, Text Revision (DSM-IV-TR). By looking at the diagnostic criteria, you can see that major depressive disorder (MDD) is a serious disorder and is more than just feeling down or sad temporarily. The disorder is only diagnosed when there are clear indications of a composite of symptoms in addition to clinical distress or impairment in social, occupational, or educational functioning.

Major depressive disorder can be diagnosed as a single episode or as recurrent, when there are two or more episodes. MDD would not be diagnosed if the symptoms were better accounted for by other disorders (such as schizoaffective disorder, schizophrenia, or other similar disorders). MDD is listed on Axis I when it is diagnosed.

These diagnostic criteria apply to both adults and children. There has never been a specific diagnosis of childhood depression in any version of *DSM*. When diagnosing a child or adolescent with *DSM-IV*, two "Notes" apply. First, children and adolescents might show irritable mood rather than depressed mood. Second, children might fail to make expected weight gains rather than losing or gaining significant amounts of weight. Although these acknowledgments of developmental differences are appropriate, they ignore the many other differences between depressive symptoms in children versus adults (see Course of the Disorder section for further information).

If children or adolescents experience a great deal of these symptoms in reaction to an identifiable stressor, but if they do not meet criteria for major depressive disorder,

TABLE 7.1 *DSM-IV* Diagnostic Criteria for Major Depressive Episode

A. Five (or more) of the following symptoms have been present during the same 2-week period and represent a change from previous functioning; at least one of the symptoms is either (1) depressed mood or (2) loss of interest or pleasure.

Note: Do not include symptoms that are clearly due to a general medical condition, or mood-incongruent delusions or hallucinations.

(1) depressed mood most of the day, nearly every day, as indicated by either subjective report (e.g., feels sad or empty) or observation made by others (e.g., appears tearful). Note: In children and adolescents, can be irritable mood.

(2) markedly diminished interest or pleasure in all, or almost all, activities most of the day, nearly every day (as indicated by either subjective account or observation made by others)

(3) significant weight loss when not dieting or weight gain (e.g., a change of more than 5% of body weight in a month), or decrease or increase in appetite nearly every day. Note: In children, consider failure to make expected weight gains.

(4) insomnia or hypersomnia nearly every day

(5) psychomotor agitation or retardation nearly every day (observable by others, not merely subjective feelings of restlessness or being slowed down)

(6) fatigue or loss of energy nearly every day

(7) feelings of worthlessness or excessive or inappropriate guilt (which may be delusional) nearly every day (not merely self-reproach or guilt about being sick)

(8) diminished ability to think or concentrate, or indecisiveness, nearly every day (either by subjective account or as observed by others)

(9) recurrent thoughts of death (not just fear of dying), recurrent suicidal ideation without a specific plan, or a suicide attempt or a specific plan for committing suicide

B. The symptoms do not meet criteria for a Mixed Episode of both highs and lows (related to Bipolar Disorder).

C. The symptoms cause clinically significant distress or impairment in social, occupational, or other important areas of functioning.

D. The symptoms are not due to the direct physiological effects of a substance (e.g., a drug of abuse, a medication) or a general medical condition (e.g., hypothyroidism).

E. The symptoms are not better accounted for by bereavement, i.e., after the loss of a loved one, the symptoms persist for longer than 2 months, or are characterized by marked functional impairment, morbid preoccupation with worthlessness, suicidal ideation, psychotic symptoms, or psychomotor retardation.

Source: American Psychiatric Association (2000).

Reprinted with permission from the *Diagnostic and Statistical Manual of Mental Disorders, Fourth Edition, Text Revision.* Copyright 2000 American Psychiatric Association.

they might meet criteria for **adjustment disorder with depressed mood.** Adjustment disorder with depressed mood would be diagnosed when a child or adolescent experiences depressed mood, tearfulness, or feelings of hopelessness in reaction to an identifiable stressor that occurred within 3 months of the psychological symptoms (American Psychiatric Association, 2000). Given that major depressive disorder is considered the more severe disorder, more attention has been paid to major depressive disorder than to adjustment disorder with depressed mood.

There has also been some recent interest in defining a new syndrome of childhood traumatic grief (Brown & Goodman, 2005). The idea is that children could be experiencing depressive-like symptoms and possibly posttraumatic-like symptoms after a trauma. These experiences could be conceptualized as normal grief or traumatic grief. For example, in an exploration of children who lost a parent in the attacks on 9/11, some children experienced what seemed to be a normative pattern of grief, whereas other children experienced an intensified and troubled grief reaction, which was considered childhood traumatic grief (Brown & Goodman, 2005). Although there is not a current effort to include childhood traumatic grief in *DSM-V*, it appears to be a viable concept for further study.

Prevalence Rates

As mentioned in chapter 1, prevalence rates refer to the number of cases of a particular disorder at any one time. Also discussed in chapter 1 was the difficulty in establishing accurate prevalence rates that are reflective

"Son, it's important to remember that it's O.K. to be depressed."

of children and adolescents of any age, race/ethnicity, gender, and socioeconomic status. Prevalence rates presented in this section refer to the diagnosis of major depressive disorder, which represents the categorical approach to defining abnormal child behavior. Based on results from the MECA study, rates of major depressive disorder range from 0.7% to 7.1% in children and adolescents (Shaffer et al., 1996). This range reflects differences in informants (i.e., youth, parent, or youth and parent combined) and reflects differences in severity of symptoms. Notably, parents tended to report greater rates of depression in adolescents than reported by the adolescents themselves (King et al., 1997).

Before the MECA study, the most commonly reported prevalence rates for depression suggested that between 2% and 5% of children and adolescents in the community experience major depressive disorder at any one time (Garrison et al., 1997; Schwartz et al., 1998). These prevalence rates are summarized in Table 7.2. Between 10% and 50% of children and adolescents in outpatient and inpatient psychiatric facilities experience MDD (Fleming & Offord, 1990; Schwartz et al., 1998).

Although these prevalence rates reflect the number of children and adolescents who meet criteria for MDD, it is important to note that groups of depressed children are very heterogeneous (i.e., they have a lot of variability of symptoms; Costello, Mustillo, Erkanli, Keeler, & Angold, 2003).

As might be expected, rates of depression increase with age. Depression in preschoolers is relatively rare, with most estimates suggesting that less than 1% of preschool children in nonclinical facilities show clinical depression (Luby, Mrakotsky et al., 2003) and less than 1% of young girls aged 5 to 8 show clinically elevated depressive symptoms (Keenan, Hipwell, Duax, Stouthamer-Loeber, & Loeber, 2004). In school-aged children, prevalence rates range from 2% to 4% (Costello et al., 2003). By the time of adolescence, prevalence rates in nonclinical facilities rise to 7% and higher (Hankin & Abela, 2005; Reynolds, 1995). These rates are all significantly higher when clinical samples are studied, such as when children are receiving mental health services on an outpatient or inpatient basis or when they are receiving help from a school psychologist (Sorensen, Nissen, Mors, & Thomsen, 2005). One review estimated that at least one out of every six adolescents receiving inpatient mental health services had a primary diagnosis related to a mood disorder (Reynolds, 1995).

When considering prevalence rates based on gender, there is an interaction between age and gender. That is, comments cannot be made on prevalence rates based on gender without also commenting on the age of the children under consideration. Before puberty, there is relatively consistent evidence that boys and girls show approximately equal rates of depression (Stark, Bronik, Wong, Wells, & Ostrander, 2000), although some reviews of the literature have argued that boys have higher rates of depression than girls before puberty (Hankin & Abela, 2005). After puberty, there is consistent evidence that girls show much higher rates of depression, usually estimated at a 2:1 ratio for girls to boys (Hankin & Abramson, 2001; Stark et al., 2000). This gender ratio continues into adulthood, with women showing at least 2 or 3 times higher

TABLE 7.2 Overview of Prevalence Information for Major Depressive Disorder

Prevalence	2–5%
Age	Adolescents > Children
Gender	Before puberty, equal rates; after puberty, girls > boys (2:1)
SES	Lower SES > Higher SES (perhaps)
Race/Ethnicity	Possibility of higher rates in African-American boys compared with Caucasian-American boys; no differences between girls

rates of depression than men (Nolen-Hoeksema, 2001; Whiffen & Demidenko, 2006). Although there are many theories as to why this gender difference occurs in adolescence, the most compelling reasons have to do with psychosocial and cognitive factors. It appears that girls are more oriented toward sociality and cooperation and are more likely to show ruminative coping styles (where they focus on their problems rather than trying to distract themselves or conversely do something about the problems; Nolen-Hoeksema & Girgus, 1994). In addition, girls' maladaptive cognitions appear to be more salient than boys' maladaptive cognitions (Hankin & Abramson, 2001), and girls tend to deal in a more reactive manner to specific stressors than boys, which is associated with depressive symptoms (Shih, Eberhart, Hammen, & Brennan, 2006). These factors may put girls at greater risk for depression in adolescence when they are faced with greater personal and social challenges that are brought about by both biological and social stressors. Based on a longitudinal study, it appears that girls have poorer outcomes than boys (Birmaher et al., 2004).

Prevalence rates based on socioeconomic status (SES) are more difficult to interpret. A number of studies have found that rates of major depression do not differ based on SES (Costello et al., 1988; Whitaker et al., 1990), but more recent studies have shown an inverse relationship between depression and SES with children from lower SES communities showing higher rates of depression (reviewed in Hammen & Rudolph, 2003). If depression is viewed as a continuous variable, however, higher rates of depressive symptoms have been consistently associated with lower levels of SES (Gore, Aseltine, & Colton, 1993; Hammen & Rudolph, 2003).

There has only been limited research into prevalence rates of depression regarding ethnicity and race (Evans & Lee, 1998). Although older studies found no differences in depression rates between African-American and Caucasian-American youth (Costello et al., 1988; Kandel & Davies, 1982), more recent studies suggest that African-American boys show higher rates of depression than Caucasian-American boys (Kistner, David, & White, 2003). African-American girls and Caucasian-American girls did not differ in their level of depressive symptoms (Kistner et al., 2003).

In a number of comprehensive reviews of race/ethnicity and adolescent depression, the only firm pattern was that Mexican-American adolescents had higher rates of depression than youth in other ethnic groups (Roberts, 2000; Twenge & Nolen-Hoeksema, 2002). These higher rates of depression appear to be due to acculturation, feelings of fatalism, and a lack of control (Roberts,

2000). For girls but not boys, low self-esteem in combination with low cultural affiliation was associated with greater depressive symptoms (E. J. McDonald et al., 2005). The higher prevalence rates in Latino/Latina children do not appear to be due to problems with the assessment measures. There is strong evidence that empirically based assessment techniques for depression are equally effective at assessing depression across many groups of adolescents, including European American, Mexican American, Cuban American, and Puerto Rican American (Crockett, Randall, Shen, Russell, & Driscoll, 2005). Overall, depression has been identified in children and adolescents in nearly every region and country, including Asia, Central America, England, Russia, the Caribbean, Sweden, and Mexico (Canino et al., 2004; Gau, Chong, Chen, & Cheng, 2005; Kopp, 2003; Meltzer, Gatward, Goodman, & Ford, 2003).

The most compelling difference in rates of major depression are found for age (with older children and adolescents showing more depression than younger children) and for gender (with postpubertal girls showing higher rates than any other group of youngsters).

Comorbidity

As mentioned in the first chapter, comorbidity is the co-occurrence of two different disorders in one individual. For many disorders, including depression, comorbidity is the rule rather than the exception. Depression is often found in children and adolescents who are also showing other clinical disorders (Marmorstein & Iacono, 2003; Rudolph, Hammen, & Daley, 2006). In fact, children who are depressed are more likely to be comorbid with another disorder than are adults who are depressed (Hammen & Rudolph, 2003). The highest rates of comorbidity are between MDD and an anxiety disorder (Angold, Costello, & Erkanli, 1999), with some reviews of the research literature suggesting that as many as 80% of depressed children also meet criteria for an anxiety disorder (Schroeder & Gordon, 2002). The high rates of comorbidity between depression and anxiety are especially noticeable in girls as opposed to boys (Joiner, Blalock, & Wagner, 1999). Comorbidity between depression and anxiety is so high that the two syndromes often cannot be distinguished as separate problems (Chorpita, Plummer, & Moffitt, 2000; Eley & Stevenson, 1999; Hinden, Compas, Howell, & Achenbach, 1997).

Relatively high rates of comorbidity have been found between depression and a number of other clinical disorders, including conduct disorder, oppositional defiant disorder, attention-deficit/hyperactivity disorder, substance use disorders, and eating disorders (Marmorstein & Iacono, 2003; Stark et al., 2000). One study found that 90% of adolescents who were in treatment for depression met criteria for at least one other clinical disorder, such as separation anxiety disorder, conduct disorder, oppositional defiant disorder, specific phobia, and social phobia (Sorensen et al., 2005). Comorbidity between depression and a substance use disorder is especially high in later adolescence (Rao, Daley, & Hammen, 2000). Overall, the overwhelming evidence shows that major depressive disorder is comorbid with a great many other disorders. Thus, high rates of comorbidity are expected for children and adolescents who are diagnosed with major depressive disorder, especially if they are seeking treatment for their depression.

Depression is also linked to the onset of other disorders, which are sometimes comorbid with depression and sometimes develop later. Later substance use is more strongly associated with conduct problems than depressive problems (Miller-Johnson, Lochman, Coie, Terry, & Hyman, 1998). Major depressive disorder and disruptive disorders, however, are associated with earlier onset of substance use and abuse and higher rates of substance use and abuse in both male and female adolescents (Costello, Erkanli, Federman, & Angold, 1999; Rao et al., 1999). For girls, there are reciprocal connections between the onset of depressive symptoms and delinquency (Wiesner, 2003). There are more mixed findings with boys, with one study finding that depressive symptoms predicted later delinquency behaviors, but delinquency did not predict later depressive symptoms (Beyers & Loeber, 2003), and another study finding that delinquency did successfully predict later depression (Weisner, 2003). Depression is notable for the disruption in current functioning as well as the link to disturbed functioning in later years.

Course of the Disorder

Symptoms of depression are likely to differ somewhat based on the age of the child (Weiss & Garber, 2003). Preschoolers and younger children are more apt to show irritability and somatic complaints rather than reporting dysphoric mood or hopelessness (Luby et al., 2002; Luby, Heffelfinger et al., 2003). Disturbed sleep patterns are less likely to be seen in preschoolers and children than in adolescents and adults (Luby, Mrakotsky, et al., 2003). Adolescents are also more likely to report depressed mood, feelings of hopelessness, and low self-esteem than are younger children (Schroeder & Gordon,

2002). Self-esteem is inversely related to age in clinical samples (Orvaschel, Beeferman, & Kabacoff, 1997). In other words, the older the child or adolescent, the lower the self-esteem. Poor self-esteem is linked strongly to depression in adolescents (Tram & Cole, 2000). The core symptoms of depression, however, remain consistent across childhood and adolescence (Birmaher, Williamson, et al., 2004).

The average length of a depressive episode varies somewhat, depending on the characteristics of the sample under investigation. Overall, the average length of a depressive episode in children and adolescents ranges from 16 weeks to 36 weeks, with longer lengths of time found for outpatient and inpatient samples of children and shorter lengths of time found for community samples of children (Kovacs, 1996; McCauley et al., 1993).

Children who have been depressed in the past are more likely to experience depression in the future (Roza, Hofstra, vander Ende, & Verhulst, 2003). For example, one study found that 25% of children and adolescents receiving mental health services for depression experienced another episode of major depression within 1 year, and a total of 54% showed a recurrence of major depression within 3 years (McCauley et al., 1993). Another study found that the recurrence rate within 2 years was as high as 69% (Emslie et al., 1997). This greater likelihood of depression also follows children into adulthood, with evidence that at least 60% of depressed children will experience at least one episode of major depression in adulthood. Depressed children are also at greater risk for other clinical disorders in adulthood (Roza et al., 2003). Overall, depression is a pervasive disorder that is apt to recur for the children and adolescents throughout their lives. The seriousness of this clinical disorder leads to the important question of etiology.

There is no sadder sight than a young pessimist.

—Mark Twain

Etiology

There are a number of theories as to why depression develops in children and adolescents, but there is no overarching theory that has been well established as the definitive explanation. Genetic factors appear to put children at risk for the development of depression, given that children of depressed parents are more likely to develop depression even if the children are raised by nondepressed adoptive parents (Goodman & Gotlib, 2002a, 2002b). In addition, monozygotic twins have higher concordance for major depression (i.e., are more

Case Study: Carly, The Distressed Adolescent

Carly Prochaski, a 15-year-old high school sophomore, had always earned As in her honors courses. In the last grading period, however, she failed all her courses. The school counselor became alarmed and recommended that Carly and her parents seek the help of a therapist.

During the first interview with the therapist, Carly stated that she did not have any problems and that her parents were "overreacting." She realized that her grades had dropped, but she felt sure that she knew the class material. Carly denied feeling sad, but did acknowledge that she did not enjoy activities (such as soccer and going to the mall) as much as she did previously. She reported that she had many friends, but when pushed, she admitted that she had not done anything with her friends for at least 2 months. Carly reported that she had gained 10 pounds recently, which concerned her greatly since she had always been thin and trim.

When asked about drug use, Carly denied any use of illicit drugs. She did say that she had tried beer at a party once, but she decided not to drink anymore because she had heard that Native Americans were at greater risk for alcoholism. Carly is Native American, and she was adopted by the Prochaskis when she was an infant. Although her biological parents were in high school when she was born, she often wishes that they had not given her up for adoption because she sometimes feels uncomfortable around so many Caucasian Americans.

Mr. and Mrs. Prochaski reported that Carly had always been a happy and healthy child. She achieved excellence in schoolwork and on the soccer field. She had lots of friends and was always appreciated by those around her. When asked about allowing Carly more access to her Native American culture, her parents stated that they had purchased books for her about Native American customs and they always had her play the part of the "Indian" in school plays. When asked if they had taken Carly to any areas, such as the local reservation, where Carly could meet more Native Americans, Carly's parents said that they had not taken her there because they did not want her to see "how lazy those people were."

With written permission from the parents and Carly, the psychologist was also able to meet with the school counselor. The school counselor was greatly concerned about Carly, as her behavior had changed rapidly in recent months. Carly, who had never previously missed soccer practice or a soccer game even when she was sick, had failed to show up at soccer practices, and she even missed one game without notifying the coach. She began withdrawing from others at school and seemed to walk the halls "in a daze." The school counselor was also terribly worried about a poem that Carly had written in her English class. The poem described the world as a cold, wintery place without love or warmth. The poem concluded with the protagonist laying down in the snow to await death.

Before the psychologist could meet with Carly for psychological testing, the psychologist received a call from Carly's parents. The previous afternoon, Carly had taken an entire bottle of aspirin. When her parents could not wake her for dinner, Carly was rushed to the hospital to have her stomach pumped. Although the amount of aspirin was not life-threatening, it was clearly an act to be taken seriously. Later at the hospital, Carly denied that she tried to kill herself, but rather stated that she had lost count of how many aspirin she had taken to alleviate her menstrual cramps.

Carly was put on antidepressant medication and was sent home with her parents. A meeting was scheduled with the psychologist, but the parents canceled the appointment because Carly had been in an excellent mood and had even played several games of Scrabble with them. In addition, Carly had planned a dinner party for a number of her friends that night.

The following week, Carly's father called the psychologist to report that Carly had killed herself the previous night. Late at night, she had filled the bathtub with water, took all her medication, and slit her wrists. Her parents found her dead in the morning. Carly's parents declined the offer for therapy to deal with their grief about Carly's death. They divorced 6 months later.

Although Carly had initially seemed like she was doing fine after being released from the hospital, it is not uncommon that an individual's mood will lighten when he or she makes the final decision to commit suicide. It may have been that Carly was trying to have a good time with her family and friends as a way of saying goodbye to them. This case illustrates the importance of taking a suicide attempt seriously.

Source: Morgan (1999).

---

similar in their rates of depression) than dizygotic twins or siblings (Rice, Harold, & Thapar, 2002). Even in nontwin siblings, there is a high concordance rate between siblings who show symptoms of depression and anxiety (Kelvin, Goodyer, & Altham, 1996). Further evidence of a strong genetic influence is provided by the following studies:

- Genetic analyses were found for twins in symptoms of both depression and anxiety (Eley & Stevenson, 1999).
- One twin study found that genetic influences accounted for over 60% of the variance in depression and anxiety (Hudziak, Rudiger, Neale, Heath, & Todd, 2000).

Depression in childhood is associated with depression in adolescence and adulthood.

• Common genetic liabilities put children at risk for depression as well as antisocial behavior (O'Connor, McGuire, Reiss, Hetherington, & Plomin, 1998).

• Children with both a depressed parent and a depressed grandparent had significantly high rates of psychopathology, including depression, anxiety disorders, and disruptive disorders (Warner, Weissman, Mufson, & Wickramaratne, 1999; Wickramaratne, Greenwald, & Weissman, 2000).

• Heritability estimates were stronger from severe levels of depression than for depressive symptoms that did not meet criteria for major depressive disorder (Eley, 1997) although another study found more genetic evidence for lower levels of depressive symptoms than higher levels (Rende, Slomkowski, Lloyd-Richardson, Stroud, & Niaura, 2006).

Overall, there is compelling evidence of a genetic component in the development of depression in children and adolescents. One comprehensive review suggested that approximately 50% of the variance accounting for the development of depression is due to genetic influences (Rutter, Silberg, O'Connor, & Simonoff, 1999a, 1999b). There is also some evidence of other biological factors in childhood depression.

With regard to biological factors, there are less consistent results for children and adolescents than there are for adults. Factors that look promising for further study include growth hormone abnormalities, elevated serum thyrotropic, and a number of the neurotransmitter systems such as acetylcholine, norepinephrine, serotonin, and neuropeptides (Rutter et al., 1999). Cerebral laterality (e.g., asymmetry between portions of the right and left hemispheres in the brain) has also been implicated in the etiology of childhood depression (Pine et al., 2000). Although these biological factors are beyond the scope of this textbook, suffice it to say that additional investigation into biological factors are warranted (Rutter et al., 1999).

There is strong evidence that a cognitive conceptualization of depression is helpful in understanding the development and maintenance of depression in children and adolescents. Like adults who are depressed, children and adolescents who are depressed tend to show maladaptive cognitions about themselves, their lives, and the future (Gencoz, Voelz, Gencoz, Pettit, & Joiner, 2001). Their attributional style for negative events shows that they have internal, stable, and global attributions for bad things that happen to them, all of which are associated with depression in adults (Hankin & Abela, 2005). Children's cognitive distortions are related to their current and future depressive symptoms (Stewart et al., 2004) and to hopelessness (Gibb & Alloy, 2006). In particular, self-critical cognitions and interpersonal concerns were linked to depressive symptomatology in a group of inpatient adolescents (Frank, Poorman, VanEgeren, & Field, 1997). Interestingly, depressed children may be relatively accurate in some of their negative views of their own social status, but they appear to exaggerate these negative views (Rudolph & Clark, 2001). There is mixed evidence as to whether or not depressed children actually engage in fewer pleasant events than nondepressed children (Hankin & Abela, 2005).

One type of cognitive theory that has received a lot of support is the interpersonal theory of depression. Originally developed by Coyne (1976) to explain depression in adults, the interpersonal theory of depression is now used to explain the development of depression in children and adolescents. A central component of the interpersonal theory of depression is that individuals who seek excessive amounts of reassurance (e.g., by asking people how they look or by looking to others for constant reassurance) tend to be rejected by others, which is then linked to greater feelings of depression. One study found that young adolescents with excessive reassurance-seeking behavior and high levels of depression received greater amounts of interpersonal rejection than adolescents who showed less reassurance-seeking behavior (Joiner, 1999). A strong cognitive component is consistent with the interpersonal theory of depression. Young adolescents who were depressed tended to show negative interpersonal representations about themselves, their family, and their peers and tended to be rejected by peers (Rudolph, Hammen, & Burge, 1997). This theory holds promise for explaining the complex cognitive, behavioral, and interpersonal factors that are related to the development of depression in children and adolescents.

Family environment and family functioning also are related to the development and maintenance of depression in children and adolescents. Figure 7.1 shows the kinetic family drawing of a 13-year-old boy who is depressed (Burns & Kaufman, 1972). In this drawing, the boy shows himself in bed, with his mother's back to him and his father in the distance. Although any interpretation would have to be validated with a more psychometrically sound measure, this kinetic family drawing could be interpreted to show the boy's disengagement from his family as well as his lethargy and depression (Burns & Kaufman, 1972).

Family dysfunction and conflict are much more prevalent in families with a depressed youngster than those with nondistressed youngsters (Merikangas, Swendsen, Preisig, & Chazan, 1998; Tamplin et al., 1998), although this type of increased dysfunction is not always found (Olsson, Nordstrom, Arinell, & von Knorring, 1999; Pavlidis & McCauley, 2001). When compared with the families of nondepressed adolescents, the families of depressed adolescents showed less supportiveness and more conflict (Sheeber & Sorensen, 1998) and poorer parental bonding (Stein et al., 2000). Parents of depressed children showed significantly higher levels of critical expressed emotion than did parents of children diagnosed with attention-deficit/hyperactivity disorder and parents of children in a nonclinical group (Asarnow, Tompson, Woo, & Cantwell, 2001). Adolescents' negative perceptions of their families were associated with increased risk for depression and antisocial behavior (Garnefski, 2000). Other family risk factors include frequent parental separations or divorces, marital satisfaction, and parental attitudes toward caregiving (Najman et al., 2005). Although genetic factors have been implicated with regard to the connection between parental depression and child depression, there is compelling evidence that this connection may be influenced by psychosocial factors within the family. Specifically, a comprehensive review of the research on children of depressed parents suggests that the presence or absence of interparental conflict influences children's outcomes (Downey & Coyne, 1990). When there were high levels of interparental conflict in families with a depressed parent, children and adolescents experienced externalizing disorders, such as conduct disorder and oppositional defiant disorder. When there were low levels of interparental conflict, children and adolescents showed internalizing problems, such as depression and anxiety disorders (Downey & Coyne, 1990). Overall, family dysfunction appears to be related to the onset and maintenance of depression in children and adolescents.

As discussed later in Box 7.3, parental depression is associated with emotional/behavioral problems in children. Specifically, both maternal and

FIGURE 7.1 Kinetic Family Drawing by a 13-year-old Boy Diagnosed with Depression.

Source: Burns & Kaufman (1972).

paternal depressive symptoms are associated with increased emotional/behavioral problems in children (Connell & Goodman, 2002; Kane & Garber, 2004; Silk, Shaw, Forbes, Lane, & Kovacs, 2006). Interestingly, these associations are found in a diversity of families, including Caucasian-American and Chinese-American families (Johnson & Jacob, 2000; Kim & Ge, 2000).

The developmental psychopathology framework can help synthesize the many factors that are related to the development of depression in children and adolescents (Hankin & Abela, 2005). As will be discussed later in the chapter, a number of risk factors, such as social/interpersonal factors, familial factors, and peer relationships, are associated with the development of depression (Garber & Carter, 2006). Within the developmental psychopathology framework, researchers view the development of depression from an ecological transactional framework, where biological, psychological, and social systems interact to affect the child's functioning (Cicchetti & Toth, 1998). For example, one study found that the combination of troubled parent–adolescent interactions and troubled relationships with peers was associated with depressive symptoms 1 year later (Allen et al., 2006).

Similar to most other clinical disorders of childhood and adolescence, there is no clear-cut understanding of why depression develops in children or adolescents. The most likely explanation encompasses multiple factors that put the child at risk for the development of depression. For example, one study found that depressed adolescents of depressed mothers showed higher levels of cognitive distortions and poorer interpersonal behaviors than did depressed adolescents without a history of maternal depression (Hammen & Brennan, 2001). Figure 7.2 provides a multifactorial, transactional model of child and adolescent depression that attempts to integrate many etiological factors into one comprehensive

model (Hammen & Rudolph, 2003). This type of integrative model provides a framework that should help further research into the etiology of depression in children and adolescents.

Noble deeds and hot baths are the best cures for depression
—Dodie Smith

Treatment

Given the sometimes devastating outcome of child and adolescent depression, it is heartening to find that there are effective treatments. Sometimes, however, it is difficult for depressed children to be identified for services. One large national study found that children reported a greater need for depressive symptoms, whereas parents reported a greater need for their children's disruptive behavior (Wu et al., 1999). Once depressed children are identified for services, there is no standard treatment that stands out as the only therapy that is effective. A number of intervention strategies appear to help alleviate depression within children and adolescents. As mentioned in the chapter on interventions, there is a strong dedication within the field to identify evidence-based therapies for children and adolescents (Hibbs & Jensen, 2005; Kazdin & Weisz, 2003; McClellan & Werry, 2003). One comprehensive meta-analysis found that cognitive treatments, cognitive–behavioral treatments, and noncognitive treatments were all about the same in decreasing depressive symptoms in children and adolescents and although the improvements were not large, they were statistically significant (Weisz, McCarty, & Valeri, 2006).

There is a recent and ongoing comprehensive study of depression called "Treatment for adolescents with depression study" (TADS), which was funded by the National Institute of Mental Health (Treatment for

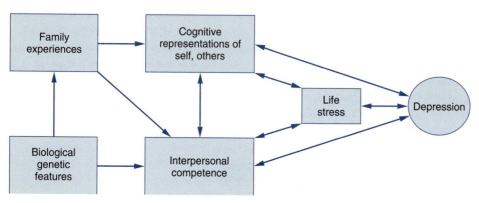

FIGURE 7.2

Multifactorial, Transactional Model of Child and Adolescent Depression.

Source: Hammen & Rudolph (2003).

Case Study: Henry, The Adolescent Dealing With Parental Alcoholism

Henry, who is 16-years-old, was identified as possibly depressed in a schoolwide screening to identify children at risk for depression. Based on both the screening questionnaire and subsequent questionnaires and interviews, Henry reported a great deal of depressive symptomatology. At about the same time, Henry's teacher recommended that he see the school psychologist because of his declining school performance, lethargy, and constant appearance of being sad.

After receiving permission from his parents, Henry was allowed to begin therapy at school for his depression. Upon meeting the therapist, Henry appeared sad, slow moving, and his speech was slow and monotone. Henry reported that he lived with his mother, who was alcoholic, and that he had a paper route to help support the family. Henry stated that he had few friends and rarely engaged in any social activities. He said that he had been feeling quite sad and down for at least 2 or 3 months. He also mentioned that he had accidentally hit a hitchhiker while he was driving the family car 3 weeks ago. The hitchhiker was in a coma. Henry described this event as yet another example of the hopelessness of life. Although Henry thought a lot about dying, he did not have any active plans to harm himself nor had he ever tried to harm himself previously.

Given the vast number of depressive symptoms that Henry exhibited (anhedonia, feelings of worthlessness, helplessness, sadness, low mood, loss of pleasure in previously enjoyable events, thoughts of death), therapy began immediately. The treatment plan called for cognitive–behavioral therapy, which was administered in 50-minute sessions twice a week for 5 weeks. The goals of therapy included helping Henry build self-help skills and social problem-solving skills that he could apply to real-life situations. Other goals were to teach Henry self-control skills, self-monitoring techniques, self-evaluation skills, and self-reinforcement skills. In addition, a major emphasis in therapy was to modify cognitive distortions and develop better cognitive strategies. Henry's treatment was administered in group format, with three other adolescents who were depressed. The group format allows adolescents to work on the development of social skills and to realize that they are not alone in many of their concerns.

After completion of treatment, Henry did not show signs of depression, and he stated that he was feeling optimistic about the future. At 5-week follow-up and at 1-year follow-up, Henry continued to show no symptoms of depression. Although the cognitive–behavioral treatment was effective for Henry, some type of intervention for his mother's alcoholism might also help Henry in the long run.

Source: Reynolds (1988).

Adolescents with Depression Study [TADS] Team, 2004). A total of 439 adolescents who were experiencing major depression were randomly assigned to one of four treatment groups: medication only (Fluoxetine/Prozac), cognitive–behavioral therapy, the combination of medication and cognitive–behavioral therapy, or inert pill placebo (Treatment for Adolescents with Depression Study [TADS] Team, 2005). The treatments were randomly assigned further as either short-term (12-weeks) or long-term (36-weeks; Treatment for Adolescents with Depression Study [TADS] Team, 2003).

Results of the TADS project (Treatment for Adolescents with Depression Study [TADS] Team, 2004) suggest that:

- The combination of medication and cognitive–behavioral therapy was superior to any other treatment.
- Medication alone was more effective than cognitive–behavioral therapy alone.
- Medication alone or medication with cognitive–behavioral therapy was more effective than placebo, but cognitive–behavioral therapy alone was not significantly better than placebo.

A total of 71.9% children and adolescents showed significant improvement with the combination of medication and cognitive–behavioral therapy. Somewhat lower percentages of children and adolescents showed significant improvement with medication alone (60.6%) or cognitive–behavioral treatment alone (43.2%). A total of 34.8% of adolescents showed significant improvement on the placebo pill (Treatment for Adolescents with Depression Study [TADS] Team, 2004).

A number of interesting issues have arisen from these results. Given that there is a wealth of research suggesting that cognitive–behavioral therapy is effective for adolescent depression (Rohde, Lewinsohn, Clarke, Hops, & Seeley, 2005; Weersing & Brent, 2003), the researchers themselves were surprised that cognitive–behavioral therapy was not more effective. Some clinical researchers have speculated that the cognitive–behavioral treatment in the TADS project was too much of an amalgamation of different aspects of the treatment (Hollon, Garber, & Shelton, 2005). Specifically, the therapy used in the TADS project was created by putting together the major components of many different cognitive–behavioral therapies, such as mood monitoring, working on cognitive distortions, social problem solving, and psychoeducational aspects while also providing optional treatments as needed, such as relaxation or affect regulation (Rohde, Feeny, & Robins, 2005). It may be that too many aspects of cognitive–behavioral therapy were being forced into the therapy sequence, which may have limited the clinicians from modifying the treatment to the needs of a particular client (Hollon et al., 2005).

In addition to these issues, note that 34.8% of adolescents who received placebo pill showed significant improvement (Treatment for Adolescents with Depression Study [TADS] Team, 2004). That is quite a sizable portion of adolescents who were able to improve just by believing that they were taking an antidepressant medication. Thus, therapies should not only be tested against each other but also against placebo to make sure that the improvements are not just due to the belief that benefits should occur. Overall, the TADS project suggests that the combination of antidepressant medication and cognitive–behavioral treatment was the most effective strategy in decreasing depression in adolescents (Ginsburg, Albano, Findling, Kratochvil, & Walkup, 2005; Treatment for Adolescents with Depression Study [TADS] Team, 2004).

There are, however, concerns that these data will be used to put more adolescents on antidepressants, which then may place them at increased risk for suicide. For example, the conclusions of the TADS project have been questioned because of the potential dangers of using antidepressant medications with children and adolescents (Antonuccio & Burns, 2004). These authors suggested that drug-free treatments such as cognitive–behavioral treatment or even psychological placebos such as exercise should be used before moving to medicate the adolescent (Antonuccio & Burns, 2004).

As noted in chapter 4 and as discussed in the "You Decide" section in this chapter, antidepressants have been linked to an increased risk for suicidal thoughts and behaviors in children and adolescents (Fortune & Hawton, 2005). There was enough concern about increased risk for suicide that the U.S. Food and Drug Administration mandated a "black box" warning for the use of antidepressant medication with youth, and the American Psychological Association created a task force to investigate the benefits and dangers of using antidepressant medication with children and adolescents (DeAngelis, 2004).

For now, the medications that have been clinically validated in double-blind studies for use with children and adolescents are Fluoxetine/Prozac and Sertraline/Zoloft, both of which are Selective Serotonin Reuptake Inhibitors (SSRIs; Phelps et al., 2002). Note that Fluoxetine/Prozac was utilized in the TADS project (Treatment for Adolescents with Depression Study [TADS] Team, 2005). Both Fluoxetine/Prozac and Sertraline/Zoloft have side effects, such as restlessness, insomnia, diarrhea, and nausea (DuPaul et al., 2003), and there is also concern about related sexual dysfunction in adolescents who are sexually active (Sharko & Reiner, 2004). These medications, however, do have the black box label that is mandated by the FDA to warn that increased suicidality may occur, especially in the early stages of taking the medication or at times when there are dramatic changes in dosages (Jick et al., 2004). Even with these warnings, however, many child psychiatrists have still supported the use of antidepressant medication with children and adolescents (Emslie et al., 2004; Richmond & Rosen, 2005; Ringold, 2005). If you or someone you care about is concerned about these types of medication issues, please consult a physician directly rather than making any decisions based on the information presented here.

In addition to the exploration of effectiveness with cognitive–behavioral therapy and antidepressants, the effectiveness of other treatments have been explored. For example, electroconvulsive therapy (ECT) has also been used for treatment of depression in youth, but the results are mixed, and the procedures are very controversial with children and adolescents (Ghaziuddin et al., 2004; Knapp, 2001; Rudnick, 2001). Moving to therapies that are not controversial, many effective therapies include a family component (Gaynor et al., 2003), and family therapy is effective in treating children who are depressed, especially in conjunction with cognitive–behavioral therapy (Diamond & Josephson, 2005). For example, 81% of adolescents who completed an attachment-based family therapy no longer met criteria for major depressive disorder after treatment, whereas only 47% of the adolescents in the wait-list control group no longer were depressed (Diamond, Reis, Diamond, Siqueland, & Isaacs, 2002). This finding is consistent with findings that adolescent depressive symptoms are related to problematic attachments with the primary caregiver, such as parental unresponsiveness, unsupportiveness, and unavailability (Shirk, Gudmundsen, & Burwell, 2005). There is some indication that family therapy for depression is more effective with children than adolescents and is more effective when at least one parent is depressed in contrast to families with no parental psychopathology (Cottrell, 2003). Interestingly, cognitive–behavioral therapy

YOU DECIDE: SHOULD ANTIDEPRESSANT MEDICATION BE USED WITH ADOLESCENTS?

<u>Yes</u>

- Antidepressant medication is effective in reducing symptoms of depression in adolescents; thus, it should be used to relive human suffering (Brown, Carpenter, & Simerly, 2005).
- When monitored closely, antidepressant medication can be used safely and effectively (Emslie et al., 2004).

<u>No</u>

- Antidepressant medication is too dangerous to give to adolescents, especially because it is associated with an increase in the likelihood of experiencing suicidal ideation (Jick et al., 2004).

- Cognitive–behavioral therapy can be very effective in decreasing adolescent depression, and it can have better long-term effects than antidepressant medication (Rohde et al., 2005; Weersing & Brent, 2003). Thus, because cognitive–behavioral treatment is effective, longer lasting, and safer than antidepressant medication, why would anyone choose antidepressant medication unless it was a last resort for adolescents who did not respond to other interventions?

So, should antidepressant medication be used with adolescents? You decide.

appears to be effective at decreasing maladaptive cognitions, whereas family therapy appears to be effective at reducing family conflict and problems within the parent–child relationship (Kolko, Brent, Baugher, Bridge, & Birmaher, 2000).

There has been some investigation of treatments for depressed children and adolescents who are also experiencing another disorder. In general, treating depressed children who are comorbid with another disorder is difficult (Kennard, Ginsburg, Feeny, Sweeney, & Zagurski, 2005). For example, treatment of depression appears to be more difficult when adolescents are also diagnosed with substance abuse or dependence (Rohde, Clarke, Lewinsohn, Seeley, & Kaufman, 2001). In contrast, cognitive–behavioral therapy appears to be effective with depressed adolescents who are conduct disordered, but the long-term gains from treatment are not well established (Rohde, Clarke, Mace, Jorgensen, & Seeley, 2004). In a sample of adolescents diagnosed with both major depressive disorder and conduct disorder, it appeared that reducing adolescents' negative thinking was the mediating factor in the effectiveness of therapy (Kaufman, Rohde, Seeley, Clarke, & Stice, 2005). Figure 7.3 shows an example from *Think Good—Feel Good: A Cognitive Behaviour Therapy Workbook for Children and Young People* (Stallard, 2002). While working with a therapist, this workbook can be used by children and adolescents to help them understand the experience of depression and the process of effective therapy. Figure 7.3 shows the reciprocal connections between cognitions (such as negative thinking), actions (such as withdrawing from your friends), and feelings (such as depression) in a manner that children and adolescents can understand.

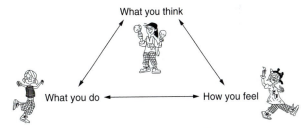

FIGURE 7.3 "The Magic Circle" from *Think Good—Feel Good: A Cognitive Behaviour Therapy Workbook for Children and Young People.*

(Stallard, 2002).

Box 7.1 highlights the types of treatment components that have been explored in outcome studies to evaluate the effectiveness of treatment for depression. Overall, these cognitive–behaviorally based therapies decrease depressive symptoms in children and adolescents.

Prevention

There have been a number of indicated prevention interventions and selective mental health prevention programs related to childhood depression. Many indicated prevention interventions have involved children who show elevated symptoms of depression, but who do not yet meet criteria for major depressive disorder. Indicated prevention intervention programs utilizing social problem-solving programs and cognitive interventions are effective in decreasing depressive symptomatology in children and adolescents (Clarke et al., 1995; Spence, Sheffield, & Donovan, 2003), although the intervention gains do not appear to remain at 1-, 2-, 3-, or

BOX 7.1

TREATMENT OF MAJOR DEPRESSIVE DISORDER IN ADOLESCENTS

A typical way of testing the effectiveness of treatments is to conduct an outcome study that compares one treatment with another (e.g., Brent, Kolko, Birmaher, Baugher, & Bridge, 1999). An integral part of conducting an outcome study is to assign clients randomly to different therapeutic interventions, rather than just reviewing how clients fared in different treatments. Random assignment helps the researcher trust the results, with the idea that if clients in one type of therapy experience better outcomes, then the better outcomes are due to the superiority of that treatment and not some other factor.

After a number of outcome studies are conducted, other researchers can synthesize the results from those studies and conduct a meta-analysis that provides a better overview of treatment effectiveness. One such meta-analysis of psychosocial treatments for adolescent depression found that 63% of clients showed improvement at the end of treatment, with an overall effect size of 1.27 (Lewinsohn & Clarke, 1999). The following treatment strategies are particularly effective:

Cognitive techniques

> Constructive thinking (rational emotive therapy, cognitive therapy)

Positive self-talk
Being your own coach
Coping skills
Self-change skills (self-monitoring, goal setting, self-reinforcement)

Family Context

> Conflict resolution
> Communication skills
> Parenting skills

Behavioral

> Problem-solving skills
> Increasing pleasant activities
> Social skills (assertiveness, making friendships, role modeling)

Affective education and management

> Relaxation
> Anger Management

Source: Lewinsohn & Clarke (1999).

4-year follow-up (Spence, Sheffield, & Donovan, 2005). In order to make indicated prevention intervention programs for adolescent depression, there has been some attention to adding "booster" sessions, such as meetings with the therapist after the completion of the preventive intervention to provide additional psychoeducational information and development of skills in adolescents (Simons, Rohde, Kennard, & Robins, 2005).

Selective mental health prevention programs often focus on children who are at risk for the development of depression because of their parents' depression or because of parental separation. Therapists often use cognitive psychoeducational programs to help children of depressed parents and children of separated parents, with components aimed at both children and their parents. These types of programs improve parenting skills and children's coping skills, both of which decrease the risk of the children developing depression themselves (Beardslee et al., 1993; Patterson, DeGarmo, & Forgatch, 2004). Interestingly, some selective prevention programs that are aimed at parent management treatment actually help reduce levels of parental depression, which in turn predicts better child outcomes at least

18 months later (Patterson et al., 2004). Although many of these prevention programs have been instituted with middle-class families, there are promising results that comparable preventive intervention programs are effective for urban, culturally diverse families (Podorefsky, McDonald-Dowdell, & Beardslee, 2001). Other types of selective prevention programs are aimed at children who have experienced some type of medical crisis, such as a bone fracture (Lewinsohn, Seeley, Hibbard, Rohde, & Sack, 1996) and pregnant teen mothers (O'Hara, 1995). Given the devastation to children, adolescents, and families when depression develops in youngsters, preventive efforts seem to be a promising way to decrease or even prevent distress in children's lives.

Unfortunately, there are not very many universal mental health prevention programs that have been tested empirically. There is some evidence that a primary care-based prevention program (Gillham, Hamilton, Freres, Patton, & Gallop, 2006) and a school-based cognitive-behavioral program (Hayes, 2004; Possel, Horn, Groen, & Hautzinger, 2004) can help prevent increases of depression in children and adolescents. One school-based universal prevention program that

Case Study: George, The Adolescent with Many Problems

George was 16-years-old when he was admitted to a juvenile detention center. Upon admission, George was withdrawn. Later that afternoon, George wrapped his neck with his shoelaces and tape, which resulted in severe breathing difficulty. When he was found by the detention center staff, he was semiconscious. When George was taken to the hospital, he continued to be withdrawn, but he did say that he would continue to try to kill himself and that no one could stop him. He also admitted that he had been depressed recently, that he had difficulty sleeping, limited appetite, feelings of guilt, and chronic suicidal ideation.

When asked about his history, George's parents reported that he had experienced a normal childhood until he was 13 years old. They reported that he began using drugs (LSD, marijuana, and sedatives), did poorly in school, ran away from home, and attempted suicide by taking an overdose of aspirin around that time. At the age of 14, George had an argument with the principal and was expelled from school. After a thorough psychological evaluation, George was placed in a group home so that he could work on self-control and so that his

relationship with his parents could be dealt with therapeutically. During his time in the group home, George's behavior improved immensely, and his relationship with his parents also improved due to family counseling. He attended school regularly and held an after-school job. In addition, he did not appear to be involved in any illegal activities or drug use.

About 6 months prior to admission to the detention center, George became involved in drugs again and began additional illegal activities (including 10 episodes of breaking and entering). George can recall feeling depressed around this time. Due to the illegal activity, he was sent to the juvenile detention center. He improved immensely in the detention center, so he was released to live with his parents again. Approximately 3 weeks before readmission to the detention center, George left with some friends to try to drive to Texas in a stolen car. After he was caught, he was readmitted to the detention center. George became terribly depressed, and he felt immense guilt over his illegal activities and how he had let down his parents. These feelings of guilt seemed to lead to his suicide attempt.

Source: Spitzer et al. (1994).

---

targeted depression showed strong effects when instituted by trained psychologists and researchers (Shochet et al., 2001), but when instituted by trained teachers, the same program showed little effectiveness in decreasing depressive symptomatology in the adolescent students (Harnett & Dadds, 2004). Other universal mental health prevention programs do not target depression specifically, but are designed in such a way that the development of depression may be prevented. For example, universal prevention programs that teach problem-solving skills and help to develop social competence may also help prevent the onset of depression in children and adolescents (Weissberg, Caplan, & Harwood, 1991).

A comprehensive meta-analysis of programs that targeted the prevention of depression in children and adolescents showed that selective prevention programs were more effective than universal prevention programs at the end of the program (Horowitz & Garber, 2006). Long after the programs were completed, selective and indicated prevention programs showed stronger effects than universal prevention programs (Horowitz & Garber, 2006). Overall, more work is needed in the area of universal mental health prevention to prevent depression from occurring in children and adolescents (Sheffield et al., 2006).

CHILD AND ADOLESCENT SUICIDE

Suicide is the third leading cause of death for youth between the ages of 10 and 19, with accidents leading to the highest numbers of deaths and homicides leading to the second highest numbers of deaths for children and adolescents (Centers for Disease Control, 2004). Suicide in younger children is relatively rare, with much higher rates in adolescents. Although the actual number of adolescents who kill themselves is relatively small (approximately 4,000 adolescents per year in the United States) and has been declining since 1992, the devastation of a completed suicide is immeasurable (Centers for Disease Control, 2004). These numbers may be an underestimate, given that some deaths due to accidents (such as a car accident or a drug overdose) may have been intentional. In addition, over 8% of high school students reported that they had made at least one suicide attempt, but did not succeed (Commission on Adolescent Suicide Prevention, 2005). At least 60% of adolescents report that they know another adolescent who tried to commit suicide (Ackerman, 1993). Being exposed to a friend's completed suicide is associated with increased rates of major depression in adolescents (Bridge, Day, Richardson, Birmaher, & Brent, 2003) and with increased risk for a suicide attempt (Gallo & Pfeffer, 2003). There is growing concern about the use of the Internet and specifically the use of chat rooms as a way of sharing ideas about suicide or about encouraging others to attempt suicide through coordinated cybersuicides (Becker & Schmidt, 2004).

Although it does not appear that gay, lesbian, bisexual, and transgendered youth are at increased risk for suicide attempts, life stressors and stressors specific to being gay were associated with suicide attempts (Savin-Williams & Ream, 2003b). Adolescent suicide is an international problem, with concerns documented in many different countries, including Trinidad and Tobago (Ali & Maharajh, 2005), China (Liu & Sun, 2005; Liu & Tein, 2005), Finland, New Zealand (Starling, Rey, & Simpson, 2004), and Australia (DeLeo, Cerin, Spathonis, & Burgis, 2005).

Instead of thinking of suicide as an all-or-none event, there are gradations of suicidality in children and adolescents. Table 7.3 shows the Pfeffer Spectrum of Suicidal Behavior, which is very useful in conceptualizing suicidality in children and adolescents (Pfeffer, 1986).

Suicide is connected with the experience of major depressive disorder (Flisher, 1999). In a review of children and adolescents who made fatal suicide attempts, between 30% and 76% experienced some type of mood disorder (Flisher, 1999). Note, however, that youth who attempt suicide are not necessarily depressed. For example, one longitudinal study in New Zealand found that youth suicide attempts had risen but rates of depression had remained unchanged (Starling et al., 2004). Separate from depression, it is striking to know that between 70% and 90% of children and adolescents who completed a suicide met criteria for some type of clinical disorder (Commission on Adolescent Suicide Prevention, 2005). Adolescents diagnosed with adjustment disorder had a more rapid suicide process (e.g., they attempted suicide with fewer warning signs or previous distress) than did adolescents with other disorders

(Portzky, Audenaert, & van Heeringen, 2005). Overall, suicides are most often completed with children and adolescents who are significantly distressed in some way, but not solely distressed by depressive symptoms.

Suicide can be conceptualized as having primarily two components: thoughts and actions. It is not uncommon for individuals of any age to have fleeting thoughts of death or suicide when significantly distressed. Adolescents who attempt suicide, however, are likely to report very high levels of **suicidal ideation** (thoughts about killing oneself; King et al., 2001). The MECA study found that the biggest differences between adolescents who thought about killing themselves and those who actually tried to commit suicide were poor family environment, low levels of parental monitoring, parental psychopathology, adolescents' own physical fighting, recent drunkenness, and smoking cigarettes (King et al., 2001).

A significant portion of adolescents (31%) expect their suicide attempt to cause their own death, and the majority of those who survive an attempt (57%) are sorry or ambivalent that they survived (Spirito & Donaldson, 1998). Approximately one third of adolescent attempts are planned and two thirds are more of an impulsive nature (Brown, Overholser, Spirito, & Fritz, 1991). Adolescents who plan their suicide seem to be more depressed, more hopeless, and to experience more suicidal ideation than those adolescents whose attempt was not planned (Brown et al., 1991). In addition, suicidal adolescents tend to demand more perfection from themselves, which they then feel they cannot live up to, which is associated with hopelessness and eventual suicidal ideation (Hewitt, Newton, Flett, & Callander, 1997).

In all age groups including adults, females are more likely than males to attempt suicide, but males are more likely than females to complete suicides (Dilsaver, Benazzi, Rihmer, Akiskal, & Akiskal, 2005; Lewinsohn, Rohde, Seeley, & Baldwin, 2001). This pattern is likely due to the method of suicide attempt, with boys using

TABLE 7.3   Pfeffer Spectrum of Suicidal Behavior

Level	Behavior Pattern
1. Nonsuicidal	No evidence of self-destructive thoughts or actions
2. Suicidal ideation	Thoughts or verbalizations of suicidal intention
3. Suicidal threat	Verbalization of impending suicidal action and/or precursor action that if carried out, would lead to harm
4. Mild attempt	Actual self-destructive act that realistically would not have endangered life and did not necessitate ICU
5. Serious attempt	Actual self-destructive action that realistically could have led to the child's death and may have necessitated ICU

Source: Pfeffer (1986).

Handguns and other firearms are extremely lethal methods for attempting suicide.

more lethal methods, such as firearms and hanging, and girls trying to overdose on drugs (Spirito & Donaldson, 1998). There are no well-established patterns of suicide attempts or completions based on race, ethnicity, or socioeconomic status (Spirito & Donaldson, 1998). There are, however, some specific findings that point to patterns of race, ethnicity, and culture. Native American and Aboriginal Canadian youth show higher rates of suicide than their peers (Evans & Lee, 1998). No other clear-cut patterns have been identified. Suicide, however, is evident in every group, including Hispanic/Latina females who were thought previously to be at low risk (Zayas, Kaplan, Turner, Romano & Gonzalez-Ramos, 2000). In fact, there is growing evidence that Hispanic/Latino/Latina adolescents show rates of attempted suicide that are higher than African-American or Caucasian youth. See Box 7.2 for more issues related to race and ethnicity patterns in suicide.

For every one completed suicide by a child or adolescent, it is estimated that 100 to 200 other youth had tried to harm themselves (American Association of Suicidology, 2004). Across all ethnicities, the majority of completed suicides by adolescents in the United States (57%) are carried out with the use of a gun (American Association of Suicidology, 2004). When suicidal adolescents have access to firearms in their home, they are 75 times more likely to kill themselves than suicidal adolescents who do not have access to firearms (Brent et al., 1991). Guns are twice as likely to be in the homes of adolescents who complete a suicide than adolescents with a failed suicide attempt or adolescents with a psychiatric problem

(Brent et al., 1991). Interestingly, preventive efforts have been targeted to get parents to remove guns from the homes of suicidal adolescents, but one study found that only 26.9% of the families removed guns from the home of their suicidal adolescent (Brent, Baugher, Birmaher, Kolko, & Bridge, 2000). The second most common method of completed suicides is hanging (Spirito & Donaldson, 1998). The most common way that adolescents attempt, but do not complete, suicide is through drug overdose (Spirito & Donaldson, 1998).

One study explored the idea that exposure to violence in the community would be associated with greater risk for depression and suicide in young inner-city adolescents (Mazza & Reynolds, 1999). Interestingly, this study found that there was not a direct link between exposure to violence and depression or suicide when posttraumatic stress disorder (PTSD) was taken into account. In other words, adolescents who were exposed to high levels of violence in the community were likely to develop PTSD. Adolescents who developed PTSD were also at risk for developing depression and for feeling suicidal (Mazza & Reynolds, 1999). This study shows the complexity of factors that are related to the development of suicidal ideation and intention.

For adolescents of all racial and ethnic backgrounds, there are a number of well-established risk factors for suicide (Brent et al., 2004; Commission on Adolescent Suicide Prevention, 2005; Ehrlich et al., 2004; Gould et al., 2004; Huey et al., 2005; Kerr, Preuss, & King, 2006; Osvath, Voros, & Fekete, 2004; Spirito, Valeri, Boergers, & Donaldson, 2003), including

BOX 7.2

RACE/ETHNICITY AND SUICIDE

As with many other topics, research into suicide has all but ignored children and adolescents from diverse racial and ethnic backgrounds. When studies have been conducted, there are a number of similarities between suicidal youth of all races and ethnicities. For example, African-American adolescents who attempted suicide had less supportive social networks, lower levels of connections in a social network, lower levels of family cohesion, and lower levels of family adaptability compared with nonsuicidal adolescents (Compton, Thompson, & Kaslow, 2005). These results tend to mirror the results of studies with adolescents from other racial and ethnic groups.

A unique challenge in working with suicidal African-American adolescents from impoverished urban areas is that traditional methods of intervention (such as individual psychotherapy) are neither feasible nor effective at addressing the root of adolescents' problems (Summerville, Kaslow, & Doepke, 1996). A case example to illustrate this point was provided for a 16-year-old African-American female whose mother was addicted to crack cocaine. The girl, named Tee, became pregnant at the age of 14. She was raped while she was pregnant with her first child. She had her second child at the age of 16. The second child died of sudden infant death syndrome at 5 months of age. Tee had wanted to

go back to school, but after the death of her second child and the overwhelming lack of support from her family or the social service system, she tried to kill herself with an overdose of Tylenol. Tee survived the suicide attempt, but it was obvious that traditional therapy would not address the essence of Tee's problems nor would the severe life stressors and life circumstances be resolved through psychotherapy (Summerville et al., 1996).

The clinical researchers who worked with Tee developed a comprehensive treatment program for suicidal adolescents in impoverished settings (Summerville et al., 1996). In addition to traditional work on cognitive–behavioral factors and interpersonal problem-solving skills with these adolescents, there is also a focus on outreach programs that get the adolescent's parent or caretaker involved in the treatment. The interventions are community-based, rather than based in a location that is difficult for the adolescent to reach, and there is an attempt to provide continuity of care between the emergency room that intervened in the suicide attempt and the community based outpatient care facility. These strategies attempt to make treatment more accessible and more comprehensive for adolescents in impoverished urban areas who already have a great many challenges in their lives.

- Clinical disorders, such as depression, drug abuse, and alcohol abuse
- Personality and interpersonal factors, such as hopelessness, depressive affect, impulsivity, cognitive distortions, and poor social skills
- Prior suicide attempt
- Family factors, such as parental clinical disorder, parental negative control, sexual abuse, physical abuse
- Stressful life events and high levels of daily hassles
- Troubled peer relationships
- Poor coping strategies
- Exposure to suicide (e.g., by a classmate, friend, or family member)
- Access to lethal methods, such as access to guns
- Primary medical concerns, such as chronic illness, concerns about pregnancy, sexually transmitted disease
- Specific suicidal plan (with concrete, realistic, accessible, and lethal plans holding the greatest concern).

- Combination of depression and white matter hyperintensities (shown through magnetic resonance imaging scans of the brain)

Overall, adolescent suicide is a serious and far-reaching problem. Children and adolescents who make suicidal statements or who make suicidal gestures should be taken very seriously. Quite often, the precipitating event is a stressor related to parents, school, friends, or dating relationships (Gould, Greenberg, Velting, & Shaffer, 2003). Even if the precipitating event is considered to be minor to an outsider, these events are of great concern to adolescents themselves. Thus, it is imperative that therapists, teachers, parents, friends, and family members take seriously a child's or adolescent's wish to die. One study did find that both fathers and mothers take adolescents' suicide attempts quite seriously (Wagner, Aiken, Mullaley, & Tobin, 2000). Based on reports about the day before the suicide attempt, the time of discovery of the attempt, and the day after the attempt, parents reported greater caring feelings, sadness, and anxiety after the suicide attempt. In addition, parents were more likely to make supportive

Case Study: Alexa, Survivor of Childhood Abuse

Alexa had been both physically and verbally abused by her mother throughout her childhood. Apparently, her father did not intervene to help her. She states

I tried to kill myself one day—it was a halfhearted attempt at best. I didn't even break the skin. That's when I left home and stayed with friends of mine. I had just graduated from high school.... My father was

eating lamb chops at the table when the police were there. Picture my father eating lamb chops while the police came—this is about as passive you get. Please don't disturb my dinner, I'm eating now. Everything chaos around him.

Source: Rhodes & Rhodes (1996, p. 202).

---

comments rather than hostile comments after discovering the suicide (Wagner et al., 2000).

In addition to traditional therapies for suicidal adolescents (such as cognitive–behavioral therapy), there is growing interest in ways to prevent adolescent suicide (Gould et al., 2003). Suicide hotlines are often set up in communities with the idea that distressed adolescents would call the hotline rather than trying to take their own life. Communities with suicide hotlines have slightly lower rates of suicide than communities without suicide hotlines (Commission on Adolescent Suicide Prevention, 2005). These patterns of prevention, however, are most evident in Caucasian females, who are the greatest users of the suicide hotlines (Shaffer, Garland, Fisher, Bacon, & Vieland, 1990). Thus, although suicide hotlines are effective in helping some adolescents, they are not effective with all groups of suicidal adolescents.

Curriculum-based prevention programs have been established in a number of school systems to try to reach large groups of adolescents (Commission on Adolescent Suicide Prevention, 2005). These programs are considered universal mental health prevention programs because they are administered to all adolescents in a particular school system regardless of whether or not the adolescents are at risk for suicide. Parents, teachers, and school administrators are often recipients of the prevention programs along with adolescents. These school-based programs often have the following goals:

- To raise awareness of adolescent suicide and associated problems
- To train participants to notice and identify adolescents who might be at risk for suicide
- To educate participants about community resources and referral processes for adolescents who are suicidal

Overall, there have been mixed results on these types of prevention programs. Although some programs are helpful in imparting information to adolescents, many programs are ineffective and even disturbing to adolescents (Commission on Adolescent Suicide Prevention, 2005). Because most of these programs were not developed with the integration of empirically based knowledge, many of the programs may inadvertently work against the goals of the program. One study reported that suicidal students found the program upsetting and distressing rather than reassuring and helpful (Shaffer et al., 1991).

Given the conflicting evidence about the effectiveness of prevention programs, there is still a great need to develop more comprehensive and more effective suicide prevention programs. Suggestions for comprehensive prevention programs include targeting the reduction of risk factors in the lives of adolescents, identifying youth with major depressive disorder or another mood disorder, increasing family support and family functioning, increasing community-based programs and community support, and decreasing the availability of guns (Brent et al., 2000; Christoffel, 2000; Duke, Resnick, & Borowsky, 2005; Pfeffer, 2002; Shaffer & Pfeffer, 2001). There is also support for using the Internet for suicide prevention efforts as another way of reaching an increasing web-savvy generation of adolescents (Becker & Schmidt, 2004). Overall, a concerted effort is needed to reduce the prevalence of suicidal ideation and suicide attempts in adolescents. Because many of the risk factors for suicide are comparable to the risk factors for other problems (such as depression, substance abuse, delinquency, teenage pregnancy), suicide prevention programs could help prevent many other problems in adolescents' lives.

As much as I hate to admit it, I have suicide potential...I hate myself. No one cares. I just want to give up. Quit facing the embarrassment and die.

—Siana, 2005, p. 42

In the context of understanding youth suicide, it is also important to understand that youth often harm themselves without the intent of death. **Self-mutilative behavior** (SMB) "refers to the direct and deliberate destruction of one's own body tissue without suicidal intent" (Nock & Prinstein, 2005, p. 140). SMB is surprisingly common in clinical samples as well as community samples. Epidemiological studies suggest that between 40% to 61% of adolescent psychiatric inpatients have engaged in self-mutilation, and between 14% and 39% of adolescents in a community sample reported engaging in self-mutilation (reviewed in Nock & Prinstein, 2005). Thus, SMB is a prevalent and alarming problem that both mental health professionals and medical personnel need to understand (Derouin & Bravender, 2004).

SMB is often misdiagnosed as suicide, and it is difficult for clinicians and other professionals to disentangle SMB and suicide attempts. When an adolescent is found to have cut him- or herself, it is important to ascertain whether or not there was suicidal intent. In one sample of youth who had cut themselves, 40.2% said that they wanted to die, but the remaining 59.8% did not intend to harm themselves with an intent to die (Rodham, Hawton, & Evans, 2004). In that same sample, girls who cut themselves were more likely than boys to say that they wanted to punish themselves and that they were trying to get relief from an awful and distressing state of mind (but without the intent of death). In addition to using SMB as a maladaptive way of coping with psychological distress, youth also appear to receive social reinforcement from other adolescents for self-mutilation

Case Study: Jenny, the Girl Who Was Sad for a Very Long Time

Jenny is a 9-year-old who attends third grade and lives with her 12-year-old brother and mother. She visits her father in a nearby town about twice a month. When Jenny was 7 years old, her parents divorced. Within the next 2 years, Jenny's mother began working full time, the family moved to an apartment in another school district, Jenny had to change schools in the middle of the year, and Jenny's mother began dating a man seriously. Two months after announcing her engagement, Jenny's mother brought Jenny in for therapy.

Jenny's mother told the therapist that Jenny had been getting more and more unhappy over the past 18 months. Jenny was lethargic, she did not seem to enjoy activities that she used to enjoy, and she no longer attempted to make any friends. Jenny had been involved in Brownies and gymnastics at her old school, but she did not want to join these activities at her new school. In addition, Jenny stated that she did not like any of the kids at her new school, so she spent her afternoons watching television and waiting for her mother to come home from work. Jenny later acknowledged to the therapist that she feared her mother would leave her when she married the new boyfriend. Jenny already felt that her mother spent all of her extra time with the boyfriend, so Jenny already felt abandoned. Jenny's school work also began to falter, with Jenny often not turning in homework and not doing well on tests. At her old school, Jenny was an above-average student, but at her new school, Jenny was barely passing her classes. In addition, although Jenny used to enjoy visiting her father twice a month, she now dreaded those visits. She reported that her father spent much of their time together berating her mother, and she felt uncomfortable being with her father now.

A full assessment showed that Jenny experienced elevated levels of sadness, but not enough to be diagnosed with major depressive disorder. Jenny had experienced feelings of sadness for a great length of time (at least 18 months), thus a diagnosis of dysthymic disorder was given.

Jenny and her mother began therapy with the following behavioral techniques in the treatment plan:

- Increase the number of pleasant activities in which Jenny engaged.
- Conduct parent training with Jenny's mother to help her learn to reward Jenny's positive interactions and other desirable behaviors.
- Institute a positive reinforcement program (token economy) for Jenny's improved school performance.
- Help Jenny learn new social skills to allow the development of friendships in the new school.

Both Jenny and her mother were very receptive to the therapeutic interventions. Jenny's mother began showing much more attention to Jenny's positive behaviors and Jenny, in turn, began getting involved in many school and social activities. Within a month of beginning therapy, Jenny's grades started to improve, and she began showing a happier disposition. At the end of the 10-week treatment, Jenny's behavior and feelings fell within the normal range of standardized assessment measures. At both 6-month and 1-year follow-up, Jenny continued to show no signs of dysthymia. She had shown some sadness when her mother got married, but she soon became adjusted to her stepfather's presence in the house. Additionally, she remained actively involved in Brownies, gymnastics, and other school activities. Jenny reported that she was busy with her new friends.

Source: Frame, Johnstone, & Giblin (1988).

TABLE 7.4 *DSM-IV* Diagnostic Criteria for Dysthymic Disorder

A. Depressed mood for most of the day, for more days than not, as indicated either by subjective account or observation by others, for a least 2 years. Note: In children and adolescents, mood can be irritable and duration must be at least 1 year.

B. Presence, while depressed, of two (or more) of the following:

    (1) poor appetite or overeating

    (2) insomnia or hypersomnia

    (3) low energy or fatigue

    (4) low self-esteem

    (5) poor concentration or difficulty making decisions

    (6) feelings of hopelessness

C. During the 2-year period (1 year for children or adolescents) of the disturbance, the person has never been without the symptoms in Criteria A and B for more than 2 months at a time.

D. No major depressive episode has been present during the first 2 years of the disturbance (1 year for children and adolescents); i.e., the disturbance is not better accounted for by chronic major depressive disorder, or major depressive disorder, in partial remission.

E. There has never been a manic episode, a mixed episode, or a hypomanic episode, and criteria have never been met for cyclothymic disorder.

F. The disturbance does not occur exclusively during the course of a chronic psychotic disorder, such as schizophrenia or delusional disorder.

G. The symptoms are not due to the direct physiological effects of a substance (e.g., a drug of abuse, a medication) or a general medical condition (e.g., hypothyroidism).

H. The symptoms cause clinically significant distress or impairment in social, occupational, or other important areas of functioning.

Specify if:
    Early Onset: if onset is before age 21 years
    Late Onset: if onset is age 21 years or older

Source: American Psychiatric Association (2000).
Reprinted with permission from the *Diagnostic and Statistical Manual of Mental Disorders, Fourth Edition, Text Revision.* Copyright 2000 American Psychiatric Association.

(Nock & Prinstein, 2005). In contrast to other methods of self-harm, self-cutters appear to be more impulsive in their acts given that they are less likely than others to have thought about self-harm before attempting self-harm (Nock & Prinstein, 2005; Rodham et al., 2004). The promising treatments for self-mutilation tend to be of a cognitive–behavioral nature (B. Walsh, 2005). Overall, self-mutilative behavior is of great concern for the well-being of adolescents and young adults. Both suicidality and self-mutiliative behavior should be taken very seriously. Professional help should be sought when adolescents or young adults display these behaviors.

DYSTHYMIC DISORDER

In contrast to major depressive disorder, which can be short-lived, but intense, dysthymic disorder is a longer-term, somewhat less intense experience of depression. As can be seen in Table 7.4, **dysthymic disorder** is diagnosed when a child experiences at least 1 year of depressed mood, during which time the child does not meet criteria for major depressive disorder. There is far less research into children's and adolescents' experience of dysthymia than there is for major depressive disorder. This point is illustrated by the fact that prevalence rates for dysthymia were not reported in the overall results of the MECA study (Shaffer et al., 1996). In fact, the MECA research group noted that dysthymic disorder is in need of further research (Schwab-Stone et al., 1996). When research has been conducted, it appears that dysthymic disorder is present in 2% to 4% of children and adolescents in community samples (Garrison et al., 1997; Kovacs, 1997).

Based on the limited information that is available, dysthymic disorder is a very distressing disorder. The average length of dysthymia is approximately 4 years (Klein, Dougherty, & Olino, 2005; Kovacs, Obrosky, Gatsonis, & Richards, 1997). It is not unusual for children and adolescents to experience dysthymic disorder for 5 years or longer (Dougherty, Klein, & Davila, 2004). One study found that 2 years after onset of dysthymic disorder, only 7% of the children had recovered from the disorder (Kovacs et al., 1997). This low rate of recovery is in contrast to an 86% recovery rate from major depressive disorder after 2 years (Kovacs et al., 1997).

Like major depressive disorder, dysthymic disorder is highly comorbid with other disorders, such as anxiety disorders, conduct disorder, and other affective disorders (Masi, Millepiedi et al., 2003). Children and adolescents with dysthymic disorder were particularly prone to also show generalized anxiety disorder and simple phobias. Before puberty, children with dysthmic disorder often also experience separation anxiety disorder (Masi, Millepiedi et al., 2003). When dysthymic disorder is comorbid with externalizing disorders (such as oppositional defiant disorder, conduct disorder, or attention-deficit/hyperactivity disorder), the length of duration of the disorder is almost $2\frac{1}{2}$ years longer than when the disorder is not comorbid with an externalizing disorder (Kovacs et al., 1997), and the disorder is more likely to be comorbid with additional disorders (Vance, Sanders, & Arduca, 2005). In addition, children who are comorbid for attention-deficit/hyperactivity disorder and dysthmia were more likely to also experience separation anxiety disorder and social phobia compared with children solely experiencing attention-deficit/hyperactivity disorder (Vance, Harris, Boots, Talbot, & Karamitsios, 2003). Children who have experienced both major depressive disorder and dysthymic disorder during their lifetime show even greater impairment than those who have just experienced one of those disorders (Goodman, Schwab-Stone, Lahey, Shaffer, & Jensen, 2000). Girls and boys appear to show similar symptom profiles of dysthymic disorder (Masi, Millepiedi et al., 2003).

Dysthymic disorder appears to be related to an adverse parent–child relationship, chronic stress, and a family history of dysthymic disorder (Dougherty et al., 2004). The combination of a problematic parent–child relationship and chronic stress appears to be particularly debilitating in terms of a prolonged experience of dysthymia (Dougherty et al., 2004).

Treatment for dysthymic disorder tends to be comparable to treatment for major depressive disorder. Antidepressant medication has been found to be somewhat helpful for some children diagnosed with dysthymic disorder (DuPaul et al., 2003), however, cognitive–behavioral treatments are also quite effective (Curry & Reinecke, 2003; Weisz, Southam-Gerow, Gordis, &

Connor-Smith, 2003). The combination of medication and psychotherapy may prove to be the most effective treatment strategy. Given that dysthymic disorder is more difficult to treat than major depressive disorder, greater efforts are needed to find effective treatments for this distressing disorder (Markowitz, 1995).

Overall, dysthymic disorder is a long-term, distressing disorder for children and adolescents. Much more research is needed into the specific course of the disorder and the etiological factors that lead to the development of dysthymic disorder. Many research projects have lumped together major depressive disorder and dysthymic disorder, which has led to a dearth of information about dysthymic disorder specifically. Interestingly, one study found that children diagnosed with major depressive disorder and children diagnosed with dysthymic disorder did not differ in any aspect other than current level of symptoms (Goodman et al., 2000). More research on dysthymic disorder is warranted.

BIPOLAR DISORDER AND CYCLOTHYMIC DISORDER

Bipolar disorder is known more commonly as manic depression. It is characterized by extreme highs (which are referred to as manic episodes) and extreme lows (which are referred to as major depressive episodes). There are two primary conceptualizations of bipolar disorder. Bipolar I disorder is characterized by one or more manic or mixed episodes and one or more major depressive episodes. Bipolar II disorder is characterized by one or more major depressive episodes along with at least one hypomanic episode. If the child or adolescent experiences at least one manic or mixed episode, then he or she would not be diagnosed with Bipolar II disorder.

Interest in bipolar disorder, and the concomitant research to explore characteristics of bipolar disorder in children, have exploded over the past few years. Here was the prevailing wisdom in early 2002 when the first edition of this textbook went to press: "Overall, bipolar disorder is considered relatively rare in children and adolescents. It is almost nonexistent in young children, and the prevalence rates in older adolescents are thought to range from 0.4% to 1.2%." (Lewinsohn, Klein, & Seeley, 1995) (p. 201; Phares, 2003)

Since that time, there has been an overwhelming interest in bipolar disorder from many different facets of society, including the professional research community, pharmaceutical companies, popular television, books, and magazines (Geller & DelBello, 2003; Kowatch &

Fristad, 2006; Youngstrom, Findling, Youngstrom, & Calabrese, 2005). For example, memoirs of individuals who have experienced bipolar disorder or mania (Behrman, 2002; Simon, 2002) and books geared toward parents with a child diagnosed with bipolar disorder (Papolos & Papolos, 2002) have become plentiful. In March of 2003, the National Institute of Mental Health even held a conference called the "Pediatric Bipolar Disorder Conference" (Biederman & James, 2004). Ironically, the prevalence of pediatric bipolar has not increased based on studies with standardized measures, but apparently the awareness of the disorder has increased significantly. Note that epidemiological studies still find that pediatric bipolar disorder is rare, with estimates ranging from 0.2% (1-month prevalence) to 1.4% (lifetime prevalence) of the child and adolescent (Commission on Adolescent Depression and Bipolar Disorder, 2005). Within clinical populations, and especially inpatient adolescent populations, there are higher rates of bipolar disorder (Harpaz-Rotem, Leslie, Martin, & Rosenheck, 2005).

Given the perceptions that there has been an increase in the research on pediatric bipolar disorder, I conducted a quick *PsycINFO* search for any articles that included the words "pediatric" or "child" and "bipolar." As can be seen in Figure 7.4, published research has exploded in the area of pediatric bipolar disorder. In fact, in the

$6\frac{1}{2}$-year period from 1994 through half of 2000 there were the same number of articles published on pediatric bipolar disorder as in just 2005 alone.

Although the diagnosis of bipolar disorder is still controversial in prepubertal children, there is clear evidence that the disorder exists and that it can be diagnosed effectively and in a valid manner (Biederman et al., 2003; Nottelmann et al., 2001). Earlier onset is linked to more maladaptive outcomes (Commission on Adolescent Depression and Bipolar Disorder, 2005). The recovery rate for an episode of bipolar disorder is relatively quick, with an average of 6 month's recovery rate in adolescents (Pavuluri, Birmaher, & Naylor, 2005). The likelihood of recurrence, however, is quite high (Pavuluri et al., 2005). Like other mood disorders, bipolar disorder is highly comorbid with other disorders, such as generalized anxiety disorder and other anxiety disorders, eating disorders, attention-deficit/hyperactivity disorder, substance use disorder, and conduct disorder (Harpold et al., 2005; Masi, Toni et al., 2003; McElroy, Kotwal, Keck, & Akiskal, 2005; Wilens et al., 2004).

As for etiology, bipolar disorder is thought to be highly genetically related, given that a large majority of adolescents diagnosed with bipolar disorder have a close relative with the disorder (Geller, Craney et al., 2002; Youngstrom et al., 2005). One study

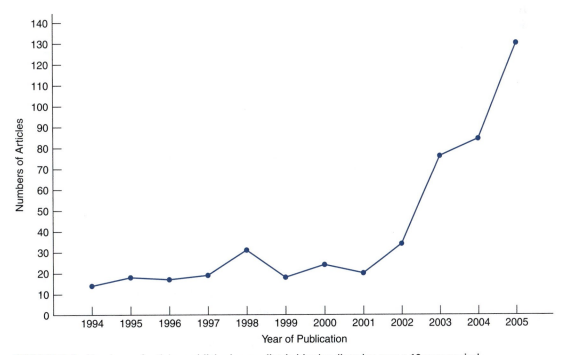

FIGURE 7.4 Numbers of articles published on pediatric bipolar disorder over a 12-year period.

found that 63% of adolescents diagnosed with bipolar disorder had a first-degree relative, most often a parent, who was diagnosed with bipolar disorder (Kafantaris, Coletti, Dicker, Padula, & Pollack, 1998). Other studies have found high concordance rates between parents and adolescents with bipolar disorder (Pavuluri et al., 2005). In particular, children of fathers with bipolar disorder are more at risk than children of mothers with bipolar disorder (Kornberg et al., 2000). There is also some evidence of brain abnormalities in children and adolescents with bipolar disorder, but it is not clear whether these abnormalities developed before or after the disorder began (Kaur et al., 2005).

In both adolescents and adults, bipolar disorder can be treated effectively with lithium carbonate (Brown et al., 2005; Kowatch et al., 2005; Pavuluri et al., 2004). Divalproex sodium appears to be equally as effective as lithium or even more so (Barzman et al., 2005; Findling et al., 2005). Once the child or adolescent is stabilized, then evidence-based cognitive–behavioral therapy can be used to augment the stabilization of the client. For example, psychoeducational strategies, skill-building programs, communication enhancement, problem solving, strategies to regulate emotions, and strategies to regulate impulses can all be used effectively once the child or adolescent is stable (Kowatch et al., 2005). There is growing evidence that cognitive–behavioral therapies, in conjunction with medication, can be effective in reducing bipolar symptoms in children and adolescents (Pavuluri et al., 2004). Similarly, family therapy in conjunction with medication management appears to be effective in decreasing symptoms of bipolar disorder (Miklowitz et al., 2004). Severe symptoms of bipolar disorder often require hospitalization to stabilize the child or adolescent (Biederman et al., 2004). Children living in a stable, intact family appeared to do better in treatment, whereas children whose mothers showed low levels of warmth were more likely to relapse after successful treatment (Geller, Craney et al., 2002).

Note, however, that there are a number of controversies about the diagnosis of bipolar disorder in youth. First, there appears to be a potential overlap between symptoms of mania and symptoms of attention-deficit/hyperactivity disorder. For example between 60% and 90% of samples of children and adolescents with bipolar disorder also meet criteria for attention-deficit/hyperactivity disorder (Commission on Adolescent Depression and Bipolar Disorder, 2005). Thus, there has been a professional debate as to whether pediatric bipolar disorder is being diagnosed accurately or whether there is too much of a confound between the

diagnostic criteria of the two disorders. This issue is related to the specificity of manic symptoms. A number of studies have suggested that when children and adolescents experience symptoms of mania, the symptoms may be related to problems other than bipolar disorder, such as attention-deficit/hyperactivity disorder (Carlson, 1998; Carlson & Kelly, 1998). Conversely, it may be that symptoms of mania in adolescents are sometimes misdiagnosed with another type of disorder, such as schizophrenia (Reynolds, 1995). Some researchers have argued that the surest way to diagnose bipolar disorder correctly in youth is to focus on the characteristic of mania with elation and or grandiosity (Geller, Zimmerman, et al., 2002; Tillman et al., 2003). Interestingly, these same issues are of concern in the adult literature because comorbidity rates between bipolar disorder and attention-deficit/hyperactivity disorder are high in adults (Wilens et al., 2003).

There has been a call for more careful and evidence-based assessment procedures for pediatric bipolar disorder to disentangle these issues (Youngstrom et al., 2005). There is some evidence that parents are more accurate raters of bipolar symptoms in their children and adolescents than are teachers or the youth themselves (Youngstrom et al., 2004). In addition, there has been a call for more careful differential diagnosis between major depressive disorder and bipolar disorder, especially in impoverished populations of adolescents (Dilsaver & Akiskal, 2005).

Another issue in the area of pediatric bipolar disorder is whether the manic phases are being evaluated correctly and from a developmentally sensitive perspective. A number of recent sets of case studies (Carlson, 2005; Dilsaver & Akiskal, 2004) and larger scale studies (Wilens et al., 2003) have suggested that high rates of bipolar disorder or at least symptoms of mania are present in clinically referred populations of preschoolers. Given the naturally mercurial and labile nature of preschoolers' behaviors and moods—with recurring highs and lows (Schaefer & DiGeronimo, 2000)—it will be important to ensure that normal childhood exuberance is not pathologized and mislabeled as mania.

Interestingly, bipolar disorder has been linked to great creativity in a number of artists, writers, performers, and musicians (Jamison, 1995). Creative individuals such as Samuel Clemens (Mark Twain), Virginia Woolf, Georgia O'Keeffe, Cole Porter, Charles Mingus, and Vincent van Gogh were all thought to experience bipolar disorder. Although it is not clear whether the symptoms of bipolar disorder were evident in childhood or adolescence, a number of these individuals did show symptoms by the time of early adulthood (Jamison, 1995). With the great burst of energy that occurs in mania, there were also devastating consequences due to despair in most of these artists. Suffice it to say that the diagnosis of bipolar disorder in children and adolescents is still in need of additional research.

Cyclothymic disorder is even more rare and less understood in children and adolescents than is bipolar disorder. Cyclothymia shows a longer-term, less-intense pattern than bipolar disorder. An analogy might help make this disorder clear. Major depressive disorder is to dysthymic disorder just as bipolar disorder is to cyclothymic disorder. In children and adolescents, cyclothymia would be diagnosed when there is evidence of numerous hypomanic symptoms and numerous depressive symptoms over the course of at least 1 year (American Psychiatric Association, 2000). If the symptoms are severe enough in that year to diagnose a major depressive episode, manic episode, or mixed episode, then cyclothymia would not be diagnosed.

Cyclothymic disorder is not highly prevalent in children and adolescents. In one study of children of parents with bipolar disorder, cyclothymic disorder was more prevalent in children of disordered parents than in children of parents in a nonclinical control group (Klein, Depue, & Slater, 1985). The average age of onset was 12 years old, with a range from 7 to 15 years old. This study suggested that cyclothymic disorder does exist in children and adolescents, albeit at low rates in the general community. Note that some recent research has focused on cyclothymic temperament, which focuses on stable characteristics of an individual's personality that cycle from high to low moods (Chiaroni, Hantouche, Gouvernet, Azorin, & Akiskal, 2005; Kochman et al., 2005). These studies, however, have tied cyclothymic temperament to bipolar disorder rather than cyclothymic disorder so they cannot help inform us of the clinical picture of children or adolescents who experience cyclothymic disorder. Given the rarity of cyclothymic disorder and the lack of research on the topic, an in-depth discussion is not warranted. It is important to keep in mind, however, that one of the biggest challenges in diagnosing cyclothymic disorder is distinguishing it from the normal highs and lows that adolescents often experience.

It is not difficult to fill a child's hand.
—Proverb of Africa

DEPRESSION CONCEPTUALIZED IN A DIMENSIONAL MANNER

The bulk of this chapter has focused on categorical conceptualizations of mood disturbances. Although there is a great deal of research on major depressive disorder and bipolar disorder, and to a lesser extent dysthymic disorder, and cyclothymic disorder in children and adolescents, there is also a great deal of concern about subclinical levels of depression. Given the pervasiveness of feelings of sadness at some point in everyone's life, it is important to understand that feelings of depression exist on a continuum from no symptoms to severe symptoms. The importance of sad feelings is illustrated in the normative data from the Child Behavior Checklist (CBCL; Achenbach & Rescorla, 2001). Based on a review of 120 parent-reported items of children's behavior in the huge normative sample, the item that most distinguished children who received clinical services from children who did not receive clinical services was the item: Unhappy, sad, or depressed. This fact suggests that parents and professionals consider sadness and depression to be a crucial symptom for which children should receive treatment.

In addition to using the CBCL to explore depression from a dimensional perspective, the Children's Depression Inventory (CDI; Kovacs, 1992) is a widely used measure of depressive symptoms in children and adolescents. Based on a downward extension of the Beck Depression Inventory for adults (Beck, Steer, & Brown, 1996; Beck, Steer, & Garbin, 1988), the CDI is used to assess children's feelings of depression, negative mood, interpersonal problems, ineffectiveness, anhedonia, and negative self-esteem. Although there has been some evidence to suggest that the CDI also assesses anxiety (Crowley & Emerson, 1996; Lerner et al., 1999) and some externalizing problems (Craighead, Smucker, Craighead, & Ilardi, 1998; Weiss et al., 1992), the measure is most often used to assess depression in children and adolescents aged 7 to 17 and can be helpful in considering depression from a dimensional perspective. Although this dimensional measure is sometimes used in a categorical fashion by instituting cutoff scores that are then compared with diagnostic interviews (Timbremont, Braet, & Dreessen, 2004), the CDI shows great promise in helping understand depression from a dimensional perspective.

There is growing evidence and support for conceptualizing depression in a dimensional manner rather than a categorical manner. For example, a comprehensive study of the structure of depression in a community sample of children and adolescents suggested that depression is dimensional (Hankin, Fraley, Lahey, & Waldman, 2005). In addition, specific symptoms of depression, such as depressed mood or loss of interest or pleasure, were best conceptualized as dimensional. Different domains of depression, such as vegetative or emotional distress, were best conceptualized as dimensional as were depressive profiles of boys versus girls and children versus adolescents (Hankin et al., 2005). These data call into question categorical diagnostic systems such as *DSM-IV-TR* (Hankin et al., 2005).

Studies that have investigated the structure of different symptoms suggest also that dimensional approaches to depression are worthwhile. Like the measures from the Achenbach System of Empirically Based Assessment (ASEBA), such as the Child Behavior Checklist (Achenbach & Rescorla, 2001), other comprehensive measures of children's and adolescents' symptoms suggest that depression is highly related to anxiety (Lahey et al., 2004). It appears that certain types of anxiety, specifically generalized anxiety and possibly social anxiety, cannot be disentangled from the experience of depression in youth (Lahey et al., 2004). Thus, depression appears to exist on a continuum with the addition of certain symptoms of anxiety.

This connection between depression and anxiety is referred to as **negative affect** (Jacques & Mash, 2004). The concept of negative affect has been around for over 20 years (Wolfe, Finch, Saylor, & Blount, 1987) and has been used with preschoolers, children, and adolescents (Turner & Barrett, 2003; Garber, Braafladt, & Weiss, 1995; Jacques & Mash, 2004; Lonigan, Phillips, & Hooe, 2003). As reflected later in the discussion of depressive syndromes, it appears that symptoms of depression and anxiety are likely to co-occur in children and adolescents (Achenbach & Rescorla, 2001; Lahey et al., 2004). In young children, both boys and girls show negative affect to approximately the same degree (Else-Quest, Hyde, Goldsmith, & Van Hulle, 2006).

With these studies as a backdrop, it should not be surprising to find that depression has been conceptualized in many different ways. One common framework is to think of depression as being conceptualized in three primary ways (Petersen et al., 1993):

- Clinical depression
- Depressive syndrome
- Depressed mood

Clinical depression has already been covered in the section on major depressive disorder. Suffice it to say that depressive syndromes and depressed mood

are thought to be somewhat less severe than clinical depression, but are no less important to understand and alleviate.

A **depressive syndrome** is less severe than major depressive disorder but more severe than depressed mood. Depressive syndromes are most often identified through empirically validated assessment measures, which identify a constellation of emotions and behaviors that co-occur with depression. Feelings and behaviors such as feeling lonely, crying, perfectionism, feeling unloved, feeling guilty, feeling sad, and worrying are all part of the depressive syndrome. Interestingly, most depressive syndromes have been linked to symptoms of anxiety, with an anxious-depressed syndrome (Achenbach & Rescorla, 2001; Hinden et al., 1997; Lahey et al., 2004). In fact, depression and anxiety often cannot be distinguished as two separate syndromes through statistical analyses (Achenbach & Rescorla, 2001; Hinden et al., 1997; Lahey et al., 2004). It is estimated that approximately 5% of nonclinical children and adolescents experience the depressive syndrome at any one time (Petersen et al., 1993).

Another way of conceptualizing the depressive syndrome is to consider subthreshold levels of depressive symptoms. Subthreshold conditions indicate that children or adolescents are experiencing a number of psychological symptoms, but they do not meet criteria for a formal disorder (Lewinsohn, Shankman, Gau, & Klein, 2004). One large community study found that 25.9% of the sample were considered subthreshold for major depressive disorder (Lewinsohn et al., 2004). A total of 47.9% of youth with subthreshold depression also showed one or more additional subthreshold conditions, such as anxiety. Other studies have found relatively high levels of subthreshold major depressive disorder and have found that these children and adolescents were psychologically distressed nonetheless (Gonzalez-Tejera et al., 2005; Keenan, Hipwell, Duax, Stouthamer-Loeber, & Loeber, 2004). Thus, whether this group is considered to show a depressive syndrome or to be subthreshold for a depressive disorder, these children and adolescents are significantly distressed and deserve attention and treatment (Lewinsohn et al., 2004).

Depressed mood is reflected when the child or adolescent experiences sadness and unhappiness (Petersen et al., 1993). Most often, depressed mood is assessed through a single item on the Child Behavior Checklist (Achenbach & Rescorla, 2001). Depressed mood is less intense and less pervasive than clinical depression or depressive syndrome. When parents of nonclinical children reported on their children's depressed mood, 10%

to 20% of boys and 15% to 20% of girls were reported to have experienced depressed mood within the past 6 months (Achenbach & Rescorla, 2001). When adolescents' self-reports are considered, 20% to 35% of boys and 25% to 40% of girls reported that they had experienced depressed mood within the past 6 months (Achenbach & Rescorla, 2001). Based on a review of the literature, it is estimated that 35% of children and adolescents experience depressed mood at any one time (Petersen et al., 1993).

Interestingly, gender differences in the depressive syndrome and depressed mood parallel gender differences found in youth with major depressive disorder. Although gender differences are even more prevalent in youth receiving clinical services than those who do not, the depressive syndrome and depressed mood are found in adolescent girls to a much greater extent than in adolescent boys (Compas et al., 1997). These findings suggest that there are more commonalities than differences between clinical depression and subclinical levels of depression. In some ways, these comparable findings support the conceptualization of depression on a dimensional basis rather than a categorical basis. Other than severity, there is little that is distinctly different between clinical depression and subclinical depression. An integral part of understanding depression from a dimensional perspective is to understand the risk and protective factors that are related to the development of depressed mood and depressive syndrome.

Risk Factors

A number of risk factors are linked to the development of increased depressive symptoms in children and adolescents. Risk factors run the gamut from familial to biological to cognitive to psychosocial characteristics (Reinecke & Simons, 2005). There are few risk factors, however, that have been linked to the development of depressive symptoms only. In other words, many of the risk factors for depressive symptoms also put children at risk for other types of problems. For example, negative body image is associated with the experience of depressive symptoms and also leads to eating disorders (Steinberg, Phares, & Thompson, 2004; Stice, Presnell, & Spangler, 2002; White & Grilo, 2005). Low self-esteem and anxiety also are precursors to the development of depressive symptoms (Reinherz, Giaconia, Hauf, Wasserman, & Paradis, 2000). High levels of parental hostility and harsh-inconsistent parenting were associated with increased risk for depression in a study of African-American

adolescents, but these factors also predicted conduct disorder (Kim et al., 2003). Community rates of criminal victimization and discrimination were associated with depressive symptoms in African-American adolescents, but this pattern appears to put youth at risk for a number of other problems (Simons et al., 2002). These risk factors appear to be somewhat comparable for children and adolescents from diverse racial and ethnic backgrounds (White & Grilo, 2005). Experiencing a negative interpersonal event related to religion was associated with greater risk for depression in adolescents (Pearce, Little, & Perez, 2003).

Comparable cognitive, peer, and familial risk factors that are associated with the onset of major depressive disorder are also associated with the development of less-severe levels of depressive symptoms (Hankin & Abela, 2005). With regard to cognitive factors, dysphoric children and adolescents, especially girls, tend to interpret events in a less supportive and less helpful manner than nondysphoric children (Calvete & Cardenoso, 2005; Shirk, Van Horn, & Leber, 1997). Sad and dysphoric youngsters also tend to have negative interpersonal schemata, which leads them to interpret events in a more negative and hopeless manner (Shirk, Boergers, Eason, & Van Horn, 1998) or to seek out reassurance from parents who are not supportive (Abela et al., 2005). Children with these maladaptive cognitive styles then appear to be more vulnerable to the effects of parental depressive symptoms (Abela, Skitch, Adams, & Hankin, 2006). Children and adolescents who show less than optimal temperamental characteristics, such as low positive emotionality or high negative emotionality, appear to be at risk for the development of depressive symptoms (Compas, Connor-Smith, & Jaser, 2004).

With regard to peer risk factors, children who were neglected by their peers or who were submissive-rejected by their peers tended to show higher rates of depression and **anhedonia** (lacking feelings of joy and happiness) than did other children (Hecht, Inderbitzn, & Bukowski, 1998; Reinherz et al., 2000). Children with higher rates of depression tend to perceive less acceptance from their peers and tended to be more inaccurate in these perceptions (Kistner, David-Ferdon, Repper, & Joiner, 2006). Notably, children's perceptions of peer acceptance had a stronger link to depressive symptoms than did actual peer acceptance (Kistner, Balthazor, Risi, & Burton, 1999). In addition, peers tend to have comparable levels of depressive symptoms with each other (Stevens & Prinstein, 2005). When adolescents seek involvement with deviant peers, their externalizing behaviors increase, which leads to

BOX *7.3*

CHILDREN OF DEPRESSED PARENTS

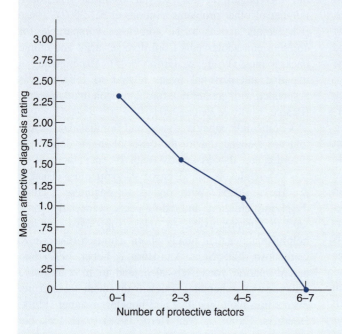

FIGURE 7.5 Lifetime Affective Disorder Ratings by Number of Protective Factors (high risk random sample; excluded children of normal mothers).

Source: Hammen (1991). Reprinted with permission from Hammen, *Depression runs in families*. Copyright 1991, Springer-Verlag New York, Inc.

Parental depression, and specifically maternal depression, is one of the most studied areas in parental psychopathology (Goodman & Gotlib, 2002a). A number of researchers have investigated parental depression, especially maternal depression, including Field's (2000) work with infants, Rohde and colleagues' (2005) work with adolescents, and Radke-Yarrow's (1998) work across the life span. With much of the focus on maternal depression, it is interesting to note that paternal depression appears to put youth at comparable risk as maternal depression (Low & Stocker, 2005).

Although children of depressed parents are at risk for the development of depression themselves, they are also at risk for a number of other problems. Children of depressed parents are eight times more likely to develop depression, five times more likely to develop conduct disorder, and three times more likely to develop an anxiety disorder (Wickramaratne & Weissman, 1998).

In an intriguing book entitled, *Depression Runs in Families,* Dr. Connie Hammen (1991) outlined the different risk and resilience factors related to children of depressed mothers. Based on extensive work with children of depressed mothers, children of chronically ill mothers, and children of nondistressed mothers, Dr. Hammen and her colleagues have found that children of depressed mothers are influenced by many of the same risk and resilience factors as

in many other adverse circumstances. Risk factors, such as genetic loading, difficult temperament, and parental distress were linked to poorer outcomes for children. Resilience or protective factors such as coping skills, social competence, at least average intelligence, lower life stress, and good problem-solving skills were linked to better outcomes for children, even in the face of parental depression. As can be seen in Figure 7.5, higher numbers of protective factors were associated with lower affective diagnosis ratings.

Even though Dr. Hammen and her colleagues have explored maternal depression primarily, it is important to note that similar findings have been established with regard to paternal depression (reviewed in Connell & Goodman, 2002; Johnson & Jacob, 2000; Kane & Garber, 2004; Phares, Duhig, & Watkins, 2002). Whether it is the father or the mother who is depressed, there are comparable risk and protective factors regarding the well-being of the children of depressed parents. When parents are comorbid for disorders (such as depression and alcohol abuse), there is an even greater likelihood for children to experience detrimental outcomes (Warner et al., 1995). In addition, children who are depressed who also have a parent who is depressed are at greater risk for maladaptive outcomes (Birmaher et al., 2004).

depressive symptoms in relation to the consequences of the externalizing behaviors (Fergusson, Wanner, Vitaro, Horwood, & Swain-Campbell, 2003). Homeless and runaway adolescents show heightened levels of depressive symptoms, which seem to be exacerbated by their peer- and nonpeer-related experiences when they are on the streets (Whitbeck, Hoyt, & Bao, 2000). Adolescent mothers who report high rates of social isolation from peers and family in addition to perceived incompetence and weight/shape concerns were related to depressive symptoms (Birkeland, Thompson, & Phares, 2005). Regarding risk factors within the family, parental depression has been identified as a salient risk factor for the development of depressive symptomatology in children and adolescents.

Other family factors that have been identified as risk factors for the development of depressive symptoms are interparental conflict and marital hostility (Birmaher et al., 2004; Grych & Fincham, 2001; Kerig, 1998; Low & Stocker, 2005), parental emotional unavailability (Lee & Gotlib, 1991), poor parental bonding or insecure attachment (Abela et al., 2005; Ingram & Ritter, 2000; Shirk et al., 2005; Stein et al., 2000; Sund & Wichstrom, 2002), parental negativity and criticism (Donenberg & Weisz, 1997; Nelson, Hammen, Brennan, & Ullman, 2003), low levels of parental support (Stice, Ragan, & Randall, 2004), avoidant coping styles within the family (Steele, Forehand, & Armistead, 1997), and stressful family events related to parental physical illness (Grant & Compas, 1995). Physical abuse within the family is linked to depressive symptoms, even when other risk factors are controlled statistically (Kaplan et al., 1998; Libby, Oroton, Novins, Beals, & Manson, 2005). Although not formally a risk factor within the family, it should be noted that adolescents' poor physical health is related to later depressive symptoms (Williams, Colder, Richards, & Scalzo, 2002).

Overall, a number of well-established risk factors are associated with the development of depressive symptoms in youngsters.

My grandma love me
Even when I'm sad
I have someone to care for me
When I'm lonely
She's there
My grandma
Is the one for me.

—Lisa, 6 years old and homeless (Children's Defense Fund—Minnesota, 1990; page 24).

Protective Factors

Just as with risk factors, few protective factors are specific to protecting against depressive symptoms only. Good parent–child relationships, stable and nonconflicted parent–parent relationships, and warm, sensitive, and responsive parenting are salient protective factors against the development of depressive symptoms (Hammen, 2003). These patterns were found in samples of inner-city African-American adolescents (Sagrestano, Paikoff, Holmbeck, & Fendrich, 2003), predominantly Caucasian-American samples (Hammen, 2003), in a sample of children and adolescents who lost at least one parent to death (Lin, Sandler, Ayers, Wolchik, & Luecken, 2004), and in a sample of children of depressed parents (Brennan, LeBrocque, & Hammen, 2003). Low parental conflict buffered girls but not boys from developing depressive symptoms in the context of living in a violent neighborhood (Forehand & Jones, 2003). Strong relationships with family members, such as grandparents, and nonfamily members, such as teachers, are also related to fewer depressive symptoms (Werner & Smith, 2001). A warm father–infant relationship can prevent maladaptive outcomes for youth with a mother who is depressed (Mezulis, Hyde, & Clark, 2004). As can be seen in Box 7.4, cognitive factors such as optimism can serve as protective factors against the development of depressive symptoms.

Other factors that are thought to protect against the development of depressive symptoms include social support, appropriate family involvement, peer acceptance, and appropriate peer values and involvement (Seidman et al., 1999). Note, however, that the stress-buffering model of depression has not received empirical support in large-scale studies (Burton, Stice, & Seeley, 2004). The stress-buffering model suggested that high levels of social support would minimize the association between stressful live events and depression in adolescent girls. There have now been large, prospective studies of this model, nearly all of which provide no strong support for the model (Burton et al., 2004).

Other protective factors, however, have been supported by research. For example, higher self-esteem in African-American male adolescents was related to decreased levels of depression in adulthood (Mizell, 1999). Peer warmth was associated with decreased risk for depressive symptoms in samples from both Los Angeles and Tianjin, People's Republic of China (Greenberger, Chen, Tally, & Dong, 2000). Higher levels of positive religiosity were related to lower levels of

BOX 7.4

THE OPTIMISTIC CHILD

Dr. Martin Seligman and colleagues (Seligman, Reivich, Jaycox, & Gillham, 1995) have studied children who are optimistic. The essence of optimism is the way in which children think about causes of events. Not only would an optimistic child engage in positive thinking, but he or she would see the causes of events in a positive manner or, at a minimum, would not see the causes of events in a negative manner. In particular, negative events would not be interpreted as permanent, pervasive, or personal. This explanatory style is the mirror image of what is found in children who are depressed. Optimistic children tend to show extraordinarily low levels of depression and distress, given that their outlook on events helps to buffer against negative events in their lives.

So, how can parents and teachers help children develop an optimistic outlook on life?

- Monitor your own attitudes—children follow the examples we set for them.
- Help children to challenge their own negative attributions by brainstorming additional ways of interpreting negative events in their lives.
- Help children learn better problem-solving skills.
- Model good social skills and help children with their social skills.
- Build positive events and interpretations of events into children's everyday lives.

Source: Seligman et al. (1995).

---

depression (Pearce et al., 2003). Overall, protective factors against the development of depression are comparable to factors that protect against the development of other disorders. These risk and protective factors are important to keep in mind when trying to prevent and treat children's and adolescents' depressive symptoms.

SUMMARY AND KEY CONCEPTS

Anaclitic Depression and Failure to Thrive in Infancy. **Anaclitic depression** is an old term that refers to infants who had lost their primary caregiver and also seemed to have lost their will to live. **Failure to thrive** is a newer term that refers to infants who show apathy, slow motor development, no interest in their surroundings, and little interest in food or liquids. More recently, the *Diagnostic Classification: 0–3R* system has identified two types of depression in infants: **prolonged bereavement/grief reaction** and **depression of infancy and early childhood.**

Masked Depression. **Masked depression** is an old concept that refers to children who show externalizing types of behavior problems but who are really depressed.

Major Depressive Disorder. According to *DSM-IV-TR,* **major depressive disorder** is a clinical disorder in which individuals experience at least 2 weeks of depressed mood, loss of interest, disturbed eating patterns, disturbed sleeping patterns, disturbed activity levels, feelings of worthlessness, diminished concentration, and possible thoughts of death and suicide. A less-severe disorder, **adjustment disorder with depressed mood** is also classified in *DSM-IV,* with the primary mood disturbance in reaction to an identifiable event. In terms of treatment, cognitive–behavioral treatments have been found to be superior to other types of treatments in reducing

depressive symptomatology. These treatments are considered empirically supported treatments because they were developed and perfected with a research base in mind.

Child and Adolescent Suicide. Between 6% and 10% of adolescents report that they have tried to commit suicide. Thoughts and feelings of wanting to kill oneself are referred to as **suicidal ideation.** Youth who harm themselves without the intent to commit suicide (e.g., cutting their skin) are engaging in **self-mutilative behavior** (SMB).

Dysthymic Disorder. According to *DSM-IV-TR,* **dysthymic disorder** is a longer term, but somewhat less-intense experience of depression than MDD.

Bipolar Disorder and Cyclothymic Disorder. **Bipolar disorder** is more commonly known as manic-depression, a disorder in which very high highs and very low lows are experienced. Although prevalence rates of bipolar disorder are relatively low, especially in younger children, the scholarly and popular interest in bipolar disorder has increased significantly over the last few years. **Cyclothymic disorder** is considered a longer lasting, but less-intense disorder than bipolar disorder.

Depression Conceptualized in a Dimensional Manner. Instead of conceptualizing depression in a categorical manner, a growing number of researchers and clinicians feel that it is important to conceptualize depression on a continuum.

Although they do not meet criteria for a major depressive disorder, these children and adolescents are significantly distressed. A number of large empirical studies have found that depression cannot be disentangled from anxiety. The combination of depressive symptoms and anxiety is known as **negative affect.** Approximately 5% of nonclinical children and adolescents experience a **depressive syndrome,** which is a constellation of depressive feelings and behaviors that are considered less severe than major depressive disorder. In addition, approximately 35% of nonclinical children and adolescents experience **depressed mood,** which is characterized by feelings of sadness, being down, and feeling depressed. One type of depressive feeling is termed **anhedonia,** which is the lack of feeling or experiencing joy and happiness.

KEY TERMS

anaclitic depression
failure to thrive
prolonged
  bereavement/grief
  reaction

depression of
  infancy and early
  childhood
masked depression
major depressive
  disorder

adjustment disorder
  with depressed
  mood
suicidal ideation
self-multilative
  behavior

dysthymic disorder
bipolar disorder
cyclothymic
  disorder
negative affect

depressive
  syndrome
depressed mood
anhedonia

SUGGESTED READINGS

Danquah, Meri Nana-Ama. *Willow Weep for Me: A Black Woman's Journey Through Depression.* New York: Random House, 1999. This powerful memoir describes the author's lifelong battle with depression and frames the struggle in terms of cultural factors that add to her struggle.

Siana, Jolene. *Go Ask Ogre: Letters from a Deathrock Cutter.* Los Angeles: Process, 2005. This book is an engaging, diary-type memoir that includes scrapbook memorabilia scattered throughout. The author describes how she began self-cutting and how she overcame her destructive impulses.

SUGGESTED VIEWINGS

In America. (2002). Loosely based on the early experiences of the co-writer/director Jim Sheridan, this film shows an immigrant family who moved to America partly to escape their depression over the death of the youngest child in the family. Resilience is evident in the young girls in the family, and strong role models are shown in the neighbor who is living with AIDS and the father who will not allow limited finances or difficult circumstances get in the way of sharing joy with his family.

Monster. (2003). After enduring years of sexual abuse, physical abuse, and depression, the protagonist in this film became a prostitute at the age of 13. During adolescence and young adulthood, she experienced drug abuse, multiple sexual assaults, and she eventually became a mass murderer. Based on a true story.

CHAPTER 8

ANXIETY DISORDERS AND PROBLEMS WITH ANXIETY

CHAPTER SUMMARY

SEPARATION ANXIETY DISORDER

SPECIFIC PHOBIAS

SOCIAL PHOBIA

OBSESSIVE-COMPULSIVE DISORDER

GENERALIZED ANXIETY DISORDER

POSTTRAUMATIC STRESS DISORDER

SELECTIVE MUTISM

ALL ANXIETY DISORDERS OF CHILDHOOD AND ADOLESCENCE

ANXIETY CONCEPTUALIZED IN A DIMENSIONAL MANNER

SUMMARY AND KEY CONCEPTS

KEY TERMS

SUGGESTED READINGS

SUGGESTED VIEWINGS

Ever since August we been livin' here. The room is either very hot or freezin' cold. When it be hot outside it's hot in here. When it be cold outside we have no heat. We used to live with my aunt but then it got too crowded there so we moved out. We went to welfare and they sent us to the shelter. Then they shipped us to Manhattan. I'm scared of the elevators. 'Fraid they be stuck. I take the stairs.
— Angie, a 12-year-old, African-American girl who lives in a homeless shelter (Kozol, 1988, p. 62)

When considering fear and anxiety, it is crucial to acknowledge that many fears are legitimate. Before diagnosing Angie for a specific phobia of elevators, it would be important to know that the elevator often breaks down between floors. Even when it is working, children in the elevator are often at risk for abuse by pedophiles in the building or are pressured to purchase drugs by dealers who frequent the shelter. This issue is imperative when considering the diagnosis of an anxiety disorder.

When fear and anxiety are experienced to more extreme degrees than expected, children may be experiencing some type of anxiety disorder. There are a number of anxiety disorders, including separation anxiety disorder, specific phobia, social phobia, obsessive-compulsive disorder, generalized anxiety disorder, posttraumatic stress disorder, and selective mutism. The main component that links these disorders together is

the experience of anxiety, fear, or worrying (Silverman & Carter, 2006; Williams, Reardon, Murray, & Cole, 2005). Note that separation anxiety disorder and selective mutism are located in the section of *DSM-IV* entitled Disorders usually first diagnosed in infancy, childhood, or adolescence. The other disorders can be diagnosed in individuals of any age. Each of these disorders will be described separately along with prevalence information. After all the disorders are described, issues related to comorbidity, course of the disorders, etiology, treatment, and prevention of anxiety disorders will be discussed for all the anxiety disorders together.

Note that there are a few anxiety disorders that will not be covered in this chapter, including panic disorders, acute stress disorder, anxiety disorder due to a general medical condition, and substance-induced anxiety disorder. These disorders tend to be relatively rare in childhood (American Psychiatric Association, 2000) and have not received a great deal of attention from researchers on developmental psychopathology. Students interested in these and other anxiety disorders should consider reading *Anxiety Disorders in Children and Adolescents, second edition* (Morris & March, 2004).

A crust eaten in peace is better than a banquet partaken in anxiety.

—Aesop

Case Study: Tiny Tina

Tina was 10 years old when she first was referred to a psychiatrist because she hated going to school. She was small in stature and had a sweet personality. On the first day of school the previous year, Tina hid in the family's basement so that she would not have to go to school. She only agreed to go to school when her mother agreed to stay with her at school and to have lunch with her. Since that time, Tina often showed somatic complaints (e.g., stomachaches and headaches). Recently, her parents had to physically pick her up out of bed, dress her, feed her, and transport her to school to get Tina to attend school. Tina was usually willing to participate in other activities, such as Girl Scout meetings and overnight sleepovers at a friend's house, but her sister usually accompanied her on these outings. Although Tina missed a great deal of school, she continued to do well in her studies.

Based on the psychiatrist's interview with Tina, it became obvious that Tina's main concern was not about school but rather was about leaving her family. Tina's mother hypothesized that these concerns began around the time of Tina's grandmother's death. Tina admitted that she worried something awful would happen to her family while she was at school. She seemed not to have these concerns when she took part in other activities, partly because her sister was with her. Overall, it appeared that Tina was not refusing to go to school as much as she was concerned about separating from her family. For this reason, she was given a provisional diagnosis of separation anxiety disorder. Provisional means that the diagnosis is not final until further information is collected. Note that this case illustrates the need to differentiate between separation anxiety disorder and a specific phobia due to fear of the school setting (which is discussed later in this chapter).

Source: Spitzer et al. (1994).

SEPARATION ANXIETY DISORDER

Separation anxiety disorder is characterized by extreme, developmentally inappropriate anxiety when separated from a primary caretaker, such as a parent. As can be seen in Table 8.1, the diagnostic criteria note that the distress can occur when the child is separated from the caretaker or can occur even when thinking about being separated from the caretaker. Children diagnosed with separation anxiety disorder often have nightmares about being separated from their parents, and they fear that something awful will happen to their parents when they are not together. Somatic complaints (such as headaches and stomachaches) are common in children with separation anxiety disorder, especially when they are about to be separated from their primary caretaker (Silverman & Dick-Niederhauser, 2004).

Although it is important to know the developmental appropriateness of behavior for any disorder, this issue is especially important with separation anxiety disorder. Normal **separation anxiety** usually occurs between the ages of 10 and 18 months, with a significant decrease in separation anxiety by the age of 2 years (American Academy of Pediatrics, 2004b). Infants and toddlers who experience normal separation anxiety tend to cling to their caretaker more often and become distressed when separated from their caretaker, even when the caretaker just leaves the room momentarily. The development of separation anxiety is considered to be positive, because it means that the infant or toddler has developed a good attachment to his or her caretaker. Separation anxiety only is considered abnormal when it occurs well after the normal developmental period or when it is in excess of what would be expected for children of that age.

It is not uncommon for separation anxiety disorder to occur after some type of major life stress, such as the death of a loved one, a severe car accident within the family, or parental separation/divorce (Cronk, Slutske, Madden, Bucholz, & Heath, 2004). For example, there was an increase in separation anxiety disorder in children in New York City 6 months after the attacks on September 11, 2001 (Hoven, Duarte, Wu, Erickson, Musa, & Mandell, 2004). Many children diagnosed with separation anxiety disorder reside in caring, loving, and well-functioning families, although it is not uncommon to find that parents of children with separation anxiety disorder have themselves had some type of anxiety or mood disorder (Kearney, Sims, Pursell, & Tillotson, 2003). Most children with separation anxiety disorder come to the attention of clinicians because of their refusal to separate from their parents and go to school (Albano, Chorpita, & Barlow, 2003). Approximately three quarters of children diagnosed with separation anxiety disorder show reluctance to attend school due to the separation from their parents (King & Bernstein, 2001).

The course of separation anxiety disorder is quite variable, with some youngsters showing **spontaneous**

TABLE 8.1   DSM-IV Diagnostic Criteria for Separation Anxiety Disorder

A. Developmentally inappropriate and excessive anxiety concerning separation from home or from those to whom the individual is attached, as evidence by three (or more) of the following:

(1) recurrent excessive distress when separation from home or major attachment figures occurs or is anticipated

(2) persistent and excessive worry about losing, or about possible harm befalling, major attachment figures

(3) persistent and excessive worry that an untoward event will lead to separation from a major attachment figure (e.g., getting lost or being kidnapped)

(4) persistent reluctance or refusal to go to school or elsewhere because of fear of separation

(5) persistently and excessively fearful or reluctant to be alone or without major attachment figures at home or without significant adults in other settings

(6) persistent reluctance or refusal to go to sleep without being near a major attachment figure or to sleep away from home

(7) repeated nightmares involving the theme of separation

(8) repeated complaints of physical symptoms (such as headaches, stomachaches, nausea, or vomiting) when separation from major attachment figures occurs or is anticipated

B. The duration of the disturbance is at least 4 weeks.

C. The onset is before age 18 years.

D. The disturbance causes clinically significant distress or impairment in social, academic (occupational), or other important areas of functioning.

E. The disturbance does not occur exclusively during the course of a Pervasive Developmental Disorder, Schizophrenia, or other Psychotic Disorder and, in adolescents and adults, is not better accounted for by Panic Disorder with Agoraphobia.

Specify if:

Early Onset: if onset occurs before age 6 years

Source: American Psychiatric Association (2000).

Reprinted with permission from the *Diagnostic and Statistical Manual of Mental Disorders, Fourth Edition, Text Revision.* Copyright 2000 American Psychiatric Association.

remission (i.e., the symptoms go away without any therapeutic intervention) and some youngsters showing many years of difficulty with separating from their parents (Kearney et al., 2003). A chronic course of separation anxiety disorder is associated with later onset, psychopathology within the family, marital distress in the parents, and comorbidity with other psychiatric disorders in the child (Foley, Pickles, Maes, Silberg, & Eaves, 2004; Kearney et al., 2003).

It is interesting to note that a number of studies have explored separation anxiety in parents. For example, mothers and fathers reported similar levels of separation anxiety when dropping off their children (aged 1 to 5) at a child-care center (Deater-Deckard, Scarr, McCartney, & Eisenberg, 1994). On the other end of the developmental spectrum, mothers and fathers of college students reported somewhat high degrees of separation anxiety (Hock, Eberly, Bartle-Haring, Ellwanger, & Widaman, 2001). Higher degrees of separation anxiety were associated with poorer parent–student attachment for both mothers and fathers.

Prevalence Rates

Separation anxiety disorder is relatively common when compared with other psychological disorders. Prevalence rates range from 2.0% to 12.9% (Albano et al., 2003), and a prevalence rate of 4% is noted in *DSM-IV* (American Psychiatric Association, 2000). The 4% prevalence rate is consistent with what was found in the Methods for the Epidemiology of Child and Adolescent Mental Disorders (MECA) study when parents' reports and children's reports were combined (Shaffer et al., 1996). The peak age of onset is between 7 and 9 years (Silverman & Dick-Niederhauser, 2004). Girls are more likely than boys to experience separation anxiety disorder (Eisen & Schaefer, 2005). There is some indication that children from lower SES groups and children whose parents have limited educations are more likely to experience separation anxiety disorder (Cronk et al., 2004). Almost no research has investigated patterns of prevalence regarding race and ethnicity, but the limited research suggests that there are no

Separation anxiety is developmentally appropriate in infants and toddlers, but can be problematic in older children and adolescents.

TABLE 8.2 Overview of Prevalence Information for Separation Anxiety Disorder

Prevalence	4%
Age	Children > Adolescents
Gender	Girls > Boys
SES	Lower > Higher
Race/Ethnicity	No differences

racial or ethnic differences in the prevalence rates of separation anxiety disorder (Silverman & Dick-Niederhauser, 2004). This information on prevalence rates is summarized in Table 8.2.

SPECIFIC PHOBIAS

Formerly known as simple phobias, **specific phobias** are represented by extreme fears of objects or situations. The diagnostic criteria are presented in Table 8.3. As

illustrated by Yoshino, many fears are very common and normal during childhood. The patterns of common childhood fears have not changed significantly for over 70 years (Schaefer & DiGeronimo, 2000). In addition to developmentally appropriate fears, there are objects and situations (e.g., having a gun pointed at you or finding yourself face-to-face with a hungry tiger) that would rightly cause concern for any individual. A fear becomes a phobia when it is excessive or unreasonable for individuals in that culture (American Psychiatric Association, 2000). The content of fears appears to be related to cultural experiences (American Psychiatric Association, 2000). For example, fear of magic or spirits are common in many cultures and would not be diagnosed as a specific phobia unless the fear exceeded the normal experience for most other individuals in that culture. Normal and common fears are discussed in more detail later in this chapter.

First of all, let me assert my firm belief that the only thing we have to fear is fear itself.

—Franklin D. Roosevelt

It is important to note the aspects of the diagnostic criteria that are unique to children and adolescents rather than adults. Anxiety related to the feared object is often represented by crying, tantrums, freezing, or clinging in children. Children often do not realize that their fear is unreasonable, whereas adults by definition must know that their fear is excessive or unreasonable. Because so many fears are transitory in children, the fear and clinical impairment or distress must be present for at least 6 months to meet criteria for a specific phobia (American Psychiatric Association, 2000).

The onset of a specific phobia is often associated with a traumatic event (e.g., developing a specific phobia, animal type after being bit by a dog or after seeing a friend bit by a dog) or is associated with repeated warnings about a certain danger (e.g., being warned repeatedly by one's parents that dogs are dangerous and they should be avoided at all costs). It is not uncommon for children to experience similar types of specific phobias as their first-degree relatives. That is, children with a specific phobia, animal type are likely to have a close relative with a specific phobia, animal type, but the feared animals are often different between family members (American Psychiatric Association, 2000).

As can be seen in Box 8.1 on page 217, **school refusal** (i.e., refusing to go to school) or **school phobia** (i.e., being fearful of going to school) can be related to a number of different problems. The families of school refusers tend to be less cohesive (i.e., less close)

TABLE 8.3 DSM-IV Diagnostic Criteria for Specific Phobia

A. Marked and persistent fear that is excessive or unreasonable, cued by the presence or anticipation of a specific object or situation (e.g., flying, heights, animals, receiving an injection, seeing blood).

B. Exposure to the phobic stimulus almost invariably provokes an immediate anxiety response, which may take the form of a situationally bound or situationally predisposed Panic Attack. *Note:* In children, the anxiety may be expressed by crying, tantrum, freezing, or clinging.

C. The person recognizes that the fear is excessive or unreasonable. *Note:* In children, this feature may be absent.

D. The phobic situation(s) is avoided or else is endured with intense anxiety or distress.

E. The avoidance, anxious anticipation, or distress in the feared situation(s) interferes significantly with the person's normal routine, occupational (or academic) functioning, or social activities or relationships, or there is marked distress about having the phobia.

F. In individuals under age 18 years, the duration is at least 6 months.

G. The anxiety, Panic Attacks, or phobic avoidance associated with the specific object or situation are not better accounted for by another mental disorder, such as Obsessive-Compulsive Disorder (e.g., fear of dirt in someone with an obsession about contamination), Posttraumatic Stress Disorder (e.g., avoidance of stimuli associated with a severe stressor), Separation Anxiety Disorder (e.g., avoidance of school), Social Phobia (e.g., avoidance of social situations because of fear of embarrassment), Panic Disorder With Agoraphobia, or Agoraphobia without History of Panic Disorder.

Specify type:
   Animal Type
   Natural Environment Type (e.g., heights, storms, water)
   Blood-Injection-Injury Type
   Situational Type (e.g., airplanes, elevators, enclosed places)
   Other Type (e.g., phobic avoidance of situations that may lead to choking, vomiting, or contracting an illness; in children, avoidance of loud sounds or costumed characters)

Source: American Psychiatric Association (2000).

Reprinted with permission from the *Diagnostic and Statistical Manual of Mental Disorders, Fourth Edition, Text Revision.* Copyright 2000 American Psychiatric Association.

and less adaptable (i.e., less flexible) than the families of nonclinical children (Bernstein, Warren, Massie, & Thuras, 1999). Note that school refusal is not always associated with being absent from school. For example, the child may refuse to go to school, but the parent makes her or him attend school anyway. In a sample of anxiety-based school refusers, there were more days of absenteeism with older children, children with lower levels of fear, and children with less-active families (Hansen, Sanders, Massaro, & Last, 1998).

Note also that there has been an attempt to disentangle children who refuse to go to school because of anxiety (known as anxious school refusal) versus children who refuse to go to school for oppositional reasons (known as truancy). Anxious school refusal was associated with other internalizing disorders such as separation anxiety disorder and depression (Egger, Costello, & Angold, 2003). Truancy school refusers, on the other hand, were more likely to also meet criteria for oppositional defiant disorder, conduct disorder, or depression (Egger et al., 2003). Overall, the symptom of not wanting to go to school must be evaluated thoroughly and the context of the child's situation must be considered. Box 8.1 provides more discussion of this issue.

Surprisingly little research has been completed with specific phobias in children and adolescents. Most children with a specific phobia tend to show all three aspects of anxiety: cognitive, behavioral, and physiological (Albano et al., 2003). Children's cognitions about the feared stimulus tend to be catastrophic (e.g., "If the dog bites me, I will get sick and die."). The behavioral aspect is usually represented by avoidance of the feared object (e.g., screaming and crying to convince their parents that they should not go to school, in the case of school phobia). Physiological characteristics are often represented by rapid heart rate, hyperventilation, shakiness, sweating, and an upset stomach when being confronted with the feared stimulus (Lichtenstein & Annas, 2000). Although specific phobias are intensely distressing to children as well as their parents, specific phobias often remit somewhat quickly during childhood (King, Muris, & Ollendick, 2004). Phobic adults, however, often identify the onset of their phobia as occurring during their childhood (Albano et al., 2003).

Prevalence Rates

Specific phobias are relatively common within childhood and adolescence. Between 2.4% and 3.6% of children

Case Study: Yoshino, the Girl Who Was Afraid of Everything

Yoshino's fears began very early in life. Within the first 6 months of her life, she showed startle responses to loud noises, cried when there was too much or unexpected sensory stimulation, and flailed her arms and legs as though she was terrified that she would be dropped. Between the ages of 6 and 9 months, Yoshino seemed to be afraid of strangers and of objects that suddenly appeared over her head. After she turned 1, Yoshino showed intense fear of being separated from her parents, of being injured, and of falling into the toilet. By the age of 2, Yoshino was terrified of large animals, loud noises, separation from her parents, and large objects or machines. When she was 3, Yoshino showed extreme distress when she was left alone. By the time she was 4, Yoshino was terrified of the dark. Between the ages of 6 and 12, Yoshino was fearful of natural events (such as earthquakes and hurricanes), she was terrified of being embarrassed, of making a mistake, and of being rejected in social situations. In her later adolescence between the ages of 13 and 18, Yoshino continued to show a great deal of fear about being injured and about being alienated in social settings.

You might be ready to diagnose Yoshino with a number of anxiety disorders given her lifelong series of fears. What you need to know, however, is that Yoshino is perfectly normal. Each of the fears listed at each age are developmentally appropriate and are experienced by the majority of children during that developmental phase. Professionals must know about these normal fears before trying to diagnose an anxiety disorder such as specific phobia. If Yoshino's fears had been excessive and debilitating, then a diagnosis might be warranted. In most cases, however, these fears are part of the normal developmental process and should not be labeled as pathological.

Adapted from (Schaefer & DiGeronimo, 2000).

TABLE 8.4 **Overview of Prevalence Information for Specific Phobia**

Prevalence	2–3%
Age	Children and young adolescents > Older adolescents
Gender	Girls > Boys
SES	Unknown patterns
Race/Ethnicity	Unknown patterns

and adolescents are thought to meet criteria for a specific phobia (Albano et al., 2003), with the MECA study finding a prevalence rate of 2.6% when parents' and children's reports were combined (Shaffer et al., 1996). Higher prevalence rates have been reported in primary care samples within the United States (Chavira, Stein, Bailey, & Stein 2004) and in some other countries such as Sweden (Lichtenstein & Annas, 2000). The average age of onset of specific phobias is between 7 and 8 years old, and specific phobias tend to peak between the ages of 10 and 13 (Silverman & Ginsburg, 1998). Girls are more likely than boys to experience a specific phobia (Hartung & Widiger, 1998; King et al., 2004). It may be that gender role orientation is more important than gender per se in the prevalence rates of specific phobias. One study found that higher levels of masculinity (regardless of whether the child was a boy or a girl) were associated with lower levels of fears (Ginsburg & Silverman, 2000). Thus, the gender pattern may have more to do with gender role orientation rather

than gender itself. Almost no research has been done to investigate differential prevalence rates regarding SES or race and ethnicity (King et al., 2004). The information about prevalence rates is summarized in Table 8.4.

SOCIAL PHOBIA

The primary characteristics of **social phobia** revolve around fear in social situations in which the child might embarrass her or himself. Increasingly, researchers and therapists think that a more descriptive name for this experience is social anxiety disorder (Ammerman, McGraw, Crosby, Beidel, & Turner, 2006; Herbert, Crittenden, & Dalrymple, 2004). As can be seen in Table 8.5, children must have the capacity for social relationships, but they become terrified at having to interact with peers in social or performance situations. This disorder must be differentiated from normal shyness or reticence in social situations, which can be quite common in children (Williams et al., 2005). Because symptoms of shyness are transient in children, a diagnosis of social phobia requires at least a 6-month duration of symptoms. Note, however, that nonclinical levels of shyness are somewhat traitlike and tend to endure for long periods of time (Hirshfeld-Becker, Biederman, & Rosenbaum, 2004).

The majority of children diagnosed with social phobia fall into the specific type of generalized social phobia (Albano et al., 2003). That is, most children who meet

TABLE 8.5 DSM-IV Diagnostic Criteria for Social Phobia

A.	A marked and persistent fear of one or more social or performance situations in which the person is exposed to unfamiliar people or to possible scrutiny by others. The individual fears that he or she will act in a way (or show anxiety symptoms) that will be humiliating or embarrassing. *Note:* In children, there must be evidence of the capacity for age-appropriate social relationships with familiar people and the anxiety must occur in peer settings, not just in interactions with adults.
B.	Exposure to the feared social situation almost invariably provokes anxiety, which may take the form of a situationally bound or situationally predisposed Panic Attack. *Note:* In children, the anxiety may be expressed by crying, tantrums, freezing, or shrinking from social situations with unfamiliar people.
C.	The person recognizes that the fear is excessive or unreasonable. *Note:* In children, this feature may be absent.
D.	The feared social or performance situations are avoided or else are endured with intense anxiety or distress.
E.	The avoidance, anxious anticipation, or distress in the feared social or performance situation(s) interferes significantly with the person's normal routine, occupational (academic) functioning, or social activities or relationships, or there is marked distress about having the phobia.
F.	In individuals under age 18 years, the duration is at least 6 months.
G.	The fear or avoidance is not due to the direct physiological effects of a substance (e.g., a drug of abuse, a medication) or a general medical condition and is not better accounted for by another mental disorder (e.g., Panic Disorder With or Without Agoraphobia, Separation Anxiety Disorder, Body Dysmorphic Disorder, a Pervasive Developmental Disorder, or Schizoid Personality Disorder).
H.	If a general medical condition or another mental disorder is present, the fear in Criterion A is unrelated to it, e.g., the fear is not of Stuttering, trembling in Parkinson's disease, or exhibiting abnormal eating behavior in Anorexia Nervosa or Bulimia Nervosa.
I. Specify if:	
	Generalized: if the fears include most social situations (also consider the additional diagnosis of Avoidant Personality Disorder)

Source: American Psychiatric Association (2000).

Reprinted with permission from the *Diagnostic and Statistical Manual of Mental Disorders, Fourth Edition, Text Revision.* Copyright 2000 American Psychiatric Association.

criteria for social phobia experience the phobia in nearly all social situations. The school setting, however, tends to result in a great deal of distress because of both unstructured and structured encounters with large groups of peers (Beidel, Morris, & Turner, 2004). Children with social phobia tend to expect themselves to do more poorly in social interaction tasks and to evaluate their performance more poorly in these tasks than do children without social phobia (Alfano, Beidel, & Turner, 2006). Quite often, social phobia develops after a traumatic event, such as falling down a flight of stairs when other children are watching (Beidel et al., 2004). A number of social situations are feared by children with social phobia (Beidel et al., 2004), including

- Reading aloud in front of the class (71% of children with social phobia feared this situation)
- Musical or athletic performances (61%)
- Joining in on a conversation (59%)
- Speaking to adults (59%)
- Starting a conversation (58%)

Given that many of these concerns are evident in the school setting, it is interesting to note that many teachers, school psychologists, and school counselors do not know a great deal about social phobia (Herbert et al., 2004). Overall, social anxiety is associated with poor peer interactions and poor social skills (Herbert et al., 2004; Morgan & Banerjee, 2006). Children and adolescents with social phobia tend to be "loners" and often do not have any friends (Albano et al., 2003). Parents of socially phobic adolescents often lament that their teens do not tie up the phone lines constantly and that their lives are not a blur of teens coming and going from the house (Albano et al., 2003). Children with social anxiety perceive their parents as socially isolating and less socially active than children with low levels of social anxiety (Caster, Inderbitzen, & Hope, 1999). Overall, it appears that children and adolescents diagnosed with social phobia are extremely afraid of being embarrassed, rejected, or evaluated negatively by their peers (Albano et al., 1996). Adults who are diagnosed with avoidant personality disorder were more likely than adults with other personality disorders or depressed adults to have

"DADDY, PLEASE DON'T MAKE ME GO TO SCHOOL"

If you were a clinician and a father reported that every morning his 9-year-old daughter said, "Daddy, please don't make me go to school," what diagnoses (if any) would you consider? School refusal (i.e., refusing to go to school) is relatively common in children (and even some college students!). The term *school phobia* is used frequently, but there is no formal diagnosis of school phobia or school refusal. Rather, the symptom of refusing to go to school could be an indication of a number of different problems:

- There is a math test and the child is not prepared.
- Specific phobia—The child is fearful of going to school, and it is not within the first month of the school year.
- Separation anxiety disorder—The child does not want to leave her parents, and it happens that school is the place she is supposed to go.
- Social phobia—The child is terrified of having to interact with his peers, and he is afraid that he will

do something embarrassing and be ridiculed by his classmates.

- It is opening day of the baseball season, and the child wants to watch the San Francisco Giants play their mid-day game.

Thus, the actual symptom of refusing to go to school or being afraid to go to school can mean very different things for different children. The process of differential diagnosis should help to clarify which disorder, if any, is appropriate for the child. This clarification is especially important for helping to treat children who refuse to go to school (Bernstein, Hektner, Borchardt, & McMillan, 2001; D'Eramo & Francis, 2004; Kearney & Hugelshofer, 2000; McShane, Walter, & Rey, 2004).

Source: Albano et al., 2003; King and Bernstein (2001).

---

shown signs of social phobia in childhood (Rettew et al., 2003).

Prevalence Rates

Prevalence rates of social phobia in childhood and adolescence range from 1% to 3%, with very low rates in childhood and higher rates in adolescence (Albano et al., 2003), although higher prevalence rates are sometime found (Chavira et al., 2004). Social phobia rarely occurs before the age of 10 (Albano et al., 2003). The average age of onset occurs between 11 and 12 years, with more adolescents diagnosed than younger children (Beidel et al., 2004). In clinical samples, girls outnumber boys for treatment of social phobia (Hartung & Widiger, 1998), although this gender difference is not found in every study (Beidel et al., 2004). Data on SES, race, and ethnicity remain unclear (Albano et al., 2003). The information about prevalence rates is summarized in Table 8.6.

TABLE 8.6 Overview of Prevalence Information for Social Phobia

Prevalence	1–3%
Age	Adolescents > Children
Gender	Girls > Boys
SES	Unknown patterns
Race/Ethnicity	Unknown patterns

OBSESSIVE-COMPULSIVE DISORDER

The case study entitled Lady MacBeth on page 222 provides an eloquent description of a client's experience with **obsessive-compulsive disorder (OCD).** OCD is a disorder that occurs when a child or adolescent has disordered thoughts, ideas, or images (called **obsessions**) or disordered, repetitive behaviors (called **compulsions**). As with all disorders, normal levels of obsessiveness and compulsiveness need to be distinguished from abnormal levels of obsessiveness and compulsiveness (Williams et al., 2005). It is not unusual for children and adolescents to have certain thoughts that could be considered obsessions (e.g., a child who thinks constantly about her beloved kitten or an adolescent who cannot get a certain girlfriend off her mind) and to show behaviors that might be considered compulsive (e.g., a young child who wants to say "goodnight, I love you" to each person in the house at his bedtime or an adolescent who insists that her clothes be in a certain order in her closet). These normal idiosyncracies should not be mistaken for OCD (Zohar & Felz, 2001).

When OCD is present, children and adolescents often have both obsessions and compulsions, but the diagnosis of OCD only requires that either obsessions or compulsions be present. The obsessions or compulsions must cause significant distress, must be time consuming

Case Study: Emily Has No Friends

Since kindergarten, Emily has shown extreme withdrawal and anxiety around peers at school and in the neighborhood. Now that she is 7 years old and in the second grade, her teacher recommended that her mother seek professional help for Emily. Emily stands alone in the corner of the playground during recess and does not interact with other children. Even when another child approaches to try to play with her, she withdraws from that child. Emily appears to be afraid of being embarrassed or humiliated by her peers. Emily's mother has often taken her by the hand to play with other children in the neighborhood, but Emily just cries and runs away from the children. Emily does not have any friends at school or

in the neighborhood. She has never been invited to another child's birthday party.

Unlike her behavior with peers at school and in the neighborhood, Emily is very socially engaged with her family. At home, she is outgoing and warm and she appears to enjoy the social connections with her family.

Based on these characteristics, a diagnosis of social phobia appears to be warranted. Emily obviously has the capacity for appropriate social interactions (as evidenced by her interactions with her family), but she appears to be afraid of social interactions with her peers in almost any situation.

Source: Spitzer et al. (1994).

(occurring for more than 1 hour per day), or must impact negatively on the child's or adolescent's life. As can be seen in Table 8.7 on page 223, the diagnostic criteria in *DSM-IV* also note a difference between OCD in children and OCD in adults. Whereas adults have to realize that the symptoms are excessive or unreasonable, children and adolescents do not.

OCD is a very distressing disorder. It appears that compulsions (behavioral excesses) are often completed to reduce the anxiety of obsessions (recurrent cognitions). Imagine a little boy who sometimes has thoughts about hurting his father and then who kneels down and prays to "undo" his bad thoughts. Each time he imagines his father being hurt, he kneels down and does a series of prayers. The prayers seem to reduce his anxiety about his thoughts, which inadvertently reinforce the likelihood that he will pray the next time he has a troubling thought about his father. In many cases of OCD, compulsions can take over the child's or adolescent's life, leaving them little time to do anything else other than their compulsive behaviors. One study found that 90% of children and adolescents receiving treatment for OCD reported at least one serious dysfunction related to their OCD (Piacentini, Bergman, Keller, & McCracken, 2003). OCD is often a long-term, debilitating problem, and at least 50% of adolescents diagnosed with OCD continue to have the problem into adulthood (Rapoport & Ismond, 1996).

Washing rituals (e.g., hand washing, washing the desk at school), repeating rituals (e.g., saying a certain phrase over and over), and checking behaviors (e.g., repeatedly making sure that their house key is in their backpack) are the most common compulsions in children and adolescents (Albano et al., 2003). The most common

obsessions include fear of contamination (e.g., getting germs from dirt, contracting AIDS or another life-threatening illness) and concerns about hurting oneself or a family member (Albano et al., 2003). Certain obsessions seem to be linked to certain compulsions in children and adolescents (March et al., 2004), for example:

- Concerns about contamination are tied to washing rituals.
- Obsessions of harm to self or others are tied to compulsions of a repeating nature.
- Obsessions with aggressive themes seem to lead to checking behavior.

Prevalence Rates

As noted in Table 8.8 on page 223, OCD is thought to be relatively rare, with a lifetime prevalence rate of 1% noted in a study of adolescents, and less than 1% in children under the age of 10 (Geffken, Pincus, & Zelikovsky, 1999; March, Franklin, Leonard, & Foa, 2004). Because of the hidden nature of the disorder (i.e., children and adolescents often try to keep their symptoms a secret), many youth experience OCD but never receive help for their problems (March et al., 2004). Thus, these prevalence rates may be an underestimate of the actual occurrence of OCD in childhood and adolescence (Geffken et al., 1999).

The average age of onset for children and adolescents diagnosed with OCD is between 8 and 11 years old (Piacentini, March, & Franklin, 2006). It is rare for a young child to develop OCD. Prevalence rates regarding gender show approximately similar numbers

Case Study: Shy Sylvia

Just like in Chapter 5 in the case of Devastated Darryl, you are going to be asked to formulate a treatment plan. Creating a treatment plan is an integral part of how clinicians help child clients.

Once you have written down your own thoughts, please refer to the suggestions reprinted from The Child Psychotherapy Treatment Planner *(Jongsma, Peterson, & McInnis, 2000b). There are few right or wrong answers to the exercise, rather you are being challenged to think creatively and to apply your knowledge to a realistic case.*

Sylvia is a 7-year-old Hispanic/Latina girl, and she is painfully shy. Although she interacts well with her mother, father, and two older brothers, she avoids contact with other children and adults. Her teachers and after-school caretakers have noted that Sylvia keeps to herself around other children and that she seems to become very nervous when forced to play with other children. She rarely makes eye contact with adults or children and tends to look at the floor whenever she is around others. Sylvia's parents report that she takes part in solitary activities frequently, such as reading and drawing. They have also noted that she needs a great deal of reassurance from them and that she tends to be very sensitive to even the slightest criticism. Her mother reported an example in which Sylvia stayed in her room, crying, for over two hours last week when Sylvia's mother suggested that she should brush her hair because it had become messy.

Sylvia's parents noted that these problems have been evident for as long as they can remember. They recall that she was a particularly clingy and sensitive child, but they assumed that she would grow out of it. Sylvia's father acknowledges that he is a bit uncomfortable around strangers, but that he manages to have good relationships with friends and co-workers. The parents appear to be very concerned about Sylvia's shyness and seem motivated to engage in treatment for these problems.

During your initial interview with Sylvia, she did not make direct eye contact with you except once when you mentioned a children's book that is one of her favorites. She smiled once when her oldest brother tried to tickle her. She sat on the couch in your office as though she were trying to disappear into the cushions. She kept her hands folded during the entire interview and although she answered questions when asked, she did not provide much more than one- or two-word answers. She seemed to be especially anxious (e.g., rigid muscles, arms folded across her chest) when you asked her questions directly.

Sylvia's medical history and developmental milestones are all reported to be normal, with the exception of her difficulties in social relationships. Her academic work is not problematic. No major traumas were reported.

TREATMENT PLAN

Imagine that you are the clinician who has been contacted by Sylvia's parents. One of your first tasks is to develop a treatment plan that will guide your assessment and treatment of Sylvia and her family. Using what you know about shyness/anxiety and therapeutic interventions, write out a treatment plan for Sylvia and her family. As you can see below, you are expected to delineate a series of behavioral definitions (e.g., the observable symptoms that are problematic), long-term goals, short-term objectives, and therapeutic interventions. Note that short-term objectives and therapeutic interventions are usually linked together so that the clinician can target specific behaviors with specific interventions. Once you have completed this section, turn to the next section to see what professional clinicians suggest for this type of case in *The Child Psychotherapy Treatment Planner* (Jongsma et al., 2000b). Make sure to compare your answers with the professionals' suggestions in order to identify ideas or concepts that you may not have considered.

BEHAVIORAL DEFINITIONS

1. _____
2. _____
3. _____
4. _____
5. _____
6. _____
7. _____
8. _____
9. _____
10. _____

LONG-TERM GOALS

1. _____
2. _____
3. _____
4. _____
5. _____
6. _____
7. _____
8. _____
9. _____
10. _____

SHORT-TERM OBJECTIVES	THERAPEUTIC INTERVENTIONS
1. _____	1. _____
2. _____	2. _____
3. _____	3. _____
4. _____	4. _____

(continued)

> ### Case Study: Shy Sylvia (*continued*)

5. _____
6. _____
7. _____
8. _____
9. _____
10. _____

5. _____
6. _____
7. _____
8. _____
9. _____
10. _____

From *The Child Psychotherapy Treatment Planner*—Jongsma, Peterson, and McInnis (2000b)

SOCIAL PHOBIA/SHYNESS

BEHAVIORAL DEFINITIONS

1. Hiding, limited or no eye contact, a refusal or reticence to respond verbally to overtures from others, and isolation in most social situations.

2. Excessive shrinking or avoidance of eye contact with unfamiliar people for an extended period of time (i.e., six months or longer).

3. Social isolation and/or excessive involvement in isolated activities (e.g., reading, listening to music in his/her room, playing, video games).

4. Extremely limited or no close friendships outside the immediate family members.

5. Hypersensitivity to criticism, disapproval, or perceived signs of rejection from other.

6. Excessive need for reassurance of being liked by others before demonstrating a willingness to get involved with them.

7. Marked reluctance to engage in new activities or take personal risks because of the potential for embarrassment or humiliation.

8. Negative self-image as evidenced by frequent self-disparaging remarks, unfavorable comparisons to others, and a perception of self as being socially unattractive.

9. Lack of assertiveness because of a fear of being met with criticism, disapproval, or rejection.

10. Heightened physiological distress in social setting manifested by increased heart rate, profuse sweating, dry mouth, muscular tension, and trembling.

LONG-TERM GOALS

1. Eliminate anxiety, shyness, and timidity in most social settings.

2. Establish and maintain long-term (i.e., six months) interpersonal or peer friendships outside of the immediate family.

3. Initiate social contacts regularly with unfamiliar people or when placed in new social settings.

4. Interact socially with peers or friends on a regular, consistent basis without excessive fear or anxiety.

5. Achieve a healthy balance between time spent in solitary activity and social interaction with others.

6. Develop the essential social skills that will enhance the quality of interpersonal relationships.

7. Resolve the core conflicts contributing to the emergence of social anxiety and shyness.

8. Elevate self-esteem and feelings of security in interpersonal peer and adult relationships.

SHORT-TERM OBJECTIVES

1. Complete psychological testing.

2. Complete psychoeducational testing.

3. Complete a speech/language evaluation.

4. Comply with the behavioral and cognitive strategies and gradually increase the frequency and duration of social contacts.

5. Agree to initiate one social contact per day.

6. Increase positive self-statements in social interactions.

7. Verbally acknowledge compliments without excessive timidity or withdrawal.

8. Increase positive statements about peer interaction and social experiences.

9. Increase participation in interpersonal or peer group activities.

10. Identify strengths and interests that can be used to initiate social contacts and develop peer friendships.

11. Increase participation in school-related activities.

12. Decrease the frequency of self-disparaging remarks in the presence of peers.

13. Increase assertive behaviors to deal more effectively and directly with stress, conflict, or intimidating peers.

14. Verbalize how current social anxiety and insecurities are associated with past rejection experiences and criticism from significant others.

15. Enmeshed or overly protective parents identify how they reinforce social anxiety and overly dependent behaviors.

16. Parents reinforce the client's positive social behaviors and set limits on overly dependent behaviors.

17. Verbally recognize the secondary gain that results from social anxiety, self-disparaging remarks, and overdependence on parents.

18. Overly critical parents verbally recognize how their negative remarks contribute to the client's social anxiety, timidity, and low self-esteem.

19. Parents set realistic and age-appropriate goals for the client.

(continued)

20. Parents comply with recommendations regarding therapy and/or medication evaluations.

21. Express fears and anxiety in individual play-therapy sessions or through mutual storytelling.

22. Identify and express feelings in art.

23. Express feelings and actively participate in group therapy.

24. Take medication as directed by the prescribing physician.

THERAPEUTIC INTERVENTIONS

1. Arrange for psychological testing to assess the severity of the client's anxiety and gain greater insight into the dynamics contributing to the symptoms.

2. Arrange for psychoeducational testing of the client to rule out the presence of a learning disability that may contribute to social withdrawal in school setting.

3. Refer the client for a comprehensive speech/language evaluation to rule out possible impairment that may contribute to social withdrawal.

4. Give feedback to the client and his/her family regarding psychological, psychoeducational, and speech/language testing.

5. Actively build the level of trust with the client through consistent eye contact, active listening, unconditional positive regard, and warm acceptance to help increase his/her ability to identify and express feelings.

6. Design and implement a systematic desensitization program in which the client gradually increases the frequency and duration of social contacts to help decrease his/her social anxiety.

7. Develop reward system or contingency contract to reinforce client for initiating social contacts and/or engaging in play or recreational activities with peers.

8. Train the client to reduce anxiety by using guided imagery in a relaxed state, with the client visualizing himself/herself dealing with various social situations in a confident manner.

9. Assist the client in developing positive self-talk as a means of managing his/her social anxiety or fears.

10. Assign the task of initiating one social contact per day.

11. Use behavioral rehearsal, modeling, and role play to reduce anxiety, develop social skills, and learn to initiate conversation.

12. Praise and reinforce any emerging positive social behaviors.

13. Ask the client to list how he/she is like his/her peers.

14. Encourage participation in extracurricular or positive peer group activities.

15. Instruct client to invite a friend for an overnight visit and/or set up an overnight visit at a friend's home; process any fears and anxiety that arise.

16. Ask the client to make a list or keep a journal of both positive and negative social experiences; process this with the therapist.

17. Explore social situations in which client interacts with others without excessive fear or anxiety. Process these successful experiences and reinforce any strengths or positive social skills that client uses to decrease fear or anxiety.

18. Consult with school officials about ways to increase the client's socialization (e.g., raising flag with group of peers, tutoring a more popular peer, pairing the client with another popular peer on classroom assignments).

19. Provide feedback on any negative social behaviors that interfere with the ability to establish and maintain friendships.

20. Teach assertiveness skills to help communicate thoughts, feelings, and needs more openly and directly.

---

of boys and girls diagnosed with OCD (March et al., 2004). An interesting pattern emerges when age and gender are explored. Boys are more likely to receive a diagnosis of OCD before puberty, whereas girls are more likely to receive a diagnosis of OCD after puberty (Piacentini et al., 2006). There has been little research on the prevalence rates of OCD regarding SES (Albano et al., 1996). Within community-based epidemiological studies, there does not appear to be any difference in the prevalence of OCD with regard to race and ethnicity (March et al., 2004). Interestingly, there are proportionally more Caucasian-American children than

African-American children who receive treatment for OCD, which suggests that Caucasian-American children might be referred for treatment of OCD more readily than are African-American children (March et al., 2004).

GENERALIZED ANXIETY DISORDER

Formerly known as overanxious disorder, **generalized anxiety disorder (GAD)** occurs when children or adolescents experience a pervasive and chronic level of

Case Study: Lady MacBeth, the Adolescent Who Had to Wash Her Hands

Following is the transcript of an interview session with a girl who meets criteria for obsessive-compulsive disorder. Note that she exhibits both disordered behavior (compulsions) and disordered thoughts (obsessions).

Interviewer: What were the things that you were doing?

Client: In the morning when I got dressed, I was real afraid that there'd be germs all over my clothes and things, so I'd stand there and I'd shake them for half an hour. I'd wash before I did anything—like if I was gonna wash my face, I'd wash my hands first; and if I was gonna get dressed, I'd wash my hands first; and then it got even beyond that point. Washing my hands wasn't enough, and I started to use rubbing alcohol. It was winter time and cold weather, and this really made my hands bleed. Even if I just held them under water, they'd bleed all over the place, and they looked terrible, and everyone thought I had a disease or something.

Interviewer: And when you were doing that much washing, how much time every day did that take, if you added up all the different parts of it?

Client: It took about 6 hours a day...

Interviewer: You also told me about other things in addition to the washing and worrying about dirt: that you would have plans about how you would do other things.

Client: Okay, well they were like set plans in my mind that if I heard the word, like, something that had to do with germs or disease, it would be considered something bad and so I had things that would go through my mind that were sort of like "cross that out and it'll make it okay" to hear that word.

Interviewer: What sort of things?

Client: Like numbers or words that seemed to be sort of like a protector.

Interviewer: What numbers and what words were they?

Client: It started out to be the number 3 and multiples of 3 and then words like "soap and water," something like that; and then the multiples of 3 got really high, they'd end up to be 123 or something like that. It got real bad then.

Interviewer: At any time did you really believe that something bad would happen if you didn't do these things? Was it just a feeling, or were you really scared?

Client: No! I was petrified that something would really happen...

Interviewer: Who were the people you'd worry most would get hurt?

Client: My family, basically my family...

Source: Spitzer et al. (1994, pp. 344–346).

Reprinted with permission from the *DSM-IV Casebook*. Copyright 1994 American Psychiatric Association.

---

anxiety and worry. The diagnostic criteria are presented in Table 8.9 on page 226. Most often, the anxiety and worry are somewhat diffuse (e.g., a child who worries about nearly everything), but sometimes the anxiety and worry are focused on a few specific events or activities (e.g., worrying about doing well in reading and feeling anxious about the dog's health and feeling distressed about a friend's parent's marriage). The anxieties and worries are considered to be unrealistic and excessive (Robin et al., 2006). Children often worry about future events (e.g., whether they will make the varsity soccer team in high school even though they are still in grade school) and sometimes worry about adult concerns (e.g., the family finances).

Children diagnosed with GAD tend to be very self-conscious and perfectionistic (Flannery-Schroeder, 2004). They tend to assume that bad things will happen to those around them, and they tend to assume that the negative consequences to events will be a lot worse than most others expect (Albano et al., 2003). Although even nonclinical children have worries about low-frequency, but highly negative, events (such as terrorism), children diagnosed with GAD do not realize that these events are infrequent and unlikely (Flannery-Schroeder, 2004).

The clinical characteristics of children and adolescents diagnosed with GAD are pervasive. In a sample of youth receiving services for GAD at an outpatient clinic, 100% reported experiencing tension, 93.6% reported apprehensive expectations, 89.9% said that they had a negative self-image, and 86.0% felt a need for reassurance from trusted adults (Masi et al., 2004). Overall, GAD is a chronic and all-encompassing problem of childhood and adolescence.

TABLE 8.7 DSM-IV Diagnostic Criteria for Obsessive-Compulsive Disorder

A.   Either obsessions or compulsions:

Obsessions as defined by (1), (2), (3), and (4):

(1) recurrent and persistent thoughts, impulses, or images that are experienced, at some time during the disturbance, as intrusive and inappropriate and that cause marked anxiety or distress

(2) the thoughts, impulses, or images are not simply excessive worries about real-life problems

(3) the person attempts to ignore or suppress such thoughts, impulses, or images, or to neutralize them with some other thought or action

(4) the person recognizes that the obsessional thoughts, impulses, or images are a product of his or her own mind (not imposed from without as in thought insertion)

Compulsions as defined by (1) and (2):

(1) repetitive behaviors (e.g., hand washing, ordering, checking) or mental acts (e.g., praying, counting, repeating words silently) that the person feels driven to perform in response to an obsession, or according to rules that must be applied rigidly

(2) the behaviors or mental acts are aimed at preventing or reducing distress or preventing some dreaded event or situation; however, these behaviors or mental acts either are not connected in a realistic way with what they are designed to neutralize or prevent or are clearly excessive

B.   At some point during the course of the disorder, the person has recognized that the obsessions or compulsions are excessive or unreasonable. *Note:* This does not apply to children.

C.   The obsessions or compulsions cause marked distress, are time consuming (take more than 1 hour a day), or significantly interfere with the person's normal routine, occupational (or academic) functioning, or usual social activities or relationships.

D.   If another Axis I disorder is present, the content of the obsessions or compulsions is not restricted to it (e.g., preoccupation with food in the presence of an Eating Disorder; hair pulling in the presence of Trichotillomania; concern with appearance in the presence of Body Dysmorphic Disorder; preoccupation with drugs in the presence of a Substance Use Disorder; preoccupation with having a serious illness in the presence of Hypochondriasis; preoccupation with sexual urges or fantasies in the presence of a Paraphilia; or guilty ruminations in the presence of Major Depressive Disorder).

E.   The disturbance is not due to the direct physiological effects of a substance (e.g., a drug of abuse, a medication) or a general medical condition.

Specify if:

With Poor Insight: if, for most of the time during the current episode, the person does not recognize that the obsessions and compulsions are excessive or unreasonable

Source: American Psychiatric Association (2000).

Reprinted with permission from the *Diagnostic and Statistical Manual of Mental Disorders, Fourth Edition, Text Revision.* Copyright 2000 American Psychiatric Association.

TABLE 8.8 Overview of Prevalence Information for Obsessive-Compulsive Disorder

Prevalence	1% of adolescents
Age	Adolescents > Children
Gender	No differences
SES	Unknown patterns
Race/Ethnicity	No differences (in epidemiological studies)

Prevalence Rates

As noted in Table 8.10, epidemiological data suggest that GAD is present in 2% to 19% of children and adolescents, with most conservative studies suggesting that GAD is present in 2% to 4% of children and adolescents (Chavira et al., 2004; Flannery-Schroeder, 2004). GAD is more prevalent in adolescents than in children (Masi et al., 2004). During adolescence and into adulthood, GAD is more common in females than in males (Williams et al., 2005). Regarding family SES, children from middle and higher SES families are found more frequently in clinical facilities than are children from lower SES families (Albano et al., 2003). There has been almost no research into the different prevalence rates of GAD within different racial and ethnic groups (Robin et al., 2006).

Oh, it's scary 'cause all this violence going on now. And I—and I just wonder if it's gonna get worse or if it's gonna be better.

> —Marie, a Dominican American teenager who lives in an impoverished urban area (Way, 1998, p. 169)

When he was 3 years old, Frank began to worry that he would die in his sleep. From that time on, he was a light sleeper, and he would awaken often during the night. Frank's father had a history of panic disorder and major depression, and Frank's mother had a history of major depression.

By the time he was 8 years old, Frank, worried about everything. For the past 3 months, he had been hearing things as he was falling asleep. He often thought that he heard "something that seemed like something mumbling" and he reported that he thought he heard someone breathing in his room. On a number of occasions at night, he thought he saw "flashes of light" and he began experiencing panic attacks (e.g., shortness of breath, tachycardia, tingling in his hands, and extreme fearfulness). The panic attacks lasted approximately 15 to 20 minutes and frightened Frank so much that he no longer would sleep in his own room. With his parents' permission, Frank began sleeping on the couch in the living room, and then Frank's father would carry Frank to bed once he was sound asleep.

During the clinical interview, Frank appeared to take pride in his knowledge of his clinical symptomatology. He was able to report each symptom and gave immense details on

his troubling experiences. He acknowledged that he worried all the time. Even though he was still in elementary school, he worried that his dropping grades would prevent him from gaining admission to a "good college." Based on interviews with Frank and his parents, Frank received the following multiaxial diagnosis:

Axis I:	Generalized Anxiety Disorder
	Panic Disorder Without Agoraphobia
Axis II:	No diagnosis (i.e., no personality disorders or developmental disabilities)
Axis III:	None (i.e., no physical illnesses)
Axis IV:	Problems with primary support group; both parents have chronic Major Depressive Disorder, In Partial Remission
Axis V:	Global Assessment of Functioning = 60 (current)

Source: Rapoport & Ismond (1996).

POSTTRAUMATIC STRESS DISORDER

Posttraumatic stress disorder (PTSD) occurs when children or adolescents experience some type of traumatic event (such as a sexual assault, sniper attack, earthquake, car accident, or death of a parent) and have even more problems related to the event than would otherwise be expected (Runyon, Deblinger, Behl, & Cooper, 2006). Symptoms of PTSD in children include depression, anxiety, emotional disturbance, somatic complaints, aggression, and acting-out (Foa, Johnson, Feeny, & Treadwell, 2001). As noted in Table 8.11 on page 227, the core features of PSTD are that the individual has experienced some type of trauma, and they show three constellations of behaviors: reexperiencing, avoidance, and arousal (Criteria B, C, and D). These three constellations of behaviors, called symptom clusters, are well established through empirical research (Williams et al., 2005).

Historically, PTSD was the focus of research on adult veterans of war. Within the past 20 years, however, a great deal of interest has focused on children's and adolescents' experience of PTSD, especially as it relates to the trauma of physical abuse, sexual abuse, community violence, and homelessness (Cloitre, Stovall-McClough,

Miranda, & Chemtob, 2004; Kaplow, Dodge, Amaya-Jackson, & Saxe, 2005; A. Stewart et al., 2004). In addition to the trauma of abuse, PTSD has been investigated with children who have experienced kidnaping, school shootings, fires, domestic violence, floods, car accidents, hurricanes, war, and other disasters (Meiser-Stedman, Yule, Smith, Glucksman, & Dalgleish, 2005; Udwin, Boyle, Yule, Bolton, & O'Ryan, 2000). There has also been a noticeable increase in research on PTSD as it relates to pediatric health issues, including diabetes diagnosis (Landolt, Vollrath, Laimbacher, Gnehm, & Sennhauser, 2005), cancer (Kazak, Alderfer, Rourke, et al., 2004; Kazak, Alderfer, Streisand, et al., 2004; Landolt, Vollrath, Ribi, Gnehm, & Sennhauser, 2003), and burns (Saxe et al., 2005). In addition, there have been a number of studies of posttraumatic symptoms in relation to terrorism and the attacks on September 11, 2001 (Brown & Goodman, 2005; Fremont, 2004; Henry, Tolan, & Gorman-Smith, 2004; La Greca, Roberts, Silverman, & Vernberg, 2002; Whalen, Henker, King, Jamner, & Levine, 2004).

Pretrauma functioning appears to be related to posttrauma functioning. For example, children in Seattle, Washington, who showed higher rates of internalizing and externalizing problems before the attacks on

Robert, why is it necessary for you to walk up and down every aisle three times whenever you go to the pencil sharpener?

September 11, 2001, showed the highest rates of post-traumatic symptoms after the attacks (Lengua, Long, Smith, & Meltzoff, 2005). In general, the severity of the trauma, the child's proximity to the traumatic event, and the duration of the trauma are all related to increased risk for PTSD (Williams et al., 2005). The criteria in *DSM-IV* are meant to highlight the extreme and maladaptive nature with which the individual reacts to the trauma.

Prevalence Rates

Although there are no good epidemiological estimates of PTSD in children and adolescents, it appears that PTSD is relatively common in childhood when compared with other psychological disorders. One review of epidemiological data suggested that 36% of all children and adolescents could meet criteria for PTSD (Fletcher, 2003). This number is the combination of interesting age trends, where 39% of preschoolers, 33% of elementary school children, and 27% of adolescents met criteria for PTSD (Fletcher, 2003). Thus, it appears that PTSD is more common in younger children when compared with adolescents. Other large-scale studies based on representative samples have suggested lower prevalence rates that are closer to 5% (Williams et al., 2005). In either case, PTSD is highly prevalent in children. As noted in Box 8.2 on page 230, children exposed to war and other atrocities are at greater risk for developing PTSD. For all children, it appears that girls are more at risk for the development of PTSD than are boys (Fletcher, 2003). Little is known about the differential prevalence rates related to SES, and there are no known differences when racial and ethnic groups are compared (Fletcher, 2003). There is surprisingly little research on

PTSD in children, other than in reaction to physical and sexual abuse. More research is needed to confirm the scant knowledge that is available currently. This type of research may be enhanced when better assessment measures are developed for PTSD (McKnight, Compton, & March, 2004). Table 8.12 on page 228 summarizes the prevalence data for PTSD.

SELECTIVE MUTISM

Formerly known as elective mutism, **selective mutism** is diagnosed when children fail to speak in one or more situations (such as school) when it is obvious that they can speak in other situations (such as home). The most typical case of selective mutism is when a child speaks well at home but does not speak at school or in other situations away from home (Freeman, Garcia, Miller, Dow, & Leonard, 2004). Current thinking suggests that these children do not speak due to high levels of anxiety, rather than to oppositional tendencies (Yeganeh, Beidel, Turner, Pina, & Silverman, 2003). The diagnostic criteria for selective mutism are presented in Table 8.13 on page 231.

Children diagnosed with selective mutism tend to be very shy, withdrawn, negative, and isolated, especially in the situations where they do not speak (American Psychiatric Association, 2000; Toppelberg, Tabors, Coggins, Lum, & Burger, 2005). After children develop selective mutism, they are often scapegoated and teased by other children (American Psychiatric Association, 2000). The disorder often lasts only a few months, although selective mutism can last several years when left untreated (American Psychiatric Association, 2000; Bergman, Piacentini, & McCracken, 2002).

TABLE 8.9 DSM-IV Diagnostic Criteria for Generalized Anxiety Disorder

A. Excessive anxiety and worry (apprehensive expectation), occurring more days than not for at least 6 months, about a number of events or activities (such as work or school performance).

B. The person finds it difficult to control the worry.

C. The anxiety and worry are associated with three (or more) of the following six symptoms (with at least some symptoms present for more days than not for the past 6 months). *Note:* Only one item is required in children.

(1) restlessness or feeling keyed up or on edge

(2) being easily fatigued

(3) difficulty concentrating or mind going blank

(4) irritability

(5) muscle tension

(6) sleep disturbance (difficult falling or staying asleep, or restless unsatisfying sleep)

D. The focus of the anxiety and worry is not confined to features of an Axis I disorder, e.g., the anxiety or worry is not about having a Panic Attack (as in Panic Disorder), being embarrassed in public (as in Social Phobia), being contaminated (as in Obsessive-Compulsive Disorder), being away from home or close relatives (as in Separation Anxiety Disorder), gaining weight (as in Anorexia Nervosa), having multiple physical complaints (as in Somatization Disorder), or having a serious illness (as in Hypochondriasis), and the anxiety and worry do not occur exclusively during Posttraumatic Stress Disorder.

E. The anxiety, worry, or physical symptoms cause clinically significant distress or impairment in social, occupational, or other important areas of functioning.

F. The disturbance is not due to the direct physiological effects of a substance (e.g., drug of abuse, a medication) or a general medical condition (e.g., hyperthyroidism) and does not occur exclusively during a Mood Disorder, a Psychotic Disorder, or a Pervasive Developmental Disorder.

Source: American Psychiatric Association (2000).

Reprinted with permission from the *Diagnostic and Statistical Manual of Mental Disorders, Fourth Edition, Text Revision.* Copyright 2000 American Psychiatric Association.

TABLE 8.10 Overview of Prevalence Information for Generalized Anxiety Disorder

Prevalence	2–4%
Age	Adolescents > Children
Gender	Females > Males
SES	Middle and Higher > Lower
Race/Ethnicity	Unknown patterns

Prevalence Rates

Selective mutism is quite rare, with far fewer than 1% of children in mental health clinics experiencing the disorder (American Psychiatric Association, 2000). Exact prevalence rates are thought to be between 0.08% and 2.0%, with the most consistent estimates falling below 1% (Freeman et al., 2004). Two well-designed studies, one in a primary care facility (Chavira et al., 2004) and one in a public school (Bergman et al., 2002), found that prevalence rates were 0.5% and 0.71%, respectively. Selective mutism is much more common with younger children than with older children or adolescents (American Psychiatric Association, 2000). Symptoms most often occur before the age of 5, but

referrals for diagnosis and treatment usually occur once the child reaches school age. Selective mutism is more common in girls than in boys (Freeman et al., 2004; Hartung & Widiger, 1998). Almost no epidemiological research has addressed the prevalence rates of selective mutism according to SES or race and ethnicity (Freeman et al., 2004). There appears to be a somewhat higher prevalence in children who are not native speakers of the language that is dominant in their current living situation (Elizur & Perednik, 2003; Toppelberg et al., 2005). Prevalence data for selective mutism are presented in Table 8.14.

I think the thing I'm most frightened of is the world ending.
—14 year old, Carleen, from England

ALL ANXIETY DISORDERS OF CHILDHOOD AND ADOLESCENCE

Although there is a great deal of uniqueness between the different anxiety disorders, many studies combine

TABLE 8.11   DSM-IV Diagnostic Criteria for Posttraumatic Stress Disorder

A. The person has been exposed to a traumatic event in which both of the following were present:
  (1) the person experienced, witnessed, or was confronted with an event or events that involved actual or threatened death or serious injury, or a threat to the physical integrity of self or others

  (2) the person's response involved intense fear, helplessness, or horror. *Note:* In children, this may be expressed instead by disorganized or agitated behavior.

B. The traumatic event is persistently reexperienced in one (or more) of the following ways:

  (1) recurrent and intrusive distressing recollections of the event, including images, thoughts, or perceptions. *Note:* In young children, repetitive play may occur in which themes or aspects of the trauma are expressed.

  (2) recurrent distressing dreams of the event. *Note:* In children, there may be frightening dreams without recognizable content.

  (3) acting or feeling as if the traumatic event were recurring (includes a sense of reliving the experience, illusions, hallucinations, and dissociative flashback episodes, including those that occur on awakening or when intoxicated). *Note:* In young children, trauma-specific reenactment may occur.

  (4) intense psychological distress at exposure to internal or external cues that symbolize or resemble an aspect of the traumatic event

  (5) physiological reactivity on exposure to internal or external cues that symbolize or resemble an aspect of the traumatic event

C. Persistent avoidance of stimuli associated with the trauma and numbing of general responsiveness (not present before the trauma), as indicated by three (or more) of the following:

  (1) efforts to avoid thoughts, feelings, or conversations associated with the trauma

  (2) efforts to avoid activities, places, or people that arouse recollections of the trauma

  (3) inability to recall an important aspect of the trauma

  (4) markedly diminished interest or participation in significant activities

  (5) feeling of detachment or estrangement from others

  (6) restricted range of affect (e.g., unable to have loving feelings)

  (7) sense of a foreshortened future (e.g., does not expect to have a career, marriage, children, or a normal life span)

D. Persistent symptoms of increased arousal (not present before the trauma), as indicated by two (or more) of the following:

  (1) difficulty falling or staying asleep

  (2) irritability or outbursts of anger

  (3) difficulty concentrating

  (4) hypervigilance

  (5) exaggerated startle response

E. Duration of the disturbance (symptoms in Criteria B, C, and D) is more than 1 month.
F. The disturbance causes clinically significant distress or impairment in social, occupational, or other important areas of functioning.

Specify if:
  Acute: if duration of symptoms is less than 3 months
  Chronic: if duration of symptoms is 3 months or more

Specify if:
  With Delayed Onset: if onset of symptoms is at least 6 months after the stressor

Source: American Psychiatric Association (2000).

Reprinted with permission from the *Diagnostic and Statistical Manual of Mental Disorders, Fourth Edition, Text Revision.* Copyright 2000 American Psychiatric Association.

Children with generalized anxiety disorder are often worried and anxious for no apparent reason.

TABLE 8.12 **Overview of Prevalence Information for Posttraumatic Stress Disorder**

Prevalence	5%–39%
Age	Younger > Older
Gender	Girls > Boys
SES	Unknown pattern
Race/Ethnicity	No differences

children with all these anxiety disorders together in one sample (Albano et al., 2003). For this reason, comorbidity, courses of the disorders, etiology, treatment, and prevention will be discussed broadly for anxiety disorders in childhood and adolescence. Where possible, specific comments will be made about specific disorders.

Comorbidity

Comorbidity is quite common with anxiety disorders in childhood and adolescence (Albano et al., 2003;

Kendall, Brady, & Verduin, 2001). The highest rates of comorbidity are between different anxiety disorders themselves (e.g., separation anxiety disorder and generalized anxiety disorder) and between anxiety disorders and mood disorders (e.g., separation anxiety disorder and major depressive disorder; Eley & Gregory, 2004). For example, within an anxiety disorders clinic, 83% of the children were found to be comorbid with at least one other disorder (Verduin & Kendall, 2003). Regarding the comorbidity of anxiety disorders with other anxiety disorders in that same study, 74% of children with a primary diagnosis of separation anxiety disorder also met criteria for generalized anxiety disorder, 48.6% of children with a primary diagnosis of generalized anxiety disorder also had a secondary diagnosis of specific phobia, and 57% of the children receiving treatment for social phobia also met criteria for generalized anxiety disorder (Verduin & Kendall, 2003). Thus, anxiety disorders are highly comorbid with other anxiety disorders.

Anxiety disorders are also highly comorbid with other internalizing disorders, such as major depression (Verduin & Kendall, 2003) and dysthymia (Masi, Millepiedi et al., 2003). For example, 56% of the children receiving treatment for generalized anxiety disorder also met criteria for major depressive disorder (Masi et al., 2004). Children who were refugees due to a war often experience both PTSD and major depression (Thabet et al., 2004). In a group of children with selective mutism, there were higher rates of comorbidity with social phobia for immigrant children when compared with nonimmigrant/native children (Elizur & Perednik, 2003). Although to a lesser extent than with internalizing disorders, children receiving treatment for anxiety disorders are also often comorbid with externalizing disorders, such as attention-deficit/hyperactivity disorder (Sukhodolsky et al., 2005) and conduct problems (Gregory, Eley, & Plomin, 2004). These patterns of comorbidty also persist into adulthood, with highly stable patterns of anxiety and depression from childhood through adolescence and into adulthood (Roza et al., 2003). Overall, comorbidity is the rule rather than the exception with anxiety disorders in childhood and adolescence, as well as adulthood (Angold et al., 1999).

Course of the Disorder

Different anxiety disorders have different courses within childhood and adolescence. The course of separation anxiety disorder is variable, with some youngsters only having brief problems with the disorder and other youngsters having chronic problems into adolescence

Case Study: Nina, a Girl Who Fears the Nighttime Visitor

At the age of 8, Nina presented as a sad, very quiet child who almost never smiled. She spends most of her time in her bedroom watching television, and she is concerned that no one at school likes her. Nina has trouble sleeping and often has nightmares about her father molesting her. She is afraid that her father (who is in jail) will come into her room and hurt her. She herself is afraid of being sent to jail for doing something wrong. Nina feels that her mother picks on her and favors her siblings. Nina's siblings, 9-year-old Sara and 11-year-old Don, often fight with Nina. When at home, Nina is often irritable and sad. When at school, Nina is often aggressive and disruptive.

Based on this clinical picture, you might be inclined to diagnose Nina with some type of anxiety disorder. Nina's history of sexual abuse by her father, however, would lead clinicians to a diagnosis of posttraumatic stress disorder.

The sexual abuse was discovered when Nina was admitted to a hospital for vaginal bleeding and a vaginal discharge. Nina was diagnosed with vaginal warts and gonorrhea. After this diagnosis, Nina confided to a social worker that her father had been sexually abusing her and (to a lesser extent) her sister, Sara, for the past 2 years. Nina's father would enter the girls' room at night and have vaginal intercourse with Nina. He threatened both girls with severe beatings if they ever told anyone. After witnessing the molestation, Nina's brother, Don, reported the abuse to their mother, who did not believe him. Nina's mother told Nina's father, who then beat Don severely

(which occurred frequently even before the abuse disclosure). Nina and Sara told their mother that Don had not been lying, but she just told them to stop "making up stories."

When the social worker finally interviewed Nina's mother about the sexual abuse, she acknowledged that she suspected that her husband was sexually abusing her daughters, but she reported that she would have feared for her life if she had confronted him about the abuse. In the past 12 years of marriage, Nina's father had beaten Nina's mother severely on several occasions. Nina's mother felt that she could not leave her husband because their religion did not allow divorce.

After the sexual abuse was confirmed, the children were put into foster care, the father was sent to jail, and the mother's parental rights were taken away temporarily due to her failure to protect her children from her husband. The children were then allowed to stay with their maternal grandmother while the case was under investigation. Nina and her siblings were finally returned to their mother after she became involved in psychological assessment and treatment for herself and her children.

This case illustrates that sexual abuse can serve as the trauma that leads to posttraumatic stress disorder. In addition, the mother's initial disbelief in the children's allegations of abuse probably exacerbated the trauma for Nina and her sister.

Source: Spitzer et al. (1994).

(Silverman & Dick-Niederhauser, 2003). Notably, it appears that although some children and adolescents no longer show separation anxiety disorder after a period of time, they tend to show some type of other anxiety disorder unless they receive treatment (Silverman & Dick-Niederhauser, 2004).

Specific phobias are often associated with a trauma and are sometimes quick to remit, but many children experience at least 1 or 2 years of intense phobic reactions, which often could be treated effectively to prevent unnecessary suffering (King et al., 2004). Having a specific phobia earlier in life appears to put children at risk for the development of other phobias throughout childhood, adolescence, and adulthood but does not appear to put the child at risk for other types of anxiety disorders (Silverman & Dick-Niederhauser, 2004).

Social phobia disorder is often a chronic problem throughout childhood and adolescence. It is not uncommon for social phobia to persist into adulthood (Williams et al., 2005).

Obsessive-compulsive disorder is also a long-term problem, and sometimes subthreshold levels of OCD in childhood or adolescence become exacerbated when the child leaves home for college or other independent activities (Albano et al., 2003). Once a child has experienced OCD, it appears that they are vulnerable to OCD throughout their life if not treated effectively, but they do not appear to be more vulnerable to other types of anxiety disorders (Silverman & Dick-Niederhauser, 2004).

Generalized anxiety disorder also tends to be a chronic, long-term problem for children and adolescents. GAD can lead into adult dysfunction unless treated effectively (Flannery-Schroeder, 2004).

Posttraumatic stress disorder is associated with a trauma (by definition) and has a variable course, with some cases remitting quickly and other cases lasting years (McKnight et al., 2004). It may be that there are trauma-specific differences in the course of the disorder, but those patterns have yet to be established.

BOX *8.2*

WAR IS NOT HEALTHY FOR CHILDREN AND OTHER LIVING THINGS

This saying from the late 1960s and early 1970s in the United States remains true currently throughout the world. There are many studies of children who have survived war atrocities, including children and adolescents in Iraq who survived the Gulf War (Dyregrov, Gjestad, & Raundalen, 2002), Palestinian children living in refugee camps (Thabet, Abed, & Vostanis, 2004), and children from Bosnia who had been exposed to both nonviolent and violent war experiences (Allwood, Bell-Dolan, & Husain, 2002). One additional study will be highlighted here to show the range of traumatic experiences that children and adolescents face throughout the world.

It is estimated that 300,000 children across 50 countries are used as child soldiers in armed conflicts. Many of these children are abducted and made to serve against their will. One study of child soldiers in Uganda highlights the plight of these children (Derluyn, Broekaert, Schuyten, & De Temmerman, 2004). A total of 301 youth (248 boys and 53 girls) participated in the study, all of whom were former soldiers for the Ugandan Lord's Resistance Army (LRA). The average age when they were abducted and forced into the army was 12.9 years, and most of the children were in the army for at least 2 years before escaping. A total of 10% of the children were orphans who had lost both parents to the armed conflict. Here are just a few of the experiences of these children:

- 77% witnessed somebody being killed
- 52% were beaten seriously
- 39% personally killed another person
- 39% had to abduct other children

- 27% of those in the Sudan had to drink urine
- 35% of the girls reported being sexually abused while in captivity ("given as wife")
- 18% of the girls gave birth to at least one child while in captivity

A total of 97% of the children reported significant symptoms of PTSD. The intensity of PTSD symptoms was not related to the number of traumatic events reported, the age of the child, or the length of time in captivity. It appears that the traumas were so chronic and pervasive that most children were impacted negatively and for many years after they escaped (Derluyn et al., 2004). If the numbers do not illustrate the horror of these children's experiences, here is a firsthand account by a girl who was made to serve as a Ugandan soldier:

> *I was abducted at night from my home. . . . On the way to Sudan, an abducted boy tried to escape. He was recaptured and I had to kill him, by beating him to death with sticks. One day, I was beaten seriously because I dropped a water container during a gunfire. . . . Several times, I went to villages to loot food and abduct other children. One day, I was given to a commander as his wife. I got pregnant and delivered a boy. In a fight . . . I managed to escape, but I had to leave my child in the bush. I don't know what happened to him. (Derluyn et al., 2004, p. 863).*

Case Study: Quiet Kevin

Kevin is a sweet, energetic, friendly 6-year-old who only speaks to members of his immediate family. Since the age of 2, Kevin has not spoken to anyone else other than his immediate family. He engages in activities outside the family (e.g., playing games at school, going to parties, singing in the grocery store, playing piano), but he will not speak to anyone other than his immediate family in these situations.

During the clinical interview, Kevin whispered answers to his mother but he would not speak to the interviewer directly. Kevin acknowledged that his lack of speaking was a problem that he would like to resolve. He was not, however, able to identify any reason that he did not speak in social situations.

This case represents a relatively clear-cut example of selective mutism. Although many cases of selective mutism do not appear until the child enters school, Kevin's case shows a particularly lengthy course of the disorder. After treatment with behavior therapy and antidepressants, Kevin began to speak periodically in school, and he began to speak to his grandparents on the phone. By the end of the second-grade, Kevin was talking to nearly everyone (except for his former kindergarten teacher), and he appeared to be a happy, exuberant child. Kevin was even voted class president for the following year.

Source: Spitzer et al. (1994).

TABLE 8.13 DSM-IV Diagnostic Criteria for Selective Mutism.

A.	Consistent failure to speak in specific social situations (in which there is an expectation for speaking, e.g., at school) despite speaking in other situations.
B.	The disturbance interferes with educational or occupational achievement or with social communication.
C.	The duration of the disturbance is at least 1 month (not limited to the first month of school).
D.	The failure to speak is not due to a lack of knowledge of, or comfort with, the spoken language required in the social situation.
E.	The disturbance is not better accounted for by a Communication Disorder (e.g., Stuttering) and does not occur exclusively during the course of a Pervasive Developmental Disorder, Schizophrenia, or other Psychotic Disorder.

Source: American Psychiatric Association (2000).

Reprinted with permission from the *Diagnostic and Statistical Manual of Mental Disorders, Fourth Edition, Text Revision.* Copyright 2000 American Psychiatric Association.

TABLE 8.14 Overview of Prevalence Information for Selective Mutism

Prevalence	< 1%
Age	Younger > Older
Gender	Girls > Boys
SES	Unknown patterns
Race/Ethnicity	Unknown patterns

Selective mutism tends to remit on its own within a few months of onset. There are, however, continuing impairments in functioning for many children who do not receive treatment (Bergman et al., 2002).

The basic anxiety, the anxiety of a finite being about the threat of non-being, cannot be eliminated. It belongs to existence itself.

—Paul Johannes Tillich

Etiology

Three primary theoretical models are used currently to help explain the development of anxiety disorders in children and adolescents: biological, behavioral, and cognitive (Albano et al., 2003). Biological models (including genetic and neurological models) have received a great deal of attention recently (Lau, Eley, & Stevenson, 2006; Vasa & Pine, 2004). Much of the support for biological models has come from family studies that have shown strong connections between anxiety disorders in children and anxiety disorders in their parents (Connell & Goodman, 2002). Specifically, children of parents who have an anxiety disorder are more likely than children of nondisordered parents to develop an anxiety disorder (McClure, Brennan, Hammen, & LeBrocque, 2001). Similarly, children diagnosed with an anxiety disorder are more likely to have parents with an anxiety disorder or with high levels of anxiety when compared with parents of nondisordered children (McClure et al., 2001). Both fathers' and mothers'

heightened anxiety levels are associated with children's anxiety (Krain & Kendall, 2000) and symptoms of OCD (Lougee, Perlmutter, Nicolson, Garvey, & Swedo, 2000). These family studies do not address whether the connection is based on genetic transmission or environmental influences. Other twin studies, however, have provided clear evidence of at least some genetic influence in the development of anxiety disorders in childhood (Eley & Gregory, 2004; Lichtenstein & Annas, 2000). There is more evidence for genetic influences in trait (i.e., stable, long-term anxiety) than in state (i.e., temporary) levels of anxiety (Lau et al., 2006).

There has also been a great deal of interest in the neurobiology of anxiety itself. Unfortunately, the majority of the research in this area has been completed with animals and with adult humans (Vasa & Pine, 2004). When children and adolescents are included in studies, there is evidence of structural brain differences between children with and without an anxiety disorder (Vasa & Pine, 2004). In addition, OCD appears to be triggered by streptococcal infections in some children. Known as pediatric autoimmune neuropsychiatric disorders (PANDAS), OCD as well as some tic disorders may be triggered by infections in some children (Lougee et al., 2000; Storch et al., 2004). There is also growing evidence based on neuroimagining through functional MRI assessments that anxious children may have selective attention to fearful or threatening concepts, and they may remember anxiety-producing situations to a greater extent than nonanxiety-producing situations (Vasa & Pine, 2004).

Taken together, these studies suggest that it is likely that both genetic and environmental factors influence the development of anxiety disorders in children and adolescents (Ammerman et al., 2006). As can be seen in Box 8.3, there is also evidence that neurobiological

BOX *8.3*

BEHAVIORAL INHIBITION: COULD IT BE THE COMMON FACTOR TO ANXIETY DISORDERS?

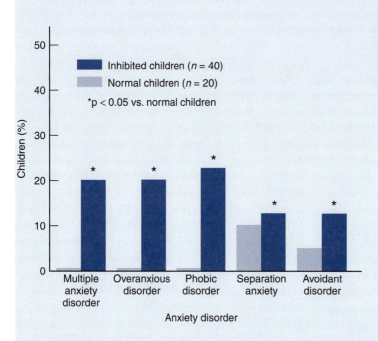

Anxiety Disorders in Inhibited and Normal Children.

Note that Overanxious Disorder is now considered to be comparable to Generalized Anxiety Disorder.
Source: Biederman et al. (1995).

Anyone who has been around a number of newborns and young infants knows that babies enter the world with different temperamental styles (i.e., the way in which they deal with their environment). As noted in chapter 5, some babies are mellow (known as easy babies), some require a high degree of maintenance (known as difficult babies), and some babies are wary of new situations but then seem to enjoy the new situation eventually (known as slow-to-warm-up babies). The study of temperamental style suggests that temperament early in life is related to psychological functioning later in life. Easy babies tend to develop into easy children. Difficult babies tend to develop into difficult children. Slow-to-warm-up babies tend to be wary of new situations throughout their lives. One example of this pattern was shown in a study that followed children for over 7 years. Seven-year olds who had been classified as highly reactive infants (i.e., with difficult temperament) showed higher rates of anxiety than infants with low reactivity levels (Kagan, Snidman, Zentner, & Peterson, 1999).

One interesting slant on temperament research is the exploration of behavioral inhibition. Behavioral inhibition is a traitlike characteristic in which youngsters show hesitation and inhibition in new situations (Biederman, Hirshfeld-Becker, et al., 2001; Fox, Henderson, Marshall, Nichols, & Ghera, 2005). Specifically, babies who show behavioral

inhibition tend to be irritable early in life, tend to be very shy during toddlerhood, and tend to be quiet, introverted, and cautious by the time they reach elementary school (Kagan, 2002). Because of the obvious similarities between inhibition and anxiety, a number of researchers have investigated the connections between behavioral inhibition and anxiety disorders in childhood and adolescence (Prior, Smart, Sanson, & Oberklaid, 2000). As can be seen in the following figure, behaviorally inhibited children are much more likely than noninhibited children to experience an anxiety disorder (Biederman, Rosenbaum, Chaloff, & Kagan, 1995).

Overall, there is compelling evidence that children who show behavioral inhibition very early in life are more at risk for the development of an anxiety disorder in childhood. Because behavioral inhibition is considered to be related primarily to biological and genetic factors, the research on behavioral inhibition provides strong evidence of at least some biological and genetic influences in the development of anxiety disorders in childhood and adolescence. Interestingly, behavioral inhibition is inversely related to the development of disruptive disorders such as oppositional defiant disorder (Biederman et al., 2001; Fox et al., 2005). Thus, behavioral inhibition seems to put children at risk for an anxiety disorder but not other disorders.

factors such as temperament and **behavioral inhibition** (i.e., infants who are irritable, shy, and fearful) are related to the onset of anxiety disorders in children and adolescents (Kagan, 2002; van Brakel, Muris, & Bogels, 2004).

Behavioral models gained a lot of attention after the founder of behaviorism, J. B. Watson, showed that phobias could be learned through classical conditioning (Watson & Rayner, 1920). Little Albert, an 11-month-old boy, developed a phobia of a white rat after the rat was paired with a loud bang that scared the child. Before the sight of the rat was paired with the loud bang, Little Albert showed no fear toward the rat and even seemed interested in playing with the rat. After the rat and the loud bang were paired together five times, Little Albert showed intense fear of the rat. This classic, albeit cruel, study showed that fears could be developed through behavioral principles. Since that time, researchers have explored both classical and operant conditioning models of anxiety disorders as well as social learning models. Operant models suggest that fears are developed from an association between a stimulus (e.g., a dog) and a negative consequence (e.g., a loud and scary bark from the dog). Classical conditioning models suggest that fears are developed from repeated pairings of a stimulus (e.g., an elevator) and an aversive experience (e.g., being trapped in an elevator).

Neither operant models nor classical conditioning models fully explain the development of phobias (King et al., 2004). To address this limitation, the **two-factor theory** (reformulated more recently into the avoidance-conditioning model) combined elements from both operant and classical conditioning (Mowrer, 1960). The initial development of the phobia is developed through classical conditioning (i.e., a previously neutral stimulus is paired with an aversive stimulus) and then the phobia is maintained through operant conditioning (i.e., avoidance of the feared stimulus is associated with reduced distress, which reinforces the avoidance of the feared object).

Social learning is one other variant of the behavioral model that suggests children learn to be fearful from observing others' fear. Much of the research on social learning and anxiety has focused on family influences. For example, the family connections in anxiety disorders is thought to be due to children's observations of their anxious parents (Moore, Whaley, & Sigman, 2004; Turner, Beidel, Roberson-Nay, & Tervo, 2003). It appears that anxious parents do not overtly restrict their children's behavior, but rather that the parents report higher levels of distress when the children are engaging in less-than-sedentary activities, and this distress appears to lead to an emotional climate of anxiety within the family, which then seems to influence children's behavior (Turner et al., 2003). Evidence of this process is seen internationally. For example, one study of Palestinian children in East Jerusalem and the West Bank found that children were more prone to develop PTSD if they witnessed a great deal of anxiety in their own home (Khamis, 2005). Although some fears and anxieties in childhood seem to be developed through behavioral principles, many fears and anxieties are not explained well by the behavioral model (King et al., 2004). The research with monkeys described in Box 8.4 suggests that certain fears may be more easily developed than others (Ohman & Mineka, 2001, 2003).

Cognitive models of anxiety disorders suggest that faulty cognitions and inappropriate focus on anxiety-producing events are at the core of anxiety disorders (Bogels & Zigterman, 2000). The cognitive theory is supported by findings that children with anxiety disorders tend to ruminate about fearful stimuli and tend to misinterpret ambiguous stimuli in an anxiety-provoking manner (Shortt, Barrett, Dadds, & Fox, 2001). There is also evidence, at least with children experiencing OCD, that metacognitions (i.e., thinking about one's own thoughts) are related to anxiety symptoms. An example of a item from a questionnaire on metacognitions is: "I pay close attention to the way my mind works" (Cartwright-Hatton, Mather, Illingworth, Brocki, Harrington, & Wells, (2004). Children and adolescents who showed higher rates of metacognitions also showed greater obsessive and compulsive symptoms (Mather & Cartwright-Hatton, 2004). Overall, there is no question that children with anxiety disorders have faulty cognitions and different cognitive processes than other children. The real question is whether or not these different cognitive processes lead to the development of anxiety disorders in the first place or whether they are a consequence of anxiety disorders that developed through other mechanisms (D'Eramo & Francis, 2004).

One interesting twist on the cognitive theory is that children who experience limited control early in their lives tend to develop cognitive styles (e.g., interpreting events as out of one's control) that are conducive to the development of anxiety disorders (Chorpita, 2001). The lack of control may also intersect with the child's temperament (e.g., behavioral inhibition) and put the child at greater risk for the development of anxiety. This theory allows the possibility that the cognitive style puts the child at risk for the development of an anxiety

BOX *8.4*

CAN A MONKEY LEARN TO FEAR A FLOWER?

Imagine seeing a rhesus monkey become terrified when shown a flower. As unusual as it sounds, a team of researchers headed by Dr. Sue Mineka (Cook & Mineka, 1989; Mineka, Davidson, Cook, & Keir, 1984; reviewed in Ohman & Mineka, 2001, 2003) wanted to explore whether fears could be developed through observational learning. One study found that adolescent monkeys who observed their parents respond fearfully to a snake also responded fearfully to a snake (Mineka et al., 1984). Another study used edited videotapes to explore the biological preparedness of monkeys to fear snakes or other stimuli (Cook & Mineka, 1989). The researchers made a videotape of a

monkey showing an extreme fear response to a snake. The monkey's fear response was then edited into four different types of videotapes, with the feared object edited in as either a toy snake, a toy crocodile, a flower, or a toy rabbit. Other monkeys then viewed these videotapes and only those monkeys who observed the videotape with the toy snake and the toy crocodile acquired a fear. This study suggests that certain stimuli (such as snakes and crocodiles for monkeys) are more conducive to developing phobias than other stimuli (Cook & Mineka, 1989; Ohman & Mineka, 2001, 2003).

disorder but does not necessarily lead to an anxiety disorder.

Related to the cognitive theories of the development of anxiety, there is growing evidence that **emotional regulation** (i.e., the ability to deal effectively with one's emotions) may also play a role in anxiety. For example, in contrast to children without an anxiety disorder, children with an anxiety disorder reported more intense feelings of worry and anger; showed less ability to regulate their emotions of worry, sadness, and anger; and felt less control over their feelings of worry, sadness, and anger (Suveg & Zeman, 2004). Thus, it appears that emotional regulation plays a role in the experience of anxiety. It is unclear whether emotional regulation leads to the development of anxiety disorders or whether it is one of the cooccurring problems associated with anxiety disorders.

Overall, there is some support for all three models of the development of anxiety disorders (biological, behavioral, and cognitive). It is likely that different anxiety disorders may be influenced to different degrees by all three of these causal mechanisms. In fact, there is growing evidence that there may be a hierarchy of risks in the development of anxiety disorders in children. First, children may have a neural network that puts them at risk for the development of an anxiety disorder, this risk may be exacerbated by cognitive or physiological characteristics that make them vulnerable to anxiety, which may then lead to broad behavioral tendencies (such as a difficult temperament), which may then lead to the specific symptoms of anxiety (Vasa & Pine, 2004). It is likely that many children are probably biologically and genetically predetermined to be at risk for the development of an anxiety disorder,

and then environmental influences, behavioral factors, and cognitive functioning influence whether or not an anxiety disorder develops in that particular child (Albano et al., 2003).

To conquer fear is the beginning of wisdom, in the pursuit of truth as in the endeavor after a worthy manner of life.
—Bertrand Russell

Treatment

Although a number of treatments are possible for anxiety disorders, only those with empirical support are discussed here. This research often separates the treatment of phobias from the treatment of other anxiety disorders. Unfortunately, there has been little controlled research to assess the effectiveness of PTSD in children and adolescents (Foa, Keane, & Friedman, 2004). There is growing evidence, however, of the effectiveness of using trauma-focused cognitive-behavioral therapy with children who have been sexually abused (Cohen, Deblinger, & Mannarino, 2005). It appears that the stronger therapeutic alliance (e.g., rapport, trust between client and therapist), the more effective the treatment can be for survivors of sexual abuse who are being treated for PTSD (Cloitre, Stovall-McClough, Miranda, & Chemtob, 2004). For most cognitive-behavioral treatments of anxiety disorders, therapists who showed more collaboration and who were not perceived as too formal were rated as having a better therapeutic alliance with the child, which was ultimately tied to more effective treatment (Creed & Kendall, 2005).

Note that an integral part of providing effective treatment to children with an anxiety disorder is to make sure that the child is first evaluated with evidence-based assessment techniques (Phares & Curley, in press; Silverman & Ollendick, 2005). Once the child is diagnosed correctly and once the child's strengths and weaknesses are identified, then the application of an evidence-based treatment is warranted.

There are a number of evidence-based treatments for specific phobias (D'Eramo & Francis, 2004), including

- Participant modeling (where the child observes others dealing appropriately with the feared stimulus and then actively participates in dealing with the feared stimulus)
- Reinforced practice (where the child interacts with the feared stimulus and is given positive reinforcement for dealing with the feared stimulus)
- Imaginal desensitization (using systematic desensitization with the fear hierarchy imagined by the client, not acted out by the client)
- In vivo desensitization (using systematic desensitization with the fear hierarchy actually experienced by the client, as discussed in the chapter on therapeutic interventions)
- Filmed modeling (where the client watches videotaped actors who are shown dealing appropriately with the feared stimulus)
- Live modeling (where the client observes a person who deals appropriately with the feared stimulus)
- Cognitive–behavioral interventions (where clients learn to challenge faulty cognitions and to replace them with more realistic cognitions)

Because it is used so frequently in evidence-based treatments for phobias, a brief description of systematic desensitization is warranted. **Systematic desensitization** is usually used to decrease anxiety symptoms and specific phobias. The main components of systematic desensitization are exposure to the feared stimulus (either in real life or imagined) and then pairing that exposure to relaxation, with some awareness of the self-talk that the child is exhibiting (Velting, Setzer, & Albano, 2004). First, clients are taught progressive muscle relaxation. Then, with the aid of their therapist, they construct a hierarchy of anxiety-provoking situations or stimuli (known as a fear hierarchy). For example, a child who is phobic of dogs might develop the following hierarchy (from least to most anxiety provoking):

- Thinking about a small dog
- Thinking about a big dog

- Being in the same building as a small dog who is on a chain
- Being in the same building as a big dog who is on a chain
- Being across the room from an unchained small dog
- Being across the room from an unchained big dog
- Having a small dog barking loudly and hovering over the child
- Having a big dog barking loudly and hovering over the child

Fear hierarchies usually have between 20 and 25 items on them, although more recently effective treatments have been conducted with fear hierarchies of about 10 items (Velting et al., 2004). After the hierarchy is established, the therapist has the child use his or her relaxation strategies while imagining each step of the hierarchy (beginning with the least-anxiety-provoking step). Children would only move on to the next item of the hierarchy once they mastered relaxation in association with the previous anxiety-provoking item. Eventually, each of the items on the hierarchy are acted out behaviorally while being paired with relaxation. Again, children would move to the next step on their hierarchy only after feeling relaxed with the previous behaviors. Systematic desensitization is quite effective in treating specific phobias and other focused anxieties in childhood and adolescence. Interestingly, the use of systematic desensitization is quite similar for adults as well as children (Donohue & Johnston, 2002).

Treatments for social phobia are somewhat similar to the treatments for specific phobia, but they are a bit more complex. One evidence-based treatment of social phobia, the Cognitive Behavioral Group Treatment for Adolescent Social Phobia, includes a number of different modules, including psychoeducation, social skills training, cognitive restructuring, problem solving, and exposure (Albano et al., 2003). Like with the treatment of specific phobias, this treatment usually includes the use of a fear hierarchy that the child then works to master without fear (Velting et al., 2004).

I'm afraid of lions and tigers, bears, bombs, fires, and very scary monsters.

—7-year-old, Yamikani, from Zimbabwe

With regard to the treatment of other anxiety disorders, cognitive–behavioral procedures (with or without family anxiety management training) have shown evidence of helping alleviate most other anxiety disorders (Chorpita, Taylor, Francis, Moffitt, & Austin, 2004;

Compton et al., 2004; Kendall & Suveg, 2006), including social phobia (Baer & Garland, 2005) and OCD (Piacentini & Langley, 2004; Piacentini et al., 2006). There are four primary components to cognitive–behavioral interventions for anxiety disorders (Kendall, Hudson, Choudhury, Webb, & Pimentel, 2005):

• Children learn to recognize feelings of anxiety and somatic complaints in response to anxiety.

• Children learn to question and clarify unrealistic and negative cognitions when exposed to an anxiety-producing scenario.

• Children are taught to make a plan for how to cope with the anxiety-provoking situation in the future.

• Children are taught to evaluate their success at dealing with an anxiety-provoking situation and to reward themselves for coping well with the situation.

Note that these techniques sound like they might be difficult to convey to a child, but the ways that the techniques are implemented tend to be very child friendly. For example, in one of the best-known cognitive–behavioral treatments for anxiety disorders, children use a "Coping Cat" workbook that shows the different ways that a frightened versus secure cat might deal with different situations. As illustrated in Figure 8.1, children can be exposed to evidence-based techniques in a way that is engaging and accessible for them (Kendall, 1992).

This cognitive–behavioral treatment program can be used with children alone (Kendall et al., 2005) or can be enhanced with **family anxiety management training** (Barrett, Duffy, Dadds, & Rapee, 2001; Barrett & Shortt, 2003). Family anxiety management training involves trying to empower parents and children to become experts in coping with anxiety. Specifically, parents are taught basic behavioral techniques so that they can respond appropriately to their child's anxiety (Dadds et al., 2004). Therapists also helped parents to identify their own concerns and anxieties as well as to learn problem-solving techniques for dealing with these concerns. Parents and children are also taught communication skills. Overall, cognitive–behavioral procedures with or without family anxiety management training have been found to be effective in alleviating anxiety disorders (Barrett et al., 2001; Kendall et al., 2005; Rapee, Abbott, & Lyneham, 2006). These treatments are effective with children, regardless of whether or not their anxiety disorder is comorbid with another disorder (Kendall, Aschenbrand, & Hudson, 2003; Shortt, Barrett, & Fox, 2001). There is also growing evidence that attachment-based family therapy, in conjunction with cognitive–behavioral therapy, can help anxious youth (Siqueland, Rynn, & Diamond, 2005).

Medication for anxiety disorders should be mentioned briefly. Although there is support for use of **anxiolytic agents** (antianxiety medications) with adults, there is limited evidence for the effectiveness of anxiolytic agents with children (Brown et al., 2005; Phelps et al., 2002). Even when medications are paired with therapeutic interventions, only modest effectiveness rates are found (Pediatric OCD Treatment Study/POTS Team, 2004). Specifically, the following effectiveness rates (i.e., what percentage of children were helped by the interventions) were found in a study of children with OCD (Pediatric OCD Treatment Study/POTS Team, 2004):

• 3.6%: Placebo

• 21.4%: Medication only (Sertraline/Zoloft)

• 39.3%: Cognitive–behavior therapy only

• 53.6%: Medication plus cognitive–behavior therapy

This study suggests that not all children with an anxiety disorder can be helped by medication, even when it is combined with a therapeutic intervention (Pediatric OCD Treatment Study/POTS Team, 2004).

FIGURE 8.1   Sample Page from *Coping Cat Workbook.*

With regard to the evaluation of medications by themselves, a number of studies showed that anxiolytic agents were no more effective than placebo pills with the treatment of a number of anxiety disorders in childhood and adolescence (Brown et al., 2005; Phelps et al., 2002). The two anxiolytic medications that have been shown to be more effective than placebo are Clonazepam/Klonopin to treat separation anxiety disorder and generalized anxiety disorder and Clomipramine/Anafranil to treat OCD. Note, however, that the serious side effects of Clomipramine/Anafranil suggest that it should not be used with children or adolescents (Phelps et al., 2002).

Antidepressants have also been used extensively to treat anxiety disorders (Brown et al., 2005). In general, there is limited empirical support for the use of antidepressants with children who are experiencing an anxiety disorder. There is, however, some empirical support for the use of Fluoxetine/Prozac or Sertraline/Zoloft in the treatment of OCD, although combinations of medication and cognitive–behavioral treatment appear to provide the most effective treatment of OCD (Liebowitz et al., 2002; Pediatric OCD Treatment Study/POTS Team, 2004). Children who have comorbid disorders, especially conduct disorder or bipolar disorder, and children who have more severe impairment at the beginning of treatment show the lowest

amount of improvement in psychopharmacological interventions for OCD (Masi et al., 2005). In chapter 4, there is a more thorough discussion of the pros and cons of using psychopharmacological interventions with children and adolescents.

Overall, therapies that are considered behavioral and cognitive–behavioral in nature have received the most empirical support for the treatment of anxiety disorders with children and adolescents. Further research is needed to establish which treatments work best for which anxiety disorders (Brown et al., 2005). In addition, a great deal more research is needed with antianxiety medications (DuPaul et al., 2003). In considering different treatments, it is also important for clinicians to remember that there are normal levels of worries in children and their parents (see Box 8.5).

Courage is resistance to fear, mastery of fear, not absence of fear.

—Mark Twain

Prevention

Before discussing human prevention programs, a brief discussion of an animal study is warranted. There has been speculation that youth can be inoculated from the extremely adverse effects of stress by being exposed to moderate levels of stress in their early life.

BOX 8.5

WHAT DO CHILDREN AND THEIR PARENTS WORRY ABOUT?

Although the specific contents of worries and fears are not usually relevant to the treatment or prevention of anxiety disorders, it is interesting to note what types of worries and fears children and their parents experience. As can be seen following, certain fears (e.g., animals) are consistent across age groups, but other fears, worries, and nightmares change developmentally. For example, the frequency of fears and nightmares related to imaginary creatures lessened with age, whereas the frequency of fears and nightmares related to test performance increased with age (Muris, Merckelbach, Gadet, & Moulaert, 2000). Other findings from this study include

- The number one fear listed for children aged 4–6, 7–9, and 10–12 was a fear of animals.
- Children aged 4–6 and 7–9 listed imaginary creatures as their second fear and their most frequent nightmare.
- Children aged 10–12 listed social threats as their second most common fear and being kidnaped as their most common nightmare.

When parents are asked about their worries about their children, they tend to report concerns over car accidents, bicycle accidents, abduction, head injuries, exposure to environmental toxins, discipline, values, affection, too much television, proper nutrition, and finances (Stickler, 1996). This study also found that parents' fears tended to be influenced by media coverage. Specifically, parents often had exaggerated or unfounded fears based on extensive media coverage on a low-frequency event (such as abduction by a stranger; Stickler, 1996). A number of authors have written about the extreme media coverage of horrific, yet rare events like child abduction, while all but ignoring other more common and equally horrific events like chronic child sexual abuse within the family (Beyer & Beasley, 2003; Renk, Liljequist, Steinberg, Bosco, & Phares, 2002; Zgoba, 2004).

It would be potentially unethical to design a study whereby infants and toddlers were intentionally exposed to moderately stressful situations, but conducting this research with nonhuman primates might help inform human researchers and clinicians. One prospective study of squirrel monkeys suggested that stress inoculation can prevent anxiety in the future (Parker, Buckmaster, Schatzberg, & Lyons, 2004). Specifically, infant squirrel monkeys were randomly assigned to either receive moderately stressful conditions early in their lives or to receive regular care. Approximately a year later, they were tested to see their reactions to a different stressful situation. The moneys who had been exposed to stressors early in life appeared to have been "inoculated," given that they showed reduced distress and better physiological functioning in the face of the later stressful situations. This type of research design might help lead researchers design safe, ethical prevention programs for humans that innoculate youngsters against negative effects from later stressful situations.

With humans, there have been a number of prevention programs in the area of anxiety disorders (Barrett & Turner, 2004; Hayes, 2004). One cognitive–behavioral program in Australia will be highlighted because it shows a nice combination of selective and indicated prevention efforts (Dadds, Spence, Holland, Barrett, & Laurens, 1997). These researchers wanted to help children who were at risk for developing anxiety disorders as well as those children who had already developed mild anxiety disorders. The prevention and early intervention efforts were completed in an urban area, with a diverse sample of children aged 7 to 14. As is consistent with prevention programs, the researchers had a series of screenings to identify children who were appropriate for the program:

- Nearly 2,000 children completed a self-report measure of anxiety (the Revised Children's Manifest Anxiety Scale; Reynolds & Richmond, 1978).

- Teachers were asked to nominate up to three children in their classroom who showed the highest levels of anxiety (as illustrated by shyness, nervousness, fearfulness, and inhibition) to possibly include these students in the program.

- Teachers were asked to nominate up to three children in their classroom who showed the highest levels of disruptive behavior (as illustrated by aggression, impulsivity, and noncompliance) to possibly exclude these students from the program.

- Children identified as appropriate in these previous steps were included in a list that was sent back to teachers to ensure that all of the students were actually appropriate for the program (e.g., the students and their parents spoke English, the students were not developmentally delayed, the students did not have a severe learning disability).

- The parents of children who remained viable program participants were then contacted to have the program explained to them. Parents were then asked to complete diagnostic interviews and behavior ratings for their children.

Based on these screening procedures, a total of 128 children were identified as at-risk for the development of an anxiety disorder or already met criteria for an anxiety disorder and had parents who were interested in the program. Half of the children received the preventive intervention program, and half of the children were put into the monitoring control condition (i.e., their progress was monitored, but they did not receive any active preventive interventions). The preventive intervention program focused on a FEAR plan:

- **F**eel good by learning to relax.

- **E**xpect good things to happen by using positive self-talk.

- **A**ctions are important, so make a plan about how to deal with anxiety-provoking stimuli.

- **R**eward yourself for trying to overcome your fears.

The program lasted for 10 weeks, with sessions that lasted 1 to 2 hours. Parents were also given three sessions that focused on helping their children cope with anxiety and on helping them deal with their own anxiety. Children's functioning was evaluated at the end of the intervention/monitoring period and then again at a 6-month follow-up. As can be seen in Figure 8.2, significant improvements emerged for the children in the prevention program, both in terms of reductions in anxiety disorders and in the prevention of onset of new anxiety disorders. Overall, this study shows that prevention and early intervention programs can be effective and are an important resource in the prevention of anxiety disorders.

Other efforts in the prevention of anxiety disorders have also been completed. One successful selective mental health prevention program identified preschool children who showed high levels of withdrawal and inhibition (Rapee, Kennedy, Ingram, Edwards, & Sweeney, 2005). Families were randomly assigned to no treatment control or to receive a 6-session parent education prevention program. At the end of the program and again at 6-month follow-up, children whose parents

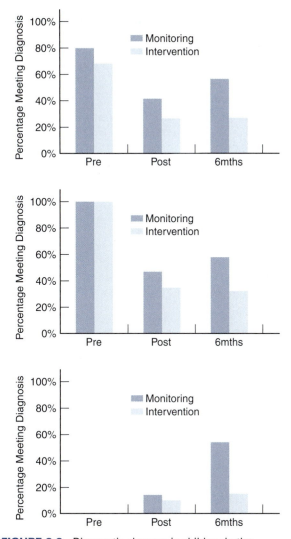

FIGURE 8.2 Diagnostic changes in children in the intervention and monitoring groups at postintervention (post) and 6-month follow-up (6 months) for all children (top panel), children who met *Diagnostic and Statistical Manual of Mental Disorders (4th ed.)* criteria for an anxiety disorder at preintervention (pre; middle panel), and children who were diagnosis-free at preintervention (bottom panel).

Source: Dadds et al. (1997).

participated in the parent education prevention program showed fewer anxiety disorder diagnoses in contrast to children in the control group (Rapee et al., 2005). This program was seen as cost effective and easily administered, so there is hope that it could be disseminated on a large-scale basis.

In terms of indicated prevention efforts, one additional benefit of effective treatment is that it can serve as an indicated prevention that prevents the onset of additional problems in the child (Knitzer, 2000). For example, in contrast to children who did not respond successfully to cognitive–behavioral treatment for anxiety disorders, children who were successfully treated for anxiety disorders were less likely to show substance use and depression 7 years later as adolescents (Kendall, Safford, Flannery-Schroeder, & Webb, 2004). Overall, there are a number of promising universal, selective, and indicated prevention strategies, but more work is needed to ascertain which programs work under which circumstances and for which children. As noted in Box 8.6, children's fears differ somewhat around the world, so prevention programs would need to address the specific concerns of the country in which the program was to be implemented.

ANXIETY CONCEPTUALIZED IN A DIMENSIONAL MANNER

The topic of anxiety has been studied extensively from a dimensional perspective. Much of the focus of this dimensional research has examined the interconnections between anxiety and depression (e.g., Chorpita, Plummer, & Moffitt, 2000). The combination of anxiety and depression has been referred to as **negative affect** (Austin & Chorpita, 2004; Jacques & Mash, 2004). It appears that the experience of negative affect is common to both anxiety and depression, but children who experience anxiety also show physiological hyperarousal (e.g., trouble breathing, nauseous, sweaty palms), whereas children who experience depression also experience anhedonia (i.e., not feeling joy or happiness; Joiner et al., 1996). In addition, studies of the discriminant validity of anxiety measures and of depression measures have shown that distinct factors of anxiety and depression can be found separately (Ruggiero, Morris, Beidel, Scotti, & McLeer, 1999), although this is not always the case. For example, in a meta-analysis of the major assessment questionnaires in the anxiety area, the measures were able to reliably distinguish between anxious youth and those with no emotional problems, and anxious youth and those with externalizing problems, but the measures could not reliably differentiate between anxious youth and depressed youth (Seligman, Ollendick, Langley, & Baldacci, 2004). Thus, there is some evidence to suggest that children's feelings of anxiety are distinguishable from their feelings of depression, but there is clearly an overlap between anxiety and depression (Lahey et al., 2004).

BOX 8.6

FEARS ACROSS THE GLOBE

What children fear depends somewhat on the country in which they live and their SES circumstances.

- Chinese children are more likely than children from Western cultures to fear social-evaluative situations (e.g., getting poor grades, performing poorly in a play).
- Children from Carribean nations are more likely than children from Western cultures to fear things related to nature (e.g., animals, darkness).
- Regarding their fears of animals, children from more impoverished settings tend to fear rats and cockroaches, whereas children from middle and upper SES settings tend to fear poisonous insects.
- Children from lower SES families tend to experience fear related to the necessities of life (e.g., having something to eat, safety), whereas children from middle and higher SES families tend not to have intense fears about the basic necessities.

Source: Barrios & O'Dell (1998).

One of the ways of understanding anxiety from a dimensional perspective is to consider two different types of anxiety: **state anxiety** (i.e., anxiety that is based on the situation and is relatively temporary) and **trait anxiety** (i.e., anxiety that is more chronic and stable across situations). This distinction was popularized by the use of the State-Trait Anxiety Inventory for Children (STAIC; Spielberger, Edwards, & Lushene, 1973), which assesses both situational and chronic levels of anxiety. Interest in state and trait distinctions in anxiety continue to be of interest to researchers and clinicians (Lau et al., 2006). Other self-report measures that are used to assess anxiety from a dimensional perspective include the Revised Children's Manifest Anxiety Scale (RCMAS; Reynolds & Richmond, 1997) and the Fear Survey Schedule for Children-Revised (FSSC-R; Ollendick, 1983). These measures assess global levels of anxiety and fear, rather than making the distinction between state and trait anxiety.

One other way that researchers and clinicians have investigated anxiety from a dimensional perspective is to explore children's and adolescents' worries and fears (Laugesen, Dugas, & Bukowski, 2003). These investigations have focused largely on developmental differences in worries and have highlighted normative developmental patterns for children and adolescents in their worries and fears. For example, in a nonclinical population, worries about separation from parents were highest with children aged 6 to 9, death and danger worries were highest with preteens aged 10 to 13, and social anxiety as well as concerns about failure and criticism were highest for adolescents aged 14 to 17 (Weems & Costa, 2005). These types of studies highlight the importance of understanding fears and worries from a dimensional and normative basis to help inform the study and treatment of clinical levels of anxiety.

Risk Factors

A number of risk factors have been identified that are associated with the development of high levels of anxiety (Donovan & Spence, 2000). In addition to the causative risk factors discussed in the etiology section earlier (e.g., behavioral inhibition, genetic predisposition, anxious parents), a number of factors seem to put children at risk for problems with anxiety.

Similar to the risk for depression, infants and preschoolers with insecure attachment with their primary caregiver are at risk for the development of high levels of anxiety (Shamir-Essakow, Ungerer, & Rapee, 2005). Early adversities in children's lives, including maternal prenatal stress and multiple father figures, were associated with greater levels of anxiety in adolescents but not greater levels of depression (Phillips, Hammen, Brennan, Najman, & Bor, 2005). Early childhood physical abuse and sexual abuse appears to put children at risk for later anxiety, and this pattern appears consistent cross-culturally (Chaffin, Silovsky, & Vaughn, 2005; Libby, Orton, Novins, Beals, & Manson, 2005; Owens & Chard, 2003). Even spanking can be associated with increased fears and anxiety in children, as evidenced in the "You Decide" section.

In addition, one study explored recent achievements and adversities in school-aged children (Goodyer, Wright, & Altham, 1990). The researchers found that children who had not had any recent social achievements (e.g., making new friends, being voted into a desirable position at school) and who also had poor friendships appeared to be at greater risk for the development of

Case Study: Jennifer—A Case Example of Fears and Anxieties

Jennifer is an 8-year-old girl who is terribly frightened by insects and who experiences extreme amounts of worry and somatic complaints. She often avoids locations where she might run across insects (such as the kitchen). Her worries center around her "not being good enough," "making mistakes," "being teased by others," and "being in accidents." The somatic complaints, which have no medical cause, include headaches, stomachaches, sweating, and a racing heart when she sees an insect.

For the assessment, Jennifer was interviewed with the Anxiety Disorders Interview Schedule for Children (ADIS-C), and she completed a number of self-report questionnaires such as the Fear Survey Schedule for Children-Revised (FSSC-R), the Revised Children's Manifest Anxiety Scale (RCMAS), and the State-Trait Anxiety Inventory for Children (STAIC). In addition, Jennifer's mother also completed the ADIS-Parent

version, the FSSC-R, and the RCMAS to report on Jennifer's fears and anxieties. During the assessment, Jennifer's mother also acknowledged that she was afraid of insects herself and that she had always been a "worrier." Based on this evaluation, Jennifer was found to have excessive levels of fear and anxiety.

Jennifer and her mother were invited to participate in a 10-week cognitive–behavioral treatment program that was geared toward the alleviation of fears and anxiety. With the use of fear hierarchies, positive reinforcement, and self-control training, Jennifer was able to conquer her fear of insects. Assessments at the end of treatment and follow-up assessments at 3, 6, and 12 months after treatment, showed that Jennifer's fears and worries had decreased significantly and had remained low even a year after treatment.

Source: Silverman & Ginsburg (1995).

---

anxiety problems as well as problems with depression (Goodyer et al., 1990).

Interestingly, some factors are related to risk for certain anxiety problems but not others. Histories of a single-parent household, family problems, low parental education, poverty, and parental antisocial problems were associated with risk for separation anxiety disorder but not generalized anxiety disorder (Costello & Angold, 1995). School failure, stressful life events, and parental psychological symptoms were associated with risk for generalized anxiety disorder but not separation anxiety disorder in children (Costello & Angold, 1995). Anxiety problems in adolescence were associated with earlier

stressful life events, continuing adversity, and parental psychopathology (Costello & Angold, 1995). Living in a violent, inner-city community was associated with heightened levels of anxiety, especially in relation to exposure to gun violence (Duncan, 1996). Overall, there are a number of risk factors associated with the development of anxiety problems.

Protective Factors

A number of factors are also associated with protecting children from the development of anxiety problems. Family support was found to protect against the

---

YOU DECIDE: SHOULD PARENTS USE SPANKING TO HELP DEAL WITH THEIR CHILDREN'S TROUBLING BEHAVIOR?

Yes

- Spanking can be effective in the short run and when it is delivered appropriately (e.g., in a controlled, planned manner rather than in a fit of parental rage), then spanking can be part of an effective parenting strategy (Barkley, 1997b).
- If used in moderation, spanking can be a salient way of gaining the child's attention and helping the child gain back his or her self-control (Baumrind, Cowan, & Larzelere, 2002).

No

- Spanking leads to fear of the parent, and it does not teach the child what to do but rather just what not to do. Spanking is associated with an increase in children's emotional/behavioral problems (Gershoff, 2002).
- Spanking is not effective in the long run. Rather, consistent consequences to behaviors and the use of rewards for appropriate behavior are more effective in the long run than spanking (American Academy of Pediatrics, 2005).

So, should parents use spanking to help deal with their children's troubling behavior? You decide.

development of anxiety problems and worries in a sample of urban children exposed to community violence (White, Bruce, Farrell, & Kliewer, 1998). Similarly, in a study of African-American sixth-graders who were exposed to family stressors, it was found that parental warmth and kin support (e.g., support from grandparents, aunts, and uncles) were associated with decreased anxiety and shyness (McCabe, Clark, & Barnett, 1999). Thus, parental warmth and kinship social support served as protective factors from the development of anxiety even in children from highly stressed family environments.

On the individual level, personal feelings of perceived competence and positive self-views were associated with decreased risk for anxiety problems in an urban sample of African-American and Caucasian-American children (Magnus, Cowen, Wyman, Fagen, & Work, 1999). In a follow-up with child survivors of Nazi Germany, personal characteristics of altruism and humor appeared to serve as protective factors against the development of PTSD (Bluglass, 2003). Overall, a number of protective factors have been found to decrease the likelihood of anxiety problems in childhood. More research is needed in this area to ascertain whether there are other protective factors that could be used to inform prevention programs (Donovan & Spence, 2000).

SUMMARY AND KEY CONCEPTS

Separation Anxiety Disorder.   **Separation anxiety disorder** occurs when a child experiences extreme levels of distress on separating from his or her primary caretakers. Often, separation anxiety disorder shows **spontaneous remission,** whereby the disorder remits without therapeutic intervention.

Specific Phobias.   **Specific phobias** are extreme and unrealistic fears of objects or situations. **School refusal** (refusing to go to school) or **school phobia** (fearing to go to school) are sometimes associated with a specific phobia, but are often associated with other anxiety disorders.

Social Phobia.   **Social phobia** occurs when children fear social situations due to concerns about being embarrassed or humiliated. The social situations must include dealing with peers and not just adults.

Obsessive-Compulsive Disorder.   **Obsessive-compulsive disorder (OCD)** occurs when children experience **obsessions** (recurrent, disordered thoughts) or **compulsions** (repetitive, disordered behaviors). Often, the compulsions are acted on to reduce anxiety related to the obsessions.

Generalized Anxiety Disorder.   **Generalized anxiety disorder (GAD)** occurs when children experience pervasive and chronic levels of anxiety. By definition, the anxiety is not focused on one object or situation (as with specific phobia) nor is it associated with social interactions (as with social phobia).

Posttraumatic Stress Disorder.   **Posttraumatic stress disorder (PTSD)** occurs when children deal with a trauma in an even more negative manner than would be expected. Traumas include sexual abuse, physical abuse, a severe car accident, or war. Children often experience psychological symptoms, nightmares, and flashbacks related to the trauma.

Selective Mutism.   **Selective mutism** occurs when children speak in one setting but do not speak in another setting. This disorder is now thought to be related to anxiety rather than oppositional behavior.

All Anxiety Disorders of Childhood and Adolescence. There are high rates of comorbidity for anxiety disorders in childhood and adolescence. The courses of anxiety disorders vary. Specific phobias and selective mutism are usually the least chronic, whereas OCD and GAD tend to last for long periods of time and often into adulthood.

The primary etiological explanations of anxiety disorders are biological, behavioral, and cognitive. Family studies, twin studies, and work on **behavioral inhibition** (a temperamental style in which infants are irritable, shy, and fearful) all support a biological explanation of many anxiety disorders of childhood. Behavioral models include classical conditioning and operant conditioning. The **two-factor theory** combines classical conditioning and operant conditioning in explaining the development and maintenance of anxiety disorders. Cognitive theories focus on maladaptive cognitions in the development of anxiety disorders. **Emotional regulation** (the ability to control one's emotions) has also been implicated in the experience of anxiety. The most likely explanation encompasses some combination of all these theoretical models.

The primary treatments for anxiety disorders in childhood and adolescence focus on behavioral and cognitive–behavioral interventions. For example, **systematic desensitization** pairs relaxation with progressively anxiety-producing situations from a hierarchy of fears. Some cognitive–behavioral interventions also include parents in the treatment, with a **family anxiety management training** component to the treatment. Medications, such as **anxiolytic agents** (which are antianxiety medications) and antidepressants have been used to treat anxiety disorders in children and adolescents. In addition to these treatments, a number of prevention programs have been found to be effective in preventing the onset and reoccurrence of anxiety disorders.

Anxiety Conceptualized in a Dimensional Manner.   A great deal of work has explored anxiety from a dimensional perspective. Much of this work has explored the overlap between anxiety and depression, which is a concept known as **negative affect.** Anxiety has also been conceptualized in a dimensional manner by exploring **state anxiety** (i.e., situationally based anxiety) and **trait anxiety** (i.e., chronic and stable levels of anxiety). There are a number of risk factors for the development of anxiety problems. Absence of social achievements, poor friendships, family adversity, school difficulties, and parental psychological problems have all been linked to the development of at least one type of anxiety disorder. Protective factors have also been identified that decrease the likelihood of developing an anxiety disorder. Family support, parental warmth, perceived competence, and positive self-views have all been identified as factors that protect against the development of anxiety problems.

KEY TERMS

separation anxiety disorder
spontaneous remission
specific phobias
school refusal
school phobia

social phobia
obsessive-compulsive disorder (OCD)
obsessions
compulsions

generalized anxiety disorder (GAD)
posttraumatic stress disorder (PTSD)
selective mutism
behavioral inhibition

two-factor theory
emotional regulation
systematic desensitization
family anxiety management training

anxiolytic agents
negative affect
state anxiety
trait anxiety

SUGGESTED READINGS

Colas, Emily. *Just Checking: Scenes from the Life of an Obsessive-Compulsive*. New York: Pocket Books, 1998. The author describes her lifetime struggle with obsessive-compulsive disorder, with special attention to overcoming the debilitating disorder.

Rothenberg, Laura. *Breathing for a Living: A Memoir*. New York: Hyperion, 2003. The author writes about her fear of death and her preoccupation with her own mortality. These characteristics may be interpreted as psychopathology until you find out that the author has cystic fibrosis and only has a life expectancy of 28 years.

SUGGESTED VIEWINGS

Lemony Snicket's A Series of Unfortunate Events. (2004). A number of themes in this movie are relevant to developmental psychopathology, including bereaved children, inconsistent parenting behaviors, and environmental chaos. The theme of anxiety in a parental figure is particularly well illustrated by the aunt who comes to an unfortunate demise with leeches. Knowing about this book and film series will also help keep you informed of child clients' interests.

Spellbound. (2002). Instead of focusing on anxiety disorders, it is also important to explore normative levels of anxiety in stressful situations. This documentary follows a series of children and adolescents who are seeking to become national champions in a spelling bee contest. In addition to the focus on anxiety, this film shows family factors that are associated with high achievement and cultural issues related to perfection.

ATTENTION-DEFICIT/HYPERACTIVITY DISORDER AND RELATED PROBLEMS

CHAPTER SUMMARY

Delay does not spoil things; it makes them better.
—Proverb of Africa

ATTENTION-DEFICIT/HYPERACTIVITY DISORDER

You have seen them in the grocery store. You have heard them in the movie theatre. You have seen them run the aisles of the airplane as you are waiting for the flight to take off. You probably even remember them from your own years in elementary school. They are children with an excessive amount of energy and a high level of activity. But are they children who meet criteria for the diagnosis of attention-deficit/hyperactivity disorder (ADHD)?

There is probably no childhood disorder that has created more controversy and more public debate than ADHD (American Academy of Pediatrics, 2004a; Milich, Balentine, & Lynam, 2001). Some professionals feel that ADHD is extremely prevalent among children and that medication is effective in reducing the symptoms (e.g., Hechtman, Abikoff, & Jensen, 2005). Other professionals feel that ADHD is overdiagnosed significantly and that medicating active children is an attempt to create docile children (e.g., Breggin, 2001b, 2002). Both of these two ends of the continuum will be discussed in this chapter. First, the current definitions of ADHD within the mainstream professional community will be presented. Later in the chapter, criticisms of these

definitions will be presented and alternative conceptualizations of high levels of activity will be proposed.

What we now know as attention-deficit/hyperactivity disorder has a long and variable history (Barkley, 2006; Conners, 2000). As early as 1902, professionals wrote about children who showed severe levels of inattention and lack of impulse control. From that time until the mid-1960s, various terms that focused on brain damage were used to describe these children, such as minimal brain damage syndrome and minimal brain dysfunction (Conners, 2000).

In the first edition of *DSM,* there were no specific diagnoses for what we now know as ADHD (American Psychiatric Association, 1952). A number of acute brain disorders could have been used to encompass minimal brain dysfunctions, but no specific diagnoses related to the constellation of hyperactivity, impulsivity, and inattention. In 1968, *DSM-II* presented the diagnostic category of **hyperkinetic reaction of childhood or adolescence** (American Psychiatric Association, 1968). The entire definition is as follows:

This disorder is characterized by overactivity, restlessness, distractibility, and short attention span, especially in young children; the behavior usually diminishes in adolescence. If this behavior is caused by brain damage, it should be diagnosed under the appropriate non-psychotic organic brain syndrome. (p. 50)
—**Reprinted with permission from the *Diagnostic and Statistical Manual of Mental Disorders, Second Edition.* Copyright 1968 American Psychiatric Association.**

Case Study: Eddie, the Boy Who Was into Everything

At the age of 9, Eddie was referred to a psychiatrist due to his behavior at school. In the past year, he had been suspended twice for hyperactive and impulsive behavior. Most recently, he climbed onto the overhead lights of the classroom and caused an uproar in the class when he could not get himself down. His teachers complain that other children cannot concentrate when Eddie is in the room because he walks around constantly. Even when he is seated, his rapid foot and hand movements are disruptive to the other children. Eddie has almost no friends and does not play games with other children due to his impulsivity and overly active behavior. He likes to play with his dog after school or ride his bike alone.

Eddie's mother reports that he has been excessively active since he was a toddler. By the age of 3, Eddie would awaken at 4:30 AM each day and go downstairs without any supervision. At times, he would "demolish" the kitchen or living room, and at other times he would leave the house by himself. Once when he was 4 years old, he was found walking alone on a busy street in the early morning. Luckily, a passerby rescued him before he got into traffic.

After being rejected by a preschool because of his hyperactivity and impulsivity, Eddie attended a kindergarten and had a very difficult year due to his behavior. For first and second grade, he attended a special behavioral program. Most recently, he was allowed to attend a regular education class, with pullout services for help with his behavior. Within his own classroom, Eddie is so impulsive and impatient that he is not able to play games with other children.

A psychological assessment of Eddie revealed that he has average intellectual functioning, with academic achievement that is slightly below average. According to the psychologist, Eddie's attention span is "virtually nonexistent." Eddie shows symptoms of hyperactivity, impulsivity, and inattention. After the evaluation, Eddie received stimulant medication (methylphenidate) and appeared to be more in control of his behavior when he took the medication.

Source: Spitzer et al. (1994).

Although this definition is somewhat similar to the current definition of ADHD, it was not until the publication of *DSM-III* that the term *attention-deficit disorder* (ADD) was publicized widely and that the constellation of hyperactivity, impulsivity, and inattention was conceptualized (American Psychiatric Association, 1980). The primary relevant diagnoses in *DSM-III* were: attention deficit disorder with hyperactivity (ADD with H) and attention deficit disorder without hyperactivity (ADD without H). Note that ADD without H was acknowledged as having limited empirical evidence, with unknown prevalence rates and etiological information (American Psychiatric Association, 1980). Partly for this reason, and partly for political reasons by the task force that wrote *DSM-III-R,* the diagnosis of ADD without H was dropped from the new diagnostic criteria in *DSM-III-R* (Barkley, 2006). The diagnosis of undifferentiated attention-deficit disorder was added to the end of the section on Disorders Usually First Evident in Infancy, Childhood, or Adolescence (American Psychiatric Association, 1987). This disorder was described the following way:

This is a residual category for disturbance in which the predominant feature is the persistence of developmentally inappropriate and marked inattention that is not a symptom of another disorder, such as Mental Retardation or Attention-Deficit Hyperactivity Disorder, or of a disorganized and chaotic environment. Some of the disturbances that in DSM-III would have been categorized as Attention Deficit Disorder without Hyperactivity would be included in this category. Research is necessary to determine if this is a valid diagnostic category and, if so, how it should be defined. (p. 95)

—**Reprinted with permission from the** *Diagnostic and Statistical Manual of Mental Disorders, Third Edition, Revised.* **Copyright 1987 American Psychiatric Association.**

By the time of the publication of *DSM-IV* (American Psychiatric Association, 1994) and *DSM-IV-TR* (American Psychiatric Association, 2000) a form of ADD without H was back in the limelight. As can be seen in Table 9.1, the three subtypes of attention-deficit/hyperactivity disorder include combined type (with both hyperactivity-impulsivity and inattention), predominantly inattentive type (which is comparable to ADD without H in *DSM-III*), and predominantly hyperactive-impulsive type (which is comparable to ADHD from *DSM-III-R*). This history shows the changes that can occur in diagnostic definitions. Although some of these decisions were based on empirical evidence, some decisions were influenced by the research and political agendas of the professionals involved in these decisions (Conners, 2000).

The most important thing to remember when reviewing the criteria for ADHD is that the behavior should

TABLE 9.1 DSM-IV Diagnostic Criteria for Attention-Deficit/Hyperactivity Disorder (ADHD)

A. Either (1) or (2):
    (1) six (or more) of the following symptoms of *inattention* have persisted for at least 6 months to a degree that is maladaptive and inconsistent with developmental level:

    Inattention

      (a) often fails to give close attention to details or makes careless mistakes in school work, work, or other activities
      (b) often has difficulty sustaining attention in tasks or play activities
      (c) often does not seem to listen when spoken to directly
      (d) often does not follow through on instructions and fails to finish schoolwork, chores, or duties in the workplace (not due to oppositional behavior or failure to understand instructions)
      (e) often has difficulty organizing tasks and activities
      (f) often avoids, dislikes, or is reluctant to engage in tasks that require sustained mental effort (such as schoolwork or home work)
      (g) often loses things necessary for tasks or activities (e.g., toys, school assignments, pencils, books, or tools)
      (h) is often easily distracted by extraneous stimuli
      (i) is often forgetful in daily activities

    (2) six (or more) of the following symptoms of *hyperactivity-impulsivity* have persisted for at least 6 months to a degree that is maladaptive and inconsistent with developmental level:

    Hyperactivity

      (a) often fidgets with hands or feet or squirms in seat
      (b) often leaves seat in classroom or in other situations in which remaining seated is expected
      (c) often runs about or climbs excessively in situations in which it is inappropriate (in adolescents or adults, may be limited to subjective feelings of restlessness)
      (d) often has difficulty playing or engaging in leisure activities quietly
      (e) is often "on the go" or often acts as if "driven by a motor"
      (f) often talks excessively

    Impulsivity

      (g) often blurts out answers before questions have been completed
      (h) often has difficulty awaiting turn
      (i) often interrupts or intrudes on others (e.g., butts into conversations or games)

B. Some hyperactive-impulsive or inattentive symptoms that caused impairment were present before age 7 years.
C. Some impairment from the symptoms is present in two or more settings (e.g., at school [or work] and at home).
D. There must be clear evidence of clinically significant impairment in social, academic, or occupational functioning.
E. The symptoms do not occur exclusively during the course of a Pervasive Developmental Disorder, Schizophrenia, or other Psychotic Disorder and are not better accounted for by another mental disorder (e.g., Mood Disorder, Anxiety Disorder, Dissociative Disorder, or a Personality Disorder).

Code based on type:
Attention-Deficit/Hyperactivity Disorder, Combined Type: if both Criteria A1 and A2 are met for the past 6 months
Attention-Deficit/Hyperactivity Disorder, Predominantly Inattentive Type: if Criterion A1 is met but Criterion A2 is not met for the past 6 months
Attention-Deficit/Hyperactivity Disorder, Predominantly Hyperactive-Impulsive Type: if Criterion A2 is met but Criterion A1 is not met for the past 6 months

Source: American Psychiatric Association (2000).

Reprinted with permission from the *Diagnostic and Statistical Manual of Mental Disorders, Fourth Edition, Text Revision.* Copyright 2000 American Psychiatric Association.

Children can only be diagnosed with ADHD if they show impairment related to the symptoms in two or more environments (such as at school and at home).

be above and beyond what is expected for a child of that age and gender. As with all other diagnoses, children only meet criteria if their behavior is beyond what would be considered developmentally appropriate. Note that there are three primary components to diagnosing ADHD: inattention, hyperactivity, and impulsivity. It is important to highlight the distinctions between these symptoms. *DSM-III* provided one of the great improvements in conceptualizing and diagnosing ADHD by separating inattention from hyperactivity and impulsivity. Like the criteria in *DSM-III,* the current criteria focus on the distinctiveness of inattention, hyperactivity, and impulsivity.

After considering these symptoms in the diagnosis of ADHD, it is also crucial to acknowledge Criteria B (age), C (settings), and D (impairment). Criterion B notes that at least some of the symptoms that cause impairment must have been present before the age of 7. This criterion is important because it shows the chronicity of ADHD. It is especially important in considering the diagnosis of ADHD in adolescents and adults. If there is no evidence that the maladaptive symptoms of hyperactivity, impulsivity, or inattention were present before the age of 7, then the diagnosis of ADHD would not be appropriate. This issue distinguishes between the chronic problem of ADHD (symptoms of which would have been present before the age of 7) and a more situational problem that only appeared at a later age.

Criterion C is of equal, if not more, importance in distinguishing between ADHD and other situational

problems. Specifically, Criterion C notes that impairment from the symptoms must be present in at least two settings. There are actually two important components to this criterion: Symptoms must be present in two or more settings, and symptoms must cause impairment in two or more settings. For children and adolescents, Criterion C is especially important to consider when evaluating behavior in school and at home. Some children appear to be very hyperactive, impulsive, and inattentive at school, but they show few or no signs of disturbance at home. Alternately, other children show significant impairment at home but do not show any symptoms at school. When children show significant symptoms that cause impairment in one setting but not the other, then a diagnosis of ADHD is not warranted. This issue is of great concern when assessing the symptoms of ADHD, as noted in Box 9.1.

The final criterion to discuss is Criterion D, which states that individuals must show clinically significant impairment in either the social, academic, or occupational domains. This criterion is important to acknowledge because children or adolescents sometimes have high levels of activity, impulsivity, or inattention, but they still are able to function well in a diverse array of settings. Often, children can use compensatory strategies for dealing with these difficulties, so they do not experience impairment in social, academic, or occupational settings. For example, a child may be quite inattentive, but she compensates for this difficulty by studying harder and using memory aids to help her learn her class material. In addition, she compensates for her inattentiveness

BOX 9.1

ASSESSMENT OF ADHD

Given the importance of a valid diagnosis of ADHD for proper treatment, it seems worthwhile to consider what should be done in a thorough assessment for the presence or absence of ADHD. There are too many examples of children being prescribed a stimulant, such as Ritalin, just because their parents reported that they are too active. A comprehensive assessment should help establish whether or not children's behaviors are out of the range of normal behavior for a child of that age and gender. In fact, a report from *Consumer Reports Best Buy Drugs,* which is an independent, nonprofit group that is not subsidized by any type of advertising, came out with a report suggesting that the most important first step before considering psychostimulant medication is to get a thorough and accurate assessment (Consumer Reports Best Buy Drugs, 2005a). In fact, the report suggests that many children who are prescribed medication for ADHD either do not meet criteria at all or only have mild symptoms that do not require medication. They suggest that a thorough evaluation and consideration of alternate treatments is warranted before putting a child on medication for symptoms of ADHD. Interestingly, in a review article in the *New England Journal of Medicine,* physicians were encouraged to suggest a thorough educational assessment to evaluate any academic problems that might exist (Rappley, 2005).

A great number of assessment tools are used to assess the symptoms of ADHD. Given that impairments from ADHD symptoms have to be present in at least two settings, it is crucial that behaviors in at least two settings are assessed. Because ADHD is highly comorbid with other disorders, a thorough and comprehensive assessment should be conducted. A number of the more established measures are listed following with a brief explanation.

Direct observation: As noted in the chapter on assessment, direct observations can be done through standardized mechanisms (e.g., the Direct Observation Form; Achenbach, 1991a) or can be done through an unstandardized observational process (e.g., watching a child's behavior and paying attention to the antecedents and consequences to his or her behavior). At a minimum, school-aged children (especially children in elementary school) should be observed in their classrooms in a number of different tasks (some structured, such as doing math, and some unstructured, such as recess) as well as at least one other setting (e.g., the home, the day care, the assessor's office, a laboratory).

Interviews: Semistructured or structured interviews are appropriate to ascertain the symptoms that are present for ADHD. One notable structured interview, which can be used for children's self-report as well as parents' report, is the Diagnostic Interview Schedule for Children (DISC; Shaffer et al., 2000). The DISC results in a comprehensive assessment of a number of diagnoses, including ADHD.

Behavior Checklists: A number of excellent behavior checklists can be used with a number of different informants, including parents, teachers, and sometimes children themselves (depending on the age of the child). The Child Behavior Checklist (CBCL) and related measures (Achenbach & Rescorla, 2001) provide a comprehensive overview of children's and adolescents' behavior. These measures include subscales for attention problems, delinquent behavior, and aggressive behavior, but do not include a specific subscale for hyperactivity and impulsivity. The measures in the Behavior Assessment System for Children (BASC; Reynolds & Kamphaus, 2005) include subscales for hyperactivity and attention problems in addition to a number of other internalizing and externalizing problems. Both the CBCL and the BASC systems of assessment provide broad measures of children's and adolescents' behavior. Other more specific measures for ADHD include the Conners' Parent Rating Scale and the Conners' Teacher Rating Scale (Conners, 1990). These measures focus on hyperactivity, inattention, and conduct problems. Many assessors use some combination of all or many of these behavior checklists (Crystal, Ostrander, Chen, & August, 2001). Like most areas of assessment, gaining perspectives from multiple informants (e.g., parents, teachers, children) is a standard practice (Steinhausen, Drechsler, Foldenyi, Imhof, & Brandeis, 2003).

In addition to these measures, other assessment tools can be used in a comprehensive assessment of ADHD. An intelligence test, for example, can be of great help in evaluating children for ADHD to ascertain the strengths and weaknesses of their intellectual functioning. Similarly, achievement tests can be invaluable in assessing children for ADHD, given that academic problems are often associated with ADHD. It is also prudent to assess for children's strengths and competencies because these factors may be helpful in treating any deficits that are found. As mentioned in the chapter on assessment, it is also important to consider factors outside the child that might relate to the child's functioning. Thus, an assessment of the school environment and the home environment would be warranted in trying to gain a thorough understanding of the child's functioning.

BOX *9.1*

(CONTINUED)

There are, of course, pros and cons to each of these assessment methods. For example, behavioral observations are time consuming and may not be realistic for clinicians in the community to conduct (Pelham et al., 2005). Structured diagnostic interviews are reliable and valid, but they are not realistic to conduct in independent practice given their length and the possibility that rapport will be damaged if the structured interview is conducted too early in the assessment process. Behavior ratings are a strength in this area, but multiple informants must be used to get an accurate depiction of the child's behavior across situations, and informants' perspectives can be altered by their own psychological symptoms (Pelham et al., 2005). There is evidence, however, that parental symptoms of ADHD do not influence parental reports of children's ADHD (Faraone, Monuteaux, Biederman, Cohan & Mick, 2003). Overall, there is no gold standard for an assessment of ADHD, but using these different techniques can lead to a more thorough and accurate diagnosis.

Source: DuPaul & Stoner, 2004; Neul, Applegate, & Drabman, 2003.

---

in other settings. In this case, she would not meet criteria for ADHD. Similarly, a child might be extremely overactive compared to his peers, but he can channel this high energy level into activities that accommodate his overactivity. In this case, he would not meet criteria for ADHD.

Criteria B (age), C (settings), and D (impairment) are important to consider because they often disallow a diagnosis of ADHD that would have otherwise been made. Note that one criterion is absent from the formal *DSM-IV* diagnosis of ADHD. There is no formal requirement that children diagnosed with ADHD must experience limitations in their schoolwork. Although academic deficits are quite common in children diagnosed with ADHD (Gresham, Lane, & Beebe-Frankenberger, 2005), these deficits are not necessary for a diagnosis of ADHD. Thus, it is possible that a child would show impairment in social functioning, for example, but would have adequate or even excellent schoolwork.

As mentioned previously, according to the American Psychiatric Association's (2000) *Diagnostic and Statistical Manual of Mental Disorders—Fourth Edition,* there are currently three types of **attention-deficit/hyperactivity disorder (ADHD). Attention-deficit/hyperactivity disorder, combined type** is thought to have three primary characteristics: hyperactivity, impulsivity, and inattention. As can be seen in the diagnostic criteria for ADHD, children must meet criteria for both hyperactivity-impulsivity and inattention to meet criteria for ADHD, combined type. Children who meet criteria for this disorder show heightened levels of inappropriate behavior and also have difficulty with sustained attention and concentration. The second type of ADHD is known as **attention-deficit/hyperactivity disorder, predominantly inattentive type,** which focuses on children who have problems with inattention but do not show inappropriate levels of hyperactivity or impulsivity. This diagnosis is comparable to the diagnosis in *DSM-III* known as attention-deficit disorder without hyperactivity (American Psychiatric Association, 1980). Children who meet criteria for this diagnosis often find it difficult to pay attention and to concentrate, but they do not exhibit high levels of energetic behavior or impulsivity. Within many school systems, these children are often still referred to as "ADD." The third type of ADHD is known as **attention-deficit/hyperactivity disorder, predominantly hyperactive-impulsive type,** which focuses on children who have problems with hyperactivity and impulsivity, but do not appear to have problems with attention or concentration. This diagnosis is comparable to the diagnosis in *DSM-III* that was known as attention-deficit disorder with hyperactivity.

These subtypes have been validated in a number of studies (Levy et al., 2005; Maedgen & Carlson, 2000), and the subtypes appear to have different associated problems (Counts, Nigg, Stawicki, Rappley, & Eye, 2005). For example, children diagnosed with ADHD, combined type or with ADHD, predominantly hyperactive-impulsive showed more social problems than children diagnosed with ADHD, predominantly inattentive (Gadow, Drabick, et al., 2004). Some researchers, however, suggest that the subtypes are actually distinctly different disorders rather than subtypes of one disorder (Barkley, 2003; Milich et al., 2001), and there are still some questions as to the validity of the subtypes (Woo & Rey, 2005). Note also that children often change from one subtype to another over the course of their lifetime. Thus, although these subtypes may be stable enough to use for research purposes, they may not be stable enough during early childhood and middle childhood to use clinically in a way that classifies the child for different services (Lahey, Pelham, Loney, Lee, & Willcutt, 2005).

Even with the specificity of criteria for subtypes of ADHD, it is important to acknowledge that ADHD is a very diverse and heterogeneous disorder (Counts et al., 2005; Jensen & Members of the MTA Cooperative Group, 2002; Wilens, Biederman, & Spencer, 2002). Two children diagnosed with any specific type of ADHD could be quite different from each other. It is for this reason that further studies into the specific characteristics of this disorder are needed.

The current diagnostic criteria appear to be well accepted within the mainstream, professional community. Both psychologists and psychiatrists, however, continue to try to refine the diagnostic criteria to clarify this disorder. For example, given the high rates of comorbidity and the distinct differences depending on the comorbid disorder, there have been suggestions that perhaps different subtypes of ADHD exist, such as ADHD, aggressive subtype and ADHD, anxious subtype (Counts et al., 2005; Jensen et al., 2001; Jensen & Members of the MTA Cooperative Group, 2002; Mannuzza, Klein, Abikoff, & Moulton, 2004; Rowland et al., 2002). Overall, ADHD commands a great deal of attention within the professional community. There is clearly a great deal of interest and concern over symptoms related to ADHD. One possible reason for the interest in this disorder relates to its high prevalence rates.

How poor are they that have not patience!
What wound did ever heal but by degrees?

—William Shakespeare

Prevalence Rates

As with so many other disorders, prevalence rates of ADHD vary widely, depending on what sample is used in the study. When clinical or special education samples are used, approximately 50% of children meet criteria for ADHD (Pihl & Nantel-Vivier, 2005). Larger epidemiological studies in the community suggest that between 2% and 10% of children meet criteria for ADHD (reviewed in Biederman, 2005). A common figure that is cited suggests that between 3% and 7% of

TABLE 9.2 Overview of Prevalence Information for Attention-Deficit/Hyperactivity Disorder

Prevalence	3–7% of school-aged children
Age	Childhood > Adolescence
Gender	Boys > Girls
SES	No differences when comorbidity is controlled statistically
Race/Ethnicity	Unclear patterns

school-aged children meet criteria for ADHD (American Psychiatric Association, 2000). Overall, ADHD is one of the most prevalent disorders in childhood (Pihl & Nantel-Vivier, 2005). See Table 9.2 for a summary of the prevalence information.

Regarding the prevalence of subtypes, it appears that the combined subtype is the most common. It is estimated that between 50% and 75% of children and adolescents diagnosed with ADHD fit into the combined type, where they experience both inattention and hyperactivity-impulsivity symptoms (Wilens et al., 2002). Approximately 20% to 30% of ADHD children meet criteria for the inattentive subtype, and less than 15% of ADHD children are estimated to meet criteria for the hyperactivity-impulsive subtype (Wilens et al., 2002).

With regard to age patterns, symptoms of ADHD tend to appear first in the preschool years (ages 3 and 4), but children tend to be referred for help between the ages of 7 and 9 (Barkley, 2003; Durston, 2003). Within clinical samples, it appears that approximately 50% to 80% of children diagnosed with ADHD will continue to meet criteria for ADHD when they are adolescents (Resnick, 2005). Regarding ADHD in adults, a number of epidemiological studies in primary health-care facilities have found that the prevalence rates of ADHD in adults ranges from 0.3% to 5% (McCann & Roy-Byrne, 2004; Montano, 2004), with 4% being the most commonly accepted prevalence rate (Resnick, 2005). Thus, although ADHD exists in adulthood, it is more prevalent in childhood and adolescence (Biederman, 2005).

With regard to gender differences, consistent differences in prevalence rates for the genders are found in nearly every country that has been studied (DuPaul et al., 2001; Newcorn et al., 2001; Wilens et al., 2002). Boys outnumber girls with the diagnosis of ADHD at least 2:1, with reports going as high as 9:1 (Barkley, 2006; Biederman, 2005). Higher ratios of boys tend to be found in clinical samples when compared with community samples, which suggests that boys with ADHD might be referred for help even more than girls with ADHD

Case Study: Beth, the Little Girl Who Did Not Follow Rules

Beth was $5\frac{1}{2}$ years old when her parents brought her to the local child guidance center for an evaluation. Her parents reported that Beth was difficult to discipline at home, and her kindergarten teacher reported that Beth was a discipline problem at school, where she showed inattentiveness, hyperactivity, and distractability.

Beth lived with her parents, a younger sister, and a younger brother in a lower-middle-class neighborhood. The prenatal period for Beth seemed unproblematic, but there were problems during labor and delivery. After 20 hours of labor, Beth had to be delivered with forceps, at which time it was discovered that her umbilical cord was wrapped around her neck. At birth, Beth was blue due to the anoxia (lack of oxygen). Although Beth had to stay in the neonatal intensive care unit, she appeared to recover well from the birth trauma.

Beth experienced somewhat slowed developmental milestones, and she experienced a series of unfortunate accidents. When she was 2 years old, Beth experienced four head injuries, all of which were due to her falling on her head. One incident occurred when Beth fell from a shopping cart, and the other incidents occurred when Beth fell down the stairs or fell off a chair at home. Beth never lost consciousness during these incidents and did not appear to suffer any immediate consequences. After these accidents, Beth continued to have somewhat delayed development (e.g., she was not toilet trained until the age of 3).

Beth's parents appeared to focus a great deal of their attention on their youngest son, much to the exclusion of Beth and her sister. Beth seemed to react to being ignored by throwing temper tantrums, becoming demanding, and running around the house chronically. When Beth was engaged in appropriate play, she would lose interest rapidly and then move onto another activity without picking up the toys with which she had just finished playing. Beth's mother reported that nearly all her interactions with Beth were negative.

Beth showed the same heightened energy levels at school. Her kindergarten teacher reported that Beth was constantly on the go and that she could not stay focused on one task for very long. Beth seemed distracted by any extraneous noise, and she was difficult to redirect back to her class work. In addition, Beth seemed to have a great deal of perceptual–motor problems that were evidenced in tasks such as drawing and cutting out paper figures.

The psychological evaluation revealed that Beth had very low intellectual functioning, with significant visual-motor deficits. Beth reported low levels of self-esteem. A neurological evaluation revealed that Beth had difficulty with fine motor coordination, but no overt brain dysfunctions were uncovered. Behavioral observations between Beth and her parents revealed that Beth's parents interacted with her primarily when she was misbehaving (e.g., being loud, refusing to do something). Notably, her parents did not interact with her to show her how to complete tasks, but rather would just point out when she was doing something wrong. Behavioral observation also confirmed Beth's heightened levels of activity, impulsivity, and inattention.

Overall, Beth met criteria for ADHD—combined type. She exhibits a common problem, in which parents' and teachers' high expectations are not realistic due to her limited functioning. It appears that Beth becomes frustrated when she does not understand directions, and she acts out when she becomes frustrated. Therapy for the parents as well as Beth was recommended.

Source: Leon (1990).

(Wilens et al., 2002). Boys diagnosed with ADHD are more likely to be comorbid with conduct disorder than are girls (Abikoff et al., 2002; Newcorn et al., 2001). An overwhelming number of studies of ADHD have intentionally included only boys in the sample, given the low numbers of girls who meet criteria for the diagnosis. The ratio of ADHD diagnoses for boys versus girls has been questioned due to the assessment process and due to the potential for underreporting of symptoms for girls (Waschbusch, King, & Northern Partners in Action for Children and Youth, 2006). For example, there is evidence that boys' and girls' behaviors are rated differently by teachers, with boys' ADHD behaviors being overemphasized (Jackson & King, 2004). Relatedly, there is concern that girls and women with similar symptoms of ADHD as boys and men are being ignored or are being missed by the professional community (Quinn, 2005). Even with these caveats, there is still clear evidence that boys experience ADHD more frequently than do girls.

When boys and girls with ADHD are compared, interesting patterns emerge. A comprehensive meta-analysis identified both differences and similarities between boys and girls diagnosed with ADHD (Gaub & Carlson, 1997). When compared with boys, girls diagnosed with ADHD showed lower intellectual functioning, lower levels of hyperactivity, and fewer comorbid externalizing problems. There were no gender differences, however, with regard to fine motor skills, social functioning, academic performance, or impulsivity. In addition, there were no gender differences on family-related variables such as parental depression and parental education (Gaub & Carlson, 1997). These results continue to be found in more recent individual studies (Abikoff et al., 2002; Graetz, Sawyer, & Baghurst, 2005; Newcorn et al., 2001). The meta-analysis and subsequent studies have not been able to ascertain whether or not the gender differences were due to some type of referral bias (e.g., brighter girls with higher levels of activity tend not to be referred for services because teachers do not perceive them to be as much of a problem as girls with lower levels of intellectual functioning). In a study that attempted to assess parents' perceptions of boys' versus girls' symptoms, parents rated most ADHD symptoms as more typical of boys and saw similar behaviors in girls as less problematic (Ohan & Johnston, 2005). In addition, when rating a hypothetical vignette about either a boy or a girl with ADHD, both mothers and fathers perceived the boys' behavior to be more intentional than the girls' behavior, and they reported that they would react more strictly to the boys' behavior than to the girls' behavior (Maniadaki, Sonuga-Barke, & Kakouros, 2005). Overall, ADHD is a serious and potentially long-standing problem in boys as well as in girls (Hinshaw, Owens, Sami, & Fargeon, 2006).

There is limited research into the prevalence patterns of ADHD with regard to socioeconomic status (SES). The studies that have been conducted suggest that all three subtypes of ADHD are somewhat more prevalent in lower SES communities (Barkley, 2003). It appears, however, that this pattern is due to factors other than SES per se. Specifically, when comorbid disorders are controlled statistically, then the differences in SES groups vanish (Barkley, 2003; Rowland, Lesesne, & Abramowitz, 2002). Thus, it appears that when other comorbid disorders, especially conduct disorder, are controlled statistically, there are no differences in ADHD across the social classes (Rowland et al., 2002).

There is a marked void of research into the issue of race/ethnicity and ADHD. One review found that out of the thousands of research articles on ADHD, only 16 articles focused on ADHD in African-American children and adolescents (Samuel et al., 1997). The research on ADHD has been criticized for focusing only on white, middle-class children and their families (Kendall & Hatton, 2002). When ratings are compared for African-American children and Caucasian-American children, teachers tend to rate African-American children higher on symptoms of ADHD (Epstein et al., 2005), whereas Caucasian-American children were rated higher than Hispanic/Latino/Latina children (Havey, Olson, McCormick, & Cates, 2005). It is unclear, however,

whether these ratings are based on perceptual biases or actual differences in behaviors.

When classroom observations are used and when random control children are used to control for teachers' ratings, then the racial/ethnic differences between African-American and Caucasian children dissipate (Epstein et al., 2005). Thus, it may be that even nonclinical African-American children are perceived to have higher rates of activity than are Caucasian children. In addition, when aggression and defiance are controlled statistically, cultural differences disappear (Evans & Lee, 1998). When samples of children in the community are evaluated, parents of African-American children report fewer symptoms of ADHD than do parents of Caucasian-American children, and African-American children are less likely to receive medication for ADHD than are Caucasian-American children (Rowland et al., 2002; Stevens, Harman, & Kelleher, 2005). Within the Asian-American community, prevalence rates of ADHD are lower than in other racial and ethnic groups (Serafica, 1997). Overall, research on differential prevalence rates based on race/ethnicity is still somewhat limited, and the results are not clear-cut.

There is, however, growing evidence of a disparity between Caucasian-American and African-American children in the identification and treatment of ADHD (Bussing, Zima, Gary, & Garvan, 2003; Rowland et al., 2002). For example, in a group of children with comparable ADHD symptoms, Caucasian children were twice as likely to have been evaluated for and treated for ADHD (Bussing et al., 2003). There is speculation that some of these racial differences in accessing health care are related to racism, whereby Caucasian-American children's hyperactivity problems are seen as medically related, and African-American children's hyperactivity problems are seen as a result of bad parenting, low intellectual functioning, substance abuse, poverty, or violent surroundings (Kendall & Hatton, 2002). There is also an indication that African-American parents are less likely to seek an evaluation and treatment for ADHD symptoms in their children (Davison & Ford, 2001). These patterns appear to be comparable for other mental health problems and appear to be evident in community samples as well as samples of children in the welfare system (Bussing et al., 2003; Raghavan et al., 2005). Within a school-based sample of children diagnosed with ADHD, African-American parents were less likely than Caucasian-American parents to see the school as a source of identification or intervention for the ADHD symptoms and were less worried about ADHD-related problems (Bussing et al., 2003). Thus, the investigation of racial/ethnic differences in prevalence rates may be complicated by cultural differences in the interpretation of ADHD symptoms and the need for assessments and interventions for these symptoms.

Researchers have also explored prevalence rates across cultures (DuPaul et al., 2001). ADHD in children as well as adults has been found and diagnosed in nearly every culture that has been studied, including Australia, Spain, Brazil, Germany, England, Italy, New Zealand, the Netherlands, Japan, the Ukraine, Uganda, China, and Ethiopia (DuPaul et al., 2001; Gadow et al., 2000; Kooij et al., 2005; Rohde et al., 2005; Wolraich et al., 2003; Yang, Wang, Qian, Biederman, & Faraone, 2004). Although there is evidence of higher rates of ADHD within the United States, this pattern may be due to the diagnostic criteria used in the study. For example, much lower prevalence rates are found in England, but this discrepancy is apparently due to the diagnostic criteria used in England. Diagnostic criteria for **hyperkinetic disorder** from the *International Classification of Diseases-10 (ICD-10;* World Health Organization, 1992) are now used within Great Britain. Hyperkinetic disorder is comparable to ADHD except that it is much more severe than ADHD, and neurological deficits must be present (Whalen & Henker, 1998). Fewer children are diagnosed with these more stringent criteria. For example, using the same sample of children from Brazil, 5.8% of children met criteria for ADHD by using *DSM-IV* criteria, whereas 1.5% of children met criteria for hyperkinetic disorder using *ICD-10* criteria (Rohde et al., 2005). Thus, the differences across cultures in the diagnosis of ADHD may be due to the use of different diagnostic criteria.

In addition to different definitions of ADHD across cultures, there is also a possibility that behaviors may be interpreted differently in different cultures (Yamamoto, Silva, Ferrari, & Nukariya, 1997). For example, children in Puerto Rico tend to show more exaggerated body movements and to interrupt each other more than Caucasian-American children (Evans & Lee, 1998). Chinese children in Hong Kong were reported to show more hyperactivity than comparison groups in the United States and in the United Kingdom, but this pattern may have been due to less tolerance for activity with these children (Evans & Lee, 1998). Overall, care should be taken to ensure that children are assessed in a manner that is culturally sensitive and that is respectful of differences across nations (Yamamoto et al., 1997). In most nations, however, ADHD is a relevant concern for the school system, as noted in Box 9.2.

Genius is nothing but a greater aptitude for patience.
—Georges Louis Leclerc de Buffon

Comorbidity

As with so many disorders in childhood and adolescence, comorbidity is the rule rather than the exception for ADHD (Levy, Hay, Bennett, & McStephen, 2005). Comorbidity estimates are higher between ADHD and conduct disorder and lower between ADHD and anxiety disorders (Biederman, 2005; Costello et al., 2003). Overall, estimates of comorbidity between ADHD and externalizing disorders range from 42% to 93%, whereas comorbidity between ADHD and internalizing disorders are estimated from 13% to 51% (Jensen et al., 1997). When children with ADHD are comorbid with dysthymic disorder, they are also more likely to be diagnosed with separation anxiety disorder and social phobia in comparison to ADHD children who are not also experiencing dysthymic disorder (Vance, Harris, Boots, Talbot, & Karamitsios, 2003). Children who were comorbid for ADHD and OCD were more impaired and had more troubled social, school, and family functioning than children who experienced either disorder alone (Sukhodolsky et al., 2005).

ADHD in childhood is associated with the development of substance abuse in adolescence (Molina & Pelham, 2003). Specifically, adolescents diagnosed with ADHD were more likely than adolescents who did not meet criteria for ADHD to drink more alcohol, use more tobacco, and use more illegal drugs. Although there were no differences in substance-use disorders between these groups, the elevated usage levels of alcohol, tobacco, and illegal substances suggest that ADHD in childhood puts children at risk for more substance problems in adolescence (Molina & Pelham, 2003). Adolescents with ADHD and conduct disorder appeared to be particularly at risk for substance use and abuse due to affiliations with deviant peers (Marshal & Molina, 2006).

Boys diagnosed with ADHD who show high levels of aggression also reported higher rates of depressive symptoms than did ADHD boys without aggression and boys in a control group (Treuting & Hinshaw, 2001). When compared with boys in a control group, boys diagnosed with ADHD showed higher levels of sadness, anger, and guilt (Braaten & Rosen, 2000).

In terms of gender differences, boys diagnosed with ADHD were more likely to be comorbid for oppositional defiant disorder, whereas girls diagnosed with ADHD were more likely to be comorbid for separation anxiety disorder (Levy et al., 2005). For both externalizing and internalizing disorders, comorbidity with ADHD

BOX *9.2*

ADHD IN THE SCHOOLS

ADHD is one of the most prevalent and challenging behavioral disorders that teachers have to deal with in the classroom (DuPaul & Stoner, 2004). Luckily, there are good teaching strategies that teachers can use and good behavioral techniques that school psychologists can use to help children with ADHD learn and behave appropriately in the classroom (DuPaul & Stoner, 2004).

Regarding assessment, referral for testing due to possible ADHD is one of the most common requests for school psychologists (DuPaul & Stoner, 2004). Luckily, there are standard assessment batteries that can be given, and there are clear diagnostic criteria that can be used. In comparison to previous diagnostic systems, it appears that *DSM-IV* is beneficial to school psychologists because the diagnostic criteria are more objective and are based on firm empirical findings (Pelham, Fabiano, & Massetti, 2005).

For children who are highly active and inattentive, teachers can design special curriculum to enhance the student's mastery of the material. For example, breaking assignments into smaller parts and providing more frequent positive reinforcement for attention and concentration can help keep students with ADHD focused and motivated (Dowdy et al., 1998). Research on psychostimulant medication suggests that making tasks more interesting to students can enhance their motivation to complete the tasks, so creating more interesting academic assignments might be a way to increase students' performance in the classroom without the use of medication (Volkow et al., 2004).

One salient issue regarding ADHD in the schools centers on teachers' expectations and feelings about children with high levels of activity. Rather than diagnosing ADHD in a particular child, another way of conceptualizing ADHD is to look at the goodness-of-fit between student and teacher (Greene, 1995, 1996). Specifically, certain children may behave in ways that are not a good "fit" for certain teachers. For example, one teacher may deal best with children who sit still and do not talk very much, whereas another teacher may deal best with inquisitive children who are very active and interactive. A child with high levels of activity would probably not fare well with the first teacher but may flourish with the second teacher. The goodness-of-fit model argues that we should look at the fit between student and teacher rather than just identifying problems within the child (Greene, 1995, 1996).

Interestingly, teachers vary a great deal on how stressful they feel it is to work with a highly active and inattentive child. In general, general education elementary teachers reported greater stress when having to deal with a child with ADHD in comparison to a child without ADHD, but they reported the most stress when having to deal with a child with ADHD who also experienced oppositional and aggressive behavior and who showed significant social impairments (Greene, Beszterczey, Katzenstein, Park, & Goring, 2002). Thus, even within the realm of teaching children diagnosed with ADHD, it appears that some children are more stressful to deal with than others from a teacher's perspective.

The school system has also become a site for the management of medications related to ADHD. Many children are required to receive dosages of their medication at school, and school nurses and other school personnel are increasingly being called on to administer psychostimulant medications and to evaluate their effectiveness. National guidelines within school psychology are suggested for monitoring the effects of psychostimulant medications in children while they are at school, but these guidelines are rarely followed (Volpe, Heick, & Guerasko-Moore, 2005).

Overall, most teachers, school psychologists, school nurses, and administrators have to deal with ADHD on a relatively frequent basis. When teachers, parents, and school professionals can work as a team to address ADHD children's academic and psychological needs, then ADHD children tend to have more success than when these collaborative efforts are not in place (Dowdy et al., 1998).

---

is associated with higher levels of impairment, greater use of mental health services, and a poorer prognosis (Biederman, 2005). These same patterns of comorbidity have been found in other countries, such as Sweden (Kadesjoe & Gillberg, 2001; Kopp, 2003) and the Ukraine (Drabick, Gadow, Carlson, & Bromet, 2004).

In addition to the high rates of comorbidity between ADHD and conduct disorder, there are also high rates of comorbidity between ADHD and learning disorders, with estimates ranging from 10% for girls and nearly 30% for boys (Biederman, 2005). ADHD, combined type, alone or in conjunction with conduct problems, tends to be more comorbid with learning disorders than are other subtypes of ADHD (Gresham et al., 2005). As can be seen in Table 9.3, children and adolescents (aged 6 to 17) diagnosed with ADHD were found to have significant academic difficulties in one community-based study (Faraone et al., 1993). Similar learning problems have been found in children as young as 3 years old and in preschoolers (Spira & Fischel, 2005). Overall, it

Is this boy in Barcelona, Spain, showing hyperactivity or acceptable amounts of activity?

TABLE 9.3 **Percentage of ADHD Children and Adolescents with School Difficulties**

Problem	ADHD (N = 140)	Control (N = 120)
Needed academic tutoring*	56%	25%
Repeated a grade*	30%	13%
Placed in special class*	35%	2%
Reading disorder*	18%	4%
Arithmetic disorder*	21%	8%

*Differed significantly between ADHD group and nonclinical control group.
Source: Adapted from Faraone et al. (1993).

appears that these difficulties may be linked to deficits in executive function, such as working memory, planning, attention, and reasoning (Biederman et al., 2004).

The high prevalence between ADHD and at least one learning disorder (LD) has led to speculation that these two problems may be intertwined permanently (Rabiner, Coie, & Conduct Problems Prevention Research Group, 2000). Specifically, problems with attention, cognitive functioning, and emotional/behavioral functioning may be common to both ADHD and LD, so it is difficult to disentangle the two disorders in any one child. For example, children who were inattentive in kindergarten

showed significant reading problems up to 5 years later, even when controlling for earlier reading problems (Rabiner et al., 2000). In addition, boys diagnosed with ADHD showed less task persistence (i.e., they gave up earlier) on academic tasks than did boys in a control group (Hoza, Pelham, Waschbusch, Kipp, & Owens, 2001). It is also possible that children are inattentive because they are frustrated by the difficult academic material. More research on specific subtypes of ADHD and LD may help clarify these issues, especially if the research samples are more homogeneous in symptom presentation (Gadow et al., 2004).

This issue relates to **differential diagnosis** (i.e., trying to establish which disorder, if any, is appropriate for a particular child). Differential diagnosis is a challenge with ADHD and a number of other disorders. Distinguishing between bipolar disorder/mania and symptoms of ADHD is especially difficult (Geller et al., 2002). One study found that inpatient children who experienced symptoms of mania also experienced more severe levels of ADHD than did inpatient children who did not experience mania (Carlson & Kelly, 1998). The symptoms that best distinguish bipolar disorder from ADHD are elation, grandiosity, flight of ideas/racing thoughts, decreased need for sleep, and hypersexuality, all of which are characteristic of bipolar but not of ADHD (Geller et al., 2002). The potential confound between the diagnosis of ADHD and bipolar is of great concern because stimulant medication is countertherapeutic to children with symptoms of mania (Phelps et al., 2002). As can be seen in the "You Decide" section, there are differing opinions about the connections between ADHD and bipolar disorder.

Another difficult differential diagnosis can occur when sexually abused children show symptoms of hyperactivity but also show symptoms of posttraumatic stress disorder (PTSD). There is a great deal of overlap between the symptoms of hyperactivity and PTSD, and in children who have been sexually abused, there is a great deal of difficulty in distinguishing between these two disorders (Weinstein, Staffelbach, & Biaggio, 2000). For this reason, it is imperative that clinicians gather a full history and conduct a comprehensive assessment in children who show signs of hyperactivity.

Other factors that are associated with inattention, hyperactivity, and impulsivity include troubled social interactions and poor peer relationships (Hoza et al., 2005). Boys and girls diagnosed with ADHD have comparable levels of impairment in their social relations and show greater problems in social interactions than do nondisordered boys and girls (Greene et al., 2001). It is not surprising to find that many children who

YOU DECIDE: IS ATTENTION-DEFICIT/HYPERACTIVITY DISORDER CONFOUNDED WITH BIPOLAR DISORDER?

Yes

- Symptoms of irritability, hyperactivity, accelerated speech, and distractibility are common in both children with ADHD and children with bipolar disorder (Geller et al., 2002).
- In contrast to children with ADHD and major depressive disorder, children with ADHD and bipolar disorder were also comorbid for many other disorders, including conduct disorder, severe oppositional defiant disorder, agoraphobia, OCD, and alcohol abuse (Wozniak et al., 2004).

No

- Although there are common symptoms, children, adolescents, and adults can be diagnosed effectively for either ADHD or bipolar disorder or both (Wilens, Biederman, Wozniak, Gunawardene, Wong, & Monuteaux, 2003; Youngstrom, Findling, Youngstrom, & Calbrese, 2005).
- There is a strong family history connection for bipolar disorder, with children of parents with bipolar disorder being five times more likely than other children to be diagnosed with bipolar disorder (Youngstrom & Duax, 2005).

So, is attention-deficit/hyperactivity disorder confounded with bipolar disorder? You decide.

---

are inattentive, hyperactive, and impulsive would have trouble making and maintaining friendships. Many of these children are actively disliked by their peers, given their difficulty with sustaining conversations and waiting their turn. There is speculation that some of the same processes that create the difficulties with attention, activity level, and impulsivity also serve to make social relationships difficult (Hoza et al., 2005). Children diagnosed with ADHD often overestimate their own competence, which may also be related to difficult interactions with peers (Hoza et al., 2004). Known as positive illusory bias, which reflects children's perceptions of personal strengths where they do not appear to exist, children with ADHD combined type and ADHD hyperactive-inattentive type were more likely than children with ADHD inattentive type in a control group to overestimate their academic and social competence (Owens & Hoza, 2003).

In the family domain, children and adolescents diagnosed with ADHD often also have difficult and conflicted relationships with their mothers and fathers (Edwards, Barkley, Laneri, Fletcher, & Metevia, 2001). Parent–child conflict appears to be elevated in families with children who experience many externalizing disorders, including ADHD, oppositional defiant disorder, and conduct disorder (Burt, Krueger, McGue, & Iacono, 2003). These elevated rates of conflict may be due to higher rates of hostility in parents of children diagnosed with ADHD and oppositional defiant disorder (Seipp & Johnston, 2005).

Overall, comorbidity is an especially difficult challenge in the diagnosis and study of ADHD. Some researchers have argued that the high rates of comorbidity between ADHD and other disorders suggest a problem in the diagnostic criteria (Achenbach, 1990/1991; Caron & Rutter, 1991). Other researchers have argued that the high rates of comorbidity between ADHD and other disorders are further evidence of the high levels of impairment that children with ADHD experience (Costello et al., 2003). Both of these explanations would suggest that further research is needed into the diagnostic specificity and accuracy of criteria for ADHD.

Course of the Disorder

The majority of ADHD diagnoses are first given between the ages of 7 and 9 (Barkley, 2003). By diagnostic definition, symptoms must have been present before the age of 7, but many children are not referred for an evaluation of ADHD symptoms until they reach school age. In fact, many children are referred for an evaluation of a learning disorder due to difficulties in the school setting and then are also found to meet criteria for ADHD (Root & Resnick, 2003). Children who develop the disorder earlier in life (i.e., before the age of 6) tend to show greater problems with cognitive functioning, higher rates of comorbidity, more family disadvantage, and a greater likelihood of having the disorder into adolescence (Spira & Fischel, 2005; Steinhausen et al., 2003). Children who have a later onset of ADHD (i.e., after the age of 6) tend to experience the symptoms after developing a reading disorder and tend to have a better prognosis than children with an earlier onset of ADHD (Barkley, 2003).

Case Study: Jonas, a Case of Comorbidity in Action

Jonas was 16 years old when he was brought in for treatment. When he was in elementary school, from grades 1 through 4, he received methylphenidate to treat symptoms of ADHD, primarily inattentive type. After that time, his symptoms were manageable without medication. Jonas' parents, however, were still concerned that he was only attaining a "C" average and that he did not show a great deal of interest in academic activities. Jonas was often inattentive in school, and when he occasionally did homework, he could not focus on his studies. Both parents were highly educated professionals, and they wanted Jonas to excel in school.

Over the past 6 months, Jonas's behavior decompensated tremendously. He used to play on a soccer team, but after missing a number of practices, he was finally kicked off the team. He had also been truant from school on a number of occasions. Jonas's parents reported that he was usually already asleep by the time they got home from work on weekdays, and he usually stayed with his friends for entire weekends. He refused to take part in family activities, and when he was at home, he would only watch television or play video games without interacting with the rest of the family. Jonas's parents were terribly concerned that he was depressed and withdrawn.

When Jonas's parents brought him in for a psychological evaluation, he appeared irritated and cynical. He denied that he was depressed, but he did acknowledge that he was often bored and tired. After a lengthy interview during which strong rapport was established, Jonas finally admitted that he had been drinking heavily for the past year. He would usually skip school and "hang out" with teenagers from the neighborhood drinking beer, playing video games, watching television, listening to music, and driving around the neighborhood. Because his parents had given him a car, Jonas was often the one who could drive his friends to get beer and to drive around the neighborhood. During the assessment interview, Jonas was most concerned that his parents would forbid him to use the car if they found out that he had been drinking alcohol. Apparently, his parents did not have any idea about his drinking behavior nor about the friends with whom he "hung out."

This case provides an example of the comorbidity between alcohol abuse and ADHD. Approximately 20% of adolescents who abuse substances also meet criteria for ADHD. Following is the 5-axis diagnosis for Jonas.

Axis I:	Attention-deficit/hyperactivity disorder, predominately inattentive type Alcohol abuse
Axis II:	No diagnosis on Axis II
Axis III:	None
Axis IV:	Problems with primary support group: parent–child communication problem
Axis V:	Global Assessment of Functioning (GAF) = 65 (current)

Source: Rapoport & Ismond (1996).

Between 50% and 80% of children diagnosed with ADHD continue to meet criteria for the disorder when they are in midadolescence (Barkley, 2003). Thus, there is a high degree of stability in ADHD symptoms (Biederman et al., 2001). Young adolescents with ADHD show riskier road-crossing behaviors (Clancy, Rucklidge, & Owen, 2006), and adolescents and young adults with ADHD show greater risk for car accidents and traffic violations (Barkley, Murphy, DuPaul, & Bush, 2002).

A significant proportion of ADHD children and adolescents also experience ADHD in adulthood. As noted in Box 9.3, different pathways lead to a diagnosis of ADHD in adulthood. One prospective study of children aged 6 to 12 years old found that 43% of the children still met criteria for ADHD 10 years later, when they were ages 16 to 22, but that only 8% met criteria 16 years later when they were aged 22 to 28 years old (Rowland et al., 2002). The continuation of ADHD symptoms from childhood to adolescence

to adulthood is more likely for children who show extremely high levels of hyperactivity and impulsivity, who experience aggression and other conduct problems, and those from distressed families (Barkley, 2003). ADHD in adulthood is associated with a number of problems, including employment as an unskilled worker, lower levels of education, and greater rates of comorbid psychopathology (McGough et al., 2005).

ADHD in childhood is also predictive of other emotional/behavioral problems in adolescence and adulthood (Steinhausen et al., 2003). Often, ADHD symptoms are identified long before conduct disorder symptoms (Patterson, DeGarmo, & Knutson, 2000). Notably, children who show impulsive, hyperactive, and attentional problems in addition to showing conduct problems are more likely to become chronic offenders than are children with conduct problems who do not experience impulsivity, hyperactivity, and attentional problems

BOX *9.3*

ADHD IN ADULTHOOD

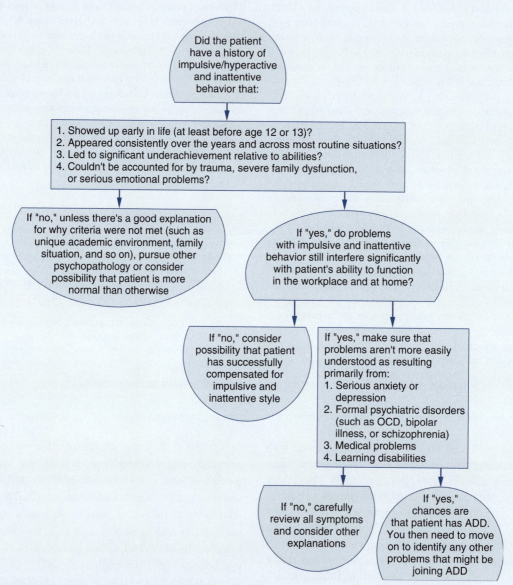

FIGURE 9.1 The Road to a Diagnosis of Adult ADHD.

Source: Barkley (1998).

The diagnosis of ADHD in adulthood used to be controversial and suspect. The most salient features of ADHD, such as physical restlessness and behavioral overactivity, are not as present in adulthood as in childhood (Barkley, 2003). Thus, many clinicians and researchers assumed that children "outgrew" their ADHD by the time they reached adulthood.

There is growing evidence, however, that some adults experience ADHD without having been diagnosed in childhood. Diagnosis of ADHD for the first time in adulthood is difficult because the diagnostic criteria require the existence of symptoms before the age of 7. Most assessments of adults rely on the adult's memory, rather than gathering other data (such as school records or

BOX *9.3*

(CONTINUED)

behavioral observations) that could confirm the existence of the symptoms at an early age. In addition, assessments of adults most often rely on the adult client as the sole informant, rather than including parents' and teachers' reports of the client's behavior. The problem is further compounded by a lack of reliable and valid assessment tools that assess symptoms of ADHD in adults. When family members are used for retrospective reports of adults, however, reliable patterns of symptoms can be collected in a valid manner (Faraone, Biederman, Feighner, & Monuteaux, 2000).

Figure 9.1 outlines the decision-making rules that can lead to a diagnosis of ADHD in adults. Because some symptoms of ADHD, especially inattention, are related to other psychological problems (such as anxiety and depression), it is imperative that the clinician conduct a careful differential diagnosis to verify that the problems are related to ADHD rather than some other disorder. Additionally, because adults with ADHD have even higher rates of comorbidity than do children with ADHD, it is important to assess for other disorders in addition to ADHD.

Sources: Barkley (2003), Faraone (2000), Resnick (2005).

(Barkley, 2006; Biederman, 2005; Lee & Hinshaw, 2004). In fact, children with the combination of impulsivity, hyperactivity, inattention, and conduct problems have been referred to as **"fledgling psychopaths"** because they appear to be destined for a troubled life if no prevention or intervention efforts are instituted (Gresham, Lane, & Lambros, 2000).

A unique feature of ADHD is that it shows **heterotypic continuity,** which means that the specific symptoms change over time but the behavior is still dysfunctional. For example, younger children tend to show gross motor movements in their overactivity, whereas older children tend to show restlessness and fidgetiness (DuPaul, McGoey, Eckert, & Van Brakle, 2001). Both types of behaviors are consistent with the diagnostic criteria, and both types of behaviors are usually dysfunctional, but the symptoms themselves change over the developmental course.

Etiology

There is no clearly established theory of the development of ADHD that has been accepted by all ADHD researchers (Nigg, 2001). However, a number of plausible etiological theories have empirical support. The majority of plausible explanations for the development of ADHD center around genetic, biological, and neurological factors. There is evidence, for example, that **family-genetic risk factors** play a role in the development and maintenance of ADHD. Parents of children with ADHD are more likely than parents of children with other disorders or nonclinical children to meet criteria for

ADHD (Biederman, 2005; Chronis et al., 2003). In fact, there is evidence that parents with ADHD show significant difficulties in their parenting role, which may exacerbate their children's risk for ADHD (Smalley et al., 2000; Sprich, Biederman, Crawford, Mundy, & Faraone, 2000; Weiss, Hechtman, & Weiss, 2000). Some, but not all, parents and siblings of children with ADHD appear to have greater neuropsychological difficulties (Nigg, Blaskey, Stawicki, & Sachek, 2004). Thus, it may be that a subset of children are more genetically vulnerable to ADHD than others, and there may be multiple etiological pathways for the development of ADHD.

Consistent with the family-genetic risk factor theory, there is also evidence from twin and adoption studies that ADHD has at least a partial genetic component (Dick, Viken, Kaprio, Pulkkinen, & Rose, 2005; Hudziak Derks, Althoff, Rettew, & Boomsma, 2005; Volk, Neuman, & Todd, 2005). For example, in a large-scale study of twins, genetic dominance was found to account for 48% of the variance in explaining symptoms of ADHD, an additional 30% of the variance was accounted for by other genetic factors, and 22% of the variance was accounted for by unique environmental factors (Hudziak et al., 2005). One longitudinal study of twins diagnosed with ADHD suggested that genetic factors contribute not only to the development but also to the maintenance over time of the ADHD symptoms (Larsson, Larsson, & Lichtenstein, 2004). Although the results of twin and adoption studies regarding ADHD are criticized occasionally (Joseph, 2000), there appears to be clear evidence of some type of genetic component in the

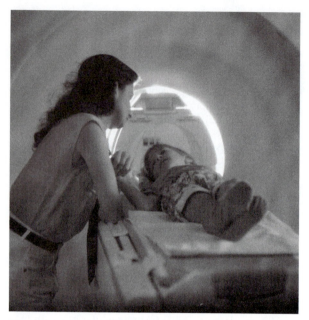

Magnetic resonance imaging is being used increasingly in research on brain structure and brain functioning in children diagnosed with ADHD.

etiology of ADHD (Biederman, 2005; Hudziak et al., 2005; Sprich et al., 2000).

Interestingly, there is evidence that the comorbidity between ADHD, oppositional defiant disorder, and conduct disorder may be influenced by environmental factors more so than the genetic factors that are related to the development of ADHD itself. Specifically, in twin studies, it appears that comorbidity with ADHD and other externalizing disorders is related to shared

environmental factors between the twins (Burt, McGue, Krueger, & Iacono, 2005). This pattern could be due to the fact that ADHD appears to have a heavier genetic loading than the other externalizing disorders with which there are high levels of comorbidity (Burt et al., 2005).

Another line of inquiry into the etiology of ADHD includes the investigation of neurobiological patterns, including investigation of dopamine and norepinephrine, which are neurotransmitters in the brain that influence behavior (Barkley, 2003; Biederman, 2005). There has also been a great deal of research into the brain structures and brain functioning of children and adolescents diagnosed with ADHD (Durston et al., 2004). A thorough review of this literature suggests that ADHD may be due to abnormalities in the portion of the brain called the frontal-striatal regions (Durston, 2003; Vaidya et al., 2005). The frontal-striatal regions are illustrated in Figure 9.2. Imaging techniques, such as functional magnetic resonance imaging (fMRI) and diffusion tensor imaging (DTI), show promise in trying to identify similarities and differences between the brain functioning of children with and without ADHD (Durston, 2003). In addition, electroencephalography (EEG) has been used for over three decades in work related to ADHD, and the technique continues to be useful in research and evaluations of children with ADHD (Loo & Barkley, 2005). Overall, there is overwhelming evidence that ADHD is at least partially due to genetic and biological factors (Biederman, 2005)

A promising etiological theory of the development and maintenance of ADHD relates to limitations in self-control, which is consistent with the evidence of abnormalities in the frontal-striatal regions of the brain. In a book entitled *ADHD and the Nature of*

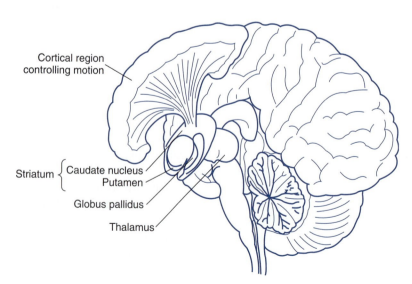

FIGURE 9.2 Diagram of the human brain showing the right hemisphere, and particularly the location of the striatum, globus pallidus, and thalamus. Most of the left hemisphere has been cut away up to the prefrontal lobes to reveal the striatum and other midbrain structures.

Source: Barkley (1998).

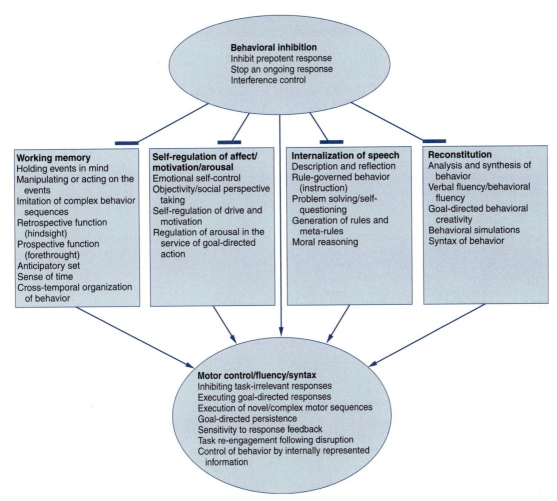

FIGURE 9.3 A schematic configuration of a conceptual model that links behavioral inhibition with the performance of the four executive functions that bring motor control, fluency, and syntax under the control of internally represented information.

Source: Barkley (1997a).

Self-Control, Dr. Russell Barkley (2005) outlined his theory that self-control and behavioral inhibition are the primary characteristics of ADHD. Further, he argued that attentional difficulties are only secondary to difficulties with self-control. As can be seen in Figure 9.3, four primary neuropsychological aspects are required for effective functioning in behavioral inhibition:

- Working memory
- Self-regulation of affect, motivation, and arousal
- Internalization of speech
- Reconstitution (i.e., behavioral analysis and synthesis)

Overall, a number of researchers (Barkley, Edwards, Laneri, Fletcher, & Metevia, 2001; Biederman, 2005;

Cepeda, Cepeda, & Kramer, 2000; Martinussen, Hayden, Hogg-Johnson, & Tannock, 2005) have found that these aspects tend to be limited in children diagnosed with ADHD. Other researchers have found that deficits in behavioral inhibition (Schachar, Mota, Logan, Tannock, & Klim, 2000) and executive functioning (Klorman et al., 1999) can even distinguish children diagnosed with ADHD from children diagnosed with conduct disorder, children comorbid for conduct disorder and ADHD, and nonclinical children. Thus, there is relatively good evidence that deficits in self-control and behavioral inhibition are a central part of the difficulties that children with ADHD face, although there appear to be many etiological factors that determine the development of ADHD (Sonuga-Barke, 2005). There is also some

BOX *9.4*

A MOTHER'S EXPERIENCE IN HER OWN WORDS

Yesterday we had a doctor's appointment. This was a nine o'clock appointment with a pediatric specialist in town. We were there at five minutes to nine. I had to take Jeremy out of school to be there. He was there for ADHD . . . and we waited and waited and waited. It got to be 9:15 and the next patient came in and said, "I'm here to see Dr. So-and-So, my appointment is for 9:15." Two minutes later the doctor came out and took him in and there we were, still sitting, waiting. . . .

Jeremy is not the most cooperative child in the world, and in the next five to ten minutes he was sitting there screaming, "My turn, my turn, my turn." . . .

After we'd had 15 or 20 minutes of extra waiting, the doctor came back out and called Jeremy. We'd been there almost an hour. We had the first appointment of the day and we were there almost an hour before we even saw the

doctor. I went in and said, "Before we get started, I have to talk to you about something. We were here for a nine o'clock appointment, and we were here on time. I have a child that I took out of school to be here. I made a nine o'clock appointment so we wouldn't have to wait and we waited anyway. . . . This is a child we are talking about, a child who is here for ADHD. He does not do well in a waiting room." He said, "Well, I made the mistake. I was running slow and I didn't read who was first."

This guy is a pediatric specialist. Why can't he be sensitive to these issues? My son was there for hyperactivity. We were there <u>because</u> he can't sit still and cooperate. It just sometimes makes me feel like I'm banging my head against a wall. (pp. 16–18)

Source: Marsh (1995).

---

indication that etiological factors of the development and maintenance of ADHD may differ for children in contrast to adults (Lijffijt, Kenemans, Verbaten, & van Engeland, 2005).

There is equivocal evidence about the impact of psychosocial family factors on the development and maintenance of ADHD. As can be seen in Box 9.4, raising a child with ADHD could be taxing on even the most patient of parents. A number of externalizing behavior problems are associated with a number of adverse family factors, such as interparental conflict, dissimilar parenting styles of mothers and fathers, parental psychopathology, a troubled parent–child relationship, and aversive parental control behaviors (Biederman, 2005; Harvey, 2000; Kashdan et al., 2004). Most of these factors, however, are associated with oppositional problems and conduct problems or with the combination of ADHD and conduct problems rather than the experience of ADHD alone. Other psychosocial and environmental factors have received some empirical support regarding the identification and maintenance of ADHD. For example, a poor goodness-of-fit between students' behavior and teachers' tolerance for activity and inattention may be related to labeling behaviors as problematic that might not be viewed as problematic in another setting (Greene, 1995, 1996; Greene, Besterezey, et al., 2002).

In addition to knowing about etiological formulations that have empirical support, it is also important to know about theories that have consistently received no

empirical support. During the 1970s, dietary habits, food additives, and sugar consumption were all implicated in the development and maintenance of what we now know as ADHD. When well-controlled studies are conducted, however, none of these factors are related to ADHD (Rojas & Chan, 2005; Waschbusch & Hill, 2003). In other words, the widely held beliefs that sugar causes hyperactivity and that food additives (such as preservatives) cause hyperactivity are not found to be true when studied carefully. Although some children have idiosyncratic responses to some foods, the majority of children who meet ADHD criteria would act similarly if they ingested sugar as if they had ingested a placebo with a nonsugar inert substance in it (Rojas & Chan, 2005).

There is also no consistent evidence that environmental toxins (such as lead) are related to the development and maintenance of ADHD. Some research with animals has suggested that when animals are exposed to high doses of lead, they become more agitated, impulsive, and distracted (Rowland et al., 2002). It is unclear, however, whether these same patterns occur in humans. Lead and other toxins can cause neurological and cognitive problems, but there is no consistent evidence that environmental toxins are in any way related to ADHD (Rojas & Chan, 2005; Rowland et al., 2002).

Some researchers have acknowledged that ADHD symptoms may be beneficial in some circumstances. Specifically, there is speculation that from an evolutionary perspective, some characteristics of ADHD were

Case Study: Mark, the Daydreamer

His mother thinks that he is depressed. His father thinks that he is lazy and unfocused. Both parents agree that he was a demanding baby who rarely slept and who cried a lot.

Mark is 11 years old, and he seems to have chronic problems with paying attention. He seems absent-minded, and he often seems to be lost in a fog. Mark has difficulty following conversations at the dinner table or following jokes with his classmates. In addition to his limited attention span, Mark has almost no friends and appears to be rigid in his social interactions (e.g., he wants to do certain things over and over again).

Until recently, Mark had been performing adequately in school. He maintained a solid "B" average for most of his subjects. In the seventh grade, however, Mark's grades began to slip. Although he tried to keep up with the schoolwork, his homework became disorganized, and he appeared to daydream a lot when he was supposed to be studying. Overall,

Mark's father reported being disappointed and irritated with him, whereas his mother reported that she felt protective and worried about him.

An evaluation showed that Mark experienced heightened levels of inattention, poor concentration, and poor memory for details. Based on the evaluation and information collected from Mark's teachers and parents, Mark was diagnosed with attention-deficit/hyperactivity disorder—predominantly inattentive type. Before he began the eighth grade, Mark was prescribed methylphenidate. During the eighth grade, Mark's grades improved dramatically, as did his behavior. He no longer seemed as inattentive or unable to concentrate as he had in the previous year. In addition, his relationship with his parents improved, and he made two new friends in a basketball program. Mark did not experience any adverse effects of the medication.

Source: Spitzer et al. (1994).

---

adaptive given the demands of survival at different times throughout history (Barkley, 2004). For example, the hunter theory would argue that impulsivity, distractability, and aggression were adaptive for someone who was hunting given the need to have rapid responses and the need to experience flexible thinking to survive as a hunter (Shelley-Tremblay & Rosen, 1996). Although evolutionary theories are speculative, there is some evidence that certain characteristics of ADHD may be adaptive in some settings.

Given that there is such diversity in the experience of ADHD, there may be different etiologies for different children diagnosed with ADHD. Clearly, further research is needed to ascertain whether different theories explain the development and maintenance of different subtypes of ADHD or whether an overarching theory helps explain the majority of ADHD cases.

Treatment

Although a number of therapies have been attempted with ADHD, only a selection of effective treatments will be reviewed here. The three primary types of treatments that will be reviewed are medication, behavioral therapies within the family, and behavioral techniques within the school system. Although other therapies, such as cognitive therapy, family therapy, play therapy, and interpersonal counseling have been attempted with children diagnosed with ADHD, the primary methods of treatment center around psychopharmacological

interventions (i.e., medication) and behavioral therapies. There has been a significant amount of research on cognitive therapies, but they have not been found to be well established as empirically supported treatments (Hinshaw, 2006; Schroeder & Gordon, 2002). In addition, there is growing interest in exploring complementary and alternative medicine treatments, such as homeopathy, yoga, massage, essential fatty acid supplementation, and use of green outdoor spaces, that could be used in conjunction with traditional treatments (Rojas & Chan, 2005). Overall, there is a need to disseminate information about effective treatments to practitioners in the community and to the public at large (Weisz, Doss, & Hawley, 2005, 2006).

The most comprehensive and largest recent study to explore treatment of ADHD is called the **Multimodal Treatment Study of Children with ADHD (MTA study;** Conners et al., 2001; Jensen et al., 2001; MTA Cooperative Group, 1999; Pelham et al., 2000). Funded by the National Institute of Mental Health, the MTA study included six sites across the United States and included 579 children diagnosed with ADHD, combined type. At the beginning of the study, children ranged in age from 7 to 9.9 years old. Children were randomly assigned to one of four conditions, which were intended to last for 14 months:

- Medication
- Intensive behavioral treatment with parent, child, and school components

By permission of Mike Luckovich and Creators Syndicate, Inc.

- Combination of medication and intensive behavioral treatment
- Treatment as usual (where children received treatment, most often medication, in the community with their regular physicians)

The study was designed to explore the immediate and long-term effects of these different treatments. There have been a number of important findings from the MTA study, including

- Children who received either medication alone or the combination of medication and behavioral treatment showed significantly more improvement in ADHD symptoms than children who received behavioral treatment alone or treatment as usual in the community (MTA Cooperative Group, 1999).
- Children who received both medication and behavioral treatment ended up needing lower doses of the medication at the end of the study in comparison with children who received medication only (Vitiello et al., 2001).
- Children with comorbid disorders like conduct problems or anxiety disorders were more effectively treated with behavioral treatment than are children with ADHD alone (Wells et al., 2000).
- The combination of medication and behavioral treatment was more effective than other treatments for low SES ethnic minority children who were comorbid with ADHD and another disorder (Arnold et al., 2003).

- Children who were in the medication only or medication plus behavioral treatment groups were less likely to improve when their parents showed high levels of depressive symptoms and when their behavior was particularly severe before treatment. Children with lower intellectual functioning were also less likely to improve in these two groups (Owens et al., 2003).
- The more effective treatments (medication for ADHD alone and the combination of medication and behavioral treatment for ADHD and another disorder) were also the most cost-effective treatments when the incremental benefit of the treatments were considered (Jensen et al., 2005).
- Even after effective treatment and a reduction in ADHD symptoms, children from all four treatment groups continued to show significant impairments in their social relationships according to reports by their peers (Hoza et al., 2005).

Overall, the MTA study has shed light on the effective treatments for ADHD and ADHD with comorbid disorders. Note, however, that the MTA study has also been criticized on a number of grounds, including the design of the study and the interpretation of results. For example, because the MTA study did not use a double-blind or placebo-controlled design (where neither prescribing physicians, parents, or children knew whether the child was receiving active medication or a placebo), the effectiveness results of the medication trials are called into question (Breggin, 2001a). Teachers and parents who reported on the children's behavior knew which type of treatment the children were receiving, so they may have been influenced by that knowledge. The main reporters of children's behavior who did not know which type of treatment the child was receiving (observers who were unaware of treatment status, peers, and the children themselves) were the ones who did not show significant differences in the superiority of psychostimulant medication (Breggin, 2001a). Thus, there is a question as to the trust in which we can interpret the results of the MTA study.

In addition, the MTA study has been criticized for not helping further the field in an understanding of which types of treatments might be best suited for different children. For example, the question, "What type of treatment by what type of therapist is most effective in dealing with what specific problems among specific children with ADHD?" was not addressed by the MTA study (Greene & Ablon, 2001, p. 119). Thus, clinicians are still left with trying to identify a treatment that will be most effective for any individual client that arrives in their office. With the overall results of the MTA study in mind, and with the acknowledgment that clinicians and consumers need to know more about these treatments, a closer look at the different treatment regimens is in order.

With regard to psychopharmacological treatments, the primary medications that are used to treat ADHD are stimulants, such as methylphenidate (Ritalin), Dextroamphetamine (Dexedrine), and Amphetamine & d-ampheamine compound (Adderall; Brown et al., 2005; DuPaul et al., 2003). Note that although pemoline (Cylert) used to be prescribed for the treatment of ADHD, it is no longer recommended because of a number of reports of acute liver failure in children (Phelps et al., 2002). Note also that a newer medication that has been used to treat ADHD, atomoxetine (Strattera), has been linked to a risk for suicidal thinking. The U.S. Food and Drug Administration has suggested caution in the administration of this medication given the potential dangers (Consumer Reports Medical Guide, 2005).

Through the use of double-blind studies, certain antidepressant medications have been shown to be effective in the treatment of ADHD. Both fluoxetine (Prozac) and bupropion (Wellbutrin) have been clinically validated as effective in the treatment of ADHD (Phelps et al., 2002). Recall from chapter 4, however, that the use of antidepressants with children has come under fire because of the potential for increased risk for suicidality.

Turning back to psychstimulant medication, effectiveness rates of stimulant medications range from 75% to 90% (Pennington, 2002), with most researchers concluding that effectiveness rates hover around 80% (Wilens et al., 2002; Rowland et al., 2002). Thus, it is reasonable to assume that approximately 80% of ADHD children who are treated with a stimulant medication will show behavioral improvements. When compared directly, both Ritalin and Adderall appeared to be equally effective (Pelham et al., 2000; Pliszka, Browne, Olvera, & Wynne, 2000). Even students who are skeptical of medication should be impressed by these rates of effectiveness. It is also important to acknowledge, however, that approximately 20% of ADHD children who are treated with stimulant medications show either no improvement or show adverse effects (Rowland et al., 2002).

Even the children who do experience positive effects from stimulant medication do not show improvement in all areas of functioning. Stimulant medications have been found to be very effective in helping to increase attention, concentration, and compliance and to decrease disruptive behavior, impulsive behavior, and aggression (Brodeur & Pond, 2001). There is some evidence that stimulant medications are effective in helping improve peer relationships, but these positive effects are not found in all studies (Hoza et al., 2005). Unfortunately, stimulant medication has been found to only have modest positive effects on academic achievement, if at all (Bussing, Zima, & Perwien, 2000; Ryan, Reid, Epstein, Ellis, & Evans, 2005). There is some evidence that methylphenidate (Ritalin) increases dopamine in the brain, which in turn makes mathematics problems more interesting and makes individuals more motivated to complete the tasks (Volkow et al., 2004). In a study of young children (aged 7 to 9 years old) who were diagnosed with ADHD but who did not have a learning disorder or a conduct disorder, children were helped equally in their academic performance by methylphenidate (Ritalin) alone; methylphenidate combined with therapy that included academic assistance, parent training, social skills training, organizational skills training, and psychotherapy; and methylphenidate and placebo therapy (known as attention control, where attention was paid to the students but no therapy was delivered; Hechtman, 2004). Thus, there is some evidence that medication can help with academic functioning, but the results are still not conclusive.

Unfortunately, the strongest behavioral effects of stimulant medications tend to disappear after the medication is withdrawn (Brown et al., 2005; Phelps et al., 2002). Overall, stimulant medication is well accepted within the field. Although psychologists cannot prescribe

BOX *9.5*

A DIFFERENT VIEW OF ADHD AND MEDICATION

Imagine an 8-year-old named James. James's mother complains that he is constantly underfoot and that he does not pay attention when she gives him lists of chores to complete. James's father complains that he chatters all the time, gets into too many things around the house, and will not sit still and play by himself. James's teacher complains that he is fidgety in class and that he will only sit still and listen to her when they are talking one-on-one. You might already have diagnosed James with ADHD. You might, however, want to consider an alternative explanation. Dr. Peter Breggin and Ginger Ross Breggin (1995) would argue that James is suffering from a lack of adult attention and that there is a mismatch between James's needs and what those in his environment wish to give him. Rather than treating highly active and inattentive children with methylphenidate or another stimulant medication, the Breggins argue that we should explore environmental changes that might help meet the child's basic needs. Rather than diagnosing and finding fault in children, we should look at the family system, the school system, and the community system to identify how the child's environment can be modified to help the child feel more secure and happy. To make their point, the Breggins identified a new "disorder" called Dad Attention Deficit Disorder (DADD), in which children do not receive enough attention from their fathers and must behave in ways to get their fathers' attention (Breggin & Breggin, 1995). Children with this disorder are "treated" effectively with loving and appropriate attention from their father.

These concepts are obviously quite a departure from mainstream psychology and psychiatry. Interestingly, Dr. Breggin is himself a psychiatrist. In his book, *Talking back to Ritalin: What Doctors Aren't Telling You about Stimulants for Children (rev ed.),* Dr. Breggin (2001b) illustrates the biochemical hazards of medications such as Ritalin and provides other alternatives to treating active children. In another book called *The Ritalin Fact Book: What Your Doctor Won't Tell you about ADHD and Stimulant Drugs,* Dr. Breggin (2002) argues that medications are used to force children into docility and submission. Medications that are used for behavioral change can be considered chemical restraints. In fact, it is as if we are trying to medicate childhood out of children (Breggin, 2002).

The use of stimulant medication or any other type of medication is potentially controversial. As described in

chapter 4, there are side effects to stimulant medication, such as stunted growth (Phelps et al., 2002). In addition, Ritalin has become even more controversial since many adolescents have started selling their own Ritalin to other children as an illicit drug. Apparently, some non-ADHD children find that Ritalin can give them a "buzz" that they enjoy. One survey of adolescents in Wisconsin and Minnesota found that selling or trading stimulant medication was quite common (Moline & Frankenberger, 2001). For adolescents who were prescribed medication:

- 34% of adolescents said that they were sometimes approached to sell or trade their medication.
- 11% said that they were almost always or always approached to sell or trade their medication.

There are a growing number of arrests and prosecutions of children and adolescents who are selling Ritalin and other psychopharmacological medications for profit. These patterns occur in college as well. A recent survey of college students found that (Hall, Irwin, Bowman, Frankenberger, & Jewett, 2005):

- 17% of male college students acknowledge using substances like Ritalin illegally (e.g., purchasing the medication from someone else who has a prescription).
- 11% of female college students report using substances like Ritalin illegally.

For college students as well as adolescents, Ritalin is thought to give individuals without ADHD a "high" that keeps them awake and able to work or study for longer periods of time. Known as "Vitamin R," students often use illegally obtained Ritalin to pull an all-nighter for studying or for partying (Hall et al., 2005). Thus, the use of Ritalin is considered problematic for a number of reasons, from social-political reasons to the use of the medication as an illicit drug.

Overall, the Breggins and other professionals have called into the question the diagnosis of ADHD as well as the treatment of ADHD. Some writers have suggested that we are pathologizing childhood by labeling overactivity as a psychiatric symptom rather than as evidence of a child being a child (Stolzer, 2005).

medications, they often refer children for an evaluation of the appropriateness of medication for symptoms of ADHD. In addition, many psychologists work in conjunction with a psychiatrist or behavioral pediatrician

to provide comprehensive treatment services for children diagnosed with ADHD (Barkley, 2006).

As can be seen in Box 9.5, however, the use of psychostimulants for the treatment of ADHD is a controversial topic. Approximately 90% of visits to a physician with complaints of hyperactivity result in prescribing a medication, usually methylphenidate (Whalen & Henker, 1998). Over the past decade, use of psychostimulants has risen dramatically in the treatment of ADHD, whereas therapy services have decreased dramatically in the treatment of ADHD within the same time period (Hoagwood, Kelleher, Feil, & Comer, 2000). The prevalence of stimulants to treat symptoms of ADHD is staggering. There has been an eightfold increase in the use of psychostimulants over the past 10 years (Diller, 1999b). This pattern is primarily within the United States. In fact, 90% of the prescriptions for methylphenidate worldwide are written in the United States (Diller, 1999b). The pattern of usage is troubling, given that many children who receive psychostimulants are not followed closely by the prescribing physician. For example, one study found that children who were diagnosed with ADHD and who were prescribed medication did not differ from other nondisordered children in the amount of follow-up visits they had with the prescribing physician (Gardner, Kelleher, Pajer, & Campo, 2004).

Among the many criticisms of the use of medications for the treatment of ADHD is that the patterns of prescriptions seems to be influenced by many factors other than the actual symptoms of the disorder. For example, girls and adolescents are less likely to receive psychostimulant medication for symptoms of ADHD than are boys and younger children (Angold, Erkanli, Egger, & Costello, 2000). African Americans are less likely than Caucasian Americans to receive psychostimulants or any other type of treatment for ADHD (Stevens et al., 2005). In a study of psychostimulant prescriptions in the state of New York, children in upstate New York were 10 times more likely to be prescribed a psychostimulant than similar children in New York City (Radigan, Lannon, Roohan, & Gesten, 2005).

The question also arises as to who is prescribing psychostimulants. Compared with pediatricians and child psychiatrists, family practitioners who prescribe psychostimulants for high levels of activity are less likely to conduct formal assessment procedures, are less likely to provide or recommend therapy services, and are less likely to suggest follow-up care for the medication (Hoagwood et al., 2000). At least 50% of children diagnosed with ADHD are treated in a way that is not consistent with the recommendations provided by the American Academy of Child and Adolescent Psychiatry (Hoagwood et al., 2000). Regardless of the effectiveness of psychostimulants for the treatment of

ADHD symptoms, these trends are of great concern. Both the American Academy of Child and Adolescent Psychiatry as well as the American Academy of Pediatrics (American Academy of Pediatrics, 2000) have established firm guidelines for the assessment and treatment of ADHD. These guidelines should be followed by physicians to make sure that children are not being overmedicated or medicated improperly. There are a number of resources for parents when considering the use of medication for ADHD. For example, *Straight Talk about Psychiatric Medications for Kids (rev. ed.)* (Wilens, 2004b) provides a scientific basis of the pros and cons of medication use and explains these issues in a way that does not require advanced medical training. On the other end of the spectrum, parents who might be questioning the use of psychostimulants will likely find *Talking back to Ritalin: What Doctors Aren't Telling You about Stimulants for Children* (Breggin, 2001b) of interest.

There are also other concerns regarding the use of stimulant medication. Given that there are relatively high rates of comorbidity between ADHD and substance abuse disorders (Molina & Pelham, 2003), a question often arises as to whether stimulant medication is associated with later substance abuse in adolescence and adulthood. Based on available research, there is no indication that stimulant medication is associated with a greater likelihood of substance abuse later in life (Wilens, 2004a). In fact, effective treatment of ADHD in childhood and adolescence with psychostimulant medication is associated with a decreased risk for substance use disorders in adulthood (Wilens, 2004a; Wilens, Faraone, Biederman, & Gunawardene, 2003). Although more longitudinal studies are needed, there is no cause for parents' concerns about stimulant medications leading to substance abuse problems.

Overall, the use of stimulant medications is well accepted within the field, but remains quite controversial for some professionals and parents (Barkley, 2003). As discussed in the therapeutic interventions chapter, the attributions of children on medication can sometimes be counterproductive to long-term behavior change. Research continues to investigate the strengths and weaknesses of the use of medications in treating ADHD. Many professionals advocate a combination of medication and behavioral therapy because improvements from behavioral therapy tend to remain even after the treatment is terminated (Barkley, 2003; MTA Cooperative Group, 1999).

There are some remedies worse than the disease.
—Publilius Syrus

In addition to medications that are used for treatment of ADHD, a number of therapies have been tried with ADHD children. **Behavioral parent training** and behavioral interventions in classrooms are considered evidence-based treatments for ADHD (Anastopoulos & Farley, 2003). The basic premise of behavioral parent training is to help parents execute good behavioral techniques that facilitate their children's behavioral control (Barkley, 1997b). In a 10-session treatment package, the following topics would be addressed each week (Barkley, 1997b):

- Teaching parents, through psychoeducational processes, why children misbehave

- Helping parents to pay attention to their children's behavior (especially teaching parents to "catch" their children behaving well so that they could provide positive reinforcement)

- Helping parents to increase their children's compliance and to help enhance children's ability for independent play

- Teaching parents about token economies, such as using poker chips, points, or a star chart to reward appropriate behavior

- Teaching parents about the appropriate use of time out and other disciplinary actions

- Helping parents to enhance many of their children's behaviors in addition to the behaviors that were part of the original referral concern

- Teaching parents how to anticipate and prevent troubled behavior in their children

- Empowering parents to work with teachers to improve their children's behavior at school

- Helping parents to prepare for the future with regard to challenges that their children will face in maintaining behavioral control

- Processing the children's behavioral progress with parents to review what strategies have worked and what strategies should be used in the future with their children

Behavioral parent training is effective for a number of externalizing problems in children, including ADHD (Anastopoulos & Farley, 2003). Most often, behavioral parent training is only recommended for children aged 2 to 11 (Barkley, 1997b), although there are now behavioral parent training programs for parents of adolescents as well (Barkley, Edwards, & Robin, 1999). Behavioral parent training has sometimes been combined with problem-solving communication training for families with an adolescent diagnosed with ADHD (Barkley, Edwards, Laneri, Fletcher, & Metevia, 2001). Both treatments (problem-solving communication training alone and behavioral parent training combined with problem-solving communication) were found to be effective (Barkley et al., 2001).

Some behavioral therapy and parent training techniques have been presented in books for parents to read themselves. Within the popular press, a book called *Ritalin Is Not the Answer: A Drug-Free, Practical Program for Children Diagnosed with ADD or ADHD* (Stein, 1999) and a companion book called *Ritalin Is Not the Answer Action Guide: An Interactive Companion to the Bestselling Drug-Free ADD/ADHD Parenting Program* (Stein, 2002) have received a great deal of attention by providing specific behavioral suggestions that parents can use in conjunction with a trained clinician. Two other books targeted at parents, *Your Defiant Child: Eight Steps to Better Behavior* (Barkley & Benton, 1998) and *Taking Charge of ADHD: The Complete Authoritative Guide for Parents (rev.)* (Barkley, 2000), also include behavioral parent training strategies. Overall, behavioral parent training has been found to be quite effective in addressing the symptoms of ADHD (Anastopoulos & Farley, 2003). Although the immediate behavioral improvements are not as notable as with medication (based on teachers' ratings), the improvements from behavioral parent training tend to remain long after treatment is completed, which is often not the case with stimulant medication (Anastopoulos & Farley, 2003). The use of both stimulants and behavioral techniques provide a multimodal treatment of ADHD that can lead to the lowest dosages of medication and good long-term results (Vitiello et al., 2001). As noted in Box 9.6, young adolescents often report wanting behaviors from their parents that are consistent with the lessons learned in behavioral parent training.

In addition to behavioral parent training programs, a number of behavioral programs are also instituted in the school system. Most of the school-based behavioral programs can be described as **contingency management strategies,** which include token economies, time-out, and response-cost procedures (Nolan & Carr, 2000). Most of these procedures fall within the domain of applied behavior analysis (Baldwin, 1999). These procedures are discussed in greater detail in the chapter on treatment and interventions. Suffice it to say that these procedures all rely on behavioral principles to help children gain control of their behavior. **Token economies** are instituted so that children receive some

BOX *9.6*

WHAT PRETEENS WANT THEIR PARENTS TO KNOW

Although a number of important lessons can be learned from behavioral parent training (Barkley, 1997b), sometimes these suggestions are surprisingly consistent with what children want from their parents. Out of the mouths of babes (or preteens, in this case):

- Encourage me when I do a good job. (p. 9)
- Give me reasons for your demands. (p. 15)
- Nagging doesn't work in the long run. (p. 53)

- Set a good example for me. (p. 64)
- Don't make any promises you might not be able to keep. (p. 85)
- Don't spend all your time on the child who's acting up. Acknowledge the good as well as the bad. (p. 92)
- When telling me about your rules, make sure I understand the consequences. (p. 104)

Source: Holladay (1994).

type of reward after successfully completing specific behaviors. For example, children with ADHD, predominantly hyperactive-impulsive type, might receive a token for every 15 minutes that they sit in their seat during quiet time in class. After receiving five tokens, they might be able to "cash in" these tokens for a prize that they want (e.g., a fancy pencil or 10 extra minutes to play a computer game). **Time-out** is used to try to decrease maladaptive behavior by removing the reinforcements for that behavior. Most often, there is a time-out chair or a time-out section of the room where the child is sent after exhibiting the maladaptive behavior. Most programs that use time-out limit the amount of time to correspond with 1 minute per year of age of the child. Thus, a 7-year-old would be put in time-out for no more than 7 minutes per infraction. **Response-cost procedures** occur when a child has to forfeit something desirable if he or she exhibits a specific maladaptive behavior. The easiest example to imagine in your own life is the fine for returning a rented video later than the deadline (i.e., you lose your precious money because of returning the video late). Within the school system, a response-cost procedure with ADHD children might be that they lose a specific amount of time at recess if they blurt out an answer during the morning lecture. There are also social skills training programs that can be implemented in the school setting that show great promise (Antshel & Remer, 2003).

Overall, contingency management strategies are considered evidence-based treatments, especially in conjunction with other treatments (Hinshaw, Klein, & Abikoff, 2002). With regard to other interventions within the school system, a number of academic interventions are effective. Specifically, peer tutoring and task modifications help ADHD children with both their attentional difficulties and their academic performance (DuPaul & Stoner, 2004). In fact, a meta-analysis of school-based interventions found that contingency management strategies, as well as academic interventions, were significantly more effective than were cognitive-behavioral treatments with ADHD children (DuPaul & Eckert, 1997).

Even with the support of empirical evidence for these specific treatments, it is important to ascertain which treatment is best for which child (Owens et al., 2003). Specifically, the individual strengths and weaknesses of each child should be identified through functional assessment to determine the treatment that would be most likely to help alleviate the symptoms of ADHD (DuPaul, Eckert, & McGoey, 1997). In addition, the goodness-of-fit between teacher and student should be considered, and treatment interventions may need to be addressed with the teacher (or the school system) rather than the student (Greene, 1996). There is a significant need for clinicians to coordinate services with school professionals to provide the most comprehensive treatment to children with ADHD (NIH Consensus Development Panel, 2000).

Outside the school system, parent support groups can also be helpful for families dealing with ADHD. The largest ADHD organization for families within the United States is called Children and Adults with Attention-Deficit/Hyperactivity Disorder (CHADD). This organization provides information, referrals, and support services for families dealing with ADHD. Many communities across the United States have local parent support groups that are affiliated with CHADD. The national organization can be located at *www.chadd.org*, and local chapters can be identified through this Web site. The primary criticism of organizations such as

Case Study: ADHD within a Family System

Although ADHD is a diagnosis for an individual child, adolescent, or adult, family systems therapists look within the entire family system to explore the etiology, maintenance, and ramifications of children with high levels of activity and impulsivity. In the Johnson family, the single mother, Sonya, has two sons, 9-year-old Jim and 7-year-old Jack. Jim was referred to a residential facility because of severe hyperactivity, aggression, cruelty to animals, and oppositional behavior.

Sonya often had her mother (the boys' grandmother) care for them. In observations of their interactions, it became obvious that Sonya did not have any control within the family, and that her mother was the one who tried to run the family. The family therapists wanted to help change the structure of the family so that Sonya could parent effectively without any interference from her mother. For this reason, only Sonya and the boys (and not the grandmother) were included in the therapy sessions. Following is a verbatim excerpt from a session where the therapists are actively trying to bolster the mother's legitimate right to parent her children. After the mother's power is restored within the family system, the therapists can help the mother with more appropriate parenting strategies that would be consistent with behavioral parent training. The transcript begins when the mother is trying to contain Jim in his chair after he has threatened to leave the session and after he has threatened to hit the therapists.

Mom to Jim:	[while putting her arm across him so he remains in the chair] Do not move! [to therapists] He does things to really get on my nerves. [to Jim] You know something. I am taking this radio away! You know that.
Jim:	[pleadingly to mom] No!
Mom:	You ain't keeping that because you can't listen.

Sonya then proceeds to tell of several incidents in which Jim hits his younger brother, Jack, with the last incident resulting in Jack crying.

Jim:	No! I told you that Jack started it.
Mom:	No! You did. I—
Jim:	[interrupting mom] I did not!
Therapist 2 to mom:	Let me ask you something. Do you mind that Jim is interrupting you when you are talking with other adults?
Mom:	See, he thinks that because I'm talking with someone else I'm not going to do anything about what he's doing.
Therapist 2:	Okay. So what are you going to do about it right now? [Jim, at this point, attempts to get out of his chair.]
Mom:	[again places her arm across Jim's chair so that he can't get up] No! You sit here when I am talking. I've come a long way to be here. You are going to sit here and you are going to listen. Because if you don't, you won't be coming home next week. I'll take everything back that I brought for you. Do you think that I can't take back everything that is here? I'm going to prove my point! [reaches for the items on the table]
Jim:	[grabbing for the items] No, no, no. Why? Why?

Sonya, in turn, proceeds to tell the therapists of more incidents in which Jim hits his younger brother.

Therapist 1 to mom:	So, what you are saying—Jim interrupts] I'm not going to listen to your son right now because you are an adult and I am talking to you. So, what you are saying is that Jim's hitting is a big problem. Do you think that he understands that this is a big problem?

Source: Kemenoff, Jachimczyk, & Fussner (1998, p. 138).

CHADD is the social or political agenda that might exist for the organization. Much of the funding for CHADD comes from pharmaceutical companies, with a majority of the funding coming from the manufacturer of Ritalin, CibaGeneva Pharmaceuticals (Breggin, 2001b). The organization has been criticized for promoting the use of psychostimulants, especially Ritalin, while ignoring other therapeutic interventions (Breggin, 2001b). For this reason, support organizations such as CHADD should be viewed with caution. Although some families may be helped by the information and support that is provided by CHADD, it is important that families learn about all of their options regarding the identification of and treatment for high levels of activity and inattention in their children.

To summarize the current knowledge base on treating ADHD effectively, a survey of 50 psychologists and 51 physicians who are experts in the field was completed (Conners, March, Frances, Wells, & Ross, 2001). This survey was completed after the main results from the MTA study were distributed, so this summary takes into account the initial results of the MTA study. Overall, the experts recommended that starting with the combination of medication and behavioral treatment was appropriate when the symptoms of ADHD were severe, when the child showed significant aggression or academic problems, when the family was disrupted significantly by the symptoms of ADHD, for children older than preschool, and when there were comorbid problems with externalizing disorders. Conversely, behavioral treatment without medication was suggested as a first step in treatment when the child was preschool age, when the ADHD symptoms were on the mild end of the continuum, when there were comorbid internalizing disorders, when there were comorbid social skills problems, and when the family preferred psychosocial treatments instead of medication (Conners et al., 2001). Overall, this survey of experts is reflective of the research data on the best practices in the treatment of ADHD.

Patience is the best remedy for every trouble.
—Titus Maccius Plautus

Prevention

Given the implications of a strong neurological etiology in the development of ADHD (Barkley, 2006), little work has been done in the prevention of ADHD. Notably, major collections of writings on prevention programs (e.g., Cicchetti, Rappaport, Sandler, & Weissberg, 2000; Price, Cowan, Lorion, & Ramos-McKay, 1988) do not address the prevention of ADHD. Although some of the work on behavioral parent training could be considered indicated prevention (i.e., the prevention of further problems related to the symptoms of ADHD), to date almost no attention has been given to the prevention of the onset of ADHD. This oversight within the professional community may be due to the assumption that ADHD cannot be prevented.

The professional writings that come closest to discussing preventive efforts for ADHD specifically address the goodness-of-fit between student and teacher (Greene, 1995, 1996). These writings suggest that ADHD primarily manifests itself when there is a poor fit between students' behavior and teachers' expectations; thus, preventive efforts could be directed at making teachers more accepting of students' diverse array of behaviors. Overall, more work is needed to be done to explore whether aspects of ADHD can be prevented or minimized in children before the disorder is full-blown.

ATTENTION-DEFICIT/HYPERACTIVITY DISORDER CONCEPTUALIZED IN A DIMENSIONAL MANNER

More than any other disorder in this book, ADHD is lacking in dimensional conceptualizations. ADHD is studied thoroughly within the framework of diagnostic criteria, but there is extraordinarily little research that conceptualizes attention and activity levels in a dimensional manner. Notably, entire volumes of professional writings that explore dimensional conceptualizations of children's behavior do not include any formal discussion of ADHD (e.g., Hankin & Abela, 2005; Luthar, 2003). One collection of writings from a dimensional perspective includes a chapter on attention, but not on activity levels that might be associated with ADHD (Taylor, 1995) and another included a chapter on disorders of action regulation (Pennington, 2002). There are, however, writings in other areas of psychology that address some of the dimensional issues related to attention, hyperactivity, and impulsivity. As can be seen in Box 9.7, even social psychology and personality psychology can help inform researchers interested in impulsivity as it relates to conceptualizing ADHD in a dimensional manner.

Information from standardized measures can help inform us about the prevalence of behaviors related to ADHD from a dimensional perspective. Based on the normative data that were used to standardize the Child Behavior Checklist and related measures (Achenbach & Rescorla, 2001), it appears that the occurrence of inattention, overactivity, and impulsivity are quite common in children of all ages. As can be seen in Figure 9.4, inattention ("can't concentrate"), overactivity ("can't sit still"), and impulsivity ("acts without thinking") are all relatively common for clinical and nonclinical boys and girls across the age span according to parents, youth, and teachers. Children who are referred for clinical services continue to show much higher levels of inattention, overactivity, and impulsivity than children in the nonclinical group, but children in the nonclinical group also show relatively high levels of these behaviors.

BOX 9.7

WAITING FOR THE MARSHMALLOW

In an intriguing series of studies, Dr. Walter Mischel and colleagues identified delay of gratification as a central component to functioning well (Mischel & Ebbesen, 1970; Mischel, Shoda, & Peake, 1988; Rodriguez, Mischel, & Shoda, 1989). In some ways, delay of gratification can be seen as being the polar opposite of impulsivity. In fact, there is evidence to suggest that attentional processes can help delay gratification, which is related to better behavioral outcomes even a decade later (Mischel et al., 1988).

How did these researchers explore this important issue? One of their research paradigms put preschool children (ages 4 and 5) in a situation where they could choose between receiving a less-desirable reward immediately or waiting for a more desirable reward (in many cases, a marshmallow). The dependent variable in these studies was how long the children waited for the desirable reward before giving in to the less-desirable reward (Mischel & Ebbesen, 1970). They found that children who waited longer (i.e., who delayed gratification longer) tended to use distraction strategies for themselves (i.e., they did not think about the marshmallow for which they were waiting anxiously). Not only was delay of gratification related to current intellectual

and attentional functioning in the preschoolers (Rodriguez et al., 1989), but also delay of gratification was also related to functioning nearly a decade later (Mischel et al., 1988). Specifically, children were followed over 10 years, and those who had delayed gratification longer in preschool were more socially competent, academically competent, and better at coping during adolescence (Mischel et al., 1988).

More recent work in this area has suggested similar results. For example, preschoolers who use distraction in the context of interesting projects can delay gratification longer than children who do not use distraction techniques and who focus on a tangible reward that is supposed to be given for waiting longer (Peake, Hebl, & Mischel, 2002). When tasks and projects are not of high interest to preschool children, then providing rewards for sustained attention can help children stay focused on their activities as long as there is not an inordinate focus on the rewards (Peake et al., 2002).

These studies suggest that children's skills in preschool are related to their functioning in adolescence. The studies further suggest that teaching children strategies to delay gratification in early childhood might help improve children's functioning in adolescence and beyond.

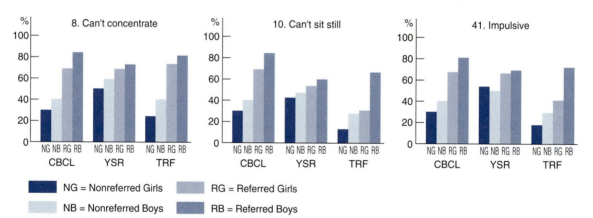

FIGURE 9.4 Percent of children for whom each problem was endorsed
NG = Nonreferred Girls   NB = Nonreferred Boys
RG = Referred Girls   RB = Referred Boys.

Source: Achenbach & Rescorla (2001).

Risk Factors

Given the lack of research into symptoms of ADHD from a dimensional perspective, it is not surprising that there is very little research into the risk factors for

symptoms of inattention, overactivity, and impulsivity. Many of the risk factors that are common to other disorders, such as parental psychopathology or low SES, are not risk factors for the development of ADHD (Ford,

Case Study: Neil, the Boy Who Was Impulsive and Aggressive

Since the age of 3, Neil had been hyperactive, inattentive, aggressive, and intrusive into others' personal space. Now, at the age of 7, Neil was admitted to a psychiatric hospital for the fourth time due to his hyperactivity and impulsivity. His impulsivity was especially focused on bothering little girls and pulling up their skirts. He had no friends, tended to get into fights both at school and in the community, and had been suspended from school on a number of occasions.

Neil lived with his biological mother, his older brother, and periodically with his mother's boyfriend. When Neil was 3 years old, his biological father died suddenly of a heart attack, and his mother became depressed and developed a substance abuse problem. Many of Neil's problems seemed to develop after the death of his father. By the age of 4, Neil had been kicked out of his preschool and was admitted to a psychiatric inpatient unit at that time. He was diagnosed with ADHD, with additional conduct problems, and he was put on medication to control the ADHD. Although the medication worked temporarily, his behavior soon began to deteriorate no matter which medication was given. Two more admissions to the psychiatric hospital were attempted when Neil's behavior worsened. No medication seemed to relieve the symptoms of hyperactivity, impulsivity, belligerence, and aggression.

During the most recent admission, the question of sexual abuse arose. Given that Neil's acting-out behavior was of a sexual nature (e.g., pulling girls' skirts up, pinching girls on the butt), the treatment team decided to explore whether there had been any incidents of sexual abuse. At first, Neil denied that anyone had touched him inappropriately or that he had been sexually abused. After a sexual abuse expert was called in, however, Neil acknowledged that his mother's boyfriend had initiated anal intercourse with him when his mother had left Neil and the boyfriend in the same bed together. Specifically, Neil reported that "He bopped me up the butt."

A report was made to child protective services, and an investigation was initiated. During the investigation, the mother's boyfriend was not allowed to have contact with Neil. Unfortunately, no one in Neil's family believed his accusations, and his mother was especially hesitant to believe the allegations. Neil's mother repeatedly questioned Neil about the allegations and apparently tried to get him to change his story. Neil eventually reported that it was his deceased father, and not the mother's boyfriend, who had sexually abused him. After further investigation, the child protective service team could not determine clearly who had sexually abused Neil. Although there was clear physical evidence that Neil had been sexually abused, there was no clear evidence that identified the perpetrator. For that reason, the case had to be closed as "unfounded" regarding the mother's boyfriend, and the family was no longer followed by child protective services.

At one year follow-up, Neil still exhibited some heightened levels of hyperactivity and aggression, but he was now functioning well in school. Neil no longer showed any acting-out behavior of a sexual nature. Neil's mother showed improved functioning and had secured a full-time job. Her health and psychological functioning had improved significantly. Neil's relationship with his mother's boyfriend was described as positive.

This case illustrates the importance of looking beyond the presenting problems of hyperactivity and impulsivity. It took four admissions to a psychiatric hospital for the professional staff to realize that Neil had been sexually abused. Although he received some treatment related to the abuse, the family refused further treatment once the child protective agency dropped the investigation. The therapy services that were received seemed to have helped Neil and his family to some degree, but more treatment is needed so the entire family can deal with the remaining issues of sexual abuse and family functioning.

Source: Kolko & Stauffer (1991).

Goodman, & Meltzer, 2004). Although certain types of psychopathology are more prevalent in parents of children with ADHD in contrast to parents of nonclinical children, these connections appear to be linked to the comorbid oppositional and conduct problems in the ADHD children rather than serving as a risk factor for the development of ADHD (Chronis et al., 2003; Wilens et al., 2005). There are indications that adversity indicators, such as marital disorder, low SES, large family size, maternal psychological distress, paternal illegal activities, and out-of-home placement are all associated with ADHD, but the directionality of these risk factors is not clear (Biederman, 2005).

One prospective study attempted to assess the nature of risk in relation to maternal smoking and stress during pregnancy (Rodriguez & Bohlin, 2005). Pregnant women were recruited into the study and then data were collected over a 7-year period. Children who had been exposed in utero to smoking and to stress were significantly more likely to show symptoms of ADHD by the age of 7. This pattern was particularly true for boys. The results were not confounded by SES or birth-related difficulties. This study suggests that prenatal exposure to smoking and stress may serve as a risk factor for the development of ADHD symptoms. In a similar series of studies, low birthweight babies appear to be a greater risk for the development of ADHD (Rowland et al., 2002). Given that maternal smoking and stress during pregnancy are related to lower birthweight in neonates, these two lines of research both converge to suggest that low birthweight babies who were exposed to maternal smoking and stress in utero are at increased risk for the development of ADHD in childhood (Rowland et al., 2002). A review of this literature came to the same conclusion—infants who are born to mothers who smoke and mothers who have high levels of stress during pregnancy are at increased risk for ADHD later in their childhood (Linnet et al., 2003).

In an intriguing prospective study of young children, television viewing was assessed at age 1 and 3 and then attention was measured at age 7 (Christakis, Zimmerman, DiGiuseppe, & McCarty, 2004). Results of the study showed that more hours of television in the early years were associated with greater attentional problems at the age of 7. Although these findings need to be replicated, this study suggests that television viewing may serve as a risk factor for later attentional problems.

Overall, there are no overarching and well-established risk factors for the development of ADHD other than these few factors and the factors that have been implicated in the etiology of ADHD, such as family history and genetic predisposition (Ford et al., 2004; Samudra & Cantwell, 1999). There are indications, however, that prenatal and early environments are potentially important in either the development of or at least the exacerbation of symptoms of ADHD, so more research is needed in this area.

Protective Factors

Like the lack of research into risk factors, there is also a lack of research into factors that would protect children from the development of ADHD. One large-scale study with 2,232 twins found that maternal warmth was associated with decreased symptoms of ADHD in children who were born with very low birthweight (Tully, Arseneault, Caspi, Moffitt, & Morgan, 2004). This study suggests that parental warmth can protect children from the development of hyperactivity even when they are at risk for the development of ADHD.

Because stable home and school environments, with consistent and fair rules and consequences, are helpful in decreasing overactivity and impulsivity (Barkley, 2003), it is not unreasonable to assume that these factors might protect children from the development or maintenance of overactivity and impulsivity.

In terms of individual characteristics, goal-directed solitary play appears to serve as a protective factor. Specifically, girls diagnosed with ADHD who showed higher levels of goal-directed solitary play were less likely than girls in a control group to show symptoms of anxiety and depression (Mikami & Hinshaw, 2003).

Overall, these potential protective factors need to be replicated in other studies related to ADHD in both boys and girls. More research is needed to establish whether there are any other factors that can protect children from the development of ADHD.

SUMMARY AND KEY CONCEPTS

Attention-Deficit/Hyperactivity Disorder. Attention-Deficit/Hyperactivity Disorder (ADHD) is characterized by three primary symptoms: hyperactivity, impulsivity, and inattention. ADHD used to be called **hyperkinetic reaction of childhood or adolescence.** Currently, there are three types of ADHD: **ADHD, combined type** (which consists of hyperactivity, impulsivity, and inattention), **ADHD, predominantly inattentive type** (which consists of inattention, but not hyperactivity and impulsivity), and **ADHD, predominantly hyperactive-impulsive type** (which consists of hyperactivity and impulsivity, but not inattention). In the ICD-10, the term **hyperkinetic disorder** is used to diagnose children who are hyperactive, impulsive, inattentive, and have neurological deficits.

ADHD has high prevalence rates and high comorbidity rates. **Differential diagnosis,** the process of establishing which disorder or disorders are relevant for a particular child, is especially difficult given the high comorbidity rates. Children who

exhibit the combination of hyperactivity, impulsivity, inattention, and conduct problems have been referred to as **fledgling psychopaths** because this constellation of behaviors has been associated with antisocial behavior in adulthood.

Family-genetic risk factors are often implicated in the development of ADHD. The frontal-striatal region of the brain has been strongly implicated in the development of ADHD.

A large, multisite study of the effectiveness of treatments for ADHD is known as the **Multimodal Treatment Study of Children With ADHD (MTA study).** Treatments for ADHD center around stimulant medication (such as methylphenidate, which is known as Ritalin), **behavioral parent training,** and **contingency management strategies** (such as **token economies, time-out,** and **response-cost procedures).**

Attention-Deficit/Hyperactivity Disorder Conceptualized in a Dimensional Manner. Unfortunately, there has been very little research into hyperactivity, impulsivity, and inattention from a dimensional perspective.

KEY TERMS

hyperkinetic reaction of childhood or adolescence	ADHD, predominantly inattentive type	hyperkinetic disorder	family-genetic risk factors	contingency management strategies
attention-deficit/hyperactivity disorder (ADHD), combined type	ADHD, predominantly hyperactive-impulsive type	differential diagnosis	Multimodal Treatment Study of Children with ADHD (MTA Study)	token economies time-out response-cost procedures
		fledgling psychopaths		
		heterotypic continuity	behavioral parent training	

SUGGESTED READINGS

Jergen, Robert. *The Little Monster: Growing Up with ADHD*. Lanham, MD: Scarecrow Education, 2004. With a history of school failure, suicide attempts, and alcoholism, it was not until he reached college that the author was diagnosed with ADHD. This memoir tells of the impact of receiving the diagnosis and details the course of treatment that followed.

Roseman, Bruce. *A Kid Just Like Me: A Father and Son Overcome the Challenges of ADD and Learning Disabilities*. New York: Perigee, 2001. Now a practicing physician, the author describes his youth that was impacted by his experience of ADD and learning difficulties. He also now has a son who has similar difficulties, so the story tells the experiences of both the father and the son.

SUGGESTED VIEWINGS

Thirteen. (2003). This film was co-written by Nikki Reed, when she was just 13 years old, and it is loosely based on her life and experiences. Many difficulties are shown in this film, including friends with ADHD, parents who abuse substances, fathers who are absent, people who cut themselves to try to deal with their emotional pain, and communities that appear to follow rules that are different than those that police officers wish to enforce. The lack of parental monitoring or adult role models is particularly noticeable in this film.

Coach Carter. (2005). Based on a true story, this film shows the inspirational story of a basketball coach who worked with students who had poor impulse control and who were disengaged from learning and life. The coach provided strong structure for the players to succeed on and off the basketball court and displayed strong mentorship qualities.

CHAPTER 10

DISRUPTIVE DISORDERS, OPPOSITIONAL PROBLEMS, AND CONDUCT PROBLEMS

CHAPTER SUMMARY

OPPOSITIONAL DEFIANT DISORDER

CONDUCT DISORDER

OPPOSITIONAL DEFIANT DISORDER AND CONDUCT DISORDER

OPPOSITIONAL PROBLEMS AND CONDUCT PROBLEMS CONCEPTUALIZED IN A DIMENSIONAL MANNER

SUMMARY AND KEY CONCEPTS

KEY TERMS

SUGGESTED READINGS

SUGGESTED VIEWINGS

. . . When I was thirteen, while robbing a man I turned my head and was hit in the face. The man tried to run, but was tripped by [my friend], who then held him for me. I stomped him for twenty minutes before leaving him unconscious in an alley. Later that night, I learned that the man had lapsed into a coma and was disfigured from my stomping. The police told bystanders that the person responsible for this was a "monster." The name stuck, and I took that as a moniker over my birth name.

——Monster Kody Scott, now known as Sanyika Shakur (1993, p. 13), a former gang member in Los Angeles.

Aggressive and violent children and adolescents are a concern to everyone. Their presence is salient in the school system as well as in society at large (Hankin, Abela, Auerbach, McWhinnie, & Skitch, 2005; Hinshaw & Lee, 2003; Loeber, Burke, Lahey, Winters, & Zera, 2000). The two primary disruptive disorders that receive attention in developmental psychopathology are oppositional defiant disorder (ODD) and conduct disorder (CD). These disorders are both considered disruptive disorders because they cause disruptions in the lives of those around children and adolescents who exhibit these problems. Both ODD and CD are considered externalizing disorders. ODD and CD will be described separately, and prevalence information will be discussed for each disorder. Because of the common characteristics of the disorders, the discussion

of comorbidity, courses of the disorders, etiology, treatment, and prevention will be combined to include both disorders together.

OPPOSITIONAL DEFIANT DISORDER

Oppositional defiant disorder (ODD) occurs when a child shows defiant, oppositional, hostile, and negative behavior for at least 6 months. Although nearly all children show defiance at some point in their lives, ODD is only diagnosed if the defiance, negativism, and hostility are beyond what would be expected for a child of that age and gender (Greene, 2006). Children with ODD are often irritating to those around them. They often defy the instructions of their parents and teachers, intentionally annoy adults and children, and are angry or spiteful. These behaviors can be evident in nearly every child (or adult!) when they are having a bad day, but ODD would only be diagnosed if these behaviors are present chronically for at least 6 months. As can be seen in Table 10.1, the diagnostic criteria for ODD are meant to distinguish this disorder from normal behavior at different developmental levels.

The more things are forbidden, the more popular they become.

—Mark Twain

Case Study: Jeremy, the Boy Who Swore at the Teacher

Jeremy's mother brought him in for an evaluation when he was 9 years old. He had been a difficult child since nursery school, but his misbehavior had escalated over the past few months. In general, he was disobedient, deceitful, and difficult to manage both at school and at home. Recently, he swore at his teacher, which resulted in a 3-day suspension. He was reprimanded by a police officer for riding his bicycle in the street. The next day, he again rode his bicycle in the street and failed to use his brakes, which resulted in him crashing through a storefront window.

Looking back on his development, Jeremy's mother acknowledged that he behaved well as long as he was supervised and he received attention. When he received good attention, he was sweet, charming, and a joy to be around. When he did not receive adequate attention, however, he created problems. He seemed to annoy other children intentionally, often teasing, tripping, and kicking them. Jeremy also has had chronic difficulties with his teachers. He often talks back to them and does not obey them. He shows oppositional behavior to nearly all adults at his school. Despite these difficulties, his grades have remained adequate.

Overall, Jeremy is a relatively classic case of oppositional defiant disorder. Although he has had police involvement (which would be expected with the more severe diagnosis of conduct disorder), this involvement has been relatively minor. The chronic nature of his negativism and defiant behavior are the hallmark signs of ODD.

Source: Spitzer et al. (1994).

Although not a formal aspect of the diagnostic criteria, children with oppositional defiant disorder often fight with other children.

As with nearly all the disorders in *DSM-IV,* ODD must cause clinically significant impairment in social, academic, or occupational functioning (Criterion B). It is possible to imagine a child who exhibits many of the symptoms of ODD, but who does not show any significant impairment in these areas. The impairment criterion, for example, might not be met for children in highly accommodating environments.

The final criterion (Criterion D) is important to keep in mind when considering children with more severe symptoms of aggression. Many children show the less-severe symptoms that are consistent with both ODD and the more severe symptoms that are consistent with CD, but these children would only be diagnosed with CD. In other words, the diagnosis of CD takes precedence over ODD.

As illustrated in the case study of Jose, oppositional behaviors can be quite normal at different developmental stages. Figure 10.1 shows that oppositional behaviors tend to be relatively frequent in nonreferred young boys and tend to decrease over time (Loeber, Lahey, & Thomas, 1991). These data highlight the importance of knowing developmental trends in children's behaviors before identifying oppositional behavior as deviant. This caveat, however, is not meant to suggest that young children can never exhibit diagnosable disruptive behavior disorders. In one clinical sample of children aged 2 through 5, 41.8% met criteria for CD (many of whom were comorbid with ADHD), and 25.3% met criteria for ODD (Keenan & Wakschlag, 2000). These researchers even named their article "More Than the Terrible Twos" to highlight the fact that even toddlers

TABLE 10.1 *DSM-IV* Diagnostic Criteria for Oppositional Defiant Disorder

A. A pattern of negativistic, hostile, and defiant behavior lasting at least 6 months, during which four (or more) of the following are present:

(1) often loses temper

(2) often argues with adults

(3) often actively defies or refuses to comply with adults' requests or rules

(4) often deliberately annoys people

(5) often blames others for his or her mistakes or misbehavior

(6) is often touchy or easily annoyed by others

(7) is often angry and resentful

(8) is often spiteful or vindictive

Note: Consider a criterion met only if the behavior occurs more frequently than is typically observed in individuals of comparable age and developmental level.

B. The disturbance in behavior causes clinically significant impairment in social, academic, or occupational functioning.

C. The behaviors do not occur exclusively during the course of a Psychotic or Mood Disorder.

D. Criteria are not met for Conduct Disorder, and, if the individual is age 18 years or older, criteria are not met for Antisocial Personality Disorder.

Source: American Psychiatric Association (2000).
Reprinted with permission from the *Diagnostic and Statistical Manual of Mental Disorders, Fourth Edition, Text Revision.* Copyright 2000 American Psychiatric Association.

can show severe behavior problems that are above and beyond what would be expected developmentally (Keenan & Wakschlag, 2000). In addition, violent fantasies evident in early play are associated with later oppositional difficulty (Dunn & Hughes, 2001).

When children meet criteria for ODD, they are often found to have other problems as well. ODD is associated with hyperactivity, academic difficulties, low self-esteem, and poor peer relationships (Costello, Mustillo, Erkanli, Keeler, & Angold, 2003; Donnellan, Trzesniewski, Robins, Moffitt, & Caspi, 2005; Loeber, Green, Lahey, Frick, & McBurnett, 2000).

A lie can give more pain than a spear.

—Proverb of Africa

Prevalence Rates

As summarized in Table 10.2, it is estimated that between 2% and 16% of children meet criteria for ODD (American Psychiatric Association, 2000). A higher percentage (20%) of adoptive children met criteria, especially those with preadoption abuse and neglect (Simmel, Brooks, Barth, & Hinshaw, 2001). The disorder is diagnosed more frequently in children as opposed to adolescents. ODD is more prevalent in boys before puberty, but there are approximately equal numbers of boys and girls who meet criteria for ODD after puberty (American Psychiatric Association, 2000). This age and gender interaction is probably due to the

TABLE 10.2 Overview of Prevalence Information for Oppositional Defiant Disorder

Prevalence	2–16%
Age	Younger > Older
Gender	Boys > Girls (before puberty); equivalent after puberty
SES	Lower SES > Higher SES
Race/Ethnicity	No consistent patterns

fact that the severe cases of ODD, who are mostly boys, tend to be diagnosed with conduct disorder rather than ODD in adolescence. Thus, the prevalence appears to be the same for girls both before and after puberty, whereas the prevalence for boys decreases after puberty because so many boys meet criteria for conduct disorder in adolescence. Children from lower SES families tend to be more at risk for a diagnosis of ODD than are children from higher SES families (Barry, Dunlap, Cotten, Lochman, & Wells, 2005; Evans, 2004; McNeil, Capage, & Bennett, 2002). Although there are mixed findings in some studies, it does not appear that there are any consistent prevalence patterns of ODD based on race and ethnicity (McNeil et al., 2002; Snyder, Reid, & Patterson, 2003). Comparable prevalence rates have been found in a number of other countries, including the Ukraine (Drabick et al., 2004) and Taiwan (Gau et al., 2005).

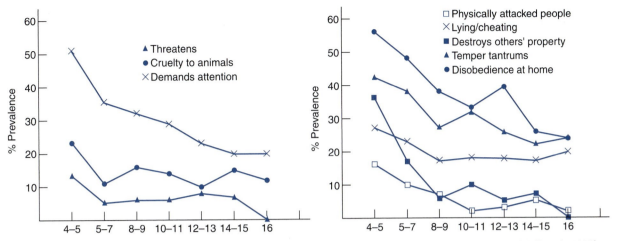

FIGURE 10.1   Prevalence of selected disruptive behaviors with age in nonreferred boys. (Data are from Edelbrock, 1989).

Source: Loeber et al. (1991).

Case Study: Jose, the Boy Who Only Said "No"

Jose exhibits a very negativistic pattern of behavior. He says "no" to nearly every request that is made of him. In addition to saying "no," Jose whines to his parents about their requests. He often cries, is irritable, is sullen, and withdraws from those around him. When he is really upset, he throws severe temper tantrums (e.g., throwing himself on the floor, screaming, crying, and begging to get his way).

Jose is also very demanding of his parents' attention. His parents have noticed that his older sister is not nearly as demanding of their attention. Of particular concern to Jose's parents is that he seems to only act up around them. They are concerned that they have reinforced these oppositional behaviors and thus have created the oppositional behavior exhibited by Jose. His parents are most concerned about his breath-

holding episodes. Sometimes Jose gets so upset when his parents forbid him from doing something, he holds his breath and gets red in the face. He has not yet fainted from these episodes, but his parents are very worried that he could incur brain damage from holding his breath for so long.

Given Jose's oppositional and negativistic behavior, you might be ready to diagnose him with oppositional defiant disorder. When you find out that he is 2 years old, however, you should be wary of diagnosing his behavior. All the behaviors described for Jose are very common among 2-year-olds. Although they are sometimes not pleasant for parents or toddlers, the "terrible twos" are not a diagnosis in *DSM-IV*.

Source: Adapted from American Academy of Pediatrics (2005).

CONDUCT DISORDER

In contrast to ODD, **conduct disorder (CD)** is a much more serious disorder. The primary characteristics of CD include violating the basic rights of others and breaking societal norms for that developmental level. As can be seen in Table 10.3, the categories of criteria include aggression to people and animals, such as bullying or cruelty, destruction of property, deceitfulness or theft, and serious violations of rules. Note that there are new forms of bullying that are being seen in the new technologies that are available. For example, one survey found that 25% of adolescents reported that they had been bullied over the Internet, and 16% of adolescents

reported that they had been bullied via a text message (Jerome & Segal, 2003). Thus, although the diagnostic criteria remain the same, clinicians need to be aware of the new ways in which bullying and other conduct problems can be shown. Symptoms need to have been present within the past year, with at least one symptom present within the past 6 months.

Because many children and adolescents live in settings where undesirable behavior is actually necessary for survival, it is imperative that the clinician take into consideration the child's or adolescent's living situation before making a diagnosis. For example, adolescents who are impoverished and living in a high-crime area may have to engage in fighting to protect themselves

Case Study: Saigon Pete from Grosse Pointe

Pete, whose mother was Vietnamese and whose father was an American serviceman, lived in Vietnam for his first 2 years of life. His biological mother put him up for adoption, and he was adopted by a family in the United States. His adoptive family abused him, including beatings and intentional burnings, and he was moved to foster care by the age of 2 1/2. He was then adopted by a family who lived in Grosse Point, a wealthy suburb of Detroit, where he grew up with three other adopted siblings.

Pete adjusted to his new family initially, but he remained somewhat shy and uncommunicative in the early years. He had a great deal of friends, but he developed a stormy and difficult relationship with his parents. When he was in junior high school, he began befriending a group of young adolescents who drank beer, smoked marijuana, tortured animals, and skipped school. Pete's academic work plummeted, and he also got in trouble for fighting with the popular teenagers at school, vandalizing the neighbors' mailboxes, and shooting at squirrels.

By the age of 14, his acting-out behaviors increased. For example, he and his friends stole a neighbor's car to go joyriding. Around this time, his parents separated, and he decided to live with his father rather than move to another state with his mother and siblings. By the age of 15, Pete skipped school more days than not, and his drug use escalated. He and his friends were now heavily involved with using LSD, mescaline,

marijuana, and glue. His parents tried to gain some control over him by sending him to a military school, but he was expelled quickly for chronic truancy.

On the day before his 16th birthday, Pete slashed his wrists with a butcher knife, which resulted in severed tendons and nerves. He became unconscious, but when he regained consciousness, he called one of his friends' mother, who then had him rushed to the hospital. While at the psychiatric hospital, Pete explained that he had not intended to kill himself. Instead, he stated that he had been dropping acid, then thought he heard police sirens outside. Rather than being arrested, Pete thought that it would be better to slash his wrists. When asked directly, Pete stated that he was not depressed. He did, however, note that his life was worthless and that it would not make a difference whether he lived or died.

The intake team at the psychiatric hospital diagnosed Pete with conduct disorder, adolescent onset type (moderate) due to Pete's illicit activities (e.g., grand theft auto, fighting). They also diagnosed Pete with hallucinogen abuse, cannabis abuse, and adjustment disorder, with depressed mood. They felt that there was not enough evidence for a diagnosis of major depressive disorder or dysthymia, although one of these disorders was probably present.

Source: Spitzer et al. (1994).

---

or youngsters from war-ravaged countries may have to be aggressive to survive. In these cases, a diagnosis of conduct disorder would not be appropriate (American Psychiatric Association, 2000).

CD can be diagnosed at any age. If the individual meets criteria for both ODD and CD, then the diagnosis of CD would prevail. If the individual is older than 18 years and he or she also meets criteria for antisocial personality disorder, then the diagnosis of antisocial personality disorder would supercede the diagnosis of CD.

There are two primary types of CD: childhood-onset type and adolescent-onset type. Childhood-onset type is considered the more serious of the two types because it is associated with chronic problems into adulthood (Hinshaw & Lee, 2003; McCabe et al., 2004; Silverthorn, Frick, & Reynolds, 2001). In fact, some researchers argue that the development of CD is distinctly different for individuals with childhood-onset CD and those with adolescent-onset (Hankin et al., 2005; Moffitt, 2003). Both types of the disorder are

based partially on reciprocal processes between the child and his/her environment. Childhood-onset CD, however, begins with very early difficulties in infant or child temperament and the parent–child relationship, whereas adolescent-onset CD is associated with exposure to troubled peers in later childhood and adolescence (Kim-Cohen et al., 2005; McCabe, Hough, Wood, & Yeh, 2001; Moffitt, 2003). Overestimates of social competence are related to greater levels of aggression, which are also related to poor peer relationships (Brendgen, Vitaro, Turgeon, Poulin, & Wanner, 2004). Based on *DSM-IV* criteria, the severity of CD can be noted as mild, moderate, or severe.

Attitudes are caught, not taught.

—Old Quaker saying

There is growing evidence that another distinction between types of CD is warranted. In addition to considering childhood-onset and adolescent-onset types of CD, there is also evidence to suggest that children and adolescents with CD also fall along a continuum

TABLE 10-3 *DSM-IV* Diagnostic Criteria for Conduct Disorder

A. A repetitive and persistent pattern of behavior in which the basic rights of others or major age-appropriate societal norms or rules are violated, as manifested by the presence of three (or more) of the following criteria in the past 12 months, with at least one criterion present in the past 6 months:

Aggression to people and animals

(1) often bullies, threatens, or intimidates others

(2) often initiates physical fights

(3) has used a weapon that can cause serious physical harm to others (e.g., a bat, brick, broken bottle, knife, gun)

(4) has been physically cruel to people

(5) has been physically cruel to animals

(6) has stolen while confronting a victim (e.g., mugging, purse snatching, extortion, armed robbery)

(7) has forced someone into sexual activity

Destruction of property

(8) has deliberately engaged in fire setting with the intention of causing serious damage

(9) has deliberately destroyed others' property (other than by fire setting)

Deceitfulness or theft

(10) has broken into someone else's house, building, or car

(11) often lies to obtain goods or favors or to avoid obligations (i.e., "cons" others)

(12) has stolen items of nontrivial value without confronting a victim (e.g., shoplifting, but without breaking and entering; forgery)

Serious violations of rules

(13) often stays out at night despite parental prohibitions, beginning before age 13 years

(14) has run away from home overnight at least twice while living in parental or parental surrogate home (or once without returning for a lengthy period)

(15) is often truant from school, beginning before age 13 years

B. The disturbance in behavior causes clinically significant impairment in social, academic, or occupational functioning.

C. If the individual is age 18 years or older, criteria are not met for Antisocial Personality Disorder.

Specify type based on age at onset:

Childhood-Onset Type: onset of at least one criterion characteristic of Conduct Disorder prior to age 10 years

Adolescent-Onset Type: absence of any criteria characteristic of Conduct Disorder prior to age 10 years

Specify severity:

Mild: few if any conduct problems in excess of those required to make the diagnosis and conduct problems cause only minor harm to others

Moderate: number of conduct problems and effect on others intermediate between "mild" and "severe"

Severe: many conduct problems in excess of those required to make the diagnosis or conduct problems cause considerable harm to others

Source: American Psychiatric Association (2000).
Reprinted with permission from the *Diagnostic and Statistical Manual of Mental Disorders, Fourth Edition, Text Revision.* Copyright 2000 American Psychiatric Association.

of **callous-unemotional traits** (Frick, Cornell, Barry, Bodin, & Dane, 2003; Frick, Stickle, Dandreaux, Farrell, & Kimonis, 2005; Kimonis, Frick, & Barry, 2004; Loney, Frick, Clements, Ellis, & Kerlin, 2003). Callous traits are characterized by a lack of empathy and the use of others for one's own gain. Unemotional traits are characterized by lack of guilt and remorse and limited affect and feelings. This concept is consistent with the idea of psychopathy in adolescents and adults (Farrington, 2005; Lynam et al., 2005; Rutter, 2003, 2005; Salekin & Frick, 2005). Children and adolescents diagnosed with CD who show high levels of callous-unemotional traits, tend to show high levels of psychopathy in adolescence, and show high levels of comorbidity with a number of other disorders (Salekin, Leistico, Neumann, DiCicco, & Duros, 2004). Youth

Case Study: Reginald, the "Handful"

Reginald has always been a "handful." He repeated both first and second grades. Due to his disruption in the classroom, Reginald usually spent more time in the principal's office than in his regular classroom. He was suspended from school recently for setting up a blockade to demand money from younger children on their way home from school.

When he was not at school, Reginald's behavior was also problematic. Reginald's mother found items in his room that she believed were stolen, he damaged the neighbor's property on more than one occasion, he lied constantly, and he often left the house late at night and would not say where he was going.

By the age of 11, Reginald's teacher asked his mother to take him for psychological help because he was bullying and fighting with other children at school. Reginald's mother is a single mother who works two part-time jobs to try to support the family. Reginald and his three siblings are often left unsupervised at home.

Reginald met criteria for conduct disorder, childhood-onset type. The evaluation also showed that Reginald had limited intellectual functioning (Full Scale IQ = 66; Verbal IQ = 57; Performance IQ = 78). Following is the multiaxial diagnosis:

Axis I:	Conduct disorder, childhood-onset type (moderate)
Axis II:	Mild mental retardation
Axis III:	None (No known physical problems)
Axis IV:	Problems with primary support group: family disruption Educational problems: academic problems
Axis V:	Global Assessment of Functioning = 45 (current)

Source: Rapoport & Ismond (1996).

---

who show high levels of callous and unemotional traits tend to focus on the positive aspects of aggressive behavior and tend ignore any concerns about hostile acts of behavior (Pardini, Lochman, & Frick, 2003). These adolescents tend to become adults with the most severe forms of antisocial behavior (Piatigorsky & Hinshaw, 2004).

Previous categorizations of CD focused on whether youth were involved in these activities with a group or alone. In *DSM-III-R* (American Psychiatric Association, 1987), CD was broken down into a group type (also known as a socialized type) and a solitary, aggressive type. In some ways, the socialized type or group type of CD was thought to be more related to youth who might become involved in gang activity rather than completing deviant acts alone. Gang activity has been found to be associated with prior reports of peer rejection and school failure in children as young as middle school (Dishion, Nelson, & Yasui, 2005). Thus, there is a need to explore gang activity and gang involvement, whether or not it is considered as part of the diagnostic classification system of *DSM*. Although the distinctions between solitary versus socialized types of CD continue to be meaningful, the age-of-onset typing and callous-unemotional conceptualizations appear to be the most useful (Frick, Cornell, Barry, Bodin, & Dane, 2003; Hinshaw & Lee, 2003).

The most severe behaviors related to CD, such as armed robbery or sexual assault, are rare at any age.

Other behaviors related to CD, however, are evident even in nonclinical samples. Specifically, truancy, alcohol use, and use of marijuana are all relatively infrequent in younger childhood but are much more prevalent in adolescence (Pennington, 2002). In general, the less-severe symptoms related to CD increase over time in nonclinical samples. Property and status offenses are more common in adolescence than in childhood (Kimonis & Frick, 2006). These patterns of behavior have lead other researchers to suggest another way to conceptualize subtypes of CD (Tackett, Krueger, Iacono, & McGue, 2005). Specifically, there is evidence that children who show aggressive behavior (e.g., bullying, fighting, sexual assault) are different than children who show nonaggressive, rule-breaking behavior (e.g., running away from home, being truant). Even in the norming process for the Child Behavior Checklist, children's behaviors naturally fell into two different narrow band subscales in this domain—aggressive and rule-breaking (Achenbach & Rescorla, 2001). Thus, there appears to be support for considering another way to conceptualize subtypes of CD.

For all different subtypes, when children or adolescents meet criteria for CD, they usually have a number of other problems as well (Loeber et al., 2000; Snyder et al., 2003). CD is associated with oppositional attitudes toward parents, teachers, and other authority figures (Snyder et al., 2003). Youth diagnosed with CD tend to have academic difficulties, such as being held back in school, scoring

TABLE 10.4 Overview of Prevalence Information
for Conduct Disorder

Prevalence	1–10% Overall; 6% to 16% for boys; 2% to 9% for girls
Age	Adolescents > Children
Gender	Boys > Girls
SES	Lower > Higher
Race/Ethnicity	No consistent patterns

poorly on academic achievement tests, and dropping out of school before graduation, especially when they are comorbid with ADHD (Gresham, Lane, & Beebe-Frankenberger, 2005). CD is also associated with peer difficulties, such as being disliked or rejected by nondeviant peers and being socially ineffective (Snyder et al., 2003). Children and adolescents diagnosed with CD also tend to show high levels of hyperactivity (Hinshaw & Lee, 2003). Substance use and early, risky sexual behavior are associated with CD as well (Dishion, French, & Patterson, 1995). For girls, peer rejection in combination with aggressive behavior were associated with later development of substance use and risky sexual behavior in adolescents (Prinstein & LaGreca, 2004). When girls were not rejected by peers, however, there was no long-term association between aggression, substance use, and risky sexual behavior (Prinstein & La Greca, 2004).

Prevalence Rates

As noted in Box 10.4, approximately 1% to 10% of adolescents experience CD (American Psychiatric Association, 2000). The prevalence rates of CD vary by gender. Between 6% and 16% of boys meet criteria for CD and between 2% and 9% of girls meet criteria for CD (American Psychiatric Association, 2000). More adolescents than children are diagnosed with CD. As is obvious from the prevalence rates, more boys than girls are diagnosed with CD (Lahey et al., 2000; Maughan, Rowe, Messer, Goodman, & Melzer, 2004). Interestingly, symptoms also vary between boys and girls (American Psychiatric Association, 2000; Cote, Zoccolillo, Tremblay, Nagin, & Vitaro, 2001; Hartung, Milich, Lynam, & Martin, 2002; Lahey et al., 2000; Loeber et al., 2000). Boys with CD tend to exhibit confrontational and aggressive behaviors, such as stealing, vandalism, fighting, and acting out at school. Girls with CD tend to exhibit more nonconfrontational behaviors, such as running away, truancy, substance use, and prostitution. Based on parents' reports, children's self-reports, and direct observations, boys show higher rates of cruelty to animals than do girls (Dadds et al., 2004).

The patterns of comorbid disorders vary for boys and girls, with boys showing higher rates of comorbid externalizing disorders and girls showing higher rates of comorbid internalizing disorders (Rowe et al., 2002). There are similar patterns, however, when boys' versus girls' illegal activities are compared. Although boys show higher prevalence of illegal activities and offending, the patterns for boys and girls appear to be similar, with the more troubled children beginning their offending behaviors earlier and continuing on to chronic offending while some offend during adolescence and then do not do so as they reach adulthood (Fergusson & Horwood, 2002).

There is consistent evidence that CD is more prevalent in youth from low SES families than youth from middle and higher SES families (Barry et al., 2005; Brody et al., 2003; Kimonis & Frick, 2006). Notably, violent activities associated with CD seem to be more biologically based in adolescents from high-SES neighborhoods, whereas violence is more associated with contextual factors such as poor parent–adolescent relationships in adolescents from low-SES neighborhoods (Beyers, Loeber, Wikstrom, & Stouthamer-Loeber, 2001).

Although the research is sometimes equivocal, there is no consistent evidence of different prevalence patterns of CD regarding race or ethnicity (Lahey et al., 1999). In a study of cultural characteristics and propensity toward delinquency and conduct disorder, Asian-American adolescents who believed more in an individual frame of reference (i.e., looking out for an individual's interests rather than the community's well-being) reported higher rates of delinquency, whereas adolescents who believed more in a collectivist frame (where the needs of the community are taken into consideration first and foremost) reported the lowest rates of delinquent acts (Le & Stockdale, 2005). Thus, there may be cultural differences in some communities regarding the propensity to show conduct disordered behavior.

Antisocial Personalty Disorder

A brief discussion of **antisocial personality disorder (APD)** is warranted. As can be seen in Table 10.5, APD can only be diagnosed in individuals over the age of 18. APD is considered a personality disorder and is noted on Axis II of a *DSM-IV* multiaxial assessment. The basic characteristics of APD are a chronic pattern of violating others' rights and a long-term disregard for others' well-being. For a diagnosis of APD, there must be evidence of these behaviors since the age of 15, and there must be evidence of CD before the age of 15. Retrospective

Case Study: Shaniqua, the "Born Liar"

Shaniqua was 16 years old when she was admitted to a psychiatric hospital for her behavioral problems. The admission to a psychiatric hospital was preceded by many years of conduct problems. By the age of 12, Shaniqua was already known to the authorities because of truancy and petty theft. Over the past 4 years, she had continued to steal from local stores, set fires in vacant lots, and lie chronically. Shaniqua had still been in junior high school because of academic difficulties. Recently, however, she was expelled after she and her friends were caught smoking marijuana in the gym.

Shaniqua's parents reported that they had lost all control of her. When they tried to reprimand her, she would leave the house and stay out all night. They stated that she was a "born liar."

During her stay in the psychiatric hospital, Shaniqua became demanding and disruptive. She befriended a number of other troubled girls and demanded that she be the center of attention. When the staff would not bow to her every request, Shaniqua would storm out of group therapy meetings and cause a scene. Although she presented a tough exterior, the staff at the hospital thought that Shaniqua felt insecure and dependent under this tough exterior. Shaniqua met criteria for CD.

Source: Spitzer et al. (1994).

TABLE 10.5 *DSM-IV* Diagnostic Criteria for Antisocial Personality Disorder

A. There is a pervasive pattern of disregard for and violation of the rights of others occurring since age 15 years, as indicated by three (or more) of the following:

   (1) failure to conform to social norms with respect to lawful behaviors as indicated by repeatedly performing acts that are grounds for arrest

   (2) deceitfulness, as indicated by repeated lying, use of aliases, or conning others for personal profit or pleasure

   (3) impulsivity or failure to plan ahead

   (4) irritability and aggressiveness, as indicated by repeated physical fights or assaults

   (5) reckless disregard for safety of self or others

   (6) consistent irresponsibility, as indicated by repeated failure to sustain consistent work behavior or honor financial obligations

   (7) lack of remorse, as indicated by being indifferent to or rationalizing having hurt, mistreated, or stolen from another

B. The individual is at least age 18 years.

C. There is evidence of Conduct Disorder...with onset before age 15 years.

D. The occurrence of antisocial behavior is not exclusively during the course of Schizophrenia or a Manic Episode.

Source: American Psychiatric Association (2000).
Reprinted with permission from the *Diagnostic and Statistical Manual of Mental Disorders,* Fourth Edition, Text Revision. Copyright 2000 American Psychiatric Association.

---

reports are often necessary to ascertain whether the adult showed symptoms of CD in childhood or adolescence. In general, retrospective reports by adults diagnosed with APD tend to be more accurate when the adult's current behavior is consistent with their past behavior (Rueter, Chao, & Conger, 2000). Approximately 25% of youth diagnosed with CD go on to develop APD in adulthood (Lemery & Doelger, 2005). APD appears to be predicted more directly from childhood conduct disorder rather than childhood ADHD, particularly in children from low SES families (Lahey, Loeber, Burke, & Applegate, 2005).

The term **psychopath** is often used to describe individuals with APD, especially those individuals who show callousness and lack of emotions (Salekin, Neumann, et al., 2004). Note that adolescents diagnosed with CD who later meet criteria for APD are also highly comorbid for substance abuse disorders (Salekin, Leistico, et al., 2004). There is evidence that children with the combination of hyperactivity, impulsivity, attention problems, and conduct problems can be considered **fledgling psychopaths** (Gresham et al., 2001). That is, children with this constellation of problems are very likely to develop severe problems with APD. There is a great deal of consistency in psychopathic traits from adolescence to adulthood (Gretton, Hare, & Catchpole, 2004). Given that approximately 50% of the known crimes are committed by 10% of families (including known juvenile and adult offenders), these severe cases of APD are important to identify and treat (Moffitt, 2005).

...It is so remarkably easy just to tell the truth in this world, that I often marvel that there are so many madly foolish, so wretchedly stupid, that they hide truth.

—Jack London

OPPOSITIONAL DEFIANT DISORDER AND CONDUCT DISORDER

A great deal of research has been completed on ODD and CD. In much of this work, the diagnoses of ODD and CD are combined and investigated together. This pattern of combining children diagnosed with ODD and those diagnosed with CD is partly due to the similarity in symptoms between ODD and CD. As can be seen in Figure 10.2, there are two primary dimensions onto which symptoms of ODD and CD fall: **covert/overt** and **destructive/nondestructive** (Frick, 1998a).

The covert/overt dimension shows that some behaviors are more secretive (covert) in nature, such as stealing, firesetting, running away, and skipping school, whereas other behaviors are more obvious to others (overt), such as fighting, being cruel, arguing, and defying adults. The destructive/nondestructive dimension suggests that some behaviors are more destructive, such as vandalism and being cruel to animals, whereas other behaviors are nondestructive, such as using substances and annoying others. Overall, this template helps to clarify the organization of symptoms of both ODD and CD.

Because of the overlap of symptoms in both ODD and CD, many researchers have tried to establish commonalities and distinctions between these two disorders. A number of researchers have argued that ODD and CD are actually just different ends of the spectrum for the same disorder (reviewed by Borduin, Henggeler, & Manley, 1995). Other researchers, however, have tried to distinguish between the symptoms of the two disorders. In support of the distinctness of the two disorders is the fact that symptoms of ODD tend to have a much earlier onset than the symptoms of CD (Rowe et al., 2002). In addition, nearly all youth diagnosed with CD have a history of ODD, but not all children with ODD go on to develop CD (Rowe et al., 2002).

Although current mainstream thinking suggests that ODD and CD are distinctly different disorders, the discussion of characteristics of ODD and CD remain intertwined in many professional publications (e.g., Hinshaw & Lee, 2003). For this reason, the remaining topics of comorbidity, courses of the disorders, etiology, treatment, prevention, risk factors, and protective factors are discussed for ODD and CD together. Where possible, specific patterns are mentioned for ODD and CD separately.

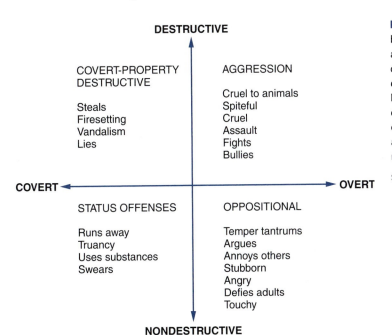

FIGURE 10.2 These clusters of behaviors are based on the meta-analysis of 60 factor analyses conducted by Frick et al. (1993). The clusters are formed from the intersection of two dimensions of behavior covariation. The horizontal dimension captures a bipolar dimension ranging from overt to covert patterns of behavior, and the vertical dimension captures a dimension ranging from destructive to nondestructive types of behavior.

Source: Frick (1998a).

Case Study: Stuart, Comorbidity in Action

When he was 8 years old, Stuart was referred for psychological evaluation and treatment due to many years of oppositional behavior, overactivity, social problems, and school problems. His mother reported that he had always been overly active and difficult to manage. When he first started school, his teachers found him to be hyperactive, aggressive, and unable to learn. He was known as a class "pest" because he would bother other children when they were working quietly, and he would talk back to the teacher. Although he attended school regularly, he could not read nor do math by the age of 8. He did, however, know the alphabet.

During the current year of school, Stuart remained aggressive, socially isolated, and impulsive. He soiled his pants frequently. At home, he refused to follow his mother's requests, and he threw temper tantrums frequently. Stuart's father was involved minimally with discipline of Stuart because the father had been battling a terminal illness for the past 2 years. Within the past 6 months, Stuart's father had been in and out of the hospital frequently. Overall, the family system was very stressed. Following is the diagnostic formulation for Stuart:

Axis I:	Oppositional defiant disorder
	Attention-deficit/hyperactivity disorder, combined type
	Encopresis, without constipation and overflow incontinence
	Reading disorder
	Mathematics disorder
Axis II:	No diagnosis on Axis II
Axis III:	None
Axis IV:	Problems with primary support group: illness in parent
	Educational problems: learning difficulties
Axis V:	Global assessment of functioning = 45 (current)
	Global assessment of functioning = 50 (highest level past year)

Source: Rapoport & Ismond (1996).

Comorbidity

By definition, ODD and CD cannot be diagnosed in the same child at the same time. However, a number of disorders are highly comorbid with both ODD and CD. In general, higher rates of comorbidity are found in clinical samples and in incarcerated samples than in nonclinical samples (Abram, Teplin, McClelland, & Dulcan, 2003). ODD co-occurs significantly with ADHD (Dick et al., 2005; Greene et al., 2002). In addition, ODD is sometimes comorbid with mood disorders, anxiety disorders, and language processing disorders (Greene et al., 2002). There is evidence that ADHD and dysthymic disorder come before the development of ODD and have a role in its development (Vance, Sanders, & Arduca, 2005).

Regarding conduct disorder, CD is very highly comorbid with ADHD (Costello et al., 2003; Greene et al., 2002). In samples of conduct disordered youth, between 65% and 90% also meet criteria for ADHD (Frick, 1998a). CD is also commonly comorbid with depression and anxiety (Costello et al., 2003; Gregory, Eley, & Plomin, 2004; Marmorstein & Iacono, 2003). Comorbidity with internalizing disorders is especially salient for girls who are diagnosed with CD (Abram et al., 2003). Interestingly, delinquency appears to predict depression in boys, whereas for girls, the connections between delinquency and depression appear to be bidirectional and reciprocal (Wiesner, 2003).

CD and substance use disorders tend to co-occur as well, and there is evidence that the CD usually occurs before the substance use disorder (Armstrong & Costello, 2002). Notably, CD appears to put children at risk for earlier onset of substance use disorders (Armstrong & Costello, 2002). In juvenile detention centers, girls show higher rates of comorbidity than do boys, and older adolescents showed higher rates of comorbidity in contrast to younger adolescents (Abram et al., 2003). As with so many other disorders, comorbidity is the rule rather than the exception with disruptive disorders.

Courses of the Disorders

Given the characteristic symptoms of ODD and CD, it is important to know that aggression and antisocial behavior are among the most stable behaviors in humans. For example, externalizing problems, poor social skills, and poor emotional regulation in toddlers and in preschoolers were associated with maladaptive social relationships in kindergarten (Keane & Calkins, 2004). Children who showed disruptive behaviors and poor adaptive functioning in preschool showed higher rates of both internalizing and externalizing problems as well as academic problems in elementary school (Barkley, Shelton, et al.,

2002). In addition, aggression in kindergarten was predictive of aggression, poor peer relationships, and dysfunctional teacher–child interactions many years later (Ladd & Burgess, 1999).

Correlations between earlier and later aggression range from .63 to .92, which suggests that aggression early in childhood is a strong predictor of aggression later in adolescence (Loeber & Stouthamer-Loeber, 1998). These stability estimates are comparable to the stability of intellectual functioning, which is also considered to be among the most stable of human characteristics.

As for the developmental course, ODD tends to develop gradually, with symptoms usually first showing up at home and then generalizing to the school setting (American Psychiatric Association, 2000). With CD, less-severe symptoms such as lying and shoplifting tend to show up first and then the more severe symptoms, such as burglary and sexual assault, tend to show up later (American Psychiatric Association, 2000). Aggression in either ODD or CD is associated with unemployment in early and middle adulthood (Kokko & Pulkkinen, 2000). In trying to predict later CD, ODD was the only disorder that significantly predicted the later development of CD, whereas depression, ADHD, and anxiety did not predict the later onset of CD in a reliable manner (Lahey, Loeber, Burke, Rathouz, & McBurnett, 2002).

Of great importance are the characteristics that are associated with the progression from ODD to CD to APD. Although not all ODD children develop CD and not all CD adolescents go on to develop APD in adulthood, there is a fair amount of continuity between these disorders (Rowe, Maughan, Pickles, Costello, & Angold, 2002). Based on an extensive review of the research literature (Frick & Loney, 1999), the stability and continuity of these disorders is associated with:

- Parental history of APD or criminal involvement
- Problematic family environments (e.g., limited parental supervision)
- Low SES and economic disadvantage
- Early onset of severe conduct problems (before the age of 11)
- Severe aggression
- High numbers and large variability of types of conduct problems
- Comorbidity with ADHD
- Lower intellectual functioning

These well-known patterns from ODD to CD to APD are noteworthy because of the implications for treatment and prevention (which are discussed later in the chapter). Note also that these connections are striking in terms of the negative lifelong impact on troubled youth who grow up to be troubled adults. For example, one large prospective study found that the most disturbed 5% of the sample of children with conduct problems showed from 1.5 to 19 times more problems than the least disturbed 50% of the sample (Fergusson, Horwood, & Ridder, 2005). These patterns included the prediction of criminal behavior, mental disorders, greater numbers of sexual partners, and higher rates of substance dependence in adulthood (Fergusson et al., 2005).

As can be seen in Box 10.1, there are strong ties between criminality in parents and children, especially between fathers and sons (Marler et al., 2005). It is

---

BOX 10.1

LIKE FATHER, LIKE SON

Whether it is due to genetic transmission, environmental factors, or more likely a combination of the two, there is a strong connection between antisocial behavior in fathers and antisocial behavior in sons (Moss, Baron, Hardie, & Vanyukov, 2001). When the fathers of CD boys are compared with fathers of nonclinical boys, the fathers of CD boys show much greater rates of APD and aggression than the fathers of nonclinical boys (Goetting, 1994; Reeves, Werry, Elkind, & Zametkin, 1987). Overall, aggression in sons is associated with aggression in fathers (Eaves et al., 2000).

When exploring these patterns based on the father's status, fathers who were diagnosed with antisocial personality disorder in combination with alcohol or drug dependence were more likely to have sons who showed oppositional defiant disorder or conduct disorder (Loukas, Zucker, Fitzgerald, & Krull, 2003; Moss et al., 2001). Overall, there is a clear connection between fathers' and sons' levels of oppositional difficulties, conduct problems, and aggression (Loukas et al., 2003; Moss et al., 2001; Phares, 1996). The connections between aggression in fathers and sons is evident in many nonhuman mammals as well (Marler, Trainor, & Davis, 2005).

Shoplifting is a common behavior in adolescents diagnosed with conduct disorder.

not surprising to learn that the progression from ODD to CD to APD is associated with parental criminality and a history of parental APD. Problematic family environments are also associated with the chronicity of these disorders. For example, parents who do not monitor their children's behavior and parents who are not involved in their children's lives tend to have children who move from ODD to CD to APD (Brody et al., 2003). Interparental conflict is also characteristic of the problematic family environments that are associated with the continuation of disruptive behaviors (Owens & Shaw, 2003), including when children move from ODD to CD to APD. For example, families that showed a great deal of **triangulation** (where parents put the child in between them when they argue) tend to have children who show high levels of aggression across time (Johnson, 2003). In general, low SES and economic disadvantage are considered risk factors for the development of ODD and CD, but

impoverishment is also associated with the chronicity of these disruptive behavior disorders (Brody et al., 2003; Evans, 2004; Wikstrom & Sampson, 2003).

As discussed already, earlier onset of severe symptoms is associated with greater chronicity of ODD, CD, and APD (McMahon & Kotler, 2006; Moffitt, 2003). Specifically, early onset of CD is associated with greater likelihood of developing APD in adulthood (American Psychiatric Association, 2000). This pattern makes a great deal of sense when you consider a young child who is already violating the rights of others before he or she even goes through puberty. Severe levels of aggression are also associated with the move from ODD, CD, to APD (McMahon & Wells, 1998). Again, this finding makes a great deal of sense given that ODD children who are aggressive are already showing more severe problems than ODD children who are not violent in their oppositional behavior. Children are also more likely to move from ODD to CD to APD when they show high levels of conduct problems and a great variety in their conduct problems (McMahon & Wells, 1998; Patterson, 1996). When children have already diversified and become engaged in a number of types of antisocial behaviors, they seem to be more entrenched in this antisocial lifestyle.

Regarding the co-occurrence of other disorders, comorbidity with ADHD is associated with a more severe and chronic outcome (Offord & Bennett, 1996). Interestingly, comorbidity with anxiety is associated with less-severe disturbance (Frick, 1998a). The combination of CD and depression is associated with significant impairments in academic functioning and was also predictive of nicotine dependance and drug dependence (Marmorstein & Iacono, 2003). Lower intellectual functioning is also associated with the chronic pattern from ODD to CD to APD (McMahon & Wells, 1998). It may be that children with lower IQs do not have the intellectual resources to find alternative outlets for their behavior, so they remain involved in antisocial activities. Overall, these characteristics are well established from years of research into the chronic patterns of ODD, CD, and APD. All these disorders are associated with cognitive processes that are associated with seeing malicious intent in others' behaviors even in ambiguous situations (see Box 10.2).

Etiology

One of the ways that etiological factors are studied is to compare and contrast the different correlates of different disorders. As can be seen in Table 10.6, the correlates of

BOX *10.2*

IS THERE MALICIOUS INTENT?

You are driving the speed limit (like every other law-abiding driver) and someone pulls up on your bumper and starts honking and waving his arms. What do you assume is going on? Do you interpret his actions as hostile, get angry at him, and consider what type of road rage you will exhibit? Do you feel differently when you realize that the man is trying to warn you that your backpack is still on the roof of your car?

Consider another scenario. You leave an acquaintance in your room for a few minutes, and when you return you find that your cell phone is broken. What do you assume happened? Was the cell phone already broken before you left the room? Did the acquaintance accidentally break the cell phone? Did she break it on purpose?

These ambiguous vignettes are presented with the idea of showing how attributions can influence reactions. In both scenarios, if your first thought was that the person was trying to do you harm, you would probably respond much more negatively than if you assumed that there was no malicious intent.

This type of research (with more age-appropriate scenarios, such as losing a ball or breaking a video game) has helped to identify dysfunctional attributions in aggressive children and adolescents. Specifically, many aggressive children and adolescents interpret ambiguous situations in a very hostile manner (Coy, Speltz, DeKlyen, & Jones,

2001; Crick & Dodge, 1994; de Castro, Slot, Bosch, Koops, & Veerman, 2003; MacBrayer, Milich, & Hundley, 2003; Shahinfar, Kupersmidt, & Matza, 2001). Known as the hostile attributional bias, children often react aggressively when they interpret their peers' behavior in a hostile manner (Dodge & Frame, 1982). This hostile attributional bias tends to be part of a vicious cycle, whereby children react aggressively, which is associated with peer rejection, which is then associated with more aggressive behaviors and seeking out deviant peers (Johnston & Ohan, 1999; MacBrayer et al., 2003). Hostile attributions appear to be exacerbated in aggressive boys who are experiencing negative feelings (de Castro et al., 2003). Boys are particularly vulnerable to acting aggressively when they interpret the situation negatively, they perceive that they are rejected by peers, and they blame the peers for their difficulties in peer relationships (Guerra, Asher, & DeRosier, 2004). Note that mothers of aggressive children also show this hostile attributional bias (MacBrayer et al., 2003).

Overall, this research on social-cognitive factors related to aggression has identified important aspects of the development of aggression in children and adolescents. This work has helped to identify prevention strategies that can challenge children's hostile attributional biases (Coie & Jacobs, 1993; MacBrayer et al., 2003).

TABLE 10.6 **Summary of the Differential Correlates to Conduct Disorder and ADHD**

Conduct Disorder	ADHD
Parental criminality/ antisocial behavior	Parental ADHD
Parental substance abuse	Poor academic achievement
Ineffective parenting practices	Poor performance on neuropsychological tests of frontal lobe functioning
Parental divorce/marital conflict	
Socioeconomic disadvantage	Poor response inhibition

Source: Frick (1998b).

CD and ADHD are different. Thus, although there is a great deal of comorbidity between CD and ADHD, there appears to be specific and different etiological correlates to each of the two disorders.

With regard to the specific etiological theories that attempt to explain the development of ODD and CD,

there are a number of compelling theories, including genetic and biological influences, familial psychosocial factors, and environmental influences (Hudziak Derks, Althoff, Copeland, & Boomsma, 2005). Unlike ADHD, there is more support for environmental influences than for genetic or biological influences in the development of ODD and CD (Gregory et al., 2004; Ingoldsby et al., 2006). For example, poor parenting during infancy is associated with risk for the development of externalizing disorders in later adolescence (Ford et al., 2004; Olson, Bates, Sandy, & Lanthier, 2000; Shaw, Owens, Giovannelli, & Winslow, 2001), aggressive interparental conflict is highly linked to childhood aggression and disruptiveness (Erath, Bierman, & the Conduct Problems Prevention Research Group, 2006), and parent–child conflict is a salient feature of ODD and CD (Burt et al., 2003; Owens & Shaw, 2003).

Support for genetic and biological influences in the development of ODD and CD comes from the connections between parental psychopathology (especially

JIMMY, SIXTH-GENERATION PAIN IN THE ASS

APD) and CD, as well as findings from studies of twins (Burt et al., 2003; Dick et al., 2005; Gelhorn et al., 2005; Gregory et al., 2004; Taylor, Iacono, & McGue, 2000). For example, identical twins tend to have higher concordance rates for CD than do fraternal twins, which suggests a genetic component in the development of CD (Burt, McGue, Krueger, & Iacono, 2005). One twin study of CD in Australia found that a high percentage of the variance was accounted for by genetic influences (Slutske et al., 1997). In addition, there is evidence that temperamental style, which is thought to be partially genetically determined, is associated with the possible development of CD. Specifically, having a difficult temperament in infancy is associated with aggression in later childhood (Lahey & Waldman, 2003). In addition, having a temperamental style that is consistent with sensation seeking (e.g., seeking out novel situations, seeking change in one's environment, etc.) is associated with disruptive behavior problems in children (Rettew, Copeland, Stanger, & Hudziak, 2004).

There has also been evidence to suggest that the brain functioning of ODD and CD children differs from that of nonclinical children. Specifically, studies of EEG recordings suggest that children with disruptive disorders show different brain functioning in the frontal lobe when compared with nonclinical children (Baving, Laucht, & Schmidt, 2000). The frontal lobe has also been implicated in a number of other disorders, including ADHD (Baving et al., 2000). Using EEG recordings, studies of P3 event-related potential have also shown that children with ODD and CD, as well as a number of other externalizing disorders, show reduced P3 amplitudes

(Iacono, Carlson, Malone, & McGue, 2002). This study suggests that there is psychophysiological evidence of brain functioning differences for children who show risk for externalizing behavior.

Other psychophysiological data also suggest a predisposition toward disruptive and antisocial behavior in children and adolescents. In comprehensive meta-analyses, children with high rates of antisocial behavior were consistently found to show lower resting heart rate and higher heart rate reactivity during a stressor when compared with children in a nonclinical control group (Ortiz & Raine, 2004). In an analysis of morning plasma cortisol levels in adolescent girls, girls diagnosed with CD showed consistently lower cortisol levels than girls in a nonclinical control group (Pajer, Gardner, Rubin, Perel, & Neal, 2001). These results are consistent with research on boys' cortisol levels (Pajer et al., 2001). Based on studies of brain functioning, heart rate, and cortisol levels, these studies suggest that there are biological predispositions toward oppositional and conduct problems in children and adolescents. The actual mechanisms of transmission for any of these differences, however, are not well established at this point.

In addition to the possibility of genetic predispositions to CD, a number of familial psychosocial factors have been implicated in the development of ODD and CD (Ford et al., 2004; Kilgore, Snyder, & Lentz, 2000). Many of these factors focus on less-than-optimal parenting practices. Some factors, such as overreactivity and hostility, are linked to parents of children who are comorbid for oppositional defiant disorder and ADHD (Seipp & Johnston, 2005). These parenting practices are found in both mothers and fathers and remain significant even after controlling for genetic effects (Meyer et al., 2000). Both mothers and fathers of ODD children showed maladaptive parenting strategies, but mothers were more appropriately responsive to their ODD children, ODD children were more compliant with their fathers, and mothers reported greater amounts of parenting stress in relation to their ODD child (Calzada, Eyberg, Rich, & Querido, 2004). One study explored the more serious aspects of ODD and CD that are specific to firesetting and cruelty to animals (Becker, Stuewig, Herrera, & McCloskey, 2004). Children were more likely to engage in firesetting when there were high levels of parental spousal abuse, paternal pet abuse, and paternal alcohol abuse. Children were more likely to show cruelty to animals when there were high levels of parental spousal abuse and harsh parenting from both mothers and fathers (Becker et al., 2004). Given that firesetting and cruelty to animals are related to delinquency, this study highlights a number of parenting characteristics that are precursors to ODD and CD.

A number of parenting characteristics are associated with disruptive behaviors in children. The following is a partial list of parenting characteristics that have been associated with the development of ODD and CD (Ford et al., 2004; Frick, 1998b; Jaffee, Caspi, Moffitt, & Taylor, 2004; Kim et al., 2003; Moffitt, 2003):

- Inadequate monitoring of the child's behavior
- Limited involvement in the child's life
- Inconsistent and harsh discipline practices
- Limited warmth and positive reinforcement of the child's accomplishments
- Inadequate problem-solving skills
- High levels of interparental conflict, especially in front of the child
- Chronic coercive and negative interactions with the child
- Physical abuse

All these factors have been studied extensively, and all of them have received support for playing a causative role in the development of ODD and CD (Cummings, Goeke-Morey, & Papp, 2004; Jaffee et al., 2004; Moffitt, 2003; Snyder et al., 2003). In a seminal book entitled, *Coercive Family Process,* Dr. Gerald Patterson (1982) described the **coercion theory** about families with an oppositional and conduct disordered child. Parents exhibit inadequate and harsh parenting practices, children react by acting out, which in turn leads to more harsh parenting. It is important to acknowledge that the family is a system and that parents influence children, but children also influence parents. Thus, the reciprocal nature of interactions within families is important to acknowledge. These patterns have been well established in over two decades of research (Snyder et al., 2003). Note that these patterns are evident in both the mother–child and father–child relationship (Denham et al., 2000).

Related to the coercion theory, a number of studies have found a strong link between physical abuse and children's aggressive behavior. It could be that physically abusive parents are passing on a genetic predisposition for aggression to their children or it could be that the physical abuse is an environmental factor that leads to greater aggression in children. In a comprehensive, prospective study of 1,116 twin pairs, one study established that it is the physical abuse itself rather than genetic loading for aggression that has a causative role in the development of aggression and

antisocial behavior in children (Jaffee et al., 2004). There was, however, a second study with this same sample where both genetic factors and the family environmental aspects of physical abuse were related. Specifically, children who were not at genetic risk for the development of aggression and antisocial behavior showed a 2% increase in the likelihood of aggression because of being physically abused, whereas children who were at genetic risk showed an increase of 24% due to the physical abuse (Jaffee et al., 2005). Thus, it appears that higher rates of aggression can be at least partially caused by physical abuse within the family, and the combination of genetic risk and child abuse puts children at much higher risk for the development of aggression and antisocial behavior than either risk factor alone (Jaffee et al., 2005).

In addition to genetic, biological, and familial influences, there is also support for environmental influences in the development of ODD and CD. The primary environmental influence that is associated with the onset of ODD and CD is living in poverty (Brody et al., 2003; Lahey et al., 1999). Socioeconomic disadvantage has been found consistently to be linked to the development of ODD and CD. The specific mechanisms are not well known, given that many children who grow up in poverty do not develop any emotional/behavioral problems (Brody et al., 2003; Evans, 2004; Lahey et al., 1999). It may be that socioeconomic disadvantage is tied to a number of other risk factors, such as exposure to violence, inadequate housing and nutrition, stress, and deviant peers (Luthar, 1999; Perez-Smith, Albus, & Weist, 2001).

Deviant peers, in particular, have been linked to conduct problems. Known as **deviancy training,** adolescents with conduct problems tend to exacerbate problem behaviors in other adolescents (Dishion, McCord, & Poulin, 1999; Dodge, 2003; Weiss et al., 2005). This pattern is particularly true for boys and for homeless youth in contrast to girls and housed youth, respectively (Heinze, Toro, & Urberg, 2004). In younger children, naming aggressive children as ones' friends is associated with increased aggression, whereas being named as a friend to aggressive children is not associated with increased levels of aggression (Mrug, Hoza, & Bukowski, 2004). Negative influences by externalizing peers seems to be more problematic for girls than for boys (Hanish, Martin, Fabes, Leonard, & Herzog, 2005). Interestingly, the combination of low self-esteem and deviant peers was related to higher conduct problems, whereas low self-esteem without a context of deviant peers was not significantly related to problematic behavior (DuBois & Silverthorn, 2004). Unfortunately, higher percentages of deviant peers are evident in impoverished neighborhoods and environments (Evans, 2004; Luthar, 1999).

Figure 10.3 shows an illustration of the many environmental influences that can be involved in the development of ODD and CD (Dishion, French, & Patterson, 1995). As can be seen in the figure, children and adolescents are influenced by interpersonal factors, relationship processes, behavior settings, and community contexts. All these factors are important to consider in the development of oppositional behavior and conduct problems (Dishion et al., 1995).

Overall, there is support for a number of etiological explanations of the development of ODD and CD, but there is no one theory that has gained support exclusively. Rather, it is probable that ODD and CD are developed due to a number of factors, including a genetic predisposition combined with inadequate parenting and less-than-optimal environmental factors (Moffitt, 2005). Box 10.3 highlights the need to conduct research in this area that is conscientious of race and ethnicity.

Note, however, that because of the potentially causative role that family factors play in the development of ODD and CD, clinicians should assess characteristics of the family as well as the child referred for an evaluation (McMahon & Frick, 2005). Thus, in addition to conducting a thorough evaluation of the child, clinicians should evaluate parental functioning (e.g., psychopathology), parenting practices (e.g., level of monitoring), interparental conflict, and relevant environmental characteristics of the family (McMahon & Frick, 2005). This type of thorough assessment will not only help delineate the nature of the problems in the child's life, but will also help in the treatment of oppositional behavior and conduct problems.

Greatness is not secured by violence.
—Proverb of Africa

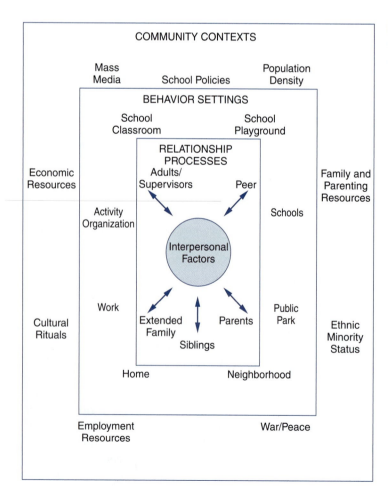

FIGURE 10.3 Framework for the Ecology of Antisocial Behavior.

Source: Dishion et al. (1995).

RACE, ETHNICITY, AND RESEARCH METHODOLOGY

No clear racial or ethnic patterns are evident regarding prevalence rates of ODD or CD. Some studies find more Caucasian-American youth evidencing CD, some studies find more African-American youth evidencing CD, and some studies find more Latino/Hispanic youth evidencing CD (Lahey et al., 1999). Thus, there are no clear patterns of CD regarding race and ethnicity.

Why, then, is there evidence of higher rates of aggression and antisocial behavior in ethnic minorities when compared to Caucasian Americans? A number of studies have documented that African Americans as a group display higher rates of aggressive and delinquent behavior than Caucasian Americans as a group (Hinshaw & Park, 1999). African-American children had more problems, like school problems, in relation to disruptive behavior disorders than did Caucasian children (Ezpeleta, Keeler, Alaatin, Costello, & Angold, 2001). Teachers' ratings of African-American youth show higher rates of aggression and misbehavior than do ratings of Caucasian youth (Downey & Pribesh, 2004). Other studies have shown that African-American adolescent boys who do not have a job are at increased risk for externalizing problems, such as juvenile delinquency (Luthar, 1999). When compared with Caucasian-American youth, African-American youth in impoverished urban neighborhoods appear to become involved in criminal activities to a greater extent and to be less cautious about others' continuing involvement in crime (Luthar, 1999). Overall, this line of research that explores aggression and criminal activity has found consistent racial and ethnic differences, especially when African Americans are compared with Caucasian Americans.

The findings from these two lines of research appear to contradict each other. That is, they contradict each other until you look closely at the research methodology that was used in the studies. Most of the studies that explore

delinquency in youth use samples of adjudicated and incarcerated youth (Yung & Hammond, 1997). Thus, when racial and ethnic differences are found in adolescents in juvenile detention facilities, a number of factors other than actual behavior could be involved. Of foremost concern are the possibly discriminatory practices regarding arrest, detention, and sentencing (Yung & Hammond, 1997). It may be that African Americans are more at risk for arrest, detention, and incarceration (rather than probation) than are Caucasian Americans (Yung & Hammond, 1997). Caucasian youth in juvenile detention facilities appear to show more comorbidity than youth of other racial/ethnic backgrounds, which suggests that Caucasian youth have to be more troubled to be incarcerated than other youth (Abram et al., 2003).

Given that there are no clear differences in CD for different racial and ethnic groups when large-scale epidemiological studies are completed, it is likely that factors other than behavior are related to the racial and ethnic differences that are found in studies of incarcerated youth (Hinshaw & Park, 1999). Teachers' ratings of African-American youth appear to be inflated in contrast to ratings of Caucasian youth (Downey & Pribesh, 2004). When children show approximately the same externalizing behaviors, African-American children are more likely to receive the more severe diagnosis of conduct disorder, whereas Caucasian children are more likely to receive the less-severe diagnosis of oppositional defiant disorder (McNeil et al., 2002). When SES level is controlled in studies that find racial and ethnic differences in diagnostic prevalence, racial and ethnic differences disappear (McNeil et al., 2002). In other words, aggressive and criminal behaviors found in samples of adjudicated youth appear to be strongly associated with poverty rather than race and ethnicity per se. These issues highlight the importance of understanding the research design in relation to the results that are found in studies.

Treatment

There are a number of evidence-based treatments for children with oppositional and conduct problems. The two treatments that have received the most support are both variants of **behavioral parent training,** which focuses on teaching parents appropriate and effective parenting strategies (Rappaport & Thomas, 2004). One treatment, known as the *Incredible Years,* is administered via videotape and allows parents to observe other parents modeling appropriate parenting skills (Webster-Stratton & Reid, 2003). Clinicians usually show groups

of parents the videotape and then lead discussions on how to implement the strategies in the parents' own families. The other treatment is usually administered with groups of parents and follows a manual called *Living with Children* (Patterson & Gullion, 1968). Both of these methods of behavioral parent training include

- Teaching parents to monitor their children's behavior and activities (e.g., knowing their children's friends, discussing where the child goes after school and when out with friends)

PROMOTING PARENTS' PROBLEM-SOLVING AND EFFECTIVE COPING STRATEGIES

Source: Webster-Stratton & Herbert (1994).

- Paying attention to good behavior (even if parents have to "catch" their child being good) and reward the good behavior

- Identify and provide consequences for inappropriate behavior (e.g., providing consistent negative consequences for maladaptive behavior, or when appropriate, ignoring bad behavior)

- Remain calm and consistent when implementing consequences to maladaptive behavior

- Instigate warm and caring interactions with children

These principles from behavioral parent training have been found to be effective in decreasing maladaptive behavior in oppositional and conduct disordered children (Chamberlain & Smith, 2003; Kazdin, 2005b; McMahon & Forehand, 2003; Webster-Stratton & Reid, 2003).

Interestingly, the *Incredible Years* program was most effective with children who had the highest level of pretreatment conduct problems and with mothers who had the highest level of critical parenting at pretreatment (Reid, Webster-Stratton, & Baydar, 2004).

At least 11 other treatments for ODD and CD have been identified as evidence-based (Brinkmeyer & Eyberg, 2003; Greene et al., 2004; Henggeler & Lee, 2003; Kazdin, 2005b; Kazdin & Whitley, 2003; Lochman, Barry, & Pardini, 2003; Nixon, Sweeney, Erickson, & Touyz, 2004; Sukhodolsky, Golub, Stone, & Orban, 2005). These treatments include

- Anger control training
- Anger coping therapy
- Assertiveness training
- Collaborative problem solving
- Delinquency prevention program

- Multisystemic therapy
- Parent–child interaction therapy
- Parent training program
- Problem solving skills training
- Rational–emotive therapy
- Time-out plus signal seat treatment

These treatments cannot be described in detail, but suffice it to say that nearly all the treatments are of a behavioral or cognitive–behavioral nature (Lochman, Powell, Whidby, & Fitzgerald, 2006; Sheldrick, Kendall, & Heimberg, 2001). Other variations on behavioral parent training also look promising. For example, in a success-based, noncoercive treatment program that is similar to behavioral parent training, mothers of young children from violent homes were able to learn appropriate parenting skills, which were associated with decreased child behavior problems (Ducharme, Atkinson, & Poulton, 2000). In addition, parent training–related treatments have been shown to improve parents' self-efficacy in their parenting skills and to reduce parenting stress, which are in turn related to decreased conduct problems in children (Feinfield & Baker, 2004). Note that these evidence-based treatments can work for many children with severe problems, including high rates of comorbidity, impoverished living conditions, and family dysfunction (Kazdin & Whitley, 2006a).

One of these treatments, **multisystemic therapy,** is highlighted to provide more insight into a comprehensive treatment for oppositional and conduct disordered youth (Henggeler & Lee, 2003; Timmons-Mitchell, Bender, Kishna, & Mitchell, 2006). The idea behind multisystemic therapy is that children and adolescents with conduct problems have difficulties at a number of different levels (personal, social/peers, familial, societal) and experience difficulties in a number of different settings (home, school, neighborhood, larger community). The therapy is designed to intervene at whatever level and in whatever context is necessary. Thus, therapists sometimes engage in individual therapy with an adolescent, family therapy, school consultation, peer interventions, or couples therapy with the adolescent's parents (Henggeler & Lee, 2003). Therapeutic interventions are equally as diverse. Although many of the interventions are of a behavioral and cognitive–behavioral nature, therapists use the therapeutic orientation that seems most appropriate for that adolescent and that family. At the core of multisystemic therapy is that children and adolescents are part of systems that must be treated (Henggeler & Lee, 2003), which is consistent with the rationale

Case Study: Partying Patricia

Just like in chapter 5 (Devastated Darryl) and chapter 8 Shy Sylvia), you get to create a treatment plan for a complex case. Clinicians often use treatment plans to help guide their therapeutic strategies and to evaluate whether or not those strategies have been successful.

After jotting down your own treatment plan for this case, take a look at the suggestions reprinted from The Family Therapy Treatment Planner *(Dattilio & Jongsma, 2000) and compare your treatment plan with one that a professional might have developed.*

Patricia is a 16-year-old Caucasian girl who lives with her biological mother, stepfather, and three younger brothers (one of whom is a biological brother and two of whom are her half-brothers, ages 13, 6, and 4, respectively). Patricia and her mother argue almost constantly about nearly every aspect of Patricia's life (e.g., school, friends, dating, caring for her younger siblings, style of clothes, and curfew). For example, Patricia has begun wearing clothes that are "like a prostitute," according to her mother. Although Patricia's stepfather tries to stay out of the arguments, he has recently found it necessary to step in and try to gain control of Patricia's behavior (which has lead to even more conflict in the family). Patricia's mother appreciates her husband's attempt to control Patricia but feels that he is taking away her authority with her daughter. Patricia's mother and stepfather find themselves arguing about Patricia with increasing frequency, and even her younger brothers seem distressed by the situation.

Patricia feels that both her mother and her stepfather are painfully out-of-date in their ideas about teenagers. For example, she reports that none of her friends have a curfew and so she feels justified in coming home at 4:00 A.M. on weekends. Most often, Patricia attends parties at the local college where her boyfriend lives in a fraternity house. Although her parents have set a curfew of midnight, they are usually unable to stay up that late to see if Patricia makes it home on time. Patricia has skipped from school frequently to spend time with her boyfriend. She plans to get an apartment with him when she is 18 so that she can escape from her parents' rules.

Patricia's parents report that she used to be a warm, friendly child who was always compliant with adults. Her biological parents divorced when she was very young, and she has limited contact with her biological father. Patricia's mother and stepfather married when Patricia was 6 and her biological brother was 3. Her youngest brothers were born when she was 10 and 12. Her parents report that she used to like helping with the babies, but that for the past few years she has withdrawn significantly from helping around the house. Although she continues to be affectionate with her younger siblings, she no longer is willing to take care of them when asked. During the past few years, the arguments between Patricia and her mother have increased. The most recent argument had to do with how Patricia wants to spend spring break. According to Patricia, "All of my friends are going to stay in a hotel on the beach for the whole week and my stupid parents won't let me go." Unbeknownst to her parents, Patricia plans to go away with her boyfriend for spring break.

During the initial interview with Patricia, her parents, and her younger brothers, it appeared obvious where the lines have been drawn. For example, Patricia sat on a chair by herself separate from the rest of the family, while her brothers and parents crowded cozily onto a large couch. Patricia was jovial with her brothers but seemed to disagree with nearly every statement made by her parents. She sighed loudly when her mother talked and said "Ugh" when her mother began to cry. When asked directly about her experiences, Patricia reported that she just wanted her parents to get off her back so that she could be an adult. She frequently cited how "uptight" her parents were and wished aloud that they were more like her friends' parents who allegedly do not set limits on their teenagers' behavior.

Patricia's medical history was significant for asthma, which has since been managed effectively. Her developmental history was notable in that she achieved major milestones (e.g., crawling, walking, talking, toilet training, reading, and writing) significantly earlier than expected.

Treatment Plan

Please create a treatment plan for Patricia and her family. You should include behavioral definitions, long-term goals, short-term objectives, and therapeutic interventions. It may be most helpful to consider this case from a family systems perspective. After you have developed your own treatment plan, please compare it with the treatment plan from *The Family Therapy Treatment Planner* (Dattilio & Jongsma, 2000).

Behavioral Definitions

1. _____
2. _____
3. _____
4. _____
5. _____
6. _____
7. _____
8. _____
9. _____
10. _____

Long-Term Goals

1. _____
2. _____
3. _____
4. _____
5. _____
6. _____

(continued)

Case Study: Partying Patricia (*continued*)

Long-Term Goals (continued)

7. _____
8. _____
9. _____
10. _____

Short-Term Objectives	*Therapeutic Interventions*
1. _____	1. _____
2. _____	2. _____
3. _____	3. _____
4. _____	4. _____
5. _____	5. _____
6. _____	6. _____
7. _____	7. _____
8. _____	8. _____
9. _____	9. _____
10. _____	10. _____

From *The Family Therapy Treatment Planner*—Dattilio and Jongsma (2000)

ADOLESCENT/PARENT CONFLICTS

BEHAVIORAL DEFINITIONS

1. Parents experience conflicts with adolescent child that begin to interfere with the family's overall functioning.
2. Parents argue with each other over how to respond to the adolescent's disruptive nonconforming behaviors.
3. Family members resent the adolescent-centered conflict, increasing tension in the home.
4. Parents feel a loss of control and the adolescent feels empowered by parent's dilemma, making his/her own rules and resisting parental intervention.
5. Adolescent acts out in areas of substance abuse, sexuality, school performance, and/or delinquency.

LONG-TERM GOALS

1. Parents arrive at some level of agreement regarding how to respond to the adolescent.
2. Parents reduce the effects of the adolescent's misbehavior on other family members.
3. Parents learn new methods for working together to achieve harmony and balance in the family.
4. Parents devise and enforce a set of rules and standards that promote peace and harmony in the family.
5. Parents feel empowered to take control of the family and react firmly to adolescent acting out.

SHORT-TERM OBJECTIVES

1. Define the specifics about what needs to change in the adolescent's behavior.
2. Parents clarify philosophy on parenting expectations for the adolescent.
3. Parents and adolescent cooperate with psychological testing to identify specific areas of parent/child conflict.
4. Identify family, school, or marital factors that may be contributing to the adolescent's undesirable behavior.
5. Parents identify their strengths and weaknesses in parenting style.
6. Parents read books and watch videotapes on parenting adolescents.
7. Parents develop and implement a monitoring system for the adolescent's whereabouts, and indicate any deficiencies in the monitoring system.
8. Parents identify and record the occurrence of a specific desirable behavior of the adolescent's that they would like to see increase in frequency.
9. Implement a behavioral contract to increase the frequency of the adolescent's target behavior.
10. Increase the frequency of positive social- or activity-oriented interactions between parents and the adolescent.
11. Establish and implement consequences for negative adolescent behavior (e.g., the use of response cost).
12. Parents identify and make an effort to terminate any undesirable behaviors that they may be modeling for the adolescent.
13. Parents confer with each other frequently to increase mutual support in parenting.
14. Parents use structured dialogue techniques to ensure good parental communication for problem solving.
15. Parents minimize criticism of the other's parenting efforts.
16. Parents discuss disagreements only at times when discussion is likely to be constructive, and not in the presence of the children.
17. Parents identify and replace distorted cognitive beliefs that relate to parenting their teenager.
18. Family members hold family meetings regularly and conform to the rules of interaction.
19. Family members demonstrate empathy and respect for other individual's points of view by paraphrasing or reflecting speaker's position before responding.
20. Parents list alternatives to their current parenting methods.
21. Parents enact alternative parenting styles and evaluate their effectiveness.
22. Identify and challenge unreasonable beliefs and expectations regarding adolescent behaviors.

(continued)

23. Parents establish consistent house rules and regulations.

24. Family establishes a regular dinner hour and sets rules regarding how often members will be present.

25. Parents go out alone at least one night per week for socialization and/or recreation.

THERAPEUTIC INTERVENTIONS

1. Open up the forum for family members to share their perception of the adolescent's behavior and discuss feelings about the adolescent's behavior.

2. Assess whether the adolescent's acting-out behavior is transient or is a more stable pattern.

3. Have parents share their philosophy on parenting and what expectations they have for their son or daughter.

4. Explore familial interaction patterns or dynamics that may be exacerbating the conflict between adolescent and parents (underlying conflicts, family-of-origin issues, unrealistic expectations, marital problems, etc.).

5. Explore familial interaction patterns or dynamics that may be exacerbating the conflict between adolescent and parents (underlying conflicts, family-of-origin issues, unrealistic expectations, marital problems, etc.).

6. Explore environmental stressors that may be exacerbating the adolescent's acting out (e.g., family transitions, inconsistent rules, school or social difficulties, peer relationships, or peer pressure).

7. Role-play a parent/adolescent conflict to assess how parents solve the problem; give parents feedback regarding the strengths and weaknesses of their approach.

8. Teach how the adolescent's strengths can be augmented and his/her weaknesses diminished.

9. Ask parents to develop monitoring for their adolescent, knowing *where* he/she is, *who* he/she is with, *what* he/she is doing, and *when* he/she will be home.

10. Assign parents to record their joint monitoring efforts with the adolescent as a homework assignment.

11. Ask parents to discuss their successes at monitoring and to identify events or situations in which monitoring requires improvement.

12. Ask parents to select a behavior of the adolescent's that they would like to see decrease or diminish. Ask them to record its occurrence every day for a week, and notice the behaviors or situations that precede it (antecedents) and follow it (consequences).

13. Have parents decide on an appropriate reward system (e.g., verbal praise, use of the car, allowance) to reinforce the positive target behavior of the adolescent; seek agreement between parents and adolescent for this behavioral contract.

14. Recommend that each parent increase the number of parent-initiated, casual, positive conversations with the adolescent.

15. Develop with parents a response cost/procedure to use in conjunction with the adolescent's targeted negative behavior; assign implementation and review success.

16. If parents are modeling for the adolescent the behavior they would like to extinguish (e.g., yelling or becoming sarcastic), have parents become aware and contract to change their own behavior before trying to change the same behavior in the adolescent.

17. Teach parents techniques of anger control to better mediate conflict.

18. Ask parents to role-play support for each other regarding their reaction to the adolescent's misbehavior; have the supportive parent ask (in a supportive, non-threatening manner) how the other parent deals with the misbehavior and whether the supportive parent can do anything in the future to help.

19. Have parents contract to support the other's parenting by not interfering during the other's parent/adolescent interactions or with the other's decisions (i.e., avoid splitting their parental unity.

20. Help each parent identify when they are engaging in criticizing the other parent in a nonconstructive manner.

21. Help parents establish a practice of meeting in private so they can discuss parenting decisions and come to a mutual agreement before presenting it to the adolescent.

---

for family therapy with delinquent adolescents (Robbins, Alexander, & Turner, 2000).

Multisystemic therapy has been found to be very effective, even with chronic juvenile offenders (Curtis, Ronan, & Borduin, 2004). The strongest improvements have been found when therapists follow the multisystemic therapy guidelines closely (Huey, Henggeler, Brondino,

& Pickrel, 2000). Adolescents who received the treatment showed fewer behavioral problems and were less likely to be rearrested than were adolescents who received "usual services." Note, however, that like other treatments for conduct problems, multisystemic therapy does not work for everyone. One follow-up study found that 71% of adolescents who received "usual services" had been rearrested within 4 years, whereas 26% of adolescents who received multisystemic therapy had been rearrested in that same time period (McMahon & Wells, 1998). In a long-term follow-up to adolescents who completed multisystemic treatment, there was a 50% recidivism rate for 28-year-olds who had completed multisystemic treatment as adolescents, whereas there was a 81% recidivism rate for adults who had been involved in individual therapy as an adolescent (Schaeffer & Borduin, 2005). These differences in rearrest and recidivism rates show the success of multisystemic therapy, but they also highlight the difficulty of treating these adolescents.

One large meta-analysis of multisystemic treatment showed that treated families were functioning 70% better than families treated with other therapies or who did not receive treatment (Curtis et al., 2004). Multisystemic treatment seemed to affect family functioning more effectively than impacting adolescents behavior directly (Curtis et al., 2004).

Multisystemic therapy has also been used with adolescents who abuse substances and adolescent sex offenders (Henggeler & Lee, 2003). The treatment was most effective when therapists were well trained and well supervised (Curtis et al., 2004). In addition, multisystemic therapy seems to work best when there is a match between client and therapist race/ethnicity, for example when African-American youth work with African-American therapists (Halliday-Boykins, Schoenwald, & Letourneau, 2005). Overall, multisystemic therapy is a promising therapy for children and adolescents who may have no other therapeutic alternatives (McMahon & Wells, 1998).

For all these treatments, a stronger therapeutic alliance between the therapist and the family is associated with greater improvements in the child's or adolescent's behavior (Kazdin, Marciano, & Whitley, 2005). Conversely, for all these treatments, it appears that treatments are less effective when clients and their families perceive barriers to the treatment (Bussing, Zima, Gary, & Garvan, 2003; Kazdin & Wassell, 1999). Barriers to treatment include stressors (such as disagreements about taking part in therapy), treatment demands (such as perceiving that treatment is too demanding or costly), relevance of treatment (such as feeling that the treatment is relevant to the child's problems), and relationship with the therapist (such as feeling supported by the therapist). Higher levels of perceived barriers to treatment were associated with less therapeutic improvement in conduct disordered children (Kazdin & Wassell, 1999).

Many studies have found that African-American families perceive greater barriers to treatment than families of other racial/ethnic backgrounds (Bussing et al., 2003; Perrino, Coatsworth, Briones, Pantin, & Szapocznik, 2001). This pattern may help explain why proportionally fewer African-American children are able to access high-quality mental health care for ODD and CD (McNeil et al., 2002). Overall, clients' perceptions of barriers to therapy should be considered when working with conduct disordered youth and their families, and more attention should be paid to engaging racial and ethnic minorities into treatment that is known to work with other groups of children (McNeil et al., 2002).

In addition to the therapeutic interventions just reviewed, medications have also been used to treat ODD and CD. Due to the high levels of comorbidity with ADHD, many ODD and CD children are treated with stimulants such as methylphenidate (Ritalin), Dextroamphetamine (Dexedrine), and Amphetamine & d-ampheamine compound (Adderall; Brown et al., 2005; DuPaul et al., 2003). Although pemoline (Cylert) used to be prescribed for the treatment of comorbid ADHD and disruptive disorders, it is no longer suggested for use with children because of a potentially lethal side effect of acute liver failure (Phelps et al., 2002).

In general, these medications tend to be most effective for children who are comorbid with ADHD, but there is some evidence that stimulants may reduce aggressive behaviors in some ODD and CD children and adolescents who are not comorbid with ADHD (Altepeter & Korger, 1999).

Other medications tend to be used for symptoms that are associated with oppositional behaviors and conduct problems. For example, lithium has been used to decrease aggression when there are also high levels of mania. Antipsychotic medications have also been used to decrease aggression (Brown et al., 2005). Antidepressant medications and antianxiety medications are used with ODD and CD children who are comorbid for depression and anxiety, respectively. One antianxiety medication, buspirone (Buspar) has received recent attention for its effectiveness in reducing aggression and assaultive behavior in children diagnosed with ODD or CD (Phelps et al., 2002). At the current time, however, buspirone (Buspar) is only clinically validated for the treatment of anxiety disorders in children, so prescribing it for aggression and assaultive behavior must be handled carefully.

Overall, there are a number of promising treatments for ODD and CD, but the disorders continue to be difficult to treat. Certain personal characteristics, such as the level of callous/unemotional traits, appear to make treatment more challenging. For example, in a parent training treatment study with an evidence-based treatment package, young boys who showed higher levels of callousness and unemotionality did not show the same improvements as boys low in these characteristics (Hawes & Dadds, 2005). Specifically, boys high in callousness and unemotionality were less responsive to the use of time-out and showed less emotion when being punished. Thus, even effective treatments may need to be modified for particularly challenging children (Hawes & Dadds, 2005).

Because of the intense parental involvement that is required in the most effective therapies, treatment effectiveness relies on parents' abilities to a large extent. For example, one treatment program was compared for work with preadolescents directly versus the preadolescents and their parents (Lochman & Wells, 2004). The treatment that included parents in addition to preadolescents was far superior to working with preadolescents alone (Lochman & Wells, 2004).

Because parents of ODD and CD children are often troubled themselves, it is difficult to get them engaged into treatment for their offspring and to get them to show up for treatment on a regular basis. For this reason, a number of interventions have been tried in the school system (Hughes, Cavell, Meehan, Zhang, & Collie, 2005; vanLier, Muthen, van der Sar, & Crijnen; Wilson, Lipsey & Derzon, 2003, 2004). One year-long psychoeducational treatment program for youngsters was not effective in reducing disruptive behavior at 2-year follow-up (Shelton et al., 2000). Conversely, one after-school treatment program for early-career juvenile

offenders was effective at reducing the likelihood of future criminal offenses (Myers et al., 2000). One research project compared parent training alone with child training, and teacher training and found that the groups that involved parent training (with or without child and teacher training) were the most beneficial in helping to improve parenting in both mothers and fathers (Webster-Stratton, Reid, & Hammond, 2004). Similarly, the groups that involved teacher training (with or without child and parent training) resulted in improvements in teachers' behavior, which ultimately resulted in improvements in the children's behavior (Webster-Stratton et al., 2004). Interestingly, mothers' but not fathers' parenting behavior also improved when the child alone or when the child and the teacher received training. Overall, this study suggests that interventions in the school can affect children's behavior, which can influence parenting behavior in the home (Webster-Stratton et al., 2004).

Overall, treatment programs that are administered in school settings are effective for the most part. One meta-analysis that evaluated the effectiveness of school-based interventions on aggressive behavior found that children who received treatment were less aggressive than children who did not receive treatment, and better-run programs showed more improvements than poorly run programs (Wilson et al., 2003). Overall, this meta-analysis and the individual studies suggest that targeting youth in a school setting is worthwhile, especially if there is a parent component to the treatment program.

Given the functional impairments that are present in the parents of many ODD and CD children (e.g.,

---

YOU DECIDE: SHOULD CHILDREN AND ADOLESCENTS BE HELD TO THE SAME LEGAL STANDARD AS ADULTS?

Yes

- Although the U.S. Supreme Court has ruled that the execution of youth who committed crimes before they were 16 years old is unconstitutional, the execution of youth who committed crimes at the age of 16 or older is allowed in many states (Steinberg & Scott, 2003).

- Many countries, including the United States, Nigeria, Pakistan, Saudi Arabia, Yemen, Iran, and the Congo, allow the execution of individuals who committed their crimes when they were juveniles (Steinberg & Scott, 2003).

No

- Children and adolescents show developmentally appropriate immaturity that suggests their crimes are not conducted in the same way as crimes by adults (Steinberg & Scott, 2003).

- Children and adolescents show diminished responsibility by definition of their age and developmental level. Family, cultural, and neighborhood factors relate strongly to their involvement in criminal activities (Ford et al., 2004; Steinberg & Scott, 2003).

So, should children and adolescents be held to the same legal standard as adults? You decide.

parental psychopathology, interparental conflict, disengaged parenting styles), it is not surprising to find that many ODD and CD children cannot be helped effectively by the treatments that are known to work, especially those without a parental component. Some children with severe conduct problems are placed in residential facilities or therapeutic foster care settings (Chamberlain & Smith, 2003). Many of these facilities use a variety of the treatments just described. The most effective residential facilities utilize multiple therapies that focus on many different aspects of adolescents, their family, their peer group, and their environment (Chamberlain & Smith, 2003). Because of the high rates of comorbidity with other disorders, treatment programs often have to address both the oppositional and conduct problems as well as the comorbid disorder such as depression (Rohde, Clarke, Mace, Jorgensen, & Seeley, 2004). These multidimensional intervention programs have been found to be effective for both boys and girls (Leve, Chamberlain, & Reid, 2005).

As noted in the "You Decide" section, there is conflicting evidence as to whether or not youth should be treated as adults when sentencing is completed. Many adolescents are mandated to attend some type of remediation program instead of serving jail time. Unfortunately, a number of interventions through the juvenile justice system are not effective. Boot camps, for example are associated with either no therapeutic gains or even higher rates of rearrest than services-as-usual (Bottcher & Ezell, 2005; Cullen, Blevins, Trager, & Gendreau, 2005). Some military-style residential treatment programs appear to work, but they tend to be voluntary rather than court ordered, and they appear to be treating a less-severe group of adolescents than court-mandated boot camps (Weis, Wilson, & Whitemarsh, 2005). Treatments, such as group therapy, that put delinquent youths with other delinquent youths in an unstructured setting appear to increase the youths' connections with deviant peers, which in turn exacerbates rather than ameliorates their problem behavior (Leve & Chamberlain, 2005). Thus, effective programs for the treatment of CD and criminal behavior require multimodal involvement from youth, families, schools, and the community (Henggeler & Lee, 2003). When children and adolescents receive effective treatments for conduct problems, there are often improvements not only in the child or adolescent, but also in the parents and in the family system (Kazdin & Wassell, 2000). Thus, the search for effective treatments for conduct problems continues, with the hope of finding ways to improve the lives of children, adolescents, their

families, and members of their social network. The connections between violence and television discussed in Box 10.4 are relevant to both treatment and prevention.

Prevention

Because of the personal and societal costs of ODD and CD, a number of prevention programs have attempted to prevent these disorders from ever developing (August, Egan, Realmuto, & Hektner, 2003; August, Realmuto, Hektner, & Bloomquist, 2001; Brotman et al., 2003, 2005; Conduct Problems Prevention Research Group, 2002, 2004; Peters, Petrunka, & Arnold, 2003; Shaw, Dishion, Supplee, Gardner, & Arnds, 2006; Tremblay, LeMarquand, & Vitaro, 1999). Prevention programs have included work with:

- Social skills and interpersonal skills training
- Academic skills training
- Parenting skills training (including individuals who were expecting their first child)
- Peer training
- Day care-worker training
- Teacher training
- School-based preventive interventions

Some of these prevention programs targeted children who were already showing low levels of conduct problems (August et al., 2003), whereas others targeted children who were not yet showing problems but who were at risk for the development of problems, such as siblings of adjudicated youth (Brotman et al., 2005). In addition to these programs that are targeted at preventing oppositional problems and conduct problems specifically, there are a host of other prevention programs that could indirectly reduce the likelihood of ODD and CD. For example, programs that attempt to prevent violence within the family, such as child physical abuse, may indirectly help to prevent ODD and CD because physical abuse is a risk factor for the development of these disorders (Jaffee et al., 2004; Jouriles et al., 2001). Many of the prevention programs try to reach very young children to prevent more serious problems from occurring (Shaw et al., 2006).

One representative prevention program that targets CD specifically is the delinquency prevention program for preschoolers at risk for the development of ODD and CD (Lacourse et al., 2002; Vitaro, Brendgen, & Tremblay, 2001). These researchers taught the basic principles of behavioral parent training to parents of preschool children who were identified as at-risk for the

BOX *10.4*

DOES TELEVISION CAUSE VIOLENCE?

Nearly every time that there is a school shooting or other horrific act of violence perpetrated by a youngster, a discussion of television violence will undoubtedly take place. There is no question that violence is pervasive in the media and that children watch a great deal of television. A total of 71.2% of television programs shown in prime time have some violent content, with an average of 5.3 violent scenes per hour (Huston & Wright, 1998). On Saturday mornings, 92.0% of programing contained violence, with 23.0 violent scenes per hour (Huston & Wright, 1998). Preschoolers, on average, watch 27 hours of television per week (Centerwall, 2000). Overall, reviews of the scholarly literature and meta-analyses conclude consistently that television violence is associated with higher levels of aggression (Browne & Hamilton-Giachritsis, 2005). But why do some television watchers become more violent than others?

One possible explanation is the context of the violence. Violence that is perceived as real is associated with higher levels of aggression than fictional violence, such as violence in cartoons (Huston & Wright, 1998). Violence that encourages viewers to identify with the aggressor is also associated with higher levels of aggression (Donnerstein, Slaby, & Eron, 1994).

There are also familial characteristics that must be considered when investigating the effects of television violence. For example, children in families with high levels of conflict appear to seek out more violent television shows (Vandewater, Lee, & Shim, 2005). Conversely, parents who communicate with their children and who show high levels of warmth toward their children tend to have children who watch less-violent television (Spears & Seydegart, 2004; Huston & Wright, 1998). Given that ODD and CD are associated with harsh parenting, it would not be surprising to find that aggressive children seek out more violent programming (Huston & Wright, 1998). Parents who monitor their children's television viewing tend to have children who seek out less-violent programming (Spears & Seydegart, 2004).

Overall, the connections between television violence and children's aggression are complex. Although there is no question about the connection between viewing violence and exhibiting aggression, the causal links have yet to be established. Note that there are additional concerns about television viewing by children and adolescents because many potentially harmful behaviors are prevalent in prime-time television, such as risky sex, use of tobacco, alcohol, and drugs, and riding in a car without a seatbelt fastened (Will, Porter, Geller, & DePasquale, 2005). In addition, violence and even graphic violence is often present on television news shows, such as after a terrorist attack or during coverage of a war conflict (Walma van der Molen, 2004). Thus, care should be taken to define the type of violence and maladaptive behaviors to which children are being exposed.

development of ODD and CD. In order to reach out to these parents, the researchers visited the families' homes, rather than expecting the families to attend meetings at the research center. This type of outreach was found to be an effective way to engage families in preventive interventions. Overall, this prevention program reduced the incidence of ODD and CD, even when children were followed up in later childhood and older adolescence (Lacourse et al., 2002; Tremblay et al., 1999)

Another far-reaching prevention program is the Families and Schools Together (FAST) program (Conduct Problems Prevention Research Group, 1992, 2002, 2004; Hill, Lochman, Coie, Greenberg, & The Conduct Problems Prevention Research Group, 2004). The FAST program targets first graders at risk for conduct problems and provides enrichment services for the child, family, and school. Specifically, first-grade teachers provide a 57-session program to promote social competence, program staff provide academic tutoring and social

skills training, and a family coordinator provides parent training and home visits (Conduct Problems Prevention Research Group, 1999a, 1999b, 2002, 2004; Orrell-Valente, Pinderhughes, Valente, & Laird, 1999). Overall, the FAST program is very effective at lowering the risk for aggression, hyperactivity, and disruptive behaviors and is effective at increasing children's social competence, academic functioning, and emotional well-being (Conduct Problems Prevention Research Group, 1999a, 1999b, 2002, 2004; Orrell-Valente et al., 1999). Interestingly, when family coordinators are matched on race/ethnicity and socioeconomic status with the families, family members are more engaged in the program (Orrell-Valente et al., 1999). Overall, the FAST program is a very useful program for the prevention of ODD and CD.

Thus, there are a number of prevention programs to decrease the risk for developing oppositional and conduct problems. The most effective prevention programs

---

Case Study: Eddie, Wally, and Deana Try to Make Sense out of "Being Bad"

The following is a verbatim transcript between a teacher and her kindergarten students. Apparently, good and bad depend on the adult's response.

Eddie: Sometimes I hate myself.
Teacher: When?
Eddie: When I'm naughty.
Teacher: What do you do that's naughty?
Eddie: You know, naughty words. Like "shit." That one.
Teacher: That makes you hate yourself?
Eddie: Yeah, when my dad washes my mouth with soap.
Teacher: What if he doesn't hear you?
Eddie: Then I get away with it. Then I don't hate myself.
Wally: If I'm bad, like take the food when it's not time to eat yet and my mom makes me leave the kitchen, then I hate myself because I want to stay with her in the kitchen.
Eddie: And here's another reason when I don't like myself. This is a good reason.

Sometimes I try to get the cookies on top of the refrigerator.
Teacher: What's the reason you don't like yourself?
Eddie: Because my mom counts to ten fast and I get a spanking and my grandma gets mad at her.
Deana: Here's when I like myself: when I'm coloring and my mommy says, "Stop coloring. We have to go out." And I tell her I'm coloring and she says "Okay, I'll give you ten more minutes."
Teacher: What if you have to stop what you're doing?
Deana: When she's in a big hurry. That's when she yells at me. Then I don't like myself.

Source: Paley (1981, p. 54–55). Reprinted by permission of the publisher from WALLY'S STORIES by Vivian G. Paley, Cambridge, Mass.: Harvard University Press, Copyright © 1981 by the President and Fellows of Harvard College.

---

tend to provide multiple levels of preventive interventions, such as working with children, parents, and teachers (Taylor et al., 1999). Based on a television series on families and the Positive Parenting Program, the mass media can be an effective tool in the prevention of defiant behaviors (Sanders, Montgomery, & Brechman-Toussaint, 2000). The home–school partnership is especially important for comprehensive prevention programs (Webster-Stratton, 1993). Decreasing associations with deviant peers is also very important for the long-term prevention of CD (Vitaro, Brendgen, Pagani, Tremblay, & McDuff, 1999; Vitaro, Brendgen, & Tremblay, 2000). More work is needed, however, to establish and institute effective prevention programs (Tremblay et al., 1999).

It is better to spend the night in irritation at an offense than in repentance for taking revenge.
—Proverb of Africa

OPPOSITIONAL PROBLEMS AND CONDUCT PROBLEMS CONCEPTUALIZED IN A DIMENSIONAL MANNER

Unlike ADHD, there has been a lot of research into the dimensional conceptualizations of oppositional problems

and conduct problems (Keane & Calkins, 2004; Lahey et al., 1999). As the case study of Jose illustrated earlier in the chapter, the "terrible twos" can look surprisingly similar to serious oppositional problems. One study found that 40% of preschoolers exhibited at least one antisocial behavior each day, such as pushing or shoving other children, and doing something sneaky (Willoughby, Kupersmidt, & Bryant, 2001). Both oppositional behaviors and mild conduct problems occur frequently throughout childhood in most children. Even within nonclinical samples, oppositional behaviors tend to decrease over time (Loeber et al., 1991) whereas conduct-related problems tend to increase over time (Loeber et al., 1991). Toddlers and preschoolers with heightened levels of externalizing problems, however, tend to show heightened levels of aggression in later childhood and adolescence (Keane & Calkins, 2004).

One example of conceptualizing oppositional and conduct problems in a dimensional manner is illustrated with the use of the Child Behavior Checklist (Achenbach & Rescorla, 2001). Based on his father's report, Figure 10.4 shows the behavior of a 15-year-old boy with aggressive problems. This profile represents a pattern of both externalizing problems (i.e., aggressive problems) and internalizing problems (i.e., anxious/depressed, withdrawn/depressed) as well

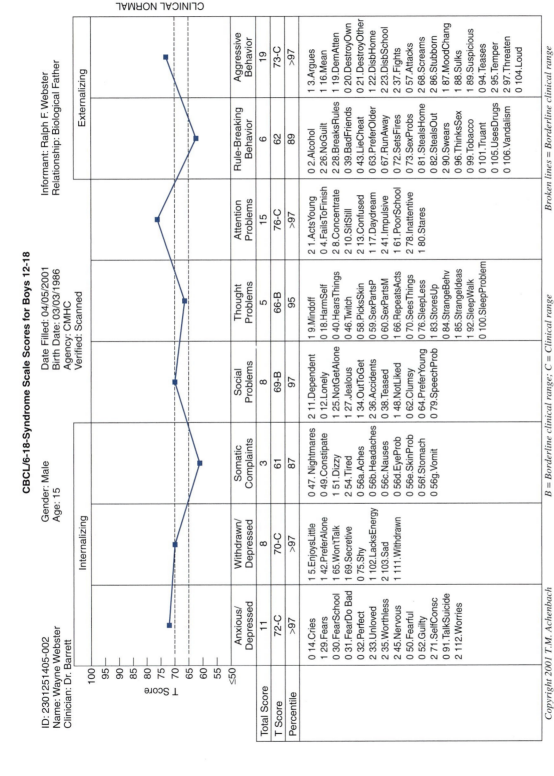

FIGURE 10.4 Computer-scored Syndrome Profile from CBCL completed for Wayne Webster by his father.

Source: Achenbach & Rescorla (2001).

as other problems (i.e., social problems, attention problems).

Overall, it is useful to conceptualize oppositional and conduct problems in a dimensional manner. Some researchers have even argued that ODD and CD should be conceptualized as a continuum of disruptive behaviors rather than two separate disorders (reviewed by Borduin et al., 1995). In either case, there are a number of risk factors that are associated with the development of oppositional and conduct problems. Many of these risk factors have been targeted for prevention efforts to decrease the likelihood that children would develop oppositional and conduct problems (Weikart & Schweinhart, 1997). Given the connections between harsh discipline and aggression in children, Box 10.5 discusses these issues.

Risk Factors

Regarding oppositional problems, children who have at least one parent with a history of mood disorder, ODD, CD, attention-deficit/hyperactivity disorder, antisocial personality disorder, or a substance-related disorder are more at risk for the development of oppositional problems (American Psychiatric Association, 2000). When there is a great deal of upheaval in the child-care procedures (e.g., changes in day care, different primary caretakers in the home), children seem to be more likely to develop oppositional problems than when there is consistency in child-care procedures (American Psychiatric Association, 2000). Maternal smoking while the baby is in utero appears to put children at risk for the eventual development of disruptive behaviors (Burke, Loeber, Mutchka, & Lahey, 2002; Wakschlag & Hans, 2002). In addition, children who experience harsh, inconsistent, or neglectful parenting are more at risk for the development of oppositional problems than are children who receive consistent, warm, and nurturing parenting (American Psychiatric Association, 2000; Heidgerken, Hughes, Cavell, & Willson, 2004; Klein, Forehand, & Family Health Project Research Group, 2000; Owens & Shaw, 2003; Stormshak, Bierman, McMahon, Lengua, & Conduct Problems Prevention Research Group, 2000).

BOX *10.5*

SPARE THE ROD, SPOIL THE CHILD?

Corporal punishment is defined as "the use of physical force with the intention of causing a child to experience pain, but not injury, for the purpose of correction or control of the child's behavior" (Straus, 1994, p. 4). The issue of corporal punishment and spanking is of great importance when working with families of oppositional and aggressive children. Given the connections between aggression in parents and aggression in children (Frick, 1998b), it is worthwhile to consider the amount and effects of corporal punishment with children. As discussed in the chapter on risk factors, there is sometimes a fine line between corporal punishment and physical abuse.

A number of reviews of corporal punishment in the United States suggested that it is quite prevalent (Gershoff, 2002; Straus & Stewart, 1999). The following patterns were found:

- Approximately 94% of parents in the United States reported that they spanked their child at least once before the child turned 3 or 4 years of age.
- More parents in the low SES group hit their children than in the high SES group.
- Even when controlling for SES, more African-American parents hit their children than parents of other ethnic/racial heritages, including Caucasian-American parents.
- More boys are hit by their parents than are girls.
- More mothers than fathers hit their children.
- More parents in the South hit their children than in the Northeast or West.

The high prevalence of corporal punishment and spanking is surprising, given that corporal punishment is not an effective method of behavior control (Gershoff, 2002; Straus & Steward, 1999). Specifically, corporal punishment is associated with higher levels of misbehavior even after controlling for initial levels of misbehavior (Mahoney, Donnelly, Lewis, & Maynard, 2000). Corporal punishment is associated with aggression and fear of the parent. Although children may learn what not to do via punishment, they do not learn the appropriate behavior with corporal punishment (Gershoff, 2002; Straus & Steward, 1999). Based on extensive research on the negative effects of corporal punishment, many scholars (Mahoney et al., 2000; Straus & Steward, 1999) as well as the American Academy of Pediatrics (2005) argue that little or no corporal punishment should be perpetrated on children.

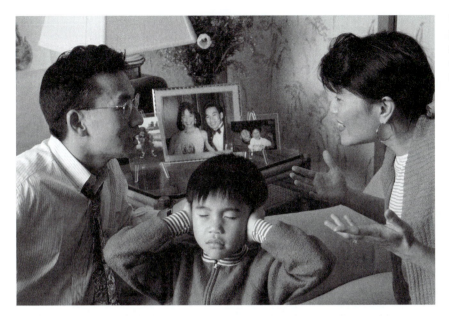

Family conflict and inconsistent parenting in early childhood can serve as risk factors for the development of conduct problems in later childhood.

Regarding conduct problems and antisocial behavior, risk factors include prenatal and perinatal difficulties, difficult infant temperament, neuropsychological deficits, inconsistent parenting, harsh discipline, parental rejection, lack of parental supervision, father absence, having a delinquent sibling, inconsistent caregiving procedures, early placement in an institution, large family size, neglect, physical abuse, sexual abuse, befriending delinquent peers, and attending a substandard school (American Psychiatric Association, 2000; Goldstein & Rider, 2005; Henry, Tolan, & Gorman-Smith, 2001; Loeber et al., 2000; Pfiffner, McBurnett, & Rathouz, 2001; Wolfe, Scott, Wekerle, & Pittman, 2001). The experience of ADHD in early childhood, especially in conjunction with aggression, serves as a risk factor for the development of conduct problems in adolescence and of antisocial personality problems in adulthood (Mannuzza, Klein, Abikoff, & Moulton, 2004). Physical fighting at an earlier age also has a strong association with physical violence at a later age (Loeber, Green, Lahey, & Kalb, 2000). A history of parental psychopathology or criminality, such as parental APD, alcohol dependence, mood disorders, schizophrenia, AD/HD, or CD, is also associated with the development of conduct problems in youth (American Psychiatric Association, 2000; Kazdin, 1997; Wakschlag & Keenan, 2001). Chronic school failure and involvement in special education services is associated with the development of CD and delinquency (Fink, 1990). Witnessing violence within the community is also associated with increased risk for developing antisocial behaviors (Halliday-Boykins & Graham, 2001; Miller, Wasserman, Neugebauer, Gorman-Smith,

& Kamboukos, 1999; Weist, Acosta, & Youngstrom, 2001). Witnessed community violence served to be a risk factor, even when there was low conflict within the family (Miller et al., 1999).

Because early pubertal timing is associated with behavioral problems in girls, an interesting study explored violent behavior in girls in relation to pubertal timing and neighborhood contexts (Obeidallah, Brennan, Brooks-Gunn, & Earls, 2004). In a racially diverse sample of adolescent girls, neighborhood disadvantage alone or early pubertal timing alone were not associated with violent behavior. The combination of early pubertal timing and neighborhood disadvantage, however, was associated with greater violent acts for adolescent girls. In fact, early maturing girls who lived in disadvantaged neighborhoods showed three times the number of violent acts when compared with early maturing girls who lived in less-disadvantaged neighborhoods (Obeidallah et al., 2004). Thus, the risk for violence and other conduct problems is multifaceted.

One study of severe delinquents illustrates the known risk factors for disruptive behaviors (Chamberlain, 1996). This was a sample of severely delinquent adolescent boys, with a mean age of 14.54 years. On average, their juvenile justice records began before the age of 12, and they had already been arrested nearly 11 times. The following risk factors were evident for a number of the boys (percentages of prevalence are noted in parentheses):

- Family violence (66%)
- Single-parent home (57%)

Case Study: One Teacher's Story of Why She Teaches

Michael was 7 years old and had never attended school on a regular basis. When he did show up for school, he was defiant, threw tantrums, and would talk back to teachers. He often ran away from school. Truant officers already knew Michael and his family quite well. Michael lived with his grandmother, aunts, and many cousins in a small apartment. His mother's whereabouts were "unknown," and his father did not have contact with him.

When Michael joined this teacher's special education classroom, the first thing she noticed was his smell and his appearance. It seems that Michael had not taken a bath in years, and his clothes were unwashed adult's clothes that hung on him like he was a hanger. His fingernails were filled with black, grimy dirt, and his hair was greasy and filthy.

Although Michael could not read or write, the first thing the teacher chose to tackle was his cleanliness and his appearance. She had new clothes donated from a local store, and she allowed Michael to choose a new item of clothes each day that he attended school. She taught him how to use soap and water, including how to wash under his fingernails and how to wash his hair. Within weeks, Michael was showing up to school consistently in clean clothes and with good hygiene.

Next, the teacher wanted to work on Michael's academic work. She knew that he could not read, so she never pressured him to read out loud with the other children. Rather, she allowed him to follow along with the reading group. Sometimes the teacher would offer Michael the chance to do "echo reading," during which she would read a short passage and then Michael would repeat what she said.

One day in reading group, Michael raised his hand to read out loud. Although he struggled a bit with the passage, he lifted his head and showed a beaming smile when he was through with the passage. During the rest of the year, Michael showed up to school every day, even when he was sick. Many years later, he continues to do well in school and to behave appropriately. As the teacher said, "He now knows he is worthy of someone's care and attention; he had only needed some encouragement, love, and guidance. Don't we all?" (Clarkson, 1999; p. 180).

- Severe poverty (53%)
- Victim of physical abuse (51%)
- Three or more siblings (28%)
- Siblings institutionalized (21%)
- Father convicted (15%)
- Victim of sexual abuse (11%)
- Mother hospitalized (9%)

On average, the boys experienced 6.96 risk factors. This sample highlights the prevalence of risk factors in groups of adolescents with conduct problems and also shows that multiple risk factors are often present in the lives of these adolescents (Chamberlain, 1996).

It is quite common that children with oppositional and conduct problems have multiple risk factors that are associated with the development of these problems (Williams, Ayers, Van Dorn, & Arthur, 2004). Risk factors are often referred to as coming in "packages" because many risk factors co-occur together, such as poverty, large family size, poor housing, overcrowding, poor parental supervision, parental criminality, and interparental conflict (Snyder et al., 2003). The neighborhood in which children and adolescents live is also thought to encompass many risk factors, such as community violence, inadequate schools, and deviant peers (Leventhal & Brooks-Gunn, 2000). Higher numbers of risk factors, also known as cumulative risk factors, are associated with a greater likelihood of experiencing oppositional and conduct problems (Forehand, Biggar, & Kotchick, 1998; McGee & Williams, 1999).

Protective Factors

Protective factors have not been studied to the same degree that risk factors have in relation to oppositional and conduct problems (Goldstein & Rider, 2005; Williams et al., 2004). However, a number of factors seem to protect children from developing oppositional and conduct problems, even in the context of adverse environments (Goldstein & Rider, 2005; Kerr, Lopez, Olson, & Sameroff, 2004; McCabe, Clark, & Barnett, 1999; Schoppe, Mangelsdorf, & Frosch, 2001; Seidman et al., 1999; Williams et al., 2004). Protective factors include

- Good relationship with consistent caregiver (either a parent or a nonparent)
- Warm, consistent, caring, and involved parents

- Low amounts of parental physical discipline
- Connections to stable adult outside the family
- Above-average intelligence
- Competence in multiple skill areas
- Good social skills
- Connections to nondeviant friends
- Being firstborn
- Easy temperament
- Internal locus of control
- Adequate school achievement
- Social support from relatives

Of all these protective factors, high IQ and good parenting skills were the most important protective factors regarding antisocial behavior (Masten et al., 1999). All these protective factors, however, have been associated with decreasing the likelihood of developing CD (Masten et al., 1999). Thus, even a child born into poverty and living in a violent community might be protected from developing oppositional and conduct problems due to these protective factors. Note that many of the protective factors interact with each other. For example, a child's good social skills may make it easier for a parent to engage in warm and caring interactions (Kazdin, 1997).

Interestingly, many of these protective factors are not specific to preventing oppositional and conduct problems. As discussed in the chapter on protective factors, most of these protective factors are associated with decreased likelihood of many emotional/behavioral problems.

SUMMARY AND KEY CONCEPTS

Oppositional Defiant Disorder (ODD). **Oppositional defiant disorder (ODD)** is a disruptive disorder that is characterized by oppositional, hostile, defiant, and negative interactions.

Conduct Disorder (CD). **Conduct disorder (CD)** is a disruptive disorder that is characterized by the violation of basic rights of others and by breaking social norms. CD is much more severe than ODD. **Callous-unemotional traits** are characterized by a lack of empathy and a lack of feelings. A subset of youth diagnosed with CD show callous-unemotional traits.

Antisocial personality disorder (APD) is only diagnosed in adulthood (over the age of 18) and is characterized by disregard for and the violation of rights of others. The term **psychopath** is often used when describing individuals diagnosed with APD. The term **fledgling psychopaths** is used to describe children and adolescents who show a combination of hyperactivity, impulsivity, attention problems, and conduct problems.

Oppositional Defiant Disorder and Conduct Disorder. Symptoms of both ODD and CD appear to fall onto two primary dimensions: **covert/overt** and **destructive/nondestructive.** There are high rates of comorbidity for both ODD and CD. Regarding the courses of the disorders, a number of characteristics are associated with the progression from ODD to CD to APD. For example, **triangulation,** where the parents put the child in between them in their arguments, often have children who show aggression over a long period of time.

No single theory explains the development of ODD or CD. **Coercion theory** suggests that coercive family processes can put a child at risk for the development of oppositional and conduct disordered behaviors. Through a process known as **deviancy training,** troubled adolescents tend to develop more problems when they associate with other troubled adolescents.

A number of effective treatments have been identified for ODD and CD, most of which are behavioral or cognitive–behavioral in nature. **Behavioral parent training** teaches parents effective parenting skills. **Multisystemic therapy** is a comprehensive treatment program that includes work with the adolescent, the family, the school system, peers, and any other important systems in the adolescent's life. A number of prevention programs have been instituted, but further research is needed in this area.

Oppositional Problems and Conduct Problems Conceptualized in a Dimensional Manner. There has been a good deal of research that explores oppositional and conduct problems from a dimensional perspective. A number of risk factors have been identified that are related to the onset of oppositional and conduct problems. Although there is less work on protective factors, a number of protective factors have been identified that decrease the risk for the onset of oppositional and conduct problems.

KEY TERMS

oppositional defiant disorder (ODD)	callous-unemotional traits	psychopath fledgling psychopaths	triangulation coercion theory	multisystemic therapy
conduct disorder (CD)	antisocial personality disorder (APD)	covert/overt destructive/nondestructive	deviancy training behavioral parent training	

SUGGESTED READINGS

Datcher, Michael, *Raising Fences: A Black Man's Love Story.* New York: Riverhead Books, 2001. With a mother who is employed full-time and a father who is nonexistent, it is not surprising that the author was engaged in minor criminal activities by the time of adolescence. This story tells the story of how the author rose out of poverty and became a poet and journalist.

Shakur, Sanyika, *Monster: The Autobiography of an L.A. Gang Member.* New York: Penguin, 1993. This eloquent memoir illustrates both risk factors for conduct disorder and antisocial personality disorder (such as living in poverty, racism, exposure to violence from an early age, and paternal absence) as well as protective factors later in life (such as faith and social support).

SUGGESTED VIEWINGS

Crash. (2005). Many risk factors are illustrated in this powerful film that shows different layers of conduct disorder and antisocial personality disorder (including from the angle of a mother of a troubled son, the victim of theft, a father trying to protect his family, and police officers who are on both sides of the law). The film deals well with issues of poverty, violence, and culture. No easy answers are in sight.

Holes. (2003). Geared toward children and adolescents, this film illustrates the story of a boy who steals a pair of sneakers and is sent to a youth detention center where there is a sadistic warden. Issues of oppositional defiant disorder and conduct disorder are evident, but there is also an overlying theme that questions when it is appropriate to stand up to authority.

CHAPTER 11

ALCOHOL AND SUBSTANCE USE, ABUSE, AND DEPENDENCE

CHAPTER SUMMARY

ALCOHOL ABUSE, ALCOHOL DEPENDENCE,
   SUBSTANCE ABUSE, AND SUBSTANCE
   DEPENDENCE
ALCOHOL AND SUBSTANCE USE AND ABUSE
   CONCEPTUALIZED IN A DIMENSIONAL
   MANNER

NICOTINE
SUMMARY AND KEY CONCEPTS
KEY TERMS
SUGGESTED READINGS
SUGGESTED VIEWINGS

Anytime is hard to be a kid.
— Pindi, 13 years old, United States

Compared with other types of developmental psychopathology in childhood and adolescence, only limited amounts of research have been completed in the areas of substance abuse and dependence with children and adolescents (Chassin, Ritter, Trim, & King, 2003). This dearth of research is ironic given that alcohol and substance use are common among adolescents and even some children. Most children and adolescents who drink alcohol and use substances do not go on to develop substance-related disorders (Kassel, Weinstein, Skitch, Veilleux, & Mermelstein, 2005). Alcohol and substance experimentation are so common during youth that some researchers have argued it is developmentally appropriate, especially in that it serves to help the process of becoming independent from parental controls and to bond more strongly with peers (Commission on Adolescent Substance and Alcohol Abuse, 2005). There is concern, however, that alcohol and substance use are always illegal for minors in the United States and that these illegal activities are often associated with other problems, such as delinquency, shoplifting, truancy, and breaking curfew (Commission on Adolescent Substance and Alcohol Abuse, 2005). For the purposes of this chapter, both ends of the spectrum will be explored. First, substance-related disorders will be discussed to show the problems that are associated with substance use gone awry, then substance use will be discussed to explore the functioning of children and adolescents who

do not develop clinical disorders but who do use illicit substances.

ALCOHOL ABUSE, ALCOHOL DEPENDENCE, SUBSTANCE ABUSE, AND SUBSTANCE DEPENDENCE

There are over 114 substance-related diagnoses in *DSM-IV* (American Psychiatric Association, 2000). These disorders can be diagnosed in adults as well as children and adolescents. The substance-related disorders that are most prevalent and are of primary concern for children and adolescents are **substance abuse** and **substance dependence.** As can be seen in Table 11.1, substance abuse requires use of a substance that harms the child or adolescent in some way by causing clinically significant impairment or distress, but without signs of tolerance or withdrawal. Table 11.2 shows that substance dependence requires use of a substance that not only harms the child or adolescent but also shows signs of tolerance or withdrawal. By definition, substance dependence is considered more severe than substance abuse. Thus, the diagnosis of substance dependence takes precedence over substance abuse. The following classes of substances can be diagnosed for both substance abuse and substance dependence:

- Alcohol

- Amphetamine (e.g., speed, diet pills, Ritalin)

- Cannabis (marijuana)
- Cocaine (including cocaine powder and crack)
- Hallucinogen (e.g., LSD, mescaline)
- Inhalant (e.g., paint thinner, glue, spray paint, Liquid Paper)
- Opioid (e.g., morphine, heroin, codeine, methadone)
- Phencyclidine (PCP)
- Sedative, hypnotic, or anxiolytic (e.g., sleeping pills, barbiturates, antianxiety medications)
- Other or unknown substances (e.g., anabolic steroids, nitrite inhalants such as "poppers," nitrous oxide)

The following substances can be diagnosed for substance dependence only and not for substance abuse:

- Nicotine dependence (e.g., cigarettes, chewing tobacco)
- Polysubstance (e.g., many substances together)

The only other substance that is covered in *DSM-IV* that has not been mentioned yet is caffeine. In addition to caffeine, all the substances mentioned previously (except nicotine and polysubstances) can be used to diagnose intoxication. Caffeine intoxication is represented by excessive ingestion of caffeine (e.g., 2 to 3 cups of brewed coffee) followed by symptoms such as nervousness, restlessness, muscle twitching, and psychomotor agitation. For intoxication to be diagnosed, clinically significant distress or impairment in social, occupational, or other areas of functioning must be present. Note that there are different symptoms of intoxication for specific substances.

The research literature on alcohol and substance abuse and dependence in children and adolescents is usually combined, rather than studying alcohol and other substances separately and rather than studying abuse and dependence separately. For that reason, alcohol abuse and dependence and substance abuse and dependence will be discussed together. This combination of disorders is often referred to as **substance use disorders** (Brown & Abrantes, 2006). Where possible, specific information will be given for alcohol and other substances separately and for abuse and dependence separately. Note that Tables 11.1 and 11.2 are used for alcohol as well as the other substances covered in this chapter. After discussing alcohol abuse, alcohol dependence, substance abuse, and substance dependence, alcohol and substance use will be discussed from a dimensional perspective. Finally, a section on nicotine use in children and adolescents is included at the end of the chapter.

Adolescents who abuse substances often befriend other adolescents who abuse substances.

Alcohol and substance abuse by children and adolescents have potentially serious negative ramifications. Within the family environment, adolescents who abuse substances often experience poor parent–child communication, poor parental supervision and discipline, and interpersonal conflict with their parents and siblings (Diamond & Josephson, 2005). Within the school environment, adolescent substance abusers often show inadequate academic performance and increased levels of emotional/behavioral problems (Windle, Mun, & Windle, 2005). Within the peer network, adolescent substance abusers often are involved with a deviant peer group, and they often are engaged in conflict with their peers (Dishion, McCord, & Poulin, 1999). Within the larger community, adolescent substance abusers are often involved in delinquent behaviors and experience legal problems (Gilvarry, 2000).

In addition to these areas of concern, there are also physiological effects of substances that can cause problems. Alcohol, sedatives, hypnotics, and opiates

TABLE 11.1   DSM-IV Diagnostic Criteria for Substance Abuse

A.   A maladaptive pattern of substance use leading to clinically significant impairment or distress, as manifested by one (or more) of the following, occurring within a 12-month period:

    (1) recurrent substance use resulting in a failure to fulfill major role obligations at work, school, or home (e.g., repeated absences or poor work performance related to substance use; substance-related absences, suspensions, or expulsions from school; neglect of children or household)

    (2) recurrent substance use in situations in which it is physically hazardous (e.g., driving an automobile or operating a machine when impaired by substance use)

    (3) recurrent substance-related legal problems (e.g., arrests for substance-related disorderly conduct)

    (4) continued substance use despite having persistent or recurrent social or interpersonal problems caused or exacerbated by the effects of the substance (e.g., arguments with spouse about consequences of intoxication, physical fights)

B.   The symptoms have never met the criteria for Substance Dependence for this class of substance.

Source: American Psychiatric Association (2000).
Reprinted with permission from the *Diagnostic and Statistical Manual of Mental Disorders, Fourth Edition, Text Revision.* Copyright 2000 American Psychiatric Association.

TABLE 11.2   DSM-IV Diagnostic Criteria for Substance Dependence

A maladaptive pattern of substance use, leading to clinically significant impairment or distress, as manifested by three (or more) of the following, occurring at any time in the same 12-month period:

(1) tolerance, as defined by either of the following:

    (a) a need for markedly increased amounts of the substance to achieve intoxication or desired effect
    (b) markedly diminished effect with continued use of the same amount of the substance

(2) withdrawal, as manifested by either of the following:

    (a) the characteristic withdrawal syndrome for the substance . . .
    (b) the same (or a closely related) substance is taken to relieve or avoid withdrawal symptoms

(3) the substance is often taken in larger amounts or over a longer period than was intended

(4) there is a persistent desire or unsuccessful efforts to cut down or control substance use

(5) a great deal of time is spent in activities necessary to obtain the substance (e.g., visiting multiple doctors or driving long distances), use the substance (e.g., chain-smoking), or recover from its effects

(6) important social, occupational, or recreational activities are given up or reduced because of substance use

(7) the substance use is continued despite knowledge of having a persistent or recurrent physical or psychological problem that is likely to have been caused or exacerbated by the substance (e.g., current cocaine use despite recognition of cocaine-induced depression, or continued drinking despite recognition that an ulcer was made worse by alcohol consumption)

Specify if:
With Physiological Dependence: evidence of tolerance or withdrawal (i.e., either Item 1 or 2 is present)
Without Physiological Dependence: no evidence of tolerance or withdrawal (i.e., neither Item 1 nor 2 is present)

Source: American Psychiatric Association (2000).
Reprinted with permission from the *Diagnostic and Statistical Manual of Mental Disorders, Fourth Edition, Text Revision.* Copyright 2000 American Psychiatric Association.

Case Study: Chelsea, the Party Girl

Chelsea began drinking alcohol at school parties when she was 12 years old. At first she did not like the taste of beer, but she felt that all her friends were drinking so she went along with them. She later learned that she preferred the vodka-spiked punch, because it had a sweeter taste. By the time she was 14, Chelsea and her friends began attending parties at a local fraternity house. Not only could they drink as much alcohol as they wanted, but the fraternity members would often give them bottles of beer to take home so they could get drunk during the week. On more than one occasion, Chelsea and her friends brought the beer to school in plastic containers and got drunk at school.

When she was 15 and a sophomore in high school, Chelsea and her friend went to a fraternity party like they did almost every weekend. Chelsea and her friend became quite drunk, and Chelsea's friend was raped while she was unconscious. Chelsea felt that it was her fault for not protecting her friend. She tried to stop drinking and stayed abstinent of alcohol for 2 days, but she was drinking with her friends at school within 72 hours. Three months later Chelsea was picked up by campus police at 3 AM while she was stumbling around campus and mumbling incoherently. She was admitted to a hospital with a blood alcohol level of 0.20, which is over twice the legal limit for driving in most states. When Chelsea was in the hospital, it became apparent that she met criteria for alcohol dependence, with physiological dependence. Chelsea reported that she had been drinking every day for quite some time and that many days she drank just to keep from getting headaches.

When her parents were contacted, they reported that they had no idea she was drinking alcohol (although Chelsea's mother reported having some suspicions of her alcohol use). They did not realize that Chelsea had been truant from school on numerous occasions, and they did not notice that Chelsea had been hiding her report cards that showed her failing grades and unexcused absences. When Chelsea's parents were able to visit her at the hospital, her father said, "Chelsea, my mother died from alcoholism and there is no way I'm going to let this get you too. We are all going to fight this together."

Chelsea and her parents began attending therapy together, and Chelsea joined an Alcoholics Anonymous group that consisted of adolescents and young adults at the university. Chelsea was abstinent of alcohol for 3 months when she attended a graduation party with her friends. She began drinking again, but called her father after she had finished three drinks. At that point, she decided not to attend any more parties with her friends.

Chelsea got a job at a local stable where she developed a great deal of interest in taking care of horses and in showing horses. She befriended a number of the other adolescents working with horses, and the owner of the stable provided her with many healthy outlets for her interest in horses.

Meanwhile, the family therapy was uncovering years of trouble within the family that had never been addressed. Chelsea and her mother had become more and more confrontational with each other, but Chelsea's father had no idea about these problems. Chelsea's mother felt that she did not want to bother Chelsea's father about her suspicions of their daughter's abuse of alcohol. Chelsea's parents also reported great concern over letting Chelsea become independent from them, although ironically they had not monitored her behavior closely before the hospitalization. The family therapist worked to help Chelsea become more independent, in an age-appropriate manner rather than by using alcohol. The therapist also worked with the family to facilitate communication and to help the parents bond together as a unit.

Chelsea was able to maintain "A" and "B" grades. In addition to working at the stable, she also became a volunteer at a local rape crisis center. She had remained sober through her high school graduation and went on to attend a college out of state.

Source: Morgan (1999).

---

such as heroin all serve to depress the central nervous system. The central nervous system is stimulated by substances such as cocaine, amphetamines, and phencyclidine. Substances such as LSD and mescaline can cause hallucinations (Gilvarry, 2000). In addition to these physiological effects, most substances serve to alter decision making and judgment and can negatively influence fine motor and gross motor skills (Bukstein & VanHasselt, 1995). In the case of overdose, substances can lead to permanent impairment and death.

I drank when I was happy and I drank when I was anxious and I drank when I was bored and I drank when I was depressed, which was often.

—Caroline Knapp (1996, p. 1)

Prevalence Rates

A number of epidemiological studies have been conducted that assess the prevalence of substance use disorders in children and adolescents. In the Methods for the Epidemiology of Child and Adolescent Mental Disorders (MECA) Study, 2% of adolescents met criteria for a substance use disorder (Kandel et al., 1997). This estimate is consistent with the prevalence rate of 2.4% found in a large community sample (Costello et al., 2003). In a study of rural youth from the southeast, 6% of the sample met criteria for a substance use disorder (Costello, Erkanli, Federman, & Angold, 1999). Other epidemiological studies have found higher rates of substance use disorders in children and adolescents, with prevalence rates ranging from 6.2% to 8.3% (Harpaz-Rotem et al., 2005; Kilpatrick et al., 2003). When looking at specific substances, the prevalence rates are lower, but all these specific substances would be included in the total prevalence rates just reported. For example, inhalant abuse and dependence was relatively prevalent in a large community sample. Specifically, 0.4% of adolescents aged 12 to 17 years old met criteria for inhalant abuse or dependence (Wu, Pilowsky, & Schlenger, 2004).

In studies of adolescents in treatment, the highest prevalence rates of substance use disorders (82.6%) were found in treatment facilities that specialized in alcohol and drug treatment, with high rates of substance use disorders also found in adolescents within the juvenile justice system (62.1%), the community mental health system (40.8%), special education classes for severely emotionally disturbed adolescents within the school system (23.6%), and in the child welfare system (19.2%; Aarons, Brown, Hough, Garland, & Wood, 2001; Abram, Teplin, McClelland, & Dulcan, 2003). Thus, clinicians working within treatment settings are likely to have adolescent clients with substance use disorders. Unfortunately, clinicians are often not aware of substance use disorders in their child and adolescent clients. One study found that of the 42 adolescents seeking mental health treatment who met criteria for a substance use disorder, only 16 (45.2%) were correctly identified by the clinician as having a substance use disorder (Kramer, Robbins, Phillips, Miller, & Burns, 2003). In a sample of adolescents who met criteria for substance abuse or dependence, only 20% reported that they needed any help with substance-related problems (Tims et al., 2002). Thus, clinicians need to be made more aware of substance use disorders in their child and adolescent clients, even if the clients are not asking for help with these issues.

Rates of alcohol abuse, alcohol dependence, substance abuse, and substance dependence increase with age. One large community study found no substance use disorders in children 11 and younger and then found a

prevalence rate of 0.1% in 12-year-olds, 0.3% in 13-year-olds, 1.4% in 14-year-olds, 5.3% in 15-year-olds, and 7.6% in 16-year-olds (Costello et al., 2003). The MECA study found comparable rates at the younger ages and found a prevalence rate of 8.7% with 17-year-olds (Kandel et al., 1997). This finding parallels the growing use of substances from early adolescence to later adolescence (Commission on Adolescent Substance and Alcohol Abuse, 2005). Childhood prevalence rates appear to reach their peak between the ages of 15 and 19 (Gilvarry, 2000).

Given that so many studies of drinking in older adolescence and early adulthood are conducted with college students, it is interesting to note that drinking patterns are relatively comparable for girls who do and who do not attend college, with the exception that binge drinking is more prevalent in girls who attend college as compared with their non-college-bound siblings (Slutske et al., 2004). Within college students, there appear to be different drinking patterns that can be assessed reliably. Over the course of the first year of undergraduate studies, students tend to fall into one of the following drinking groups: light-stable (53%), light-stable plus high holiday (9%), medium-increasing (8%), high-decreasing (20%), and heavy-stable (10%; Greenbaum Del Boca, Darkes, Wang, & Goldman, 2005). All groups except the light-stable group increased their drinking during Thanksgiving, the winter break between Christmas and New Year's Eve, and spring break. Students in this sample ranged in age from 17 to 20, so all the drinking that was reported was considered underage drinking (Greenbaum et al., 2005). These patterns are related to gender, race/ethnicity, alcohol expectancies, sensation seeking, and where the students lived. Specifically, Caucasians boys who lived in an off-campus apartment showed higher rates of drinking as did individuals who had positive alcohol expectancies and those who were high in sensation-seeking orientations (Del Boca, Darkes, Greenbaum, & Goldman, 2004). These patterns of drinking can help inform prevention and intervention programs (Greenbaum et al., 2005), and it would not be surprising to find similar types of subtyping in groups of high school students.

Findings from studies on substance use disorders and gender effects are complicated. Many studies have found comparable rates of substance use disorders for boys and girls when substances are combined (Costello et al., 2003; Duncan, Strycker, & Duncan, 1999; Kilpatrick et al., 2003). Specific substances, however, often show gender differences in use. For example, boys were more likely than girls to smoke marijuana and to use crack cocaine, but it is unclear whether these usage patterns were related to patterns of abuse and dependence (Costello et al., 1999). Boys and girls did not differ, however, in their reported inhalant abuse and dependence (Wu et al., 2004). More family dysfunctions, such as more conflict and less cohesion, were found in substance-abusing girls when compared with substance-abusing boys (Dakof, 2000). In general, girls who show substance abuse and dependence tend to be more debilitated than are boys who show similar problems (Johnson & Pandina, 2000; Kilpatrick et al., 2003). Both girls and boys, however, show similar patterns of risk factors for the development of substance abuse (Beatty, Wetherington, Jones & Roman, 2006; Costello et al., 1999).

Children and adolescents from the lower socioeconomic bracket tend to show higher rates of substance use disorders (Boothroyd, Gomez, Armstrong, Haynes, & Ort, 2005). Note, however, that substance use and abuse have been documented in all SES groups, including adolescents from affluent, suburban neighborhoods (McMahon & Luthar, 2006).

Regarding race and ethnicity, Hispanic/Latino/Latina children and adolescents showed the lowest rates of substance use disorders, whereas African-American children and adolescents showed the highest rates of substance use disorders (Kandel et al., 1997). Prevalence rates for Caucasian-American children and adolescents fell between these two groups. High rates of alcohol abuse and dependence are found within samples of Native American youth (Novins & Baron, 2004) and Native Hawaiian adolescents (Hishinuma et al., 2005). These prevalence rates are summarized in Table 11.3.

Note that there has also been concern about higher rates of substance abuse disorders among gay, lesbian, bisexual, transgendered, and questioning adolescents and young adults (Eisenberg & Wechsler, 2003;

Jordan, 2000; E. Olson, 2000). Children and adolescents within a sexual minority seem to be at risk for developing substance use disorders, so efforts have been made to highlight the need for preventive programs for these youth (Cochran, Stewart, Ginzler, & Cauce, 2002; Jordan, 2000). In addition, gay-sensitive treatments have been encouraged for this population (Olson, 2000).

There are also higher rates of substance abuse and dependence in adolescents who have run away from home and those who are homeless (Whitbeck & Hoyt, 1999). Although the direction of causality is not clear (i.e., Did they become homeless and then start abusing substances, or did they start abusing substances and then become homeless?), there are significant negative ramifications for adolescents' substance abuse in this vulnerable population (Whitbeck & Hoyt 1999). There are particularly high rates of substance abuse for sexual minority youth who are homeless (Cochran et al., 2002).

Studies have also been conducted to explore different groups of children in high school. One study explored self-identified "jocks" and compared their use of substances compared with youth who did not report themselves to be jocks (Miller et al., 2003). In a large sample from a public school system in western New York, adolescents who reported themselves to be jocks were significantly more likely to engage in excessive drinking, regardless of gender, race, physical maturity, age, SES, or type of athletic activity. African-American girls who considered themselves to be jocks were at the highest risk for abusing substances (Miller et al., 2003).

The issue of caffeine dependence has begun receiving attention in research with adolescents. Although not as potentially life-threatening or as harmful as many other substances, caffeine can be associated with negative health outcomes (Bernstein, Carroll, Thuras, Cosgrove, & Roth, 2002). One study of adolescents aged 13 to 17 found that 77.8% of adolescents stated that they felt withdrawal symptoms when they did not ingest caffeine, 41.7% reported tolerance to caffeine, 38.9% said that they either wanted to or had tried to reduce their caffeine intake, and 16.7% said that they ingested high amounts of caffeine even though they knew that it was not good for them (Bernstein et al., 2002). Adolescents who reported higher levels of caffeine use also reported significantly higher levels of anxiety. This study suggests that health advocates and clinical child psychologists should explore the ramifications of high levels of caffeine use in adolescents and should consider

TABLE 11.3 Overview of Prevalence Information for Substance Use Disorders

Prevalence	2.0%
Age	Adolescents > Children
Gender	No consistent pattern
SES	Lower > Higher
Race/Ethnicity	African Americans > Caucasian Americans and Hispanic/Latino/Latina Americans

preventive efforts to reduce the use of caffeine (Bernstein et al., 2002).

> *A few hours ago I was at the bank, and a nice woman came up to me and said, "Oh, you're the comedian who doesn't use the F-word."*
> *"I use it all the time," I said. " 'Family.' It's the dirtiest word I know."*
> *She laughed and said, "No, not that one. The other F-word."*
> *"You couldn't mean me," I smiled, "because I use that one all the time, too."*
> *"You do?"*
> *"Sure." I nodded. " 'Father.' It's right up there with 'family.' Almost interchangeable."*
> —Louie Anderson, a comedian whose father was alcoholic (Anderson, 1991, p. 21).

Comorbidity

Rates of comorbidity for substance use disorders (including alcohol abuse and dependence) are quite high. One review of research done in the community found that 60% of youth who met criteria for a substance use disorder were comorbid with another psychiatric disorder (Armstrong & Costello, 2002). These high comorbidity rates between substance use disorders and other disorders are evident across all racial/ethnic groups (Robbins et al., 2002). The large majority of adolescents in treatment for substance abuse have abused multiple substances (Chung & Martin, 2005).

Comorbidity is common between substance use disorders and conduct disorder, with suggestions that up to half of substance abusing adolescents also meet criteria for conduct disorder (Armstrong & Costello, 2002). Although there appears to be a connection between substance use disorders and attention-deficit/hyperactivity disorder (ADHD), this connection disappears when conduct problems are controlled statistically (Armstrong & Costello, 2002; Disney, Elkins, McGue, & Iacono, 1999; Weinberg & Glantz, 1999). In other words, there is not a strong connection between ADHD and substance abuse or dependence (Disney et al., 1999).

A connection between depression and substance abuse in late adolescence is found in many studies (Armstrong & Costello, 2002; Kandel et al., 1999; Rao, Daley, & Hammen, 2000), but not others (Weinberg & Glantz, 1999). The conflicting findings regarding the connection between substance abuse and depression may be due to differential patterns for boys versus girls. One large community study found that the comorbidity rates between a substance use disorder and major depression varied for girls and boys, with girls showing a 38.5% rate of comorbidity and boys showing a 16.6% rate of comorbidity (Kilpatrick et al., 2003). Another study found that alcohol use was associated with depression for girls but not boys (Poulin, Hand, Boudreau, & Santor, 2005). Alcohol dependence, however, is related to suicidal behavior (Hufford, 2001).

There is evidence that substance use disorders are linked to bipolar disorder. Specifically, 32% of adolescents diagnosed with bipolar disorder also met criteria for a substance use disorder, whereas only 7% of adolescents who were not diagnosed with bipolar disorder met criteria for a substance use disorder (Wilens et al., 2004). There is a strong relationship between binge eating disorders (such as bulimia) and substance use disorders (Ross & Ivis, 1999). Most anxiety disorders do not appear to be well established as comorbid features of substance use disorders (Weinberg & Glantz, 1999), but there is evidence of comorbidity between substance use disorders and posttraumatic stress disorder in adolescents (Giaconia et al., 2000). Again, patterns for girls and boys differ in the comorbidity between substance use disorders and PTSD. A total of 24.6% of adolescent girls with a substance use disorder also met criteria for PTSD, whereas only 13.5% of boys with a substance use disorder did (Kilpatrick et al., 2003). These patterns suggest the need to explore comorbidity patterns for girls and boys separately.

In samples of adolescents in treatment, inhalant abuse was associated with depression, suicidality, and abuse of other substances (e.g., alcohol, hallucinogens, cocaine, amphetamines, and nicotine; Sakai, Hall, Mikulich-Gilbertson, & Crowley, 2004). Adolescents who abused inhalants did not differ significantly on any measures when compared with adolescents who used inhalants but who did not abuse them (Sakai et al., 2004).

Comorbidity has ramifications for future functioning. One longitudinal study followed African-American youth from 6th grade to 10th grade (Miller-Johnson, Lochman, Coie, Terry, & Hyman, 1998). This study found that the combination of depression and conduct disorder in 6th grade was highly related to alcohol and marijuana use in 10th grade. Conduct disorder alone was also related to higher levels of substance use later in adolescence, but depression alone was not related to later substance use (Miller-Johnson et al., 1998). Overall, comorbidity is associated with lower levels of functioning and greater rates of impairment (Windle & Davies, 1999; Zeitlin, 1999).

Course of the Disorder

As noted earlier, most adolescents use substances but do not develop substance use disorders. Adolescents who do not go on to develop problems with substances tend not to make the substances part of their everyday life and do not commit to the use of substances as part of their own self-identity (Kassel et al., 2005). In general, earlier use of substances is associated with higher rates of substance abuse and dependence (Flory, Lynam, Milich, Leukefeld, & Clayton, 2004; McGue & Iacono, 2004; Rey, Martin, & Krabman, 2004; Wu et al., 2004). These patterns differ somewhat for different disorders, with early onset of alcohol abuse showing greater long-term problems than late onset of alcohol abuse but both early-onset and late-onset abuse of marijuana showing maladaptive patterns of adjustment into young adulthood (Flory et al., 2004).

Adolescents who go on to abuse substances tend to follow a relatively common progression, from using alcohol and cigarettes, to smoking marijuana, to using hard drugs such as cocaine or heroine (Commission on Adolescent Substance and Alcohol Abuse, 2005). This process has been referred to as the **gateway phenomenon,** with the idea that earlier drug use (e.g., use of marijuana) provides a gateway to using harder substances. It is important to note, however, that a great many adolescents use marijuana without developing more severe substance abuse or dependence problems (Rey et al., 2004). The section on risk factors is helpful in identifying who is at risk for developing substance abuse and who is less likely to.

In general, children and adolescents might pass through a number of stages before developing a substance use disorder (Sattler, 1998):

- Experimental stage—where adolescents' use of substances is due to curiosity, interest in risk-taking, and sometimes related to peer pressure
- Social stage—where adolescents' use is only within the context of being with friends who are also experimenting with the substances
- Instrumental stage—where adolescents use substances to alter their feelings and behavior, such as to feel more calm in response to stress or to feel more loose in a situation that causes them anxiety
- Habitual stage—where adolescents develop the habit of using substances and ignore other facets of their life
- Compulsive stage—where adolescents become focused on gaining access to their substance of

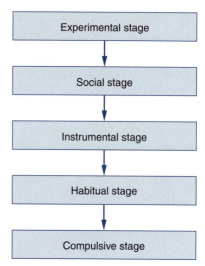

FIGURE 11.1 Stages in Becoming a Substance Abuser.

Source: Sattler (1998).

choice and neglect nearly all other aspects of their life.

These stages are illustrated in Figure 11.1. Although not all adolescents progress through these stages, it is typical that adolescents who abuse substances have passed through the earlier stages of less-severe substance use (Sattler, 1998). Substance dependence is usually evident at the habitual stage and the compulsive stage, but interventions are appropriate at a much earlier stage whenever possible (Sattler, 1998).

In addition to these stages of substance abuse and dependence, other factors are associated with the course of substance abuse and dependence. With regard to comorbidity, the majority of comorbid disorders seem to appear well before the onset of substance use disorders. For example, conduct disorder, ADHD, and oppositional defiant disorder were found to occur many years before the onset of substance use and abuse (Armstrong & Costello, 2002; Hahesy, Wilens, Biederman, Van Patten, & Spencer, 2002). Earlier generalized anxiety disorder was associated with increased risk for alcohol abuse, but earlier separation anxiety disorder was associated with a decreased risk for alcohol abuse (Kaplow, Curran, Angold, & Costello, 2001; Hahesy et al., 2002). There is conflicting evidence as to the pattern with major depression, with some studies finding that depression tends to occur before the onset of a substance use disorder (Armstrong & Costello, 2002), and other studies finding that depression comes after the substance use disorder (Hahesy et al., 2002).

Persistent delinquency in early childhood predicted substance use in early adolescence as well as later adolescence (Loeber, Stouthamer-Loeber, & White, 1999). Social impairment (e.g., lacking social skills, difficulty in maintaining friendships) was predictive of alcohol abuse and drug abuse in a 4-year follow-up of young adolescents (Greene et al., 1999). Boys whose father abused substances were at greater risk for oppositional defiant disorder, conduct disorder, an anxiety disorder, and a mood disorder, which in turn were related to increased risk for developing a substance use disorder (Clark, Parker, & Lynch, 1999). Overall, a number of precursors exist to the development of substance abuse and dependence.

It is important to note that substance use disorders have ramifications for the physical health of children and adolescents. Adolescents who use substances and who show risk-taking behavior are likely to report physical injuries related to the substance use (Spirito, Jelalian, Rasile, Rohrbeck, & Vinnick, 2000). Another study found that substance-abusing adolescents engaged in more HIV-risk behaviors than adolescents diagnosed with another psychiatric disorder and adolescents in a nonclinical control group (Deas-Nesmith, Brady, White, & Campbell, 1999).

Unfortunately, even with treatment, substance abuse tends to reoccur. As can be seen in Figure 11.2, relapse after treatment (i.e., going back to abusing a substance) is quite common as early as 3 months after intensive therapeutic services (Pagliaro & Pagliaro, 1996). Ways to prevent relapse are discussed in the treatment section of this chapter. If treatment and relapse prevention are not effective, adolescents with alcohol abuse problems are at risk for substance use disorders, major depression,

borderline personality disorder, and antisocial personality disorder in early adulthood (Rohde, Lewinsohn, Kahler, Seeley, & Brown, 2001).

Etiology

Like so many other disorders, it is likely that multiple etiological factors lead to the development of alcohol and substance abuse and dependence (Cicchetti & Rogosch, 1999b). A number of factors have been implicated in the development of alcohol and substance abuse and dependence, including biological, familial, interpersonal (cognitive), cultural, and societal factors (Waldron, 1998).

Biological theories have gained support from family studies and twin studies (Hicks, Krueger, Iacono, McGue, & Patrick, 2004; Hopfer, Crowley, & Hewitt, 2003; Siewert, Stallings, & Hewitt, 2003). In general, there are high concordance rates between parents' and adolescents' alcohol and substance abuse (Kassel et al., 2005). Biological theories, however, rarely account for a huge portion of the variance that explains the development of alcohol and substance abuse and dependence (Chassin et al., 2003). One review of behavioral genetics research concluded that genetic factors provide a moderate amount of influence in the development of alcohol abuse in boys, but only a modest amount of influence in girls (Vik et al., 1997). Similarly, environmental factors play a role in the development of substance abuse problems, but are influenced by biological factors. One comprehensive study of twins found that 77% of the variance in early substance use was accounted for by the environmental factors of peer deviance and a maladaptive parent–child relationship (Walden, McGue, Iacono, Burt, & Elkins, 2004).

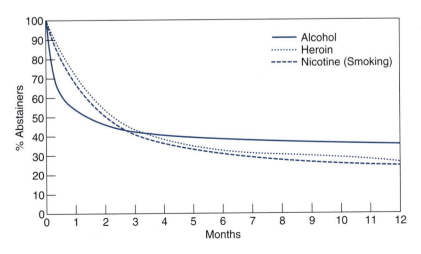

FIGURE 11.2 Typical relapse rates following treatment for problematic patterns of substance use.

Source: Pagliaro & Pagliaro (1996).

BOX *11.1*

ALCOHOL AND THE FAMILY

Research on parents who abuse alcohol has focused almost exclusively on fathers, while neglecting mothers (Leonard et al., 2000; Ohannessian et al., 2004; Phares, 1996). This pattern is unusual, given that nearly all other types of psychopathology have been investigated in mothers more than in fathers. This pattern is probably due to the higher prevalence of alcohol abuse and dependence in men when compared with women (American Psychiatric Association, 2000).

Overall, there is strong evidence that parents (especially fathers) who abuse substances are more likely to have children (especially boys) who abuse substances (Chassin, Pitts, DeLucia, & Todd, 1999; Chen & Weitzman, 2005; Leonard et al., 2000; Loukas, Fitzgerald, Zucker, & von Eye, 2001; Windle & Davies, 1999; Windle & Tubman, 1999). Children of alcoholic parents are four to nine times more likely to experience alcohol abuse or dependence at some point in their lives than are children of nonalcoholic parents (Windle & Tubman, 1999). These patterns are particularly true when the parents are experiencing a comorbid disorder in addition to the alcohol abuse or dependence (Ohannessian et al., 2004). This risk appears to remain to some degree even after fathers stop drinking (DeLucia, Belz, & Chassin, 2001). Note, however, that the majority of children of parents who are alcohol dependent do not go on to abuse alcohol. Thus, although there is a connection between alcohol misuse in parents and children, this connection does not mean that children of alcoholic parents are set to abuse alcohol in their own lives (Chen & Weitzman, 2005; Windle & Tubman, 1999).

The higher rates of alcohol abuse and dependence in children of alcoholics are related to genetic predisposition in the children, physiological vulnerabilities in the children, and parenting behaviors that create a less-than-optimal environment for the child (Fals-Stewart, Kelley, Fincham, Golden, & Logsdon, 2004; Vik, Brown, & Myers, 1997).

The genetic predisposition seems stronger for boys than girls, although there is some evidence that paternal drinking is associated with increased depression in boys and in increased depression and drinking in girls (Chen & Weitzman, 2005). Physiological vulnerabilities are apparent in children of alcoholics in that they seem to need more alcohol to achieve the same effects as their peers, which is known as sensitivity (Vik et al., 1997). Thus, children of alcoholics often drink more alcohol to achieve the same state as their peers, which in turn is related to more problematic drinking.

Even when children of alcoholic parents show problems, they do not always show problems with alcohol. Parental alcoholism was associated with heightened drinking in adolescents when the adolescents also showed high levels of externalizing problems but not when the adolescents showed high levels of internalizing problems (Hussong, Curran, & Chassin, 1998). In young children, fathers' drinking was associated with sons' externalizing behavior, especially when the drinking was in the context of family conflict (Loukas, Zucker, Fitzgerald, & Krull, 2003). There may be multiple factors that are related to adolescents' heightened risk for problems when they have a parent with alcohol dependence.

Other research in this area has also highlighted the risk for having a father who abuses substances other than alcohol. In a study that compared children who lived with their father who either abused alcohol, abused illicit drugs, or did not abuse any substance, children of fathers who abused illicit drugs showed more emotional/behavioral problems than children in the other two groups (Fals-Stewart et al., 2004). This pattern was especially true when there were high levels of interparental conflict and dysfunctional parenting by the father (Fals-Stewart et al., 2004). Overall, this research suggests that children of fathers who abuse alcohol or other substances are at greater risk for maladjustment.

. . . [The] delivery of my premature son was unlikely to have been a joyous occasion. Most fetal alcohol babies emerge not in a tide, the facsimile of saline, primordial, life-granting sea, but instead enter this world tainted with stale wine. Their amniotic fluid literally reeks of Thunderbird or Ripple . . .

—Michael Dorris (1989, p. 261) about his adopted son, Adam, who was diagnosed with fetal alcohol syndrome.

Children of alcoholics provide an interesting test of behavioral genetics theories. As discussed in Box 11.1,

higher alcohol use in children of alcoholics appears to be related to genetic predisposition, physiological differences, and environmental factors, such as limited parental control (Leonard et al., 2000). Children of parents who abuse other substances may be subjected to even more pernicious physiological effects (Morrow et al., 2004). For example, children born to mothers who use cocaine during pregnancy experience neurological deficits and language delays that are related to abnormal brain development while in utero (Morrow et al., 2004).

Case Study: David, Whose Father Abused Alcohol

David was 15 years old when his grades began dropping and he was causing problems at school. David's father was alcoholic, and his mother devoted nearly all her time to trying to take care of David's father. Although David and his mother had been close, he felt ignored by her now that his father's alcoholism had worsened. David was very concerned about his parents, and he was motivated to keep them together.

Around the age of 15, David began smoking marijuana. His teachers and other school personnel noticed extreme changes in his behavior. After his substance use was discovered, he was admitted to an inpatient unit for treatment of substance abuse and dependence. After he was discharged from the inpatient facility, he again began drinking alcohol and smoking marijuana. His guidance counselor suggested that he get involved in therapy and that his parents take an active role in the therapy.

The therapist helped the family see that David might be using his self-destructive behavior and substance use to gain attention from his mother. The therapist also helped the parents to see that David's behavior was tied closely to his parents' functioning. David's father finally became motivated to address his own alcoholism. After individual treatment and involvement in Alcoholics Anonymous, David's father stopped drinking.

David had one more relapse with excessive drinking and smoking marijuana, but then remained sober at a 3-year follow-up. His parents' marriage improved significantly after David's father's treatment for alcoholism. David's mother also found that she had more time to spend with David, rather than dealing with her husband's alcoholism.

Source: Sweet (1991).

These children begin life at a disadvantage and are often exposed to less-than-optimal environments that can further limit their potential for good functioning. For that reason, a growing number of treatment programs are meant to help the substance-abusing mother, which will in turn hopefully improve her functioning and her parenting skills to prevent maladaptive outcomes in the baby (Dakof et al., 2003).

Parental substance use disorders that are comorbid with other disorders appear to put offspring at risk for the development of increased emotional/behavioral problems. For example, 3% of parents without any clinical disorder had a child who met criteria for ADHD, 13% of parents with a substance use disorder had a child who met criteria for ADHD, 25% of parents who met criteria for ADHD also had a child with ADHD, and 50% of parents who were comorbid for a substance use disorder and ADHD had a child with ADHD (Wilens et al., 2005). The combination of substance use disorders and antisocial personality disorder in fathers put children at risk for oppositional defiant disorder, conduct disorder, ADHD, major depressive disorder, and separation anxiety disorder (Moss, Baron, Hardie, & Vanyukov, 2001). Thus, parental psychopathology and especially parental comorbidity have been linked to increased risk for emotional/behavioral problems in children. These patterns have been seen across multiple generations within families (Bailey, Hill, Oesterle, & Hawkins, 2006).

Regarding familial factors, the connections between parents' and adolescents' substance abuse and dependence may be due to a number of different factors. Parents' drug use can influence adolescents directly through a genetic predisposition and through modeling the behavior, but it can also influence adolescents indirectly through impaired parenting and limited control when the parent is under the influence of the substance (Hopfer et al., 2003; Siewert et al., 2003). Parents' attitudes toward alcohol use, and especially fathers' attitudes toward alcohol use, are associated closely with young children's attitudes toward alcohol use (Brody, Ge, Katz, & Arias, 2000).

Note that authoritative parenting (i.e., warm, nurturing interactions combined with age-appropriate structure and limits) is associated with decreased likelihood of substance use disorders in adolescents (Fletcher & Jefferies, 1999). Conversely, parental rejection is associated with adolescents' favorable attitudes toward substance use and intent to use substances (Teichman & Kefir, 2000). Adolescents who feel rejected by their father are at even greater risk for substance use and abuse than adolescents who feel rejected by their mother (Teichman & Kefir, 2000).

One theory that has tied these factors together is the **dynamic diathesis-stress model** of developmental psychopathology (Ingram & Luxton, 2005). The dynamic diathesis-stress model suggests that individuals are vulnerable to psychopathology due to personal characteristics (such as biological risk or maladaptive coping skills), but do not develop psychopathology unless they are challenged with significant stressors. As can be seen in Figure 11.3, a family history of alcoholism can be related to many factors (such as

Intravenous drug use is often associated with adolescents at the habitual and compulsive stages in the development of substance use disorders.

biological risk, temperament/cognitive factors, family environment, and extrafamilial environment) that can influence stressors and be related to a diverse array of adverse outcomes (e.g., externalizing problems, internalizing problems, and health problems; Windle & Tubman, 1999). Thus, parental alcohol abuse and dependence can be related to a number of problems within children's lives.

When connections are found between parental alcohol consumption and children's behavior, it is important to remember the reciprocity of interactions between parents and children. Rather than assuming that high parental alcohol intake "causes" emotional/behavioral problems in children, it may also be that difficult behaviors in children lead parents to ingest more alcohol. As discussed in the chapter on oppositional and conduct problems, a series of studies have suggested that children who show externalizing behavior problems can lead adults with whom they interact to drink more alcohol (Pelham et al., 1997). Thus, the reciprocity of parent–child effects is important to keep in mind when considering etiologies related to parental alcohol abuse.

Cognitive theoretical models of substance abuse and dependence focus on adolescents' perceptions of benefits of using substances (e.g., peer acceptance) and costs to using substances (e.g., harmful effects, parental disapproval; Chassin et al., 2003). As can be seen in Box 11.2 on page 324, expectancies of the effects of alcohol and drug use have also been implicated in the development of substance abuse and dependence patterns.

Behavioral models of substance abuse and dependence have focused on the antecedents and consequences of using and abusing substances. For example, if using a substance decreases anxiety in a stressful situation, then use of that substance is reinforced by the pleasant effects from the substance (Kassel et al., 2005). Some researchers have argued that adolescents may use substances to cope with stress, which initially helps the adolescent feel better, but then leads to more problems (Commission on Adolescent Substance and Alcohol Abuse, 2005).

A number of etiological factors show which children and adolescents are at risk for developing alcohol dependence in adulthood. Specifically, many of these studies have followed children and adolescents who abuse substances into adulthood to find which children and adolescents develop substance dependence (Windle et al., 2005; Zucker, Fitzgerald, & Moses, 1995). Children and adolescents are most likely to develop alcohol dependence in adulthood when the following characteristics are present (Chassin, Flora, & King, 2004; Lillehoj, Trudeau, & Spoth, 2005; Windle et al., 2005; Zucker et al., 1995):

- Childhood antisocial behavior and aggression
- Childhood problems with academic achievement
- Poor social and interpersonal connections in childhood
- Higher levels of activity in childhood
- Higher levels of impulsivity in childhood and adolescence

Case Study: T.S., Who Likes Drag Racing and Cocaine

T.S., a 19-year-old inner-city youth, was picked up by an ambulance that his friend called after he had snorted a great deal of cocaine. He was belligerent and argumentative and showed signs of cocaine intoxication (e.g., his eyes were dilated, his breathing was irregular, and his pulse was rapid and irregular). After he was stabilized, T.S., acknowledged that he had been using alcohol and many different drugs since the age of 13. He began using alcohol and marijuana around that time, then added speed and cocaine to his usage, then finally settled on cocaine as his drug of choice by the age of 17.

He would often steal money from his mother or steal car stereos to purchase cocaine. His mother, who herself had a drinking problem, seemed unaware of her son's problems. He told her that he received good grades and that he played on the high school basketball team, neither of which were true. T.S.'s mother, however, did not question these accomplishments,

even though she had no evidence in support of T.S.'s claims. In fact, T.S. had already dropped out of high school and would spend his days and nights getting high with his friends. T.S. and his friends would often get high and then go drag racing into the early morning hours.

When he was admitted to the emergency room, T.S. was asked if he could control his drug use. He replied angrily, "Of course I could. No problem. I just don't see any damn good reason to stop." The hospital staff diagnosed T.S. with cocaine abuse. If they could have gathered more information, they might have diagnosed T.S. with cocaine dependence. Given the history of conduct problems and current antisocial behavior, T.S. also received a provisional diagnosis of antisocial personality disorder.

Source: Spitzer et al. (1994).

- Poor or inadequate parenting and low levels of parent–child contact
- Parental psychopathology and parental inadequacy as a role model

Thus, there are characteristics in early childhood that are associated with risk for developing alcohol dependence in adulthood (Cassin et al., 2004; Tarter et al., 2003; Windle et al., 2005; Zucker et al., 1995).

Foolishness often precedes wisdom.

—Proverb of Africa

Treatment

Compared with research on treatment for other types of developmental psychopathology, the research is limited regarding evidence-based treatments for children and adolescents with substance use disorders (Kazdin & Weisz, 2003). In general, adolescents are difficult to treat for substance abuse and dependence because they often lack motivation to change their behaviors (Kramer et al., 2003; Walker, Roffman, Stephens, Berghuis, & Kim, 2006). Overall, the average rate of abstaining from substances after treatment is 38% at 6-month follow-up and 32% at 1-year follow-up (Williams & Chang, 2000). These numbers show the difficulty in treating adolescent substance abuse and dependence effectively.

Although a number of treatments are being utilized for adolescent substance abuse, little empirical work has been completed to establish the most effective

treatments. Most treatments are better than no treatments in reducing substance abuse and in reducing other emotional/behavioral problems (Waldron, Slesnick, Brody, Turner, & Peterson, 2001; Williams & Chang, 2000). There are a diverse array of treatments, including psychosocial treatments (which range from needle exchange to outpatient therapy to inpatient therapeutic communities), traditional and 12-step models (which include Alcoholics Anonymous and other abstinence-focused treatments), cognitive–behavioral models (which focus on cognitions as well as behaviors as the point of intervention), family therapy models (which focus on the family as a unit, rather than focusing on the individual substance abuser), and psychopharmacological treatments (American Academy of Child and Adolescent Psychiatry, 2005; Kamon, Budney, & Stanger, 2005; Waldron et al., 2001).

In general, little research has been done into the differential effectiveness of these treatments to test which one is more effective than another (American Academy of Child and Adolescent Psychiatry, 2005). Most of the outcome research in this area has focused on family-based interventions and cognitive–behavioral interventions (Chassin et al., 2003; Kamon et al., 2005; Waldron et al., 2001). Family therapies that involve multiple systems in the adolescent's life (such as peers, the family, and school personnel) are more effective than individual treatments with adolescents (Cormack & Carr, 2000). One such treatment has involved intensive engagement of families of substance-abusing Hispanic/Latino adolescents (Santisteban et al.,

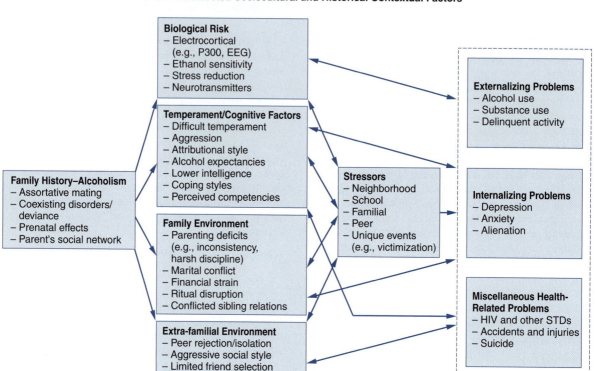

FIGURE 11.3 Dynamic diathesis-stress model of developmental psychopathology: An application to children of alcoholics (COA's).

Source: Windle & Tubman (1999).
Wendy K. Silverman & Thomas H. Ollendick, *Developmental issues in the clinical treatment of children*, Copyright © 1999 by Allyn & Bacon. Reprinted by permission.

2003; Szapocznik et al., 1988). This treatment paradigm, known as brief strategic family therapy, has been shown to be effective with very challenging adolescents in very challenging circumstances (Robbins, Bachrach, & Szapocznik, 2002). Overall, the treatment outcome research suggests that families and other systems (e.g., peer networks and the educational system) need to receive attention when treating adolescents who abuse substances (American Academy of Child and Adolescent Psychiatry, 2005; Myers, Brown, & Vik, 1998). When adolescents are involved in juvenile drug court, there is evidence that mandating evidence-based treatments can help reduce future use and abuse of substances (Henggeler et al., 2006).

Cognitive–behavioral interventions tend to focus on adolescents' cognitions in relation to their behaviors of engaging in substance use and abuse. Typical cognitive–behavioral interventions might include (Dennis et al., 2004; Myers et al., 1998; Walker et al., 2006):

- Motivational enhancement
- Introduction of functional analysis (such as using a behavioral chain worksheet)
- Cognitive–behavioral skills training modules
- Assertiveness training
- Training on giving and receiving criticism and expressing feelings
- Dealing with conflict, anger, and frustration
- Managing negative emotions
- **Relapse prevention** (i.e., trying to prevent the reoccurrence of substance abuse after treatment), including identifying high-risk situations that are likely to lead to substance use, coping with high-risk situations, refusal skills to say "no" to substances when they are offered, setting positive goals, and selecting alternative activities (Witkiewitz & Marlatt, 2004)

Case Study: Doug, the "Booze Brother"

Doug's childhood was relatively normal. His father sold insurance, and his mother was a full-time homemaker. Doug played basketball in grade school and was quite popular. He never spent very much time on schoolwork and tended to earn "Cs" in most of his subjects.

Doug's family appeared "normal" from the outside, but Doug felt a great deal of problems within the family. His father was away from home a great deal, and he drank a fair amount when he was home. Doug's father was a dominant person, and he verbally abused Doug when he was drunk or when he had a bad day. Doug's mother was anxious and stressed much of the time. She smoked cigarettes incessantly and was prescribed tranquilizers to help with her anxiety.

Doug had to attend a different middle school than most of his friends. He tried to gain his old popularity by playing basketball, but he did not make the school basketball team. Not only was he ridiculed at school for not making the team, but his father was very vocal about his disappointment in Doug's failure to make the team. Doug spent less and less time with his old friends in the neighborhood and began spending more time with kids at school who also showed no interest in their academic work. Doug became more and more rebellious. He stole a carton of his mother's cigarettes and gave them to his new friends at school. He began smoking at that point and continues smoking to this day.

Doug also became rebellious in middle school and in early high school. He would talk back to teachers and refuse to follow his parents' commands. His father became even more domineering in reaction to Doug's rebelliousness, which led to even more rebellions by Doug.

Around the beginning of high school, Doug got a job in a local garage. He continued to socialize with other disenfranchised youth and would often "party" with them. Doug became known as a "Booze Brother" because of his frequent alcohol use. He was suspended from school twice for being drunk and once for having marijuana in his locker. He was expelled from school when he was found to be selling marijuana to other students. After being expelled, he was put in a drug and alcohol rehabilitation facility. Doug stated that he "served his time" in this facility, but that it did not change his mind about any of this behaviors.

Once he was discharged, he continued to "party" and to sell drugs. He had found that the job at the garage did not provide enough money for his growing drug habit, nor was it exciting enough for him. He enjoyed being the supplier at parties and felt that he was popular again. Doug's parents, and especially his father, continued to berate him for his poor schoolwork. Doug dealt with the difficulties at home by "partying" with his friends.

One night at a friend's party, Doug had made a lot of money selling drugs to other teenagers. He decided to splurge on himself, so he bought some high-quality bourbon, marijuana, and a number of pills. After finishing a fifth of bourbon, smoking marijuana, and taking a number of pills, Doug was walking down the stairs, slipped, and fell through a plate glass window. He broke his arm, fractured his leg, and received gashes that led to permanent scars all over his face and body. The paramedics were amazed that he survived the drug overdose as well as the fall.

After being stabilized medically, Doug was admitted into another inpatient unit that specialized in drug and alcohol treatment. He did well in the hospital and was allowed to live at home during his senior year of high school. Unfortunately, Doug's parents did not supervise his activities closely nor did they spend very much time with him, and he got involved with his old friends again. Within 2 months of his discharge from the hospital, Doug was caught selling drugs at school again. His parents put him into a drug rehabilitation center again. He did well in the treatment center and was doing well on discharge, but it remains to be seen if his improvements are long term.

Source: Meyer (1989).

One cognitive–behavioral strategy is to focus on the antecedents and consequences of substance use and abuse. A sample **behavioral chain** worksheet is shown in Figure 11.5 on page 326 to illustrate how adolescents can gain awareness of what comes before and after their substance use. The behavioral chain worksheet is used to help adolescents identify a triggering event, their thoughts, feelings, behavior, and positive as well as negative consequences to any alcohol or drug use (Myers et al., 1998).

Note that relapse prevention is of great importance in the treatment of substance abuse and dependence (Witkiewitz & Marlatt, 2004). Many adolescents can be treated effectively when they are away from home (e.g., in a residential facility), but then begin to abuse substances once they are home again. Relapse prevention helps adolescents identify their own high-risk situations (e.g., the graduation party where they know all their friends will be drinking), to cope with these high-risk situations, to learn effective refusal skills

BOX *11.2*

IS WHAT YOU BELIEVE, WHAT YOU GET?

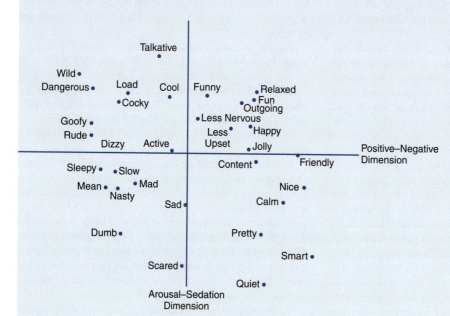

FIGURE 11.4 Individual differences scaling stimulus configuration for alcohol expectancy words representing modes of meaning within a hypothetical expectancy memory network for children in grades 3–12. The horizontal dimension represents evaluation (positive–negative), and the vertical dimension represents arousal–sedation.

Source: Dunn & Goldman (1998).

If you thought that alcohol would make your face look grotesque and ugly every time you drank it, would you drink alcohol? Probably not. If, on the other hand, you thought that alcohol would make you attractive and funny every time you drank it, then you might be more inclined to drink alcohol on a regular basis. This is the premise of the research on expectancies.

Expectancies can be defined as what an individual expects or anticipates from ingesting a substance (Goldman & Darkes, 2004). Expectancies relate to the expected reinforcing qualities of the substance and to the outcomes that are anticipated from use of the substance. Most individuals' expectancies are developed through observational learning (e.g., watching parents, peers, or characters in the media using the substance) and through direct experience (Goldman & Darkes, 2004).

Expectancies can be measured meaningfully in children even before they begin drinking (Dunn & Goldman, 1996, 1998; Miller, Smith, & Goldman, 1990). A sample question is: How often do adults feel HAPPY when they drink alcohol? The possible answers are: Never, Sometimes, Usually, and Always (Dunn & Goldman, 1998). Expectancies are correlated with drinking from very early elementary school

into adulthood (Deas, Riggs, Langenbucher, Goldman, & Brown, 2000; Dunn & Goldman, 1998).

In children from 3rd through 12th grades, expectancies are represented by two dimensions: arousal–sedation and positive–negative. As can be seen in Figure 11.4, these dimensions are characterized by feelings and experiences that children and adolescents expect to occur when someone drinks alcohol (Dunn & Goldman, 1998).

In general, younger children expect more negative and sedating effects, but as they age, they begin to expect more positive and arousing effects. This change appears to be related to greater exposure to peer and adult drinking (Cumsille, Sayer, & Graham, 2000). Children and adolescents who expect more positive effects and who expect more arousing effects are more likely to drink alcohol than those children and adolescents who expect negative and sedating effects (Cruz & Dunn, 2003). This pattern is evident at all ages and becomes especially salient in adolescence and young adulthood. Of great importance is that alcohol expectancies are better at predicting problem drinking than are demographic and background variables (Christiansen & Goldman, 1983).

BOX *11.2*

(CONTINUED)

Research on alcohol expectancies has great relevance to preventive interventions. Because children's expectancies can influence their likelihood of drinking alcohol, providing early preventive interventions that challenge expectancies for positive and arousing effects of alcohol could help prevent alcohol use and abuse in childhood, adolescence, and early adulthood (Cumsille et al., 2000; Goldman, 1999). This type of expectancy challenge prevention program has been effective with older adolescent college students (Darkes & Goldman, 1998; Dunn, Lau, & Cruz, 2000) and has now been established as effective with children as young as 4th grade (Cruz & Dunn, 2003; Stewart et al., 2005). Specifically, children who are exposed to the expectancy challenge reported more negative and sedating qualities of alcohol, which are associated with decreased likelihood of using alcohol at an early age (Cruz & Dunn, 2003).

---

for when they are offered substances, and to develop alternative interests that would put them in less high-risk situations (Myers et al., 1998). Many relapse prevention interventions focus on the need to develop a new peer network that is not engaged in substance use and abuse.

Maintenance of therapeutic gains can be difficult. Having siblings who abuse substances can decrease the likelihood of maintaining therapeutic gains after treatment (Latimer, Winters, Stinchfield, & Traver, 2000). Poorer therapeutic outcome is also associated with a longer history of substance abuse, lower family support, lower self-esteem, and more delinquent behavior (Myers et al., 1998). Treatments tend to work best with adolescents who have at least one protective factor in their favor, who receive peer and parental support, who had low rates of substance use before treatment, who receive sufficiently long treatment, who complete treatment, and who participate in aftercare (Latimer, Newcomb, Winters, & Stinchfield, 2000; Williams & Chang, 2000). Treatment gains are also better when adolescents have a strong working alliance with their therapists during therapy (Tetzlaff et al., 2005), and they are particularly good when both parents and adolescents have a strong therapeutic alliance with the therapist (Shelef, Diamond, Diamond, & Liddle, 2005).

Overall, the most effective treatments of substance abuse and dependence in adolescents focus on a wide variety of facets of adolescents' lives, including individual characteristics (such as cognitions and motivations), familial characteristics (such as parental monitoring), issues related to the peer network (e.g., the need to find friends who do not abuse substances), and aftercare or relapse maintenance issues (Myers et al., 1998).

One reason why I don't drink is because I wish to know when I am having a good time.

—Nancy Astor

Prevention

As can be seen in the "You Decide" section on page 327, there is an ongoing debate about whether substance abuse can be prevented in children and adolescents. Overall, a number of effective prevention programs help to decrease the likelihood that children and adolescents will abuse substances in the future (e.g., Spoth, Redmond, & Shin, 2001; Spoth, Reyes, Redmond, & Shin, 1999). These programs can be administered in schools, in communities, and via mass media (Hawkins, Van Horn, & Arthur, 2004; Spoth, Redmond, Shin, & Azevedo, 2004). One prevention program called the Strong African American Families Program showed success at preventing alcohol use and abuse in a sample of rural young adolescents (Brody et al., 2006). School-based prevention programs are often disseminated throughout an entire school system and can also involve parents in the prevention program (Brown, Catalano, Fleming, Haggerty, & Abbott, 2005; Spoth et al., 2001, 2004). Typical substance use prevention programs in schools include the following aspects (Botvin & Dusenbury, 1989; Dusenbury & Falco, 1997; Meyers & Nastasi, 1999; Spoth et al., 2004):

- Teaching children factual information about the harmful effects of alcohol and illicit drugs
- Teaching children drug refusal skills (e.g., how to say "no" when offered a substance and still feel good about yourself)
- Enhancing children's and adolescents' feelings of personal and social competence
- Training teachers, aides, and parents how to talk with children about substance use, as well as teaching them the warning signs of substance use

Trigger	Thought	Feeling	Behavior	Consequences	
				Positive	Negative
1. Gathering with friends, offered drugs	I'll feel left out if I don't use They'll think I'm lame if I say no	Anxious, uncomfortable	Use drugs	Feel comfortable with peers, have a good time, enjoy high	Guilt, feel like failure Hangover Spent money Punishment, loss of privileges Parents upset
2. Argument with parents	They don't listen or understand I'm sick of being blamed for everything	Angry, frustrated	Use drugs	Forget about argument, feel relaxed, feel less angry	Parents more angry Problems not addressed

FIGURE 11.5 Sample behavior chain worksheet.

Source: Myers et al. (1998).

- Maintaining follow-up on the prevention program, often with booster sessions that are implemented on a recurrent basis
- Helping to create a substance-intolerant social climate within the school system

Many of these programs have been found to be effective in decreasing use of substances, especially nonalcohol substances (Brown et al., 2005; Spoth et al., 2004). A program called Life Skills Training, which teaches personal and social skills, has been especially effective at preventing substance use (Botvin & Griffin, 2004; Dusenbury, Brannigan, Hansen, Walsh, & Falco, 2005; Foxcroft, 2005; Gorman, 2005). Note, however, that information-based programs and fear-inducing tactics alone are not effective in reducing substance use (Botvin & Griffin, 2004). The Drug Abuse Resistance Education (DARE) program is an example of a widespread, but ineffective, program for prevention of substance use (West & O'Neal, 2004). The DARE program, which is often provided by law enforcement agencies, is very popular but shows few positive effects. A number of long-term follow-up studies have found no differences in use of drugs, attitudes toward drugs, or self-esteem between youth who did or did not participate in the DARE program (West & O'Neal, 2004). Efforts are underway to improve the effectiveness of the DARE program, but to date, the program has been unsuccessful at preventing substance use and abuse (West & O'Neal, 2004). Interactive programs in schools, where the staff can interact with students, are more effective than noninteractive programs. Noninteractive prevention programs reduced substance abuse rates by 4%, whereas interactive prevention programs reduced substance abuse rates by 21% (Tobler, 2000).

Community-based universal prevention programs have often been instituted with groups of parents, especially parents of adolescents (Guyll, Spoth, Chao, Wickrama, & Russell, 2004; Pantin, Schwartz, Sullivan, Coatsworth, & Szapocznik, 2003). Prevention programs often work with parents to prevent drinking and drug use in their own children. Trying to make the prevention program specific to families' needs is associated with more effective preventive efforts (Hogue & Liddle, 1999). For example, in a prevention program known as Familias Unidas (Families United), Hispanic immigrant parents of adolescents take part in participatory-learning groups and learn about communicating effectively with their adolescent, develop skills in dealing with the school system, and learn about how to monitor their adolescents' behavior and how to respond appropriately to it (Pantin, Coatsworth et al., 2003; Pantin, Schwartz et al., 2003). All these factors are thought to serve as protective factors against the development of substance use problems in adolescents, and the program has been found to be effective (Pantin et al., 2003). There have also been effective prevention programs developed specifically for American Indian and Alaska Native youth (Hawkins, Cummins, & Marlatt, 2004).

In addition to working with parents regarding their own children, many prevention programs help parents to become more involved in community efforts that prevent the misuse of substances. One of the most well known prevention groups is Mothers Against Drunk Driving (MADD).

Another version of a community-based program, which is not really meant as a prevention strategy, has to do with the cost of substances. A number of communities have shown that when prices of alcohol and cigarettes are raised, adolescent rates of alcohol and cigarette use decrease significantly, and adolescents report being

Case Study: Family Therapy and Treatment for Drug and Alcohol Dependence

Bob and Mary have four children, ages 8, 6, 4, and 2. Bob was recently released from prison and has a lengthy drug and alcohol abuse history. Bob and Mary had been separated for 4 months, and just reunited 2 weeks ago. Within the last 2 weeks, Bob has had two "setbacks" where he began drinking again and using drugs. This family therapy session includes Bob, Mary, and their two oldest children, 8-year-old Susie and 6-year-old Alicia. The therapist is using a solution-focused brief family therapy. Bob is in individual treatment for his drug and alcohol problems. The current therapy is meant to deal with the harm that has been caused within the family. In this session, the therapist has just noted that the children look bored (as a way of engaging them in the therapy session), when the following interactions took place:

Bob:	[nodding toward Susie] She's probably a lot more interested in it. It affects her a lot more than it does the younger ones.
Therapist:	Is that right?
Bob:	Yes.
Therapist:	How does it affect her?
Bob:	She mentioned to me—actually, she has, too [pointing to Alicia]—that they don't like me drinking. They've seen what it's done.

Therapist:	Let me ask you, Susie, how is your dad different when he doesn't drink?
Susie:	He's nicer. He takes us places.
Therapist:	You like that, going places with your dad.
Susie:	Yesterday we went to the beach.
Therapist:	You went to the beach.
Susie:	My dad is always nice, but I don't like when he drinks. I can tell. My mom always tells me when he drinks, but I can tell sometimes by myself because I can tell when he gets home in the morning...
Therapist:	And you went to the beach yesterday. How was it?
Susie:	Fun.
Therapist:	[to Bob] How did you manage to take the kids to the beach yesterday? How did that happen?
Susie:	We went jet skiing, but I took a friend to the beach. It was just my dad and me and my friend. He went jet skiing with my uncle.
Therapist:	So you and Dad and your friend went to the beach. I'll bet that was very special for you...

Source: Klar & Berg (1999, pp. 255–256).

YOU DECIDE: DO ALCOHOL AND DRUG PREVENTION PROGRAMS WORK?

Yes

- Life Skills Training, which combines teaching young adolescents personal and social skills, is very effective at preventing substance use and abuse (Botvin & Griffin, 2004; Dusenbury et al., 2005).
- The Strengthening Families Program and the Focus on Families Program are effective in reducing substance use and abuse in children of parents who abuse substances (Commission on Adolescent Substance and Alcohol Abuse, 2005).

No

- Campaigns such as "Just Say No" were found to be ineffective in reducing adolescent drinking (Schwebel, 1998). These results are found consistently (Commission on Adolescent Substance and Alcohol Abuse, 2005).
- Widely established programs like the Drug Abuse Resistance Education (DARE) program are not effective in reducing substance use or abuse (West & O'Neal, 2004).

So, do alcohol and drug prevention programs work? You decide.

concerned about the costs of these substances (Beyers, Toumbourou, Catalano, Arthur, & Hawkins, 2004; Riedel, Robinson, Klesges, & McLain-Allen, 2002). Although raising prices has rarely been intended for preventive reasons, the decrease in adolescent substance use after raised prices is a welcome benefit to the higher cost of substances.

Mass-media prevention programs have been used extensively; however, there are inconsistent results on their effectiveness (Derzon & Lipsey, 2002). Most of these prevention campaigns have used public service announcements (PSAs) to caution children and adolescents about using alcohol and illicit drugs. Some PSAs have been found to be effective, especially ones that target adolescents at risk. For example, one PSA campaign was targeted at sensation-seeking adolescents, and the program was effective in reducing the use of marijuana even several months after the program was completed (Palmgreen, Donohew, Lorch, Hoyle, & Stephenson, 2002; Stephenson, 2003). On the negative side, PSA campaigns that provide explicit messages about not doing drugs are perceived by adolescents as controlling (Burgoon et al., 2002). When adolescents perceived that they were being told what to do, rather than being allowed to make an informed decision, they were likely to show reactance to the prevention message, which was related to an increase in substance use (Burgoon et al., 2002).

The inconsistency in these results may be due to the lack of controlled studies of these public service announcements. There is a need to dismantle prevention programs that are administered through the mass media to identify components of the program that work and components of the program that are not successful (Derzon & Lipsey, 2002).

Overall, some prevention programs have been found to be effective, but many others appear to miss those most in need of the services. For example, many prevention programs have helped to decrease the onset of substance use among nonabusers, but have not decreased the likelihood for intensified substance use among children and adolescents who are already abusing the substance (Commission on Adolescent Substance and Alcohol Abuse, 2005). Given that over $2.45 billion are spent on drug abuse prevention and research programs each year, it is surprising that more effective prevention programs have not been identified and implemented (Arthur & Blitz, 2000). More efforts are needed to tie together research findings with prevention programs that are instituted nationwide to try to reduce the number of adolescents who use and abuse substances (Stoil, Hill,

Jansen, Sambrano, & Winn, 2000). As can be seen in Box 11.3, these issues are of concern internationally.

ALCOHOL AND SUBSTANCE USE AND ABUSE CONCEPTUALIZED IN A DIMENSIONAL MANNER

In contrast to most of the disorders discussed in this book, the use and abuse of alcohol and substances have been studied extensively from a dimensional perspective. It should come as no surprise that alcohol and substance use is relatively prevalent among children and especially adolescents. In the Methods for the Epidemiology of Child and Adolescent Mental Disorders (MECA) Study of children aged 9 to 18, 47.8% reported having had an alcoholic beverage, 5% reported having smoked marijuana, and 0.5% reported having used cocaine at some point in their lives (Kandel et al., 1997). The MECA study tended to find somewhat lower rates of substance use than other studies, which was probably due to the style of data collection (i.e., interviews). Specifically, studies with confidential self-report questionnaires tend to find higher rates of substance use than do studies that use interviews (Kandel et al., 1997). In an interview-based study of rural children from the southeast, 54.1% of girls and 50.2% of boys reported using alcohol by the age of 16 (Costello et al., 1999). This same study found that 10.5% of girls and 14.9% of boys had tried marijuana by the age of 16. Higher rates of usage are often found in anonymous surveys. In a national, anonymous survey, 80.7% of high school seniors reported having drunk alcohol sometime within their lives, and 48.4% reported having used some type of illicit drug (Johnston, O'Malley, & Bachman, 1995). Other estimates are comparable in terms of illicit drug use, with a common estimate being that approximately 40% to 50% of high school students have tried marijuana at least once (Rey et al., 2004). In terms of changes over time, one study found that use of illicit drugs (mainly marijuana) hit a peak usage of 54% with high school students in 1981 then declined to 27% in 1992 and then rose to the current level of 40% (Maughan et al., 2005). Thus, exposure to illicit drugs is relatively common in samples of high school students.

As with substance abuse, patterns of substance use suggest that substance use increases with age (Costello et al., 2003). There are interesting developmental differences when adolescents are compared with adults. In contrast to adults, adolescents who use substances (especially alcohol) tend to use less frequently and tend to

BOX *11.3*

SUBSTANCE USE AND ABUSE AROUND THE GLOBE

Substance use and abuse is problematic for adolescents throughout the world. Following are some brief highlights of research findings with adolescents from a diverse array of cultures.

- A review of research on Arab adolescents in Israel, Jordan, and the Palestinian authority found that drug abuse was more prevalent in Israeli Arab adolescents than in Israeli Jewish adolescents and that Jordanian adolescents who were dependent on substances showed higher levels of education than did Palestinian adolescents who were dependent on substances (Weiss, Sawa, Abdeen, & Yanai, 1999).
- A total of 11% of adolescents in Taiwan reported having a substance use disorder. The highest rates of substance

use disorders were found for boys, adolescents living in rural communities, and adolescents from academically impoverished backgrounds (Chong, Chan, & Cheng, 1999).
- Chinese youth who live in Hong Kong show similarly moderate rates of drinking alcohol as Chinese youth who live in mainland China (Lo & Globetti, 2000).
- Within the United States, African-American adolescents from low-income urban areas who received high levels of parental monitoring were less likely to engage in substance use, selling drugs, sexual behavior, school truancy, and violence (Li, Feigelman, & Stanton, 2000).

have lower overall intake, but tend to ingest more of the substance at one time (Deas et al., 2000). With alcohol, this trend has been termed **binge drinking** (Morawska & Oei, 2005). Binge drinking is defined as having five or more alcoholic drinks on one occasion, and it has been associated with psychosocial, neurological, and physical health problems (Naimi et al., 2003). Approximately 30% of high school students report binge drinking, with many more boys than girls reporting that they are likely to binge drink (Dryfoos, 1997). Based on national surveys in the United States, binge drinking was seen in over 40% of high school seniors in the late 1970s and early 1980s and then decreased rapidly down to 28% in 1992 (Maughan, Iervolino, & Collishaw, 2005). Since that time, rates of binge drinking have increased slightly but have not risen to the high of 40% that was seen in the late 1970s and early 1980s (Maughan et al., 2005). In a study of female twins, binge drinking was found to be environmentally determined and to be more prevalent in girls attending college in contrast to same-aged girls who were not attending college (Slutske et al., 2004). Interestingly, approximately 22% of young adults who binge drink eventually reduce their alcohol consumption while still in college without any professional treatment or interventions (Vik, Cellucci, & Ivers, 2003). Adolescents who continue to binge drink or to be chronic heavy drinkers into young adulthood are more likely to have high blood pressure and to be overweight or obese at the age of 24 (Oesterle, Hill, Hawkins, Guo, Catalano, & Abbott, 2004). Thus, binge

drinking has both psychological as well as physical consequences.

Substance use varies with gender, but the patterns are complex. In very young samples of children from first through seventh grades, children who said that they intended to use a substance when they were older were more likely to try the substance at an earlier age than children who reported that they did not intend to use the substance (Andrews Tildesley, Hops, Duncan, & Severson, 2003). Boys were more likely than girls to report an intention to drink alcohol and to use tobacco eventually (Andrews et al., 2003). When exploring the gender differences in patterns of usage, younger adolescent boys (12–13 years old) and older adolescent boys (16–18 years old) drink more alcohol than their same-aged female peers, but middle school adolescent boys and girls (14–15 years old) show similar levels of drinking alcohol (Farrell, Kung, White, & Valois, 2000; Vik et al., 1997).

Substance use is often more prevalent in lower SES communities, but the types of substances may vary. For example, the use of cocaine power appears to be more prevalent among middle-class and wealthy adolescents, whereas crack cocaine is more prevalent in adolescents from more impoverished backgrounds (Luthar, 1999).

With regard to substance use patterns and race/ethnicity, different patterns are evident when use rather than abuse is explored. Although abuse patterns tend to show the highest rates in African Americans, usage patterns

In her own words, Errica Erikson describes her experience as an adolescent in a small Northwestern town:

We drank one beer, then a few more, soon I was stumbling around looking for Jessica.

"What time is it?" I asked her when I saw her getting warm by the fire.

"Eleven-fifty, why?" she said in a slurred voice.

"We have to be home by twelve!" I cried with wide eyes.

The two of us then stumbled toward her car and drove away from the music and noise.

"Be careful, but try to hurry!" I said.

The road had a lot of turns and corners on it. As soon as it became straight, the car began to pick up speed. I closed my eyes because everything was becoming blurry and hard to see.

All of a sudden I felt myself flying through the air. Jessica screamed and my eyes shot open. We were in the air, then the car rolled, stopping only because it hit a fence post. Our heads hit the windshield so hard, we were knocked out.

I sat there in the dark, blood running down my face. I reached over and shook Jessica.

"Jessica wake up!" I cried. "Wake up! Please, Jessica!" I shook her so hard, yet she made no response. "Jessica!" I cried again in desperation. Moments passed, then she groaned.

Source: Shandler (1999, p. 38–39).

---

tend to show the highest rates in Caucasian Americans and Native Americans (Sattler, 1998; Vik et al., 1997). African-American high school seniors report significantly lower levels of alcohol use than Caucasian Americans and Hispanic/Latino/Latina Americans (Nettles & Pleck, 1994; Vik et al., 1997). Caucasian-American high school students report higher usage of hallucinogens, amphetamines, inhalants, barbiturates, and tranquilizers than do African-American and Hispanic/Latino/Latina youth (Vik et al., 1997).

Even subclinical levels of substance use are associated with difficulties in functioning. Adolescents who use substances show poorer academic achievement, more negative affect, and poorer psychosocial functioning than adolescents who do not use substances (Vik et al., 1997; Windle et al., 2005).

Risk Factors

Theories of adolescent substance use have focused on risk factors that are associated with the onset of subclinical substance use. These theories often focus on three types of influence: social, attitudinal, and intrapersonal (Petraitis, Flay, & Miller, 1995).

A great deal of research has investigated risk factors for alcohol and substance use and abuse. The following are some of the primary risk factors that have been identified throughout diverse communities in the United States and in other countries (Allison et al., 1999; Beyers et al., 2004; Goldman, 1999; Griffin, Botvin, Scheier, Diaz, & Miller, 2000; Hoffmann, Cerbone, & Su, 2000; Hussong & Hicks, 2003; Koss et al., 2003; Lau et al., 2005; Leonard et al., 2000; Sullivan & Farrell, 1999):

- High levels of externalizing problems or delinquent behavior
- Spending time with peers after school, with no adult supervision
- Peer pressure to use drugs
- Peers who engaged in drinking and using drugs
- Peer approval of substance use
- Family approval of substance use
- Poor parenting practices, with little monitoring of children's behaviors
- Physical abuse
- Low self-esteem
- History of sexual activity
- High rates of stressful life events
- High emotional distress (such as depression and anger)
- High sensation-seeking needs
- Positive expectancies about the effects of substances
- Low academic achievement
- School norms for drug use
- Drug and alcohol availability
- Extreme poverty
- Disorganized and disenfranchised neighborhood

Many of these risk factors co-occur for the same children. For example, parents who abuse substances

BOX *11.4*

PEER PRESSURE

A common concern is that peers will pressure children and adolescents into using and abusing substances. There is a great deal of evidence, however, that children and adolescents choose friends who are consistent with their own attitudes toward substance use and abuse (Engels, Knibbe, DeVries, Drop, & Van Breukelen, 1999). This process is known as selective association, meaning that adolescents actively select a social network that is consistent with their attitudes about substance use rather than being influenced by the peers who happen to be in their social network (Engels et al., 1999).

There is no question, however, that patterns of substance use and abuse are remarkably similar within peer groups. In fact, there is more similarity among friends regarding substance use than there is for academic orientation and ethnic identity, especially for Caucasian-American and Asian-American adolescents (Hamm, 2000). Part of this connection may be due to the effects of peers' sensation-seeking behavior. Pairs of friends who had a high degree of sensation seeking tended to influence each other to use alcohol and marijuana more so than when pairs of friends did not desire high levels of sensation seeking (Donohew et al., 1999). Peers' alcohol use appears to relate in a bidirectional manner with other adolescents. Specifically, when viewed over time, individual adolescents appear to be influenced by their peers' level of alcohol consumption but the peers are also influenced by the adolescent's alcohol consumption (Bray et al., 2003).

Overall, substance using and abusing adolescents tend to socialize with other substance using and abusing adolescents (Bray et al., 2003). This socializing can lead to additional "deviancy training," whereby troubled adolescents engage in even more troubling behavior (such as substance use and abuse) due to peer influences (Dishion et al., 1999).

The issue of differential influences of peers versus parents is important. One study found that peer and sibling substance use and abuse were more strongly related to adolescents' substance use and abuse than were parents' patterns of substance use and abuse (Windle, 2000). Both sibling and peer deviance are associated with the onset of substance use in middle childhood, but sibling deviance appears to be even more strongly tied to later substance use than does peer deviance (Stormshak, Comeau, & Shepard, 2004). The parent–child relationship can help prevent adolescents from using and abusing substances, but parental influences are strongest when adolescents are not involved with a substance-using peer group (Gerrard, Gibbons, Zhao, Russell, & Reis-Bergan, 1999). Further, parental social support seems to protect girls more so than boys from the deleterious effects of deviant peers (Marshal & Chassin, 2000).

How children and adolescents spend their time is also related to substance use and abuse. In a study of sixth and seventh graders, adolescents who spent time after school with peers reported higher rates of substance use than did adolescents who spent time after school alone at home, or with their parents, or in organized after-school activities (Flannery, Williams, & Vazsonyi, 1999). This pattern was also true for increased levels of delinquency and aggression.

Note that in addition to pressure from peers to use or not use substances, the norms for substance use in the particular school are related to adolescents' substance use (Allison et al., 1999). Specifically, school norms for drug use accounted for variance above and beyond peer influences and parental influences in predicting adolescents' substance use (Allison et al., 1999). Thus, the norms for use or nonuse of substances that are present in the adolescent's school are important to assess.

---

tend to show poorer monitoring of their children's behavior, inconsistent discipline, low rates of positive parenting, and low rates of involvement, which are all related to externalizing problems in children (Stanger, Dumenci, Kamon, & Burstein, 2004). Parents who abuse substances are also more likely to physically abuse their children (Kerwin, 2005). The risk factors related to peers and peer pressure are discussed further in Box 11.4, and the issues related to substance use and pregnancy are discussed in Box 11.5.

Note that many of these risk factors can be considered individual or interpersonal, such as high sensation-seeking needs and low self-esteem, whereas other risk factors can be considered contextual, such as extreme poverty, and living in a disorganized neighborhood (Wright & Masten, 2005). In addition, some of these risk factors covary to put children at more or less risk. For example, boys who showed high levels of anger and low levels of fear were at greater risk for alcohol use initiation when they also showed lower levels of

BOX *11.5*

SEX, DRUGS, AND BABIES

A national survey of high school students found that 51% of the students reported that they had experienced sexual intercourse at least once, with more boys acknowledging having had intercourse than girls (Huszti, Hoff, & Johnson, 2003). More sexual partners in adolescence are related to a higher risk for pregnancy in adolescence (Valois, Oeltmann, Waller, & Hussey, 1999). The use of safer sex methods has increased over the past two decades, but 22% of adolescents still report not using contraception during their first experience with sexual intercourse (Huszti et al., 2003). Sexually active adolescent girls who do not use contraception have a 90% chance of becoming pregnant within 12 months (Huszti et al., 2003).

Although rates of sexual intercourse have decreased somewhat over the past decade, and the teen birthrate has decreased somewhat, 10.8% of babies born each year in the United States are born to a teenage mother (Children's Defense Fund, 2005d). Younger siblings of pregnant adolescents are also at increased risk for becoming pregnant (East & Jacobson, 2001). Poor parental supervision and monitoring, a distant parent–child relationship, prior sexual abuse, low SES, and living in a dangerous neighborhood are also risk factors for pregnancy during adolescence (Miller, Benson, & Galbraith, 2001).

The teen birthrate is much higher in the United States than in most other industrialized countries. The teen birthrate is twice as high in the United States as in Great Britain, four times as high as in Spain and Sweden, seven times as high as in the Netherlands and Denmark, and 15 times higher than in Japan (Coley & Chase-Lansdale, 1998). Overall, a great many infants are born to adolescent mothers and fathers. Parenthetically, fathers of babies born to adolescent mothers are on average 2 to 3 years older than the mothers (Coley & Chase-Lansdale, 1998). Thus, the fathers are not always still in adolescence, but rather may have already reached adulthood.

Alcohol and drug use and abuse are related to adolescent pregnancy (Coley & Chase-Lansdale, 1998; Kellogg, Hoffman, & Taylor, 1999). Although the directionality is not well established, it appears that alcohol and drugs can limit adolescents' judgement and decision-making processes and may allow them to be less concerned about having unprotected sex.

Unfortunately, alcohol and drug use do not always cease when adolescents realize that they are pregnant. One study found significant alcohol usage among pregnant teenagers and found that the amount of alcohol ingested during pregnancy was related directly to lower functioning and growth in the babies born to these mothers (Cornelius, Goldshmidt, Taylor, & Day, 1999). In addition, the timing of alcohol use during pregnancy can have differential negative ramifications on the fetus (Cornelius et al., 1999). Extreme levels of alcohol use during pregnancy are related to fetal alcohol syndrome, and any amount of alcohol use during pregnancy can be harmful to the fetus (Dorris, 1989). Smoking (Albrecht et al., 1999) and drug abuse (Farrow, Watts, Krohn, & Olson, 1999) are also quite prevalent with pregnant adolescents.

Overall, there is a disturbing connection between substance use and pregnancy in adolescence. Prevention efforts have been focused at many levels of this problem, including prevention of unprotected sexual activities, prevention of pregnancy, and programs for parenting teenagers once the baby is born (Coley & Chase-Lansdale, 1998). Prevention efforts are particularly important because of the connections between teen pregnancy and child maltreatment (Kaufman & Zigler, 1992). Teen pregnancy is linked to child maltreatment, especially for adolescents who live in poverty. For these reasons, programs targeted at preventing substance use and unprotected sex may also help prevent some cases of child abuse.

Source: Kaufman & Zigler (1992).

---

inhibitory control (Pardini, Lochman, & Wells, 2004). Depression, however, was predictive of early use of alcohol regardless of the boys' level of inhibitory control (Pardini et al. 2004).

In a comprehensive study of risk factors for substance use in an urban African-American population, five primary risk factors were identified: intentions to use substances, having a history of sexual intercourse, showing externalizing and delinquent behaviors, feeling peer pressure to use substances, and having peers who used substances (Bray, Adams, Getz, & McQueen, 2003; Sullivan & Farrell, 1999). It appears that the more risk factors that were present (from 0 to 5), the more alcohol, substance, and tobacco use reported.

In urban minority communities, girls' substance use appears to be tied to sexual development and eventual risk for sexually transmitted diseases and pregnancy. For example, early menarche (i.e., beginning their period earlier than other girls) is associated with drinking alcohol at an earlier age and with drinking a higher quantity of alcohol (Dick, Rose, Viken, & Kaprio, 2000). Substance use in conjunction with conduct problems appears to be urban minority girls at risk for sexually transmitted diseases and for pregnancy (Bachanas et al., 2002). For example, in one study of impoverished ethnic minority girls, substance abuse was associated with greater risk for pregnancy, and 17.0% of the adolescent girls already had children of their own compared with a national average of 2.9% (Boothroyd et al., 2005).

Girls who have been sexually abused also seem to be at greater risk for the development of substance use disorders. Even when controlling for the girls' age, other experiences of child abuse, depression, aggression, family SES, parental behavior, and maternal substance use, girls who had been sexually abused in childhood showed higher rates of substance abuse than girls who had not been sexually abused (Bailey & McCloskey, 2005).

Different risk factors are sometimes related to increased risk of use or abuse of specific substances. In a national sample, adolescents who had a history of familial alcohol problems, who had been physically assaulted, been sexually assaulted, or witnessed violence were at an increased risk for alcohol abuse/dependence (Kilpatrick et al., 2000). Adolescents with a history of familial drug problems, those who had been physically assaulted, those who witnessed violence, or those who had experienced posttraumatic stress disorder were more at risk for marijuana abuse/dependence (Kilpatrick et al., 2000). Similar risk factors were found for adolescents who were at risk for abuse and dependence on harder drugs than marijuana, with the addition of a history of familial alcohol problems and having experienced a sexual assault (Kilpatrick et al., 2000).

Note that many of these risk factors, especially lack of parental monitoring and high rates of family conflict, are associated with a number of emotional/behavioral problems in children and adolescents (Ary et al., 1999). These risk factors seem to be especially salient for the development of externalizing problems (Ary et al., 1999). The risk factors that are most strongly connected to substance use disorders (and not other internalizing disorders) are larger family size, lower SES, hyperactivity, attention problems, and aggression (Reinherz, Giaconia, Hauf, Wasserman, & Paradis, 2000). Overall, a number of risk factors have been identified that are associated with increased use and abuse of substances.

As mentioned in chapter 9, there has been a great deal of research to investigate whether the use of medication, such as psychostimulant medication for the treatment of ADHD, serves as a risk factor for greater use of substances in adolescence and adulthood. Based on a number of studies and meta-analyses, there is no causal link between taking psychostimulant medication earlier in life and developing a substance use disorder in later adolescence or adulthood (Wilens, 2004; Wilens et al., 2003). In fact, effective treatment for ADHD, such as with psychostimulant medication, is associated with a decreased risk for substance use disorders later in adolescence and in early adulthood (Wilens, 2004b; Wilens et al., 2003). When ADHD symptoms are not treated and when they persist, they are linked to an increased risk for substance use disorders, although this link is no longer evident when symptoms of conduct disorder are controlled statistically (Armstrong & Costello, 2002; Molina & Pelham, 2003).

Protective Factors

In addition to the wealth of knowledge about risk factors, there is also a great deal of information available on factors that seem to protect children and adolescents from developing alcohol and substance abuse problems. The following is a list of some of the major protective factors that have been identified (Dunn, 2005; Elder, Leaver-Dunn, Wang, Nagy, & Green, 2000; El-Sheikh & Buckhalt, 2003; Miller, Davies, & Greenwald, 2000; Pilowsky, Zybert, & Vlahov, 2004; Wills, Sandy, Yaeger, & Shinar, 2001):

- Feeling committed to school
- Being involved in extracurricular activities (such as sports and activity clubs)
- Attending a place of worship (such as church, synagogue, or mosque)
- Had a strong religious belief system (regardless of attendance at a place of worship)
- Communicating with parents when distressed
- Getting involved in demanding activities when distressed
- Showing positive emotions
- Expecting success in one's future endeavors
- Not having any close adult role models who use substances inappropriately
- Feeling intolerant of deviant behaviors in others
- Having a supportive family
- Having a family that is high in adaptability and cohesion

A number of prevention programs try to discourage children and adolescents from starting to smoke and try to help children and adolescents discontinue smoking if they have already started.

- Experiencing a positive parent–child relationship
- Having parents who expect positive academic achievement
- Having peers who expect positive academic achievement
- Living with two parents (whether biological or stepparents)
- Showing good school attendance

These protective factors have been identified as helpful for a diverse array of populations. In a study of urban African-American youth, a number of protective factors were found to decrease the likelihood of alcohol and drug use (Sullivan & Farrell, 1999). Notably, protective factors that kept adolescents involved in school and community activities served to prevent the use and abuse of alcohol and other substances. In addition, family commitment to abstaining from alcohol and drugs served as a protective factor for African-American and Hispanic/Latino/Latina adolescents (Johnson & Johnson, 1999). Family sanctions against any use of substances (including nicotine) were also found to prevent the use of substances in both rural and urban adolescents (Scheer, Borden, & Donnermeyer, 2000).

These protective factors can often prevent the maladaptive pattern that is present in children of parents who abuse alcohol. For example, one study found that children of alcoholics who perceived their family to be adaptive and cohesive and who felt that they had a good attachment to their mother and father were protected from the adverse effects of parental alcohol abuse (El-Sheikh & Buckhalt, 2003).

Many of these protective factors also serve to protect children and adolescents from other problematic behaviors in addition to protecting them from abusing substances themselves. For example, factors that protect children and adolescents from developing alcohol and substance use problems also seem to protect children and adolescents from delinquency and sexual involvement (Wright & Masten, 2005).

Never let me smoke.
—Advice from a preteen to parents (Holladay, 1994, p. 133)

NICOTINE

Teen smoking has received a great deal of attention recently, largely due to the settlements from lawsuits that have been brought against tobacco manufacturers. Although prevalence of smoking has decreased with adults, it has not decreased among adolescents (Kassel et al., 2005). Studies vary somewhat in prevalence, but it is estimated that 54% of high school seniors have used tobacco, 24% of high school seniors smoke cigarettes on a regular basis, and 4% of adolescents have chewed smokeless tobacco (Kassel et al., 2005; Moolchan, Ernst, & Henningfield, 2000). Caucasian-American youth are significantly more likely to smoke cigarettes, with African-American youth reporting the lowest rates of smoking cigarettes during adolescence (Scarinci, Robinson, Alfano, Zbikowski, & Klesges,

2002). The prevalence rates of smoking among Hispanic/Latino/Latina youth fall in the middle of these two groups. Whereas the rates of smoking in Caucasian adolescents tend to decrease as they reach adulthood, rates of smoking appear to increase into young adulthood for African-American youth (Blitstein, Robinson, Murray, Klesges, & Zbikowski, 2003; Scarinci et al., 2002). In other words, Caucasian adolescents appear to begin smoking at an earlier age than African-American adolescents, but smoking rates in African-Americans reach and surpass the smoking rates of Caucasians as they reach older adolescence and early adulthood. Across all racial and ethnic groups, it is estimated that 75% of adolescent smokers will continue to smoke as adults (Moolchan et al., 2000).

A number of risk factors are associated with use of tobacco products. Smoking in adolescence is associated with adverse childhood experiences, such as sexual abuse, physical abuse, emotional abuse, domestic violence, parental divorce, having a substance-abusing household member, having a household member with psychiatric problems, having an incarcerated household member, having parents who smoke, having parents who do not show high levels of monitoring behavior, and having a family with low levels of bonding (Anda et al., 1999; Hill, Hawkins, Catalano, Abbott, & Guo, 2005). Youth who live in risky neighborhoods and who have a lack of hope are at risk for smoking as well as marijuana and alcohol use (Wilson, Syme, Boyce, Battistich, & Selvin, 2005). Smoking is also associated with binge drinking (Ramsey et al., 2005). Based on behavioral genetics research, it appears that smoking is related to both genetic and environmental causes (Rende, Slomkowski, McCaffery, Lloyd-Richardson, & Niaura, 2005).

Comorbidity of psychiatric disorders also appears to be a risk factor for smoking cigarettes. Depressive symptoms and emotional distress, in particular, are associated with smoking in adolescence (Orlando, Ellickson, & Jinnett, 2001; Stevens, Colwell, Smith, Robinson, & McMillan, 2005; Windle & Windle, 2001). In a longitudinal study that followed African-American youth from 6th grade to 10th grade, the researchers found that comorbidity between depression and conduct disorder in early adolescence was related strongly to tobacco use in later adolescence (Miller-Johnson et al., 1998). Another study found that depression and anxiety predicted smoking in 14- and 15-year-old adolescents and also made them vulnerable to peers' prosmoking influences (Patton et al., 1998). Smoking is linked to the use of marijuana and alcohol as well (Wilson et al., 2005).

The majority of research on adolescents and nicotine has focused on use of nicotine rather than nicotine dependence. One study, however, did explore adolescents who met criteria for nicotine dependence (Riggs, Mikulich, Whitmore, & Crowley, 1999). Referring back to Table 11.2, recall that nicotine dependence would be evidenced by adolescents who showed a maladaptive pattern of nicotine use (such as smoking) where they either show tolerance (such as needing to smoke more to be as satisfied as before) or showing signs of withdrawal (such as irritability, anger, insomnia, depressed mood, restlessness, difficulty concentrating, decreased heart rate, and increased appetite when not smoking for long periods of time; American Psychiatric Association, 2000). Results from the study on nicotine dependence showed that adolescents who met criteria for nicotine dependence also were highly comorbid for other disorders, such as conduct disorder, attention-deficit/hyperactivity disorder, major depression, and other substance use disorders (Riggs et al., 1999).

Relatively little research has been done on smoking cessation in children and adolescents. There is conflicting evidence about the use of nicotine replacement therapy. One review suggested that nicotine replacement therapy (such as using a nicotine patch or nicotine gum) was potentially problematic and had limited effectiveness with adolescents (Patten, 2000). Another more recent study, however, found that the nicotine patch with or without an antidepressant was effective at reducing the adolescents' smoking behavior (Killen et al., 2004). In that study, adolescents tended not to completely quit smoking but rather decreased smoking so that they were not smoking on a daily basis (Killen et al., 2004).

A number of effective treatment programs have been identified for adults who wish to quit smoking, but very little work has been done to treat children and adolescents who smoke. Studies with adults have suggested that following up smoking cessation programs with direct mailings to the clients can help them remain abstinent from tobacco, especially when the mailings are tailored to the specific situation of the client (Webb, Simmons, & Brandon, 2005). These types of studies could be fruitful with treatment of child and adolescent smokers. Interestingly, parental smoking cessation is associated with decreased risk for adolescent smoking as long as the other parent does not smoke (Chassin, Presson, Rose, Sherman, & Prost, 2002). Thus, smoking cessation programs with adults who are parents may also serve as a preventive intervention for youth smoking.

When compared with treatment, comparatively more work has been done on prevention of smoking in children and adolescents. Attitudes toward smoking and tobacco use are important to understand before instituting prevention programs. One study used videotapes of a child actor to assess attitudes of middle school students toward the use of tobacco (Kury, Rodrigue, & Perri, 1998). Students were shown a videotape and told that this student would be joining the school. The videotape showed the child smoking, using smokeless (chewing) tobacco, or not using any tobacco product. Students were then asked to complete measures that assessed their attitudes toward the peer. This study found that the nonsmoking peer was rated most favorably, followed by the peer who was using smokeless tobacco. The results of this study suggest that, at least in middle school, attitudes toward smokers tend to be less favorable than to nonsmokers (Kury et al., 1998). When prevention programs do not work, it may be because they assume that adolescents begin smoking intentionally rather than the more likely case that adolescents begin smoking because of contextual reasons rather than as a planned activity (Kremers, Mudde, de Vries, Brug, & de Vries, 2004).

Other factors have been effective in reducing the prevalence of smoking by children and adolescents. For example, enforcement of youth access laws to cigarettes has been associated with significant decreases in the rates of youth smoking (Jason, Berk, Schnopp-Wyatt, & Talbot, 1999). Nationwide, the minimum legal age for purchasing cigarettes is 18. Most communities, however, inadvertently allow children and adolescents access to tobacco products. One study found that 70% of stores allowed the sale of tobacco products to minors (Jason et al., 1999). In communities that enforce the laws that limit youth access to cigarettes, youth smoking decreases dramatically. One community that enforced youth access laws was able to show a reduction in smoking by seventh and eighth graders from 16% to 5% (Jason et al., 1999). Overall, communities that show regular enforcement of youth access laws show underage smoking rates that average 8.1%, whereas approximately 15.5% of youth smoke in communities that do not regularly enforce youth access laws (Jason et al., 1999). It appears that the behavior of store clerks is more predictive of tobacco sales to minors than the behavior of the minors when they are trying to purchase cigarettes (Klonoff & Landrine, 2004). Thus, preventive interventions and training with store clerks might be another avenue of decreasing underage smoking. In addition, when prices of cigarettes are increased, smoking decreases in adolescents (Riedel et al., 2002). Conversely, youth can buy cigarettes via the Internet with almost no ramifications and at a cheaper price. One study found that 23 out of 29 (79.3%) confederate minors in the study purchased cigarettes off the Internet, and nearly all the purchases (91%) were provided without asking about the child's age (Jensen, Hickman, Landrine, & Klonoff, 2004). Given that raising prices and making cigarettes less accessible to minors are both strategies that decrease smoking behavior in youth, these studies have important implications for the prevention of smoking.

Words are, of course, the most powerful drug used by [human]kind.

—Rudyard Kipling

SUMMARY AND KEY CONCEPTS

Alcohol Abuse, Alcohol Dependence, Substance Abuse, and Substance Dependence. **Substance abuse** is diagnosed when children or adolescents use a substance (such as alcohol, marijuana, or cocaine) to such an extent that it impairs their functioning in some way. **Substance dependence** is diagnosed when children or adolescents not only abuse a substance but also show either tolerance or withdrawal symptoms. Substance abuse and substance dependence are often referred to collectively as **substance use disorders.** Substance use disorders are relatively common in adolescence and are highly comorbid with other disorders.

Substance use disorders usually begin with less severe substances (such as alcohol or marijuana) and move on to harder substances (such as cocaine or heroin). This process is known as the **gateway phenomenon.** Substance use disorders are thought to have multiple etiologies, with the **dynamic diathesis-stress model** providing an integrative theory of substance use disorders.

A number of treatments have been attempted with substance use disorders in adolescents. Family-based interventions and cognitive–behavioral interventions show the most promise in the treatment of adolescent substance abuse and dependence. Even after effective treatment of a substance use disorder, it is important to try to prevent the reoccurrence of the problem with **relapse prevention** programs. Many universal prevention programs have been instituted to prevent the onset of substance use and abuse.

Alcohol and Substance Use and Abuse Conceptualized in a Dimensional Manner. Unlike many other disorders, substance problems have received extensive attention from a dimensional perspective. A number of risk factors are related to the development of substance problems. A great deal of protective factors also decrease the likelihood of developing substance use problems.

Nicotine.   A significant percentage of children and adolescents have tried cigarettes or smokeless chewing tobacco.

Although treatment programs for smoking cessation are rare for children and adolescents, there are a number of programs to prevent the onset of smoking early in life.

KEY TERMS

substance abuse

substance dependence

substance use disorders

gateway phenomenon

dynamic diathesis-stress model

relapse prevention

behavioral chain

binge drinking

SUGGESTED READINGS

Dobie, Kathy. *The Only Girl in the Car*. New York: Delta Trade Paperbacks, 2003. At the age of 14, the author decided to lose her virginity. After that, many of the boys in town assumed that she was "easy." With beer flowing freely, the author went for a ride with a group of boys who ended up gang raping her. This story describes her struggles with the aftermath of this trauma and describes her ultimate triumph over these difficulties.

LeBlanc, Adrian Nicole. *Random Family: Love, Drugs, Trouble, and Coming of Age in the Bronx*. New York: Simon and Schuster, 2003. This compilation of case studies shows the complications that arise for girls growing up in an impoverished community that has extensive amounts of drugs and alcohol available to them.

SUGGESTED VIEWINGS

Upside of Anger. (2005). An absent father and a mother who abuses alcohol are the central themes in this family drama, which focuses on the resilience of youth even in difficult circumstances.

Ray. (2005). Based on the life of singer-songwriter Ray Charles, this film shows the devastation of alcohol and substance abuse in adulthood and illustrates how these difficulties may be related to adversity in childhood, including visual impairments, bereavement, poverty, and racism.

CHAPTER 12

PERVASIVE DEVELOPMENTAL DISORDERS AND SCHIZOPHRENIA IN CHILDHOOD AND ADOLESCENCE

CHAPTER SUMMARY

PERVASIVE DEVELOPMENTAL DISORDERS

PERVASIVE DEVELOPMENTAL DISORDERS CONCEPTUALIZED IN A DIMENSIONAL MANNER

SCHIZOPHRENIA

SCHIZOPHRENIA CONCEPTUALIZED IN A DIMENSIONAL MANNER

SUMMARY AND KEY CONCEPTS

KEY TERMS

SUGGESTED READINGS

SUGGESTED VIEWINGS

Children have but little charity for one another's defects.
—Mark Twain

This chapter combines two primary areas of concern, pervasive developmental disorders and schizophrenia, both of which are considered severe problems. Although these areas have common issues of severity and limited prognosis for independent living, they are distinctly separate syndromes that should not be confused with one another. For example, in the 1950s and 1960s, there was a great deal of confusion about whether autistic disorder and schizophrenia in childhood were the same disorder or distinctly different disorders (Pennington, 2002). It is now clearly understood that these two disorders are distinctly different, with different treatments and prognoses. Thus, it is important to identify the specific symptoms and characterizations of these disorders. Clinicians are often faced with the challenge of having to use differential diagnoses to tease apart these difficult disorders. These disorders are important for psychiatrists, clinical psychologists, and school psychologists to understand, given that both mental health professionals and professionals within the school system will be likely to encounter children with these severe disorders (Commission on Adolescent Schizophrenia, 2005). In addition, pediatricians are often the first professionals to identify problems in these children. For this reason, clinical practice guidelines have been developed so that pediatricians

and mental health professionals can work cooperatively with children who might be experiencing autism, pervasive developmental disorders, or other difficulties (The Interdisciplinary Council on Developmental and Learning Disorders, 2000).

PERVASIVE DEVELOPMENTAL DISORDERS

Pervasive developmental disorders are all characterized by long-standing and overarching deficits in functioning. Five primary pervasive developmental disorders will be covered in this section (autistic disorder, Asperger's disorder, Rett's disorder, childhood disintegrative disorder, and pervasive developmental disorder not otherwise specified). Many researchers now refer to this constellation of disorders as autistic spectrum disorders (Siegel & Ficcaglia, 2006). Of these five disorders, autistic disorder is probably the best known.

Autistic Disorder

First identified by Leo Kanner in 1943 as early infantile autism (Kanner, 1943), **autistic disorder** is characterized by impairments in social interaction, communication, and stereotyped or atypical behavior (American Psychiatric Association, 2000). As can be seen in

Case Study: Jimmy, a Young Boy Who Was Diagnosed with Autistic Disorder

When Jimmy was 5 years old, his parents took him to an inpatient psychiatric facility to have him evaluated. Jimmy lived with his parents, Mr. and Mrs. Peterson, and his 15-year-old sister. There was no history of psychiatric or psychological problems within the family.

Although Jimmy was 5, he could only use a few words and tended to scream or gesture to get what he wanted. In addition, his parents described him as "impossible to manage," given his high activity level. So far, he was unable to be toilet trained. Jimmy's parents kept thinking that he would outgrow these difficulties, but they finally realized that some type of formal evaluation might help identify Jimmy's problems.

The pregnancy with Jimmy, birth, and his subsequent early years were all considered "normal." Jimmy had not experienced any major medical illness or injuries. Mr. and Mrs. Peterson did, however, note that Jimmy did not like to be held when he was an infant. When he was held, Jimmy would often arch his back and scream until he was put down again. He did not make eye contact as an infant and almost never smiled. By the age of 3, Jimmy still seemed to prefer the company of objects rather than the company of people.

Currently, Jimmy did little else other than run around the house, spin a toy for hours at a time, bang objects incessantly, or rock back and forth in a chair for hours at a time. He only had about 20 words in his vocabulary, and he continued to communicate by making shrill crying noises when he wanted something.

The 3-week evaluation on the inpatient unit confirmed a diagnosis of autistic disorder. Given his impairment in social interactions, impairment in communication skills, and stereotyped patterns of behavior, the diagnosis of autistic disorder appeared to be appropriate.

Jimmy was admitted to the treatment facility for 3 months, with a goal of improving his social interactions, compliance with commands, and behavioral control. Jimmy's parents were also taught behavioral management skills that could help them with Jimmy's behavior once he returned home. A special education school near Jimmy's home was identified as an appropriate educational placement for him, and the special education teacher coordinated with the staff of the treatment facility to maintain the behavioral system that they had instituted.

Based on a 1-year follow-up, there was evidence that Jimmy had improved somewhat in his communication skills and in his social interactions. These improvements, however, did not negate a continued diagnosis of autistic disorder. Jimmy continued to have severe impairments in communication and social interactions. His intensive treatment through the special education school and through his parents' interventions at home were maintained.

Source: Leon (1990).

Table 12.1, autistic disorder is a severe disorder that is evident from very early in a child's life. As should also be evident in the diagnostic criteria, a thorough assessment is needed that includes an evaluation of the child, the family, and the school environment (Ozonoff, Goodlin-Jones, & Solomon, 2005).

Prevalence Rates Although there has been a great deal of attention in the media and in research given to autistic disorder (Gernsbacher, Dawson, & Goldsmith, 2006; Vastag, 2004), it is interesting to note that autistic disorder is quite rare. The prevalence rate is usually estimated at 5 cases per 10,000, which is the equivalent of 0.05% of the population (American Psychiatric Association, 2000). More recent estimates suggest a prevalence rate of 30 to 60 cases per 10,000 (0.3% to 0.6%), but even with these higher numbers, the prevalence of autistic disorder continues to be quite rare (Maughan et al., 2005). This slight increase in cases appears to be due to better detection and evaluation methods in combination with a greater awareness of the disorder in the lay public (Gernsbacher, Dawson,

& Goldsmith, 2005). In contrast to popular media accounts, there is no epidemic of autism (Gernsbacher et al., 2006).

Although some parents do not begin to suspect problems until children reach the age of 3 or 4, it is thought that children are born with autistic disorder and that more subtle signs of autism can be identified as young as in infancy (Klinger, Dawson, & Renner, 2003; Zwaigenbaum et al., 2005). Autism is much more common in boys than in girls, with most estimates suggesting a 4:1 ratio of boys to girls (American Psychiatric Association, 2000; Yeargin-Allsopp et al., 2003). Girls with autistic disorder are thought to show even more severe impairments in intellectual functioning than boys with the disorder, with higher rates of mental retardation in girls with autism than boys with autism (American Psychiatric Association, 2000). There are no known patterns of autistic disorder with regard to SES or race/ethnicity. In fact, autism has been identified in every socioeconomic status group and in nearly every race/ethnicity (Yeargin-Allsopp et al., 2003). Box 12.1 on page 343 explains how autism is an equal-opportunity disorder.

TABLE 12.1 DSM-IV Diagnostic Criteria for Autistic Disorder

A.	A total of six (or more) items from (1), (2), and (3), with at least two from (1), and one each from (2) and (3):

(1) qualitative impairment in social interaction, as manifested by at least two of the following:

    (a) marked impairment in the use of multiple nonverbal behaviors such as eye-to-eye gaze, facial expression, body postures, and gestures to regulate social interaction

    (b) failure to develop peer relationships appropriate to developmental level

    (c) a lack of spontaneous seeking to share enjoyment, interests, or achievements with other people (e.g., by a lack of showing, bringing, or pointing out objects of interest)

    (d) lack of social or emotional reciprocity

(2) qualitative impairments in communication as manifested by at least one of the following:

    (a) delay in, or total lack of, the development of spoken language (not accompanied by an attempt to compensate through alternative modes of communication such as gesture or mime)

    (b) in individuals with adequate speech, marked impairment in the ability to initiate or sustain a conversation with others

    (c) stereotyped and repetitive use of language or idiosyncratic language

    (d) lack of varied, spontaneous make-believe play or social imitative play appropriate to developmental level

(3) restricted repetitive and stereotyped patterns of behavior, interests, and activities, as manifested by at least one of the following:

    (a) encompassing preoccupation with one or more stereotyped and restricted patterns of interest that is abnormal either in intensity or focus

    (b) apparently inflexible adherence to specific, nonfunctional routines or rituals

    (c) stereotyped and repetitive motor mannerisms (e.g., hand or finger flapping or twisting, or complex whole-body movements)

    (d) persistent preoccupation with parts of objects

B.	Delays or abnormal functioning in at least one of the following areas, with onset prior to age 3 years: (1) social interaction, (2) language as used in social communication, or (3) symbolic or imaginative play.
C.	The disturbance is not better accounted for by Rett's Disorder or Childhood Disintegrative Disorder.

Source: American Psychiatric Association (2000).
Reprinted with permission from the *Diagnostic and Statistical Manual of Mental Disorders, Fourth Edition, Text Revision.* Copyright 2000 American Psychiatric Association.

Cross-cultural studies have also shown that symptoms of autism and prevalence rates of autism are consistent across Western and Eastern cultures (Durham, 2000; Fombonne, 2003; Klinger et al., 2003; Micheli, 2000).

There has been a great deal of media attention given to children with a unique aspect of autistic disorder that has been referred to as **autistic savant.** Children identified as autistic savant are diagnosed with autistic disorder, but also show a unique set of skills that are often beyond imagination (McMahon, 2002; Rimland, 2003). Known as **splinter skills,** these unique abilities are often not even present in the most intellectually gifted nonautistic individuals. Some of these skills include the ability to perform complex mathematical problems quickly and with perfect accuracy, being able to identify the day of the week that a particular date landed on within the past 200 years, being able to count objects within a rapid amount of time, or being able to recreate a musical composition after only hearing the music once (Klin & Volkmar, 1997; McMahon, 2002; Rimland, 2003). These fascinating splinter skills are not well understood, especially given that many of the individuals with these skills test within the mentally retarded range on traditional intelligence tests. Although there has been a great fascination with individuals who are autistic savant, they represent only about 5% of all individuals diagnosed with autistic disorder (Klin & Volkmar, 1997). Thus, the overwhelming majority of individuals with autistic disorder do not show evidence of any extraordinary skills. Prevalence rates are summarized in Table 12.2.

Comorbidity. The most common comorbid disorder that co-occurs with autistic disorder is mental retardation. Although it is difficult to get an accurate IQ on children with autism, the majority of autistic individuals (with estimates as high as 75%) also meet criteria for mental retardation (American Psychiatric Association,

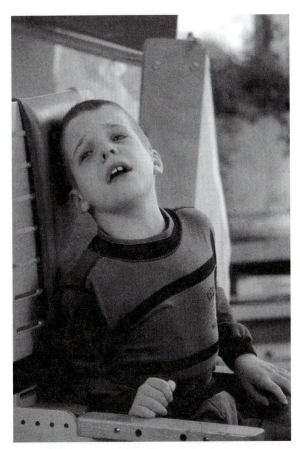

Autistic disorder is a serious disorder that is associated with severe impairments in many, but not all, diagnosed children and adolescents.

TABLE 12.2 **Overview of Prevalence Information for Autistic Disorder**

Prevalence	< 1% (30–60 cases per 10,000 or .3% to .6%)
Age	Usually identified in early toddlerhood or in preschool
Gender	Males > Females (4:1 Ratio Males to Females)
SES	No known patterns
Race/Ethnicity	No known patterns

2000; Morgan, Campbell, & Jackson, 2003). Their IQs usually fall in the moderate range of retardation, with a common range of 35 to 50. IQ appears to increase with age in samples of younger versus older children diagnosed with autism (Mayes & Calhoun, 2003). This pattern, however, may be due to children with higher intellectual functioning not being detected and diagnosed with autism until later in childhood rather than in early childhood (Mayes & Calhoun, 2003). Other developmental and congenital disorders are also more prevalent in children with autism than other samples of children, including cerebral palsy and tuberous sclerosis (Fombonne, 2003). Note that nearly half of children diagnosed with autistic disorder are nonverbal (i.e., mute), and the remaining children show language deficits such as **echolalia** (i.e., repeating what is said to them) or show severely limited language abilities (Foxx, Schreck, Garito, Smith, & Weisenberger, 2004).

There are other associated features to autistic disorder, such as hyperactivity, aggression, self-injurious behavior, mood problems, and compulsive type behaviors, but these features are thought to be part of the associated sequelae to the disorder rather than representing distinctly different comorbid disorders (American Psychiatric Association, 2000; Gadow, Devincent, Pomeroy, & Azizian, 2005). One study did find higher rates of ADHD in a sample of children with autism, and they argued that the ADHD symptoms were distinctive from the symptoms of autism and thus should be considered a comorbid disorder (Goldstein & Schwebach, 2004). Disruptive behaviors in boys with autism were found to be associated with attempts to curtail their repetitive behaviors or to prevent access to an object that was used in repetitive rituals, or to try to get away from sensory stimulation that was unwelcome, such as the noise of a vacuum cleaner or a toilet flushing (Reese, Richman, Belmont, & Morse, 2005).

Depression and anxiety disorders are common in children with autism, especially those who are higher functioning and who can verbalize these concerns (Ozonoff et al., 2005). One study of fears found that children with autism showed higher rates of situational phobias and fears related to medical procedures in contrast to children with Down syndrome and children with comparable mental ages or chronological ages (Evans, Canavera, Kleinpeter, Maccubbin, & Taga, 2005). In general, children with autism and other pervasive developmental disorders appear to have heightened rates of psychopathology just like other clinical samples of youth (Gadow et al., 2005). Unfortunately, evidence-based assessment techniques for other psychiatric and psychological problems have not been well normed with children with autism, so care must be taken in trying to diagnose other disorders in children with autism.

To take care of Noah for twenty minutes is to know how radically ill he is.

—Josh Greenfeld about his son who is autistic

YOU DECIDE: ARE AUTISTIC DISORDER AND ASPERGER'S DISORDER DISTINCTLY DIFFERENT DISORDERS?

Yes

- Children diagnosed with autistic disorder show different patterns of functioning than children diagnosed with Asperger's disorder. Autistic children show more severe behavioral problems and more repetitive behavior movement problems than do children with Asperger's disorder (Starr et al., 2003).
- Children diagnosed with autistic disorder show higher rates of comorbidity than do children diagnosed with Asperger's disorder, with Asperger's disordered children showing higher rates of oppositional defiant disorder than children with autistic disorder (Gadow et al., 2004).

No

- A review of the characteristics of children diagnosed with autism and children diagnosed with Asperger's disorder does not show any significant differences in functioning between the two groups of children (Macintosh & Dissanayake, 2004).
- Parents, clinicians, and some researchers have argued that Asperger's does not capture the true essence of children with problems and think that Asperger's disorder is really just reflective of high-functioning autism (Mayes & Calhoun, 2004; Szatmari, 2000).

So, are autistic disorder and Asperger's disorder distinctly different disorders? You decide.

Course of the Disorder. It is commonly thought that children are born with autism, rather than developing it at the time the symptoms become more evident. One interesting study of videotapes of children's 1-year-old birthday parties found that subtle differences can even be seen at that early age (Osterling, Dawson, & Munson, 2002). Videotapes for first-year birthday parties were compared for children who were later diagnosed with autistic disorder, children who were later diagnosed with mental retardation (without autism), and typically developing children. Research assistants who did not know the later status of the children rated the videotapes on a number of dimensions. Results showed that children who were later diagnosed with autism were less likely to look at other children or adults at the birthday celebration and were less likely to respond to their name in comparison with children who were typically developing or those who later were diagnosed with mental retardation (Osterling et al., 2002). Compared with typically developing children, children later diagnosed with autism and children later diagnosed with mental retardation were more likely to show repetitive behaviors and were less likely to use nonverbal gestures to convey their wishes (Osterling et al., 2002). Overall, this study suggests that there are subtle signs as early as 1 year old that distinguish children with autism from typically developing children.

By the age of 2, there are a number of "red flags" in toddlers that have been associated with eventual identification of autism or autistic-like disorders. These red flags include impaired social interactions (such as inappropriate gaze, lack of warm expression with

gaze, lack of response to own name), unconventional gestures (such as lack of pointing and lack of showing another individual something), unconventional sounds and words (such as limited use of consonants), repetitive behaviors and restricted interests (such as hand flapping, repeatedly moving objects in the same pattern, playing with only one toy), and emotional regulation (such as being difficult to calm when distressed; Wehterby, Woods, Allen, Cleary, Dickinson, & Lord, 2004). These characteristics differentiated children under the age of 2 who went on to be diagnosed with autism or another pervasive developmental disorder from developmentally delayed children and from children showing typical development (Wehterby et al., 2004).

Longitudinal research, and careful research at different developmental levels, has identified characteristics of autism throughout the life span. Although some of these symptoms can be decreased or alleviated by intensive behavioral therapy, the typical developmental course of autism is as follows (Capps, Losh, & Thurber, 2000; Dyck, Piek, Hay, Smith, & Hallmayer, 2006; Gross, 2004; Seltzer, Shattuck, Abbeduto, & Greenberg, 2004; Spector & Volkmar, 2006):

- Infants with autism appear to be limited in their social responsiveness (such as avoiding eye-to-eye contact and not seeking out social interactions with caregivers), tend to focus on idiosyncratic pieces of objects (e.g., only looking at the hand of a teddy bear and never exploring the rest of the teddy bear), and often show extreme distress when any routines are changed.

BOX *12.1*

AUTISM IS AN EQUAL OPPORTUNITY DISORDER

Although some disorders differ in prevalence based on race/ethnicity, autism is consistently found to have comparable rates across all races and ethnicities. For example, in a study of the prevalence of autism in the city of Atlanta, Georgia, 3.4% of Caucasian children were found to meet criteria for autistic disorder, and 3.4% of African-American children met criteria for autistic disorder (Yeargin-Allsopp et al., 2003). In addition, children from immigrant families are no more likely to meet criteria for autsim than are children from native-born families (Fombonne, 2003). Overall, there is no evidence of differential rates of autism based on race/ethnicity or immigrant status.

- Toddlers with autism show significant delays and deficits in verbal language. These delays are often the first signs that "something is wrong," which often motivates parents to seek a formal evaluation of their child. Approximately 90% of parents of children who are ultimately diagnosed with autism reported some type of significant abnormality in their child by the age of 2 (Volkmar, Chawarska, & Klin, 2005).

- Children with autism continue to show significant deficits in social interactions and may also appear to display poor coordination and gross motor movements. It is not uncommon for children with autism to show nonfunctioning routines and rituals (such as touching all the shiny objects within one room) and stereotyped movements (such as hand flapping, rocking, and spinning). If redirected from these behaviors or if forbidden from engaging in these behaviors, children with autism often become very distressed and frustrated. Children with autism are often not able to detect facial features and emotions that others are feeling.

- Puberty may be somewhat delayed for individuals with autism. Other features (e.g., social deficits, limited language abilities, stereotyped behaviors) usually continue through adolescence and into adulthood. There is a trend for some of the symptoms of autism to decrease somewhat in adolescence and into adulthood. For autistic individuals who are somewhat verbal, their language tends to focus on concrete objects rather than abstract conceptualizations (e.g., reporting what others ate at lunch rather than joining in on a discussion about a television show).

Unless intensive therapeutic interventions are completed, most of these deficits continue into adulthood. Adults with autism are rarely able to live independently, but rather most often live with family members or in group homes and other structured and protected environments (Seltzer et al., 2004). In some longitudinal studies, most children with autism (85%–90%) grow up to be adults who continue to have significant deficits in language and intellectual functioning, which necessitates some type of sheltered living arrangement (Seltzer et al., 2004). Another long-term follow-up study of children with autism who were followed into adulthood found that 78% of the sample showed a poor outcome in adulthood (Billstedt, Gillberg, & Gillberg, 2005). Only 4 out of the 120 participants (3.3%) lived independently, and their lives were quite isolated.

There is a subset of individuals with autism (approximately 15%) who show significant improvements of their symptoms and who show less impairment in adulthood (Seltzer et al., 2004). The large majority of adults with autism continue to show deficits in social interactions. Over half of the adults with autism in one study did not have any friend or acquaintance (Howlin et al., 2004). Although better outcomes are expected for individuals with an IQ above 50 and with language skills that developed by the age of 5, the overwhelming majority of children with autism will continue to show signs of autism throughout their lives (American Psychiatric Association, 2000; Billstedt et al., 2005).

Etiology. The early theoretical work on autism is replete with blaming parents, and especially mothers, for the development of autism. Parents were thought to be "refrigerator" parents who showed emotional distance and coldness toward their child, which led to the development of autism (Kanner, 1943). These parent-blaming theories have never been supported by empirical evidence and are handily dismissed in current discussions of the etiology of autism (Hooley, 2004; Simpson, 2004). More recently, there has been interest in the **theory of mind,** which suggests that children with autism do not develop appropriate cognitive functioning and cannot conceptualize mental representations of individuals in a way that allows them to predict others' behavior (Josehph & Tager-Flusberg, 2004). Although this

---

Case Study: The Mother of a Child Diagnosed with Autism (in Her Own Words)

Asher was seen twice before my husband and I got the diagnosis. It took every ounce of courage I could muster to go that day. The therapist delivered the original diagnosis of "pervasive developmental disorder with autistic tendencies." The first words out of his mouth are forever etched in my psyche: "I want you to know that nothing you could possibly have done could cause your son to do the things he does." I will always be grateful to him for these words. Here we were, hearing one

of the most difficult diagnoses, and both my husband and I remember our most prominent emotion on that day was relief. We were not crazy. We had not irreparably damaged our son. There was a professional who understood his behavior and was willing to support our family through the harrowing days ahead. Our thanks go out to him. (p. 31)

Source: Marsh (1995).

---

hypothesis is intriguing, there has been limited evidence to support the theory of mind (Klinger et al., 2003; Wellman, Cross, & Watson, 2001).

The most overwhelming evidence currently suggests that autism is due to some type of organic deficit (Morgan et al., 2003; Rutter, 2005; Wassink, Brzustowicz, Bartlett, & Szatmari, 2004). The exact nature of those organic deficits, however, remains unclear. There is some evidence that autism is already established in a fetus by the point of 30 to 32 weeks of gestation (Beversdorf et al., 2005). In studies of prenatal stressors, mothers of children with autism reported greater levels of stressors from 25 to 28 weeks of gestation compared with mothers of children with Down syndrome or mothers of children without any known disorders (Beversdorf et al., 2005). The timing of these prenatal stressors is consistent with the gestational period for brain development that is found to be abnormal in children with autism. As mentioned in chapter 1, there is also promising new evidence that mirror neurons, which fire similarly whether children are conducting a behavior or they are observing someone conduct the behavior, may help explain the lack of empathy in children with autism (Dingfelder, 2005).

There is also evidence of a genetic component in autism, given that there are high concordance rates for monozygotic twins who have autism (Ho, Todd, & Constantino, 2005). Even in subthreshold levels of autistic behaviors, there is evidence of genetic influences, but the connection is not large (Ronald, Happe, & Plomin, 2005). There is some evidence to suggest a slightly higher risk for autism in individuals with chromosomal abnormalities. Specifically, children with a chromosomal abnormality known as 22q11.2 deletion are at an increased risk for a number of different disorders, including autism (Fine et al., 2005). Unlike other disorders, like Down syndrome, where there is a direct link between the chromosomal abnormality and

the disorder, the 22q11.2 deletion only appears to put some children at risk for autism whereas most children with the chromosomal abnormality do not develop autism (Niklasson, Rasmussen, Oskarsdottir, & Gillberg, 2002; Oskarsdottie, Belfrage, Sandstedt, Viggedal, & Uvebrant, 2005; Yagi et al., 2003).

There is also evidence of some underlying problems in neurochemical, neuroanatomical, and other central nervous system functions (Hendren, DeBacker, & Pandina, 2000; Nicolson & Szatmari, 2003; Wassink et al., 2004). These deficits most often seem to occur during the prenatal period (Eigsti & Shapiro, 2003). To date, there is still a great deal of confusion about what actually causes autism. Although research on etiology appears to point to organic deficits, more research is needed before identifying what specific organic deficits put children at risk for autistic disorder.

For the purposes of treatment, however, a clearly established etiology may not be crucial. Even without a clear understanding of etiology, it appears possible to treat the symptoms of autism. In order to use behavioral therapies, the focus should be on the antecedents and consequences to specific behaviors rather than trying to find the overall etiology of the development of autism (Lovaas & Smith, 2003).

Treatment. Nearly all the effective treatments for the symptoms of autism have been behavioral in nature. Behavioral interventions have been used to increase the use of appropriate language, increase social skills, increase social connections, increase attention, decrease aggression, decrease self-injurious behavior, and decrease hyperactivity (Simpson, 2001, 2004; Yoder & Stone, 2006). The Treatment and Education of Autistic and Related Communication Handicapped Children (TEACCH) program is a well-known and effective behavioral teaching system for working with autistic children, which has been used in the United States as well as countries such as France, Sweden, Italy, and Israel (Durham, 2000; Durnik et al., 2000; Erba, 2003; Micheli, 2000; Shulman, 2000; Siegel, 2004). The TEACCH program has also been used effectively with adults with autism, although improvements were related to decreased behavioral problems rather than increased skills (VanBourgondien, Reichle, & Schopler, 2003). As can be seen in Box 12.2, behavioral therapies for autistic disorder are extremely time intensive and extremely involved. Based on years of research, these behavior therapies can help alleviate a great many deficits in children with autism (Wolery, Barton, & Hine, 2005).

Regarding other treatment strategies, antipsychotic medication (such as haloperidol/Haldol) has been used to control severe aggressive behavior with children with autism (DuPaul et al., 2003; Tanguay, 2000). Risperidone (Risperdal) has been used increasingly with children diagnosed with autism or other pervasive developmental disorders (Masi, Cosenza, Mucci, & Brovedani, 2003). Risperidone significantly decreased the symptoms of autism, but the children were still severely impaired (Masi et al., 2003). Note also that Risperidone is an antipsychotic medication, so signs of adverse reactions are important to monitor (Brown et al., 2005; Phelps et al., 2002). Selective serotonin reuptake inhibitor (SSRI) medication, which is a type of antidepressant, has been found to be effective in decreasing aggression and hyperactivity in children diagnosed with autism (Tanguay, 2000). These medications have not been validated in double-blind clinical trials for the treatment of autism, and there are concerns about their use given the potential for increased suicidality in youth (Phelps et al., 2002). There is some evidence that the combination of behavioral treatments and antipsychotic medication is far superior to the use of medication alone in controlling severe aggression in children with autism (Brown et al., 2005; Phelps et al., 2002). There have been no effective medications, however, for increasing social interactions or language abilities in children with autism (DuPaul et al., 2003). Use of medication increases as youth with autism grow into adulthood, but there are limited studies of the effectiveness of the medication (Seltzer et al., 2004). Overall, the most promising treatments for autism are the intensive behavioral therapies that have shown effective results with a subset of children with autism. Although not every child with autism can be helped with evidence-based treatments, there are new techniques to try to match children's characteristics with the treatment that will be most effective for them (Sherer & Schreibman, 2005).

As noted in the research methods chapter, the concept of facilitated communication (where a facilitator "helps" autistic children convey their inner thoughts and feelings through typing on a keyboard) has been shown to be completely inappropriate (Jacobson, Foxx, & Mulick, 2005; Romanczyk, Arnstein, Soorya, & Gillis, 2003). In reviews of all of the empirical research on facilitated communication, the overwhelming conclusion has been that facilitators, and not autistic individuals, were conveying the messages on the keyboards (Jacobson et al., 2005; Rimland, 1994). Although there were initial hopes that facilitated communication was a way to "unlock" the mysteries of autism, facilitated communication is completely useless in trying to communicate with children and adults with autism. There are a number of other treatments that are popular but appear to be ineffective. For example, sensory integration therapy, where there is an attempt to improve the functioning of the vestibular system (inner-ear structure), the tactile sensory system (touch), and the proprioceptive system (muscles and joints), has not received any empirical support (Romanczyk et al., 2003). Another popular and expensive treatment, dolphin-assisted therapy, where children with autism are immersed in the world of dolphins has not been shown to be effective by objective researchers (Romanczyk et al., 2003). Although the operators of dolphin-assisted therapy sites claim a 97% success rate, no formal independent studies have been completed to assess the effectiveness of this time-consuming and expensive treatment (Romanczyk et al., 2003). Other treatments, such as diet therapies and vitamin B treatments, are also not shown to be effective (Romanczyk et al., 2003). Overall, the majority of effective treatments for autism are of a behavioral nature, but even the best behavioral treatments cannot help every child with this debilitating disorder (Lovaas & Smith, 2003).

Prevention. Given that the actual etiology of autistic disorder is so poorly understood, it has been virtually impossible to identify prevention strategies related to autism. There has been a great deal of media attention to the possibility that certain vaccinations, such as measles-mumps-rubella (MMR) vaccinations, are responsible for the onset of autism in children (Harvey, 2003). Given that there has been a slight rise in the incidence of autism in the United States that has been associated with the use of these vaccinations, many parents and professionals have expressed concern about a causal link (Thrower, 2004). In fact, there have been a great number of lawsuits especially in the United Kingdom related to the link between MMR vaccinations and autism (Elphinstone, 2004).

BOX *12.2*

INTENSIVE BEHAVIORAL THERAPY FOR AUTISM

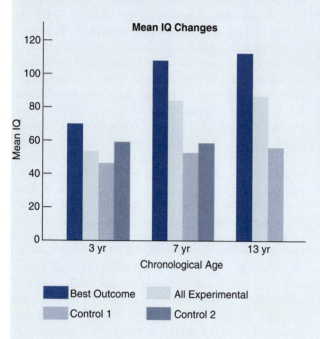

FIGURE 12.1 Measured intelligence of children in the Experimental and Control Groups in the UCLA early intervention studies. The black bars represent all Experimental Group children combined; the white bars represent the subset of the Experimental Group with the best outcomes. The two types of gray bars represent the Control Groups. Control Group 2 was lost to follow-up after the assessment of 7-year-olds.

Source: Newsom (1998). The data are from Lovaas (1987) and McEachlin, Smith, and Lovaas (1993).

One of the most promising findings to come out of research on the treatment of autistic disorder is the work by Ivar Lovaas and his colleagues at the University of California, Los Angeles (Lovaas, 1987; Lovaas & Smith, 2003; McEachlin, Smith, & Lovaas, 1993). Based on over 35 years of research, Dr. Lovaas and his research group have established an intensive treatment program that utilizes behavioral strategies to treat the symptoms of autism. Although there are slight variations in the treatment strategies, some of the common characteristics of these treatments are

- Intensive one-on-one behavioral therapy for more than 40 hours per week for over 2 years.
- Therapeutic interventions are most often delivered by college students, though parents are also trained in the behavioral methods.
- Operant teaching techniques (such as rewarding successive approximations toward the goal of making eye contact with the therapist) are used.
- Some use of punishment techniques are used to decrease severe aversive behaviors (e.g., bitter lemon juice is squirted in the child's mouth when he bites his hand).

- Behaviors that are targeted include social skills/social interactions, language skills, cognitive functioning, and self-care skills.
- Treatment is usually completed in the child's home, in order to maximize generalizability of the effects of treatment. As treatment gains are made, treatment is then moved to other settings (such as the preschool or school setting) to address generalizability issues even more.

Many studies have assessed the effectiveness of these treatment strategies (reviewed in Lovaas & Smith, 2003). Overall, approximately half of the children who received this intensive treatment have shown significant gains, whereas children in control groups have shown almost no significant gains. For example, children who received treatment had an average increase in IQ of 25 to 30 points compared to children in the control groups (Lovaas, 1987). Nearly half of the children who received treatment were able to attend regular education classrooms all the way through high school, whereas none of the children in the control groups were able to attend regular education classrooms (McEachlin et al., 1993). As can be seen in Figure 12.1, children in the experimental conditions showed vast improvements over a number of years, especially for those children identified as showing the best outcomes.

The remarkable results for some of these children continued into adulthood. At follow-up in young adulthood, many of the successfully treated young adults cannot be distinguished from other young adults who did not have a history of autism. Using the same treatment methods, other research groups have found comparable results (Newsom, 1998). Overall, this treatment modality appears to be very promising for at least a subset of children diagnosed with autistic disorder. Better results have been found for children who received treatment earlier and who had somewhat higher functioning before beginning treatment (Lovaas & Smith, 2003; Rogers, 1998). Further research is needed to establish why some children respond so remarkably to the treatment and why some do not. In addition, the practicality of the treatments (e.g., both in time and effort) must be considered in relation to the effects of the treatment. Overall, however, these behavioral treatment methods are the most promising treatments for autistic disorder that have been identified.

A number of reviews of this research literature shows that there is no link between MMR vaccinations and autism (Murch, 2003, 2004; Steffenburg, Steffenburg, & Gillberg, 2003). Nearly all the lawsuits in the United Kingdom have also been unsuccessful in showing a causal role between MMR vaccinations and the development of autism (Elphinstone, 2004). One study was able to look at a quasi-experimental test of these connections. Given that the initial concern for a link between MMR and autism was developed partly because of the slight rise in autism and the increased use of MMR vaccinations, it was an interesting coincidence that an area in Yokohama, Japan, allowed for a test of these connections. Specifically, in the Kohoku Ward, which has approximately 300,000 residents, MMR vaccines were given for a period of time but then were not given in 1993 and in later years (Honda, Shimizu, & Rutter, 2005). If there was a link between MMR and autism, then one would expect that the rates of autism would have been high in the years after the vaccinations were given but that the rates would have tapered off when the children born in 1993 and after grew to early childhood and middle childhood when autism would have been clearly evident if it existed. In fact, the opposite was true. Like the United States and the U.K., rates of autism increased steadily over these periods of time and continued to increase even after children without MMR vaccines were old enough to attend school (Honda et al., 2005). This study provides further epidemiological evidence that the MMR vaccine is not associated with an increased risk for autism. Rather, there is evidence that the rates of autism appear to be increasing slightly (although still staying below 1% prevalence rate) because there are better evaluation and diagnostic techniques through which to identify autism, so the apparent raise in prevalence rates may be an artifact of better evaluation procedures (Gernsbacher et al., 2005, 2006; Murch, 2003, 2004).

Stopping vaccinations will likely have no impact on the prevalence of autism (and would likely be associated with more physical illness in children because they would not be immunized from mumps, measles, or rubella). Thus, the best hope for prevention of the devastating effects of autism is in early identification and intensive treatment at an early age (Erba, 2003; Lovaas & Smith, 2003). Until the mechanisms of the disorder are better understood, true prevention programs will probably be impossible to develop. Early identification and early intensive intervention, however, provide hope for preventing the severe complications and limited prognosis for children with autism (Lovaas & Smith, 2003). Thus, conducting thorough assessments of very young children who are showing some of the "red flags" delineated earlier in this chapter may help identify children in need of early intensive intervention services (Wehterby et al., 2004).

Human kind cannot bear very much reality.

—T. S. Eliot

Asperger's Disorder

Like autistic disorder, Asperger's disorder is also considered a pervasive developmental disorder. **Asperger's disorder** is comparable to autistic disorder, but without the severe language deficits. It appeared as a formal diagnosis for the first time in *DSM-IV* (American Psychiatric Association, 1994). As can be seen in Table 12.3, Asperger's disorder is a chronic disorder that affects many facets of a child's life. See also the "You Decide" section to reflect on the separateness and overlapping qualities of Asperger's disorder with autistic disorder.

First identified in the 1940s by a psychiatrist in Austria named Hans Asperger, the early descriptions of these children were very comparable to descriptions of children with autistic disorder (reviewed in Klinger et al., 2003). Later, Asperger's cases were reviewed with more current cases that did not fully meet criteria for autistic disorder, and the following differences were noted (Wing, 1981) and have been noted more recently (Starr, Szatmari, Bryson, & Zwaigenbaum, 2003):

TABLE 12.3 DSM-IV Diagnostic Criteria for Asperger's Disorder

A. Qualitative impairment in social interaction, as manifested by at least two of the following:

(1) marked impairment in the use of multiple nonverbal behaviors such as eye-to-eye gaze, facial expression, body postures, and gestures to regulate social interaction

(2) failure to develop peer relationships appropriate to developmental level

(3) a lack of spontaneous seeking to share enjoyment, interests, or achievements with other people (e.g., by a lack of showing, bringing, or pointing out objects of interest to other people)

(4) lack of social or emotional reciprocity

B. Restricted repetitive and stereotyped patterns of behavior, interests, and activities, as manifested by at least one of the following:

(1) encompassing preoccupation with one or more stereotyped and restricted patterns of interest that is abnormal either in intensity or focus

(2) apparently inflexible adherence to specific, nonfunctional routines or rituals

(3) stereotyped and repetitive motor mannerisms (e.g., hand or finger flapping or twisting, or complex whole-body movements)

(4) persistent preoccupation with parts of objects

C. The disturbance causes clinically significant impairment in social, occupational, or other important areas of functioning.

D. There is no clinically significant general delay in language (e.g., single words used by age 2 years, communicative phrases used by age 3 years).

E. There is no clinically significant delay in cognitive development or in the development of age-appropriate self-help skills, adaptive behavior (other than in social interaction), and curiosity about the environment in childhood.

F. Criteria are not met for another specific Pervasive Developmental Disorder or Schizophrenia.

Source: American Psychiatric Association (2000). Reprinted with permission from the *Diagnostic and Statistical Manual of Mental Disorders, Fourth Edition, Text Revision*. Copyright 2000 American Psychiatric Association.

- Intellectual functioning appears to be average or above average in children with Asperger's disorder, whereas children with autistic disorder tend to show significantly impaired intellectual functioning.

- Language development tends not to be delayed in children with Asperger's disorder, but use of language can still be somewhat idiosyncratic or unusual. For example, children with Asperger's disorder may be able to carry on a conversation, but they might not make adjustments for the social context of these conversations (e.g., they might talk to a 2-year old the same way they talk with an adult).

- The physical gait and motor skills of children with Asperger's disorder tend to be limited and can be described as clumsy, whereas the physical abilities of children with autistic disorder tend not to be problematic.

- Social interactions of children with Asperger's disorder tend to be limited (e.g., these children may be seen as peculiar or naive in their social interactions), but not as severely limited as children diagnosed with autistic disorder. Many children with

Asperger's disorder seem to desire social interactions, but lack the skills with which to engage in smooth social interactions. Children with autistic disorder, on the other hand, rarely have any desire for seeking out social interactions.

Overall, Asperger's disorder is less severe than autism. There are many similarities in the clinical presentation but there are also consistent differences. For example, in a prospective study of children diagnosed with autism or Asperger's disorder, children with autism showed more severe behavioral problems and repetitive movement activities (such as hand flapping or rocking) than did children with Asperger's disorder (Starr et al., 2003). Like children with Asperger's disorder, children with autism showed increased communication and socialization skills, but the differences in the groups were still evident with children in the autistic group showing consistently more problems in all domains (Starr et al., 2003).

Given the similar trajectories between these two disorders, some researchers have questioned whether Asperger's disorder and autistic disorder are really two separate and distinct disorders or whether Asperger's

Impaired social interactions are a cornerstone of Asperger's disorder.

disorder is merely a reflection of children with autistic disorder who are high functioning (Ghaziuddin, 2005; Mayes & Calhoun, 2004). In addition, the criterion that no significant delay in language be present has been criticized (Fitzgerald, 1999) as has the distinction between cognitive functioning in autistic disorder versus Asperger's disorder (Mayes & Calhoun, 2004). Some researchers have even questioned the actual existence of Asperger's disorder (Mayes, Calhoun, & Crites, 2001; Mayes & Calhoun, 2004). For example, based on a thorough literature review, one set of researchers concluded that "there is currently insufficient evidence to establish the validity of Asperger's disorder as a syndrome distinct from high-functioning autism" (Macintosh & Dissanayake, 2004, p. 421). Others have criticized the entire conceptualization of pervasive developmental disorders like autistic disorder and Asperger's disorder because they do not reflect the "true" nature of the experiences of children (Szatmari, 2000).

Because Asperger's disorder only first appeared as a formal diagnosis in 1994 with the publication of *DSM-IV* (American Psychiatric Association, 1994), there has not been extensive research on the disorder. Asperger's disorder is thought to be a rare disorder (with less than 1% of the population showing the disorder). There is conflicting evidence, however, as to whether Asperger's disorder or autistic disorder is more prevalent. For example, some researchers have suggested that Asperger's disorder is more prevalent than autistic disorder, with estimates that Asperger's disorder is three to five times as common as autistic disorder (Treffert, 1999). A number of other more recent studies have suggested that Asperger's disorder is similar to or less

prevalent than autistic disorder with estimates ranging from a low of 0.025% to a high of .5% (Fombonne, 2003; Ozonoff, Dawson, & McPartland, 2002). The bottom line is that prevalence rates are still woefully unknown for Asperger's disorder and more research is needed on this interesting disorder (Fombonne, 2003). Suffice it to say that both autism and Asperger's disorder continue to show prevalence rates of less than 1% of the population, thus they both continue to be rare disorders (Fombonne, 2003). Like autistic disorder, Asperger's disorder is much more common in boys than in girls (Fombonne, 2003; Ozonoff et al., 2002; Wing, 1981).

Comorbidity rates have also not been well established for Asperger's disorder. By diagnostic definition, Asperger's disorder is not comorbid with mental retardation because cognitive functioning should be within the normal range or higher. It is not clear if children with Asperger's disorder are at risk for other psychiatric disorders. One study of preschoolers found that both teachers and parents rated children with Asperger's disorder as having significantly more oppositional behavior problems than children with autism (Gadow, DeVincent, Pomeroy, & Azizian, 2004). Another study, in a community-based mental health facility, showed that children with Asperger's disorder and other autism-like disorders were likely to be referred for problems in social interactions and for "strange" behavior but were less likely than other children to be referred for drug use, truancy, or running away (Mandell, Walrath, Manteuffel, Sgro, & Pint-Martin, 2005).

There is some evidence that symptoms of Asperger's disorder are consistent with symptoms of nonverbal learning disorders (Rourke & Tsatsanis, 2000). One study of 100 boys with Asperger's disorder found that 51% met criteria for a nonverbal learning disorder (Cederlund & Gillberg, 2004). Children with Asperger's disorder often need specialized attention in the school setting given their unique way of interacting with others and their different way of learning (Griswold, Barnhill, Myles, Hagiwara, & Simpson, 2002; Myles & Simpson, 2002).

Like autistic disorder, Asperger's disorder is thought to be a lifelong and pervasive problem. Asperger's disorder is thought to exist from birth, but early diagnosis is difficult given that the symptoms are not striking at early ages and given that there is a wide variability in social interactions and repetitive behaviors that occur in early childhood (McConachie, LeCouteur, & Honey, 2005). Given that Asperger's disorder is less severe than autistic disorder, however, the prognosis is less bleak than with autistic disorder. Although individuals with Asperger's disorder often continue to show deficits in social interactions and other functioning throughout their lives, they can often live independently and lead productive lives (Ozonoff et al., 2002).

The etiology of Asperger's disorder continues to remain a mystery. Like autistic disorder, there is evidence that Asperger's disorder is due to some type of organic pathology (Klinger et al., 2003). The exact nature of the etiology of Asperger's disorder, however, has not been well established. Prenatal or perinatal problems were evident in 13% of children with Asperger's disorder, 11% had a combination of pre- or perinatal difficulties and family history of an autistic-like disorder, 55% had a family history of an autistic-like disorder and no other risk factors, 8% had some type of chromosomal abnormality, and there was no risk factor identified in 13% of the sample (Gillberg & Cederlund, 2005). Relatives of children with Asperger's disorder are more likely than relatives of children with autism to have depression, schizophrenia, and Asperger's disorder (Ghaziuddin, 2005). A family history of autism, Asperger's disorder, or other pervasive developmental disorders was evident in 50% of boys with Asperger's disorder (Gillberg & Cederlund, 2005). In addition, siblings of children of with Asperger's disorder are at greater risk for Asperger's disorder (Ghaziuddin, 2005).

Treatment and prevention of Asperger's disorder also remain understudied. The best hypotheses suggest that effective treatments for autistic disorder would be effective for Asperger's disorder. Specifically, behavioral therapy and social skills training in a group therapy format have been suggested as effective treatments for the symptoms of Asperger's disorder (Ozonoff et al., 2002). In addition, medications (such as selective serotonin reuptake inhibitor antidepressants and antipsychotics) may be helpful in treating any aggression and behavioral difficulties associated with Asperger's disorder (Tanguay, 2000).

Overall, there is still very limited information about children diagnosed with Asperger's disorder. The disorder itself remains a bit controversial, given that some researchers consider Asperger's disorder to be a mild form of autistic disorder (Mayes et al., 2001; Mayes & Calhoun, 2004). Now that Asperger's disorder is a formal diagnosis in *DSM-IV*, it is possible that increased research into the disorder will clarify these complex issues regarding diagnostic definitions, etiology, treatment, and prevention.

Other Pervasive Developmental Disorders

Three other primary pervasive developmental disorders are listed in *DSM-IV*: Rett's disorder, childhood disintegrative disorder, and pervasive developmental disorder—not otherwise specified (PDD–NOS). Both **Rett's disorder** and **childhood disintegrative disorder** are new entries into *DSM-IV* and were not included in previous versions of the *DSM*. As can be seen by their descriptions in Tables 12.4 and 12.5, both Rett's disorder and childhood disintegrative disorder are similar in that the infant's neonatal and early infancy months appear to be normal. In Rett's disorder, there are usually significant deficits that appear somewhere before the age of 4 years old. In childhood disintegrative disorder, significant deficits appear somewhere before the age of 10.

Rett's disorder is very rare and continues to be poorly understood. To date, only girls have been diagnosed with Rett's disorder (American Psychiatric Association, 2000). There is some indication that the etiology for Rett's disorder is related to neurological complications and it appears to be genetically linked to other autism-like disorders (Mount, Charman, Hastings, Reilly, & Cass, 2003; Naidu, 1997; Werry, 1996). Given that the disorder has only been identified in girls, an early hypothesis was that the disorder was somehow linked to the X chromosome (Kalat & Wurm, 1999). This hypothesis, however, has not been supported by further research (Kalat & Wurm, 1999). In the few cases of Rett's disorder that have been followed into adulthood, prognosis appears to be even poorer than in autistic disorder (Naidu, 1997; Werry, 1996). Individuals with

TABLE 12.4 DSM-IV Diagnostic Criteria for Rett's Disorder

A. All of the following:

(1) apparently normal prenatal and perinatal development

(2) apparently normal psychomotor development through the first 5 months after birth

(3) normal head circumference at birth

B. Onset of all of the following after the period of normal development:

(1) deceleration of head growth between ages 5 and 48 months

(2) loss of previously acquired purposeful hand skills between ages 5 and 30 months with the subsequent development of stereotyped hand movements (e.g., handwringing or hand washing)

(3) loss of social engagement early in the course (although often social interaction develops later)

(4) appearance of poorly coordinated gait or trunk movements

(5) severely impaired expressive and receptive language development with severe psychomotor retardation

Source: American Psychiatric Association (2000). Reprinted with permission from the *Diagnostic and Statistical Manual of Mental Disorders, Fourth Edition, Text Revision*. Copyright 2000 American Psychiatric Association.

Rett's disorder can usually only function within a very structured and sheltered environment, and their psychomotor problems often continue to worsen (Mount et al., 2003). With more attention to this disorder now that it is included in *DSM-IV*, more research may lead to a better understanding of this debilitating disorder. The same can be said for childhood disintegrative disorder, which is described in Table 12.5.

Also known as Heller's disease, childhood disintegrative disorder is extraordinarily rare (Hendry, 2000). Internationally, estimates ranged from 11.1 to 64.5 per million (Fombonne, 2002). A common prevalence rate is quoted as 1 out of every 10,000 individuals, which suggests a prevalence rate of 0.01% (Fombonne, 2002). Thus, childhood disintegrative disorder is extremely rare. In the few documented cases that exist, the average age of onset was between 3.3 years and 4 years, and there were approximately four times as many boys than girls with the disorder (Fombonne, 2002; Volkmar, 1992; Werry, 1996). There is so little research on this disorder that the course of the disorder, etiological factors, treatment of the disorder, and prevention of the disorder are not well understood. The symptoms of childhood disintegrative disorder often appear to be very similar to autistic disorder, but the age of onset and the loss of previously normal functioning set childhood disintegrative disorder apart from autistic disorder (Fombonne, 2002). There is some evidence that childhood disintegrative disorder is a neurological disorder and that there is no formal recovery from the disorder (Werry, 1996). With the inclusion of childhood disintegrative disorder

in *DSM-IV*, it is hoped that more research attention will be given to this troubling and perplexing disorder.

The final disorder in *DSM-IV* related to this topic is **pervasive developmental disorder not otherwise specified (PDD—NOS)** (American Psychiatric Association, 2000). PDD—NOS is diagnosed when a child shows significant impairments in their social interactions, communication skills, or repetitive behaviors but does not meet criteria for another pervasive developmental disorder like autistic disorder, Asperger's disorder, Rett's disorder, or childhood disintegrative disorder. One study of 216 children diagnosed with PDD—NOS found that the children fell into one of three subgroups:

- Children who almost fit criteria for Asperger's disorder but who did not meet criteria because they had some level of language difficulties or a slight amount of cognitive impairment

- Children who almost met criteria for autistic disorder but who did not meet criteria for some reason (e.g., the onset of their problems was after the age of 3, or they were too young to fully meet the criteria for autism)

- Children who almost met criteria for autism but who did not have severe impairments in stereotyped behaviors and repetitive movements (Walker et al., 2004).

The use of the PDD—NOS diagnosis can be helpful when children do not meet full criteria for a pervasive developmental disorder but who show significant impairments nonetheless. The category of PDD—NOS lends

TABLE 12.5   DSM-IV Diagnostic Criteria for Childhood Disintegrative Disorder

A.	Apparently normal development for at least the first 2 years after birth as manifested by the presence of age-appropriate verbal and nonverbal communication, social relationships, play, and adaptive behavior.
B.	Clinically significant loss of previously acquired skills (before age 10 years) in at least two of the following areas:

    (1) expressive or receptive language

    (2) social skills or adaptive behavior

    (3) bowel or bladder control

    (4) play

    (5) motor skills

C.	Abnormalities of functioning in at least two of the following areas:

    (1) qualitative impairment in social interaction (e.g., impairment in nonverbal behaviors, failure to develop peer relationships, lack of social or emotional reciprocity)

    (2) qualitative impairments in communication (e.g., delay or lack of spoken language, inability to initiate or sustain a conversation, stereotyped and repetitive use of language, lack of varied make-believe play)

    (3) restricted, repetitive, and stereotyped patterns of behavior, interests, and activities, including motor stereotypies and mannerisms

D.	The disturbance is not better accounted for by another specific Pervasive Developmental Disorder or by Schizophrenia.

Source: American Psychiatric Association (2000). Reprinted with permission from the *Diagnostic and Statistical Manual of Mental Disorders, Fourth Edition, Text Revision*. Copyright 2000 American Psychiatric Association.

itself well to the discussion of dimensional levels of pervasive developmental problems because many children show significant problems in social interactions, communication skills, or stereotyped behaviors, but do not meet criteria for a specific disorder.

PERVASIVE DEVELOPMENTAL DISORDERS CONCEPTUALIZED IN A DIMENSIONAL MANNER

In some ways, the mere existence of the diagnoses of Asperger's disorder and autistic disorder is helpful in conceptualizing pervasive developmental disorders in a dimensional manner (Tanguay, 2004; Klin & Volkmar, 1997). Given that Asperger's disorder can be considered a less-severe disorder than autistic disorder, these two disorders are clearly on the same continuum of pervasive developmental disorders. Some researchers consider Asperger's disorder a mild version of autism (Rutter & Schopler, 1992) and even question whether Asperger's disorder exists as a distinct disorder that is different from autistic disorder (Mayes et al., 2001).

Pervasive developmental disorders can also be conceptualized in a dimensional manner because of common deficits across the disorders. Shared attention (i.e.,

paying attention to two different tasks at once such as looking at a ball and sharing the ball with someone), for example, is a common limitation among children with both autistic disorder and Asperger's disorder (Tanguay, 2004). Deficits in social responses and social interactions are also common among most of the pervasive developmental disorders (Tanguay, 2004). Deficits in cognitive functioning and executive functioning may underlie the deficits in social understanding (Verte, Geurts, Roeyers, Oosterlaan, & Sergeant, 2005). These types of deficits can be seen in children at different developmental stages, so there must be severe deficits before applying one of the pervasive developmental disorder diagnoses (Klin & Volkmar, 1997).

Risk Factors

Unlike many other psychological problems, it is difficult to identify risk factors for pervasive developmental disorders, other than those that are associated with the etiology of the disorder. Organic factors (such as CNS abnormalities, neuroanatomical abnormalities, neurological deficits, chromosomal deficits) have been associated with autism, for example, but few other risk factors have been identified (Klinger et al., 2003).

Protective Factors

The same limited information can be said for protective factors in relation to the pervasive developmental disorders. Other than intensive early intervention, there are no known factors that can help prevent the severe sequelae to pervasive developmental disorders. Early intervention programs tend to focus on extremely structured and intensive training programs, so it may be that more structured environments serve a protective function (Lovaas & Smith, 2003). It is clear, however, that even the most structured environment cannot protect children from the onset of pervasive developmental disorders, nor can it ensure a better prognosis for these children.

Be it life or death, we crave only reality.
—Henry David Thoreau

SCHIZOPHRENIA

Although the term *schizophrenia* was originally meant to signify a "split mind," the diagnosis of schizophrenia has nothing to do with split or multiple personalities (unless you consider the "split" from reality). As can be seen in Table 12.6, schizophrenia is a severe disorder that encompasses being out of touch with reality (such as having beliefs that are not true, hearing voices that no one else can hear, or seeing things that others cannot see) and having significant deficits in social, occupational, or academic functioning due to the limited contact with reality. Note that **delusions** refer to beliefs that are inaccurate (such as a 16-year-old boy believing that he is the rap star Usher), and **hallucinations** are sensory/perceptual occurrences that are inaccurate (such as hearing voices, seeing visions, or smelling odors that do not exist).

Prevalence Rates

Given the devastating effects of schizophrenia, it is heartening to find that early onset schizophrenia in children and adolescents is quite rare. Prevalence rates suggest that fewer than 1% of children under the age of 19 experience schizophrenia, with most estimates as low as 0.25% (Pennington, 2002; McClellan et al., 2001). Even in inpatient hospital settings for children and adolescents, the prevalence of schizophrenia is only 2.1% (Harpaz-Rotem et al., 2005).

Schizophrenia has almost never been documented in children under the age of 5, and it is very rare before

TABLE 12.6 DSM-IV Diagnostic Criteria for Schizophrenia

A. *Characteristic symptoms:* Two (or more) of the following, each present for a significant portion of time during a 1-month period (or less if successfully treated):
(1) delusions
(2) hallucinations
(3) disorganized speech (e.g., frequent derailment or incoherence)
(4) grossly disorganized or catatonic behavior
(5) negative symptoms, i.e., affective flattening, alogia, or avolition

Note: Only one Criterion A symptom is required if delusions are bizarre or hallucinations consist of a voice keeping up a running commentary on the person's behavior or thoughts, or two or more voices conversing with each other.

B. *Social/occupational dysfunction:* For a significant portion of the time since the onset of the disturbance, one or more major areas of functioning such as work, interpersonal relations, or self-care are markedly below the level achieved prior to the onset (or when the onset is in childhood or adolescence, failure to achieve expected level of interpersonal, academic, or occupational achievement).

C. *Duration:* Continuous signs of the disturbance persist for at least 6 months. This 6-month period must include at least 1 month of symptoms (or less if successfully treated) that meet Criterion A (i.e., active-phase symptoms).

Types:
Paranoid Type
Disorganized Type
Catatonic Type
Undifferentiated Type
Residual Type

Source: American Psychiatric Association (2000). Reprinted with permission from the *Diagnostic and Statistical Manual of Mental Disorders, Fourth Edition, Text Revision.* Copyright 2000 American Psychiatric Association.

the age of 15 (Ballageer, Malla, Manchanda, Takhar, & Haricharan, 2005). For boys, the first psychotic break of early onset schizophrenia is often between the ages of 15 and 24, whereas females often experience their first psychotic break between the ages of 20 and 29 (Commission on Adolescent Schizophrenia, 2005). As with so many of the other disorders in this chapter, early onset schizophrenia is much more common in boys, with most estimates suggesting a 2:1 ratio of boys to girls (Commission on Adolescent Schizophrenia, 2005). This gender distribution, however, tends to equal out after adolescence, whereby older adolescents and adults do not show gender differences in the prevalence rates of schizophrenia (American Psychiatric Association, 2000). Within childhood and adolescence, there are no strong patterns of prevalence related to SES or race/ethnicity (Asarnow & Asarnow, 2003). Within adults, however, schizophrenia appears to be inappropriately overdiagnosed in African-American communities (Carter & Neufeld, 1998). The prevalence rates of schizophrenia are relatively consistent worldwide, including in developed and developing countries (Pennington, 2002).

Note that children and adolescents are sometimes misdiagnosed with schizophrenia when other disorders would have been more appropriate (Stayer et al., 2004). The severity of the diagnosis dictates that care be taken before formally diagnosing a child or adolescent or even an adult with schizophrenia (Stayer et al., 2004). An overview of prevalence rates is provided in Table 12.7.

Comorbidity

Schizophrenia in childhood and adolescence commonly co-occurs with other psychiatric disorders. One study found that 69% of children with schizophrenia also met criteria for another psychiatric disorder (Russell, Bott, & Sammons, 1989). The most common comorbid disorders were conduct disorder, oppositional defiant disorder, and depression. Within samples of adolescents in treatment for schizophrenia, estimates for comorbid substance abuse diagnoses range from 42.8% to 54% (Kumra, Thaden, DeThomas, & Kranzler, 2005; Werry,

TABLE 12.7 Overview of Prevalence Information for Schizophrenia in Childhood and Adolescence

Prevalence	< 1% (approximately 0.25%)
Age	Adolescence and older (very rare in children)
Gender	Boys > Girls (2:1 ratio of boys to girls)
SES	No known patterns
Race/Ethnicity	No known patterns

McClellan, Andrews, & Ham, 1994). It is estimated that 26% of adolescents receiving inpatient treatment for schizophrenia also are comorbid for obsessive compulsive disorder (Nechmad et al., 2003). Although lower IQ scores are found in children and adolescents diagnosed with schizophrenia, the IQ scores are rarely in the range that would justify a diagnosis of mental retardation, and the IQ scores tend to be higher than those found with children and adolescents diagnosed with autistic disorder (Asarnow & Asarnow, 2003). Overall, comorbidity is the rule rather than the exception in children and adolescents diagnosed with schizophrenia. Note, however, that schizophrenia and autism rarely co-occur in the same individuals, which is further evidence of their diagnostic distinctions (Asarnow & Asarnow, 2003).

Course of the Disorder

Schizophrenia that first appears in childhood and adolescence is a severe and often lifelong disorder. Although schizophrenia rarely is identified in young children, there is some evidence that there are early subtle signs in children who develop schizophrenia in later childhood or adolescence. Delayed developmental milestones (such as walking later than usual or developing language later than usual), poor early academic work, high levels of impulsivity, and high levels of social withdrawal are often identified retrospectively in children who develop schizophrenia in later childhood or adolescence (Asarnow & Asarnow, 2003).

Most often, the first psychotic break in later childhood or adolescence is followed by multiple other breaks throughout the child's life (Ballageer et al., 2005). After schizophrenia develops, many other noticeable complications often arise, such as social isolation, academic deficits, and economic impairment (McClellan et al., 2001). The long-term prognosis for children and adolescents who are diagnosed with schizophrenia is not especially promising. Earlier onset of schizophrenia is related to even poorer prognosis than later onset (Ballageer et al., 2005). Childhood-onset schizophrenia shows a fair amount of continuity into adulthood (Nicolson & Rapoport, 2000; Poulton et al., 2000). Overall, there is rarely a full "recovery" from schizophrenia. The best hope that many individuals with schizophrenia have is for remission from active symptoms through intensive therapeutic and psychopharmacological interventions (Commission on Adolescent Schizophrenia, 2005).

Etiology

Although there is less research in children and adolescents with schizophrenia than there is for adults, certain patterns of etiology have been found for children, adolescents, and adults diagnosed with schizophrenia. There is strong evidence of a genetic component to the development of schizophrenia (Ban, 2004; Jang, 2005; Pennington, 2002). For example, there is evidence that specific genes (G72/G30) are responsible for the development of schizophrenia as well as bipolar disorder (Maier, Hofgen, Zobel, Rietschel, 2005). There is not perfect matching, however, between those genes and the occurrence of schizophrenia or bipolar disorder, so the search for other genetic processes continues.

Based on behavioral genetics research, the more genetic comparability between individuals, the higher the concordance for schizophrenia. Concordance rates for schizophrenia are approximately 9% for nontwin siblings, 13% when one biological parent is diagnosed with schizophrenia, 17% in dizygotic (nonidentical) twins, 46% when both biological parents are diagnosed with schizophrenia, and 46% in monozygotic (identical) twins (Gottesman, 1991; Moises, Zoega, Li, & Hood, 2004). Children of schizophrenia parents were at greater risk for the onset of schizophrenia, as well as other disorders, regardless of whether they were reared by the schizophrenic parent or by psychologically healthy adoptive parents (Erlenmeyer-Kimling, Roberts, & Rock, 2004; Ross & Compagnon, 2001). Higher paternal age is also associated with greater risk for schizophrenia (Raschka, 2000). Relatives of individuals with schizophrenia also show more limited neuropsychological functioning, which may be another indication of a genetic link in the development of schizophrenia (Szoke et al., 2005).

There is also strong evidence of prenatal and other biological factors that lead to the development of schizophrenia (Susser, Brown, & Matte, 2000). Specifically, disruptions in brain development during the prenatal period are associated with greater risk for schizophrenia in childhood and adulthood (Susser et al., 2000). Significantly more complications during pregnancy were found for children and adolescents who later developed schizophrenia than for the prenatal period of children and adolescents in a control group (Nicolson & Rapoport, 2000). Studies using magnetic resonance imaging (MRI) and positron-emission tomography (PET) suggest that brain abnormalities are evident in children and adolescents with schizophrenia (Crow, 2004; Hendren et al., 2000; Nicolson & Rapoport, 2000). A decrease in cortical gray matter in the frontal and temporal regions is evident in children with schizophrenia (Rapoport et al., 1999). Other biological markers, such as eye-tracking dysfunction, are notable in the families of children with early onset schizophrenia (Sporn et al., 2005). Thus, there is compelling evidence of a strong genetic and biological link toward the predisposition for schizophrenia. Note that there is some evidence that genetic and biological factors play a stronger role in childhood-onset schizophrenia in contrast to adult onset schizophrenia (Sporn et al., 2005).

Note, however, that genetic and biological factors do not explain all the variance accounted for in the development of schizophrenia in children and adolescents. Other biological markers and neurodevelopmental markers have been studied, but to date there is no strong evidence of other clear etiologies of schizophrenia in these areas (Asarnow & Asarnow, 2003). There has been some promising work in the area of communication deviance and expressed emotion within families. **Communication deviance** is characterized by a confusing and unclear communication style within the family, and **expressed emotion** is characterized by hostile, critical, and overinvolved levels of emotional communication within the family (Hooley, 2004). Both communication deviance and expressed emotion are found at higher levels in families with offspring who are schizophrenic than in families without schizophrenic offspring (Asarnow & Asarnow, 2003). Although it is not thought that communication deviance or expressed emotion could be the sole etiological factor that would lead to the development of schizophrenia, these factors may exacerbate the likelihood that a child or adolescent with a genetic predisposition toward schizophrenia could end up developing the disorder (Hooley, 2004).

Given the preponderance of studies that suggest a genetic component to the development of schizophrenia, it is interesting to know that some researchers still question the search for a gene for schizophrenia. In a series of comprehensive and thoughtful critiques of the research literature on genetic influences in schizophrenia, the question has been raised as to why no specific genes have been found that are specific to schizophrenia (Joseph, 2004a, 2004b). Specifically, one researcher commented that "researchers rarely consider the possibility that they have found no schizophrenia genes because there are no schizophrenia genes" (p. 167; Joseph, 2004a). Research into the genetic and biological causes of schizophrenia will likely continue (Commission on Adolescent Schizophrenia, 2005), but the critique of this research is also warranted to keep researchers on track.

Case Study: Cathy, a 14-Year Old with Psychotic Symptoms

Cathy was found by a classmate in the restroom at school. Cathy had slit her wrists and was taken to an inpatient psychiatric ward for evaluation. Upon her initial interview, Cathy reported that the "troops" were taking over the school and that they were trying to get to her. She reported that most of the children at school had already been invaded by the troops and that their brains had been taken out and replaced by washing machines. Although no one else could hear the noise, Cathy reported that the constant noise of helicopters outside of the hospital was proof of the invasion of the troops. Cathy reported that she did not really want to die, but that death was better than invasion by the troops. Cathy was diagnosed with schizophrenia, paranoid type.

Cathy's parents reported that she had become more reclusive in the past year. Although she had one friend in the past, this friendship had apparently been cut off about 1 year ago. Cathy's father (who showed up to the interview wearing military fatigues) reported that Cathy just needed a "good swat on the butt" to stop her nonsense and attention-seeking behavior. He also stated that he would be leaving the country shortly for paramilitary training in South America to train for militia duties when war was declared on the U.S. government.

Regarding her developmental history, Cathy's mother reported that she had been a sickly baby and that she had been slow to achieve some developmental milestones. Of note, Cathy's father thought that Cathy was jealous of her younger sister, who often met developmental milestones before Cathy. In addition to her sister, Shelly, who was 13 years old, Cathy also had a younger brother who was 4 years old.

During the family interviews, it became obvious that certain alliances existed within the family. Neither parent seemed especially close to Cathy. Cathy's father was very attentive and complementary about Cathy's sister, whereas Cathy's mother was very close to Cathy's little brother. It became obvious that there were some boundary issues and possible sexual abuse issues within the family when Cathy's sister complained that her father helped her dry herself off after showers, slept in the same bed with her, and touched her breasts occasionally. Cathy's mother reported that she was not concerned about her husband's behavior as long as he did not touch her (the mother). Cathy's mother went on to report that she allowed her 4-year-old son to sleep with her and to breast-feed frequently, but that she had not allowed her husband to sleep with her since their son was born 4 years previously.

Treatment was planned from a three-pronged approach. First, antipsychotic medication was given to Cathy in order to decrease her symptoms of schizophrenia (e.g., delusions, hallucinations, illogical thinking, and paranoia). Second, Cathy became involved in individual therapy sessions to deal with her personal concerns and lack of friends. Finally, family therapy was conducted with the entire family. The medication and individual sessions with Cathy appeared to be successful. Her symptoms of schizophrenia decreased significantly and she became more social with peers. The family therapy sessions, however, became problematic. After the report that Cathy's father touched the girls' breasts, a report had to be made with child protective services. Cathy's sister and her mother denied any problems when child protective services investigated the report, so the case could not be pursued. The family discontinued family therapy after the abuse report was made, which was also around the same time that Cathy's father left for militia training in South America. Cathy's mother stated that the father was not sure if or when he would return to the family.

After 6 months, Cathy had to be hospitalized again with active symptoms of schizophrenia. She was later discharged to a group home that specialized in the treatment of adolescents with severe psychological problems. At a 2-year follow-up, Cathy was still living in the group home and had not experienced any active symptoms of schizophrenia in the previous 2 years.

Source: Morgan (1999).

Treatment

Treatment for schizophrenia in children and adolescents tends to take a multimodal approach. That is, children and adolescents diagnosed with schizophrenia tend to be involved in a number of different interventions, including medication, behavior therapy, social skills training, special educational services, and family therapy (Commission on Adolescent Schizophrenia, 2005; McCellan & Werry, 2003). The primary treatment of choice for schizophrenia at any age is the use of antipsychotic medications. Antipsychotic medications (such as haloperidol/Haldol, clozapine/Clozaril, thioridazine/Mellaril, thiothixene/Navane, loxapine/Daxlin) are more effective than placebo pills and psychotherapy for alleviating the active symptoms of schizophrenia, such as hallucinations, delusions, and illogical thinking (DuPaul et al., 2003; Kranzler et al., 2005; Phelps et al., 2002; McCellan & Werry, 2003). More research is needed, however, to investigate the optimal medications for children and adolescents with schizophrenia and to explore the long-term effects of using antipsychotic medication with youngsters (Commission on Adolescent

Schizophrenia, 2005). One step in the direction of more careful medication management of children and adolescents diagnosed with schizophrenia was the development of training guidelines and practice parameters for child psychiatrists (Liberman, Glick, & Kopelowicz, 2004). Unfortunately, these practice parameters are often not instituted in actual practice (Liberman et al., 2004).

Other types of therapy in combination with medications are also helpful for children with schizophrenia (Dunn & McDougle, 2001). Behavior therapy can be used to help youngsters with schizophrenia modify their behavior (such as increasing self-help skills and compliance with medication regimens; Zimmermann, Favrod, Trieu, & Pomini, 2005). Social skills training can be used to improve the social connections that children with schizophrenia might not otherwise develop (Lauriello, Lenroot, & Bustillo, 2003). Special educational services can help children and adolescents gain more academic skills (Commission on Adolescent Schizophrenia, 2005).

Given the connections between communication deviance in families and the exacerbation of symptoms of schizophrenia, it is not surprising to learn that family therapy has been used with children and adolescents with schizophrenia. When there are high levels of negative expressed emotion and communication deviance, family therapy is highly effective in addition to medication (Miklowitz, 2004).

Overall, multimodal treatments (especially in conjunction with antipsychotic medications) have been found to help manage some of the symptoms of schizophrenia in childhood and adolescence, but no actual "cures" for schizophrenia have been found to date (Miklowitz, 2004). Even with intensive treatment, children and adolescents need to be monitored closely and supervised to ensure that their symptoms of schizophrenia do not become exacerbated.

Prevention

Given the high genetic loading for a predisposition toward schizophrenia, it is worthwhile to consider targeting prevention efforts at children who are at risk of developing schizophrenia due to their parents' own diagnosis of schizophrenia (Commission on Adolescent Schizophrenia, 2005). Only limited attention has been given to preventive efforts with children of schizophrenic parents, but this work often centers around increasing the structure in the child's environment, providing other adult role models outside the family for the child, and decreasing adverse communication styles within the family (Asarnow & Asarnow, 2003; Hooley,

2004). Efforts to prevent the development of schizophrenia are sorely in need of attention, given the devastating effects of this disorder once it develops (Commission on Adolescent Schizophrenia, 2005).

Don't part with your illusions. When they are gone, you may still exist, but you have ceased to live.

—Mark Twain

SCHIZOPHRENIA CONCEPTUALIZED IN A DIMENSIONAL MANNER

Unfortunately, little attention has been given to conceptualizing schizophrenia from a dimensional standpoint. Partly because the disorder is so severe, it is rare that children or adolescents show different levels of gradation of schizophrenic symptoms. It may be worthwhile, however, for researchers to try to conceptualize schizophrenia from a dimensional standpoint. Viewing symptoms of schizophrenia in a dimensional manner may help elucidate the meaning and experience of children's and adolescents' symptoms.

Risk Factors

Like so many of the other problems discussed in this chapter, the risk factors that are linked to the development of schizophrenia are closely tied to the hypothesized etiologies for the disorder. Children and adolescents of parents with schizophrenia are at an increased risk for the development of schizophrenia as well as other psychological disorders. Specifically, children who have at least one biological parent (and especially children who have two biological parents) diagnosed with schizophrenia are at increased risk for the development of schizophrenia (Asarnow & Asarnow, 2003). These findings are connected to both a genetic risk (i.e., having a genetic predisposition toward the development of schizophrenia) and an environmental risk (i.e., being raised by a parent who is disordered; Asarnow & Asarnow, 2003). Children from families where there are high levels of communication deviance and expressed emotion are also at high risk for the development of schizophrenia, especially in the context of a genetic predisposition to schizophrenia (Asarnow & Asarnow, 2003).

Another possible marker for the development of schizophrenia is having an attentional problem (Pantelis et al., 2004). Although attentional problems are common among many developmental psychopathologies (such as attention-deficit/hyperactivity disorder, major depressive disorder), the attentional difficulties related to schizophrenia tend to be more fundamental and may be related to additional sensory stimulation (such as hallucinations or delusions) that are not found commonly in other disorders (Cornblatt, Dworkin, Wolf, & Erlenmeyer-Kimling, 1996). This area is clearly in need of more research because promising findings have been identified when looking for attentional difficulties as a risk factor for the development of schizophrenia in childhood and adolescence (Pantelis et al., 2004). Few other risk factors have been identified that put children and adolescents at risk for the development of symptoms related to schizophrenia.

There has been a great deal of work in exploring family factors in the maintenance of schizophrenia symptoms after treatment. Many studies have found that higher levels of conflict, criticism, emotional overinvolvement, and communication deviance in the family are associated with relapse in youth who have made improvements due to treatment of schizophrenia (Hooley, 2004; Lopez et al., 2004). There is also some evidence that psychosocial factors that are related to family socioeconomic status may put youth at increased risk for the experience of schizophrenia. Although rates of schizophrenia do not differ significantly for children in different SES groups, one study found that children were at greater risk for psychotic disorders if they lived in a family that received public assistance, where there was parental unemployment, where there was only one parent in the household, and when there were lower levels of SES (Wicks, Hjern, Gunnell, Lewis, & Dalman, 2005).

Protective Factors

Unfortunately, there has been little research into factors that might protect children from developing schizophrenia when they are exposed to the risk factors just discussed. There is some evidence that providing a stable home environment, offering access to stable mentors and role models outside the family, and increasing appropriate communication skills within the family will help protect at-risk children from developing symptoms of schizophrenia (Asarnow & Asarnow, 2003). There is also evidence that providing a warm family environment will help protect against the reoccurrence of schizophrenia (Lopez et al., 2004). These findings are evident in families from many racial/ethnic backgrounds, including Caucasian, Hispanic/Latino/Latina, and African American (Lopez et al., 2004).

SUMMARY AND KEY CONCEPTS

Pervasive Developmental Disorders. The first pervasive developmental disorder covered in this chapter was **autistic disorder** (which is a disorder characterized by severe limitations in social interaction, communication, and stereotyped or atypical behavior). A small subset of children (5%) diagnosed with autistic disorder also can be referred to as **autistic savant** because they show special abilities known as **splinter skills** in addition to their symptoms of autism. There are no clearly known etiologies for autism, but one theory that has received attention recently (with only limited support) was the **theory of mind,** which suggests that children with autism have significant limitations in cognitive functioning and mental representation that limit their ability to predict others' behavior.

The second pervasive developmental disorder that was covered is known as **Asperger's disorder,** which is considered a mild form of autistic disorder. Children with Asperger's disorder show adequate language abilities, but show deficits in social interactions and stereotyped behavior. **Rett's disorder** and **childhood disintegrative disorder,** both of which are very rare disorders, were also included in the discussion of pervasive developmental disorders. Rett's disorder is characterized by adequate development through the first 5 months of life, which then begins to deteriorate before the age of 48 months

(4 years old). Childhood disintegrative disorder is characterized by normal development for the first 2 years of life, with decompensation in language, social behavior, bowel or bladder control, play skills, or motor skills before the age of 10 years old. **Pervasive developmental disorder not otherwise specified (PDD—NOS)** is a diagnosis that is used when the child has significant impairments in social interactions, communication skills, or repetitive behaviors but does not meet criteria for any disorder specifically.

Pervasive Developmental Disorders Conceptualized in a Dimensional Manner. There has been some argument that the distinction between Asperger's disorder and autistic disorder is one of severity rather than distinct differences. Thus, Asperger's disorder may be seen as falling lower on the continuum of severity than autistic disorder.

Schizophrenia. Schizophrenia is characterized by being out of touch with reality, such as hearing voices or seeing things (known as **hallucinations**) and believing things that are not true (known as **delusions**), and showing significant deficits in academic, occupational, or social functioning due to these symptoms. Most etiological factors focus on organic deficits, but there is also evidence that **communication deviance** (maladaptive, confusing, and unclear communication within the family) and **expressed emotion** (hostile, critical, and over-involved emotions within the family) can increase the risk for the development of schizophrenia in children and adolescents.

Schizophrenia Conceptualized in a Dimensional Manner. Because of the severity of the symptoms of schizophrenia, it is rare to find children or adolescents with only low levels of symptoms of schizophrenia.

KEY TERMS

autistic disorder
autistic savant
splinter skills
theory of mind
Asperger's disorder

Rett's disorder
childhood
    disintegrative
    disorder

pervasive
    developmental
    disorder not
    otherwise
    specified

hallucinations
delusions
communication
    deviance
expressed emotion

SUGGESTED READINGS

Williams, Donna. *Everyday Heaven: Journeys Beyond the Stereotypes of Autism*. New York: Kingsley, 2004. This is the fourth book in a series of memoirs that explain the life of a woman who was autistic as a child but who has overcome the odds and triumphed over this potentially debilitating disorder. The other books in the series are *Nobody Nowhere* (Williams, 1994), *Somebody Somewhere* (Williams, 1995), and *Like Colour to the Blind* (Williams, 2001).

Fling, Echo R. *Eating an Artichoke: A Mother's Perspective on Asperger's Syndrome*. New York: Kingsley, 1999. This book explains the struggle of one family to find out why their son's behavior in class was "not normal." The diagnosis of Asperger's syndrome was made when the child was 5 years old.

SUGGESTED VIEWINGS

Millions. (2005). If a young boy sees things and hears things of a religious nature that others can not see or hear, is he schizophrenic? This lighthearted film tells the story of two brothers who find a great deal of money and follows them as they decide how best to use it. One of the brothers is doing his best to follow the visions that come to visit him periodically.

Napoleon Dynamite. (2004). It is possible that some of the characters in this amusing film could be diagnosed with Asperger's disorder but it is also possible that they just have quirky social skills. With themes of friendship, self-improvement, and trying to fit in, the popularity of this film with adolescents should be telling us something about their experiences.

CHAPTER 13

LEARNING DISORDERS AND DEVELOPMENTAL DISABILITIES

CHAPTER SUMMARY

Learning is not attained by chance, it must be sought for with ardor and attended to with diligence.

—Abigail Adams

Imagine that you are 9 years old and you have to read the following passage out loud to your class. Your classmates and your teacher would all expect you to be able to read the following passage clearly and without pausing too much between words. Go ahead and try it:

Many words look funny when they are reversed. You may find that you have to inspect words letter-by-letter. Then, you run into letters that are especially difficult because they seem reversible, like a and s, or h and n, or b and d. There are words that look reversible too, like on-no, was-saw, and dog-god. It is especially embarrassing if you finally figure out a word, just to see it again without recognizing the word. Words like "and," "the," and "but" are likely to be difficult each time they are encountered.

Even for the most academically gifted college students, that passage was probably a bit of a challenge. For many students, even when they could identify words, it was hard to maintain their train of thought with regard to the meaning of the sentence (e.g., toward the end of

the sentence you may have already forgotten what the beginning of the sentence had said). You may have also found that it required a great deal of concentration to read and comprehend the passage. Now try reading the same passage in a slightly different format:

Many words look funny when they are reversed. You may find that you have to inspect words letter-by-letter. Then, you run into letters that are especially difficult because they seem reversible, like a and s, or h and n, or b and d. There are words that look reversible too, like on-no, was-saw, and dog-god. It is especially embarrassing if you finally figure out a word, just to see it again without recognizing the word. Words like "and," "the," and "but" are likely to be difficult each time they are encountered.

For most college students, this passage probably was not a significant challenge to read and comprehend. In some ways, this example is the closest that some college students will get to remembering how difficult it is to learn to read. Unless you have learning difficulties, or unless you have begun studying a foreign language recently, you probably take your reading abilities for granted given the high level of reading skills that have developed over the years. This example is meant to remind students what it might be like to have a problem with reading. Not only is the difficulty with reading a problem for the individual, but many school exercises make it a social problem as well (especially with regard to possible teasing from classmates or feelings of personal embarrassment).

Please note that this exercise was meant to allow you to experience difficulty with reading. The mirror-image text shown at the beginning of the chapter is *not* meant to imply that children with learning disorders see everything in reverse—they do not. Although some children reverse numbers and letters occasionally, it is almost unheard of to have everything reversed in mirror-image (Lyon, Fletcher, & Barnes, 2003).

Note that after discussing learning disorders, the next section of this chapter deals with developmental disabilities. These two topics are included together because of the common issues surrounding intelligence and learning, but these two topics should not be confused with one another. The large majority of individuals with a learning disorder have average intelligence or higher. By definition, individuals with a developmental disability such as mental retardation have low intelligence and problems in adaptive functioning. Thus, although there are some small common issues in both of these topics, they are largely representing two distinctly different populations of children with two distinctly different sets of research literatures.

Oh, what a tangled web do parents weave When they think that their children are naive.

—Ogden Nash

LEARNING DISORDERS

Formerly known as academic skills disorders, **learning disorders** (LD) are identified when children or adolescents are unable to perform academically up to the level that would be expected based on their intellectual potential. There are three primary types of learning disorders listed in *DSM-IV:* reading disorder, mathematics disorder, and disorder of written expression (American Psychiatric Association, 2000). There is also a diagnosis known as learning disorder not otherwise specified, which could be diagnosed when a child is having extraordinary difficulties with learning but does not meet criteria for any of the other three diagnoses of learning disorders.

As can be seen in Table 13.1, the three primary diagnoses for learning disorders all focus on a significant discrepancy between a child's academic achievement and intellectual functioning. Known as the **discrepancy method,** a learning disorder is diagnosed if academic achievement falls significantly below what

would be expected for that level of intellectual functioning (Flanagan, 2005; Reynolds, 2003). Note that these discrepancies must be documented through individual standardized testing, rather than relying on measures that might be administered in large groups or in classrooms of children. The discrepancy between academic achievement and intellectual functioning must interfere significantly with academic functioning or with other daily activities that require those skills. Note also that if sensory deficits are present (e.g., visual impairments, hearing impairments), the academic limitations must be in excess of what would be expected for an individual with that sensory deficit. As will be discussed later, this discrepancy score system is still utilized for diagnoses with *DSM-IV,* but educational systems and specifically the federal government mandate for education systems has moved toward a different model of defining learning disorders (Kavale, 2002).

Based on these diagnostic criteria, children with learning difficulties must be assessed individually to ascertain their level of intellectual functioning and their level of academic achievement in the specific areas of difficulties. An example of an individual intelligence test is the Wechsler Intelligence Schedule for Children-Fourth edition (WISC-IV), and an example of an individual achievement test is the Woodcock-Johnson-III: Tests of Achievement (WJ-III). Note that, although these diagnoses are listed in the section of *DSM-IV* entitled "Disorders Usually First Diagnosed in Infancy, Childhood, or Adolescence," the diagnoses of learning disorders can be applied to adults as well as children. In fact, a number of young adults first request testing for learning disorders when they find it difficult to master college-level material (Birch & Chase, 2004; Troiano, 2003).

Terms that are consistent with the *DSM-IV* criteria for learning disorders are used throughout this chapter. Note, however, that some researchers use other terminology to describe the same disorders. Reading disorder is often referred to as **dyslexia,** mathematics disorder is often referred to as **dyscalculia,** and disorder of written expression is often referred to as **dysgraphia** (Lyon et al., 2003; Shalev, 2004; Voeller, 2004). Although there are slight variations as to why professionals might use these different terminologies, for all intents and purposes, these terminologies are comparable. This point is especially important to keep in mind regarding dyslexia. Often nonprofessionals think of dyslexia as a certain problem with reading (e.g., reversing letters). Dyslexia, however, is currently thought to be consistent

TABLE 13.1 DSM-IV Diagnostic Criteria for Three Types of Learning Disorders

DIAGNOSTIC CRITERIA FOR READING DISORDER

A. Reading achievement, as measured by individually administered standardized tests of reading accuracy or comprehension, is substantially below that expected given the person's chronological age, measured intelligence, and age-appropriate education.

B. The disturbance in Criterion A significantly interferes with academic achievement or activities of daily living that require reading skills.

C. If a sensory deficit is present, the reading difficulties are in excess of those usually associated with it.

DIAGNOSTIC CRITERIA FOR MATHEMATICS DISORDER

A. Mathematical ability, as measured by individually administered standardized tests, is substantially below that expected given the person's chronological age, measured intelligence, and age-appropriate education.

B. The disturbance in Criterion A significantly interferes with academic achievement or activities of daily living that require mathematical ability.

C. If a sensory deficit is present, the difficulties in mathematical ability are in excess of those usually associated with it.

DIAGNOSTIC CRITERIA FOR DISORDER OF WRITTEN EXPRESSION

A. Writing skills, as measured by individually administered standardized tests (or functional assessments of writing skills), are substantially below those expected given the person's chronological age, measured intelligence, and age-appropriate education.

B. The disturbance in Criterion A significantly interferes with academic achievement or activities of daily living that require the composition of written texts (e.g., writing grammatically correct sentences and organized paragraphs).

C. If a sensory deficit is present, the difficulties in writing skills are in excess of those usually associated with it.

Source: American Psychiatric Association (2000).

Reprinted with permission from the *Diagnostic and Statistical Manual of Mental Disorders, Fourth Edition, Text Revision*. Copyright 2000 American Psychiatric Association.

Reading aloud in front of the classroom can be terrifying for children with a reading disorder.

with the overarching diagnosis of reading disorder (Bishop & Snowling, 2004).

Although it is not formally reflected in *DSM-IV*, a number of researchers have identified a fourth type of learning disorder. **Social-emotional learning disorders,** also known as nonverbal learning disorders, are experienced by children who show problems with social perception, spatial skills, time orientation, and directionality (Rourke & Tsatsanis, 2000; Rubenstein, 2005). Children with nonverbal learning disorders also show deficits in spatial and emotional aspects of language, such as understanding the content of stories

YOU DECIDE: IS THE NO CHILD LEFT BEHIND ACT WORKING?

Yes

- Since 2001, federal law has mandated that schools need to be accountable to show improvements in students' learning, that parents and students should have more choices in educational settings including private and faith-based settings, and that states should have more flexibility in how federal dollars are spent toward education (Executive Summary, 2001). The fiscal year budget proposal for 2006 requests that 104 million dollars be set aside for an early reading program and that 1.1 billion dollars be set aside for educational programs in reading (U.S. Department of Education, 2005).

- Currently, the reading test scores of 9-year-olds in the United States are the highest ever recorded on the Nation's Report Card (U.S. Department of Education, 2005).

No

- Children who were born to single mothers with less than a 12th-grade education who initiated prenatal care after the first trimester of the pregnancy or who were born with a low birth weight were 1.2 to 3.4 times as likely to have a learning disorder than children who were not exposed to any of these risk factors (Blair & Scott, 2002). A total of 91.2% of Caucasian-American children graduate from high school, whereas only 83.5% of African-American children and 63.4% of Hispanic/Latino/Latina children graduate from high school in the United States (Richman, Bowen, & Wooley, 2004).

- Moving from a high-poverty area into a low-poverty area was associated with increased academic achievement (Leventhal & Brooks-Gunn, 2004). There are over 13 million children in the United States currently being raised in poverty (Children's Defense Fund, 2005d).

So, is the No Child Left Behind Act Working? You decide.

and being able to identify the main character's feelings in a story (Worling, Humphries, & Tannock, 1999). Overall, these children show significant deficits in nonverbal abilities.

If these symptoms sound familiar to you, try rereading the diagnostic symptoms for Asperger's disorder that are listed in the chapter on severe and persistent disorders. A number of researchers and clinicians have argued that nonverbal learning disabilities and Asperger's Disorder are either highly related or even the same disorder (Rourke & Tsatsanis, 2000; Volkmar & Klin, 1998). The symptoms of both disorders are very similar, and there is confusion as to whether these two disorders are really describing the same phenomenon. It is not completely clear whether social–emotional learning disorders are a distinct disorder or whether they are a learning disorder that is combined with social skills deficits (Rourke & Tsatsanis, 2000). In either case, there is a great deal of empirical research into the ramifications of social–emotional learning disorders, with a focus on trying to understand this troubling problem.

Stepping back from the *DSM-IV* definition of learning disorders, it is important to note that there has been a strong movement to discard the discrepancy between intellectual functioning and academic achievement (Fletcher, Coulter, Reschly, & Vaughn, 2004).

These changes have been initiated in the research community and are being instituted at the federal level in the United States (Francis et al., 2005; Lewis, Hudson, Richter, & Johnson, 2004). All public school systems in the country have to follow the Individuals with Disabilities in Education Act (IDEA), which provides mandates for who receives services, what types of services should be received, and what types of outcomes should be expected (Lewis et al., 2004). Based on the most recent revision, the IDEA no longer uses the discrepancy score between IQ and achievement to define children with a learning disorder (Federal Register, 2005). Children who have significant trouble in their academic achievement, regardless of their IQ, should qualify for services for learning disorders (Wright & Wright, 2005). There is also a move toward using **responsiveness to intervention** as part of the process in identifying children who have a learning disorder. Responsiveness to intervention is used to ascertain whether a child who is struggling academically can be helped by enhanced educational services (Kavale, Holdnack, & Mostert, 2005). Thus, children who are still not able to achieve even when they are being exposed to teaching methods that are usually effective with others would be classified as learning disordered (Fletcher, Francis, Morris, & Lyon, 2005).

When the discrepancy method and the newer method in the IDEA are compared, different children are identified as in need of services. Using the discrepancy method in *DSM-IV,* children who have higher IQs and who are in higher socioeconomic brackets are identified as meeting criteria for a learning disorder, whereas using the IDEA criteria means that children with lower IQs and from more impoverished backgrounds meet criteria for a learning disorder (Swanson et al., 2000). This pattern makes sense when you think about the two definitions. Based on *DSM-IV,* children's academic achievement has to be significantly lower than their intellectual functioning, so children with low academic achievement who also have modest intellectual functioning would not meet criteria for a learning disorder and hence they would not be eligible for LD services in most school districts. The new IDEA definition, on the other hand, explores the actual level of academic achievement rather than the achievement in comparison to the intellectual functioning, so children with lower levels of achievement are identified as having a learning disorder and thus are eligible for remedial services. Overall, this change is thought to be for the better, and it should help more children gain access to educational services that they need (Swanson et al., 2000).

A child who asks questions isn't stupid.

—Proverb of Africa

Prevalence Rates

According to *DSM-IV,* the prevalence of learning disorders ranges from 2% to 10%, with approximately 5% of children and adolescents meeting criteria for a learning disorder (American Psychiatric Association, 2000). These numbers are considered an underestimate. Learning disorders researchers find higher rates, with estimates of 2% to 10% of the general population having some type of learning disorder. Based on estimates in *DSM-IV,* approximately 4% of school-age children and adolescents meet criteria for a reading disorder, but again those numbers appear to be an underestimate. In this area of research, a more widely used prevalence rate for reading disorders is between 10% and 15% of school-age children (Lyon et al., 2003). As for mathematics disorder, a total of 5% to 6% of school-aged children meet criteria for mathematics disorders, although many of these children also have a comorbid reading disorder (Fuchs & Fuchs, 2002; Shalev, 2004). Estimates are as high as 8% for children who have cognitive deficits that make mathematics difficult for them (Geary, 2004). Although there are no strong studies to estimate the prevalence rates, it is thought that disorders of written expression (without comorbid reading disorders) are relatively rare with an estimated prevalence of less than 1% of school-aged children (American Psychiatric Association, 2000).

Reading disorders encompass the overwhelming majority of learning disorders, with four out of five learning disorders being diagnosed as a reading disorder or a reading disorder in combination with a mathematics disorder or a disorder of written expression. Note that mathematics disorders and disorders of written expression are usually diagnosed in addition to reading disorders (American Psychiatric Association, 2000). In other words, it is rare to find a child with a mathematics disorder or a disorder of written expression who does not also meet criteria for a reading disorder. Figure 13.1 on page 366 provides a writing sample of an 8-year-old girl who ultimately was diagnosed with both a reading disorder and a disorder of written expression.

Age patterns are difficult to synthesize because learning problems often become evident as academic tasks become more difficult. Although learning disorders can be diagnosed at any age, it is rare that learning disorders are identified before children enter kindergarten because these academic tasks are not required before they enter formal schooling (Lyon et al., 2003). A common age for the first referral for a reading disorder is 7 years old, given that reading tasks become more formalized around this age (Turner & Rack, 2004). Mathematics disorders are usually first identified around the age of 8, when arithmetic assignments become more rigorous (Geary, 2004). Disorders of written expression are less well documented, but there is some evidence that first referrals can occur around the age of 7 (Ryan et al., 2005). Overall, the older children are when they are first referred for an LD evaluation, the less severe their impairments tend to be (Geary, 2004; Lipka & Siegel, 2006). In other words, children with less-severe learning problems can usually show adequate, albeit limited, academic achievement in the early grades but may begin to show significant deficits as academic material gets even more difficult in the middle school years.

With regard to gender, most clinical studies find that learning disorders of all types are more common in boys than in girls. These studies find that between 60% and 80% of children referred for help with reading disorders are boys (American Psychiatric Association, 2000). Note, however, that when more rigorous epidemiological studies are conducted, the gender differences are not as evident (American Psychiatric Association, 2000; Shalev, 2004). This difference may be due to the fact that boys are referred more quickly for services or are more disruptive and thus are identified for services earlier than

Case Study: Janet, Who Is a "Slow Learner"

Janet is 13 years old and attends the 6th grade in a regular classroom (not a special education classroom). Her current teacher describes her as a "slow learner with a poor memory." The teacher goes further to say that Janet learns almost nothing in group settings and that she must be attended to on an individual basis for her to grasp any new concepts. Janet is currently failing reading and is almost failing English, arithmetic, and spelling. Her academic strengths appear to be in art and sports.

Janet did not show any significant problems in her developmental history. She had her tonsils out when she was 5 years old, and she had a number of ear infections (known as chronic otitis) when she was young. Her other developmental milestones, such as crawling, walking, and talking, all appeared to be on time.

Janet, however, has had school problems almost from the very beginning of school. She failed the first grade and noted that her teacher was "mean." After being placed into a special education classroom in first grade, she was removed from the special education classroom due to chronic fighting with her classmates.

Now that Janet is in 6th grade, she continues to have some interpersonal problems at school in addition to her academic difficulties. Although she seems to be a friendly child, she is quite sensitive about her academic difficulties. She feels that she gets "bossed around" at school, but she does report having a great many friends in her neighborhood.

An evaluation for a learning disorder revealed that Janet has intelligence in the Average range and that she has significant deficits in her reading achievement scores. She currently reads at the 4th-grade level. Her other academic achievement scores, such as spelling and arithmetic, were somewhat delayed but did not show significant deficits.

Janet meets criteria for a reading disorder. Her other academic achievements were not significantly delayed, so no other learning disorder diagnoses were appropriate. Janet's behavioral difficulties were thought to be associated with her reading disorder, so no other emotional/behavioral disorders were appropriate.

Source: Spitzer et al. (1994).

---

are girls (Liederman, Kantrowitz, & Flannery, 2005). In addition, it may be that teachers confuse learning disorders with limited achievement, and thus, refer boys for services more often than girls (Liederman et al., 2005). Overall, there is evidence that boys are somewhat more susceptible to learning disorders than are girls, but the gender difference in prevalence rates is not as strong as originally thought (Shalev, 2004).

With regard to epidemiological patterns in socioeconomic status and race/ethnicity, surprisingly little research has addressed these issues. Although children from lower SES homes and children from ethnic minority groups are disproportionately represented in special education classes, it is not clear whether these patterns are due to actual epidemiological rates or due to biases within the referral and identification process (Rea, McLaughlin, & Walther-Thomas, 2002; Sattler, 2002). There are concerns that the overrepresentation of ethnic minorities in special education classes may be due to discriminatory practices in identifying children with learning problems and then by putting them in a more restrictive environment than needed (Ferri & Connor, 2005; Grossman, 2002).

One study found that boys' school achievement improved when their family moved from a high-poverty

to a low-poverty area, but this study focused on achievement gains rather than learning disorders per se (Leventhal & Brooks-Gunn, 2004). This study does suggest that boys who are in safer school environments and who are encouraged to spend more of their time completing homework appear to do much better in school than their peers in less-safe, impoverished schools where there is not a philosophy of expecting students to complete their homework (Leventhal & Brooks-Gunn, 2004). Note that there is almost no research on ethnic and racial groups other than African American and Latino/Latina/Hispanic (Lyon et al., 2003). Learning disorders have been documented in nearly every country that has completed research on the topic, including Italy, Japan, Belgium, and Spain (Casas & Castellar, 2004; Cornoldi & Lucangeli, 2004; Desoete, Roeyers, & DeClercq, 2004; Woodward & Ono, 2004). It is interesting to note that learning disorders are more common in English-speaking countries, whereas the lowest rates are found in Japan and China (Loomis, 2006). Table 13.2 provides an overview of the prevalence information for learning disorders.

Comorbidity

As with so many other disorders, comorbidity with a learning disorder is the rule rather than the exception.

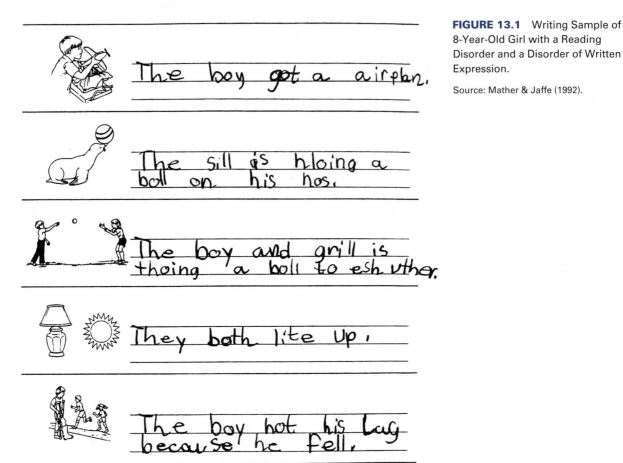

FIGURE 13.1 Writing Sample of 8-Year-Old Girl with a Reading Disorder and a Disorder of Written Expression.

Source: Mather & Jaffe (1992).

TABLE 13.2 Overview of Prevalence Information for Learning Disorders

Prevalence	
Overall LD	2–10% of all children
Reading	10–15% of school-age children
Mathematics	5–6% of school-age children
Written expression	< 1% of school-age children
Age	
Reading	Onset by age 7
Mathematics	Onset by age 8
Written expression	Onset by age 7
Gender	Boys (although there is equivocal evidence)
SES	Unknown
Race/Ethnicity	Unknown

It is not uncommon for children, adolescents, and even adults who experience a learning disorder to also experience one or more other psychiatric disorders (Shalev, 2004). Although the range of estimated comorbidity with LD has varied from 10% to 92%, it appears that a more realistic range is from 19% to 26% (Barkley, 2006; Culbertson, 1998). Reading disorders are associated with greater risk for both internalizing and externalizing disorders (Arnold et al., 2005; Carroll, Maughan, Goodman, & Meltzer, 2005). Disorders that co-occur commonly with LD are language disorders and ADHD (Shalev, 2004).

The high comorbidity rates between LD and language disorders have received a lot of empirical attention. Language disorders and communication disorders appear to be highly related to learning disorders, especially reading disorders (Tallal, 2003). Given that language and communication skills are central to the ability to read, it is not surprising that language disorders, communication disorders, and learning disorders co-occur in the same children quite often (Lewis, Freebairn, & Taylor, 2000). Language and communication disorders also show high comorbidity rates with other psychological disorders (Toppelberg & Shapiro, 2000). It is likely that the high comorbidity rates between language disorders, communication disorders, and reading disorders are due to the common mechanisms involved in the development of all of these disorders (Tallal, 2003; Toppelberg & Shapiro, 2000).

Comorbidity between LD and ADHD has also received a great deal of attention given the high rates of comorbidity between these two disorders (Doyle, Faraone, DuPre, & Biederman, 2001; Monuteaux, Faraone, Herzig, Navsaria, & Biederman, 2005; Shalev, 2004). In general, children who are comorbid for both LD and ADHD tend to have significant impairments in both areas of functioning (i.e., learning and attention/behavioral control). For example, children in grades 2 through 4 who met criteria for both LD and ADHD showed more significant impairment in their learning problems than did children without the comorbid diagnosis of ADHD (Bussing, Zima, Belin, & Forness, 1998). Even children diagnosed with LD who did not meet criteria for ADHD were shown to have comparable deficits in attention as children diagnosed with ADHD (Mayes, Calhoun, & Crowell, 1998). As can be seen in Figure 13.2, children with learning disorders sometimes also have high levels of aggression, which can be reflected in their writing samples (Mather & Jaffe, 1992).

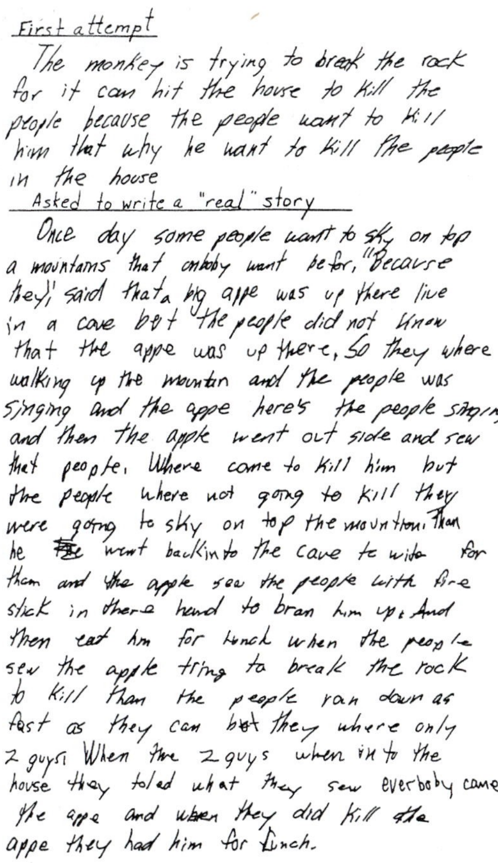
First attempt
The monkey is trying to break the rock for it can hit the house to kill the people because the people want to kill him that why he want to kill the people in the house
Asked to write a "real" story
Once day some people want to sky on top a mountains that onboby want befor, "Because they," said that a big appe was up there live in a cave bot the people did not know that the appe was up there, So they where walking up the mountin and the people was singing and the appe here's the people singing and then the apple went out side and sew that people. Where come to kill him but the people where not going to kill they were going to sky on top the mountoni Than he went backinto the cave to wite for them and the apple sew the people with fire stick in there hand to bran him up. And then eat him for lunch when the people sew the apple tring to break the rock to kill than the people ran down as fast as they can but they where only 2 guys. When the 2 guys when in to the house they toled what they sew everboby came to kill the appe and when they did kill the appe they had him for lunch.

FIGURE 13.2 Flavio's Writing Sample Illustrating Good Story Grammar but Poor Language and Visual Recall Skills. (Note also the aggressive themes in the writing sample.)

Source: Mather & Jaffe (1992).

Criticisms of high comorbidity rates (especially between LD and ADHD) have been discussed in the professional literature. Referred to as the "Balkanization process" (i.e., the tendency to create new and independent diagnostic categories when using currently existing categories might be more appropriate), the high rates of comorbidity have been criticized as an indication of the limitations in the current diagnostic system (Kavale & Forness, 1998). Specifically, researchers have suggested identifying co-occurring problems across many different disorders (such as problems in social skills or attention) rather than developing new and more complex disorders (Kavale & Forness, 1998; Kavale & Forness, 2000). In addition, an empirical method should be used to assess whether disorders are really distinctly different from one another rather than just assuming that disorders are distinctly different from one another (Lahey et al., 2004).

In addition to all these comorbid problems and the diagnostic issues associated with them, there is evidence that children diagnosed with LD are prone to have social deficits and interpersonal problems, which in turn appear to increase their learning difficulties (Fleming, Cook, & Stone, 2002). These interpersonal difficulties may be related to the higher levels of difficulty that children with a learning disorder experience in processing social information (Bauminger, Edelsztein, Schorr, & Morash, 2005). For example, in contrast to children without a learning disorder, children with a learning disorder showed greater difficulty in understanding that individuals can experience two conflicting emotions at the same time, such as love and hate (Bauminger et al., 2005). Thus, there are many other disorders and problems that children with learning disorders experience in addition to their learning difficulties.

Help me with my homework when I need you to.
—Advice from preteens to their parents (Holladay, 1994, p. 119)

Course of the Disorder

As noted in the prevalence section that discussed age patterns of onset, learning disorders are usually not identified until first or second grade for most children, with reading disorders and disorders of written expression usually being identified earlier than mathematics disorders (American Psychiatric Association, 2000; Shalev, 2004). Children with higher intelligence and children

Case Study: Matt's Mother Advocates for Him (in Her Own Words)

My son Matt is going to middle school next year, so I started to activate the process to change schools, to transition him. I was told by our learning strategist and everybody else that we had to make an appointment with the principal. So I called the office and asked to make the appointment with the principal, and I was told they don't do that. They said that I had to go through the guidance office, so they switched me to the guidance office. I told them that my son would be coming there next year and I wanted to make an appointment with the principal. The guidance office told me they couldn't do that until I talked with a guidance counselor, so a little later a woman called me and asked why on earth would I want to talk to the principal and what was the problem. I tried to explain to her that my son would be coming there next year and that he was a rather unique child, that he has attention deficit hyperactivity disorder (ADHD), learning disorder (LD), and is gifted...

I tried to explain to this guidance counselor how difficult things are for him and that he needs a computer in the classroom. Her response was that the transition team would decide that. She asked if this was in his Individualized Education Program (IEP) and I said, "Yes, it is, that he needs a computer in the classroom. He is totally mainstreamed with a computer.

He has attention deficit and it is very difficult for him to make transitions of any kind." She said, "Well, we do a wonderful job of transitioning all the students, this is what we do, and I'm sure he will be just fine. Why do you really think you want to talk to the principal?" "I want to talk to him about the type of student he is getting next year," I said. She said, "Well, I really don't think that's necessary." "Well then," I said, "I'd like to at least come in and observe the classrooms." She answered, "Well, I don't know if I can arrange it. We'll see if I can arrange it. Call me back in March...."

So I started over. I called the school again and I said, "I want to speak to the principal." I got the principal and I said, "I would like to have a meeting with you." So I go in this Friday. It's just an example of how we are handled. The guidance counselor just wasn't listening at all to anything I was saying: the fact that what my son has is debilitating enough to make him non-functional in the regular classroom, that he has to see psychiatrists, talk to counselors, work as a team; and this is her way of trying to help him prepare? So I decided what he needed and just did it without her.

Source: Marsh (1995, pp. 13–16).

---

with less severe learning disorders tend not to be identified as having a learning disorder until later in their academic schooling and sometimes not until college (Birch & Chase, 2004; Lipka & Siegel, 2006).

There are often long-term ramifications to learning disorders. At least half of the children diagnosed with a mathematics disorder tend to have the disorder into early adolescence (Shalev, 2004). Nearly 40% of children or adolescents diagnosed with LD drop out of school before high school graduation (American Psychiatric Association, 2000). This rate is over 1.5 times higher than the average dropout rate. Thus, in addition to the high rates of comorbidity, a number of other academically related problems are associated with learning disorders. Even in adulthood, a large number of adults with LD experience difficulty in their occupational pursuits and in their social interactions (American Psychiatric Association, 2000). Specifically, adults with LD often have difficulty obtaining and maintaining satisfying jobs and often have difficulties in their social lives (American Psychiatric Association, 2000).

Early identification and early intervention, however, are thought to prevent a lifetime of difficulties (American Psychiatric Association, 2000; Gersten, Jordan, & Flojo, 2005). Without some type of educational intervention

(e.g., tutoring, special educational services, teaching intensive educational strategies), it is rare that a severe learning disorder would dissipate over time (Lyon et al., 2003). Given that later learning in most academic subjects relies on earlier fundamental information, once children fall significantly behind in a school subject it is difficult for them to "catch up" without intensive intervention strategies. With these educational enhancement strategies in place, however, children and adolescents with LD can expect to continue their education into college and even graduate school if they so desire (Turner & Rack, 2005). See Box 13.1 to consider where America stands on a number of indicators in relation to education.

Etiology

No single etiological factor has been identified in the development of learning disorders (Lyon et al., 2003; Plomin & Kovas, 2005). The three factors that have been identified most often as leading to a greater risk for the development of a learning disorder are

- Genetic factors
- Biological factors
- Ineffective learning strategies (Sattler, 2002)

HOW AMERICA STANDS

Among industrialized countries, the United States ranks

1st	in military technology		1st	in defense expenditures
1st	in gross domestic product		10th	in eighth-grade science scores
1st	in the number of millionaires and billionaires		21st	in eighth-grade math scores

Source: Children's Defense Fund (2005d).

Studies in behavioral genetics suggest that learning disorders may be genetically related. Notably, there is often a strong family history of learning disorders in children with documented learning disorders (Cutting & Denckla, 2004; Doyle et al., 2001; Geary, 2004; Olson, 2004; Plomin & Kovas, 2005). Studies of monozygotic twins and dizygotic twins have shown higher concordance rates for learning disorders in monozygotic twins, which suggests a genetic component to the disorder (Geary, 2004; Willcutt, DeFries, Pennington, Smith, Cardon, & Olson, 2003). In addition, children with learning disorders are more likely to have experienced prenatal and perinatal complications and to show electrophysiological abnormalities (Watson & Westby, 2003). Relatedly, babies who are very low birth weight are at increased risk for learning disorders (Litt, Taylor, Klein, & Hack, 2005; Stanton-Chapman, Chapman, & Scott, 2001) as are children born in the summer (Martin,

Foels, Clanton, & Moon, 2004). Molecular genetics studies suggest that a gene mutation may be related to learning disorders, and that chromosomal abnormalities may be involved as well (Galaburda, 2005).

These studies of genetic and prenatal differences, however, are far from conclusive. For example, the family history of learning disorders may put a child at greater risk for developing a learning disorder due to genetic factors, but it also may put a child at greater risk due to environmental factors (such as a parent who cannot help with homework or who is ambivalent about the need for academic excellence or who does not expect academic success in the child). Notably, children whose parents do not read to them frequently tend to have higher rates of reading disorders than children whose parents read to them more often (Rashid, Morris, & Sevcik, 2005).

Teachers can be an integral part of helping identify children with learning problems and in helping to remedy those problems.

Biological factors, such as problems in perceptual systems, perceptual–motor functioning, neurological organization, and oculomotor functioning, may be related to the development of a learning disorder (Kooistra, Crawford, Dewey, Cantell, & Kaplan, 2005; Voeller, 2004). It is not uncommon for children with a learning disorder to show a number of these difficulties. Although no clear-cut basis for these problems has been identified, there is speculation that children with learning disorders may have experienced some type of minor birth trauma or may have experienced chronic middle ear infection before the age of 4 years old (Shalev, 2004). These factors may have put the child at risk for the development of a learning disorder due to biologically related deficits. It may be that these biological factors lead to abnormalities in cognitive processing.

Limitations in visual perception, attention, memory, and linguistic processes, all of which have the common element of cognitive processing, appear to be pervasive among children and adolescents diagnosed with a learning disorder (American Psychiatric Association, 2000). Most notably, children who develop reading disorders tend to have deficits in word recognition, which seem to be related to deficits in **phonological awareness** (Tallal, 2003; Voeller, 2004). Children with deficits in phonological awareness appear to have limited abilities to "notice, think about, or manipulate sounds in words" (Lyon & Cutting, 1998, p. 481). Children with a reading disorder do not differ from children with regular reading abilities in their visuospatial abilities, but when the task demands more phonological awareness, then children with a reading disorder show greater deficits than children without a reading disorder (Voeller, 2004). The connections between phonological awareness and the development of reading skills and language skills has been found in nearly every language that has been studied internationally (Ziegler & Goswami, 2005).

Note that these phonological deficits and language disorders are thought to be a key feature of reading disorders (Bishop & Snowling, 2004; Lovett, Steinbach, & Frijters, 2000). Specifically, children with language deficits and phonological deficits are highly likely to develop reading disorders (Lewis, Freebairn, & Taylor, 2000; McArthur, Hogben, Edwards, Heath, & Mengler, 2000). Although phonological deficits are also common in other disorders (such as autism), it appears that phonological deficits are a key factor in the development of reading disorders (Bishop & Snowling, 2004). Phonological deficits are thought to have both genetic and environmental etiologies (Tiu, Wadsworth, Olson, & DeFries, 2004).

Using an ineffective learning strategy has also been identified as a factor that may lead to a learning disorder (Obiakor & Ford, 2002; Sattler, 2002). Children may not learn the most effective ways of solving academic problems and thus, may fall behind in their academic achievement. Specifically, they may not learn how to analyze problems effectively, how to relate a current problem with problems that were solved in the past, how to implement a strategy for conceptualizing a problem that is to be solved, or how to evaluate their own performance and adjust their performance accordingly (Sattler, 2002). A related problem is that children with learning disorders overestimate their performance in academic tasks, which is known as positive illusory bias (Heath & Glen, 2005). Apparently positive illusory bias serves a self-protection function whereby children are protecting themselves from adverse academic feedback. One study found that when children were given positive feedback for their effort, their estimations of their own work became much more accurate, even though their actual performance did not improve (Heath & Glen, 2005).

Overall, there are no clear etiological factors that are known to lead consistently to the development of a learning disorder. Like so many other disorders, learning disorders are likely to be developed from a complex combination of factors that result in children's and adolescents' inability to learn in the way that other youth learn.

Treatment

Interventions for learning disorders are usually some combination of educational and psychological interventions, so the classic conceptualization of "treatment" does not always apply to helping children and adolescents with learning disorders. For example, although psychostimulant medication (such as Ritalin) is effective in reducing aversive behavior in children diagnosed with ADHD, it has little effectiveness in raising achievement scores or in increasing study skills in children diagnosed with both LD and ADHD (Brown et al., 2005).

Overall, the school system is probably the most salient site for interventions with learning disorders. An individualized education program (IEP) should be developed for any child who meets criteria for a learning disorder or who has a mental health problem that is in need of services (Siegel, 2005). From the perspective of the federal government in the United States, public schools are mandated to use assessment, intervention, and prevention strategies that are effective. Specifically,

Case Study: Nigel, the Boy Who Showed Problems in Reading

Nigel is 13 years old, but still in the 5th grade. He had been held back for two different academic years because of his difficulties with mastering academic work. He shows particular difficulty with reading and spelling, but also shows problems in math. Nigel did not show any major developmental problems or academic problems until he reached the third grade. Behaviorally, Nigel appears to be somewhat anxious and withdrawn, but he does not show any conduct problems at school or at home.

Nigel lives with his four brothers and sisters as well as his parents. He receives special educational services once a week, due to his academic difficulties. He is also involved in speech therapy, which began when he was 3 years old. His parents monitor his homework each night and try to help in any way they can. Both of Nigel's parents, all of his aunts and uncles, and nearly all of his siblings have had significant learning problems.

Based on a request from his teachers and parents, Nigel was evaluated by a school psychologist to determine whether or not Nigel had any learning disorders. A comprehensive assessment was completed, including intellectual functioning, academic achievement functioning, and behavioral assessment. Nigel's Intelligent Quotient (IQ) was in the average range, but there was a significant discrepancy between his Verbal IQ and Performance IQ. Specifically, Nigel's Verbal IQ fell into the Borderline Range (which is below the Low Average category), whereas his Performance IQ fell into the Superior Range. Nigel had difficulty with verbal tasks, especially vocabulary, and he had strengths in putting blocks and puzzles together. His academic achievement tests showed that he was performing at or below the third-grade level in nearly all areas (including reading, spelling, arithmetic, word recognition, comprehension, and listening skills). Behaviorally, Nigel was quiet and shy. During the classroom observation, Nigel tended to work by himself or ask other children for help, and he rarely asked the teacher for help.

Based on the results of this evaluation, Nigel was diagnosed with a reading disorder. Although he showed significant deficits in mathematics as well, he did not meet criteria for mathematics disorder. A treatment and educational plan was developed that addressed Nigel's difficulties in reading and spelling. After Nigel's difficulties in reading and spelling were addressed, the treatment plan focused on Nigel's difficulties in mathematics. Nigel received 30 weeks of intensive intervention from his reading teacher who was trained in special education. Interventions included developing better skills in sight reading, focusing on words that were frequently misspelled, correcting reading and spelling errors, and finding reading materials that were of interest to Nigel to enhance his motivation to learn to read better. After the intervention, Nigel improved significantly in his reading and spelling abilities. The reading teacher planned to continue to provide additional help to Nigel in the classroom setting, but it was determined that he no longer required this intensive one-on-one intervention. Nigel's mathematics difficulties were to be addressed in the following school year.

At 6-month follow-up, Nigel was still reading at about 6 months behind his classmates, but this delay was a significant improvement on his previous 2-year delay in reading. Behaviorally, he showed more self-confidence in the classroom, and he began to interact socially with more of his peers. His parents had also taken a much more active role with Nigel and his siblings to ensure that reading assignments and other homework assignments were completed each evening.

This case illustrates a classic example of a reading disorder. Although Nigel's reading problems were not identified until third grade, he probably had been having difficulties even before third grade. In addition to interventions regarding the reading disorder, it is important to consider the social–emotional functioning of children and adolescents with learning disorders. As a 13-year-old in a class with mostly 10-year-olds, the social ramifications of being held back due to learning difficulties should be addressed in addition to intervening with the learning disorder.

Source: Singh, Beale, & Snell (1988).

both the No Child Left Behind Act and the Individuals with Disabilities Education Act mandate that schools use evidence-based techniques in classrooms and throughout the school system (Lewis et al., 2004). These mandates have trickled down to education training programs, with an emphasis on identifying evidence-based practices within the school system (Bauer, Johnson, & Sapona, 2004). See the "You Decide" section to consider the current effectiveness of the No Child Left Behind Act.

As can be seen in Box 13.2, over half the children receiving special education services through the Individuals with Disabilities Education Act (IDEA) were receiving services for learning disorders (Sattler, 1998). The majority of these children received services either with special pullout programs from their regular education classroom or they received part-time services within an educational resource room. Because of mainstreaming, there has been a strong push to keep special education

BOX *13.2*

SPECIAL EDUCATIONAL SERVICES IN SCHOOLS

Who receives services through the Individuals with Disabilities Education Act (IDEA)?

- 51.1% had specific learning disorders.
- 21.1% had speech and language impairments.
- 11.6% were diagnosed with mental retardation.
- 8.6% experienced severe emotional disturbances.
- 7.6% fell into other categories (such as multiple disabilities, hearing impairments, heath problems, orthopedic disabilities, autism, or traumatic brain injury).

Where did these children receive special education services?

- 39.8% were in a regular classroom (most of whom received brief "pullout" services for their special education needs, which totaled no more than 21% of the school day).
- 31.7% were in a resource room (which means that they received special services in a resource room for between 21% and 60% of the school day).

- 23.5% were in a separate class (which means that these students received special education services for 60% or more of the day, usually in a self-contained special education classroom).
- 3.7% were in a separate day school (these separate schools usually were designed to serve the needs of children and adolescents with either learning, physical, or severe emotional difficulties).
- 0.8% were in a residential facility (which includes children and adolescents who lived in a full-time facility and received special education services through this facility).
- 0.5% were homebound or in a hospital environment (which means that the students were receiving special education services within the home setting, usually because they could not function in a school setting, or they received special education services in a hospital environment, where they were receiving additional mental health services).

Source: Sattler (1998).

---

children in regular education classrooms rather than in special education classrooms (Kavale, 2002).

Although empirical studies of the effectiveness of this diverse array of services are limited, there is some evidence that special education services can help children and adolescents overcome their learning disorders (Alexander & Slinger-Constant, 2004; Shalev, 2004). Most special educational services try to incorporate some of the following interventions (Elliott, Busse, & Shapiro, 1999):

- Instructional interventions (e.g., using special education teaching methods that maximize children's ability to learn new material)
- School–home notes (e.g., sending notes home so that teachers and parents can communicate about what work needs to be done and how they can work together to help children).
- Performance feedback (e.g., providing children with direct feedback about their academic performance).
- Self-management (e.g., helping children learn how to manage their own time and behavior within the academic setting).

- Contingency management interventions (e.g., teachers providing reinforcement to increase on-task behaviors, work completion, and accuracy).
- Cognitive-based interventions (e.g., self-instructional training to help increase on-task behavior and self-control in academic activities).
- Peer tutoring (e.g., having peers help peers on academic tasks).
- Group contingencies (e.g., rewarding the entire classroom for maximal efforts by most children in the classroom).
- Cooperative learning (e.g., having students work together in small groups or in teams to maximize the learning of all students in the group;

In addition, there are examples of unique and innovative intervention programs, such as one called "I Don't Like to Write but I Love to Get Published," which helps motivate reluctant writers to work on their writing skills by working for a classroom newspaper (Alber, 1999). These techniques are somewhat effective in intervening with children who have a learning disorder. The majority of these techniques can be instituted in regular education classrooms or in special education

classrooms. There is a small, but significant advantage for children to be mainstreamed (Kavale, 2002; Rea et al., 2002).

A great deal of attention has also been paid to the effectiveness of phonological training for children with reading disorders. Phonological training uses techniques like word identification training to help children gain mastery over reading and writing (Alexander & Slinger-Constant, 2004; Lovett et al., 2000). Given the connection between language deficits and reading disorders, it is not surprising to find that programs like phonological training are effective in treating reading disorders (Calhoon, 2005). There is evidence that longer periods of phonological training are associated with the greatest benefits, especially for children with severe reading difficulties (Alexander & Slinger-Constant, 2004).

Note, however, that not all summaries of special educational efforts have been promising. Based on a thorough meta-analysis of five types of special education interventions for LD, few of the interventions were found to have a strong impact on educational functioning (Kavale & Forness, 1999). As can be seen in Table 13.3, only one of the interventions (applied behavior analysis) achieved a large mean effect size (.80 and above), and the majority showed medium to small mean effect sizes. Overall, this research suggests that some special educational strategies, such as applied behavior analysis, early intervention, and psycholinguistic training, are more promising than others, such as modality instruction or perceptual–motor training (Kavale & Forness, 1999).

Other studies have identified effective interventions that can be conducted in the school system. Children with learning disorders who have poor self-concepts can be helped significantly at their school by cognitive–behavioral treatment for poor self-concept (Elbaum & Vaughn, 2003). Previous work on self-concept interventions had shown modest effects, but a finer-grained analysis shows that many of those interventions were done with children diagnosed with LD but who did not have any problems with their self-concept. A meta-analysis showed that interventions for poor self-concept show significant improvements with children who had poor self-concept at the beginning of the intervention, but not for those who had average or above average self-concept at the beginning of the study (Elbaum & Vaughn, 2003). Thus, these interventions should be targeted at children with learning disorders who have shown significantly poor self-concept.

Given that most special education interventions are conducted in the school system, it is important to look at the match between children's needs and the services they receive within the school system. There are concerns about what types of children are placed in special education classrooms that are meant for children diagnosed with LD. One study of second through fourth graders found that a majority of children diagnosed with ADHD or who had other serious emotional/behavioral disorders were placed in special education services for LD, even though they did not need primary services for LD (Lopez, Forness, MacMillan, & Bocian, 1996). In

TABLE 13.3 Summary of Meta-Analyses in Special Education Services for LD

Interventions	Number of Studies	Mean Effect Size	Standard Deviation of Effect Size
Perceptual–motor training	180	.08	.27
Psycholinguistic training	34	.39	.54
Modality instruction	39	.15	.28
Early intervention	74	.40	.62
Applied behavior analysis	41	.93*	1.16

* Large effect size.

Source: Kavale and Forness (1999).

FIGURE 13.3 Picture Drawn by a Boy (Age 12 years, 10 months) Who Was a Foster Child in a Deplorable Home.

Source: DiLeo (1973).

general, it appeared that child study teams (who place children in special educational services) were hesitant about placing children in classrooms for severely emotionally disturbed (SED) children and instead placed these children in services for LD. This placement pattern can work against the best interests of both behaviorally troubled children and children diagnosed with LD. In LD classrooms, children with severe behavioral problems may be helped by the extra attention on learning problems, but there will be little intervention for their behavioral problems. Conversely, non–behaviorally disordered children diagnosed with LD will experience a more troubling classroom environment because of the inclusion of children who might be better served in an SED classroom (Lopez et al., 1996). Overall, additional attention to appropriate services for both LD and non-LD children within the special education system is needed.

In addition to attention to services within the school setting, there has been increasing interest in helping teachers and school psychologists utilize the home environment more than it has been in the past. The thought is that teachers, special educators, and school psychologists only have access to children for a limited portion of the day (usually about 6 or 7 hours of the school day), but parents and other caretakers have access to children for the remainder of the day and all day on weekends (Berger, 2003; Shaywitz, 2005). There has been growing interest in trying to engage parents in the educational system to enhance their children's learning and educational attainments. This perspective is also held by professional in children's protective agencies who are concerned about the home lives of children with learning disorders (James, 2004). Judging from the drawing in Figure 13.3, you might imagine that the child's best interests would be served if the teacher could work with the foster parents to provide a more stable and enriching home environment.

Historically, parents were often only contacted by school personnel if something was wrong (e.g., the child was failing a course or was truant). Often, the relationship between parents and school personnel was strained because of a lack of common goals and an adversarial atmosphere rather than an atmosphere of cooperation (Christenson & Buerkle, 1999). More recently, many school personnel have made a concerted effort to connect with families in a cooperative manner that works to benefit children and adolescents who are struggling with their academic functioning. In keeping with this new emphasis, the following suggestions have been made to help school psychologists become educational partners with families to enhance children's school success (Christenson & Buerkle, 1999):

- Disseminate information to parents about the school curriculum and the ideal home curriculum.
- Establish parent–educator problem solving to create a partnership between parents and educators so that

the home environment can become more conducive to educational activities.

- Engage in solution-oriented family–school meetings so that parents feel their time in school meetings is productive and works toward the best interests of their child.

- Engage in conjoint behavioral consultation, which allows the school psychologist to serve as a consultant between parents and teachers to develop mutually agreed upon solutions for the child's academic difficulties.

- Develop family–school teams so that parents can become more involved in setting policies and can help within the school system

Overall, this new focus on families as educational partners has been effective. When teachers, special educators, school psychologists, and parents work together to enhance children's school success, the best interests of the child are facilitated. One study of parents and students involved in collaborative teaching models that included a parent–teacher partnership showed that parents and students were highly satisfied with this model and reported that students' self-esteem and academic understanding increased because of the collaborative methods (Gerber & Popp, 1999). Treatments that are more psychological in nature, such as cognitive behavioral treatments, can also be effective with children who have a learning disorder in addition to psychological problems (Willner, 2005). More research is needed in this area to ascertain the specific mechanisms of change, but the empirical work so far has been promising. Note also that books that are specifically geared toward parents with a child struggling with a learning disorder are available, including *Overcoming Dyslexia* (Shaywitz, 2005) and *How to Reach and Teach Children and Teens with Dyslexia: A Parent and Teacher Guide to Helping Students of All Ages Academically, Socially, and Emotionally* (Stowe, 2000).

The love of learning, the sequestered nooks, and all the sweet serenity of books.
—Henry Wadsworth Longfellow

Prevention

Because there has been only limited success with educational interventions to treat learning disorders, there has been a renewed focus on the prevention of learning difficulties. On the national front, there has been a recent movement toward state-funded universal education for children before they reach kindergarten. Known as universal pre-K, these programs are instituted with the idea that children of preschool age need to be exposed to an enhanced educational learning environment to make sure that they are ready academically for kindergarten. A comprehensive evaluation of universal pre-K programs in Oklahoma found that children who attended pre-K programs showed significant academic improvements and that these improvements were consistent across diverse SES and racial/ethnic groups (Gormley, Gayer, Phillips, & Dawson, 2005). Thus, universal pre-K programs appear to be worthwhile if the classrooms are run from an educational perspective by highly talented

Educationally enriching environments, such as those in Head Start programs, can be beneficial for children when the programs are maintained for an extended period of time.

early education teachers (Gormley et al., 2005). These programs are thought to prevent a whole host of potential problems, including academic, social–emotional, and psychological.

In terms of the specific prevention of learning disorders, the majority of empirical work has focused on the prevention of reading disorders, and the majority of the work has focused on early education (Rabiner, Malone, & the Conduct Problems Prevention Research Group, 2004; Stipek, 2001). Because reading disorders are thought to be due to difficulties with word recognition, which are brought about by difficulties with phonological awareness, most preventive interventions seek to train students in phonological awareness at an early age (Alexander & Slinger-Constant, 2004; Speece & Ritchey, 2005). Many prevention programs work with children in kindergarten and first grade to enhance their phonological awareness (Coyne, Kame'enui, Simmons, & Harn, 2004; Rabiner et al., 2004). These early intervention and prevention programs have been found to be effective in reducing the risk for development of a reading disorder (Calhoon, 2005; Speece & Ritchey, 2005). Phonological awareness prevention programs tend to present the information in a gamelike format so that children can learn how to analyze words and synthesize or blend parts of words into the entire word (Lyon & Cutting, 1998). Overall, a number of prevention and early intervention programs are effective in preventing the onset of diagnosable reading disorders (Calhoon, 2005).

Unfortunately, prevention programs may not be helpful for children who have both reading problems and attentional problems. For example, an early intervention program was found to be successful with children who had difficulty reading but who were not inattentive and children who were inattentive but who did not have difficulty reading (Rabiner et al., 2004). Both of these groups of children were found to have gained significantly after the prevention program. The prevention program, however, did little to improve the reading capabilities of children who were both inattentive and poor readers (Rabiner et al., 2004). Thus, prevention programs still need to be improved to find ways to help provide effective services to children who are most in need. In addition, preventive interventions should target the specific needs of children, given that reading difficulties can be due a diverse array of problems such as inattention, poor phonological skills, or difficulties with English as a second language (Jitendra et al., 2004).

In terms of prevention of mathematics disorders and disorders of written expression, very few prevention programs have been tested empirically. There is some evidence, however, that early identification and early interventions for students with math difficulties can prevent the onset of a mathematics disorder (Fuchs, 2005; Gersten et al., 2005).

Other prevention programs have been instituted that address the school environment itself. Given that ineffective schools are a risk factor for learning problems in children, preventive efforts to improve schools themselves are ultimately aimed at decreasing the risk for learning problems in children (Berninger, Dunn, Lin, & Shimada, 2004; Obiakor & Ford, 2002).

With all these prevention programs that have been shown to work, why isn't every school using them? Many of these prevention programs were funded by a specific grant, and then once the grant runs out and the academic papers are written, the prevention program disappears (Adelman & Taylor, 2003). There is a need for sustained preventive efforts for all children, and many scholars argue that preventive efforts should be mandated in schools alongside academic efforts (Adelman & Taylor, 2000; Greenberg et al., 2003).

LEARNING DISORDERS AND LEARNING PROBLEMS CONCEPTUALIZED IN A DIMENSIONAL MANNER

Even in *DSM-IV*, there is an acknowledgment that learning problems might not be due to a learning disorder within the individual. To diagnose a learning disorder, other characteristics such as normal variations in academic attainment, lack of educational opportunity, poor teaching methods, and cultural factors must be ruled out first (American Psychiatric Association, 2000).

In terms of conceptualizing learning problems in a dimensional manner, it is important to acknowledge that lots of children have problems in learning at different times in their academic endeavors. A total of 8.8% of Caucasian-American children, 16.5% of African-American children, and 36.6% of Hispanic/Latino/Latina children never finish high school, but only a small subset of these children have documented learning disorders (Richman et al., 2004). Thus, many problems that children experience with learning are not encompassed by the diagnostic criteria of learning disorders. Although categorical conceptualizations of learning disorders are used in most Western countries, there is growing interest in conceptualizing learning problems in a dimensional manner to serve children's needs more directly (Ghesquiere & Ruijssenaars, 1998).

BOX *13.3*

GETTING A HEAD START ON EDUCATION (AND LIFE)

One of the most well known prevention programs is the Head Start Program, which has been in existence for almost 40 years. Although Head Start was begun initially to enhance social competence in preschool children from impoverished backgrounds (Zigler, 1979), it quickly became a prevention program that addressed many needs of children from economically disadvantaged circumstances and children from ethnic minority groups.

In its original conceptualization, Head Start programs involved a brief summer school experience for preschoolers before they began kindergarten. The initial program focused on development of social competence and social skills to help children get along with one another. The program soon developed into a longer and more intensive program that addressed social–emotional needs, academic needs, and family enhancement needs (Murray, Guerra, & Williams, 1997). Short-term gains were noted in children's social–emotional, intellectual, and academic functioning (Darlington, Royce, Snipper, Murray, & Lazar, 1980). Research on Head Start programs suggests that the longer the intervention is offered, the more positive the effects for children and families involved in the programs (Darlington et al., 1980). Unfortunately, the gains based on short-term Head Start programs with no follow-up or sustained enrichment activities tend to be short lived (Lee, Brooks-Gunn, Schnur, & Liaw, 1990). There is consistent evidence that enrichment activities should be given on a longer term basis for maximal preventive effects for academic, intellectual, and social–emotional functioning (Lee et al., 1990). These findings of the need for longer-term and sustained enrichment efforts have been known for over 15 years, but there is still limited progress toward implementing these changes nationally (Zigler & Styfco, 2004).

Current changes in the Head Start program include an emphasis on helping fathers become engaged in their children's lives (McAllister, Wilson, & Burton, 2004) and helping decrease the likelihood of children's emotional/behavioral problems through parent training (Reid, Webster-Stratton, & Baydar, 2004).

Rather than focusing on specific learning disorders, it may be more meaningful to explore learning problems and difficulties that are associated with learning problems. For example, assessing functional skills (such as orientation, attention, basic sensory functions, modality-specific learning, cross-modal sensory integration, higher-level linguistic and phonological skills, and higher-order cognitive abilities) and using criterion-referenced tests (where the child's actual abilities are compared with where their abilities should be) may be more appropriate than assessing specific academic areas (Hambleton & Zenisky, 2003). In other words, there might be cognitive impairments and deficits in processing that are more relevant to learning problems and are more amenable to interventions than the overarching diagnoses of learning disorders.

Although most school systems require formal diagnoses to classify children as in need of special education services, comparable educational interventions might be appropriate whether or not children meet formal diagnostic criteria for learning disorders (Adelman & Taylor, 1993). For example, a treatment plan for a child diagnosed with a learning disorder would look very similar to a treatment plan for a child who was showing underachievement in the school setting (Jongsma, Peterson, & McInnis, 1996).

Overall, the diagnoses of learning disorders are similar to other diagnoses discussed in this book. Although there are advantages to using formal diagnostic criteria, there are also disadvantages to these criteria. It is important to keep a broad view of learning and educational problems to prevent focusing solely on diagnostic definitions of learning disorders. Too often, children struggle with their academic work and yet do not meet criteria for a learning disorder based on *DSM-IV*. Although the new IDEA criteria may help with this issue, these children may not be able to receive special services for their learning difficulties because they do not meet diagnostic criteria for a learning disorder. They may continue to struggle and then eventually quit school, or they may finally find some type of additional remedial educational services (e.g., a dedicated teacher who wants to help them, a parent who helps them each night with homework, or a tutor who can provide additional academic enrichment activities). Overall, children's learning difficulties are no less tolerable just because they do not meet formal diagnostic criteria for a learning disorder.

Risk Factors

Historically, researchers of learning problems and learning disorders did not conceptualize these problems from

Case Study: Darryl, the Boy Who Showed Problems with Reading

Darryl was a fifth grader who had already experienced three different teachers since school began that year. Before this year, he had never attended any school for longer than a few months. He attended elementary school in an impoverished area within San Francisco. Like many of his impoverished classmates, Darryl seemed to always wear clothes that were either too big or too little for him, and his clothes were almost always wrinkled and dirty.

At school, his desk was located near the teacher's desk because he had a habit of reaching out and touching or hitting other children who were seated near him. He also refused to participate in classroom activities and was especially adamant about not participating in oral reading activities. His handwriting was atrocious, and he never seemed to be able to stay within the lines on the paper.

Athletically, Darryl did not fare much better. He could not seem to kick the ball straight in kickball, nor could he hit a baseball. He tended to be ignored or teased by other children. Even the loners in his class seemed to stay away from him.

From all these accounts, it might have made sense to refer Darryl to a school psychologist for an evaluation for a learning disorder. One day, however, a new teacher noticed that Darryl put his book up to his face (nearly touching his nose) when he tried to look at pictures in the book. The teacher referred Darryl for an eye exam with the school nurse the very next day. Based on this exam, the school nurse referred Darryl to an optometrist who provided eyeglasses to low-income children. Although Darryl's mother could not drive, she was able to take Darryl to the optometrist's office on public transportation.

When Darryl showed up at school with his "Coke bottle" glasses, his entire outlook on life appeared to be different. He was able to read in class. He kicked the ball on his first try and made it to first base in a game of kickball. He stopped hitting and grabbing children because he could see them now. He began reading everything in sight, including multiple books from the school library. His writing improved significantly because he could see the lines on the paper.

This case illustrates the need to look at basic functioning and sensory issues before diagnosing a learning disorder. Given his poor eyesight, Darryl may have missed valuable educational experiences and could have continued to miss these experiences had his new teacher not been perceptive enough to notice his difficulties with sight. This case also illustrates how a small intervention (i.e., helping a child get affordable reading glasses) can change the child's outlook on reading and on the educational experience tremendously.

Source: Wright (1999).

---

a risk and resilience framework (Wong, 2003). Increasingly, researchers and educators are exploring risk and protective factors in relation to the development of learning difficulties (Wong, 2003).

A number of factors appear to put children at risk for educational and learning deficits. As mentioned in the section on etiology, children who experience prenatal and perinatal complications appear to be at greater risk for learning disorders (Taylor & Rogers, 2005; Watson & Westby, 2003). Relatedly, children who were exposed to alcohol or cocaine in utero are at greater risk for the development of a learning disorder (Watson & Westby, 2003). Other early factors relate to later learning disorders as well. For example, difficult temperament early in life appears to be related to a greater risk for learning disorders in children once they begin attending school (Teglasi, Cohn, & Meshbesher, 2004).

Individual child characteristics appear to be related to their learning difficulties once they reach school age. Children who believe that intellectual functioning and academic achievement are fixed and stable tend to do more poorly in school than children who believe that functioning is related to effort (Stipek, 2005). Attentional problems and problems in self-regulation are consistently identified as risk factors for the development of learning problems (reviewed in Wright & Masten, 2005). Emotional/behavioral problems are also evident in a large number of children with learning problems, but it is not clear if emotional/behavioral problems put children at risk for learning problems or if learning problems put children at risk for emotional/behavioral problems (Carroll et al., 2005; Sorenson et al., 2003). Children and adolescents who have emotional/behavioral problems are significantly more likely to drop out of school before high school graduation than their counterparts without emotional/behavioral problems, even after controlling for rates of educational achievement (Wright & Masten, 2005). Similarly, children who show poor engagement and low expectations for academic success in the early years of school are significantly more likely to drop out of school when they reach the high school years (Hauser-Cram, Sirin, & Stipek, 2003).

Some physical illnesses also put children at risk for learning disorders and other academic difficulties. For example, sickle cell disease is associated with cognitive and learning deficits because of the impact of the disease on the neuropsychological system. Children with sickle cell disease are at greater risk than physically healthy children to experience learning disorders and to fail at least one grade in school (Peterson, Palermo, Swift, Beebe, & Drotar, 2005). Thus, children with sickle cell disease should be evaluated early and often for academic difficulties that could be treated.

Many environmental conditions, such as poverty, large family size, and limited parental education are associated with greater learning problems and limited educational attainment (Arnold & Doctoroff, 2003; Sattler, 2002; Stanton-Chapman et al., 2001). Children who are raised in impoverished households, where there is little focus on education, reading, or correct use of language, appear to be at an increased risk for the development of a learning disorder (Voeller, 2004).

A number of factors within the school setting appear to put children at risk for learning problems. Attending schools that are ineffective and overcrowded can serve as a risk factor for limited educational achievement (Mather & Ofiesh, 2005; Obiakor & Ford, 2002). Having teachers who do not have high expectations can also serve as a risk factor for limited educational attainment. In particular, teachers showed less hope for success for students whose parents had different educational values than the teachers (Hauser-Cram et al., 2003). This pattern was particularly relevant for low SES families, which then put children at even greater risk for learning problems.

Overall, a number of personal, familial, environmental, and educational risk factors are associated with the development of learning problems. Many of these risk factors also put the child at risk for the development of other emotional/behavioral problems (Wright & Masten, 2005). Prevention programs (such as Head Start) target these overarching risk factors to try to prevent myriad problems that might develop in children and adolescents, rather than solely focusing on the prevention of learning difficulties. Box 13.4 provides some additional ideas for how the educational system can be changed in order to help enhance students' well-being.

What one knows is, in youth, of little moment; they know enough who know how to learn.

—Henry Brooks Adams.

Protective Factors

A number of factors appear to protect children from the development of a learning disorder. On the individual level of the student, children who attribute their academic success to their own hard work and who attribute academic failures to lack of effort tend to show better academic functioning and fewer academic problems (reviewed in Wright & Masten, 2005). When children are at risk for the development of a learning disorder due to a parental learning disorder, they seem to be buffered from the increased risk when they have high intellectual functioning and strong language skills (Voeller, 2004). Children who are at risk for learning

---

BOX *13.4*

AN EDUCATIONAL SYSTEM THAT NEEDS AN OVERHAUL

Given the difficulty that exists in remediation and prevention of learning problems, a number of scholars have proposed sweeping changes within the educational system to reduce institutional barriers to learning. Some suggestions include

- Looking beyond the diagnosis of learning disorder to explore the many learning problems that children encounter (Adelman, 1992)
- Focusing on institutional barriers to learning that are inherent in the structure of the current educational system (Adelman & Taylor, 2003)
- Expanding the concept of intervention beyond teaching (Adelman & Taylor, 2002)

- When teaching is the intervention of choice, personalizing instruction for children in order to enhance their individual motivational and educational needs (Taylor & Adelman, 1999)
- Tying together social policy issues and practice issues in order to form school–home–community partnerships that will reduce barriers to learning within the school system (Adelman & Taylor, 1997; Adelman, Taylor, & Schnieder, 1999)
- Reconceptualizing learning disorders from being within the individual child to a more accurate reflection of the problems that are inherent in the educational system, social system, and political system (Adelman & Taylor, 1993)

difficulties but who have strong social relationships with peers seem to be buffered from the development of severe learning disorders (Wiener, 2004).

In relation to the school environment, school success and academic attainment appear to be enhanced by the following characteristics (Al-Yagon & Mikulincer, 2004; Wright & Masten, 2005):

- Access to success experiences by students early in their educational experiences
- Teachers who have high expectations of success for their students
- Teachers who are seen as supportive by students and who can provide an emotionally close and stable base for the child
- Students who have been encouraged to develop self-confidence in their ability to learn new material
- Students with high expectations and firm goals for themselves within the educational setting
- Teachers who communicate individual and personal regard for students, especially teachers who express positive unconditional regard for their students.

In addition to these school-related protective factors, there are also familial factors that appear to protect children from the development of learning disorders. Authoritative parenting (in which parents provide age-appropriate structure with warmth, concern, and high expectations for their children) has been associated with better academic functioning (Davis-Kean, 2005). Relatedly, parents' beliefs and expectations for academic success and their amount of reading with their children are strongly related to children's academic success, even when SES is controlled statistically (Davis-Kean, 2005). This pattern differed somewhat for children of different racial/ethnic backgrounds. Specifically, in African-American families, parental education and family income were not directly related to academic achievement but rather were mediated by parental educational expectations. Parental warmth was also positively related to higher levels of academic achievement. For Caucasian-American families, parental educational expectations were related to academic achievement, but parental education was also directly related to children's academic achievement. Interestingly, parental warmth was not related significantly to children's academic achievement (Davis-Kean, 2005). This study shows the complexity of familial factors that predict academic achievement and that protect against the development of learning disorders. There is consistent and strong evidence for children from all races that high parental

expectations and high levels of parental reading behavior to children serve as protective factors against the development of learning problems.

Parental involvement in the educational process has also been linked to better academic outcomes and fewer learning disorders for children (Pantin, Coatsworth et al., 2003; Pantin, Schwartz et al., 2003). One interesting prevention study suggested that increasing parental involvement in the school system had direct effects on increasing children's academic functioning (Steinberg, Lamborn, Dornbusch, & Darling, 1992). Overall, a number of protective factors within the school system, within the family, and within children themselves serve to protect children from developing learning problems. There is still a need to identify more protective factors so that greater attention can be paid to preventive programs that would enhance protective factors in the lives of children at risk for learning disorders (Wong, 2003). See Box 13.5 for more information on how schools can serve as a protective factor.

A coconut shell full of water is a sea to an ant.

—Proverb of Africa

DEVELOPMENTAL DISABILITIES

The term **developmental disability** is now often used to describe the disorder that is also known as mental retardation. Although the formal diagnostic criteria continue to use the term *mental retardation,* many advocates working within the field prefer the term *developmental disability* because it is less stigmatizing, and it has less of a negative history than the term *mental retardation* (Koger, Schettler, & Weiss, 2005). In addition, the term *developmental disability* suggests that limitations of a developmental nature characterize this disorder. In essence, the terms *developmental disability* and *mental retardation* can be used interchangeably. Table 13.4 provides the diagnostic criteria for Mental Retardation that are found in *DSM-IV* (American Psychiatric Association, 2000).

Note that the primary characteristics of mental retardation include low intellectual functioning and limited adaptive functioning. This combination of symptoms is crucial in diagnosing mental retardation correctly. Individuals who have an IQ below 70 but who are otherwise able to show adequate adaptive functioning would not be diagnosed with mental retardation. Note also that the diagnostic criteria present categories of mental retardation, depending on the severity of the intellectual deficits.

BOX 13.5

EFFECTIVE SCHOOLS AS A PROTECTIVE FACTOR

There is growing evidence that children who attend effective schools are better off on a number of academic and behavioral indices than children who attend less-effective schools. In particular, attendance at an effective school appears to serve as a protective factor against the development of learning disorders. The characteristics of effective schools that are consistent across a number of countries include

- Leadership in the school that is strong and positive
- A focus and emphasis on academic learning
- High expectations for the success of students

- Consistent expectations for students, with the use of collegial and joint planning for students' academic activities
- Active involvement of students in the daily functioning of the school and in the overall life of the school
- Active involvement of parents in the overall functioning and life of the school
- Consistent monitoring of students' academic progress
- Incentives and rewards for academic excellence and for high levels of effort

Source: Mortimore (1995).

TABLE 13.4   DSM-IV Diagnostic Criteria for Mental Retardation

A. Significantly subaverage intellectual functioning: an IQ of approximately 70 or below on an individually administered IQ test (for infants, a clinical judgment of significantly subaverage intellectual functioning).

B. Concurrent deficits or impairments in present adaptive functioning (i.e., the person's effectiveness in meeting the standards expected for his or her age by his or her cultural group) in at least two of the following areas: communication, self-care, home living, social/interpersonal skills, use of community resources, self-direction, functional academic skills, work, leisure, health, and safety.

C. The onset is before age 18 years.

Degree of severity reflecting level of intellectual impairment:

Mild Mental Retardation:	IQ level 50–55 to approximately 70
Moderate Mental Retardation:	IQ level 35–40 to 50–55
Severe Mental Retardation:	IQ level 20–25 to 35–40
Profound Mental Retardation:	IQ level below 20 or 25
Mental Retardation, Severity Unspecified	

Source: American Psychiatric Association (2000).

Reprinted with permission from the *Diagnostic and Statistical Manual of Mental Disorders, Fourth Edition, Text Revision.* Copyright 2000 American Psychiatric Association.

Within the educational system, the following terms are used to signify severity level (Sattler, 2001):

- Mild mental retardation is referred to as **educable** within the educational field. Children with this severity of mental retardation can develop social skills and communication skills and can often achieve academic skills up to the sixth-grade level. Higher academic functioning is often limited, even with intensive special education services in the higher grades. With proper support, these individuals can develop vocational skills and may be able to live somewhat independently as adults.

- Moderate mental retardation is referred to as **trainable** within the field of education. Individuals with this level of severity can develop communication and

social skills and can often achieve academic work that is consistent with the fourth grade if special education services are provided. With some support, these individuals can be employed in unskilled and semiskilled jobs as adults. Independent living is rare for individuals with moderate mental retardation, but structured group settings are not uncommon for individuals with this level of impairment.

- Severe mental retardation is referred to as **severely/ profoundly handicapped** within the educational field. Individuals with this level of severity often have limited language abilities, poor motor skills, severely limited self-help skills, and little hope for academic achievement. In older adolescence and early adulthood, individuals with severe mental retardation

Case Study: Natasha, a Girl Diagnosed with Mild Mental Retardation

Natasha was referred for an evaluation when she was 9 years old and in the third grade. Although she had been slow in her preschool, kindergarten, first grade, and second grade activities, no formal evaluations had been recommended until she reached the third grade.

Natasha lived with her parents and three older siblings. Her parents were both employed full time, and none of her siblings had any academic or intellectual difficulties. The pregnancy with Natasha had been uneventful and in her early years, she was characterized as a happy and healthy child. Natasha's parents did, however, note that she had been delayed in some of her developmental milestones. For example, Natasha was approximately 1 year behind in her language abilities, play activities, toilet training, and self-help skills (such as tying her shoes and dressing herself).

Natasha attended preschool for 3 years, partly because the preschool teacher did not think she was ready for kindergarten. Once she began kindergarten, she lagged behind other children in her academic and physical abilities. In first grade, she fell even further behind her classmates in reading, and by the second grade she still could not read, even though she was receiving tutoring on a daily basis. By third grade, Natasha could only read at the first-grade level, whereas her classmates were reading third- and fourth-grade material. At this time, Natasha was also beginning to be teased by her classmates. Although she had always been friendly and social, Natasha seemed especially vulnerable to the cruel comments of her classmates.

The formal evaluation by the school psychologist revealed that Natasha had a Full Scale IQ of 65, that she was in the 6th percentile of achievement in reading, and that she was in the 4th percentile of achievement in mathematics. Based on an assessment of her adaptive functioning, Natasha scored within the normal range on activities related to social interactions, but scored nearly 2 years below her chronological age in physical skills and adaptive skills. Based on these assessment results, Natasha was diagnosed with mental retardation, mild.

Natasha remained in regular education classes for the majority of the day, but was pulled out of her class for special education services in reading and math. The special education teacher also coordinated with Natasha's regular education teachers over the years to provide appropriate in-class assignments. This arrangement was continued until Natasha reached the end of the twelfth grade. In addition, Natasha's parents enrolled her in a special resource program on Saturday mornings that taught adaptive skills to children and adolescents with developmental disabilities. Children were taught to make simple purchases (e.g., buying gifts for their parents), to cook simple meals (such as macaroni and cheese), to read a schedule for public transportation, to balance a checkbook, and to vote. Natasha seemed very receptive to learning these new skills, and she thrived in these classes.

After twelfth grade, Natasha was given a special diploma that acknowledged her 12 years of attendance at school and her involvement in special education services, but that clarified her inability to receive a regular high school diploma. She got a job in a factory after high school, where she worked for 2 years. She then married and had children and became a stay-at-home mother.

Source: Morgan (1999).

---

may be able to work within a sheltered workshop setting, but their work and caretaking habits would need to be supervised closely.

- Profound mental retardation is referred to as **severely/ profoundly handicapped** or **custodial** within the educational field. Individuals with this level of severity most often do not show any self-care skills, verbal abilities, or motor skills. Care and supervision by others is almost always necessary. Many individuals with profound mental retardation never develop basic skills that would be expected of young children (such as bowel and bladder control, the ability to feed oneself, the ability to clothe oneself).

The diagnostic criteria in *DSM-IV* (American Psychiatric Association, 2000) have been widely accepted, but there are growing concerns about referring to a developmental disability as a type of psychopathology (Bebko & Weiss, 2006). A number of scholars are beginning to conceptualize developmental disabilities as a naturally occurring part of development whereby some individuals are at the lower end of the normal distribution and others are at the higher end of the distribution (Bebko & Weiss, 2006). This philosophy is consistent with the current definition of mental retardation provided by the American Association on Mental Retardation (AAMR; 2002). The IQ cutoff and requirement of adaptive skills deficits are comparable in both diagnostic definitions. There are, however, no subcategories of mental retardation based on the severity of intellectual deficits or of functional abilities. In contrast to the *DSM-IV* definition, the AAMR focuses more on the child's environment before diagnosing mental retardation within the individual.

The tone of the AAMR definition is important to consider, given that there is a focus on both strengths and weaknesses within individuals with developmental disabilities. Directly quoted from the AAMR (2002), here are the "five assumptions that are essential to the application of the definition:

1. Limitations in present functioning must be considered within the context of community environments typical of the individual's age peers and culture.

2. Valid assessment considers cultural and linguistic diversity as well as differences in communication, sensory, motor, and behavioral factors.

3. Within an individual, limitations often coexist with strengths.

4. An important purpose of describing limitations is to develop a profile of needed supports.

5. With appropriate personalized supports over a sustained period, the life functioning of the person with mental retardation generally will improve." (p. 1)

In addition to acknowledging the tone of the AAMR definition and the statement about assumptions, it is important to know that the AAMR definition focuses on supports that children, adolescents, and adults have in their life. Supports are "the resources and individual strategies necessary to promote the development, education, interests, and personal well-being of a person with mental retardation. Supports can be provided by a parent, friend, teacher, psychologist, doctor or by any appropriate person or agency" (AAMR, 2002, p. 4). Support activities and areas of interest can include (AAMR, 2002)

- Human development activities, such as physical, cognitive, social, and emotional development

- Teaching and educational activities, such as having an active role in the learning process, using technology for educational pursuits, and developing problem-solving strategies

- Home living activities, such as being able to bathe and groom oneself, being able to use the toilet effectively, being able to dress oneself, and being able to cook and clean

- Community living activities, such as being able to utilize the transportational system, being able to visit friends or to take part in recreational activities, and being able to interact with members of the community

- Employment activities, such as having skills that fit the needs of a job, being able to complete the tasks of the job effectively, dealing with coworkers, and dealing with supervisors

- Health and safety activities, such as accessing health care and taking medications, being able to communicate effectively with a health-care provider, trying to eat in a healthy manner, trying to maintain physical health, and trying to maintain emotional health

- Behavioral activities, such as dealing effectively with emotions like anger, behaving appropriately in different contexts, and making good decisions for one's own well-being

- Social activities, such as engaging in social activities both within and outside the family, making appropriate and responsible decisions regarding sexuality, and caring for others

- Protection and advocacy activities, such as keeping one's self safe from exploitation, knowing how to gain access to legal services, and dealing effectively with finances

Thus, the AAMR places a lot of emphasis on the individual's support system and argues that we all have a responsibility for children, adolescents, and adults who experience mental retardation. Rather than focusing on a diagnosis within the person, the AAMR organizations attempts to consider the individual as one part of a larger system that should be utilized to maximize the functioning of everyone regardless of their fundamental abilities. Because the diagnostic definitions of mental retardation are largely the same for *DSM-IV* and the AAMR, prevalence rates tend to be assessed similarly through both systems of diagnosis.

Prevalence Rates

The overall prevalence rates of mental retardation average around 1% of the population (American Psychiatric Association, 2000). These rates, however, vary depending on the severity of the disorder. The overwhelming majority of individuals with mental retardation (85%) fall into the mild category of mental retardation, which represents an IQ ranging from 50 or 55 to 70. The next most prevalent group falls within the moderate range, with approximately 10% of individuals diagnosed with mental retardation showing an IQ between 35 or 40 and 50 or 55. The other categories of mental retardation, severe (3%–4% of individuals with mental retardation) and profound (1%–2% of individuals with mental retardation) are much rarer (American Psychiatric Association, 2000; Morgan, Campbell, & Jackson, 2003).

Given that mental retardation is thought to be evident from birth in most cases, there are no known patterns that show differences in prevalence across age. In other words, although mental retardation (especially mild mental retardation) may not be identified until childhood, it is thought that the rates of mental retardation remain constant throughout the life span (Heikura et al., 2003).

Like many of the other disorders discussed in this chapter, boys are much more likely to be diagnosed with mental retardation than girls. The ratio of boys to girls is approximately 1.6:1 (American Psychiatric Association, 2002; Leonard & Wen, 2002). The prevalence rates based on SES and race/ethnicity are somewhat dependent on what type of etiology is responsible for the development of the mental retardation. Higher rates of mild mental retardation, which are thought to be due to environmental influences, tend to be found in children from lower SES families and children from ethnic minority populations who are living in poverty (Hatton, 2002; Reijneveld, Brugman, Verhulst, & Verloove-Vanhorick, 2005). These same patterns, however, are not evident in genetically related and organically related causes of mental retardation (Hatton, 2002; Reijneveld et al., 2005). As mentioned in more depth in the etiology section, it appears that low SES is a risk factor for the development of mild retardation. A number of scholars have noted the irony of high rates of mild mental retardation, which are tied to lower SES environments, in some of the richest countries in the world (Emerson, 2004). For overall prevalence rates as well as the issue of the links between lower SES and mild mental retardation, comparable rates of mental retardation have been found internationally, including in South Africa, England, Finland, and the Netherlands (Christianson et al., 2002; Hatton, 2002; Heikura et al., 2003; Reijneveld et al., 2005). Table 13.5 provides an overview of the prevalence information for mental retardation.

Comorbidity

A great number of neurological disorders and psychological disorders co-occur frequently with mental retardation (Dekker & Koot, 2003; Dosen & Day, 2001). Epilepsy is quite commonly found in individuals with mental retardation, and the rates of epilepsy appear to be higher for individuals with more severe levels of mental retardation (Besag, 2002). Cerebral palsy, motor impairments, visual impairments (e.g., blindness), and hearing impairments (e.g., deafness) are also much more common in individuals diagnosed with mental retardation than in individuals who are of normal intelligence

TABLE 13.5 Overview of Prevalence Information for Mental Retardation

Prevalence	1.0% overall
Mild	2.7% of population, 85% of individuals with MR
Moderate	0.2% of population, 10% of individuals with MR
Severe	0.1% of population, 3–4% of individuals with MR
Profound	0.05% of population, 1–2% of individuals with MR
Age	Usually evident from birth, except in mild category
Gender	Boys > Girls (Approximately 1.6:1 ratio boys to girls)
SES	Mixed pattern based on hypothesized etiology
Race/Ethnicity	Mixed pattern based on hypothesized etiology

(Beckung & Hagberg, 2002; Mervis, Boyle, & Yeargin-Allsopp, 2002).

There are also high rates of comorbidity with pervasive developmental disorders, such as autistic disorder and Rett's disorder. Depending on the sample and the severity of the mental retardation, rates of comorbidity between mental retardation and pervasive developmental disorders range from 1.8% to 82.2% (de Bildt, Sytema, Kraijer, & Minderaa, 2005). Lower rates tend to be found with community samples of higher functioning children and adolescents, such as those with mild severity of mental retardation, whereas the highest rates of comorbidity are found with individuals who are at the profound level of severity of mental retardation and who are in a clinical or residential setting (de Bildt, Sytema, Kraijer, & Minderaa, 2005). One study found that the prevalence between mental retardation and a pervasive developmental disorder ranged from 7.8% to 19.8%, with the most reliable figure being 16.7% (de Bildt, et al., 2005). Thus, it is quite common for mental retardation, especially severe and profound mental retardation, to co-occur with pervasive developmental disorders such as autistic disorder and Rett's disorder (de Bildt, et al., 2005; Kent, Evans, Paul, & Sharp, 1999; Mount, Charman, Hastings, Reilly, & Cass, 2003).

With regard to psychopathology other than the pervasive developmental disorders, estimates range from 1.0% to 21.9% of disorders that co-occur with mental retardation (Dekker & Koot, 2003; Hodapp & Dykens, 2003). This range occurs due to different studies and different methodologies of identifying psychological disorders that are comorbid with mental retardation. Specifically, studies that use case files of children and adolescents with mental retardation find that lower rates are diagnosed with both mental retardation and another psychological disorder (Hodapp & Dykens, 2003). When studies use psychopathology rating scales of children and adolescents in institutional settings or clinical settings, then the prevalence rates of comorbidity are much higher (Dekker & Koot, 2003). In either case, it is clear that a substantial number of children and adolescents are diagnosed with mental retardation in addition to another type of psychopathology. Types of comorbid psychopathologies include attention-deficit/hyperactivity disorder, major depressive disorder, anxiety disorder, and oppositional defiant disorder (Dekker & Koot, 2003; Sturmey, 2002). The term, **dual diagnosis** is often used to refer to individuals who are diagnosed with both mental retardation and another type of psychopathology (Bebko & Weiss, 2006; Dekker, Koot, vanderEnde, & Verhulst, 2002; Fabry, Reitz, & Luster, 2002).

When dimensional conceptualizations of emotional/behavioral problems are explored, a high percentage of children and adolescents continue to show emotional/behavioral problems (Dekker & Koot, 2003; Maes, Broekman, Dosen, & Nauts, 2003). A wide range of problems are common in children and adolescents with mental retardation, including

- Aggression and antisocial behavior (Dickson, Emerson, & Hatton, 2005; Dosen, 2004; Emerson, Robertson, & Wood, 2005)
- Compulsive-like behaviors (Evans & Gray, 2000)
- Self-injurious behavior with no apparent intent of suicide (Petty & Oliver, 2005)
- Suicidality (Lunsky, 2004)
- Academic difficulties (Palermo et al., 2002)
- Speech and language problems (Lerman et al., 2005; Tallal & Benasich, 2002)
- Sleep problems (Didden, Korzilius, van Aperlo, van Overloop, & de Vries, 2002)
- Social problems and social skills deficits (Bellanti, Bierman, & Conduct Problems Prevention Research Group, 2000; de Bildt, Serra, Luteijn, Kraijer, Sytema, & Minderaa, 2005)
- Attachment difficulties (Ganiban, Barnett, & Cicchetti, 2000; Janssen, Schuengel, & Stolk, 2002)
- Physical health problems and obesity (Lin, Yen, Li, & Wu, 2005; Zijlstra & Vlaskamp, 2005).

Overall, it is not uncommon for other psychological, behavioral, and social problems to co-occur with mental retardation. Recall, however, that individuals with mental retardation also have many strengths, and they can sometimes show high levels of adaptive functioning in certain areas (de Bildt, et al., 2005). For example, when compared with normally developing children and children with unspecified mental retardation, children with Down's syndrome were more likely to look at another child who was distressed and were more likely to comfort a distressed child (Kasari, Freeman, & Bass, 2003). Thus, children and adolescents with mental retardation and other intellectual disabilities should be evaluated for both their deficits as well as their strengths (Mohr & Gray, 2005).

> *I often hear people comment on how happy kids with Down's syndrome are and how loving.... That image of "dumb and happy" is so unfair. Joel is a typical child; sometimes he's happy and loving and sometimes he's downright miserable.... Sounds like a typical six-year-old, doesn't it?*
>
> —Mother of a child with Down's syndrome (Marsh, 1995, pp. 10–11)

Course of the Disorder

Some mental retardation, such as Down's syndrome, is detected at birth (or earlier through genetic testing), whereas other more subtle forms of mental retardation are not detected or confirmed until later in childhood (Hodapp & Dykens, 2003). With the more subtle forms of mental retardation, there do appear to be differences that are evident by the age of 1. As mentioned in chapter 12, a study of videotapes of children's first-year birthday parties shed light into subtle differences in functioning between children later diagnosed with mental retardation, autism, or no disorder (Osterling et al., 2002). This study showed that children who were later diagnosed with mental retardation or autism used nonverbal gestures less than typically developing children, and they looked at objects held by others less frequently than typically developing children (Osterling et al., 2002). Children who were later diagnosed with mental retardation showed greater ability to respond to their name and to look at other children and adults than did children who were later diagnosed with autism (Osterling et al., 2002). This study suggested that subtle differences in children with mental retardation can be perceived as early as 1 year of age.

Regarding functional deficits, children and adolescents with developmental disabilities will continue to

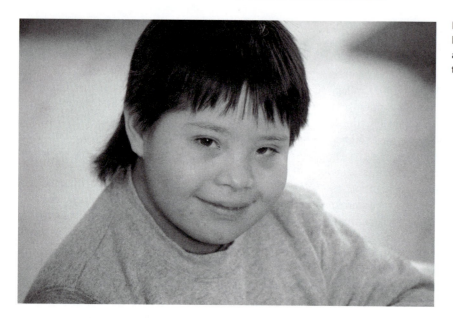

Like most children, children with Down's syndrome can have many assets and strengths in addition to their limitations.

show delays throughout their lifetimes. Interestingly, individuals with mental retardation show even more consistency across time in their intellectual functioning (based on standardized IQ tests) than do individuals with normal or above-average intelligence (Sattler, 2002). Behavior problems also appear to be very consistent across the lives of children and adolescents, whereby children with high levels of behavior problems will likely be the adolescents who show high levels of behavior problems (Chadwick, Kusel, Cuddy, & Taylor, 2005). Long-term prospective studies have found that lower intellectual functioning is predictive of a whole host of negative outcomes, such as crime, substance use disorders, mental disorders, poor educational outcomes, limited occupational outcomes, and riskier sexual practices in terms of more partners and more pregnancies (Fergusson, Horwood, & Ridder, 2005). Most of these outcomes, however, appear to be more related to childhood behavior problems and family dysfunction rather than intellectual functioning per se. Lower intellectual functioning was predictive of poorer educational and occupational outcomes, even when controlling statistically for earlier behavior problems and family circumstances (Fergusson et al., 2005).

Regardless of the chronic nature of intellectual deficits and behavior problems, children and adolescents with mental retardation can continue to learn new skills and challenge themselves for greater accomplishments throughout their lifetimes, but they usually will continue to show developmental delays and behavioral difficulties when compared to same-aged peers (Hodapp, Kazemi, Rosner, & Dykens, 2006; Sattler, 2002).

Within the family context, it is important to consider developmental changes and challenges in raising a child with mental retardation. When parents of preschool children with or without intellectual disabilities are compared, there are few differences on parental depression or marital adjustment (Baker, Blacher, & Olsson, 2005). Interestingly, parents of both intellectually delayed children and nondelayed children reported greater levels of distress when there were higher levels of child behavior problems (Baker et al., 2005). Thus, there may be more commonalities between parents of delayed and nondelayed children than previously thought.

Parents' stress levels do, however, covary in relation to their children's functioning. Parents of children with autism reported higher levels of stress than parents of children with Down's syndrome, cerebral palsy, intellectual delays not related to Down's syndrome, and typically developing children (Eisenhower, Baker, & Blacher, 2005). Relatedly, children with Down's syndrome showed significantly less behavioral problems than children with autism (Eisenhower et al., 2005). In contrast to parents of typically developing children, however, parents of children with intellectual disabilities tend to report greater stress. These differences appear to be related to the children's level of problem behavior rather than the intellectual disability per se, given that the differences disappear when the children's behavioral problems are controlled statistically (Blacher, Neece, & Paczkowski, 2005). These patterns have been found in families with adopted children as well as in families with biological children (Leung & Erich, 2002). Thus, parental functioning and stress level should be evaluated to help families who might be struggling with a special-needs child.

In addition to considering the course of mental retardation in childhood and adolescence, there is a great deal of attention given to the functioning of adults with mental retardation and other intellectual disabilities. A number of life skills are needed for adults to live independently or semi-independently. Skills such as financial decision making or even balancing a checkbook are important to consider if someone with mild mental retardation wishes to live semi-independently (Suto, Clare, Holland, & Watson, 2005). There has also been a focus on quality of life in individuals with mental retardation as they grow into adulthood and older age. Although interventions of remedial skills may still be in place, the goals of researchers and practitioners who focus on quality of life are to ensure that individuals with intellectual disabilities can lead fulfilling and enjoyable lives no matter what their level of functioning (Verdugo, Schalock, Keith, & Stancliff, 2005). There are a number of valid assessments of quality of life, and these assessments can be tied to appropriate prevention or intervention services (Verdugo et al., 2005).

As individuals with mental retardation approach their later years, other complications may arise. There is a shortened life expectancy for individuals with Down's syndrome (Bittles & Glasson, 2004); however, it has increased steadily over the past century. For example, in 1929 children with Down's syndrome were only expected to live to the age of 9. This number rose to 12 years old in 1949, 18 in 1963, 30 in 1973, 35 in 1982, 56 in 1991, and 60 in 2002 (Bittles & Glasson, 2004). Figure 13.4 shows this trend graphically. Thus, although there continues to be a shortened life expectancy for individuals with Down's syndrome, the gap in life expectancy between those with and without Down's syndrome has decreased substantially over the past century.

With that time frame in mind, it is important to know that individuals with Down's syndrome who are over 45 years old have a significant risk for the onset of Alzheimer's disease, especially if they have epilepsy that started later in their life (Menendez, 2005). Both congenital heart defects and environmentally based heart functioning issues are also of concern to adults with mental retardation. Approximately 48% of individuals with Down's syndrome have some type of congenital heart defect (Bittles & Glasson, 2004). In addition, because of heightened levels of obesity in individuals with mental retardation, there is also a heightened risk for coronary artery disease and heart attacks in later life (Walsh, 2005). Thus, a number of health-related complications and neurological difficulties as expressed through Alzheimer's disease and epilepsy are important to be considered when providing services to adults and the elderly who have intellectual disabilities. Like programs geared at intellectually adequate individuals of all ages, prevention

FIGURE 13.4 Life expectancy (in years) of Down's syndrome individuals over the past three-quarters of a century.

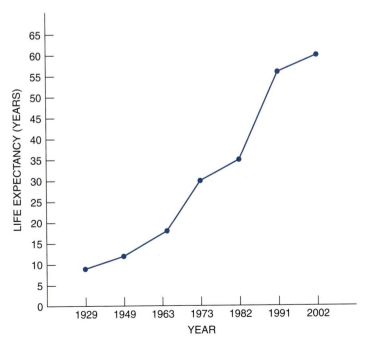

programs to increase the physical exercise of older adults with mental retardation show benefits in both physical health and in adaptive functioning (Walsh, 2005).

Etiology

Many possible etiologies lead to mental retardation, but between 30% and 40% of the cases of mental retardation have no known risk factor or genetic marker that explains its occurrence (American Psychiatric Association, 2000). It is likely that different types of mental retardation have different etiologies (Morgan et al., 2003). As can be seen in Table 13.6, possible known etiologies of mental retardation include hereditary disorders that are based on parental genotype, early alterations of embryonic development, problems in later pregnancy and perinatal problems, acquired childhood diseases or accidents, and environmental influences. Although prenatal testing (such as amniocentesis or chorionic villus sampling) can be used to detect some chromosomal abnormalities before birth, the majority of etiologies of mental retardation cannot be detected before the birth of a child. In general, children who show severe or profound mental retardation are most likely to have hereditary reasons for the mental retardation or to have experienced early alterations in their embryonic development (Stromme & Hagberg, 2000).

A great wealth of information, and some implications for prevention programs, is contained in the knowledge of etiological factors for the development of mental retardation. In terms of hereditary disorders, only 5% of the cases of mental retardation are known to be due to factors such as errors of metabolism (e.g., Tay-Sachs disease, phenylketonuria), other single-gene abnormalities (e.g., neurofibromatosis), or other chromosomal aberrations (e.g., fragile X syndrome; Plomin & Walker, 2003). Some of these disorders could be prevented with genetic testing of parents before pregnancy (such as Tay-Sachs), but genetic counseling in relation to the prevention of mental retardation is complicated, especially when dealing with adolescents and young adults (Harel, Abuelo, & Kazura, 2003; Tercyak, 2003).

Approximately 30% of the cases of mental retardation are due to early alterations of embryonic development. Probably the best known example is Down's syndrome (which is a chromosomal abnormality related to trisomy 21), but prenatal exposure to toxins such as maternal alcohol abuse or substance abuse and intrauterine infections are also known to cause mental retardation (Plomin & Walker, 2003). Down's syndrome appears to be related directly to abnormalities within the physical structure of the brain, which lead to limited intellectual functioning (Pennington, Moon, Edgin, Stedron, & Nadel, 2003). As for prenatal exposure to alcohol, a specific disorder known as fetal alcohol syndrome develops when the fetus is exposed to large quantities of alcohol during certain crucial developmental periods during the pregnancy (Cone-Wesson, 2005). Fetal alcohol

TABLE 13.6 Etiological Factors Associated with Mental Retardation

Predisposing Factor	Approx. % of population with MR	Examples of specific disorder or condition
Hereditary disorders	5%	Inborn errors of metabolism (e.g., Tay-Sachs disease, phenylketonuria), other single-gene abnormalities (e.g., neurofibromatosis), chromosomal aberrations (e.g., fragile X syndrome).
Early alterations of embryonic development	30%	Chromosomal abnormalities (e.g., Down's syndrome related to trisomy 21), prenatal exposure to toxins (e.g., maternal alcohol consumption or substance abuse, intrauterine infections).
Later pregnancy and perinatal problems	10%	Fetal malnutrition, placental insufficiency, prematurity, hypoxia, trauma, low birth weight, intracranial hemorrhage.
Acquired childhood diseases/accidents	5%	Infections (e.g., meningitis, encephalitis), demyelinating or degenerative disorders (e.g., leukodystrophies), malnutrition, head trauma (e.g., car or household accidents, child abuse), poisoning (e.g., lead, mercury), environmental deprivation (e.g., psychosocial disadvantage, neglect, or deprivation).
Environmental influences and other mental disorders	15–20%	Deprivation, child abuse, severe mental disorders.
Unknown	30–40%	

Source: Hodapp & Dykens (2003, 2005); Morgan et al. (2003).

syndrome results in a number of problems, including mental retardation, attention-deficit/hyperactivity disorder, cerebral palsy, learning disorders, language disorders, and epilepsy (Burd, Cotsanas-Hassler, Martsolf, & Kerbeshian, 2003). Approximately 15% to 20% of children with FAS meet criteria for mental retardation (Burd et al., 2003). Prenatal exposure to other substances, such as cocaine, is also deleterious. Children who were exposed to cocaine prenatally may have limited cognitive abilities, language difficulties, behavioral problems, and limited intellectual functioning (Cone-Wesson, 2005). Overall, most of these cases of mental retardation could have been prevented either through prenatal genetic testing or through prevention of alcohol and substance abuse in pregnant women (Bono et al., 2005; Burd et al., 2003).

Problems in later pregnancy and perinatal problems represent approximately 10% of the cases of mental retardation. Physical health issues such as fetal malnutrition, placental insufficiency, prematurity, hypoxia, trauma, low birth weight, and intracranial hemorrhage are all potentially responsible for limited intellectual functioning in children (Baumeister & Baumeister, 2000; Shenkin, Starr, & Deary, 2004). Note that some of these problems could be prevented by better prenatal health care, which is often not accessible to impoverished women (Graham, 2005).

Acquired childhood diseases or accidents account for 5% of the cases of mental retardation. This category includes infections such as meningitis and encephalitis, demyelinating or degenerative disorders such as leukodystrophies, malnutrition, head trauma from events like car or household accidents or child abuse, poisoning by toxic environmental agents like lead or mercury, and environmental deprivation from psychosocial disadvantage, neglect, or deprivation (Hodapp & Dykens, 2005). A number of scholars have called for psychologists and other mental health professionals to be more active in the fight against environmental toxins, given that the ramifications of such toxins are often seen in intellectual, developmental, behavioral, and learning difficulties (Koger, Schettler, & Weiss, 2005).

An additional 15% to 20% of cases of mental retardation are documented as being due to environmental influences and other mental disorders. For example, physical deprivation and child abuse (even when there is not head trauma) are related to the potential onset of mental retardation (Cicchetti, 2004). Deprivation due to being raised in an impoverished area has been documented widely and has been criticized widely given that it is a preventable reason for intellectual disabilities (Emerson

2004; Graham, 2005). In terms of abuse, not only is child physical abuse related to mental retardation, but being raised in a household with domestic violence (involving only adult-to-adult violence with no abuse directed toward a child) is also associated with decreased intellectual functioning (Koenen, Moffitt, Caspi, Taylor, & Purcell, 2003). Framed within a model of exposure to extreme stress, children who witness domestic violence have an average of 8 IQ points less than children not exposed to domestic violence. This pattern is evident even when controlling for genetic and other environmental factors (Koenen et al., 2003). In terms of other etiological factors, severe forms of mental disorders, such as autism and Rett's disorder, have already been discussed in terms of their co-occurrence with mental retardation (deBildt, Sytema, Kraijer, & Minderaa, 2005).

Finally, between 30% and 40% of the cases of mental retardation have no known cause. It is likely that some of the cases can be attributed to the factors already listed, but this high rate of unknown etiology suggests the need for greater research into the causes of and prevention of intellectual disabilities (Hodapp & Dykens, 2005).

Overall, many of the known etiologies for mental retardation are preventable, but prevention efforts have been difficult to fund and sustain. For example, the prevention of alcohol and substance use in pregnant women, increased funding for prenatal care, the prevention of child abuse, and the prevention of poverty would all be strategies that could reduce the incidence of mental retardation, but these efforts are not receiving a concerted national effort at this time (Emerson, 2004). Regardless of the etiology of a specific case of mental retardation, a number of treatments and interventions can improve specific functioning in children and adults with mental retardation.

Treatment

Consistent with federal statutes (such as PL 94-142 and the Individuals with Disabilities Education Act) that support education and treatment in the least-restrictive environment, there is a fair amount of consensus that children and adolescents with developmental disabilities should be included in public educational systems whenever possible. Although many countries including the United States have had a history of relegating children and adolescents with mental retardation to the back wards of state hospitals and residential facilities, there has been a concerted effort to bring children and adolescents with mental retardation into the mainstream over the past 40 years (Zucker, Perras, Gartin, &

Case Study: Behavioral Treatment of Susan's Self-Injurious Behavior

At the age of 19, Susan was placed in an institution for severely and profoundly developmentally delayed adolescents and young adults. She was the 9th of 14 children and grew up in an impoverished, rural setting with her parents and siblings. Susan has a very diminutive stature and is African American. Susan's prenatal history, infancy, and childhood were marred with many physical and health-related complications (including spina bifida, hydrocephalus, malnutrition, and pneumonia). Her developmental milestones were either met extraordinarily late or were not met at all. She continues to have no verbal language abilities and communicates with a series of grunts and moans. Her intellectual functioning is estimated to be below 20 and she is classified as experiencing profound mental retardation.

Throughout her life, Susan has hit herself and bit herself with increasing frequency as she got older. She often has bruises on her face and body that were self-inflicted. The treatment team at the institution designed a behavioral therapy program to decrease this self-injurious behavior. Specifically, hitting (operationally defined as hitting or slapping her own body with her hand or elbow) and biting (operationally defined as putting any part of her hand or fingers into her mouth) were identified as the target behaviors for intervention. After baseline observation to quantify the occurrence of these behaviors, two patterns were noted. Susan's self-injurious behaviors were only evidenced when she was not involved in any other activity, and she would hit herself when asked to wake up in the morning, which was often inadvertently rewarded by staff who let her stay in bed for a longer period of time.

Treatment strategies encompassed two primary techniques. Differential reinforcement of other behaviors (DRO) was used to reinforce behaviors other than the target behaviors. For the DRO treatment, Susan's behavior was observed every 5 minutes for a period of 5 seconds. If Susan did not hit or bite herself during this 5-second period, she was given a desirable food reward (e.g., raisins, nuts, or M&Ms) and was given a social reward (e.g., the staff person would say "Good playing, Susan" or would pat her on the back). Overcorrection was also used, which includes positive practice (i.e., teaching an appropriate behavior and reinforcing the desired behavior through many repetitions). Overcorrection for hitting required that staff move Susan's arms down to her side then above her head when she hit herself, and then have Susan rub lotion on the area she just hit. This process was repeated 5 times after each time she hit herself. Overcorrection for biting was instituted by having a staff member brush Susan's teeth, tongue, and gums lightly for 3 minutes with a toothbrush soaked in oral antiseptic after each instance of biting.

As can be seen in the figure, the baseline of hitting was quite high, it was successfully decreased during active treatment, and treatment gains were relatively well maintained at 3-month follow-up. Even better success was shown with the decrease and eventual disappearance of Susan's biting behaviors.

Source: Matson & Friedt (1988).

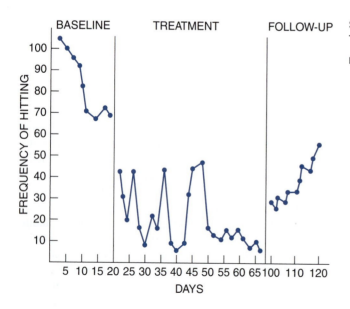

Susan's Rate of Hitting during Baseline, Training, and at Three-Month Follow-up.

Note: Each data point is the average of 2 days.

Fidler, 2005). For example, in 1964 a total of 91,592 children and adolescents under the age of 21 were housed within state institutions across the United States which represented 47.6% of all of the residents of these institutions (Breedlove et al., 2005). As of 2004, a total of 1,641 youth were housed within state institutions, which represented 4.1% of all residents (Breedlove et al., 2005). Thus, there has been a substantial and successful move to find treatment facilities, group homes, and community-based living arrangements in the mainstream of society for children and adolescents with intellectual disabilities (Breedlove et al., 2005). For many different difficulties, children and adolescents who receive services and who live in the mainstream of society show greater educational and behavioral improvements than those who receive more confined services (Kavale, 2002; Rea et al., 2002).

The majority of educational interventions for children and adolescents with mental retardation occur within public school systems (Biasini et al., 1999; Zucker et al., 2005). Many higher functioning children with mental retardation can be mainstreamed in regular education classrooms, whereas lower functioning children are often provided educational services in special education classrooms (Biasini et al., 1999).

With regard to psychological and behavioral issues, treatments for mental retardation vary according to the level of severity of the child's or adolescent's functioning and what specific symptoms are being addressed in the treatment. The majority of effective treatments are of a behavioral nature (e.g., operant behavioral techniques and other skills training techniques to teach self-help skills, communication skills, vocational techniques, and social skills; Butz, Bowling, & Bliss, 2000). Applied behavior analysis techniques (i.e., the operant conditioning principles discussed in the therapeutic interventions chapter) have been especially useful with teaching basic skills to children with severe limitations in their behavioral repertoire (Morgan et al., 2003; Zucker et al., 2005). Treatments can also include family interventions to help families deal with the challenges of having a child or adolescent with a developmental disability (Blacher et al., 2005).

Antipsychotic medication has been used with some developmentally delayed children who show severe signs of aggression. The evidence is unclear as to whether antipsychotic medication is helpful in maintaining behavioral control over children with mental retardation (Brown et al., 2005; Gray & Mohr, 2004). Other medications, such as antidepressants, anti-anxiety, and psychostimulant medications have been used with

developmentally delayed children and adolescents, but there is little empirical evidence to support the continued use of these medications (Brown et al., 2005; Filho et al., 2005; Pearson et al., 2004). In fact, one study found that there were no positive benefits to the use of antidepressants in 40% of cases and an actual deterioration of behavior in an additional 25% of cases (Branford et al., 1998). Because of past overreliance on medications in residential facilities for children with developmental disabilities, strict guidelines must now be followed before placing children in residential facilities on psychotropic or other medications (Brown et al., 2005).

Prevention

Given the varied etiologies for different types of mental retardation, there are a number of possible avenues for the prevention of mental retardation. Mental retardation due to hereditary disorders (such as Tay-Sachs) might be prevented by early genetic counseling with parents who are carriers of the disorder (Harel et al., 2003; Plomin & Walker, 2003). Prenatal testing can identify some types of abnormal embryonic development (such as Down's syndrome) so that decisions can be made regarding the continuation of the pregnancy. The risk for neural tube defects, which are associated with mental retardation, can be reduced from 50% to 70% by taking folic acid supplements before and during pregnancy (Morgan et al., 2003). Other problems related to abnormal embryonic development (such as maternal alcohol use and maternal substance use) can be prevented by educating pregnant women about the harmful effects of these substances and by allowing pregnant women better access to treatment for alcohol and drug problems (Kopfstein, 2002). Many problems in later pregnancy and perinatal problems (such as fetal malnutrition, low birth weight) can be prevented by good prenatal care for pregnant women. Some childhood diseases related to the development of mental retardation (such as meningitis) can be prevented or at least controlled through public health interventions (Kopfstein, 2002). Many childhood accidents (such as head injuries from car accidents, poisoning) can be prevented by creating a child-safe environment (e.g., always having children use a car seat or seat belt when in a car, mandating use of helmets for activities such as bike riding, rollerblading, skateboarding, and certain contact sports, storing household cleaners and other poisons well out of the reach of children). Certain environmental influences, such as lead and mercury poisoning, can be prevented by changing laws regarding the use of these products.

Case Study: The Mother of a Child Diagnosed with Down's Syndrome (in Her Own Words)

My first real acknowledgment that something was different came when one of our doctors arrived to examine our son, Joel.... It was Easter morning, and unfortunately my husband had returned home to gather our other two children and to share the good news of the birth of his new son with our closest friends. So I was alone when our pediatrician came in for the initial exam. At first I thought nothing of his questions about Joel's appearance being different from that of our other two children, and even joked about the fact that we had finally gotten a child with a small nose. When he finally shared his suspicions with me that Joel had Down's syndrome, he was holding the baby.

The warm memories of his caring and concern helped carry me through many of the difficult times ahead.... I was immediately moved into a private room, and for me that was very important. I had only needed to listen to my roommate make one phone call to be convinced that I simply could not bear to listen to another person share their joy right now. My world had just fallen apart. I had been on top of the world with my wonderful Easter gift one moment, and suddenly crashed to the depths the next....

The days I spent in the hospital were a time when rules were bent a bit and the staff was sensitive to what I needed. There was one afternoon when I think there were about 15 people in my room ... I realize that it's often difficult to know what to say, but I appreciated those people who took the risk and didn't avoid me. (pp. 45–47)

Source: Marsh (1995).

For example, mental retardation related to lead poisoning decreased by 98% when the federal government in the United States limited the use of lead in paint and gasoline (Morgan et al., 2003). Even with that decrease, however, studies still suggest that children, especially those in impoverished urban settings, are exposed to lead. For example, the rates of elevated blood levels of lead are double in African-American children when compared with Caucasian-American children (Children's Defense Fund, 2005d). Finally, other environmental influences (such as child abuse, deprivation) can be prevented by communitywide universal prevention programs and selective prevention programs that target parents who are at risk for maltreatment of their children (Cicchetti, Toth, & Rogosch, 2000; Fisher et al., 2000; Sicher et al., 2000). Although not all causes of mental retardation can be eliminated, there are a number of prevention strategies that can reduce the incidence of mental retardation (Morgan et al., 2003).

DEVELOPMENTAL DISABILITIES CONCEPTUALIZED IN A DIMENSIONAL MANNER

Intellectual functioning clearly exists on a continuum. Although the diagnostic criteria for mental retardation are important for research and classification purposes, there is growing awareness of the importance of considering developmental disabilities from a dimensional perspective. In fact, there are signs of progress in trying to humanize the conceptualizations of intellectual functioning. A number of current themes are of special importance in considering the dimensional conceptualization of developmental disabilities (Robinson, Zigler, & Gallagher, 2000; Sattler, 2002):

- Focusing on the commonalities between lower intelligence and higher intelligence individuals, rather than focusing on the differences between these two groups

- Highlighting the fact that children and adolescents with limited intellectual abilities can still make improvements in their lives and can challenge themselves to strive to higher expectations if they are given the proper guidance and support

- Questioning the concept of mental retardation, given the dimensional nature of intellectual functioning and given the importance of so many human characteristics other than intelligence

- De-emphasizing and even abandoning the use of labeling, given that individuals' functioning is better conceptualized by their strengths and weaknesses rather than a formal diagnostic label

- Increasing the acceptance of individual differences and the tolerance for deviance from societal norms

- Highlighting the need for continued protection and expansion of the legal rights of children and adolescents with limited intellectual abilities

- Highlighting the importance of prevention of intellectual limitations, especially due to the environmental influences that are associated with some etiologies of mental retardation

A CLASSIC STUDY THAT HIGHLIGHTS "CHANGES" IN INTELLECTUAL FUNCTIONING

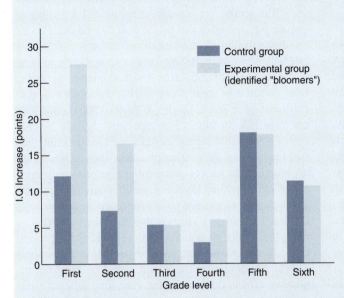

FIGURE 13.5 I.Q. score gains: Grades 1 through 6.

Source: *Forty studies that changed psychology* (3rd ed.) By Hock, © 1999. Reprinted by permission of Prentice-Hall, Inc., Upper Saddle River, NJ.

Although intellectual functioning is thought to be relatively stable throughout life, a number of studies have shown that enrichment programs can help raise intellectual functioning in children and adolescents (Hodapp & Zigler, 1995). In an interesting study with an experimental design, it was also established that teachers' expectations about children's intellectual functioning can alter children's scores on standardized intelligence tests (Rosenthal & Jacobson, 1966). For this study, students in grades 1 through 6 were given an intelligence test at the beginning of the school year and again at the end of the school year. Teachers were told that the test would identify children who were "blooming" and "spurting" and thus would be expected to show significant increasing in their intellectual functioning over the course of the academic year. In actuality, the test was an IQ test and did not have any predictive validity about intellectual growth spurts.

After the IQ testing at the beginning of the year, teachers were given a list of the top 10 students in their class who were expected to "bloom" that year. In actuality, children were placed on this list of "bloomers" randomly (i.e., there were no IQ differences between the children on the list and children not placed on the list). The design of the study was intended to see if teachers' expectations about children's performance could actually change IQ functioning in the children after 1 year of working with those teachers. Note that this type of deception would probably not be allowed under the current regulations for ethical treatment of human subjects. In 1966, however, this type of study was thought to be harmless and thought to provide exceedingly important information about teachers' expectations.

As can be seen in Figure 13.5, children in the experimental group (who had been randomly assigned to be "bloomers") did in fact show significant increases in IQ by the end of the year. This pattern was especially notable for first- and second-grade children. This study suggested that, especially in younger children, teachers' expectations for intellectual growth can actually lead to greater intellectual growth in children. It may have been that teachers saw younger children's intelligence as more malleable and less set than older children's intelligence, and thus, the impact of expectations had a larger effect in the earlier grades.

Source: Hock (1999); Rosenthal & Jacobson (1966)

• Emphasizing the coordination and planned implementation of educational and psychological services for children and adolescents with limited intellectual functioning and adaptive skills

These themes are present in a number of professional settings (e.g., school systems, training programs in psychology, medical facilities) and should continue to be the focus of attention in this area. More research is needed on exploring developmental disabilities from a truly developmental perspective (Pennington, 2002).

Risk Factors

The risk factors for the development of limited intellectual functioning and limited adaptive behavior are confounded with the etiologies that are thought to lead to these deficits. Risk factors include genetic abnormalities, biological predispositions, maternal alcohol and drug use during pregnancy, poor prenatal health care, childhood accidents, child abuse, deprivation, poverty, malnutrition, and the existence of other severe forms of psychopathology (Hodapp & Dykens, 2003; Pennington, 2002). In addition, children born to mothers with an intellectual disability are at increased risk for intellectual disability themselves (McConnell, Llewellyn, Mayes, Russo, & Honey, 2003). This risk appears to be due to genetic or organic factors, because when those factors were controlled statistically, the children did not differ from children born to mothers of average intelligence (McConnell et al., 2003). This study points to the importance of genetic counseling and pregnancy prevention services for women with limited intellectual functioning if they are interested. As noted in the section on prevention, many of the risk factors for mental retardation can be decreased or even eliminated, but other risk factors cannot be eliminated.

Protective Factors

Depending on the etiology of developmental disabilities, some protective factors can lead to better outcomes for children who have limited intellectual and adaptive abilities. The section on prevention mentioned a number of preventive strategies that might lead to a decrease in the incidence of limited intellectual and adaptive functioning (such as genetic counseling, better prenatal care, prevention of poverty). In addition, enriched environments can help children of nearly any intellectual ability to perform at higher levels (Zigler & Styfco, 2004). Box 13.6 on page 393 illustrates how teachers' beliefs in children's intellectual capabilities can enhance their intellectual functioning. Prevention programs such as Head Start are based on the idea of overcoming environmental deprivations by providing intensive, enriched environments for children who might not otherwise receive educationally and intellectually enriching activities in the home (Zigler & Styfco, 2004). As noted earlier in Box 13.3, the preventive effects of Head Start are strong as long as educational enrichment continues for a long period of time, but the positive effects do not last for very long without some type of educational enhancement (Zigler & Styfco, 2004).

Because the etiology of many cases of mental retardation has not been identified, it is difficult to clarify specific protective factors. In general, however, providing enriched and stable environments for children of all intellectual and adaptive levels should only serve to help them in their continued growth.

SUMMARY AND KEY CONCEPTS

Learning Disorders. **Learning disorders** are diagnosed when children's academic achievement is significantly lower than what would be expected based on their intellectual functioning. This method of defining a learning disorder is called the **discrepancy method** because the discrepancy or difference between intellectual functioning and academic achievement are used to determine whether or not the child has a learning disorder. There are three primary types of learning disorders: reading disorder (also known as **dyslexia**), mathematics disorder (also known as **dyscalculia**), and disorder of written expression (also known as **dysgraphia**). For each of these disorders, there must be a significant discrepancy between intellectual functioning and academic achievement (both of which were assessed by individually administered standardized tests), the deficits in achievement must impact negatively on academic functioning or daily activities, and the deficits must be in excess of any problems that might be expected for any sensory deficit that is present. A newer learning disorder that has not yet been included in *DSM-IV* is a **social-emotional learning disorder.** Children with a social-emotional learning disorder show significant deficits in nonverbal abilities, social perception, spatial skills, time orientation, and directionality. Learning disorders are often comorbid with other disorders, especially language disorders and ADHD.

In addition to using the discrepancy method for determining learning disorders, there is a move toward using the child's actual academic achievement as the main consideration in determining who is learning disordered. Specifically, if children have substandard academic achievement scores and substandard academic functioning, then they would be qualified for services for learning disordered children. As part of this movement, there is also interest in the **responsiveness to intervention,** which helps determine the severity of a learning disorder based on whether or not the child can be helped (i.e., is responsive to) academic and educational services.

Although there are no clear-cut etiologies that lead to LD, there is evidence that some combination of genetic factors, biological factors (including cognitive processing problems), and ineffective learning strategies put children at risk for the development of a learning disorder. Links between difficulties in **phonological awareness** (the ability to know sounds within words) and reading disorders are receiving particular attention from an etiological perspective.

Learning Disorders and Learning Problems Conceptualized in a Dimensional Manner.   Many children experience significant problems with learning but do not meet criteria for a formal diagnosis of a learning disorder. Certain features that are consistent across learning problems (such as attentional abilities, phonological skills, and higher-order cognitive abilities) may be more useful to identify and remediate than learning disorders per se.

Developmental Disabilities.   Currently, the term **developmental disability** is used interchangeably with mental retardation. According to the diagnostic criteria, mental retardation

is diagnosed when children show significant impairments in intellectual functioning (i.e., an IQ lower than 70) and show limitations in their adaptive functioning. Categories of mental retardation include mild mental retardation (known as **educable** within the education field), moderate mental retardation (known as **trainable** within the education field), severe mental retardation (known as **severely/profoundly handicapped** in the educational system), and profound mental retardation (known as severely/profoundly handicapped or **custodial** within the education field). Comorbidity is common in children diagnosed with mental retardation, and the term **dual diagnosis** is often used to refer to comorbidity within this group.

Developmental Disabilities Conceptualized in a Dimensional Manner.   Intellectual functioning occurs on a continuum, so it is not uncommon to consider the range of intellectual functioning in children rather than focusing on whether or not they meet criteria for mental retardation.

KEY TERMS

learning disorders	dysgraphia	responsiveness to	developmental	severely/profoundly
discrepancy method	social-emotional	intervention	disability	handicapped
dyslexia	learning disorders	phonological	educable	custodial
dyscalculia		awareness	trainable	dual diagnosis

SUGGESTED READINGS

Beck, Martha. *Expecting Adam: A Ture Story of Birth, Rebirth, and Everyday Magic.* New York: Berkeley Books, 1999. In this compelling memoir, two high-achieving professionals have to rethink their priorities when they learn through prenatal testing that their child will be born with Down's syndrome.

Weinstein, Lissa. *Reading David: A Mother and Son's Journey Through the Labrynth of Dyslexia.* New York: Penguin Group, 2004. This book describes the experiences of a mother and her son who struggled for years to get the boy help for a learning disorder.

SUGGESTED VIEWINGS

Radio. (2003). This story of a developmentally disabled man and the high school football team that adopts him is based on a true story. The strengths of individuals with or without developmental disabilities are highlighted as are issues of loyalty, friendship, and good music playing on the radio.

I Am Sam. (2002). Should someone with the intellectual capabilities of a 7-year-old be allowed to raise his daughter alone? What about when the daughter says that she does not want to learn to read because her father cannot? This film portrays the challenges faced by a developmentally delayed single father raising a bright and precocious young daughter.

CHAPTER 14

PEDIATRIC PSYCHOLOGY AND HEALTH PSYCHOLOGY FOR CHILDREN AND ADOLESCENTS

CHAPTER SUMMARY

I have cerebral palsy. For me, it's a lot easier to make friends on the computer than it is to make friends on Earth. But I don't want to meet my e-mail friends. It's nice to have the mystery.

—Tamara, 14, South Africa

PEDIATRIC PSYCHOLOGY

In some ways, **pediatric psychology** is where the field of psychology meets the field of medicine. Also known as child health psychology, pediatric psychology encompasses several aspects of child functioning in relation to physical health and well-being (Roberts, Mitchell, & McNeal, 2003). The focus of pediatric psychology includes research, consultation, assessment, and treatment (Drotar, 2000; Roberts et al., 2003). Prevention programs, such as health promotion, are an integral part of pediatric psychology (Durlak, 2000; Fuemmeler, 2004; McDonald et al., 2005). As can be seen in Box 14.1, a diverse array of topics are covered within the field of pediatric psychology.

Some psychological disorders (such as eating disorders, elimination disorders) tend to be discussed within pediatric psychology because of their connections with health-involved behaviors (i.e., eating and elimination, respectively). Other psychological or physical disorders (such as somatoform disorders, factitious disorders, and genetic chromosomal disorders) are almost always tied to the discussion of pediatric psychology or health psychology because of their direct relevance to physical health and symptoms. Within the field of pediatric psychology, however, there is also a great deal of attention to issues that are not specific to psychological disorders. For example, pediatric psychology focuses on how chronic illness in children (e.g., diabetes, sickle-cell anemia, cancer, and AIDS) and how chronic illness in parents (e.g., cancer, AIDS) influence children's emotional/behavioral functioning. There is an emphasis on treatment and prevention of problems within the area of pediatric psychology (Fuemmeler, 2004; Roberts et al., 2003). In particular, there is a strong focus on maintaining health and on promoting positive health behaviors (Brown, Boeving, LaRosa, & Carpenter, 2006; Durlak, 2000; Holden, 2003). Thus, pediatric psychology is the application of developmental psychopathology to the physical well-being of children, adolescents, and families.

BOX *14.1*

SELECTED TOPICS COVERED IN THE HANDBOOK OF PEDIATRIC PSYCHOLOGY (3RD ED.)

Issues That Cut Across the Field

Health promotion
Prevention of injuries and disease
Adherence to prescribed medical regimens
Psychosocial adjustment of children with chronic physical conditions
Families and other systems in pediatric psychology
Management of pain and distress
Psychopharmacology

Chronic Medical Conditions

Prematurity and the neonatal intensive care unit
Pediatric asthma
Cystic fibrosis
Childhood diabetes
Sickle cell disease and hemophilia
Pediatric oncology
HIV/AIDS in children and adolescents
Brain and spinal cord injury
Juvenile rheumatoid arthritis
Cardiovascular disease
Pediatric burns
Pediatric abdominal disorders

Developmental, Behavioral, and Cognitive/Affective Conditions

Pediatric feeding problems
Failure to thrive
Autism and mental retardation
Pediatric obesity
Elimination disorders (enuresis and encopresis)
Habit disorders (bruxism, trichotillomania, and tics)
Pediatric sleep disorders
Attention-deficit/hyperactivity disorder
Anorexia nervosa and bulimia nervosa
Child maltreatment

Emerging Issues

Racial and ethnic health disparity and access to care
Quality of life
Genetic disorders and genetic testing
Telehealth
International pediatric psychology

Source: Roberts (2003).

Pediatric psychology is a relatively new area of study in relation to other fields of study. The *Journal of Pediatric Psychology* was first published in 1976, which can be compared with a more established journal such as the *Journal of Abnormal Psychology,* which was first published in 1906. As can be seen in Table 14.1, a wide variety of physical, health, and emotional issues are covered in the *Journal of Pediatric Psychology.* Another indication of the breadth, and newly established status of pediatric psychology is that the Society of Pediatric Psychology was recognized formally as a division of the American Psychological Association (Division 54) in 1999. Obviously, work in pediatric psychology had taken place before these two events. Establishing a journal and a division within APA, however, were symbolic of the formal existence of pediatric psychology as an area of specialty. Most often, pediatric psychologists are trained first as clinical child psychologists and researchers, and then they specialize in pediatric issues throughout their training. Given this new area of study, various disorders and issues within pediatric psychology will be covered in this chapter.

my hand holds the taco
against the will of my anorexic mind.
but most days I'm strong
the self I know as my Flesh
is the winner.
it fights my other self,
the irrational self that is my Thoughts,
that tells me not to consume,
that tells me that food is evil.
—E.G.K.Z., 17, Northeastern United States (Shandler, 1999, p. 16)

EATING DISORDERS AND OBESITY

Anorexia nervosa and bulimia nervosa are the two primary eating disorders that occur in childhood or adolescence. Both problems are associated with a severe pattern of maladaptive eating. In the case of **anorexia nervosa,** the pattern of maladaptive eating is characterized by extremely limited intake of food, whereas **bulimia nervosa** is characterized by the intake and then purging of excessive amounts of food. Both disorders are extremely serious and are potentially life-threatening (American Psychiatric Association, 2000).

TABLE 14.1 Topics of Empirical Papers Published in the *Journal of Pediatric Psychology* in 2004

Topic	% of studies
Chronic pediatric conditions	
Childhood cancer	13.2%
Sickle cell disease	11.3%
Diabetes	7.6%
Asthma	1.9%
Cystic fibrosis	3.7%
Parental arthritis	1.9%
"Chronic" health issues	5.7%
High-risk infants and toddlers	5.7%
Adherence	1.9%
Acute medical conditions	1.9%
Unintentional pediatric injury	17.0%
Body image/obesity	3.7%
Painful medical procedures	1.9%
Addictions: Smoking and cocaine	3.7%
Stress and coping	7.6%
Sleeping	1.9%
Other (such as recurrent pain, medical procedures)	9.4%

Anorexia Nervosa

As can be seen in Table 14.2, anorexia nervosa is characterized by being underweight, being terrified of gaining more weight, experiencing body image disturbance, and experiencing **amenorrhea** (which means that a previously menstruating female has not experienced at least three consecutive menstrual cycles). There are two types of anorexia nervosa: restricting type, in which individuals solely restrict their diet and do not engage in any binging or purging behavior, and binge-eating/purging type, in which individuals regularly engage in binge-eating or purging to maintain their low weight. Note that the primary distinction between anorexia nervosa, binge-eating/purging type and bulimia nervosa is that individuals with anorexia nervosa remain significantly underweight, whereas individuals with bulimia nervosa remain at a normal weight or at a heavier weight than normal.

Prevalence Rates Although anorexia nervosa has received a lot of media attention in the past, the prevalence of the full-blown disorder is actually quite low. As summarized in Table 14.3, approximately 0.5% of adolescent females and young adult women experience anorexia nervosa (American Psychiatric Association, 2000). As will be discussed in the section on dimensional conceptualizations of eating disorders, the experience of

Gymnast Christy Henrich died of complications related to anorexia nervosa.

body image problems and some level of food restrictions is much higher than the prevalence rate of anorexia nervosa. The average age of onset for anorexia nervosa is between 14 and 18 years old (American Psychiatric Association, 2000). It is extremely rare to see the onset of anorexia nervosa before puberty or after the age of 40.

In terms of gender, the overwhelming majority of individuals who experience anorexia nervosa are female. Most estimates suggest that 90% of diagnosed cases of anorexia nervosa are girls and women (American Psychiatric Association, 2000). Note, however, that anorexia nervosa does occur in boys and men and is often overlooked because of the focus on girls and women with this disorder. For males diagnosed with anorexia nervosa, it is not unusual to see extreme exercise as the primary modality of weight control (Ray, 2004; Ricciardelli & McCabe, 2004).

TABLE 14.2   DSM-IV Diagnostic Criteria for Anorexia Nervosa

A. Refusal to maintain body weight at or above a minimally normal weight for age and height (e.g., weight loss leading to maintenance of body weight less than 85% of that expected; or failure to make expected weight gain during period of growth, leading to body weight less than 85% of that expected).

B. Intense fear of gaining weight or becoming fat, even though underweight.

C. Disturbance in the way in which one's body weight or shape is experienced, undue influence of body weight or shape on self-evaluation, or denial of the seriousness of the current low body weight.

D. In postmenarcheal females, amenorrhea, i.e., the absence of at least three consecutive menstrual cycles. (A woman is considered to have amenorrhea if her periods occur only following hormone, e.g., estrogen, administration.)

Specify type:

  Restricting Type: during the current episode of Anorexia Nervosa, the person has not regularly engaged in binge-eating or purging behavior (i.e., self-induced vomiting or the misuse of laxatives, diuretics, or enemas)

  Binge-Eating/Purging Type: during the current episode of Anorexia Nervosa, the person has regularly engaged in binge-eating or purging behavior (i.e., self-induced vomiting or the misuse of laxatives, diuretics, or enemas)

Source: American Psychiatric Association (2000).

Reprinted with permission from the *Diagnostic and Statistical Manual of Mental Disorders, Fourth Edition, Text Revision.* Copyright 2000 American Psychiatric Association.

TABLE 14.3   Overview of Prevalence Information for Anorexia Nervosa

Prevalence	0.5% of adolescent females and young adult females
Age	Adolescence and young adulthood > childhood or adulthood
Gender	Females > males
SES	Middle and higher SES > Lower SES
Race/Ethnicity	Caucasian American > Other races/ethnicities

Regarding SES, anorexia nervosa tends to be associated with individuals from middle and higher SES groups (Wilson, Becker, & Heffernan, 2003). Race and ethnicity have not been studied thoroughly, but the majority of cases tend to be within the Caucasian-American community, and there are higher rates of dietary restraint in Caucasian-American samples than in racial and ethnic minority samples (White & Grilo, 2005). Interestingly, anorexia nervosa is much more prevalent in industrialized countries where there is an abundance of food and an emphasis on being thin (American Psychiatric Association, 2000). Worldwide, the highest prevalence rates for anorexia nervosa occur in the United States, Canada, the European countries, Australia, Japan, New Zealand, and South Africa (American Psychiatric Association, 2000).

Bulimia Nervosa

In contrast to the severe restrictive eating patterns that occur with anorexia nervosa, bulimia nervosa is characterized by frequent episodes of binging and purging. As can be seen in Table 14.4, binge eating occurs when individuals consume large quantities of food within short amounts of time and when individuals have a subjective sense of being out of control regarding their food intake. In conjunction with the binge eating, individuals also partake in inappropriate purging activities, such as intentional vomiting, use of laxatives, fasting, or excessive exercise to try to compensate for their binge eating. Although nearly everyone has binged or purged at some point in their lives, the diagnosis of bulimia nervosa is only appropriate when the binge–purge cycle occurs at least twice a week for over 3 months and when there is significant negative body image. The two types of bulimia nervosa include purging type, in which individuals use self-induced vomiting or laxatives as their compensatory strategy, and nonpurging type, in which individuals use other compensatory strategies, such as fasting or excessive exercise.

Prevalence Rates   Although bulimia nervosa is slightly more prevalent than anorexia nervosa, it is still relatively infrequent when other types of developmental psychopathology are considered. As noted in Table 14.5, bulimia nervosa is thought to occur in approximately 1% to 3% of adolescent and young adult females (American Psychiatric Association, 2000). Bulimia nervosa is much more likely to occur in adolescence and young adulthood. Over 90% of individuals diagnosed with bulimia nervosa are female, thus, it is quite rare to diagnose bulimia nervosa in boys and men. When boys and men are diagnosed with bulimia nervosa,

Case Study: "I Just Want to Lose a Few More Pounds"

When Janet was 12 years old, she began dieting because her friends and family had teased her about being "pudgy." At the age of 12, Janet weighed 110 pounds and measured over 5 feet tall. By the age of 14, Janet was admitted to a psychiatric hospital weighing only 62 pounds (with a height of 5 feet, 2 inches). She had long since stopped menstruating, and she looked like a skeleton. At that time, Janet lived with her parents, an older sister, and a younger brother. Janet's father was a very successful engineer, who worked long hours and who brought work home frequently in the evenings and on weekends. Janet considered her family to be very high in achievement motivation, with a lot of pressure to excel at every aspect of their lives. Expression of strong feelings was not supported within the family, given that Janet's parents felt that talking about feelings was a sign of immaturity. Sexual issues and sex education were also taboo subjects within the family.

Janet had appeared to be a well-adjusted, healthy young girl when she was growing up. She had a number of friends and maintained a straight "A" average in school. Janet reported that she studied extensively to earn her high grades, and that she was happy with her academic achievements. As Janet became more concerned about her weight loss between the ages of 12 and 14, she seemed to withdraw from her friends. She was still able to maintain her straight "A" grades.

At the time of admission to the psychiatric hospital, Janet was distressed about her appearance and felt that her weight loss had become too severe. She reported, however, that she could no longer control her weight loss and admitted to only consuming 400 calories or less per day in addition to excessive amounts of exercise. Psychological assessment revealed that Janet did not show any severe signs of psychopathology, but that she had ambivalence about separating from the family and growing up.

A behavioral program was established in the hospital so that Janet would be encouraged to gain weight. Janet was given meals in her room alone and she was weighed each morning. If she lost weight from one day to the next, she was not allowed to leave her hospital room for the entire day. If she maintained or gained weight, then she was allowed to interact with other clients at the hospital and to get involved with enjoyable activities for the rest of that day. During the 10-week hospitalization, Janet did not maintain or gain weight on only five separate occasions. Janet was involved in individual therapy to address her concerns about weight, her developing autonomy from her parents, and her social involvement with friends. Janet's family was involved in family therapy to help the family express feelings and to help family members develop their own standards of achievement. By the end of the hospitalization, Janet weighed 93 pounds and reported that she felt happier and more self-confident.

Upon discharge, Janet went back to school and reestablished a number of friendships. She began dating and reported a great deal of satisfaction in attending dances and going out with friends. Although there were a few times when her eating behavior became too restrictive, Janet was able to maintain appropriate food intake with the help of her therapist and her parents. At 18-month follow-up, Janet had achieved a normal weight and had continued to participate in social activities as well as maintaining good academic progress.

Source: Leon (1990).

---

they appear to be more likely than girls and women to have had premorbid obesity (American Psychiatric Association, 2000). Little is known about patterns of bulimia nervosa based on SES; however, bulimia nervosa appears to be more prevalent in individuals from middle and higher SES families (Stice, Wonderlich, & Wade, 2006; Wilson et al., 2003).

Within the United States, bulimia nervosa has a much higher prevalence in Caucasian American girls and women than in girls and women from other ethnic and racial groups (American Psychiatric Association, 2000). There is some indication that eating disorders may be equivalent between Caucasian-American and Hispanic/Latina-American girls, but there is consistent evidence that eating disorders are less prevalent in African-American girls in the United States (Granillo, Jones-Rodriguez, & Carvajal. 2005).

Worldwide, bulimia nervosa tends to be most prevalent in industrialized countries, such as the United States, Canada, the European countries, Australia, Japan, New Zealand, and South Africa (American Psychiatric Association, 2000).

For the remainder of issues regarding eating disorders (comorbidity, course of the disorder, etiology, treatment, prevention, and dimensional conceptualizations), both anorexia nervosa and bulimia nervosa will be combined in the discussion. Although there are patterns that will be highlighted for each disorder separately, a number of the issues that deserve attention are comparable for both anorexia nervosa and bulimia nervosa.

Comorbidity of Eating Disorders

Anorexia nervosa is often associated with higher rates of depressive symptoms and specific symptoms of major

TABLE 14.4   DSM-IV Diagnostic Criteria for Bulimia Nervosa

A. Recurrent episodes of binge eating. An episode of binge eating is characterized by both of the following:

   (1) eating, in a discrete period of time (e.g., within any 2-hour period), an amount of food that is definitely larger than most people would eat during a similar period of time and under similar circumstances

   (2) a sense of lack of control over eating during the episode (e.g., a feeling that one cannot stop eating or control what or how much one is eating)

B. Recurrent inappropriate compensatory behavior in order to prevent weight gain, such as self-induced vomiting; misuse of laxatives, diuretics, enemas, or other medications; fasting; or excessive exercise.

C. The binge eating and inappropriate compensatory behaviors both occur, on average, at least twice a week for 3 months.

D. Self-evaluation is unduly influenced by body shape and weight.

E. The disturbance does not occur exclusively during episodes of Anorexia Nervosa.

Specify type:

   Purging Type: during the current episode of Bulimia Nervosa, the person has regularly engaged in self-induced vomiting or the misuse of laxatives, diuretics, or enemas

   Nonpurging Type: during the current episode of Bulimia Nervosa, the person has used other inappropriate compensatory behaviors, such as fasting or excessive exercise, but has not regularly engaged in self-induced vomiting or the misuse of laxatives, diuretics, or enemas

Source: American Psychiatric Association (2000).

Reprinted with permission from the *Diagnostic and Statistical Manual of Mental Disorders, Fourth Edition, Text Revision.* Copyright 2000 American Psychiatric Association.

TABLE 14.5   Overview of Prevalence Information for Bulimia Nervosa

Prevalence	1%–3% of adolescent females and young adult females
Age	Adolescence and young adulthood > childhood and adulthood
Gender	Females > males
SES	Middle and higher SES > Lower SES
Race/Ethnicity	Caucasian American > Other races/ethnicities

depressive disorder (such as difficulty sleeping, irritability, and social withdrawal). These symptoms, however, are also present in nonanorexic individuals who are experiencing starvation, so it is not clear whether these depressive symptoms are related to the anorexic behavior or the actual self-starvation (American Psychiatric Association, 2000). For this reason, depressive symptoms must be assessed carefully in individuals with anorexia nervosa. Even with this caveat, however, there is evidence of higher rates of depression and anxiety in older adolescents and young adults diagnosed with anorexia nervosa (Kaye, Bulik, Thornton, Barbarich, & Masters, 2004; Lewinsohn, Striegel-Moore, & Seeley, 2000). For example, between 50% and 70% of clients diagnosed with an eating disorder also meet criteria for either major depressive disorder or dysthymia (Linscheid & Butz, 2003; Wilson et al., 2003). Symptoms of obsessive–compulsive disorder (OCD) are also fairly common

in individuals diagnosed with anorexia nervosa, especially when these behaviors are related to food (American Psychiatric Association, 2000). Note, however, that comorbidity appears to be less prevalent in anorexia nervosa than in bulimia nervosa (Bean, Maddocks, Timmel, & Weltzin, 2005).

Bulimia nervosa is associated with higher rates of depression and anxiety (Bisaga et al., 2005; Lewinsohn et al., 2000; Stice, Burton, & Shaw, 2004). Substance abuse and dependence (especially alcohol and stimulant abuse and dependence) are comorbid in approximately one third of individuals with bulimia nervosa (American Psychiatric Association, 2000). The connections between bulimia nervosa and substance use disorders may be due to an underlying tendency to act impulsively (Favaro et al., 2005; Kane, Loxton, Staiger, & Dawe, 2004). Personality disorders, such as borderline personality disorder, are relatively common in individuals diagnosed with bulimia nervosa as well as anorexia nervosa (Bruce & Steiger, 2005). There have been suggestions that there are two subtypes of bulimia nervosa—one that is comorbid with depression and another that is comorbid with a host of disorders including antisocial personality disorder, anxiety disorder, and substance dependence (Duncan et al., 2005). When young adult women have a history of both anorexia nervosa and bulimia nervosa, they are at significantly greater risk for alcohol abuse in comparison with young adult women who have experienced just one of these eating disorders (Bulik et al., 2004).

Course of the Disorders

Both anorexia nervosa and bulimia nervosa are more likely to first appear during adolescence or young adulthood. The average age of onset of anorexia nervosa is between 14 and 18 years old (American Psychiatric Association, 2000). Anorexia nervosa rarely occurs before puberty or after the age of 40. Anorexia nervosa often first develops after a traumatic or stressful event, such as leaving home to go to college. There are concerns that the earlier the onset of anorexia nervosa, the more physical harm that can occur for the adolescent (Sokol et al., 2005). Specifically, anorexia nervosa is not healthy at any age, but there appear to be more health-related complications when it begins in adolescents as opposed to when the onset is in early adulthood (Sokol et al., 2005).

Bulimia nervosa usually has an onset in late adolescence or early adulthood. Like anorexia nervosa, bulimia nervosa is rarely first diagnosed in young children or older adults (American Psychiatric Association, 2000). The first occurrence of bulimia nervosa is often linked to the end of a period of dieting or restricted eating. Bulimia nervosa may come and go throughout an individual's life. In fact, bulimia nervosa is quite persistent across many individuals' lives (Fairburn et al., 2003). Most often, there have been years of maladaptive eating patterns before individuals seek treatment for bulimia nervosa (American Psychiatric Association, 2000).

Etiology of Eating Disorders

A number of theories have been proposed to help explain the development and maintenance of eating disorders. Genetic theories have found support in the higher rates of eating disorders among monozygotic twins when compared with dizygotic twins or other relatives (Kortegaard, Hoerder, Joergensen, & Kyvik, 2001). Specifically, monozygotic twins tend to have a concordance rate of 50% for eating disorders, whereas dizygotic twins tend to have a concordance rate of only 10%. These data suggest a genetic link in the development of eating disorders (Garner & Myerholtz, 1998). Behavioral genetics studies have implicated both genetic and environmental characteristics in the development of eating disorders (Klump, McGue, & Iacono, 2000). Biological theories have also suggested a link in the development of eating disorders. Some biological mechanisms that have

been implicated in the development of eating disorders are disturbances in neurotransmitters and disturbances in hormone regulation (Mizes & Miller, 2000; Wilson et al., 2003). Although biological theories can help explain a part of the development of eating disorders, they do not fully explain the development and maintenance of both anorexia nervosa and bulimia nervosa.

Recent theories regarding the development of eating disorders have focused on psychosocial etiologies for the disorders. Included in these theories are societal pressures for thinness, cognitive internalizations of unrealistic images that are portrayed in the media, and familial factors related to appearance and achievement (Johnson & Wardel, 2005; Linscheid & Butz, 2003; Polivy & Herman; Wilson et al., 2003). In particular, there has been a great deal of interest recently on the internalization of the thin ideal as it relates to media exposure (Gilbert, Keery, & Thompson, 2005). For example, in a study with an experimental design, older adolescent girls reported significantly more body dissatisfaction and low mood when they were exposed to media that showed a thin model (Birkeland et al., 2005). Body image-related messages are also routine in children's videos but less so in children's books (Herbozo, Tantleff-Dunn, Gokee-Larose, & Thompson, 2004).

Regarding family factors, the father–daughter relationship appears to be particularly salient in the development of body dissatisfaction and eating disorders (Berg, Crosby, Wonderlich, & Hawley, 2000; Huon & Walton, 2000; Vincent & McCabe, 2000). As can be seen in Figure 14.1, a number of factors can lead to the development of anorexia nervosa and bulimia nervosa. There is some evidence that bulimia nervosa is more culture-bound and less genetically related than anorexia nervosa (Keel & Klump, 2003).

Overall, there is no one theory that helps explain the development and maintenance of eating disorders. Many of the risk factors illustrated in Figure 14.1 seem to add to the vulnerability of girls and women to develop an eating disorder. The best explanation of the actual etiology of both anorexia nervosa and bulimia nervosa is likely to be a combination of many of these theories, including genetic vulnerability, biological disturbances, and psychosocial risk factors.

Treatment of Eating Disorders

A number of treatments for eating disorders have been established, including nutritional counseling, individual therapy, group therapy, family therapy, pharmacotherapy, and behavioral contracts (Eisler et al., 2000; Gore,

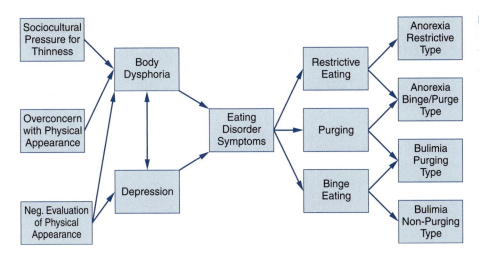

FIGURE 14.1 Psychosocial risk factor model for anorexia and bulimia nervosa.

Source: Williamson et al. (1998).

VanderWal, & Thelen, 2001; Holtkamp et al., 2005; Lock, Agras, Bryson, & Kraemer, 2005; Mizes & Miller, 2000; Pritchard, Bergin, & Wade, 2004). The most consistently effective results have come from cognitive–behavioral therapies that focus both on individuals' behavior and also their cognitions (Russell, 2004; Wegner & Wegner, 2001; Wilfley, Passi, Cooperberg, & Stein, 2006). As can be seen in Box 14.2, a number of cognitive distortions are present in individuals with eating disorders and body image problems. Cognitive–behavioral therapies can address these cognitive distortions to replace the troubled thinking with more realistic thoughts and beliefs.

Overall, eating disorders are highly treatable, but distressed individuals must first try to access treatment (or have their parents access treatment for them). Like any other problem, clients must want to change their lives or at least to reduce the distress related to their problems before they can be helped by treatment.

Prevention of Eating Disorders

Given the distress and sometimes life-threatening ramifications of eating disorders, it is not surprising to learn that many scholars have discussed the need for preventive efforts. Unfortunately, there are few universal prevention programs aimed at preventing eating disorders and body image disturbance in children and adolescents (Stewart, 2004). Although treatment programs often include a preventive component (known as indicated prevention to prevent the reoccurrence of an eating disorder), there are few formal large-scale programs for the prevention of eating disorders in children and adolescents (Levine & Smolak, 2001; Stice et al., 2006). For example, one prevention program that had teachers administer the preventive educational program showed promising results after 1-year follow-up but the sample size was quite modest (Favaro, Zanettin, Huon, & Santonastaso, 2005). In addition, one preventive intervention used the Internet to administer a preventive intervention that showed promising results (Luce et al., 2005). Unfortunately, some prevention programs that show promising results at the end of treatment are not able to maintain those results at follow-up (Ghaderi, Martensson, & Schwan, 2005; Weiss & Wertheim, 2005).

Although there are not a huge number of prevention programs for children and adolescents, there are a number of evidence-based prevention programs aimed at college students. In a comprehensive meta-analysis of prevention programs, the more effective programs were found to be selected prevention programs rather than targeted prevention programs, to be interactive rather than didactic, to be administered only to females and not to both males and females, to have more than one session, and to use well-established measures (Stice & Shaw, 2004). The effective programs were found to significantly decrease body image dissatisfaction, which is a risk factor for the development of an eating disorder (Stice & Shaw, 2004). Interestingly, the weight of the person (i.e., overweight, average weight, or underweight) administering the prevention program does not appear to influence the effectiveness of the program (Sperry, Thompson, Roehrig, & Vandello, 2005).

Dimensional Conceptualizations of Body Image Problems

More than any other disorders in this textbook, eating disorders have been evaluated extensively from a dimensional conceptualization (Williamson, Leaves, &

BOX *14.2*

COMMON COGNITIVE DISTORTIONS AMONG INDIVIDUALS WITH EATING DISORDERS AND BODY IMAGE PROBLEMS

"I just can't control myself. Last night when I had dinner in a restaurant, I ate everything I was served, although I had decided ahead of time that I was going to be very careful. I am so weak."

"I've gained 2 pounds, so I can't wear shorts anymore."

"If I gain one pound, I'll go on and gain a hundred pounds."

"Two people laughed and whispered something to each other when I walked by. They were probably saying that I looked unattractive. I <u>have</u> gained 3 pounds..."

"If I eat a sweet, it will be converted instantly into stomach fat."

Source: Garner & Bemis (1982).

Stewart, 2005). There have been strong cases against using the *DSM-IV* diagnostic criteria with children and adolescents because of the poor reliability of the diagnoses (Nicholls, Chater, & Lask, 2000). In particular, there has been a great deal of attention to the development of body image problems and body dissatisfaction from a dimensional perspective. Even without meeting criteria for an eating disorder, body image problems and body dissatisfaction can be very distressing and disturbing.

Over half of average-weight adolescent girls have tried dieting, and one study found that 29.3% of the 10- to 14-year-old girls were dieting at the time of the study (McVey, Tweed, & Blackmore, 2004; Stice et al., 2006). The majority of girls who diet begin dieting before the age of 15 (Wilson et al., 2003). Given this high prevalence of dieting, it is not surprising to learn that the overwhelming majority of adolescent girls report feeling dissatisfied with their body. This phenomenon has been referred to as "normative discontent," given the high prevalence of body image dissatisfaction within groups of adolescent girls (Rodin, Silberstein, Striegel-Moore, 1985). High levels of body image dissatisfaction have also been found in samples of young children (Steinberg, Phares, & Thompson, 2004; Thompson & Smolak, 2001) and younger preadolescent girls (Wood, Becker, & Thompson, 1996). Body image dissatisfaction has been hypothesized as the most important psychosocial characteristic that puts youth at risk for eating disorders (Johnson & Wardle, 2005; Smolak, 2004, 2006).

It appears that higher levels of internalization of cultural norms of thinness are associated with higher levels of body image dissatisfaction (Thompson & Stice, 2001). Weight concerns are associated with higher rates of psychological distress and lower rates of well-being, even when actual weight is controlled statistically (McHale, Corneal, Crouter, & Birch, 2001). It appears,

however, that body image concerns may occur prior to the development of depressive symptoms rather than the other way around. Specifically, a 4-year longitudinal study found that body image concerns and eating disturbances during early adolescence were associated with higher rates of depression 4 years later (Stice, Hayward, Cameron, Killen, & Taylor, 2000).

There are a number of risk factors associated with poor body image and with the development of full-blown eating disorders. These risk factors include being female, coming from a higher socioeconomic status family, early gastrointestinal problems, early eating problems in childhood, engaging in competitive appearance-related sports (such as dance or gymnastics), and having a close relative (such as a mother) who experienced an eating disorder or other body image problems (Jacobi, Hayward, Zwaan, Kraemer, & Agras, 2004; Neumaerker, Bettle, Neumaerker, & Bettle, 2000).

Given the high prevalence of body image dissatisfaction, it is unfortunate that there are few factors known to protect adolescent girls from developing poor body image. Interestingly, some researchers have suggested that populations with low amounts of body image dissatisfaction (such as African-American girls and women in the United States, lesbian girls and women in the United States, or girls and women in some nonindustrialized countries) should be explored to identify protective factors (Austin et al., 2004; Franko, 2002; Warren, Gleaves, Cepeda-Benito, del Carmen, Rodriguez-Ruiz, 2005). This type of work has suggested that the cultural values placed on thinness and weight restriction serve to put adolescent girls at risk for body image dissatisfaction, so preventive efforts are needed to change the sociocultural values regarding weight and beauty (Thompson, Heinberg, & Tantleff-Dunn, 2004; Thompson & Stice, 2001). Another study suggested that both sociocultural and individual factors served to protect children from developing disordered eating, including having high self-esteem, achieving in school, being connected to the family, and experiencing emotional well-being (Croll, Neumark-Sztainer, Story, & Ireland, 2002). Having parents who show authoritative parenting is also associated with healthy eating and lower risk of developing an eating disorder (Kremers, Brug, de Vries, & Engles, 2003). These factors could be used to help develop more preventive programs.

Overall, eating disorders and body image dissatisfaction appear to be related to a number of factors, including genetic, biological, psychosocial, and sociocultural factors. Prevention and treatment of eating disorders and body image disturbances are of great importance, given the often devastating effects of these problems. Interested readers are encouraged to read *Handbook of Eating Disorders and Obesity* (Thompson, 2003) and *Exacting Beauty: Theory, Assessment, and Treatment of Body Image Disturbance* (Thompson et al., 2004), both of which provide a comprehensive discussion of these issues.

To be fat is to be ignored, made fun of, scoffed at, disparaged, joked about, condescended to, mocked, and belittled—not every minute of every day, not unequivocally, not by every person, but often enough, by enough people, and in enough situations that it takes a toll on the person's very soul

—Wilensky (2004, p. 83).

Obesity

Both in the professional literature and in the popular press, there has been an astronomical increase in attention to childhood as well as adult obesity recently (Evans, Finkelstein, Kamerow, & Renaud, 2005). In 2001, the surgeon general of the United States published a report entitled, "Call to Action to Prevent and Decrease Overweight and Obesity" (U.S. Department of Health and Human Services, 2001). Similarly, obesity has been referred to as the "disease of the twenty-first century" (Rossner, 2002). Children and adolescents are defined as being overweight when their mass-body index (BMI) is at or above the 95th percentile compared with same-age and same-gender children (Dietz, 2004).

Note that there is no formal psychiatric diagnosis of obesity in *DSM-IV* (American Psychiatric Association, 2000). The most relevant disorder is known as **binge-eating disorder,** which is defined as when an individual has repeated episodes of binge eating that seem out of control (American Psychiatric Association, 2000). This disorder is not formally included in *DSM-IV* but rather is

in Appendix B as a criteria set that is provided for further study. Binge-eating disorder may or may not become a formalized disorder in *DSM-V,* and the disorder is not considered synonymous with being overweight or obese because many times individuals are overweight even without binge eating. Thus, this section will focus on children and adolescents who are overweight or who are obese, rather than restricting the discussion to the underresearched area of binge-eating disorder.

In terms of prevalence of overweight status and obesity, one study of over 8,300 adolescents found 11.6% of Caucasian girls and 26.1% of Caucasian boys were overweight or obese (Boutelle, Newmark-Sztainer, Story, & Resnick, 2002). For African-American children in that sample, the prevalence rates for being overweight or obese were 31.4% and 32.3% for girls and boys, respectively (Boutelle et al., 2002). Within the Hispanic/Latino/Latina group in this study, 29.4% of girls and 32.2% of boys were overweight or obese (Boutelle et al., 2002). These numbers tend to increase throughout childhood into adolescence and then rise even further in adulthood (Dietz, 2004). Other estimates of overweight status and obesity have ranged from 22.0% to 43% of children and adolescents who are overweight or obese (Jelalian & Mehlenbeck, 2003; Thorpe et al., 2004). Thus, there is great concern about the high number of children who are significantly overweight or obese.

Epidemiological data suggest that boys show higher rates of being overweight or being obese than do girls (Boutelle et al., 2002). It appears that higher rates of overweight status and obesity are seen in lower SES communities, although this pattern is not always found (Jelalian & Mehlenbeck, 2003; Taylor et al., 2005). One national study, however, found that 31.9% of children living in poverty were obese or at risk for obesity, compared with 26.7% of children who were not living in poverty (Children's Defense Fund, 2005d). In terms of race/ethnicity within the United States, higher rates of obesity are seen in African-American and Mexican-American children and adolescents when compared with Caucasian-American children and adolescents (Dietz, 2004). Binge eating is most common in African-American boys and girls in contrast to Caucasian boys and girls (Johnson, Rohan, & Kirk, 2002). When looking internationally, obesity is seen in nearly every country studied, but the prevalence rates in the United States and other Western cultures are significantly higher than other countries (Hsieh & Fitzgerald, 2005; Lamerz et al., 2005; Moreno et al., 2004; Taylor et al., 2005).

The issue of comorbid disorders with obesity has not been studied extensively. There is evidence that obesity co-occurs with attention-deficit/hyperactivity quite often, at least in clinical samples (Agranat-Megedger et al., 2005). Other disorders have not been investigated thoroughly in association with obesity. In terms of associated factors that are not full-blown disorders, children who experience obesity tend to show lower self-esteem and poorer body image satisfaction than their normal weight peers (Young-Hyman, Schlundt, Herman-Wenderoth, & Bozylinski, 2003).

When considering the course of the disorder, children and adolescents who are obese tend to remain obese without some type of change in their activities and eating habits. Approximately 80% of adolescents who are overweight will develop obesity during adulthood (Dietz, 2004).

The etiology of obesity is not extremely well understood, but it appears to be determined by multiple factors, such as genetics, shared environment, and cultural variables (Jelalian & Mehlenbeck, 2003). More work is needed in this area to provide a better understanding of the etiological factors that lead to overweight status and obesity in children and adolescents.

With regard to treatment and prevention, both types of efforts have been increasing in recent years (Rolland-Cachera et al., 2004; Wilfley et al., 2006). Treatments tend to be psychoeducational in nature, and some include medication when the children are extremely obese (Chanoine, Hampl, Jensen, Boldrin, & Hauptman, 2005). Unfortunately, no medications have been found to be effective consistently, nor are there approved weight-control medications for children and adolescents (Zametkin, Zoon, Klein, & Munson, 2004). Some interventions include what are referred to as diets (Butryn & Wadden, 2005). Given that there is concern about dieting in the eating disorder literature, it is heartening to know that helping overweight and obese youth use diets to develop sensible eating habits is not associated with later risk for an eating disorder (Butryn & Wadden, 2005).

Note that some intervention programs have found that the factor most predictive of children's and adolescents' weight loss is their parents' life satisfaction and family satisfaction (White et al., 2004). In fact, in a 7-year follow-up to a treatment study, children whose parents received the intervention were significantly better off than children who received the intervention themselves (Golan & Crow, 2004). Overall, family-based interventions, especially those with a behavioral focus, are particularly effective for reducing obesity in children as well as in their families (Berry et al., 2004; Epstein, 2003;

Kitzmann & Beech, 2006). Thus, parental involvement in these treatment programs appears to be crucial.

Many successful treatment and prevention programs have the same components that focus on nutritional status and eating healthy, increasing physical activity and physical fitness, finding ways to make these lifestyle changes permanent, teaching parents about healthy eating and the importance of physical activities, and actual group exercise (Baranowski et al., 2000; Kirk et al., 2005; Robinson & Sirard, 2005). Other aspects of prevention programs include reduction of passive activities, such as watching television and playing video games, in addition to helping children become health advocates (Caballero, 2004; Robinson & Killen, 2001). One study found that girls and boys enjoyed different physical activities, with boys liking baseball, soccer, and football more than girls, who liked swimming and Rollerblading more than boys (Wilson, Williams, Evans, Mixon, & Rheaume, 2005). This type of study of children's preferences can help inform preventionists as they develop the specific activities included in prevention programs (Wilson et al., 2005).

Prevention efforts have been directed at many different groups, including youth who use the Internet (White et al., 2004) and youth who are receiving routine medical care (Rand, Auinger, Klein, & Weitzman, 2005). Many different groups of adults have been engaged into preventive efforts, including parents (Wardle et al., 2001), teachers (Yager & O'Dea, 2005) and school administrators (Veugelers & Fitzgerald, 2005). Television, which is ironically a culprit in increased risk for obesity, has been identified as an ideal resource for reaching sedentary children and adolescents (Caroli, Argentieri, Cardone, & Masi, 2004). Thus, there are a number of effective treatments and prevention programs to decrease the likelihood of obesity in children and adolescents.

Because weight is by definition a dimensional characteristic, most of the work in this area has conceptualized weight in a dimensional manner. Thus, although there are cutoffs for which children and adolescents are considered overweight and which ones are obese, the focus in this area has been to consider weight from a dimensional perspective, where higher BMI scores are potentially problematic (Dietz, 2004). There are a number of risk factors for becoming overweight or obese. You might first jump to the conclusion that eating high-fat, high-calorie foods is the only real reason that obesity develops, but there is evidence that eating habits are not terribly predictive of the onset of obesity. For example, in one study comparing children of lean and obese parents, the children's self-reported intake of high-fat foods did not differ between the two groups, but children's preference for high-fat foods, their preference for passive activities, and their participation in passive activities differed between the two groups, and these factors were predictive of overweight status in the child (Wardle, Guthrie, Sanderson, Birch, & Plomin, 2001). This finding was confirmed in a prospective study that found neither the consumption of high-fat food nor binge eating served as risk factors for obesity (Stice, Presnell, Shaw, & Rohde, 2005).

Risk factors include more attempts at dieting, greater utilization of radical weight-loss methods, more weight-related concerns, parental obesity, depressive symptoms, and lower self-esteem (Burrows & Cooper, 2002; Stice et al., 2005). Other risk factors include watching television and playing video games for extended periods of time and lack of physical activity (Vandewater, Shim, & Caplovitz, 2004).

A number of protective factors appear to decrease the likelihood that children will become overweight or obese, including high self-esteem, strong school achievement, strong connections to the family, good emotional well-being, authoritative parenting, and parents who model good eating and physical activity behavior (Croll et al., 2002; Kremers et al., 2003). In summary, there is a great deal of attention to the issue of childhood obesity currently, and hopefully this focus will lead to additional preventive efforts to help decrease the likelihood of children becoming overweight or obese.

Alison told me she finally knew she was really losing weight when for the first time in fifteen years she could look down and see her own feet.... a year later she called to tell me she had just crossed one leg over the other while sitting in a chair

—Wilensky, (2004 pp. 84–85).

Feeding Disorders

The final set of disorders that will be discussed in relation to eating disorders occurs in infancy and early childhood. **Feeding and eating disorder of infancy or early childhood** is diagnosed in an infant or child under the age of 6 who fails to make expected weight gains and shows a consistent failure to eat enough (American Psychiatric Association, 2000). Feeding problems are common in infancy and toddlerhood (Chatoor & Ganiban, 2003), but this disorder is only diagnosed when there is significant weight loss or failure to make expected weight gains. If there is a known medical condition that is causing the problem, then the diagnosis of feeding and eating disorder of infancy or early childhood would not be made.

This disorder is relatively rare, with estimates of approximately 1.5% of infants in the general population. Approximately 1% to 5% of admissions for pediatric cases have to do with failure to thrive, which is when the infant is brought to the hospital because he or she seems to be wasting away. About half of those admissions for failure to thrive are thought to be for a feeding and eating disorder of infancy or early childhood (American Psychiatric Association, 2000). Earlier onset (i.e., before the age of 2) is associated with more problems than later onset, such as developmental delays and malnutrition. Boys and girls are equally vulnerable to this disorder. Little is known about different prevalence rates due to SES or race/ethnicity.

Another type of feeding or eating disorder that occurs early in life is **pica.** This disorder is diagnosed when an infant, toddler, child, adolescent, or adult eats substances that are not meant to be edible, such as dirt or paper, on a regular basis for at least 1 month (American Psychiatric Disorder, 2000). The type of substance appears to vary by age, with infants, toddlers, and young children diagnosed with pica being more likely to eat paint, string, cloth, hair, or plaster, older children being more likely to eat animal droppings, bugs, sand, small rocks, or leaves, and adolescents or adults being more likely to eat clay or dirt (American Psychiatric Association, 2000). Because these behaviors are not uncommon in young childhood, this disorder would only be diagnosed if the eating behaviors were out of the norm for that developmental level and if the behavior was not part of a cultural practice. For example, some cultures value eating dirt from certain locations, so these behaviors would not be diagnosed in that culture.

Pica is quite rare in nonclinical populations after childhood, but pregnant women sometimes engage in eating nonnutritive substances. Although there are not good epidemiological studies of pica, there appear to be more cases of pica in infants and toddlers, in individuals with mental retardation or pervasive developmental disorders, and in youth from impoverished backgrounds, where there is limited parental supervision (American Psychiatric Association, 2000). For children or adolescents with mental retardation, the prevalence of pica increases with the severity of the retardation. For example, there are estimates of pica in 15% of adults who experience severe mental retardation. There are no known patterns that suggest gender differences or racial/ethnic differences (American Psychiatric Association, 2000).

The final feeding or eating disorder to discuss for infancy and young childhood is **rumination disorder,** which is diagnosed when infants or children regurgitate their food and rechew it repeatedly (American Psychiatric Association, 2000). This diagnosis would only be made if the child showed the behavior persistently for at least a month and if the behavior was not due to some type of medical condition. The disorder is rare, but when it occurs it is more common in infants and in individuals with mental retardation (American Psychiatric Association, 2000). The onset of the disorder is most often from 3 to 12 months of age. Rumination disorder appears to be more common in boys as opposed to girls and in children from impoverished backgrounds. There are no known patterns of racial/ethnic differences. When rumination disorder occurs in infants, they are at risk for malnutrition, and 25% of infants with severe and recurrent rumination disorder die from the associated malnutrition (American Psychiatric Association, 2000).

For all these feeding and eating disorders of infancy and early childhood, comorbidity is common for mental retardation and especially severe mental retardation (American Psychiatric Association, 2000). These disorders often remit on their own without intervention, but some cases continue for a long period of time if interventions are not attempted. Etiology is not well known, but the preponderance of evidence points to a troubled relationship between the primary caregiver and the infant or child (Feldman, Keren, Gross-Rozval, & Tyano, 2004). Given this assumed etiology, it is not surprising to find that the main treatments (other than medical stabilization) are geared toward improving the parenting skills and decreasing the parent negativity and hostility toward the infant or toddler (Chatoor, 2005). There

are no known prevention programs, but it would not be unreasonable to assume that preventive programs to enhance parenting skills and parental positive engagement with their infants might reduce the occurrence of these feeding and eating disorders of infancy and early childhood (Chatoor, 2005). In summary, these disorders are rare but potentially life-threatening when they occur in infants and toddlers, so professional medical and psychological help is warranted.

ELIMINATION DISORDERS

Enuresis and **encopresis** are two types of elimination disorders that have been identified. Enuresis occurs when children cannot or will not control their urinary functioning (e.g., wetting the bed or wetting themselves at school). Encopresis occurs when children cannot or will not control their bowel functioning (e.g., soiling themselves at night or during the day). Both of these disorders are diagnosed only if there are no medical causes for the behavior and if the child is older than 5 (in the case of enuresis) or 4 (in the case of encopresis).

Enuresis

As can be seen in Table 14.6, the diagnostic criteria for enuresis are very clear about the behavioral manifestations of the disorder. That is, the voiding of urine has to be repeated (e.g., at least twice a week for at least 3 consecutive months) or there has to be clear distress or impairment related to the lack of urinary control (American Psychiatric Association, 2000). Given that many urinary accidents are due to physiological

TABLE 14.6 DSM-IV Diagnostic Criteria for Enuresis

A. Repeated voiding of urine into bed or clothes (whether involuntary or intentional).

B. The behavior is clinically significant as manifested by either a frequency of twice a week for at least 3 consecutive months or the presence of clinically significant distress or impairment in social, academic (occupational), or other important areas of functioning.

C. Chronological age is at least 5 years (or equivalent developmental level).

D. The behavior is not due exclusively to the direct physiological effect of a substance (e.g., a diuretic) or a general medical condition (e.g., diabetes, spina bifida, a seizure disorder).

Specify type:

Nocturnal Only

Diurnal Only

Nocturnal and Diurnal

Source: American Psychiatric Association (2000).

Reprinted with permission from the *Diagnostic and Statistical Manual of Mental Disorders, Fourth Edition, Text Revision.* Copyright 2000 American Psychiatric Association.

causes, it is imperative that clinicians first verify that children have had a thorough medical exam before diagnosing and treating enuresis from a psychological or behavioral standpoint. There are three types of enuresis: nocturnal only (i.e., only at night), diurnal only (i.e., only during the day), and both nocturnal and diurnal (i.e., both at night and during the day). Although not noted in *DSM-IV*, most researchers consider that there are two additional categorizations in the understanding of enuresis: primary and secondary. Primary enuresis occurs when children have never gained urinary control (i.e., they were never dry for an extended period of time). Secondary enuresis occurs when children had previously gained control over their urinary functioning, but have subsequently lost that control (i.e., they used to be potty trained, but now meet criteria for enuresis; Christophersen & Mortweet, 2001). The primary ages for secondary enuresis to appear are between the ages of 5 and 8 (Walker, 2003). Nearly 80% to 85% of cases of enuresis are considered primary (Houts, 2003).

Prevalence Rates   Nocturnal enuresis is much more common than diurnal enuresis. *DSM-IV* cites prevalence rates for enuresis at 5% to 10% for children at the age of 5, 3% to 5% for 10-year-olds, and 1% for adolescents older than 14 (American Psychiatric Association, 2000). More often, prevalence rates are estimated to be 15% to 20% for 5-year-olds and 1% to 2% for adolescents (Houts, 2003; Walker, 2003). Understandably, rates of enuresis tend to decrease with age. It is estimated that rates of enuresis in young adult populations average approximately 1% (Houts, 2003). Boys tend to be diagnosed with enuresis more so than girls, with the ratio of boys to girls in clinical treatment settings for enuresis averages 2:1 (Houts, 2003). Children from families in the lower socioeconomic bracket tend to show more enuresis than do children from middle and higher socioeconomic brackets (Walker, 2003). To date, there are no clear data on differential patterns of enuresis based on race or ethnicity. Internationally, however, studies have shown both similar and different patterns with the United States. For example, many Western countries show similar prevalence rates of enuresis when compared with the United States (Hackett, Hackett, Bhakta, & Gowers, 2001). There is evidence, however, that children in China gain urinary control at an earlier age than American children and that there is a lower prevalence of enuresis in China than in the United States (Liu, Sun, Uchiyama, Li, & Okawa, 2000). Regardless of the specific details in different countries, enuresis exists worldwide.

TABLE 14.7   Overview of Prevalence Information for Enuresis

Prevalence	15–20% of 5-year-olds
Age	Younger > Older
Gender	Boys > Girls
SES	Lower SES > Middle or higher SES
Race/Ethnicity	Unknown patterns

Other Characteristics of Enuresis   Enuresis is not linked with other comorbid disorders for most children. Although there were early conceptualizations of a triad of enuresis, fire setting, and cruelty to animals, this hypothesis has not been supported by empirical investigations (Walker, 2003). There is some evidence that developing later bladder control, for example not until age 5, is associated with later suicidal behavior in adolescence (Lie & Sun, 2005). Enuresis is more common in children with sickle cell disease than physically healthy children (Barakat et al., 2001). In terms of etiology, primary nocturnal enuresis is highly heritable. When both parents have a history of enuresis, 77% of their children meet criteria for enuresis, and when one parent has a history of enuresis, 42% of their children can be diagnosed with enuresis (Luxem & Christophersen, 1999).

There are a number of treatments for enuresis, especially for nocturnal enuresis. Interventions include support and encouragement, periodic awaking, retention control and sphincter exercises, psychotherapy, family therapy, hypnosis, pharmacological treatments, cognitive interventions, and behavioral treatments (Walker, 2003). The most successful treatment for nocturnal enuresis is through behavioral treatments such as the urine alarm system (formerly known as the bell-and-pad; Houts, 2003), which is consistent with an applied behavior analysis perspective. Approximately 75% of children can be helped by a urine alarm system (Brown et al., 2005). This method is illustrated in the case study of Sophie. Psychopharmacological treatments, especially in conjunction with behavioral techniques, have also been found to be effective (Fritz et al., 2004). Overall, enuresis is very treatable, assuming that there are no other significant factors that affect the child's or family's functioning.

Prevention efforts have been aimed at helping parents learn better ways of toilet training their children, without traumatizing themselves or their children in the process (Ondersma & Walker, 1998). Overall, there are many ways to help children learn control over their urinary functioning before enuresis occurs and there are many effective treatments of enuresis once it occurs.

Case Study: Sophie, the 9-Year-Old Who Still Wet the Bed

Although Sophie was referred originally for learning problems, her problems with nocturnal enuresis soon became apparent during the initial assessment. Sophie lived with her father, mother, and two older siblings. She had achieved appropriate bladder and bowel control during the day (i.e., diurnal) by the age of 2. She never mastered bladder control at night (i.e., nocturnal) and had wet the bed almost every night of her life. A recent medical evaluation indicated that there were no medical or physical problems that were contributing to Sophie's enuresis. A family history showed that Sophie's mother had wet the bed until she was 14 years old, at which time she stopped wetting the bed with no outside intervention.

Sophie's parents had tried a number of interventions to help her remain dry at night, including restricting liquid intake late at night, waking her up periodically during the night to use the toilet, and giving her rewards for remaining dry all night. To date, none of these strategies had worked. Sophie expressed a strong desire to remain dry during the night because her bedwetting problems limited her from spending the night with friends and going camping. Other than the enuresis and school difficulties, Sophie was a well-adjusted girl with lots of friends and a good relationship with her parents and siblings. Formal evaluation revealed that Sophie had average intelligence and average academic functioning.

Evaluation of the enuresis began with collecting baseline data before treatment began. For 2 weeks, Sophie and her parents were asked to keep track of how many nights she wet the bed. For those 2 weeks, Sophie wet the bed every night.

A behavioral treatment, sometimes known as the bell-and-pad, was chosen because of the effectiveness of this treatment. The rationale behind this treatment is to wake children as soon as they urinate even a little at night. This feedback is meant to help children develop their own internal "alarms" when they have the urge to urinate at night. A device is placed in the child's bed that sounds an alarm when any moisture (such as urine) is placed on it. After being awoken by the alarm, children are to go to the toilet to complete their urination, and they also are told to remove and replace the wet bed sheets and to reset the alarm before going back to sleep. In addition, the first week of treatment includes scheduled wake-up appointments when the child is woken up and told to try to use the toilet. It should be noted that the bell-and-pad system is developed in such a way that children cannot get shocked by the electrical wires that are in the device.

As can be seen in Figure 14.2, the treatment with Sophie progressed in a typical manner. During the first week, while Sophie was still getting used to the equipment, she wet the bed 6 of the 7 nights. During the second week, she had 4 wet nights. During the third week, she had no wet nights. During the following 10 weeks, she did not wet the bed once. Follow-up was conducted at 3, 6, and 12 months, which showed that Sophie had not wet the bed once after successful completion of treatment.

This case represents a typical treatment program for nocturnal enuresis. Sophie and her family were very motivated toward treatment, and they showed a great deal of compliance with the treatment regimen. When other issues are present in the family (such as inconsistency in parental compliance with treatment or other difficulties in the family), treatment can be more difficult to institute.

Source: Caddy & Bollard (1988).

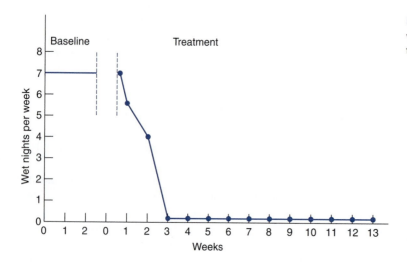

FIGURE 14.2 Number of wet nights per week during baseline and throughout treatment.

Encopresis

The other elimination disorder to consider is encopresis. As illustrated in Table 14.8, encopresis occurs when children do not control their bowel functioning either unintentionally or intentionally over a period of at least 3 months (American Psychiatric Association, 2000). Children must be at least 4 years old (or the equivalent developmentally) before the diagnosis would be appropriate. Like enuresis, a full physical exam should be completed before diagnosing encopresis to verify that no medical problems are resulting in the lack of bowel control.

Most often, children with encopresis show signs of fecal retention and constipation (i.e., not being able to defecate; Christophersen & Mortweet, 2001). As the children retain their feces, the feces become hard and compacted in the colon, which makes it painful to expel the feces. As the colon becomes more and more full, the child has less and less control over when the feces will be expelled. Thus, the passage of feces into inappropriate places (such as clothing) can occur without the child's intentional control (Cox et al., 2003). Although not formally categorized in DSM-IV, there appear to be three primary types of encopresis: children who soil in a manipulative and intentional manner, children who experience diarrhea and loose stools due to excessive stress, and children who unintentionally retain their feces and become constipated (Walker, 2003). The overwhelming majority of children with encopresis (80% to 90%) show this latter pattern, where they retain their feces and become constipated and unable to control their bowel functioning any longer (Cox et al., 2003; Walker, 2003).

Prevalence Rates   Approximately 1% to 2% of children experience encopresis (American Psychiatric Association, 2000). Within pediatric populations of children, the prevalence is about 3% (Luxem & Christophersen, 1999). Studies of age patterns have not been conducted in a thorough manner, but it appears that younger children are more likely than older children to experience encopresis (Luxem & Christophersen, 1999). Most cases of encopresis do not last into adolescence, and encopresis is extremely rare in adulthood (Walker, 2003). Boys are more likely than girls to experience encopresis, with estimates as high as a 6:1 ratio of boys to girls (Luxem & Christophersen, 1999). There are no clearly established patterns of encopresis based on SES, race, or ethnicity (Ondersma & Walker, 1998).

Other Characteristics of Encopresis   Although encopresis is not known to be comorbid with other psychiatric disorders, approximately 30% of children with encopresis also are diagnosed with enuresis (Walker, 2003). Children with encopresis show a slightly higher level of emotional problems, but it is not clear whether these problems are comorbid disorders or whether these emotional problems are related to the distress over encopresis itself (Walker, 2005). One study found that, in comparison with children in a nonclinical control group, children with encopresis showed higher rates of anxiety, higher rates of depression, poorer family environment, greater attentional difficulties, more social difficulties, a greater degree of disruptive behaviors, and lower school performance (Cox et al., 2002).

Regarding the course of the disorder, encopresis tends to be more prevalent in children as opposed to adolescents. Most cases of encopresis remit by the time of adolescence (Ondersma & Walker, 1998), even without treatment.

Unlike enuresis, there is no link between encopresis in children and their parents. That is, parents of encopretic children are no more likely to have experienced encopresis than parents of nonencopretic children (Walker, 2003). There are, however, other etiological factors that appear to be associated with the development of encopresis (Christophersen & Mortweet, 2001; Walker, 2003), including

- Not enough roughage in the diet
- A diet with too many dairy products and cheeses

TABLE 14.8   DSM-IV Diagnostic Criteria for Encopresis

A. Repeated passage of feces into inappropriate places (e.g., clothing or floor) whether involuntary or intentional.

B. At least one such event a month for at least 3 months.

C. Chronological age is at least 4 years (or equivalent developmental level).

D. The behavior is not due exclusively to the direct physiological effects of a substance (e.g., laxatives) or a general medical condition except through a mechanism involving constipation.

Source: American Psychiatric Association (2000).

Reprinted with permission from the *Diagnostic and Statistical Manual of Mental Disorders, Fourth Edition, Text Revision.* Copyright 2000 American Psychiatric Association.

TABLE 14.9 Overview of Prevalence Information for Encopresis

Prevalence	1–2%
Age	Younger children > Adolescents
Gender	Boys > Girls
SES	No patterns
Race/Ethnicity	No patterns

- Not enough intake of fluids
- Intentional fecal retention by the child (to avoid painful stools)
- Medications that may lead to constipation
- Troubling emotional factors in the child

Treatment of encopresis depends somewhat on the type of encopresis the child is experiencing. Children who show manipulative soiling would be most appropriate for some type of psychological, behavioral, or family therapy to deal with children's manipulations and children's need to control the environment (Christophersen & Mortweet, 2001). Children who show encopresis through diarrhea or who show the more common type of encopresis through constipation tend to be appropriate for somewhat similar types of treatment. Treatments include medical interventions, changes of diet, biofeedback, and behavioral treatments (Walker, 2003). Medical interventions and behavioral treatments have been found to be the most effective treatments for encopresis (Ritterband et al., 2003). All of these treatments seek to reduce the retention of feces and to increase the likelihood of defecating in the toilet when appropriate. A number of successful studies have now shown that treatment for encopresis can be delivered via the Internet after just a few brief meetings with the clinician (Ritterband et al., 2003). Overall, encopresis is a very treatable disorder.

Prevention of encopresis has focused primarily on appropriate toilet training and appropriate eating habits. Because the cycle of encopresis often begins with a poor diet (e.g., not enough roughage, too many dairy products, too little intake of liquids), prevention efforts have focused on increasing appropriate eating habits and subsequent toileting habits with children (Christophersen & Mortweet, 2001; Walker, 2003).

Dimensional Conceptualizations of Elimination Disorders

In most Western cultures, toilet training is accomplished between the ages of $1\frac{1}{2}$ and $2\frac{1}{2}$ (Walker, 2003). Of course, "accidents" can occur after that time. It has been estimated that 40% of 3-year-olds, 22% of 5-year-olds, 10% of 10-year-olds, and 3% of 15-year-olds have some type of elimination "accident" (Luxem & Christophersen, 1999). Although these "accidents" do not qualify for the diagnosis of enuresis or encopresis, they can be quite distressing to the child and the parents. When asked about their primary concerns, parents of young children cite toileting as their second most common concern, with negative behaviors being their most common concern (Mesibov, Schroeder, & Wesson, 1993). It appears that parents have higher expectations about toilet training than do professionals. In a survey of parents and pediatricians, parents reported that their children should be able to remain dry throughout the night consistently by the age of 3, whereas pediatricians did not expect dry nights consistently until children were over 5 years old (Luxem & Christophersen, 1999). Although parents have a great deal of concerns about their children's development of appropriate toileting practices, it is relatively rare that these minor problems develop into formally diagnosable disorders such as enuresis and encopresis.

SOMATOFORM DISORDERS AND FACTITIOUS DISORDERS

Both somatoform disorders and factitious disorders provide intense challenges for pediatricians and for pediatric psychologists. In the most simple terms, **somatoform disorders** are characterized by the existence of medically unexplained physical symptoms that seem to get worse over time and seem to persist for long periods of time. Physical symptoms that are expressed through somatoform disorders are thought to be exaggerated, but not intentionally made up (Bursch, 2006). That is, symptoms do not appear to be under the voluntary control of the client (American Psychiatric Association, 2000). **Factitious disorders,** on the other hand, are thought to be intentional falsifications of physical symptoms to meet some psychological need of the client and to maintain the client in the "sick role." Physical symptoms are often manufactured by the client, such as with the ingestion of foreign substances or injections of chemicals (Libow, 1998). The biggest challenge with both somatoform disorders and factitious disorders is to establish that there really is no legitimate medical explanation for the symptoms that are being presented.

Within the category of somatoform disorders, there are actually a number of diagnoses in the *DSM-IV,* including somatization disorder, pain disorder, hypochondriasis, and body dysmorphic disorder. **Somatization disorder** is a combination of pain, gastrointestinal, sexual, and pseudoneurological symptoms that persist over long periods of time and that have no known medical cause (American Psychiatric Association, 2000). **Pain disorder** is present when the primary complaints are related to pain and when psychological symptoms seem to be enhancing the development, maintenance, or exacerbation of the experience of pain (American Psychiatric Association, 2000). **Hypochondriasis** occurs when individuals believe that they have or fear that they have a serious medical disorder based on their misinterpretation of physical symptoms or bodily sensations (American Psychiatric Association, 2000). **Body dysmorphic disorder** is present when individuals are preoccupied or even obsessed with negative aspects of their body, such as a large nose or short fingers (American Psychiatric Association, 2000). All these somatoform disorders also require that there either be clinically significant distress related to the physical symptoms or that the symptoms impair social, academic, occupational, or other important areas of functioning.

There are no clear-cut prevalence rates for somatoform disorders in children and adolescents. Estimates suggest that between 2.7% and 11.0% of children and adolescents have met criteria for a somatoform disorder at some point in their lives (Bursch, 2006). The rates of comorbidity between somatoform disorders and other psychiatric disorders are quite high, but there is limited research into the comorbidity rates of somatoform disorders (Lieb, Pfister, Mastaler, & Wittchen, 2000). There is a pattern whereby children whose parents show somatoform disorders or who are highly focused on health issues are more at risk for somatoform disorders (Craig, Bialas, Hodson, & Cox, 2004). In addition, somatoform disorders are more prevalent in children who have been maltreated (Haugaard, 2004). Although physical symptoms without known medical causes are actually quite common in children, there is still limited research on the formal diagnosis of any of the somatoform disorders within child and adolescent populations.

There has been an attempt to create a body of knowledge that is separate for each of the somatoform disorders. Unfortunately, there is extraordinarily little research on somatoform disorders in childhood and adolescents (Bursch, 2006). In terms of pain disorder, the most common symptom expression in pain disorder is severe and persistent headaches (Nanke & Rief, 2004). There is evidence that biofeedback can be very effective for headaches that are part of the experience of pain disorder (Nanke & Rief, 2004). Regarding

hypochondriasis, there is very little substantive research with child and adolescent populations (Bursch, 2006).

When considering body dysmorphic disorder, there is somewhat more research than with the other somatoform disorders. Interestingly, many researchers who usually study eating disorders or body image difficulties have taken an interest in body dysmorphic disorder, and it is often discussed in books written about body image disturbances (Phillips & Castle, 2002). Body dysmorphic disorder is still considered a somatoform disorder rather than a disorder of body image, but the connections are understandable. In terms of the research on body dysmorphic disorder, an in-depth investigation into 33 children and adolescents diagnosed with body dysmorphic disorder showed that this disorder is quite debilitating (Albertini & Phillips, 2003). The majority of children and adolescents had concerns about their skin (61%) and/or their hair (55%). They evidenced a great deal of compulsive behaviors in relation to their body concerns, including trying to camouflage their perceived inadequacies, comparing oneself to others, and checking the mirror routinely. These behaviors are relatively common in adolescents in general, but youth with body dysmorphic disorder engaged in the behaviors so often that they experienced negative personal, social, educational, and occupational ramifications. A sizable portion of the sample (39%) had to be hospitalized due to the disorder, and many (21%) had attempted suicide (Albertini & Phillips, 2003). Overall, body dysmorphic disorder is relatively rare, but when it occurs, it has devastating consequences for the child and family (Phillips & Castel, 2002).

Across many of these specific disorders, one strategy that has been used in both the assessment of somatoform disorders and the eventual treatment of somatoform disorders is to have the child or adolescent self-monitor their own symptoms. Figure 14.3 provides an example of a self-monitoring protocol that could be used to assess recurrent stomach pain in relation to eating and other daily activities. Treatments of somatoform disorders tend to focus on behavioral treatments, cognitive–behavioral treatments, relaxation, and biofeedback (Bursch, 2006; Nanke & Rief, 2004). Many of these treatments are effective, with children and adolescents experiencing some type of somatoform disorder (Bursch, 2006). Usually, a pediatric psychologist would work in conjunction with a pediatrician to institute these treatments.

In contrast to somatoform disorders, factitious disorders occur when physical symptoms are manufactured or created by children and adolescents intentionally (American Psychiatric Association, 2000). The motivation

Time	Stomach Pain Rating (0–4)	Check how long your stomachache lasted	What were you doing when you had your stomachache?
Breakfast		— about a few minutes — about 1/2 hour — about 1 hour — about 2 hours or more	
Lunch		— about a few minutes — about 1/2 hour — about 1 hour — about 2 hours or more	
Dinner		— about a few minutes — about 1/2 hour — about 1 hour — about 2 hours or more	
Bedtime		— about a few minutes — about 1/2 hour — about 1 hour — about 2 hours or more	

Code#_____ Daily Monitoring Form Date:_____

FIGURE 14.3 Example of a Self-Monitoring Diary for Children.

Source: Edwards and Finney (1994).
Roberta A. Olson et al., *The sourcebook of pediatric psychology,* Copyright © 1994 by Allyn & Bacon. Reprinted by permission.

behind the symptoms is assumed to be so that the child or adolescent can remain in the "sick role," from which they receive attention and caring behaviors. If symptoms are produced or feigned intentionally and if there are external incentives (e.g., receiving financial gains, avoiding legal responsibility for one's actions), then the diagnosis would be **malingering** (which is a V-Code), rather than factitious disorder.

Factitious disorders are very rare in children and adolescents (Bursch, 2006; Donders, 2005) and are primarily investigated through case studies (Libow, 2002). For this reason, little is known about the presentation, epidemiology, assessment, and treatment of factitious disorders in children. It is crucial, however, to provide a thorough medical evaluation of children's and adolescents' physical symptoms before concluding that clients are showing factitious disorder (Donders, 2005; Kozlowska, 2003; O'Shea, 2003).

Factitious disorder by proxy, also known as Munchausen by proxy, occurs when physical symptoms are created in children or adolescents by another person, usually a parent (Mart, 2002; Rogers, 2004). Factitious disorder by proxy is included in *DSM-IV* in Appendix B, which provides diagnoses for further study (American Psychiatric Association, 2000). Factitious disorder by proxy is similar to factitious disorder in that symptoms are created intentionally to remain in the sick role. The primary difference between factitious disorder and factitious disorder by proxy is that the parents are the ones who serve in the sick role by proxy (or who serve in the role of a long-suffering parent, in many cases). Most often, parents or other caretakers use some type of drug or substance to induce symptoms in the child. The

results are potentially life-threatening, as evidenced by a case study that describes a 3-year-old boy who died after his mother allegedly gave him a toxic substance that caused chronic diarrhea (Schreier & Ricci, 2002). One study found that parents with factitious disorder by proxy are more likely than other parents to kill their child through covert means (Meadow, 2000).

The disorder would be diagnosed in the parent or caretaker, rather than in the child or adolescent. In the majority of documented cases, the perpetrator is the mother (Sheridan, 2003). On average, it takes between 1 and 2 years to identify factitious disorder by proxy correctly, given that numerous medical tests and treatments are usually given before realizing that it is the parent or caretaker who is causing the symptoms intentionally (Ayoub, Deutsch, & Kinscherff, 2000; Meadow, 2002; Sheridan, 2003).

Although factitious disorder by proxy is relatively rare, it has gained a great deal of attention in the professional literature, in the media, and in fictional stories. A number of case studies have been published to describe interesting cases of factitious disorder by proxy (Awadallh et al., 2005; Ayoub, Schreier, & Keller, 2002; Schreier, 2001, 2002; Schreier & Ricci, 2002; van Hahn et al., 2001), and some of these case studies have been criticized for appearing to be implausible (Albrecht, 2001). Characters illustrating factitious disorder by proxy have shown up in many diverse popular venues such as the movie *The Sixth Sense,* in the detective novel *Devil's Waltz* by Jonathan Kellerman (1993), and in a book for the popular press called *Sickened: The Memoir of a Munchausen by Proxy Childhood* (Gregory 2003). Although factitious disorder by proxy is quite rare, the media attention has lead to some researchers fearing that the disorder will be overdiagnosed and that real physical illnesses in children will be overlooked (Mart, 2004; Rogers, 2004). In addition, there are suggestions that the name of the disorder itself is confusing. There has been a recommendation to refer to the problem in terms of medically abuse behavior rather than as an actual disorder in the parent (Mart, 2004).

Overall, both somatoform disorders and factitious disorders are quite rare in children and adolescents. The diagnostic conceptualization of these disorders has been questioned, given that clients or parents of clients often do not want to consider that their physical complaints do not have a physical basis (Sharep & Mayou, 2004). Thus, care must be taken when diagnosing these disorders to help clients receive the best care. When these disorders are present, they provide a unique challenge for physicians and pediatric psychologists, given the difficulty in accurate diagnosis and the care that needs to be taken in treating ostensibly medical illnesses with psychological and behavioral techniques (Bursch, 2006).

Dimensional Conceptualizations of Somatoform and Factitious Disorders

Somatoform disorders are not well documented within child and adolescent populations, but physical symptoms without any known medical cause are actually quite common among children and adolescents (Campo & Fritz, 2001). Nearly half of children and adolescents complain of some physical symptom within any 2-week time period, and approximately 15% report four or more symptoms within a 2-week time period (Campo & Reich, 1999). Within any 3-month period, approximately 15% to 20% of children and adolescents report significant stomach pain (Bursch, 2006). Age patterns of symptom complaints vary according to the symptoms. Complaints of recurrent abdominal pain tend to be most prevalent with younger children, complaints of headaches tend to be more prevalent among older children, and complaints of many physical symptoms at one time tend to increase with age (Bursch, 2006). Regarding gender, girls tend to report more physical complaints than do boys (Achenbach & Rescorla, 2001). There are indications that children and adolescents from impoverished areas report higher rates of physical symptom complaints than children and adolescents in better living circumstances (Chapman, 2005; Grant et al., 2004). There have been equivocal findings regarding physical symptom complaints and race/ethnicity (Campo &

Reich, 1999). Children's somatic complaints appear to show comparable rates across most industrialized nations (Domenech-Llaberia et al., 2004; Garralda & Rangel, 1999; Rollman, 1998). There appears to be a fair amount of continuity in complaints of physical symptoms across the life span (Garralda & Rangel, 1999). Higher somatic complaints are associated with exposure to a violent trauma (Hilker, Murphy, & Kelley, 2005), with having low reading skills (Arnold et al., 2005), with high levels of family hostility (Jacobvitz, Hazen, Curran, & Hitchens, 2004), and higher levels of anxiety (American Academy of Pediatrics, 2004).

Note that reports of somatic complaints differ based on who is asked about the symptoms. For example, in the normative samples for the Child Behavior Checklist, Youth Self-Report, and Teacher Report Form, children and adolescents reported much higher rates of somatic complaints, including stomachaches, headaches, and nausea than their parents and teachers reported about them (Achenbach & Rescorla, 2001).

Factitious disorders and factitious disorder by proxy have been less well investigated in terms of the dimensional conceptualizations of these problems (Bursch, 2006). Although feigning physical symptoms is commonplace during childhood and adolescence, these behaviors are not thought to be related to factitious disorders (O'Shea, 2003). Overall, much more research is needed to understand the diagnostic conceptualizations as well as the dimensional conceptualizations of factitious disorders and factitious disorder by proxy.

GENETIC CHROMOSOMAL DISORDERS

A number of genetic chromosomal disorders should be mentioned briefly to provide examples of the breadth of problems with which pediatric psychologists work. **Turner's syndrome** is a rare, sex-linked chromosomal abnormality that occurs in girls. The prevalence rate is reported to be 1 in 2,500 to 1 in 5,000 girls (Rovet, 2004). The disorder occurs when genetic material is lost from the X-chromosome (Rovet, 2004). Girls with Turner's syndrome are short in stature, tend to lack secondary sexual characteristics (such as breast development, pubic hair growth), and are prone to kidney and heart defects (Haverkamp, Zerres, Rietz, Noeker, & Ruenger, 2004). In addition to these consistent problems, other characteristics are also associated with Turner's syndrome occasionally. Girls with Turner's syndrome tend to show learning disorders, spatial skill deficits, motor impairment, mathematical skill deficits, social isolation, and social skills deficits (Denckla & Cutting, 2004; Lesniak-Karpiak, Mazzocco, & Ross, 2003; Mazzocco, 2001; Nijhuis-vanderSanden, Smits-Engelsman, & Eling, 2000; Temple, 2002). In one study of 101 girls with Turner's syndrome, their intellectual functioning was found to average 86.4, whereas their nonaffected sisters' intellectual functioning averaged 99.3 (Haverkamp et al., 2004). Girls with Turner's syndrome are also at greater risk for being teased by their peers (especially teasing about body appearance), and this teasing is associated with depression and self-image problems (Rickert, Hassed, Hendon, & Cunniff, 1996). Although many difficulties are faced by girls with Turner's syndrome, many of these difficulties (such as educational achievement, occupational status, and personal well-being) tend to resolve themselves by adulthood, whereas the cognitive deficits often continue throughout the life span (Ross et al., 2002).

Another disorder of interest to pediatric psychologists is **Klinefelter's syndrome,** which is a sex-linked disorder that occurs in males who have an XXY chromosomal structure (Geschwind & Dykens, 2004). Other variations of Klinefelter's syndrome show 2 or more X chromosomes and 1 or more Y chromosomes in males. The prevalence of Klinefelter's syndrome is estimated to be 1 in 500 to 1 in 1,000 newborn boys (Geschwind & Dykens, 2004). Boys with this syndrome used to be thought to show higher rates of criminality and psychiatric problems than boys without the syndrome, but well-controlled studies have shown this pattern to be incorrect (Geschwind & Dykens, 2004). Boys with Klinefelter's syndrome do, however, show language deficits, learning disorders, academic problems, emotional/behavioral problems, and neuromaturational lags more than other boys (Denckla & Cutting, 2004; Fales et al., 2003; Geschwind & Dykens, 2004).

Turner's syndrome and Klinefelter's syndrome are just two of the many genetic and chromosomal problems that occur in children. Although these types of syndromes are rare, pediatric psychologists often work with these children given their need for intensive medical and psychological services.

OTHER DISORDERS

There are a number of other disorders with which pediatric psychologists get involved. Two important disorders in pediatric psychology are **sleep disorders** and **tic disorders.**

Sleep Disorders

Sleep disorders include narcolepsy (unintentionally falling asleep), insomnia (not being able to fall asleep), and hypersomnia (sleeping too much; Streisand & Efron, 2003). Approximately 9% to 14% of parents report that their child experiences some type of sleep disturbance, but the majority of these disturbances do not qualify as sleep disorders (Schreck, Mulick, & Rojahn, 2005). In fact, formal sleep disorders like narcolepsy, insomnia, and hypersomnia are quite rare in childhood (Davey, 2005; Streisand & Efron, 2003). One study of sleep disorders in adolescents reported a prevalence rate of 4% for insomnia, but much lower rates of other sleep disorders (Ohayon, Roberts, Zulley, Smirme, & Priest, 2000). Other difficulties, such as not sleeping through the night, not wanting to take naps, and experiencing nightmares are much more common in infancy and early childhood (Owens, Spirito, McGuinn, & Nobile, 2000). Sleep difficulties in infancy (especially difficulties in self-soothing at night) are associated with sleep difficulties in toddlerhood (Gaylor, Burnham, Goodlin-Jones, & Anders, 2005). Common sleep problems in childhood include children being tired when they wake up, being confused when woken up, severe nightmares not wanting to go to bed, and too much sleeping (Glaze, Rosen, & Owens, 2002; Spruyt O'Brien, Cluydts, Verleye, & Ferri, 2005).

Sleep difficulties are associated with other mental health problems, such as attention-deficit/hyperactivity disorder (Bullock & Schall, 2005; Owens, 2005) and many types of pervasive developmental disorders (Couturier et al., 2005; McDougall, Kerr, & Espie, 2005; Oyane & Bjorvatn, 2005; Polimeni, Richdale, & Francis, 2005; Williams, Sears, & Allard, 2004). The combination of sleep disturbances and difficult temperament in early childhood is particularly predictive of emotional/behavioral problems in later childhood (Scher, Zukerman, & Epstein, 2005). The connections between sleep disturbances and children's emotional/behavioral problems appears to be due to psychosocial risk factors more than any genetic predisposition to these difficulties (Gregory, Eley, O'Connor, & Plomin, 2004).

Sleep problems are associated with greater risk for injuries, presumably because the child is sleep deprived and makes careless mistakes that put them at risk for injury (Owens, Fernando, & McGuinn, 2005). For that reason, as well as for the well-being of everyone in the household, a great deal of attention has gone into finding effective treatments for sleep difficulties in infants, children, and adolescents. The majority of the effective treatments work from a behavioral method. One particularly good book on helping parents with their children's sleep difficulties is Dr. Richard Ferber's (1985) classic book called *Solve Your Child's Sleep Problems.* Another popular book, *Take Charge of Your Child's Sleep,* was written by a leading researcher in the field of sleep disturbance (Owens & Mindell, 2005). Medications have also been tried with some success in decreasing sleep disturbances in children and adolescence (Ingrassia & Turk, 2005). Dealing with sleep problems has the added benefit of improving children's daytime behavior (Aronen, Paavonen, Fjaellberg, Soininen, & Toerroenen, 2000).

Tic Disorders

Known as a type of habit disorder, tic disorders are also of concern to pediatric psychologists. Tics are a stereotyped, sudden, unintentional, recurrent movement or vocalization. Tics that are seen commonly in children with tic disorders include blinking of the eyes, puckering of the nose, shrugging of the shoulder, grimacing of the face, and turning of the head (Glaros & Epkins, 2003). Tics and ultimately tic disorders are thought to be relatively common in childhood, with an estimated prevalence rate of 18% in children under the age of 10 and then with lower prevalence rates of about 2% to 3% by the time of adolescence (Peterson, Pine, Cohen, & Brook, 2001). Chronic tics that do not go away even in adulthood are thought to occur in approximately 1.6% of the population (Glaros & Epkins, 2003). Approximately two or three times more boys than girls are diagnosed with tic disorders (Peterson et al., 2001).

Tic disorders are often comorbid with other psychiatric disorders, such as mood disorders (Coffey et al., 2000a), anxiety disorders (Coffey et al., 2000b), and attention-deficit/hyperactivity disorder (Woods, Himle, & Osmon, 2005). One prospective longitudinal study suggested that tics in childhood were predictive of obsessive compulsive disorder in late adolescence and early adulthood (Peterson et al., 2001). Overall, there were many associations between tics, attention-deficit/hyperactivity disorder, and obsessive compulsive disorder (Peterson et al., 2001).

Although rare in childhood, Tourette's disorder is probably the best-known tic disorder due to its severity (Glaros & Epkins, 2003). Children with Tourette's disorder show both motor and verbal tics and often make vocalizations that are considered quite inappropriate (e.g., unintentionally saying a curse word in the middle of a conversation; American Psychiatric Association, 2000). Tourette's disorder and other tic and movement disorders appear to have significant genetic and biological etiologies, although there are also behavioral components to the maintenance of tics for some children (Carr, Sidener, Sidener, & Cummings, 2005; Giedd, Rapoport, Garvey, Perlmutter, & Swedo, 2000). Medications, such as risperidone (Risperdal), clonidine (Catapres), or haloperidol (Haldol) can be effective in reducing the occurrence of tics in about 80% of children with relatively few side effects (Brown et al., 2005; Kim, Lee, Hwang, Shin, & Cho, 2005).

I am having a midlife crisis. Tomorrow I will be nineteen. It sounds melodramatic. But technically I should have had this crisis five years ago—my life expectancy according to average statistics is twenty-eight years
—Laura Rothenberg (2003, p. 1), explaining her experiences of cystic fibrosis

CHRONIC ILLNESS IN CHILDREN AND CHILDREN'S WELL-BEING

Although all of the problems discussed thus far in this chapter are relevant to pediatric psychology, the overwhelming majority of work in pediatric psychology focuses on the connections between physical illness and children's well-being. Children with chronic physical illnesses show significantly more internalizing and externalizing emotional/behavioral problems than their physically healthy peers (Peterson, Reach, & Grabe, 2003). In general, poorer psychological outcome is associated with physical illnesses that (Peterson et al., 2003; Wallander, Thompson, & Alriksson-Schmidt, 2003):

- Are unpredictable or recurrent (such as sickle cell anemia, asthma, or epilepsy)
- Are severe and chronic (such as sickle cell anemia or cystic fibrosis)
- Require frequent monitoring and self- or parent-administered medical treatments as well as frequent medical visits or rehabilitation (such as diabetes or cystic fibrosis)
- Lead to multiple hospitalizations or that require constant bed rest (such as cancer)
- Are life-threatening (such as some types of cancer or renal disease)
- Are obvious to others (such as illnesses or treatments that lead to scars or hair loss)

- Are related to some type of social stigma (such as AIDS or some physical differences)
- Require numerous painful treatments.

There are too many chronic illnesses to cover in this chapter, so a few selected topics are reviewed. Interested readers are referred to a number of excellent books on pediatric psychology, including *Handbook of Pediatric Psychology* (3rd ed) (Roberts, 2003), *Handbook of Pediatric and Adolescent Health Psychology* (Goreczny & Hersen, 1999), and *Handbook of Research in Pediatric and Clinical Child Psychology* (Drotar, 2000), In addition, review of the *Journal of Pediatric Psychology* is likely to increase students' interest in this fascinating area.

For the purposes of this chapter, the chronic childhood illnesses of diabetes, sickle-cell anemia, cancer, and HIV/AIDS will be covered. These illnesses provide some indication of the type of work in which pediatric psychologists get involved and also highlight the need for multidisciplinary teams of pediatricians, specialist physicians, nurses, psychiatrists, educators, physical therapists, nutritionists, and pediatric psychologists to work together to help children cope with these difficult illnesses. As you can see in Box 14.3, chronic illness in children can also impact the family significantly.

Juvenile Onset Diabetes

Formally known as insulin-dependent diabetes or Type I diabetes, juvenile onset diabetes is a lifelong disease for which there is no complete cure (Wysocki, Greco, & Buckloh, 2003). Diabetes that first appears in adulthood is known as noninsulin-dependent diabetes, or Type II diabetes. Common symptoms that are associated with the diagnosis of diabetes in childhood are frequent need to urinate, excessive thirst, eating large quantities of food and still feeling hungry, and rapid weight loss. These symptoms, in addition to a medical evaluation that shows ketonuria (ketones in the urine) and blood glucose level greater than 200 mg/dL, suggest that the child has insulin-dependent diabetes.

Approximately 1 out of 500 to 600 children will develop diabetes in childhood (Wysocki et al., 2003). This figure is relatively consistent within the United States and non-Scandinavian European countries, but rates are higher in the Scandinavian countries and lower than in the Asian countries. Within the United States, girls and boys are at equal risk for juvenile onset diabetes, and Caucasian Americans are 1.5 times more likely to develop the disease than are African Americans. Although there are no formal age stipulations when

---

BOX *14.3*

PARENTS OF CHILDREN WITH CHRONIC PHYSICAL PROBLEMS (IN THEIR OWN WORDS)

One of the most difficult aspects of parenting a child with special needs is the feeling of isolation that many of us experience. Many times, family and friends, not knowing what to say or do, will avoid conversation regarding the child, or even avoid the parents altogether. (p. 118)

What you said didn't help, you know; your snappy, "Look, Kathy, you've just got to learn to accept this" stunned me. Accept it? I wanted to scream, accept it? I'll never accept this, never ever accept that my baby has cerebral palsy, is "developmentally delayed"...or might never walk or talk. It's just not acceptable to me that she will have pain, be "different"...and may have a reduced life span. (pp. 2–3)

Being heard is the single most important idea...Jeremy has cancer and no one would listen to me saying that this kid was sick. I went here, I went there, we took him to the hospital, we were told, "There's nothing to worry about."...A biopsy was all I wanted! If the pediatrician hadn't listened to me, things would not have happened the way they did. The cancer wouldn't have been found in time, the chemotherapy wouldn't have worked, and Jeremy

wouldn't be here. What it boils down to is an instinct. (pp. 3–4)

It is always music to my ears when I hear a health professional or a teacher acknowledge the different aspects of my daughter that are positive. It acknowledges her wholeness, rather than her brokenness. (p. 68)

One evening after eight, our pediatrician stopped in to say hello after doing rounds visiting his patients. We had been admitted by the pediatric oncologist, so we were not officially considered our pediatrician's patients. He looked tired to me. Unexpectedly, he came over and asked me if he could hold Jeremy and sit and rock him for a few minutes—and he did...It was the most striking act of kindness by a physician I have ever seen. (pp. 35–36)

I am a very private person. I am not one to share my tears easily with others. But I am finding that I need to share my sadness and anger with others, those who understand feelings about parenting a child with special needs. (p. 129)

Source: Marsh (1995).

diagnosing the disease, the average age of diagnosis is between 5 and 11 years old (Peterson et al., 2003).

Medical treatment of diabetes is complicated, and many issues arise related to compliance with the treatment regimen. Management of diabetes includes monitoring blood glucose levels at least twice a day (which means drawing blood twice a day), receiving shots of insulin once or more per day, following strict dietary rules (such as eating at regular times during the day and limiting or deleting sugar and saturated fats from the diet), and routine exercise (Wysocki et al., 2003). Depending on the age of the diagnosed child, either parents or children themselves are responsible for completing these daily management techniques. Normal developmental processes, such as gaining independence and autonomy, can sometimes be hampered by parents' attempts to control adolescents' eating behavior to control symptoms of diabetes (Maharaj, Rodin, Connolly, Olmsted, & Daneman, 2001; Miller & Drotar, 2003).

Severe complications can occur when there is chronic noncompliance with treatment (and even sometimes when there is complete compliance with treatment), including cognitive deficits, blindness, renal failure, nerve disease, amputation of a limb due to associated vascular disease, heart disease, coma, and death (Wysocki et al., 2003). Given the severity of complications related to juvenile onset diabetes, compliance with treatment is considered crucial for the wellbeing of the child. Treatment compliance decreases with more complex medical regimens, when children and families must make lifestyle changes, and as children grow

older (Peterson et al., 2003). Treatment adherence, as evidenced by metabolic control, is enhanced when mothers are seen as collaborative with their child rather than uninvolved (Wiebe et al., 2005) and when the family shows high level of cohesion (Cohen, Lumley, Naar-King, Patridge, & Cakan, 2004). As can be seen in Figure 14.4, adherence to the medical management of diabetes in children is conceptualized as a central component in the control of diabetes (Johnson, 1995).

When significant patterns of noncompliance or nonadherence with treatment are evident, then children and their families are often referred to a pediatric psychologist. Pediatric psychologists can engage in a variety of psychological treatments (Johnson, 1998; LaGreca & Bearman, 2003), but the most common are

- Education
- Behavioral or social-learning interventions
- Relaxation and biofeedback training
- Family therapy

Treatment for medical nonadherence and noncompliance can be very effective and helpful for children and families (La Greca & Bearman, 2003). As illustrated in the case study of Alli, the higher functioning the family unit, the less likelihood of medical nonadherence.

Sickle Cell Disease

Sickle cell disease is a genetic disorder that occurs in approximately 1 out of every 500 African Americans within the United States (Chen, Cole, & Kato, 2004).

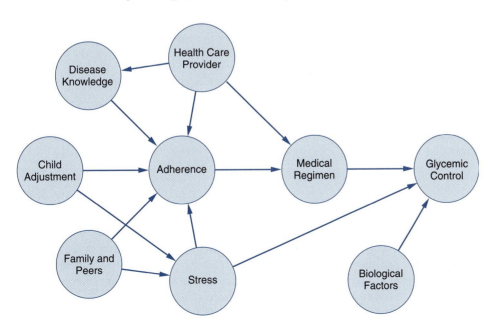

FIGURE 14.4 A Hypothetical Model of Psychological Predictors of Glycemic Control in Insulin-Dependent Diabetes Mellitus.

Source: Johnson (1995).

Case Study: The Family of a Child with Diabetes

Alli was 8 years old when she was diagnosed with insulin-dependent diabetes mellitus. She lives with her biological mother (Patty), father (Jeff), and brother (aged 14). Alli was described as an average student, with a strong will, and excellent skills as a soccer player. She had been quite healthy until one week when she began feeling ill. After being diagnosed with diabetes by her pediatrician, Alli was admitted to the hospital to be stabilized.

While in the hospital, the psychologist who worked on the diabetes team worked with the family from a psychoeducational model to help the family cope with the demands of the disease. First, the psychologist made initial contact with the family (which is known as engagement) and assessed the family for potential problems with adherence to the medical regimen. The psychologist was especially interested in the family's level of knowledge about diabetes, their willingness to learn about the disease, their willingness to develop problem-solving strategies related to the chronic care of diabetes, and their ability to work cooperatively with each other on shared tasks. The psychologist also assessed the family for any underlying issues that would create resistance to the effective treatment of the diabetes. From a psychoeducational stand point, the psychologist helped share information with the family in a way that the family could understand and also tried to develop additional skills within the family. The psychologist also emphasized the need to prevent problems before they occurred. The following transcript was from an early session with the family. As can be seen in the transcript, the family is relatively healthy in dealing with each other and with the adjustment to Alli's diagnosis.

Therapist: At this point, you may be feeling overwhelmed with all the information you have been getting.

Patty: Yes—how are we going to do all of this? The consequences for not keeping her diabetes in control are devastating. And she is already so strong willed, how will we be able to make sure that she will do what she is supposed to? Maybe I should quit work.

Alli: I don't want to give shots.

Jeff: Maybe we should cancel our spring vacation and stay at home.

Therapist: Yes, you do sound like this has been overwhelming. We'll take one point at a time. First, you should know that how you are feeling is very typical. It takes awhile to sort through all the information and figure out how the new routines will work in your family. That's why the care team is here, to answer questions and offer advice. And you will be able to do all of this, including giving yourself shots when you are ready. What usually happens is that at first, families stick to the routine precisely. Then, as you get more familiar with the routine, it may slip a little. Then what usually happens is that you develop a routine that works for your family and in different situations. While you have to change routines to care for the diabetes, you want to hold off on making other major changes for awhile.

Patty: But if the routine slips, won't that have major consequences down the road?

Therapist: There is a little room for tolerance in the routine. We'll make sure you have time to talk with Dr. Smith regarding the short-term and long-term consequences. Would that be helpful?

Patty: Yes, thanks.

Therapist: Are there any areas that you feel might be a problem?

Alli: Shots!

Therapist: Wow, that really seems to be worrying you. What are you doing for your care right now?

Alli: I am doing finger sticks. I did two today.

Patty: Yes, she did, and she read the meter as well.

Therapist: How do you do a finger stick? Can you show me?

Alli: Sure. [demonstrates]

Patty: And she only had to be shown this once.

Therapist: Really. You sure are a fast learner.

Jeff: Yes, she can be.

Therapist: What else have you been learning?

Alli: About diet. The diet lady brought by fake food for us to see.

Therapist: There is a lot to learn about that too.

Alli: Yep.

Source: Fournier & Rae (1999, p. 320).

The disease can also occur in individuals descended from Italy, Greece, Asia Minor, and other countries around the Mediterranean Sea and the Caribbean Sea. Sickle cell anemia is the most severe form of sickle cell disease. The disease is usually not identified until after the age of 6 months. After that age, symptoms begin to occur such as severe episodes of pain, severe infections, strokes, and anemia. In later childhood, retarded growth and delays in sexual maturity are present (Lemanek, Ranalli, Green, Biega, & Lupia, 2003). Medical interventions related to sickle cell disease have included newborn screening, pain management, transfusion therapy, surgery, and comprehensive care (Chen et al., 2004; Koontz, Short, Kalinyak, & Noll, 2004).

Pediatric psychologists often get involved in helping children with sickle cell disease because of the emotional/behavioral sequelae to this disease. Children with sickle cell disease often exhibit poorer self-esteem, poorer peer relationships, delayed academic competence, more internalizing problems, and more externalizing behavior problems than their physically healthy peers (Lemanek et al., 2003; Schatz, 2004). There are also limitations that are evident in the cognitive and intellectual functioning of children with sickle cell disease (Grueneich et al., 2004; Schatz, Finke, Kellett, & Kramer, 2002; Thompson et al., 2003). In addition to pediatric psychologists working to intervene with these emotional/behavioral problems, they can also get involved in trying to help the family cope with this devastating illness. Family conflict and distress are associated with greater emotional/behavioral problems in children with sickle cell disease (Gil et al., 2003; Logan, Radcliffe, & Smith-Whitley, 2002). Thus, working to find more effective coping mechanisms within the family would help to reduce the maladaptive functioning of children with sickle cell disease (Chen et al., 2004; Harbeck-Weber, Fisher, & Dittner, 2003; Logan et al., 2002).

Overall, sickle cell disease is a severe illness that influences not only children but the entire family. Pediatric psychologists have been actively involved in trying to help children and families cope with this lifelong disease.

Healing is a matter of time, but it is sometimes also a matter of opportunity.

—Hippocrates

Childhood Cancer

Cancer occurs in approximately 1 out of 330 children before the age of 19 (Vannatta & Gerhardt, 2003). Close to 40% of childhood cancer is diagnosed between the ages of birth and 4 years old. Boys are more at risk for cancer than are girls, and Caucasian-American children have slightly higher rates of cancer than do African-American children (Vannatta & Gerhardt, 2003).

A number of different types of cancer occur in childhood, including acute leukemia, brain tumors, lymphoma, neuroblastoma, soft tissue sarcomas, and bone tumors. Although many cancers that occur in adults are associated with lifestyle choices (such as smoking) and environmental toxins (such as exposure to radioactive materials), cancers in childhood tend to be associated with genetic predispositions, chromosomal abnormalities, immune deficiencies, or other developmental abnormalities (Peterson et al., 2003). Medical interventions are geared toward treating the cancer directly, but pediatric psychologists often become involved with helping the child and family cope with the medical treatments and the diagnosis of cancer itself (Clarke, Davies, Jenney, Glaser, & Eiser, 2005; Friedman, Latham, & Dahlquist, 1998; Kazak, 2005; Kazak et al., 2004). There have been many interventions developed to help children deal with aversive and sometimes extremely painful treatment regimens that are necessary to battle cancer. Most of these interventions utilize behavioral and cognitive behavioral techniques to help the child deal with these stressful and painful

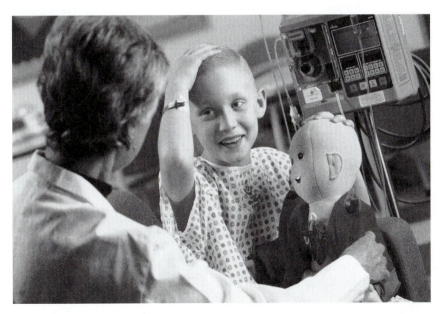

Physicians and psychologists often try to help pediatric cancer patients cope with the effects of treatment, such as hair loss.

Case Study: A Teenager Who Is Battling Cancer

Penny is 15 years old and lives with her parents and older brother. She was diagnosed with leukemia when she was 10 years old, endured 3 years of chemotherapy, which led to a 2-year remission of the leukemia, and then relapsed at the age of 15. A bone marrow transplant was completed when she was 15 years old, with the donor marrow coming from Penny's 18-year-old brother.

Penny's parents had both been successful attorneys in a small town when Penny was first diagnosed with leukemia. After the diagnosis, the family moved to a larger city to be closer to a cancer treatment center. In addition, Penny's mother quit her job to be able to focus on Penny's doctor's appointments and prolonged treatment. When Penny relapsed at the age of 15, Penny, her mother, and her father all reported no psychological difficulties. Penny had been a good student and even with home-schooling (which was necessitated by the medical treatments and side effects of treatment), Penny had continued to excel in her academic work. Both Penny and her mother reported exceedingly good mental health, and Penny's father reported some mild levels of psychological distress. The psychologists on staff at the oncology unit hypothesized that Penny and her mother, and to a lesser extent her father, were still in denial about the seriousness of Penny's medical condition. For example, Penny denied any concerns about her own mortality, and she refused to be part of any discussions with the medical staff. In addition, both parents reported significant dissatisfaction with their marriage.

After the bone marrow transplant, Penny and her parents began to show more signs of distress. Penny's usual style of coping with medical procedures deteriorated, and she began clinging to her mother during her hospital stay. Penny's mother seemed to deal with her own distress by trying to control the medical procedures, so much so that the medical staff often refused to care for Penny because of their aversive interactions with Penny's mother. During the 6-month hospital stay, Penny and her mother were inseparable, and Penny refused to go anywhere (even down the hall for a walk) without her mother. Once treatment was completed, Penny was discharged with directions not to see anyone outside the family because of concerns about her weakened immune system. After

4 months passed, Penny's mother called the psychological staff to request help in transitioning Penny back to school.

Penny's mother reported that Penny had concerns about her appearance, though Penny correctly noted that she had an expensive blond wig that looked real and that hid her limited hair growth. Penny did, however, express a great deal of concern about leaving her mother and going to school alone. She had not seen any peers for over 1 year and she had not been actively involved with friends for a number of years. She expressed a great desire to become more actively involved with peers and with learning to drive by herself, but she also expressed extreme anxiety about separation from her mother.

Penny began cognitive–behavioral therapy, with a focus on short-term anxiety management. An anxiety hierarchy was developed and then mastered, that began with Penny riding the elevator with a staff person (but without her mother) in the hospital for a medical appointment and ended with Penny driving alone to a fast-food restaurant during daylight hours by herself. Penny was taught progressive muscle relaxation and cognitive reframing to deal with her anxious thoughts.

After 2 months of therapy, Penny had conquered her fears and was able to function independently from her parents at an age-appropriate level. She also developed a number of friendships at school, which also increased Penny's feelings of autonomy. Penny's parents were offered marital and individual therapy, but neither parent reported any interest. Penny's mother and father seemed to remain somewhat in denial of their own distress, and both appeared to have resigned themselves to an unhappy and unsupportive marriage.

This case study illustrates how lifesaving medical treatments can impact negatively on normal developmental milestones. Developmentally, it would have been important to encourage Penny to become more involved with friends before, during, and after medical treatment. Medically, however, Penny would have been at risk for further medical problems had she begun socializing extensively. In many cases within the realm of pediatric psychology, medical treatments must (by necessity) take precedence before psychological treatments.

Source: Friedman et al. (1998).

---

procedures (Dahlquist & Pendley, 2005). School psychologists and other educational professionals also can become involved in helping children diagnosed with cancer, given that some types of cancer and treatment for cancer are associated with academic deficits and neuropsychological deficits (Poggi et al., 2005).

Not surprisingly, childhood cancer is associated with emotional/behavioral problems in children and

distress in their parents (Patenaude & Kupst, 2005). Survey studies suggest that the most stressful time for families in the process of childhood cancer is at the time of diagnosis (Clarke et al., 2005; Sahler et al., 2005; Steele, Long, Reddy, Luhr, & Phipps, 2003), although there are also increased rates of parental distress during painful medical procedures (Dahlquist & Pendley, 2005; Manne et al., 2001). Children and adolescents do surprisingly well during cancer treatment, but there are some factors that are associated with better emotional/behavioral functioning related to childhood cancer. Families that were well functioning before the diagnosis of cancer and families in which there is a strong and nonconflicted parental relationship tend to fare better throughout the treatment process for childhood cancer (Vannatta & Gerhardt, 2003). A strong and nonconflicted parent–child relationship (especially the mother–child relationship) is associated with less distress among adolescents with cancer and a higher quality of life (Manne & Miller, 1998; Orbuch, Parry, Chesler, Fritz, & Repetto, 2005). Better emotional/behavioral outcomes are also associated with the way in which medical staff members deal with the family. Specifically, parents report better outcomes when they are provided clear and direct information about the cancer and cancer treatment, when they are provided support from a liaison who serves to facilitate the relationship between the family and the medical staff, and when they receive help with utilizing and maximizing their own coping resources (Friedman et al., 1998; Norberg, Lindblad, & Boman, 2005). Good communication between parents and pediatric oncology researchers is also important to make sure that parents understand the research in which they are being asked to participate (Fisher, 2005).

In terms of parental distress, parents' rates of trait anxiety before the diagnosis of cancer in their child were associated with greater rates of distress after cancer treatment (Hoekstra-Weebers, Jasper, Kamps, & Klip, 1999). Parents of children with cancer report greater unintentional weight gain after their child is diagnosed, and this weight gain appears to be due to a reduction in physical activities (Smith, Baum, & Wing, 2005). Parents whose children have functional limitations due to the illness (e.g., not being able to play with friends, limited self-care skills) experienced more psychological distress than parents whose children did not show functional limitations (Silver, Westbrook, & Stein, 1998). Parental distress is related to children's emotional and somatic distress (Steele, Dreyer, & Phipps, 2004). Both mothers and fathers report heightened distress regarding their child's cancer, and both mothers and fathers report significantly greater caretaking duties for their child with cancer (Clarke, 2005).

Given that one fourth of children with cancer do not survive, continued involvement by pediatric psychologists is important through the dying process of the child and through the grieving process for the family. Although the research is limited in how best to help parents cope with losing a child to cancer, pediatric psychologists are often involved in helping support the family during the grieving process and to help serve as a liaison between the family and the medical staff after losing a child.

Although there have been significant advances in the treatment of childhood cancer, the impact of this disease is still overwhelming for many families. This topic has been and continues to be of central focus for pediatric psychologists due to the severity of the disease and the impact that it has on the child and family.

My main message is that I want these kids to learn from my mistake, so that what happened to me doesn't happen to them.
—Earvin "Magic" Johnson (1992, p. 356) regarding his HIV+ status due to unprotected sex

HIV and AIDS in Children and Adolescents

Worldwide, over 2.2 million children and adolescents under the age of 15 are infected with human immunodeficiency virus (HIV; UNAIDS/WHO, 2004). Although this number is devastating, it is even more devastating to realize that the percentage of children infected with HIV is still very small compared to the large number of adults infected with HIV. Worldwide, children and adolescents under the age of 15 make up only 5.6% of the known cases of persons living with HIV (UNAIDS/WHO, 2004). When deaths from AIDS are analyzed worldwide, children under the age of 15 years make up 16.5% of the deaths from AIDS-related illnesses (UNAIDS/WHO, 2004).

Of all of the cases of acquired immune deficiency syndrome (AIDS) documented within the United States, only 4.7% of the individuals are children under the age of 18 (Centers for Disease Control, 2005). Within the United States, 73% of the individuals who have HIV or AIDS are males and 65% are African American or Hispanic/Latino/Latina (Centers for Disease Control, 2005).

HIV targets the immune system and destroys T4 cells (also known as helper T cells). Once HIV is in the immune system, it may not manifest into symptoms for 8 years or more (Rounds, 2004). HIV leaves the child's immune system weakened and unable to defend itself against opportunistic infections and other problems. One prevalent infection is pneumocystis carinii pneumonia, which is one of the markers that allows the formal diagnosis of AIDS (Armstrong, Willen, & Sorgen, 2003).

There are a number of ways in which children and adolescents can become infected with HIV. In the early days of the AIDS epidemic, some children became infected through transmission of tainted blood. Children with hemophilia and other illnesses that required a large amount of blood infusions were particularly at risk for receiving blood that was HIV+. Since the advent of stringent testing protocols for donated blood in 1985, it is thought that the blood supply within the United States is relatively free from tainted blood (Armstrong et al., 2004). More recently, there have been two primary ways in which children and adolescents are at risk for HIV infection. Infants born to HIV+ mothers or mothers who have been diagnosed with AIDS have an increased risk of becoming HIV+ themselves. The other way in which children and adolescents can become HIV+ is through transmission of bodily fluids, usually through unprotected sexual contact with an infected individual. Although there have been some rare cases of young children becoming infected through the sexual contact of sexual abuse (Armistead, Forehand, Steele, & Kotchick, 1998), the majority of HIV and AIDS cases are of adolescents who have engaged in consensual unprotected sex with an infected partner (Armstrong et al., 2003; Bachanas et al., 2002). Because the two primary mechanisms of transmission are so different from one another, children who are infected through maternal transmission will be discussed separately from adolescents who are infected through unprotected sexual contact.

The overwhelming majority of children under the age of 13 who are HIV+ (91%) were infected from their HIV+ mother (Wolters et al., 1999). Most of the mothers who are HIV+ were infected from intravenous drug use or from unprotected sex with an infected partner (who is sometimes the father of the infected infant). Infants who are HIV infected from their mothers usually are infected in utero through HIV passage through the placenta, through maternal secretions at the time of birth, or through breast feeding (Bhatta, Stringer, Phanuphak, & Vermund, 2003; Cocu et al., 2005). This form of transmission (from mother to infant) is known as **vertical transmission.** Medical treatment of mothers who are pregnant, such as the use of AZT and other antiviral drugs, decreases the risk of transmission to the infant down to 8% to 10% (Rounds, 2004; Taha et al., 2004). Unfortunately, these preventive measures are not always taken in the United States or in other countries, largely because pregnant women may not know that they are HIV+ (Cocu et al., 2005).

Infants who are infected through vertical transmission seem to fall into two categories, one that shows rapid disease progression and one that shows slower disease progression. Infants who are diagnosed early as HIV+ and who show early symptoms within the first year of life tend to experience a more aggressive form of HIV and subsequent development of AIDS (Wolters et al., 1999). These children show many more medical problems (such as opportunistic infections, growth retardation, hepatitis, fever, anemia, and diarrhea) and have a much shorter life span than children who show a later onset of symptoms. It remains unclear why some infants develop symptoms earlier and why some experience a slower disease progression, but it may be that there are different strains of HIV or that there are other genetic or biological factors at work (Wolters et al., 1999). Regardless of the age of onset of AIDS-related symptoms, children often experience central nervous system difficulties and cognitive deficits in addition to the severe physical problems associated with AIDS (Brown et al., 2000). Shortened life span is characteristic of children diagnosed with AIDS. Approximately 65% of children diagnosed with AIDS will live to the age of 5 (Brown et al., 2000).

No one ever told me that, as a 15 year old kid, I could end up . . . having someone for a partner who was [HIV]-infected.
—Kerri, who died of AIDS-related complications before reaching adulthood (Fisher & Fisher, 1994)

The other primary mode of transmission of HIV and AIDS is through unprotected sex during adolescence. Within the United States, approximately 20% of individuals who are HIV+, but who have not yet developed AIDS, are in the age range of 13 to 24 years old (Samples, Goodman, & Woods, 1998). The overwhelming majority of girls who became HIV+ during adolescence were infected through heterosexual unprotected sex (Centers for Disease Control, 2005). Boys infected during adolescence are more likely to have become infected by having sex with other boys or men, but they are also at risk for HIV transmission through sex with girls or women (Centers for Disease Control, 2005).

AIDS has become a leading cause of death in adolescents and young adults (Brown et al., 2000). Complications related to HIV and AIDS are the third most common cause of death for African-American adolescent girls (behind homicide and accidents), the fifth most common cause of death for African-American adolescent boys (behind homicide, accidents, suicide, and heart disease), and the seventh most common cause of death among Caucasian-American adolescent girls and boys (behind accidents, suicide, homicide, malignancies, heart disease, and congenital anomalies; Becker, Rankin, & Rickel, 1998; Donenberg & Pao, 2005). There is no doubt that HIV and AIDS are serious problems with the adolescent age group. There are also more and more children who were infected with HIV through vertical transmission or through early blood transfusions with tainted blood who have reached adolescence and who are sexually active (Centers for Disease Control, 2005). This group provides another complexity in the mission to prevent transmission of HIV and AIDS. There is evidence to suggest that HIV+ adolescents whose parents discuss sexual issues with them are more likely to disclose their HIV status to their sexual partners than those adolescents whose parents do not discuss sexual issues with them (Perrino, Gonzalez-Soldevilla, Pantin, & Szapocznik, 2000; Wilson & Donenberg, 2004).

Pediatric psychologists have gotten involved in child and adolescent HIV and AIDS cases primarily through research, assessment, and therapeutic treatments. Because of the cognitive and psychological ramifications of AIDS, psychologists often conduct psychosocial assessments and family assessments to determine how children and their families might be helped most (Blanchette, Smith, Fernandes-Penney, King, & Read, 2001). Adolescents with psychological problems (especially those with conduct problems) are at an increased risk for HIV infection due to increased risky sexual behavior (Bachanas et al., 2002; Donenberg, Emerson, Bryant, Wilson, & Weber-Shifrin, 2001). For adolescents with or without preexisting psychological problems, treatments include individual therapy with children and family therapy. Therapy can focus on many issues, including anxiety, depression, medical compliance, and bereavement in families who lose a child to AIDS (Freeman, 2004).

Within pediatric psychology and social psychology, there has also been a great deal of attention to prevention of HIV and AIDS transmission, especially with the prevention of transmission through adolescents' unprotected sex. Unfortunately, simple education programs (e.g., teaching adolescents about the dangers of unprotected sex) are not effective in getting them to adopt abstinence or safer sex practices (Rounds, 2004). Successful prevention programs have targeted mothers of adolescents and have helped them to talk with their children about sexuality and AIDS-related issues (Lefkowitz, Sigman, & Au, 2000; Perrino et al., 2000). This program

was successful in reducing risk of HIV transmission in adolescents. Overall, effective prevention programs to reduce adolescents' risk of HIV transmission need to be multidimensional and thorough (Bryan, Fisher, & Fisher, 2002; Fisher, Fisher, Bryan, & Misovich, 2002), including topics such as:

- Perceiving yourself as a sexual being
- Learning the behaviors that are necessary for protecting yourself from HIV transmission (e.g., abstinence, use of a latex condom with antispermicidal agents such as Nonoxynol-9 that are associated with killing HIV, outercourse sexual activities rather than intercourse activities)
- Learning to negotiate the use of safer sex methods with a potential sexual partner
- Finding the strength to not begin a relationship or to leave a relationship with someone who is not willing to use safer sex methods
- Buying latex condoms or finding public health facilities where latex condoms are available at no cost
- Seeking out and receiving HIV testing, if appropriate
- Sticking with HIV risk reduction practices, even when remaining with the same partner for a long period of time
- Self-reinforcement for good risk reduction practices in order to prevent relapse into riskier behaviors.

These behaviors can be conceptualized within an **Information-Motivation-Behavioral Skills (IMB) model** of AIDS risk behavior change (Fisher et al., 2002). AIDS risk reduction has been advanced with prevention programs that include all these elements (Bryan et al., 2002; Fisher et al., 2002). More programs are needed in this area, given the risk in which sexually active adolescents find themselves these days (Bachanas et al., 2002; Prinstein, Meade, & Cohen, 2003).

In fifty years, I think there will be a cure for AIDS. Many people in Zimbabwe are dying because of that dangerous disease and there is no cure yet. AIDS does not choose—elderly, young, poor, it will kill. When I grow up, I can invent that medicine. I can study a lot and then I can cure the people and they will live a long life.

—Trust, 13, Zimbabwe

CHRONIC ILLNESS IN PARENTS AND CHILDREN'S WELL-BEING

Just like the research designs that have investigated children of psychologically distressed parents, there is also a long line of research into the functioning of children of medically ill parents. In fact, children of medically ill parents have sometimes been used as a control group to compare and contrast functioning with children of psychologically distressed parents (Hammen, 1991). Some of this work has also been extended to evaluate the process of parental illness and parental death, as in the case of research on parental cancer (Faulkner & Davey, 2002) and parental AIDS (Rotheram-Borus, Weiss, Alber, & Lester, 2005; Pelton & Forehand, 2005). Although the research literature is too large to summarize for the purposes of this chapter, a few studies are highlighted to provide examples of research in this area.

Parental Cancer

Parental cancer has received some attention, although not as much as cancer in children or the ramifications of cancer in adults regardless of their parental status (Faulkner & Davey, 2002). Regarding parental cancer, there is evidence that adolescents who lose a parent to cancer are no more psychologically distressed than adolescents whose parents continue to survive with cancer (Mireault & Compas, 1996). When comparing anxiety, depression, and stress-related symptoms of adolescents with either a mother or a father diagnosed with cancer, the most significant effects emerged for adolescent girls who were dealing with maternal cancer (Compas et al., 1994). Specifically, adolescent girls whose mothers were battling cancer showed the highest level of distress when compared with younger or older girls, boys of all ages, and children of all ages who were dealing with their fathers' cancer. This pattern is consistent into adulthood, where adult daughters struggle more with their mothers' cancer than adult sons (Mosher & Danoff-Burg, 2005).

One study compared the psychosocial functioning of children who had lost a parent to cancer in comparison to children who had lost a parent to suicide 18 months earlier. Based on children's self-reports, children who lost a parent to suicide reported greater negative mood, depressive symptoms, anhedonia, and interpersonal problems (Pfeffer, Karus, Siegel, & Jiang, 2000). When the surviving parent's reports were used, no differences were found between children in the two

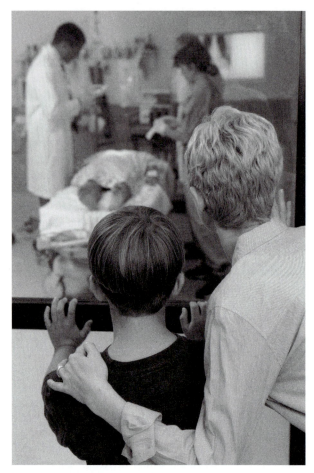

The ramifications of parental illness often vary according to the protective resources that children have in their lives (such as a strong and stable caretaker who is not ill).

bereavement groups. Additionally, children in the two bereavement groups did not differ from children in a nonbereavement group when compared on parent-reported competence and emotional/behavioral problems (Pfeffer et al., 2000). Thus, at least in some samples, it appears that children who lose a parent are quite resilient, and they either experience minor psychological symptoms or no symptoms at all 18 months after the loss of a parent. Taken together, these studies highlight the need to look at gender differences, developmental differences, and family functioning differences within the broad spectrum of parental cancer.

Although mechanisms of effects may differ depending on the parental medical illness that is studied, there are certain themes that provide clues as to how parental medical illness may relate to children's functioning. The primary pathways of influence appear to be social learning and modeling, changes in the parent–child relationship, family functioning, interparental conflict, appraisals of illness-related stressors, and coping styles (Compas, Worsham, Ey, & Howell, 1996; Finney & Miller, 1999). There continues to be a great need for further research into the influences of parental medical illness, especially with attention to helping children cope with parental illness.

> The baby . . . was due in February. The American Cancer Society's web site said that, all things considered, I had a 70 percent chance of being alive to witness the birth.
> —Movie critic Joel Siegel (2003, p. 3) writes
> about the upcoming birth of his son, Dylan

Parental AIDS

Regarding parental AIDS, there are growing numbers of "AIDS orphans" who have lost parents to the disease (Pelton & Forehand, 2005; Rotheram-Borus, 2005; Rotheram-Borus, Stein, & Lin, 2001). In some countries, especially in many African nations, entire generations of adults have been wiped out by the AIDS pandemic, and huge numbers of infants and children have become orphans because of this disease (Walders & Drotar, 2000). Even prior to parental death, children whose parents are battling AIDS may have inadvertently been abandoned emotionally given the devastating medical complications related to the disease. Parents who experience AIDS often find it more difficult to maintain a strong parent–child bond, to provide appropriate nurturing for their children, and to protect their children from the stigma associated with AIDS (Rotheram-Borus et al., 2002). It is not unusual to find higher rates of depression and anxiety in parents with AIDS as well as in their children, regardless of whether or not the children are infected with HIV (Rotheram-Borus et al., 2001). Because many parents with AIDS were infected through intravenous drug use, parental substance abuse and dependence add to the difficulties that might influence the parent–child relationship. These familial issues are further complicated by the social and economic isolation that often occurs as a result of the AIDS diagnosis in parents (Pilowsky et al., Zybert, Hsieh, Vlahov, & Susser, 2003). Unfortunately, children whose parents are diagnosed with AIDS are not likely to receive psychological help even when they need it because of economic and social barriers that prevent access to mental health services. More work is needed to understand the influence of parental AIDS and to allow easier access to therapeutic interventions

for children who are in need of help (Rotheram-Borus, 2005; Rotheram-Borus et al., 2001). Interventions with HIV+ parents and even HIV+ grandparents have shown promising psychosocial benefits for children and grandchildren (Rotheram-Borus et al., 2006), but more work is needed to help this vulnerable group of youth.

TREATMENT ISSUES IN PEDIATRIC PSYCHOLOGY

Treatment and intervention issues have been discussed throughout the chapter, but a few overarching points are necessary to understand the context of therapeutic treatment in pediatric psychology. Because there is a correspondence between high health care utilization and higher rates of psychological distress in children, it is important for physicians and other medical personnel to be aware of the need to refer their pediatric patients for psychological help when necessary (Kinsman, Wildman, & Smucker, 1999).

There are a variety of effective treatments in the area of pediatric psychology. Empirically supported treatments have been identified for many specific illnesses within the realm of pediatric psychology. Most of the treatments that have been well established are within the cognitive–behavioral and behavioral orientations (McQuaid & Nassau, 1999). In addition to these more traditional treatments, there have been a number of innovative treatments that add to the multidisciplinary approach taken within the field of pediatric psychology. The use of pediatric summer camps (Briery & Rabian, 1999), parent-to-parent support groups (Ainbinder et al., 1998), and family-centered treatments (King, King, Rosenbaum, & Goffin, 1999) have all been associated with reductions in psychological symptoms of children and their families who are dealing with medical illnesses. Overall, there is a great deal of concern within the field of pediatric psychology to lessen children's and families' psychological distress when dealing with medical illness. As noted in the "You Decide" section, children may or may not have access to these services, but if they do gain access to evidence-based treatments, then they can often be relieved of the psychological ramifications to physical illnesses.

PREVENTION ISSUES IN PEDIATRIC PSYCHOLOGY

In addition to the treatment of psychological distress related to medical illnesses, pediatric psychologists

Case Study: A Family Dealing with AIDS

Rochelle is 7 years old and is living with AIDS. Both her mother and her father were diagnosed with AIDS. Rochelle's father was a chronic IV drug user, who apparently became infected through the use of tainted needles. Rochelle's father apparently infected her mother long before Rochelle's birth and unbeknownst to either parent. Rochelle has a younger sister, Alicia, who is not HIV-positive. By the age of 2, Rochelle was diagnosed as HIV-positive. When Rochelle was 5 years old, her mother was diagnosed with AIDS. When Rochelle was 6 years old, her father (with whom she had only limited contact) was shot to death outside his home.

As a single parent, Rochelle's mother (Maggie) relies primarily on her family of origin for social and financial support. Rochelle's maternal grandmother learned of Maggie's and Rochelle's initial HIV-infection after an argument with Rochelle's father. Maggie's brother (Rochelle's uncle) still has not been informed about the family's HIV and AIDS status, but rather has been told that Maggie is battling cancer. Maggie has become increasingly ill, and her medical condition is getting more difficult to hide.

When she first learned of her daughter's and her own diagnosis (when Rochelle was 2 years old), Maggie became so depressed that she could not care for her children. At that time, Maggie's mother (Rochelle's grandmother) cared for the two girls. After approximately 1 year, Maggie was able to care for her children again. For the next 2 years (when Rochelle was aged 3 to 5), the family functioned without any major crises. Maggie was able to care for the girls and was able to maintain her own health in a relatively stable manner. Rochelle had still not been informed of her own HIV-status nor had she been told about why her mother was so sick periodically. Although the medical and psychological staff had encouraged that Rochelle be told the truth about her mother's and her own illness, Maggie chose against telling Rochelle the truth.

By the age of 5, Rochelle and her younger sister were enrolled in a Head Start program. Rochelle's health began to deteriorate somewhat (with frequent ear infections and sinusitis), but Rochelle reported that she loved going to the Head Start program even though she had to miss many days because of feeling bad. In particular, Rochelle and her sister seemed to show a strong and supportive bond with each other. When Rochelle was 6, the school district recommended that she move on to a kindergarten class, but her mother, pediatrician, and social worker all felt that Rochelle would be traumatized by being separated from her sister. Although Rochelle was academically ready to be advanced to the next grade, socially, emotionally, and physically, she was still quite vulnerable. In addition, because Rochelle was not expected to survive to adulthood, her academic pursuits were thought to be less important than her current emotional well-being. Thus, Rochelle was allowed to stay in the Head Start program with her sister.

Now at age 7, Rochelle's health and her mother's health have deteriorated significantly. Rochelle is no longer able to attend Head Start because she has to receive multiple daily infusion treatments, and she has to be fed through a tube. Maggie is also severely limited because of her health problems and can no longer care for her children. Presently, Maggie's mother (Rochelle's grandmother) is taking care of the girls as well as Maggie. Maggie is not expected to live any longer than 1 or 2 months, and Rochelle is expected to live no longer than 1 year. Although Rochelle's grandmother is willing to take care of both girls for now, she is only willing to take permanent custody of Rochelle's younger sister and not Rochelle. Maggie wants the girls to remain together, but after her death, the girls may be separated due to the grandmother's desire to care only for Rochelle's sister. If this situation occurs, Rochelle would have to be placed in a special medical foster home away from her sister and other relatives.

Source: Armistead et al. (1998).

---

place a great deal of emphasis on the prevention of psychological distress. Universal prevention programs often attempt to prevent the occurrence of medical illnesses before they occur (e.g., prevention of HIV transmission, promotion of healthy lifestyles to prevent obesity, heart disease, and some types of cancer later in life; Wilson & Evans, 2003). Universal prevention programs are geared toward the entire population of children and adolescents, rather than just children and adolescents who are at risk for the development of psychological problems, and they are also known as health-promotion programs (Wilson & Evans, 2003).

Health-promotion programs for children and adolescents often focus on:

- Increasing physical activity and fitness
- Improving nutrition
- Reducing the use of tobacco
- Reducing the use of alcohol and other drugs
- Enhancing health-related programs in schools and in the community

In addition, many AIDS risk-reduction programs have been instituted that not only target the reduction of

YOU DECIDE: DO CHILDREN HAVE EQUAL ACCESS TO HEALTH CARE AND MENTAL HEALTH CARE?

<u>Yes</u>

- Basic, mandatory health care like immunizations show few differences between groups in compliance rates (Brown, Fuemmeler, & Forti, 2003). In addition, most children and adolescents can access some level of health care in the school setting (Wiecha et al., 2004).
- Rates of insurance coverage are approximately equal in samples of children seeking preventive health care, with the main difference being that Caucasian-American children are more likely to have private health insurance, and African-American children are more likely to have public health insurance (Alio & Salihu, 2005).

<u>No</u>

- One study found that African-American children were significantly less likely to receive preventive health services than Caucasian-American children (Alio & Salihu, 2005).
- Many of the neediest children, for example, those in impoverished circumstances with challenging environmental circumstances, are not able to access health care and mental health care because of barriers such as cost, access, and perceived importance of these services (Brown et al., 2003).

So, do children have equal access to health care and mental health care? You decide.

HIV transmission, but also target transmission of other sexually transmitted diseases and the prevention of teenage pregnancy (Fisher et al., 2002; Lefkowitz et al., 2000). A number of effective universal prevention programs related to pediatric psychology have been instituted within the United States and worldwide (McDonald et al., 2005; Wilson & Evans, 2003).

In contrast to universal prevention programs within the area of pediatric psychology, selective prevention programs attempt to prevent the occurrence of psychological distress in relation to physical illnesses that have already occurred (Harbeck-Weber et al., 2003). Remember that selective prevention programs tend to focus on groups of children and adolescents who are at risk for the development of emotional/behavioral problems. In the area of pediatric psychology, children and adolescents are considered at risk due to their medical illness or their parents' medical illness. Selective prevention programs can also focus on early intervention and early identification of children and adolescents who are likely to develop psychological problems (Harbeck-Weber et al., 2003). The majority of selective prevention efforts within the field of pediatric psychology have

focused on preventing distress related to hospitalization and aversive medical procedures such as injections, chemotherapy, lumbar punctures, and surgery (Woznick & Goodheart, 2002). Many of these prevention strategies utilize cognitive–behavioral techniques (such as guided imagery, visualization, progressive relaxation, cognitive restructuring, modeling, and stress inoculation) and the development of other coping strategies to help children deal with aversive medical procedures (Woznick & Goodheart, 2002). Other strategies, such as anticipatory guidance, social support, and support for the family have also been utilized. Overall, a number of effective selective prevention techniques are used routinely with children who are undergoing aversive medical procedures and who are experiencing either acute or chronic medical illnesses.

The area of pediatric psychology has been involved in prevention efforts to a greater extent than many other areas in developmental psychopathology. The focus on health promotion and on prevention of psychological distress could be used as a model for professionals within other areas in developmental psychopathology.

SUMMARY AND KEY CONCEPTS

Pediatric Psychology.   **Pediatric psychology** is the application of psychological methods to health issues and behaviors.

Eating Disorders.   There are two primary types of eating disorders. **Anorexia nervosa** occurs when an individual is significantly underweight due to restrictive eating methods and when there is great fear of gaining more weight. **Bulimia nervosa** occurs when an individual eats large quantities of food (i.e., binges) and then tries to eliminate the food intake through artificial methods such as use of laxatives or self-induced vomiting (i.e., purging). **Binge-eating disorder** is proposed as a diagnosis that would be made when prodigious amounts of food are ingested routinely. **Feeding and eating disorder of infancy or early childhood** occurs when an infant or young child fails to eat enough food and does not make expected weight gains. **Pica** is diagnosed when an individual eats nonfood items such as paper, paint, or dirt. **Rumination disorder** occurs when an infant or child regurgitates food and rechews it repeatedly.

Elimination Disorders.   There are two primary types of elimination disorders. **Enuresis** occurs when individuals over the age of 5 cannot or will not control their urinary functioning for at least 3 consecutive months. **Encopresis** occurs when individuals over the age of 4 cannot or will not control their bowel functioning for at least 3 months.

Somatoform Disorders and Factitious Disorders. **Somatoform disorders** occur when medically unexplained physical or medical symptoms seem to get worse over time. Within the category of somatoform disorders, there are a number of specific disorders, including **somatization disorder** (the combination of pain, gastrointestinal, sexual, and pseudoneurological symptoms), **pain disorder** (the existence of pain that seems to be heightened by psychological distress), **hypochondriasis** (the belief in or fear of a serious medical disorder based on misinterpretation of physical symptoms), and **body dysmorphic disorder** (the preoccupation or obsession with negative aspects of one's body). Although symptoms within somatoform disorders are thought to be exaggerated, they are not falsified intentionally. Physical symptoms in **factitious disorders,** on the other hand, are thought to be falsified intentionally with the end goal of serving in the "sick role." If physical symptoms are feigned for external incentives (such as money), then the diagnosis would be **malingering,** which is a V-Code. If parents or other caretakers create symptoms in their children, to receive sympathy or to serve in the sick role through their child, then the parents or caretakers would be diagnosed with **factitious disorder by proxy.**

Genetic Chromosomal Disorders.   A number of genetic chromosomal disorders are of concern to pediatric psychologists. **Turner's syndrome** occurs in girls and creates short stature, limited secondary sexual characteristics, and potentially life-threatening medical problems such as heart and kidney problems. **Klinefelter's syndrome** occurs in boys who are born with an XXY chromosomal structure (or some other chromosomal structure with 2 or more X chromosomes and 1 or more Y chromosomes). Boys with Klinefelter's syndrome tend to show deficits in language, academic functioning, emotional/behavioral functioning, and neuromaturational functioning.

Other Disorders.   **Sleep disorders** and **tic disorders** are additional problems that are of concern to pediatric psychologists.

Chronic Illness in Children and Children's Well-Being. Children and adolescents with chronic illnesses (such as diabetes, sickle cell disease, cancer, and HIV/AIDS) tend to experience heightened emotional/behavioral problems. Within the area of HIV/AIDS, infants can become infected from their HIV+ mother through **vertical transmission,** or children and adolescents can become infected through sexual contact with an infected individual. One model for the prevention of HIV and AIDS, the **Information-Motivation-Behavioral Skills (IMB) model,** suggests that adolescents must receive comprehensive prevention programs to reduce their risk for transmission of HIV and AIDS.

Chronic Illness in Parents and Children's Well-Being. Just like parental psychological problems, children of parents with chronic medical illnesses (such as HIV/AIDS and cancer) are at risk for heightened emotional/behavioral problems.

Treatment Issues in Pediatric Psychology.   A number of empirically supported treatments have been documented within the field of pediatric psychology. The majority of the treatments are within the behavioral and cognitive–behavioral orientation.

Prevention Issues in Pediatric Psychology.   More than any other area within the study of developmental psychopathology, pediatric psychology has been dedicated to prevention efforts. Universal prevention efforts have focused on health promotion.

KEY TERMS

pediatric psychology	feeding and eating disorder of infancy or early childhood	somatoform disorders	body dysmorphic disorder	tic disorders
anorexia nervosa		factitious disorders	malingering	vertical transmission
bulimia nervosa		somatization disorder	factitious disorder by proxy	Information-Motivation-Behavioral Skills (IMB) model
amerorrhea	pica		Turner's syndrome	
binge-eating disorder	rumination disorder	pain disorder	Klinefelter's syndrome	
	enuresis	hypochondriasis	sleep disorders	
	encopresis			

SUGGESTED READINGS

Wilensky, Amy. *The Weight of It: A Story of Two Sisters*. New York: Henry Holt and Company, 2004. This book illustrates how lives within the same family can be separated by the experience of obesity and how drastic weight reduction through surgery has both pros and cons for the functioning of the family.

Wooten, Jim. *We Are All the Same: A Story of a Boy's Courage and a Mother's Love*. New York: Penguin Books, 2004. This powerful book describes the amazing life and early death of Nkosi, who was born HIV+ and who became a symbol of strength to others in Africa as well as throughout the world.

SUGGESTED VIEWINGS

Super Size Me. (2004). With obesity rates higher than ever in children, adolescents, and adults, this documentary shows the results of trying to eat every meal at McDonalds for 1 month. Although the film has been criticized for being light on the "documentary" aspects of filmmaking, there is a point to be learned about healthy eating habits and what children and families are exposed to during their fast-food meals that are ingested while traveling from school to soccer practice to the ballet recital.

Real Women Have Curves. (2002). Because most adolescent girls and women in Hollywood films do not have enough body fat to produce curves without the help of a plastic surgeon, this movie takes a refreshing look at what it is to be an adolescent girl with curves. Issues of body image, connections with a traditional family, and potential conflicts with cultural values are all highlighted in this heartwarming film.

WAYS TO HELP CHILDREN

CHAPTER SUMMARY

The future promise of any nation can be directly measured by the present prospects of its youth.

—President John F. Kennedy.

One of the most compelling reasons to understand abnormal child behavior is to find ways to help children in need. In every level of society and every level of educational pursuit, there are many ways to prevent problems from developing in children and additional ways to help children and families once problems appear. As is evident from the African proverb that Senator Hillary Clinton (1996) used for the title of her book, it takes a village to help children grow up to be healthy, strong, well-functioning, and self-fulfilled members of society.

HOW NONPROFESSIONALS AND PARAPROFESSIONALS CAN HELP CHILDREN

Even as an untrained caring individual or as a college student, there are a number of ways that children can be helped. As seen in the chapter on protective factors, one of the most salient protective factors against the development of problem behavior in children is having strong and stable role models in their lives. In one's own personal life, often there are opportunities to make a difference. For example, there was a public broadcasting campaign to help adults see that helping children can be easily integrated into their own lives. In this ad campaign directed toward parents, the commentator suggested that parents take another child with them and their child when going on outings or when involved in activities. The idea behind this ad campaign was to help expand the network of caring adults in children's lives. Likewise, as a caring individual you can take a special interest in children in your neighborhood, in your apartment complex, or at your place of worship. You could even have a strong positive impact on the lives of many infants, toddlers, and children by babysitting or by working within a day-care setting. Children often thrive on positive attention from competent, caring adults, and you can easily be one of those important adults in a child's life.

There are a number of programs nationwide (such as Big Brothers/Big Sisters and Boys and Girls Clubs of America), as well as local programs through Police Departments, Recreations Centers, and local schools that provide opportunities to mentor children who might otherwise find it difficult to have stable role models in their lives. Most communities also have other programs that allow volunteers to impact positively on the lives of children. For example, most communities have some type of protected living environment (often called a shelter) for children and their parents who have been exposed to domestic violence. Similarly, nearly every community has some type of protected living

Case Study: Community Elders as Co-Parents and Mentors

In her eloquent memoir, Dr. Marion Wright Edelman (1999), president of the Children's Defense Fund, writes about the co-parents and elders that were central to the community in which she grew up. In describing two particularly wonderful role models, she stated "They had no children of their own but mothered many children as if we belonged to them" (p. 10).

From taking special interest in the neighborhood children, to always having food to give to hungry children, to providing care and supervision when the children's parents were unable to watch them, these community elders provided the structure and warmth that are necessary to allow children to thrive. There are many such examples in many communities across the world.

---

environment for children who themselves have been abused or neglected by their parents. Often individuals from the community are encouraged to volunteer in these settings (after a rigorous background check) to help the children have positive influences and experiences in their lives. There is also a nationwide organization that allows individuals to advocate for abused and neglected children in the court system. These individuals are referred to as a guardian ad litem or a court-appointed special advocate. Although many states require that a court appointed guardian or special advocate be an attorney, many other states allow for trained volunteers to become court appointed advocates for children in the court system. As an attorney who has been involved in child advocacy across the nation, V. G. Weisz (1995) described in detail ways in which children can be helped through volunteer activities and through the legal system. Figure 15.1 shows the process by which allegations of child abuse are processed (Azar, 1992). Even nonprofessionals (such as a concerned neighbor or a clerk in a store) can make formal reports of child abuse to the local child protective agency, and the report will be processed appropriately. Note that many professionals, including clinical psychologists, pediatricians, social workers, and teachers in most states, are required by law to report their suspicions of child abuse and neglect (Renninger, Veach, & Bagdade, 2002).

Many inpatient and residential facilities also have opportunities for either volunteer or paid workers to help children who are distressed. Different states have different credentialing and licensing requirements for these positions, which are often referred to as psychiatric technicians, residential aids, or houseparents. A few phone calls to local facilities should help interested students understand the requirements for opportunities in their local area.

As mentioned in the chapter on protective factors, coaches of various sports can have a positive influence on children's well-being. Competent, caring, and supportive coaches can have numerous beneficial effects for both the quality of athletic development and for the psychological well-being of children involved in those opportunities (Smith & Smoll, 1997).

A number of nonprofit social and political organizations are also involved in advocating for children's mental health needs. The Society for Prevention of Child Abuse was originally an offshoot of the Society for the Prevention of Cruelty to Animals. As noted in the first chapter, the first legal case of child abuse was prosecuted in 1874 under the domain of protection of animals because there was no society for the protection of children. Since that time, the Society for the Prevention of Child Abuse and other national and local organizations have become very active in protecting the rights of abused children and in attempting to prevent child abuse internationally. Within the United States, the Children's Defense Fund is a nonprofit organization that serves as a watchdog for the rights and well-being of children. Through activities such as "Beat the Odds" and other national and international campaigns, the Children's Defense Fund tracks and publicizes the plight of children and families. The organization often publishes voting records of politicians regarding child-oriented legislation and publishes rankings of each state regarding child poverty, educational opportunities, and other relevant issues for children and families. Dr. Marian Wright Edelman (2005), the president of the Children's Defense Fund, made the following observations after the devastating hurricane that hit New Orleans and the Gulf Coast:

One of the unexpected side effects of Hurricane Katrina is that the storm opened up a national conversation on a piece of the tragedy that wasn't caused by the wind or water: poverty. Katrina ripped the blinders of denial off on the chronic quiet invisible tsunami of poverty that afflicts 37 million Americans, including 13 million children. People were forced to see what poverty

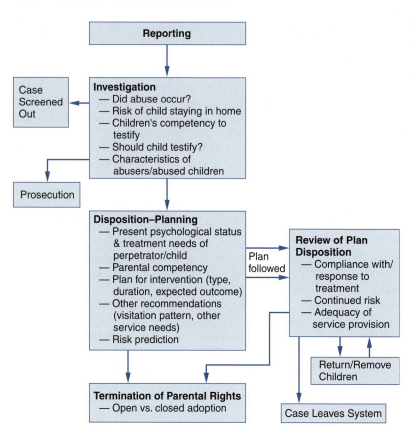

FIGURE 15.1 Movement of child abuse cases through social service and legal systems.

Source: Azar (1992).

looked like on the clear pictures on their television screens: families who didn't have enough money to own a car or have a credit card or enough cash to pay for another way out of the hurricane's path, families left stranded without food, water, or shelter when the storm came.... The day after Hurricane Katrina hit, the U.S. Census Bureau released the latest data on American poverty showing that in 2004, poverty increased in our rich country for the fourth year in a row. The number of American children living in poverty has grown by 12.8 percent over the last four years, and is now over 13 million. This means 1.5 million more children were poor in 2004 than in 2000.

The Children's Defense Fund, in addition to many other local, state, and national programs, is dedicated to trying to improve the lives of children and families in the United States and throughout the world.

In addition to helping children and families, volunteers often find that their experience enriches their own lives. Working as a volunteer or paid paraprofessional can help individuals learn more about their profession of interest. A colleague of mine (who is now a developmental psychologist studying language development) tells the story that she knew she wanted to work with children when she was an undergraduate student. She wisely tested out this interest by volunteering as a student teacher at a local elementary school. What she found was that she was fascinated by the children, but had no interest in teaching them on a full-time basis. This volunteer experience helped her identify appropriate career goals that might have been quite different had she not had the volunteer experience. Not only can this type of volunteer work help a student identify their professional interests, but this work can also help to make students more desirable candidates for jobs or graduate training programs in their area of interest.

Respect depends on reciprocity.

—Proverb of Africa

Transitioning from a Paraprofessional to a Professional

In addition to the many ways that students, nonprofessionals, and paraprofessionals can help children, there are also myriad careers through which children can be helped. Although most of these careers require a graduate degree, there are often paid positions in the

BOX 15.1

ADVICE FROM SENIOR PSYCHOLOGY MAJORS TO STUDENTS JUST STARTING IN PSYCHOLOGY

In an intriguing study, graduating senior psychology undergraduate students at the University of Scranton were asked to write a letter to an incoming freshman/freshwoman. The seniors were told to "summarize your own experiences, share some advice, and perhaps share some regrets about your years as a University of Scranton psychology student" (Norcross, Slotterback, & Krebs, 2001, p. 27). Common pieces of advice and recommendations included

- Get involved in psychology student organizations.
- Cultivate good study skills.
- Secure research experience.
- Seek help of psychology faculty.
- Get to know your professors.
- Prepare for graduate school.
- Realize that other students can help.
- Balance academic and social life.
- Obtain practical experience.
- Choose classes related to your projected career.
- Enjoy college to the fullest.

These are all excellent recommendations, and I would like to add my own recommendations (which are consistent with these recommendations). Think about your ultimate professional goals and then find ways to work toward those goals. Professors can help you in this direction, but you can also search out information for yourself. The more preparation you have done on your career of choice, the more a faculty member can help give you pointers to lead you in that direction. For seeking out information on your own, you might start with an online search engine such as Google. You could start with typing in the name of your ideal career or job and then read what appears meaningful. With all online searches, you need to be conscious of finding legitimate sources of information that are not tainted by commercialism or the funding source of the Web site.

Undergraduate as well as graduate students are also encouraged to read helpful books, such as *The Portable Mentor: Expert Guide to a Successful Career in Psychology* (Prinstein & Patterson, 2003) and *Your Career in Psychology* (Kuther, 2006). With these books and the other resources throughout this chapter, you should be well on your way to a fulfilling and meaningful career. And my final piece of advice? Have fun (and help a few kids along the way)!

community that can be found for students who have completed a bachelor's degree and who have adequate experience for the job. These positions are too variable to mention, but doing some homework in your community should highlight some of these opportunities. In addition, while doing volunteer work (for example in a mental health facility or in a shelter for abused children), students often learn about paid positions that are available before and after completing their bachelor's degree. Note the advice from senior psychology students listed in Box 15.1.

It is likely that a number of students study developmental psychopathology because they want to enter careers where they can dedicate their lives to helping children in need. There are a great diversity of careers and settings in which these goals can be met. From the mental health system, to the school system, to the criminal justice system, to the medical system, professionals from a diversity of disciplines have helped troubled children. These different professionals often provide varying levels of help to children. Specifically, within most of these professions, there is the ability to become a direct-service provider such as a clinician or therapist, a consultant or supervisor who works with direct-service providers, or a researcher who studies developmental psychopathology and the many ways in which to help children.

It is also important to note that there are many different career paths to reach the same goal. For example, if you wish to become a therapist to help children through direct services, you could become a psychologist (either at the master's or doctoral level), a social worker (either at the master's or doctoral level), or a psychiatrist (after going to medical school and completing a residency in psychiatry and a fellowship in child psychiatry). Some school psychologists also conduct therapy, especially group therapy, within the school setting. Conversely, all these disciplines, with the addition of criminology, provide opportunities to conduct research that is meaningful for children, adolescents, and families. There are a great many career paths with a wealth of options, so it is heartening to know that there are lots of ways to help children through professional careers.

After Hurricane Katrina devastated the Gulf Coast, many volunteers rushed to the area to help children and families in need.

HOW HAVING A CAREER IN PSYCHOLOGY CAN HELP CHILDREN

Within the field of psychology, there are many ways to help children. A common mistake that undergraduates make when first identifying their interests is to say that they want to be a "child psychologist." The reason this statement is potentially a mistake is that most students making this statement mean that they want to work clinically with children (e.g., doing therapy and psychological evaluations). The statement, however, actually would translate to a graduate program in developmental psychology where students learn about research with children but do not learn about therapy or assessment of children. Thus, if you are interested in becoming a psychologist who works therapeutically with children or a psychologist who conducts research on clinically oriented problems, chances are that you should be exploring clinical psychology and counseling psychology programs.

Many years ago, a doctoral degree (e.g., a Ph.D. or Psy.D.) was required to conduct therapy with children, adolescents, and families (see Box 15.4 for a further discussion of graduate degrees). Because of the changing health-care system and due to many other factors, it is now possible to plan a career as a therapist with a master's degree in clinical or counseling psychology (Hays-Thomas, 2000; Levant, Moldawsky, & Stigall, 2000). Although the salaries of master's-level therapists remain lower (on average) than the salaries of doctoral-level therapists, master's-level therapists have a great deal of opportunities for working with children, adolescents, and families. In fact, many health maintenance organizations (HMOs) and other institutions prefer hiring master's-level therapists because they can reimburse for therapy at a lower rate than for doctoral-level therapists. Note, however, that master's-level clinicians cannot be licensed as independent psychologists in most states. Rather, they can be licensed at a lower level of certification (such as a licensed mental health counselor or a marriage and family counselor). Box 15.3 gives more details on the licensure process for different graduate degrees.

An increasing number of doctoral-level therapists have begun supervising master's-level (and sometimes bachelor's-level) therapists without conducting direct therapy themselves. The pros and cons of this trend are beyond the scope of this textbook, but there are a number of other resources that discuss this issue for students who are interested in further understanding the ramifications of master's-level therapists and health maintenance organizations (Deal, Shiono, & Behrman, 1998; Hays-Thomas, 2000; Trull, 2005).

In general, the options for graduate work within psychology center around receiving a master's, Ph.D., or Psy.D. in clinical psychology or receiving a master's, Ph.D., or Ed.D. in counseling psychology (Mayne et al., 2006). Unfortunately, there is a great deal of variation on which degrees are offered at different universities. Students may find some slight variations at different graduate programs. For example, clinical psychology

Case Study: AIDS Orphans in Africa

If you keep up with the news, you are well aware of the AIDS crisis in many countries around the world. In particular, many countries in Africa have lost entire generations to HIV and AIDS. The result has been that millions of children have been orphaned due their parents' and other caretakers' deaths due to AIDS. For example, in the sub-Saharan region of Africa, over 11 million children younger than 15 years old have had at least one of their parents die from AIDS-related illnesses (Atwine, Cantor-Graae, & Bajunirwe, 2005). A number of scholarly works have highlighted the desperation of this situation (Atwine et al., 2005; Rotheram-Borus, 2005).

These issues have also been explored closer to home, in communities such as New Orleans (Pelton & Forehand, 2005). Specifically, orphans of the AIDS epidemic in the United States showed increased emotional/behavioral problems while their infected mothers were still alive and then showed an even higher increase in problems up to 2 years after their mother's death (Pelton & Forehand, 2005). Similarly, in Uganda, AIDS orphans showed a number of significant problems compared to children in their neighborhoods who had not lost a parent to AIDS, including higher rates of depression, anxiety, and anger (Atwine et al., 2005). These research findings are disturbing enough, but to read about the plight of real children is even more troubling.

In an eloquent book entitled *Love in the Driest Season: A Family Memoir,* journalist Neely Tucker (2004) provided a compelling case for why we should all care about the AIDS orphan crisis in Africa. The story begins with these haunting images:

> *By noon, the ants found the girl-child. Left to die on the day she was born, she had been placed in the tall brown grass that covers the highlands of Zimbabwe in the dry season . . . Patches of dried blood and placenta streaked her body. Her umbilical cord was still attached, a bloody stump dangling from the navel . . . The ants came from everywhere . . . Dozens, if not hundreds, poured over the fleshy stump of the umbilical cord. They began to eat her right ear. The girl-child screamed . . . The hours passed"* (Tucker, 2004, pp. 1–2).

The girl-child is taken to an overburdened and underfunded orphanage. She is named Chipo, which means "gift" in Shona. She has many near-brushes with death, but ultimately survives. Although the bureaucracy of the country and the fact that Tucker is a Caucasian foreigner nearly prevent a happy ending to this story, Tucker and his wife are able to adopt Chipo eventually. As Tucker stated at the end of the book, "Life is sweet" (Tucker, 2004, p. 266).

But what about the millions of other AIDS orphans around the globe?

---

programs tend to be housed in departments of psychology, whereas counseling psychology programs tend to be housed in departments of education. These patterns may differ at some universities, so interested students should try to use the resources listed in Box 15.2 to identify the location and availability of appropriate programs that match their interests. Note also that, historically, clinical psychology has focused on more severe problems than did counseling psychology. Some of these distinctions have been blurred over the years (Cobb et al., 2004), but in general, counseling psychology programs tend to focus a bit more on clients with less-severe psychopathology who are seeking services through schools or mental health clinics, whereas clinical psychology programs focus on the wide range of psychopathology that is presented in many different settings (such as inpatient facilities, Veteran's Administration hospitals, children's hospitals, outpatient settings, and schools).

Ph.D. or Master's in Clinical Psychology

The doctoral degree in clinical psychology is meant to be a **scientist–practitioner** degree. The training model that encompasses scientist–practitioner training suggests that students must learn to be both scientists (i.e., trained in research techniques) and practitioners (i.e., trained in clinical therapy and assessment techniques). Some doctoral programs focus more on the research side, and some programs focus more on the practice side, but in general, most doctoral clinical psychology programs attempt to train students in both research and clinical skills. Programs that are predominantly focused on training students to conduct research on clinical issues, while also training students to conduct evidence-based services, are often referred to as having a focus on **clinical science** (McFall, 2006). Clinical science is defined as "a psychological science directed at the

Providing care and comfort to children in need can be accomplished with or without advanced training.

promotion of adaptive functioning; at the assessment, understanding, amelioration, and prevention of human problems in behavior, affect, cognition or health; and at the application of knowledge in ways consistent with scientific evidence" (Academy of Psychological Clinical Science, 2006). Thus, clinical science programs are meant for students who wish to apply rigorous research methods to clinically oriented problems. The clinical doctoral programs at universities like the University of South Florida, the University of California, Berkeley, and Indiana University espouse the clinical science model. As can be seen in the "You Decide" section, there are ongoing debates between clinical scientists and practitioners on how best to provide effective treatment for children, adolescents, and families in need.

For accreditation by the American Psychological Association (APA), graduate programs must now define their specific goals (e.g., as primarily research programs, primarily therapy or assessment programs, or as hybrid programs that focus equally on research and practice), and then the programs are evaluated on the success with which these goals are reached. For students who are interested in doctoral programs in clinical psychology, it is highly advantageous to attend a graduate program that is accredited by the American Psychological Association. Many internships, which are completed after graduate course work but before the Ph.D. degree is conferred, require that students come from an APA accredited graduate program. There are also other accreditation entities, such as the Academy of Psychological Clinical Science (which is affiliated with the American Psychological Society, with an emphasis on clinical science rather than clinical practice) as well as regional and state accreditation entities, but the American Psychological Association remains the most visible and potent accrediting entity in clinical psychology at this time.

The idea behind scientist–practitioner programs (which are also referred to as **Boulder model programs** named after a conference in Boulder, Colorado) is that research knowledge is needed to treat and assess clients effectively and clinical knowledge is needed to conduct relevant research (Baker & Benjamin, 2000; Drabick & Goldfried, 2002). This textbook is written from a scientist–practitioner model, with emphasis on the importance of both research knowledge and clinical knowledge. For a more thorough discussion of the scientist–practitioner model, as well as other models of training within clinical psychology, see *Introduction to Clinical Psychology* (7th ed.) (Nietzel, Bernstein, Kramer, & Milich, 2003) or *Introduction to Clinical Psychology: Science and Practice* (Compas & Gotlib, 2002).

Courses in doctoral scientist–practitioner programs usually include theory, psychometrics, psychopathology, assessment, therapy, ethics, core courses within psychology (such as biological aspects of behavior, cognitive and affective aspects of behavior, social aspects of behavior, history and systems of psychology, human development, individual differences in behavior), research methodology, and statistics courses. Most programs require the completion of an empirical master's thesis and an empirical dissertation. Most programs also

BOX *15.2*

USEFUL RESOURCES FOR APPLYING TO GRADUATE SCHOOL AND IDENTIFYING APPROPRIATE GRADUATE PROGRAMS

If you are interested in attending graduate school, a number of resources might be helpful in identifying appropriate graduate programs and in elucidating the application process. Most universities also have career counseling centers, advising offices, and resource centers where additional information might be available. In addition, professors and current graduate students who serve as teaching assistants can help speak to your individual interests and needs for graduate training. It takes some homework on the part of the student, but informed applicants to graduate programs usually receive much better outcomes than uninformed and ill-prepared applicants. Some of the nationally available resources that you might find helpful include

- *Insider's Guide to Graduate Programs in Clinical and Counseling Psychology: 2006/2007 Edition* (Mayne, Norcross, & Sayette, 2006)
- *Graduate Study in Psychology: 2007 Edition* (American Psychological Association, 2006)
- *Directory of Graduate Programs in Clinical Child and Pediatric Psychology* (3rd ed.) (Tarnowski & Simonian, 1999)
- *Getting In: A Step-By-Step Plan for Gaining Admission to Graduate School in Psychology* (American Psychological Association, 1993)
- *Preparing for Graduate Study in Psychology: 101 Questions and Answers* (Burke & Buskist, 2006)
- *Doctoral Programs in Family Psychology* (American Psychological Association, 1997a)
- *Directory of School Psychology Graduate Programs* (Thomas, 1998)
- *Graduate Study in Educational and Psychological Measurement, Quantitative Psychology and Related Fields* (Collins, 2000)

- *Credentialing Requirements for School Psychologists* (Curtis, Hunley, & Prus, 1998)
- *Graduate Training in Behavior Therapy and Experimental-Clinical Psychology* (Association for the Advancement of Behavior Therapy, 1997)
- *Summary Information on Master's of Social Work Programs* (Council on Social Work Education, 1999)
- *Selecting a Doctoral Research Education Program in Communication Sciences and Disorders* (American Speech-Language-Hearing Association, 2000)
- *Directory of Graduate Programs in Applied Sport Psychology* (Burke, Sachs, Smission, & Smisson, 2004)
- *Career Paths in Psychology: Where Your Degree Can Take You* (Sternberg, 1997)
- *Psychology: Scientific Problem Solvers/Careers for the 21st Century* (American Psychological Association, 2003)
- *Negotiating Graduate School: A Guide for Graduate Students* (2nd ed.) (Rossman, 2002)
- *Succeeding in Graduate School: The Career Guide for Psychology Students* (Walfish & Hess, 2001)
- *Internship, Practicum, and Field Placement Handbook: A Guide for the Helping Professions* (Baird, 2004)
- *Compleat Academic: A Practical Guide for the Beginning Social Scientist* (2nd ed.) (Darley, Zanna, & Roediger, 2004)

There are also a number of Web sites that are helpful in learning about career opportunities and graduate education in the field:

Organization	Web Site
American Psychological Association	www.apa.org
American Psychological Society	www.psychologicalscience.org
Society for a Science of Clinical Psychology (APA, Division 12, Section III)	http://pantheon.yale.edu/~tat22/
Society for Research in Child Development	www.srcd.org
Society of Clinical Child and Adolescent Psychology (APA, Division 53)	www.clinicalchildpsychology.org
Society of Pediatric Psychology	www.apa.org/divisions/div54
National Association of School Psychologists	www.nasponline.org
Association for Advancement of Behavior Therapy (AABT, now known as Association for Behavioral and Cognitive Therapies (ABCT)	www.aabt.org

BOX *15.2*

(CONTINUED)

Organization	Web Site
Association for Behavior Analysis	www.abainternational.org
Council on Social Work Education	www.cswe.org
American Psychiatric Association	www.psych.org
American Academy of Child and Adolescent Psychiatry	www.aacap.org
American Academy of Pediatrics	www.aap.org
Society for Developmental and Behavioral Pediatrics	www.sdbp.org
American Art Therapy Association	www.arttherapy.org
American Music Therapy Association	www.musictherapy.org
Society for Neuroscience	www.sfn.org
Social Psychology Network (with resources for clinical child psychology)	www.socialpsychology.org

SUPPORTING AND ADVOCATING FOR PARENTS

Source: Webster-Stratton & Herbert (1994).

require between 1 and 4 years of supervised clinical practicum work in addition to a 1-year full-time clinical internship. Within most clinical psychology programs, students can gravitate toward work with children, adolescents, and families along with learning about adult functioning. Some programs (such as the University of Kansas, the University of Miami, and West Virginia University) have specific programs in clinical child psychology that do not require a great deal of training in adult functioning. Many other programs allow students to focus their clinical work and research on children, adolescents, and families along with learning about adult functioning. Box 15.5 provides a greater discussion of the pros and cons of choosing a program that focuses on children primarily.

The Ph.D. in clinical psychology allows students to pursue a number of different career paths, including research careers, academic careers (such as being a professor), independent practice, practice within an organization (such as a community mental health center, health maintenance organization, or hospital), and consultation. Research careers and academic careers require a great deal of research experience and scholarly publications for successful job applicants (Darley et al., 2004; Ilardi, Rodriguez-Hanley, Roberts, & Seigel, 2000). In addition to excellence in research, university-based professor positions also require teaching experience so that they can teach undergraduate and graduate courses. Note that there is a desperate need for researchers and professors who represent ethnic minority backgrounds and who study issues related to ethnic minority psychology (American Psychological Association, 2003; Bronstein & Quina, 2003; Jones & Rhee, 2004). There also continues to be a need for women to enter academia (Park & Nolen-Hoeksema, 2004). Practice-oriented careers require a great deal of supervised clinical experience in a particular area of expertise (such as working clinically with children diagnosed with attention-deficit/hyperactivity disorder). Careers within consultation require supervised experience within the consultant's area of expertise (such as consulting on the burn-unit of a children's hospital). In general, the Ph.D. in clinical psychology affords more career options than does the master's in clinical psychology.

Note, however, that admission into a doctoral program in clinical psychology is extremely competitive. Many doctoral programs receive 300 or 400 applications and only accept 6 or 7 students. Thus, having a strong

BOX *15.3*

A WORD ABOUT LICENSURE AND CERTIFICATION

Because there are no national or international licensure or certification boards, specific information about licensure and certification varies from state to state and country to country. The following information can be used as a general guideline, but interested students should contact the licensing board in their state to identify the specific requirements and options within that state. These governing bodies are often located in the same city as the state capital and are often housed within a department of professional regulation. For psychology, the national organization that provides links to the licensing boards of all 50 states and Canadian provinces is called the Association of State and Provincial Psychology Boards (www.asppb.org).

Licence or Certification	Training Requirements and Practice Options
Licensed Psychologist	Ph.D. or Psy.D. in clinical or counseling psychology required in nearly all states. Postdoctoral supervised hours required. Can practice independently and can use the term "psychologist" to describe professional status.
Licensed Mental Health Counselor (or comparable term)	Usually minimum of master's degree required. Degree can often be in clinical or counseling psychology, guidance counseling, rehabilitation counseling, or related area. Postmaster's supervised hours required. Can practice usually within a group practice, though some independent practice is allowed.
Marriage and Family Counselor	Usually minimum of master's degree required, with specialization in children, marriage, and families.
Licensed Clinical Social Worker	Master's degree (or higher) in social work required. Postgraduate supervised hours required. Can usually practice independently, but often work is within group practice or organization.
Licensed School Psychologist	Ph.D. or Ed.D. in school psychology or educational psychology required. Postgraduate supervised hours required. Most often, practice is within school system.
Certified Educational Specialist	Master's degree (or higher) in school psychology or educational psychology required. Postgraduate supervised hours required. Most often, practice is within school system.
Psychiatrist	M.D. from medical school plus 4-year residency in psychiatry are required. Specialization as a child psychiatrist requires another 1-year fellowship in child psychiatry. Practices can be independent, in group settings, or in hospital settings.

YOU DECIDE: SHOULD CLINICIANS BE MORE RESPONSIVE TO EVIDENCE FROM TREATMENT OUTCOME STUDIES?

Yes

- There is strong evidence of which treatments work for which child problems, so clinicians in the community should utilize the treatments that work the best to end children's suffering (Weisz, Doss, & Hawley, 2005; Weisz, Sandler, Durlak, & Anton, 2005).

- Effective treatments can be instituted in the community, along with attention to other systems of care like the school setting and the family (Burns, 2002).

No

- Controlled clinical studies of treatment are not representative of clients in the real world, so the results of these studies are not useful to clinicians in the real world (Westen, 2006).

- "Evidence" from outcome studies is not any more meaningful than "evidence" from clinical expertise that guides clinicians on how best to provide services to their clients (Reed, 2006).

So, should clinicians be more responsive to evidence from treatment outcome studies? You decide.

Clinical psychologists are trained to help children by using evidence-based treatments.

grade point average (usually 3.5 or better), strong Graduate Record Exam scores (usually well above 1300 when Verbal and Quantitative are combined), stellar letters of recommendation, and a strong record of research (with conference presentations and publications) are highly desirable when applying to these programs. Although students can gain admission with lower credentials, most APA-accredited doctoral programs in clinical psychology are looking for students who fit this profile. Parenthetically, note that Graduate Record Exam (GRE) scores and undergraduate grade point average (GPA) are associated with success in graduate school. Specifically, higher GREs and GPAs were associated with higher GPAs in graduate school, comprehensive examination scores, ratings by faculty, and numbers of publications (Kuncel, Hezlett, & Ones, 2001). The subject test of the GRE (also known as the advanced test) was even more predictive of success in graduate school than were the verbal and quantitative scores on the general GRE (Kuncel et al., 2001).

Master's programs in clinical psychology mirror doctoral programs in their emphasis, but they tend to be 2-year programs rather than 5-year programs, and they tend to have less-stringent requirements for admission. Master's programs often offer similar types of course work, but the empirical requirements end with the master's thesis rather than continuing on for the doctoral dissertation. Graduate programs that offer a master's degree are referred to as **terminal master's programs.** Students who wish to receive their master's without continuing in the program for a Ph.D. would be

looking for a terminal master's program that is meant to end when the student earns the master's degree. Doctoral programs, on the other hand, award the master's degree on the way to the doctoral degree, but students are expected to continue in the program after the master's is earned. Thus, the master's is not considered "terminal" (or the final degree) in a doctoral program.

There is great variability in the focus of master's programs within clinical psychology. Some are more practice oriented, some are more research oriented, and some are consistent with a scientist–practitioner model. Students should try to match their interests with the focus of the masters program. The American Psychological Association does not accredit master's level programs, nor do they accredit programs (such as developmental, industrial/organizational, or behavioral neuroscience) outside of the realm of clinical, counseling, or school psychology.

If students are interested in the doctoral degree, it is in their best interest to gain admission to a doctoral program from the start (if possible). In general, it is difficult to "transfer" from a terminal master's program straight into a doctoral program without first going through the admissions process for the doctoral program. If students are interested in the doctoral degree, but cannot gain admission into a doctoral program, then using the master's degree as a stepping-stone into a doctoral program is a viable option. These students, however, would probably find that only a small portion of their course work and clinical work from their masters program would transfer to a doctoral program once they

BOX *15.4*

ACADEMIC DEGREES AT A GLANCE

In order to familiarize students with various academic degrees, selected degrees are presented here that are relevant to helping children. Note that the time frames of these degrees are approximate. Programs nearly always require a set of classes or minimum credit hours or specific requirements (such as an internship, thesis, or dissertation) rather than requiring a certain number of years of schooling.

Associate of Arts (A.A.): The Associate of Arts degree is earned after 2 years of college, which are usually completed at a community college.

Bachelor of Arts (B.A.) or Bachelor of Sciences (B.S.) or Bachelor of Social Work (B.S.W.): Bachelors degrees are earned after 4 years of undergraduate work (either with an A.A. and 2 additional years, or 4 years at a college or university). The Bachelor of Arts is usually awarded for disciplines in liberal arts and the social sciences (e.g., psychology, criminology, education), the Bachelor of Sciences is usually awarded for disciplines in the hard sciences (e.g., biology, chemistry), and the Bachelor of Social Work is solely for a bachelor's degree completed in social work. Note that some universities offer both the B.A. and the B.S. within the same discipline, depending on the content of the course work (e.g., a general psychology major may lead to a B.A., but a psychology major with heavy emphasis in biology and physiology may lead to a B.S.). Schooling after the bachelor's degree is considered to be graduate work. Nearly all master's and doctoral programs require a bachelor's degree before entering into the graduate program.

Master of Arts (M.A.) or Master of Sciences (M.S.): Master's degrees are usually 2-year graduate degrees that are completed after the bachelor's degree. As with the B.A. and B.S., the Master of Arts is usually awarded in most liberal arts and social science disciplines whereas the Master of Sciences is awarded when the hard sciences are represented in the discipline. A thesis is usually required for both the M.A. and the M.S. degrees.

Master of Social Work (M.S.W.): The Master of Social Work is usually a 2-year graduate degree in social work. In addition to course requirements, there are usually a fair amount of clinical practicum requirements.

Educational Specialist (Ed.S.): The educational specialist is usually a 2-year graduate program that is comparable to the M.A. in education, but without the thesis requirement. Many students can work toward both the Ed.S. and the M.A. in education at the same time. Some jobs within the school system require the Ed.S., even if applicants already have their M.A. in education.

Doctorate of Education (Ed.D.): The Doctorate of Education degree is a doctoral graduate degree that usually requires 4 to 5 years of graduate work in education (either an M.A. in education plus 2 to 3 years of additional graduate work or 4 to 5 years of graduate training in a doctoral program). A dissertation is usually required.

Doctorate of Philosophy (Ph.D.): The Doctorate of Philosophy is a doctoral graduate degree that usually requires 5 to 6 years of graduate work. Ph.D. degrees are offered in most social science disciplines (e.g., psychology, criminology, women's studies) and hard science disciplines (e.g., biology and chemistry). The requirements for the Ph.D. in psychology vary depending on the area of specialization, with primarily research requirements in developmental psychology and both research and clinical practicum requirements (including a 1-year, full-time clinical internship) in clinical psychology. A dissertation is usually required.

Doctorate of Psychology (Psy.D.): The Doctorate of Psychology is a doctoral graduate degree that usually requires 5 years of graduate work. Course requirements focus on the practice of psychology, and there are heavy clinical practicum requirements (including a 1-year clinical internship). Although a master's and dissertation are often required, these projects tend to be literature reviews rather than original empirical research.

Doctorate of Social Work (D.S.W.): The Doctorate of Social Work is a 5-year graduate degree in social work (or an M.S.W. with 3 additional years of graduate work). Within the field of social work, the M.S.W. is considered the practice-oriented degree, whereas the D.S.W. is primarily for those who want to conduct research and who want to teach in the discipline of social work.

Medical Doctorate (M.D.): The Medical Doctorate is completed after 4 years of medical school. After medical school, students complete a residency in their area of specialization. Residencies vary in length depending on the area of specialization, with psychiatry residencies lasting 4 years. Specialization as a child psychiatrist requires an additional 1-year fellowship in child psychiatry.

Case Study: Coping with Divorce

Here are some examples of the many ways that adults and therapists can help children cope with parental divorce.

A 12-year-old boy said, "We had to go see a counselor after my parents got their separation but not because of that. It was because my brother and I started fighting really bad, and they thought I had hurt him" (p. 191).

A 19-year-old young woman stated, "I think my brother took the pain inside himself. He'd go off and hang out with his friends a lot, but I know that he didn't talk with them about it. He was dealing with it on his own without anybody else, and I think that's just the way some people have to deal with it. I think he wouldn't have known what to do if somebody had come to him and said, 'Hey, let's sit down and talk about this.' If it were, say, my mom's best friend, I think he would have felt like he was going against my dad, being a traitor. So I think you have to figure out what type of a person

they are and then help them out accordingly" (p. 184).

A 12-year-old boy wrote, "The therapist I see, I tell him whatever happened, and then at the end he'll scribble something in his notebook, really short, and say, 'Okay, that's it for today.' I like him. It's just the helpfulness that I get from him that feels good" (p. 184).

A 19-year-old young woman reflected, "I guess it was good that I had a lot of adult influences. My mom's best friend's a pastor. I talked to her a lot . . . My fifth grade teacher is still my favorite teacher I ever had, and he was the one I had when I was going through the separation. He was somebody else that I could go and talk to, and I had a really close best friend at the time. I'd hang out with her a lot and try to get out of the house. It helped." (p. 192).

Source: Royko (1999)

---

gained admission. Many of the references in Box 15.2 detail the pros and cons of gaining admission into a doctoral versus master's program.

Psy.D. in Clinical Psychology

In contrast to the scientist–practitioner model in most doctoral and master's programs in clinical psychology, a number of professional schools of psychology have been developed that offer the **Psy.D. (Doctorate of Psychology)** in clinical psychology. These programs focus almost exclusively on the practice side of psychology (e.g., therapy, assessment, consultation). The first Psy.D. program was developed in 1968 (Peterson, 1971), and there are Psy.D. programs found in nearly every state in the union. Some Psy.D. programs are housed within academic universities (such as Rutgers and Baylor Universities), but the majority are found at self-sustained professional schools that are not affiliated directly with any university (such as the Alliant International University/California Schools of Professional Psychology or the Illinois Schools of Professional Psychology). Although some Psy.D. and professional school programs in clinical psychology have obtained accreditation from the American Psychological Association (APA), the majority have not obtained this accreditation (Cobb et al., 2004; Trull, 2005).

Course work in Psy.D. programs tends to focus more on theory and clinical applications than on research

methodology and statistics. In addition, a great deal of time is focused on direct clinical experience (e.g., clinical practica in assessment and therapy). Graduation from a professional school and the degree of Psy.D. should enable most students to seek licensure as a psychologist in most states. Some states, however, are moving to the requirement that the graduate training must have taken place in an APA-accredited program, so students must be cognizant of the accreditation of these professional schools and of the licensure requirements in their state. Interested students can read more about the differences between Psy.D. programs and Ph.D. practice-oriented programs to make more informed decisions on which training path to take (Norcross, Castle, Sayette, & Mayne, 2004).

Ph.D. in Experimental Psychopathology

On the other end of the spectrum, programs in **experimental psychopathology** focus solely on research rather than on clinical training. Although programs in experimental psychopathology are somewhat rare, some universities (such as Harvard University and the University of Hawaii at Manoa) have extraordinary training programs in research on issues related to psychopathology. The idea behind programs in experimental psychopathology is that empirical research can be conducted on clinical issues without spending time learning clinical

Case Study: In Praise of Teachers

A special education teacher wrote, "These extraordinary children arrived filled with invisible gifts in hand, just for me. They challenged me to emerge from my cocoon of complacency and ignorance" (p. 150; Wright, 1999).

A current teacher wrote about her own drama teacher from high school, "Mr. Emmelhainz made the finest contribution a teacher can make; he helped his students help themselves. He believed in them, in their ability and in their worthiness of respect" (p. 154; Wright, 1999).

A teacher on the verge of retiring after a long and successful career stated, "Each day I witness the competence of my fellow teachers who are dedicated and excellent role models. They are like candles that light others while consuming themselves" (p. 91; Wright, 1999).

Speaking of her student, a sixth grade teacher noted, "Formally, I was Andrew's mentor. Informally, he was mine" (p. 7; Wright, 1999).

BOX *15.5*

SPECIFICITY VERSUS BREADTH IN TRAINING

One choice that students must make when considering options in graduate training is the extent to which they wish to specialize in their early graduate training. Students who know they wish to work only with children might seek graduate training that specializes in children (e.g., a clinical child psychology Ph.D. program rather than a more general clinical psychology Ph.D. program or graduate training in early education, special education, or school psychology rather than a more general education program). Students who want broader training, with advanced specialization in children might seek a more general program that allows some specialization with children (e.g., a clinical psychology M.A., Ph.D., or Psy.D. program that teaches skills related to both children and adults). Within the field of psychiatry, general medical skills are taught in medical school before students can specialize in psychiatry while on residency (which usually focuses on all age groups), and then further specialization is required in a child fellowship. Thus, students interested in psychiatry are mandated to gain general medical and psychiatric skills before specializing in child psychiatry.

When considering the specificity versus breadth issue, there are pros and cons to both types of programs. Ultimately, this decision should be made based on the student's own interests. It should be noted, however, that working with children often means working with adults (i.e., parents). In order to feel completely competent in working with children and adolescents, it behooves students to gain some type of training and research knowledge in work with adults and families.

skills (such as therapy or assessment techniques). Overall, a program in experimental psychopathology would be excellent for students who wish to conduct research in the field of developmental psychopathology but who do not wish to spend time learning clinical skills. Applying developmental and clinical science to real-world issues can be a very powerful mechanism through which to improve the lives of children (Lerner, Fisher, & Weinberg, 2000; McCall & Groark, 2000).

Ph.D., Ed.D. or Master's in Counseling Psychology

As mentioned previously, programs in counseling psychology tend to focus on less-severe types of problems than in clinical psychology programs. There are exceptions to this rule, but in general, counseling psychology programs train students to work within school settings, outpatient mental health settings, and university counseling center settings. Because many counseling psychology programs are housed within departments of education, much of the training tends to focus on the educational side of emotional/behavioral problems. Within many counseling psychology programs at the doctoral and master's level, there is a focus on scientist–practitioner models of training.

Ph.D. or Master's in Developmental Psychology

When students say that they want to specialize in "child psychology," they are (usually unknowingly) referring to the field of developmental psychology. This scholarly discipline, however, is not well suited for students who wish to work clinically and therapeutically with children, adolescents, and families. Both the Ph.D. and the master's in developmental psychology are academic, research-oriented degrees. Programs in developmental psychology tend to be housed within departments of psychology and tend to focus on research on very specific issues related to development (e.g., language development, social development). Although developmental programs focused on children under the age of 18 in the past, there has been increasing focus on life span development that addresses developmental processes from conception until death.

The Ph.D. or master's degree in developmental psychology would afford successful students to conduct research in areas related to developmental psychology. Many researchers within the field of developmental psychopathology have degrees in developmental psychology, with an emphasis on developmental psychopathology. Still other researchers within the field of developmental psychopathology have doctoral degrees in clinical psychology or have medical degrees with specialization in child psychiatry. Overall, the field of developmental psychology is an important one for students interested in conducting research with children, adolescents, and families.

Some students are interested in pursuing training in specific techniques, such as family therapy. There are many ways to go about receiving training in family therapy, including finding a clinical psychology or counseling psychology doctoral or master's program that specializes in family therapy (Kasloe, Celano, & Stanton, 2005) or by finding a program that focuses solely on marriage and family counseling (which is offered at the master's level more frequently than at the doctoral level; (Nelson & Smock, 2005)). The effectiveness of family therapy (Curtis et al., 2004; Diamond & Josephson, 2005) and couples counseling (Baucom, Epstein, & Gordon, 2000) have been supported by empirical evidence, especially when framed within a cognitive–behavioral or behavioral orientation.

Students also sometimes ask about other specific techniques, such as art therapy (Haeseler, 2004) and music therapy (Hanser, 2000). These techniques are sometimes offered within psychology or counseling programs and they are sometimes offered in graduate programs specific to the technique (such as a master's in art therapy). Note that these types of techniques are not thought of highly by many psychologists because of the limited evidence to support the use of those techniques (Bellmer et al., 2003).

HOW HAVING A CAREER IN SOCIAL WORK CAN HELP CHILDREN

Historically, the field of social work has dealt with children through social and administrative institutions (e.g., child protection agencies, adoption agencies). Although the emphasis in training continues to focus on administrative mechanisms of helping, social work is now a diverse field that allows career opportunities in many different settings. Like psychologists, social workers can be found helping children in hospitals, schools, community mental health centers, and private outpatient clinics as well as in governmental agencies such as child protective agencies and adoption agencies. Different graduate programs focus on different aspects of the field (e.g., direct clinical services versus work within a child protective agency), so students should try to match their career interests with the focus of the graduate program.

Bachelor's of Social Work

As can be seen in Box 15.4, there are three degrees possible within social work—the B.S.W., the M.S.W., and the D.S.W. The B.S.W. is completed at the undergraduate level and often affords students the opportunity to work at entry-level positions within governmental agencies (e.g., child protective services). Although the B.S.W. is not required for admission into an M.S.W. program, the B.S.W. gives extensive training in the field of social work and often requires direct practicum experience for the completion of the degree.

Master's of Social Work

The M.S.W. is the most prevalent degree within the field of social work. Whether the student's bachelor's degree is in social work, psychology, education, or another related area, applicants to M.S.W. programs are expected to have an extensive amount of practicum or work experience in the field. The M.S.W. allows students to work toward licensure after graduation. Most states require additional supervised hours to be licensed as a clinical social worker. Licensed clinical social workers can conduct therapy, complete social history and functional assessments, work as child advocates,

BOX *15.6*

PRESCRIPTION PRIVILEGES FOR CLINICAL PSYCHOLOGISTS?

Historically, one of the primary differences between clinical psychologists and psychiatrists was the ability to prescribe medication (known as prescription privileges). Psychiatrists have the medical training that allows them to prescribe medication, whereas clinical psychologists are not allowed to prescribe medication, even if they have a lot of course work in psychopharmacology (the study of drugs and behavior). Recently, however, some clinical psychologists have argued that prescription privileges should be available to psychologists who complete enough training in psychopharmacology (Welsh, 2003). In fact, the American Psychological Association Council of Representatives is in favor of prescription privileges for practicing psychologists, and a number of states have introduced legislation that would allow psychologists to prescribe medication after sufficient training (Hanson et al., 1999). One study, known as the Psychopharmacology Demonstration Project, showed that with appropriate training, clinical psychologists can be trained to prescribe medications in an effective and ethical manner (Newman, Phelps, Sammons, Dunivin, & Cullen, 2000).

There are strongly held beliefs on both sides of this issue (Heiby, DeLeon, & Anderson, 2004; Klusman, 2001; Sammons, Gorny, Zinner, & Allen, 2000; Welsh, 2003). In general, clinical psychologists have a thorough understanding of behavior, they usually have a good understanding of their clients' problems, and they could help their clients with both psychotherapy and medication when needed (Gutierrez & Silk, 1998). In addition, allowing clinical psychologists to prescribe medications would enable more clients to have access to services (Sammons et al., 2000; Welsh, 2003). These points help support the option of prescription privileges for clinical psychologists. In contrast, a number of

questions have been raised about prescription privileges for clinical psychologists. Because clinical psychologists do not have formal medical training (other than some course work in psychopharmacology that would be required for obtaining prescription privileges), they may put clients in danger due to their lack of thorough medical knowledge (Heiby et al., 2004). In addition, clinical psychologists would be furthering their involvement in the medical model rather than exploring environmental and behavioral interventions that could help alleviate suffering (Albee, 1998). Give people a hammer and all they see are nails. There is concern that prescription privileges will hamper clinical psychologists' therapeutic interventions and will dissuade them from exploring preventive strategies for psychological problems.

In addition, there is a raging debate as to whether psychoactive medications should be prescribed to children (De Angelis, 2004). As mentioned in the chapter on interventions, there are great concerns about using antidepressants with children because of the potential for suicide. In addition, other than medications for ADHD, most medications have not been tested thoroughly on children but rather have been tested on adults and then are still prescribed for children (De Angelis, 2004). Given the different physical makeup of children versus adults, this practice may put children in danger of medications that are safe for adults but that are potentially harmful to adults (De Angelis, 2004).

Overall, there is no easy answer to the issue of prescription privileges. Those in the psychological and medical communities have strongly held beliefs on both sides of the issue (Barnett & Neel, 2000; Plante et al., 1998; Resnick & Norcross, 2002; Sammons et al., 2000). Where do you stand?

---

provide counseling services in schools, and serve as consultants in hospitals. The M.S.W. degree does not usually require any research training, so the M.S.W. is considered more of a practice degree than a research degree.

Doctorate of Social Work

The D.S.W., on the other hand, is considered a research degree. The D.S.W. degree is most often sought by individuals who wish to become a professor and those who wish to conduct research.

Overall, the lines between social work and psychology have blurred over the years. In general, social workers are trained to consider child and adolescent functioning

within a broader context (e.g., the community, the school, the family) than are psychologists. These distinctions, however, have blurred as more and more social workers conduct individual therapy and more and more psychologists work within different contexts related to children, adolescents, and families.

HOW HAVING A CAREER IN EDUCATION CAN HELP CHILDREN

There are a variety of ways to help children through the educational system. From general education teachers, to special education teachers, to guidance counselors, to school psychologists, there are a number of different professionals within the school system who affect children daily.

Teachers

Teachers in regular education classrooms have a phenomenal impact on generations of children. Teachers in regular education classrooms are not expected to have specialized training in children with special needs, but they have to deal with behavioral difficulties in children occasionally. Teachers are often the first individuals to identify children who might be in need of help and they can play an important role in helping children gain access to appropriate specialists (e.g., school psychologists, speech therapists). Teachers can help intervene with one child or hundreds of children, depending on their interests and activities (Gruwell, 1999). Even by supporting children, teachers can affect the well-being of youth. For example, one longitudinal study found that higher rates of middle school students' perceptions of teacher support were associated with lower rates of depression and higher rates of self-esteem (Reddy, Rhodes, & Mulhall, 2003). Depending on the state or country requirements, most teachers can be certified after completion of a bachelor's degree with approximately 1 year of additional certification courses (if the bachelor's degree was not in education) and a series of practicum experiences as a student teacher.

Special Education Teachers

Special education teachers are not only trained in educational teaching methods but they also complete training in helping children with special needs. Special education teachers often specialize in one type of special education service (e.g., children with severe physical disabilities, children with emotional difficulties, or children with limited intellectual functioning). Depending on their specialty, special education teachers could work in a resource room and provide pullout services for children for a limited amount of time per week or they could have their own classroom for children with whom they are assigned to work full time. Depending on the state or country, special education teachers are expected to have completed their bachelor's degree, specialized credentialing course work in special education, and student teaching experiences in special education classes. Although it is not usually required, some special education teachers also have obtained a master's degree in special education.

Guidance Counselors

Guidance counselors can also have a meaningful impact on many children. Guidance counselors often provide a wealth of services for children and adolescents, ranging from scheduling academic classes, to teaching anger management classes, to helping with college applications, to talking with troubled children and their parents. The types of activities in which guidance counselors engage depend on the needs of the school and the students in that school system. Guidance counselors most often have a master's in counselor education.

School Psychologists and Educational Specialists

School psychologists and educational specialists can help children who, for the most part, are having emotional/behavioral difficulties. Many school psychologists also do a great deal of testing and evaluation (e.g., to determine if a child has a learning disorder). School psychologists and educational specialists, therefore, can serve in roles to help evaluate children or to help treat children. Evaluations for specific learning disorders or emotional/behavioral problems are almost always done in a one-on-one situation with children. On the other hand, many school psychologists and educational specialists conduct group interventions (such as prevention programs, group therapy, behavioral management classes) to help children change their behavior. For example, school psychologists are increasingly being asked to provide school-based programs to prevent youth violence (Evans & Rey, 2001) and to implement home–school–community partnerships to promote resilience in children and adolescents (Smith, Boutte, Zigler, & Finn-Stevenson, 2004). School psychologists and educational specialists also can serve as consultants to teachers who need help with behavioral issues in their classrooms. In general, educational specialists would have earned either an Ed.S. or master's degree in school psychology. School psychologists, on the other hand, often have earned a Ph.D. or an Ed.D. in school psychology or educational psychology. There is a great deal of overlap in the training of school psychologists and clinical child psychologists, but school psychologists usually receive more intensive training in educational and school-system issues than do clinical child psychologists (Mattison, 2000; Tryon, 2000).

Other Professionals

In addition to the training that occurs in departments of education, it should be noted that many other

Special education teachers have advanced training in effective teaching techniques for children with special needs.

professionals can help children within the school system. Mental health counselors (with a master's in clinical or counseling psychology), clinical psychologists (with a Ph.D. or Psy.D. in clinical psychology), and social workers (with an M.S.W.) often work within the school system to help children through counseling or, in the case of clinical psychologists, through therapy and assessments. An increasing amount of government funding for mental health services will be targeted for school systems across the United States (Oakland & Cunningham, 1999). There may be even greater opportunities for professionals to help children through work within the school system in the future.

HOW HAVING A CAREER IN MEDICINE CAN HELP CHILDREN

Within the field of medicine, there are many avenues through which to help children with psychological problems. In addition to trained medical professionals, there are also a number of other professionals who work in medical settings to help children who are medically and emotionally challenged.

Psychiatric Nurses

Within the nursing profession, there is a specialization of psychiatric nursing through which training is gained in mental health issues. Psychiatric nurses often work within psychiatric hospitals or inpatient units where children and adolescents receive intensive treatment for psychological problems. Psychiatric nurses can deal with the medical side of mental health (e.g., administering medications that have been prescribed) as well as the psychological side of mental health (e.g., conducting a mental health history assessment, providing therapeutic interventions).

Psychiatrists

Probably the best-known professionals within the field of medicine in terms of helping children with emotional/behavioral difficulties are child psychiatrists. As mentioned earlier, child psychiatrists have completed their bachelor's degree (usually in biology or another premed major), have completed medical school (which allows rotations through all the various specialties including psychiatry), have completed their 4-year psychiatric residency, and most often have completed another 1-year child fellowship. Given their training, psychiatrists can prescribe medications and can conduct therapy. Although it is relatively rare, some psychiatrists also are involved actively in research with children, adolescents, and families. Note that one of the biggest differences between clinical psychologists and psychiatrists surrounds the use of medications, the completion of research, and the ability to conduct psychological testing. Psychiatrists (and not clinical psychologists) can prescribe medication for psychological difficulties. As can be seen in Box 15.6 on page 447, however, this difference is under review. Clinical psychologists from Ph.D. programs (and not psychiatrists or most clinical psychologists from Psy.D. programs) are trained in

Case Study: The Girl Who Wouldn't Talk

Jadie was nearly 8 years old when she entered the classroom for severely emotionally disturbed children that was run by Torey Hayden (1991). She had the diagnosis of what is now known as selective mutism. Jadie spoke at home, but would not utter a word or whisper at school. She never had spoken in school. Upon meeting Jadie, her teacher noticed that she walked in a manner that suggested she was carrying a very heavy load of books (i.e., she remained hunched over constantly, whether walking or sitting).

After a somewhat brief time in this classroom, Jadie began speaking with her teacher. Although previous professionals had tried hard to get Jadie to speak, Ms. Hayden worked with her in a nonconfrontational manner and allowed her to begin communicating on her own terms. After she was speaking for a while, Ms. Hayden asked Jadie to try to stand up straight. Jadie had already been evaluated by the school nurse and by her pediatrician who both ascertained that she did not have a medical problem that was causing her to bend over constantly. When Ms. Hayden was trying gently to coax Jadie to stand up straight, Jadie replied that she had to keep bent over "To keep my insides from falling out" (p. 34).

With long and intensive work by this caring teacher, it became clear that Jadie had experienced severe abuse. Ms. Hayden was able to uncover Jadie's troubling experiences and to help her deal with these issues. Eventually, Jadie was placed into a foster care setting and she grew up to be a competent, yet still somewhat withdrawn young woman. She was able to attend high school without any additional special educational help and she went on to attend college and study English literature. This case illustrates the impact of a caring and competent special education teacher who had the patience and determination that were necessary to reach into the world of a troubled young girl.

Source: Hayden (1991).

research methods and can conduct empirical research with children, adolescents, and families. Clinical psychologists (both from Ph.D. and Psy.D. programs) are usually trained in conducting psychological assessments and evaluations. Although psychiatrists are trained in the use of some assessment techniques (e.g., interviews, mental status exams), they are not usually trained in how to administer or interpret standardized psychological tests such as intelligence testing, achievement testing, or emotional/behavioral measures. Both clinical psychologists and psychiatrists are trained in therapy and various interventions. There is a great need for child psychiatrists currently, and especially research-oriented child psychiatrists, who could help test medications effectively with children and adolescents (Ringold, 2005).

Developmental Pediatricians

Another somewhat lesser known specialization within the medical field is developmental pediatrics. Developmental pediatricians usually specialize in pediatrics for their 3-year residency (after medical school), then complete a fellowship in developmental pediatrics. Like child psychiatrists, developmental pediatricians can prescribe medications and can conduct therapy. Their special knowledge of pediatrics and developmental processes allows them to focus more on the normative side of development as well as the abnormal side of development.

Other Professionals

In addition to these professionals within the medical field, a number of other professionals can work within medical settings. The psychological management of health and disease is a growing area for clinical psychologists (Levant et al., 2001; Mullins et al., 2003). In addition to working in hospitals, pediatric psychologists are increasingly working in primary care settings, such as with a group practice of pediatricians (Frank, McDaniel, Bray, & Heldring, 2003; Pisani, Berry, & Goldfarb, 2005). The area of health promotion is very active for pediatric psychologists who focus on prevention programs to help enhance healthy outcomes for children (Durlak, 2000; Fuemmeler, 2004; Power, Shapiro, & DuPaul, 2003). Clinical psychologists (especially pediatric psychologists) and social workers often work within pediatric settings (e.g., an oncology unit for children) or children's hospitals to help children who are experiencing medical difficulties. Any type of inpatient setting for children must somehow address the educational needs of the children on the unit, so special educators and school psychologists often work within inpatient settings to help disturbed children with their educational needs. Overall, there are a number of diverse disciplines through which children can be helped in medical settings. Hospitals and other medical settings often utilize **multidisciplinary teams** (consisting of professionals from multiple and diverse disciples) to help children, adolescents, and families. There is increasing emphasis for professionals to involve multiple systems (i.e., multiple areas of the child's life) into the evaluation and treatment of serious emotional disorders (Hansen, Litzelman, Marsh, & Milspaw, 2004). These multiple systems would include families (see also Box 15.7), schools, and the community (Hansen et al., 2004).

Increasingly, psychologists and other professionals in medical settings are using technology to provide services that might be too expensive or difficult to administer in person. Called **telehealth** because of its origins in using the telephone for outreach services to clients who could not reach a medical center, these services are now provided via the Internet, and this technology has allowed many children to receive services that they would not have otherwise been able to access (Wasem & Puskin, 2000). Internet-based services have been used to assess clients, to provide entire evidence-based treatment packages, and to provide enhanced services to clients who are receiving services in traditional medical settings (Naglieri et al., 2004; Ritterband, Gonder-Frederick, et al., 2003). There is great promise in using the Internet as an adjunct to traditional in-person treatment. For example, Ritterband, Cox, and colleagues (2003) randomly assigned encopretic children to treatment as usual with no Internet utilization or the same treatment but with enhanced toilet training via the Internet. They found significant improvements in both groups, but children in the treatment group who also received the enhanced Internet treatment showed significantly better progress in managing their encopresis (Ritterband, Cox, et al., 2003). Overall, Web-based services are here to stay, but like all other treatments, psychologists will need to ensure that these services are provided in an ethical and evidence-based manner (Fisher & Fried, 2003).

Anybody who is in a position to discipline others should first learn to accept discipline himself [or herself].
—Malcolm X

HOW HAVING A CAREER IN THE JUDICIAL JUSTICE SYSTEM CAN HELP CHILDREN

There are a number of ways in which to help children through a career in the judicial justice system. Some professionals may even start out in law enforcement and then find that they can serve children in many ways.

School Resource Officers

Resource officers in elementary, middle, and high schools often play a vital role in the well-being of children and adolescents. Although their training is usually within law enforcement (such as training as a police officer or a sheriff), resource officers tend to also deal with emotional/behavioral issues that arise for troubled children and adolescents. Many resource officers make it a point to serve in a preventive role, by getting to know students well enough to know when they are at risk for showing problematic behavior. In addition, resource officers can serve as role models for children and adolescents who might not have contact with stable adults other than their teachers. Individuals trained in law enforcement also often have the opportunity to work with adjudicated youth (e.g., youngsters who are serving time in a juvenile detention center, who are living at a therapeutic "boot camp," or who are in a diversionary program to help prevent future criminal activities). These opportunities tend to arise for law enforcement officers who receive additional training regarding children and adolescents and those who show a special proclivity toward helping children, adolescents, and families.

Criminologists

The field of criminology offers interested students wonderful training and opportunities. Although graduate work in criminology does not allow professionals to conduct therapy or assessments, criminologists can conduct research on criminal behavior or other legal issues related to children and adolescents. **Criminologists** usually earn a master's or doctoral degree in criminology. Criminologists might study patterns of violence within schools or within the community and might serve as consultants to prevention programs to decrease this violence. Criminologists can also get involved in studying issues related to juvenile crime and the etiologies of such criminal behavior. The juvenile justice system often employs criminologists in many different capacities.

Forensic Psychologists

Within the field of psychology, there is specialized training in forensic psychology that is most consistent with work done in the criminal justice system. **Forensic psychologists,** who usually earn a Ph.D. in clinical psychology with a specialization in forensic psychology, can engage in a wide variety of activities related to children's mental health. They can conduct assessments, such as custody evaluations or evaluations to ascertain competency to stand trial. They can conduct therapy with individual troubled youngsters, with groups of troubled youngsters, or with youth and their families.

BOX 15.7

WORKING WITH FAMILIES

As noted throughout this chapter, there are many ways to achieve the same goal. Working with families is a perfect example. Many professionals, such as clinical psychologists, social workers, psychiatrists, pediatricians, and school psychologists, and even many nonprofessionals can work to help families function better. Table 15.1 delineates strategies to help deal with family systems issues. These strategies can be used by any professionals who have training and competence in this area. Overall, professionals' specific discipline is often not as meaningful as their area of expertise.

TABLE 15-1 Parent education strategies for different family dynamics

Family System Issues	Parent Education Approaches
1. Family communication Dysfunctional communication patterns	Active listening Confrontation and problem-solving skills Examination of irrational beliefs
2. Emotional distance between family members Enmeshed families (too little distance) messages Disengaged families (too much distance)	Analysis of children's mistaken goals Use of logical consequences Confrontation skills Communication skills Family meetings
3. Family role structuring Inverted hierarchy (lack of parental authority) Split parental team	Assertive discipline Behavior modification Use of logical consequences Parental communication and negotiation

Source: Gunn & Fisher (1999).

They often are involved in investigations related to allegations of child physical or sexual abuse (Bruck & Ceci, 2004). Forensic psychologists often serve as expert witnesses in court cases that have both psychological and legal ramifications. They also can get involved in consulting on legal cases, such as consulting with attorneys on mental health issues regarding children or with providing information about a child's ability to understand the charges against him or her. Increasingly, forensic psychologists are being asked to consult on the development of programs that would help lessen the problem behavior of incarcerated youth (Cowles & Washburn, 2005). Overall, a doctoral degree in clinical psychology with a specialization in forensic psychology can open the door to many opportunities in helping children. There are also a few select graduate programs (e.g., University of Virginia, University of Nebraska) that offer joint programs in clinical psychology and the law. Graduates of these programs have training both as clinical psychologists and as attorneys, so they have extraordinary professional credentials through which to help children.

Attorneys and Judges

Attorneys and judges are also in a position to help children through the judicial system. Attorneys are needed to represent children in custody disputes, child protective litigation, juvenile criminal charges, and other legal issues. Organized programs, such as Guardian ad Litem programs and child protective services, usually have a staff of attorneys (paid and volunteer) who try to ensure that the best interests of the child are represented in legal proceedings. Likewise, judges in family court, dependency court, and juvenile criminal court also make the decisions that have direct ramifications for children. Judges who understand the needs of children and families (and who understand that sometimes the needs of children are different than the needs of their parents) are likely to help children immensely through the legal decisions that they make.

It is easier to build strong children than to repair broken men [and women].

—Frederick Douglass

HOW HAVING A CAREER IN PREVENTION CAN HELP CHILDREN

Any book on developmental psychopathology would not be complete without a discussion of helping children through preventive efforts. There is no specific field or discipline that trains preventionists. Historically, programs with the term "community" in them (e.g., community psychology or community psychiatry) were more involved in prevention efforts (Rappaport & Seidman, 2000). More recently, however, prevention has been integrated into a diverse array of fields and training activities. Within clinical psychology, graduate students can even focus on preventive interventions during their clinical internship (Humphreys, 2000). Most training programs in prevention also integrate training on multicultural issues and strengths within diverse communities (Hall & Barongan, 2002; Harrison-Hale, McLoyd, & Smedley, 2004). Increasingly, there is awareness of the continuum of prevention and intervention programs, with a focus on multiple systems of care and evidence-based programs that are culturally sensitive (Weisz, Sandler, Durlak, & Anton, 2005).

Professionals who are dedicated to the prevention of developmental psychopathology can be trained in a variety of other disciplines, including behavioral medicine, social work, education, medicine, criminology, and law. For example, many prevention programs are run by psychologists and educators in the school system (Noam & Hermann, 2002; Romer & McIntosh, 2005). Other disciplines, such as public health, communication, and sociology can also be involved in prevention efforts by studying issues related to prevention and by consulting on prevention programs. Applying research findings from prevention programs can be one way of improving the lives of children through communitywide efforts that focus on public policy and social justice (Lerner et al., 2000; McCall & Groark, 2000). There is even room in the political arena for psychologists, who can affect children's lives through legislation and public policy (Sullivan & Reedy, 2005) Overall, there are many avenues to the goal of helping children through prevention efforts.

SUMMARY AND KEY CONCEPTS

How Nonprofessionals and Paraprofessionals Can Help Children. Volunteering in local organizations, serving as a mentor for a child, and coaching a sports team are just a few of the ways that nonprofessionals can become an important part of children's lives. Serving as a role model can help add to the protective features found in a child's otherwise troubled life.

How Having a Career in Psychology Can Help Children. Within the field of psychology, the primary specialization through which graduate students learn therapy, assessment, and research skills is clinical psychology. Programs that focus on both clinical skills (e.g., therapy and assessment skills) and research skills (e.g., developing, conducting, and disseminating empirical research) are called **scientist–practitioner** programs. Programs that are focused more on research than on direct clinical work are referred to as programs in **clinical science**. Scientist–practitioner programs are also known as **Boulder model programs** (after a conference held in Boulder, Colorado). These programs have the philosophy that good clinical practice is informed by research knowledge and good research practice is informed by clinical practice. If students wish to obtain a master's degree without proceeding to the doctoral degree, then they should seek a **terminal master's program.** In contrast to scientist–practitioner programs, **Psy.D. (Doctorate of Psychology)** programs focus solely on clinical practice without much or any focus on the development of research skills. On the other end of the spectrum, programs in **experimental psychopathology** focus on the development of empirical research skills with little to no training in clinical skills. Other training programs within the field of psychology include counseling psychology (which historically has focused on less-severe mental health problems than clinical psychology) and developmental psychology (which focuses on the empirical study of children and normative developmental processes without any training in clinical skills).

How Having a Career in Social Work Can Help Children. Within the field of social work, students can seek the bachelor's degree (B.S.W.), the master's degree (M.S.W.), or the doctoral degree (D.S.W.). Social workers often work within governmental agencies (such as child protective agencies), but they can also work in their own independent practices, or in schools, hospitals, or mental health clinics.

How Having a Career in Education Can Help Children. The field of education is replete with opportunities to help children. Teachers in general education classrooms, special education teachers, guidance counselors, school psychologists, and educational specialists all have training within the field of education and can have a significant impact on the lives of many children.

How Having a Career in Medicine Can Help Children. The medical field also affords many opportunities through which to help children. Psychiatric nurses, psychiatrists, and developmental pediatricians all receive specialized training to help individuals with mental health and psychiatric problems. More than most other settings, medical settings often utilize **multidisciplinary teams** and **telehealth** to provide comprehensive services.

How Having a Career in the Judicial Justice System Can Help Children. Although many individuals may think of the judicial justice system as a system that punishes children and adolescents for criminal transgressions, there are actually a number of career opportunities that allow professionals in the judicial system to help children when they need it most. School resource officers, **criminologists, forensic**

psychologists, attorneys and judges can impact significantly on children's lives when children are involved in criminal, family, or dependency court proceedings.

How Having a Career in Prevention Can Help Children. Although there is not one specific discipline that trains professionals to work on prevention projects regarding children, a number of fields can lead to work in prevention. Many disciplines, including psychology, social work, education, medicine, criminology, law, public health, communication, and sociology can lead to careers in prevention programs and the empirical study of prevention of psychopathology.

KEY TERMS

scientist–practitioner	terminal masters	experimental	telehealth
clinical science	program	psychopathology	criminologists
Boulder model	Psy.D. (Doctorate	multidisciplinary	forensic
programs	of Psychology)	teams	psychologists

SUGGESTED READINGS

Hinshaw, Stephen P. *The Years of Silence Are Past: My Father's Life with Bipolar Disorder.* New York: Cambridge University Press, 2002. In this powerful memoir of growing up with a father who shows unpredictable behavior, Dr. Stephen Hinshaw helps the reader understand the life experiences of children in this situation. As a leading researcher in developmental psychopathology, Dr. Hinshaw also helps to explain the importance of destigmatizing mental health problems and therapy for both children and adults.

Freedom Writers & Gruwell, E. *Freedom Writers Diary: How a Teacher and 150 Teens Used Writing to Change Themselves and the World Around Them.* New York: Broadway Books, 2006). Based on the powerful true life story of a teacher who used writing to help her high school students pull themselves out of violent and impoverished surroundings, this book shows how one person (in this case a dedicated teacher) can make a difference.

SUGGESTED VIEWINGS

School of Rock. (2003). This lighthearted film shows a teacher who may not be the best at teaching in a traditional manner, but who provides his students with joy and passion for a subject in which they may have previously been disinterested.

Harry Potter and the Sorcerer's Stone. (2001); Harry Potter and the Chamber of Secrets. (2002); Harry Potter and the Prisoner of Azkaban. (2004); Harry Potter and the Goblet of Fire. (2005); Harry Potter and the Order of the Phoenix. (2007). Whether as a volunteer, a clinician, a researcher, a teacher, or a pediatrician, if you work

with children and adolescents, you need to know something about what they enjoy. The *Harry Potter* series, including the books and the films, are wildly popular with children, adolescents, and even adults. Depending on the age group with whom you work, you may need to spend time watching different films or television shows, but suffice it to say that your child clients or students will think that you are an idiot if you do not know about the popular trends for that age group.

REFERENCES

Aarons, G. A., Brown, S. A., Hough, R. L., Garland, A. F., & Wood, P. A. (2001). Prevalence of adolescent substance use disorders across five sectors of care. *Journal of the American Academy of Child and Adolescent Psychiatry, 40,* 419–426.

Abela, J. R. Z., Hankin, B. L., Haigh, E. A. P., Adams, P., Vinokuroff, T., & Trayhern, L. (2005). Interpersonal vulnerability to depression in high-risk children: The role of insecure attachment and reassurance seeking. *Journal of Clinical Child and Adolescent Psychology, 34,* 182–192.

Abela, J. R. Z., Skitch, S. A., Adams, P., & Hankin, B. L. (2006). The timing of parent and child depression: A hopelessness theory perspective. *Journal of Clinical Child and Adolescent Psychology, 35,* 253–263.

Aber, M. S., & Nieto, M. (2000). In D. Cicchetti, J. Rappaport, I. Sandler, & R. P. Weissberg (Eds.), *The promotion of wellness in children and adolescents* (pp. 185–219). Washington, D.C.: CWLA Press.

Abbott, M. W. (1992). Television violence: A proactive prevention campaign. In G. W. Albee, L. A. Bond, & T. V. C. Monsey (Eds.), *Improving children's lives: Global perspectives on prevention* (pp. 263–278). Newbury Park, CA: Sage.

Abikoff, H. B., Jensen, P. S., Arnold, L. L. E., Hoza, B., Hechtman, L., Pollack, S., Martin, D., Alvir, J., March, J. S., Hinshaw, S., Vitiello, B., Newcorn, J., Greiner, A., Cantwell, D. P., Conners, C. K., Elliot, G., Greenhill, L. L., Kraemer, H., Pelham, W. E., Severe, J. B., Swanson, J. M., Wells, K., & Wigal, T. (2002). Observed classroom behavior of children with ADHD: Relationship to gender and comorbidity. *Journal of Abnormal Child Psychology, 30;* 349–359.

Abram, K. M., Teplin, L. A., McClelland, G. M., & Dulcan, M. K. (2003). Comorbid psychiatric disorders in youth in juvenile detention. *Archives of General Psychiatry, 60,* 1097–1108.

Achenbach, T. M. (1974). *Developmental psychopathology.* New York: Wiley.

Achenbach, T. M. (1982). *Developmental psychopathology* (2nd ed.). New York: Wiley.

Achenbach, T. M. (1990/1991). "Comorbidity" in child and adolescent psychiatry: Categorical and quantitative perspectives. *Journal of Child and Adolescent Psychopharmacology, 1,* 271–278.

Achenbach, T. M. (1991a). *Integrative guide for the 1991 CBCL/4–18, YSR, and TRF Profiles.* Burlington, VT: University of Vermont Department of Psychiatry.

Achenbach, T. M. (1991b). *Manual for the Child Behavior Checklist/4–18 and 1991 Profile.* Burlington, VT: University of Vermont Department of Psychiatry.

Achenbach, T. M. (1991c). *Manual for the Teacher's Report Form and 1991 Profile.* Burlington, VT: University of Vermont Department of Psychiatry.

Achenbach, T. M. (1991d). *Manual for the Youth Self-Report and 1991 Profile.* Burlington, VT: University of Vermont Department of Psychiatry.

Achenbach, T. M. (1992). *Manual for the Child Behavior Checklist/2–3 and 1992 Profile.* Burlington, VT: University of Vermont Department of Psychiatry.

Achenbach, T. M. (1997). *Manual for the Young Adult Behavior Checklist and Young Adult Self-Report.* Burlington, VT: University of Vermont Department of Psychiatry.

Achenbach, T. M. (1998). Diagnosis, assessment, taxonomy, and case formulations. In T. H. Ollendick & M. Hersen (Eds.), *Handbook of child psychopathology* (3rd ed. pp. 63–87). New York: Plenum.

Achenbach, T. M. (2002). Empirically based assessment and taxonomy across the life span. In J. E. Helzer & J. J. Hudziak (Eds.), *Defining psychopathology in the 21st century: DSM-V and beyond* (pp. 155–166). Washington, DC: American Psychiatric Publishing.

Achenbach, T. M. (2005). Advancing assessment of children and adolescents: Commentary on evidence-based assessment of child and adolescent disorders. *Journal of Clinical Child and Adolescent Psychology, 34,* 541–547.

Achenbach, T. M., & Dumenci, L. (2001). Advances in empirically based assessment: Revised cross-informant syndromes and new *DSM*-oriented scales for the CBCL, YSR, and TRF: Comment on Lengua, Sadowksi, Friedrich, and Fisher (2001). *Journal of Consulting and Clinical Psychology, 69,* 699–702.

Achenbach, T. M., Dumenci, L., & Rescorla, L. A. (2003). Are American children's problems still getting worse? A 23-year comparison. *Journal of Abnormal Child Psychology, 31,* 1–11.

Achenbach, T. M., Dumenci, L., & Rescorla, L. A. (2003). *DSM*-oriented and empirically based approaches to constructing scales from the same item pools. *Journal of Clinical Child and Adolescent Psychology, 32,* 328–340.

Achenbach, T. M., & Edelbrock, C. (1983). *Manual for the Child Behavior Checklist and Revised Child Behavior Profile.* Burlington, VT: University of Vermont Department of Psychiatry.

Achenbach, T. M., Howell, C. T., McConaughy, S. H., & Stanger, C. (1995a). Six-year predictors of problems in a national sample of children and youth: I. Cross-informant syndromes. *Journal of the American Academy of Child and Adolescent Psychiatry, 34,* 336–347.

Achenbach, T. M., Howell, C. T., McConaughy, S. H., & Stanger, C. (1995b). Six-year predictors of problems in a national sample of children and youth: II. Signs of disturbance. *Journal of the American Academy of Child and Adolescent Psychiatry, 34,* 488–498.

Achenbach, T. M., Howell, C. T., McConaughy, S. H., & Stanger, C. (1995c). Six-year predictors of problems in a national sample of children and youth: III. Transitions to young adult syndromes. *Journal of the American Academy of Child and Adolescent Psychiatry, 34,* 658–669.

Achenbach, T. M., Howell, C. T., Quay, H. C., & Conners, C. K. (1991). National survey of problems and competencies among four- to sixteen-year-olds. *Monographs of the Society for Research in Child Development, 56,* (3, Serial No. 225).

Achenbach, T. M., Krukowski, R. A., Dumenci, L., & Ivanova, M. Y. (2005). Assessment of adult psychopathology: Meta-analyses and implications of cross-informant correlations. *Psychological Bulletin, 131,* 361–382.

Achenbach, T. M. & McConaughy, S. H. (1997). *Empirically based assessment of child and adolescent psychopathology: Practical applications* (2nd ed.). Thousand Oaks, CA: Sage.

Achenbach, T. M. & McConaughy, S. H. (2003). The Achenbach System of Empirically Based Assessment. In C. R. Reynolds & R. W. Kamphaus (Eds.), *Handbook of psychological and educational assessment of children: Personality, behavior, and context* (2nd ed.) (pp. 406–430). New York: Guilford.

Achenbach, T. M., McConaughy, S. H., & Howell, C. T. (1987). Child/adolescent behavioral and emotional problems: Implications of cross-informant correlations for situational specificity. *Psychological Bulletin, 101,* 213–232.

Achenbach, T. M., Newhouse, P. A., & Rescorla, L. A. (2004). *Manual for ASEBA Older Adult Forms & Profiles.* Burlington, VT: University of Vermont, Research Center for Children, Youth, and Families.

Achenbach, T. M., & Rescorla, L. A. (2000). *Manual for the Achenbach System of Empirically Based Assessment (ASEBA) Preschool Forms and Profiles.* Burlington, VT: University of Vermont, Research Center for Children, Youth, and Families.

Achenbach, T. M., & Rescorla, L. A. (2001). *Manual for the Achenbach System of Empirically Based Assessment (ASEBA) School-Age Forms and Profiles.* Burlington, VT: University of Vermont, Research Center for Children, Youth, and Families.

Achenbach, T. M., & Rescorla, L. A. (2003). *Manual for ASEBA Adult Forms & Profiles.* Burlington, VT: University of Vermont, Research Center for Children, Youth, and Families.

Ackerman, B. P., Kogos, J., Youngstrom, E., Schoff, K., & Izard, C. (1999). Family instability and the problem behaviors of children from economically disadvantaged families. *Developmental Psychology, 35,* 258–268.

Ackerman, G. L. (1993). A congressional view of youth suicide. *American Psychologist, 48,* 183–184.

Ackerman, N. W. (1958). *The psychodynamics of family life.* New York: Basic Books.

Adam, E. K. (2004). Beyond quality: Parental and residential stability and children's adjustment. *Current Directions in Psychological Science, 13,* 210–213.

Adelman, H. S. (1992). LD: The next 25 years. *Journal of Learning Disabilities, 25,* 17–22.

Adelman, H. S., & Taylor, L. (1993). *Learning problems and learning disabilities: Moving forward.* Pacific Grove, CA: Brooks/Cole.

Adelman, H. S., & Taylor, L. (1997). Addressing barriers to learning: Beyond school-linked services and full-service schools. *American Journal of Orthopsychiatry, 67,* 408–421.

Adelman, H. S., & Taylor, L. (2000). Moving prevention from the fringes into the fabric of school improvement. *Journal of Educational and Psychological Consultation, 11,* 7–36.

Adelman, H. S., & Taylor, L. (2002). School counselors and school reform: New directions. *Professional School Counseling, 5,* 235–248.

Adelman, H. S., & Taylor, L. (2003). On sustainability of project innovations as systemic change. *Journal of Educational and Psychological Consultation, 14,* 1–25.

Adelman, H. S., Taylor, L., & Schnieder, M. V. (1999). A school-wide component to address barriers to learning. *Reading and Writing Quarterly: Overcoming Learning Difficulties, 15,* 277–302.

Agranat-Megedger, A. N., Deitcher, C., Goldzweig, G., Leibenson, L., Stein, M. & Galili-Weisstub, E. (2005). Childhood obesity and attention deficit/hyperactivity disorder: A newly described comorbidity in obese hospitalized children. *International Journal of Eating Disorders, 37,* 357–359.

Ainbinder, J. G., Blanchard, L. W., Singer, G. H. S., Sullivan, M. E., Powers, L. K., Marquis, J. G., Santelli, B., & the Consortium to Evaluate Parent to Parent. (1998). A qualitative study of parent to parent support for parents of children with special needs. *Journal of Pediatric Psychology, 23,* 99–109.

Ainsworth, M. D. S., Blehar, M. C., Waters, E., & Wall, S. (1978). *Patterns of attachment: A psychological study of the strange situation.* Hillsdale, NJ: Erlbaum.

Alarcon, R. D., Bell, C. C., Kirmayer, L. J., Lin, K. M., Ustun, B., & Wisner, K. L. (2002). In D. J. Kupfer (Ed.), *A research agenda for DSM-V* (pp. 219–281). Washington, DC: American Psychiatric Association.

Albano, A. M. (2003). Treatment of social anxiety disorder. In M. A. Reinecke, F. M. Dattilio, & A. Freeman (Eds.), *Cognitive therapy with children and adolescents: A casebook for clinical practice* (2nd ed. pp. 128–161). New York: Guilford.

Albano, A. M., Chorpita, B. F. & Barlow, D. H. (2003). Childhood anxiety disorders. In E. J. Mash, & B. A. Barkley (Eds.), *Child psychopathology* (2nd ed. pp. 279–329). New York: Guilford.

Albano, A. M., & Silverman, W. K. (1996). *Anxiety Disorders Interview Schedule for DSM-IV: Clinician Manual.* New York: Psychological Corporation.

Albee, G. W. (1982). Preventing psychopathology and promoting human potential. *American Psychologist, 37,* 1043–1050.

Albee, G. W. (1998). Fifty years of clinical psychology: Selling our soul to the devil. *Applied and Preventive Psychology, 7,* 189–194.

Albee, G. W., Bond, L. A., & Monsey, T. V. C. (Eds.) (1992). *Improving children's lives: Global perspectives on prevention.* Newbury Park, CA: Sage.

Alber, S. R. (1999). "I don't like to write but I love to get published": Using a classroom newspaper to motivate reluctant writers. *Reading and writing quarterly: Overcoming learning difficulties, 15,* 355–360.

Albertini, R. S., & Phillips, K. A. (2003). Thirty-three cases of body dysmorphic disorder in children and adolescents. In M. E. Hertzig & E. A. Farber (Ed.), *Annual progress in child psychiatry and child development: 2000–2001* (pp. 335–348). New York: Brunner-Routledge.

Albrecht, F. (2001). Factitious disorder by proxy. *Journal of the American Academy of Child and Adolescent Psychiatry, 40,* 4.

Albrecht, S. A., Cornelius, M. D., Braxter, B., Reynolds, M. D., Stone, C., & Cassidy, B. (1999). An assessment of nicotine dependence among pregnant adolescents. *Journal of Substance Abuse Treatment, 16,* 337–344.

Albrecht, S. L., Amey, C., & Miller, M. K. (1996). Patterns of substance abuse among rural black adolescents. *Journal of Drug Issues, 26,* 751–781.

Aldridge, J., Lamb, M. E., Sternberg, K. J., Orbach, Y., Esplin, P. W., & Bowler, L. (2004). Using a human figure drawing to elicit information from alleged victims of child sexual abuse. *Journal of Consulting and Clinical Psychology, 72,* 304–316.

Alexander, A. W., & Slinger-Constant, A. M. (2004). Current status of treatments for dyslexia: Critical review. *Journal of Child Neurology, 19,* 744–758.

Alfano, C. A., Beidel, D. C., & Turner, S. M. (2006). Cognitive correlates of social phobia among children and adolescents. *Journal of Abnormal Child Psychology, 34,* 189–201.

Ali, A., & Maharajh, H. D. (2005). Social predictors of suicidal behaviour in adolescents in Trinidad and Tobago. *Social Psychiatry and Psychiatric Epidemiology, 40,* 186–191.

Alio, A. P., & Salihu, H. M. (2005). Maternal determinants of pediatric preventive care utilization among Blacks and Whites. *Journal of the National Medical Association, 97,* 792–797.

Allen, J. P., Insabella, G., Porter, M. R., Smith, F. D., Land, D., & Phillips, N. (2006). A social-interactional model of the development of depressive symptoms in adolescence. *Journal of Consulting and Clinical Psychology, 74,* 55–65.

Allison, K. W., Crawford, I., Leone, P. E., Trickett, E., Perez-Febles, A., Burton, L. M., & LeBlanc, R. (1999). Adolescent substance use: Preliminary examinations of school and neighborhood context. *American Journal of Community Psychology, 27,* 111–141.

Allwood, M. A., Bell-Dolan, D., & Husain, S. A. (2002). Children's trauma and adjustment reactions to violent and nonviolent war experiences. *Journal of the American Academy of Child and Adolescent Psychiatry, 41,* 450–457.

Altepeter, T. S., & Korger, J. N. (1999). Disruptive behavior: Oppositional defiant disorder and conduct disorder. In S. D. Netherton, D. Holmes, & C. E. Walker (Eds.), *Child and adolescent psychological disorders: A comprehensive textbook* (pp. 118–138). New York: Oxford University Press.

Alva, S. A. (1995). Academic invulnerability among Mexican American students: The importance of protective resources and appraisals. In A. M. Padilla (Ed.), *Hispanic psychology: Critical issues in theory and research* (pp. 288–302). Thousand Oaks, CA: Sage.

Alvord, M. K., & Grados, J. J. (2005). Enhancing resilience in children: A proactive approach. *Professional Psychology: Research and Practice, 36,* 238–245.

Al-Yagon, M., & Mikulincer, M. (2004). Socioemotional and academic adjustment among children with learning disorders: The mediational role of attachment-based factors. *Journal of Special Education, 38,* 111–123.

Amato, P. R. (2001). Children of divorce in the 1990s: An update of the Amato and Keith (1991) meta-analysis. *Journal of Family Psychology, 15,* 355–370.

Ambrosini, P. J. (2000). Historical development and present status of the schedule for affective disorders and schizophrenia for school-age children (K-SADS). *Journal of the American Academy of Child and Adolescent Psychiatry, 39,* 39–48.

American Academy of Child and Adolescent Psychiatry. (2002). Practice parameters for the use of stimulant medications in the treatment of children, adolescents, and adults. *Journal of the Academy of Child and Adolescent Psychiatry, 41 (Suppl.),* 26S–49S.

American Academy of Child and Adolescent Psychiatry. (2005). Practice parameter for the assessment and treatment of children and adolescents with substance use disorders. *Journal of the American Academy of Child and Adolescent Psychiatry, 44,* 609–621.

American Academy of Pediatrics (2000). Diagnosis and evaluation of the child with Attention-Deficit/Hyperactivity Disorder. *Pediatrics, 105,* 1158–1170.

American Academy of Pediatrics (2001). Clinical practice guidelines: Treatment of the school-aged child with ADHD. *Pediatrics, 106,* 1033–1044.

American Academy of Pediatrics. (2004a). *ADHD: A complete and authoritative guide.* Elk Grove Village, IL: Author.

American Academy of Pediatrics. (2004b). *Baby and child health.* New York: DK Publishing.

American Academy of Pediatrics (2005). *Caring for your baby and young child: Birth to age 5* (4th ed). New York: Bantam Books.

American Association of Suicidology (2004). Youth suicide fact sheet. Retrieved March 19, 2004, from www.suicidology.org

American Association on Mental Retardation. (2002). *Mental retardation: Definition, classification, and systems of support.* Washington, DC: Author.

American Psychiatric Association. (1952). *Diagnostic and statistical manual of mental disorders.* Washington, DC: Author.

American Psychiatric Association. (1968). *Diagnostic and statistical manual of mental disorders* (2nd ed.). Washington, DC: Author.

American Psychiatric Association. (1980). *Diagnostic and statistical manual of mental disorders* (3rd ed.). Washington, DC: Author.

American Psychiatric Association. (1987). *Diagnostic and statistical manual of mental disorders* (3rd ed. rev.). Washington, DC: Author.

American Psychiatric Association. (1994). *Diagnostic and statistical manual of mental disorders* (4th ed.) Washington, DC: Author.

American Psychiatric Association. (1998). *DSM-IV Sourcebook (Vol 4).* Washington, DC: Author.

American Psychiatric Association. (2000). *Diagnostic and statistical manual of mental disorders* (4th ed.): *Text Revision (DSM-IV-TR).* Washington, DC: Author.

American Psychological Association. (1987). *Casebook on ethical principles of psychologists.* Washington, DC: Author.

American Psychological Association. (1993). *Getting in: A step-by-step plan for gaining admission to graduate school in psychology.* Washington, DC: Author.

American Psychological Association. (1997a). *Doctoral programs in family psychology.* Washington, DC: Author.

American Psychological Association. (1997b). *Journals in psychology: A resource for authors* (5th ed.) Washington, DC: Author.

American Psychological Association. (2001). *Publication manual of the American Psychological Association* (5th ed.). Washington, DC: Author.

American Psychological Association. (2002). Ethical principles of psychologists and code of conduct. *American Psychologist, 57,* 1060–1073.

American Psychological Association. (2003a). Guidelines on multicultural education, training, research, practice, and organizational change for psychologists. *American Psychologist, 58,* 377–402.

American Psychological Association. (2003b). *Psychology: Scientific problem solvers/Careers for the twenty-first century.* Washington, DC: Author.

American Psychological Association. (2006). *Graduate study in psychology: 2007 edition.* Washington, DC: Author.

American Speech-Language-Hearing Association. (2000). *Selecting a doctoral research education program in communication sciences and disorders.* Rockville, MD: Fulfillment Operations.

Ammerman, R. T., McGraw, K. L., Crosby, L. E., Beidel, D. C., & Turner, S. M. (2006). Social anxiety disorder. In R. T. Ammerman (Ed.), *Comprehensive handbook of personality and psychopathology: Child psychopathology (Vol 3)* (pp. 135–147). Hoboken, NJ: Wiley.

Ammerman, R. T., & Patz, R. J. (1996). Determinants of child abuse potential: Contribution of parent and child factors. *Journal of Clinical Child Psychology, 25,* 300–307.

Anastopoulos, A. D., Barkley, R. A., & Sheldon, T. L. (1996). Family based treatment: Psychosocial intervention for children and adolescents with Attention Deficit Hyperactivity Disorder. In E. D. Hibbs & P. S. Jensen (Eds.), *Psychosocial treatments for child and adolescent disorders: Empirically based strategies for clinical practice* (pp. 267–284). Washington, DC: American Psychological Association.

Anastopoulos, A. D., & Farley, S. E. (2003). A cognitive-behavioral training program for parents of children with attention-deficit/hyperactivity disorder. In A. E. Kazdin & J. R. Weisz (Eds.), *Evidence-based psychotherapies for children and adolescents* (pp. 187–203). New York: Guilford.

Anda, R. F., Croft, J. B., Felitti, V. J., Nordenberg, D., Giles, W. H., Williamson, D. F., & Giovino, G. A. (1999). Adverse childhood experiences and smoking during adolescence and adulthood. *JAMA: Journal of the American Medical Association, 282,* 1652–1658.

Anderson, C. A., Berkowitz, L., Donnerstein, E., Huesmann, L. R., Johnson, J. D., Linz, D., Malamuth, N. M., & Wartella, E. (2003). *The influence of media violence on youth, 4,* 81–110.

Anderson, E. R., & Greene, S. M. (1999). Children of stepparents and blended families. In W. K. Silverman & T. H. Ollendick (Eds.), *Developmental issues in the clinical treatment of children* (pp. 342–357). Boston: Allyn and Bacon.

Anderson, L. (1991). *Dear Dad: Letters from an adult child.* New York: Penguin Books.

Anderson, N. B., & Nickerson, K. J. (2005). Genes, race, and psychology in the genome era: An introduction. *American Psychologist, 60,* 5–8.

Andrade, A. R., Lambert, E. W., & Bickman, L. (2000). Dose effect in psychotherapy: Outcomes associated with negligible treatment. *Journal of the American Academy of Child and Adolescent Psychiatry, 39,* 161–168.

Andrews, J. A., Tildesley, E., Hops, H., Duncan, S. C., & Severson, H. H. (2003). Elementary school age children's future intentions and use of substances. *Journal of Clinical Child and Adolescent Psychology, 32,* 556–567.

Angelou, M. (2004). *The collected autobiographies of Maya Angelou.* New York: Random House.

Angold, A., Costello, E. J., & Erkanli, A. (1999). Comorbidity. *Journal of Child Psychology and Psychiatry, 40,* 57–87.

Angold, A., Erkanli, A., Egger, H. L., & Costello, E. J. (2000). Stimulant treatment for children: A community perspective. *Journal of the American Academy of Child and Adolescent Psychiatry, 39,* 975–984.

Anthony, E. J. (1974). The syndrome of the psychologically invulnerable child. In E. J. Anthony & C. Koupernik (Eds.), *The child in his family: Children at psychiatric risk* (pp. 529–545). New York: Wiley.

Anthony, E. J., & Cohler, B. J. (Eds.), (1987). *The invulnerable child.* New York: Guilford.

Antonuccio, D., & Burns, D. (2004). Fluoxetine, cognitive-behavioral therapy, and their combination for adolescents with depression: Treatment for adolescents with depression study (TADS) randomized controlled trial: Comment. *Journal of the American Medical Association, 292,* 2577.

Antshel, K. M., & Remer, R. (2003). Social skills training in children with attention deficit hyperactivity disorder: A randomized-controlled clinical trial. *Journal of Clinical Child and Adolescent, 32,* 153–165.

APA Presidential Task Force on Evidence-Based Practice. (2006). Evidence-based practice in psychology. *American Psychologist, 61,* 271–285.

Appleyard, K., Egeland, B., van Dulmen, M. H. M., & Sroufe, L. A. (2005). When more is not better: The role of cumulative risk in child behavior outcomes. *Journal of Child Psychology and Psychiatry, 46,* 235–245.

Apted, M., & Robinson, H. T. (2003). Narratives and documentaries: An encounter with Michael Apted and his films. In A. Sabbadini (Ed.), *The couch and the silver screen: Psychoanalytic reflections on European cinema* (pp. 159–180). New York: Brunner-Routledge.

Archer, R. P. (2005). *MMPI-A: Assessing adolescent psychopathology.* Mahwah, NJ: Lawrence Erlbaum Associates, Publishers.

Armistead, L., Forehand, R., Steele, R., & Kotchick, B. (1998). Pediatric AIDS. In T. H. Ollendick & M. Hersen (Eds.), *Handbook of child psychopathology* (3rd ed., pp. 463–481). New York: Plenum Press.

Armstrong, F. D., & Drotar, D. (2000). Multi-institutional and multidisciplinary research collaboration: Strategies and lessons from cooperative trials. In D. Drotar (Ed.), *Handbook of research in pediatric and clinical child psychology* (pp. 281–303). New York: Plenum Press.

Armstrong, T. D., & Costello, E. J. (2002). Community studies on adolescent substance use, abuse, or dependence and psychiatric comorbidity. *Journal of Consulting and Clinical Psychology, 70,* 1224–1239.

Arnett, J. J. (2000). Emerging adulthood: A theory of development from the late teens through the twenties. *American Psychologist, 55,* 469–480.

Arnold, D. H., & Doctoroff, G. L. (2003). The early education of socioeconomically disadvantaged children. *Annual Review of Psychology, 54,* 517–545.

Arnold, D. S., O'Leary, S. G., Wolff, L. S., & Acker, M. M. (1993). The Parenting Scale: A measure of dysfunctional parenting in discipline situations. *Psychological Assessment, 5,* 137–144.

Arnold, E. M., Goldston, D. B., Walsh, A. K., Reboussin, B. A., Daniel, S. S., Hickman, E., & Wood, F. B. (2005). Severity of emotional and behavioral problems among poor and typical readers. *Journal of Abnormal Child Psychology, 33,* 205–217.

Arnold, L. E., Chuang, S., Davies, M., Abikoff, H. B., Conners, C. K., Elliott, G. R., Greenhill, L. L., Hechtman, L., Hinshaw, S. P., Hoza, B., Jensen, P. S., Kraemer, H. C., Langworthy-Lam, K. S., March, J. S., Newcorn, J. H., Pelham, W. E., Severe, J. B., Swanson, J. M., Vitiello, B., Wells, K. C., & Wigal, T. (2004). Nine months of multicomponent behavioral treatment for ADHD and effectiveness of MTA fading procedures. *Journal of Abnormal Child Psychology, 32,* 39–51.

Arnold, L. E., Elliott, M., Sachs, L., Bird, H., Kraemer, H. C., Wells, K. C., Abikoff, H. B., Comarda, A., Conners, C. K., Elliott, G. R., Greenhill, L. L., Hechtman, L., Hinshaw, S. P., Hoza, B., Jensen, P. S., March, J. S., Newcorn, J. H., Pelham, W. E., Severe, J. B., Swanson, J. M., Vitiello, B., & Wigal, T. (2003). *Journal of Consulting and Clinical Psychology, 71,* 713–727.

Aronen, E. T., Paavonen, E. J., Fjaellberg, M., Soininen, M. & Toerroenen, J. (2000). Sleep and psychiatric symptoms in school-age children. *Journal of the American Academy of Child and Adolescent Psychiatry, 39,* 502–508.

Arrington, E. G., & Wilson, M. N. (2000). A re-examination of risk and resilience during adolescence: Incorporating culture and diversity. *Journal of Child and Family Studies, 9,* 221–230.

Arseneault, L., Moffitt, T. E., Caspi, A., Taylor, P. J., & Silva, P. A. (2000). Mental disorders and violence in a total birth cohort: Results from the Dunedin Study. *Archives of General Psychiatry, 57,* 979–986.

Arthur, M. W., & Blitz, C. (2000). Bridging the gap between science and practice in drug abuse prevention through needs assessment and strategic community planning. *Journal of Community Psychology, 28,* 241–255.

Ary, D. V., Duncan, T. E., Biglan, A., Metzler, C. W., Noell, J. W., & Smolkowski, K. (1999). Development of adolescent problem behavior. *Journal of Abnormal Child Psychology, 27,* 141–150.

Ary, D. V., Duncan, T. E., Duncan, S. C., & Hops, H. (1999). Adolescent problem behavior: The influence of parents and peers. *Behaviour Research and Therapy, 37,* 217–230.

Asarnow, J. R., & Asarnow, R. F. (2003). Childhood-onset schizophrenia. In E. J. Mash, & B. A. Barkley (Eds.), *Child psychopathology* (2nd ed., pp. 455–485). New York: Guilford.

Asarnow, J. R., Tompson, M., Woo, S., & Cantwell, D. P. (2001). Is expressed emotion a specific risk factor for depression or a nonspecific correlate of psychopathology? *Journal of Abnormal Child Psychology, 29,* 573–583.

Associated Press (2001). Deaths of Gaza children inflame Mideast. *USA Today,* 11/23/2001, pp. 1–3.

Association for the Advancement of Behavior Therapy. (1997). *Graduate training in behavior therapy and experimental-clinical psychology.* New York: Author.

Atwine, B., Cantor-Graae, E., & Bajunirwe, F. (2005). Psychological distress among AIDS orphans in rural Uganda. *Social Science and Medicine, 61,* 555–564.

Auerbach, C. F., & Silverstein, L. B. (2003). *Qualitative data: An introduction to coding and analysis.* New York: New York University Press.

August, G. J., Egan, E. A., Realmuto, G. M., & Hektner, J. M. (2003). Parceling component effects of a multifaceted prevention program for disruptive elementary school children. *Journal of Abnormal Child Psychology, 31,* 515–527.

August, G. J., Realmuto, G. M., Hektner, J. M., & Bloomquist, M. L. (2001). An integrated components preventive intervention for aggressive elementary school children: The early risers program. *Journal of Consulting and Clinical Psychology, 69,* 614–626.

Austin, A. A., & Chorpita, B. F. (2004). Temperament, anxiety, and depression: Comparisons across five ethnic groups of children. *Journal of Clinical Child and Adolescent, 33,* 216–226.

Austin, S. B., Ziyadeh, N., Kahn, J., Camargo, C. A., Colditz, G. A., & Field, A. E. (2004). Sexual orientation, weight concerns, and eating-disordered behaviors in adolescent girls and boys. *Journal of the American Academy of Child and Adolescent Psychiatry, 43,* 1115–1123.

Awadallah, N., Vaughan, A., Franco, K., Munir, F., Sharaby, N., & Goldfarb, J. (2005). Munchausen by proxy: A case, chart series, and literature review of older victims. *Child Abuse and Neglect, 29,* 931–941.

Ayoub, C. C., Deutsch, R. M., & Kinscherff, R. (2000). Munchausen by proxy: Definitions, identification, and evaluation. In R. M. Reece (Ed.), *Treatment of child abuse: Common ground for mental health, medical, and legal practitioners* (pp. 213–226). Baltimore nd: Johns Hopkins University Press.

Ayoub, C. C., Schreier, H. A. & Keller, C. (2002). Munchausen by proxy: Presentations in special education. *Child Maltreatment: Journal of the American Professional Society on the Abuse of Children, 7,* 149–159.

Azar, S. T. (1992). Legal issues in the assessment of family violence involving children. In R. T. Ammerman & M. Hersen (Eds.), *Assessment of family violence: A clinical and legal sourcebook* (pp. 47–70). New York: Wiley.

Azar, S. T., Ferraro, M. H., & Breton, S. J. (1998). Intrafamilial child maltreatment. In T. H. Ollendick & M. Hersen (Eds.), *Handbook of child psychopathology* (3rd ed., pp. 483–504). New York: Plenum Press.

Bachanas, P. J., Morris, M. K., Lewis-Gess, J. K., Sarett-Cuasay, E. J., Fores, A. L., Sirl, K. S., & Sawyer, M. K. (2002). Psychological adjustment, substance use, HIV knowledge, and risky sexual behavior in at-risk minority females: Developmental differences during adolescence. *Journal of Pediatric Psychology, 27,* 373–384.

Baer, S., & Garland, E. J. (2005). Pilot study of community-based cognitive behavioral group therapy for adolescents with social phobia. *Journal of the American Academy of Child and Adolescent Psychiatry, 44,* 258–264.

Baer, R. A., & Nietzel, M. T. (1991). Cognitive and behavioral treatment of impulsivity in children: A meta-analytic review of the outcome literature. *Journal of Clinical Child Psychology, 20,* 400–412.

Bagner, D. M., & Eyberg, S. M. (2003). Father involvement in parent training: When does it matter? *Journal of Clinical Child and Adolescent Psychology, 32,* 599–605.

Bailey, J. A., Hill, K. G., Oesterle, S., & Hawkins, J. D. (2006). Linking substance use and problem behavior across three generations. *Journal of Abnormal Child Psychology, 34,* 273–292.

Bailey, J. A., & McCloskey, L. A. (2005). Pathways to adolescent substance use among sexually abused girls. *Journal of Abnormal Child Psychology, 33,* 39–53.

Baird, B. N. (2004). *Internship, practicum, and field placement handbook: A guide for the helping professions* (4th ed.). Upper Saddle River, NJ: Prentice Hall.

Baker, B. L., Blacher, J., & Olsson, M. B. (2005). Preschool children with and without developmental delay: Behaviour problems, parents' optimism and well-being. *Intellectual Disability Research, 49,* 575–590.

Baker, D. B., & Benjamin, L. T. (2000). The affirmation of the scientist-practitioner: A look back at Boulder. *American Psychologist, 55,* 241–247.

Bakermans-Kranenburg, M. J., van IJzendoorn, M. H., & Juffer, F. (2003). Less is more: Meta-analyses of sensitivity and attachment interventions in early childhood. *Psychological Bulletin, 129,* 195–215.

Baldwin, S. (1999). Applied behavior analysis in the treatment of ADHD: A review and rapprochement. *Ethical Human Sciences and Services, 1,* 35–59.

Ballageer, T., Malia, A., Manchanda, R., Takhar, J., & Haricharan, R. (2005). Is adolescent-onset first-episode psychosis different from adult onset? *Journal of the American Academy of Child and Adolescent Psychiatry, 44,* 782–789.

Balsam, K. F., Rothblum, E. D., & Beauchaine, T. P. (2005). Victimization over the life span: A comparison of lesbian, gay, bisexual, and heterosexual siblings. *Journal of Consulting and Clinical Psychology, 73,* 477–487.

Ban, T. A. (2004). Neuropsychopharmacology and the genetics of schizophrenia: A history of the diagnosis of schizophrenia. *Progress in Neuro-Psychopharmacology & Biological Psychiatry, 28,* 753–762.

Bandura, A. (1986). *Social foundations of thought and action: A social cognitive theory.* Englewood Cliffs, NJ: Prentice Hall.

Bandura, A., Ross, D., & Ross, S. A. (1961). Transmission of aggression through imitation of aggressive models. *Journal of Abnormal and Social Psychology, 63,* 575–582.

Barakat, L. P., Smith-Whitley, K., Schulman, S., Rosenberg, D., Puri, R., & Ohene-Frempong, K. (2001). Nocturnal enuresis in pediatric sickle cell disease. *Journal of Developmental & Behavioral Pediatrics, 22,* 300–305.

Baranowski, T., Mendlein, J., Resnicow, K., Frank, E., Cullen, K. W., & Baranowski, J. (2000). Physical activity and nutrition in children and youth: An overview of obesity prevention. *Preventive Medicine: An International Journal Devoted to Practice and Theory, 31,* S1–S10.

Barkley, R. A. (1997a). Behavioral inhibition, sustained attention, and executive functions: Constructing a unifying theory of ADHD. *Psychological Bulletin, 121,* 65–94.

Barkley, R. A. (1997b). *Defiant children: A clinician's manual for assessment and parent training* (2nd ed.). New York: Guilford.

Barkley, R. A. (1998). *Attention-deficit hyperactivity disorder: A handbook for diagnosis and treatment* (2nd ed.). New York: Guilford.

Barkley, R. A. (2000). *Taking charge of ADHD: The complete authoritative guide for parents* (rev ed.). New York: Guilford.

Barkley, R. A. (2003). Attention-deficit/hyperactivity disorder. In E. J. Mash, & B. A. Barkley (Eds.), *Child psychopathology* (2nd ed., pp. 75–143). New York: Guilford.

Barkley, R. A. (2004). Attention-deficit/hyperactivity disorder and self-regulation: Taking an evolutionary perspective on executive functioning. In R. F. Baumeister & K. D. Vohs (Eds.), *Handbook of self-regulation: Research, theory, and applications* (pp. 301–323). New York: Guilford.

Barkley, R. A. (2005). *ADHD and the nature of self-control.* New York: Guilford.

Barkley, R. A. (2006). *Attention-deficit hyperactivity disorder: A handbook for diagnosis and treatment* (3rd ed.). New York: Guilford.

Barkley, R. A., & Benton, C. M. (1998). *Your defiant child: Eight steps to better behavior.* New York: Guilford.

Barkley, R. A., Edwards, G. H., Laneri, M., Fletcher, K., & Metevia, L. (2001). The efficacy of problem-solving communication training alone, behavior management training alone, and combination for parent-adolescent conflict in teenagers with ADHD and ODD. *Journal of Consulting and Clinical Psychology, 69,* 926–941.

Barkley, R. A., Edwards, G. H., Laneri, M., Fletcher, K., & Metevia, L. (2001). Executive functioning, temporal discounting, and sense of time in adolescents with attention deficit hyperactivity disorder (ADHD) and oppositional defiant disorder (ODD). *Journal of Abnormal Child Psychology, 29,* 541–556.

Barkley, R. A., Edwards, G. H., & Robin, A. L. (1999). *Defiant teens: A clinician's manual for assessment and family intervention.* New York: Guilford.

Barkley, R. A., & Murphy, K. R. (2005). *Attention-deficit hyperactivity disorder: A clinical workbook* (3rd ed.). New York: Guilford.

Barkley, R. A., Murphy, K. R., DuPaul, G. J., & Bush, T. (2002). Driving in young adults with attention deficit hyperactivity disorder: Knowledge, performance, adverse outcomes, and the role of executive functioning. *Journal of the International Neuropsychological Society, 8,* 655–672.

Barkley, R. A., Shelton, T. L., Crosswait, C., Moorehouse, M., Fletcher, K., Barrett, S., Jenkins, L., & Metevia, L. (2002). Preschool children with disruptive behavior: Three-year outcome as a function of adaptive disability. *Development and Psychopathology, 14,* 45–67.

Barkmann, C. & Schulte-Markwort, M. (2005). Emotional and behavioral problems of children and adolescents in Germany: An epidemiological screening. *Social Psychiatry and Psychiatric Epidemiology, 40,* 357–366.

Barmish, A. J., & Kendall, P. C. (2005). Should parents be co-clients in cognitive-behavioral therapy for anxious youth? *Journal of Clinical Child and Adolescent Psychology, 34,* 569–581.

Barnett, J. E., & Neel, M. L. (2000). Must all psychologists study psychopharmacology? *Professional Psychology: Research and Practice, 31,* 619–627.

Bar-Or, O. (Ed.). (1996). *The child and adolescent athlete*. New York: Blackwell Science.

Baron, I. S. (2004). *Neuropsychological evaluation of the child*. New York: Oxford University Press.

Barrett, P. M., Duffy, A. L., Dadds, M. R., & Rapee, R. M. (2001). Cognitive-behavioral treatment of anxiety disorders in children: Long-term (6-year) follow-up. *Journal of Consulting and Clinical Psychology, 69*, 135–141.

Barrett, P. M., & Shortt, A. L. (2003). Parental involvement in the treatment of anxious children. In A. E. Kazdin & J. R. Weisz (Eds.), *Evidence-based psychotherapies for children and adolescents* (pp. 101–119). New York: Guilford.

Barrett, P. M., & Turner, C. M. (2004). Prevention strategies. In T. L. Morris & J. S. March (Eds.), *Anxiety disorders in children and adolescents* (2nd ed, pp. 371–386). New York: Guilford.

Barrios, B. A., & O'Dell, S. L. (1998). Fears and anxieties. In E. J. Mash & R. A. Barkley (Eds.), *Treatment of childhood disorders* (2nd ed., pp. 249–298). New York: Guilford.

Barry, T. D., Dunlap, S. T., Cotten, S. J., Lochman, J. E., & Wells, K. C. (2005). The influence of maternal stress and distress on disruptive behavior problems in boys. *Journal of the American Academy of Child and Adolescent Psychiatry, 44*, 265–273.

Barzman, D. H., McConville, B. J., Masterson, B., McElroy, S., Sethuraman, G., Moore, K., Kahwaty, A., & Nelson, D. (2005). Impulsive aggression with irritability and responsive to divalproex: A pediatric bipolar spectrum disorder phenotype? *Journal of Affective Disorders, 88*, 279–285.

Bateson, G., Jackson, D. D., Haley, J., & Weakland, J. (1956). Towards a theory of schizophrenia. *Behavioral Science, 1*, 251–264.

Baucom, D. H., Epstein, N., & Gordon, K. C. (2000). Marital therapy: Theory, practice, and empirical status. In C. R. Snyder & R. E. Ingram (Eds.). *Handbook of psychological change: Psychotherapy processes & practices for the 21st century* (pp. 280–308). Hoboken, NJ: Wiley.

Bauer, A. M., Johnson, L. J., & Sapona, R. H. (2004). Reflections on 20 years of preparing special education teachers. *Exceptionality, 12*, 239–246.

Baumeister, A. A. & Baumeister, A. A. (2000). Mental retardation: Causes and effects. In M. Hersen, & R. T. Ammerman (Eds.). *Advanced abnormal child psychology* (2nd ed., pp. 327–355). Mahwah, NJ: Lawrence Erlbaum Associates.

Bauminger, N., Edelsztein, H. S., & Morash, J. (2005). Social information processing and emotional understanding in children with LD. *Journal of Learning Disabilities, 38*, 45–60.

Baumrind, D. (1971). Current patterns of parental authority. *Developmental Psychology Monographs, 4 (1, part 2)*.

Baumrind, D., Cowan, P. A., & Larzelere, R. E. (2002). Ordinary physical punishment: Is it harmful? Comment on Gershoff (2002). *Psychological Bulletin, 128*, 580–584.

Baving, L., Laucht, M., & Schmidt, M. H. (2000). Oppositional children differ from healthy children in frontal brain activation. *Journal of Abnormal Child Psychology, 28*, 267–275.

Bayley, N. (2005). *Bayley Scales of Infant and Toddler Development (3rd ed.; Bayley-III)*. San Antonio, TX: Harcourt Assessment.

Bean, P., Maddocks, M. B., Timmel, P., & Weltzin, T. (2005). Gender differences in the progression of co-morbid psychopathology symptoms of eating disordered patients. *Eating and Weight Disorders, 10*, 168–174.

Beardslee, W. R., Salt, P., Porterield, K., Rothberg, P. S., van de Velde, P., Swatling, S., Hoke, L., Moilanen, D. L., & Wheelock, I. (1993). Comparison of preventive interventions for families with parental affective disorder. *Journal of the American Academy of Child and Adolescent Psychiatry, 32*, 254–263.

Beatty, L. A., Wetherington, C. L., Jones, D. J., & Roman, A. B. (2006). Substance use and abuse by girls and women. In J. Worell & C. D. Goodheart (Eds.), *Handbook of girls' and women's psychological health* (pp. 113–121). New York: Oxford University Press.

Beauchaine, T. P. (2003). Taxometrics and developmental psychopathology. *Development and Psychopathology, 15*, 501–527.

Bebko, J. M., & Weiss, J. A. (2006). Mental retardation. In R. T. Ammerman (Ed.), *Comprehensive handbook of personality and psychopathology: Child psychopathology (Vol 3)* (pp. 233–253). Hoboken, NJ: Wiley.

Beck, A. T. (1976). *Cognitive therapy and emotional disorders*. New York: International Universities Press.

Beck, A. T., Steer, R. A., & Brown, G. K. (1996). *Manual for the Beck Depression Inventory—II*. San Antonio, TX: Psychological Corporation.

Beck, A. T., Steer, R. A., & Garbin, M. G. (1988). Psychometric properties of the Beck Depression Inventory: Twenty-five years of evaluation. *Clinical Psychology Review, 8*, 77–100.

Beck, M. (1999). *Expecting Adam: A true story of birth, rebirth, and everyday magic*. New York: Berkley Books.

Becker, E., Rankin, E., & Rickel, A. U. (1998). *High-risk sexual behavior: Interventions with vulnerable populations*. New York: Plenum Press.

Becker, K., & Schmidt, M. H. (2004). Internet chat rooms and suicide. *Journal of the American Academy of Child and Adolescent Psychiatry, 43*, 246–247.

Becker, K. D., Stuewig, J., Herrera, V. M., & McCloskey, L. A. (2004). A study of firesetting and animal cruelty in children: Family influences and adolescent outcomes. *Journal of the American Academy of Child and Adolescent Psychiatry, 43*, 905–912.

Beckung, E., & Hagberg, G. (2002). Neuroimpairments, activity limitations, and participation restrictions in children with cerebral palsy. *Developmental Medicine & Child Neurology, 44*, 309–316.

Behrman, A. (2002). *Electroboy: A memoir of mania*. New York: Random House.

Beidel, D. C., Morris, T. L., & Turner, M. W. (2004). Social phobia. In T. L. Morris & J. S. March (Eds.), *Anxiety disorders in children and adolescents* (2nd ed., pp. 141–163). New York: Guilford.

Belgrave, F. Z., Townsend, T. G., Cherry, V. R., & Cunningham, D. M. (1997). The influence of an Africentric worldview and demographic variables on drug knowledge, attitudes, and use among African American youth. *Journal of Community Psychology, 25*, 421–433.

Bell, L. G., & Bell, D. C. (2005). Family dynamics in adolescence affect midlife well-being. *Journal of Family Psychology, 19*, 198–207.

Bellak, L. (1993). *The T.A.T., C.A.T., and S.A.T. in clinical use* (5th ed). Boston: Allyn & Bacon.

Bellanti, C. J., Bierman, K. L., & Conduct Problems Prevention Research Group. (2000). Disentangling the impact of low cognitive ability and inattention on social behavior and peer relationships. *Journal of Clinical Child Psychology, 29*, 66–75.

Bellmer, E. A., Hoshino, J., Schrader, B., Strong, M., & Hutzler, J. B. (2003). Perception of the art therapy field by psychology professors. *Art Therapy, 20*, 163–169.

Belsky, J. (2001). Emanuel Miller Lecture: Developmental risks (still) associated with early child care. *Journal of Child Psychology and Psychiatry, 42*, 845–859.

Belsky, J. (2002). Quantity counts: Amount of child care and children's socioemotional development. *Journal of Developmental & Behavioral Pediatrics, 23*, 167–170.

Belsky, J. (2005). Attachment Theory and Research in Ecological Perspective: Insights from the Pennsylvania Infant and Family Development Project and the NICHD Study of Early Child Care. In K. E. Grossmann, K. Grossmann, & E. Waters (Eds.), *Attachment from infancy to adulthood: The major longitudinal studies* (pp. 71–97). New York: Guilford.

Bemporad, J. R. (1994). Dynamic and interpersonal theories of depression. In W. M. Reynolds & H. F. Johnston (Eds.), *Handbook of depression in children and adolescents* (pp. 81–95). New York: Plenum Press.

Bengtson, V. L., Acock, A. C., Allen, K. R., Dilworth-Anderson, P., & Klein, D. M. (Eds.) (2005). *Sourcebook of family theory and research*. Thousand Oaks, CA: Sage.

Berg, M. L., Crosby, R. D., Wonderlich, S. A., & Hawley, D. (2000). Relationship of temperament and perceptions of nonshared environment in bulimia nervosa. *International Journal of Eating Disorders, 28*, 148–154.

Berger, E. H. (2003). *Parents as partners in education: Families and schools working together* (6th ed.). Upper Saddle River, NJ: Prentice Hall.

Bergman, R. L., Piacentini, J., & McCracken, J. T. (2002). Prevalence and description of selective mutism in a school-based sample. *Journal of the American Academy of Child and Adolescent Psychiatry, 41*, 938–946.

Berman, S. L., Kurtines, W. M., Silverman, W. K., & Serafini, L. T. (1996). The impact of exposure to crime and violence on urban youth. *American Journal of Orthopsychiatry, 66*, 329–336.

Berninger, V. W., Dunn, A., Lin, S. C., & Shimada, S. (2004). School evolution: scientist–practitioner educators creating optimal learning environments for all students. *Journal of Learning Disabilities, 37*, 500–508.

Bernstein, G. A., Carroll, M. E., Thuras, P. D., Cosgrove, K. P., & Roth, M. E. (2002). Caffeine dependence in teenagers. *Drug & Alcohol Dependence, 66*, 1–6.

Bernstein, G. A., Hektner, J. M., Borchardt, C. M., & McMillan, M. H. (2001). Treatment of school refusal: One-year follow-up. *Journal of the American Academy of Child and Adolescent Psychiatry, 40*, 206–213.

Bernstein, G. A., Warren, S. L., Massie, E. D., & Thuras, P. D. (1999). Family dimensions in anxious-depressed school refusers. *Journal of Anxiety Disorders, 13*, 513–528.

Berry, D., Sheehan, R., Heschel, R., Knafl, K., Melkus, G., & Grey, M. (2004). Family-based interventions for childhood obesity: A review. *Journal of Family Nursing, 10*, 429–449.

Bersoff, D. N. (2003). *Ethical Conflicts in Psychology* (3rd ed.). Washington, DC: American Psychological Association.

Besag, Frank M. C. (2002). Childhood epilepsy in relation to mental handicap and behavioural disorders. *Journal of Child Psychology and Psychiatry, 43*, 103–131.

Besharov, D. J. (1998). *Recognizing child abuse: The trainer's manual.* New York: American Enterprise Institute for Public Policy Research.

Beutler, L. E., & Moleiro, C. (2001). Clinical versus reliable and significant change. *Clinical Psychology: Science and Practice, 8*, 441–445.

Beversdorf, D. Q., Manning, S. E., Hillier, A., Anderson, S. L., Nordgren, R. E., Walters, S. E., Nagaraja, H. N. Cooley, W. C., Gaelic, S. E., & Bauman, M. L. (2005). Timing of prenatal stressors and autism. *Journal of Autism and Developmental Disorders, 35*, 471–478.

Beyer, K. R., & Beasley, J. O. (2003). Nonfamily child abductors who murder their victims: Offender demographics from interviews with incarcerated offenders. *Journal of Interpersonal Violence, 18*, 1167–1188.

Beyers, J. M., & Loeber, R. (2003). Untangling developmental relations between depressed mood and delinquency in male adolescents. *Journal of Abnormal Child Psychology, 31*, 247–266.

Beyers, J. M., Loeber, R., Wikstrom, P. H., & Stouthamer-Loeber, M. (2001). What predicts adolescent violence in better-off neighborhoods? *Journal of Abnormal Child Psychology, 29*, 369–381.

Beyers, J. M., Toumbourou, J. W., Catalano, R. F., Arthur, M. W., & Hawkins, J. D. (2004). A cross-national comparison of risk and protective factors for adolescent substance use: The United States and Australia. *Journal of Adolescent Health, 35*, 3–16.

Bhatta, M. P., Stringer, J. S. A., Phanuphak, P., & Vermund, S. H. (2003). Mother-to-child HIV transmission prevention in Thailand: Physician zidovudine use and willingness to provide care. *International Journal of STD & AIDS, 14*, 404–410.

Biasini, F. J., Grupe, L., Huffman, L., & Bray, N. W. (1999). Mental retardation: A symptom and a syndrome. In S. D. Netherton, D. Holmes, & C. E. Walker (Eds.), *Child and adolescent psychological disorders: A comprehensive textbook* (pp. 6–23). New York: Oxford University Press.

Bickman, L., Guthrie, P. R., Foster, E. M., Lambert, E. W., Summerfelt, W. T., Breda, C. S., & Heflinger, C. A. (1995). *Evaluating managed mental health services: The Fort Bragg experiment*. New York: Plenum Press.

Bickman, L., Lambert, E. W., Andrade, A. R., & Penaloza, R. V. (2000). The Fort Bragg continuum of care for children and adolescents: Mental health outcomes over 5 years. *Journal of Consulting and Clinical Psychology, 68*, 710–716.

Biederman, J. (2005). Attention-deficit/hyperactivity disorder: A selective overview. *Biological Psychiatry, 57*, 1215–1220.

Biederman, J., Faraone, S. V., Wozniak, J., Mick, E., Kwon, A., & Aleardi, M. (2004). Further evidence of unique developmental phenotypic correlates of pediatric bipolar disorder: Findings from a large sample of clinically referred preadolescent children assessed over the last 7 years. *Journal of Affective Disorders, 82S,* S45–S58.

Biederman, J., Hirshfeld-Becker, D. R., Rosenbaum, J. F., Herot, C., Friedman, D., Snidman, N., Kagan, J., & Faraone, S. V. (2001). Further evidence of association between behavioral inhibition and social anxiety in children. *American Journal of Psychiatry, 158,* 1673–1679.

Biederman, J., & James, R. S. (2004). Furthering the scientific foundation of pediatric bipolar disorder. *Journal of Affective Disorders, 82S,* S1–S3.

Biederman, J., Kwon, A., Aleardi, M., Chouinard, V., Marino, T., Cole, H., Mick, E., & Faraone, S. V. (2005). Absence of gender effects on Attention Deficit Hyperactivity Disorder: Findings in nonreferred subjects. *American Journal of Psychiatry, 162,* 1083–1089.

Biederman, J., Mick, E., Faraone, S. V., & Burback, M. (2001). Patterns of remission and symptom decline in conduct disorder: A four-year prospective study of an ADHD sample. *Journal of the American Academy of Child and Adolescent Psychiatry, 40,* 290–298.

Biederman, J., Mick, E., Faraone, S. V., Spencer, T., Wilens, T. E., & Wozniak, J. (2003). Current concepts in the validity, diagnosis and treatment of paediatric bipolar disorder. *International Journal of Neuropsychopharmacology, 6,* 293–300.

Biederman, J., Monuteaux, M. C., Doyle, A. E., Seidman, L. J., Wilens, T. E., Ferrero, F., Morgan, C. L., & Faraone, S. V. (2004). Impact of executive function deficits and attention-deficit/hyperactivity disorder (ADHD) on academic outcomes in children. *Journal of Consulting and Clinical Psychology, 72,* 757–766.

Biederman, J., Monuteaux, M. C., Greene, R. W., Braaten, E., Doyle, A. E., & Faraone, S. V. (2001). Long-term stability of the Child Behavior Checklist in a clinical sample of youth with attention deficit hyperactivity disorder. *Journal of Clinical Child Psychology, 30,* 492–502.

Biederman, J., Rosenbaum, J. F., Chaloff, J., & Kagan, J. (1995). Behavioral inhibition as a risk factor. In. J. S. March (Ed.), *Anxiety disorders in children and adolescents* (pp. 61–81). New York: Guilford.

Bijttebier, P., Vasey, M. W., & Braet, C. (2003). The information-processing paradigm: A valuable framework for clinical child and adolescent psychology. *Journal of Clinical Child and Adolescent Psychology, 32,* 2–9.

Biklen, D. (1990). Communication unbound: Autism and praxis. *Harvard Educational Review. 60,* 291–314.

Biklen, D., & Cardinal, D. N. (1997). *Contested words, contested science: Unraveling the facilitated communication controversy.* New York: Teachers College Press.

Biklen, D., Morton, M. W., Saha, S. N., & Duncan, J. (1991). I AMN NOT A UTISTIVC ON THJE TYP" ("I'm not autistic on the typewriter"). *Disability, Handicap and Society, 6,* 161–180.

Billsteadt, E., Gillberg, C., & Gillberg, C. (2005). Autism after adolescence: Population-based 13- to 22-year follow-up study of 120 individuals with Autism diagnosed in childhood. *Journal of Autism and Developmental Disorder, 35,* 351–360.

Birch, S., & Chase, C. (2004). Visual and language processing deficits in compensated and uncompensated college students with dyslexia. *Journal of Learning Disabilities, 37,* 389–410.

Bird, H. R. (1996). Epidemiology of childhood disorders in a cross-cultural context. *Journal of Child Psychology and Psychiatry, 37,* 35–49.

Bird, H. R., Canino, G. J., Davies, M., Zhang, H., Ramirez, R., & Lahey, B. B. (2001). Prevalence and correlates of antisocial behaviors among three ethnic groups. *Journal of Abnormal Child Psychology, 29,* 465–478.

Birkeland, R., Thompson, J. K., Herbozo, S., Roehrig, M., Cafri, G., & van den Berg, P. (2005). Media exposure, mood, and body image dissatisfaction: An experimental test of person versus product priming. *Body Image, 2,* 53–61.

Birkeland, R., Thompson, J. K., & Phares, V. (2005). Adolescent motherhood and postpartum depression. *Journal of Clinical Child and Adolescent Psychology, 34,* 292–300.

Birmaher, B., Bridge, J. A., Williamson, D. E., Brent, D. A., Dahl, R. E., Axelson, D. A., Dorn, L. D., & Ryan, N. (2004). Psychosocial functioning in youths at high risk to develop major depressive disorder. *Journal of the American Academy of Child and Adolescent Psychiatry, 43,* 839–846.

Birmaher, B., Williamson, D. E., Dahl, R. E., Axelson, D. A., Kaufman, J., Dorn, L., & Ryan, N. D. (2004). Clinical presentation and course of depression in youth: Does onset in childhood differ from onset in adolescence? *Journal of the American Academy of Child and Adolescent Psychiatry, 43,* 63–70.

Bisaga, K., Whitaker, A., Davies, M., Chuang, S., Feidman, J., & Walsh, B. T. (2005). Eating disorder and depressive symptoms in urban high school girls from different ethnic backgrounds. *Journal of Developmental & Behavioral Pediatrics, 26,* 257–266.

Bishop, D. V. M., & Snowling, M. J. (2004). Developmental dyslexia and specific language impairment: Same or different? *Psychological Bulletin, 130,* 858–886.

Bittles, A. H., & Glasson, E. J. (2004). Clinical, social, and ethical implications of changing life expectancy in Down syndrome. *Developmental Medicine & Child Neurology, 46,* 282–286.

Blacher, J., Neece, C. L., & Paczkowski, E. (2005). Families and intellectual disability. *Current Opinion in Psychiatry, 18,* 507–513.

Black, M. M., Dubowitz, H., & Starr, R. H. (1999). African American fathers in low income, urban families: Development, behavior, and home environment of their three-year-old children. *Child Development, 70,* 967–978.

Black, M. M., & Nitz, K. (1996). Grandmother co-residence, parenting, and child development among low income, urban teen mothers. *Journal of Adolescent Health, 18,* 218–226.

Blair, C., & Scott, K. G. (2002). Proportion of LD placements associated with low socioeconomic status: Evidence for a gradient? *Journal of Special Education, 36,* 14–22.

Blanchette, N., Smith, M. L., Fernandes-Penney, A., King, S., & Read, S. (2001). Cognitive and motor development in children with vertically transmitted HIV infection. *Brain and Cognition, 46,* 50–53.

Blatt, S. J. (2004). *Experiences of depression: Theoretical, clinical, and research perspectives.* Washington, DC: American Psychological Association.

Blitstein, J. L., Robinson, L. A., Murray, D. M., Klesges, R. C., & Zbikowski, S. M. (2003). Rapid progression to regular cigarette smoking among nonsmoking adolescents: interactions with gender and ethnicity. *Preventive Medicine, 36,* 455–463.

Block, J., & Block, J. H. (2006). Venturing a 30-year longitudinal study. *American Psychologist, 61,* 315–327.

Bluglass, K. (2003). *Hidden from the Holocaust: Stories of resilient children who survived and thrived.* Westport, CT: Praeger Publishers.

Bogels, S. M., & Zigterman, D. (2000). Dysfunctional cognitions in children with social phobia, separation anxiety disorder, and generalized anxiety disorder. *Journal of Abnormal Child Psychology, 28,* 205–211.

Bolger, K. E., & Patterson, C. J. (2001). Developmental pathways from child maltreatment to peer rejection. *Child Development, 72,* 549–568.

Bono, K. E., Dinehart, L. H. B., Claussen, A. H., Scott, K. G., Mundy, P. C., & Katz, L. F. (2005). Early intervention with children prenatally exposed to cocaine: Expansion with multiple cohorts. *Journal of Early Intervention, 27,* 268–284.

Boothroyd, R. A., Gomez, A., Armstrong, M. L., Haynes, D., & Ort, R. (2005). Young and poor: The well-being of adolescent girls living in families receiving temporary assistance for needy families program. *Journal of Child and Family Studies, 14,* 141–154.

Borden, K. A., & Brown, R. T. (1989). Attributional outcomes: The subtle messages of treatment for attention deficit disorder. *Cognitive Therapy and Research, 13,* 147–160.

Bordens, K. S., & Abbott, B. B. (2003). *Research design and methods: A process approach* (5th ed.). New York: McGraw-Hill.

Borduin, C. M., Henggeler, S. W., & Manley, C. M. (1995). Conduct and oppositional disorders. In V. B. VanHasselt & M. Hersen (Eds.), *Handbook of adolescent psychopathology* (pp. 349–383). New York: Lexington Books.

Borduin, C. M., Schaeffer, C. M., & Heiblum, N. (1999). Relational problems: The social context of child and adolescent disorders. In S. D. Netherton, D. Holmes, & C. E. Walker (Eds.), *Child and adolescent psychological disorders: A comprehensive textbook* (pp. 498–519). New York: Oxford University Press.

Bostic, J. Q., & Pataki, C. (2000). All the world's a stage. *Journal of the American Academy of Child and Adolescent Psychiatry, 39,* 1565–1567.

Bottcher, J., & Ezell, M. E. (2005). Examining the effectiveness of boot camps: A randomized experiment with a long-term follow up. *Journal of Research in Crime and Delinquency, 42,* 309–332.

Botvin, G. J., & Dusenbury, L. (1989). Substance abuse prevention and the promotion of competence. In L. A. Bond & B. E. Compas (Eds.), *Primary prevention and promotion in the schools* (pp. 146–178). Newbury Park, CA: Sage.

Botvin, G. J., & Griffin, K. W. (2004). Life skills training: Empirical findings and future directions. *Journal of Primary Prevention, 25,* 211–232.

Bouchard, T. J. (2004). Genetic influence on human psychological traits: A survey. *Current Directions in Psychological Science, 13,* 148–151.

Boutelle, K., Neumark-Sztainer, D., Story, M., & Resnick, M. (2002). Weight control behaviors among obese, overweight, and nonoverweight adolescents. *Journal of Pediatric Psychology, 27,* 531–540.

Bow, J. N., & Quinnell, F. A. (2001). Psychologists' current practices and procedures in child custody evaluations: Five years after American Psychological Association guidelines. *Professional Psychology: Research and Practice, 32,* 261–268.

Bowen, M. (1978). *Family therapy in clinical practice.* Northvale, NY: Jason Aronson.

Bowers, W. A., Evans, K., LeGrange, D., & Andersen, A. E. (2003). Treatment of adolescent eating disorders. In M. A. Reinecke, F. M. Dattilio, & A. Freeman (Eds.), *Cognitive therapy with children and adolescents: A casebook for clinical practice* (2nd ed. pp. 247–280). New York: Guilford.

Bowlby, J. (1969). *Attachment.* New York: Basic Books.

Bowlby, J. (1973). *Attachment and loss (Vol. 2) Separation anxiety and anger.* New York: Basic Books.

Boxer, P., & Butkus, M. (2005). Individual social-cognitive intervention for aggressive behavior in early adolescence: An application of the cognitive-ecological framework. *Clinical Case Studies, 4,* 277–294.

Boyce, W. T., Frank, E., Jensen, P. S., Kessler, R. C., Nelson, C. A., Steinberg, L., & The MacArthur Foundation Research Network on Psychopathology and Development. (1998). Social context in developmental psychopathology: Recommendations for future research from the MacArthur Network on Psychopathology and Development. *Development and Psychopathology, 10,* 143–164.

Boyd-Franklin, N. (2003). *Black families in therapy: Understanding the African American experience* (2nd ed.). New York: Guilford.

Braaten, E. B., & Rosen, L. A. (2000). Self-regulation of affect in attention deficit-hyperactivity disorder (ADHD) and non-ADHD boys: Differences in empathic responding. *Journal of Consulting and Clinical Psychology, 68,* 313–321.

Brady, S. S., & Matthews, K. A. (2002). The influence of socioeconomic status and ethnicity on adolescents' exposure to stressful life events. *Journal of Pediatric Psychology, 27,* 575–583.

Bradley, R. H., & Corwyn, R. F. (2002). Socioeconomic status and child development. *Annual Review of Psychology, 53,* 371–399.

Brandenburg, N. A., Friedman, R. M., & Silver, S. E. (1990). The epidemiology of childhood psychiatric disorders: Prevalence findings from recent studies. *Journal of the American Academy of Child and Adolescent Psychiatry, 29,* 76–83.

Brandon, T. H., Collins, B. N., Juliano, L. M., & Lazev, A. B. (2000). Preventing relapse among former smokers: A comparison of minimal interventions through telephone and mail. *Journal of Consulting and Clinical Psychology, 68,* 103–113.

Branford, D., Bhaumik, S., & Naik, B. (1998). Selective serotonin reuptake inhibitors for the treatment of perseverative and maladaptive behaviours of people with intellectual disability. *Journal of Intellectual Disability Research, 42,* 301–396.

Brassard, M. R., Germain, R., & Hart, S. N. (1987). *Psychological maltreatment of children and youth.* Elmsford, NY: Pergamon Press.

Brassard, M. R., Hart, S. N., & Hardy, D. B. (1991). Psychological and emotional abuse of children. In R. T. Ammerman & M. Hersen (Eds.), *Case studies in family violence* (pp. 255–270). New York: Plenum Press.

Braswell, L., August, G. J., Bloomquist, M. L., Realmuto, G. M., Skare, S. S., & Crosby, R. D. (1997). School-based secondary prevention for children with disruptive behavior: Initial outcomes. *Journal of Abnormal Child Psychology, 25,* 197–208.

Bratton, S. C., Ray, D., Rhine, T., & Jones, L. (2005). The efficacy of play therapy with children: A meta-analytic review of treatment outcomes. *Professional Psychology: Research and Practice, 36,* 376–390.

Bray, J. H., Adams, G. J., Getz, J. G., & McQueen, A. (2003). Individuation, peers, and adolescent alcohol use: A latent growth analysis. *Journal of Consulting and Clinical Psychology, 71,* 553–564.

Breedlove, L., Decker, C., Lakin, K. C., Prouty, R., Coucouvanis, K., Braddock, D., & Smith, G. (2005). Placement of children and youth in state institutions: 40 years after the high point, it is time to just stop. *Mental Retardation, 43,* 235–238.

Breen, M. J., & Fiedler, C. R. (2003). *Behavioral approach to assessment of youth with emotional/behavioral disorders: A handbook for school-based practitioners* (2nd ed.). Austin, TX: Pro-ed, Inc.

Breggin, P. R. (2001a). MTA study has flaws. *Archives of General Psychiatry, 58,* 1184–1188.

Breggin, P. R. (2001b). *Talking back to Ritalin: What doctors aren't telling you about stimulants for children* (2nd ed. rev.). Cambridge, MA: Da Capo Press.

Breggin, P. R. (2002). *The ritalin fact book: What your doctor won't tell you about ADHD and stimulant drugs.* New York: Perseus Publishing.

Breggin, P. R., & Breggin, G. R. (1995). The hazards of treating "attention-deficit/hyperactivity disorder" with methylphenidate (Ritalin). *Journal of College Student Psychotherapy, 10,* 55–72.

Brendgen, M., Vitaro, F., Turgeon, L., Poulin, F., & Wanner, B. (2004). Is there a dark side of positive illusions? Overestimation of social competence and subsequent adjustment in aggressive and nonaggressive children. *Journal of Abnormal Child Psychology, 32,* 305–320.

Brennan, P. A., LeBrocque, R. & Hammen, C. (2003). Maternal depression, parent-child relationships, and resilient outcomes in adolescence. *Journal of the American Academy of Child and Adolescent Psychiatry, 42,* 1469–1477.

Brent, D. A., Baugher, M., Birmaher, B., Kolko, D. J., & Bridge, J. (2000). Compliance with recommendations to remove firearms in families participating in a clinical trail for adolescent depression. *Journal of the American Academy of Child and Adolescent Psychiatry, 39,* 1220–1226.

Brent, D. A., Kolko, D. J., Birmaher, B., Baugher, M., & Bridge, J. (1999). A clinical trial for adolescent depression: Predictors of additional treatment in the acute and follow-up phases of the trial. *Journal of the American Academy of Child and Adolescent Psychiatry, 38,* 263–270.

Brent, D. A., Oquendo, M., Birmaher, B., Greenhill, L., Kolko, D., Stanley, B., Zelazny, J., Brodsky, B., Melhem, N., Ellis, S., & Mann, J. J. (2004). Familial transmission of mood disorders: Convergence and divergence with transmission of suicidal behavior. *Journal of*

the American Academy of Child and Adolescent Psychiatry, 43, 1259–1266.

Brent, D. A., Perper, J., Allman, C., Moritz, G., Wartella, M., & Zelenak, J. (1991). The presence and availability of firearms in the homes of adolescent suicides: A case-control study. *Journal of the American Medical Association, 266,* 2989–2995.

Bridge, J. A., Day, N. L., Richardson, G. A., Birmaher, B., & Brent, D. A. (2003). Major depressive disorder in adolescents exposed to a friend's suicide. *Journal of the American Academy of Child and Adolescent Psychiatry, 42,* 1294–1300.

Briery, B. G., & Rabian, B. (1999). Psychosocial changes associated with participation in a pediatric summer camp. *Journal of Pediatric Psychology, 24,* 183–190.

Briggs-Gowan, M. J., Horwitz, S. M., Schwab-Stone, M. E., Leventhal, J. M., & Leaf, P. J. (2000). Mental health in pediatric settings: Distribution of disorders and factors related to service use. *Journal of the American Academy of Child and Adolescent Psychiatry, 39,* 841–849.

Brinkmeyer, M. Y., & Eyberg, S. M. (2003). Parent-child interaction therapy for oppositional children. In A. E. Kazdin & J. R. Weisz (Eds.), *Evidence-based psychotherapies for children and adolescents* (pp. 204–223). New York: Guilford.

Brodeur, D. A., & Pond, M. (2001). The development of selective attention in children with attention deficit hyperactivity disorder. *Journal of Abnormal Child Psychology, 29,* 229–239.

Brody, G. H. (2004). Siblings' direct and indirect contributions to child development. *Current Directions in Psychological Science, 13,* 124–126.

Brody, G. H., Ge, X., Conger, R., Gibbons, F. X., Murry, V. M., Gerrard, M., & Simons, R. L. (2001). The influence of neighborhood disadvantage, collective socialization, and parenting on African American children's affiliation with deviant peers. *Child Development, 72,* 1231–1246.

Brody, G. H., Ge, X., Katz, J., & Arias, I. (2000). A longitudinal analysis of internalization of parental alcohol-use norms and adolescent alcohol use. *Applied Developmental Science, 4,* 71–79.

Brody, G. H., Ge, X., Kim, S. Y., Murry, V. M., Simons, R. L., Gibbons, F. X., Gerrard, M., & Conger, R. D. (2003). Neighborhood disadvantage moderates associations of parenting and older sibling problem attitudes and behavior with conduct disorders in African American children. *Journal of Consulting and Clinical Psychology, 71,* 211–222.

Brody, G. H., Murry, V. M., Kogan, S. M., Gerrard, M., Gibbons, F. X., Molgaard, V., Brown, A. C., Anderson, T., Chen, Y. F., Luo, Z., & Wills, T. A. (2006). The Strong African American Families Program: A cluster-randomized prevention trial of long-term effects and a mediational model.. *Journal of Consulting and Clinical Psychology, 74,* 356–366.

Brody, G. H., Murry, V. M., Gerrard, M., Gibbons, F. X., McNair, L., Brown, A. C., Wills, T. A., Molgaard, V., Spoth, R. L., Luo, Z., & Cehn, Y. F. (2006). The Strong African American Families Program: Prevention of youths' high-risk behavior and a test of a model of change. *Journal of Family Psychology, 20,* 1–11.

Bronfenbrenner, U. (1979). *The ecology of human development: Experiments by nature and design.* Cambridge, MA: Harvard University Press.

Bronstein, P., & Quina, K. (Eds.) (2003). *Teaching gender and multicultural awareness: Resources for the psychology classroom.* Washington, DC: American Psychological Association.

Brook, J. S., Whiteman, M., Brook, D. W., & Gordon, A. S. (1982). Paternal and peer characteristics: Interactions and association with male college students' marijuana use. *Psychological Reports, 51,* 1319–1330.

Brotman, L. M., Gouley, K. K., Chesir-Teran, D., Dennis, T., Klein, R. G., & Shrout, P. (2005). Prevention for preschoolers at high risk for conduct problems: Immediate outcomes on parenting practices and child social competence. *Journal of Clinical Child and Adolescent Psychology, 34,* 724–734.

Brotman, L. M., Klein, R. G., Kamboukos, D., Brown, E. J., Coard, S. I., & Sosinsky, L. S. (2003). Preventive intervention for urban, low-income preschoolers at familial risk for conduct problems: A randomized pilot study. *Journal of Clinical Child and Adolescent Psychology, 32,* 246–257.

Brown, E. C., Catalano, R. F., Fleming, C. B., Haggerty, K. P., & Abbott, R. D. (2005). Adolescent substance use outcomes in the raising healthy children project: A two-part latent growth curve analysis. *Journal of Consulting and Clinical Psychology, 73,* 699–710.

Brown, E. J., & Goodman, R. F. (2005). Childhood traumatic grief: An exploration of the construct in children bereaved on September 11. *Journal of Clinical Child and Adolescent Psychology, 34,* 248–259.

Brown, L., Overholser, J., Spirito, A., & Fritz, G. (1991). The correlates of planning in adolescent suicide attempts. *Journal of the American Academy of Child and Adolescent Psychiatry, 30,* 95–99.

Brown, L. K., Lourie, K. J., & Pao, M. (2000). Children and adolescents living with HIV and AIDS: A review. *Journal of Child Psychology and Psychiatry, 41,* 81–96.

Brown, L. M., & Gilligan, C. (1998). *Meeting at the crossroads: Women's psychology and girls' development.* Collingdale, PA: Diane Publishing Company.

Brown, L. S. (2006). The neglect of lesbian, gay, bisexual, and transgendered clients. In J. C. Norcross, L. E. Beutler, & R. F. Levant (Eds.), *Evidence-based practices in mental health: Debate and dialogue on the fundamental questions* (pp. 346–353). Washington, DC: American Psychological Association.

Brown, R. T., Boeving, A., LaRosa, A., & Carpenter, L. A. (2006). Health and chronic illness. In D. A. Wolfe & E. J. Mash (Eds.), *Behavioral and emotional disorders in adolescents: Nature, assessment, and treatment* (pp. 505–531). New York: Guilford Press.

Brown, R. T., Carpenter, L. A., & Simerly, E. (2005). *Mental health medications for children: A primer.* New York: Guilford Press.

Brown, R. T., Fuemmeler, B., & Forti, E. (2003). Racial and ethnic health disparity and access to care. In M. C. Roberts (Ed.), *Handbook of pediatric psychology* (3rd ed., pp. 683–695). New York: Guilford Press.

Brown, S. A., & Abrantes, A. M. (2006). Substance use disorders. In D. A. Wolfe & E. J. Mash (Eds.), *Behavioral and emotional disorders in adolescents: Nature, assessment, and treatment* (pp. 226–256). New York: Guilford Press.

Browne, K. D., & Hamilton-Giachritsis, C. (2005). The influence of violent media on children and adolescents: A public-health approach. *Lancet, 365,* 702–710.

Bruce, K. R., & Steiger, H. (2005). Treatment implications of Axis-II comorbidity in eating disorders. *Eating Disorders: The Journal of Treatment & Prevention, 13,* 93–108.

Bruene-Butler, L., Hampson, J., Elias, M. J., Clabby, J. F. & Schuyler, T. (1997). The improving social awareness-social problem solving project. In G. W. Albee & T. P. Gullotta (Eds.), *Primary prevention works* (pp. 239–267). Thousand Oaks, CA: Sage.

Bruinink, R. H., Woodcock, R. W., Weatherman, R. F., & Hill, B. K. (1996). *The Scales of Independent Behavior—Revised.* Chicago: Riverside.

Bryan, A., Fisher, J. D., & Fisher, W. A. (2002). Tests of the mediational role of preparatory safer sexual behavior in the context of the theory of planned behavior. *Health Psychology, 21,* 71–80.

Bryant-Davis, T. (2005). Coping strategies of African American adult survivors of childhood violence. *Professional Psychology: Research and Practice, 36,* 409–414.

Buck, J. N. (1985). *The House-Tree-Person technique: Revised manual.* Los Angeles: Western Psychological Services.

Buckner, J. C., Bassuk, E. L., Weinreb, L. F., & Brooks, M. G. (1999). Homelessness and its relation to the mental health and behavior of low-income school-age children. *Developmental Psychology, 35,* 246–257.

Buckner, J. C., Mezzacappa, E., & Beardslee, W. R. (2003). Characteristics of resilient youths living in poverty: The role of self-regulatory process. *Development and Psychopathology, 15,* 139–162.

Budman, S. H. (2000). Behavioral health care dot-com and beyond: Computer-mediated communications in mental health and substance abuse treatment. *American Psychologist, 55,* 1290–1300.

Bukstein, O. G., & VanHasselt, V. B. (1995). Substance use disorders. In V. B. VanHasselt & M. Hersen (Eds.), *Handbook of adolescent psychopathology: A guide to diagnosis and treatment* (pp. 384–406). New York: Lexington Books.

Bulik, C. M., Klump, K. L., Thornton, L., Kaplan, A. S., Devlin, B., Fichter, M. M., Halmi, K. A., Strober, M., Woodside, D. B., Crow, S., Mitchell, J. E., Rotondo, A., Mauri, M., Cassano, G. B., Keel, P. K., Berrettini, W. H., & Kaye, W. H. (2004). Alcohol use disorder comorbidity in eating disorders: A multicenter study. *Journal of Clinical Psychiatry, 65,* 1000–1006.

Bullock, G. L., & Schall, U. (2005). Dyssomnia in children diagnosed with attention deficit hyperactivity disorder: A critical review. *Australian and New Zealand Journal of Psychiatry, 39,* 373–377.

Burd, L., Cotsonas-Hassler, T. M., Martsolf, J. T., & Kerbeshian, J. (2003). Recognition and management of fetal alcohol syndrome. *Neurotoxicology and Teratology, 25,* 681–688.

Burgoon, M., Alvaro, E. M., Broneck, K., Miller, C., Grandpre, J. R., Hall, J. R., & Frank, C. A. (2002). Using interactive media tools to test substance abuse prevention messages. In W. D. Crano & M. Burgoon (Eds.). *Mass media and drug prevention: Classic and contemporary theories and research.* (pp. 67–87). Mahwah, NJ: Lawrence Erlbaum Associates.

Burke, J. D., Loeber, R., Mutchka, J.S., & Lahey, B. B. (2002). A question for DSM-V: Which better predicts persistent conduct disorder-delinquent acts or conduct symptoms? *Criminal Behaviour & Mental Health, 12,* 37–52.

Burke, K. L., Sachs, M. L., & Smission, C. P. (Eds.) (2004). *Directory of graduate programs in applied sport psychology* (7th ed). Morgantown, WV: Fitness Information Technology, Incorporated.

Burns, B. J. (2002). Reasons for hope for children and families: A perspective and overview. In B. J. Burns & K. Hoagwood (Eds.), *Community treatment for youth: Evidence-based interventions for severe emotional and behavioral disorders* (pp. 3–15). New York: Oxford University Press.

Burns, B. J., Compton, S. N., Egger, H. L., Farmer, E. M. Z., & Robertson, E. B. (2002). An annotated review of the evidence base for psychosocial and psychopharmacological interventions for children with selected disorders. In B. J. Burns & K. Hoagwood (Eds.), *Community treatment for youth: Evidence-based interventions for severe emotional and behavioral disorders* (pp. 212–276). New York: Oxford University Press.

Burns, B. J., Phillips, S. D., Wagner, H. R., Barth, R. P., Kolko, D. J., Campbell, Y., & Landsverk, J. (2004). Mental health need and access to mental health services by youths involved with child welfare: A national survey. *Journal of the American Academy of Child and Adolescent Psychiatry, 43,* 960–970.

Burns, C. W. (2003). Assessing the psychological and educational needs of children with moderate and severe mental retardation. In C. R. Reynolds & R. W. Kamphaus (Eds.), *Handbook of psychological and educational assessment of children: Intelligence, aptitude, and achievement* (2nd ed.) (pp. 671–684). New York: Guilford.

Burns, R. C. (1982). *Self-growth in families: Kinetic Family Drawings (K-F-D) research and application.* New York: Brunner/Mazel.

Burns, R. C., & Kaufman, S. H. (1972). *Actions, styles and symbols in kinetic family drawings (KFD-D): An interpretative manual.* New York: Brunner/Mazel.

Burns, T. G., & O'Leary, S. D. (2004). Wechsler intelligence scale for children-IV: Test Review. *Applied Neuropsychology, 11,* 233–236.

Burrows, A., & Cooper, M. (2002). Possible risk factors in the development of eating disorders in overweight pre-adolescent girls. *International Journal of Obesity, 26,* 1268–1273.

Bursch, B. (2006). Somatization disorders. In R. T. Ammerman (Ed.), *Comprehensive handbook of personality and psychopathology: Child psychopathology (Vol 3)* (pp. 403–421). Hoboken, NJ: Wiley.

Burt, S. A., Krueger, R. F., McGue, M., & Iacono, W. (2003). Parent-child conflict and the comorbidity among childhood externalizing disorders. *Archives of General Psychiatry, 60,* 505–513.

Burt, S. A., McGue, M., Krueger, R. F., & Iacono, W. G. (2005). Sources of covariation among the child-externalizing disorders: Informant effects and the shared environment. *Psychological Medicine, 35,* 1133–1144.

Burton, E., Stice, E., & Seeley, J. R. (2004). A prospective test of the stress-buffering model of depression in adolescent girls: No support once again. *Journal of Consulting and Clinical Psychology, 72,* 689–697.

Bushman, B. J., & Anderson, C. A. (2001). Media violence and the American public: Scientific facts versus media misinformation. *American Psychologist, 56,* 477–489.

Burke, C., & Buskist, W. (2006). *Preparing for graduate study in psychology: 101 questions and answers.* Needham Heights, MA: Allyn and Bacon.

Bussing, R., Gary, F. A., Mills, T. I., & Garvan, C. W. (2003). Parental explanatory models of ADHD: Gender and cultural variations. *Social Psychiatry and Psychiatric Epidemiology, 38,* 563–575.

Bussing, R., Zima, B. T., Belin, T. R., & Forness, S. R. (1998). Children who qualify for LD and SED programs: Do they differ in level of ADHD symptoms and comorbid psychiatric conditions. *Behavioral Disorders, 23,* 85–97.

Bussing, R., Zima, B. T., Gary, F. A., & Garvan, C. W. (2003). Barriers to detection, help-seeking, and service use for children with ADHD symptoms. *Journal of Behavioral Health Services and Research, 30,* 176–189.

Bussing, R., Zima, B. T., & Perwien, A. R. (2000). Self-esteem in special education children with ADHD: Relationship to disorder characteristics and medication use. *Journal of the American Academy of Child and Adolescent Psychiatry, 39,* 1260–1269.

Butcher, J. N., Dahlstrom, W. G., Graham, J. R., Tellegen, A., & Kaemmer, B. (1989). *Minnesota Multiphasic Personality Inventory-2 (MMPI-2): Manual for administration and scoring.* Minneapolis, MN: University of Minnesota Press.

Butcher, J. N., & Williams, C. L. (2000). *Essentials of the MMPI-2 and MMPI-A interpretation* (2nd ed.). Minneapolis: University of Minnesota Press.

Butryn, M. L., & Wadden, T. A. (2005). Treatment of overweight in children and adolescents: Does dieting increase the risk of eating disorders? *International Journal of Eating Disorders, 37,* 285–293.

Butz, M. R., Bowling, J. B., & Bliss, C. A. (2000). Psychotherapy with the mentally retarded: A review of the literature and the implications. *Professional Psychology: Research and Practice, 31,* 42–47.

Caballero, B. (2004). Obesity prevention in children: Opportunities and challenges. *International Journal of Obesity, 28,* S90–S95.

Cacioppo, J. T., Berntson, G. G., Sheridan, J. F., & McClintock, M. K. (2000). Multilevel integrative analyses of human behavior: Social neuroscience and the complementing nature of social and biological approaches. *Psychological Bulletin, 126,* 829–843.

Caddy, G. R., & Bollard, J. (1988). Enuresis. In M. Hersen & C. G. Last (Eds.), *Child behavior therapy casebook* (pp. 347–357). New York: Plenum Press.

Cai, X., Kaiser, A. P., & Hancock, T. B. (2004). Parent and teacher agreement on child behavior checklist items in a sample of preschoolers from low-income and predominantly African American families. *Journal of Clinical Child and Adolescent, 33,* 303–312.

Calhoon, M. B. (2005). Effects of a peer-mediated phonological skill and reading comprehension program on reading skill acquisition for middle school students with reading disabilities. *Journal of Learning Disabilities, 38,* 424–433.

Calhoun, S. L., & Mayes, S. D. (2005). Processing speed in children with clinical disorders. *Psychology in the Schools, 42,* 333–343.

Calkins, S. D., & Degnan, K. A. (2006). Temperament in early development. In R. T. Ammerman (Ed.), *Comprehensive handbook of personality and psychopathology: Child psychopathology (Vol 3)* (pp. 64–84). Hoboken, NJ: Wiley.

Calvete, E., & Cardenoso, O. (2005). Gender differences in cognitive vulnerability to depression and behavior problems in adolescents. *Journal of Abnormal Child Psychology, 33,* 179–192.

Calzada, E. J., Eyberg, S. M., Rich, B., & Querido, J. G. (2004). Parenting disruptive preschoolers: Experiences of mothers and fathers. *Journal of Abnormal Child Psychology, 32,* 203–213.

Campbell, S. B. (1998). Developmental perspectives. In T. H. Ollendick & M. Hersen (Eds.), *Handbook of child psychopathology* (3rd ed., pp. 3–35). New York: Plenum Press.

Campbell, S. B. (2000). Editor's note. *Journal of Abnormal Child Psychology, 28,* 481.

Campbell, S. B., & Davies, P. T. (2002). *Developmental psychopathology and family process: Theory, research, and clinical implications.* New York: Guilford.

Campo, J. V., & Fritz, G. (2001). A management model for pediatric somatization. *Psychosomatics: Journal of Consultation Liaison Psychiatry, 42,* 467–476.

Campo, J. V., & Reich, M. D. (1999). Somatoform disorders. In S. D. Netherton, D. Holmes, & C. E. Walker (Eds.), *Child and adolescent psychological disorders: A comprehensive textbook* (pp. 320–343). New York: Oxford.

Canino, G., Shrout, P. E., Rubio-Stipec, M., Bird, H. R., Bravo, M., Ramirez, R., Chavez, L., Alegria, M., Bauermeister, J. J., Hohmann, A., Ribera, J., Garcia, P., & Martinez-Taboas, A. (2004). The *DSM-IV* rates of child and adolescent disorders in Puerto Rico. *Archives of General Psychiatry, 61,* 85–93.

Cantwell, D. P., Lewinsohn, P. M., Rohde, P., & Seeley, J. R. (1997). Correspondence between adolescent report and parent report of psychiatric diagnostic data. *Journal of the American Academy of Child and Adolescent Psychiatry, 36,* 610–619.

Caplan, P. J. (1995). *They say you're crazy: How the world's most powerful psychiatrists decide who's normal.* Reading, MA: Addison-Wesley.

Caplan, P. J., & Cosgrove, L., (2004). *Bias in psychiatric diagnosis.* Northvale, NJ: Jason Aronson, Inc.

Caplan, R., Guthrie, D., Tang, B., Komo, S., & Asarnow, R. F. (2000). Thought disorder in childhood schizophrenia: Replication and update of concept. *Journal of the American Academy of Child and Adolescent Psychiatry, 39,* 771–778.

Capps, L., Losh, M., & Thurber, C. (2000). "The frog ate the bug and made his mouth sad": Narrative competence in children with autism. *Journal of Abnormal Child Psychology, 28,* 193–204.

Carlson, C. I. (2003). Assessing the family context. In C. R. Reynolds & R. W. Kamphaus (Eds.), *Handbook of psychological and educational assessment of children: Personality, behavior, and context* (2nd ed., pp. 473–492). New York: Guilford

Carlson, G. A. (1998). Mania and ADHD: Comorbidity or confusion. *Journal of Affective Disorders, 51,* 177–187.

Carlson, G. A. (2005). Early onset bipolar disorder: Clinical and research considerations. *Journal of Clinical Child and Adolescent Psychology, 34,* 333–343.

Carlson, G. A., & Kelly, K. L. (1998). Manic symptoms in psychiatrically hospitalized children—what do they mean? *Journal of Affective Disorders, 51,* 123–135.

Caroli, M., Argentieri, L., Cardone, M., & Masi, A. (2004). Role of television in childhood obesity prevention. *International Journal of Obesity, 28,* S104–S108.

Caron, C., & Rutter, M. (1991). Comorbidity in child psychopathology: Concepts, issues and research strategies. *Journal of Child Psychology and Psychiatry, 32,* 1063–1080.

Carothers, S. S., Borkowski, J. G., Lefever, J. B., & Whitman, T. L. (2005). Religiosity and the socioemotional adjustment of adolescent mothers and their children. *Journal of Family Psychology, 19,* 263–275.

Carr, J. E., Sidener, T. M., Sidener, D. W., & Cummings, A. R. (2005). Functional analysis and habit-reversal treatment of Tics. *Behavioral Interventions, 20,* 185–202.

Carroll, J. M., Maughan, B., Goodman, R., & Meltzer, H. (2005). Literacy difficulties and psychiatric disorders: Evidence for comorbidity. *Journal of Child Psychology and Psychiatry, 46,* 524–532.

Carson, B., & Murphey, C. (1990). *Gifted hands: The Ben Carson story.* Grand Rapids, MI: Zondervan Publishing House.

Carter, J. R., & Neufeld, R. W. J. (1998). Cultural aspects of understanding people with schizophrenic disorders. In S. S. Kazarian & D. R. Evans (Eds.), *Cultural clinical psychology: Theory, research, and practice* (pp. 246–266). New York: Oxford University Press.

Cartwright-Hatton, S., Mather, A., Illingworth, V., Brocki, J., Harrington, R., & Wells, A. (2004). Development and preliminary validation of the Meta-cognitions Questionnaire—Adolescent Version. *Journal of Anxiety Disorders, 18,* 411–422.

Casas, A. M., & Castellar, R. G. (2004). Mathematics education and learning disabilities in Spain. *Journal of Learning Disabilities, 37,* 62–73.

Casey, R. J., & Berman, J. S. (1985). The outcome of psychotherapy with children. *Psychological Bulletin, 98,* 388–400.

Caspi, A. (2000). The child is father of the man: Personality continuities from childhood to adulthood. *Journal of Personality and Social Psychology, 78,* 158–172.

Caspi, A., & Moffitt, T. E. (1995). The continuity of maladaptive behavior: From description to understanding in the study of antisocial behavior. In D. Cicchetti & D. J. Cohen (Eds.), *Developmental psychopathology (Vol 2): Risk, disorder, and adaptation* (pp. 472–511). New York: Wiley.

Caspi, A., Taylor, A., Moffitt, T. E., & Plomin, R. (2000). Neighborhood deprivation affects children's mental health: Environmental risks identified in a genetic design. *Psychological Science, 11,* 338–342.

Cassidy, J., & Mohr, J. J. (2001). Unsolvable fear, trauma, and psychopathology: Theory, research, and clinical considerations related to disorganized attachment across the life span. *Clinical Psychology: Science and Practice, 8,* 275–298.

Cassidy, J., & Shaver, P. R. (Eds.). (1999). *Handbook of attachment: Theory, research, and clinical applications.* New York: Guilford Press.

Caster, J. B., Inderbitzen, H. M., & Hope, D. (1999). Relationship between youth and parent perceptions of family environment and social anxiety. *Journal of Anxiety Disorders, 13,* 237–251.

CDF Reports (1999). Gun violence: Nearly thirteen children die from gunfire every day in America. *CDF Reports, 20,* 1–2, 12–13.

Ceballo, R., Ramirez, C., Hearn, K. D., & Maltese, K. L. (2003). Community violence and children's psychological well-being: Does parental monitoring matter? *Journal of Clinical Child and Adolescent Psychology, 32,* 586–592.

Ceci, S. J., & Papierno, P. B. (2005). The rhetoric and reality of gap closing: When the "have-nots" gain but the "haves" gain even more. *American Psychologist, 60,* 149–160.

Cederlund, M., & Gillberg, C. (2004). One hundred males with Asperger syndrome: A clinical study of background and associated factors. *Developmental Medicine & Child Neurology, 46,* 652–660.

Centers for Disease Control. (2004). Suicide among children, adolescents, and young adults—United States, 1980–1992. *Morbidity and Mortality Weekly Report, 44,* 289–291.

Centerwall, B. S. (2000). Television and violent crime. In D. S. Del Campo & R. L. Del Campo (Eds.), Taking sides: *Clashing views on controversial issues in childhood and society* (3rd ed.) (pp. 148–155). Guilford, CT: Dushkin/McGraw-Hill.

Cepeda, N. J., Cepeda, M. L., & Kramer, A. F. (2000). Task switching and attention deficit hyperactivity disorder. *Journal of Abnormal Child Psychology, 28,* 213–226.

Cerel, J., Fristad, M. A., Verducci, J., Weller, R. A., & Weller, E. B. (2006). Childhood bereavement: Psychopathology in the 2 years postparental death. *Journal of the American Academy of Child and Adolescent Psychiatry, 45,* 681–690.

Chabrol, B., Decarie, J. C., & Fortin, G. (1999). The role of cranial MRI in identifying patients suffering from child abuse and presenting with unexplained neurological findings. *Child Abuse and Neglect, 23,* 217–228.

Chadwick, O., Kusel, Y., Cuddy, M., & Taylor, E. (2005). Psychiatric diagnoses and behaviour problems from childhood to early adolescence in young people with severe intellectual disabilities. *Psychological Medicine, 35,* 751–760.

Chaffin, M., Silovsky, J. F., Funderburk, B., Valle, L. A., Brestan, E. V., Balachova, T., Jackson, S., Lensgraf, J., & Bonner, B. L. (2004). Parent-child interaction therapy with physically abusive parents: Efficacy for reducing future abuse reports. *Journal of Consulting and Clinical Psychology, 72,* 500–510.

Chaffin, M., Silovsky, J. F., & Vaughn, C. (2005). Temporal concordance of anxiety disorders and child sexual abuse: Implications for direct versus artifactual effects of sexual abuse. *Journal of Clinical Child and Adolescent Psychology, 34,* 210–222.

Chamberlain, P. (1996). Community-based residential treatment for adolescents with conduct disorder. In T. H. Ollendick & R. J. Prinz (Eds.), *Advances in clinical child psychology (Vol. 18)* (pp. 63–90). New York: Plenum Press.

Chamberlain, P., & Smith, D. K. (2003). Antisocial behavior in children and adolescents: The Oregon multidimensional treatment foster care model. In A. E. Kazdin & J. R. Weisz (Eds.), *Evidence-based psychotherapies for children and adolescents* (pp. 282–300). New York: Guilford Press.

Chamberlain, P., & Smith, D. K. (2005). Multidimensional treatment foster care: A community solution for boys and girls referred from juvenile justice. In E. D. Hibbs & P. S. Jensen (Eds.), *Psychosocial treatment for child and adolescent disorders: Empirically based strategies for clinical practice* (2nd ed., pp. 557–573). Washington, DC: American Psychological Association.

Chambless, D. L., Baker, M. J., Baucom, D. H., Beutler, L. E., Calhoun, K. S., Crits-Christoph, P., Daiuto, A., DeRubeis, R., Detweiler, J., Haaga, D. A. F., Johnson, S. B., McCurry, S., Mueser, K. T., Pope, K. S., Sanderson, W. C., Shoham, V., Stickle, T., Williams, D. A., & Woody, S. (1998). Update on empirically validated therapies, II. *The Clinical Psychologist, 51,* 3–16.

Chambless, D. L., & Hollon, S. D. (1998). Defining empirically supported therapies. *Journal of Consulting and Clinical Psychology, 66,* 7–18.

Chandler, L. K., & Dahlquist, C. (2005). *Functional assessment: Strategies to prevent and remediate challenging behavior in school settings.* Upper Saddle River, NJ: Pearson Education.

Chang, D. F., & Sue, S. (2003). The effects of race and problem type on teachers' assessments of student behavior. *Journal of Consulting and Clinical Psychology, 71,* 235–242.

Chang, L., Schwartz, D., Dodge, K. A., & McBride-Chang, C. (2003). Harsh parenting in relation to child emotion regulation and aggression. *Journal of Family Psychology, 17,* 598–606.

Chanoine, J., Hampi, S., Jensen, C., Boldrin, M., & Hauptman, J. (2005). Effect of Orlistat on weight and body composition in obese adolescents: A randomized controlled trial. *JAMA: Journal of the American Medical Association, 293,* 2873–2883.

Chapman, E., & Bilton, D. (2004). Patients' knowledge of cystic fibrosis: Genetic determinism and implications for treatment. *Journal of Genetic Counseling, 13,* 369–385.

Chapman, M. V. (2005). Neighborhood quality and somatic complaints among American youth. *Journal of Adolescent Health, 36,* 244–252.

Chappell, K. (2003). Dr. Ben Carson: Top surgeon's life-and-death struggle with prostate cancer. *Ebony,* January 2003.

Chassin, L., Flora, D. B., & King, K. M. (2004). Trajectories of alcohol and drug use and dependence from adolescence to adulthood: The effects of familial alcoholism and personality. *Journal of Abnormal Psychology, 113,* 483–498.

Chassin, L., Pitts, S. C., DeLucia, C., & Todd, M. (1999). A longitudinal study of children of alcoholics: Predicting young adult substance use disorders, anxiety, and depression. *Journal of Abnormal Psychology, 108,* 106–119.

Chassin, L., Presson, C., Rose, J., Sherman, S. J., & Prost, J. (2002). Parental smoking cessation and adolescent smoking. *Journal of Pediatric Psychology, 27,* 485–496.

Chassin, L., Ritter, J., Trim, R. S., & King, K. M. (2003). Adolescent substance use disorders. In E. J. Mash, & B. A. Barkley (Eds.). *Child psychopathology* (2nd ed., pp. 199–230). New York: Guilford Press.

Chatoor, I. (2005). Evaluation and treatment of infantile anorexia. In E. D. Hibbs, & P. S. Jensen (Eds.). *Psychosocial treatments for child and adolescent disorders: Empirically based strategies for clinical practice* (2nd ed., pp. 295–320). Washington, DC: American Psychological Association.

Chatoor, I., & Ganiban, J. (2003). Food refusal by infants and young children: Diagnosis and treatment. *Cognitive and Behavioral Practice, 10,* 138–146.

Chavira, D. A., Stein, M. B., Bailey, K., & Stein, M. T. (2004). Child anxiety in primary care: prevalent but untreated. *Depression and Anxiety, 20,* 155–164.

Chen, E. (2004). Why socioeconomic status affects the health of children: A psychosocial perspective. *Current Directions in Psychological Science, 13,* 112–115.

Chen, E., Cole, S. W., & Kato, P. M. (2004). A review of empirically supported psychosocial interventions for pain and adherence outcomes in sickle cell disease. *Journal of Pediatric Psychology, 29,* 197–209.

Chen, J. Q., & Chen, D. G. (2005). Awareness of child sexual abuse prevention education among parents of Grade 3 elementary school pupils in Fuxin City, China. *Health Education Research, 20,* 540–547.

Chen, Y., & Weitzman, E. R. (2005). Depressive symptoms, DSM-IV alcohol abuse and their comorbidity among children of problem drinkers in a national survey: Effects of parent and child gender and parent recovery status. *Journal of Studies on Alcohol, 66,* 66–73.

Chi, T. C., & Hinshaw, S. P. (2002). Mother-child relationships of children with ADHD: The role of maternal depressive symptoms and depression-related distortions. *Journal of Abnormal Child Psychology, 30,* 387–400.

Chiaroni, P., Hantouche, E. G., Gouvernet, J., Azorin, J. M., & Akiskal, H. S. (2005). The cyclothymic temperament in healthy controls and familially at risk individuals for mood disorder: endophenotype for genetic studies? *Journal of Affective Disorders, 85,* 135–145.

Children's Defense Fund. (1999). *The state of America's children yearbook.* Washington, DC: Author.

Children's Defense Fund. (2005a). *Beat the odds reunion participants.* Washington, DC: Author.

Children's Defense Fund. (2005b). *Child abuse and neglect fact sheet.* Washington, DC: Author.

Children's Defense Fund. (2005c). *A moral outrage: One American child or teen killed by gunfire nearly every 3 hours.* Washington, DC: Author.

Children's Defense Fund. (2005d). *The state of America's children—2005.* Washington, DC: Author.

Children's Defense Fund—Minnesota. (1990). *157,000 children: Facts and feelings about being on welfare in Minnesota.* St. Paul, MN: Author.

Chong, M. Y., Chan, K. W., & Cheng, A. T. A. (1999). Substance use disorders among adolescents in Taiwan: Prevalence, sociodemographic correlates and psychiatric comorbidity. *Psychological Medicine, 29,* 1387–1396.

Chorpita, B. F. (2001). Control and the development of negative emotions. In M. W. Vasey & M. R. Dadds (Eds.), *The developmental psychopathology of anxiety* (pp. 112–142). New York: Oxford University Press.

Chorpita, B. F., Plummer, C. M., & Moffitt, C. E. (2000). Relations of tripartite dimensions of emotion to childhood anxiety and mood disorders. *Journal of Abnormal Child Psychology, 28,* 299–310.

Chorpita, B. F., Taylor, A. A., Francis, S. E., Moffitt, C., & Austin, A. A. (2004). Efficacy of modular cognitive behavior therapy for childhood anxiety disorders. *Behavior Therapy, 35,* 263–287.

Christakis, D. A., Zimmerman, F. J., Di Giuseppe, D. L., & McCarty, C. A. (2004). Early television exposure and subsequent attentional problems in children. *Pediatrics, 113,* 708–713.

Christiansen, B. A., & Goldman, M. S. (1983). Alcohol-related expectancies versus demographic/background variables in the prediction of adolescent drinking. *Journal of Consulting and Clinical Psychology, 51,* 249–257.

Christianson, A. L., Zwane, M. E., Manga, P., Rosen, E., Venter, A., Downs, D., & Kromberg, J. G. R. (2002). Children with intellectual disability in rural South Africa: Prevalence and associated disability. *Intellectual Disability Research, 46,* 179–186.

Christenson, S. L., & Buerkle, K. (1999). Families as educational partners for children's school success: Suggestions for school psychologists. In C. R. Reynolds & T. B. Gutkin (Eds.), *The handbook of school psychology* (3rd ed., pp. 707–744). New York: Wiley.

Christenson, S. L., & Thurlow, M. L. (2004). School dropouts: Prevention considerations, interventions, and challenges. *Current Directions in Psychological Science, 13,* 36–39.

Christoffel, K. K., (2000). Commentary: When counseling parents on guns doesn't work: Why don't they get it? *Journal of the American Academy of Child and Adolescent Psychiatry, 39,* 1226–1228.

Christophersen, E. R., & Mortweet, S. L. (2001). Diagnosis and management of encopresis. In E. R. Christophersen, & S. L. Mortweet (Eds.). *Treatments that work with children: Empirically supported strategies for managing childhood problems* (pp. 123–143). Washington, DC: American Psychological Association.

Christophersen, E. R., & Mortweet, S. L. (2001). Diagnosis and management of nocturnal enuresis. In E. R. Christophersen, & S. L. Mortweet (Eds.). *Treatments that work with children: Empirically supported strategies for managing childhood problems* (pp. 145–158). Washington, DC: American Psychological Association.

Chronis, A. M., Lahey, B. B., Pelham, W. E., Kipp, H. L., Baumann, B. L., & Lee, S. S. (2003). Psychopathology and substance abuse in parents of young children with attention-deficit/hyperactivity disorder. *Journal of the American Academy of Child and Adolescent Psychiatry, 42,* 1424–1432.

Chung, T., & Martin, C. S. (2005). Classification and short-term course of *DSM-IV* cannabis, hallucinogen, cocaine, and opioid disorders in treated adolescents. *Journal of Consulting and Clinical Psychology, 73,* 995–1004.

Cicchetti, D. (1990). A historical perspective on the discipline of developmental psychopathology. In J. Rolf, A. Masten, D. Cicchetti, K. Nuechterlein, & S. Weintraub (Eds.), *Risk and protective factors in the development of psychopathology* (pp. 2–28). New York: Cambridge University Press.

Cicchetti, D. (2004). An odyssey of discovery: Lessons learned through three decades of research on child maltreatment. *American Psychologist, 59,* 731–741.

Cicchetti, D., Rappaport, J., Sandler, I., & Weissberg, R. P. (Eds.). (2000). *The promotion of wellness in children and adolescents.* Washington, DC: CWLA Press.

Cicchetti, D., & Rogosch, F. A. (1999a). Conceptual and methodological issues in developmental psychopathology research. In P. C. Kendall, J. N. Butcher, & G. N Holmbeck (Eds.), *Handbook of research methods in clinical psychology* (2nd ed., pp. 433–465). New York: Wiley.

Cicchetti, D., & Rogosch, F. A. (1999b). Psychopathology as risk for adolescent substance use disorders: A developmental psychopathology perspective. *Journal of Clinical Child Psychology, 28,* 355–365.

Cicchetti, D., Rogosch, F. A., & Toth, S. L. (1997). Ontogenesis, depressotypic organization, and the depressive spectrum. In S. S. Luthar, J. A. Burack, D. Cicchetti, & J. R. Weisz (Eds.), *Developmental psychopathology: Perspectives on adjustment, risk, and disorder* (pp. 273–313). New York: Cambridge University Press.

Cicchetti, D., & Toth, S. L. (1995). Developmental psychopathology and disorders of affect. In D. Cicchetti & D. J. Cohen (Eds.), *Developmental psychopathology (Vol 2): Risk, disorder, and adaptation* (pp. 369–420). New York: Wiley.

Cicchetti, D., & Toth, S. L. (1997). Transactional ecological systems in developmental psychopathology. In S. S. Luthar, J. A. Burack, D. Cicchetti, & J. R. Weisz (Eds.), *Developmental psychopathology: Perspectives on adjustment, risk, and disorder* (pp. 317–349). New York: Cambridge University Press.

Cicchetti, D., & Toth, S. L. (1998). The development of depression in children and adolescents. *American Psychologist, 53,* 221–241.

Cicchetti, D., Toth, S. L., & Rogosch, F. A. (2000). The development of psychological wellness in maltreated children. In D. Cicchetti, J. Rappaport, I. Sandler, & R. P. Weissberg (Eds.), *The promotion of wellness in children and adolescents* (pp. 395–426). Washington, DC: CWLA Press.

Cicchetti, D., & Walker, E. (2003). *Neurodevelopmental mechanisms in psychopathology.* New York: Cambridge University Press.

Cillessen, A. H. N., & Rose, A. J. (2005). Understanding popularity in the peer system. *Current Directions in Psychological Science, 14,* 102–105.

Clancy, T. A., Rucklidge, J. J., & Owen, D. (2006). Road-crossing safety in virtual reality: A comparison of adolescents with and without ADHD. *Journal of Clinical Child and Adolescent Psychology, 35,* 203–215.

Clark, D. B., Parker, A. M., & Lynch, K. G. (1999). Psychopathology and substance-related problems during early adolescence: A survival analysis. *Journal of Clinical Child Psychology, 28,* 333–341.

Clark, L. A., Watson, D., & Reynolds, S. (1995). Diagnosis and classification of psychopathology: Challenges to the current system and future directions. *Annual Review of Psychology, 46,* 121–153.

Clarke, G. N., DeBar, L. L., & Lewinsohn, P. M. (2003). Cognitive-behavioral group treatment for adolescent depression. In A. E. Kazdin & J. R. Weisz (Eds.), *Evidence-based psychotherapies for children and adolescents* (pp. 120–134). New York: Guilford.

Clarke, G. N., Hawkins, W., Murphy, M., Sheeber, L. B., Lewinsohn, P. M., & Seeley, J. R. (1995). Targeted prevention of unipolar depressive disorder in an at-risk sample of high school adolescents: A randomized trial of a group cognitive intervention. *Journal of the American Academy of Child and Adolescent Psychiatry, 34,* 312–321.

Clarke, J. N. (2005). Fathers' home health care work when a child has cancer: I'm her Dad; I have to do it. *Men and Masculinities, 7,* 385–404.

Clarke, S., Davies, H., Jenney, M., Glaser, A., & Eiser, C. (2005). Parental communication and children's behaviour following diagnosis of childhood Leukaemia. *Psycho-Oncology, 14,* 274–281.

Clarke-Stewart, K. A., Vandell, D. L., McCartney, K., Owen, M. T., & Booth, C. (2000). Effects of parental separation and divorce on very young children. *Journal of Family Psychology, 14,* 304–326.

Clarkson, S. (1999) Beyond street smarts. In E. Wright (Ed.), *Why I teach* (pp. 177–180). Rocklin, CA: Prima Publishing.

Clay, D. L., Mordhorst, M. J., & Lehn, L. (2002). Empirically supported treatments in pediatric psychology: Where is the diversity? *Journal of Pediatric Psychology, 27,* 325–337.

Clinton, H. R. (1996). *It takes a village and other lessons children teach* us. New York: Simon and Schuster.

Cloitre, M., Stovall-McClough, K. C., Miranda, R., & Chemtob, C. M. (2004). Therapeutic alliance, negative mood regulation, and treatment outcome in child abuse-related posttraumatic stress disorder. *Journal of Consulting and Clinical Psychology, 72,* 411–416.

Cloud, J. (2005, October 10). The battle over gay teens. *Time,* 42–51.

Cobb, H. C., Reeve, R. E., Shealy, C. N., Norcross, J. C., Schare, M. L., Rodolfa, E. R., Hargrove, D. S., Hall, J. E., & Allen, M. (2004). Overlap among clinical, counseling, and school psychology: Implications for the profession and combined-integrated training. *Journal of Clinical Psychology, 60,* 939–955.

Cochran, B. N., Stewart, A. J., Ginzler, J. A., & Cauce, A. M. (2002). Challenges faced by homeless sexual minorities: Comparison of gay, lesbian, bisexual, and transgender homeless adolescents with their heterosexual counterparts. *American Journal of Public Health, 92,* 773–777.

Cocu, M., Thorne, C., Matusa, R., Tica, V., Florea, C., Asandi, S., & Giaquinto, C. (2005). Mother-to-child transmission of HIV infection in Romania: Results from an education and prevention programme. *AIDS Care, 17,* 76–84.

Coffey, B. J., Biederman, J., Geller, D. A., Spencer, T. J., Kim, G. S., Bellordre, C. A., Frazier, J. A., Cradock, K., & Magovcevic, M. (2000a). Distinguishing illness severity from tic severity in children and adolescents with Tourette's disorder. *Journal of the American Academy of Child and Adolescent Psychiatry, 39,* 556–561.

Coffey, B. J., Biederman, J., Smoller, J. W., Geller, D. A., Sarin, P., Schwartz, S., & Kim, G. S. (2000b). Anxiety disorders and tic severity in juveniles with Tourette's disorder. *Journal of the American Academy of Child and Adolescent Psychiatry, 39,* 562–568.

Cohen, D. M., Lumley, M. A., Naar-King, S., Partridge, T., & Cakan, N. (2004). Child behavior problems and family functioning as predictors of adherence and glycemic control in economically disadvantaged children with Type 1 diabetes: A prospective study. *Journal of Pediatric Psychology, 29,* 171–184.

Cohen, J. A., Deblinger, E., & Mannarino, A. P. (2005). Trauma-focused cognitive-behavioral therapy for sexually abused children. In E. D. Hibbs & P. S. Jensen (Eds.), *Psychosocial treatment for child and adolescent disorders: Empirically based strategies for clinical practice* (2nd ed., pp. 743–765). Washington, DC: American Psychological Association.

Coie, J. D., Dodge, K. A., Terry, R., & Wright, V. (1991). The role of aggression in peer relations: An analysis of aggression episodes in boys' play groups. *Child Development, 62*, 812–826.

Coie, J. D., & Jacobs, M. R. (1993). The role of social context in the prevention of conduct disorder. *Development and Psychopathology, 5*, 263–275.

Colapinto, J. (2001). *As nature made him: The boy who was raised as a girl.* New York: Perennial.

Colas, E. (1998). *Just checking: Scenes from the life of an obsessive-compulsive.* New York: Pocket Books.

Coley, R. L. (2001). (In)visible men: Emerging research on low-income, unmarried, and minority fathers. *American Psychologist, 56*, 743–753.

Coley, R. L., & Chase-Lansdale, P. L. (1998). Adolescent pregnancy and parenthood: Recent evidence and future directions. *American Psychologist, 53*, 152–166.

Collins, L. (2000). *Graduate study in educational and psychological measurement, quantitative psychology, and related fields.* Pennsylvania State University, University Park, PA: Author.

Collins, W. A., Maccoby, E. E., Steinberg, L., Hetherington, E. M., & Bornstein, M. H. (2000). Contemporary research on parenting: The case for nature and nurture. *American Psychologist, 55*, 218–232.

Commission on Adolescent Depression and Bipolar Disorder. (2005). Depression and bipolar disorder. In D. L. Evans, E. B. Foa, R. E. Gur, H. Hendin, C. P. O'Brien, M. E. P. Seligman, & B. T. Walsh (Eds.), *Treating and preventing adolescent mental health disorders: What we know and what we don't know* (pp. 3–74). New York: Oxford University Press.

Commission on Adolescent Schizophrenia. (2005). Schizophrenia. In D. L. Evans, E. B. Foa, R. E. Gur, H. Hendin, C. P. O'Brien, M. E. P. Seligman, & B. T. Walsh (Eds.), *Treating and preventing adolescent mental health disorders: What we know and what we don't know* (pp. 77–158). New York: Oxford University Press.

Commission on Adolescent Substance and Alcohol Abuse. (2005). Substance use disorders. In D. L. Evans, E. B. Foa, R. E. Gur, H. Hendin, C. P. O'Brien, M. E. P. Seligman, & B. T. Walsh (Eds.), *Treating and preventing adolescent mental health disorders: What we know and what we don't know* (pp. 335–429). New York: Oxford University Press.

Commission on Adolescent Suicide Prevention. (2005). Youth suicide. In D. L. Evans, E. B. Foa, R. E. Gur, H. Hendin, C. P. O'Brien, M. E. P. Seligman, & B. T. Walsh (Eds.), *Treating and preventing adolescent mental health disorders: What we know and what we don't know* (pp. 433–493). New York: Oxford University Press.

Compas, B. E., Connor-Smith, J., & Jaser, S. S. (2004). Temperament, stress reactivity, and coping: Implications for depression in childhood and adolescence. *Journal of Clinical Child and Adolescent Psychology, 33*, 21–31.

Compas, B. E., Connor-Smith, J. K., Saltzman, H., Thomsen, A. H., & Wadsworth, M. E. (2001). Coping with stress during childhood and adolescence: Problems, progress, and potential in theory and research. *Psychological Bulletin, 127*, 87–127.

Compas, B. E., & Gotlib, I. H. (2002). *Introduction to clinical psychology: Science and practice.* Boston: McGraw-Hill.

Compas, B. E., Hinden, B. R., & Gerhardt, C. A. (1995). Adolescent development: Pathways and processes of risk and resilience. *Annual Review of Psychology, 46*, 265–293.

Compas, B. E., Oppedisano, G., Connor, J. K., Gerhardt, C. A., Hinden, B. R., Achenbach, T. M., & Hammen, C. (1997). Gender differences in depressive symptoms in adolescence: Comparison of national samples of clinically referred and nonreferred youths. *Journal of Consulting and Clinical Psychology, 65*, 617–626.

Compas, B. E., Worsham, N. L., Epping-Jordan, J. E., Grant, K. E., Mireault, G., Howell, D. C., & Malcarne, V. L. (1994). When Mom or Dad has cancer: Markers of psychological distress in cancer patients, spouses, and children. *Health Psychology, 13*, 507–515.

Compas, B. E., Worsham, N. L., Ey, S., & Howell, D. C. (1996). When Mom or Dad has cancer II: Coping, cognitive appraisals, and psychological distress in children of cancer patients. *Health Psychology, 15*, 167–175.

Compton, M. T., Thompson, N. J., & Kaslow, N. J. (2005). Social environment factors associated with suicide attempt among low-income African Americans: The protective role of family relationships and social support. *Social Psychiatry and Psychiatric Epidemiology, 40*, 175–185.

Compton, S. N., March, J. S., Bretn, D., Albano, A. M., Weersing, R., & Curry, J. (2004). Cognitive-behavioral psychotherapy for anxiety and depressive disorders in children and adolescents: An evidence-based medicine review. *Journal of the American Academy of Child and Adolescent Psychiatry, 43*, 930–959.

Compton, S. N., Nelson, A. H., & March, J. S. (2000). Social phobia and separation anxiety symptoms in community and clinical samples of children and adolescents. *Journal of the American Academy of Child and Adolescent Psychiatry, 39*, 1040–1046.

Conduct Problems Prevention Research Group. (1992). A developmental and clinical model for the prevention of conduct disorder. The FAST Track Program. *Development and Psychopathology, 4*, 509–527.

Conduct Problems Prevention Research Group. (1999a). Initial impact of the fast track prevention trial for conduct problems: I. The high-risk sample. *Journal of Consulting and Clinical Psychology, 67*, 631–647.

Conduct Problems Prevention Research Group. (1999b). Initial impact of the fast track prevention trial for conduct problems: II. Classroom effects. *Journal of Consulting and Clinical Psychology, 67*, 648–657.

Conduct Problems Prevention Research Group. (2002). Evaluation of the first 3 years of the Fast Track prevention trial with children at high risk for adolescent conduct problems. *Journal of Abnormal Child Psychology, 30*, 19–35.

Conduct Problems Prevention Research Group. (2004). The effects of the fast track program on serious problem outcomes at the end of elementary school. *Journal of Clinical Child and Adolescent Psychology, 33*, 650–661.

Cone-Wesson, B. (2005). Prenatal alcohol and cocaine exposure: Influences on cognition, speech, language, and hearing. *Journal of Communication Disorders, 38*, 279–302.

Connell, A. M., & Goodman, S. H. (2002). The association between psychopathology in fathers versus mothers and children's internalizing and externalizing behavior problems: A meta-analysis. *Psychological Bulletin, 128*, 746–773.

Conners, C. K. (1990). *Conners' Teacher Rating Scales/Conners' Parent Rating Scales Manual*. North Tonawanda, NY: Multi-Health Systems, Inc.

Conners, K. C. (2000). Attention-deficit/hyperactivity disorder: Historical development and overview. *Journal of Attention Disorders, 3*, 173–191.

Conners, C. K., Epstein, J. N., March, J. S., Angold, A., Wells, K. C., Klaric, J., Swanson, J. M., Arnold, L. E., Abikoff, H. B., Elliott, G. R., Greenhill, L. L., Hechtman, L., Hinshaw, S. P., Hoza, B., Jensen, P. S., Kraemer, H. C., Newcorn, J. H., Pelham, W. E., Severe, J. B., Vitiello, B. & Wigal, T. (2001). Multimodal treatment of ADHD in the MTA: An alternative outcome analysis. *Journal of the American Academy of Child and Adolescent Psychiatry, 40*, 159–167.

Conners, C. K., March, J. S., Frances, A., Wells, K. C., & Ross, R. (2001). Treatment of attention deficit-hyperactivity disorder: Expert consensus guidelines. *Journal of Affective Disorders, 4S*, 1S–128S.

Connolly, C. (2005, March 25). Native Americans criticize Bush's silence. *Washington Post*. Retrieved September 27, 2005, from www.washingtonpost.com

Consortium on the School-based Promotion of Social Competence. (1994). The school-based promotion of social competence: Theory, research, practice, and policy. In R. J. Haggerty, L. R. Sherrod, N. Garmezy, & M. Rutter (Eds.), *Stress, risk, and resilience in children and adolescents: Processes, mechanisms, and interventions* (pp. 268–316). New York: Cambridge University Press.

Consumer Reports. (1995). Mental health: Does therapy help? *Consumer Reports*, November, 734–739.

Consumer Reports. (2004). Drugs versus talk therapy. *Consumer Reports*, October, 22–29.

Consumer Reports Best Buy Drugs. (2005a, September). Treating attention deficit hyperactivity disorder. Retrieved from http://www.crbestbuydrugs.org/drugreport_DR_ADHD.html

Consumer Reports Best Buy Drugs. (2005b September 30). Safety alert: New warning on attention-deficit drug. Retrieved from http://mg.consumerreports.org/mg/safetyalert/strattera.htm

Consumer Reports Medical Guide (2005, September 30). Safety alert: New warning on attention-deficit drug. *Consumer Reports Medical Guide*. Retrieved January 2, 2007, from www.consumerreports.org

Conte, J. R., Wolf, S., & Smith, T. (1989). What sexual offenders tell us about prevention strategies. *Child Abuse and Neglect, 13*, 293–301.

Coohey, C. (2000). The role of friends, in-laws, and other kin in father-perpetrated child physical abuse. *Child Welfare, 79*, 373–402.

Cook, M., & Mineka, S. (1989). Observational conditioning of fear to fear-relevant versus fear-irrelevant stimuli in rhesus monkeys. *Journal of Abnormal Psychology, 98*, 448–459.

Cook, W. L., & Kenny, D. A. (2004). Application of the social relations model to family assessment. *Journal of Family Psychology, 18*, 361–371.

Cormack, C., & Carr, A. (2000). Drug abuse. In A. Carr (Ed.), *What works with children and adolescents?: A critical review of psychological interventions with children, adolescents and their families* (pp. 155–177). New York: Routledge.

Cornblatt, B. A., Dworkin, R. H., Wolf, L. E., & Erlenmeyer-Kimling, L. (1996). Markers, developmental processes, and schizophrenia.

In M. F. Lenzenweger & J. J. Haugaard (Eds.), *Frontiers of developmental psychopathology* (pp. 125–147). New York: Oxford University Press.

Cornelius, M. D., Goldshmidt, L., Taylor, P. M., & Day, N. L. (1999). Prenatal alcohol use among teenagers: Effects on neonatal outcomes. *Alcoholism: Clinical and Experimental Research*, 23, 1238–1244.

Cornoldi, C., & Lucangeli, D. (2004). Arithmetic education and learning disabilities in Italy. *Journal of Learning Disabilities, 37*, 42–49.

Costello, E. J., & Angold, A. (1995). Epidemiology. In J. S. March (Ed.), *Anxiety disorders in children and adolescents* (pp. 109–124). New York: Guilford.

Costello, E. J., & Angold, A. (1996). Developmental psychopathology. In R. B. Cairns, G. H. Elder, & E. J. Costello (Eds.), *Developmental science* (pp. 168–189). New York: Cambridge University Press.

Costello, E. J., Costello, A. J., Edelbrock, C., Burns, B. J., Dulcan, M. K., Brent, D., & Janiszewski, S. (1988). Psychiatric disorders in pediatric primary care. *Archives of General Psychiatry, 45*, 1107–1116.

Costello, E. J., Erkanli, A., Federman, E., & Angold, A. (1999). Development of psychiatric comorbidity with substance abuse in adolescents: Effects of timing and sex. *Journal of Clinical Child Psychology, 28*, 298–311.

Costello, E. J., Mustillo, S., Erkanli, A., Keeler, G., & Angold, A. (2003). Prevalence and development of psychiatric disorders in childhood and adolescence. *Archives of General Psychiatry, 60*, 837–844.

Costigan, C. L., & Cox, M. J. (2001). Father's participation in family research: Is there a self-selection bias? *Journal of Family Psychology, 15*, 706–720.

Cote, S., Zoccolillo, M., Tremblay, R. E., Nagin, D., & Vitaro, F. (2001). Predicting girls' conduct disorder in adolescence from childhood trajectories of disruptive behaviors. *Journal of the American Academy of Child and Adolescent Psychiatry, 40*, 678–684.

Cottrell, D. (2003). Outcome studies of family therapy in child and adolescent depression. *Journal of Family Psychology, 25*, 406–416.

Council on Social Work Education. (1999). *Summary information on Master of Social Work programs*. Alexandria, VA. Author.

Counts, C. A., Nigg, J. T., Stawicki, J. A., Rappley, M. D., & Eye, A. V. (2005). Family adversity in *DSM-IV* ADHD combined and inattentive subtypes and associated disruptive behavior problems. *Journal of the American Academy of Child and Adolescent Psychiatry, 44*, 690–698.

Couturier, J. L., Speechley, K. N., Steele, M., Norman, R., Stringer, B., & Nicolson, R. (2005). Parental perception of sleep problems in children of normal intelligence with pervasive developmental disorders: Prevalence, severity, and pattern. *Journal of the American Academy of Child and Adolescent Psychiatry, 44*, 815–822.

Cowles, C. A., & Washburn, J. J. (2005). Psychological consultation on program design of intensive management units in juvenile correctional facilities. *Professional Psychology: Research and Practice, 36*, 44–50.

Cowen, E. L., Work, W. C., & Wyman, P. A. (1997). The Rochester Child Resilience Project (RCRP): Facts found, lessons learned, future directions divined. In S. S. Luthar, J. A. Burack,

D. Cicchetti, & J. R. Weisz (Eds.), *Developmental psychopathology: Perspectives on adjustment, risk, and disorder* (pp. 527–547). New York: Cambridge University Press.

Cowen, E. L., Wyman, P. A., Work, W. C., Kim, J. Y., Fagen, D. B., & Magnus, K. B. (1997). Follow-up study of young stress-affected and stress-resilient urban children. *Development and Psychopathology, 9*, 565–577.

Cox, D. J., Morris, J. B., Barowitz, S. M., & Sutphen, J. L. (2002). Psychological differences between children with and without chronic encopresis. *Journal of Pediatric Psychology, 27*, 585–591.

Cox, D. J., Ritterband, L. M., Quillian, W., Kovatchev, B., Morris, J., Sutphen, J., & Borowitz, S. (2003). Assessment of behavioral mechanisms maintaining encopresis: Virginia encopresis-constipation apperception test. *Journal of Pediatric Psychology, 28*, 375–382.

Cox, M. J., & Paley, B. (2003). Understanding families as systems. *Current Directions in Psychological Science, 12*, 193–196.

Coy, K., Speltz, M. L., DeKlyen, M., & Jones, K. (2001). Social-cognitive processes in preschool boys with and without oppositional defiant disorder. *Journal of Abnormal Child Psychology, 29*, 107–119.

Coyne, J. C. (1976). Toward an interactional description of depression. *Psychiatry, 39*, 28–40.

Coyne, M. D., Kame'enui, E. J., Simmons, D. C., & Harn, B. A. (2004). Beginning reading intervention as inoculation or insulin: First-grade reading performance of strong responders to kindergarten intervention. *Journal of Learning Disabilities, 37*, 90–104.

Craig, T. K. J., Bialas, I., Hodson, S., & Cox, A. D. (2004). Intergenerational transmission of somatization behaviour: 2. Observations of joint attention and bids for attention. *Psychological Medicine, 34*, 199–209.

Craighead, W. E., Smucker, M. R., Craighead, L. W., & Ilardi, S. S. (1998). Factor analysis of the Children's Depression Inventory in a community sample. *Psychological Assessment, 10*, 156–165.

Crawford, I., McLeod, A., Zamboni, B. D., & Jordan, M. B. (1999). Psychologists' attitudes toward gay and lesbian parenting. *Professional Psychology: Research and Practice, 30*, 394–401.

Creed, T. A., & Kendall, P. C. (2005). Therapist alliance-building behavior within a cognitive-behavioral treatment for anxiety in youth. *Journal of Consulting and Clinical Psychology, 73*, 498–505.

Crick, N. R., & Dodge, K. A. (1994). A review and reformulation of social information processing mechanisms in children's social adjustment. *Psychological Bulletin, 15*, 74–101.

Crick, N. R., & Zahn-Waxler, C. (2003). The development of psychopathology in females and males: Current progress and future challenges. *Development and Psychopathology, 15*, 719–742.

Crits-Christoph, P., Wilson, G. T., & Hollon, S. D. (2005). Empirically supported psychotherapies: Comment on Westen, Novotny, and Thompson-Brenner (2004). *Psychological Bulletin, 131*, 412–417.

Crockett, L. J., Randall, B. A., Shen, Y. L., Russell, S. T., & Driscoll, A. K. (2005). Measurement equivalence of the center for epidemiological studies depression scale for Latino and Anglo adolescents: A national study. *Journal of Consulting and Clinical Psychology, 73*, 47–58.

Croll, J. K., Neumark-Sztainer, D., Story, M., & Ireland, M. (2002). Prevalence and risk and protective factors related to disordered eating behaviors among adolescents: Relationship to gender and ethnicity. *Journal of Adolescent Health, 31*, 166–175.

Cronk, N. J., Slutske, W. S., Madden, P. A. F., Bucholz, K. K., & Heath, A. C. (2004). Risk for separation anxiety disorder among girls: Paternal absence, socioeconomic disadvantage, and genetic vulnerability. *Journal of Abnormal Psychology, 113*, 237–247.

Crow, T. J. (2004). Cerebral asymmetry and the lateralization of language: Core deficits in schizophrenia as pointers to the gene. *Current Opinion in Psychiatry, 17*, 97–106.

Crowley, S. L., & Emerson, E. N. (1996). Discriminant validity of self-reported anxiety and depression in children: Negative affectivity or independent constructs? *Journal of Clinical Child Psychology, 25*, 139–146.

Cruz, I. Y., & Dunn, M. E. (2003). Lowering risk for early alcohol use by challenging alcohol expectancies in elementary school children. *Journal of Consulting and Clinical Psychology, 71*, 493–503.

Crystal, D. S., Ostrander, R., Chen, R. S., & August, G. J. (2001). Multimethod assessment of psychopathology among *DSM-IV* subtypes of children with attention-deficit/hyperactivity disorder: Self-, parent, and teacher reports. *Journal of Abnormal Child Psychology, 29*, 189–205.

Cuffe, S. P., McKeown, R. E., Addy, C. L., & Garrison, C. Z. (2005). Family and psychosocial risk factors in a longitudinal epidemiological study of adolescents. *Journal of the American Academy of Child and Adolescent Psychiatry, 44*, 121–129.

Culbertson, J. L. (1998). Learning disabilities. In T. H. Ollendick & M. Hersen (Eds.), *Handbook of child psychopathology* (3rd ed., pp. 117–156). New York: Plenum Press.

Culbertson, J. L., & Schellenbach, C. J. (1992). Prevention of maltreatment in infants and young children. In D. J. Willis, E. W. Holden, & M. Rosenberg (Eds.), *Prevention of child maltreatment: Developmental and ecological perspectives* (pp. 47–77). New York: Wiley.

Cullen, F. T., Blevins, K. R., Trager, J. S., & Gendreau, P. (2005). The rise and fall of boot camps: A case study in common-sense corrections. In B. B. Benda & N. J. Pallone (Eds.), *Rehabilitation issues, problems, and prospects in boot camp* (pp. 53–70). New York: Haworth Press.

Cullinan, D. (2007). *Students with emotional and behavioral disorders: An introduction for teachers and other helping professionals* (2nd ed.). Upper Saddle River, NJ: Pearson.

Cummings, E. M., & Davies, P. (1994). *Children and marital conflict: The impact of family dispute and resolution.* New York: Guilford Press.

Cummings, E. M., Davies, P., & Campbell, S. B. (2000). *Developmental psychopathology and family process: Theory, research, and clinical implications.* New York: Guilford Press.

Cummings, E. M., Goeke-Morey, M. C., & Papp, L. M. (2004). Everyday marital conflict and child aggression. *Journal of Abnormal Child Psychology, 32*, 191–202.

Cummings, E. M., Goeke-Morey, M. C., & Raymond, J. (2004). Fathers in family context: Effects of marital quality and marital conflict. In M. E. Lamb (Ed.), *The role of the father in child development* (4th ed., pp. 196–221). Hoboken, NJ: Wiley.

Cumsille, P. E., Sayer, A. G., & Graham, J. W. (2000). Perceived exposure to peer and adult drinking as predictors of growth in positive alcohol expectancies during adolescence. *Journal of Consulting and Clinical Psychology, 68*, 531–536.

Cunningham, C. E., Boyle, M., Offord, D., Racine, Y., Hundert, J., Scord, M., & McDonald, J. (2000). Tri-ministry study: Correlates of school-based parenting course utilization. *Journal of Consulting and Clinical Psychology, 68*, 928–933.

Curry, J. F., & Reinecke, M. A. (2003). Modular therapy for adolescents with major depression. In M. A. Reinecke, F. M. Dattilio, & A. Freeman (Eds.), *Cognitive therapy with children and adolescents: A casebook for clinical practice* (2nd ed., pp. 95–127). New York: Guilford Press.

Curtis, M. J., Hunley, S. A., & Prus, J. R. (1998). *Credentialing requirements for school psychologists*. Bethesda, MD: National Association of School Psychologists Publications.

Curtis, N. M., Ronan, K. R., & Borduin, C. M. (2004). Multisystemic treatment: A meta-analysis of outcome studies. *Journal of Family Psychology, 18*, 411–419.

Curtis, W. J., & Cicchetti, D. (2003). Moving research on resilience into the 21st century: Theoretical and methodological considerations in examining the biological contributors to resilience. *Development and Psychopathology, 15*, 773–810.

Cutting, L., & Denckla, M. B. (2004). Genetic disorders and learning disabilities: Closing remarks and future research questions. *Learning Disabilities Research & Practice, 19*, 174–175.

Cytryn, L., & McKnew, D. H. (1972). Proposed classification of childhood depression. *American Journal of Psychiatry, 129*, 149–155.

Cytryn, L., & McKnew, D. H. (1979). Affective disorders. In J. Noshpitz (Ed.), *Basic handbook of child psychiatry (Vol. 2)* (pp. 300–340). New York: Basic Books.

Dadds, M. R., Spence, S. H., Holland, D. E., Barrett, P. M., & Laurens, K. R. (1997). Prevention and early intervention for anxiety disorders: A controlled trial. *Journal of Consulting and Clinical Psychology, 65*, 627–635.

Dadds, M. R., Whiting, C., Bunn, P., Fraser, J. A., Charlson, J. H., & Pirola-Merlo, A. (2004). Measurement of cruelty in children: The cruelty to animals inventory. *Journal of Abnormal Child Psychology, 32*, 321–334.

Dahlquist, L. M., & Pendley, J. S. (2005). When distraction fails: Parental anxiety and children's responses to distraction during cancer procedures. *Journal of Pediatric Psychology, 30,* 623–628.

Dakof, G. A. (2000). Understanding gender differences in adolescent drug abuse: Issues of comorbidity and family functioning. *Journal of Psychoactive Drugs, 32,* 25–32.

Dakof, G. A., Quille, T. J., Tejeda, M. J., Alberga, L. R., Bandstra, E., & Szapocznik, J. (2003). Enrolling and retaining mothers of substance-exposed infants in drug abuse treatment. *Journal of Consulting and Clinical Psychology, 71*, 764–772.

Dalgleish, T., Taghavi, R., Neshat-Doost, H., Moradi, A., Canterbury, R., & Yule, W. (2003). Patterns of processing bias for emotional information across clinical disorders: A comparison of attention, memory, and prospective cognition in children and adolescents with depression, generalized anxiety, and posttraumatic stress disorder. *Journal of Clinical Child Psychology, 32,* 10–21.

Dallam, S. J., Gleaves, D. H., Cepeda-Benito, A., Silberg, J. L., Kraemer, H. C., & Spiegel, D. (2001). The effects of child sexual abuse: Comment on Rind, Tromovitch, and Bauserman (1998). *Psychological Bulletin, 127*, 715–733.

D'Amato, R. C., Reynolds, C. R., & Fletcher-Janzen, E. (2005). *Handbook of school neuropsychology*. Hoboken, NJ: Wiley.

D'Amato, R. C., Rothlisberg, B. A., & Rhodes, R. L. (1997). Utilizing a neuropsychological paradigm for understanding common educational and psychological tests. In C. R. Reynolds & E. Fletcher-Janzen (Eds.), *Handbook of clinical child neuropsychology* (2nd ed., pp. 270–295). New York: Plenum Press.

Danquah, M. N. (1999). *Willow Weep for Me: A Black Woman's Journey through Depression*. New York: Random House.

Darkes, J., & Goldman, M. S. (1998). Expectancy challenge and drinking reduction: Process and structure in the alcohol expectancy network. *Experimental and Clinical Psychopharmacology, 6,* 64–76.

Darley, J. M., & Zanna, M. P. (2004). The hiring process in academia. In J. M. Darley, M. P. Zanna, & H. L. Roediger (Eds.). *The compleat academic: A career guide* (2nd ed., pp. 31–56). Washington, DC: American Psychological Association.

Darley, J. M., Zanna, M. P., & Roediger, H. L. (Eds.) (2004). *The compleat academic: A career guide* (2nd ed.). Washington, DC: American Psychological Association.

Darlington, R. B., Royce, J. M., Snipper, A. S., Murray, H. W., & Lazar, I. (1980). Preschool programs and later school competence of children from low-income families. *Science, 208,* 202–204.

Datcher, M. (2001). *Raising fences: A black man's love story*. New York: Riverhead Books.

Dattilio, F. M., & Jongsma, A. E. (2000). *The family therapy treatment planner*. New York: Wiley.

Davies, P. T., & Cicchetti, D. (2004). Toward an integration of family systems and developmental psychopathology approaches. *Development and Psychopathology, 16*, 477–481.

Davies, P. T., Cummings, E. M., & Winter, M. A. (2004). Pathways between profiles of family functioning, child security in the interparental subsystem, and child psychological problems. *Development and Psychopathology, 16*, 525–550.

Davila, J., Ramsay, M., Stroud, C. B., & Steinberg, S. J. (2005). Attachment as vulnerability to the development of psychopathology. In B. L. Hankin & J. R. Z. Abela (Eds.), *Development of psychopathology: A vulnerability-stress perspective* (pp. 215–242). Thousand Oaks, CA: Sage.

Davis, M. K., & Gidycz, C. A. (2000). Child sexual abuse prevention programs: A meta-analysis. *Journal of Clinical Child Psychology, 29,* 257–265.

Davis-Kean, P. E. (2005). The influence of parent education and family income on child achievement: The indirect role of parental expectations and the home environment. *Journal of Family Psychology, 19,* 294–304.

Davison, J. C., & Ford, D. Y. (2001). Perceptions of attention deficit hyperactivity disorder in one African American community. *Journal of Negro Education, 70,* 264–274.

Dawson-McClure, S. R., Sandler, I. N., Wolchik, S. A., & Millsap, R. E. (2004). Risk as a moderator of the effects of prevention programs for children from divorced families: A six-year longitudinal study. *Journal of Abnormal Child Psychology, 32,* 175–190.

Deal, L. W., Shiono, P. H., & Behrman, R. E. (1998). Children and managed health care: Analysis and recommendations. *The Future of Children, 8,* 4–24.

DeAngelis, T. (2004). Should our children be taking psychotropics? *Monitor on Psychology, 35,* 42–45.

DeAngelis, T. (2005). Shaping evidence-based practice. *Monitor on Psychology, 36,* 26–31.

Deas, D., Riggs, P., Langenbucher, J., Goldman, M., & Brown, S. (2000). Adolescents are not adults: Developmental considerations in alcohol users. *Alcoholism: Clinical and Experimental Research, 24,* 232–237.

Deas-Nesmith, D., Brady, K. T., White, R., & Campbell, S. (1999). HIV-risk behaviors in adolescent substance abusers. *Journal of Substance Abuse Treatment, 16,* 169–172.

Deater-Deckard, K. (2000). Parenting and child behavioral adjustment in early childhood: A quantitative genetic approach to studying family processes. *Child Development, 72,* 468–484.

Deater-Deckard, K., Fulker, D. W., & Plomin, R. (1999). A genetic study of the family environment in the transition to early adolescence. *Journal of Child Psychology and Psychiatry, 40,* 769–775.

Deater-Deckard, K., Scarr, S., McCartney, K., & Eisenberg, M. (1994). Paternal separation anxiety: Relationships with parenting stress, child-rearing attitudes, and maternal anxieties. *Psychological Science, 5,* 341–346.

DeBildt, A., Serra, M., Luteijn, E., Kraijer, D., Sytema, S., & Minderaa, R. (2005). Social skills in children with intellectual disabilities with and without autism. *Intellectual Disability Research, 49,* 317–328.

DeBildt, A., Sytema, S., Kraijer, D., & Minderaa, R. (2005). Prevalence of pervasive developmental disorders in children and adolescents with mental retardation. *Journal of Child Psychology and Psychiatry, 46,* 275–286.

DeBildt, A., Sytema, S., Kraijer, D., Sparro, S., & Minderaa, R. (2005). Adaptive functioning and behaviour problems in relation to level of education in children and adolescents with intellectual disability. *Intellectual Disability Research, 49,* 672–681.

de Castro, B. O., Slot, N. W., Bosch, J. D., Koops, W., & Veerman, J. W. (2003). Negative feelings exacerbate hostile attributions of intent in highly aggressive boys. *Journal of Clinical Child and Adolescent Psychology, 32,* 56–65.

Dekker, M. C., Koot, H. M., van der Ende, J., & Verhulst, F. C. (2002). Emotional and behavioral problems in children and adolescents with and without intellectual disability. *Journal of Child Psychology and Psychiatry, 43,* 1087–1098.

Dekker, M. C., & Koot, H. M. (2003). *DSM-IV* disorders in children with borderline to moderate intellectual disability. I: Prevalence and impact. *Journal of the American Academy of Child and Adolescent Psychiatry, 42,* 915–922.

Dekker, M. C., & Koot, H. M. (2003). *DSM-IV* disorders in children with borderline to moderate intellectual disability. II: Child and family predictors. *Journal of the American Academy of Child and Adolescent Psychiatry, 42,* 923–931.

Del Boca, F. K., Darkes, J., Greenbaum, P. E., & Goldman, M. S. (2004). Up close and personal: Temporal variability in the drinking of individual college students during their first year. *Journal of Consulting and Clinical Psychology, 72,* 155–164.

De Leo, D., Cerin, E., Spathonis, K., & Burgis, S. (2005). Lifetime risk of suicide ideation and attempts in an Australian community: Prevalence, suicidal process, and help-seeking behaviour. *Journal of Affective Disorders, 86,* 215–224.

De Los Reyes, A. & Kazdin, A. E. (2004). Measuring informant discrepancies in clinical child research. *Psychological Assessment, 16,* 330–334.

De Los Reyes, A. & Kazdin, A. E. (2005). Informant discrepancies in the assessment of childhood psychopathology: A critical review, theoretical framework, and recommendations for further study. *Psychological Bulletin, 131,* 483–509.

DeLucia, C., Belz, A., & Chassin, L. (2001). Do adolescent symptomatology and family environment vary over time with fluctuations in paternal alcohol impairment? *Developmental Psychology, 37,* 207–216.

Denckla, M. B., & Cutting, L. E. (2004). Genetic disorders with a high incidence of learning disabilities: Introduction to special series. *Learning Disabilities Research & Practice, 19,* 131–132.

Denham, S. A., Workman, E., Cole, P. M., Weissbrod, C., Kendziora, K. T., & Zahn-Waxler, C. (2000). Prediction of externalizing behavior problems from early to middle childhood: The role of parental socialization and emotion expression. *Development and Psychopathology, 12,* 23–45.

Dennis, M., Godley, S. H., Diamond, G., Tims, F. M., Babor, T., Donaldson, J., Liddle, H., Titus, J.C., Kaminer, Y., Webb, C., Hamilton, N. R., & Funk, R. (2004). The Cannabis Youth Treatment (CYT) Study: Main findings from two randomized trials. *Journal of Substance Abuse Treatment, 27,* 197–213.

D'Eramo, K. S., & Francis, G. (2004). Cognitive-behavioral psychotherapy. In T. L. Morris & J. S. March (Eds.), *Anxiety disorders in children and adolescents* (2nd ed., pp. 305–328). New York: Guilford Press.

Derluyn, I., Broekaert, E., Schuyten, G., & De Temmerman, E. (2004). Post-traumatic stress in former Ugandan child soldiers. *The Lancet, 363,* 861–863.

Derouin, A., & Bravender, T. (2004). Living on the edge: The current phenomenon of self-mutilation in adolescents. *MCN: The American Journal of Maternal/Child Nursing, 29,* 12–18.

Derzon, J. H., & Lipsey, M. W. (2002). A meta-analysis of the effectiveness of mass-communication for changing substance-use knowledge, attitudes, and behaviour. In W. D. Crano, & M. W. Lipsey (Eds.), *Mass media and drug prevention: Classic and contemporary theories and research* (pp. 231–258). Mahwah, NJ: Lawrence Erlbaum Associates.

Desoete, A., Roeyers, H., & DeClercq, A. (2004). Children with mathematics learning disabilities in Belgium. *Journal of Learning Disabilities, 37,* 50–61.

Dexheimer Pharris, M., Resnick, M. D., & Blum, R. W. (1997). Protecting against hopelessness and suicidality in sexually abused American Indian adolescents. *Journal of Adolescent Health, 21,* 400–406.

Diamond, G., & Josephson, A. (2005). Family-based treatment research: A 10-year update. *Journal of the American Academy of Child and Adolescent Psychiatry, 44,* 872–887.

Diamond, G. S., Reis, B. F., Diamond, G. M., Siqueland, L., & Isaacs, L. (2002). Attachment-based family therapy for depressed adolescents: A treatment development study. *Journal of the American Academy of Child and Adolescent Psychiatry, 41,* 1190–1196.

Dick, D. M., Rose, R. J., Viken, R. J., & Kaprio, J. (2000). Pubertal timing and substance use: Associations between and within families across late adolescence. *Developmental Psychology, 36,* 180–189.

Dick, D. M., & Todd, R. D. (2006). Genetic contributions. In R. T. Ammerman (Ed.), *Comprehensive handbook of personality and psychopathology: Child psychopathology (Vol 3)* (pp. 16–28). Hoboken, NJ: Wiley.

Dick, D. M., Viken, R. J., Kaprio, J., Pulkkinen, L., & Rose, R. J. (2005). Understanding the covariation among childhood externalizing symptoms: Genetic and environmental influences on conduct disorder, attention deficit hyperactivity disorder, and oppositional defiant disorder symptoms. *Journal of Abnormal Child Psychology, 33,* 219–229.

Dickson, K., Emerson, E., & Hatton, C. (2005). Self-reported antisocial behaviour: Prevalence and risk factors amongst adolescents with and without intellectual disability. *Intellectual Disability Research, 49,* 820–826.

Didden, R., Korzilius, H., van Aperlo, B., van Overloop, C., & de Vries, M. (2002). Sleep problems and daytime problem behaviours in children with intellectual disability. *Intellectual Disability Research, 46,* 537–547.

Diener, E. (2000). Subjective well-being: The science of happiness and a proposal for a national index. *American Psychologist, 55,* 34–43.

Diener, E., Oishi, S., & Lucas, R. E. (2003). Personality, culture, and subjective well-being: Emotional and cognitive evaluations of life. *Annual Review of Psychology, 54,* 403–425.

Dietz, T. L. (1998). An examination of violence and gender role portrayals in video games: Implications for gender socialization and aggressive behavior. *Sex Roles, 38,* 425–442.

Dietz, W. H. (2004). Overweight in childhood and adolescence. *New England Journal of Medicine, 350,* 855–857.

Di Lalla, L. F. (2004). (Ed.). *Behavior genetics principles: Perspectives in development, personality, and psychopathology.* Washington, DC: American Psychological Association.

Di Leo, J. H. (1973). *Children's drawings as diagnostic aids.* New York: Brunner/Mazel.

Diller, L. H. (1999a). Attention-deficit/hyperactivity disorder. *New England Journal of Medicine, 340,* 1766.

Diller, L. H. (1999b). *Running on ritalin: A physician reflects on children, society, and performance in a pill.* New York: Bantam Books.

Diller, L. H. (2003). *Should I medicate my child? Sane solutions for troubled kids with and without psychiatric drugs.* New York: Perseus Publishing.

Dilsaver, S. C., & Akiskal, H. S. (2004). Preschool-onset mania: Incidence, phenomenology and family history. *Journal of Affective Disorders, 82S,* S35–S43.

Dilsaver, S. C., & Akiskal, H. S. (2005). High rate of unrecognized bipolar mixed states among destitute Hispanic adolescents for "major depressive disorder." *Journal of Affective Disorders, 84,* 179–186.

Dilsaver, S. C., Benazzi, F., Rihmer, Z., Akiskal, K. K., & Akiskal, H. S. (2005). Gender, suicidality and bipolar mixed states in adolescents. *Journal of Affective Disorders, 87,* 11–16.

Dingfelder, S. F. (2005). Autism's smoking gun? *Monitor on Psychology, 36,* 52–53.

Dishion, T. J., French, D. C., & Patterson, G. R. (1995). The development and ecology of antisocial behavior. In D. Cicchetti & D. J. Cohen (Eds.), *Developmental psychopathology (Vol 2): Risk, disorder, and adaptation* (pp. 421–471). New York: Wiley.

Dishion, T. J., McCord, J., & Poulin, F. (1999). When interventions harm: Peer groups and problem behavior. *American Psychologist, 54,* 755–764.

Dishion, T. J., Nelson, S. E., & Yasui, M. (2005). Predicting early adolescent gang involvement from middle school adaptation. *Journal of Clinical Child and Adolescent Psychology, 33,* 62–73.

Disney, E. R., Elkins, I. J., McGue, M., & Iacono, W. G. (1999). Effects of ADHD, conduct disorder, and gender on substance use and abuse in adolescence. *American Journal of Psychiatry, 156,* 1515–1521.

Division 44. (2000). Guidelines for psychotherapy with lesbian, gay, and bisexual clients. *American Psychologist, 55,* 1440–1451.

Dixon, L., Browne, K., & Hamilton-Giachritsis, C. (2005). Risk factors of parents abused as children: A mediational analysis of the intergenerational continuity of child maltreatment (Part I). *Journal of Child Psychology and Psychiatry, 46,* 47–57.

Dixon, W. E. (2003). *Twenty studies that revolutionized child psychology.* Upper Saddle River, NJ: Prentice Hall.

Dobie, K. (2003). *The only girl in the car: A memoir.* New York: Delta Trade Paperbacks.

Dodge, K. A. (2003). Do social information-processing patterns medicate aggressive behavior? In B. B. Lahey, T. E. Moffitt, & A. Caspi (Eds.), *Causes of conduct disorder and juvenile delinquency* (pp. 254–274). New York: Guilford Press.

Dodge, K. A., & Frame, C. L. (1982). Social cognitive biases and deficits in aggressive boys. *Child Development, 53,* 620–635.

Doherty, W. J., Kouneski, E. F., & Erickson, M. F. (1998). Responsible fathering: An overview and conceptual framework. *Journal of Marriage and the Family, 60,* 277–292.

Doll, B., Zucker, S., & Brehm, K. (2004). *Resilient classrooms: Creating healthy environments for learning.* New York: Guilford Press.

Domenech-Llaberia, E., Jane, C., Canals, J., Ballespi, S., Esparo, G., & Garralda, E. (2004). Parental reports of somatic symptoms in preschool children: Prevalence and associations in a Spanish sample. *Journal of the American Academy of Child and Adolescent Psychiatry, 43,* 598–604.

Donders, J. (2005). Performance on the test of memory malingering in a mixed pediatric sample. *Child Neuropsychology, 11,* 221–227.

Donenberg, G. R., Emerson, E., Bryant, F. B., Wilson, H., & Weber-Shifrin, E. (2001). Understanding AIDS-risk behavior among adolescents in psychiatric care: Links to psychopathology and peer relationships. *Journal of the American Academy of Child and Adolescent Psychiatry, 40,* 642–653.

Donenberg, G. R., & Pao, M. (2005). Youths and HIV/AIDS: Psychiatry's role in a changing epidemic. *Journal of the American Academy of Child and Adolescent Psychiatry, 44,* 728–747.

Donenberg, G. R., & Weisz, J. R. (1997). Experimental task and speaker effects on parent-child interactions of aggressive and depressed/anxious children. *Journal of Abnormal Child Psychology, 25*, 367–387.

Donnellan, M. B., Trzesniewski, K. H., Robins, R. W., Moffitt, T. E., & Caspi, A. (2005). Low self-esteem is related to aggression, antisocial behavior, and delinquency. *Psychological Science, 16*, 328–335.

Donnerstein, E., Slaby, R. G., & Eron, L. D. (1994). The mass media and youth aggression. In L. D. Eron, J. H. Gentry, & P. Schlegel (Eds.), *Reason to hope: A psychosocial perspective on violence and youth* (pp. 219–250). Washington, DC: American Psychological Association.

Donohew, R. L., Hoyle, R. H., Clayton, R. R., Skinner, W. F., Colon, S. E., & Rice, R. E. (1999). Sensation seeking and drug use by adolescents and their friends: Models for marijuana and alcohol. *Journal of Studies on Alcohol, 60*, 622–631.

Donohue, B., Hersen, M., & Ammerman, R. T. (2000). Historical overview. In M. Hersen & R. T. Ammerman (Eds.), *Advanced abnormal child psychology* (2nd ed.) (pp. 3–14). Hillsdale, NJ: Lawrence Erlbaum Associates.

Donohue, B., & Johnston, J. (2002). Specific phobia. In M. Hersen & L. K. Porzelius (Eds.), *Diagnosis, conceptualization, and treatment planning for adults: A step-by-step guide* (pp. 133–146). Mahwah, NJ: Lawrence Erlbaum Associates.

Donovan, C. L., & Spence, S. H. (2000). Prevention of childhood anxiety disorders. *Clinical Psychology Review, 20*, 509–531.

Doss, A. J., & Weisz, J. R. (2006). Syndrome co-occurrence and treatment outcomes in youth mental health clinics. *Journal of Consulting and Clinical Psychology, 74*, 416–425.

Dorris, M. (1989). *The broken cord*. New York: Harper Perennial.

Dosen, A. (2004). The developmental psychiatric approach to aggressive behavior among persons with intellectual disabilities. *Mental Health Aspects of Developmental Disabilities, 7*, 57–68.

Dosen, A., & Day, K. (2001). Epidemiology, etiology, and presentation of mental illness and behavior disorders in persons with mental retardation. In A. Dosen, & K. Day (Eds.). *Treating mental illness and behavior disorders in children and adults with mental retardation* (pp. 3–24). Washington, DC: American Psychiatric Publishing.

Doucette, A. (2002). Child and adolescent diagnosis: The need for a model-based approach. In L. E. Beutler, & M. L. Malik (Eds.). *Rethinking the DSM: A psychological perspective* (pp. 201–220). Washington, DC: American Psychological Association.

Dougherty, L. R., Klein, D. N., & Davila, J. (2004). A growth curve analysis of the course of dysthymic disorder: The effects of chronic stress and moderation by adverse parent-child relationships and family history. *Journal of Consulting and Clinical psychology, 72*, 1012–1021.

Dowdney, L., (2000). Childhood bereavement following parental death. *Journal of Child Psychology and Psychiatry and Allied Disciplines, 41*, 819–830.

Dowdy, C. A., Patton, J. R., Smith, T. E. C., & Polloway, E. A. (1998). *Attention-deficit/hyperactivity disorder in the classroom*. Austin, TX: Pro-Ed.

Downey, D. B., & Pribesh, S. (2004). When race matters: Teachers' evaluations of students' classroom behavior. *Sociology of Education, 77*, 267–282.

Downey, G., & Coyne, J. C. (1990). Children of depressed parents: An integrative review. *Psychological Bulletin, 108*, 50–76.

Doyle, A. E., Faraone, S. V., DuPre, E. P., & Biederman, J. (2001). Separating attention deficit hyperactivity disorder and learning disabilities in girls: A familial risk analysis. *American Journal of Psychiatry, 158*, 1666–1672.

Dozier, M., Manni, M., & Lindhiem, O. (2005). Lessons from the longitudinal studies of attachment. In K. E. Grossmann, K. Grossmann, & E. Waters (Eds.), *Attachment from infancy to adulthood: The major longitudinal studies* (pp. 305–319). New York: Guilford.

Drabick, D. A. G., Gadow, K. D., Carlson, G. A., & Bromet, E. J. (2004). ODD and ADHD symptoms in Ukrainian children: External validators and comorbidity. *Journal of the American Academy of Child and Adolescent Psychiatry, 43*, 735–743.

Drabick, D. A. G., & Goldfried, M. R. (2002). Training with Boulder model: More relevant now that ever. In S. P. Shohov (Ed.), *Advances in psychology research, Vol. 9* (pp. 185–207). Hauppauge, NY: Nova Science Publishers, Inc.

Drew, C. J., Hardman, M. L., & Hart, A. W. (1996). *Designing and conducting research: Inquiry in education and social science* (2nd ed.). Boston: Allyn and Bacon.

Drotar, D. (Ed.). (2000). *Handbook of research in pediatric and clinical child psychology: Practical strategies and methods*. New York: Plenum Press.

Drotar, D., Overholser, J. C., Levin, R., Walders, N., Robinson, J. R., Palermo, T. M., & Riekert, K. A. (2000). Ethical issues in conducting research with pediatric and clinical child populations in applied settings. In D. Drotar (Ed.), *Handbook of research in pediatric and clinical child psychology* (pp. 305–326). New York: Plenum Press.

Drotar, D., Timmons-Mitchell, J., Williams, L. L., Palermo, T. M., Levi, R., Robinson, J. R., Riekert, K. A., & Walders, N. (2000). Conducting research with children and adolescents in clinical and applied settings: Practical lessons from the field. In D. Drotar (Ed.), *Handbook of research in pediatric and clinical child psychology* (pp. 261–280). New York: Plenum Press.

Dryfoos, J. G. (1997). The prevalence of problem behaviors: Implications for programs. In R. P. Weissberg, T. P. Gullotta, R. L. Hampton, B. A. Ryan, & G. R. Adams (Eds.), *Healthy children 2010: Enhancing children's wellness* (pp. 17–46). Thousand Oaks, CA: Sage.

DuBois, D. L., & Silverthorn, N. (2004). Do deviant peer associations mediate the contributions of self-esteem to problem behavior during early adolescence? A 2-year longitudinal study. *Journal of Clinical Child and Adolescent Psychology, 33*, 382–388.

Ducharme, J. M., Atkinson, L., & Poulton, L. (2000). Success-based, noncoercive treatment of oppositional behavior in children from violent homes. *Journal of the American Academy of Child and Adolescent Psychiatry, 39*, 995–1004.

Dudley-Grant, G. R. (2001). Eastern Caribbean family psychology with conduct-disordered adolescents from the Virgin Islands. *American Psychologist, 56*, 47–57.

Duhig, A. M., Phares, V., & Birkeland, R. W. (2002). Involvement of fathers in therapy: A survey of clinicians. *Professional Psychology: Research and Practice, 33,* 389–395.

Duhig, A. M., & Phares, V. (2003). Adolescents', mothers's, and fathers' perspectives of emotional and behavioral problems: Distress, control, and motivation to change: *Child and Family Behavior Therapy, 25,* 39–52.

Duke, N., Resnick, M. D., & Borrowsky, I. W. (2005). Adolescent firearm violence: Position paper of the Society for Adolescent Medicine. *Journal of Adolescent Health, 37,* 171–174.

Dumas, J. E., Nissley, J., Nordstrom, A., Smith, E. P., Prinz, R. J., & Levine, D. W. (2005). Home chaos: Sociodemographic, parenting, interactional, and child correlates. *Journal of Clinical Child and Adolescent Psychology, 34,* 93–104.

Dumont, M., & Provost, M. A. (1999). Resilience in adolescents: Protective role of social support, coping strategies, self-esteem, and social activities on experience of stress and depression. *Journal of Youth and Adolescence, 28,* 343–363.

Duncan, A. E., Neuman, R. J., Kramer, J., Kuperman, S., Hesselbrock, V., Reich, T., & Bucholz, K. K. (2005). Are there subgroups of bulimia nervosa based on comorbid psychiatric disorders? *International Journal of Eating Disorder, 37,* 19–25.

Duncan, D. F. (1996). Growing up under the gun: Children and adolescents coping with violent neighborhoods. *Journal of Primary Prevention, 16,* 343–356.

Duncan, S. C., Strycker, L. A., & Duncan, T. E. (1999). Exploring associations in developmental trends of adolescent substance use and risky sexual behavior in a high-risk population. *Journal of Behavioral Medicine, 22,* 21–34.

Dunn, D. W., & McDougle, C. J. (2001). Childhood-onset schizophrenia. In A. Breier, P. V. Tran, J. M. Herrera, G. D. Tollefson, & F. P. Bymaster (Eds.), *Current issues in the psychopharmacology of schizophrenia* (pp. 375–388). Philadelphia: Lippincott Williams & Wilkins.

Dunn, J., & Hughes, C. (2001). "I got some swords and you're dead!": Violent fantasy, antisocial behavior, friendship, and moral sensibility in young children. *Child Development, 72,* 491–505.

Dunn, J., & Plomin, R. (1990). *Separate lives: Why siblings are so different.* New York: Basic Books.

Dunn, M. E., & Goldman, M. S. (1996). Empirical modeling of an alcohol expectancy memory network in elementary school children as a function of grade. *Experimental and Clinical Psychopharmacology, 4,* 209–217.

Dunn, M. E., & Goldman, M. S. (1998). Age and drinking-related differences in the memory organization of alcohol expectancies in 3rd, 6th, 9th, and 12th grade children. *Journal of Consulting and Clinical Psychology, 66,* 579–585.

Dunn, M. E., Lau, H. C., & Cruz, I. Y. (2000). Changes in activation of alcohol expectancies in memory in relation to changes in alcohol use after participation in an expectancy challenge program. *Experimental and Clinical Psychopharmacology, 8,* 566–575.

Dunn, M. S. (2005). The relationship between religiosity, employment, and political beliefs on substance use among high school seniors. *Journal of Alcohol and Drug Education, 49,* 73–88.

DuPaul, G. J., & Eckert, T. L. (1997). The effects of school-based interventions for attention deficit hyperactivity disorder: A meta-analysis. *School Psychology Review, 26,* 5–27.

DuPaul, G. J., & Eckert, T. L. (1998). Academic interventions for students with attention deficit hyperactivity disorder: A review of the literature. *Reading and Writing Quarterly: Overcoming Learning Difficulties, 14,* 59–82.

DuPaul, G. J., Eckert, T. L., & McGoey, K. E. (1997). Interventions for students with attention deficit hyperactivity disorder: One size does not fit all. *School Psychology Review, 26,* 369–381.

DuPaul, G. J., McGoey, K. E., Eckert, T. L., & Var Brakle, J. (2001). Preschool children with attention-deficit/hyperactivity disorder: Impairments in behavioral, social, and school functioning. *Journal of the American Academy of Child and Adolescent Psychiatry, 40,* 508–515.

DuPaul, G. J., McGoey, K. E., & Mautone, J. A. (2003). Pediatric pharmacology and psychopharmacology. In M. C. Roberts (Ed.), *Handbook of pediatric psychology* (pp. 234–250). New York: Guilford Press.

DuPaul, G. J., Schaughency, E. A., Weyandt, L. L., Tripp, G., Kiesner, J., Ota, K., & Stanish, H. (2001). Self-report of ADHD symptoms in university students: Cross-gender and cross-national prevalence. *Journal of Learning Disabilities, 34,* 370–379.

DuPaul, G. J., & Stoner, G. (2004). *ADHD in the schools: Assessment and intervention strategies* (2nd ed.). New York: Guilford Press.

Durbin, C. E., Klein, D. N., Hayden, E. P., Buckley, M. E., & Moerk, K. C. (2005). Temperamental emotionality in preschoolers and parental mood disorders. *Journal of Abnormal Psychology, 114,* 28–37.

Durham, C. (2000). Evolution of services for people with autism and their families in France: Influence of the TEACCH program. *International Journal of Mental Health, 29,* 22–34.

Durlak, J. A. (1999). Meta-analytic research methods. In P. C. Kendell, J. N. Butcher, & G. N. Holmbeck (Eds.), *Handbook of research methods in clinical psychology* (2nd ed., pp. 419–429). New York: Wiley.

Durlak, J. A. (2000). Health promotion as a strategy in primary prevention. In D. Cicchetti, J. Rappaport, I. Sandler, & R. P. Weissberg (Eds.), *The promotion of wellness in children and adolescents* (pp. 221–241). Washington, DC: CWLA Press.

Durnik, M., Dougherty, J. M., Andersson, T., Persson, B., Bjorevall, G., & Emilsson, B. (2000). Influence of the TEACCH program in Sweden. *International Journal of Mental Health, 29,* 72–87.

Durston, S. (2003). A review of the biological bases of ADHD: What have we learned from imaging studies? *Mental Retardation and Development Disabilities Research Reviews, 9,* 184–195.

Durston, S., Hulshoffpol, H. E., Schnack, H. G., Kahn, R. S., & van Engeland, H. (2004). Magnetic resonance imaging of boys with attention-deficit/hyperactivity disorder and their unaffected siblings. *Journal of the American Academy of Child and Adolescent Psychiatry, 43,* 332–340.

Dusenbury, L., Brannigan, R., Hansen, W. B., Walsh, J., & Falco, M. (2005). Quality of implementation: Developing measures crucial to understanding the diffusion of preventive interventions. *Health Education Research, 20,* 308–313.

Dusenbury, L., & Falco, M. (1997). School-based drug abuse prevention strategies: From research to policy and practice. In R. P. Weissberg, T. P. Gullotta, R. L. Hampton, B. A. Ryan, & G. R. Adams (Eds.), *Healthy children 2010: Enhancing children's wellness* (pp. 47–75). Thousand Oaks, CA: Sage.

Dyck, M. J., Piek, J. P., Hay, D., Smith, L., & Hallmayer, J. (2006). Are abilities abnormally interdependent in children with autism? *Journal of Clinical Child and Adolescent Psychology, 35,* 20–33.

Dykens, E. M., & Hodapp, R. M. (2001). Research in mental retardation: Toward an etiologic approach. *Journal of Child Psychology and Psychiatry and Allied Disciplines, 42,* 49–71.

Dyregrov, A., Gjestad, R., & Raundalen, M. (2002). Children exposed to warfare: A longitudinal study. *Journal of Traumatic Stress, 15,* 59–68.

East, P. L., & Jacobson, L. J. (2001). The younger siblings of teenage mothers: A follow-up of their pregnancy risk. *Developmental Psychology, 37,* 254–264.

Eaves, L., Rutter, M., Silberg, J. L., Shillady, L., Maes, H., & Pickles, A. (2000). Genetic and environmental causes of covariation in interview assessments of disruptive behavior in child and adolescent twins. *Behavior Genetics, 30,* 321–334.

Eddy, J. M., & Chamberlain, P. (2000). Family management and deviant peer association as mediators of the impact of treatment condition on youth antisocial behavior. *Journal of Consulting and Clinical Psychology, 68,* 857–863.

Edelbrock, C. (1989). [Prevalence of externalizing behaviors]. Unpublished data, Department of Psychiatry, University of Massachusetts Medical Center, Worcester. Reported in Loeber, Lahey, & Thomas (1991).

Edelman, M. W. (1999). *Lanterns: A memoir of mentors.* Boston: Beacon Press.

Edelman, M. W. (2005). *Making poverty a priority.* Washington, DC: Children's Defense Fund.

Edwards, G. H., Barkley, R. A., Laneri, M., Fletcher, K., & Metevia, L. (2001). Parent-adolescent conflict in teenagers with ADHD and ODD. *Journal of Abnormal Child Psychology, 29,* 557–572.

Edwards, M. C., & Finney, J. W. (1994). Somatoform disorders: Psychological issues. In R. A. Olson, L. L. Mullins, J. B. Gillman, & J. M. Chaney (Eds.), *The sourcebook of pediatric psychology* (pp. 380–391). Boston: Allyn and Bacon.

Egger, H. L., Costello, E. J., & Angold, A. (2003). School refusal and psychiatric disorders: A community study. *Journal of the American Academy of Child and Adolescent Psychiatry, 42,* 797–807.

Ehntholt, K. A., Smith P. A., & Yule, W. (2005). School-based cognitive-behavioural therapy group intervention for refugee children who have experienced war-related trauma. *Clinical Child Psychology and Psychiatry, 10,* 235–250.

Ehrensaft, M. K., Cohen, P., Brown, J., Smailes, E., Chen, H., & Johnson, J. G. (2003). Intergenerational transmission of partner violence: A 20-year prospective study. *Journal of Consulting and Clinical Psychology, 71,* 741–753.

Ehringer, M. A., Rhee, S. H., Young, S., Corley, R., & Hewitt, J. K. (2006). Genetic and environmental contributions to common psychopathologies of childhood and adolescence: A study of twins and their siblings. *Journal of Abnormal Child Psychology, 34,* 1–17.

Ehrlich, S., Noam, G. G., Lyoo, I. K., Kwon, B. J., Clark, M. A. & Renshaw, P. F. (2004). White matter hyperintensities and their associations with suicidality in psychiatrically hospitalized children and adolescents. *Journal of the American Academy of Child and Adolescent Psychiatry, 43,* 770–776.

Eigsti, I., & Shapiro, T. (2003). A systems neuroscience approach to Autism: Biological, cognitive, and clinical perspectives. *Mental Retardation and Developmental Disabilities Research Reviews, 9,* 206–216.

Eisen, A. R., & Schaefer, C. E. (2005). *Separation anxiety in children and adolescents: An individualized approach to assessment and treatment.* New York: Guilford Press.

Eisenberg, M. E., & Wechsler, H. (2003). Social influences on substance-use behaviors of gay, lesbian, and bisexual college students. *Social Science & Medicine, 57,* 1913–1923.

Eisenberg, N., Spinrad, T. L., & Cumberland, A. (1998). The socialization of emotion: Reply to commentaries. *Psychological Inquiry, 9,* 317–333.

Eisenhower, A. S., Baker, B. L., & Blacher, J. (2005). Preschool children with intellectual disability: Syndrome specificity, behaviour problems, and maternal well-being. *Intellectual Disability Research, 49,* 657–671.

Eisler, I., Dare, C., Hodes, M., Russell, G., Dodge, E., & LeGrange, D. (2000). Family therapy for adolescent anorexia nervosa: The results of a controlled comparison of two family interventions. *Journal of Child Psychology and Psychiatry and Allied Disciplines, 41,* 727–736.

Elbaum, B., & Vaughn, S. (2003). For which students with learning disabilities are self-concept interventions effective? *Journal of Learning Disabilities, 36,* 101–108.

Elder, C., Leaver-Dunn, D., Wang, M. Q., Nagy, S., & Green, L. (2000). Organized group activity as a protective factor against adolescent substance use. *American Journal of Health Behavior, 24,* 108–113.

Eley, T. C. (1997). Depressive symptoms in children and adolescents: Etiological links between normality and abnormality: A research note. *Journal of Child Psychology and Psychiatry, 38,* 861–865.

Eley, T. C., & Gregory, A. M. (2004). Behavioral genetics. In T. L. Morris & J. S. March (Eds.), *Anxiety disorders in children and adolescents* (2nd ed., pp. 71–97). New York: Guilford Press.

Eley, T. C., & Stevenson, J. (1999). Exploring the covariation between anxiety and depression symptoms: A genetic analysis of the effects of age and sex. *Journal of Child Psychology and Psychiatry, 40,* 1273–1282.

Elias, M. J., & Clabby, J. F. (1989). *Social decision making skills: A curriculum guide for the elementary grades.* Rockville, MD: Aspen.

Elias, M. J., & Clabby, J. F. (1991). *School-based enhancement of children and adolescents' social problem solving skills.* San Francisco: Jossey-Bass.

Elias, M. J., Parker, S., & Rosenblatt, J. L. (2005). Building educational opportunity. In S. Goldstein & R. B. Brooks (Eds.), *Handbook of resilience in children* (pp. 315–336). New York: Kluwer Academic/Plenum.

Eliez, S., & Reiss, A. L. (2000). MRI neuroimaging of childhood psychiatric disorders: A selective review. *Journal of Child Psychology and Psychiatry and Allied Disciplines, 41,* 679–694.

Elizur, Y., & Perednik, R. (2003). Prevalence and description of selective mutism in immigrant and native families: A controlled study. *Journal of the American Academy of Child and Adolescent Psychiatry, 42*, 1451–1459.

Elkin, T. D., Tye, V. L., Hudson, M., & Crom, D. (1998). Participation in sports by long-term survivors of childhood cancer. *Journal of Psychosocial Oncology, 16*, 63–73.

Elliott, S. N., Busse, R. T., & Shapiro, E. S. (1999). Intervention techniques for academic performance problems. In C. R. Reynolds & T. B. Gutkin (Eds.), *The handbook of school psychology* (3rd ed., pp. 664–685). New York: Wiley.

Ellis, B. J. (2004). Timing of pubertal maturation in girls: An integrated life history approach. *Psychological Bulletin, 130*, 920–958.

Elphinstone, P. (2004). MMR and autism: The debate continues. *Lancet, 363*, 569.

El-Sheikh, M., & Buckhalt, J. A. (2003). Parental problem drinking and children's adjustment: Attachment and family functioning as moderators and mediators of risk. *Journal of Family Psychology, 17*, 510–520.

El-Sheikh, M., & Whitson, S. A. (2006). Longitudinal relations between marital conflict and child adjustment: Vagal regulation as a protective factor. *Journal of Family Psychology, 20*, 30–39.

Else-Quest, N. M., Hyde, J. S., Goldsmith, H. H., & van Hulle, C. A. (2006). Gender differences in temperament: A meta-analysis. *Psychological Bulletin, 132*, 33–72.

Embry, L. E., Vander Stoep, A., Evens, C., Ryan, K. D., & Pollock, A. (2000). Risk factors for homelessness in adolescents released from psychiatric residential treatment. *Journal of the American Academy of Child and Adolescent Psychiatry, 39*, 1293–1299.

Emerson, E. (2005). Poverty and children with intellectual disabilities in the world's richer countries. *Journal of Intellectual & Developmental Disability, 29*, 319–338.

Emerson, E., Robertson, J., & Wood, J. (2005). Emotional and behavioural needs of children and adolescents with intellectual disabilities in an urban conurbation. *Intellectual Disability Research, 49*, 16–24.

Emery, R. E., & Laumann-Billings, L. (1998). An overview of the nature, causes, and consequences of abusive family relationships: Toward differentiating maltreatment and violence. *American Psychologist, 53*, 121–135.

Emery, R. E., Laumann-Billings, L., Waldron, M. C., Sbarra, D. A., & Dillon, P. (2001). Child custody mediation and litigation: Custody, contact, and coparenting 12 years after initial dispute resolution. *Journal of Consulting and Clinical Psychology, 69*, 323–332.

Emshoff, J., Avery, E., Raduka, G., & Anderson, D. J. (1996). Findings from Super Stars: A health promotion program for families to enhance multiple protective factors. *Journal of Adolescent Research, 11*, 68–96.

Emslie, G. J., Hughes, C. W., Crismon, M. L., Lopez, M., Pliszka, S., Toprac, M. G., & Boemer, C. (2004). A feasibility study of the childhood depression medication algorithm: The Texas children's medication algorithm project (CMAP). *Journal of the American Academy of Child and Adolescent Psychiatry, 43*, 519–527.

Emslie, G. J., Rush, A. J., Weinberg, W. A., Gullion, C. M., Rintelmann, J., & Hughes, C. W. (1997). Recurrence of major depressive disorder in hospitalized children and adolescents. *Journal of the American Academy of Child and Adolescent Psychiatry, 36*, 785–792.

Emslie, G. J., Weinberg, W. A., Kennard, B. D., & Kowatch, R. A. (1994). Neurobiological aspects of depression in children and adolescents. In W. M. Reynolds & H. F. Johnston (Eds.), *Handbook of depression in children and adolescents* (pp. 143–165). New York: Plenum Press.

Engels, R. C. M. E., Knibbe, R. A., DeVries, H., Drop, M. J., & Van Breukelen, G. J. P. (1999). Influences of parental and best friends' smoking and drinking on adolescent use: A longitudinal study. *Journal of Applied Social Psychology, 29*, 337–361.

Epstein, J. N., Willoughby, M., Valencia, E. Y., Tonev, S. T., Abikoff, H. B., Arnold, L. E., & Hinshaw, S. P. (2005). The role of children's ethnicity in the relationship between teacher ratings of attention-deficit/hyperactivity disorder and observed classroom behavior. *Journal of Consulting and Clinical Psychology, 73*, 424–434.

Epstein, L. H. (2003). Development of evidence-based treatment for pediatric obesity. In A. E. Kazdin & J. R. Weisz (Eds.), *Evidence-based psychotherapies for children and adolescents* (pp. 374–388). New York: Guilford.

Erath, S. A., Bierman, K. L., and the Conduct Problems Prevention Research Group. (2006). Aggressive marital conflict, maternal harsh punishment, and child aggressive-disruptive behavior: Evidence for direct and mediated relations.. *Journal of Family Psychology, 20*, 217–226.

Erba, H. W. (2003). Early intervention programs for children with autism: Conceptual frameworks for implementation. In M. E. Hertzig, & E. A. Farber (Eds.), *Annual progress in child psychiatry and child development: 2000–2001* (pp. 433–453). New York: Brunner-Routledge.

Erienmeyer-Kimling, L., Hans, S., Ingraham, L., Marcus, J., Wynne, L., Rehman, A., Roberts, S. A., & Auerbach, J. (2005). Handedness in children of schizophrenic parents: Data from three high-risk studies. *Behavior Genetics, 35*, 351–358.

Erlenmeyer-Kimling, L., Roberts, S. A., & Rock, D. (2004). Longitudinal prediction of schizophrenia in a prospective high-risk study. In L. F. DiLalla (Eds.), *Behavior genetics principles: Perspectives in development, personality, and psychopathology* (pp. 135–144). Washington, DC: American Psychological Association.

Evans, B., & Lee, B. K. (1998). Culture and child psychopathology. In S. S. Kazarian & D. R. Evans (Eds.), *Cultural clinical psychology: Theory, research, and practice* (pp. 289–315). New York: Oxford University Press.

Evans, D. L., Foa, E. B., Gur, R. E., Hendin, H., O'Brien, C. P., Seligman, M. E. P., & Walsh, B. T. (Eds.). (2005). *Treating and preventing adolescent mental health disorders: What we know and what we don't know*. New York: Oxford University Press.

Evans, D. L., & Seligman, M. E. P. (2005). Introduction. In D. L. Evans, E. B. Foa, R. E. Gur, H. Hendin, C. P. O'Brien, M. E. P. Seligman, & B. T. Walsh (Eds.), *Treating and preventing adolescent mental health disorders: What we know and what we don't know* (pp. xxv–xl). New York: Oxford University Press.

Evans, D. W., Canavera, K., Kleinpeter, F. L., Maccubbin, E., & Taga, K. (2005). The fears, phobias and anxieties of children with autism spectrum disorders and Down syndrome: Comparisons with developmentally and chronologically age matched children. *Child Psychiatry and Human Development, 36*, 3–26.

Evans, D. W., & Gray, F. L. (2000). Compulsive-like behavior in individuals with Down syndrome: Its relation to mental age level, adaptive and maladaptive behavior. *Child Development, 71*, 288–300.

Evans, G. D., & Rey, J. (2001). In the echoes of gunfire: Practicing psychologists' responses to school violence. *Professional Psychology: Research and Practice, 32*, 157–164.

Evans, G. W. (2004). The environment of childhood poverty. *American Psychologist, 59*, 77–92.

Evans, G. W., Gonnella, C., Marcynyszyn, L. A., Gentile, L., & Salpekar, N. (2005). The role of chaos in poverty and children's socioemotional adjustment. *Psychological Science, 16*, 560–565.

Evans, H. L., & Sullivan, M. A. (1993). Children and the use of self-monitoring, self-evaluation, and self-reinforcement. In A. J. Finch, W. M. Nelson, & E. S. Ott (Eds.), *Cognitive-behavioral procedures with children and adolescents: A practical guide* (pp. 67–89). Boston: Allyn and Bacon.

Evans, W. D., Finkelstein, E. A., Kamerow, D. B., & Renaud, J. M. (2005). Public perceptions of childhood obesity. *American Journal of Preventive Medicine, 28*, 26–32.

Ezpeleta, L., Keeler, G., Alaatin, E., Costello, E. J., & Angold, A. (2001). Epidemiology of psychiatric disability in childhood and adolescence. *Journal of Child Psychology and Psychiatry, 42*, 901–914.

Fabry, B. D., Reitz, A. L., & Luster, W. C. (2002). Community treatment of extremely troublesome youth with dual mental health/mental retardation diagnoses: A data based case study. *Education & Treatment of Children, 25*, 339–355.

Fairburn, C. G., Stice, E., Cooper, Z., Doll, H. A., Norman, P. A., & O'Connor, M. E. (2003). Understanding persistence in bulimia nervosa: A 5-year naturalistic study. *Journal of Consulting and Clinical Psychology, 71*, 103–109.

Fales, C. L., Knowlton, B. I., Holyoak, K. J., Geschwind, D. H., Swerdloff, R. S., & Gonzalo, I. G. (2003). Working memory and relational reasoning in Klinefelter syndrome. *Journal of the International Neurophychological Society, 9*, 839–846.

Fals-Stewart, W., Kelly, M. L., Fincham, F. D., Golden, J., & Logsdon, T. (2004). Emotional and behavioral problems of children living with drug-abusing fathers: Comparisons with children living with alcohol-abusing and non-substance-abusing fathers. *Journal of Family Psychology, 18*, 319–330.

Fantuzzo, J., Grim, S., Mordell, M., McDermott, P., Miller, L., & Coolahan, K. (2001). A multivariate analysis of the Revised Conners' Teacher Rating Scale with low-income, urban preschool children. *Journal of Abnormal Child Psychology, 29*, 141–152.

Faraone, S. V. (2000). Attention deficit hyperactivity disorder in adults: Implications for theories of diagnosis. *Current Directions in Psychological Science, 9*, 33–36.

Faraone, S. V., & Biederman, J. (2000). Nature, nurture, and attention deficit hyperactivity disorder. *Developmental Review, 20*, 568–581.

Faraone, S. V., Biederman, J., Feighner, J. A., & Monuteaux, M. C. (2000). Assessing symptoms of attention deficit hyperactivity disorder in children and adults: Which is more valid? *Journal of Consulting and Clinical Psychology, 68*, 830–842.

Faraone, S. V., Biederman, J., Lehman, B. K., Spencer, T., Norman, D., Seidman, L. J., Kraus, H., Perrin, J., Chen, W. J., & Tsuang, M. T. (1993). Intellectual performance and school failure in children with attention deficit hyperactivity disorder and in their siblings. *Journal of Abnormal Psychology, 102*, 616–623.

Faraone, S. V., Monuteaux, M. C., Biederman, J., Cohan, S. L., & Mick, E. (2003). Does parental ADHD bias maternal reports of ADHD symptoms in children? *Journal of Consulting and Clinical Psychology, 71*, 168–175.

Farmer, A. (2004). Bad luck and bad genes in depression. In L. F. Di Lalla (Ed.), *Behavior genetics principles: Perspectives in development, personality, and psychopathology* (pp. 107–121). Washington, DC: American Psychological Association.

Farrell, A. D., Kung, E. M., White, K. S., & Valois, R. F. (2000). The structure of self-reported aggression, drug use, and delinquent behaviors during early adolescence. *Journal of Clinical Child Psychology, 29*, 282–292.

Farrell, A. D., Meyer, A. L., Kung, E. M., & Sullivan, T. N. (2001). Development and evaluation of school-based violence prevention programs. *Journal of Clinical Child Psychology, 30*, 207–220.

Farrell, A. D., Meyer, A. L., & White, K. S. (2001). Evaluation of responding in peaceful and positive ways (RIPP): A school-based prevention program for reducing violence among urban adolescents. *Journal of Clinical Child Psychology, 30*, 451–463.

Farrington, D. P. (2005). The importance of child and adolescent psychopathy. *Journal of Abnormal Child Psychology, 33*, 489–497.

Farrow, J. A., Watts, D. H., Krohn, M. A., & Olson, H. C. (1999). Pregnant adolescents in chemical dependency treatment: Description and outcomes. *Journal of Substance Abuse Treatment, 16*, 157–161.

Faulkner, R. A., & Davey, M. (2002). Children and adolescents of cancer patients: The impact of cancer on the family. *American Journal of Family Therapy, 30*, 63–72.

Favaro, A., Zanetti, T., Huon, G., & Santonastaso, P. (2005). Engaging teachers in an eating disorder preventive intervention. *International Journal of Eating Disorders, 38*, 73–77.

Favaro, A., Zanetti, T., Tenconi, E., Degortes, D., Ronzan, A., Veronese, A., & Santonastaso, P. (2005). The relationship between temperament and impulsive behaviors in eating disordered subjects. *Eating Disorders: The Journal of Treatment & Prevention, 13*, 61–70.

Federal Drug Administration. (2004, October 15). FDA launches a multi-pronged strategy to strengthen safeguards for children treated with antidepressant medications. Retrieved from http://www.fda.gov/bbs/topics/news/2004/NEW01124.html

Federal Drug Administration. (2004, October 28). Labeling change request letter for antidepressant medications. Retrieved from http://www.fda.gov/cder/drug/antidepressants/SSRIlabelChange.htm

Feinberg, M. E., & Hetherington, E. M. (2000). Sibling differentiation in adolescence: Implications for behavioral genetic theory. *Child Development, 71*, 1512–1524.

Feinberg, M. E., Neiderhiser, J. M., Simmens, S., Reiss, D., & Hetherington, E. M. (2000). Sibling comparison of differential parental treatment in adolescence: Gender, self-esteem, and emotionality as mediators of the parenting-adjustment association. *Child Development, 71*, 1611–1628.

Feinfield, K. A., & Baker, B. L. (2004). Empirical support for a treatment program for families of young children with externalizing problems. *Journal of Clinical Child and Adolescent Psychology, 33*, 182–195.

Feldman, R., Keren, M., Gross-Rozval, O., & Tyano, S. (2004). Mother-child touch patterns in infant feeding disorders: Relation to maternal, child, and environmental factors. *Journal of the American Academy of Child and Adolescent Psychiatry, 43*, 1089–1097.

Felner, R. D., Favazza, A., Shim, M., Brand, S., Gu, K., & Noonan, N. (2001). Whole school improvement and restructuring as prevention and promotion: Lessons from STEP and the project on High Performance Learning Communities. *Journal of School Psychology, 39*, 177–202.

Felner, R. D., Felner, T. Y., & Silverman, M. M. (2000). Prevention in mental health and social intervention: Conceptual and methodological issues in the evolution of the science and practice of prevention. In J. Rappaport, J. & E. Seidman (Eds.), *Handbook of community psychology* (pp. 9–42). New York: Kluwer Academic/Plenum Press.

Felner, R. D., Ginter, M., & Primavera, J. (2002). Primary prevention during school transitions: Social support and environmental structure. In T. A. Revenson, A. R. D, Augelli, S. E. French, D. L. Hughes, & D. Livert (Eds.), *A quarter century of community psychology: Readings from the American Journal of Community Psychology* (pp. 147–161). New York: Kluwer Academic/Plenum Press.

Ferber, R. (1985). *Solve your child's sleep problems*. New York: Simon and Schuster.

Ferdinand, R. F., van der Ende, J., & Verhulst, F. C. (2004). Parent-adolescent disagreement regarding psychopathology in adolescents from the general population as a risk factor for adverse outcome. *Journal of Abnormal Psychology, 113*, 198–206.

Ferdinand, R. F., Visser, J. H., Hoogerheide, K. N., van der Ende, J., Kasius, M. C., Koot, H. M., & Verhulst, F. C. (2004). Improving estimation of the prognosis of childhood psychopathology: Combination of DSM-IIIR/DISC diagnoses and CBCL scores. *Journal of Child Psychology and Psychiatry, 45*, 599–608.

Fergusson, D. M., & Horwood, L. J. (2002). Male and female offending trajectories. *Development and Psychopathology, 14*, 159–177.

Fergusson, D. M., & Horwood, L. J. (2003). Resilience to childhood adversity: Results of a 21-year study. In S. S. Luthar (Ed.), *Resilience and vulnerability: Adaptation in the context of childhood adversities* (pp. 130–155). New York: Cambridge University Press.

Fergusson, D. M., Horwood, L. J., & Ridder, E. M. (2005). Show me the child at seven: The consequences of conduct problems in childhood for psychosocial functioning in adulthood. *Journal of Child Psychology and Psychiatry, 46*, 837–849.

Fergusson, D. M., Horwood, L. J., & Ridder, E. M. (2005). Show me the child at seven II: Childhood intelligence and later outcomes in adolescence and young adulthood. *Journal of Child Psychology and Psychiatry, 46*, 850–858.

Fergusson, D. M., Wanner, B., Vitaro, F., Horwood, L. J., & Swain-Campbell, N. (2003). Deviant peer affiliations and depression: Confounding or causation? *Journal of Abnormal Child Psychology, 31*, 605–618.

Ferrando, P. J., & Lorenzo-Seva, U. (2005). IRT-Related factor analytic procedures for testing the equivalence of paper-and-pencil and internet-administered questionnaires. *Psychological Methods, 10*, 193–205.

Ferri, B. A., & Connor, D. J. (2005). In the shadow of Brown: Special education and overrepresentation of students of color. *Remedial and Special Education, 26*, 93–100.

Fewster, G. (2002). The DSM IV you, but not IV me. *Child & Youth Care Forum, 31*, 365–380.

Field, T. M. (2000). Infants of depressed mothers. In S. L. Johnson & A. M. Hayes (Eds.), *Stress, coping, and depression* (pp. 3–22). Mahwah, NJ: Lawrence Erlbaum Associates.

Filho, A. G. C., Bodanese, R., Silva, T. L., Alvares, J. P., Aman, M., & Rohde, L. A. (2005). Comparison of risperidone and methylphenidate for reducing ADHD symptoms in children and adolescents with moderate mental retardation. *Journal of the American Academy of Child and Adolescent Psychiatry, 44*, 748–755.

Filipek, P. A. (1999). Neuroimaging in the developmental disorders: The state of the science. *Journal of Child Psychology and Psychiatry, 40*, 113–128.

Finch, A. J., Nelson, W. M., & Moss, J. H. (1993). Childhood aggression: Cognitive-behavioral therapy strategies and interventions. In A. J. Finch, W. M. Nelson, & E. S. Ott (Eds.), *Cognitive-behavioral procedures with children and adolescents: A practical guide* (pp. 148–205). Boston: Allyn and Bacon.

Findling, R. L., McNamara, N. K., Youngstrom, E. A., Stansbrey, R., Gracious, B. L., Reed, M. D., & Calabrese, J. R. (2005). Double-blind 18-month trial of lithium versus divalproex maintenance treatment in pediatric bipolar disorder. *Journal of the American Academy of Child and Adolescent Psychiatry, 44*, 409–417.

Fine, S. E., Weissman, A., Gerdes, M., Pinto-Martin, J., Zackai, E. H., McDonald-McGinn, D. M., & Emanuel, B. S. (2005). Autism spectrum disorders and symptoms in children with molecularly confirmed 22q 11.2 deletion syndrome. *Journal of Autism and Developmental Disorders, 35*, 461–470.

Fink, C. M. (1990). Special education students at risk: A comparative study of delinquency. In P. E. Leone (Ed.), *Understanding troubled and troubling youth* (pp. 61–81). Newbury Park, CA: Sage.

Finkelhor, D. (1988). The trauma of sexual abuse: Two models. In G. E. Wyatt & G. J. Powell (Eds.), *Lasting effects of child sexual abuse* (pp. 61–82). Newbury Park, CA: Sage.

Finkelhor, D., Asdigian, N., & Dziuba-Leatherman, J. (1995). The effectiveness of victimization prevention instruction: An evaluation of children's responses to actual threats and assaults. *Child Abuse and Neglect, 19*, 141–153.

Finkelhor, D., Ormrod, R., Turner, H., & Hamby, S. L. (2005). The victimization of children and youth: A comprehensive, national survey. *Child Maltreatment, 10*, 5–25.

Finney, J. W., & Miller, K. M. (1999). Children of parents with medical illness. In W. K. Silverman & T. H. Ollendick (Eds.), *Developmental issues in the clinical treatment of children* (pp. 433–442). Boston: Allyn and Bacon.

First, M. B. (2002). The DSM-IV Text Revision: Rationale and potential impact on clinical practice. *Psychiatric Services, 53*, 288–292.

Fischer, M., Barkley, R. A., Smallish, L., & Fletcher, K. (2005). Executive functioning in hyperactive children as young adults:

Attention, inhibition, response perseveration, and the impact of comorbidity. *Developmental Neuropsychology, 27,* 107–133.

Fisher, C. B. (2003). *Decoding the ethics code: A practical guide for psychologists.* Thousand Oaks, CA: Sage.

Fisher, C. B. (2005). Commentary: SES, ethnicity, and goodness-of-fit in clinician-parent communication during pediatric cancer trials. *Journal of Pediatric Psychology, 30,* 231–234.

Fisher, C. B. (2004). Informed consent and clinical research involving children and adolescents: Implications of the revised APA ethics code and HIPAA. *Journal of Clinical Child and Adolescent Psychology, 33,* 832–839.

Fisher, C. B., & Fried, A. L. (2003). Internet-mediated psychological services and the American Psychological Association Ethics Code. *Psychotherapy: Theory, Research, Practice, Training, 40,* 103–111.

Fisher, C. B., Hatashita-Wong, M., & Greene, L. I. (1999). Ethical and legal issues. In W. K. Silverman & T. H.Ollendick (Eds.), *Developmental issues in the clinical treatment of children* (pp. 470–486). Boston: Allyn and Bacon.

Fisher, C. B., Hoagwood, K., Boyce, C., Duster, T., Frank, D. A., Grisso, T., Levine, R. J., Macklin, R., Spencer, M. B., Takanishi, R., Trimble, J. E., & Zayas, L. H. (2002). Research ethics for mental health science involving ethnic minority children and youths. *American Psychologist, 57,* 1024–1040.

Fisher, J. D., & Fisher, W. A. (1994). *People like us-Revised (video).* The AIDS Risk Reduction Projects at the University of Connecticut and the University of Western Ontario. Original copyright 1992 Storrs, CT: The University of Connecticut.

Fisher, J. D., Fisher, W. A., Bryan, A. D., & Misovich, S. J. (2002). Information-motivation-behavioral skills model-based HIV risk behavior change intervention for inner-city high school youth. *Health Psychology, 21,* 177–186.

Fisher, P. A., Gunnar, M. R., Chamberlain, P., & Reid, J. B. (2000). Preventive intervention for maltreated preschool children: Impact on children's behavior, neuroendocrine activity, and foster parent functioning. *Journal of the American Academy of Child and Adolescent Psychiatry, 39,* 1356–1364.

Fitzgerald, M. (1999). Criteria for Asperger's disorder. *Journal of the American Academy of Child and Adolescent Psychiatry, 38,* 1071.

Fitzpatrick, K. M. (1997). Fighting among America's youth: A risk and protective factors approach. *Journal of Health and Social Behavior, 38,* 131–148.

Flanagan, D. P., & Mascolo, J. T. (2005). Psychoeducational assessment and learning disability diagnosis. In D. P. Flanagan & P. L. Harrison (Eds.), *Contemporary intellectual assessment: Theories, tests, and issues* (2nd ed.) (pp. 521–544). New York: Guilford Press.

Flanagan, R., Miller, J. A., & Jacob, S. (2005). The 2002 Revision of the American Psychological Association's Ethics Code: Implications for school psychologists. *Psychology in the Schools, 42,* 433–445.

Flannery, D. J., Williams, L. L., & Vazsonyi, A. T. (1999). Who are they with and what are they doing? Delinquent behavior, substance use, and early adolescents' after-school time. *American Journal of Orthopsychiatry, 69,* 247–253.

Flannery-Schroeder, E. C. (2004). Generalized anxiety disorder. In T. L. Morris & J. S. March (Eds.), *Anxiety disorders in children and adolescents* (2nd ed.) (pp. 125–140). New York: Guilford Press.

Fleming, J. E., Cook, T. D., & Stone, C. A. (2002). Interactive influences of perceived social contexts on the reading achievement of urban middle schoolers with learning disabilities. *Learning Disabilities Research & Practice, 17,* 47–64.

Fleming, J. E., & Offord, D. R. (1990). Epidemiology of childhood depressive disorders: A critical review. *Journal of the American Academy of Child and Adolescent Psychiatry, 29,* 571–580.

Fleming, K. (2000). *The boy with the thorn in his side: A memoir.* New York: Perennial.

Fletcher, A. C., & Jefferies, B. C. (1999). Parental mediators of associations between perceived authoritative parenting and early adolescent substance use. *Journal of Early Adolescence, 19,* 465–487.

Fletcher, J. M., Coulter, W. A., Reschly, D. J., & Vaughn, S. (2004). Alternative approaches to the definition and identification of learning disabilities: Some questions and answers. *Annals of Dyslexia, 54,* 304–331.

Fletcher, J. M., Francis, D. J., Morris, R. D., & Lyon, G. R. (2005). Evidence-based assessment of learning disabilities in children and adolescents. *Journal of Clinical Child and Adolescent Psychology, 34,* 506–522.

Fletcher, K. E. (2003). Childhood posttraumatic stress disorder. In E. J. Mash, & B. A. Barkley (Eds.), *Child psychopathology* (2nd ed.), (pp. 330–371). New York: Guilford Press.

Fling, E. R. (1999). *Eating an artichoke: A mother's perspective on Asperger's syndrome.* Philadelphia: Jessica Kingsley.

Flisher, A. J. (1999). Annotation: Mood disorder in suicidal children and adolescents: Recent developments. *Journal of Child Psychology and Psychiatry, 40,* 315–324.

Flisher, A. J., Kramer, R. A., Grosser, R. C., Alegria, M., Bird, H. R., Bourdon, K. H., Goodman, S. H., Greenwald, S., Horwitz, S. M., Moore, R. E., Narrow, W. E., & Hoven, C. W. (1997). Correlates of unmet need for mental health services by children and adolescents. *Psychological Medicine, 27,* 1145–1154.

Flisher, A. J., Kramer, R. A., Hoven, C. W., Greenwald, S., Alegria, M., Bird, H. R., Canino, G., Connell, R., & Moore, R. E. (1997). Psychosocial characteristics of physically abused children and adolescents. *Journal of the American Academy of Child and Adolescent Psychiatry, 36,* 123–131.

Flory, K., Lynam, D., Milich, R., Leukefeld, C., & Clayton, R. (2004). Early adolescent through young adult alcohol and marijuana use trajectories: Early predictors, young adult outcomes, and predictive utility. *Development and Psychopathology, 16,* 193–213.

Flouri, E. (2005). *Fathering and child outcomes.* Hoboken, NJ: Wiley.

Foa, E. B., Johnson, K. M., Feeny, N. C., & Treadwell, K. R. H. (2001). The child PTSD symptom scale: A preliminary examination of its psychometric properties. *Journal of Clinical Child Psychology, 30,* 376–384.

Foa, E. B., Keane, T. M., & Friedman, M. J. (Eds.) (2004). *Effective treatments for PTSD: Practice guidelines from the International Society for Traumatic Stress Studies.* New York: Guilford.

Fogas, B. S., Oesterheld, J. R., & Shader, R. I. (2001). A retrospective study of children's perceptions of participation as clinical research subjects in a minimal risk study. *Journal of Developmental & Behavioral Pediatrics, 22,* 211–216.

Foley, D. L., Pickles, A., Maes, H. M., Silberg, J. L., & Eaves, L. J. (2004). Course and shortterm outcomes of separation anxiety disorder in a community sample of twins. *Journal of the American Academy of Child and Adolescent Psychiatry, 43,* 1107–1114.

Foley, D. L., Pickles, A., Simonoff, E., Maes, H. H., Silberg, J. L., Hewitt, J. K. & Eaves, L. J. (2001). Parental concordance and comorbidity for psychiatric disorder and associate risks for current psychiatric symptoms and disorders in a community sample of juvenile twins. *Journal of Child Psychology and Psychiatry and Allied Disciplines, 42,* 381–394.

Fombonne, E. (2003). The prevalence of autism. *Journal of the American Medical Association, 289,* 87–89.

Foot, H. C., Morgan, M. J., & Shute, R. H. (1990). *Children helping children.* New York: Wiley.

Ford, T., Goodman, R., & Meltzer, H. (2004). The relative importance of child, family, school and neighbourhood correlates of childhood psychiatric disorder. *Social Psychiatry and Psychiatric Epidemiology, 39,* 487–496.

Forehand, R., Biggar, H., & Kotchick, B. A. (1998). Cumulative risk across family stressors: Short- and long-term effects for adolescents. *Journal of Abnormal Child Psychology, 26,* 119–128.

Forehand, R., & Jones, D. J. (2003). Neighborhood violence and coparent conflict: Interactive influence on child psychosocial adjustment. *Journal of Abnormal Child Psychology, 31,* 591–604.

Forman, E. M., & Davies, P. T. (2003). Family instability and young adolescent maladjustment: The mediating effects of parenting quality and adolescent appraisals of family security. *Journal of Clinical Child and Adolescent Psychology, 32,* 94–105.

Fortune, S. A., & Hawton, K. (2005). Deliberate self-harm in children and adolescents: A research update. *Current Opinion in Psychiatry, 18,* 401–406.

Fournier, C. J., & Rae, W. A. (1999). Psychoeducational family therapy. In D. M. Lawson & F. F. Prevatt (Eds.), *Casebook in family therapy* (pp. 310–326). Belmont, CA: Wadsworth.

Fox, N. A., Henderson, H. A., Marshall, P. J., Nichols, K. E., & Ghera, M. M. (2005). Behavioral inhibition: Linking biology and behavior within a developmental framework. *Annual Review of Psychology, 56,* 235–262.

Foxcroft, D. (2005). International Center for alcohol policies (ICAP)'s latest report on alcohol education: A flawed peer review process. *Addiction, 100,* 1066–1068.

Foxx, R. M., Schreck, K. A., Garito, J., Smith, A., & Weisenberger, S. (2004). Replacing the echolalia of children with autism with functional use of verbal labeling. *Journal of Developmental and Physical Disabilities, 16,* 307–320.

Frame, C. L., Johnstone, B., & Giblin, M. S. (1988). Dysthymia. In M. Hersen & C. G. Last (Eds.), *Child behavior therapy casebook* (pp. 71–83). New York: Plenum Press.

Francis, D. J., Fletcher, J. M., Stuebing, K. K., Lyon, G. R., Shaywitz, B. A., & Shaywitz, S. E. (2005). Psychometric approaches to the identification of LD: IQ and achievement scores are not sufficient. *Journal of Learning Disabilities, 38,* 98–108.

Frank, R. G., McDaniel, S. H., Bray, J. H., & Heldring, M. (2003). *Primary care psychology.* Washington, DC: American Psychological Association.

Frank, S. J., Poorman, M. O., VanEgeren, L. A., & Field, D. T. (1997). Perceived relationships with parents among adolescent inpatients with depressive preoccupations and depressed mood. *Journal of Clinical Child Psychology, 26,* 205–215.

Franklin, M. E., Rynn, M., Foa, E. B., & March, J. S. (2003). Treatment of obsessive-compulsive disorder. In M. A. Reinecke, F. M. Dattilio, & A. Freeman (Eds.), *Cognitive therapy with children and adolescents: A casebook for clinical practice* (2nd ed., pp. 162–188). New York: Guilford Press.

Franko, D. L., & Striegel-Moore, R. H. (2002). The role of body dissatisfaction as a risk factor for depression in adolescent girls: Are differences Black and White? *Journal of Psychosomatic Research, 53,* 975–983.

Fraser, M. W. (2004). *Risk and resilience in childhood: An ecological perspective* (2nd ed.). Washington, DC: National Association of Social Workers Press.

Frauenglass, S., Routh, D. K., Pantin, H. M., & Mason, C. A. (1997). Family support decreases influence of deviant peers on Hispanic adolescents' substance use. *Journal of Clinical Child Psychology, 26,* 15–23.

Freeman, J. B., Garcia, A. M., Miller, L. M., Dow, S. P., & Leonard, H. L. (2004). Selective mutism. In T. L. Morris & J. S. March (Eds.), *Anxiety disorders in children and adolescents* (2nd ed., pp. 280–301). New York: Guilford Press.

Freeman, M. (2004). Mental health impacts of HIV/AIDS on children. *Journal of Child and Adolescent Mental Health, 16,* iii–iv.

Fremont, W. P. (2004). Childhood reactions to terrorism-induced trauma: A review of the past 10 years. *Journal of the American Academy of Child and Adolescent Psychiatry, 43,* 381–392.

Freud, S. (1894/1962). *Standard edition of the complete psychological works of Sigmund Freud* (Vol 3.). London: Hogarth.

Frick, P. J. (1998a). Conduct disorders. In T. H. Ollendick & M. Hersen (Eds.), *Handbook of child psychopathology* (3rd ed., pp. 213–237). New York: Plenum Press.

Frick, P. J. (1998b). *Conduct disorders and severe antisocial behavior.* New York: Plenum Press.

Frick, P. J. (2004). Integrating research on temperament and childhood psychopathology: Its pitfalls and promise. *Journal of Clinical Child and Adolescent Psychology, 33,* 2–7.

Frick, P. J., Cornell, A. H., Barry, C. T., Bodin, S. D., & Dane, H. E. (2003). Callous-unemotional traits and conduct problems in the prediction of conduct problem severity, aggression, and self-report of delinquency. *Journal of Abnormal Child Psychology, 31,* 457–470.

Frick, P. J., Lahey, B. B., Loeber, R., Tannenbaum, I. E., VanHorn, Y., Christ, M. A. G., Hart, E. L., & Hanson, K. (1993). Oppositional defiant disorder and conduct disorder: A meta-analytic review of factor analyses and cross-validation in a clinic sample. *Clinical Psychology Review, 13,* 319–340.

Frick, P. J., & Loney, B. R. (1999). Outcomes of children and adolescents with oppositional defiant disorder and conduct disorder. In H. C. Quay & A. E. Hogan (Eds.), *Handbook of disruptive behavior disorders* (pp. 507–524). New York: Kluwer Academic/Plenum Press.

Frick, P. J., & Loney, B. R. (2000). The use of laboratory and performance-based measures in the assessment of children and adolescents with conduct disorders. *Journal of Clinical Child Psychology, 29,* 540–554.

Frick, P. J., & Morris, A. S. (2004). Temperament and developmental pathways to conduct problems. *Journal of Clinical Child and Adolescent Psychology, 33,* 54–68.

Frick, P. J., Stickle, T. R., Dandreaux, D. M., Farrell, J. M., & Kimonis, E. R. (2005). Callous-unemotional traits in predicting the severity and stability of conduct problems and delinquency. *Journal of Abnormal Child Psychology, 33,* 471–487.

Friedman, A. G., Latham, S. A., & Dahlquist, L. M. (1998). Childhood cancer. In T. H. Ollendick & M. Hersen (Eds.), *Handbook of child psychopathology* (3rd ed., pp. 435–461). New York: Plenum Press.

Frisby, C. L., & Reynolds, C. R. (2005). *Comprehensive handbook of multicultural school psychology.* Hoboken, NJ: Wiley.

Fritz, G., Rockney, R., Bernet, W., Arnold, V., Beitchman, J., Benson, R. S., Bukstein, O., Kinlan, J., McClellan, J., Rue, D., Shaw, J. A., Stock, S., Work Group on Quality Issues, & Kroeger-Ptakowski, K. (2004). Practice parameter for the assessment and treatment of children and adolescents with enuresis. *Journal of the American Academy of Child and Adolescent Psychiatry, 43,* 1540–1550.

Fromm-Reichmann, F. (1948). Notes on the development of treatment of schizophrenics by psychoanalytic psychotherapy. *Psychiatry, 11,* 263–273.

Frontline Documentary. (1993, October 19). *Prisoners of silence.* Written, produced, and directed by Jon Palfreman. Corporation for Public Broadcasting.

Frye, A. A., & Garber, J. (2005). The relations among maternal depression, maternal criticism, and adolescents' externalizing and internalizing symptoms. *Journal of Abnormal Child Psychology, 33,* 1–11.

Fuchs, L. S. (2005). Prevention research in mathematics: Improving outcomes, building identification models, and understanding disability. *Journal of Learning Disabilities, 38,* 350–352.

Fuchs, L. S., & Fuchs, D. (2002). Mathematical problem-solving profiles of students with mathematics disabilities with and without comorbid reading disabilities. *Journal of Learning Disabilities, 35,* 564–571.

Fuemmeler, B. F. (2004). Bridging disciplines: An introduction to the special issue on public health and pediatric psychology. *Journal of Pediatric Psychology, 29,* 405–414.

Fuligni, A. J. (1998). The adjustment of children from immigrant families. *Current Directions in Psychological Science, 7,* 99–103.

Fuligni, A. J., Tseng, V., & Lam, M. (1999). Attitudes toward family obligations among American adolescents with Asian, Latin American, and European backgrounds. *Child Development, 70,* 1030–1044.

Gadow, K. D., DeVincent, C. J., Pomeroy, J., & Azizian, A. (2004). Psychiatric symptoms in preschool children with PDD and clinic and comparison samples. *Journal of Autism and Developmental Disorders, 34,* 379–393.

Gadow, K. D., DeVincent, C. J., Pomeroy, J., & Azizian, A. (2005). Comparison of DSM-IV symptoms in elementary school-age children with PDD versus clinic and community samples. *Autism, 9,* 392–415.

Gadow, K. D., Drabick, D. A. G., Loney, J., Sprafkin, J., Salisbury, H., Azizian, A., & Schwartz, J. (2004). Comparison of ADHD symptom subtypes as source-specific syndromes. *Journal of Child Psychology and Psychiatry, 45,* 1135–1149.

Gadow, K. D., Nolan, E. E., Litcher, L., Carlson, G. A., Panina, N., Golovakha, E., Sprafkin, J., & Bromet, E. J. (2000). Comparison of attention-deficit/hyperactivity disorder symptoms subtypes in Ukrainian school children. *Journal of the American Academy of Child and Adolescent Psychiatry, 39,* 1520–1527.

Galaburda, A. M. (2005). Neurology of learning disabilities: What will the future bring? The answer comes from the successes of the recent past. *Learning Disability Quarterly, 28,* 107–109.

Gallo, C. L., & Pfeffer, C. R. (2003). Children and adolescents bereaved by a suicidal death: Implications for psychosocial outcomes and interventions. In R. A. King, & A. Apter (Eds.), *Suicide in children and adolescents* (pp. 294–312). New York: Cambridge University Press.

Gallucci, N. T. (1997). On the identification of patterns of substance abuse with the MMPI-A. *Psychological Assessment, 9,* 224–232.

Ganiban, J., Barnett, D., & Cicchetti, D. (2000). Negative reactivity and attachment: Down syndrome's contribution to the attachment-temperament debate. *Development and Psychopathology, 12,* 1–21.

Garb, H. N., Wood, J. M., Lilienfeld, S. O., & Nezworski, M. T. (2002). Effective use of projective techniques in clinical practice: Let the data help with selection and interpretation. *Professional Psychology: Research and Practice, 33,* 454–463.

Garber, B. D. (2004). Directed co-parenting intervention: Conducting child-centered interventions in parallel with highly conflicted co-parents. *Professional Psychology: Research and Practice, 35,* 55–64.

Garber, J., Braafladt, & Weiss, B. (1995). Affect regulation in depressed and nondepressed children and young adolescents. *Development and Psychopathology, 7,* 93–115.

Garber, J., & Carter, J. S. (2006). Major depression. In R. T. Ammerman (Ed.), *Comprehensive handbook of personality and psychopathology: Child psychopathology (Vol 3)* (pp. 165–216). Hoboken, NJ: Wiley.

Garber, J., & Kaminski, K. M. (2000). Laboratory and performance-based measures of depression in children and adolescents. *Journal of Clinical Child Psychology, 29,* 509–525.

Gardner, W., Pajer, K. A., Kelleher, K. J., Scholle, S. H., & Wasserman, R. LC. (2002). Child sex differences in primary care clinicians' mental health care of children and adolescents. *Archives of Pediatric Adolescent Medicine, 156,* 454–459.

Gardner, W., Kelleher, K. J., Pajer, K., & Campo, J. V. (2004). Follow-up care of children identified with ADHD by primary care clinicians: A prospective cohort study. *Journal of Pediatrics, 145,* 767–771.

Garmezy, N. (1974). The study of competence in children at risk for severe psychopathology. In E. J. Anthony & C. Koupernik (Eds.), *The child in his family: Children at psychiatric risk* (pp. 77–97). New York: Wiley.

Garnefski, N. (2000). Age differences in depressive symptoms, antisocial behavior, and negative perceptions of family, school, and peers among adolescents. *Journal of the American Academy of Child and Adolescent Psychiatry, 39,* 1175–1181.

Garner, D. M., & Bemis, K. M. (1982). A cognitive-behavioral approach to anorexia nervosa. *Cognitive Therapy and Research, 6,* 123–150.

Garner, D. M., & Myerholtz, L. E. (1998). Eating disorders. In T. Ollendick (Ed.), *Comprehensive clinical psychology (Vol. 5)* (pp. 591–628). Kidlington, Oxford: Elsevier Science Ltd.

Garralda, M. E., & Rangel, L. A. D. (1999). Somatoform disorders and chronic physical illness. In H. C. Steinhausen & F. C. Verhulst (Eds.), *Risks and outcomes in developmental psychopathology* (pp. 231–249). New York: Oxford University Press.

Garrison, C. Z., Waller, J. L., Cuffe, S. P., McKeon, R. E., Addy, C. L., & Jackson, K. L. (1997). Incidence of major depressive disorder and dysthymia in young adolescents. *Journal of the American Academy of Child and Adolescent Psychiatry, 36*, 458–465.

Gau, S. S. F., Chong, M. Y., Chen, T. H. H., & Cheng, A. T. A. (2005). A 3-year panel study of mental disorders among adolescents in Taiwan. *American Journal of Psychiatry, 162*, 1344–1350.

Gaub, M., & Carlson, C. L. (1997). Gender differences in ADHD: A meta-analysis and critical review. *Journal of the American Academy of Child and Adolescent Psychiatry, 36*, 1036–1045.

Gaylor, E. E., Burnham, M. M., Goodlin-Jones, B. L., & Anders, T. F. (2005). A longitudinal follow-up study of young children's sleep patterns using a developmental classification system. *Behavioral Sleep Medicine, 3*, 44–61.

Gaylor, E. E., Goodlin-Jones, B. L., & Anders, T. F. (2001). Classification of young children's sleep problems: A pilot study. *Journal of the American Academy of Child and Adolescent Psychiatry, 40*, 61–67.

Gaynor, S. T., Weersing, V. R., Kolko, D. J., Birmaher, B., Heo, J., & Brent, D. A. (2003). The prevalence and impact of large sudden improvements during adolescent therapy for depression: A comparison across cognitive-behavioral, family, and supportive therapy. *Journal of Consulting and Clinical Psychology, 71*, 386–393.

Geary, D. C. (2004). Mathematics and learning disabilities. *Journal of Learning Disabilities, 37*, 4–15.

Geffken, G. R., Pincus, D. B., & Zelikovsky, N. (1999). Obsessive compulsive disorder in children and adolescents: Review of background, assessment, and treatment. *Journal of Psychological Practice, 5*, 15–31.

Geisinger, K. F. (2000). Psychological testing at the end of the millennium: A brief historical review. *Professional Psychology: Research and Practice, 31*, 117–118.

Gelhorn, H. L., Stallings, M. C., Young, S. E., Corley, R. P., Rhee, S. H., & Hewitt, J. K. (2005). Genetic and environmental influences on conduct disorder: Symptom, domain and fullscale analyses. *Journal of Child Psychology and Psychiatry, 46*, 580–591.

Geller, B., Craney, J. L., Bolhofner, K., Nickelsburg, M. J., Williams, M., & Zimerman, B. (2002). Two-year prospective follow-up of children with a prepubertal and early adolescent bipolar disorder phenotype. *American Journal of Psychiatry, 159*, 927–933.

Geller, B., & DelBello, M. (2003). *Bipolar disorder in childhood and early adolescence*. New York: Guilford Press.

Geller, B., Zimerman, B., Williams, M., DelBello, M. P., Bolhofner, K., Craney, J. L., Frazier, J., Beringer, L., & Nickelsburg, M. J. (2002). *DSM-IV* mania symptoms in a prepubertal and early adolescent bipolar disorder phenotype compared to attention-deficit hyperactive and normal controls. *Journal of Child and Adolescent Psychopharmacology, 12*, 11–25.

Geller, D. A., Hoog, S. L., Heiligenstein, J. H., Ricardi, R. K., Tamura, R., Kluszynski, S., & Jacobson, J. G. (2001). Fluoxetine treatment for obsessive-compulsive disorder in children and adolescents: A placebo-controlled clinical trial. *Journal of the American Academy of Child and Adolescent Psychiatry, 40*, 773–779.

Gencoz, T., Voelz, Z. R., Gencoz, F., Pettit, J. W., & Joiner, T. E. (2001). Specificity of information processing styles to depressive symptoms in youth psychiatric inpatients. *Journal of Abnormal Child Psychology, 29*, 255–262.

Gerber, P. J., & Popp, P. A. (1999). Consumer perspectives on the collaborative teaching model: Views of students with and without LD and their parents. *Remedial and Special Education, 20*, 288–296.

Gernsbacher, M. A., Dawson, M., & Goldsmith, H. H. (2005). Three reasons not to believe in an autism epidemic. *Current Directions in Psychological Science, 14*, 55–58.

Gerrard, M., Gibbons, F. X., Zhao, L., Russell, D. W., & Reis-Bergan, M. (1999). The effect of peers' alcohol consumption on parental influence: A cognitive mediational model. *Journal of Studies on Alcohol, Supplement 13*, 32–44.

Gershoff, E. T. (2002). Corporal punishment by parents and associated child behaviors and experiences: A meta-analytic and theoretical review. *Psychological Bulletin, 128*, 539–544.

Gersten, R., Jordan, N. C., & Flojo, J. R. (2005). Early identification and interventions for students with mathematics difficulties. *Journal of Learning Disabilities, 38*, 293–304.

Geschwind, D. H., & Dykens, E. (2004). Neurobehavioral and psychosocial issues in Klinefelter syndrome. *Learning Disabilities Research & Practice, 19*, 166–173.

Ghaderi, A., Martensson, M., & Schwan, H. (2005). "Everybody's different": A primary prevention program among fifth grade school children. *Eating Disorders: The Journal of Treatment & Prevention, 13*, 245–259.

Ghaziuddin, M. (2005). A family history study of Asperger syndrome. *Journal of Autism and Developmental Disorders, 35*, 177–182.

Ghaziuddin, N., Kutcher, S. P., Knapp, P., Bernet, W., Arnold, V., Beitchman, J., Benson, R. S., Bukstein, O., Kinlan, J., McClellan, J., Rue, D., Shaw, J. A., Stock, S., Work Group on Quality Issues, & Kroeger-Ptakowski, K. (2004). Practice parameter for use of electroconvulsive therapy with adolescents. *Journal of the American Academy of Child and Adolescent Psychiatry, 43,*, 1521–1539.

Ghesquiere, P., & Ruijssenaars, A. J. J. M. (1998). Does categorical special education make sense? The Flemish special education system in the international debate. *British Journal of Developmental Disabilities, 44*, 53–63.

Giaconia, R. M., Reinherz, H. Z., Hauf, A. C., Paradis, A. D., Wasserman, M. S., & Langhammer, D. M. (2000). Comorbidity of substance use and post-traumatic stress disorders in a community sample of adolescents. *American Journal of Orthopsychiatry, 70*, 253–262.

Gibb, B. E., & Alloy, L. B. (2006). A prospective test of the hopelessness theory of depression in children. *Journal of Clinical Child and Adolescent Psychology, 35*, 264–274.

Giedd, J. N., Rapoport, J. L., Garvey, M. A., Perlmutter, S., & Swedo, S. E. (2000). MRI assessment of children with obsessive-compulsive disorder or tics associated with streptococcal infection. *American Journal of Psychiatry, 15*, 281–283.

Gifford-Smith, M., Dodge, K. A., Dishion, T. J., & McCord, J. (2005). Peer influence in children and adolescents: Crossing the bridge from developmental to intervention science. *Journal of Abnormal Child Psychology, 33,* 255–265.

Gil, K. M., Carson, J. W., Porter, L. S., Ready, J., Valrie, C., Redding-Lallinger, R., & Daeschner, C. (2003). Daily stress and mood and their association with pain, health-care use, and school activity in adolescents with sickle cell disease. *Journal of Pediatric Psychology, 28,* 363–373.

Gilbert, S. C., Keery, H., & Thompson, J. K. (2005). The media's role in body image and eating disorders. In E. Cole & J. H. Daniel (Eds.), *Featuring females: Feminist analyses of media* (pp. 41–56). Washington, DC: American Psychological Association.

Gillberg, C., & Cederlund, M. (2005). Asperger syndrome: Familial and pre- and perinatal factors. *Journal of Autism and Developmental Disorders, 35,* 159–166.

Gillham, J. E., Hamilton, J., Freres, D. R., Patton, K., & Gallop, R. (2006). Preventing depression among early adolescents in the primary care setting: A randomized controlled study of the Penn Resiliency Program. *Journal of Abnormal Child Psychology, 34,* 203–219.

Gilligan, C. (1993). *In a different voice: Psychological theory and women's development.* Cambridge, MA: Harvard University Press.

Gilvarry, E. (2000). Substance abuse in young people. *Journal of Child Psychology and Psychiatry, 41,* 55–80.

Ginsburg, G. S., Albano, A. M., Findling, R. L., Kratochvil, C. & Walkup, J. (2005). Integrating cognitive behavioral therapy and pharmacotherapy in the treatment of adolescent depression. *Cognitive and Behavioral Practice, 12,* 252–262.

Ginsburg, G. S., & Silverman, W. K. (2000). Gender role orientation and fearfulness in children with anxiety disorders. *Journal of Anxiety Disorders, 14,* 57–67.

Gladwell, M. (1998). Do parents matter? *The New Yorker,* August 17, 54–65.

Glaros, A. G., & Epkins, C. C. (2003). Habit disorders: Bruxism, trichotillomania, and tics. In M. C. Roberts (Ed.), *Handbook of pediatric psychology* (3rd ed., pp. 561–577). New York: Guilford Press.

Glaser, D. (2000). Child abuse and neglect and the brain—A review. *Journal of Child Psychology and Psychiatry, 41,* 97–116.

Glaser, K. (1968). Masked depression in children and adolescents. In S. Chess and A. Thomas (Eds.), *Annual progress in child psychiatry and child development (Vol. 1)* (pp. 345–355). New York: Brunner/Mazel.

Glaze, D. G., Rosen, C. L., & Owens, J. A. (2002). Toward a practical definition of pediatric insomnia. *Current Therapeutic Research, 63,* B4–B17.

Gliner, J. A., Morgan, G. A., & Harmon, R. J. (2000). Single-subject designs. *Journal of the American Academy of Child and Adolescent Psychiatry, 39,* 1327–1329.

Goetting, A. (1994). The parenting-crime connection. *Journal of Primary Prevention, 14,* 169–186.

Golan, M., & Crow, S. (2004). Targeting parents exclusively in the treatment of childhood obesity: Long-term results. *Obesity Research, 12,* 357–361.

Goldman, M. S. (1999). Risk for substance abuse: Memory as a common etiological pathway. *Psychological Science, 10,* 196–198.

Goldman, M. S., & Darkes, J. (2004). Alcohol expectancy multiaxial assessment: A memory network-based approach. *Psychological Assessment, 16,* 4–15.

Goldstein, S., & Brooks, R. B. (2005) (Eds.). *Handbook of resilience in children.* New York: Kluwer Academic/Plenum Press.

Goldstein, S., & Rider, R. (2005). Resilience and the disruptive disorders of childhood. In S. Goldstein & R. B. Brooks (Eds.), *Handbook of resilience in children* (pp. 203–222). New York: Kluwer Academic/Plenum Press.

Goldstein, S., & Schwebach, A. J. (2004). The comorbidity of pervasive developmental disorder and attention deficit hyperactivity disorder: Results of a retrospective chart review. *Journal of Autism and Developmental Disorders, 34,* 329–339.

Goldston, D. B., Daniel, S. S., Reboussin, B. A., Reboussin, D. M., Frazier, P. H., & Harris, A. E. (2001). Cognitive risk factors and suicide attempts among formerly hospitalized adolescents: A prospective naturalistic study. *Journal of the American Academy of Child and Adolescent Psychiatry, 40,* 91–99.

Gonzalek-Tejera, G., Canino, G., Ramirez, R., Chavez, L., Shrout, P., Bird, H., Bravo, M., Martinez-Taboas, A., Ribera, J., & Bauermeister, J. (2005). Examining minor and major depression in adolescents. *Journal of Child Psychology and Psychiatry, 46,* 888–899.

Goodman, G. (2002). *The internal world and attachment.* Hillsdale, NJ: Analytic Press.

Goodman, S. H. (2003). Genesis and epigenesis of psychopathology in children with depressed mothers: Toward an integrative biopsychosocial perspective. In D. Cicchetti & E. Walker (Eds.), *Neurodevelopmental mechanisms in psychopathology* (pp. 428–460). New York: Cambridge University Press.

Goodman, S. H., & Gotlib, I. H. (Eds.). (2002a). *Children of depressed parents: Mechanisms of risk and implications for treatment.* Washington, DC: American Psychological Association.

Goodman, S. H., & Gotlib, I. H. (2002b). Transmission of risk to children of depressed parents: Integration and conclusions. In S. H. Goodman & I. Gotlib (Eds.), *Children of depressed parents: Mechanisms of risk and implications for treatment* (pp. 307–326). Washington, DC: American Psychological Association.

Goodman, S. H., Hoven, C. W., Narrow, W. E., Cohen, P., Fielding, B., Alegria, M., Leaf, P. J., Kandel, D., Horwitz, S. M., Bravo, M., Moore, R., & Dulcan, M. K. (1998). Measurement of risk for mental disorders and competence in a psychiatric epidemiologic community survey: The National Institute of Mental Health Methods for the Epidemiology of Child and Adolescent Mental Disorders (MECA) study. *Social Psychiatry, 33,* 162–173.

Goodman, S. H., Lahey, B. B., Fielding, B., Dulcan, M., Narrow, W., & Regier, D. (1997). Representativeness of clinical samples of youths with mental disorders: A preliminary population-based study. *Journal of Abnormal Psychology, 106,* 3–14.

Goodman, S. H., Schwab-Stone, M., Lahey, B. B., Shaffer, D., & Jensen, P. S. (2000). Major depression and dysthymia in children and adolescents: Discriminant validity and differential consequences in a community sample. *Journal of the American Academy of Child and Adolescent Psychiatry, 39*, 761–770.

Goodwin, R. D., Fergusson, D. M., & Horwood, L. J. (2005). Childhood abuse and familial violence and the risk of panic attacks and panic disorder in young adulthood. *Psychological Medicine, 35*, 881–890.

Goodyer, I. M., Wright, C., & Altham, P. (1990). Recent achievements and adversities in anxious and depressed school age children. *Journal of Child Psychology and Psychiatry and Allied Disciplines, 31*, 1063–1077.

Gordon, E. F. (2000). *Mockingbird years: A life in and out of therapy.* New York: Basic Books.

Gordon, R. A., Savage, C., Lahey, B. B., Goodman, S. H., Jensen, P. S., Rubio-Stipec, M., & Hoven, C. W. (2003). Family and neighborhood income: Additive and multiplicative associations with youths' well-being. *Social Science Research, 32*, 191–219.

Gore, S., Aseltine, R. H., & Colton, M. E. (1993). Gender, social-relational involvement, and depression. *Journal of Research on Adolescence, 3*, 101–125.

Gore, S. A., Vander Wal, J. S., & Thelen, M. H. (2001). Treatment of eating disorders in children and adolescents. In J. K. Thompson, & L. Smolak (Eds.), *Body image, eating disorders, and obesity in youth: Assessment, prevention, and treatment* (pp. 293–311). Washington, DC: American Psychological Association.

Goreczny, A. J., & Hersen, M. (1999). *Handbook of pediatric and adolescent health psychology.* Boston: Allyn and Bacon.

Gorman, D. M. (2005). Does measurement dependence explain the effects of the life skills training program on smoking outcomes? *Preventive Medicine: An International Journal Devoted to Practice and Theory, 40*, 479–487.

Gorman-Smith, D., Tolan, P. H., Henry, D. B., & Florsheim, P. (2000). Patterns of family functioning and adolescent outcomes among urban African American an Mexican American families. *Journal of Family Psychology, 14*, 436–457.

Gormley, W. T., Gayer, T., Phillips, D. & Dawson, B. (2005). The effects of universal Pre-K on cognitive development. *Developmental Psychology, 41*, 1–13.

Gosling, S. D., Vazire, S., Srivastava, S., & John, O. P. (2004). Should we trust web-based studies? A comparative analysis of six preconceptions about internet questionnaires. *American Psychologist, 59*, 93–104.

Gothelf, D., Apter, A., Brand-Gothelf, A., Offer, N., Ofek, H., Tano, S., & Pfeffer, C. R. (1998). Death concepts in suicidal adolescents. *Journal of the American Academy of Child and Adolescent Psychiatry, 37*, 1279–1286.

Gottesman, I. I. (1991). *Schizophrenia genesis: The origins of madness.* New York: Freeman.

Gottesman, I. I., & Gould, T. D. (2003). The endophenotype concept in psychiatry: Etymology and strategic intentions. *American Journal of Psychiatry, 160*, 636–645.

Gould, M. S., Greenberg, T., Velting, D. M., & Shaffer, D. (2003). Youth suicide risk and preventive interventions: A review of the past 10 years. *Journal of the American Academy of Child and Adolescent Psychiatry, 42*, 386–405.

Gould, M. S., Velting, D., Kleinman, M., Lucas, C., Thomas, J. G., & Chung, M. (2004). Teenager's attitudes about coping strategies and help-seeking behavior for suicidality. *Journal of the American Academy of Child and Adolescent Psychiatry, 43*, 1124–1133.

Graetz, B. W., Sawyer, M. G., & Baghurst, P. (2005). Gender differences among children with *DSM-IV* ADHD in Australia. *Journal of the American Academy of Child and Adolescent Psychiatry, 44*, 159–168.

Graham, H. (2005). Intellectual disabilities and socioeconomic inequalities in health: An overview of research. *Journal of Applied Research in Intellectual Disabilities, 18*, 101–111.

Graham, S. (1992). "Most of the subjects were white and middle class": Trends in published research on African Americans in selected APA journals, 1979–1989. *American Psychologist, 47*, 629–639.

Granillo, T., Jones-Rodriguez, G., & Carvajal, S. C. (2005). Prevalence of eating disorders in Latina adolescents: Associations with substance use and other correlates. *Journal of Adolescent Health, 36*, 214–220.

Grant, K. E., & Compas, B. E. (1995). Stress and anxious-depressed symptoms among adolescents: Searching for mechanisms of risk. *Journal of Consulting and Clinical Psychology, 63*, 1015–1021.

Grant, K. E., Compas, B. E., Stuhlmacher, A. F., Thurm, A. E., McMahon, S. D., & Halpert, J. A. (2003). Stressors and child and adolescent psychopathology: Moving from markers to mechanisms of risk. *Psychological Bulletin, 129*, 447–466.

Grant, K. E., Katz, B. N., Thomas, K. J., O'Koon, J. H., Meza, C. M., DiPasquale, A., Rodriguez, V. O., & Bergen, C. (2004). Psychological symptoms affective low-income urban youth. *Journal of Adolescent Research, 19*, 613–634.

Gray, K. M., & Mohr, C. (2004). Mental health problems in children and adolescents with intellectual disability. *Current Opinion in Psychiatry, 17*, 365–370.

Green, A. H. (1991). Child neglect. In R. T. Ammerman & M. Hersen (Eds.), *Case studies in family violence* (pp. 135–152). New York: Plenum Press.

Green, J. (1999). *The velveteen father: An unexpected journey to parenthood.* New York: Ballantine.

Green, J., Kroll, L., Imrie, D., Frances, F. M., Begum, K., Harrison, L., & Anson, R. (2001). Health gain and outcome predictors during inpatient and related day treatment in child and adolescent psychiatry. *Journal of the American Academy of Child and Adolescent Psychiatry, 40*, 325–332.

Greenbaum, P. E., Del Boca, F., Darkes, J., Wang, C. P., & Goldman, M. S. (2005). Variation in the drinking trajectories of freshmen college students. *Journal of Consulting and Clinical Psychology, 73*, 229–238.

Greenberg, M. T., Weissberg, R. P., O'Brien, M. U., Zins, J. E., Fredericks, L., Resnik, H., & Elias, M. J. (2003). Enhancing school-based prevention and youth development through coordinated social, emotional, and academic learning. *American Psychologist, 58*, 466–474.

Greenberger, E., Chen, C., Tally, S. R., & Dong, Q. (2000). Family, peer, and individual correlates of depressive symptomatology among

U.S. and Chinese adolescents. *Journal of Consulting and Clinical Psychology, 68,* 209–219.

Greene, R. W. (1995). Students with ADHD in school classrooms: Teacher factors related to compatibility, assessment, and intervention. *School Psychology Review, 24,* 81–93.

Greene, R. W. (1996). Students with attention-deficit hyperactivity disorder and their teachers: Implications of a goodness-of-fit perspective. In T. H. Ollendick & R. J. Prinz (Eds.), *Advances in clinical child psychology (Vol. 18)* (pp. 205–230). New York: Plenum Press.

Greene, R. W. (2006). Oppositional defiant disorder. In R. T. Ammerman (Ed.), *Comprehensive handbook of personality and psychopathology: Child psychopathology (Vol 3)* (pp. 285–298). Hoboken, NJ: Wiley.

Greene, R. W., & Ablon, J. S. (2001). What does the MTA study tell us about effective psychosocial treatment for ADHD? *Journal of Clinical Child Psychology, 30,* 114–121.

Greene, R. W., Ablon, J. S., Goring, J. C., Raezer-Blakely, L., Markey, J., Monuteaux, M. C., Henin, A., Edwards, G., & Rabbitt, S. (2004). Effectiveness of collaborative problem solving in affectively dysregulated children with oppositional-defiant disorder: Initial findings. *Journal of Consulting and Clinical Psychology, 72,* 1157–1164.

Greene, R. W., Beszterczey, S. K., Katzenstein, T., Park, K., & Goring, J. (2002). Are students with ADHD more stressful to teach? Patterns of teacher stress in an elementary school sample. *Journal of Emotional and Behavioral Disorders, 10,* 79–89.

Greene, R. W., Biederman, J., Faraone, S. V., Monuteaux, M. C., Mick, E., DuPre, E. P., Fine, C. S., & Goring, J. G. (2001). Social impairment in girls with ADHD: Patterns, gender comparisons, and correlates. *Journal of the American Academy of Child and Adolescent Psychiatry, 40,* 704–710.

Greene, R. W., Biederman, J., Faraone, S. V., Wilens, T. E., Mick, E., & Blier, H. K. (1999). Further validation of social impairment as a predictor of substance use disorders: Findings from a sample of siblings of boys with and without ADHD. *Journal of Clinical Child Psychology, 28,* 349–354.

Greene, R. W., Biederman, J., Zerwas, S., Monuteaux, M., Goring J. C., & Faraone, S. V. (2002). Psychiatric comorbidity, family dysfunction, and social impairment in referred youth with oppositional defiant disorder. *American Journal of Psychiatry, 159,* 1214–1224.

Greening, L., Stoppelbein, L., Dhossche, D., & Martin, W. (2005). Psychometric evaluation of a measure of Beck's negative cognitive triad for youth: Applications for African-American and Caucasian. *Depression and Anxiety, 21,* 161–169.

Gregory, A. M., Eley, T. C., O'Connor, T. G., & Plomin, R. (2004). Etiologies of associations between childhood sleep and behavioral problems in a large twin sample. *Journal of the American Academy of Child and Adolescent Psychiatry, 43,* 744–751.

Gregory, A. M., Eley, T. C., & Plomin, R. (2004). Exploring the association between anxiety and conduct problems in a large sample of twins aged 2–4. *Journal of Abnormal Child Psychology, 32,* 111–122.

Gregory, J. (2003). *Sickened: The memoir of a Munchausen by proxy childhood.* New York: Bantam Books.

Gresham, F. M., Lane, K. L., & Beebe-Frankenberger, M. (2005). Predictors of hyperactive-impulsive-inattention and conduct problems: A comparative follow-back investigation. *Psychology in the Schools, 42,* 721–736.

Gresham, F. M., Lane, K. L., & Lambros, K. M. (2000). Comorbidity of conduct problems and ADHD: Identification of "fledgling psychopaths." *Journal of Emotional and Behavioral Disorders, 8,* 83–93.

Gresham, F. M., Lane, K. L., McIntyre, L. L., Olson-Tinker, H., Dolstra, L., MacMillan, D. M., Lambros, M. M., & Bocian, K. (2001). Risk factors associated with the co-occurrence of hyperactivity-impulsivity-inattention and conduct problems. *Behavioral Disorders, 26,* 189–199.

Gretton, H. M., Hare, R. D., & Catchpole, R. E. H. (2004). Psychopathy and offending from adolescence to adulthood: A 10-year follow-up. *Journal of Consulting and Clinical Psychology, 72,* 636–645.

Griffin, K. W., Botvin, G. J., Scheier, L. M., Diaz, T., & Miller, N. L. (2000). Parenting practices as predictors of substance use, delinquency, and aggression among urban minority youth: Moderating effects of family structure and gender. *Psychology of Addictive Behaviors, 14,* 174–184.

Griswold, D. E., Barnhill, G. P., Myles, B. S., Hagiwara, T., & Simpson, R. L. (2002). Asperger syndrome and academic achievement. *Focus on Autism and Other Developmental Disabilities, 17,* 94–102.

Grizenko, N., & Pawliuk, N. (1994). Risk and protective factors for disruptive behavior disorders in children. *American Journal of Orthopsychiatry, 64,* 534–544.

Gross, D., Fogg, L., Webster-Stratton, C., Garvey, C., Julion, W., & Grady, J. (2003). Parent training of toddlers in day care in low-income urban communities. *Journal of Consulting and Clinical Psychology, 71,* 261–278.

Gross, T. F. (2004). The perception of four basic emotions in human and nonhuman faces by children with autism and other developmental disabilities. *Journal of Abnormal Child Psychology, 32,* 469–480.

Grossman, H. (2002). *Ending discrimination in special education* (2nd ed.). Springfield, IL: Charles C. Thomas.

Group for the Advancement of Psychiatry. (1999). Violent behavior in children and youth: Preventive intervention from a psychiatric perspective. *Journal of the American Academy of Child and Adolescent Psychiatry, 38,* 235–241.

Gruenberg, A. M., & Goldstein, R. D. (2003). Multiaxial assessment in the twenty-first century. In K. A. Phillips & M. B. First (Eds.), *Advancing DSM: Dilemmas in psychiatric diagnosis* (pp. 145–152). Washington, DC: American Psychiatric Association.

Grueneich, R., Ris, M. D., Ball, W., Kalinyak, K. A., Noll, R., Vannatta, K., & Wells, R. (2004). Relationship of structural magnetic resonance imaging, magnetic resonance perfusion, and other disease factors to neuropsychological outcome in sickle cell disease. *Journal of Pediatric Psychology, 29,* 83–92.

Gruwell, E. (1999). *The freedom writers diary.* New York: Random House.

Grych, J. H., & Fincham, F. D. (2001). *Interparental conflict and child development: Theory, research, and application.* Cambridge, England: Cambridge University Press.

Grych, J. H., Fincham, F. D., Jouriles, E. N., & McDonald, R. (2000). Interparental conflict and child adjustment: Testing the mediational role of appraisals in the cognitive-contextual framework. *Child Development, 71,* 1648–1661.

Grych, J. H., Jouriles, E. N., Swank, P. R., McDonald, R., & Norwood, W. D. (2000). Patterns of adjustment among children of battered women. *Journal of Consulting and Clinical Psychology, 68,* 84–94.

Guerra, V. S., Asher, S. R., & DeRosier, M. E. (2004). Effect of children's perceived rejection on physical aggression. *Journal of Abnormal Child Psychology, 32,* 551–563.

Gunn, W. B., & Fisher, B. L. (1999). Systemic approaches—Family therapy. In *Counseling and psychotherapy with children and adolescents: Theory and practice for school and clinical settings* (3rd ed., pp. 351–375). New York: Wiley.

Gurman, A. S. (2001). Brief therapy and family/couple therapy: An essential redundancy. *Clinical Psychology: Science and Practice,* 8, 51–65.

Guthrie, R. V. (2003). *Even the rat was white: A historical view of psychology* (2nd ed.). Boston: Allyn and Bacon.

Gutierrez, P. M., Osman, A., Kopper, B. A., & Barrios, F. X. (2000). Why young people do not kill themselves: The reasons for living inventory for adolescents. *Journal of Clinical Child Psychology, 29,* 177–187.

Gutierrez, P. M., & Silk, K. R. (1998). Prescription privileges for psychologists: A review of the psychological literature. *Professional Psychology: Research and Practice, 29,* 213–222.

Guyll, M., Spoth, R. L., Chao, W., Wickrama, K. A. S., & Russell, D. (2004). Family-focused preventive interventions: Evaluating parental risk moderation of substance use trajectories. *Journal of Family Psychology, 18,* 293–301.

Haavisto, A., Sourander, A., Ellila, H., Valimaki, M., Santaiahti, P., & Helenius, H. (2003). Suicidal ideation and suicide attempts among child and adolescent psychiatric inpatient Finland. *Journal of Affective Disorders, 76,* 211–221.

Hackett, R., Hackett, L., Bhakta, P., & Gowers, S. (2001). Enuresis and encopresis in a South Indian population of children. *Child: Care, Health and Development, 27,* 35–46.

Haeseler, M. P. (2004). Ethical issues in art therapy. *Art Therapy, 21,* 231–232.

Hagan, M. A., & Castagna, N. (2001). The real numbers: Psychological testing in custody evaluations. *Professional Psychology: Research and Practice, 32,* 269–271.

Hahesy, A. L., Wilens, T. E., Biederman, J., Van Patten, S. L., & Spencer, T. (2002). Temporal association between childhood psychopathology and substance use disorder from a sample of adults with opioid or alcohol dependency. *Psychiatry Research, 109,* 245–254.

Haight, W. L. (1998). "Gathering the spirit" at First Baptist Church: Spirituality as a protective factor in the lives of African American children. *Social Work, 43,* 213–221.

Haley, J. (1976). *Problem-solving therapy.* San Francisco: Jossey-Bass.

Hall, G. C. N., & Barongan, C. (2002). *Multicultural psychology.* Upper Saddle River, NJ: Prentice Hall.

Hall, G. C. N., & Maramba, G. G. (2001). In search of cultural diversity: Recent literature in cross-cultural and ethnic minority psychology. *Cultural Diversity and Ethnic Minority Psychology, 7,* 12–26.

Hall, G. S. (1904). *Adolescence.* New York: Appleton.

Hall, K. M., Irwin, M. M., Bowman, K. A., Frankenberger, W., & Jewett, D. C. (2005). Illicit use of prescribed stimulant medication among college students. *Journal of American College Health, 53,* 167–174.

Halliday-Boykins, C. A., & Graham, S. (2001). At both ends of the gun: Testing the relationship between community violence exposure and youth violent behavior. *Journal of Abnormal Child Psychology, 29,* 383–402.

Halliday-Boykins, C. A., Schoenwald, S. K., & Letourneau, E. J. (2005). Caregiver-therapist ethnic similarity predicts youth outcomes from an empirically based treatment. *Journal of Consulting and Clinical Psychology, 73,* 808–818.

Halpern, E. (2001). Family psychology from an Israeli perspective. *American Psychologist, 56,* 58–64.

Hamarman, S., Pope, K. H., & Czaja, S. J. (2002). Emotional abuse in children: Variations in legal definitions and rates across the United States. *Child Maltreatment, 7,* 303–311.

Hamarman, S., & Bernet, W. (2000). Evaluating and reporting emotional abuse in children: Parent-based, action-based focus aids in clinical decision-making. *Journal of the American Academy of Child and Adolescent Psychiatry, 39,* 928–930.

Hambleton, R. K., & Zenisky, A. (2003). Advances in criterion-referenced testing methods and practices. In C. R. Reynolds & R. W. Kamphaus (Eds.), *Handbook of psychological and educational assessment of children: Intelligence, aptitude, and achievement* (2nd ed., pp. 377–404). New York: Guilford Press.

Hamby, S. L., & Finkelhor, D. (2000). The victimization of children: Recommendations for assessment and instrument development. *Journal of the American Academy of Child and Adolescent Psychiatry, 39,* 829–840.

Hamerman, S., & Ludwig, S. (2000). Emotional abuse and neglect. In R. M. Reece (Ed.), *Treatment of child abuse: Common ground for mental health, medical, and legal practitioners* (pp. 201–210). Baltimore MD: Johns Hopkins University Press.

Hamilton, C. E. (2000). Continuity and discontinuity of attachment from infancy through adolescence. *Child Development, 71,* 690–694.

Hamm, J. V. (2000). Do birds of a feather flock together? The variable bases for African American, Asian American, and European American adolescents' selection of similar friends. *Developmental Psychology, 36,* 209–219.

Hammen, C. (1991). *Depression runs in families: The social context of risk and resilience in children of depressed mothers.* New York: Springer-Verlag.

Hammen, C. (2003). Risk and protective factors for children of depressed parents. In S. S. Luthar (Ed.), *Resilience and vulnerability: Adaptation in the context of childhood adversities* (pp. 50–75). New York: Cambridge University Press.

Hammen, C., & Brennan, P. A. (2001). Depressed adolescents of depressed and nondepressed mothers: Tests of an interpersonal impairment hypothesis. *Journal of Consulting and Clinical Psychology, 69,* 284–294.

Hammen, C., & Rudolph, K. D. (2003). Childhood depression. In E. J. Mash & R. A. Barkley (Eds.), *Child psychopathology* (2nd ed., pp. 233–278). New York: Guilford Press.

Hampton, B. R., & Gottlieb, M. C. (1997). Ethical concerns regarding gender in family practice. In D. T. Marsh & R. D. Magee (Eds.), *Ethical and legal issues in professional practice with families* (pp. 50–74). New York: Wiley.

Hanish, L. D., Martin, C. L., Fabes, R. A., Leonard, S., & Herzog, M. (2005). Exposure to externalizing peers in early childhood: Homophily and peer contagion processes. *Journal of Abnormal Child Psychology, 33,* 267–281.

Hankin, B. L., & Abela, J. R. Z. (2005). Depression from childhood through adolescence and adulthood. In B. L. Hankin & J. R. Z. Abela (Eds.), *Development of psychopathology: A vulnerability-stress perspective* (pp. 245–288). Thousand Oaks, CA: Sage.

Hankin, B. L., Abela, J. R. Z., Auerbach, R. P., McWhinnie, C. M., & Skitch, S. A. (2005). Development of behavioral problems over the life course: A vulnerability and stress perspective. In B. L. Hankin & J. R. Z. Abela (Eds.), *Development of psychopathology: A vulnerability-stress perspective* (pp. 385–416). Thousand Oaks, CA: Sage.

Hankin, B. L., & Abramson, L. Y. (2001). Development of gender differences in depression: An elaborated cognitive vulnerability-transactional stress theory. *Psychological Bulletin, 127,* 773–796.

Hankin, B. L., Fraley, R. C., Lahey, B. B., & Waldman, I. D. (2005). Is depression best viewed as a continuum or discrete category? A taxometric analysis of childhood and adolescent depression in a population-based sample. *Journal of Abnormal Psychology, 114,* 96–110.

Hansen, C., Sanders, S. L., Massaro, S., & Last, C. G. (1998). Predictors of severity of absenteeism in children with anxiety-based school refusal. *Journal of Clinical Child Psychology, 27,* 246–254.

Hansen, M., Litzelman, A., Marsh, D. T., & Milspaw, A. (2004). Approaches to serious emotional disturbance: Involving multiple systems. *Professional Psychology: Research and Practice, 35,* 457–465.

Hanser, S. B. (2000). *The New Music Therapist's Handbook* (2nd ed.). Milwaukee, WI: Hal Leonard Corporation.

Hanson, K. M., Louie, C. E., Van Male, L. M., Pugh, A. O., Karl, C., Muhlenbrook, L., Lilly, R. L., & Hagglund, K. J. (1999). Involving the future: The need to consider the views of psychologists-in-training regarding prescription privileges for psychologists. *Professional Psychology: Research and Practice, 30,* 203–208.

Harbeck-Weber, C., Fisher, J. L., & Dittner, C. A. (2003). Promoting coping and enhancing adaptation to illness. In M. C. Roberts (Ed.), *Handbook of pediatric psychology* (3rd ed., pp. 99–118). New York: Guilford Press.

Harel, A., Abuelo, D., & Kazura, A. (2003). Adolescents and genetic testing: What do they think about it? *Journal of Adolescent Health, 33,* 489–494.

Harnett, P. H., & Dadds, M. R. (2004). Training school personnel to implement a universal school-based prevention of depression program under real-world conditions. *Journal of School Psychology, 42,* 343–357.

Harpaz-Rotem, I., Leslie, D. L., Martin, A., & Rosenheck, R. A. (2005). Changes in child and adolescent inpatient psychiatric admission diagnoses between 1995 and 2000. *Social Psychiatry and Psychiatric Epidemiology, 40,* 642–647.

Harpold, T. L., Wozniak, J., Kwon, A., Gilbert, J., Wood, J., Smith, L., & Biederman, J. (2005). Examining the association between pediatric bipolar disorder and anxiety disorders in psychiatrically referred children and adolescents. *Journal of Affective Disorders, 88,* 19–26.

Harris, J. G., & Liorente, A. M. (2004). Cultural considerations in the use of the Wechsler Intelligence Scale for Children-Fourth Edition (WISC-IV). In A. Prifitera, D. H. Saklofske, & L. G. Weiss (Eds.), *WISC-IV clinical use and interpretation: Scientist-practitioner perspectives* (pp. 381–413). San Diego, CA: Elsevier Academic Press.

Harris, J. R. (1995). Where is the child's environment? A group socialization theory of development. *Psychological Review, 102,* 458–489.

Harris, J. R. (1998a). *The nurture assumption: Why children turn out the way they do.* New York: Free Press.

Harris, J. R. (1998b). The trouble with assumptions. *Psychological Inquiry, 9,* 294–297.

Harrison-Hale, A. O., McLoyd, V. C., & Smedley, B. (2004). Racial and ethnic status: Risk and protective processes among African American families. In K. I. Maton, C. J. Schellenbach, B. J. Leadbeater, & A. L. Solarz (Eds.), *Investing in children, youth, families, and communities: Strengths-based research and policy* (pp. 269–283). Washington, DC: American Psychological Association.

Harrop, C., & Trower, P. (2001). Why does schizophrenia develop at late adolescence? *Clinical Psychology Review, 21,* 241–266.

Hart, K. J., & Morgan, J. R. (1993). Cognitive-behavioral procedures with children: Historical context and current status. In A. J. Finch, W. M. Nelson, & E. S. Ott (Eds.), *Cognitive-behavioral procedures with children and adolescents: A practical guide* (pp. 1–24). Boston: Allyn and Bacon.

Harter, S. (1985). *Manual for the Self-Perception Profile for Children.* Denver: University of Denver.

Harter, S. (1988). *Manual for the Self-Perception Profile for Adolescents.* Denver: University of Denver.

Hartung, C. M., Milich, R., Lynam, D. R., & Martin, C. A. (2002). Understanding the relations among gender, disinhibition, and disruptive behavior in adolescents. *Journal of Abnormal Psychology, 111,* 659–664.

Hartung, C. M., & Widiger, T. A. (1998). Gender differences in the diagnosis of mental disorders: Conclusions and controversies of the *DSM-IV. Psychological Bulletin, 123,* 260–278.

Harvey, E. A. (2000). Parenting similarity and children with attention-deficit/hyperactivity disorder. *Child and Family Behavior Therapy, 22,* 39–54.

Harvey, P. (2004). "MMR and autism: The debate continues": Comment. *Lancet, 363,* 568.

Hatton, C. (2002). People with intellectual disabilities from ethnic minority communities in the United States and the United Kingdom. In L. M. Glidden (Ed.), *International review of research in mental retardation* (pp. 209–239). San Diego, CA: Academic Press.

Haugaard, J. J. (2000). The challenge of defining child sexual abuse. *American Psychologist, 55*, 1036–1039.

Haugaard, J. J. (2004). Recognizing and treating uncommon behavioral and emotional disorders in children and adolescents who have been severely maltreated: Somatization and other somatoform disorders. *Child Maltreatment: Journal of the American Professional Society on the Abuse of Children, 9*, 169–176.

Hauser-Cram, P., Sirin, S. R., & Stipek, D. (2003). When teachers' and parents' values differ: Teachers' rating of academic competence in children from low-income families. *Journal of Educational Psychology, 95*, 813–820.

Haverkamp, F., Zerres, K., Rietz, C., Noeker, M., & Ruenger, M. (2004). Risk analyses for the cognitive phenotype in Turner's syndrome: Evidence of familial influence as a decisive factor. *Journal of Child Neurology, 19*, 183–190.

Havey, J. M., Olson, J. M., McCormick, C., & Cates, G. L. (2005). Teachers' perceptions of the incidence and management of attention-deficit hyperactivity disorder. *Applied Neuropsychology, 12*, 120–127.

Hawes, D. J., & Dadds, M. R. (2005). The treatment of conduct problems in children with callous-unemotional traits. *Journal of Consulting and Clinical Psychology, 73*, 737–741.

Hawker, D. S. J., & Boulton, M. J. (2000). Twenty years' research on peer victimization and psychosocial maladjustment: A meta-analytic review of cross-sectional studies. *Journal of Child Psychology and Psychiatry, 41*, 441–455.

Hawkins, E. H., Cummins, L. H., & Marlatt, G. A. (2004). Preventing substance abuse in American Indian and Alaska native youth: Promising strategies for healthier communities. *Psychological Bulletin, 130*, 304–323.

Hawkins, J. D. (1997). Academic performance and school success: Sources and consequences. In R. P. Weissberg, T. P. Gullotta, R. L. Hampton, B. A. Ryan, & G. R. Adams (Eds.), *Healthy children 2010: Enhancing children's wellness* (pp. 278–305). Thousand Oaks, CA: Sage.

Hawkins, J. D., Van Horn, M. L., & Arthur, M. W. (2004). Community variation in risk and protective factors and substance use outcomes. *Prevention Science, 5*, 213–220.

Hawley, K. M., & Weisz, J. R. (2003). Child, parent, and therapist (dis)agreement on target problems in outpatient therapy: The therapist's dilemma and its implications. *Journal of Consulting and Clinical Psychology, 71*, 62–70.

Hawley, K. M., & Weisz, J. R. (2005). Youth versus parent working alliance in usual clinical care: Distinctive associations with retention, satisfaction, and treatment outcome. *Journal of Clinical Child and Adolescent Psychology, 34*, 117–128.

Hayden, T. L. (1991). *Ghost girl*. New York: Avon Books.

Hayden, T. L. (2003). *Beautiful Child*. New York: Harper Collins.

Hayden, T. L. (2005). *Twilight children: Three voices no one heard until a therapist listened*. New York: William Morrow.

Hayes, C. (2004). Prevention of depression and anxiety in children and adolescents. In K. N. Dwivedi & P. B. Harper (Eds.), *Promoting the emotional well-being of children and adolescents and preventing their mental ill health: A handbook* (pp. 149–172). Philadelphia: Jessica Kingsley.

Hays-Thomas, R. L. (2000). The silent conversation: Talking about the master's degree. *Professional Psychology: Research and Practice, 31*, 339–345.

Healy, D. (2004). *Let them eat Prozac: The unhealthy relationship between the pharmaceutical industry and depression*. New York: New York University Press.

Heath, N. L., & Glen, T. (2005). Positive illusory bias and the self-protective hypothesis in children with learning disabilities. *Journal of Clinical Child and Adolescent Psychology, 34*, 272–281.

Hecht, D. B., Inderbitzen, H. M., & Bukowski, A. L. (1998). The relationship between peer status and depressive symptoms in children and adolescents. *Journal of Abnormal Child Psychology, 26*, 153–160.

Hechtman, L., Abikoff, H. B., & Jensen, P. S. (2005). Multimodal therapy and stimulants in the treatment of children with attention-deficit/hyperactivity disorder. In E. D. Hibbs & P. S. Jensen (Eds.), *Psychosocial treatment for child and adolescent disorders: Empirically based strategies for clinical practice* (2nd ed. pp. 411–437). Washington, DC: American Psychological Association.

Hechtman, L., Abikoff, H., Klein, R. G., Weiss, G., Respitz, C., Kouri, J., Blum, C., Greenfield, B., Etcovitch, J., Fleiss, K., & Pollack, S. (2004). Academic achievement and emotional status of children with ADHD treated with long-term methylphenidate and multimodal psychosocial treatment. *Journal of the American Academy of Child and Adolescent Psychiatry, 43*, 812–819.

Heiby, E. M., DeLeon, P. H., & Anderson, T. (2004). A debate on prescription privileges for psychologists. *Professional Psychology: Research and Practice, 35*, 336–344.

Heidgerken, A. D., Hughes, J. N., Cavell, T. A., & Willson, V. L. (2004). Direct and indirect effects of parenting and children's goals on child aggression. *Journal of Clinical Child and Adolescent Psychology, 33*, 684–693.

Heikura, U., Taanila, A., Olsen, P., Hartikainen, A., von Wendt, L., & Jarvelin, M. (2003). Temporal changes in incidence and prevalence of intellectual disability between two birth cohorts in Northern Finland. *American Journal on Mental Retardation, 108*, 19–31.

Heinze, H. J., Toro, P. A., & Urberg, K. A. (2004). Antisocial behavior and affiliation with deviant peers. *Journal of Clinical Child and Adolescent Psychology, 33*, 336–346.

Helzer, J. E., & Hudziak, J. J. (2002). *Defining psychopathology in the 21st century: DSM-V and beyond*. Washington, DC: American Psychiatric Association.

Hendren, R. L., DeBacker, I., & Pandina, G. J. (2000). Review of neuroimaging studies of child and adolescent psychiatric disorders from the past 10 years. *Journal of the American Academy of Child and Adolescent Psychiatry, 39*, 815–828.

Hendry, C. N. (2000). Childhood disintegrative disorder: Should it be considered a distinct diagnosis? *Clinical Psychology Review, 20*, 77–90.

Henggeler, S. W., Halliday-Boykins, C. A., Cunningham, P. B., Randall, J., Shapiro, S. B., & Chapman, J. E. (2006). Juvenile drug court: Enhancing outcomes by integrating evidence-based treatments. *Journal of Consulting and Clinical Psychology, 74*, 42–54.

Henggeler, S. W., & Lee, T. (2003). Multisystemic treatment of serious clinical problems. In A. E. Kazdin & J. R. Weisz (Eds.), *Evidence-based psychotherapies for children and adolescents* (pp. 301–322). New York: Guilford.

Henggeler, S. W., & Randall, J. (2000). Conducting randomized treatment studies in real-world settings. In D. Drotar (Ed.), *Handbook of research in pediatric and clinical child psychology* (pp. 447–461). New York: Plenum Press.

Henrich, C. C., Schwab-Stone, M., Fanti, K., Jones, S. M., & Ruchkin, V. (2004). The association of community violence exposure with middle-school achievement: A prospective study. *Journal of Applied Developmental Psychology, 25,* 327–348.

Henry, B., Caspi, A., Moffitt, T. E., Harrington, H. L., & Silva, P. A. (1999). Staying in school protects boys with poor self-regulation in childhood from later crime: A longitudinal study. *International Journal of Behavioral Development, 23,* 1049–1073.

Henry, D. B., Tolan, P. H., & Gorman-Smith, D. (2001). Longitudinal family and peer group effects on violence and nonviolent delinquency. *Journal of Clinical Child Psychology, 30,* 172–186.

Henry, D. B., Tolan, P. H., & Gorman-Smith, D. (2004). Have there been lasting effects associated with the September 11, 2001, terrorist attacks among inner-city parents and children? *Professional Psychology: Research and Practice, 35,* 542–547.

Herbert, J. D., Crittenden, K., & Dalrymple, K. L. (2004). Knowledge of social anxiety disorder relative to attention deficit hyperactivity disorder among educational professionals. *Journal of Clinical Child and Adolescent, 33,* 366–372.

Herbozo, S., Tantleff-Dunn, S., Gokee-Larose, J., & Thompson, J. K. (2004). Beauty and thinness messages in children's media: A content analysis. *Eating Disorders: The Journal of Treatment and Prevention, 12,* 21–34.

Hetherington, E. M., Bridges, M., & Insabella, G. M. (1998). What matters? What does not? Five perspectives on the association between marital transitions and children's adjustment. *American Psychologist, 53,* 167–184.

Hetherington, E. M., & Clingempeel, W. G. (1992). Coping with marital transitions. *Monographs of the Society for Research in Child Development, 57,* (2–3, Serial No. 227).

Hetherington, E. M., & Stanley-Hagan, M. (1999). The adjustment of children with divorced parents: A risk and resiliency perspective. *Journal of Child Psychology and Psychiatry, 40,* 129–140.

Heubeck, B. G. (2000). Cross-cultural generalizability of CBCL syndromes across three continents: From the USA and Holland to Australia. *Journal of Abnormal Child Psychology, 28,* 439–450.

Hewitt, P. L., Newton, J., Flett, G. L., & Callander, L. (1997). Perfectionism and suicide ideation in adolescent psychiatric patients. *Journal of Abnormal Child Psychology, 25* 95–101.

Hibbs, E. D., & Jensen, P. S. (Eds.). (2005). *Psychosocial treatments for child and adolescent disorders: Empirically based strategies for clinical practice* (2nd ed.) Washington, DC: American Psychological Association.

Hicks, B. M., Krueger, R. F., Iacono, W. G., McGue, M., & Patrick, C. J. (2004). Family transmission and heritability of externalizing disorders: A twin-family study. *Archives of General Psychiatry, 61,* 922–928.

Hilker, K. A., Murphy, M. A., & Kelley, M. L. (2005). Violence exposure, somatic complaints, and health care utilization in a pediatric sample. *Children's Health Care, 34,* 35–46.

Hill, K. G., Hawkins, J. D., Catalano, R. F., Abbott, R. D., & Guo, J. (2005). Family influences on the risk of daily smoking initiation. *Journal of Adolescent Health, 37,* 202–210.

Hill, L. G., Lochman, J. E., Coie, J. D., Greenberg, M. T., & The Conduct Problems Prevention Research Group. (2004). *Journal of Consulting and Clinical Psychology, 72,* 809–820.

Hill, N. E., & Taylor, L. C. (2004). Parental school involvement and children's academic achievement: Pragmatics and issues. *Current Directions in Psychological Science, 13,* 161–164.

Hinden, B. R., Compas, B. E., Howell, D. C., & Achenbach, T. M. (1997). Covariation of the anxious-depressed syndrome during adolescence: Separating fact from artifact. *Journal of Consulting and Clinical Psychology, 65,* 6–14.

Hines, M., Heinlen, K., Enochs, W. K., Etzbach, C. A., & Etzbach, W. (2005). The case of 9-year-old Janelle and her mother. In K. Eriksen & V. E. Kress (Eds.), *Beyond the DSM Story: Ethical quandaries, challenges, and best practices* (pp. 141–159). Thousand Oaks, CA: Sage.

Hinshaw, S. P. (2002). *The years of silence are past: My father's life with bipolar disorder.* New York: Cambridge University Press.

Hinshaw, S. P. (2006). Treatment for children and adolescents with attention-deficit/hyperactivity disorder. In P. C. Kendall (Ed.), *Child and adolescent therapy: Cognitive-behavioral procedures* (3rd ed., pp. 82–113). New York: Guilford Press.

Hinshaw, S. P., Klein, R. G., & Abikoff, H. B. (2002). Childhood attention-deficit hyperactivity disorder: nonpharmacological treatments and their combination with medication. In P. E. Nathan & J. M. Gorman (Eds.), *A guide to treatments that work* (2nd ed., pp. 3–23). New York: Oxford University Press.

Hinshaw, S. P., & Lee, S. S. (2003). Conduct and oppositional defiant disorders. In E. J. Mash, & B. A. Barkley (Eds.), *Child psychopathology* (2nd ed., pp. 279–329). New York: Guilford Press.

Hinshaw, S. P., Owens, E. B., Sami, N., & Fargeon, S. (2006). Prospective follow-up of girls with attention-deficit/hyperactivity disorder into adolescence: Evidence for continuing cross-domain impairment. *Journal of Consulting and Clinical Psychology, 74,* 489–499.

Hinshaw, S. P., & Park, T. (1999). Research problems and issues: Toward a more definitive science of disruptive behavior disorders. In H. C. Quay & A. E. Hogan (Eds.), *Handbook of disruptive behavior disorders* (pp. 593–620). New York: Kluwer Academic/Plenum Press.

Hintze, J. M., & Shapiro, E. S. (1999). School. In W. K. Silverman & T. H. Ollendick (Eds.), *Developmental issues in the clinical treatment of children* (pp. 156–170). Boston: Allyn and Bacon.

Hirsch, B. J. (2005). *A place to call home: After-school programs for urban youth.* Washington, DC: American Psychological Association.

Hirshfeld-Becker, D. R., Biederman, J., & Rosenbaum, J. F. (2004). Behavioral inhibition. In T. L. Morris & J. S. March (Eds.), *Anxiety disorders in children and adolescents* (2nd ed., pp. 27–58). New York: Guilford Press.

Hishinuma, E. S., Johnson, R. C., Kim, S. P., Nishimura, S. T., Makini Jr., G. K., Andrade, N. N., Yates, A., Goebert, D. A.,

Mark, G. Y., Mayeda, D. T., & Revilla, L. A. (2005). Prevalence and correlates of misconduct among ethnically diverse adolescents of Native Hawaiian/Part-Hawaiian and Non-Hawaiian Ancestry. *International Journal of Social Psychiatry, 51*, 242–258.

Ho, A., Todd, R. D., & Constantino, J. N. (2005). Brief report: Autistic traits in twins vs. non-twins—a preliminary study. *Journal of Autism and Developmental Disorders, 35*, 129–133.

Hoagwood, K., Kelleher, K. J., Feil, M., & Comer, D. M. (2000). Treatment services for children with ADHD: A national perspective. *Journal of the American Academy of Child and Adolescent Psychiatry, 39*, 198–206.

Hobbs, N. (1975). *The futures of children: Categories, labels, and their consequences*. San Francisco: Jossey-Bass.

Hock, R. R. (1999). *Forty studies that changed psychology: Explorations into the history of psychological research* (3rd ed.). Upper Saddle River, NJ: Prentice-Hall.

Hock, R. R. (2004). *Forty studies that changed psychology: Explorations into the history of psychological research* (4th ed.). Upper Saddle River, NJ: Prentice Hall.

Hock, E., Eberly, M., Bartle-Haring, S., Ellwanger, P., & Widaman, K. F. (2001). Separation anxiety in parents of adolescents: Theoretical significance and scale development. *Child Development, 72*, 284–298.

Hodapp, R. M. (1997). Developmental approaches to children with disabilities: New perspectives, populations, prospects. In S. S. Luthar, J. A. Burack, D. Cicchetti, & J. R. Weisz (Eds.), *Developmental psychopathology: Perspectives on adjustment, risk, and disorder* (pp. 189–207). New York: Cambridge University Press.

Hodapp, R. M., & Dykens, E. M. (2003). Mental retardation (intellectual disabilities). In E. J. Mash, & B. A. Barkley (Eds.), *Child psychopathology* (2nd ed., pp. 486–519). New York: Guilford Press.

Hodapp, R. M., & Dykens, E. M. (2005). Measuring behavior in genetic disorders of mental retardation. *Mental Retardation and Developmental Disabilities Research Reviews, 11*, 340–346.

Hodapp, R. M., Kazemi, E., Rosner, B. A., & Dykens, E. M. (2006). Mental retardation. In D. A. Wolfe & E. J. Mash (Eds.), *Behavioral and emotional disorders in adolescents: Nature, assessment, and treatment* (pp. 383–409). New York: Guilford Press.

Hodapp, R. M., & Zigler, E. (1995). Past, present, and future issues in the developmental approach to mental retardation and developmental disabilities. In D. Cicchetti & D. J. Cohen (Eds.), *Developmental psychopathology (Vol. 2): Risk, disorder, and adaptation* (pp. 299–331). New York: Wiley.

Hodges, E. V. E., Boivin, M., Vitaro, F., & Bukowski, W. M. (1999). The power of friendship: Protection against an escalating cycle of peer victimization. *Developmental Psychology, 35*, 94–101.

Hodges, K. (1997). *Child adolescent schedule (CAS)*. Ypsilanti, MI: Eastern Michigan University.

Hoekstra-Weebers, J. E. H. M., Jasper, J. P. C., Kamps, W. A., & Klip, E. C. (1999). Risk factors for psychological maladjustment of parents of children with cancer. *Journal of the American Academy of Child and Adolescent Psychiatry, 38*, 1526–1535.

Hoffman, A. (1996). Advice from my grandmother. In S. S. Fiffer & S. Fiffer (Eds.), *Family: American writers remember their own* (pp. 3–9). New York: Pantheon Books.

Hoffman, B. (1972). *Albert Einstein: Creator and rebel*. New York: Viking Press.

Hoffmann, J. P., Cerbone, F. G., & Su, S. S. (2000). A growth curve analysis of stress and adolescent drug use. *Substance Use and Misuse, 35*, 687–716.

Hofstra, M. B., Vander Ende, J., & Verhulst, F. C. (2000). Continuity and change of psychopathology from childhood into adulthood: A 14-year follow-up study. *Journal of the American Academy of Child and Adolescent Psychiatry, 39*, 850–858.

Hoge, R. D., Andrews, D. A., & Leschied, A. W. (1996). An investigation of risk and protective factors in a sample of youthful offenders. *Journal of Child Psychology and Psychiatry and Allied Disciplines, 37*, 419–424.

Hogue, A., & Liddle, H. A. (1999). Family-based preventive intervention: An approach to preventing substance use and antisocial behavior. *American Journal of Orthopsychiatry, 69*, 278–293.

Holden, E. W. (2003). Pediatric psychology and public health: Opportunities for further integration in the 21st century. In M. C. Roberts (Ed.), *Handbook of pediatric psychology* (3rd ed., pp. 710–718). New York: Guilford.

Holladay, R., & Friends. (1994). *What preteens want their parents to know*. New York: McCracken Press.

Hollon, S. D., & Beck, A. T. (1994). Cognitive and cognitive-behavioral therapies. In A. E. Bergin & S. L. Garfield (Eds.), *Handbook of psychotherapy and behavior change* (4th ed., pp. 428–466). New York: Wiley.

Hollon, S. D., Garber, J., & Shelton, R. C. (2005). Treatment of depression in adolescents with cognitive behavior therapy and medications: A commentary of the TADS Project. *Cognitive and Behavioral Practice, 12*, 149–155.

Holmbeck, G. N., Friedman, D., Abad, M., & Jandasek, B. (2006). Development and psychopathology in adolescence. In D. A. Wolfe & E. J. Mash (Eds.), *Behavioral and emotional disorders in adolescents: Nature, assessment, and treatment* (pp. 21–55). New York: Guilford Press.

Holmbeck, G. N., & Shapera, W. E. (1999). Research methods with adolescents. In P. C. Kendall, J. N. Butcher, & G. N. Holmbeck (Eds.), *Handbook of research methods in clinical psychology* (2nd ed., pp. 634–661). New York: Wiley.

Holtkamp, K., Konard, K., Kaiser, N., Ploenes, Y., Heussen, N., Grzella, I., & Hewrpertz-Dahlmann, B. (2005). A retrospective study of SSRI treatment in adolescent anorexia nervosa: Insufficient evidence for efficacy. *Journal of Psychiatric Research, 39*, 303–310.

Honda, H., Shimizu, Y., & Rutter, M. (2005). No effect of MMR withdrawal on the incidence of autism: A total population study. *Journal of Child Psychology and Psychiatry, 46*, 572–579.

Hood, K. K., & Eyberg, S. M. (2003). Outcomes of parent-child interaction therapy: Mothers' reports of maintenance three to six years after treatment. *Journal of Clinical Child and Adolescent, 32*, 419–429.

Hooley, J. M. (2004). Do psychiatric patients do better clinically if they live with certain kinds of families? *Current Directions in Psychological Science, 13*, 202–205.

Hopfer, C. J., Crowley, T. J., & Hewitt, J. K. (2003). Review of twin and adoption studies of adolescent substance use. *Journal of the American Academy of Child and Adolescent Psychiatry, 42,* 710–719.

Horn, W. F. (2006). Healthy marriages provide numerous benefits to adults, children, and society. In D. S. Del Campo & R. L. Del Campo (Eds.), *Taking sides: Clashing views in childhood and society* (6th ed., pp. 198–201). Dubuque, IA: McGraw-Hill.

Horowitz, J. L., & Garber, J. (2006). The prevention of depressive symptoms in children and adolescents: A meta-analytic review. *Journal of Consulting and Clinical Psychology, 74,* 401–415.

House, A. E., Elliott, S. N., & Witt, J. C. (2002). *DSM-IV Diagnosis in the Schools* (2nd ed.). New York: Guilford Press.

Houts, A. C. (2003). Behavioral treatment for enuresis. In A. E. Kazdin & J. R. Weisz (Eds.), *Evidence-based psychotherapies for children and adolescents* (pp. 389–406). New York: Guilford Press.

Hoven, C. W., Duarte, C. S., Wu, P., Erickson, E. A., Musa, G. J., & Mandell, D. J. (2004). Exposure to trauma and separation anxiety in children after the WTC attack. *Applied Developmental Science, 8,* 172–183.

Howard, M., & Hodes, M. (2000). Psychopathology, adversity, and service utilization of young refugees. *Journal of the American Academy of Child and Adolescent Psychiatry, 39,* 368–377.

Hoza, B., Gerdes, A. C., Hinshaw, S. P., Arnold, L. E., Pelham, W. E., Molina, B. S. G., Abikoff, H. B., Epstein, J. N., Greenhill, L. L., Hechtman, L., Odbert, C., Swanson, J. M., & Wigal, T. (2004). Self-perceptions of competence in children with ADHD and comparison children. *Journal of Consulting and Clinical Psychology, 72,* 382–391.

Hoza, B., Gerdes, A. C., Mrug, S., Hinshaw, S. P., Bukowski, W. M., Gold, J. A., Arnold, L. E., Abikoff, H. B., Conners, C. K., Elliott, G. R., Greenhill, L. L., Hechtman, L., Jensen, P. S., Kraemer, H. C., March, J. S., Newcorn, J. H., Severe, J. B., Swanson, J. M., Vitiello, B., Wells, K. C., & Wigal, T. (2005). Peer-assessed outcomes in the multimodal treatment study of children with attention deficit hyperactivity disorder. *Journal of Clinical Child and Adolescent, 34,* 74–86.

Hoza, B., Mrug, S., Gerdes, A. C., Hinshaw, S. P., Bukowski, W. M., Gold, J. A., Kraemer, H. C., Pelham, W. E., Wigal, T., & Arnold, L. E. (2005). What aspects of peer relationships are impaired in children with attention-deficit/hyperactivity disorder? *Journal of Consulting and Clinical Psychology, 73,* 411–423.

Hoza, B., Pelham, W. E., Waschbusch, D. A., Kipp, H., & Owens, J. S. (2001). Academic task persistence of normally achieving ADHD and control boys: Performance, self-evaluations, and attributions. *Journal of Consulting and Clinical Psychology, 69,* 271–283.

Hsieh, P., & FitzGerald, M. (2005). Childhood obesity in Taiwan: Review of the Taiwanese literature. *Nursing & Health Sciences, 7,* 134–142.

Hudson, A. (1998). Applied behavior analysis. In T. Ollendick (Ed.), *Comprehensive clinical psychology (Vol. 5)* (pp. 107–130). Kidlington, Oxford: Elsevier Science Ltd.

Hudson, A., Melita, B., & Arnold, N. (1993). Brief report: A case study assessing the validity of facilitated communication. *Journal of Autism and Developmental Disorders, 23,* 165–173.

Hudziak, J. J. (2002). Importance of phenotype definition in genetic studies of child psychopathology. In J. E. Helzer & J. J. Hudziak (Eds.), *Defining psychopathology in the 21st century: DSM-V and beyond* (pp. 211–230). Washington, DC: American Psychiatric Publishing.

Hudziak, J. J., Derks, E., Althoff, R. R., Copeland, W., & Boomsma, D. I. (2005). The genetic and environmental contributions to oppositional defiant behavior: A multi-informant twin study. *Journal of the American Academy of Child and Adolescent Psychiatry, 44,* 907–914.

Hudziak, J. J., Derks, E. M., Althoff, R. R., Rettew, D. C., & Boomsma, D. I. (2005). The genetic and environmental contributions to attention deficit hyperactivity disorder as measured by the Conners' rating scales-revised. *American Journal of Psychiatry, 162,* 1614–1620.

Hudziak, J. J., Rudiger, L. P., Neale, M. C., Heath, A. C., & Todd, R. D. (2000). A twin study of inattentive, aggressive, and anxious/depressed behaviors. *Journal of American Academy of Child and Adolescent Psychiatry, 39,* 469–476.

Huey, S. J., Henggeler, S. W., Brondino, M. J., & Pickrel, S. G. (2000). Mechanisms of change in multisystemic therapy: Reducing delinquent behavior through therapist adherence and improved family and peer functioning. *Journal of Consulting and Clinical Psychology, 68,* 451–467.

Huey, S. J., Henggeler, S. W., Rowland, M. D., Halliday-Boykins, C. A., Cunningham, P. B., & Pickrel, S. G. (2005). Predictors of treatment response for suicidal youth referred for emergency psychiatric hospitalization. *Journal of Clinical Child and Adolescent Psychology, 34,* 582–589.

Hufford, M. R. (2001). Alcohol and suicidal behavior. *Clinical Psychology Review, 21,* 797–811.

Hughes, J. N., Cavell, T. A., & Jackson, T. (1999). Influence of the teacher-student relationship on childhood conduct problems: A prospective study. *Journal of Clinical Child Psychology, 28,* 173–184.

Hughes, J. N., Cavell, T. A., Meehan, B. T., Zhang, D., & Collie, C. (2005). Adverse school context moderates the outcomes of selective interventions for aggressive children. *Journal of Consulting and Clinical Psychology, 73,* 731–736.

Humphreys, K. (2000). Beyond the mental health clinic: New settings and activities for clinical psychology internships. *Professional Psychology: Research and Practice, 31,* 300–304.

Hunsley, J., & Bailey, J. M. (1999). The clinical utility of the Rorschach: Unfulfilled promises and an uncertain future. *Psychological Assessment, 11,* 266–277.

Hunsley, J., & Bailey, J. M. (2001). Whither the Rorschach? An analysis of the evidence. *Psychological Assessment, 13,* 472–485.

Hunsley, J., Lee, C. M., & Wood, J. M. (2003). Controversy and questionable assessment techniques. In S. O. Lilienfeld, S. J. Lynn, & J. M. Lohr (Eds.), *Science and pseudoscience in clinical psychology* (pp. 39–76). New York: Guilford Press.

Hunter, W. M., Jain, D., Sadowski, L. S., & Sanhueza, A. I. (2000). Risk factors for severe child discipline practices in rural India. *Journal of Pediatric Psychology, 25,* 435–447.

Huon, G. F., & Walton, C. J. (2000). Initiation of dieting among adolescent females. *International Journal of Eating Disorders, 28,* 226–230.

Hupp, S. D. A., & Adams, S. L. (2004). Making diagnostic labels reflective of environmental influences: A rose by any other name may not be so thorny. *Behavior Therapist, 27,* 4–7.

Hussong, A. M., Curran, P. J., & Chassin, L. (1998). Pathways of risk for accelerated heavy alcohol use among adolescent children of alcoholic parents. *Journal of Abnormal Child Psychology, 26,* 453–466.

Hussong, A. M., & Hicks, R. E. (2003). Affect and peer context interactively impact adolescent substance use. *Journal of Abnormal Child Psychology, 31,* 413–426.

Huston, A. C., Donnerstein, E., Fairchild, H., Feshbach, N. D., Katz, P. A., Murray, J. P., Rubinstein, E. A., Wilcox, B. L., & Zuckerman, D. (1992). *Big world, small screen: The role of television in American society.* Lincoln: University of Nebraska Press.

Huston, A. C., & Wright, J. C. (1998). Mass media and children's development. In I. E. Sigel & K. A. Renninger (Eds.), *Handbook of child psychology. Volume 4: Child psychology in practice* (5th ed., pp. 999–1058). New York: Wiley.

Huszti, H., Hoff, A., & Johnson, C. (2003). Sexual behaviors and problems of adolescents. In M. C. Roberts (Ed.), *Handbook of pediatric psychology* (3rd ed.; pp. 664–679). New York: Guilford.

Hyde, J. S. (2005). The gender similarities hypothesis. *American Psychologist, 60,* 581–592.

Iacono, W. G., Carlson, S. R., Malone, S. M., & McGue, M. (2002). P3 event-related potential amplitude and the risk for disinhibitory disorders in adolescent boys. *Archives of General Psychiatry, 59,* 750–757.

Ialongo, N. S., Kellam, S. G., & Poduska, J. (2000). A developmental epidemiological framework for clinical child and pediatric psychology research. In D. Drotar (Ed.), *Handbook of research in pediatric and clinical child psychology* (pp. 3–19). New York: Plenum Press.

Ilardi, S. S., Rodriguez-Hanley, A., Roberts, M. C., & Seigel, J. (2000). On the origins of clinical psychology faculty: Who is training the trainers. *Clinical Psychology: Science and Practice, 7,* 346–354.

Ingoldsby, E. M., Shaw, D. S., Winslow, E., Schonberg, M., Gilliom, M., & Criss, M. M. (2006). Neighborhood disadvantage, parent-child conflict, neighborhood peer relationships, and early antisocial behavior problem trajectories. *Journal of Abnormal Child Psychology, 34,* 303–319.

Ingram, R. E., Hayes, A., & Scott, W. (2000). Empirically supported treatments: A critical analysis. In C. R. Snyder, & R. E. Ingram (Eds.), *Handbook of psychological change: Psychotherapy processes and practices for the 21st century* (pp. 40–60). New York: Wiley.

Ingram, R. E., & Luxton, D. D. (2005). Vulnerability-stress models. In B. L. Hankin & J. R. Z. Abela (Eds.), *Development of psychopathology: A vulnerability-stress perspective* (pp. 32–46). Thousand Oaks, CA: Sage.

Ingram, R. E., & Ritter, J. (2000). Vulnerability to depression: Cognitive reactivity and parental bonding in high-risk individuals. *Journal of Abnormal Psychology, 109,* 588–596.

Ingrassia, A., & Turk, J. (2005). The use of clonidine for severe and intractable sleep problems in children with neurodevelopmental disorders: A case series. *European Child & Adolescent Psychiatry, 14,* 34–40.

Institute of Medicine. (1994). *Reducing risk for mental disorders: Frontiers for prevention intervention research.* Washington, DC: National Academy Press.

Interdisciplinary Council on Developmental and Learning Disorders. (2000). *Clinical practice guidelines.* Bethesda, MD: Author.

Irvine, M. (2001, November 19). Attention disorder drug abuse up among youth. *Detroit News.* Retrieved November 14, 2005, from www.detnews.com

Isley, S. L., O'Neil, R., Clatfelter, D., & Parke, R. D. (1999). Parent and child expressed affect and children's social competence: Modeling direct and indirect pathways. *Developmental Psychology, 35,* 547–560.

Jackson, D. A., & King, A. R. (2004). Gender differences in the effects of oppositional behavior on teachers ratings of ADHD symptoms. *Journal of Abnormal Child Psychology, 32,* 215–224.

Jackson, H., & Nuttall, R. L. (2001). A relationship between childhood sexual abuse and professional sexual misconduct. *Professional Psychology: Research and Practice, 32,* 200–204.

Jacobi, C., Hayward, C., de Zwaan, M., Kraemer, H. C., & Agras, W. S. (2004). Coming to terms with risk factors for eating disorders: Application of risk terminology and suggestions for a general taxonomy. *Psychological Bulletin, 130,* 19–65.

Jacobson, J. W., Foxx, R. M., & Mulick, J. A. (Eds.). (2004). Facilitated communication: The ultimate fad treatment. *Controversial therapies for developmental disabilities: Fad, fashion and science in professional practice* (pp. 363–383). Mahwah, NJ: Lawrence Erlbaum Associates.

Jacobson, K. C., & Rowe, D. C. (1999). Genetic and environmental influences on the relationships between family connectedness, school connectedness, and adolescent depressed mood: Sex differences. *Developmental Psychology, 35,* 926–939.

Jacobvitz, D., Hazen, N., Curran, M., & Hitchens, K. (2004). Observations of early triadic family interactions: Boundary disturbances in the family predict symptoms of depression, anxiety, and attention-deficit/hyperactivity disorder in middle childhood. *Development and Psychopathology, 16,* 577–592.

Jacques, H. A. K., & Mash, E. J. (2004). A test of the tripartite model of anxiety and depression in elementary and high school boys and girls. *Journal of Abnormal Child Psychology, 32,* 13–25.

Jaffee, S. R., Caspi, A., Moffitt, T. E., Dodge, K. A., Rutter, M., Taylor, A., & Tully, L. A. (2005). Nature X nurture: Genetic vulnerabilities interact with physical maltreatment to promote conduct problems. *Development and Psychopathology, 17,* 67–84.

Jaffee, S. R., Caspi, A., Moffitt, T. E., & Taylor, A. (2004). Physical maltreatment victim to antisocial child: Evidence of an environmentally mediated process. *Journal of Abnormal Psychology, 113,* 44–55.

Jaffee, S. R., Harrington, H., Cohen, P., & Moffitt, T. E. (2005). Cumulative prevalence of psychiatric disorder in youths. *Journal of the American Academy of Child and Adolescent Psychiatry, 44,* 406–407.

Jaffee, S. R., Moffitt, T. E., Caspi, A., & Taylor, A. (2003). Life with (or without) father: The benefits of living with two biological parents depend on the father's antisocial behavior. *Child Development, 74,* 109–126.

James, H. (2004). Promoting effective working with parents with learning disabilities. *Child Abuse Review, 13,* 31–41.

Jamison, K. R. (1995). Manic-depressive illness and creativity. *Scientific American, Feb,* 62–67.

Jang, K. L. (2005). *The behavioral genetics of psychopathology: A clinical guide.* Mahway, NJ: Lawrence Erlbaum Associates.

Janicke, D. M., & Finney, J. W. (2001). Children's primary health care services: A social-cognitive model of sustained high use. *Clinical Psychology: Science and Practice, 8,* 228–241.

Janssen, C. G. C., Schuengel, C., & Stolk, J. (2002). Understanding challenging behaviour in people with severe and profound intellectual disability: A stress-attachment model. *Intellectual Disability Research, 46,* 445–453.

Jason, L. A., Berk, M., Schnopp-Wyatt, D. L., & Talbot, B. (1999). Effects of enforcement of youth access laws on smoking prevalence. *American Journal of Community Psychology, 27,* 143–160.

Jelalian, E., & Mehlenbeck, R. (2003). Pediatric obesity. In M. C. Roberts (Ed.), *Handbook of pediatric psychology* (3rd ed., pp. 529–543). New York: Guilford Press.

Jensen, J. A., Hickman III, N. J., Landrine, H., & Klonoff, E. A. (2004). Availability of tobacco to youth via the internet. *JAMA: Journal of the American Medical Association, 291,* 1837.

Jensen, P. S. (2001). Clinical equivalence: A step, a misstep, or just a misnomer? *Clinical Psychology: Science and Practice, 8,* 436–440.

Jensen, P. S. (2003). Comorbidity and child psychopathology: Recommendations for the next decade. *Journal of Abnormal Child Psychology, 31,* 293–300.

Jensen, P. S., Garcia, J. A., Glied, S., Crowe, M., Foster, M., Schlander, M., Hinshaw, S., Vitiello, B., Arnold, L. E., Elliott, G., Hechtman, L., Newcorn, J. H., Pelham, W. E., Swanson, J., & Wells, K. (2005). Cost-effectiveness of ADHD treatments: Findings from the multimodal treatment study of children with ADHD. *American Journal of Psychiatry, 162,* 1628–1636.

Jensen, P. S., Hinshaw, S. P., Kraemer, H. C., Lenora, N., Newcorn, J. H., Abikoff, H. B., March, J. S., Arnold, L. E., Cantwell, D. P., Conners, C. K., Elliott, G. R., Greenhill, L. L., Hechtman, L., Hoza, B., Pelham, W. E., Severe, J. B., Swanson, J. M., Wells, K. C., Wigal, T., & Vitiello, B. (2001). ADHD comorbidity findings from the MTA study: Comparing comorbid subgroups. *Journal of the American Academy of Child and Adolescent Psychiatry, 40,* 147–158.

Jensen, P. S., Martin, D., & Cantwell, D. P. (1997). Comorbidity in ADHD: Implications for research, practice, and *DSM-V. Journal of the American Academy of Child and Adolescent Psychiatry, 36,* 1065–1079.

Jensen, P. S., & Members of the MTA Cooperative Group. (2002). ADHD comorbidity findings from the MTA study: New diagnostic subtypes and their optimal treatments. In J. E. Helzer, & J. J. Hudziak (Eds.), *Defining psychopathology in the 21st century: DSM-V and beyond* (pp. 169–192). Washington, DC: American Psychiatric Publishing,.

Jensen, P. S., & Watanabe, H. K. (1999). Sherlock Holmes and child psychopathology assessment approaches: The case of the false-positive. *Journal of the American Academy of Child and Adolescent Psychiatry, 38,* 138–146.

Jensen, P. S., Watanabe, H. K., & Richters, J. E. (1999). Who's up first? Testing for order effects in structured interviews using a counterbalanced experimental design. *Journal of Abnormal Child Psychology, 27,* 439–445.

Jergen, R. (2004). *The little monster: Growing up with ADHD.* Lanham, MD: Scarecrow Education.

Jerome, L., & Segal, A. (2003). Bullying by internet. *Journal of the American Academy of Child & Adolescent Psychiatry, 42,* 751.

Jessor, R., Turbin, M. S., & Costa, F. M. (1998). Protective factors in adolescent health behavior. *Journal of Personality and Social Psychology, 75,* 788–800.

Jewell, J., Handwerk, M., Almquist, J., & Lucas, C. (2004). Comparing the validity of clinician-generated diagnosis of conduct disorder to the diagnostic interview schedule for children. *Journal of Clinical Child and Adolescent Psychology, 33,* 536–546.

Jick, H., Kaye, J. A., & Jick, S. S. (2004). Antidepressants and the risk of suicidal behaviors. *Journal of the American Medical Association, 292,* 338–343.

Jitendra, A. K., Edwards, L. L., Starosta, K., Sacks, G., Jacobson, L. A., & Choutka, C. M. (2004). Early reading instruction for children with reading difficulties: Meeting the needs of diverse learners. *Journal of Learning Disabilities, 37,* 421–439.

Johnson, D. B., Pedro-Carroll, J. L., & Demanchick, S. P. (2005). The Primary Mental Health Project: A play intervention for school-age children. In L. A. Reddy, T. M. Files-Hall, & C. E. Schaefer (Eds.), *Empirically based play interventions for children* (pp. 13–30). Washington, DC: American Psychological Association.

Johnson, D. L. (1988). Primary prevention of behavior problems in young children: The Houston parent-child development center. In R. H. Price, E. L. Cowen, R. P. Lorion, & J. Ramos-McKay (Eds.), *14 ounces of prevention: A casebook for practitioners* (pp. 44–52). Washington, D.C.: American Psychological Association.

Johnson, D. L., & Blumenthal, J. (2004). The parent child development centers and school achievement: A follow-up. *Journal of Primary Prevention, 25,* 195–209.

Johnson, E. M. (1992). *My life.* New York: Fawcett Crest.

Johnson, F., & Wardle, J. (2005). Dietary restraint, body dissatisfaction, and psychological distress: A prospective analysis. *Journal of Abnormal Psychology, 114,* 119–125.

Johnson, J. G., McGeoch, P. G., Caskey, V. P., Abhary, S. G., Sneed, J. R., & Bornstein, R. F. (2005). The developmental psychopathology of personality disorders. In B. L. Hankin & J. R. Z. Abela (Eds.), *Development of psychopathology: A vulnerability-stress perspective* (pp. 417–464). Thousand Oaks, CA: Sage.

Johnson, M. H., Halit, H., Grice, S. J., & Karmiloff-Smith, A. (2002). Neuroimaging of typical and atypical development: A perspective from multiple levels of analysis. *Development and Psychopathology, 14,* 521–536.

Johnson, P. B., & Johnson, H. L. (1999). Cultural and familial influences that maintain the negative meaning of alcohol. *Journal of Studies on Alcohol, Supplement 13,* 79–83.

Johnson, S. B. (1995). Insulin-dependent diabetes mellitus in child-hood. In M. C. Roberts (Ed.), *Handbook of pediatric psychology* (pp. 263–285). New York: Guilford.

Johnson, S. B. (1998). Juvenile diabetes. In T. H. Ollendick & M. Hersen (Eds.), *Handbook of child psychopathology* (3rd ed., pp. 417–434). New York: Plenum Press.

Johnson, S. L., & Jacob, T. (2000). Moderators of child outcome in families with depressed mothers and fathers. In S. L. Johnson & A. M. Hayes (Eds.), *Stress, coping, and depression* (pp. 51–67). Mahwah, NJ: Lawrence Erlbaum Associates.

Johnson, V., & Pandina, R. J. (2000). Alcohol problems among a community sample: Longitudinal influences of stress, coping, and gender. *Substance Use and Misuse, 35,* 669–686.

Johnson, V. K. (2003). Linking changes in whole family functioning and children's externalizing behavior across the elementary school years. *Journal of Family Psychology, 17,* 499–509.

Johnson, W. G., Rohan, K. J., & Kirk, A. A. (2002). Prevalence and correlates of binge eating in White and African American adolescents. *Eating Behaviors, 3,* 179–189.

Johnston, C., & Leung, D. W. (2001). Effects of medication, behavioral, and combined treatments on parents' and children's attributions for the behavior of children with attention-deficit hyperactivity disorder. *Journal of Consulting and Clinical Psychology, 69,* 67–76.

Johnston, C., & Murray, C. (2003). Incremental validity in the psychological assessment of children and adolescents. *Psychological Assessment, 15,* 496–507.

Johnston, C., & Ohan, J. L. (1999). Externalizing disorders. In W. K. Silverman & T. H. Ollendick (Eds.), *Developmental issues in the clinical treatment of children* (pp. 279–294). Boston: Allyn and Bacon.

Johnston, L. D., O'Malley, P. M., & Bachman, J. G. (1995). *National survey results on drug use from Monitoring the Future Study, 1975–1994: Vol. 1 Secondary school students.* Rockville, MD: U.S. Department of Health and Human Services.

Joiner, T. E. (1999). A test of interpersonal theory of depression in youth psychiatric inpatients. *Journal of Abnormal Child Psychology, 27,* 77–85.

Joiner, T. E., Blalock, J. A., & Wagner, K. D. (1999). Preliminary examination of sex differences in depressive symptoms among adolescent psychiatric inpatients: The role of anxious symptoms and generalized negative affect. *Journal of Clinical Child Psychology, 28,* 211–219.

Joiner, T. E., Catanzaro, S. J., & Laurent, J. (1996). Tripartite structure of positive and negative affect, depression, and anxiety in child and adolescent psychiatric inpatients. *Journal of Abnormal Psychology, 105,* 401–409.

Joiner, T. E., & Lonigan, C. J. (2000). Tripartite model of depression and anxiety in youth psychiatric inpatients: Relations with diagnostic status and future symptoms. *Journal of Clinical Child Psychology, 29,* 372–382.

Joiner, T. E., Rudd, M. D., Rouleau, M. R., & Wagner, K. D. (2000). Parameters of suicide crises vary as a function of previous suicide attempts in youth inpatients. *Journal of the American Academy of Child and Adolescent Psychiatry, 39,* 876–880.

Jones, C. (2001). An agonizing road for kids of Sept. 11. *USA Today,* 10/19/2001, pp. 1–8.

Jones, M. (1997). Is less better? Boot camp, regular probation and rearrest in North Carolina. *American Journal of Criminal Justice, 21,* 147–161.

Jones, S. E. (2001). Ethics code draft published for comment. *Monitor on Psychology, 32,* 1–3.

Jongsma, A. E., Peterson, L. M., & McInnis, W. P. (1996). *The child and adolescent Psychotherapy treatment planner.* New York: Wiley.

Jongsma, A. E., Peterson, L. M., & McInnis, W. P. (2000a). *The adolescent psychotherapy treatment planner.* New York: Wiley.

Jongsma, A. E., Peterson, L. M., & McInnis, W. P. (2000b). *The child psychotherapy treatment planner.* New York: Wiley.

Jordan, K. M. (2000). Substance abuse among gay, lesbian, bisexual, transgender, and questioning adolescents. *School Psychology Review, 29,* 201–206.

Jorm, A. F., Dear, K. B. G., Rodgers, B., & Christensen, H. (2003). Interaction between mother's and father's affection as a risk factor for anxiety and depression symptoms: Evidence for increased risk in adults who rate their father as having been more affectionate than their mother. *Social Psychiatry and Psychiatric Epidemiology, 38,* 173–179.

Joseph, J. (2000). Not in their genes: A critical view of the genetics of attention-deficit hyperactivity disorder. *Developmental Review, 20,* 539–567.

Joseph, J. (2005). The fruitless search for schizophrenia genes. *Ethical Human Psychology and Psychiatry, 6,* 167–181.

Joseph, J. (2004). *The gene illusion: Genetic research in psychiatry and psychology under the microscope.* New York: Algora Publishing.

Joseph, R. M., & Tager-Flusberg, H. (2004). The relationship of theory of mind and executive functions to symptom type and severity in children with autism. *Development and Psychopathology, 16,* 137–155.

Jouriles, E. N., McDonald, R., Spiller, L., Norwood, W. D., Swank, P. R., Stephens, N. Ware, H., & Buzy, W. M. (2001). Reducing conduct problems among children of battered women. *Journal of Consulting and Clinical Psychology, 69,* 774–785.

Kadesjoe, B., & Gillberg, C. (2001). The comorbidity of ADHD in the general population of Swedish school-age children. *Journal of Child Psychology and Psychiatry and Allied Disciplines, 42,* 487–492.

Kafantaris, V., Coletti, D. J., Dicker, R., Padula, G., & Pollack, S. (1998). Are childhood psychiatric histories of bipolar adolescents associated with family history, psychosis, and response to lithium treatment? *Journal of Affective Disorders, 51,* 153–164.

Kagan, J. (2002). Temperamental contributions to affective and behavioral profiles in childhood. In S. G. Hofmann, & P. M. DiBartolo (Eds.), *From social anxiety to social phobia: Multiple perspectives* (pp. 216–234). Needham Heights, MA: Allyn & Bacon.

Kagan, J., Snidman, N., McManis, M., Woodward, S., & Hardway, C. (2002). One measure, one meaning: Multiple measures, clearer meaning. *Development and Psychopathology, 14,* 463–475.

Kagan, J., Snidman, N., Zentner, M., & Peterson, E. (1999). Infant temperament and anxious symptoms in school age children. *Development and Psychopathology, 11,* 209–224.

Kalat, J. W., & Wurm, T. (1999). Implications of recent research in biological psychology for school psychology. In C. R. Reynolds &

T. B. Gutkin (Eds.), *The handbook of school psychology* (3rd ed., pp. 271–290). New York: Wiley.

Kameguchi, K., & Murphy-Shigematsu, S. (2001). Family psychology and family therapy in Japan. *American Psychologist, 56,* 65–70.

Kamon, J., Budney, A., & Stanger, C. (2005). A contingency management intervention for adolescent marijuana abuse and conduct problems. *Journal of the American Academy of Child and Adolescent Psychiatry, 44,* 513–521.

Kamon, J., Tolan, P. H., & Gorman-Smith, D. (2006). Interventions for adolescent psychopathology: Linking treatment and prevention. In D. A. Wolfe & E. J. Mash (Eds.), *Behavioral and emotional disorders in adolescents: Nature, assessment, and treatment* (pp. 56–88). New York: Guilford Press.

Kamphaus, R. W., & Frick, P. J. (2005). *Clinical assessment of child and adolescent personality and behavior* (2nd ed). New York: Springer-Verlag.

Kamphaus, R. W., Petoskey, M. D., & Rowe, E. W. (2000). Current trends in psychological testing of children. *Professional Psychology: Research and Practice, 31,* 155–164.

Kandel, D. B., & Davies, M. (1982). Epidemiology of depressive mood in adolescents. *Archives of General Psychiatry, 39,* 1205–1212.

Kandel, D. B., Johnson, J. G., Bird, H. R., Canino, G., Goodman, S. H., Lahey, B. B., Regier, D. A., & Schwab-Stone, M. (1997). Psychiatric disorders associated with substance use among children and adolescents: Findings from the Methods for the Epidemiology of Child and Adolescent Mental Disorders (MECA) Study. *Journal of Abnormal Child Psychology, 25,* 121–132.

Kandel, D. B., Johnson, J. G., Bird, H. R., Weissman, M. M., Goodman, S. H., Lahey, B. B., Regier, D. A., & Schwab-Stone, M. (1999). Psychiatric comorbidity among adolescents with substance use disorders: Findings from the MECA study. *Journal of the American Academy of Child and Adolescent Psychiatry, 38,* 693–699.

Kane, E. (2005). 7-year-old's gun death is tragic, inevitable. *Milwaukee Journal Sentinel,* April 18, 2005.

Kane, P., & Garber, J. (2004). The relations among depression in fathers, children's psychopathology, and father-child conflict: A meta-analysis. *Clinical Psychology Review, 24,* 339–360.

Kane, T. A., Loxton, N. J., Staiger, P. K., & Dawe, S. (2004). Does the tendency to act impulsively underlie binge eating and alcohol use problems?: Empirical investigation. *Personality and Individual Differences, 36,* 83–94.

Kanner, L. (1943). Autistic disturbances of affective contact. *Nervous Child, 2,* 217–250.

Kaplan, S. J., Pelcovitz, D., Salzinger, S., Weiner, M., Mandel, F. S., Lesser, M. L., & Labruna, V. E. (1998). Adolescent physical abuse: Risk for adolescent psychiatric disorders. *American Journal of Psychiatry, 155,* 954–959.

Kaplow, J. B., Curran, P. J., Angold, A., & Costello, E. J. (2001). The prospective relation between dimensions of anxiety and the initiation of adolescent alcohol use. *Journal of Clinical Child Psychology, 30,* 316–326.

Kaplow, J. B., Dodge, K. A., Amaya-Jackson, L., & Saxe, G. N. (2005). Pathways to PTSD, Part II: Sexually abused children. *American Journal of Psychiatry, 162,* 1305–1310.

Karen, R. (1994). *Becoming attached.* New York: Warner Books.

Karver, M. S. (2006). Determinants of multiple informant agreement on child and adolescent behavior. *Journal of Abnormal Child Psychology, 34,* 251–262.

Kasari, C., Freeman, S. F. N., & Bass, W. (2003). Empathy and response to Distress in children with Down syndrome. *Journal of Child Psychology and Psychiatry, 44,* 424–431.

Kashdan, T. B., Jacob, R. G., Pelham, W. E., Lang, A. R., Hoza, B., Blumenthal, J. D., & Gnagy, E. M. (2004). Depression and anxiety in parents of children with ADHD and varying levels of oppositional defiant behaviors: Modeling relationships with family functioning. *Journal of Clinical Child and Adolescent, 33,* 169–181.

Kaslow, F. W. (2001). Families and family psychology at the millennium: Intersecting crossroads. *American Psychologist, 56,* 37–46.

Kaslow, N. J., Celano, M. P., & Stanton, M. (2005). Training in family psychology: A competencies-based approach. *Family Process, 44,* 337–353.

Kassel, J. D., Weinstein, S., Skitch, S. A., Veilleux, J., & Mermelstein, R. (2005). The development of substance abuse in adolescence: Correlates, causes, and consequences. In B. L. Hankin & J. R. Z. Abela (Eds), *Development of psychopathology: A vulnerability-stress perspective* (pp. 355–384). Thousand Oaks, CA: Sage.

Katz, L. F., & Low, S. M. (2004). Marital violence, co-parenting, and family-level processes in relation to children's adjustment. *Journal of Family Psychology, 18,* 372–382.

Kaufman, J., & Zigler, E. (1992). The prevention of child maltreatment: Programming, research, and policy. In D. J. Willis, E. W. Holden, & M. Rosenberg (Eds.), *Prevention of child maltreatment: Developmental and ecological perspectives* (pp. 269–295). New York: Wiley.

Kaufman, N. K., Rohde, P., Seeley, J. R., Clarke, G. N., & Stice, E. (2005). Potential mediators of cognitive-behavioral therapy for adolescents with comorbid major depression and conduct disorder. *Journal of Consulting and Clinical psychology, 73,* 38–46.

Kaufmann, K. M., & Lay, J. C. (2004). Four commentaries: Looking to the future: Commentary 3. *Future of Children, 14,* 150–154.

Kaur, S., Sassi, R. B., Axelson, D., Nicoletti, M., Brambilla, P., Monkul, E. S., Hatch, J. P., Keshavan, M. S., Ryan, N., Birmaher, B., & Soares, J. C. (2005). Cingulate cortex anatomical abnormalities in children and adolescents with bipolar disorder. *American Journal of Psychiatry, 162,* 1637–1643.

Kavale, K. A. (2003). Discrepancy models in the identification of learning disability. In R. Bradley, L. Danielson, & D. P. Hallahan (Eds.), *Identification of learning disabilities: Research to practice* (pp. 369–426). Mahwah, NJ: Lawrence Erlbaum Associates.

Kavale, K. A. (2002). Mainstreaming to full inclusion: From orthogenesis to pathogenesis of an idea. *International Journal of Disability, Development and Education, 49,* 201–214.

Kavale, K. A., & Forness, S. R. (1998). Covariance in learning disability and behavior disorder: An examination of classification and placement issues. In T. E. Scruggs & M. A. Mastropieri (Eds.), *Advances in learning and behavioral disabilities (Vol. 12)* (pp. 1–42). Greenwich, CT: Jai Press.

Kavale, K. A., & Forness, S. R. (1999). Effectiveness of special education. In C. R. Reynolds & T. B. Gutkin (Eds.), *The handbook of school psychology* (3rd ed., pp. 984–1024). New York: Wiley.

Kavale, K. A., & Forness, S. R. (2000). What definitions of learning disability say and don't say: A critical analysis. *Journal of Learning Disabilities, 33,* 239–256.

Kavale, K. A., Holdnack, J. A., & Mostert, M. P. (2005). Responsiveness to intervention and the identification of specific learning disability: A critique and alternative proposal. *Learning Disability Quarterly, 28,* 2–16.

Kaye, W. H., Bulik, C. M., Thornton, L., Barbarich, N., & Masters, K. (2004). Comorbidity of anxiety disorders with anorexia and bulimia nervosa. *American Journal of Psychiatry, 161,* 2215–2221.

Kaysen, S. (1993). *Girl, interrupted.* New York: Turtle Bay Books.

Kazak, A. E. (2005). Evidence-based interventions for survivors of childhood cancer and their families. *Journal of Pediatric Psychology, 30,* 29–39.

Kazak, A. E., Alderfer, M., Rourke, M. T., Simms, S., Streisand, R., & Grossman, J. R. (2004). Posttraumatic stress disorder (PTSD) and posttraumatic stress symptoms (PTSS) in families of adolescent childhood cancer survivors. *Journal of Pediatric Psychology, 29,* 211–219.

Kazak, A. E., Alderfer, M. A., Streisand, R., Simms, S. Rourke, M. T., Barakat, L. P., Gallagher, P., & Cnaan, A. (2004). Treatment of posttraumatic stress symptoms in adolescent survivors of childhood cancer and their families: A randomized clinical trail. *Journal of Family Psychology, 18,* 493–504.

Kazarian, S. S., & Evans, D. R. (Eds.). (1998). *Cultural clinical psychology: Theory, research, and practice.* New York: Oxford University Press.

Kazdin, A. E. (1989). Developmental psychopathology: Current research, issues, and directions. *American Psychologist, 44,* 180–187.

Kazdin, A. E. (1996). Developing effective treatments for children and adolescents. In E. D. Hibbs & P. S. Jensen (Eds.), *Psychosocial treatments for child and adolescent disorders: Empirically based strategies for clinical practice* (pp. 9–18). Washington, DC: American Psychological Association.

Kazdin, A. E. (1997). Conduct disorder across the life-span. In S. S. Luthar, J. A. Burack, D. Cicchetti, & J. R. Weisz (Eds.), *Developmental psychopathology: Perspectives on adjustment, risk, and disorder* (pp. 248–272). New York: Cambridge University Press.

Kazdin, A. E. (2001). Almost clinically significant ($p < .10$): Current measures may only approach clinical significance. *Clinical Psychology: Science and Practice, 8,* 455–462.

Kazdin, A. E. (2005a). Evidence-based assessment for children and adolescents: Issues in measurement development and clinical application. *Journal of Clinical Child and Adolescent Psychology, 34,* 548–558.

Kazdin, A. E. (2005b). *Parent management training: Treatment for oppositional, aggressive, and antisocial behavior in children and adolescents.* New York: Oxford University Press.

Kazdin, A. E., Marciano, P. L., & Whitley, M. K. (2005). The therapeutic alliance in cognitive-behavioral treatment of children referred for oppositional, aggressive, and antisocial behavior. *Journal of Consulting and Clinical Psychology, 73,* 726–730.

Kazdin, A. E., & Wassell, G. (1999). Barriers to treatment participation and therapeutic change among children referred for conduct disorder. *Journal of Clinical Child Psychology, 28,* 160–172.

Kazdin, A. E., & Wassell, G. (2000). Therapeutic changes in children, parents, and families resulting from treatment of children with conduct problems. *Journal of the American Academy of Child and Adolescent Psychiatry, 39,* 414–420.

Kazdin, A. E., & Weisz, J. R. (1998). Identifying and developing empirically supported child and adolescent treatments. *Journal of Consulting and Clinical Psychology, 66,* 19–36.

Kazdin, A. E., & Weisz, J. R. (2003). *Evidence-based psychotherapies for children and adolescents.* New York: Guilford Press.

Kazdin, A. E., & Whitley, M. K. (2003). Treatment of parental stress to enhance therapeutic change among children referred for aggressive and antisocial behavior. *Journal of Consulting and Clinical Psychology, 71,* 504–515.

Kazdin, A. E., & Whitley, M. K. (2006a). Comorbidity, case complexity, and effects of evidence-based treatment for children referred for disruptive behavior. *Journal of Consulting and Clinical Psychology, 74,* 455–467.

Kazdin, A. E., & Whitley, M. K. (2006b). Pretreatment social relations, therapeutic alliance, and improvements in parenting practices in parent management training. *Journal of Consulting and Clinical Psychology, 74,* 346–355.

Keane, S. P., & Calkins, S. D. (2004). Predicting kindergarten peer social status from toddler and preschool problem behavior. *Journal of Abnormal Child Psychology, 32,* 409–423.

Keane, T. M., Friedman, M. J., & Foa, E. B. (Eds.). (2004). *Effective treatments for PTSD: Practice guidelines from the International Society for Traumatic Stress Studies.* New York: Guilford Press.

Kearney, C. A., & Hugelshofer, D. S. (2000). Systemic and clinical strategies for preventing school refusal behavior in youth. *Journal of Cognitive Psychotherapy, 14,* 51–65.

Kearney, C. A., Sims, K. E., Pursell, C. R., & Tillotson, C. A. (2003). Separation anxiety disorder in young children: A longitudinal and family analysis. *Journal of Clinical Child and Adolescent, 32,* 593–598.

Keating, K. A. (1998). Sexual abuse of persons with disabilities. *Advances in Special Education, 11,* 279–289.

Keel, P. K., & Klump, K. L. (2003). Are eating disorders culture-bound syndromes? Implications for conceptualizing their etiology. *Psychological Bulletin, 129,* 747–769.

Keenan, K., Hipwell, A., Duax, J., Stouthamer-Loeber, M. & Loeber, R. (2004). Phenomenology of depression in young girls. *Journal of the American Academy of Child and Adolescent Psychiatry, 43,* 1098–1106.

Keenan, K., & Wakschlag, L. S. (2000). More than the terrible twos: The nature and severity of behavior problems in clinic-referred preschool children. *Journal of Abnormal Child Psychology, 28,* 33–46.

Keiley, M. K., Bates, J. E., Dodge, K. A., & Pettit, G. S. (2000). A cross-domain growth analysis: Externalizing and internalizing behaviors during 8 years of childhood. *Journal of Abnormal Child Psychology, 28,* 161–179.

Keller, T. E., Spieker, S. J., & Gilchrist, L. (2005). Patterns of risk and trajectories of preschool problem behaviors: A person-oriented analysis of attachment in context. *Development and Psychopathology, 17,* 349–384.

Kellerman, J. (1993). *Devil's waltz.* New York: Bantam.

Kellogg, N. D., Hoffman, T. J., & Taylor, E. R. (1999). Early sexual experiences among pregnant and parenting adolescents. *Adolescence, 34,* 293–303.

Kelly, J. B. (2000). Children's adjustment in conflicted marriage and divorce: A decade review of research. *Journal of the American Academy of Child and Adolescent psychiatry, 39,* 963–973.

Kelly, J. A., Somlai, A. M., Benotsch, E. G., Amirkhanian, Y. A., Fernandez, M. I., Stevenson, L. Y., Sitzler, C. A., McAuliffe, T. L., Brown, K. D., & Opgenorth, K. M. (2006). Programmes, resources, and needs of HIV-prevention nongovernmental organizations (NGOs) in Africa, Central/Eastern Europe and Central Asia, Latin American and the Caribbean. *AIDS Care, 18,* 12–21.

Keltner, D., Caps, L., Kring, A. M., Young, R. C., & Heerey, E. A. (2001). Just teasing: A conceptual analysis and empirical review. *Psychological Bulletin, 127,* 229–248.

Kelvin, R. G., Goodyer, I. M., & Altham, P. M. E. (1996). Temperament and psychopathology amongst siblings of probands with depressive and anxiety disorders. *Journal of Child Psychology and psychiatry and Allied Disciplines, 37,* 543–550.

Kemenoff, S., Jachimczyk, J., & Fussner, A. (1998). Structural family therapy. In D. M. Lawson & F. F. Prevatt (Eds.), *Casebook in family therapy* (pp. 111–145). Belmont, CA: Brooks/Cole.

Kendall, J., & Hatton, D. (2002). Racism as a source of health disparity in families with children with attention deficit hyperactivity disorder. *Advances in Nursing Science, 25,* 22–39.

Kendall, P. C. (1992). *Coping cat workbook.* Ardmore, PA: Workbook Publishing.

Kendall, P. C. (Ed.). (2006). *Child and adolescent therapy: Cognitive-behavioral procedures* (3rd ed.). New York: Guilford Press.

Kendall, P. C., Aschenbrand, S. G., & Hudson, J. L. (2003). Child-focused treatment of anxiety. In A. E. Kazdin & J. R. Weisz (Eds.), *Evidence-based psychotherapies for children and adolescents* (pp. 81–100). New York: Guilford Press.

Kendall, P. C., Brady, E. U., & Verduin, T. L. (2001). Comorbidity in childhood anxiety disorders and treatment outcome. *Journal of the American Academy of Child and Adolescent Psychiatry, 40,* 787–794.

Kendall, P. C., & Braswell, L. (1993). *Cognitive-behavioral therapy for impulsive children* (2nd ed.). New York: Guilford Press.

Kendall, P. C., Flannery-Schroeder, E. C., & Ford, J. D. (1999). Therapy outcome research methods. In P. C. Kendall, J. N. Butcher, & G. N. Holmbeck (Eds.), *Handbook of research methods in clinical psychology* (2nd ed., pp. 330–363). New York: Wiley.

Kendall, P. C., Hudson, J. L., Choudhury, M., Webb, A., & Pimentel, S. (2005). Cognitive-behavioral treatment for childhood anxiety disorders. In E. D. Hibbs & P. S. Jensen (Eds.), *Psychosocial treatment for child and adolescent disorders: Empirically based strategies for clinical practice* (2nd ed., pp. 47–73). Washington, DC: American Psychological Association.

Kendall, P. C., Marrs, A. L., & Chu, B. C. (1998). Cognitive-behavioral therapy. In T. Ollendic (Ed.), *Comprehensive clinical psychology (Vol. 5)* (pp. 131–148). Kidlington, Oxford: Elsevier Science.

Kendall, P. C., Safford, S., Flannery-Schroeder, E., & Webb, A. (2004). Child anxiety treatment: Outcomes in adolescence and impact on substance use and depression at 7.4-year follow-up. *Journal of Consulting and Clinical Psychology, 72,* 276–287.

Kendall, P. C., & Suveg, C. (2006). Treating anxiety disorders in youth. In P. C. Kendall (Ed.), *Child and adolescent therapy: Cognitive-behavioral procedures* (3rd ed., pp. 243–294). New York: Guilford Press.

Kennard, B. D., Ginsburg, G. S., Feeny, N. C., Sweeney, M., & Zagurski, R. (2005). Implementation challenges to TADS cognitive-behavioral therapy. *Cognitive and Behavioral Practice, 12,* 230–239.

Kent, L., Evans, J., Paul, M., & Sharp, M. (1999). Comorbidity of autistic spectrum disorders in children with Down syndrome. *Developmental Medicine & Child Neurology, 41,* 153–158.

Kerig, P. K. (1998). Moderators and mediators of the effects of interparental conflict on children's adjustment. *Journal of Abnormal Child Psychology, 26,* 199–212.

Kerns, K. A., Aspelmeier, J. E., Gentzler, A. L., & Grabill, C. M. (2001). Parent-child attachment and monitoring in middle childhood. *Journal of Family Psychology, 15,* 69–81.

Kerr, D. C. R., Lopez, N. L., Olson, S. L., & Sameroff, A. J. (2004). Parental discipline and externalizing behavior problems in early childhood: The roles of moral regulation and child gender. *Journal of Abnormal Child Psychology, 32,* 369–383.

Kerr, D. C. R., Preuss, L. J., & King, C. A. (2006). Suicidal adolescents' social support from family and peers: Gender-specific associations with psychopathology. *Journal of Abnormal Child Psychology, 34,* 103–114.

Kerwin, M. E. (2005). Collaboration between child welfare and substance-abuse fields: Combined treatment programs for mothers. *Journal of Pediatric Psychology, 30,* 581–597.

Khamis, V. (2005). Post-traumatic stress disorder among school age Palestinian children. *Child Abuse and Neglect, 29,* 81–95.

Kiesler, C. A. (2000). The next wave of change for psychology and mental health services in the health care revolution. *American Psychologist, 55,* 481–487.

Kilgore, K., Snyder, J., & Lentz, C. (2000). The contribution of parental discipline, parental monitoring, and school risk to early-onset conduct problems in African American boys and girls. *Developmental Psychology, 36,* 835–845.

Killen, J. D., Robinson, T. N., Ammerman, S., Hayward, C., Rogers, J., Stone, C., Samuels, D., Levin, S. K., Green, S., & Schatzberg, A. F. (2004). Randomized clinical trial of the efficacy of bupropion combined with nicotine patch in the treatment of adolescent smokers. *Journal of Consulting and Clinical Psychology, 72,* 729–735.

Kilpatrick, D. G., Acierno, R., Saunders, B., Resnick, H. S., Best, C. L., & Schnurr, P. P. (2000). Risk factors for adolescent substance abuse and dependence: Data from a national sample. *Journal of Consulting and Clinical Psychology, 68,* 19–30.

Kilpatrick, D. G., Ruggiero, K. J., Acierno, R., Saunders, B. E., Resnick, H. S., & Best, C. L. (2003). Violence and risk of PTSD, major depression, substance abuse/dependence, and comorbidity: Results from the national survey of adolescents. *Journal of Consulting and Clinical Psychology, 71,* 692–700.

Kim, B., Lee, C., Hwang, J., Shin, M., & Cho, S. (2005). Effectiveness and safety of Risperidone for children and adolescents with chronic tic or Tourette disorders in Korea. *Journal of Child and Adolescent Psychopharmacology, 15,* 318–324.

Kim, I. J., Ge, X., Brody, G. H., Conger, R. D., Gibbons, F. X., & Simons, R. L. (2003). Parenting behaviors and the occurrence and co-occurrence of depressive symptoms and conduct problems among African American children. *Journal of Family Psychology, 17,* 571–583.

Kim, S., & Brody, G. H. (2005). Longitudinal pathways to psychological adjustment among Black youth living in single-parent households. *Journal of Family Psychology, 19,* 305–313.

Kim, S. Y., & Ge, X. (2000). Parenting practices and adolescent depressive symptoms in Chinese American families. *Journal of Family Psychology, 14,* 420–435.

Kim, W. J., Kim, L. I., & Rue, D. S. (1997). Korean American children. In G. Johnson-Powell & J. Yamamoto (Eds.), *Transcultural child development: Psychological assessment and treatment* (pp. 183–207). New York: Wiley.

Kim-Cohen, J., Arseneault, L., Caspi, A., Tomas, M. P., Taylor, A., & Moffitt, T. E. (2005). Validity of DSM-IV conduct disorder in $4\frac{1}{2}$–5-year-old children: A longitudinal epidemiological study. *American Journal of Psychiatry, 162,* 1108–1117.

Kimonis, E. R., & Frick, P. J. (2006). Conduct disorder. In R. T. Ammerman (Ed.), *Comprehensive handbook of personality and psychopathology: Child psychopathology (Vol 3)* (pp. 299–315). Hoboken, NJ: Wiley.

Kimonis, E. R., Frick, P. J., & Barry, C. T. (2004). Callous-unemotional traits and delinquent peer affiliation. *Journal of Consulting and Clinical Psychology, 72,* 956–966.

King, C. A., Katz, S. H., Ghaziuddin, N., Brand, E., Hill, E., & McGovern, L. (1997). Diagnosis and assessment of depression and suicidality using the NIMH Diagnostic Interview Schedule for children (DISC-2.3). *Journal of Abnormal Child Psychology, 25,* 173–181.

King, G., King, S., Rosenbaum, P., & Goffin, R. (1999). Family-centered caregiving and well-being of parents of children with disabilities: Linking process with outcome. *Journal of Pediatric Psychology, 24,* 41–53.

King, N. J., & Bernstein, G. A. (2001). School refusal in children and adolescents: A review of the past 10 years. *Journal of the Academy of Child and Adolescent Psychiatry, 40,* 197–205.

King, N. J., Muris, P., & Ollendick, T. H. (2004). Specific phobia. In T. L. Morris & J. S. March (Eds.), *Anxiety disorders in children and adolescents* (2nd ed., pp. 263–279). New York: Guilford Press.

King, N. J., Tonge, B. J., Mullen, P., Myerson, N., Heyne, D., Rollings, S., Martin, R., & Ollendick, T. H. (2000). Treating sexually abused children with posttraumatic stress symptoms: A randomized clinical trail. *Journal of the American Academy of Child and Adolescent Psychiatry, 39,* 1347–1355.

King, R. A., Schwab-Stone, M., Flisher, A. J., Greenwald, S., Kramer, R. A., Goodman, S. H., Lahey, B. B., Shaffer, D., & Gould, M. S. (2001). Psychosocial and risk behavior correlates of youth suicide attempts and suicidal ideation. *Journal of the American Academy of Child and Adolescent Psychiatry, 40,* 837–846.

Kinsfogel, K. M., & Grych, J. H. (2004). Interparental conflict and adolescent dating relationships: Integrating cognitive, emotional, and peer influences. *Journal of Family Psychology, 18,* 505–515.

Kinsman, A. M., Wildman, B. G., & Smucker, W. D. (1999). Brief report: Parent report about health care use: Relationship to child's and parent's psychosocial problems. *Journal of Pediatric Psychology, 24,* 435–439.

Kirk, S., Zeller, M., Claytor, R., Santangelo, M., Khoury, P. R., & Daniels, S. R. (2005). The relationship of health outcomes to improvement in BMI in children and adolescents. *Obesity Research, 13,* 876–882.

Kirkland, K., & Kirkland, K. L. (2001). Frequency of child custody evaluation complaints and related disciplinary action: A survey of the Association of State and Provincial Psychology Boards. *Professional Psychology: Research and Practice, 32,* 171–174.

Kirmayer, L. J., Boothroyd, L. J., & Hodgins, S. (1998). Attempted suicide among Inuit youth: Psychosocial correlates and implications for prevention. *Canadian Journal of Psychiatry, 43,* 816–822.

Kistner, J., Balthazor, M., Risi, S., & Burton, C. (1999). Predicting dysphoria in adolescence from actual and perceived peer acceptance in childhood. *Journal of Clinical Child Psychology, 28,* 94–104.

Kistner, J. A., David, C. F., & White, B. A. (2003). Ethnic and sex differences in children's depressive symptoms: Mediating effects of perceived and actual competence. *Journal of Clinical Child and Adolescent, 32,* 341–350.

Kistner, J. A., David-Ferdon, C. F., Repper, K. K., & Joiner, T. E. (2006). Bias and accuracy of children's perceptions of peer acceptance: Prospective associations with depressive symptoms. *Journal of Abnormal Child Psychology, 34,* 349–361.

Kitzmann, K. M., & Beech, B. M. (2006). Family-based interventions for pediatric obesity: Methodological and conceptual challenges from family psychology. *Journal of Family Psychology, 20,* 175–189.

Kitzmann, K. M., Gaylord, N. K., Holt, A. R., & Kenny, E. D. (2003). Child witnesses to domestic violence: A meta-analytic review. *Journal of Consulting and Clinical Psychology, 71,* 339–352.

Klar, H., & Berg, I. K. (1999). Solution-focused brief therapy. In D. M. Lawson & F. F. Prevatt (Eds.), *Casebook in family therapy* (pp. 232–258). Belmont, CA: Brooks/Cole.

Klein, D. N., Depue, R. A., & Slater, J. F. (1985). Cyclothymia in the adolescent offspring of parents with bipolar disorder. *Journal of Abnormal Psychology, 94,* 115–127.

Klein, D. N., Dougherty, L. R., & Olino, T. M. (2005). Toward guidelines for evidence-based assessment of depression in children and adolescents. *Journal of Clinical Child and Adolescent Psychology, 34,* 412–432.

Klein, K., Forehand, R., & Family Health Project Research Group. (2000). Family processes as resources for African American children exposed to a constellation of sociodemographic risk factors. *Journal of Clinical Child Psychology, 29,* 53–65.

Klein, M. (1957). *Envy and gratitude*. New York: Basic Books.

Kliewer, W., Murrelle, L., Mejia, R., Torres Y., & Angold, A. (2001). Exposure to violence against a family member and internalizing symptoms in Colombian adolescents: The protective effects of family support. *Journal of Consulting and Clinical Psychology, 69*, 971–982.

Klin, A., & Volkmar, F. R. (1997). The pervasive developmental disorders: Nosology and profiles of development. In S. S. Luthar, J. A. Burack, D. Cicchetti, & J. R. Weisz (Eds.), *Developmental psychopathology: Perspectives on adjustment, risk, and disorder* (pp. 208–226). New York: Cambridge University Press.

Klinger, L. G., Dawson, G., & Renner, P. (2003). Autistic disorder. In E. J. Mash, & B. A. Barkley (Eds.), *Child psychopathology* (2nd ed., pp. 409–454). New York: Guilford Press.

Klonoff, E. A., & Landrine, H. (2004). Predicting youth access to tobacco: The role of youth versus store-clerk behavior and issues of ecological validity. *Health Psychology, 23*, 517–524.

Klorman, R., Hazel-Fernandez, L. A., Shaywitz, S. E., Fletcher, J. M., Marchione, K. E., Holahan, J. M., Stuebing, K. K., & Shaywitz, B. A. (1999). Executive functioning deficits in attention-deficit/hyperactivity disorder are independent of oppositional defiant or reading disorder. *Journal of the American Academy of Child and Adolescent Psychiatry, 38*, 1148–1155.

Klump, K. L., McGue, M., & Iacono, W. G. (2000). Age differences in genetic and environmental influences on eating attitudes and behaviors in preadolescent and adolescent female twins. *Journal of Abnormal Psychology, 109*, 239–251.

Klusman, L. E. (2001). Prescribing psychologists and patients' medical needs: Lessons from clinical psychiatry. *Professional Psychology: Research and Practice, 32*, 496–500.

Knapp, C. (1996). *Drinking: A love story*. New York: Delta/Dell Publishing.

Knapp, P. (2001). Ethics of ECT for children: Reply. *Journal of the Academy of Child and Adolescent Psychiatry, 40*, 387–388.

Knell, S. M. (1998). Cognitive-behavioral play therapy. *Journal of Clinical Child Psychology, 27*, 28–33.

Knitzer, J. (2000). Helping troubled children and families: A paradigm of public responsibility. In J. Rappaport & E. Seidman (Eds.), *Handbook of community psychology* (pp. 541–563). New York: Kluwer Academic/Plenum Publishers.

Kochman, F. J., Hantouche, E. G., Ferrari, P., Lancrenon, S., Bayart, D., & Akiskal, H. S. (2005). Cyclothymic temperament as a prospective predictor of bipolarity and suicidality in children and adolescents with major depressive disorder. *Journal of Affective Disorders, 85*, 181–189.

Kodish, E. (2005). *Ethics and research with children: A case-based approach*. New York: Oxford University Press.

Koenen, K. C., Moffitt, T. E., Caspi, A., Taylor, A., & Purcell, S. (2003). Domestic violence is associated with environmental suppression of IQ in young children. *Development and Psychopathology, 15*, 297–311.

Koger, S. M., Schettler, T., & Weiss, B. (2005). Environmental toxicants and developmental disabilities: A challenge for psychologists. *American Psychologist, 60*, 243–255.

Kokko, K., & Pulkkinen, L. (2000). Aggression in childhood and long-term unemployment in adulthood: A cycle of maladaptation and some protective factors. *Developmental Psychology, 36*, 463–472.

Kolko, D. J. (1988). Educational programs to promote awareness and prevention of child sexual victimization: A review and methodological critique. *Clinical Psychology Review, 8*, 195–209.

Kolko, D. J., & Ammerman, R. T. (1988). Firesetting. In M. Hersen & C. G. Last (Eds.), *Child behavior therapy casebook* (pp. 243–262). New York: Plenum Press.

Kolko, D. J., Brent, D. A., Baugher, M., Bridge, J., & Birmaher, B. (2000). Cognitive and family therapies for adolescent depression: Treatment specificity, mediation, and moderation. *Journal of Consulting and Clinical Psychology, 68*, 603–614.

Kolko, D. J., & Stauffer, J. (1991). Child sexual abuse. In R. T. Ammerman & M. Hersen (Eds.), *Case studies in family violence* (pp. 153–170). New York: Plenum.

Koocher, G. P., & Keith-Spiegel, P. (1998). *Ethics in psychology: Professional standards and cases* (2nd ed.). New York: Oxford University Press.

Kooij, J. J. S., Buitelaar, J. K., van den Oord, E. J., Furer, J. W., Rijnders, E. A., & Hodiamont, P. P. G. (2005). Internal and external validity of attention-deficit hyperactivity disorder in a population-based sample of adults. *Psychological Medicine, 35*, 817–827.

Kooistra, L., Crawford, S., Dewey, D., Cantell, M., & Kaplan, B. J. (2005). Motor correlates of ADHD: Contribution of reading disability and oppositional defiant disorder. *Journal of Learning Disabilities, 38*, 195–206.

Koontz, K., Short, A. D., Kalinyak, K., & Noll, R. B. (2004). A randomized, controlled pilot trail of a school intervention for children with sickle cell anemia. *Journal of Pediatric Psychology, 29*, 7–17.

Kopfstein, R. (2003). Early intervention and prevention: Issues and services. In R. L. Schalock, P. C. Baker, & M. D. Croser (Eds.), *Embarking on a new century: Mental retardation at the end of the 20th century* (pp. 153–166). Washington, DC: American Association on Mental Retardation.

Kopp, S. (2003). Swedish child and adolescent psychiatric out-patients: A five-year cohort. *European Child and Adolescent Psychiatry, 12*, 30–35.

Korbin, J. E., Coulton, C. J., Chard, S., Platt-Houston, C., & Su, M. (1998). Impoverishment and child maltreatment in African American and European American neighborhoods. *Development and Psychopathology, 10*, 215–233.

Korchin, S. J. (1976). *Modern clinical psychology*. New York: Basic Books.

Kornberg, J. R., Brown, J. L., Sadovnick, A. d., Remick, R. A., Keck, P. E., McElroy, S. L., Rapaport, M. H., Thompson, P. M., Kaul, J. B., Vrabel, C. M., Schommer, S. C., Wilson, T., Pizzuco, D., Jameson, S., Schibuk, L., & Kelsoe, J. R. (2000). Evaluating the parent-of-origin effect in bipolar affective disorder. Is a more penetrant subtype transmitted paternally. *Journal of Affective Disorders, 59*, 183–192.

Kortegaard, L. S., Hoerder, K., Joergensen, J., Gillberg, C., & Kyvik, K. O. (2001). A preliminary population-based twin study of self-reported eating disorder. *Psychological Medicine, 31*, 361–365.

Koss, M. P., Yuan, N. P., Dightman, D., Prince, R. J., Polacca, M., Sanderson, B., & Goldman, D. (2003). Adverse childhood exposures and alcohol dependence among seven Native American tribes. *American Journal of Preventive Medicine, 25*, 238–244.

Kovacs, M. (1992). *Children's Depression Inventory Manual*. North Tonawanda, NY: Multi-Health Systems.

Kovacs, M. (1996). Presentation and course of major depressive disorder during childhood and later years of the life span. *Journal of the American Academy of Child and Adolescent Psychiatry, 35*, 705–715.

Kovacs, M. (1997). Chronic depression in childhood. In H. S. Akiskal & G. B. Cassano (Eds.), *Dysthymia and the spectrum of chronic depressions* (pp. 208–219). New York: Guilford Press.

Kovacs, M., Obrosky, S., Gatsonis, C., & Richards, C. (1997). First-episode major depressive and dysthymic disorder in childhood: Clinical and sociodemographic factors in recovery. *Journal of the American Academy of Child and Adolescent Psychiatry, 36*, 777–784.

Kowatch, R. A., & Fristad, M. A. (2006). Bipolar disorders. In R. T. Ammerman (Ed.), *Comprehensive handbook of personality and psychopathology: Child psychopathology* (Vol. 3, pp. 217–232). Hoboken, NJ: Wiley.

Kowatch, R. A., Fristad, M., Birmaher, B., Wagner, K. D., Findling, R. L., Hellander, M., & The Child Psychiatric Workgroup on Bipolar Disorder. (2005). Treatment guidelines for children and adolescents with bipolar disorder. *Journal of the American Academy of Child and Adolescent Psychiatry, 44,,* 213–235.

Kozlowska, K. (2003). Good children with conversion disorder: Breaking the silence. *Clinical Child Psychology and Psychiatry, 8*, 73–90.

Kozol, J. (1988). *Rachel and her children: Homeless families in America*. New York: Fawcett Columbine.

Kozol, J. (2000). *Ordinary resurrections: Children in the years of hope*. New York: HarperCollins.

Krahn, G. L., & Eisert, D. (2000). Qualitative methods in clinical psychology. In D. Drotar (Ed.), *Handbook of research in pediatric and clinical child psychology* (pp. 145–164). New York: Plenum Press.

Krain, A. L., & Kendall, P. C. (2000). The role of parental emotional distress in parent report of child anxiety. *Journal of Clinical Child Psychology, 29*, 328–335.

Kramer, J. R., Loney, J., Ponto, L. B., Roberts, M. A., & Grossman, S. (2000). Predictors of adult height and weight in boys treated with methylphenidate for childhood behavior problems. *Journal of the American Academy of Child and Adolescent Psychiatry, 39*, 517–524.

Kramer, T. L., Robbins, J. M., Phillips, S. D., Miller, T. L., & Burns, B. J. (2003). Detection and outcomes of substance use disorders in adolescents seeking mental health treatment. *Journal of the American Academy of Child and Adolescent Psychiatry, 42*, 1318–1326.

Kranzler, H., Roofeh, D., Gerbino-Rosen, G., Dombrowski, C., McMeniman, M., DeThomas, C., Frederickson, A., Nusser, L., Bienstock, M. D., Fisch, G. S., & Kimra, S. (2005). Clozapine: Its impact on aggressive behavior among children and adolescents with schizophrenia. *Journal of the American Academy of Child and Adolescent Psychiatry, 44,* 55–63.

Kratochvil, C. J., Newcorn, J. H., Arnold, L. E., Duesenberg, D., Emslie, G. J., Quintana, H., Sarkis, E. H., Wagner, K. D., Gao, H., Michelson, D., & Biederman, J. (2005). Atomoxetine alone or combined with fluoxetine for treating ADHD with comorbid depressive or anxiety symptoms. *Journal of the American Academy of Child and Adolescent Psychiatry, 44*, 915–924.

Kratochwill, T. R., Sheridan, S. M., Carlson, J., & Lasecki, K. L. (1999). Advances in behavioral assessment. In C.R. Reynolds & T. B. Gutkin (Eds.), *The handbook of school psychology* (3rd ed., pp. 350–382). New York: Wiley.

Kremers, S. P. J., Brug, J., de Vries, H., & Engels, R. C. M. E. (2003). Parenting style and adolescent fruit consumption. *Appetite, 41*, 43–50.

Kremers, S. P. J., Mudde, A. N., de Vries, N. K., Brug, J., & de Vries, H. (2004). Unplanned smoking initiation: New insights and implications for interventions. *Patient Education and Counseling, 55*, 345–352.

Kress, V. E. W., Eriksen, K. P., Rayle, A. D., & Ford, S. J. W. (2005). The DSM-IV-TR and culture: Considerations for counselors. *Journal of Counseling & Development, 83*, 97–104.

Krol, N. P. C. M., De Bruyn, E. E. J., Coolen, J. C., & van Aarle, E. J. M. (2006). From CBCL to *DSM*: A comparison of two methods to screen for *DSM-IV* diagnoses using CBCL data. *Journal of Clinical Child Psychology, 35*, 127–135.

Kumra, S. Thaden, E. DeThomas, C., & Kranzier, H. (2005). Correlates of substance abuse in adolescents with treatment-refractory schizophrenia and schizoaffective disorder. *Schizophrenia Research, 73*, 369–371.

Kuncel, N. R., Hezlett, S. A., & Ones, D. S. (2001). A comprehensive meta-analysis of the predictive validity of the Graduate Record Examinations: Implications for graduate student selection and performance. *Psychological Bulletin, 127*, 162–181.

Kunkel, D., Wilson, B. J., Linz, D., Potter, J., Donnerstein, E., Smith, S. L., Blumenthal, E., & Gray, T. (1996). *The national television violence study*. Studio City, CA: Mediascope.

Kuperminc, G. P., & Brookmeyer, K. A. (2006). Developmental psychopathology. In R. T. Ammerman (Ed.), *Comprehensive handbook of personality and psychopathology: Child psychopathology* (Vol. 3, pp. 100–113). Hoboken, NJ: Wiley.

Kupfer, D. J., First, M. B., & Regier, D. A. (Eds.) (2002). *A research agenda for DSM-V*. Washington, DC: American Psychiatric Association.

Kurtz-Costes, B. E., Meece, J. L., & Floryan, J. A. (1999, August). *Children's out-of-school activities and academic achievement: A longitudinal study*. Poster presented at the American Psychological Association, Boston, MA.

Kury, S. P., Rodrigue, J. R., & Perri, M. G. (1998). Smokeless tobacco and cigarettes: Differential attitudes and behavioral intentions of young adolescents toward a hypothetical new peer. *Journal of Clinical Child Psychology, 27*, 415–422.

Kutash, K., & Rivera, V. R. (1996). *What works in children's mental health services?*. Baltimore: Paul H. Brookes.

Kutchins, H., & Kirk, S. A. (1997). *Making us crazy: DSM: The psychiatric bible and the creation of mental disorders*. New York: Free Press.

Kuther, T. L. (2006). *Your career in psychology: Clinical and counseling psychology*. Belmont, CA: Thomson Wadsworth.

Kwok, O., Haine, R. A., Sandler, I. N., Ayers, T. S., Wolchik, S. A., & Tein, J. Y. (2005). Positive parenting as a mediator of the relations between parental psychological distress and mental health problems of parentally bereaved children. *Journal of Clinical Child and Adolescent Psychology, 34*, 260–271.

Kwong, M. J., Bartholomew, K., Henderson, A. J. Z., & Trinke, S. J. (2003). The intergenerational transmission of relationship violence. *Journal of Family Psychology, 17*, 288–301.

L'Abate, L. (Ed.) (1998). *Family psychopathology: The relational roots of dysfunctional behavior*. New York: Guilford Press.

Lachar, D., & Gruber, C. P. (2001). *Personality Inventory for Children—Second Edition (PIC—2)*. Los Angeles: Western Psychological Services.

Lacourse, E., Cote, S., Nagin, D. S., Vitaro, F., Brendgen, M., & Tremblay, R. E. (2002). A longitudinal-experimental approach to testing theories of antisocial behavior development. *Development and Psychopathology, 14*, 909–924.

Ladd, G. W., & Burgess, K. B. (1999). Charting the relationship trajectories of aggressive, withdrawn, and aggressive/withdrawn children during early grade school. *Child Development, 70*, 910–929.

La Greca, A. M., & Bearman, K. J. (2003). Adherence to pediatric treatment regimens. In M. C. Roberts (Ed.), *Handbook of pediatric psychology* (3rd ed., pp. 119–140). New York: Guilford Press.

La Greca, A. M., Roberts, M. C., Silverman, W. K., & Vernberg, E. M. (2002). *Helping children cope with disasters and terrorism*. Washington, DC: American Psychological Association.

Lahey, B. B., Applegate, B., Waldman, I. D., Loft, J. D., Hankin, B. L., & Rick, J. (2004). The structure of child and adolescent psychopathology: Generating new hypotheses. *Journal of Abnormal Psychology, 113*, 358–385.

Lahey, B. B., Flagg, E. W., Bird, H. R., Schwab-Stone, M. E., Canino, G., Dulcan, M. K., Leaf, P. J., Davies, M., Brogan, D., Bourdon, K., Horwitz, S. M., Rubio-Stipec, M., Freeman, D. H., Lichtman, J. H., Shaffer, D., Goodman, S. H., Narrow, W. E., Weissman, M. M., Kandel, D. B., Jensen, P. S., Richters, J. E., & Regier, D. A. (1996). The NIMH Methods for the Epidemiology of Child and Adolescent Mental Disorders (MECA) Study: Background and methodology. *Journal of the American Academy of Child and Adolescent Psychiatry, 35*, 855–864.

Lahey, B. B., Loeber, R., Burke, J. D., & Applegate, B. (2005). Predicting future antisocial personality disorder in males from a clinical assessment in childhood. *Journal of Consulting and Clinical Psychology, 73*, 389–399.

Lahey, B. B., Loeber, R., Burke, J., Rathouz, P. J., & McBurnett, K. (2002). Waxing and waning in concert: Dynamic comorbidity of conduct disorder with other disruptive and emotional problems over 7 years among clinic-referred boys. *Journal of Abnormal Psychology, 111*, 556–567.

Lahey, B. B. Miller, T. L., Gordon, R. A., & Riley, A. W. (1999). Developmental epidemiology of the disruptive behavior disorders. In H. C. Quay & A. E. Hogan (Eds.), *Handbook of disruptive behavior disorders* (pp. 23–48). New York: Kluwer Academic/Plenum Press.

Lahey, B. B., Pelham, W. E., Loney, J., Lee, S. S., & Willcutt, E. (2005). Instability of the *DSM-IV* subtypes of ADHD from preschool through elementary school. *Archives of General Psychiatry, 62*, 896–902.

Lahey, B. B., Schwab-Stone, M., Goodman, S. H. Waldman, I. D., Canino, G. Rathouz, P. J., Miller, T. L., Dennis, K. D., Bird, H., & Jensen, P.S. (2000). Age and gender differences in oppositional behavior and conduct problems: A cross-sectional household study of middle childhood and adolescence. *Journal of Abnormal Psychology, 109*, 488–503.

Lahey, B. B., & Waldman, I. D. (2003). A developmental propensity model of the origins of conduct problems during childhood and adolescence. In B. B. Lahey, T. E. Moffitt, & A. Caspi (Eds.), *Causes of conduct disorder and juvenile delinquency* (pp. 76–117). New York: Guilford Press.

Lahey, B. B., Waldman, I. D., & McBurnett, K. (1999). The development of antisocial behavior: An integrative causal model. *Journal of Child Psychology and Psychiatry, 40*, 669–682.

Laing, R. D., & Esterson, A. (1965). *Sanity, madness and the family*. London: Tavistock.

Lamerz, A., Kuepper-Nybelen, J., Wehle, C., Bruning, N., Trost-Brinkhues, G., Brenner, H., Hebebrand, J., & Herpertz-Dahlmann, B. (2005). Social class, parental education, and obesity prevalence in a study of six-year-old children in German. *International Journal of Obesity, 29*, 373–380.

Landolt, M. A., Vollrath, M., Laimbacher, J., Gnehm, H. E., & Sennhauser, F. H. (2005). Prospective study of posttraumatic stress disorder in parents of children with newly diagnosed Type 1 diabetes. *Journal of the American Academy of Child and Adolescent Psychiatry, 44*, 682–689.

Landolt, M. A., Vollrath, V., Ribi, K., Gnehm, H. E., & Sennhauser, F. H. (2003). Incidence and associations of parental and child posttraumatic stress symptoms in pediatric patients. *Journal of Child Psychology and Psychiatry, 44*, 1199–1207.

Larsson, J. O., Larsson, H., & Lichtenstein, P. (2004). Genetic and environmental contributions to stability and change of ADHD symptoms between 8 and 13 years of age: A longitudinal twin study. *Journal of the American Academy of Child and Adolescent Psychiatry, 43*, 1267–1275.

Latimer, W. W., Newcomb, M., Winters, K. C., & Stinchfield, R. D. (2000). Adolescent substance abuse treatment outcome: The role of substance abuse problem severity, psychosocial, and treatment factors. *Journal of Consulting and Clinical Psychology, 68*, 684–696.

Latimer, W. W., Winters, K. C., Stinchfield, R., & Traver, R. E. (2000). Demographic, individual, and interpersonal predictors of adolescent alcohol and marijuana use following treatment. *Psychology of Addictive Behaviors, 14*, 162–173.

Lau, A. S., Litrownik, A. J., Newton, R. R., & Landsverk, J. (2003). Going home: The complex effects of reunification on internalizing problems among children in foster care. *Journal of Abnormal Child Psychology, 31*, 345–359.

Lau, A. S., & Weisz, J. R. (2003). Reported maltreatment among clinic-referred children: Implications for presenting problems, treatment attrition, and long-term outcomes. *Journal of the American Academy of Child and Adolescent Psychiatry, 42*, 1327–1334.

Lau, J. Y. F., Eley, T. C., & Stevenson, J. (2006). Examining the state-trait anxiety relationship: A behavioural genetic approach. *Journal of Abnormal Child Psychology, 34,* 19–27.

Lau, J. Y. F., Kim, J. H., Tsui, H., Cheung, A., Lau, M., & Yu, A. (2005). The relationship between physical maltreatment and substance use among adolescents: A survey of 95,788 adolescents in Hong Kong. *Journal of Adolescent Health, 37,* 110–119.

Lauck, J. (2000). *Blackbird: A childhood lost and found.* New York: Pocket Books.

Laugesen, N., Dugas, M. J., & Bukowski, W. M. (2003). Understanding adolescent worry: The application of a cognitive model. *Journal of Abnormal Child Psychology, 31,* 55–64.

Lauriello, J., Lenroot, R., & Bustillo, J. R. (2003). Maximizing the synergy between pharmacotherapy and psychosocial therapies for schizophrenia. *Psychiatric Clinics of North America, 26,* 191–211.

Lawrence, B. K. (1999). *Bitter ice: A memoir of love, food, and obsession.* New York: William Morrow.

Lawrence, C. M., & Thelen, M. H. (1995). Body image, dieting, and self-concept: Their relation in African-American and Caucasian children. *Journal of Clinical Child Psychology, 24,* 41–48.

Lawrence, E. C. (1999). The humanistic approach of Virginia Satir. In D. M. Lawson & F. F. Prevatt (Eds.), *Casebook in family therapy* (pp. 169–187). Belmont, CA: Wadsworth Publishing Company.

Le, T. N., & Stockdale, G. D. (2005). Individualism, collectivism, and delinquency in Asian American adolescents. *Journal of Clinical Child and Adolescent Psychology, 34,* 681–691.

Leaf, P. J., Alegia, M., Cohen, P., Goodman, S. H., Horwitz, S. M., Hoven, C. W., Narrow, W. E., Vaden-Kiernan, M., & Regier, D. A. (1996). Mental health service use in the community and schools: Results from the four-community MECA Study. *Journal of the American Academy of Child and Adolescent Psychiatry, 35,* 889–897.

LeBlanc, A. N. (2003). *Random family, love, drugs, trouble and coming of age in the Bronx.* New York: Scribner.

LeBlanc, M., & Ritchie, M. (1999). Predictors of play therapy outcomes. *International Journal of Play Therapy, 8,* 19–34.

Lebow, J. (2003). Integrative family therapy for disputes involving child custody and visitation. *Journal of Family Psychology, 17,* 181–192.

LeCroy, C. W. (1994). *Handbook of child and adolescent treatment manuals.* New York: Lexington Books.

Lee, C. M., Beauregard, C., & Bax, K. A. (2005). Child-related disagreements, verbal aggression, and children's internalizing and externalizing behavior problems. *Journal of Family Psychology, 19,* 237–245.

Lee, C. M., & Gotlib, I. H. (1991). Family disruption, parental availability and child adjustment. In R. Prinz (Ed.), *Advances in behavioral assessment of children and families* (Vol. 5), (pp. 173–202). New York: Kingsley.

Lee, S. S., & Hinshaw, S. P. (2004). Severity of adolescent delinquency among boys with and without attention deficit hyperactivity disorder: Predictions from early antisocial behavior and peer status. *Journal of Clinical Child and Adolescent, 33,* 705–716.

Lee, V. E., Brooks-Gunn, J., Schnur, E., & Liaw, F. (1990). Are Head Start effects sustained? A longitudinal follow-up comparison of disadvantaged children attending Head Start, no preschool, and other preschool programs. *Child Development, 61,* 495–507.

Lefkowitz, E. S., Sigman, M., & Au, T. K. (2000). Helping mothers discuss sexuality and AIDS with adolescents. *Child Development, 71,* 1383–1394.

Leifer, M., Kilbane, T., Jacobsen, T., & Grossman, G. (2004). A three-generational study of transmission of risk for sexual abuse. *Journal of Clinical Child and Adolescent Psychology, 33,* 662–672.

Lemanek, K. L., Ranalii, M. A., Green, K., Biega, C., & Lupia, C. (2003). Diseases of the blood: Sickle cell disease and hemophilia. In M. C. Roberts (Ed.), *Handbook of pediatric psychology* (3rd ed., pp. 321–341). New York: Guilford Press.

Lemery, K. S., & Doelger, L. (2005). Genetic vulnerabilities to the development of psychopathology. In B. L. Hankin & J. R. Z. Abela (Eds.), *Development of psychopathology: A vulnerability-stress perspective* (pp. 161–198). Thousand Oaks, CA: Sage.

Lengua, L. J., Long, A. C., Smith, K. I., & Meltzoff, A. N. (2005). Pre-attach symptomatology and temperament as predictors of children's responses to the September 11 terrorist attacks. *Journal of Child Psychology and Psychiatry, 46,* 631–645.

Lenzenweger, M. F., & Haugaard, J. J. (Eds.). (1996). *Frontiers of developmental psychopathology.* New York: Oxford University Press.

Leon, G. R. (1990). *Case histories of psychopathology* (4th ed.). Boston: Allyn and Bacon.

Leonard, H., & Wen, X. (2002). The epidemiology of mental retardation: Challenges and opportunities in the new millennium. *Mental Retardation and Developmental Disabilities Research Reviews, 8,* 117–134.

Leonard, K. E., Elden, R. D., Wong, M. M., Zucker, R. A., Puttler, L. I., Fitzgerald, H. E., Hussong, A., Chassin, L., & Mudar, P. (2000). Developmental perspectives on risk and vulnerability in alcoholic families. *Alcoholism: Clinical and Experimental Research, 24,* 238–240.

Lerman, D. C., Parten, M., Addison, 1. R., Vorndran, C. M., Volkert, V. M., & Kodak, T. (2005). A methodology for assessing the functions of emerging speech in children with developmental disabilities. *Journal of Applied Behavior Analysis, 38,* 303–316.

Lerner, J., Safren, S. A., Henin, A., Warman, M., Heimberg, R. G., & Kendall, P. C. (1999). Differentiating anxious and depressive self-statements in youth: Factor structure of the Negative Affect Self-Statement Questionnaire among youth referred to an anxiety disorders clinic. *Journal of Clinical Child Psychology, 28,* 82–93.

Lerner, R. M., Fisher, C. B., & Weinberg, R. A. (2000). Toward a science for and of the people: Promoting civil society through the application of developmental science. *Child Development, 71,* 11–20.

Lerner, R. M., Walsh, M. E., & Howard, K. A. (1998). Developmental-contextual considerations: Person-context relations as the bases for risk and resiliency in child and adolescent development. In T. Ollendick (Ed.), *Comprehensive clinical psychology* (Vol. 5, pp. 1–24). Kidlington, Oxford: Elsevier Science.

Leslie, L. K., Hurlburt, M. S., James, S., Landsverk, J., Slymen, D. J., & Zhang, J. (2005). Relationship between entry into child welfare and mental health service use. *Psychiatric Services, 56,* 981–987.

Leslie, L. K., Weckerly, J., Landsverk, J., Hough, R. L., Hurlburt, M. S., & Wood, P. (2003). Racial/ethnic differences in the use of psychotropic medication in high-risk children and adolescents. *Journal of the American Academy of Child and Adolescent Psychiatry, 42*, 1433–1442.

Lesniak-Karpiak, K., Mazzocco, M. M. M., & Ross, J. L. (2003). Behavioral assessment of social anxiety in females with Turner or fragile X syndrome. *Journal of Autism and Developmental Disorders, 33*, 55–67.

Leung, P., & Erich, S. (2002). Family functioning of adoptive children with special needs: Implications of familial supports and child characteristics. *Children and Youth Services Review, 24*, 799–816.

Leung, D. W., & Slep, A. M. S. (2006). Predicting inept discipline: The role of parental depressive symptoms, anger, and attributions. *Journal of Consulting and Clinical Psychology, 74*, 524–534.

Levant, R. F., Moldawsky, S., & Stigall, T. T. (2000). The evolving profession of psychology: Comment on Lowe Hayes-Thomas's (2002) "The silent conversation." *Professional Psychology: Research and Practice, 31*, 346–348.

Levant, R. F., Reed, G. M., Ragusea, S. A., DiCowden, M., Murphy, M. J., Sullivan, F. Craig, P. L., & Stout, C. E. (2001). Envisioning and accessing new roles for professional psychology. *Professional Psychology: Research and Practice, 32*, 79–87.

Levant, R. F., & Silverstein, L. B. (2006). Gender is neglected by both evidence-based practices and treatment as usual. In J. C. Norcross, L. E. Beutler, & R. F. Levant (Eds.), *Evidence-based practices in mental health: Debate and dialogue on the fundamental questions* (pp. 338–345). Washington, DC: American Psychological Association.

Leve, L. D., & Chamberlain, P. (2005). Association with delinquent peers: Intervention effects for youth in the juvenile justice system. *Journal of Abnormal Child Psychology, 33*, 339–347.

Leve, L. D., Chamberlain, P., & Reid, J. B. (2005). Intervention outcomes for girls referred from juvenile justice: Effects on delinquency. *Journal of Consulting and Clinical Psychology, 73*, 1181–1185.

Levendosky, A. A., Huth-Bocks, A. C., Semel, M. A., & Shapiro, D. L. (2002). Trauma symptoms in preschool-age children exposed to domestic violence. *Journal of Interpersonal Violence, 17*, 150–164.

Leventhal, T., & Brooks-Gunn, J. (2000). The neighborhoods they live in: The effects of neighborhood residence on child and adolescent outcomes. *Psychological Bulletin, 126*, 309–337.

Leventhal, T., & Brooks-Gunn, J. (2003). Children and youth in neighborhood contexts. *Current Directions in Psychological Science, 12*, 27–31.

Levanthal, T., & Brooks-Gunn, J. (2004). A randomized study of neighborhood effects on low-income children's educational outcomes. *Developmental Psychology, 40*, 488–507.

Levine, M. P., & Smolak, L. (2001). Primary prevention of body image disturbances and disordered eating in childhood and early adolescence. In J. K. Thompson, & L. Smolak (Eds.), *Body image, eating disorders, and obesity in youth: Assessment, prevention, and treatment* (pp. 237–260). Washington, DC: American Psychological Association.

Levy, F., Hay, D. A., Bennett, K. S., & McStephen, M. (2005). Gender differences in ADHD subtype comorbidity. *Journal of the American Academy of Child and Adolescent Psychiatry, 44*, 368–376.

Lewinsohn, P. M., & Clarke, G. N. (1999). Psychosocial treatments for adolescent depression. *Clinical Psychology Review, 19*, 329–342.

Lewinsohn, P. M., Klein, D., & Seeley, J. R. (1995). Bipolar disorders in a community sample of older adolescents: Prevalence, phenomenology, comorbidity, and course. *Journal of the American Academy of Child and Adolescent Psychiatry, 34*, 454–463.

Lewinsohn, P. M., Rohde, P., Seeley, J. R., & Baldwin, C. L. (2001). Gender differences in suicide attempts from adolescence to young adulthood. *Journal of the American Academy of Child and Adolescent Psychiatry, 40*, 427–434.

Lewinsohn, P. M., Seeley, J. R., Hibbard, J., Rohde, P., & Sack, W. H. (1996). Cross-sectional and prospective relationships between physical morbidity and depression in older adolescents. *Journal of the American Academy of Child and Adolescent Psychiatry, 35*, 1120–1129.

Lewinsohn, P. M., Shankman, S. A., Gau, J. M., & Klein, D. N. (2004). The prevalence and comorbidity of subthreshold psychiatric conditions. *Psychological Medicine, 34*, 613–622.

Lewinsohn, P. M., Striegel-Moore, R. H., & Seeley, J. H. (2000). Epidemiology and natural course of eating disorders in young women from adolescence to young adulthood. *Journal of the American Academy of Child and Adolescent Psychiatry, 39*, 1284–1292.

Lewis, B. A., Freebairn, L. A., & Taylor, H. G. (2000). Academic outcomes in children with histories of speech sound disorders. *Journal of Communication Disorders, 33*, 11–30.

Lewis, B. A., Freebairn, L. A., & Taylor, H. G. (2000). Follow-up of children with early expressive phonology disorders. *Journal of Learning Disabilities, 33*, 433–444.

Lewis, T. J., Hudson, S., Richter, M., & Johnson, N. (2004). Scientifically supported practices in emotional and behavioral disorders: A proposed approach and brief review of current practices. *Behavioral Disorders, 29*, 247–259.

Li, X., Feigelman, S., & Stanton, B. (2000). Perceived parental monitoring and health risk behaviors among urban low-income African-American children and adolescents. *Journal of Adolescent Health, 27*, 43–48.

Liang, B., Bogat, G. A., & McGrath, M. P. (1993). Differential understanding of sexual abuse prevention concepts among preschoolers. *Child Abuse and Neglect, 17*, 641–650.

Libby, A. M., Orton, H. D., Novins, D. K., Beals, J., & Manson, S. M. (2005). Childhood physical and sexual abuse and subsequent depressive and anxiety disorders for two American Indian tribes. *Psychological Medicine, 35*, 329–340.

Liberman, R. P., Glick, I. D., & Kopelowicz, A. (2004). Drug and psychosocial curricula for psychiatry residents for treatment of schizophrenia: Part I. *Psychiatric Services, 55*, 1217–1219.

Libow, J. A. (1998). Factitious disorders. In T. Ollendick (Ed.), *Comprehensive clinical psychology* (Vol. 5, pp. 683–702). Kidlington, Oxford: Elsevier Science.

Libow, J. A. (2002). Beyond collusion: Active illness falsification. *Child Abuse and Neglect, 26*, 525–536.

Lichtenstein, P., & Annas, P. (2000). Heritability and prevalence of specific fears and phobias in childhood. *Journal of Child Psychology and Psychiatry, 41*, 927–937.

Lichtenstein, P., & Pedersen, N. L. (1997). Does genetic variance for cognitive abilities account for genetic variance in educational achievement and occupational status? A study of twins reared apart and twins reared together. *Social Biology, 44*, 77–90.

Lieb, R., Pfister, H., Mastaler, M., & Wittchen, H. (2000). Somatoform syndromes and disorders in a representative population sample of adolescents and young adults: Prevalence, comorbidity and impairments. *Acta Psychiatrica Scandinavica, 101*, 194–208.

Liebowitz, M. R., Turner, S. M., Piacentini, J., Beidel, D. C., Clarvit, S. R., Davies, S. O., Graae, F., Jaffer, M., Lin, S. H., Sallee, F. R., Schmidt, A. B., & Simpson, H. B. (2002). Fluoxetine in children and adolescents with OCD: A placebo-controlled trial. *Journal of the American Academy of Child and Adolescent Psychiatry, 41*, 1431–1438.

Liederman, J., Kantrowitz, L., & Flannery, K. (2005). Male vulnerability to reading disability is not likely to be a myth: A call for new data. *Journal of Learning Disabilities, 38*, 109–129.

Lijffijt, M., Kenemans, J. L., Verbaten, M. N., & van Engeland, H. (2005). A meta-analytic review of stopping performance in attention-deficit/hyperactivity disorder: Deficient inhibitory motor control? *Journal of Abnormal Psychology, 114*, 216–222.

Lilienfeld, S. O. (2003). Comorbidity between and within childhood externalizing and internalizing disorders: Reflections and directions. *Journal of Abnormal Child Psychology, 31*, 285–291.

Lillehoj, C. J., Trudeau, L., & Spoth, R. (2005). Longitudinal modeling of adolescent normative beliefs and substance initiation. *Journal of Alcohol and Drug Education, 49*, 7–41.

Lin, J., Yen, C., Li, C., & Wu, J. (2005). Patterns of obesity among children and adolescents with intellectual disabilities in Taiwan. *Journal of Applied Research in Intellectual Disabilities, 18*, 123–129.

Lin, K. K., Sandler, I. N., Ayers, T. S., Wolchik, S. A., & Luecken, L. J. (2004). Resilience in parentally bereaved children and adolescents seeking preventive services. *Journal of Clinical Child and Adolescent Psychology, 33*, 673–683.

Linares, L. O., Heeren, T., Bronfman, E., Zuckerman, B., Augustyn, M., & Tronick, E. (2001). A mediational model for the impact of exposure to community violence on early child behavior problems. *Child Development, 72*, 639–652.

Linnet, K. M., Dalsgaard, S., Obel, C., Wisborg, K., Henriksen, T. B., Rodriguez, A., Kotimaa, A., Moilanen, I., Thomsen, P. H., Olsen, J., & Jarvelin, M. (2003). Maternal lifestyle factors in pregnancy risk of attention deficit hyperactivity disorder and associated behaviors: Review of the current evidence. *American Journal of Psychiatry, 160*, 1028–1040.

Linscheid, T. R. (2000). Case studies and case series. In D. Drotar (Ed.), *Handbook of research in pediatric and clinical child psychology* (pp. 429–445). New York: Plenum Press.

Linscheid, T. R., & Butz, C. (2003). Anorexia nervosa and bulimia nervosa. In M. C. Roberts (Ed.), *Handbook of pediatric psychology* (3rd ed., pp. 636–651). New York: Guilford Press.

Lipka, O., & Siegel, L. S. (2006). Learning disabilities. In D. A. Wolfe & E. J. Mash (Eds.), *Behavioral and emotional disorders in adolescents: Nature, assessment, and treatment* (pp. 410–443). New York: Guilford Press.

Lipschitz, D. S., Rasmusson, A. M., Anyan, W., Cromwell, P., & Southwick, S. M. (2000). Clinical and functional correlates of posttraumatic stress disorder in urban adolescent girls at a primary care clinic. *Journal of the American Academy of Child and Adolescent Psychiatry, 39*, 1104–1111.

Litrownik, A. J., & Castillo-Canez, I. (2000). Childhood maltreatment: Treatment of abuse/incest survivors. In C. R. Snyder & R. E. Ingram (Eds.), *Handbook of psychological change* (pp. 520–545). New York: Wiley.

Litt, J., Taylor, H. G., Klein, N., & Hack, M. (2005). Learning disabilities in children with very low birthweight: Prevalence, neuropsychological correlates, and educational interventions. *Journal of Learning Disabilities, 38*, 130–141.

Little, L. (1999). The misunderstood child: The child with a nonverbal learning. *Journal of the Society of Pediatric Nurses, 4*, 113–121.

Liu, X., Guo, C., Okawa, M., Zhai, J., Li, Y., Uchiyama, M., Neiderhiser, J. M., & Kurita, H. (2000). Behavioral and emotional problems in Chinese children of divorced parents. *Journal of the American Academy of Child and Adolescent Psychiatry, 39*, 896–903.

Liu, X., & Sun, Z. (2005). Age of attaining nocturnal bladder control and adolescent suicidal behavior. *Journal of Affective Disorders, 87*, 281–289.

Liu, X., Sun, Z., Uchiyama, M. Li, Y., & Okawa, M. (2000). Attaining nocturnal urinary control, nocturnal enuresis, and behavioral problems in Chinese children aged 6 through 16 years. *Journal of the American Academy of Child and Adolescent Psychiatry, 39*, 1557–1564.

Liu, X., & Tein, J. (2005). Life events, psychopathology, and suicidal behavior in Chinese adolescents. *Journal of Affective Disorders, 86*, 195–203.

Lo, C. C., & Globetti, G. (2000). Gender differences in drinking patterns among Hong Kong Chinese youth: A pilot study. *Substance Use and Misuse, 35*, 1297–1306.

Lochman, J. E., Barry, T. D., & Pardini, D. A. (2003). Anger control training for aggressive youth. In A. E. Kazdin & J. R. Weisz (Eds.), *Evidence-based psychotherapies for children and adolescents* (pp. 263–281). New York: Guilford Press.

Lochman, J. E., Powell, N. R., Whidby, J. M., & Fitzgerald, D. P. (2006). Aggressive children: Cognitive-behavioral assessment and treatment. In P. C. Kendall (Ed.), *Child and adolescent therapy: Cognitive-behavioral procedures* (3rd ed., pp. 33–81). New York: Guilford Press.

Lochman, J. E., & Wells, K. C. (2004). The coping power program for preadolescent aggressive boys and their parents: Outcome effects at the 1-year- follow-up. *Journal of Consulting and Clinical Psychology, 72*, 571–578.

Lock, J., Agras, W. S., Bryson, S., & Kraemer, H. C. (2005). A comparison of short- and long-term family therapy for adolescent anorexia nervosa. *Journal of the American Academy of Child and Adolescent Psychiatry, 44*, 632–639.

Lock, J. & Steiner, H. (1999). Gay, lesbian, and bisexual youth risks for emotional, physical, and social problems: Results from a community-based survey. *Journal of the Academy of Child and Adolescent Psychiatry, 38*, 297–304.

Loeber, R., Burke, J. D., Lahey, B. B., Winters, A., & Zera, M. (2000). Oppositional defiant and conduct disorder: A review of the past 10 years, Part I. *Journal of the Academy of Child and Adolescent Psychiatry, 39*, 1468–1484.

Loeber, R., Drinkwater, M., Yin, Y., Anderson, S. J., Schmidt, L. C., & Crawford, A. (2000). Stability of family interaction from ages 6 to 18. *Journal of Abnormal Child Psychology, 28*, 353–369.

Loeber, R., Green, S. M., Lahey, B. B., Frick, P. J., & McBurnett, K. (2000). Findings on disruptive behavior disorders from the first decade of the Developmental Trends Study. *Clinical Child and Family Psychology Review, 3*, 37–60.

Loeber, R., Green, S. M., Lahey, B. B., & Kalb, L. (2000). Physical fighting in childhood as a risk factor for later mental health problems. *Journal of the American Academy of Child and Adolescent Psychiatry, 39*, 421–428.

Loeber, R., Lahey, B. B., & Thomas, C. (1991). Diagnostic conundrum of oppositional defiant disorder and conduct disorder. *Journal of Abnormal Psychology, 100*, 379–390.

Loeber, R., & Stouthamer-Loeber, M. (1998). Development of juvenile aggression and violence: Some common misconceptions and controversies. *American Psychologist, 53*, 242–259.

Loeber, R., Stouthamer-Loeber, M., & White, H. R. (1999). Developmental aspects of delinquency and internalizing problems and their association with persistent juvenile substance use between ages 7 and 18. *Journal of Clinical Child Psychology, 28*, 322–332.

Logan, D. E., & King, C. A. (2001). Parental facilitation of adolescent mental health services utilization: A conceptual and empirical review. *Clinical Psychology: Science and Practice, 8*, 319–333.

Logan, D. E., Radcliffe, J., & Smith-Whitley, K. (2002). Parent factors and adolescent sickle cell disease: Associations with patterns of health service use. *Journal of Pediatric Psychology, 27*, 475–484.

Lombroso, P. J., Pauls, D. L., & Leckman, J. F. (1994). Genetic mechanisms in childhood psychiatric disorders. *Journal of the American Academy of Child and Adolescent Psychiatry, 33*, 921–938.

Loney, B. R., Frick, P. J., Clements, C. B., Ellis, M. L., & Kerlin, K. (2003). Callous-unemotional traits, impulsivity, and emotional processing in adolescents with antisocial behavior problems. *Journal of Clinical Child and Adolescent Psychology, 32*, 66–80.

Lonigan, C. J., Phillips, B. M., & Hooe, E. S. (2003). Relations of positive and negative affectivity to anxiety and depression in children: Evidence from a latent variable longitudinal study. *Journal of Consulting and Clinical Psychology, 71*, 465–481.

Loo, S. K., & Barkley, R. A. (2005). Clinical utility of EEG in attention deficit hyperactivity disorder. *Applied Neuropsychology, 12*, 64–76.

Loomis, J. W. (2006). Learning disabilities. In R. T. Ammerman (Ed.), *Comprehensive handbook of personality and psychopathology: Child psychopathology* (Vol 3, pp. 272–284). Hoboken, NJ: Wiley.

Lopez, M. F., Forness, S. R., MacMillan, D. L., & Bocian, K. M. (1996). Children with attention deficit hyperactivity disorder and emotional or behavioral disorders in primary grades: Inappropriate placement in the learning disorder category. *Education and Treatment of Children, 19*, 286–299.

Lopez, S. R., & Guarnaccia, P. J. J. (2000). Cultural psychopathology: Uncovering the social world of mental illness. *Annual Review of Psychology, 51*, 571–598.

Lopez, S. R., Hipke, K. N., Polo, A. J., Jenkins, J. H., Karno, M., Vaughn, C., & Snyder, K. S. (2004). Ethnicity, expressed emotion, attributions, and course of schizophrenia: Family warmth matters. *Journal of Abnormal Psychology, 113*, 428–439.

Lorber, M. F. (2004). Psychophysiology of aggression, psychopathology, and conduct problems: A meta-analysis. *Psychological Bulletin, 130*, 531–552.

Lougee, L., Perlmutter, S. J., Nicolson, R., Garvey, M. A., & Swedo, S. E. (2000). Psychiatric disorders in first-degree relatives of children with pediatric autoimmune neuropsychiatric disorders associated with streptococcal infections (PANDAS). *Journal of the American Academy of Child and Adolescent Psychiatry, 39*, 1120–1126.

Loukas, A., Fitzgerald, H. E., Zucker, R. A., & von Eye, A. (2001). Parental alcoholism and co-occurring antisocial behavior: Prospective relationships to externalizing behavior problems in their young sons. *Journal of Abnormal Child Psychology, 29*, 91–106.

Loukas, A., Zucker, R. A., Fitzgerald, H. E., & Krull, J. L. (2003). Developmental trajectories of disruptive behavior problems among sons of alcoholics: Effects of parent psychopathology, family conflict, and child undercontrol. *Journal of Abnormal Psychology, 112*, 119–131.

Lovaas, O. I. (1987). Behavioral treatment and normal educational and intellectual functioning in young autistic children. *Journal of Consulting and Clinical Psychology, 55*, 3–9.

Lovaas, O. I., & Smith, T. (1989). A comprehensive behavioral theory of autistic children: Paradigm for research and treatment. *Journal of Behavioral Therapy and Experimental Psychiatry, 20*, 17–29.

Lovaas, O. I., & Smith, T. (2003). Early and intensive behavioral intervention in autism. In A. E. Kazdin & J. R. Weisz (Eds.), *Evidence-based psychotherapies for children and adolescents* (pp. 325–340). New York: Guilford Press.

Lovejoy, M. C., Verda, M. R., & Hays, C. E. (1997). Convergent and discriminant validity of measures of parenting efficacy and control. *Journal of Clinical Child Psychology, 26*, 366–376.

Lovett, M. W., Steinbach, K. A., & Frijters, J. C. (2000). Remediating the core deficits of developmental reading disability: A double-deficit perspective. *Journal of Learning Disabilities, 33*, 334–358.

Low, S. M., & Stocker, C. (2005). Family functioning and children's adjustment: Associations among parents' depressed mood, marital hostility, parent-child hostility, and children's adjustment. *Journal of Family Psychology, 19*, 394–403.

Luby, J. L., Heffelfinger, A. K., Mrakotsky, C., Brown, K M., Hessler, M. J., Wallis, J., & Spitznagel, E. L. (2003). The clinical picture of depression in preschool children. *Journal of the American Academy of Child and Adolescent Psychiatry, 42*, 340–348.

Luby, J. L., Heffenlfinger, A. K., Mrakotsky, C., Hessler, M. J., Brown, K. M., & Hildebrand, T. (2002). Preschool major depressive disorder: Preliminary validation for developmentally modified *DSM-V* criteria. *Journal of the American Academy of Child and Adolescent Psychiatry, 41*, 928–937.

Luby, J. L., Mrakotsky, C., Heffelfinger, A., Brown, K., Hessler, M., & Spitznagel, E. (2003). Modification of DSM-IV criteria for depressed preschool children. *American Journal of Psychiatry, 160,* 1169–1172.

Luce, K. H., Osborne, M. I., Winzelberg, A. J., Das, S., Abascal, L. B., Celio, A. A., Wilfley, D. E., Stevenson, D., Dev, P., & Taylor, C. B. (2005). Application of an algorithm-driven protocol to simultaneously provide universal and targeted prevention programs. *International Journal of Eating Disorders, 37,* 220–226.

Lum, J. J., & Phares, V. (2005). Assessing the emotional availability of parents. *Journal of Psychopathology and Behavioral Assessment, 27,* 211–226.

Lunsky, Y. (2004). Suicidality in a clinical and community sample of adults with mental retardation. *Research in Developmental Disabilities, 25,* 231–243.

Luo, S., & Klohnen, E. C. (2005). Assortative mating and marital quality in newlyweds: A couple-centered approach. *Journal of Personality and Social Psychology, 88,* 304–326.

Luthar, S. S. (1999). *Poverty and children's adjustment.* Thousand Oaks, CA: Sage.

Luthar, S. S. (2003). *Resilience and vulnerability: Adaptation in the context of childhood adversities.* New York: Cambridge University Press.

Luthar, S. S., Burack, J. A., Cicchetti, D. & Weisz, J. R. (Eds.) (1997). *Developmental psychopathology: Perspectives on adjustment, risk, and disorder.* New York: Cambridge University Press.

Luthar, S. S., Cicchetti, D., & Becker, B. (2000). The construct of resilience: A critical evaluation and guidelines for future work. *Child Development, 71,* 543–562.

Luthar, S. S., & Latendresse, S. J. (2005a). Children of the affluent: Challenges to well-being. *Current Directions in Psychological Science, 14,* 49–53.

Luthar, S. S., & Latendresse, S. J. (2005b). Comparable "risks" at the socioeconomic status extremes: Preadolescents' perceptions of parenting. *Development and Psychopathology, 17,* 207–230.

Lutzker, J. R., & Whitaker, D. J. (2005). The expanding role of behavior analysis and support: Current status and future direction. *Behavior Modification, 29,* 575–594.

Luxem, M. C., & Christophersen, E. R. (1999). Elimination disorders. In S. D. Netherton, D. Holmes, & C. E. Walker (Eds.), *Child and adolescent psychological disorders: A comprehensive textbook* (pp. 195–223). New York: Oxford.

Luyten, P. Blatt, S. J., & Corveleyn, J. (Eds.), (2005). The convergence among psychodynamic and cognitive-behavioral theories of depression: theoretical overview. In *The theory and treatment of depression: Towards a dynamic interactionism model* (pp. 67–94). Mahwah, NJ: Leuven University Press.

Lynam, D. R., Caspi, A., Moffitt, T. E., Raine, A., Loeber, R., & Stouthamer-Loeber, M. (2005). Adolescent psychopathy and the Big Five: Results from two samples. *Journal of Abnormal Child Psychology, 33,* 431–443.

Lynch, M., & Cicchetti, D. (1998). An ecological-transactional analysis of children and contexts: The longitudinal interplay among child maltreatment, community violence, and children's symptomatology. *Development and Psychopathology, 10,* 235–257.

Lynch, S. K., Turkheimer, E., D'Onofrio, B. M., Mendle, J., Emery, R. E., Slutske, W. S., & Martin, N. G. (2006). A genetically informed study of the association between harsh punishment and offspring behavioral problems. *Journal of Family Psychology, 20,* 190–198.

Lyon, G. R., & Cutting, L. E. (1998). Learning disabilities. In E. J. Mash & R. A. Barkley (Eds.), *Treatment of childhood disorders* (2nd ed., pp. 468–498). New York: Guilford Press.

Lyon, G. R., Fletcher, J. M., & Barnes, M. C. (2003). Learning disabilities. In E. J. Mash, & B. A. Barkley (Eds.), *Child psychopathology* (2nd ed., pp. 520–586). New York: Guilford Press.

Lyons, J. S., Uziel-Miller, N. D., Reyes, F., & Sokol, P. T. (2000). Strengths of children and adolescents in residential settings: Prevalence and associations with psychopathology and discharge placement. *Journal of the American Academy of Child and Adolescent Psychiatry, 39,* 176–181.

MacBrayer, E. K., Milich, R., & Hundley, M. (2003). Attributional biases in aggressive children and their mothers. *Journal of Abnormal Psychology, 112,* 698–708.

Maccoby, E. E. (2000). Parenting and its effects on children: On reading and misreading behavior genetics. *Annual Review of Psychology, 51,* 1–27.

Macintosh, K. E., & Dissanayake, C. (2004). Annotation: The similarities and differences between autistic disorder and Asperger's disorder: A review of the empirical evidence. *Journal of Child Psychology and Psychiatry, 45,* 421–434.

MacNaughton, K. L., & Rodrigue, J. R. (2001). Predicting adherence to recommendations by parents of clinic-referred children. *Journal of Consulting and Clinical Psychology, 69,* 262–270.

Maedgen, J. W., & Carlson, C. L. (2000). Social functioning and emotional regulation in the Attention Deficit Hyperactivity Disorder subtypes. *Journal of Clinical Child Psychology, 29,* 30–42.

Maes, B., Broekman, T. G., Dosen, A., & Nauts, J. (2003). Caregiving burden of families looking after persons with intellectual disability and behavioural or psychiatric problems. *Intellectual Disability Research, 47,* 447–455.

Magnus, K. B., Cowen, E. L., Wyman, P. A., Fagen, D. B., & Work, W. C. (1999). Correlates of resilient outcomes among highly stressed African-American and White urban children. *Journal of Community Psychology, 27,* 473–488.

Maharaj, S., Rodin, G., Connolly, J., Olmsted, M., & Daneman, D. (2001). Eating problems and the observed quality of mother-daughter interactions among girls with Type 1 diabetes. *Journal of Consulting and Clinical Psychology, 69,* 950–958.

Mahler, M. (1968). *On human symbiosis and the vicissitudes of individuation.* New York: International Universities Press.

Mahoney, A., Donnelly, W. O., Lewis, T., & Maynard, C. (2000). Mother and father self-reports of corporal punishment and severe physical aggression toward clinic-referred youth. *Journal of Clinical Child Psychology, 29,* 266–281.

Mahoney, A., Pargament, K. I., Tarakeshwar, N., & Swank, A. B. (2001). Religion in the home in the 1980s and 1990s: A meta-analytic review and conceptual analysis of links between religion, marriage, and parenting. *Journal of Family Psychology, 15,* 559–596.

Maier, W., Hofgen, B., Zobel, A., & Rietschel. M. (2005). Genetic models of schizophrenia and bipolar disorder: Overlapping inheritance or discrete genotypes? *European Archives of Psychiatry and Clinical Neuroscience, 255,* 159–166.

Malcarne, V. L., Hamilton, N. A., Ingram, R. E., & Taylor, L. (2000). Correlates of distress in children at risk for affective disorder: Exploring predictors in the offspring of depressed and nondepressed mothers. *Journal of Affective Disorders, 59*, 243–251.

Mandell, D. S., Walrath, C. M., Manteuffel, B., Sgro, G., & Pinto-Martin, J. (2005). Characteristics of children with autistic spectrum disorders served in comprehensive community-based mental health settings. *Journal of Autism and Developmental Disorders, 35*, 313–321.

Maniadaki, K., Sonuga-Barke, E., & Kakouros, E. (2005). Parents' causal attributions about attention deficit/hyperactivity disorder: The effect of child and parent sex. *Child: Care, Health and Development, 31*, 331–340.

Manne, S., & Miller, D. (1998). Social support, social conflict, and adjustment among adolescents with cancer. *Journal of Pediatric Psychology, 23*, 121–130.

Manne, S., Nereo, N., DuHamel, K., Ostroff, J., Parsons, S., Martini, R., Williams, S., Mee, L., Sexson, S., Lewis, J., Vickberg, S. J., & Redd, W. H. (2001). Anxiety and depression in mothers of children undergoing bone marrow transplant: Symptom prevalence and use of the Beck Depression and Beck Anxiety Inventories as screening instruments. *Journal of Consulting and Clinical Psychology, 69*, 1037–1047.

Mannheim, C. I., Sancilio, M., Phipps-Yonas, S., Brunnquell, D., Somers, P., Farseth, G., & Ninonuevo, F. (2002). Ethical ambiguities in the practice of child clinical psychology. *Professional Psychology: Research and Practice, 33*, 24–29.

Mannuzza, S., Klein, R. G., Abikoff, H., & Moulton, J. L. (2004). Significance of childhood conduct problems to later development of conduct disorder among children with ADHD: A prospective follow-up study. *Journal of Abnormal Child Psychology, 32*, 565–573.

March, J. S., Franklin, M., & Foa, E. (2005). Cognitive-behavioral psychotherapy for pediatric obsessive-compulsive disorder. In E. D. Hibbs & P. S. Jensen (Eds.), *Psychosocial treatment for child and adolescent disorders: Empirically based strategies for clinical practice* (2nd ed., pp. 121–148). Washington, DC: American Psychological Association.

March, J. S., Franklin, M. E., Leonard, H. L., & Foa, E. B. (2004). Obsessive-compulsive disorder. In T. L. Morris & J. S. March (Eds.), *Anxiety disorders in children and adolescents* (2nd ed., pp. 212–240). New York: Guilford Press.

March, J. S., Silva, S. G., Compton, S., Anthony, G., DeVeaugh-Geiss, J., Califf, R., & Krishnan, R. (2004). The child and adolescent psychiatry trials network (CAPTN). *Journal of the American Academy of Child and Adolescent Psychiatry, 43*, 515–518.

Margolin, G., & Gordis, E. B. (2004). Children's exposure to violence in the family and community. *Current Directions in Psychological Science, 13*, 152–155.

Margolin, G., Gordis, E. B., & John, R. S. (2001). Coparenting: A link between marital conflict and parenting in two-parent families. *Journal of Family Psychology, 15*, 3–21.

Markowitz, J. C. (1995). Psychotherapy of dysthymic disorder. In J. H. Kocsis & D. N. Klein (Eds.), *Diagnosis and treatment of chronic depression* (pp. 146–168). New York: Guilford Press.

Marler, C., Trainor, B. C., & Davis, E. (2005). Paternal behavior and offspring aggression. *Current Directions in Psychological Science, 14*, 163–166.

Marmorstein, N., & Iacono, W. G. (2003). Major depression and conduct disorder in a twin sample: Gender, functioning, and risk for future psychopathology. *Journal of the American Academy of Child and Adolescent Psychiatry, 42*, 225–233.

Marsh, D. B. (1995). *From the heart: On being the mother of a child with special needs*. Bethesda, MD: Woodbine House.

Marshal, M. P., & Chassin, L. (2000). Peer influence on adolescent alcohol use: The moderating role of parental support and discipline. *Applied Developmental Science, 4*, 80–88.

Marshal, M. P., & Molina, B. S. G. (2006). Antisocial behaviors moderate the deviant peer pathway to substance use in children with ADHD. *Journal of Clinical Child and Adolescent Psychology, 35*, 216–226.

Mart, E. G. (2002). Munchausen's syndrome (factitious disorder) by proxy: A brief review of its scientific and legal status. *Scientific Review of Mental Health Practice, 1*, 55–61.

Mart, E. G. (2004). Factitious disorder by proxy: A call for the abandonment of an outmoded diagnosis. *Journal of Psychiatry and Law, 32*, 297–314.

Martin, R. P., Foels, P., Clanton, G., & Moon, K. (2004). Season of birth is related to child retention rates, achievement, and rate of diagnosis of specific LD. *Journal of Learning Disabilities, 37*, 307–317.

Martin, S. (2005). Healthy kids make better students. *Monitor on Psychology, 36*, 24–26.

Martinez, C. R., & Forgatch, M. S. (2001). Preventing problems with boys' noncompliance: Effects of a parent training intervention for divorcing mothers. *Journal of Consulting and Clinical Psychology, 69*, 416–428.

Martinussen, R., Hayden, J. D. C., Hogg-Johnson, S., & Tannock, R. (2005). A meta-analysis of working memory impairments in children with attention-deficit/hyperactivity disorder. *Journal of the American Academy of Child and Adolescent Psychiatry, 44*, 377–384.

Mash, E. J., & Barkley, R. A. (Eds.) (2006). *Treatment of childhood disorders* (3rd ed.). New York: Guilford Press.

Mash, E. J., & Dozois, D. J. A. (2003). Child psychopathology: A developmental-systems perspective. In E. J. Mash & R. A. Barkley (Eds.), *Child psychopathology* (2nd ed., pp. 3–71). New York: Guildford Press.

Mash, E. J., & Hunsley, J. (2005). Evidence-based assessment of child and adolescent disorders: Issues and challenges. *Journal of Clinical Child and Adolescent Psychology, 34*, 362–379.

Masi, G., Cosenza, A., Mucci, M., & Brovedani, P. (2003). A 3-year naturalistic study of 53 preschool children with pervasive developmental disorders treated with Risperidone. *Journal of Clinical Psychiatry, 64*, 1039–1047.

Masi, G., Millepiedi, S., Mucci, M., Bertini, N., Milantoni, L., & Arcangeli, F. (2005). A naturalistic study of referred children and adolescents with obsessive-compulsive disorder. *Journal of the American Academy of Child and Adolescent Psychiatry, 44*, 673–681.

Masi, G., Millepiedi, S., Mucci, M., Pascale, R. R., Perugi, G., & Akiskal, H. S. (2003). Phenomenology and comorbidity of dysthymic disorder in 100 consecutively referred children and adolescents: Beyond *DSM-IV. Canadian Journal of Psychiatry, 48,* 99–105.

Masi, G., Millepiedi, S., Mucci, M., Poli, P., Bertini, N., & Milantoni, L. (2004). Generalized anxiety disorder in referred children and adolescents. *Journal of the American Academy of Child and Adolescent Psychiatry, 43,* 752–760.

Masi, G., Toni, C., Perugi, G., Travierso, M. C., Millepiedi, S., Mucci, M., & Akiskal, H. S. (2003). Externalizing disorders in consecutively referred children and adolescents with bipolar disorder. *Comprehensive Psychiatry, 44,* 184–189.

Mason, C. A. (2003). Developmental epidemiology: Issues, application, and relevance for clinical child psychologists. *Journal of Clinical Child and Adolescent Psychology, 32,* 178–180.

Masten, A. S. (2005). Peer relationships and psychopathology in developmental perspective: Reflections on progress and promise. *Journal of Clinical Child and Adolescent Psychology, 34,* 87–92.

Masten, A. S., Burt, K. B., Roisman, G. I., Obradovic, J., Long, J. D., & Tellegen, A. (2004). Resources and resilience in the transition to adulthood: Continuity and change. *Development and Psychopathology, 16,* 1071–1094.

Masten, A. S., & Coatsworth, J. D. (1998). The development of competence in favorable and unfavorable environments: Lessons from research on successful children. *American Psychologist, 53,* 205–220.

Masten, A. S., Hubbard, J. J., Gest, S. D., Tellegen, A., Garmezy, N., & Ramirez, M. (1999). Competence in the context of adversity: Pathways to resilience and maladaptation from childhood to late adolescence. *Development and Psychopathology, 11,* 143–169.

Masten, A. S., Miliotis, D., Graham-Bermann, S. A., Ramirez, M., & Neemann, J. (1993). Children in homeless families: Risks to mental health and development. *Journal of Consulting and Clinical Psychology, 61,* 335–343.

Masten, A. S., & Powell, J. L. (2003). A resilience framework for research, policy, and practice. In S. S. Luthar (Ed.), *Resilience and vulnerability: Adaptation in the context of childhood adversities* (pp. 1–25). New York: Cambridge University Press.

Mather, A., & Cartwright-Hatton, S. (2004). Cognitive predictors of obsessive-compulsive symptoms in adolescence: A preliminary investigation. *Journal of Clinical Child and Adolescent Psychology, 33,* 743–749.

Mather, N., & Jaffe, L. E. (1992). *Woodcock-Johnson Psychoeducational Battery-Revised: Recommendations and reports.* New York: Wiley.

Mather, N., & Ofiesh, N. (2005). Resilience and the child with learning disabilities. In S. Goldstein & R. B. Brooks (Eds.), *Handbook of resilience in children* (pp. 239–255). New York: Kluwer Academic/Plenum Press.

Matson, J. L., & Friedt, L. R. (1988). Severe and profound mental retardation. In M. Hersen & C. G. Last (Eds.), *Child behavior therapy casebook* (pp. 113–127). New York: Plenum Press.

Mattison, R. E. (2000). School consultation: A review of research on issues unique to the school environment. *Journal of the American Academy of Child and Adolescent Psychiatry, 39,* 402–413.

Maughan, B., Iervolino, A. C., & Collishaw, S. (2005). Time trends in child and adolescent mental disorders. *Current Opinion in Psychiatry, 18,* 381–385.

Maughan, B., Rowe, R., Messer, J., Goodman, R., & Meltzer, H. (2004). Conduct disorder of oppositional defiant disorder in a national sample: Developmental epidemiology. *Journal of Child Psychology and Psychiatry, 45,* 609–621.

Maughan, B., & Rutter, M. (1998). Continuities and discontinuities in antisocial behavior from childhood to adult life. In T. H. Ollendick & R. J. Prinz (Eds.), *Advances in clinical child psychology* (Vol. 20, pp. 1–47). New York: Plenum Press.

Mayes, S. D., & Calhoun, S. L. (2003). Ability profiles in children with autism: Influence of age and IQ. *Autism, 7,* 65–80.

Mayes, S. D., & Calhoun, S. L. (2004). Influence of IQ and age in childhood autism: Lack of support for DSM-IV Asperger's disorder. *Journal of Developmental and Physical Disabilities, 16,* 257–272.

Mayes, S. D., Calhoun, S. L., & Crites, D. L. (2001). Does *DSM-IV* Asperger's disorder exist? *Journal of Abnormal Child Psychology, 29,* 263–271.

Mayes, S. D., Calhoun, S. L., & Crowell, E. W. (1998). WISC-III profiles for children with and without learning disabilities. *Psychology in the Schools, 35,* 309–316.

Mayne, T. J., Norcross, J. C., & Sayette, M. A. (2006). *Insider's guide to graduate programs in clinical and counseling psychology: 2006/2007 Edition.* New York: Guilford Press.

Mazza, J. J., & Reynolds, W. M. (1999). Exposure to violence in young inner-city adolescents: Relationships with suicidal ideation, depression, and PTSD symptomatology. *Journal of Abnormal Child Psychology, 27,* 203–213.

Mazzocco, M. M. M. (2001). Math learning disability and math LD subtypes: Evidence from studies of Turner syndrome, fragile X syndrome, and neurofibromatosis type 1. *Journal of Learning Disabilities, 34,* 520–533.

McAllister, C. L., Wilson, P. C., & Burton, J. (2004). From sports fans to nurturers: An early Head Start program's evolution toward father involvement. *Fathering, 2,* 31–59.

McArthur, G. M., Hogben, J. H., Edwards, V. T., Heath, S. M., & Mengler, E. D. (2000). On the "specifics" of specific reading disability and specific language impairment. *Journal of Child Psychology and Psychiatry and Allied Disciplines, 41,* 869–874.

McCabe, K. M., Clark, R., & Barnett, D. (1999). Family protective factors among urban African American youth. *Journal of Clinical Child Psychology, 28,* 137–150.

McCabe, K. M., Hough, R., Wood, P. A., & Yeh, M. (2001). Childhood and adolescent onset conduct disorder: A test of the developmental taxonomy. *Journal of Abnormal Child Psychology, 29,* 305–316.

McCabe, K. M., Rodgers, C., Yeh, M., & Hough, R. (2004). Gender differences in childhood onset conduct disorder. *Development and Psychopathology, 16,* 179–192.

McCall, R. B., & Groark, C. J. (2000). The future of applied child development research and public policy. *Child Development, 71,* 197–204.

McCann, B. S., & Roy-Byrne, P. (2004). Screening and diagnostic utility of self-report attention deficit hyperactivity disorder in adults. *Comprehensive Psychiatry, 45,* 175–183.

McCarty, C. A., Lau, A. S., Valeri, S. M., & Weisz, J. R. (2004). Parent-child interactions in relation to critical and emotionally overinvolved expressed emotion (EE): Is EE a proxy for behavior? *Journal of Abnormal Child Psychology, 32*, 83–93.

McCarty, C. A., McMahon, R. J., & Conduct Problems Prevention Research Group (2003). Mediators of the relation between maternal depressive symptoms and child internalizing and disruptive behavior disorders. *Journal of Family Psychology, 17*, 545–556.

McCaskill, P. A., Toro, P. A., & Wolfe, S. M. (1998). Homeless and matched housed adolescents: A comparative study of psychopathology. *Journal of Clinical Child Psychology, 27*, 306–319.

McCauley, E., Myers, K., Mitchell, J., Calderon, R., Schloredt, K., & Treder, R. (1993). Depression young people: Initial presentation and clinical course. *Journal of the American Academy of Child and Adolescent Psychiatry, 32* 714–722.

McClellan, J., & Werry, J. (2003). Evidence-based treatments in child and adolescent psychiatry: An inventory. *Journal of the American Academy of Child and Adolescent Psychiatry, 42*, 1388–1400.

McClellan, J., Werry, J., Bernet, W., Arnold, V., Beitchman, J., Benson, S., Bukstein, O., Kinlan, J., Rue, D., & Shaw, J. (2001). Practice parameter for the assessment and treatment of children and adolescents with schizophrenia. *Journal of the American Academy of Child and Adolescent Psychiatry, 40* (Supplement 7), 4S–23S.

McCloskey, L. A., & Bailey, J. A. (2000). The intergenerational transmission of risk for child sexual abuse. *Journal of Interpersonal Violence, 15*, 1019–1035.

McCloskey, L. A., & Walker, M. (2000). Posttraumatic stress in children exposed to family violence and singe-event trauma. *Journal of the American Academy of Child and Adolescent Psychiatry, 39*, 108–115.

McClure, E. B., Brennan, P. A., Hammen, C., & LeBrocque, R. M. (2001). Parental anxiety disorders, child anxiety disorders, and the perceived parent-child relationship in an Australian high-risk sample. *Journal of Abnormal Child Psychology, 29*, 1–10.

McClure, E. B., Connell, A. M., Zucker, M., Griffith, J. R., & Kaslow, N. J. (2005). The adolescent depression empowerment project (ADEPT): A culturally sensitive family treatment for depressed African American girls. In E. D. Hibbs & P. S. Jensen (Eds.), *Psychosocial treatment for child and adolescent disorders: Empirically based strategies for clinical practice* (2nd ed., pp. 149–164). Washington, DC: American Psychological Association.

McConachie, H., Le Couteur, A., & Honey, E. (2005). Can a diagnosis of Asperger syndrome be made in very young children with suspected autism spectrum disorder? *Journal of Autism and Developmental Disorders, 35*, 167–176.

McConaughy, S. H. (2000). Self-report: Child clinical interviews. In E. S. Shapiro & T. R. Kratochwill (Eds.), *Conducting school-based assessments of child and adolescent behavior* (pp. 170–202). New York: Guildford.

McConaughy, S. H. (2005). *Clinical interviews for children and adolescents: Assessment to intervention.* New York: Guilford Press.

McConaughy, S. H., & Achenbach, T. M. (2001). *Manual for the Semistructured Clinical Interview for Children and Adolescents* (2nd ed.). Burlington, VT: University of Vermont, Center for Children, Youth, and Families.

McConnell, D., Llewellyn, G., Mayes, R., Russo, D., & Honey, A. (2003). Developmental profiles of children born to mothers with intellectual disability. *Journal of Intellectual & Developmental Disability, 28*, 122–134.

McCubbin, H. I., Thompson, E. A., Thompson, A. I., & Fromer, J. E. (1998). *Resiliency in Native American and immigrant families.* Thousand Oaks, CA: Sage.

McDermott, B. M., McKelvey, R., Roberts, L., & Davies, L. (2002). Severity of children's psychopathology and impairment and its relationship to treatment setting. *Psychiatric Services, 53*, 57–62.

McDonald, E. J., McCabe, K., Yeh, M., Lau, A., Garland, A., & Hough, R. L. (2005). Cultural affiliation and self-esteem as predictors of internalizing symptoms among Mexican American adolescents. *Journal of Clinical Child and Adolescent Psychology, 34*, 163–171.

McDonald, E. M., Solomon, B., Shields, W., Serwint, J. R., Jacobsen, H., Weaver, N. L., Kreuter, M., & Gielen, A. C. (2005). Evaluation of kiosk-based tailoring to promote household safety behaviors in an urban primary care practice. *Patient Education and Counseling, 58*, 168–181.

McDonald, L., & Sayger, T. V. (1998). Impact of a family and school based prevention program on protective factors for high risk youth. *Drugs and Society, 12*, 61–85.

McDougall, A., Kerr, A. M., & Espie, C. A. (2005). Sleep disturbance in children with Rett syndrome: A qualitative investigation of the parental experience. *Journal of Applied Research in Intellectual Disabilities, 18*, 201–215.

McEachlin, J. J., Smith, T., & Lovaas, O. I. (1993). Long-term outcome for children with autism who received early intensive behavioral treatment. *American Journal Mental Retardation, 97*, 359–372.

McElroy, S. L., Kotwal, R., Keck, P. E., & Akiskal, H. S. (2005). Comorbidity of bipolar and eating disorders: Distinct or related disorders with shared dysregulations? *Journal of Affective Disorders, 86*, 107–127.

McFall, R. M. (2006). Doctoral training in clinical psychology. *Annual Review of Clinical Psychology, 2*, 21–49.

McGee, R., & Williams, S. (1999). Environmental risk factors in oppositional-defiant disorder and conduct disorder. In H. C. Quay & A. E. Hogan (Eds.), *Handbook of disruptive behavior disorders* (pp. 419–440). New York: Kluwer Academic/Plenum Press.

McGoldrick, M., Gerson, R., & Shellenberger, S. (1999). *Genograms: Assessment and intervention* (2nd ed.). New York: Norton.

McGoldrick, M., Giordano, J., & Garcia-Preto, N. (Eds.) (2005). *Ethnicity and family therapy* (3rd ed.). New York: Guilford Press.

McGough, J. J., Smalley, S. L., McCracken, J. T., Yang, M., Del'Homme, M., Lynn, D. E., & Loo, S. (2005). Psychiatric comorbidity in adult attention deficit hyperactivity disorder: Findings from multiplex families. *American Journal of Psychiatry, 162*, 1621–1627.

McGue, M., & Iacono, W. G. (2004). The initiation of substance use in adolescence: A behavioral genetics perspective. In L. F. DiLalla (Ed.). *Behavior genetics principles: perspectives in development, personality, and psychopathology* (pp. 41–57). Washington, DC: American Psychological Association.

McGuigan, W. M., Vuchinich, S., & Pratt, C. C. (2000). Domestic violence, parents' view of their infant, and risk for child abuse. *Journal of Family Psychology, 14*, 613–624.

McHale, J. P., & Rasmussen, J. L. (1998). Coparental and family group-level dynamics during infancy: Early family precursors of child and family functioning during preschool. *Development and Psychopathology, 10,* 39–59.

McHale, S. M., Corneal, D. A., Crouter, A. C., & Birch, L. L. (2001). Gender and weight concerns in early and middle adolescence: Links with well-being and family characteristics. *Journal of Clinical Child Psychology, 30,* 338–348.

McHolm, A. E., Cunningham, C. E., & Vanier, M. K. (2005). *Helping your child with selective mutism: Practical steps to overcome a fear of speaking.* Oakland, CA: New Harbinger Publications, Inc.

McKillop, T. (2003). The statin wars. *The Lancet, 362,* 1498.

McKnight, C. D., Compton, S. N., & March, J. S. (2004). Posttraumatic stress disorder. In T. L. Morris & J. S. March (Eds.), *Anxiety disorders in children and adolescents* (2nd ed., pp. 241–262). New York: Guilford Press.

McLeod, B. D., & Weisz, J. R. (2004). Using dissertations to examine potential bias in child and adolescent clinical trials. *Journal of Consulting and Clinical Psychology, 72,* 235–251.

McLeod, B. D., & Weisz, J. R. (2005). The Therapy Process Observational Coding System—Alliance Scale: Measure characteristics and prediction of outcome in usual clinical practice. *Journal of Consulting and Clinical Psychology, 73,* 323–333.

McLoyd, V. C. (1998). Socioeconomic disadvantage and child development. *American Psychologist, 53,* 185–204.

McLoyd, V. C., & Steinberg, L. (Eds.) (1998). *Studying minority adolescents: Conceptual, methodological, and theoretical issues.* Mahwah, NJ: Lawrence Erlbaum Associates.

McMahon, J. A. (2002). An explanation for normal and anomalous drawing ability and some implications for research on perception and imagery. *Visual Arts Research, 28,* 38–52.

McMahon, R. J., & Forehand, R. L. (2003). *Helping the noncompliant child: Family-based treatment for oppositional behavior* (2nd ed.). New York: Guilford Press.

McMahon, R. J., & Frick, P. J. (2005). Evidence-based assessment of conduct problems in children and adolescents. *Journal of Clinical Child and Adolescent Psychology, 34,* 477–505.

McMahon, R. J., & Kotler, J. S. (2006). Conduct problems. In D. A. Wolfe & E. J. Mash (Eds.), *Behavioral and emotional disorders in adolescents: Nature, assessment, and treatment* (pp. 153–225). New York: Guilford Press.

McMahon, R. J., & Wells, K. C. (1998). Conduct problems. In E. J. Mash & R. A. Barkley (Eds.), *Treatment of childhood disorders* (2nd ed., pp. 111–207). New York: Guilford Press.

McMahon, S. D., Singh, J. A., Garner, L. S., & Benhorin, S. (2004). Taking advantage of opportunities: Community involvement, well-being, and urban youth. *Journal of Adolescent Health, 34,* 262–265.

McMahon, T. J., & Luthar, S. S. (2006). Patterns and correlates of substance use among affluent, suburban high school students. *Journal of Clinical Child and Adolescent Psychology, 35,* 72–89.

McMillen, J. C., Zima, B. T., Scott, L. D., Auslander, W. F., Munson, M. R., Ollie, M. T., & Spitznagel, E. L. (2005). Prevalence of psychiatric disorders among older youths in the foster care system. *Journal of the American Academy of Child and Adolescent Psychiatry, 44,* 88–95.

McNeil, C. B., Capage, L. C., & Bennett, G. M. (2002). Cultural issues in the treatment of young African American children diagnosed with disruptive behavior disorders. *Journal of Pediatric Psychology, 27,* 339–350.

McQuaid, E. L., & Nassau, J. H. (1999). Empirically supported treatments of disease-related symptoms in pediatric psychology: Asthma, diabetes, and cancer. *Journal of Pediatric Psychology, 24,* 305–328.

McShane, G., Walter, G., & Rey, J. M. (2004). Functional outcome of adolescents with "school refusal." *Clinical Child Psychology and Psychiatry, 9,* 53–60.

McVey, G., Tweed, S., Blackmore, E. (2004). Dieting among preadolescent and young female adolescents. *Canadian Medical Association Journal, 170,* 1559–1561.

Meadow, R. (2000). The dangerousness of parents who have abnormal illness behaviour. *Child Abuse Review, 9,* 62–67.

Meadow, R. (2002). Different interpretations of Munchausen syndrome by proxy. *Child Abuse and Neglect, 26,* 501–508.

Meehl, P. E. (2001). Comorbidity and taxometrics. *Clinical Psychology: Science and Practice, 8,* 507–519.

Meiser-Stedman, R., Yule, W., Smith, P., Glucksman, E., & Dalgleish, T. (2005). Acute stress disorder and posttraumatic stress disorder in children and adolescents involved in assaults or motor vehicle accidents. *American Journal of Psychiatry, 162,* 1381–1383.

Melton, G. B. (1992). The improbability of prevention of sexual abuse. In D. J. Willis, E. W. Holden, & M. Rosenberg (Eds.), *Prevention of child maltreatment: Developmental and ecological perspectives.* New York: Wiley.

Melton, G. B., & Ehrenreich, N. S. (1992). Ethical and legal issues in mental health services for children. In C. E. Walker & M. C. Roberts (Eds.), *Handbook of clinical child psychology* (2nd ed., pp. 1035–1055). New York: Wiley.

Meltzer, H., Gatward, R., & Goodman, R., & Ford, T. (2003). Mental health of children and adolescents in Great Britain. *International Review of Psychiatry, 15,* 185–187.

Menard, C., Bandeen-Roche, K. J., & Chilcoat, H. D. (2004). Epidemiology of multiple childhood traumatic events: Child abuse, parental psychopathology, and other family-level stressors. *Social Psychiatry and Psychiatric Epidemiology, 39,* 857–865.

Menendez, M. (2005). Down syndrome, Alzheimer's disease and seizures. *Brain & Development, 27,* 246–252.

Merikangas, K. R., Swendsen, J. D., Preisig, M. A., & Chazan, R. Z. (1998). Psychopathology and temperament in parents and offspring: Results of a family study. *Journal of Affective Disorders, 51,* 63–74.

Merikangas, K., Weissman, M., Prusoff, B. A., & Johns, K. (1988). Assortative mating and affective disorders: Psychopathology in offspring. *Psychiatry, 51,* 48–57.

Merrens, M. R., & Brannigan, G. G. (Eds.). (1996). *The developmental psychologists: Research adventures across the life span.* New York: McGraw-Hill.

Merrill, L. L., Guimond, J. M., Thomsen, C. J., & Milner, J. S. (2003). Child sexual abuse and number of sexual partners in young women: The role of abuse severity, coping style, and sexual functioning. *Journal of Consulting and Clinical Psychology, 71,* 987–996.

Merrill, L. L., Thomsen, C. J., Sinclair, B. B., Gold, S. R., & Milner, J. S. (2001). Predicting the impact of child sexual abuse on women:

The role of severity, parental support, and coping strategies. *Journal of Consulting and Clinical Psychology, 69*, 992–1006.

Mervis, C. A., Boyle, C. A., & Yeargin-Allsopp, M. (2002). Prevalence and selected characteristics of childhood vision impairment. *Developmental Medicine & Child Neurology, 44*, 538–541.

Mesibov, G. B., Schroeder, C. S., & Wesson, L. (1993). Parental concerns about their children. In M. C. Roberts, G. P. Koocher, D. K. Routh, & D. J. Willis (Eds.), *Readings in pediatric psychology* (pp. 307–316). New York: Plenum Press.

Mesman, J., & Koot, H. M. (2000). Common and specific correlates of preadolescent internalizing and externalizing psychopathology. *Journal of Abnormal Psychology, 109*, 428–437.

Meyer, G. J., Finn, S. E., Eyde, L. D., Kay, G. G., Moreland, K. L., Dies, R. R., Eisman, E. J., Kubiszyn, T. W., & Reed, G. M. (2001). Psychological testing and psychological assessment: A review of evidence and issues. *American Psychologist, 55*, 128–165.

Meyer, I. H. (2003). Prejudice, social stress, and mental health in lesbian, gay, and bisexual populations: Conceptual issues and research evidence. *Psychological Bulletin, 129*, 674–697.

Meyer, J. M., Rutter, M., Silberg, J. L., Maes, H. H., Simonoff, E., Shillady, L. L., Pickles, A., Hewitt, J. K., & Eaves, L. J. (2000). Familial aggregation for conduct disorder symptomatology: The role of genes, marital discord and family adaptability. *Psychological Medicine, 30*, 759–774.

Meyer, R. G. (1989). *Cases in developmental psychology and psychopathology*. Boston: Allyn and Bacon.

Meyers, J. (1989). The practice of psychology in the schools for the primary prevention of learning and adjustment problems in children: A perspective from the field of education. In L. A. Bond & B. E. Compas (Eds.), *Primary prevention and promotion in the schools* (pp. 391–422). Newbury Park, CA: Sage.

Meyers, J., & Nastasi, B. K. (1999). Primary prevention in school settings. In C. R. Reynolds & T. B. Gutkin (Eds.), *The handbook of school psychology* (3rd ed., pp. 764–799). New York: Wiley.

Mezulis, A. H., Hyde, J. S., & Clark, R. (2004). Father involvement moderates the effect of maternal depression during a child's infancy on child behavior problems in kindergarten. *Journal of Family Psychology, 18*, 575–588.

Micheli, E. (2000). Dealing with the reality of autism: A psychoeducational program in Milan, Italy. *International Journal of Mental Health, 29*, 50–71.

Mikami, A. Y., & Hinshaw, S. P. (2003). Buffers of peer rejection among girls with and without ADHD: The role of popularity with adults and goal-directed solitary play. *Journal of Abnormal Child Psychology, 31*, 381–397.

Miklowitz, D. J. (2004). The role of family systems in severe and recurrent psychiatric disorders: A developmental psychopathology view. *Development and Psychopathology, 16*, 667–688.

Miklowitz, D. J., George, E. L., Axelson, D. A., Kim, E. Y., Birmaher, B., Schneck, C., Beresford, C., Craighead, W. E., & Brent, D. A. (2004). Family-focused treatment for adolescents with bipolar disorder. *Journal of Affective Disorders, 82S*, S113–S128.

Milan, S., Lewis, J., Ethier, K., Kershaw, T., & Ickovics, J. R. (2004). The impact of physical maltreatment history on the adolescent mother-infant relationship: Mediating and moderating effects during the transition to early parenthood. *Journal of Abnormal Child Psychology, 32*, 249–261.

Milan, S., Pinderhughes, E. E., and the Conduct Problems Prevention Research Group. (2006). Family instability and child maladjustment trajectories during elementary school. *Journal of Abnormal Child Psychology, 34*, 43–56.

Milich, R., Balentine, A. C., & Lynam, D. R. (2001). ADHD combined type and ADHD predominantly inattentive type are distinct and unrelated disorders. *Clinical Psychology: Science and Practice, 8*, 463–488.

Milin, R., Coupland, K., Walker, S., & Fisher-Bloom, E. (2000). Outcome and follow-up study of an adolescent psychiatric day treatment school program. *Journal of the American Academy of Child and Adolescent Psychiatry, 39*, 320–328.

Miller, B. C., Benson, B., & Galbraith, K. A. (2001). Family relationships and adolescent pregnancy risk: A research synthesis. *Developmental Review, 21*, 1–38.

Miller, B. C., Fan, X., Christensen, M., Grotevant, H. D., & van Dulmen, M. (2000). Comparisons of adopted and nonadopted adolescents in a large, nationally representative sample. *Child Development, 71*, 1458–1473.

Miller, B. C., Fan, X., Grotevant, H. D., Christensen, M., Coyl, D., & van Dulmen, M. (2000). Adopted adolescents' overrepresentation in mental health counseling: Adoptees' problems or parents' lower threshold for referral? *Journal of the American Academy of Child and Adolescent Psychiatry, 39*, 1504–1511.

Miller, K. E., Hoffman, J. H., Barnes, G. M., Farrell, M. P., Sabo, D., & Melnick, M. J. (2003). Jocks, gender, race, and adolescent problems drinking. *Journal of Drug Education, 33*, 445–462.

Miller, L., Davies, M., & Greenwald, S. (2000). Religiosity and substance use and abuse among adolescents in the National Comorbidity Survey. *Journal of the American Academy of Child and Adolescent Psychiatry, 39*, 1190–1197.

Miller, L. S., Wasserman, G. A., Neugebauer, R., Gorman-Smith, D., & Kamboukos, D. (1999). Witnessed community violence and antisocial behavior in high-risk, urban boys. *Journal of Clinical Child Psychology, 28*, 2–11.

Miller, M. J., Bigler, E. D., & Adams, W. V. (2003). Comprehensive assessment of child and adolescent memory: The Wide Range Assessment of Memory and Learning, the Test of Memory and Learning, and the California Verbal Learning Test—Children's Version. In C. R. Reynolds, & R. W. Kamphaus (Eds.). *Handbook of psychological and educational assessment of children: Intelligence, aptitude, and achievement* (2nd ed., pp. 275–304). New York: Guilford Press.

Miller, P. M., Smith, G. T., & Goldman, M. S. (1990). Emergence of alcohol expectancies in childhood: A possible critical period. *Journal of Studies on Alcohol, 51*, 343–349.

Miller, V. A., & Drotar, D. (2003). Discrepancies between mother and adolescent perceptions of diabetes-related decision-making autonomy and their relationship to diabetes-related conflict and adherence to treatment. *Journal of Pediatric Psychology, 28*, 265–274.

Miller-Johnson, S., Lochman, J. E., Coie, J. D., Terry, R. & Hyman, C. (1998). Comorbidity of conduct and depressive problems at sixth grade: Substance use outcomes across adolescence. *Journal of Abnormal Child Psychology, 26*, 221–232.

Millman, H. L., Schaefer, C. E., & Cohen, J. J. (2004). *Therapies for School Behavior Problems: A Handbook of Practical Interventions.* Hoboken, NJ: Wiley.

Milner, J. S. (1986). *The Child Abuse Potential Inventory* (2nd ed.). Webster, NC: Psytec.

Milner, J. S. (1994). Assessing physical child abuse risk: The Child Abuse Potential Inventory. *Clinical Psychology Review, 14,* 547–583.

Mineka, S., Davidson, M., Cook, M., & Keir, R. (1984). Observational conditioning of snake fear in rhesus monkeys. *Journal of Abnormal Psychology, 93,* 355–372.

Minuchin, S. (1974). *Families and family therapy.* Cambridge, MA: Harvard University Press.

Minuchin, S., Montalvo, B., Guerney, B., Rosman, B., & Schumer, F. (1967). *Families of the slums.* New York: Basic Books.

Mireault, G. C., & Compas, B. E. (1996). A prospective study of coping and adjustment before and after a parent's death from cancer. *Journal of Psychosocial Oncology, 14,* 1–18.

Mischel, W., & Ebbesen, E. B. (1970). Attention in delay of gratification. *Journal of Personality and Social Psychology, 16,* 329–337.

Mischel, W., Shoda, Y., & Peake, P. K. (1988). The nature of adolescent competencies predicted by preschool delay of gratification. *Journal of Personality and Social Psychology, 54,* 687–696.

Mitchell, R. (2003). Ideological reflections on the *DSM-IV. Child and Youth Care Forum, 31,* 365–380.

Mizell, C. A. (1999). Life course influences on African American men's depression: Adolescent parental composition, self-concept, and adult earnings. *Journal of Black Studies, 29,* 467–490.

Mizes, J. S., & Miller, K. J. (2000). Eating disorders. In M. Hersen & R. T. Ammerman (Eds.), *Advanced abnormal child psychology* (pp. 441–465). Mahwah, NJ: Lawrence Erlbaum Associates, Publishers.

Moffitt, T. E. (2003). Life-course-persistent and adolescence-limited antisocial behavior: A 10-year research review and a research agenda. In B. B. Lahey, T. E. Moffitt, & A. Caspi (Eds.), *Causes of conduct disorder and juvenile delinquency* (pp. 49–75). New York: Guilford Press.

Moffitt, T. E. (2005). The new look of behavioral genetics in developmental psychopathology: Gene-environment interplay in antisocial behaviors. *Psychological Bulletin, 131,* 533–554.

Moffitt, T. E., Caspi, A., & Rutter, M. (2005). Strategy for investigating interactions between measured genes and measured environments. *Archives of General Psychiatry, 62,* 473–481.

Moffitt, T. E., Caspi, A., & Rutter, M. (2006). Measured gene-environment interactions in psychopathology: Concepts, research strategies, and implications for research, intervention, and public understanding of genetics. *Perspectives on Psychological Science, 1,* 5–27

Mohr, C., & Gray, K. M. (2005). Assessment in intellectual disability. *Current Opinion in Psychiatry, 18,* 476–483.

Moises, H., Zoega, T., Li, L., & Hood, L. (2004). Genes and neurodevelopment in schizophrenia. In L. F. DiLalla (Eds.), *Behavior genetics principles: Perspectives in development, personality, and psychopathology* (pp. 145–157). Washington, DC: American Psychological Association.

Mojtabai, R. (2005). Patental psychopathology and childhood atopic disorders in the community. *Psychosomatic Medicine, 67,* 448–453.

Molina, B. S. G., & Pelham, W. E. (2003). Childhood predictors of adolescent substance use in a longitudinal study of children with ADHD. *Journal of Abnormal Psychology, 112,* 497–507.

Moline, S., & Frankenberger, W. (2001). Use of stimulant medication for treatment of attention-deficit/hyperactivity disorder: A survey of middle and high school students' attitudes. *Psychology in the Schools, 38,* 569–584.

Molnar, B. E., Berkman, L. F., & Buka, S. L. (2001). Psychopathology, childhood sexual abuse and other childhood adversities: Relative links to subsequent suicidal behaviour in the US. *Psychological Medicine, 31,* 965–977.

Montano, B. (2004). Diagnosis and treatment of ADHD in adults in primary care. *Journal of Clinical Psychiatry, 65,* 18–21.

Monuteaux, M. C., Faraone, S. V., Herzig, K., Navsaria, N., & Biederman, J. (2005). ADHD and Dyscalculia: Evidence for independent familial transmission. *Journal of Learning Disabilities, 38,* 86–93.

Moolchan, E. T., Ernst, M., & Henningfield, J. E. (2000). A review of tobacco smoking in adolescents: Treatment implications. *Journal of the American Academy of Child and Adolescent Psychiatry, 39,* 682–693.

Moore, P. S., Whaley, S. E., & Sigman, M. (2004). Interactions between mothers and children: Impacts of maternal and child anxiety. *Journal of Abnormal Psychology, 113,* 471–476.

Moore, S., Donovan, B., Hudson, A., & Dykstra, J. (1993). Evaluation of eight case studies of facilitated communication. *Journal of Autism and Developmental Disorders, 23,* 531–539.

Moos, R. H., & Moos, B. S. (1994). *Family Environment Scale Manual* (rev. ed.). Palo Alto, CA: Consulting Psychologists Press.

Moran, P. M., Bifulco, A., Ball, C., & Campbell, C. (2001). Predicting onset of depression: The vulnerability to depression questionnaire. *British Journal of Clinical Psychology, 40,* 411–427.

Morawska, A., & Oei, T. P. S. (2005). Binge drinking in university students: A test of the cognitive model. *Addictive Behaviors, 30,* 203–218.

Moreno, L. A., Tomas, C., Gonzalez-Gross, M., Bueno, G., Perez-Gonzalez, J. M., & Bueno, M. (2004). Micro-environmental and socio-demographic determinants of childhood obesity. *International Journal of Obesity, 28,* S16–S20.

Morgan, D. L., & Morgan, R. K. (2001). Single-participant research design: Bringing science to managed care. *American Psychologist, 55,* 119–127.

Morgan, G. A., Gliner, J. A., & Harmon, R. J. (2000). Quasi-experimental designs. *Journal of the American Academy of Child and Adolescent Psychiatry, 39,* 794–796.

Morgan, J., & Banerjee, R. (2006). Social anxiety and self-evaluation of social performance in a nonclinical sample of children. *Journal of Clinical Child and Adolescent Psychology, 35,* 292–301.

Morgan, M. (1995). *How to interview sexual abuse victims.* Thousand Oaks, CA: Sage.

Morgan, R. K. (1999). *Case studies in child and adolescent psychopathology*. Upper Saddle River, NJ: Prentice Hall.

Morgan, S. B., Campbell, J. M., & Jackson, J. N. (2003). Autism and mental retardation. In M. C. Roberts (Ed.), *Handbook of pediatric psychology* (3rd ed., pp. 510–528). New York: Guilford Press.

Morris, T. L., & March, J. S. (Eds.) (2004). *Anxiety disorders in children and adolescents* (2nd ed.). New York: Guilford.

Morrow, C. E., Vogel, A. L., Anthony, J. C., Ofir, A. Y., Dausa, A. T., & Bandstra, E. S. (2004). Expressive and receptive language functioning in preschool children with prenatal cocaine exposure. *Journal of Pediatric Psychology, 29*, 543–554.

Mortimore, P. (1995). The positive effects of schooling. In M. Rutter (Ed.), *Psychosocial disturbances in young people: Challenges for prevention* (pp. 333–363). Cambridge, UK: Cambridge University Press.

Mosher, C. E., & Danoff-Burg, S. (2005). Psychosocial impact of parental cancer in adulthood: A conceptual and empirical review. *Clinical Psychology Review, 25*, 365–382.

Moss, H. B., Baron, D. A., Hardie, T. L., & Vanyukov, M. M. (2001). Preadolescent children of substance-dependent fathers with antisocial personality disorder: Psychiatric disorders and problem behaviors. *American Journal on Addictions, 10*, 269–278.

Murch, S. (2003). Separating inflammation from speculation in autism. *The Lancet, 362*, 1498–1499.

Mount, R. H., Charman, T., Hastings, R. P., Reilly, S., & Cass. H. (2003). Features of autism in Rett syndrome and severe mental retardation. *Journal of Autism and Developmental Disorders, 33*, 435–442.

Mowrer, O. H. (1960). *Learning theory and behavior*. New York: Wiley.

Mrug, S., Hoza, B., & Bukowski, W. M. (2004). Choosing or being chosen by aggressive-disruptive peers: Do they contribute to children's externalizing and internalizing problems? *Journal of Abnormal Child Psychology, 32*, 53–65.

MTA Cooperative Group. (1999). A 14-month randomized clinical trial of treatment strategies for attention-deficit/hyperactivity disorder. *Archives of General Psychiatry, 56*, 1073–1086.

Mulholland, A. M., & Mintz, L. B. (2001). Prevalence of eating disorders among African American women. *Journal of Counseling Psychology, 48*, 111–116.

Mullick, M. S. I., & Goodman, R. (2005). The prevalence of psychiatric disorders among 5–10 year olds in rural, urban and slum areas in Bangladesh: An exploratory study. *Social Psychiatry and Psychiatric Epidemiology, 40*, 663–671.

Mullins, L. L., Hartman, V. L., Chaney, J. M., Balderson, B. H. K., & Hoff, A. L. (2003). Training experiences and theoretical orientations of pediatric psychologists. *Journal of Pediatric Psychology, 28*, 115–122.

Mulvey, E. P., & Cauffman, E. (2001). The inherent limits of predicting school violence. *American Psychologist, 55*, 797–802.

Muratori, F., Picchi, L., Bruni, G., Patarnello, M., & Romagnoli, G. (2003). A two-year follow-up of psychodynamic psychotherapy for internalizing disorders in children. *Journal of the American Academy of Child and Adolescent Psychiatry, 42*, 331–339.

Muris, P., Merckelbach, H., Gadet, B., & Moulaert, V. (2000). Fears, worries, and scary dreams in 4- to 12-year-old children: Their content, developmental pattern, and origins. *Journal of Clinical Child Psychology, 29*, 43–52.

Muris, P., Schmidt, H., Engelbrecht, P., & Perold, M. (2002). DSM-IV-defined anxiety disorder symptoms in South African children. *Journal of the American Academy of Child and Adolescent Psychiatry, 41*, 1360–1368.

Murray, D. M., & Fisher, J. D. (2002). The internet: A virtually untapped tool for research. *Journal of Technology in Human Services, 19*, 5–18.

Murray, M. E., Guerra, N. G., & Williams, K. R. (1997). Violence prevention for the 21st century. In R. P. Weissberg, T. P. Gullotta, R. L. Hampton, B. A. Ryan, & G. R. Adams (Eds.), *Healthy children 2010: Enhancing children's wellness* (pp. 105–128). Thousand Oaks, CA: Sage.

Murry, V. M., & Brody, G. H. (1999). Self-regulation and self-worth of Black children reared in economically stressed, rural, single mother-headed families: The contribution of risk and protective factors. *Journal of Family Issues, 20*, 458–484.

Myers, J. E. B. (1996). Societal self-defense: New laws to protect children from sexual abuse. *Child Abuse and Neglect, 20*, 255–258.

Myers, M. G., Brown, S. A., & Vik, P. W. (1998). Adolescent substance use problems. In E. J. Mash & R. A. Barkley (Eds.), *Treatment of childhood disorders* (2nd ed., pp. 692–729). New York: Guilford Press.

Myers, W. C., Burton, P. R. S., Sanders, P. D., Donat, K. M., Cheney, J., Fitzpatrick, T. M., & Monaco, L. (2000). Project Back-on-Track at 1 year: A delinquency treatment program for early-career juvenile offenders. *Journal of the American Academy of Child and Adolescent Psychiatry, 39*, 1127–1134.

Myles, B. S., & Simpson, R. L. (1994). Facilitated communication with children diagnosed as autistic in public school settings. *Psychology in the Schools, 31*, 208–220.

Myles, B. S., & Simpson, R. L. (2002). Asperger syndrome: An overview of characteristics. *Focus on Autism and Other Developmental Disabilities, 17*, 132–137.

Naglieri, J. A., Drasgow, F., Schmit, M., Handler, L., Prifitera, A., Margolis, A., & Velasquez, R. (2004). Psychological testing on the internet: New problems, old issues. *American Psychologist, 59*, 150–162.

Naidu, S. B. (1997). Rett syndrome. *Indian Journal of Pediatrics, 64*, 651–659.

Naimi, T., Brewer, B., Mokdad, A., Denny, C., Serdula, M., & Marks, J. (2003). Definitions of binge drinking. *Journal of the American Medical Association, 289,* 1636.

Najman, J. M., Hallam, D., Bor, W., O'Callaghan, M., Williams, G. M., & Shuttlewood, G. (2005). Predictors of depression in very young children: A prospective study. *Social Psychiatry and Psychiatric Epidemiology, 40*, 367–374.

Najman, J. M., Williams, G. M., Nikles, J., Spence, S., Bor, W., O'Callaghan, M., LeBrocque, R., & Andersen, M. J. (2000). Mothers' mental illness and child behavior problems: Cause-effect association or observation bias? *Journal of the American Academy of Child and Adolescent Psychiatry, 39*, 592–602.

Nanke, A., & Rief, W. (2004). Biofeedback in somatoform disorders and related syndromes. *Current Opinion in Psychiatry, 17*, 133–138.

Nathan, P. E. (1997). In the final analysis, it's the data that count. *Clinical Psychology: Science and Practice, 4*, 281–284.

National Institutes of Health. (2000). National Institutes of Health consensus development conference statement: Diagnosis and treatment of attention-deficit/hyperactivity disorder. *Journal of the American Academy of Child and Adolescent Psychiatry, 39*, 182–193.

Nechman, A., Ratzoni, G., Poyurovsky, M., Meged, S., Avidan, G., Fuchs, C., Bloch, Y., & Weizman, R. (2003). Obsessive-compulsive disorder in adolescent schizophrenia patients. *American Journal of Psychiatry, 160*, 1002–1004.

Nelson, D. R., Hammen, C., Brennan, P. A., & Ullman, J. B. (2003). The impact of maternal depression on adolescent adjustment: The role of expressed emotion. *Journal of Consulting and Clinical Psychology, 71*, 935–944.

Nelson, T. S., & Smock, S. A. (2005). Challenges of an outcome-based perspective for marriage and family therapy education. *Family Process, 44*, 355–362.

Nettles, S. M., & Pleck, J. H. (1994). Risk, resilience, and development: The multiple ecologies of black adolescents in the United States. In R. J. Haggerty, L. R. Sherrod, N. Garmezy, & M. Rutter (Eds.), *Stress, risk, and resilience in children and adolescents: Processes, mechanisms, and interventions* (pp. 147–181). New York: Cambridge University Press.

Neugebauer, R. (1979). Medieval and early modern theories of mental illness. *Archives of General Psychiatry, 36*, 477–483.

Neul, S., Applegate, H., & Drabman, R. (2003). Assessment of attention-deficit/hyperactivity disorder. In C. R. Reynolds & R. W. Kamphaus (Eds.), *Handbook of psychological and educational assessment of children: Personality, behavior, and context* (2nd ed., pp. 320–334). New York: Guilford Press.

Neumaerker, K. J., Bettle, N., Neumaerker, U. & Bettle, O. (2000). Age- and gender-related psychological characteristics of adolescent ballet dancers. *Psychopathology, 33*, 137–142.

Nevas, D. B., & Farber, B. A. (2001). Parents' attitudes toward their child's therapist and therapy. *Professional Psychology: Research and Practice, 32*, 165–170.

New York Times. (1874). Mr. Bergh enlarging his sphere of usefulness: Inhuman treatment of a little waif—her treatment—a mystery to be cleared up. P. 8.

Newcomb, A. F., & Bagwell, C. L. (1995). Children's friendship relations: A meta-analytic review. *Psychological Bulletin, 117*, 306–347.

Newcorn, J. H., Halperin, J. M., Jensen, P. S., Abikoff, H. B., Arnold, E., Cantwell, D. P., Conners, C. K., Elliott, G. R., Epstein, J. N., Greenhill, L. L., Hechtman, L., Hinshaw, S. P., Hoza, B., Kraemer, H. C., Pelham, W. E., Severe, J. B., Swanson, J. M., Wells, K. C., Wigal, T., & Vitiello, B. (2001). Symptom profiles in children with ADHD: Effects of comorbidity and gender. *Journal of the American Academy of Child and Adolescent Psychiatry, 40*, 137–146.

Newland, M. C., & Rasmussen, E. B. (2003). Behavior in adulthood and during aging is affected by contaminant exposure in utero. *Current Directions in Psychological Science, 12*, 212–217.

Newman, R. (2005). APA's resilience initiative. *Professional Psychology: Research and Practice, 36*, 227–229.

Newman, R., Phelps, R., Sammons, M. T., Dunivin, D. L., & Cullen, E. A. (2000). Evaluation of the psychopharmacology demonstration project: A retrospective analysis. *Professional Psychology: Research and Practice, 31*, 598–603.

Newsom, C. (1998). Autistic disorder. In E. J. Mash & R. A. Barkley (Eds.), *Treatment of childhood disorders* (2nd ed.) (pp. 416–467). New York: Guilford.

NICHD Early Child Care Research Network, Allhusen, V., Appelbaum, M., Belsky, J., Booth, C. L., Bradley, R., Brownell, C., Burchinal, P., Caldwell, B., Campbell, S., Clarke-Stewart, A., Cox, M., DeHart, G., Friedman, S. L., Hirsh-Pasek, K., Huston, A., Jaeger, E., Johnson, D., Kelly, J., Knoke, B., Marshall, N., McCartney, K., O'Brien, M., Owen, M. T., Payne, C. C., Phillips, D., Pianta, R., Randolph, S., Robeson, W. W., Spicker, S. J., Vandell, D. L., Wallner-Allen, K. E., & Weinraub, M. (2001). Nonmaternal care and family factors in early development: An overview of the NICHD early child care. *Journal of Applied Developmental Psychology, 22*, 457–492.

Nicholls, D., Chater, R., & Lask, B. (2000). Children into DSM don't go: A comparison of classification systems for eating disorders in childhood and early adolescence. *International Journal of Eating Disorders, 28*, 317–324.

Nichols, M. P., & Schwartz, R. C. (2004). *Essentials of Family Therapy*. Boston: Allyn and Bacon.

Nicholson, J. M., Fergusson, D. M., & Horwood, L. J. (1999). Effects on later adjustment of living in a stepfamily during childhood and adolescence. *Journal of Child Psychology and psychiatry, 40*, 405–416.

Nicolotti, L., E.-Sheikh, M., & Whitson, S. M. (2003). Children's coping with marital conflict and their adjustment and physical health: Vulnerability and protective functions. *Journal of Family Psychology, 17*, 315–326.

Nicolson, R., & Rapoport, J. L. (2000). Childhood-onset schizophrenia: What can it teach us? In J. L. Rapoport (Ed.), *Childhood onset of "adult" psychopathology: Clinical and research advances* (pp. 167–192). Washington, D.C.: American Psychiatric Press.

Nicolson, R., & Szatmari, P. (2003). Genetic and neurodevelopmental influences in autistic disorder. *Canadian Journal of Psychiatry, 48*, 526–537.

Nietzel, M. T., Bernstein, D. A., Kramer, G. P., & Milich, R. (2003). *Introduction to clinical psychology* (6th ed.). Upper Saddle River, NJ: Prentice Hall.

Nigg, N. T. (2001). Is ADHD a disinhibitory disorder? *Psychological Bulletin, 127*, 571–598.

Nigg, J. T., Blaskey, L. G., Stawicki, J. A., & Sachek, J. (2004). Evaluating the endophenotype model of ADHD neuropsychological deficit: Results for parents and siblings of children with ADHD combined and inattentive subtypes. *Journal of Abnormal Psychology, 113*, 614–625.

Nigg, J. T., Glass, J. M., Wong, M. M., Poon, E., Jester, J. M., Fitzgerald, H. E., Puttler, L. I., Adams, K. M., & Zucker, R. A. (2004). Neuropsychological executive functioning in children at elevated risk for alcoholism: Findings in early adolescence. *Journal of Abnormal Psychology, 113*, 302–314.

Nigg, J. T., Goldsmith, H. H., & Sachek, J. (2004). Temperament and attention deficit hyperactivity disorder: The development of a multiple pathway model. *Journal of Clinical Child and Adolescent Psychology, 33*, 42–53.

NIH Consensus Development Panel. (2000). National Institutes of Health Consensus Development Conference statement: Diagnosis and treatment of attention-deficit/hyperactivity disorder (ADHD). *Journal of the American Academy of Child and Adolescent Psychiatry, 39,* 182–193.

Niiya, Y., Crocker, J., & Bartmess, E. N. (2004). From vulnerability to resilience: Learning orientations buffer contingent self-esteem from failure. *Psychological Science, 15,* 801–805.

Nijhuis-van der Sanden, R. W. G., Smits-Engelsman, B. C. M., & Eling, P. A. T. M. (2000). Motor performance in girls with Turner syndrome. *Developmental Medicine & Child Neurology, 42,* 685–690.

Niklasson, L., Rasmussen, P., Oskarsdottir, S., & Gillberg, C. (2002). Chromosome 22q11 deletion syndrome (CATCH 22): Neuropsychiatric and neuropsychological aspects. *Developmental Medicine & Child Neurology, 44,* 44–50.

Nishith, P., Mechanic, M. B., & Resick, P. A. (2000). Prior interpersonal trauma: The contribution to current PTSD symptoms in female rape victims. *Journal of Abnormal Psychology, 109,* 20–25.

Nixon, R. D. V., Sweeney, L., Erickson, D. B., & Touyz, S. W. (2003). Parent-child interaction therapy: A comparison of standard and abbreviated treatments for oppositional defiant preschoolers. *Journal of Consulting and Clinical Psychology, 71,* 251–260.

Nixon, R. D. V., Sweeney, L., Erickson, D. B., & Touyz, S. W. (2004). Parent-child interaction therapy: One- and two-year follow-up of standard and abbreviated treatments for oppositional preschoolers. *Journal of Abnormal Child Psychology, 32,* 263–271.

Noam, G. G., & Hermann, C. A. (2002). Where education and mental health meet: Developmental prevention and early intervention in schools. *Development and Psychopathology, 14,* 861–875.

Nock, M. K., & Prinstein, M. J. (2005). Contextual features and behavioral functions of self-mutilation among adolescents. *Journal of Abnormal Psychology, 114,* 140–146.

Nolan, M., & Carr, A. (2000). Attention deficit hyperactivity disorder. In A. Carr (Ed.), *What works with children and adolescents?: A critical review of psychological interventions with children, adolescents and their families* (pp. 65–101). Florence, KY: Taylor and Frances/Routledge.

Nolen-Hoeksema, S. (2001). Gender differences in depression. *Current Directions in Psychological Science, 10,* 173–180.

Nolen-Hoeksema, S., & Girgus, J. S. (1994). The emergence of gender differences in depression during adolescence. *Psychological Bulletin, 114,* 424–443.

Noll, J. G., Trickett, P. K., & Putnam, F. W. (2003). A prospective investigation of the impact of childhood sexual abuse on the development of sexuality. *Journal of Consulting and Clinical Psychology, 71,* 575–586.

Norberg, A. L., Lindblad, F., & Boman, K. K. (2005). Coping strategies in parents of children with cancer. *Social Science & Medicine, 60,* 965–975.

Norcross, J. C., Castle, P. H., Sayette, M. A., & Mayne, T. J. (2004). The PsyD: Heterogeneity in practitioner training. *Professional Psychology: Research and Practice, 35,* 412–419.

Norcross, J. C., Slotterback, C. S., & Krebs, P. M. (2001). Senior advice: Graduating seniors write to psychology freshmen. *Teaching of Psychology, 28,* 27–29.

Nottelmann, E., Biederman, J., Birmaher, B., Carlson, G. A., Chang, K. D., Fenton, W. S., Geller, B., Hoagwood, K. E., Hyman, S. E., Kendler, K. S., Koretz, D. S., Kowatch, R. A., Kupfer, D. J., Leibenluft, E., Nakmura, R. K., Nottelmann, E. D., Stover, E., Vitiello, B., Weiblinger, G., & Weller, E. (2001). National Institute of Mental Health Research roundtable on prepubertal bipolar disorder. *Journal of the American Academy of Child and Adolescent Psychiatry, 40,* 871–878.

Novins, D. K., & Baron, A. E. (2004). American Indian substance use: The hazards for substance use initiation and progression for adolescents aged 14 to 20 years. *Journal of the American Academy of Child and Adolescent Psychiatry, 43,* 316–324.

Nyborg, V. M., & Curry, J. F. (2003). The impact of perceived racism: Psychological symptoms among African American boys. *Journal of Clinical Child and Adolescent Psychology, 32,* 258–266.

Oakland, T., & Cunningham, J. (1999). The futures of school psychology: Conceptual models for its development and examples of their applications. In C.R. Reynolds & T. B. Gutkin (Eds.), *The handbook of school psychology* (3rd ed., pp. 34–53). New York: Wiley.

Obama, B. (2004). *Dreams from my father: A story of race and inheritance.* New York: Three Rivers Press.

Obeidallah, D., Brennan, R. T., Brooks-Gunn, J., & Earls, F. (2004). Links between pubertal timing and neighborhood contexts: Implications for girls' violent behavior. *Journal of the American Academy of Child and Adolescent Psychiatry, 43,* 1460–1468.

Obiakor, F. E., & Ford, B. A. (Eds., 2002). *Creating successful learning environments for African American learners with exceptionalities.* Thousand Oaks, CA: Corwin Press, Inc.

O'Connor, T. G., Caspi, A., DeFries, J. C., & Plomin, R. (2000). Are associations between parental divorce and children's adjustment genetically mediated? An adoption study. *Developmental Psychology, 36,* 429–437.

O'Connor, T. G., McGuire, S., Reiss, D., Hetherington, E. M., & Plomin, R. (1998). Co-occurrence of depressive symptoms and antisocial behavior in adolescence: A common genetic liability. *Journal of Abnormal Psychology, 107,* 27–37.

Odonovan, A., Bain, J. D., & Dyck, M. J. (2005). Does clinical psychology education enhance the clinical competence of practitioners? *Professional Psychology: Research and Practice, 36,* 104–111.

Oesterle, S., Hill, K. G., Hawkins, J. D., Guo, J., Catalano, R. F., & Abbott, R. D. (2004). Adolescent heavy episodic drinking trajectories and health in young adulthood. *Journal of Studies on Alcohol, 65,* 204–212.

Offord, D. R., & Bennett, K. J. (1996). Conduct disorder. In L. Hechtman (Ed.), *Do they grow out of it? Long-term outcomes of childhood disorders* (pp. 77–99). Washington, DC: American Psychiatric Press.

Ohan, J. L., & Johnston, C. (2005). Gender appropriateness of symptom criteria for attention-deficit/hyperactive disorder, oppositional-defiant disorder, and conduct disorder. *Child Psychiatry and Human Development, 35,* 359–381.

Ohannessian, C. M., Hesselbrock, V. M., Kramer, J., Kuperman, S., Bucholz, K. K., Schuckit, M. A., & Nurnberger, J. I. (2004). The relationship between parental alcoholism and adolescent psychopathology: A systematic examination of parental comorbid psychopathology. *Journal of Abnormal Child Psychology, 32,* 519–533.

O'Hara, M. W. (1995). *Postpartum depression: Causes and consequences.* New York: Springer-Verlag.

Ohayon, M. M., Roberts, R. E., Zulley, J., Smirne, S., & Priest, R. G. (2000). Prevalence and patterns of problematic sleep among older adolescents. *Journal of the American Academy of Child and Adolescent Psychiatry, 39,* 1549–1556.

Ohman, A., & Mineka, S. (2001). Fears, phobias, and preparedness: Toward an evolved module of fear and fear learning. *Psychological Review, 108,* 483–522.

Ohman, A., & Mineka, S. (2003). The malicious serpent: Snakes as a prototypical stimulus for an evolved module of fear. *Current Directions in Psychological Science, 12,* 5–9.

Oldehinkel, A. J., Hartman, C. A., DeWinter, A. F., Veenstra, R., & Ormel, J. (2004). Temperament profiles associated with internalizing and externalizing problems in preadolescence. *Development and Psychopathology, 16,* 421–440.

Olds, D. L. (1988). The prenatal/early infancy project. In R. H. Price, E. L. Cowen, R. P. Lorion, & J. Ramos-McKay (Eds.), *14 ounces of prevention: A casebook for practitioners* (pp. 9–23). Washington, DC: American Psychological Association.

Olds, D. L. (1997). The prenatal/early infancy project: Fifteen years later. In G. W. Albee & T. P. Gullotta (Eds.), *Primary prevention works* (pp. 41–67). Thousand Oaks, CA: Sage.

O'Leary, S. G., & Vidair, H. B. (2005). Marital adjustment, child-rearing disagreements, overreactive parenting: Predicting child behavior problems. *Journal of Family Psychology, 19,* 208–216.

Olkin, R., & Pledger, C. (2003). Can disability studies and psychology join hands? *American Psychologist, 58,* 296–304.

Olkin, R., & Taliaferro, G. (2006). Evidence-based practices have ignored people with disabilities. In J. C. Norcross, L. E. Beutler, & R. F. Levant (Eds.), *Evidence-based practices in mental health: Debate and dialogue on the fundamental questions* (pp. 353–359). Washington, DC: American Psychological Association.

Ollendick, T. H. (1983). Reliability and validity of the Revised Fear Survey Schedule for Children (FSSC-R). *Behaviour Research and Therapy, 21,* 685–692.

Ollendick, T. (Ed.) (1998). *Comprehensive clinical psychology* (Vol. 5). Kidlington, Oxford: Elsevier Science.

Olson, D. H. (2000). Circumplex model of marital and family systems. *Journal of Family Therapy, 22,* 144–167.

Olson, E. D. (2000). Gay teens and substance use disorders: Assessment and treatment. In J. R. Guss, & J. Drescher (Eds.) *Addictions in the gay and lesbian community* (pp. 69–80). New York: Haworth Press.

Olson, R. K. (2004). Genetic and environmental causes of reading disabilities: Results from the Colorado Learning Disabilities Research Center. In M. Turner, & J. Rack (Eds.) *The study of dyslexia* (pp. 23–33). New York: Kluwer Academic/Plenum Press.

Olson, S. L., Bates, J. E., Sandy, J. M., & Lanthier, R. (2000). Early developmental precursors of externalizing behavior in middle childhood and adolescence. *Journal of Abnormal Child Psychology, 28,* 119–133.

Olsson, G. I., Nordstrom, M. L., Arinell, H., & von Knorring, A. L. (1999). Adolescent depression: Social network and family

climate—A case-control study. *Journal of Child Psychology and Psychiatry, 40,* 227–237.

Oman, D., Thoresen, C. E., & McMahon, K. (1999). Volunteerism and mortality among the community-dwelling elderly. *Journal of Health Psychology, 4,* 301–316.

Omigbodun, O. O. (2004). Psychosocial issues in a child and adolescent psychiatric clinic population in Nigeria. *Social Psychiatry and Psychiatric Epidemiology, 39,* 667–672.

Ondersma, S. J., Chaffin, M., Berliner, L., Cordon, I., Goodman, G. S., & Barnett, D. (2001). Sex with children is abuse: Comment on Rind, Tromovitch, and Bauserman (1998). *Psychological Bulletin, 127,* 707–714.

Ondersma, S. J., & Walker, C. E. (1998). Elimination disorders. In T. H. Ollendick & M. Hersen (Eds.), *Handbook of child psychopathology* (3rd ed., pp. 355–378). New York: Plenum Press.

Orbuch, T. L., Parry, C., Chesler, M., Fritz, J., & Repetto, P. (2005). Parent-child relationships and quality of life: Resilience among childhood cancer survivors. *Family Relations: Interdisciplinary Journal of Applied Family Studies, 54,* 171–183.

Orlando, M., Ellickson, P. L., & Jinnett, K. (2001). The temporal relationship between emotional distress and cigarette smoking during adolescence and young adulthood. *Journal of Consulting and Clinical Psychology, 69,* 959–970.

Orrell-Valente, J. K., Pinderhughes, E. E., Valente, E., & Laird, R. D. (1999). If it's offered, will they come? Influences on parents' participation in a community-based conduct problems prevention program. *American Journal of Community Psychology, 27,* 753–783.

Ortiz, J., & Raine, A. (2004). Heart rate level and antisocial behavior in children and adolescents: A meta-analysis. *Journal of the American Academy of Child and Adolescent Psychiatry, 43,* 154–162.

Orvaschel, H., Beeferman, D., & Kabacoff, R. (1997). Depression, self-esteem, sex, and age in a child and adolescent clinical sample. *Journal of Clinical Child Psychology, 26,* 285–289.

O'Shea, B. (2003). Factitious disorders: The Baron's legacy. *International Journal of Psychiatry in Clinical Practice, 7,* 33–39.

Oskarsdottir, S., Belfrage, M., Sandstedt, E., Viggedal, G., & Uvebrant, P. (2005). Disabilities and cognition in children and adolescents with 22q11 deletion syndrome. *Developmental Medicine & Child Neurology, 47,* 177–184.

Osterling, J. A., Dawson, G., & Munson, J. A. (2002). Early recognition of 1-year-old infants with autism spectrum disorder versus mental retardation. *Development and Psychopathology, 14,* 239–251.

Osvath, P., Voros, V., & Fekete, S. (2004). Life events and psychopathology in a group of suicide attempters. *Psychopathology, 37,* 36–40.

Owens, E. B., Hinshaw, S. P., Kraemer, H. C., Arnold, L. E., Abikoff, H. B., Cantwell, D. P., Conners, C. K., Elliott, G., Greenhill, L. L., Hechtman, L., Hoza, B., Jensen, P. S., March, J. S., Newcorn, J. H., Pelham, W. E., Severe, J. B., Swanson, J. M., Vitiello, B. Wells, K. C., & Wigal, T. (2003). Which treatment for whom for ADHD? Moderators of treatment response in the MTA. *Journal of Consulting and Clinical Psychology, 71,* 540–552.

Owens, G. P., & Chard, K. M. (2003). Comorbidity and psychiatric diagnoses among women reporting child sexual abuse. *Child Abuse and Neglect, 27,* 1075–1082.

Owens, J. A. (2005). The ADHD and sleep conundrum: A review. *Journal of Developmental & Behavioral Pediatrics, 26,* 312–322.

Owens, J. A., Fernando, S., & McGuinn, M. (2005). Sleep disturbance and injury risk in young children. *Behavioral Sleep Medicine, 3,* 18–31.

Owens, J. A., Mindell, J., & Owens, J. (2005). *Take charge of your child's sleep: The all-in-one resource for solving sleep problems in kids and teens.* Emeryville, CA: Avalon Publishing.

Owens, J. A., Spirito, A., McGuinn, M., & Nobile, C. (2000). Sleep habits and sleep disturbance in elementary school-aged children. *Journal of Developmental and Behavioral Pediatrics, 21,* 27–36.

Owens, J. S., & Hoza, B. (2003). The role of inattention and hyperactivity/impulsivity in the positive illusory bias. *Journal of Consulting and Clinical Psychology, 71,* 680–691.

Owens, E. B., & Shaw, D. S. (2003). Predicting growth curves of externalizing behavior across the preschool years. *Journal of Abnormal Child Psychology, 31,* 575–590.

Oyane, N. M. F., & Bjorvatn, B. (2005). Sleep disturbances in adolescents and young adults with autism and Asperger syndrome. *Autism, 9,* 83–94.

Ozer, E. J., Richards, M. H., & Kliewer, W. (2004). Introduction to the special section on protective factors in the relation between community violence exposure and adjustment in youth. *Journal of Clinical Child and Adolescent Psychology, 33,* 434–438.

Ozonoff, S., Dawson, G., & McPartland, J. (2002). *A parent's guide to Asperger syndrome and high-functioning autism.* New York: Guilford Press.

Ozonoff, S., Goodlin-Jones, B. L., & Solomon, M. (2005). Evidence-based assessment of autism spectrum disorders in children and adolescents. *Journal of Clinical Child and Adolescent Psychology, 34,* 523–540.

Pacifici, C., Stoolmiller, M., & Nelson, C., (2001). Evaluating a prevention program for teenagers on sexual coercion: A differential effectiveness approach. *Journal of Consulting and Clinical Psychology, 69,* 552–559.

Pagliaro, A. M., & Pagliaro, L. A. (1996). *Substance use among children and adolescents: Its nature, extent, and effects from conception to adulthood.* New York: Wiley.

Pajer, K., Gardner, W., Rubin, R. T., Perel, J., & Neal, S. (2001). Decreased cortisol levels in adolescent girls with conduct disorder. *Archives of General Psychiatry, 58,* 297–302.

Palermo, T. M., Childs, G., Burgess, E. S., Kaugars, A. S., Comer, D., & Kelleher, K. (2002). Functional limitations of school-aged children seen in primary care. *Child: Care, Health and Development, 28,* 379–389.

Paley, V. G. (1981). *Wally's stories.* Cambridge, MA: Harvard University Press.

Palmgreen, P., Donohew, L., Lorch, E. P., Hoyle, R. H., & Stephenson, M. T. (2002). Television campaigns and sensation seeking targeting of adolescent marijuana use: A controlled time series approach. In R. C. Ornik (Ed.) *Public health communication: Evidence for behavior change* (pp. 35–56). Mahwah, NJ: Lawrence Erlbaum Associates.

Paniagua, F. A. (1998). *Assessing and treating culturally diverse clients: A practical guide* (2nd ed.). Thousand Oaks, CA: Sage.

Pantelis, C., Harvey, C. A., Plant, G., Fossey, E., Maruff, P., Stuart, G. W., Brewer, W. J., Nelson, H. E., Robbins, T. W., & Barnes, T. R. E. (2004). Relationship of behavioural and symptomatic syndromes in schizophrenia to spatial working memory and attentional set-shifting ability. *Psychological Medicine, 34,* 693–703.

Pantin, H., Coatsworth, J. D., Feaster, D. J., Newman, F. L., Briones, E., Prado, G., Schwartz, S. J., & Szapocznik, J. (2003). Familias Unidas: the efficacy of an intervention to promote parental investment in Hispanic immigrant families. *Prevention Science, 4,* 189–201.

Pantin, H., Schwartz, S. J., Sullivan, S., Coatsworth, J. D., & Szapocznik, J. (2003). Preventing substance abuse in Hispanic immigrant adolescents: An ecodevelopmental, parent-centered approach. *Hispanic Journal of Behavioral Sciences, 25,* 469–500.

Papolos, D., & Papolos, J. (2002). *Bipolar child: The definitive and reassuring guide to childhood's most misunderstood disorder* (2nd ed.). New York: Random House.

Pardini, D. A., Lochman, J. E., & Frick, P. J. (2003). Callous/unemotional traits and social-cognitive processes in adjudicated youths. *Journal of the American Academy of Child and Adolescent Psychiatry, 42,* 364–371.

Pardini, D., Lochman, J., & Wells, K. (2004). Negative emotions and alcohol use initiation in high-risk boys: The moderating effect of good inhibitory control. *Journal of Abnormal Child Psychology, 32,* 505–518.

Parke, R. D. (1996). Fathers, play, and emotion: A research odyssey. In M. R. Merrens & G. G. Brannigan (Eds.), *The developmental psychologists* (pp. 136–150). New York: McGraw-Hill.

Parke, R. D. (2000). Beyond white and middle class: Cultural variations in families—Assessments, processes, and policies. *Journal of Family Psychology, 14,* 331–333.

Parke, R. D. (2004). Fathers, families, and the future: A plethora of plausible predictions. *Merrill-Palmer Quarterly, 50,* 456–470.

Parker, H., & Parker, S. (1986). Father-daughter sexual abuse: An emerging perspective. *American Journal of Orthopsychiatry, 56,* 531–549.

Parker, K. J., Buckmaster, C. L., Schatzberg, A. F., & Lyons, D. M. (2004). Prospective investigation of stress inoculation in young monkeys. *Archives of General Psychiatry, 61,* 933–941.

Parks, G. (2006). The High/Scope Perry preschool project. In D. Del Campo & R. Del Campo (Eds.), *Taking sides: Clashing views in childhood and society* (6th ed.). Dubuque, IA: McGraw-Hill.

Patel, N. C., Crismon, M. L., Hoagwood, K., Johnsrud, M. T., Rascatie, K. L., Wilson, J. P., & Jensen, P. S. (2005). Trends in the use of typical and atypical antipsychotics in children and adolescents. *Journal of the American Academy of Child and Adolescent Psychiatry, 44,* 548–556.

Patenaude, A. F., & Kupst, M. J. (2005). Psychosocial functioning in pediatric cancer. *Journal of Pediatric Psychology, 30,* 9–27.

Patten, C. A. (2000). A critical evaluation of nicotine replacement therapy for teenage smokers. *Journal of Child and Adolescent Substance Abuse, 9,* 51–75.

Patterson, G. R. (1982). *Coercive family process.* Eugene, OR: Castalia.

Patterson, G. R. (1996). Some characteristics of a developmental theory for early-onset delinquency. In M. F. Lenzenweger & J. J. Haugaard (Eds.), *Frontiers of developmental psychopathology* (pp. 81–124). New York: Oxford University Press.

Patterson, G. R., DeGarmo, D., & Forgatch, M. S. (2004). Systematic changes in families following prevention trials. *Journal of Abnormal Child Psychology, 32,* 621–633.

Patterson, G. R., DeGarmo, D. S., & Knutson, N. (2000). Hyperactive and antisocial behaviors: Comorbid or two points in the same process? *Development and Psychopathology, 12,* 91–106.

Patterson, G. R., & Gullion, M. E. (1968). *Living with children: New methods for parents and teachers.* Champaign, IL: Research Press.

Patterson, T. E., & Lusterman, D. (1996). The relational reimbursement dilemma. In F. W. Kaslow (Ed.), *Handbook of relational diagnosis and dysfunctional family patterns* (pp. 46–58). New York: Wiley.

Patton, G. C., Carlin, J. B., Coffey, C., Wolfe, R., Hibbert, M., & Bowes, G. (1998). Depression, anxiety, and smoking initiation: A prospective study over 3 years. *American Journal of Public Health, 88,* 1518–1522.

Pavlidis, K., & McCauley, E. (2001). Autonomy and relatedness in family interactions with depressed adolescents. *Journal of Abnormal Child Psychology, 29,* 11–21.

Pavuluri, M. N., Birmaher, B., & Naylor, M. W. (2005). Pediatric bipolar disorder: A review of the past 10 years. *Journal of the American Academy of Child and Adolescent Psychiatry, 44,* 846–871.

Pavuluri, M. N., Graczyk, P. A., Henry, D. B., Carbray, J. A., Heidenreich, J., & Miklowitz, D. J. (2004). Child- and family-focused cognitive-behavioral therapy for pediatric bipolar disorder: Development and preliminary results. *Journal of the American Academy of Child and Adolescent Psychiatry, 43,* 528–537.

Pavuluri, M. N., Henry, D. B., Devineni, B., Carbray, J. A., Naylor, M. W., & Janicak, P. (2004). A pharmacotherapy algorithm for stabilization and maintenance of pediatric bipolar disorder. *Journal of the American Academy of Child and Adolescent Psychiatry, 43,* 859–867.

Peake, P. K., Hebl, M., & Mischel, W. (2002). Strategic attention deployment for delay of gratification in working and waiting situations. *Developmental Psychology, 38,* 313–326.

Pearce, M. J., Little, T. D., & Perez, J. E. (2003). Religiousness and depressive symptoms among adolescents. *Journal of Clinical Child and Adolescent Psychology, 32,* 267–276.

Pearson, D. A., Lane, D. M., Santos, C. W., Casat, C. D., Jerger, S. W., Loveland, K. A., Faria, L. P., Mansour, R., Henderson, J. A., Payne, C. D., Roache, J. D., Lachar, D., & Cleveland, L. A. (2004). Effects of methylphenidate treatment in children with mental retardation and ADHD: Individual variation in medication response. *Journal of the American Academy of Child and Adolescent Psychiatry, 43,* 686–698.

The Pediatric OCD Treatment Study (POTS) Team. (2004). Cognitive-behavior therapy, sertraline, and their combination for children and adolescents with obsessive-compulsive disorder: The pediatric OCD treatment study (POTS) randomized controlled trial. *Journal of the American Medical Association, 292,* 1969–1976.

Pedro-Carroll, J. (2001). The promotion of wellness in children and families: Challenges and opportunities. *American Psychologist, 56,* 993–1004.

Pelcovitz, D., Adler, N. A., Kaplan, S., Packman, L., & Krieger, R. (1992). The failure of a school-based child sexual abuse prevention program. *Journal of the American Academy of Child and Adolescent Psychiatry, 31,* 887–892.

Pelham, W. E., Fabiano, G. A., & Massetti, G. M. (2005). Evidence-based assessment of attention deficit hyperactivity disorder in children and adolescents. *Journal of Clinical Child and Adolescent, 34,* 449–476.

Pelham, W. E., Gnagy, E. M., Greiner, A. R., Hoza, B., Hinshaw, S. P., Swanson, J. M., Simpson, S., Shapiro, C., Bukstein, O., Baron-Myak, C., & McBurnett, K. (2000). Behavioral versus behavioral and pharmacological treatment in ADHD children attending a summer treatment program. *Journal of Abnormal Child Psychology, 28,* 507–525.

Pelham, W. E., Lang, A. R., Atkeson, B., Murphy, D. A., Gnagy, E. M., Greiner, A. R., Vodde-Hamilton, M., & Greenslade, K. E. (1997). Effects of deviant child behavior on parental distress and alcohol consumption in laboratory interactions. *Journal of Abnormal Child Psychology, 25,* 413–424.

Pelkonen, M., Marttunen, M., Laippala, P., & Loennqvist, J. (2000). Factors associated with early dropout from adolescent psychiatric outpatient treatment. *Journal of the American Academy of Child and Adolescent Psychiatry, 39,* 329–336.

Pelton, J., & Forehand, R. (2005). Orphans of the AIDS epidemic: An examination of clinical level problems of children. *Journal of the American Academy of Child and Adolescent Psychiatry, 44,* 585–591.

Pelzer, D. (1995). *A child called "It."* Deerfield Beach, FL: Health Communications.

Pelzer, D. (1997). *The lost boy: A foster child's search for the love of a family.* Deerfield Beach, FL: Health Communications.

Pelzer, D. (1999). *A man named Dave.* Deerfield Beach, FL: Health Communications.

Penfold, P. S. (1985). Parent's perceived responsibility for children's problems. *Canadian Journal of Psychiatry, 30,* 255–258.

Penn, D. L., Judge, A., Jamieson, P., Garczynski, J., Hennessy, M., & Romer, D. (2005). Stigma. In D. L. Evans, E. B. Foa, R. E. Gur, H. Hendin, C. P. O'Brien, M. E. P. Seligman, & B. T. Walsh (Eds.), *Treating and preventing adolescent mental health disorders: What we know and what we don't know* (pp. 532–543). New York: Oxford University Press.

Pennington, B. F. (2002). *The development of psychopathology: Nature and nurture.* New York: Guilford Press.

Pennington, B. F., Moon, J., Edgin, J., Stedron, J., & Nadel, L. (2003). The neuropsychology of Down syndrome: Evidence for hippocampal dysfunction. *Child Development, 74,* 75–93.

Perez-Smith, A. M., Albus, K. E., & Weist, M. D. (2001). Exposure to violence and neighborhood affiliation among inner-city youth. *Journal of Clinical Child Psychology, 30,* 464–472.

Perkins, D. D., Crim, B., Silberman, P., & Brown, B. B. (2004). Community development as a response to community-level adversity: Ecological theory and research and strengths-based policy. In K. I. Maton, C. J. Schellenbach, B. J. Leadbeater, & A. L. Solarz (Eds.), *Investing in children, youth, families, and communities: Strengths-based research and policy* (pp. 321–340). Washington, DC: American Psychological Association.

Perrino, T., Coatsworth, J. D., Briones, E., Pantin, H., & Szapocznik, J. (2001). Initial engagement in parent-centered preventive interventions: A family systems perspective. *Journal of Primary Prevention, 22,* 21–44.

Perrino, T., Gonzalez-Soldevilla, A., Pantin, H., & Szapocznik, J. (2000). The role of families in adolescent HIV prevention: A review. *Clinical Child and Family Psychology Review, 3,* 81–96.

Peters, R. D., McMahon, R., & Leadbeater, B. (Eds.) (2004). *Resilience in children, families, communities: Linking context to practice and policy.* New York: Kluwer Academic/Plenum.

Peters, R. D., Petrunka, K., & Arnold, R. (2003). The Better Beginnings, Better Futures Project: A universal, comprehensive, community-based prevention approach for primary school children and their families. *Journal of Clinical Child and Adolescent Psychology, 32,* 215–227.

Petersen, A. C., Compas, B. E., Brooks-Gunn, J., Stemmler, M., Ey, S., & Grant, K. E. (1993). Depression in adolescence. *American Psychologist, 48,* 155–168.

Peterson, B. S., Pine, D. S., Cohen, P., & Brook, J. S. (2001). Prospective, longitudinal study of tic, obsessive-compulsive, and attention-deficit/hyperactivity disorders in an epidemiological sample. *Journal of the Academy of Child and Adolescent Psychiatry, 40,* 685–695.

Peterson, C. C., Palermo, T. M., Swift, E., Beebe, A., & Drotar, D. (2005). Assessment of psycho-educational needs in a clinical sample of children with sickle cell disease. *Children's Health Care, 34,* 133–148.

Peterson, D. R. (1971). Status of the doctor of psychology program. *Professional Psychology, 2,* 271–275.

Peterson, J. L., & Newman, R. (2000). Helping to curb youth violence: The APA-MTV "Warning Signs" initiative. *Professional Psychology: Research and Practice, 31,* 509–514.

Peterson, L., Reach, K., & Grabe, S. (2003). Health-related disorders. In E. J. Mash, & B. A. Barkley (Eds.), *Child psychopathology* (2nd ed., pp. 716–749). New York: Guilford Press.

Peterson, L., & Tremblay, G. (1999). Importance of developmental theory and investigation to research in clinical child psychology. *Journal of Clinical Child Psychology, 28,* 448–456.

Petraitis, J., Flay, B. R., & Miller, T. Q. (1995). Reviewing theories of adolescent substance use: Organizing pieces in the puzzle. *Psychological Bulletin, 117,* 67–86.

Pettit, G. S., Bates, J. E., Dodge, K. A., & Meece, D. W. (1999). The impact of after-school peer contact of early adolescent externalizing problems is moderated by parental monitoring, perceived neighborhood safety, and prior adjustment. *Child Development, 70,* 768–778.

Petty, J., & Oliver, C. (2005). Self-injurious behaviour in individuals with intellectual disabilities. *Current Opinion in Psychiatry, 18,* 484–489.

Pfeffer, C. R. (1986). *The suicidal child.* New York: Guilford Press.

Pfeffer, C. R. (2002). Suicide in mood disordered children and adolescents. *Child and Adolescent Psychiatric Clinics of North America, 11,* 639–648.

Pfeffer, C. R., Karus, D., Siegel, K., & Jiang, H. (2000). Child survivors of parental death from cancer or suicide: Depressive and behavioral outcomes. *Psycho-Oncology, 9,* 1–10.

Pfiffner, L. J., McBurnett, K., & Rathouz, P. J. (2001). Father absence and familial antisocial characteristics. *Journal of Abnormal Child Psychology, 29,* 357–367.

Phares, V. (1992). Where's Poppa?: The relative lack of attention to the role of fathers in child and adolescent psychopathology. *American Psychologist, 47,* 656–664.

Phares, V. (1996). *Fathers and developmental psychopathology.* New York: Wiley.

Phares, V. (1999). *Poppa psychology: The role of fathers in children's mental well-being.* Westport, CT: Praeger.

Phares, V. (2003). *Understanding abnormal child psychology.* New York: Wiley.

Phares, V., & Compas, B. E. (1990). Adolescents' subjective distress over their emotional/behavioral problems. *Journal of Consulting and Clinical Psychology, 58,* 596–603.

Phares, V., & Curley, J. (In press). Evidence-based assessment for children and adolescents. In R. G. Steele, T. D. Elkin, & M. C. Roberts (Eds.), *Handbook of evidence-based therapies for children and adolescents.* Springer Publishers.

Phares, V., & Danforth, J. S. (1994). Adolescents', parents', and teachers' distress over adolescents' behavior. *Journal of Abnormal Child Psychology, 22,* 721–732.

Phares, V., Duhig, A. M., & Watkins, M. M. (2002). Family context: Fathers and other supports. In S. H. Goodman, & I. H. Gotlib (Eds.), *Children of depressed parents: Mechanisms of risk and implications for treatment* (pp. 203–225). Washington, DC: American Psychological Association.

Phares, V., Fields, S., & Binitie, I. (2006). Getting fathers involved in child-related therapy. *Cognitive and Behavioral Practice, 13,* 42–52.

Phares, V., Fields, S., Kamboukos, D., & Lopez, L. (2005). Still looking for Poppa. *American Psychologist, 60,* 735–736.

Phares, V., Lopez, E., Fields, S., Kamboukos, D., & Duhig, A. M. (2005). Are fathers involved in pediatric psychology research and treatment? *Journal of Pediatric Psychology, 30,* 631–643.

Phares, V., & Lum, J. J. (1996). Family demographics of clinically referred children: What we know and what we need to know. *Journal of Abnormal Child Psychology, 24,* 787–801.

Phelps, L., Brown, R. T., & Power, T. J. (2002). *Pediatric psychopharmacology: Combining medical and psychosocial interventions.* Washington, DC: American Psychological Association.

Phillips, B. N. (1999). Strengthening the links between science and practice: Reading, evaluating, and applying research in school psychology. In C. R. Reynolds & T. B. Gutkin (Eds.), *The handbook of school psychology* (3rd ed., pp. 56–77). New York: Wiley.

Phillips, K. A., & Castle, D. J. (Eds.). (2002). Body dysmorphic disorder. In *Disorders of body image* (pp. 101–120). Petersfield, England: Wrightson Biomedical Publishing.

Phillips, N. K., Hammen, C. L., Brennan, P. A., Najman, J. M., & Bor, W. (2005). Early adversity and the prospective prediction of depressive and anxiety disorders in adolescents. *Journal of Abnormal Child Psychology, 33,* 13–24.

Piacentini, J., Bergman, R. L., Keller, M., & McCracken, J. (2003). Functional impairment in children and adolescents with obsessive-compulsive disorder. *Journal of Child and Adolescent Psychopharmacology, 13,* S61–S69.

Piacentini, J., & Langley, A. K. (2004). Cognitive-behavioral therapy for children who have obsessive-compulsive disorder. *Journal of Clinical Psychology, 60,* 1181–1194.

Piacentini, J. C., March, J. S., & Franklin, M. E. (2006). Cognitive-behavioral therapy for youth with obsessive-compulsive disorder. In P. C. Kendall (Ed.), *Child and adolescent therapy: Cognitive-behavioral procedures* (3rd ed., pp. 297–321). New York: Guilford Press.

Piatigorsky, A., & Hinshaw, S. P. (2004). Psychopathic traits in boys with and without attention-deficit/hyperactivity disorder: Concurrent and longitudinal correlates. *Journal of Abnormal Child Psychology, 32*, 535–550.

Pihl, R. O., & Nantel-Vivier, A. (2005). Biological vulnerabilities to the development of psychopathology. In B. L. Hankin & J. R. Z. Abela (Eds.), *Development of psychopathology: A vulnerability-stress perspective* (pp. 75–103). Thousand Oaks, CA: Sage.

Pilgrim, C., Luo, Q., Urberg, K. A., & Fang, X. (1999). Influence of peers, parents, and individual characteristics on adolescent drug use in two cultures. *Merrill-Palmer Quarterly, 45*, 85–107.

Pilowsky, D. J., Zybert, P. A., Hsieh, P. W., Vlahov, D., & Susser, E. (2003). Children of HIV-positive drug-using parents. *Journal of the American Academy of Child and Adolescent Psychiatry, 42*, 950–956.

Pilowsky, D. J., Zybert, P. A., & Vlahov, D. (2004). Resilient children of injection drug users. *Journal of the American Academy of Child and Adolescent Psychiatry, 43*, 1372–1379.

Pina, A. A., Silverman, W. K., Alfano, C. A., & Saavedra, L. M. (2002). Diagnostic efficiency of symptoms in the diagnosis of DSM-IV: generalized anxiety disorder in youth. *Journal of Child Psychology and Psychiatry, 4*, 959–967.

Pincus, H. A., McQueen, L. E., & Elinson, L. (2003). Subthreshold mental disorders: Nosological and research recommendations. In K. A. Phillips, & M. B. First (Eds.) *Advancing DSM: Dilemmas in psychiatric diagnosis* (pp. 129–144). Washington, DC: American Psychiatric Association.

Pine, D. S., Kentgen, L. M., Bruder, G. E., Leite, P., Bearman, K., Ma, Y., & Klein, R. G. (2000). Cerebral laterality in adolescent major depression. *Psychiatry Research, 93*, 135–144.

Pisani, A. R., Berry, S. L., & Goldfarb, M. (2005). A predoctoral field placement in primary care: Keeping it simple. *Professional Psychology: Research and Practice, 36*, 151–157.

Plante, T. G., Boccaccini, M., & Andersen, E. (1998). Attitudes concerning professional issues impacting psychotherapy practice among members of the American Board of Professional Psychology. *Psychotherapy, 35*, 34–42.

Plante, T. G., Yancey, S., Sherman, A., & Guertin, M. (2000). The association between strength of religious faith and psychological functioning. *Pastoral Psychology, 48*, 405–412.

Pliszka, S. R., Browne, R. G., Olvera, R. L., & Wynne, S. K. (2000). A double-blind, placebo-controlled study of Adderall and methylphenidate in the treatment of attention-deficit/hyperactivity disorder. *Journal of the American Academy of Child and Adolescent Psychiatry, 39*, 619–626.

Plomin, R., & Crabbe, J. (2000). DNA. *Psychological Bulletin, 126*, 806–828.

Plomin, R., & Kovas, Y. (2005). Generalist genes and learning disabilities. *Psychological Bulletin, 131*, 592–617.

Plomin, R., & Walker, S. O. (2003). Genetics and educational psychology. *British Journal of Educational Psychology, 73*, 3–14.

Podorefsky, D. L., McDonald-Dowdell, M., & Beardslee, W. R. (2001). Adaptation of preventive interventions for a low-income, culturally diverse community. *Journal of the American Academy of Child and Adolescent Psychiatry, 40*, 879–886.

Poduska, J. M. (2000). Parents' perceptions of their first graders' need for mental health and educational services. *Journal of the American Academy of Child and Adolescent Psychiatry, 39*, 584–591.

Poggi, G., Liscio, M., Galbiati, S., Adduci, A., Massimino, M., Gandola, L., Spreafico, F., Clerici, C. A., Fossati-Bellani, F., Sommovigo, M., & Castelli, E. (2005). Brain tumors in children and adolescents: Cognitive and psychological disorders at different ages. *Psycho-Oncology, 14*, 386–395.

Poland, J., & Caplan, P. J. (2004). The deep structure of bias in psychiatric diagnosis. In P. J. Caplan, & L. Cosgrove (Eds.) *Bias in psychiatric diagnosis* (pp. 9–23). Northvale, NJ: Jason Aronson.

Polimeni, M. A., Richdale, A. L., & Francis, A. J. P. (2005). A survey of sleep problems in autism, Asperger's disorder and typically developing children. *Intellectual Disability Research, 49*, 260–268.

Polivy, J., & Herman, C. P. (2002). Causes of eating disorders. *Annual Review of Psychology, 53*, 187–213.

Popenoe, D. (2004). *War over the family*. Somerset, NJ: Transaction.

Portzky, G., Audenaert, K., & van Heeringen, K. (2005). Adjustment disorder and the course of the suicidal process in adolescents. *Journal of Affective Disorders, 87*, 265–270.

Posner, J. K., & Vandell, D. L. (1999). After-school activities and the development of low-income urban children: A longitudinal study. *Developmental Psychology, 35*, 868–879.

Possel, P., Horn, A. B., Groen, G., & Hautzinger, M. (2004). School-based prevention of depressive symptoms in adolescents: A 6-month follow-up. *Journal of the American Academy of Child and Adolescent Psychiatry, 43*, 1003–1010.

Pottick, K. J., Barber, C. C., Hansell, S., & Coyne, L. (2001). Changing patterns of inpatient care for children and adolescents at the Menninger Clinic, 1988–1994. *Journal of Consulting and Clinical Psychology, 69*, 573–577.

Pottick, K. J., McAlpine, D. D., & Andelman, R. B. (2000). Changing patterns of psychiatric inpatient care for children and adolescents in general hospitals, 1988–1995. *American Journal of Psychiatry, 157*, 1267–1273.

Poulin, C., Hand, D., Boudreau, B., & Santor, D. (2005). Gender differences in the association between substance use and elevated depressive symptoms in a general adolescent population. *Addiction, 100*, 525–535.

Poulton, R., Caspi, A., Moffitt, T. E., Cannon, M., Murray, R., & Harrington, H. L. (2000). Children's self-reported psychotic symptoms and adult schizophreniform disorder: A 15-year longitudinal study. *Archives of General Psychiatry, 57*, 1053–1058.

Power, T. J., Costigan, T. E., Leff, S. S., Eiraldi, R. B., & Landau, S. (2001). Assessing ADHD across settings: Contributions of behavioral assessment to categorical decision making. *Journal of Clinical Child Psychology, 30*, 399–412.

Power, T. J., Shapiro, E. S., & DuPaul, G. J., (2003). Preparing psychologists to link systems of care in managing and preventing children's health problems. *Journal of Pediatric Psychology, 28*, 147–155.

Prevatt, F. F. (1999a). Milan systemic therapy. In D. M. Lawson & F. F. Prevatt (Eds.), *Casebook in family therapy* (pp. 188–209). Belmont, CA: Wadsworth.

Prevatt, F. F. (1999b). Personality assessment in the schools. In C. R. Reynolds & T. B. Gutkin (Eds.), *The handbook of school psychology* (3rd ed., pp. 434–451). New York: Wiley.

Price, J. M., & Glad, K. (2003). Hostile attributional tendencies in maltreated children. *Journal of Abnormal Child Psychology, 31*, 329–343.

Price, R. H., Cowen, E. L., Lorion, R. P., & Ramos-McKay, J. (Eds.). (1988). *14 ounces of prevention: A casebook for practitioners.* Washington, D. C.: American Psychological Association.

Prinstein, M. J., & La Greca, A. M. (2004). Childhood peer rejection and aggression as predictors of adolescent girls' externalizing and health risk behaviors: A 6-year longitudinal study. *Journal of Consulting and Clinical Psychology, 72*, 103–112.

Prinstein, M. J., Meade, C. S., & Cohen, G. L. (2003). Adolescent oral sex, peer popularity, and perceptions of best friends' sexual behavior. *Journal of Pediatric Psychology, 28*, 243–249.

Prinstein, M. J., & Patterson, M. D. (Eds.). (2003). *The portable mentor: Expert guide to a successful career in psychology.* New York: Kluwer Academic/Plenum Press.

Prior, M., & Cummins, R. (1992). Questions about facilitated communication and autism. *Journal of Autism and Developmental Disorders, 22*, 331–338.

Prior, M., Smart, D., Sanson, A., & Oberklaid, F. (2000). Does shy-inhibited temperament in childhood lead to anxiety problems in adolescence? *Journal of the American Academy of Child and Adolescent Psychiatry, 39*, 461–468.

Pritchard, B. J., Bergin, J. L., & Wade, T. D. (2004). A case series evaluation of guided self-help for bulimia nervosa using a cognitive manual. *International Journal of Eating Disorders, 36*, 144–156.

Proctor, R. W., & Capaldi, E. J. (2001). Empirical evaluation and justification of methodologies in psychological science. *Psychological Bulletin, 127*, 759–772.

Pruett, M. K., Williams, T. Y., Insabella, G., & Little, T. D. (2003). Family and legal indicators of child adjustment to divorce among families with young children. *Journal of Family Psychology, 17*, 169–180.

Pryzwansky, W. B., & Wendt, R. N. (1999). *Professional and ethical issues in psychology: Foundations of practice.* New York: W. W. Norton.

Psychological Corporation. (1997). *Wechsler Adult Intelligence Scale-Third edition (WAIS-III).* San Antonio, TX: Author.

Putnam, F. W. (2003). Ten-year research update review: Child sexual abuse. *Journal of the American Academy of Child and Adolescent Psychiatry, 42*, 269–278.

Quinn, P. O. (2005). Treating adolescent girls and women with ADHD: Gender-specific issues. *Journal of Clinical Psychology, 61*, 579–587.

Rabiner, D., Coie, J. E., & Conduct Problems Prevention Research Group. (2000). Early attention problems and children's reading achievement: A longitudinal investigation. *Journal of the American Academy of Child and Adolescent Psychiatry, 39*, 859–867.

Rabiner, D. L., Malone, P. S., & Conduct problems prevention Research Group. (2004). The impact of tutoring of early reading achievement for children with and without attention problems. *Journal of Abnormal Child Psychology, 32*, 273–284.

Radecki, T. E. (1990). Cartoon monitoring. *National Coalition on Television Violence News*. April–June, p. 9.

Radigan, M., Lannon, P., Roohan, P., & Gesten, F. (2005). Medication patterns for attention-deficit/hyperactivity disorder and comorbid psychiatric conditions in a low-income population. *Journal of Child and Adolescent Psychopharmacology, 15*, 44–56.

Radke-Yarrow, M. (1998). *Children of depressed mothers: From early childhood to maturity.* New York: Cambridge University Press.

Raghavan, R., Zima, B. T., Andersen, R. M., Leibowitz, A. A., Schuster, M. A., & Landsverk, J. (2005). Psychotropic medication use in a national probability sample of children in the child welfare system. *Journal of Child and Adolescent Psychopharmacology, 15*, 97–106.

Rahman, A., Mubbashar, M., Harrington, R., & Gater, R. (2000). Annotation: Developing child mental health services in developing countries. *Journal of Child Psychology and Psychiatry, 41*, 539–546.

Ramsey, S. E., Brown, R. A., Strong, D. R., Stuart, G. L., Weinstock, M. C., & Myers, M. G. (2005). Cigarette smoking and substance use among adolescents in psychiatric treatment. *Journal of Child & Adolescent Substance Abuse, 14*, 1–13.

Rand, C. M., Auinger, P., Klein, J. D., & Weitzman, M. (2005). Preventive counseling at adolescent ambulatory visits. *Journal of Adolescent Health, 37*, 87–93.

Rao, U., Daley, S. E., & Hammen, C. (2000). Relationship between depression and substance use disorders in adolescent women during the transition to adulthood. *Journal of the American Academy of Child and Adolescent Psychiatry, 39*, 215–222.

Rao, U., Ryan, N. D., Dahl, R. E., Birmaher, B., Rao, R., Williamson, D. E., & Perel, J. M. (1999). Factors associated with the development of substance use disorder in depressed adolescents. *Journal of the American Academy of Child and Adolescent Psychiatry, 38*, 1109–1117.

Rapee, R. M., Abbott, M. J., & Lyneham, H. J. (2006). Bibliotherapy for children with anxiety disorders using written materials for parents: A randomized controlled trial. *Journal of Consulting and Clinical Psychology, 74*, 436–444.

Rapee, R. M., Kennedy, S., Ingram, M. Edwards, S., & Sweeney, L. (2005). Prevention and early intervention of anxiety disorders in inhibited preschool children. *Journal of Consulting and Clinical Psychology, 73*, 488–497.

Rapoport, J. L., Giedd, J. N., Blumenthal, J., Hamburger, S., Jeffries, N., Fernandez, T., Nicolson, R., Bredwell, J., Lenane, M., Zijdenbos, A., Paus, T., & Evans, A. (1999). Progressive cortical change during adolescence in childhood-onset schizophrenia: A longitudinal magnetic resonance imaging study. *Archives of General Psychiatry, 56*, 649–654.

Rapoport, J. L., & Ismond, D. R. (1996). *DSM-IV training guide for diagnosis of childhood disorders.* New York: Brunner/Mazel.

Rappaport, J., & Seidman, E. (Eds.) (2000). *Handbook of community psychology.* New York: Kluwer Academic/Plenum Press.

Rappaport, N., & Thomas, C. (2004). Recent research findings on aggressive and violent behavior in youth: Implications for clinical assessment and intervention. *Journal of Adolescent Health, 35*, 260–277.

Rappaport, N., & Chubinsky, P. (2000). The meaning of psychotropic medications for children, adolescents, and their families. *Journal of the American Academy of Child and Adolescent Psychiatry, 39*, 1198–1200.

Rappley, M. D. (2005). Attention deficit-hyperactivity disorder. *New England Journal of Medicine, 352*, 165–173.

Rapport, M. D. (2001). Bridging theory and practice: Conceptual understanding of treatments for children with attention deficit hyperactivity disorder (ADHD), obsessive-compulsive disorder (OCD), autism, and depression. *Journal of Clinical Child Psychology, 30*, 3–7.

Rapport, M. D., & Chung, K. M. (2000). Attention deficit hyperactivity disorder. In M. Hersen & R. T. Ammerman (Eds.), *Advanced abnormal child psychology* (pp. 413–440). Mahwah, NJ: Lawrence Erlbaum Associates.

Rapport, M. D., Chung, K., Shore, G., Denney, C. B., & Isaacs, P. (2000). Upgrading the science and technology of assessment and diagnosis: Laboratory and clinic-based assessment of children with ADHD. *Journal of Clinical Child Psychology, 29*, 555–568.

Raschka, L. B. (2000). Paternal age and schizophrenia in dizygotic twins. *British Journal of Psychiatry, 176*, 400–401.

Rashid, F. L., Morris, R. D., & Sevcik, R. A. (2005). Relationship between home literacy environment and reading achievement in children with reading disabilities. *Journal of Learning Disabilities, 38*, 2–11.

Rathvon, N., Witt, J. C., & Elliott, S. N. (2004). *Effective school interventions: Strategies for enhancing academic achievement and social competence* (2nd ed.). New York: Guilford Press.

Ray, S. L. (2004). Eating disorders in adolescent males. *Professional School Counseling, 8*, 98–101.

Rea, P. J., McLaughlin, V. L., & Walther-Thomas, C. (2002). Outcomes for students with learning disabilities in inclusive and pullout programs. *Exceptional Children, 68*, 203–222.

Read, J., Agar, K., Barker-Collo, S., Davies, E., & Moskowitz, A. (2001). Assessing suicidality in adults: Integrating childhood trauma as a major risk factor. *Professional Psychology: Research and Practice, 32*, 367–372.

Reagan, T. (2000). *Non-western educational traditions: Alternative approaches to educational thought and practice* (2nd ed.). Mahwah, NJ: Lawrence Erlbaum Associates.

Reddy, L. A., Files-Hall, T. M., & Schaefer, C. E. (2005). Announcing empirically based play interventions for children. In L. A. Reddy, T. M. Files-Hall, & C. E. Schaefer (Eds.), *Empirically based play interventions for children* (pp. 3–10). Washington, DC: American Psychological Association.

Reddy, R., Rhodes, J. E., & Mulhall, P. (2003). The influence of teacher support on student adjustment in the middle school years: A latent growth curve study. *Development and Psychopathology, 15*, 119–138.

Reder, P., McClure, M., & Jolley, A. (Eds.) (2000). *Family matters: Interfaces between child and adult mental health.* Philadelphia: Routledge.

Reed, G. M. (2006). What qualifies as evidence of effective practice? In J. C. Norcross, L. E. Beutler, & R. F. Levant (Eds.), *Evidence-based practices in mental health: Debate and dialogue on the fundamental questions* (pp. 13–55). Washington, DC: American Psychological Association.

Reed, G. M., Levant, R. F., Stout, C. E., Murphy, M. J., & Phelps, R. (2001). Psychology in the current mental health marketplace. *Professional Psychology: Research and Practice, 32*, 65–70.

Reese, R. M., Richman, D. M., Belmont, J. M., & Morse, P. (2005). Functional characteristics of disruptive behavior in developmentally disabled children with and without Autism. *Journal of Autism and Developmental Disorders, 35*, 419–428.

Reeves, J. C., Werry, J. S., Elkind, G. S., & Zametkin, A. (1987). Attention deficit, conduct, oppositional, and anxiety disorders in children: II. Clinical characteristics. *Journal of the American Academy of Child and Adolescent Psychiatry, 26*, 144–155.

Reich, W. (2000). Diagnostic interview for children and adolescents (DICA). *Journal of the American Academy of Child and Adolescent Psychiatry, 39*, 59–66.

Reid, M. J., Webster-Stratton, C., & Baydar, N. (2004). Halting the development of conduct problems in Head Start children: The effects of parent training. *Journal of Clinical Child and Adolescent Psychology, 33*, 279–291.

Reijneveld, S. A., Brugman, E., Verhulst, F. C., & Verloove-Vanhorick, S. P. (2005). Area deprivation and child psychosocial problems: A national cross-sectional study among school-aged children. *Social Psychiatry and Psychiatric Epidemiology, 40*, 18–23.

Reinecke, M. A., & Simons, A. (2005). Vulnerability to depression among adolescents: Implications for cognitive-behavioral treatment. *Cognitive and Behavioral Practice, 12*, 166–176.

Reinherz, H. Z., Giaconia, R. M., Hauf, A. M. C., Wasserman, M. S., & Paradis, A. D. (2000). General and specific childhood risk factors for depression and drug disorders by early adulthood. *Journal of the American Academy of Child and Adolescent Psychiatry, 39*, 223–231.

Reiss, D. (2005). The interplay between genotypes and family relationships: Reframing concepts of development and prevention. *Current Directions in Psychological Science, 14*, 139–143.

Reivich, K., Gillham, J. E., Chaplin, T. M., & Seligman, M. E. P. (2005). From helplessness to optimism: The role of resilience in treating and preventing depression in youth. In S. Goldstein & R. B. Brooks (Eds.), *Handbook of resilience in children* (pp. 223–237). New York: Kluwer Academic/Plenum Press.

Rende, R., Slomkowski, C., Lloyd-Richardson, E., Stroud, L., & Niaura, R. (2006). Estimating genetic and environmental influences on depressive symptoms in adolescence: Differing effects on higher and lower levels of symptoms. *Journal of Clinical Child and Adolescent Psychology, 35*, 237–243.

Rende, R., Slomkowski, C., McCaffery, J., Lloyd-Richardson, E. E., & Niaura, R. (2005). A twin-sibling study of tobacco use in adolescence: Etiology of individual differences and extreme scores. *Nicotine & Tobacco Research, 7*, 413–419.

Renk, K., Liljequist, L., Steinberg, A., Bosco, G., & Phares, V. (2002). Prevention of child sexual abuse: Are we doing enough? *Trauma, Violence, and Abuse, 3*, 68–84.

Renninger, S. M., Veach, P. M., & Bagdade, P. (2002). Psychologists' knowledge, opinions, and decision-making processes regarding child abuse and neglect reporting laws. *Professional Psychology: Research and Practice, 33*, 19–23.

Reschly, D. J., & Bersoff, D. N. (1999). Law and school psychology. In C. R. Reynolds & T. B. Gutkin (Eds.), *The handbook of school psychology* (3rd ed., pp. 1077–1112). New York: Wiley.

Resnick, R. J. (2005). Attention deficit hyperactivity disorder in teens and adults: They don't all outgrow it. *Journal of Clinical Psychology/In Session, 61*, 529–533.

Resnick, R. J., & Norcross, J. C. (2002). Prescription privileges for psychologists: Scared to death? *Clinical Psychology: Science and Practice, 9*, 270–274.

Rettew, D. C., Copeland, W., Stanger, C., & Hudziak, J. J. (2004). Associations between temperament and DSM-IV externalizing disorders in children and adolescents. *Journal of Developmental and Behavioral Pediatrics, 25*, 383–391.

Rettew, D. C., Zanarini, M. C., Yen, S., Grilo, C. M., Skodol, A. E., Shea, M. T., McGlashan, T. H., Morey, L. C., Culhane, M. A., & Gunderson, J. G. (2003). Childhood antecedents of avoidant personality disorder: A retrospective study. *Journal of the American Academy of Child and Adolescent Psychiatry, 42*, 1122–1130.

Rey, J. M. Martin, A., & Krabman, P. (2004). Is the party over? Cannabis and juvenile psychiatric disorder: The past 10 years. *Journal of the American Academy of Child and Adolescent Psychiatry, 43*, 1194–1205.

Rey, J. M., Peng, R., Morales-Blanquez, C., Widyawati, I., Peralta, V., & Walter, G. (2000). Rating the quality of the family environment in different cultures. *Journal of the American Academy of Child and Adolescent Psychiatry, 39*, 1168–1174.

Reynolds, C. R. (2003). Conceptual and technical problems in learning disability diagnosis. In C. R. Reynolds & R. W. Kamphaus (Eds.), *Handbook of psychological and educational assessment of children: Intelligence, aptitude, and achievement* (2nd ed., pp. 475–497). New York: Guilford Press.

Reynolds, C. R., & Kamphaus, R. W. (2003). *Handbook of psychological and educational assessment of children: Intelligence, aptitude, and achievement* (2nd ed.). New York: Guilford.

Reynolds, C. R., & Kamphaus, R. W. (2005). *Behavior Assessment System for Children Manual-2.* Circle Pines, MN: American Guidance Service, Inc.

Reynolds, C. R., & Richmond, B. O. (1978). What I think and feel: A revised measure of children's manifest anxiety. *Journal of Abnormal Child Psychology, 6*, 271–280.

Reynolds, C. R., & Richmond, B. O. (1997). What I think and feel: A revised measure of children's manifest anxiety. *Journal of Abnormal Child Psychology, 25*, 15–20.

Reynolds, W. M. (1988). Major depression. In M. Hersen & C. G. Last (Eds.), *Child behavior therapy casebook* (pp. 85–100). New York: Plenum Press.

Reynolds, W. M. (1995). Depression. In V. B. Van Hasselt & M. Hersen (Eds.), *Handbook of adolescent psychopathology: A guide to diagnosis and treatment* (pp. 297–348). New York: Lexington Books.

Rhee, S. H., Hewitt, J. K., Corley, R. P., Willcutt, E. G., & Pennington, B. F. (2005). Testing hypotheses regarding the causes of comorbidity: Examining the underlying deficits of comorbid disorders. *Journal of Abnormal Psychology, 114*, 346–362.

Rhodes, G., & Rhodes, R. (1996). *Trying to get some dignity: Stories of triumph over childhood abuse.* New York: William Morrow.

Ricciardelli, L. A., & McCabe, M. P. (2004). A biopsychosocial model of disordered eating and the pursuit of muscularity in adolescent boys. *Psychological Bulletin, 130*, 179–205.

Riccio, C. A., & Wolfe, M. E. (2003). Neuropsychological perspectives on the assessment of children. In C. R. Reynolds, & R. W. Kamphaus, R. W. (Eds.). *Handbook of psychological and educational assessment of children: Intelligence, aptitude, and achievement* (2nd ed., pp. 305–324). New York: Guilford Press.

Rice, F., Harold, G. T., & Thapar, A. (2002). Assessing the effects of age, sex and shared environment on the genetic aetiology of depression in childhood and adolescence. *Journal of Child Psychology and Psychiatry, 43*, 1039–1051.

Richards, M. H., Larson, R., Miller, B. V., Luo, Z., Sims, B., Parrella, D. P., & McCauley, C. (2004). Risky and protective contexts and exposure to violence in urban African American young adolescents. *Journal of Clinical Child and Adolescent Psychology, 33*, 138–148.

Richman, J. M., Bowen, G. L., & Woolley, M. E. (2004). School failure: An eco-interactional developmental perspective. In M. W. Fraser (Ed.), *Risk and resilience in childhood: An ecological perspective* (2nd ed., pp. 133–160). Washington, DC: National Association of Social Workers Press.

Richmond, M. K., & Stocker, C. M. (2003). Siblings' differential experiences of marital conflict and differences in psychological adjustment. *Journal of Family Psychology, 17*, 339–350.

Richmond, T. K., & Rosen, D. S. (2005). The treatment of adolescent depression in the era of the black box warning. *Current Opinion in Pediatrics, 17*, 466–472.

Richters, J. E., & Martinez, P. E. (1993). Violent communities, family choices, and children's chances: An algorithm for improving the odds. *Development and Psychopathology, 5*, 609–627.

Rickert, V. I., Hassed, S. J., Hendon, A. E., & Cunniff, C. (1996). The effects of peer ridicule on depression and self-image among adolescent females with Turner syndrome. *Journal of Adolescent Health, 19*, 34–38.

Riddle, M. A., Kastelic, E. A., & Frosch, E. (2001). Pediatric psychopharmacology. *Journal of Child Psychology and Psychiatry, 42*, 73–90.

Rie, H. E. (1971). Historical perspective of concepts of child psychopathology. In H. E. Rie (Ed.), *Perspectives in child psychopathology* (pp. 3–50). Chicago: Aldine-Atherton.

Riedel, B. W., Robinson, L. A., Klesges, R. C., & McLain-Allen, B. (2002). What motivates adolescent smokers to make a quit attempt? *Drug and Alcohol Dependence, 68*, 167–174.

Riggs, P. D., Mikulich, S. K., Whitmore, E. A., & Crowley, T. J. (1999). Relationship of ADHD, depression and non-tobacco substance use disorders to nicotine dependence in substance-dependent delinquents. *Drug and Alcohol Dependence, 54*, 195–205.

Rimland, B. (1994). Facilitated communication update. *Autism Research Review International, 8*, 6.

Rimland, B. A. (2003). Commentary: Autism-related language, personality, and cognition in people with absolute pitch: Results of the preliminary study. *Journal of Autism and Developmental Disorders, 33*, 169.

Rind, B., Tromovitch, P., & Bauserman, R. (1998). A meta-analytic examination of assumed properties of child sexual abuse using college samples. *Psychological Bulletin, 124*, 22–53.

Ringold, S. (2005). Antidepressant warning focuses attention on unmet need for child psychiatrists. *Journal of the American Medical Association, 293,* 537–538.

Ripple, C. H., & Zigler, E. (2003). Research, policy, and the federal role in prevention initiatives for children. *American Psychologist, 58,* 482–490.

Ritterband, L. M., Cox, D. J., Walker, L. S., Kovatchev, B., McKnight, L., Patel, K., Borowitz, S., & Sutphen, J. (2003). An internet intervention as adjunctive therapy for pediatric encopresis. *Journal of Consulting and Clinical Psychology, 71,* 910–917.

Ritterband, L. M., Gonder-Frederick, L. A., Cox, D. J., Clifton, A. D., West, R. W., & Borwitz, S. M. (2003). Internet interventions: In review, in use, and into the future. *Professional Psychology: Research and Practice, 34,* 527–534.

Robbins, M. S., Alexander, J. F., & Turner, C. W. (2000). Disrupting defensive family interactions in family therapy with delinquent adolescents. *Journal of Family Psychology, 14,* 688–701.

Robbins, M. S., Bachrach, K., & Szapocznik, J. (2002). Bridging the research-practice gap in adolescent substance abuse treatment: The case of brief strategic family therapy. *Journal of Substance Abuse Treatment, 23,* 123–132.

Robbins, M. S., Kumar, S., Walker-Barnes, C., Feaster, D. J., Briones, E., & Szapocznik, J. (2002). Ethnic differences in comorbidity among substance-abusing adolescents referred to outpatient therapy. *Journal of the American Academy of Child and Adolescent Psychiatry, 41,* 394–401.

Robbins, M. S., Szapocznik, J., Santisteban, D. A., Hervis, O. E., Mitrani, V. B., & Schwartz, S. J. (2003). Brief strategic family therapy for Hispanic youth. In A. E. Kazdin & J. R. Weisz (Eds.), *Evidence-based psychotherapies for children and adolescents* (pp. 407–424). New York: Guilford Press.

Roberts, M. C. (Ed.) (2003). *Handbook of pediatric psychology* (3rd ed.). New York: Guilford Press.

Roberts, M. C., & Ilardi, S. S. (Eds.) (2005) *Handbook of research methods in clinical psychology.* Malden, MA: Blackwell.

Roberts, M. C., Mitchell, M. C., & McNeal, R. (2003). The evolving field of pediatric psychology: Critical issues and future challenges. In M. C. Roberts (Ed.), *Handbook of pediatric psychology* (3rd ed., pp. 3–18). New York: Guilford Press.

Roberts, M. C., Vernberg, E. M., & Jackson, Y. (2000). Psychotherapy with children and families. In C. R. Snyder, & R. E. Ingram (Eds.), *Handbook of psychological change: Psychotherapy processes and practices for the 21st century* (pp. 500–519). New York: Wiley.

Roberts, R. E. (2000). Depression and suicide behaviors among adolescents: The role of ethnicity. In I. Cuellar & F. A. Paniagua (Eds.), *Handbook of multicultural mental health: Assessment and treatment of diverse populations* (pp. 359–388). San Diego: Academic Press.

Robin, J. A., Puliafico, A. C., Creed, T. A., Comer, J. S., Hofflich, S. A., Barmish, A. J., Suveg, C., & Kendall, P. C. (2006). Generalized anxiety disorder. In R. T. Ammerman (Ed.), *Comprehensive handbook of personality and psychopathology: Child psychopathology* (Vol. 3, pp. 117–134). Hoboken, NJ: Wiley.

Robins, L. N., & Regier, D. A. (1991). *Psychiatric disorders in America.* New York: Free Press.

Robins, R. W., & Trzesniewski, K. H. (2005). Self-esteem development across the lifespan. *Current Directions in Psychological Science, 14,* 158–162.

Robinson, N. M., Zigler, E., & Gallagher, J. J. (2000). Two tails of the normal curve: Similarities and differences in the study of mental retardation and giftedness. *American Psychologist, 55,* 1413–1424.

Robinson, T. N., & Killen, J. D. (2001). Obesity prevention for children and adolescents. In J. K. Thompson, & L. Smolak (Eds.) *Body image, eating disorders, and obesity in youth: Assessment, prevention, and treatment* (pp. 261–292). Washington, DC: American Psychological Association.

Robinson, T. N., & Sirard, J. R. (2005). Preventing childhood obesity: A solution-oriented research paradigm. *American Journal of Preventive Medicine, 28,* 194–201.

Rock, D. A., & Stenner, A. J. (2005). Assessment issues in the testing of children and school entry. *Future of Children, 15,* 15–34.

Rodham, K., Hawton, K., & Evans, E. (2004). Reasons for deliberate self-harm: Comparison of self-poisoners and self-cutters in a community sample of adolescents. *Journal of the American Academy of Child and Adolescent Psychiatry, 43,* 80–87.

Rodin, J., Silberstein, L. R., & Striegel-Moore, R. H. (1985). Woman and weight: A normative discontent. In T. B. Sonderegger (Ed.), *Psychology and gender: Nebraska symposium on motivation* (pp. 267–307). Lincoln: University of Nebraska Press.

Rodriquez, A., & Bohlin, G. (2005). Are maternal smoking and stress during pregnancy related to ADHD symptoms in children? *Journal of Child Psychology and Psychiatry, 46,* 246–254.

Rodriquez, D., & Audrain-McGovern, J. (2004). Team sport participation and smoking: Analysis with general growth mixture modeling. *Journal of Pediatric Psychology, 29,* 299–308.

Rodriguez, M. L., Mischel, W., & Shoda, Y. (1989). Cognitive person variables in the delay of gratification of older children at risk. *Journal of Personality and Social Psychology, 57,* 358–367.

Rogers, R. (2004). Diagnostic, explanatory, and detection models of Munchausen by proxy: Extrapolations from malingering and deception. *Child Abuse and Neglect, 28,* 225–238.

Rogers, S. J. (1998). Empirically supported comprehensive treatments for young children with autism. *Journal of Clinical Child Psychology, 27,* 168–179.

Rohde, L. A., Szobot, C., Polanczyk, G., Schmitz, M., Martins, S., & Tramontina, S. (2005). Attention-deficit/hyperactivity disorder in a diverse culture: Do research and clinical findings support the notion of a cultural construct for the disorder? *Biology Psychiatry, 57,* 1436–1441.

Rohde, P., Clarke, G. N., Lewinsohn, P. M., Seeley, J. R., & Kaufman, N. K. (2001). Impact of comorbidity on a cognitive-behavioral group treatment for adolescent depression. *Journal of the American Academy of Child and Adolescent Psychiatry, 40,* 795–802.

Rohde, P., Clarke, G., Mace, D., Jorgensen, J., & Seeley, J. R. (2004). An efficacy/effectiveness study of cognitive-behavioral treatment for adolescents with comorbid major depression and conduct disorder. *Journal of the American Academy of Child and Adolescent Psychiatry, 43,* 660–668.

Rohde, P., Feeny, N. C., & Robins, M. (2005). Characteristics and components of the TADS CBT approach. *Cognitive and Behavioral Practice, 12*, 186–197.

Rohde, P., Lewinsohn, P. M., Clarke, G. N., Hops, H., & Seeley, J. R. (2005). The adolescent coping with depression course: A cognitive-behavioral approach to the treatment of adolescent depression. In E. D. Hibbs & P. S. Jensen (Eds.), *Psychosocial treatment for child and adolescent disorders: Empirically based strategies for clinical practice* (2nd ed., pp. 219–237). Washington, DC: American Psychological Association.

Rohde, P., Lewinsohn, P. M., Kahler, C. W., Seeley, J. R., & Brown, R. A. (2001). Natural course of alcohol use disorders from adolescence to young adulthood. *Journal of the American Academy of Child and Adolescent Psychiatry, 40*, 83–90.

Rohde, P., Lewinsohn, P. M., Klein, D. N., & Seeley, J. R. (2005). Association of parental depression with psychiatric course from adolescence to young adulthood among formerly depressed individuals. *Journal of Abnormal Psychology, 114*, 409–420.

Roid, G. H. (2003). *Stanford-Binet Intelligence Scales* (5th ed.; SB5). Rolling Meadows, IL: Riverside Publishing.

Rojas, N. L., & Chan, E. (2005). Old and new controversies in the alternative treatment of attention-deficit hyperactivity disorder. *Mental Retardation and Developmental Disabilities Research Reviews, 11*, 116–130.

Rolland-Cachera, M. F., Thibault, H., Souberbielle, J. C., Soulie, D., Carbonel, P., Deheeger, M., Roinson, D., Longueville, E., Bellisle, F., & Serog, P. (2004). Massive obesity in adolescents: Dietary interventions and behaviours associated with weight regain at 2y follow-up. *International Journal of Obesity, 28*, 514–519.

Rollman, G. B. (1998). Culture and pain. In S. S. Kazarian & D. R. Evans (Eds.), *Cultural clinical psychology: Theory, research, and practice* (pp. 267–286). New York: Oxford University Press.

Romanczyk, R. G., Arnstein, L., Soorya, L. V., & Gillis, J. (2003). The myriad of controversial treatments for autism: A critical evaluation of efficacy. In S. O. Lilienfeld, S. J. Lynn, & J. M. Lohr (Eds.), *Science and pseudoscience in clinical psychology* (pp. 363–395). New York: Guilford.

Romer, D., & McIntosh, M. (2005). The roles and perspectives of school mental health professionals in promoting adolescent mental health. In D. L. Evans, E. B. Foa, R. E. Gur, H. Hendin, C. P. O'Brien, M. E. P. Seligman, & B. T. Walsh (Eds.), *Treating and preventing adolescent mental health disorders: What we know and what we don't know* (pp. 579–615). New York: Oxford University Press.

Ronald, A., Happe, F., & Plomin, R. (2005). The genetic relationship between individual differences in social and nonsocial behaviours characteristic of autism. *Developmental Science, 8*, 444–458.

Root, R. W., & Resnick, R. J. (2003). An update on the diagnosis and treatment of attention-deficit/hyperactivity disorder in children. *Professional Psychology: Research and Practice, 34*, 34–41.

Rorschach, H. (1942). *Psychodiagnostics*. Bern, Switzerland: Hans Huber (Original work published in 1921).

Roseman, B. (2001). *A kid just like me: A father and son overcome the challenges of ADD and learning disabilities*. New York: Perigee/Penguin.

Rosemond, J. K. (2005). The diseasing of America's children: The politics of diagnosis. In R. H. Wright, & N. A. Cummings (Eds.) *Destructive trends in mental health: The well-intentioned path to harm* (pp. 219–233). New York: Routledge.

Rosenthal, R., & Jacobson, L. (1966). Teachers' expectancies: Determinants of pupils' IQ gains. *Psychological Reports, 19*, 115–118.

Ross, H. E., & Ivis, F. (1999). Binge eating and substance use among male and female adolescents. *International Journal of Eating Disorders, 26*, 245–260.

Ross, J. L., Stefanatos, G. A., Kushner, H., Zinn, A., Bondy, C., & Roeltgen, D. (2002). Persistent cognitive deficits in adult women with Turner syndrome. *Neurology, 58*, 218–225.

Ross, R. G., & Compagnon, N. (2001). Diagnosis and treatment of psychiatric disorders in children with a schizophrenic parent. *Schizophrenia Research, 50*, 121–129.

Rossman, M. H. (2002). *Negotiating graduate school: A guide for graduate students* (2nd ed.). Thousand Oaks, CA: Sage.

Rossner, S. (2002). Obesity: The disease of the twenty-first century. *International Journal of Obesity, 26*, S2–S4.

Rothbaum, F., Morelli, G., Pott, M., & Liu-Constant, Y. (2000). Immigrant-Chinese and Euro-American parents' physical closeness with young children: Themes of family relatedness. *Journal of Family Psychology, 14*, 334–348.

Rothbaum, F., Weisz, J., Pott, M., Miyake, K., & Morelli, G. (2000). Attachment and culture: Security in the United States and Japan. *American Psychologist, 55*, 1093–1104.

Rothenberg, L. (2003). *Breathing for a living: A memoir*. New York: Hyperion.

Rotheram-Borus, M. J. (2005). Children of AIDS: Africa's orphans crisis. *Culture, Health, and Sexuality, 7*, 74–76.

Rotheram-Borus, M. J., & Duan, N. (2003). Next generation of preventive interventions. *Journal of the American Academy of Child and Adolescent Psychiatry, 42*, 518–526.

Rotheram-Borus, M. J., Leonard, N. R., Lightfoot, M., Franzke, L. H., Tottenham, N., & Lee, S. (2002). Picking up the pieces: Caregivers of adolescents bereaved by parental AIDS. *Clinical Child Psychology and Psychiatry, 7*, 115–124.

Rotheram-Borus, M. J., Lester, P., Song, J., Lin, Y. Y., Leonard, N. R., Beckwith, L., Ward, M. J., Sigman, M., & Lord, L. (2006). Intergenerational benefits of family-based HIV interventions. *Journal of Consulting and Clinical Psychology, 74*, 622–627.

Rotheram-Borus, M. J., Stein, J. A., & Lin, Y. Y. (2001). Impact of parent death and an intervention on the adjustment of adolescents whose parents have HIV/AIDS. *Journal of Consulting and Clinical Psychology, 69*, 763–773.

Rotheram-Borus, M. S., Weiss, R., Alber, S., & Lester, P. (2005). Adolescent adjustment before and after HIV-related parental death. *Journal of Consulting and Clinical Psychology, 73*, 221–228.

Rotter, J. B., Lah, M. I., & Rafferty, J. E. (1992). *Manual: Rotter Incomplete Sentences Blank* (2nd ed.) Orlando, FL: Psychological Corporation.

Rounds, K. A. (2004). Preventing sexually transmitted infections among adolescents. In M. W. Fraser (Ed.), *Risk and resilience in childhood: An ecological perspective* (2nd ed., pp. 251–279). Washington, DC: National Association of Social Workers Press.

Rourke, B. P., & Tsatsanis, K. D. (2000). Nonverbal learning disabilities and Asperger syndrome. In A. Klin, F. R. Volkmar, & S. S. Sparrow (Ed.), *Asperger syndrome* (pp. 231–253). New York: Guilford Press.

Rovet, J. (2004). Turner syndrome: Genetic and hormonal factors contributing to a specific learning disability profile. *Learning Disabilities Research & Practice, 19,* 133–145.

Rowe, R., Maughan, B., Pickles, A., Costello, E. J., & Angold, A. (2002). The relationship between DSM-IV oppositional defiant disorder and conduct disorder: Findings from the Great Smoky Mountains Study. *Journal of Child Psychology and Psychiatry, 43,* 365–373.

Rowland, A. S., Lesesne, C. A., & Abramowitz, A. J. (2002). The epidemiology of attention-deficit/hyperactivity disorder (ADHD): A public health view. *Mental Retardation and Developmental Disabilities Research Reviews, 8,* 162–170.

Royko, D. (1999). *Voices of children of divorce.* New York: Golden Books.

Roza, S. J., Hofstra, M. B., vander Ende, J., & Verhulst, F. C. (2003). Stable prediction of mood and anxiety disorders based on behavioral and emotional problems in childhood: A 14-year follow-up during childhood, adolescence, and young adulthood. *American Journal of Psychiatry, 160,* 2116–2121.

Rubinstien, M. B., & Tanguay, P. B. (2005). *Raising NLD superstars: What families with nonverbal learning disabilities need to know about nurturing confident, competent kids.* Philadelphia: Jessica Kingsley.

Rudnick, A. (2001). Ethics of ECT for children. *Journal of the Academy of Child and Adolescent Psychiatry, 40,* 387.

Rudolph, K. D., & Clark, A. G. (2001). Conceptions of relationships in children with depressive and aggressive symptoms: Social-cognitive distortion or reality? *Journal of Abnormal Child Psychology, 29,* 41–56.

Rudolph, K. D., & Hammen, C. (1999). Age and gender as determinants of stress exposure, generation, and reactions in youngsters: A transactional perspective. *Child Development, 70,* 660–677.

Rudolph, K. D., Hammen, C., & Burge, D. (1997). A cognitive-interpersonal approach to depressive symptoms in preadolescent children. *Journal of Abnormal Child Psychology, 25,* 33–45.

Rudolph, K. D., Hammen, C., & Daley, S. E. (2006). Mood disorders. In D. A. Wolfe & E. J. Mash (Eds.), *Behavioral and emotional disorders in adolescents: Nature, assessment, and treatment* (pp. 300–342). New York: Guilford Press.

Rueter, M. A., Chao, W., & Conger, R. D. (2000). The effect of systematic variation in retrospective conduct disorder reports on antisocial personality disorder diagnoses. *Journal of Consulting and Clinical Psychology, 68,* 307–312.

Ruggiero, K. J., Morris, T. L., Beidel, D. C., Scotti, J. R., & McLeer, S. V. (1999). Discriminant validity of self-reported anxiety and depression in children: Generalizability to clinic-referred and ethnically diverse populations. *Assessment, 6,* 259–267.

Ruggiero, K. J., Morris, T. L., & Scotti, J. R. (2001). Treatment for children with posttraumatic stress disorder: Current status and future directions. *Clinical Psychology: Science and Practice, 8,* 210–227.

Rumstein-McKean, O., & Hunsley, J. (2001). Interpersonal and family functioning of female survivors of childhood sexual abuse. *Clinical Psychology Review, 21,* 471–490.

Runyon, M. K., Deblinger, E., Behl, L., & Cooper, B. (2006). Post-traumatic stress disorder. In R. T. Ammerman (Ed.), *Comprehensive handbook of personality and psychopathology: Child psychopathology* (Vol. 3, pp. 148–164). Hoboken, NJ: Wiley.

Russ, S. W. (1998). Psychodynamically based therapies. In T. H. Ollendick & M. Hersen (Eds.), *Handbook of child psychopathology* (pp. 537–556). New York: Plenum Press.

Russell, A. T., Bott, L., & Sammons, C. (1989). The phenomenology of schizophrenia occurring in childhood. *Journal of the American Academy of Child and Adolescent Psychiatry, 28,* 399–407.

Russell, J. (2004). Management of anorexia nervosa revisited: Early intervention can help—but some cases still need tertiary inpatient care. *BMJ: British Medical Journal, 328,* 479–480.

Rutter, M. (1979). Protective factors in children's responses to stress and disadvantage. In M. W. Kent & J. E. Rolf (Eds.), *Primary prevention of psychopathology: Vol. 3. Social competence in children* (pp. 49–74). Hanover, NH: University Press of New England.

Rutter, M. (1996). Developmental psychopathology: Concepts and prospects. In M. F. Lenzeneger & J. J. Haugaard (Eds.), *Frontiers of developmental psychopathology* (pp. 209–237). New York: Oxford University Press.

Rutter, M. (1999). Resilience concepts and findings: Implications for family therapy. *Journal of Family Therapy, 21,* 119–144.

Rutter, M. (2003). Crucial paths from risk indicator to causal mechanism. In B. B. Lahey, T. E. Moffitt, & A. Caspi (Eds.), *Causes of conduct disorder and juvenile delinquency* (pp. 3–24). New York: Guilford Press.

Rutter, M. (2005). Aetiology of autism: Findings and questions. *Intellectual Disability Research, 49,* 231–238.

Rutter, M., & Schopler, E. (1992). Classification of pervasive developmental disorders: Some concepts and practical considerations. *Journal of Autism and Developmental Disorders, 22,* 459–482.

Rutter, M., Silberg, J., O'Connor, T., & Simonoff, E. (1999a). Genetics and child psychiatry: I Advances in quantitative and molecular genetics. *Journal of Child Psychology and Psychiatry, 40,* 3–18.

Rutter, M., Silberg, J., O'Connor, T., & Simonoff, E. (1999b). Genetics and child psychiatry: II Empirical research findings. *Journal of Child Psychology and Psychiatry, 40,* 19–55.

Ryan, J. B., Reid, R., Epstein, M. H., Ellis, C., & Evans, J. H. (2005). Pharmacological intervention research for academic outcomes for students with ADHD. *Behavioral Disorders, 30,* 135–154.

Sadler, J. Z. (2004). Should patients and their families contribute to the DSM-V process? *Psychiatric Services, 55,* 133–138.

Sagrestano, L. M., Paikoff, R. L., Holmbeck, G. N., & Fendrich, M. (2003). A longitudinal examination of familial risk factors for depression among inner-city African American adolescents. *Journal of Family Psychology, 17,* 108–120.

Sahler, O. J. Z., Fairclough, D. L., Phipps, S., Mulhern, R. K., Dolgin, M. J., Noll, R. B., Katz, E. R., Varni, J. W., Copeland, D. R., & Butler, R. W. (2005). Using problem-solving skills training to reduce negative affectivity in mothers of children with newly diagnosed cancer: Report of a multisite randomized trial. *Journal of Consulting and Clinical Psychology, 73,* 272–283.

Sakai, J. T., Hall, S. K., Mikulich-Gilbertson, S. K., & Crowley, T. J. (2004). Inhalant use, abuse, and dependence among adolescent patients: Commonly comorbid problems. *Journal of the American Academy of Child and Adolescent Psychiatry, 43,* 1080–1088.

Salekin, R. T., & Frick, P. J. (2005). Psychopathy in children and adolescents: The need for a developmental perspective. *Journal of Abnormal Child Psychology, 33,* 403–409.

Salekin, R. T., Leistico, A. M. R., Neumann, C. S., DiCicco, T. M., & Duros, R. L. (2004). Psychopathy and comorbidity in a young offender sample: Taking a closer look at psychopathy's potential importance over disruptive behavior disorders. *Journal of Abnormal Psychology, 113,* 416–427.

Salekin, R. T., Neumann, C. S., Leistico, A. M. R., DiCicco, T. M., & Duros, R. L. (2004). Psychopathy and comorbidity in a young offender sample: Taking a closer look at psychopathy's potential importance over disruptive behavior disorders. *Journal of Abnormal Psychology, 113,* 416–427.

Samaan, R. A. (2000). The influences of race, ethnicity, and poverty on the mental health of children. *Journal of Health Care for the Poor and Underserved, 11,* 100–110.

Sammons, M. T., Gorny, S. W., Zinner, E. S., & Allen, R. P. (2000). Prescriptive authority for psychologists: A consensus of support. *Professional Psychology: Research and Practice, 31,* 604–609.

Samples, C. L., Goodman, E., & Woods, E. R. (1998). Epidemiology and medical management of adolescents. In P. A. Pizzo & C. M. Wilfert (Eds.), *Pediatric AIDS: The challenge of HIV infection in infants, children, and adolescents* (3rd ed., pp. 615–643). Baltimore: Williams and Wilkins.

Samudra, K., & Cantwell, D. P. (1999). Risk factors for attention-deficit/hyperactivity disorder. In H. C. Quay & A. E. Hogan (Eds.), *Handbook of disruptive behavior disorders* (pp. 199–220). New York: Kluwer Academic.

Samuel, V. J., Curtis, S., Thornell, A., George, P., Taylor, A., Brome, D. R., Biederman, J., & Faraone, S. V. (1997). The unexplored void of ADHD and African-American research: A review of the literature. *Journal of Attention Disorders, 1,* 197–207.

Sanders, M. R., Markie-Dadds, C., Tully, L. A., & Bor, W. (2000). The triple P-Positive Parenting Program: A comparison of enhanced, standard, and self-directed behavioral family intervention for parents of children with early onset conduct problems. *Journal of Consulting and Clinical Psychology, 68,* 624–640.

Sanders, M. R., Montgomery, D. T., & Brechman-Toussaint, M. L. (2000). The mass media and the prevention of child behavior problems: The evaluation of a television series to promote positive outcomes for parents and their children. *Journal of Child Psychology and Psychiatry, 41,* 939–948.

Sandler, I. N., Ayers, T. S., Wolchik, S. A., Tein, J. Y., Kwok, O. M., Haine, R. A., Twohey-Jacobs, J., Suter, J., Lin, K., Padgett-Jones, S., Weyer, J. L., Cole, E., Kriege, G., & Griffin, W. A. (2003). The family bereavement program: Efficacy evaluation of a theory-based prevention program for parentally bereaved children and adolescents. *Journal of Consulting and Clinical Psychology, 71,* 587–600.

Sanger, J., Wilson, J., Davies, B., & Whitakker, R. (1997). *Young children, videos and computer games: Issues for teachers and parents.* Washington, DC: The Falmer Press.

Santisteban, D. A., Coatsworth, J. D., Perez-Vidal, A., Kurtines, W. M., Schwartz, S. J., LaPerriere, A., & Szapocznik, J. (2003). Efficacy of brief strategic family therapy in modifying Hispanic adolescent behavior problems and substance use. *Journal of Family Psychology, 17,* 121–133.

Satcher, D. (2000). Mental health: a report of the Surgeon General—Executive summary. *Professional Psychology: Research and Practice, 31,* 5–13.

Satcher, D. (2001). *Surgeon General releases a national action agenda on children's mental health.* Bethesda, MD: U.S. Department of Health and Human Services.

Satir, V. (1983). *Conjoint family therapy.* Palo Alto, CA: Science and Behavior Books.

Sattler, J. M. (1998). *Clinical and forensic interviewing of children and families.* San Diego, CA: Jerome M. Sattler.

Sattler, J. M. (2001). *Assessment of children: Cognitive applications* (4th ed.). San Diego: Jerome M. Sattler.

Sattler, J. M. (2002). *Assessment of children: Behavioral and clinical applications* (4th ed.). San Diego: Jerome M. Sattler.

Savin-Williams, R. C. (1994). Verbal and physical abuse as stressors in the lives of lesbian, gay male, and bisexual youths: Associations with school problems, running away, substance abuse, prostitution, and suicide. *Journal of Consulting and Clinical Psychology, 62,* 261–269.

Savin-Williams, R. C. (2001a). *"Mom, Dad—I'm Gay": How Families Negotiate Coming Out.* Washington, DC: American Psychological Association.

Savin-Williams, R. C. (2001b). Suicide attempts among sexual-minority youths: Population and measurement issues. *Journal of Consulting and Clinical Psychology, 69,* 983–991.

Savin-Williams, R. C. (2005). *New gay teenager.* Cambridge, MA: Harvard University Press.

Savin-Williams, R. C., & Diamond, L. M. (1999). Sexual orientation. In W. K. Silverman & T. H. Ollendick (Eds.), *Developmental issues in the clinical treatment of children* (pp. 241–258). Boston: Allyn and Bacon.

Savin-Williams, R. C., & Ream, G. L. (2003a). Sex variations in the disclosure to parents of same-sex attractions. *Journal of Family Psychology, 17,* 429–438.

Savin-Williams, R. C., & Ream, G. L. (2003b). Suicide attempts among sexual-minority male youth. *Journal of Clinical Child and Adolescent Psychology, 32,* 509–522.

Saxe, G. N., Stoddard, F., Hall, E., Chawla, N., Lopez, C., Sheridan, R., King, D., King, L., & Yehuda, R. (2005). Pathways to PTSD, Part I: Children with burns. *American Journal of Psychiatry, 162,* 1299–1304.

Saywitz, K. J., Mannarino, A. P., Berliner, L., & Cohen, J. A. (2000). Treatment for sexually abused children and adolescents. *American Psychologist, 55,* 1040–1049.

Scarinci, I. C., Robinson, L. A., Alfano, C. M., Zbikowski, S. M., & Klesges, R. C. (2002). The relationship between socioeconomic status, ethnicity, and cigarette smoking in urban adolescents. *Preventive Medicine, 34,* 171–178.

Scaturo, D. J. (2001). The evolution of psychotherapy and the concept of manualization: An integrative perspective. *Professional Psychology: Research and Practice, 32*, 522–530.

Schachar, R., Mota, V. L., Logan, G. D., Tannock, R., & Klim, P. (2000). Confirmation of an inhibitory control deficit in Attention-Deficit/Hyperactivity Disorder. *Journal of Abnormal Child Psychology, 28*, 227–235.

Schaefer, C. E., & DiGeronimo, T. F. (2000). *Ages and stages: A parent's guide to normal childhood development.* New York: Wiley.

Schaeffer, C. M., & Borduin, C. M. (2005). Long-term follow-up to a randomized clinical trail of multisystemic therapy with serious and violent juvenile offenders. *Journal of Consulting and Clinical Psychology, 73*, 445–453.

Schatz, J. (2004). Brief report: Academic attainment in children with sickle cell disease. *Journal of Pediatric Psychology, 29*, 627–633.

Schatz, J., Finke, R., Kellett, J. M., & Kramer, J. H. (2002). Cognitive functioning in children with sickle cell disease: A meta-analysis. *Journal of Pediatric Psychology, 27*, 739–748.

Scheer, S. D., Borden, L. M., & Donnermeyer, J. F. (2000). The relationship between family factors and adolescent substance use in rural, suburban, and urban settings. *Journal of Child and Family Studies, 9*, 105–115.

Scher, A, Zukerman, S., & Epstein, R. (2005). Persistent night waking and settling difficulties across the first year: Early precursors of later behavioural problems? *Journal of Reproductive and Infant Psychology, 23*, 77–88.

Schmidt, F., & Taylor, T. K. (2002). Putting empirically supported treatments into practice: Lessons learned in a children's mental health center. *Professional Psychology: Research and Practice, 33*, 483–489.

Scholle, S. H., & Kelleher, K. J. (1998). Managed care: Opportunities and threats for children with serious emotional disturbance and their families. In M. H. Epstein & K. Kutash (Eds.), *Outcomes for children and youth with emotional and behavioral disorders and their families: Programs and evaluation best practices* (pp. 659–684). Austin, TX: Pro-Ed.

Schoppe, S. J., Mangelsdorf, S. C., & Frosch, C. A. (2001). Coparenting, family process, and family structure: Implications for preschoolers' externalizing behavior problems. *Journal of Family Psychology, 15*, 526–545.

Schreck, K. A., Mulick, J. A., & Rojahn, J. (2005). Parent perception of elementary school aged children's sleep problems. *Journal of Child and Family Studies, 14*, 101–109.

Schreier, H. (2002). On the importance of motivation in Munchausen by proxy: The case of Kathy Bush. *Child Abuse and Neglect, 26*, 537–549.

Schreier, H. A. (2000). Factitious disorder by proxy in which the presenting problem is behavioral or psychiatry. *Journal of the American Academy of Child and Adolescent Psychiatry, 39*, 668–670.

Schreier, H. A. (2001). Factitious disorder by proxy: Reply. *Journal of the American Academy of Child and Adolescent Psychiatry, 40*, 4–5.

Schreier, H., & Ricci, L. R. (2002). Follow-up of a case of Munchausen by proxy syndrome. *Journal of the American Academy of Child and Adolescent Psychiatry, 41*, 1395–1396.

Schroeder, C. S., & Gordon, B. N. (2002). *Assessment and treatment of childhood problems: A clinician's guide* (2nd ed.). New York: Guilford Press.

Schultz, M. S., Waldinger, R. J., Hauser, S. T., & Allen, J. P. (2005). Adolescents' behavior in the presence of interparental hostility: Developmental and emotion regulatory influences. *Development and Psychopathology, 17*, 489–507.

Schwab-Stone, M. E., Shaffer, D., Dulcan, M. K., Jensen, P. S., Fisher, P., Bird, H. R., Goodman, S. H., Lahey, B. B., Lichtman, J. H., Canino, G., Rubio-Stipec, M. & Rae, D. S. (1996). Criterion validity of the NIMH Diagnostic Interview Schedule for Children Version 2.3 (DISC-2.3). *Journal of the American Academy of Child and Adolescent Psychiatry, 35*, 878–888. ·

Schwartz, J. A. J., Gladstone, T. R. G., & Kaslow, N. J. (1998). Depressive disorders. In T. H. Ollendick & M. Hersen (Eds.), *Handbook of child psychopathology* (3rd ed., pp. 269–289). New York: Plenum Press.

Schwartz, S. (1992). *Cases in abnormal psychology.* New York: Wiley.

Schwarzchild, M. (2000). Alienated youth. Help from families and schools. *Professional Psychology: Research and Practice, 31*, 95–96.

Schwebel, R., & Spock, B. (1998). *Saying no is not enough: Helping your kids make wise decisions about alcohol, tobacco, and other drugs* (2nd ed.). New York: Newmarket Press.

Sefa-Dedeh, A. (1992). Improving children's lives: The case for primary prevention in Ghana. In G. W. Albee, L. A. Bond, & T. V. C. Monsey (Eds.), *Improving children's lives: Global perspectives on prevention* (pp. 63–72). Newbury Park: Sage.

Segal, N. L. (2003). "Two" quiet: Monozygotic female twins with selective mutism. *Clinical Child Psychology and Psychiatry, 8*, 473–488.

Seidman, E., Chesir-Teran, D., Friedman, J. L., Yoshikawa, H., Allen, L., Roberts, A., & Aber, J. L. (1999). The risk and protective functions of perceived family and peer microsystems among urban adolescents in poverty. *American Journal of Community Psychology, 27*, 211–237.

Seipp, C. M., & Johnston, C. (2005). Mother-son interactions in families of boys with attention-deficit/hyperactivity disorder with and without oppositional behavior. *Journal of Abnormal Child Psychology, 33*, 87–98.

Sek, H., Bleja, A., & Sommerfeld, A. (1992). Fostering parental competence in Poland. In G. W. Albee, L. A. Bond, & T. V. C. Monsey (Eds.), *Improving children's lives: Global perspectives on prevention* (pp. 253–260). Newbury Park: Sage.

Seligman, L. D., Ollendick, T. H., Langley, A. K., & Baldacci, H. B. (2004). The utility of measures of child and adolescent anxiety: A meta-analytic review of the Revised Children's Manifest Anxiety Scale, the State-Trait Anxiety Inventory for Children, and the Child Behavior Checklist. *Journal of Clinical Child and Adolescent Psychology, 33*, 557–565.

Seligman, M. E. P., Reivich, K., Jaycox, L., & Gillham, J. (1995). *The optimistic child.* Boston: Houghton Mifflin.

Selvini-Palazzoli, M., Boscolo, L., Cecchin, G., & Prata, G. (1978). *Paradox and counterparadox*. New York: Jason Aronson.

Serafica, F. C. (1997). Psychopathology and resilience in Asian American children and adolescents. *Applied Developmental Science, 1*, 145–155.

Serbin, L., & Karp, J. (2003). Intergenerational studies of parenting and the transfer of risk from parent to child. *Current Directions in Psychological Science, 12*, 138–142.

Shaffer, D., Fisher, P., Dulcan, M. K., Davies, M., Piacentini, J., Schwab-Stone, M. E., Lahey, B. B., Bourdon, K., Jensen, P. S., Bird, H. R., Canino, G., & Regier, D. A. (1996). The NIMH Diagnostic Interview Schedule for Children Version 2.3 (DISC-2.3): Description, acceptability, prevalence rates, and performance in the MECA Study. *Journal of the American Academy of Child and Adolescent Psychiatry, 35*, 865–877.

Shaffer, D., Fisher, P., Lucas, C. P., Dulcan, M. K., & Schwab-Stone, M. E. (2000). NIMH Diagnostic Interview Schedule for Children Version IV (NIMH DISC-IV): Description, differences from previous versions, and reliability of some common diagnoses. *Journal of the American Academy of Child and Adolescent Psychiatry, 39*, 28–38.

Shaffer, D., Garland, A., Fisher, P., Bacon, K., & Vieland, V. (1990). Suicide crisis centers: A critical reappraisal with special reference to the prevention of youth suicide. In F. E. Goldston, C. M. Heinicke, R. S. Pynoos, & J. Yager (Eds.), *Prevention of mental health disturbance in childhood* (pp. 135–166). Washington, DC: American Psychiatric Association Press.

Shaffer, D., Garland, A., Vieland, V., Underwood, M., & Busner, C. (1991). The impact of curriculum-based suicide prevention programs for teenagers. *Journal of the American Academy of Child and Adolescent Psychiatry, 30*, 588–596.

Shaffer, D., & Pfeffer, C. R. (2001). Practice parameter for the assessment and treatment of children and adolescents with suicidal behavior. *Journal of the American Academy of Child and Adolescent Psychiatry, 40* (Supplement 7), 24S–51S.

Shahinfar, A., Kupersmidt, J. B., & Matza, L. S. (2001). The relation between exposure to violence and social information processing among incarcerated adolescents. *Journal of Abnormal Psychology, 110*, 136–141.

Shakur, S. (1993). *Monster: The autobiography of an L.A. gang member*. New York: Penguin Books.

Shaley, R. S. (2004). Developmental dyscalculia. *Journal of Child Neurology, 19*, 765–771.

Shamir-Essakow, G., Ungerer, J. A., & Rapee, R. M. (2005). Attachment, behavioral inhibition, and anxiety in preschool children. *Journal of Abnormal Child Psychology, 33*, 131–143.

Shandler, S. (1999). *Ophelia speaks*. New York: Harper Perennial.

Shapiro, E. S., & Kratochwill, T. R. (Eds., 2002). *Conducting school-based assessments of child and adolescent behavior*. New York: Guilford Press.

Sharko, A. M., & Reiner, W. G. (2004). SSRI-induced sexual dysfunction in adolescents. *Journal of the American Academy of Child and Adolescent Psychiatry, 43*, 1067.

Sharpe, M., & Mayou, R. (2004). Somatoform disorder: A help or hindrance to good patient care? *British Journal of Psychiatry, 184*, 465–467.

Shaw, D. S., Dishion, T. J., Supplee, L., Gardner, F., & Arnds, K. (2006). Randomized trial of a family-centered approach to the prevention of early conduct problems: 2-year effects of the family check-up in early childhood. *Journal of Consulting and Clinical Psychology, 74*, 1–9.

Shaw, D. S., Owens, E. B., Giovannelli, J., & Winslow, E. B. (2001). Infant and toddler pathways leading to early externalizing disorders. *Journal of the American Academy of Child and Adolescent Psychiatry, 40*, 36–43.

Shaywitz, S. (2005). *Overcoming dyslexia*. New York: Knopf.

Sheeber, L., & Sorensen, E. (1998). Family relationships of depressed adolescents: A multimethod assessment. *Journal of Clinical Child Psychology, 27*, 268–277.

Sheehan, W., & Garfinkel, B. D. (1988). Adolescent autoerotic deaths. *Journal of the American Academy of Child and Adolescent Psychiatry, 27*, 367–370.

Sheffield, J. K., Spence, S. H., Rapee, R. M., Kowalenko, N., Wignall, A., Davis, A., & McLoone, J. (2006). Evaluation of universal, indicated, and combined cognitive-behavioral approaches to the prevention of depression among adolescents. *Journal of Consulting and Clinical Psychology, 74*, 66–79.

Sheldrick, R. C., Kendall, P. C., & Heimberg, R. G. (2001). The clinical significance of treatments: A comparison of three treatments for conduct disordered children. *Clinical Psychology: Science and Practice, 8*, 418–430.

Shelef, K., Diamond, G. M., Diamond, G. S., & Liddle, H. A. (2005). Adolescent and parent alliance and treatment outcome in multidimensional family therapy. *Journal of Consulting and Clinical Psychology, 73*, 689–698.

Shelley-Tremblay, J. F., & Rosen, L. A. (1996). Attention deficit hyperactivity disorder: An evolutionary perspective. *Journal of Genetic Psychology, 157*, 443–453.

Shelton, T. L., Barkley, R. A., Crosswait, C., Moorehouse, M., Fletcher, K., Barrett, S., Jenkins, L., & Metevia, L. (2000). Multimethod psychoeducational intervention for preschool children with disruptive behavior: Two-year post-treatment follow-up. *Journal of Abnormal Child Psychology, 28*, 253–266.

Shenkin, S. D., Starr, J. M., & Deary, I. J. (2004). Birth weight and cognitive ability in childhood: A systematic review. *Psychological Bulletin, 130*, 989–1013.

Shepherd, M., Oppenheim, B., & Mitchell, S. (1971). *Childhood behavior and mental health*. New York: Grune and Stratton.

Sherer, M. R., & Schreibman, L. (2005). Individual behavioral profiles and predictors of treatment effectiveness for children with autism. *Journal of Consulting and Clinical Psychology, 73*, 525–538.

Sheridan, M. S. (2003). The deceit continues: An updated literature review of Munchausen syndrome by proxy. *Child Abuse and Neglect, 27*, 431–451.

Sherrill, J. T., & Kovacs, M. (2000). Interview schedule for children and adolescents (ISCA). *Journal of the American Academy of Child and Adolescent Psychiatry, 39*, 67–75.

Shields, A., & Cicchetti, D. (2001). Parental maltreatment and emotion dysregulation as risk factors for bullying and victimization in middle childhood. *Journal of Clinical Child Psychology, 30*, 349–363.

Shih, J. H., Eberhart, N. K., Hammen, C. L., & Brennan, P. A. (2006). Differential exposure and reactivity to interpersonal stress predict sex differences in adolescent depression. *Journal of Clinical Child and Adolescent Psychology, 35*, 103–115.

Shirk, S. R., Boergers, J., Eason, A., & Van Horn, M. (1998). Dysphoric interpersonal schemata and preadolescents' sensitization to negative events. *Journal of Clinical Child Psychology, 27*, 54–68.

Shirk, S. R., Burwell, R., & Harter, S. (2003). Strategies to modify low self-esteem in adolescents. In M. A. Reinecke, F. M. Dattilio, & A. Freeman (Eds.), *Cognitive therapy with children and adolescents: A casebook for clinical practice* (2nd ed., pp. 189–213). New York: Guilford Press.

Shirk, S. R., Gudmundsen, G. R., & Burwell, R. A. (2005). Links among attachment—related cognitions and adolescent depressive symptoms. *Journal of Clinical Child and Adolescent Psychology, 34*, 172–181.

Shirk, S. R., & Karver, M. (2003). Prediction of treatment outcome from relationship variables in child and adolescent therapy: A meta-analytic review. *Journal of Consulting and Clinical Psychology, 71*, 452–464.

Shirk, S., & Karver, M. (2006). Process issues in cognitive-behavioral therapy for youth. In P. C. Kendall (Ed.), *Child and adolescent therapy: Cognitive-behavioral procedures* (3rd ed., pp. 465–491). New York: Guilford Press.

Shirk, S. R., VanHorn, M., & Leber, D. (1997). Dysphoria and children's processing of supportive interactions. *Journal of Abnormal Child Psychology, 25*, 239–249.

Shochet, I. M., Dadds, M. R., Ham, D., & Montague, R. (2006). School connectedness is an underemphasized parameter in adolescent mental health: Results of a community prediction study. *Journal of Clinical Child and Adolescent Psychology, 35*, 170–179.

Shochet, I. M., Dadds, M. R., Holland, D., Whitefield, K., Harnett, P. H., & Osgarby, S. M. (2001). The efficacy of a universal school-based program to prevent adolescent depression. *Journal of Clinical Child Psychology, 30*, 303–315.

Shonk, S. M., & Cicchetti, D. (2001). Maltreatment, competency deficits, and risk for academic and behavioral maladjustment. *Developmental Psychology, 37*, 3–17.

Shortt, A. L., Barrett, P. M., Dadds, M. R., & Fox, T. L. (2001). The influence of family and experimental context on cognition in anxious children. *Journal of Abnormal Child Psychology, 29*, 585–596.

Shortt, A. L., Barrett, P. M., & Fox, T. L. (2001). Evaluating the FRIENDS Program: A cognitive-behavioral group treatment for anxious children and their parents. *Journal of Clinical Child Psychology, 30*, 525–535.

Shulman, C. (2000). Services for persons with autism in Israel. *International Journal of Mental Health, 29*, 88–97.

Siana, J. (2005). *Go ask ogre: Letters from a deathrock cutter.* Los Angeles: Process.

Sicher, P., Lewis, O., Sargent, J., Chaffin, M., Friedrich, W. N., Cunningham, N., Thomas, R., Thomas, P., & Villani, V. S. (2000). Developing child abuse prevention, identification, and treatment systems in Eastern Europe. *Journal of the American Academy of Child and Adolescent Psychiatry, 39*, 660–667.

Siegel, B. (2003). *Helping children with autism learn: Treatment approaches for parents and professionals.* New York: Oxford University Press.

Siegel, B., & Ficcaglia, M. (2006). Pervasive developmental disorders. In R. T. Ammerman (Ed.), *Comprehensive handbook of personality and psychopathology: Child psychopathology* (Vol 3, pp. 254–271). Hoboken, NJ: Wiley.

Siegel, L. M. (2005). *The complete IEP guide: How to advocate for your special ed child* (4th ed.). Berkeley, CA: Nolo.

Siegert, R. J., & Ward, T. (2002). Clinical psychology and evolutionary psychology: Toward a dialogue. *Review of General Psychology, 6*, 235–259.

Siewert, E. A., Stallings, M. C., & Hewitt, J. K. (2003). Genetic and environmental analysis of behavioral risk factors for adolescent drug use in a community twin sample. *Twin Research, 6*, 490–496.

Silk, J. S., Shaw, D. S., Forbes, E. E., Lane, T. L., & Kovacs, M. (2006). Maternal depression and child internalizing: The moderating role of child emotion regulation. *Journal of Clinical Child and Adolescent Psychology, 35*, 116–126.

Silver, E. J., Westbrook, L. E., & Stein, R. E. K. (1998). Relationship of parental psychological distress to consequences of chronic health conditions in children. *Journal of Pediatric Psychology, 23*, 5–15.

Silverman, W. K., & Albano, A. M. (1996). *The Anxiety Disorders Interview Schedule for DSM-IV: Child version.* New York: Psychological Corporation.

Silverman, W. K., & Carter, R. (2006). Anxiety disturbance in girls and women. In J. Worell & C. D. Goodheart (Eds.), *Handbook of girls' and women's psychological health* (pp. 60–68). New York: Oxford University Press.

Silverman, W. K., & Dick-Niederhauser, A. (2004). Separation anxiety disorder. In T. L. Morris & J. S. March (Eds.), *Anxiety disorders in children and adolescents* (2nd ed., pp. 164–188). New York: Guilford Press.

Silverman, W. K., & Ginsburg, G. S. (1995). Specific phobia and generalized anxiety disorder. In J. S. March (Ed.), *Anxiety disorders in children and adolescents* (pp. 151–180). New York: Guilford Press.

Silverman, W. K., & Ginsburg, G. S. (1998). Anxiety disorders. In T. H. Ollendick & M. Hersen (Eds.), *Handbook of child psychopathology* (3rd ed., pp. 239–268). New York: Plenum Press.

Silverman, W. K., & Ollendick, T. H. (2005). Evidence-based assessment of anxiety and its disorders in children and adolescents. *Journal of Consulting and Clinical Psychology, 34*, 380–411.

Silverstein, L. B., & Phares, V. (1996). Expanding the parenting paradigm: An examination of dissertation research 1986–1994. *Psychology of Women Quarterly, 20*, 39–53.

Silverthorn, P., Frick, P. J., & Reynolds, R. (2001). Timing of onset and correlates of severe conduct problems in adjudicated girls and boys. *Journal of Psychopathology and Behavioral Assessment, 23*, 171–181.

Simmel, C., Brooks, D., Barth, R. P., & Hinshaw, S. P. (2001). Externalizing symptomatology among adoptive youth: Prevalence and preadoption risk factors. *Journal of Abnormal Child Psychology, 29*, 57–69.

Simola, S. K., Parker, K. C. H., & Froese, A. P. (1999). Relational V-code conditions in a child and adolescent population do warrant treatment. *Journal of Marriage and Family Counseling, 25*, 225–236.

Simon, L. (2002). *Detour: My bipolar road trip in 4-D*. New York: Washington Square Press.

Simonoff, E. (2000). Extracting meaning from comorbidity: Genetic analyses that make sense. *Journal of Child Psychology and Psychiatry, 41*, 667–674.

Simons, A. D., Rohde, P., Kennard, B. D., & Robins, M. (2005). Relapse and recurrence prevention in the treatment for adolescents with depression study. *Cognitive and Behavioral Practice, 12*, 240–251.

Simons, R. L., Murry, V., McLoyd, V., Lin, K. H., Cutrona, C., & Conger, R. D. (2002). Discrimination, crime, ethnic identity, and parenting as correlates of depressive symptoms among African American children: A multilevel analysis. *Development and Psychopathology, 14*, 371–393.

Simpson, R. L. (2001). ABA and students with autism spectrum disorders: Issues and considerations for effective practice. *Focus on Autism and Other Developmental Disabilities, 16*, 68–71.

Simpson, R. L., Myles, B. S., Adams, L. G., Ben-Arieh, J., & Cook, K. T. (2004). *Autism spectrum disorders: Interventions and treatments for children and youth*. Thousand Oaks, CA: Sage.

Singh, N. N., Beale, I. L., & Snell, D. L. (1988). Learning disorders. In M. Hersen & C. G. Last (Eds.), *Child behavior therapy casebook* (pp. 193–206). New York: Plenum Press.

Siqueland, L., Rynn, M., & Diamond, G. S. (2005). Cognitive behavioral and attachment based family therapy for anxious adolescents: Phase I and II studies. *Journal of Anxiety Disorders, 19*, 361–381.

Skinner, C. H., Freeland, J. T., & Shapiro, E. S. (2003). Procedural issues associated with the behavioral assessment of children. In C. R. Reynolds & R. W. Kamphaus (Eds.), *Handbook of psychological and educational assessment of children: Personality, behavior, and context* (2nd ed., pp. 30–47). New York: Guilford Press.

Skinner, C. H., Rhymer, K. N., & McDaniel, E. C. (2000). Naturalistic direct observation in educational settings. In E. S. Shapiro & T. R. Kratochwill (Eds.), *Conducting school-based assessments of child and adolescent behavior* (pp. 21–54). New York: Guilford.

Skopp, N. A., McDonald, R., Manke, B., & Jouriles, E. N. (2005). Siblings in domestically violent families: Experiences of interparent conflict and adjustment problems. *Journal of Family Psychology, 19*, 324–333.

Skuse, D. H. (2000). Behavioural neuroscience and child psychopathology: Insights from model systems. *Journal of Child Psychology and Psychiatry, 41*, 3–31.

Slutske, W. S., Heath, A. C., Dinwidde, S. H., Madden, P. A. F., Bucholz, K. K., Dunne, M. P., Statham, D. J., & Martin, N. G. (1997). Modeling genetic and environmental influences in the etiology of conduct disorder: A study of 2,682 adult twin pairs. *Journal of Abnormal Psychology, 106*, 266–279.

Slutske, W. S., Hunt-Carter, E. E., Nabors-Oberg, R. E., Sher, K. J., Bucholz, K. K., Madden, P. A. F., Anokhin, A., & Heath, A. C. (2004). Do college students drink more than their non-college-attending peers? Evidence from a population-based longitudinal female twin study. *Journal of Abnormal Psychology, 113*, 530–540.

Smalley, S. L., McGough, J. J., Del'Homme, M., NewDelman, J., Gordon, E., Kim, T., Liu, A., & McCracken, J. T. (2000). Familial clustering of symptoms and disruptive behaviors in multiplex families with attention-deficit/hyperactivity disorder. *Journal of the American Academy of Child and Adolescent Psychiatry, 39*, 1135–1143.

Smedley, A., & Smedley, B. D. (2005). Race as biology is fiction, racism as a social problem is real: Anthropological and historical perspectives on the social construction of race. *American Psychologist, 60*, 16–26.

Smith, A. W., Baum, A., & Wing, R. R. (2005). Stress and weight gain in parents of cancer patients. *International Journal of Obesity, 29*, 244–250.

Smith, B. H., Pelham, W. E., Gnagy, E., Molina, B., & Evans, S. (2000). The reliability, validity, and unique contributions of self-report by adolescents receiving treatment for attention-deficit/hyperactivity disorder. *Journal of Consulting and Clinical Psychology, 68*, 489–499.

Smith, E. P., Boutte, G. S., Zigler, E., & Finn-Stevenson, M. (2004). Opportunities for schools to promote resilience in children and youth. In K. I. Maton, C. J. Schellenbach, B. J. Leadbeater, & A. L. Solarz (Eds.), *Investing in children, youth, families, and communities: Strengths-based research and policy* (pp. 213–231). Washington, DC: American Psychological Association.

Smith, L. (2005). Psychotherapy, classism, and the poor: Conspicuous by their absence. *American Psychologist, 60*, 687–696.

Smith, M. A., & Senior, C. (2001). The internet and clinical psychology: A general review of the implications. *Clinical Psychology Review, 21*, 129–136.

Smith, R. E., & Smoll, F. L. (1997). Coaching the coaches: Youth sports as a scientific and applied behavioral setting. *Current Directions in Psychological Science, 6*, 16–21.

Smolak, L. (2004). Body image in children and adolescents: Where do we go from here? *Body Image, 1*, 15–28.

Smolak, L. (2006). Body image. In J. Worell & C. D. Goodheart (Eds.), *Handbook of girls' and women's psychological health* (pp. 69–76). New York: Oxford University Press.

Snow, D. L., Grady, K., & Goyette-Ewing, M. (2000). A perspective on ethical issues in community psychology. In J. Rappaport & E. Seidman (Eds.), *Handbook of community psychology* (pp. 897–917). New York: Kluwer Academic/Plenum Press.

Snyder, C. R., & Ingram, R. E. (Eds.). (2000). *Handbook of psychological change: Psychotherapy processes and practices for the 21st century*. New York: Wiley.

Snyder, J., Reid, J., & Patterson, G. (2003). A social learning model of child and adolescent antisocial behavior. In B. B. Lahey, T. E. Moffitt, & A. Caspi (Eds.), *Causes of conduct disorder and juvenile delinquency* (pp. 27–48). New York: Guilford Press.

Sokol, M. S., Jackson, T. K., Selser, C. T., Nice, H. A., Christiansen, N. D., & Carroll, A. K. (2005). Review of clinical research in child and adolescent eating disorders. *Primary Psychiatry, 12*, 52–58.

Solomon, J., & George, C. (Eds.). (1999). *Attachment disorganization*. New York: Guilford Press.

Sonty, N. (1992). A multimodal approach to prevention: A review of India's integrated child development scheme. In G. W. Albee, L. A. Bond, & T. V. C. Monsey (Eds.), *Improving children's lives: Global perspectives on prevention* (pp. 191–199). Newbury Park: Sage.

Sonuga-Barke, E. J. S. (1998). Categorical models of childhood disorder: A conceptual and empirical analysis. *Journal of Child Psychology and Psychiatry, 39*, 115–133.

Sonuga-Barke, E. J. S. (2005). Causal models of attention-deficit/hyperactivity disorder: From common simple deficits to multiple developmental pathways. *Biological Psychiatry, 57*, 1231–1238.

Sorensen, L. G., Forbes, P. W., Bernstein, J. H., Weiler, M. D., Mitchell, W. M., & Waber, D. P. (2003). Psychosocial adjustment over a two-year period in children referred for learning problems: Risk, resilience and adaptation. *Learning Disabilities Research & Practice, 18*, 10–24.

Sorensen, M. J., Nissen, J. B., Mors, O., & Thomsen, P. H. (2005). Age and gender differences in depressive symptomatology and comorbidity: An incident sample of psychiatrically admitted children. *Journal of Affective Disorders, 84*, 85–91.

Southam-Gerow, M. A., Kendall, P. C., & Weersing, V. R. (2001). Examining outcome variability: Correlates of treatment response in a child and adolescent anxiety clinic. *Journal of Clinical Child Psychology, 30*, 422–436.

Southam-Gerow, M. A., Weisz, J. R., & Kendall, P. C. (2003). Youth with anxiety disorders in research and service clinics: Examining client differences and similarities. *Journal of Clinical Child and Adolescent Psychology, 32*, 375–385.

Spaccarelli, S. (1994). Stress, appraisal, and coping in child sexual abuse: A theoretical and empirical review. *Psychological Bulletin, 116*, 340–362.

Sparrow, S. S., Cicchetti, D. V., & Balla, D. A. (2005). *Vineland Adaptive Behavior Scales—Second Edition (Vineland-II)*. Circle Pines, MN: American Guidance Service.

Spears, G., & Seydegart, K. (2004). Kids' views on violence in the media. *Canadian Child and Adolescent Psychiatry Review, 13*, 7–12.

Spector, S. G., & Volkmar, F. R. (2006). Autism spectrum disorders. In D. A. Wolfe & E. J. Mash (Eds.), *Behavioral and emotional disorders in adolescents: Nature, assessment, and treatment* (pp. 444–460). New York: Guilford Press.

Speece, D. L., & Ritchey, K. D. (2005). A longitudinal study of the development of oral reading fluency in young children at risk for reading failure. *Journal of Learning Disabilities, 38*, 387–399.

Spence, S. H., Holmes, J. M., March, S., & Lipp, O. V. (2006). The feasibility and outcome of clinic plus internet delivery of cognitive-behavior therapy for childhood anxiety. *Journal of Consulting and Clinical Psychology, 74*, 614–621.

Spence, S. H., Sheffield, J. K., & Donovan, C. L. (2003). Preventing adolescent depression: An evaluation of the problem solving for life program. *Journal of Consulting and Clinical Psychology, 71*, 3–13.

Spence, S. H., Sheffield, J. K., & Donovan, C. L. (2005). Long-term outcome of a school-based, universal approach to prevention of depression in adolescents. *Journal of Consulting and Clinical Psychology, 73*, 160–167.

Sperry, S., Thompson, J. K., Roehrig, M., & Vandello, J. (2005). The influence of communicator weight on psychoeducational message acceptance in females with high vs. low levels of body image disturbance. *Eating Behaviors, 6*, 247–258.

Spielberger, C. D., Edwards, D. C., & Luschene, R. E. (1973). *Manual for the State-Trait Anxiety Inventory for Children*. Palo Alto, CA: Consulting Psychologists Press.

Spira, E. G., & Fischel, J. E. (2005). The impact of preschool inattention, hyperactivity, and impulsivity on social and academic development: A review. *Journal of Child Psychology and Psychiatry, 46*, 755–773.

Spirito, A., & Donaldson, D. (1998). Suicide and suicide attempts during adolescence. In T. Ollendick (Ed.), *Comprehensive clinical psychology* (Vol. 5, pp. 463–485). Kidlington, Oxford: Elsevier Science.

Spirito, A., Jelalian, E., Rasile, D., Rohrbeck, C., & Vinnick, L. (2000). Adolescent risk taking and self-reported injuries associated with substance use. *American Journal of Drug and Alcohol Abuse, 26*, 113–123.

Spirito, A., Valeri, S., Boergers, J., & Donaldson, D. (2003). Predictors of continued suicidal behavior in adolescents following a suicide attempt. *Journal of Clinical Child and Adolescent Psychology, 32*, 284–289.

Spitz, R. A. (1946). Anaclitic depression: An inquiry into the genesis of psychiatric conditions in early childhood, II. *Psychoanalytic Study of the Child, 2*, 313–342.

Spitzer, R. L., Gibbon, M., Skodol, A. E., Williams, J. B. W., & First, M. B. (1994). *DSM-IV casebook*. Washington, DC: American Psychiatric Press.

Sporn, A., Greenstein, D., Gogtay, N., Sailer, F., Hommer, D. W., Rawlings, R., Nicolson, R., Egan, M. F., Lenane, M., Gochman, P., Weinberger, D. R., & Rapoport, J. L. (2005). Childhood-onset schizophrenia: Smooth pursuit eye-tracking dysfunction in family. *Schizophrenia Research, 73*, 243–252.

Spoth, R. L., Redmond, C., & Shin, C. (2001). Randomized trial of brief family interventions for general populations: Adolescent substance use outcomes 4 years following baseline. *Journal of Consulting and Clinical Psychology, 69*, 627–642.

Spoth, R., Redmond, C., Shin, C., & Azevedo, K. (2004). Brief family intervention effects on adolescent substance initiation: School-level growth curve analyses 6 years following baseline. *Journal of Consulting and Clinical Psychology, 72*, 535–542.

Spoth, R., Reyes, M. L., Redmond, C., & Shin, C. (1999). Assessing a public health approach to delay onset and progression of adolescent substance use: Latent transition and log-linear analyses of longitudinal family preventive intervention outcomes. *Journal of Consulting and Clinical Psychology, 67*, 619–630.

Sprich, S., Biederman, J., Crawford, M. H., Mundy, E., & Faraone, S. V. (2000). Adoptive and biological families of children and adolescents with ADHD. *Journal of the American Academy of Child and Adolescent Psychiatry, 39*, 1432–1437.

Spruyt, K., O'Brien, L. M., Cluydts, R., Verleye, G. B., & Ferri, R. (2005). Odds, prevalence and predictors of sleep problems in school-age normal children. *Journal of Sleep Research, 14*, 163–176.

Srebnik, D., Cauce, A. M., & Baydar, N. (1996). Help-seeking pathways for children and adolescents. *Journal of Emotional and Behavioral Disorders, 4*, 210–220.

Sroufe, L. A. (1989). Pathways to adaptation and maladaptation: Psychopathology as developmental deviation. In D. Cicchetti (Ed.), *The emergence of a discipline: Rochester symposium on developmental psychopathology: Vol. 1* (pp. 13–40). Hillsdale, NJ: Lawrence Erlbaum Associates.

Sroufe, L. A. (1997). Psychopathology as an outcome of development. *Development and Psychopathology, 9*, 251–268.

Sroufe, L. A., Carlson, E. A., Levy, A. K., & Egeland, B. (1999). Implications of attachment theory for developmental psychopathology. *Development and Psychopathology, 11*, 1–13.

Stallard, P. (2002). *Think good—feel good: A cognitive behaviour therapy workbook for children and young people*. Hoboken, NJ: Wiley.

Stanger, C., Dumenci, L., Kamon, J., & Burstein, M. (2004). Parenting and children's externalizing problems in substance-abusing families. *Journal of Clinical Child and Adolescent Psychology, 33*, 590–600.

Stanton-Chapman, T. L., Chapman, D. A., & Scott, K. G. (2001). Identification of early risk factors for learning disabilities. *Journal of Early Intervention, 24*, 193–206.

Stark, K. (1990). *Childhood depression: School-based intervention*. New York: Guilford Press.

Stark, K. D., Bronik, M. D., Wong, S., Wells, G., & Ostrander, R. (2000). Depressive disorders. In M. Hersen & R. T. Ammerman (Eds.), *Advanced abnormal child psychology* (pp. 291–326). Mahwah, NJ: Lawrence Erlbaum Associates.

Stark, K. D., Sander, J. B., Yancy, M. G., Bronik, M. D., & Hoke, J. A. (2000). Treatment of depression in childhood and adolescence: Cognitive-behavioral procedures for the individual and family. In P. C. Kendall (Ed.), *Child and adolescent therapy: Cognitive-behavioral procedures* (2nd ed., pp. 173–234). New York: Guilford Press.

Starling, J., Rey, J. M., & Simpson, J. M. (2004). Depressive symptoms and suicidal behaviour: Changes with time in an adolescent clinic cohort. *Australian and New Zealand Journal of Psychiatry, 38*, 732–737.

Starr, E., Szatmari, P., Bryson, S., & Zwaigenbaum, L. (2003). Stability and change among high-functioning children with pervasive developmental disorders: A 2-year outcome study. *Journal of Autism and Developmental Disorders, 33*, 15–22.

State, M. W., Lombroso, P. J., Pauls, D. L., & Leckman, J. F. (2000). The genetics of childhood psychiatric disorders: A decade of progress. *Journal of the American Academy of Child and Adolescent Psychiatry, 39*, 946–962.

Stayer, C., Sporn, A., Gogtay, N., Tossell, J., Lenane, M., Gochman, P., & Rapoport, J. L. (2004). Looking for childhood schizophrenia: Case series of false positive. *Journal of the American Academy of Child and Adolescent Psychiatry, 43*, 1029–1029.

Steege, M. W., & Watson, T. S. (2003). *Conducting school-based functional behavioral assessments: A practitioner's guide*. New York: Guilford Press.

Steele, R. G., Dreyer, M. L., & Phipps, S. (2004). Patterns of maternal distress among children with cancer and their association with child emotional and somatic distress. *Journal of Pediatric Psychology, 29*, 507–517.

Steele, R. G., Forehand, R., & Armistead, L. (1997). The role of family processes and coping strategies in the relationship between parental chronic illness and childhood internalizing problems. *Journal of Abnormal Child Psychology, 25*, 83–94.

Steele, R. G., Long, A., Reddy, K. A., Luhr, M., & Phipps, S. (2003). Changes in maternal distress and child-rearing strategies across treatment for pediatric cancer. *Journal of Pediatric Psychology, 28*, 447–452.

Steffenburg, S., Steffenburg, U., & Gillberg, C. (2003). Autism spectrum disorders in children with active epilepsy and learning disability: Comorbidity, pre- and perinatal background, and seizure characteristics. *Developmental Medicine & Child Neurology, 45*, 724–730.

Stein, B. D., Zima, B. T., Elliott, M. N., Burnam, M. A., Shahinfar, A., Fox, N. A., & Leavitt, L. A. (2001). Violence exposure among school-age children in foster care: Relationship to distress symptoms. *Journal of the American Academy of Child and Adolescent Psychiatry, 40*, 588–594.

Stein, D., Williamson, D. E., Birmaher, B., Brent, D. A., Kaufman, J., Dahl, R. E., Perel, J. M., & Ryan, N. D. (2000). Parent-child bonding and family functioning in depressed children and children at high risk and low risk for future depression. *Journal of the American Academy of Child and Adolescent Psychiatry, 39*, 1387–1395.

Stein, D. B. (1999). *Ritalin is not the answer: A drug-free, practical program for children diagnosed with ADD or ADHD*. San Francisco: Jossey-Bass.

Stein, D. B. (2002). *Ritalin is not the answer action guide: An interactive companion to the bestselling drug-free ADD/ADHD parenting program*. New York: Wiley.

Steinberg, A. R., Phares, V., & Thompson, J. K. (2004). Gender differences in peer and parental influences: Body image disturbance, self-worth, and psychological functioning in preadolescent children. *Journal of Youth and Adolescence, 33*, 421–429.

Steinberg, L. (2004). *The ten basic principles of good parenting*. New York: Simon and Schuster.

Steinberg, L., & Avenevoli, S. (2000). The role of context in the development of psychopathology: A conceptual framework and some speculative propositions. *Child Development, 71*, 66–74.

Steinberg, L., Lamborn, S. D., Darling, N., Mounts, N. S., & Dornbusch, S. M. (1994). Overtime changes in adjustment and competence among adolescents from authoritative, authoritarian, indulgent, and neglectful families. *Child Development, 65*, 754–770.

Steinberg, L., Lamborn, S. D., Dornbusch, S. M., & Darling, N. (1992). Impact of parenting practices on adolescent achievement: Authoritative parenting, school involvement, and encouragement to succeed. *Child Development, 63*, 1266–1281.

Steinberg, L., & Scott, E. S. (2003). Less guilty by reason of adolescence: Developmental immaturity, diminished responsibility, and the juvenile death penalty. *American Psychologist, 58*, 1009–1018.

Steinhausen, H. C., Drechsler, R., Foldenyi, M., Imhof, K., & Brandeis, D. (2003). Clinical course of attention-deficit/hyperactivity disorder from childhood toward early adolescence. *Journal of the American Academy of Child and Adolescent Psychiatry, 42*, 1085–1092.

Stephens, T., Braithwaite, R. L., & Taylor, S. E. (1998). Model for using hip-hop music for small group HIV/AIDS prevention counseling with African American adolescents and young adults. *Patient Education and Counseling, 35*, 127–137.

Stephenson, M. T. (2003). Mass media strategies targeting high sensation seekers: What works and why. *American Journal of Health Behavior, 27*, S233–S238.

Sternberg, R. J. (1997). *Career paths in psychology: Where your degree can take you.* Washington, DC. American Psychological Association.

Sternberg, R. J., & Grigorenko, E. (2000). *Our labeled children: What every parent and teacher needs to know about learning disabilities.* New York: Perseus Books.

Stetson, E. G. (1992). Clinical child psychology and educational assessment. In C. E. Walker & M. C. Roberts (Eds.), *Handbook of clinical child psychology* (2nd ed., pp. 101–131). New York: Wiley.

Stevens, E. A., & Prinstein, M. J. (2005). Peer contagion of depressogenic attributional styles among adolescents: A longitudinal study. *Journal of Abnormal Child Psychology, 33,* 25–37.

Stevens, J., Harman, J. S., & Kelleher, K. J. (2005). Race/ethnicity and insurance status as factors associated with ADHD treatment patterns. *Journal of Child and Adolescent Psychopharmacology, 15,* 88–96.

Stevens, S. L., Colwell, B., Smith, D. W., Robinson, J., & McMillan, C. (2005). An exploration of self-reported negative affect by adolescents and a reason for smoking: Implications for tobacco prevention and intervention programs. *Preventive Medicine: An International Journal Devoted to Practice and Theory, 41,* 589–596.

Stevenson, J. (1999). The treatment of the long-term sequelae of child abuse. *Journal of Child Psychology and Psychiatry, 40,* 89–111.

Stewart, A. (2004). Prevention of eating disorders. In K. N. Dwivedi, & P. B. Harper (Eds.) *Promoting the emotional well-being of children and adolescents and preventing their mental ill health: A handbook* (pp. 173–197). Philadelphia: Jessica Kingsley.

Stewart, A., Steiman, M., Cauce, A. M., Cochran, B. N., Whitbeck, L. B., & Hoyt, D. R. (2004). Victimization and posttraumatic stress disorder among homeless adolescents. *Journal of the American Academy of Child and Adolescent Psychiatry, 43,* 325–331.

Stewart, S. H., Conrod, P. J., Marlatt, G. A., Comeau, M. N., Thush, C., & Krank, M. (2005). New developments in prevention and early intervention for alcohol abuse in youths. *Alcoholism: Clinical and Experimental Research, 29,* 278–286.

Stewart, S. M., Kennard, B. D., Lee, P. W. H., Hughes, C. W., Mayes, T. L., Emslie, G. J., & Lewinsohn, P. M. (2004). A cross-cultural investigation of cognitions and depressive symptoms in adolescents. *Journal of Abnormal Psychology, 113,* 248–257.

Stice, E., Burton, E. M., & Shaw, H. (2004). Prospective relations between bulimic pathology, depression, and substance abuse: Unpacking comorbidity in adolescent girls. *Journal of Consulting and Clinical Psychology, 72,* 62–71.

Stice, E., Hayward, C., Cameron, R. P., Killen, J. D., & Taylor, C. B. (2000). Body-image and eating disturbances predict onset of depression among female adolescents: A longitudinal study. *Journal of Abnormal Psychology, 109,* 438–444.

Stice, E., Presnell, K., Shaw, H., & Rohde, P. (2005). Psychological and behavioral risk factors for obesity onset in adolescent girls: A prospective study. *Journal of Consulting and Clinical Psychology, 73,* 195–202.

Stice, E., Presnell, K., & Spangler, D. (2002). Risk factors for binge eating onset in adolescent girls: A 2-year prospective investigation. *Health Psychology, 21,* 131–138.

Stice, E., Ragan, J., & Randall, P. (2004). Prospective relations between social support and depression: Differential direction of effects for parent and peer support? *Journal of Abnormal Psychology, 113,* 155–159.

Stice, E., & Shaw, H. (2004). Eating disorder prevention programs: A meta-analytic review. *Psychological Bulletin, 130,* 206–227.

Stice, E., Wonderlich, S., & Wade, E. (2006). Eating disorders. In R. T. Ammerman (Ed.), *Comprehensive handbook of personality and psychopathology: Child psychopathology* (Vol. 3, pp. 330–347). Hoboken, NJ: Wiley.

Stickler, G. B. (1996). Worries of parents and their children. *Clinical Pediatrics, 35,* 84–90.

Stipek, D. J. (2001). Pathways to constructive lives: The importance of early school success. In A. C. Bohart, & D. J. Stipek (Eds.) *Constructive & destructive behavior: Implications for family, school, & society* (pp. 291–315). Washington, DC: American Psychological Association.

Stipek, D. (2005). Children as unwitting agents in their developmental pathways. In C. R. Cooper, C. T. G. Coll, W. T. Bartko, H. Davis, & C. Chatman (Eds.) *Developmental pathways through middle childhood: Rethinking contexts and diversity as resources* (pp. 99–120). Mahwah, NJ: Lawrence Erlbaum Associates.

Stoil, M. J., Hill, G. A., Jansen, M. A., Sambrano, S., & Winn, F. J. (2000). Benefits of community-based demonstration efforts: Knowledge gained in substance abuse prevention. *Journal of Community Psychology, 28,* 375–389.

Stolzer, J. (2005). ADHD in American: A bioecological analysis. *Ethical Human Psychology and Psychiatry, 7,* 65–75.

Stoolmiller, M., Eddy, J. M., & Reid, J. B. (2000). Detecting and describing preventive intervention effects in a universal school-based randomized trial targeting delinquent and violent behavior. *Journal of Consulting and Clinical Psychology, 68,* 296–306.

Stoppelbein, L., & Greening, L. (2000). Posttraumatic stress symptoms in parentally bereaved children and adolescents. *Journal of the American Academy of Child and Adolescent Psychiatry, 39,* 1112–1119.

Storch, E. A., Gerdes, A. C., Adkins, J. W., Geffken, G. R., Star, J., & Murphy, T. (2004). Behavioral treatment of a child with PANDAS. *Journal of the American Academy of Child and Adolescent Psychiatry, 43,* 510–511.

Stormshak, E. A., Bierman, K. L., McMahon, R. J., Lengua, L. J., & Conduct Problems Prevention Research Group. (2000). Parenting practices and child disruptive behavior problems in early elementary school. *Journal of Clinical Child Psychology, 29,* 17–29.

Stormshak, E. A., Comeau, C. A., & Shepard, S. A. (2004). The relative contribution of sibling deviance and peer deviance in the prediction of substance use across middle childhood. *Journal of Abnormal Child Psychology, 32,* 635–649.

Stowe, C. M. (2000). *How to reach and teach children and teens with dyslexia: A parent and teacher guide to helping students of all ages academically, socially, and emotionally.* San Francisco: Jossey-Bass.

Straus, M. A. (1994). *Beating the devil out of them: Corporal punishment in American families.* San Francisco: Jossey-Bass/Lexington Books.

Straus, M. A., & Stewart, J. H. (1999). Corporal punishment by American Parents: National data on prevalence, chronicity, severity, and duration, in relation to child and family characteristics. *Clinical Child and Family Psychology Review, 2,* 55–70.

Streisand, R., & Efron, L. A. (2003). Pediatric sleep disorders. In M. C. Roberts (Ed.), *Handbook of pediatric psychology* (3rd ed., pp. 578–598). New York: Guilford Press.

Stromme, P., & Hagberg, G. (2000). Aetiology in severe and mild mental retardation: A population-based study of Norwegian children. *Developmental Medicine & Child Neurology, 42,* 76–86.

Sturmey, P. (2002). Mental retardation and concurrent psychiatric disorder: Assessment and treatment. *Current Opinion in Psychiatry, 15,* 489–495.

Sue, S. (2003). In defense of cultural competency in psychotherapy and treatment. *American Psychologist, 58,* 964–970.

Sue, S., Kurasaki, K. S., & Srinivasan, S. (1999). Ethnicity, gender, and cross-cultural issues in clinical research. In P. C. Kendall, J. N. Butcher, & G. N. Holmbeck (Eds), *Handbook of research methods in clinical psychology* (2nd ed., pp. 54–71). New York: Wiley.

Sue, S., & Zane, N. (2006). Ethnic minority populations have been neglected by evidence-based practices. In J. C. Norcross, L. E. Beutler, & R. F. Levant (Eds.), *Evidence-based practices in mental health: Debate and dialogue on the fundamental questions* (pp. 329–337). Washington, DC: American Psychological Association.

Sukhodolsky, D. G., do Rosario-Campos, M. C., Scahill, L., Katsovich, L., Pauls, D. L., Peterson, B. S., King, R. A., Lombroso, P. J., Findley, D. B., & Leckman, J. F. (2005). Adaptive, emotional, and family functioning of children with obsessive-compulsive disorder and comorbid attention deficit hyperactivity disorder. *American Journal of Psychiatry, 162,* 1125–1132.

Sukhodolsky, D. G., Golub, A., Stone, E. C., & Orban, L. (2005). Dismantling anger control training for children: A randomized pilot study of social problem-solving versus social skills training components. *Behavior Therapy, 36,* 15–23.

Sullivan, T. N., & Farrell, A. D. (1999). Identification and impact of risk and protective factors for drug use among urban African American adolescents. *Journal of Clinical Child Psychology, 28,* 122–136.

Summerville, M. B., Kaslow, N. J., & Doepke, K. J. (1996). Psychopathology and cognitive and family functioning in suicidal African-American adolescents. *Current Directions in Psychological Science, 5,* 7–11.

Sund, A. M., & Wichstrom, L. (2002). Insecure attachment as a risk factor for future depressive symptoms in early adolescence. *Journal of the American Academy of Child and Adolescent Psychiatry, 41,* 1478–1485.

Susser, E., Brown, A., & Matte, T. (2000). Prenatal antecedents of neuropsychiatric disorder over the life course: Collaborative studies of United States birth cohorts. In J. L. Rapoport (Ed.), *Childhood onset of "adult" psychopathology: Clinical and research advances* (pp. 121–146). Washington, DC: American Psychiatric Press.

Suto, W. M. I., Clare, I. C. H., Holland, A. J., & Watson, P. C. (2005). The relationships among three factors affecting the financial decision-making abilities of adults with mild intellectual disabilities. *Intellectual Disability Research, 49,* 210–217.

Suveg, C., & Zeman, J. (2004). Emotion regulation in children with anxiety disorders. *Journal of Clinical Child and Adolescent Psychology, 33,* 750–759.

Swan, K., Meskill, C. & DeMaio, S. (Eds.) (1998). *Social learning from broadcast television.* Cresskill, NJ: Hampton Press.

Swanson, J. M., Hanley, T., Simpson, S., Davies, M., Schulte, A., Wells, K., Hinshaw, S., Abikoff, H., Hechtman, L., Pelham, W., Hoza, B., Severe, J., Molina, B., Odbert, C., Forness, S., Gresham, F., Arnold, L. E., Wigal, T., Wasdell, M., & Greenhill, L. L. (2000). Evaluation of learning disorders in children with a psychiatric disorder: An example from the multimodal treatment study for ADHD (MTA study). In L. L. Greenhill (Ed.) *Learning disabilities: Implications for psychiatric treatment* (pp. 97–128). Washington, DC: American Psychiatric Publishing, Inc.

Sweet, E. S. (1991). What do adolescents want? What do adolescents need? Treating the chronic relapser. *Journal of Adolescent Chemical Dependency, 1,* 1–8.

Swendsen, J. D., & Merikangas, K. R. (2000). The comorbidity of depression and substance use disorders. *Clinical Psychology Review, 20,* 173–189.

Szapocznik, J., Perez-Vidal,, A., Brickman, A. L., Foote, F., Santisteban, D., Hervis, O., & Kurtines, W. A. (1988). Engaging adolescent drug abusers and their families in treatment: A strategic structural systems approach. *Journal of Consulting and Clinical Psychology, 56,* 552–557.

Szatmari, P. (2000). The classification of autism, Asperger's syndrome, and pervasive developmental disorder. *Canadian Journal of Psychiatry, 45,* 731–738.

Szoke, A., Schurhoff, F., Mathieu, F., Meary, A., Ionescu, S., & Leboyer, M. (2005). Tests of executive functions in first-degree relatives of schizophrenic patients: A meta-analysis. *Psychological Medicine, 35,* 771–782.

Tackett, J. L., Krueger, R. F., Iacono, W. G., & McGue, M. (2005). Symptom-based subfactors of *DSM*-defined conduct disorder: Evidence for etiologic distinctions. *Journal of Abnormal Psychology, 114,* 483–487.

Taha, T. E., Kumwenda, N. I., Hoover, D. R., Fiscus, S. A., Kafulafula, G., Nkhoma, C., Nour, S., Chen, S., Liomba, G., Miotti, P. G., & Broadhead, R. L. (2004). Nevirapine and Zidovudine at birth to reduce perinatal transmission of HIV in an African setting a randomized controlled trial. *JAMA: Journal of the American Medical Association, 292,* 202–209.

Tallal, P. (2003). Language learning disabilities: Integrated research approaches. *Current Directions in Psychological Science, 12,* 206–211.

Tallal, P., & Benasich, A. A. (2002). Developmental language learning impairments. *Development and Psychopathology, 14,* 559–579.

Tamplin, A., Goodyer, I. M., & Herbert, J. (1998). Family functioning and parent general health in families of adolescents with major depressive disorder. *Journal of Affective Disorders, 48,* 1–13.

Tanguay, P. E. (2000). Pervasive developmental disorders: A 10-year review. *Journal of the American Academy of Child and Adolescent Psychiatry, 39,* 1079–1095.

Tanguay, P. E. (2004). Commentary: Categorical versus spectrum approaches to classification in pervasive developmental disorders. *Journal of the American Academy of Child and Adolescent Psychiatry, 43,* 181–182.

Target, M., & Fonagy, P. (1998). Psychodynamic therapy. In T. Ollendick (Ed.), *Comprehensive clinical psychology* (Vol. 5, pp. 245–266). Kidlington, Oxford: Elsevier Science.

Tarnowski, K. J., & Simonian, S. (1999). *Directory of graduate programs in clinical child and pediatric psychology* (3rd ed.). Hillsdale, NJ: Lawrence Erlbaum Associates.

Tarter, R. E., Kirisci, L., Mezzich, A., Cornelius, J. R., Pajer, K., Vanyukov, M., Gardner, W., Blackson, T., & Clark, D. (2003). Neurobehavioral disinhibition in childhood predicts early age at onset of substance use disorder. *American Journal of Psychiatry, 160*, 1078–1085.

Tasbihsazan, R., Nettelbeck, T., & Kirby, N. (2003). Predictive validity of the Fagan test of infant intelligence. *British Journal of Developmental Psychology, 21*, 585–597.

Task Force on Promotion and Dissemination of Psychological Procedures. (1995). Training in and dissemination of empirically-validated psychological treatments: Report and recommendations. *Clinical Psychologist, 48*, 3–24.

Taylor, E. (1995). Dysfunctions of attention. In D. Cicchetti & D. J. Cohen (Eds.), *Developmental psychopathology (Vol. 2): Risk, disorder, and adaptation* (pp. 243–273). New York: Wiley.

Taylor, E., & Rogers, J. W. (2005). Practitioner review: Early adversity and developmental disorders. *Journal of Child Psychology and Psychiatry, 46*, 451–467.

Taylor, J., Iacono, W. G., & McGue, M. (2000). Evidence for a genetic etiology of early-onset delinquency. *Journal of Abnormal Psychology, 109*, 634–643.

Taylor, J., Loney, B. R., Bobadilla, L., Iacono, W. G., & McGue, M. (2003). Genetic and environmental influences on psychopathology trait dimensions in a community sample of male twins. *Journal of Abnormal Child Psychology, 31*, 633–645.

Taylor, L., & Adelman, H. S. (1999). Keeping reading and writing problems in broad perspective. *Reading and Writing Quarterly: Overcoming Learning Difficulties*, 15, 351–353.

Taylor, S. J. C., Viner, R., Booy, R., Head, J., Tate, H., Brentnall, S. L., Haines, M., Bhui, K., Hillier, S., & Stansfeld, S. (2005). Ethnicity, socio-economic status, overweight and underweight in East London adolescents. *Ethnicity & Health, 10*, 113–128.

Taylor, T. K., Eddy, J. M., & Biglan, A. (1999). Interpersonal skills training to reduce aggressive and delinquent behavior: Limited evidence and the need for an evidence-based system of care. *Clinical Child and Family Psychology Review, 2*, 169–182.

Teglasi, H., Cohn, A., & Meshbesher, N. (2004). Temperament and learning disability. *Learning Disability Quarterly, 27*, 9–20.

Teichman, M., & Kefir, E. (2000). The effects of perceived parental behaviors, attitudes, and substance-use on adolescent attitudes toward and intent to use psychoactive substances. *Journal of Drug Education, 30*, 193–204.

Tein, J., Sandler, I. N., MacKinnon, D. P., & Wolchik, S. A. (2004). How did it work? Who did it work for? Mediation in the context of a moderated prevention effect for children of divorce. *Journal of Consulting and Clinical Psychology, 72*, 617–624.

Temple, C. M. (2002). Oral fluency and narrative production in children with Turner's syndrome. *Neuropsychologia, 40*, 1419–1427.

Tercyak, K. P. (2003). Genetic disorders and genetic testing. In M. C. Roberts (Ed.), *Handbook of pediatric psychology* (3rd ed., pp. 719–734). New York: Guilford Press.

Testa, M., Van Zile-Tamsen, C., & Livingston, J. A. (2005). Childhood sexual abuse, relationship satisfaction, and sexual risk taking in a community sample of women. *Journal of Consulting and Clinical Psychology, 73*, 1116–1124.

Tetzlaff, B. T., Kahn, J. H., Godley, S. H., Godley, M. D., Diamond, G. S., & Funk, R. R. (2005). Working alliance, treatment satisfaction, and patterns of posttreatment use among adolescent substance users. *Psychology of Addictive Behaviors, 19*, 199–207.

Thabet, A. A. M., Abed, Y., & Vostanis, P. (2004). Comorbidity of PTSD and depression among refugee children during war conflict. *Journal of Child Psychology and Psychiatry, 45*, 433–542.

Thabet, A. A. M., & Vostanis, P. (1999). Post-traumatic stress reactions in children of war. *Journal of Child Psychology and Psychiatry, 40*, 385–391.

Thomas, A. (1998). *Directory of school psychology graduate programs*. Bethesda, MD: National Association of School Psychologists Publications.

Thomas, A., & Chess, S. (1977). *Temperament and development*. New York: Brunner/Mazel.

Thompson, J. K. (2003). *Handbook of eating disorders and obesity*. Hoboken, NJ: Wiley.

Thompson, J. K., Heinberg, L. J., Altabe, M., & Tantleff-Dunn, S. (2004). *Exacting beauty: Theory, assessment, and treatment of body image disturbance*. Washington, DC: American Psychological Association.

Thompson, J. K., & Smolak, L. (Eds.) (2001). *Body image, eating disorders, and obesity in youth: Assessment, prevention, and treatment*. Washington, DC: American Psychological Association.

Thompson, J. K., & Stice, E. (2001). Thin-ideal internalizing: Mounting evidence for a new risk factor for body-image disturbance and eating pathology. *Current Directions in Psychological Science, 10*, 181–183.

Thompson, M. P., Kaslow, N. J., Kingree, J. B., King, M., Bryant, L., & Rey, M. (1998). Psychological symptomatology following parental death in a predominantly minority sample of children and adolescents. *Journal of Clinical Child Psychology, 27*, 434–441.

Thompson, R. J., Armstrong, F. D., Link, C. L., Pegelow, C. H., Moser, F., & Wang, W. C. (2003). A prospective study of the relationship over time of behavior problems, intellectual functioning, and family functioning in children with sickle cell disease: A report from the cooperative study of sickle cell disease. *Journal of Pediatric Psychology, 28*, 59–65.

Thorpe, J., Kamphaus, R. W., & Reynolds, C. R. (2003). The behavior assessment system for children. In C. R. Reynolds & R. W. Kamphaus (Eds.), *Handbook of psychological and educational assessment of children: Personality, behavior, and context* (2nd ed., pp. 387–405). New York: Guilford Press.

Thorpe, L. E., List, D. G., Marx, T., May, L., Helgerson, S. D., & Frieden, T. R. (2004). Childhood obesity in New York City Elemental School students. *American Journal of Public Health, 94*, 1496–1500.

Thrower, D., Harvey, P., Murch, S., & Elphinstone, P. (2004). MMR and autism: the debate continues. *The Lancet, 363*, 567–569.

Tillman, R., Geller, B., Bolhofner, K., Craney, J. L., Williams, M., & Zimerman, B. (2003). Ages of onset and rates of syndromal and subsyndromal comorbid *DSM-IV* diagnoses in a prepubertal and early adolescent bipolar disorder phenotype. *Journal of the American Academy of Child and Adolescent Psychiatry, 42*, 1486–1493.

Timbremont, B., Braet, C., & Dreessen, L. (2004). Assessing depression in youth: Relation between the Children's Depression Inventory and a structured interview. *Journal of Clinical Child and Adolescent Psychology, 33*, 149–157.

Timmons-Mitchell, J., Bender, M. B., Kishna, M. A., & Mitchell, C. C. (2006). An independent effectiveness trial of multisystemic therapy with juvenile justice youth. *Journal of Clinical Child and Adolescent Psychology, 35*, 227–236.

Tims, F. M., Dennis, M. L., Hamilton, N., Buchan, B. J., Diamond, G., Funk, R., & Brantley, L. B. (2002). Characteristics and problems of 600 adolescent cannabis abusers in outpatient treatment. *Addiction, 97*, 46–57.

Tiu, R. D., Wadsworth, S. J., Olson, R. K., & DeFries, J. C. (2004). Causal models of reading disability: A twin study. *Twin Research, 7*, 275–283.

Tobler, N. S. (2000). Lessons learned. *Journal of Primary Prevention, 20*, 261–274.

Tolan, P., Gorman-Smith, D., & Henry, D. (2004). Supporting families in a high-risk setting: Proximal effects of the SAFEChildren preventive intervention. *Journal of Consulting and Clinical Psychology, 72*, 855–869.

Toppelberg, C. O., & Shapiro, T. (2000). Language disorders: A 10-year research update review. *Journal of the American Academy of Child and Adolescent Psychiatry, 39*, 143–152.

Toppelberg, C. O., Tabors, P., Coggins, A., Lum, K., & Burger, C. (2005). Differential diagnosis of selective mutism in bilingual children. *Journal of the American Academy of Child and Adolescent Psychiatry, 44*, 592–595.

Tram, J. M., & Cole, D. A. (2000). Self-perceived competence and the relation between life events and depressive symptoms in adolescence: Mediator or moderator? *Journal of Abnormal Psychology, 109*, 753–760.

Treatment for Adolescents with Depression Study (TADS) Team. (2003). Treatment for adolescents with depression study (TADS): Rationale, design, and methods. *Journal of the American Academy of Child and Adolescent Psychiatry, 42*, 531–542.

Treatment for Adolescents with Depression Study (TADS) Team. (2004). Fluoxetine, cognitive-behavioral therapy, and their combination for adolescents with depression: Treatment for adolescents with depression study (TADS) randomized controlled trial. *Journal of the American Medical Association, 292*, 807–820.

Treatment for Adolescents with Depression Study (TADS) Team. (2005). The treatment for adolescents with depression study (TADS): Demographic and clinical characteristics. *Journal of the American Academy of Child and Adolescent Psychiatry, 44*, 28–40.

Treffert, D. A. (1999). Pervasive developmental disorders. In S. D. Netherton, D. Holmes, & C. E. Walker (Eds.), *Child and adolescent psychological disorders: A comprehensive textbook* (pp. 76–97). New York: Oxford University Press.

Tremblay, R. E., LeMarquand, D., & Vitaro, F. (1999). The prevention of oppositional defiant disorder and conduct disorder. In H. C. Quay & A. E. Hogan (Eds.), *Handbook of disruptive behavior disorders* (pp. 525–555). New York: Kluwer Academic/Plenum Press.

Treuting, J. J., & Hinshaw, S. P. (2001). Depression and self-esteem in boys with attention-deficit/hyperactivity disorder: Associations with comorbid aggression and explanatory attributional mechanisms. *Journal of Abnormal Child Psychology, 29*, 23–39.

Treutler, C. M., & Epkins, C. C. (2003). Are discrepancies among child, mother, and father reports on children's behavior related to parents' psychological symptoms and aspects of parent-child relationships? *Journal of Abnormal Child Psychology, 31*, 13–27.

Troiano, P. F. (2003). College students and learning disability: Elements of self-style. *Journal of College Student Development, 44*, 404–419.

Trudell, B., & Whatley, M. H. (1988). School sexual abuse prevention: Unintended consequences and dilemmas. *Child Abuse and Neglect, 12*, 103–113.

Trull, T. J. (2005). *Clinical psychology* (7th ed.). Belmont, CA: Wadsworth.

Tryon, G. S. (2000). Doctoral training issues in school and clinical child psychology. *Professional Psychology: Research and Practice, 31*, 85–87.

Tucker, N. (2004). *Love in the driest season: A family memoir.* New York: Three Rivers Press.

Tully, L. A., Arseneault, L., Caspi, A., Moffitt, T. E., & Morgan, J. (2004). Does maternal warmth moderate the effects of birth weight on twins' attention-deficit/hyperactivity disorder (ADHD) symptoms and low IQ? *Journal of Consulting and Clinical Psychology, 72*, 218–226.

Turner, C. M., & Barrett, P. M. (2003). Does age play a role in the structure of anxiety and depression in children and youths? An investigation of the tripartite model in three age cohorts. *Journal of Consulting and Clinical Psychology, 71*, 826–833.

Turner, M., & Rack, J. (Eds., 2004) *The study of dyslexia.* New York: Kluwer Academic/Plenum Press.

Turner, S. L., Hamilton, H., Jacobs, M., Angood, L. M., & Dwyer, D. H. (1997). The influence of fashion magazines on the body image satisfaction of college women: An exploratory analysis. *Adolescence, 32*, 603–614.

Turner, S. M., Beidel, D. C., & Roberson-Nay, R. (2005). Offspring of anxious parents: Reactivity, habituation, and anxiety-proneness. *Behaviour Research and Therapy, 43*, 1263–1279.

Turner, S. M., Beidel, D. C., Roberson-Nay, R., & Tervo, K. (2003). Parenting behaviors in parents with anxiety disorders. *Behaviour Research and Therapy, 41*, 541–554.

Tutty, L. M. (1991). Child sexual abuse: A range of prevention options. *Journal of Child and Youth Care, Fall*, 23–41.

Twenge, J. M., & Nolen-Hoeksema, S. (2002). Age, gender, race, socioeconomic status, and birth cohort differences on the Children's Depression Inventory: A meta-analysis. *Journal of Abnormal Psychology, 111*, 578–588.

Udwin, O., Boyle, S., Yule, W., Bolton, D., & O'Ryan, D. (2000). Risk factors for long-term psychological effects of a disaster experienced in adolescence: Predictors of post traumatic stress disorder. *Journal of Child Psychology and Psychiatry and Allied Disciplines, 41,* 969–979.

Ungar, M. (2004). The importance of parents and other caregivers to the resilience of high-risk adolescents. *Family Process, 43,* 23–41.

Updegraff, K. A., McHale, S. M., & Crouter, A. C. (2000). Adolescents' sex-typed friendship experiences: Does having a sister versus a brother matter? *Child Development, 71,* 1597–1610.

Urban Institute. (1999a). Adults' environment and behavior: Mental health and parents. *Snapshots of America's Families,* January, 1999. Washington, DC: Author.

Urban Institute. (1999b). Children's environment and behavior: Behavioral and emotional problems in children. *Snapshots of America's Families,* January, 1999. Washington, DC: Author.

Urban Institute. (2004). Race, ethnicity, and economic well-being. *Snapshots of America's Families,* March, 2004. Washington, DC: Author.

U.S. Department of Health and Human Services. (2001). *The Surgeon General's call to action to prevent and decrease overweight and obesity.* Rockville, MD: U.S. Department of Health and Human Services, Public Health Service, Office of the Surgeon General.

Vaidya, C. J., Bunge, S. A., Dudukovic, N. M., Zalecki, C. A., Elliott, G. R., & Gabrieli, J. D. E. (2005). Altered neural substrates of cognitive control in childhood ADHD: Evidence from functional magnetic resonance imaging. *American Journal of Psychiatry, 162,* 1605–1613.

Valois, R. F., Oeltmann, J. E., Waller, J., & Hussey, J. R. (1999). Relationship between number of sexual intercourse partners and selected health risk behaviors among public high school adolescents. *Journal of Adolescent Health, 25,* 328–335.

VanBourgondien, M. E., Reichle, N. C., & Schopler, E. (2003). Effects of a model treatment approach on adults with autism. *Journal of Autism and Developmental Disorders, 33,* 131–140.

Van Brakel, A. M. L., Muris, P., & Bogels, S. M. (2004). Relations between parent- and teacher-reported behavioral inhibition and behavioral observations of this temperamental trait. *Journal of Consulting and Clinical Psychology, 33,* 579–589.

Vance, A., Harris, K., Boots, M., Talbot, J., & Karamitsios, M. (2003). Which anxiety disorders may differentiate attention deficit hyperactivity disorder, combined type with dysthymic disorder from attention deficit hyperactivity disorder, combined type alone? *Australian and New Zealand Journal of Psychiatry, 37,* 563–569.

Vance, A., Sanders, M., & Arduca, Y. (2005). Dysthymic disorder contributes to oppositional defiant behaviour in children with attention-deficit/hyperactivity disorder, combined type (ADHD—CT). *Journal of Affective Disorders, 86,* 329–333.

Vanden Bos, G. R., & Williams, S. (2000). The internet versus the telephone: What is telehealth anyway? *Professional Psychology: Research and Practice, 31,* 490–492.

Vandewater, E. A., Lee, J. H., & Shim, M. (2005). Family conflict and violent electronic media use in school-aged children. *Media Psychology, 7,* 73–86.

Vandewater, E. A., Shim, M., & Capiovitz, A. G. (2004). Linking obesity and activity level with children's television and video game use. *Journal of Adolescence, 27,* 71–85.

Van Evra, J. (1998). *Television and child development* (2nd ed.). Mahwah, NJ: Lawrence Erlbaum Associates.

Van Lier, P. A. C., Muthen, B. O., van der Sar, R. M., & Crijnen, A. A. M. (2004). Preventing disruptive behavior in elementary schoolchildren: Impact of a universal classroom-based intervention. *Journal of Consulting and Clinical Psychology, 72,* 467–478.

Varela, R. E., Vernberg, E. M., Sanchez-Sosa, J. J., Riveros, A., Mitchell, M., & Mashunkashey, J. (2004). Parenting style of Mexican, Mexican American, and Caucasian-Non-Hispanic families: Social context and cultural influences. *Journal of Family Psychology, 18,* 651–657.

Vasa, R. A., & Pine, D. S. (2004). Neurobiology. In T. L. Morris & J. S. March (Eds.), *Anxiety disorders in children and adolescents* (2nd ed., pp. 3–26). New York: Guilford Press.

Vasey, M. W., & Lonigan, C. J. (2000). Consider the clinical utility of performance-based measures of childhood anxiety. *Journal of Clinical Child Psychology, 29,* 493–508.

Vastag, B. (2004). National autism summit charts a path trough a scientific, clinical wilderness. *JAMA: The Journal of the American Medical Association, 291,* 29–31.

Velting, O. N., Setzer, N. J., & Albano, A. M. (2004). Update on and advances in assessment and cognitive-behavioral treatment of anxiety disorders in children and adolescents. *Professional Psychology: Research and Practice, 35,* 42–54.

Verburg, H., Janssen, H., Rikken, M., Hoefnagels, C., & van Willensward, E. M. (1992). The Dutch way of prevention. In G. W. Albee, L. A. Bond, & T. V. C. Monsey (Eds.), *Improving children's lives: Global perspectives on prevention* (pp. 177–190). Newbury Park, CA: Sage.

Verdugo, M. A., Schalock, R. L., Keith, K. D., & Stancliffe, R. J. (2005). Quality of life and its measurement: Important principles and guidelines. *Intellectual Disability Research, 49,* 707–717.

Verduin, T. L., & Kendall, P. C. (2003). Differential occurrence of comorbidity within childhood anxiety disorders. *Journal of Clinical Child and Adolescent, 32,* 290–295.

Verhulst, F. C., Achenbach, T. M., van der Ende, J., Erol, N., Lambert, M. C., Leung, P. W. L., Silva, M. A., Zilber, N., & Zubrick, S. (2003). Comparisons of problems reported by youths from seven countries. *American Journal of Psychiatry, 160,* 1479–1485.

Vernberg, E. M., Jacobs, A. K., Nyre, J. E., Puddy, R. W., & Roberts, M. C. (2004). Innovative treatment for children with serious emotional disturbance: Preliminary outcomes for a school-based intensive mental health program. *Journal of Clinical Child and Adolescent, 33,* 359–365.

Verte, S., Geurts, H. M., Roeyers, H., Oosterlaan, J., & Sergeant, J. A. (2005). Executive functioning in children with autism and Tourette syndrome. *Development and Psychopathology, 17,* 415–445.

Veugelers, P. J., & Fitzgerald, A. L. (2005). Effectiveness of school programs in preventing childhood obesity: A multilevel comparison. *American Journal of Public Health, 95,* 432–435.

Vik, P. W., Brown, S. A., & Myers, M. G. (1997). Adolescent substance use problems. In E. J. Mash & L. G. Terdal (Eds.), *Assessment of childhood disorders* (3rd ed., pp. 717–748). New York: Guilford.

Vik, P. W., Cellucci, T., & Ivers, H. (2003). Natural reduction of binge drinking among college students. *Addictive Behaviors, 28*, 643–655.

Villani, S. (2001). Impact of media on children and adolescents: A 10-year review of the research. *Journal of the Academy of Child and Adolescent Psychiatry, 40*, 392–401.

Vincent, M. A., & McCabe, M. P. (2000). Gender differences among adolescents in family, and peer influences on body dissatisfaction, weight loss, and binge eating behaviors. *Journal of Youth and Adolescence, 29*, 205–221.

Vitaro, F., Brendgen, M., Pagani, L., Tremblay, R. E., & McDuff, P. (1999). Disruptive behavior, peer association, and conduct disorder: Testing the developmental links through early intervention. *Development and Psychopathology, 11*, 287–304.

Vitaro, F., Brendgen, M., & Tremblay, R. E. (2000). Influence of deviant friends on delinquency: Searching for moderator variables. *Journal of Abnormal Child Psychology, 28*, 313–325.

Vitaro, F., Brendgen, M., & Tremblay, R. E. (2001). Preventive intervention: Assessing its effects on the trajectories of delinquency and testing for mediational processes. *Applied Developmental Science, 5*, 201–213.

Vitiello, B., Severe, J. B., Greenhill, L. L., Arnold, L. E., Abikoff, H. B., Bukstein, O. G., Elliott, G. R., Hechtman, L., Jesnen, P. S., Hinshaw, S. P., March, J. S., Newcorn, J. H., Swanson, J. M., & Cantwell, D. P. (2001). Methylphenidate dosage for children with ADHD over time under controlled conditions: Lessons from the MTA. *Journal of the American Academy of Child and Adolescent Psychiatry, 40*, 188–196.

Voeller, K. K. S. (2004). Dyslexia. *Journal of Child Neurology, 19*, 740–744.

Volk, H. E., Neuman, R. J., & Todd, R. D. (2005). A systematic evaluation of ADHD and comorbid psychopathology in a population-based twin sample. *Journal of the American Academy of Child and Adolescent Psychiatry, 44*, 768–775.

Volkmar, F. R. (1992). Childhood disintegrative disorder: Issues for *DSM-IV. Journal of Autism and Developmental Disorders, 22*, 625–642.

Volkmar, F. R., Chaawarska, K., & Klin, A. (2005). Autism in infancy and early childhood. *Annual Review of Psychology, 56*, 315–336.

Volkmar, F. R., & Klin, A. (1998). Asperger syndrome and nonverbal learning disabilities. In E. Schopler & G. B. Mesibov (Eds.), *Asperger syndrome or high functioning autism? Current issues in autism* (pp. 107–121). New York: Plenum Press.

Volkow, N. D., Wang, G., Fowler, J. S., Telang, F., Maynard, L., Logan, J., Gately, S. J., Pappas, N., Wong, C., Vaska, P., Zhu, W., & Swanson, J. M. (2004). Evidence that methylphenidate enhances the saliency of a mathematical task by increasing dopamine in the human brain. *American Journal of Psychiatry, 161*, 1173–1180.

Volpe, R. J., Heick, P. F., & Guerasko-Moore, D. (2005). An agile behavioral model for monitoring the effects of stimulant medication in school settings. *Psychology in the Schools, 42*, 509.

Voydanoff, P., & Donnelly, B. W. (1999). Risk and protective factors for psychological adjustment and grades among adolescents. *Journal of Family Issues, 20*, 328–349.

Vygotsky, L. S. (1978). *Mind in society: The development of higher psychological processes*. Cambridge, MA: Harvard University Press.

Waddell, C., McEwan, K., Shepherd, C. A., Offord, D. R., & Hua, J. M. (2005). A public health strategy to improve the mental health of Canadian children. *Canadian Journal of Psychiatry, 50*, 226–233.

Wadsworth, M. E., & Achenbach, T. M. (2005). Explaining the link between low socioeconomic status and psychopathology: Testing two mechanisms of the social causation hypothesis. *Journal of Consulting and Clinical Psychology, 73*, 1146–1153.

Wadsworth, M. E., & Compas, B. E. (2002). Coping with family conflict and economic strain: The adolescent perspective. *Journal of Research on Adolescence, 12*, 243–274.

Wadsworth, M. E., Raviv, T., Compas, B. E., & Connor-Smith, J. K. (2005). Parent and adolescent responses to poverty-related stress: Tests of mediated and moderated coping models. *Journal of Child and Family Studies, 14*, 283–298.

Wagner, B. M., Aiken, C., Mullaley, P. M., & Tobin, J. J. (2000). Parents' reactions to adolescents' suicide attempts. *Journal of the American Academy of Child and Adolescent Psychiatry, 39*, 429–436.

Waizenhofer, R. N., Buchanan, C. M., & Jackson-Newsom, J. (2004). Mothers' and fathers' knowledge of adolescents' daily activities: Its sources and its links with adolescent adjustment. *Journal of Family Psychology, 18*, 348–360.

Wakschlag, L. S., & Hans, S. L. (2002). Maternal smoking during pregnancy and conduct problems in high-risk youth: A developmental framework. *Development and Psychopathology 14*, 351–369.

Wakschlag, L. S., & Keenan, K. (2001). Clinical significance and correlates of disruptive behavior in environmentally at-risk preschoolers. *Journal of Clinical Child Psychology, 30*, 262–275.

Walden, B., McGue, M., Iacono, W. G., Burt, S. A., & Elkins, I. (2004). Identifying shared environmental contributions to early substance use: The respective roles of peers and parents. *Journal of Abnormal Psychology, 113*, 440–450.

Walders, N., & Drotar, D. (2000). Understanding cultural and ethnic influences in research with child clinical and pediatric psychology populations. In D. Drotar (Ed.), *Handbook of research in pediatric and clinical child psychology* (pp. 165–188). New York: Kluwer Academic/Plenum Press.

Waldman, I. D., & Lilienfeld, S. O. (2001). Applications of taxometric methods to problems of comorbidity: Perspectives and challenges. *Clinical Psychology: Science and Practice, 8*, 520–527.

Waldron, H. B. (1998). Substance abuse disorders. In T. Ollendick (Ed.), *Comprehensive clinical psychology* (Vol. 5, pp. 539–563). Kidlington, Oxford: Elsevier Science.

Waldron, H. B., Slesnick, N., Brody, J. L., Turner, C. W., & Peterson, T. R. (2001). Treatment outcomes for adolescent substance abuse at 4- and 7-month assessment. *Journal of Consulting and Clinical Psychology, 69*, 802–813.

Walfish, S., & Hess, A. K. (Eds.). (2001). *Succeeding in graduate school: The career guide for psychology students*. Manwah, NJ: Lawrence Erlbaum Associates.

Walker, C. E. (2003). Elimination disorders: Enuresis and encopresis. In M. C. Roberts (Ed.), *Handbook of pediatric psychology* (3rd ed., pp. 544–560). New York: Guilford Press.

Walker, D. D., Roffman, R. A., Stephens, R. S., Berghuis, J., & Kim, W. (2006). Motivational enhancement therapy for adolescent marijuana users: A preliminary randomized controlled trial. *Journal of Consulting and Clinical Psychology, 74*, 628–632.

Walker, D. R., Thompson, A., Zwaigenbaum, L., Goldberg, J., Bryson, S. E., Mahoney, W. J., Strawbridge, C. P., & Szatmari, P. (2004). Specifying PDD-NOS: A comparison of PDD-NOS, Asperger syndrome, and autism. *Journal of the American Academy of Child and Adolescent Psychiatry, 43*, 172–180.

Walker, E., Downey, G., & Bergman, A. (1989). The effects of parental psychopathology and maltreatment on child behavior: A test of the diathesis-stress model. *Child Development, 60*, 15–24.

Walker-Barnes, C. J. (2003). Developmental epidemiology: The perfect partner for clinical practice. *Journal of Clinical Child and Adolescent Psychology, 32*, 181–186.

Walma van der Molen, J. H. (2004). Violence and suffering in television news: toward a broader conception of harmful television content for children. *Pediatrics, 113*, 1771–1775.

Walsh, B. W. (2005). *Treating self-injury: A practical guide*. New York: Guilford Press.

Walsh, P. N. (2005). Ageing and health issues in intellectual disabilities. *Current Opinion in Psychiatry, 18*, 502–506.

Wamboldt, M. Z., & Wamboldt, F. S. (2000). Role of the family in the onset and outcome of childhood disorders: Selected research findings. *Journal of the Academy of Child and Adolescent Psychiatry, 39*, 1212–1219.

Wardle, J., Guthrie, C., Sanderson, S., Birch, L., & Plomin, R. (2001). Food and activity preferences in children of lean and obese parents. *International Journal of Obesity, 25*, 971–977.

Warner, V., Mufson, L., & Weissman, M. M. (1995). Offspring at high and low risk for depression and anxiety: Mechanisms of psychiatric disorder. *Journal of the American Academy of Child and Adolescent Psychiatry, 34*, 786–797.

Warner, V., Weissman, M. M., Mufson, L., & Wickramaratne, P. J. (1999). Grandparents, parents, and grandchildren at high risk for depression: A three-generation study. *Journal of American Academy of Child and Adolescent Psychiatry, 38*, 289–296.

Warren, C. S., Gleaves, D. H., Cepeda-Benito, A., del Carmen Fernandez, M., & Rodriguez-Ruiz, S. (2005). Ethnicity as a protective factor against internalization of a thin ideal and body dissatisfaction. *International Journal of Eating Disorders, 37*, 241–249.

Waschbusch, D. A., & Hill, G. P. (2003). Empirically supported, promising, and unsupported treatments for children with attention-deficit/hyperactivity disorder. In S. O. Lilienfeld, S. J. Lynn, & J. M. Lohr (Eds.), *Science and pseudoscience in clinical psychology* (pp. 333–362). New York: Guilford Press.

Waschbusch, D. A., King, S., & Northern Partners in Action for Children and Youth. (2006). Should sex-specific norms be used to assess attention-deficit/hyperactivity disorder or oppositional defiant disorder?. *Journal of Consulting and Clinical Psychology, 74*, 179–185.

Wasem, C., & Puskin, D., (2000). High-tech with the human touch: Using telehealth to reach America's children. *Professional Psychology: Research and Practice, 31*, 3–4.

Wassink, T. H., Brzustowicz, I. M., Bartlett, C. W., & Szatmari, P. (2004). The search for autism disease genes. *Mental Retardation and Developmental Disabilities Research Reviews, 10*, 272–283.

Waters, E., Hamilton, C. E., & Weinfield, N. S. (2000). The stability of attachment security from infancy to adolescence and early adulthood: General introduction. *Child Development, 71*, 678–683.

Waters, E., Merrick, S., Treboux, D., Crowell, J., & Albersheim, L. (2000). Attachment security in infancy and early adulthood: A twenty-year longitudinal study. *Child Development, 71*, 684–689.

Watson, J. (1986). Parental attributions of emotional disturbance and their relation to the outcome of therapy: Preliminary findings. *Australian Psychologist, 21*, 271–282.

Watson, J. B. (1913). Psychology as the behaviourist views it. *Psychological Review, 20*, 158–177.

Watson, J. B., & Rayner, R. (1920). Conditioned emotional reactions. *Journal of Experimental Psychology, 3*, 1–14.

Watson, S. M. R., & Westby, C. E. (2003). Strategies for addressing the executive function impairments of students prenatally exposed to alcohol and other drugs. *Communication Disorders Quarterly, 24*, 194–204.

Way, N. (1998). *Everyday courage: The lives and stories of urban teenagers*. New York: New York University Press.

Webb, M. S., Simmons, V. N., & Brandon, T. H. (2005). Tailored interventions for motivating smoking cessation: Using placebo tailoring to examine the influence of expectancies and personalization. *Health Psychology, 24*, 179–188.

Webster-Stratton, C. (1993). Strategies for helping early school-aged children with oppositional defiant and conduct disorders: The importance of home-school partnerships. *School Psychology Review, 22*, 437–457.

Webster-Stratton, C., & Herbert, M. (1994). Troubled families/problem children. New York: Wiley.

Webster-Stratton, C., & Hooven, C. (1998). Parent training for child conduct problems. In T. Ollendick (Ed.), *Comprehensive clinical psychology* (Vol. 5, pp. 185–219). Kidlington, Oxford: Elsevier Science.

Webster-Stratton, C., & Reid, M. J. (2003). The incredible years parents, teachers, and children training series: A multifaceted treatment approach for young children with conduct problems. In A. E. Kazdin & J. R. Weisz (Eds.), *Evidence-based psychotherapies for children and adolescents* (pp. 224–240). New York: Guilford Press.

Webster-Stratton, C., Reid, M. J., & Hammond, M. (2001). Preventing conduct problems, promoting social competence: A parent and teacher training partnership in Head Start. *Journal of Clinical Child Psychology, 30*, 283–302.

Webster-Stratton, C., Reid, M. J., & Hammond, M. (2004). Treating children with early-onset conduct problems: Intervention outcomes for parent, child, and teacher training. *Journal of Clinical Child and Adolescent Psychology, 33*, 105–124.

Wechsler, D. (2002). *WPPSI-III: Administration and scoring manual*. San Antonio: The Psychological Corporation.

Wechsler, D. (2003). *Wechsler Intelligence Scale for Children–Fourth Edition: Administration and scoring manual*. San Antonio: The Psychological Corporation.

Weems, C. F., & Costa, N. M. (2005). Developmental differences in the expression of childhood anxiety symptoms and fears. *Journal of the American Academy of Child and Adolescent Psychiatry, 44*, 656–663.

Weems, C. F., Silverman, W. K., & LaGreca, A. M. (2000). What do youth referred for anxiety problems worry about? Worry and its relation to anxiety and anxiety disorders in children and adolescents. *Journal of Abnormal Child Psychology, 28*, 63–72.

Weersing, V. R., & Brent, D. A. (2003). Cognitive-behavioral therapy for adolescent depression: Comparative efficacy, mediation, moderation, and effectiveness. In A. E. Kazdin & J. R. Weisz (Eds.), *Evidence-based psychotherapies for children and adolescents* (pp. 135–147). New York: Guilford Press.

Wegner, J. T., & Wegner, A. Z. (2001). Cognitive-behavioral therapy and other short-term approaches in the treatment of eating disorders. In B. P. Kinoy (Ed.), *Eating disorders: New directions in treatment and recovery* (2nd ed., pp. 112–126). New York: Columbia University Press.

Weikart, D. P., & Schweinhart, L. J. (1997). High/Scope Perry preschool program. In G. W. Albee & T. P. Gullotta (Eds.), *Primary prevention works* (pp. 146–166). Thousand Oaks, CA: Sage.

Weinberg, N. Z., & Glantz, M. D. (1999). Child psychopathology risk factors for drug abuse: Overview. *Journal of Clinical Child Psychology, 28*, 290–297.

Weindrich, D., Jennen-Steinmetz, C., Laucht, M., Esser, G., & Schmidt, M. H. (2000). Epidemiology and prognosis of specific disorders of language and scholastic skills. *European Child and Adolescent Psychiatry, 9*, 186–194.

Weiner, I. B. (2001). Advancing the science of psychological assessment: The Rorschach Inkblot Method as exemplar. *Psychological Assessment, 13*, 423–432.

Weiner, I. B., & Kuehnle, K. (1998). Projective assessment of children and adolescents. In C. R. Reynolds (Ed.), *Comprehensive clinical psychology: Assessment* (Vol. 4, pp. 431–458). Kidlington, Oxford: Elsevier Science.

Weinstein, D., Staffelbach, D., & Biaggio, M. (2000). Attention-deficit hyperactivity disorder and post-traumatic stress disorder: Differential diagnosis in childhood sexual abuse. *Clinical Psychology Review, 20*, 359–378.

Weinstein, L. (2004). *Reading David: A mother and son's journey through the labyrinth of dyslexia.* New York: Penguin.

Weis, R., Wilson, N. L., & Whitemarsh, S. M. (2005). Evaluation of a voluntary, military-style residential treatment program for adolescents with academic and conduct problems. *Journal of Clinical Child and Adolescent Psychology, 34*, 692–705.

Weiss, B., Caron, A., Ball, S., Tapp, J., Johnson, M., & Weisz, J. R. (2005). Iatrogenic effects of group treatment for antisocial youth. *Journal of Consulting and Clinical Psychology, 73*, 1036–1044.

Weiss, B., Catron, T., & Harris, V. (2000). A 2-year follow-up of the effectiveness of traditional child psychotherapy. *Journal of Consulting and Clinical Psychology, 68*, 1094–1101.

Weiss, B., & Garber, J. (2003). Developmental differences in the phenomenology of depression. *Development and Psychopathology, 15*, 403–430.

Weiss, B., Harris, V., Catron, T., & Han, S. S. (2003). Efficacy of the RECAP intervention program for children with concurrent internalizing and externalizing problems. *Journal of Consulting and Clinical Psychology, 71*, 364–374.

Weiss, B., Weisz, J. R., Politano, M., Carey, M., Nelson, W. M., & Finch, A. J. (1992). Relations among self-reported depressive symptoms in clinic-referred children versus adolescents. *Journal of Abnormal Psychology, 101*, 391–397.

Weiss, K., & Wertheim, E. H. (2005). An evaluation of a prevention program for disordered eating in adolescent girls: examining responses of high- and low-risk girls. *Eating Disorders: The Journal of Treatment & Prevention, 13*, 143–156.

Weiss, M., Hechtman, L., & Weiss, G. (2000). ADHD in parents. *Journal of the American Academy of Child and Adolescent Psychiatry, 39*, 1059–1061.

Weiss, S., Sawa, G. H., Abdeen, Z., & Yanai, J. (1999). Substance abuse studies and prevention efforts among Arabs in the 1990s in Israel, Jordan and the Palestinian authority: A literature review. *Addiction, 94*, 177–198.

Weissberg, R. P. (2000). Improving the lives of millions of school children. *American Psychologist, 55*, 1360–1373.

Weissberg, R. P., Caplan, M. Z., & Harwood, R. L. (1991). Promoting competent young people in competence-enhancing environments: A systems-based perspective on primary prevention. *Journal of Consulting and Clinical Psychology, 59*, 830–841.

Weissberg, R. P., Kumpfer, K. L., & Seligman, M. E. P. (2003). Prevention that works for children and youth: An introduction. *American Psychologist, 58*, 425–432.

Weist, M. D., Acosta, O. M., & Youngstrom, E. A. (2001). Predictors of violence exposure among inner-city youth. *Journal of Clinical Child Psychology, 30*, 187–198.

Weist, M. D., Evans, S., & Lever, N. (2003). *Handbook of School Mental Health Programs.* New York: Kluwer Academic/Plenum Press.

Weisz, J. R., Doss, A. J., & Hawley, K. M. (2005). Youth psychotherapy outcome research: A review and critique of the evidence base. *Annual Review of Psychology, 56*, 337–363.

Weisz, J. R., Doss, A. J., & Hawley, K. M. (2006). Evidence-based youth psychotherapies versus usual clinical care: A meta-analysis of direct comparisons. *American Psychologist, 61*, 671–689.

Weisz, J. R., & Hawley, K. M. (1998). Finding, evaluating, refining, and applying empirically supported treatments for children and adolescents. *Journal of Clinical Child Psychology, 27*, 206–216.

Weisz, J. R., McCarty, C. A., Eastman, K. L., Chaiyasit, W., & Suwanlert, S. (1997). Developmental psychopathology and culture: Ten lessons from Thailand. In S. S. Luthar, J. A. Burack, D. Cicchetti, & J. R. Weisz (Eds.), *Developmental psychopathology: Perspectives on adjustment, risk, and disorder* (pp. 568–592). New York: Cambridge University Press.

Weisz, J. R., McCarty, C. A., & Valeri, S. M. (2006). Effects of psychotherapy for depression in children and adolescents: A meta-analysis. *Psychological Bulletin, 132*, 132–149.

Weisz, J. R., Sandler, I. N., Durlak, J. A., & Anton, B. S. (2005). Promoting and protecting youth mental health through evidence-based prevention and treatment. *American Psychologist, 60*, 628–648.

Weisz, J. R., Southam-Gerow, M. A., Gordis, E. B., & Connor-Smith, J. (2003). Primary and secondary control enhancement training for youth depression. In A. E. Kazdin & J. R. Weisz (Eds.), *Evidence-based psychotherapies for children and adolescents* (pp. 165–183). New York: Guilford Press.

Weisz, J. R., Suwanlert, S., Chaiyasit, W., Weiss, B., Achenbach, T. M., & Trevathan, D. (1988). Epidemiology of behavioral and emotional problems among Thai and American Children: Teacher reports of ages 6–11. *Journal of Child Psychology and Psychiatry, 30*, 471–484.

Weisz, J. R., Suwanlert, S., Chaiyasit, W., Weiss, B., Walter, B., & Anderson, W. (1988). Thai and American perspectives on over- and undercontrolled child behavior problems: Exploring the threshold model among parents, teachers, and psychologists. *Journal of Consulting and Clinical Psychology, 56*, 601–609.

Weisz, J. R., Weersing, V. R., & Henggeler, S. W. (2005). Jousting with straw men: Comment on Westen, Novotny, and Thompson-Brenner (2004). *Psychological Bulletin, 131*, 418–426.

Weisz, J. R., & Weiss, B. (1991). Studying the referability of child clinical problems. *Journal of Consulting and Clinical Psychology, 59*, 266–273.

Weisz, J. R., & Weiss, B. (1993). *Effects of psychotherapy with children and adolescents*. Newbury Park, CA: Sage.

Weisz, J. R., Weiss, B., Alicke, M. D., & Klotz, M. L. (1987). Effectiveness of psychotherapy with children and adolescents: A meta-analysis for clinicians. *Journal of Consulting and Clinical Psychology, 55*, 542–549.

Weisz, J. R., Weiss, B., Han, S. S., Granger, D. A., & Morton, T. (1995). Effects of psychotherapy with children and adolescents revisited: A meta-analysis of treatment outcome studies. *Psychological Bulletin, 117*, 450–468.

Weisz, J. R., Weiss, B., Suwanlert, S., & Chaiyasit, W. (2003). Syndromal structure of psychopathology in children of Thailand and the United States. *Journal of Consulting and Clinical Psychology, 71*, 375–385.

Weisz, V. G. (1995). *Children and adolescents in need: A legal primer for the helping professional*. Thousand Oaks, CA: Sage.

Wekerle, C., & Wolfe, D. A. (1996). Child maltreatment. In E. J. Mash & R. A. Barkley (Eds.), *Child psychopathology* (pp. 492–537). New York: Guilford Press.

Wellman, H. M., Cross, D., & Watson, J. (2001). Meta-analysis of theory-of-mind development: The truth about false belief. *Child Development, 72*, 655–684.

Wells, K. C., Pelham, W. E., Kotkin, R. A., Hoza, B., Abikoff, H. B., Abramowitz, A., Arnold, L. E., Cantwell, D. P., Conners, C. K., Del Carmen, R., Elliott, G., Greenhill, L. L., Hechtman, L., Hibbs, E., Hinshaw, S. P., Jensen, P. S., March, J. S., Swanson, J. M., & Schiller, E. (2000). Psychosocial treatment strategies in the MTA Study: Rationale, methods, and critical issues in design and implementation. *Journal of Abnormal Child Psychology, 28*, 483–505.

Welsh, J. A., & Bierman, K. L. (2003). Using the clinical interview to assess children's interpersonal reasoning and emotional understanding. In C. R. Reynolds & R. W. Kamphaus (Eds.), *Handbook of psychological and educational assessment of children: Personality, behavior, and context* (2nd ed., pp. 219–234). New York: Guilford Press.

Welsh, R. S. (2003). Prescription privileges: Pro or con. *Clinical Psychology: Science and Practice, 10*, 371–372.

Werner, E. E. (1995). Resilience in development. *Current Directions in Psychological Science, 4*, 81–85.

Werner, E. E. (2005). What can we learn about resilience from large-scale longitudinal studies? In S. Goldstein & R. B. Brooks (Eds.), *Handbook of resilience in children* (pp. 91–105). New York: Kluwer Academic/Plenum Press.

Werner, E. E., & Smith, R. S. (1982). *Vulnerable but invincible: A study of resilient children*. New York: McGraw-Hill.

Werner, E. E., & Smith, R. S. (1992). *Overcoming the odds: High risk children from birth to adulthood*. Ithaca, NY: Cornell University Press.

Werner, E. E., & Smith, R. S. (2001). *Journeys from childhood to midlife: Risk, resilience, and recovery*. Ithaca, NY: Cornell University Press.

Werry, J. S. (1996). Pervasive developmental, psychotic, and allied disorders. In L. Hechtman (Ed.), *Do they grow out of it? Long-term outcomes of childhood disorders* (pp. 195–223). Washington, DC: American Psychiatric Press.

Werry, J. S., McClellan, J. M., Andrews, L. K., & Ham, M. (1994). Clinical features and outcome of child and adolescent schizophrenia. *Schizophrenia Bulletin, 20*, 619–630.

West, S. L., & O'Neal, K. K. (2004). Project D.A.R.E. outcome effectiveness revisited. *American Journal of Public Health, 94*, 1027–1029.

Westcott, H. L., & Jones, D. P. H. (1999). Annotation: The abuse of disabled children. *Journal of Child Psychology and Psychiatry, 40*, 497–506.

Westen, D. (2006). Patients and treatments in clinical trials are not adequately representative of clinical practice. In J. C. Norcross, L. E. Beutler, & R. F. Levant (Eds.), *Evidence-based practices in mental health: Debate and dialogue on the fundamental questions* (pp. 161–171). Washington, DC: American Psychological Association.

Westen, D., Novotny, C. M., & Thompson-Brenner, H. (2004). The empirical status of empirically supported psychotherapies: Assumptions, findings, and reporting in controlled clinical trials. *Psychological Bulletin, 130*, 631–663.

Westen, D., Novotny, C. M., & Thompson-Brenner, H. (2005). EBP does not equal EST: Reply to Crits-Christoph et al. (2005) and Weisz et al. (2005). *Psychological Bulletin, 131*, 427–433.

Wetherby, A. M., Woods, J., Allen, L., Cleary, J., Dickinson, H., & Lord, C. (2004). Early indicators of autism spectrum disorders in the second year of life. *Journal of Autism and Developmental Disorders, 34*, 473–493.

Whalen, C. K., & Henker, B. (1998). Attention-deficit/hyperactivity disorder. In T. H. Ollendick & M. Hersen (Eds.), *Handbook of child psychopathology* (3rd ed., pp. 181–211). New York: Plenum Press.

Whalen, C. K., Henker, B., King, P. S., Jamner, L. D., & Levine, L. (2004). Adolescents react to the events of September 11, 2001: Focused versus ambient impact. *Journal of Abnormal Child Psychology, 32*, 1–11.

Whiffen, V. E., & Demidenko, N. (2006). Mood disturbance across the life span. In J. Worell & C. D. Goodheart (Eds.), *Handbook of girls' and women's psychological health* (pp. 51–59). New York: Oxford University Press.

Whitaker, A., Johnson, J., Saffer, D., Rapoport, J. L., Kalikow, K., Walsh, B. T., Davies, M., Braiman, S., & Dolinsky, A. (1990). Uncommon troubles in young people: Prevalence estimates of selected psychiatric disorders in a nonreferred adolescent population. *Archives of General Psychiatry, 47*, 487–496.

Whitbeck, L. B., & Hoyt, D. R. (1999). *Nowhere to grow: Homeless and runaway adolescents and their families.* New York: Aldine de Gruyter.

Whitbeck, L. B., Hoyt, D. R., & Bao, W. N. (2000). Depressive symptoms and co-occurring depressive symptoms, substance abuse, and conduct problems among runaway and homeless adolescents. *Child Development, 71*, 721–732.

White, E. (2000). *Boy's own story.* New York: Knopf.

White, K. S., Bruce, S. E., Farrell, A. D., & Kliewer, W. (1998). Impact of exposure to community violence on anxiety: A longitudinal study of family social support as a protective factor for urban children. *Journal of Child and Family Studies, 7*, 187–203.

White, K. S., & Farrell, A. D. (2001). Structure of anxiety symptoms in urban children: Competing factor models of the Revised Children's Manifest Anxiety Scale. *Journal of Consulting and Clinical Psychology, 69*, 333–337.

White, M. A., & Grilo, C. M. (2005). Ethnic differences in the prediction of eating and body image disturbances among female adolescent psychiatric inpatients. *International Journal of Eating Disorders, 38*, 78–84.

White, M. A., Martin, P. D., Newton, R. L., Walden, H. M., York-Crowe, E. E., Gordon, S. T., Ryan, D. H., & Williamson, D. A. (2004). Mediators of weight loss in a family-based intervention presented over the internet. *Obesity Research, 12*, 1050–1059.

Wickramaratne, P. J., Greenwald, S., & Weissman, M. M. (2000). Psychiatric disorders in the relatives of probands with prepubertal-onset or adolescent-onset major depression. *Journal of the American Academy of Child and Adolescent Psychiatry, 39*, 1396–1405.

Wickramaratne, P. J., & Weissman, M. M. (1998). Onset of psychopathology in offspring by developmental phase and parental depression, *Journal of the Academy of Child and Adolescent Psychiatry, 37*, 933–942.

Wicks, S., Hjern, A., Gunnell, D., Lewis, G., & Dalman, C. (2005). Social adversity in childhood and the risk of developing psychosis: A national cohort study. *American Journal of Psychiatry, 162*, 1652–1657.

Widiger, T. A., & Clark, L. A. (2000). Toward *DSM-V* and the classification of psychopathology. Psychological Bulletin, 126, 946–963.

Wiebe, D. J., Berg, C. A., Korbel, C., Palmer, D. L., Beveridge, R. M., Upchurch, R., Lindsay, R., Swinyard, M. T., & Donaldson, D. L. (2005). Children's appraisals of maternal involvement in coping with diabetes: Enhancing our understanding of adherence, metabolic control, and quality of life across adolescence. *Journal of Pediatric Psychology, 30*, 167–178.

Wiecha, J. L., El-Ayadi, A. M., Fuemmeler, B. F., Carter, J. E., Handler, S., Johnson, S., Strunk, N., Korzec-Ramirez, D., & Gortmaker, S. L. (2004). Diffusion of an integrated health education program in an urban school system: Planet Health. *Journal of Pediatric Psychology, 29*, 467–474.

Wiener, J. (2004). Do peer relationships foster behavioral adjustment in children with learning disabilities? *Learning Disability Quarterly, 27*, 21–30.

Wiener, J. M. (1999). Violence and mental illness in adolescence. In R. L. Hendren (Ed.) *Disruptive behavior disorders in children and adolescents* (Vol. 18, pp. 175–189). Washington, DC: American Psychiatric Press.

Wiesner, M. (2003). A longitudinal latent variable analysis of reciprocal relations between depressive symptoms and delinquency during adolescence. *Journal of Abnormal Psychology, 112*, 633–645.

Wikstrom, P. H., & Sampson, R. J. (2003). Social mechanisms of community influences on crime and pathways in criminality. In B. B. Lahey, T. E. Moffitt, & A. Caspi (Eds.), *Causes of conduct disorder and juvenile delinquency* (pp. 118–148). New York: Guilford Press.

Wilens, T. E. (2004a). Attention-deficit/hyperactivity disorder and the substance use disorders: The nature of the relationship, who is at risk, and treatment issues. *Primary Psychiatry, 11*, 63–70.

Wilens, T. E. (2004b). *Straight talk about psychiatric medications for kids* (rev. ed.). New York: Guilford Press.

Wilens, T. E., Biederman, J., Forkner, P., Ditterline, J., Morris, M., Moore, H., Galdo, M., Spencer, T. J., & Wozniak, J. (2003). Patterns of comorbidity and dysfunction in clinically referred preschool and school-age children with bipolar disorder. *Journal of Child and Adolescent Psychopharmacology, 13*, 495–505.

Wilens, T. E., Biederman, J., Kwon, A., Ditterline, J., Forkner, P., Moore, H., Swezey, A., Snyder, L., Henin, A., Wozniak, J., & Faraone, S. V. (2004). Risk of substance use disorders in adolescents with bipolar disorder. *Journal of the American Academy of Child and Adolescent Psychiatry, 43*, 1380–1386.

Wilens, T. E., Biederman, J., & Spencer, T. J. (2002). Attention deficit/hyperactivity disorder across the lifespan. *Annual Review of Medicine, 53*, 113–131.

Wilens, T. E., Biederman, J., Wozniak, J., Gunawardene, S., Wong, J., & Monuteaux, M. (2003). Can adults with attention-deficit/hyperactivity disorder be distinguished from those with comorbid bipolar disorder? Findings from a sample of clinically referred adults. *Biological Psychiatry, 54*, 1–8.

Wilens, T. E., Faraone, S. V., Biederman, J., & Gunawardene, S. (2003). Does stimulant therapy of attention-deficit/hyperactivity disorder beget later substance abuse? A meta-analytic review of the literature. *Pediatrics, 111*, 179–185.

Wilens, T. E., Hahesy, A. L., Biederman, J., Bredin, E., Tanguay, S., Kwon, A., & Faraone, S. V. (2005). Influence of parental SUD and ADHD on ADHD in their offspring: Preliminary results from a pilot-controlled family study. *American Journal on Addictions, 14*, 179–187.

Wilensky, A. (2004). *The weight of it: A story of two sisters.* New York: Henry Holt and Company.

Wilfley, D. E., Passi, V. A., Cooperberg, J., & Stein, R. I. (2006). Cognitive-behavioral therapy for youth with eating disorders and obesity. In P. C. Kendall (Ed.), *Child and adolescent therapy: Cognitive-behavioral procedures* (3rd ed., pp. 322–355). New York: Guilford Press.

Will, K. E., Porter, B. E., Geller, E. S., & DePasquale, J. P. (2005). Is television a health and safety hazard? A cross-sectional analysis of at-risk behavior on primetime television. *Journal of Applied Social Psychology, 35*, 198–222.

Willcutt, E. G., DeFries, J. C., Pennington, B. F., Smith, S. D., Cardon, L. R., & Olson, R. K. (2003). Genetic etiology of comorbid reading difficulties and ADHD. In R. Plomin, J. C. DeFries, I. W. Craig, & P. McGuffin (Eds.), *Behavioral genetics in the postgenomic era* (pp. 227–246). Washington, DC: American Psychological Association.

Willcutt, E. G., & Pennington, B. F. (2000). Psychiatric comorbidity in children and adolescents with reading disability. *Journal of Child Psychology and Psychiatry and Allied Disciplines, 41,* 1039–1048.

Williams, D. (2001). *Like colour to the blind: Soul searching and soul finding.* Philadelphia: Jessica Kingsley.

Williams, G. J. R. (1983). Responsible sexuality and the primary prevention of child abuse. In G. W. Albee, S. Gordon, & H. Leitenberg (Eds.), *Promoting sexual responsibility and preventing sexual problems* (pp. 251–272). Hanover, NH: University Press of New England.

Williams, J. H., Ayers, C. D., Van Dorn, R. A., & Arthur, M. W. (2004). Risk and protective factors in the development of delinquency and conduct disorder. In M. W. Fraser (Ed.), *Risk and resilience in childhood: An ecological perspective,* (2nd ed., pp. 209–249). Washington, DC: National Association of Social Workers Press.

Williams, N. L., Reardon, J. M., Murray, K. T., & Cole, T. M. (2005). Anxiety disorders: A developmental vulnerability-stress perspective. In B. L. Hankin & J. R. Z. Abela (Eds.), *Development of psychopathology: A vulnerability-stress perspective* (pp. 289–327). Thousand Oaks, CA: Sage.

Williams, P. G., Colder, C. R., Richards, M. H., & Scalzo, C. A. (2002). The role of self-assessed health in the relationship between gender and depressive symptoms among adolescents. *Journal of Pediatric Psychology, 27,* 509–517.

Williams, P. G., Sears, L. L., & Allard, A. (2004). Sleep problems in children with autism. *Journal of Sleep Research, 13,* 265–268.

Williams, R. J., & Chang, S. Y. (2000). A comprehensive and comparative review of adolescent substance abuse treatment outcome. *Clinical Psychology: Science and Practice, 7,* 138–166.

Williamson, D. A., Bentz, B. G., & Rabalais, J. Y. (1998). Eating disorders. In T. H. Ollendick & M. Hersen (Eds.), *Handbook of child psychopathology* (3rd ed., pp. 291–305). New York: Plenum Press.

Williamson, D. A., Duchmann, E. G., Barker, S. E., & Bruno, R. M. (1998). Anorexia nervosa. In V. B. Van Hasselt & M. Hersen (Eds.), *Handbook of psychological treatment protocols for children and adolescents* (pp. 413–434). Mahwah, NJ: Lawrence Erlbaum Associates.

Willner, P. (2005). The effectiveness of psychotherapeutic interventions for people with learning disabilities: A critical overview. *Intellectual Disability Research, 49,* 73–85.

Willoughby, M., Kupersmidt, J., & Bryant, D. (2001). Overt and covert dimensions of antisocial behavior in early childhood. *Journal of Abnormal Child Psychology, 29,* 177–187.

Wills, T. A., & Cleary, S. D. (2000). Testing theoretical models and frameworks in child health research. In D. Drotar (Ed.), *Handbook of research in pediatric and clinical child psychology* (pp. 21–49). New York: Plenum Press.

Wills, T. A., & Dishion, T. J. (2004). Temperament and adolescent substance use: A transactional analysis of emerging self-control. *Journal of Clinical Child and Adolescent Psychology, 33,* 69–81.

Wills, T. A., Sandy, J. M., Yaeger, A., & Shinar, O. (2001). Family risk factors and adolescent substance use: Moderation effects for temperament dimensions. *Developmental Psychology, 37,* 283–297.

Wilmshurst, L. (2005). *Essentials of child psychopathology.* Hoboken, NJ: Wiley.

Wilson, D. K., & Evans, A. E. (2003). Health promotion in children and adolescents: An integration of psychosocial and environmental approaches. In M. C. Roberts (Ed.), *Handbook of pediatric psychology* (3rd ed., pp. 69–83). New York: Guilford Press.

Wilson, D. K., Williams, J., Evans, A., Mixon, G., & Rheaume, C. (2005). Brief report: A qualitative study of gender preferences and motivational factors for physical activity in underserved adolescents. *Journal of Pediatric Psychology, 30,* 293–297.

Wilson, G. T., Becker, C. B., & Heffernan, K. (2003). Eating disorder. In E. J. Mash, & B. A. Barkley (Eds.), *Child psychopathology* (2nd ed., pp. 687–715). New York: Guilford Press.

Wilson, H. W., & Donenberg, G. (2004). Quality of parent communication about sex and its relationship to risky sexual behavior among youth in psychiatric care: A pilot study. *Journal of Child Psychology and Psychiatry, 45,* 387–395.

Wilson, N., Syme, S. L., Boyce, W. T., Battistich, V. A., & Selvin, S. (2005). Adolescent alcohol, tobacco, and marijuana use: The influence of neighborhood disorder and hope. *American Journal of Health Promotion, 20,* 11–19.

Wilson, S. J., Lipsey, M. W., & Derzon, J. H. (2003). The effects of school based intervention programs on aggressive behavior: A meta-analysis. *Journal of Consulting and Clinical Psychology, 71,* 136–149.

Windle, M. (2000). Parental, sibling, and peer influences on adolescent substance use and alcohol problems. *Applied Developmental Science, 4,* 98–110.

Windle, M., & Davies, P. T. (1999). Depression and heavy alcohol use among adolescents: Concurrent and prospective relations. *Development and Psychopathology, 11,* 823–844.

Windle, M., Mun, E. Y., & Windle, R. C. (2005). Adolescent-to-young adulthood heavy drinking trajectories and their prospective predictors. *Journal of Studies on Alcohol, 66,* 313–322.

Windle, M., & Tubman, J. G. (1999). Children of alcoholics. In W. K. Silverman & T. H. Ollendick (Eds.), *Developmental issues in the clinical treatment of children* (pp. 393–414). Boston: Allyn and Bacon.

Windle, M., & Windle, R. C. (2001). Depressive symptoms and cigarette smoking among middle adolescents: Prospective associations and intrapersonal and interpersonal influences. *Journal of Consulting and Clinical Psychology, 69,* 215–226.

Winerman, L. (2005). The mind's mirror. *Monitor on Psychology, 36,* 48–50.

Wing, L. (1981). Asperger's syndrome: A clinical account. *Psychological Medicine, 11,* 115.

Winsor, A. P. (2003). Direct behavioral observation for classrooms. In C. R. Reynolds & R. W. Kamphaus (Eds.), *Handbook of psychological and educational assessment of children: Personality, behavior, and context* (2nd ed., pp. 248–255). New York: Guilford Press.

Winstead, B. A., & Sanchez, J. (2005). Gender and psychopathology. In J. E. Maddux & B. A. Winstead (Eds.), *Psychopathology: Foundations for a contemporary understanding* (pp. 39–61). Mahwah, NJ: Lawrence Erlbaum Associates.

Witkiewitz, K., & Marlatt, G. A. (2004). Relapse prevention for alcohol and drug problems: That was Zen, this is Tao. *American Psychologist, 59,* 224–235.

Witt, J. C., Elliott, S. N., Daly, E. J., Gresham, F. M., & Kramer, J. J. (1998). *Assessment of at-risk and special needs children* (2nd ed.). New York: McGraw-Hill.

Wolchik, S. A., Tein, J. Y., Sandler, I. N., & Ayers, I. S. (2006). Stressors, quality of the child-caregiver relationship, and children's mental health problems after parental death: The mediating role of self-system beliefs. *Journal of Abnormal Child Psychology, 34,* 221–238.

Wolery, M., Barton, E. E., & Hine, J. F. (2005). Evolution of applied behavior analysis in the treatment of individuals with autism. *Exceptionality, 13,* 11–23.

Wolfe, D. A., Rawana, J. S., & Chiodo, D. (2006). Abuse and trauma. In D. A. Wolfe & E. J. Mash (Eds.), *Behavioral and emotional disorders in adolescents: Nature, assessment, and treatment* (pp. 642–671). New York: Guilford Press.

Wolfe, D. A., Scott, K., Wekerle, C., & Pittman, A. L. (2001). Child maltreatment: Risk of adjustment problems and dating violence in adolescence. *Journal of the American Academy of Child and Adolescent Psychiatry, 40,* 282–289.

Wolfe, D. A., Wekerle, C., Scott, K., Straatman, A. L., & Grasley, C. (2004). Predicting abuse in adolescent dating relationships over 1 year: The role of child maltreatment and trauma. *Journal of Abnormal Psychology, 113,* 406–415.

Wolfe, V. V., Finch, A. J., Saylor, C. F., & Blount, R. L. (1987). Negative affectivity in children: A multitrait-multimethod investigation. *Journal of Consulting and Clinical Psychology, 55,* 245–250.

Wolraich, M. L., Lambert, E. W., Baumgaertel, A., Garcia-Tornel, S., Feurer, I. D., Bickman, L., & Doffing, M. A. (2003). Teachers' screening for attention deficit/hyperactivity disorder: Comparing multinational samples on teacher ratings of ADHD. *Journal of Abnormal Child Psychology, 31,* 445–455.

Wolters, P. L., Brouwers, P., & Perez, L. A. (1999). Pediatric HIV infection. In R. T. Brown (Ed.), *Cognitive aspects of chronic illness in children* (pp. 105–141). New York: Guilford Press.

Wong, B. Y. L. (2003). General and specific issues for researchers' consideration in applying the risk and resilience framework to the social domain of learning disabilities. *Learning Disabilities Research & Practice, 18,* 68–76.

Woo, B. S. C., & Rey, J. M. (2005). The validity of the DSM-IV subtypes of attention-deficit/hyperactivity disorder. *Australian and New Zealand Journal of Psychiatry, 39,* 344–353.

Wood, J. M., Nezworski, T., Lilienfeld, S. O., & Garb, H. N. (Eds.). (2003). *What's wrong with the Rorschach: Science confronts the controversial inkblot test.* San Francisco: Jossey-Bass.

Wood, K. C., Becker, J. A., & Thompson, J. K. (1996). Body image dissatisfaction in preadolescent children. *Journal of Applied Developmental Psychology, 17,* 85–100.

Woodcock, R. W., McGrew, K. S., & Mather, N. (2000). *Woodcock-Johnson psycho-educational battery-III.* Itasca, IL: Riverside Publishing.

Woods, D. W., Himie, M. B., & Osman, D. C. (2005). Use of the impact on family scale in children with Tic disorders: Descriptive data, validity, and tic severity impact. *Child & Family Behavior Therapy, 27,* 11–21.

Woodward, J., & Ono, Y. (2004). Mathematics and academic diversity in Japan. *Journal of Learning Disabilities, 37,* 74–82.

Woodward, L. J., & Fergusson, D. M. (1999). Childhood peer relationship problems and psychosocial adjustment in late adolescence. *Journal of Abnormal Child Psychology, 27,* 87–104.

World Health Organization. (1992). *The ICD-10 classification of mental and behavioural disorders: Clinical descriptions and diagnostic guidelines.* Geneva, Switzerland: Author.

Worling, D. E., Humphries, T., & Tannock, R. (1999). Spatial and emotional aspects of language inferencing in nonverbal learning disabilities. *Brain and Language, 70,* 220–239.

Wozniak, J., Spencer, T., Biederman, J., Kwon, A., Monuteaux, M., Rettew, J., & Lail, K. (2004). The clinical characteristics of unipolar vs. bipolar major depression in ADHD youth. *Journal of Affective Disorders, 82S,* S59–S69.

Woznick, L. A., & Goodheart, C. D. (2002). Relieving pain and side effects. *Living with childhood cancer: A practical guide to help families cope* (pp. 197–228). Washington, DC: American Psychological Association.

Wright, E. (1999). *Why I teach.* Rocklin, CA: Prima.

Wright, J. C., Zakriski, A. L., & Drinkwater, M. (1999). Developmental psychopathology and the reciprocal patterning of behavior and environment: Distinctive situational and behavioral signatures of internalizing, externalizing, and mixed-syndrome children. *Journal of Consulting and Clinical Psychology, 67,* 95–107.

Wright, J. C., & Zakriski, A. L. (2001). A contextual analysis of externalizing and mixed syndrome boys: When syndromal similarity obscures functional dissimilarity. *Journal of Consulting and Clinical Psychology, 69,* 457–470.

Wright, M. O., & Masten, A. S. (2005). Resilience processes in development: Fostering positive adaptation in the context of adversity. In S. Goldstein & R. B. Brooks (Eds.), *Handbook of resilience in children* (pp. 17–37). New York: Kluwer Academic/Plenum Press.

Wright, P. W. D., & Wright, P. D. (2005). *IDEA 2004.* Hartfield, VA: Harbor House Law Press.

Wu, L., Pilowsky, D. J., & Schlenger, W. E. (2004). Inhalant abuse and dependence among adolescents in the United States. *Journal of the American Academy of Child & Adolescent Psychiatry, 43,* 1206–1214.

Wu, P., Hoven, C. W., Bird, H. R., Moore, R. E., Cohen, P., Alegria, M., Dulcan, M. K., Goodman, S. H., Horwitz, S. M., Lichtman, J. H., Narrow, W. E., Rae, D. S., Regier, D. A., & Roper, M. T. (1999). Depressive and disruptive disorders and mental health service utilization in children and adolescents. *Journal of the American Academy of Child and Adolescent Psychiatry, 38*, 1081–1090.

Wyman, P. A., Cowen, E. L., Work, W. C., Hoyt-Meyers, L., Magnus, K. B., & Fagen, D. B. (1999). Caregiving and developmental factors differentiating young at-risk urban children showing resilient versus stress-affected outcomes: A replication and extension. *Child Development, 70*, 645–659.

Wyman, P. A., Sandler, I., Wolchik, S., & Nelson, K. (2000). Resilience as cumulative competence promotion and stress protection: Theory and intervention. In D. Cicchetti, J. Rappaport, I. Sandler, & R. P. Weissberg (Eds.). *The promotion of wellness in children and adolescents* (pp. 133–184). Washington, DC: CWLA Press.

Wysocki, T., Greco, P., & Buckloh, L. M. (2003). Childhood diabetes in psychological context. In M. C. Roberts (Ed.), *Handbook of pediatric psychology* (3rd ed., pp. 304–320). New York: Guilford Press.

Xue, Y., Hodges, K., & Wotring, J. (2004). Predictors of outcome for children with behavior problems served in public mental health. *Journal of Clinical Child and Adolescent Psychology, 33*, 516–523.

Yager, Z., & O'Dea, J. A. (2005). The role of teachers and other educators in the prevention of eating disorders and child obesity: *What are the issues? Eating Disorders: The Journal of Treatment & Prevention, 13*, 261–278.

Yagi, H., Furutani, Y., Hamada, H., Sasaki, T., Asakawa, S., Minoshima, S., Ichida, F., Joo, K., Kimura, M., Imamura, S., Kamatani, N., Momma, K., Takao, A., Nakazawa, M., Shimizu, N., & Matsuoka, R. (2003). Role of TBX1 in human del22q11.2 syndrome. *The Lancet, 362*, 1366–1373.

Yale, M. E., Scott, K. G., Gross, M., & Gonzalez, A. (2003). Using developmental epidemiology to choose the target population for an intervention program in a high-risk neighborhood. *Journal of Clinical Child and Adolescent Psychology, 32*, 236–242.

Yamamoto, J., Silva, J. A., Ferrari, M., & Nukariya, K. (1997). Culture and psychopathology. In G. Johnson-Powell & J. Yamamoto (Eds.), *Transcultural child development: Psychological assessment and treatment* (pp. 34–57). New York: Wiley.

Yanagida, E. H. (1998). Ethical dilemmas in the clinical practice of child psychology. In R. M. Anderson, T. I. Needels, & H. V. Hall (Eds.), *Avoiding ethical misconduct in psychology specialty areas.* Springfield, IL: Charles C. Thomas.

Yang, L., Wang, Y. F., Qian, Q. J., Biederman, J., & Faraone, S. V. (2004). DSM-IV subtypes of ADHD in a Chinese outpatient sample. *Journal of the American Academy of Child and Adolescent Psychiatry, 43*, 248–250.

Yeargin-Allsopp, M., Rice, C., Karapukar, T., Doernberg, N., Boyle, C., & Murphy, C. (2003). Prevalence of autism in a US metropolitan area. *American Medical Association, 289*, 49–55.

Yeganeh, R., Beidel, D. C., Turner, S. M., Pina, A. A., & Silverman, W. K. (2003). Clinical distinctions between selective mutism and social phobia: An investigation of childhood psychopathology. *Journal of the American Academy of Child and Adolescent Psychiatry, 42*, 1069–1075.

Yeh, M., Hough, R. L., McCabe, K., Lau, A., & Garland, A. (2004). Parental beliefs about the causes of child problems: Exploring racial/ethnic patterns. *Journal of the American Academy of Child and Adolescent Psychiatry, 43*, 605–612.

Yeh, M., & Weisz, J. R. (2001). Why are we here at the clinic? Parent-child (dis)agreement on referral problems at outpatient treatment entry. *Journal of Consulting and Clinical Psychology, 69*, 1018–1025.

Yoder, P., & Stone, W. L. (2006). Randomized comparison of two communication interventions for preschoolers with autism spectrum disorders. *Journal of Consulting and Clinical Psychology, 74*, 426–435.

Young-Hyman, D., Schlundt, D. G., Herman-Wenderoth, L., & Bozylinski, K. (2003). Obesity, appearance, and psychosocial adaptation in young African American children. *Journal of Pediatric Psychology, 28*, 463–472.

Youngstrom, E. A., & Duax, J. (2005). Evidence-based assessment of pediatric bipolar disorder Part I: Base rate and family history. *Journal of the American Academy of Child Adolescent Psychiatry, 44*, 712–717.

Youngstrom, E. A., Findling, R. L., Calabrese, J. R., Gracious, B. L., Demeter, C., Del Porto-Bedoya, D. & Price, M. (2004). Comparing the diagnostic accuracy of six potential screening instruments for bipolar disorder in youths aged 5 to 17 years. *Journal of the American Academy of Child and Adolescent Psychiatry, 43*, 847–858.

Youngstrom, E. A., Findling, R. L., & Calabrese, J. R. (2003). Who are the comorbid adolescents? Agreement between psychiatric diagnosis, youth, parent, and teacher report. *Journal of Abnormal Child Psychology, 31*, 231–245.

Youngstrom, E. A., Findling, R. L., Youngstrom, J. K., & Calabrese, J. R. (2005). Toward an evidence-based assessment of pediatric bipolar disorder. *Journal of Clinical Child and Adolescent Psychology, 34*, 433–448.

Yung, B. R., & Hammond, W. R. (1997). Antisocial behavior in minority groups: Epidemiological and cultural perspectives. In D. M. Stoff, J. Breiling, & J. D. Maser (Eds.), *Handbook of antisocial behavior* (pp. 474–495). New York: Wiley.

Zalsman, G., Netanel, R., Fischel, T., Freudenstein, O., Landau, E., Orbach, I., Weizman, A., Pfeffer, C. R., & Apter, A. (2000). Human figure drawings in the evaluation of severe adolescent suicidal behavior. *Journal of the American Academy of Child and Adolescent Psychiatry, 39*, 1024–1031.

Zametkin, A. J., Zoon, C. K., Klein, H., & Munson, S. (2004). Psychiatric aspects of child and adolescent obesity: A review of the past 10 years. *Journal of the American Academy of Child and Adolescent Psychiatry, 43*, 134–150.

Zayas, L. H., Kaplan, C., Turner, S., Romano, K., & Gonzalez-Ramos, G. (2000). Understanding suicide attempts by adolescent Hispanic females. *Social Work, 45*, 53–63.

Zeanah, C. H. (Ed.) (2005). *Handbook of infant mental health* (3rd ed.). New York: Guilford Press.

Zeanah, C. H., Larrieu, J. A., Heller, S. S., Valliere, J., Hinshaw-Fuselier, S., Aoki, Y., & Drilling, M. (2001). Evaluation of a preventive intervention for maltreated infants and toddlers in foster care. *Journal of the American Academy of Child and Adolescent Psychiatry, 40*, 214–221.

Zeiglser, D. W., Wang, C. C., Yoast, R. A., Dickinson, B., McCaffree, M. A., Robinowitz, C. B., Sterling, M. L. (2005). The neurocognitive effects of alcohol on adolescents and college students. *Preventive Medicine: An International Journal Devoted to Practice and Theory, 40*, 23–32.

Zeitlin, H. (1999). Psychiatric comorbidity with substance misuse in children and teenagers. *Drug and Alcohol Dependence, 55*, 225–234.

Zero to Three (2005). *Diagnostic classification of mental health and developmental disorders of infancy and early childhood: Revised Edition (DC: 0–3R)*. Washington, DC: Zero to Three Press.

Zgoba, K. (2004). The Amber alert: The appropriate solution to preventing child abduction? *Journal of Psychiatry and Law, 32*, 71–88.

Ziegler, J. C., & Goswami, U. (2005). Reading acquisition, developmental dyslexia, and skilled reading across languages: A psycholinguistic grain size theory. *Psychological Bulletin, 131*, 3–29.

Zigler, E. (1979). Project Head Start: Success or failure? In E. Zigler & J. Valentine (Eds.), *Project Head Start: A legacy of the War on Poverty* (pp. 495–507). New York: Free Press.

Zigler, E., & Phillips, L. (1961). Psychiatric diagnosis: A critique. *Journal of Abnormal and Social Psychology, 63*, 607–618.

Zigler, E., & Styfco, S. (2004). *Head Start debates*. Baltimore: Paul H. Brookes.

Zijistra, H. P., & Viaskamp, C. (2005). The impact of medical conditions on the support of children with profound intellectual and multiple disabilities. *Journal of Applied Research in Intellectual Disabilities, 18*, 151–161.

Zimmermann, G., Favrod, J., Trieu, V. H., & Pomini, V. (2005). The effect of cognitive behavioral treatment on the positive symptoms of schizophrenia spectrum disorders: A meta-analysis. *Schizophrenia Research, 77*, 1–9.

Zinsmeister, K. (2006). Divorce's toll on children. In D. S. Del Campo & R. L. Del Campo (Eds.), *Taking sides: Clashing views in childhood and society* (6th ed., pp. 152–158). Dubuque, IA: McGraw-Hill.

Zohar, A. H., & Felz, L. (2001). Ritualistic behavior in young children. *Journal of Abnormal Child Psychology, 29*, 121–128.

Zucker, N. L., Womble, L. G., Williamson, D. A., & Perrin, L. A. (1999). Protective factors for eating disorders in female college athletes. *Eating Disorders: The Journal of Treatment and Prevention, 7*, 207–218.

Zucker, R. A., Fitzgerald, H. E., & Moses, H. D. (1995). Emergence of alcohol problems and the several alcoholisms: A developmental perspective on etiologic theory and life course trajectory. In D. Cicchetti & D. J. Cohen (Eds.), *Developmental psychopathology (Vol 2): Risk, disorder, and adaptation* (pp. 677–711). New York: Wiley.

Zucker, S. H., Perras, C., Gartin, B., & Fidler, D. (2005). Best practices for practitioners. *Education and Training in Developmental Disabilities, 40*, 199–201.

Zwaigenbaum, L., Bryson, S., Rogers, T., Roberts, W., Brian, J., & Szatmari, P. (2005). Behavioral manifestations of autism in the first year of life. *International Journal of Developmental Neuroscience, 23*, 143–152.

PHOTO CREDITS

Putnam Inc. Page 375: Bob Daemmrich/The Image Works. Page 386: Ellen Senisi/The Image Works.

Chapter 14

Page 398: © AP/Wide World Photos. Page 421: Zigy Kaluzny/Stone/Getty Images. Page 426: SUPERSTOCK.

Chapter 15

Page 436: © AP/Wide World Photos. Page 438: Laura Dwight/Peter Arnold, Inc. Page 440: Webster-Stratton & Herbert (1994). Page 442: Michael Newman/PhotoEdit. Page 449: Will Hart/PhotoEdit.

INDEX